Research Methods for Business Students

RESEARCH METHODS FOR BUSINESS STUDENTS

EIGHTH EDITION

MARK N.K. SAUNDERS

PHILIP LEWIS • ADRIAN THORNHILL

Pearson

Harlow, England • London • New York • Boston • San Francisco • Toronto • Sydney • Dubai • Singapore • Hong Kong
Tokyo • Seoul • Taipei • New Delhi • Cape Town • São Paulo • Mexico City • Madrid • Amsterdam • Munich • Paris • Milan

PEARSON EDUCATION LIMITED
KAO Two
KAO Park
Harlow CM17 9SR
United Kingdom
Tel: +44 (0)1279 623623
Web: www.pearson.com/uk

First published under the Pitman Publishing imprint in 1997
Second edition published 2000
Third edition published 2003
Fourth edition published 2007
Fifth edition published 2009
Sixth edition published 2012
Seventh edition published 2016
Eighth edition published 2019

© Pearson Professional Limited 1997
© Pearson Education Limited 2000, 2003, 2007, 2009, 2012, 2016
© Mark N.K. Saunders, Philip Lewis and Adrian Thornhill 2019

ISBN: 978-1-292-20878-7

British Library Cataloguing-in-Publication Data
A catalogue record for the print edition is available from the British Library

Library of Congress Cataloging-in-Publication Data
Names: Saunders, M. N. K., author. | Lewis, Philip author. |
   Thornhill, Adrian, author.
Title: Research methods for business students / Mark Saunders, Philip Lewis,
   Adrian Thornhill.
Description: Eighth Edition. | New York : Pearson, [2019] | Revised edition
   of the authors' Research methods for business students, 2015.
Identifiers: LCCN 2018058370 | ISBN 9781292208787 (print) | ISBN 9781292208800
   (pdf) | ISBN 9781292208794 (epub)
Subjects: LCSH: Business—Research. | Business—Research—Data processing.
Classification: LCC HD30.4 .S28 2019 | DDC 650.072—dc23
LC record available at https://urldefense.proofpoint.com/v2/url?u=https-3A__lccn.loc.gov_2018058
370&d=DwIFAg&c=0YLnzTkWOdJlub_y7qAx8Q&r=zKTI3XC-TUJM0AsOJA2Iy8zK9anF7moqCccCkWx
1Ygs&m=aFJFa_On9Bwi_ZE496eRa0RzNQg4o0hbQsJmY60F4S4&s=jnj_MFTdyrU7pKlt5YX8gCup6Yt
YmmqllMUMXs1Og7w&e=

10 9 8 7 6 5 4 3 2 1
23 22 21 20 19

Front cover image © Mark N.K. Saunders

Print edition typeset in 9.5/12 ITC Slimbach Std by Pearson CSC
Printed and bound by L.E.G.O. S.p.A., Italy

NOTE THAT ANY PAGE CROSS REFERENCES REFER TO THE PRINT EDITION

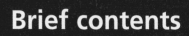

Brief contents

v

Contents

Contents

Contents

Supporting resources

Visit **www.pearsoned.co.uk/saunders** to find valuable online resources:

Companion Website for students
- Multiple-choice questions to test your learning
- Tutorials and datasets for Excel and SPSS
- Updated research datasets to practise with
- Updated additional case studies with accompanying questions
- Smarter Online Searching Guide – how to make the most of the Internet in your research
- Online glossary

For instructors
- Complete, downloadable Instructor's Manual
- PowerPoint slides that can be downloaded and used for presentations

Also: The regularly maintained Companion Website provides the following features:
- Search tool to help locate specific items of content
- Email results and profile tools to send results of quizzes to instructors
- Online help and support to assist with website usage and troubleshooting

For more information please contact your local Pearson Education sales representative or visit **www.pearsoned.co.uk/saunders**.

How to use this book

This book is written with a progressive logic, which means that terms and concepts are defined when they are first introduced. One implication of this is that it is sensible for you to start at the beginning and to work your way through the text, various boxes, self-check questions, review and discussion questions, case studies and case study questions. You can do this in a variety of ways depending on your reasons for using this book. However, this approach may not necessarily be suitable for your purposes, and you may wish to read the chapters in a different order or just dip into particular sections of the book. If this is true for you then you will probably need to use the glossary to check that you understand some of the terms and concepts used in the chapters you read. Suggestions for three of the more common ways in which you might wish to use this book follow.

As part of a research methods course or for self-study for your research project

If you are using this book as part of a research methods course the order in which you read the chapters is likely to be prescribed by your tutors and dependent upon their perceptions of your needs. Conversely, if you are pursuing a course of self-study for your research project, dissertation or consultancy report, the order in which you read the chapters is your own choice. However, whichever of these you are, we would argue that the order in which you read the chapters is dependent upon your recent academic experience.

For many students, such as those taking an undergraduate degree in business or management, the research methods course and associated project, dissertation or consultancy report comes in either the second or the final year of study. In such situations it is probable that you will follow the chapter order quite closely (see Figure P.1). Groups of chapters within which we believe you can switch the order without affecting the logic of the flow too much are shown on the same level in this diagram and are:

- those associated with data collection (Chapters 8, 9, 10 and 11);
- those associated with data analysis (Chapters 12 and 13).

Within the book we emphasise the importance of beginning to write early on in the research process as a way of clarifying your thoughts. In Chapter 1 we encourage you to keep a reflective diary, notebook or journal throughout the research process so it is helpful to read this chapter early on. We recommend you also read the sections in Chapter 14 on writing prior to starting to draft your critical review of the literature (Chapter 3).

Alternatively, you may be returning to academic study after a gap of some years, to take a full-time or part-time course such as a Master of Business Administration, a Master of Arts or a Master of Science with a Business and Management focus. Many students in such situations need to refresh their study skills early in their programme, particularly

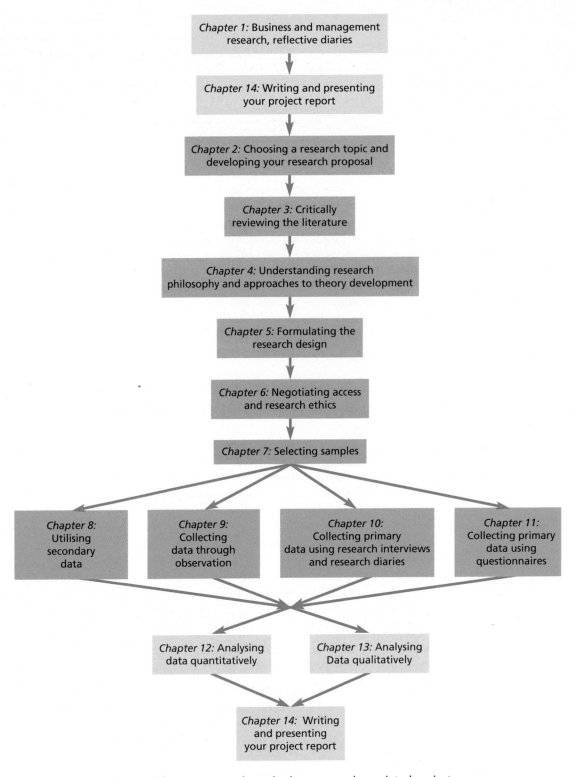

Figure P.1   Using this book for your research methods course and associated project

those associated with critical reading of academic literature and academic writing. If you feel the need to do this, you may wish to start with those chapters that support you in developing and refining these skills (Chapters 3 and 14), followed by Chapter 8, which introduces you to the range of secondary data sources available that might be of use for other assignments (Figure P.2). Once again, groups of chapters within which we believe

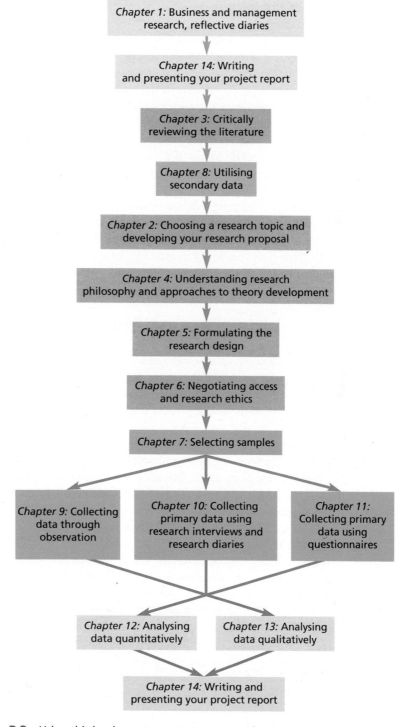

Figure P.2 Using this book as a new returner to academic study

you can switch the order without affecting the logic of the flow too much are shown on the same level in the diagram and are:

- those chapters associated with primary data collection (Chapters 9, 10 and 11);
- those associated with data analysis (Chapters 12 and 13).

In addition, we would recommend that you re-read Chapter 14 prior to starting to write your project report, dissertation or consultancy report, or if you need to undertake a presentation.

Whichever order you choose to read the chapters, we would recommend that you attempt all the self-check questions, review and discussion questions and those questions associated with the case studies. Your answers to the self-check questions can be self-assessed using the answers at the end of each chapter. However, we hope that you will actually attempt each question prior to reading the answer! If you need further information on an idea or a technique, then first look at the references in the further reading section.

At the end of each chapter, the section headed 'Progressing your research project' lists a number of tasks. Such tasks might involve you in just planning a research project or, alternatively, designing and distributing a questionnaire of your own. They all include making an entry in your reflective diary or notebook. When completed, these tasks will provide a useful aide-mémoire for assessed work (including a reflective essay or learning log) and can be used as the basis for the first draft of your project report. It is worth pointing out here that many consultancy reports for organisations do not require you to include a review of the academic literature.

As a guide through the research process

If you are intending to use this book to guide you through the research process for a research project you are undertaking, such as your dissertation, we recommend that you read the entire book quickly before starting your research. In that way you will have a good overview of the entire process, including a range of techniques available, and will be better able to plan your work.

After you have read the book once, we suggest that you re-read Section 1.5 on keeping a reflective diary or notebook and Sections 14.2–14.8 on writing first. Then work your way through the book again following the chapter order. This time you should attempt the self-check questions, review and discussion questions and those questions associated with each case study to ensure that you have understood the material contained in each chapter prior to applying it to your own research project. Your responses to self-check questions can be assessed using the answers at the end of each chapter.

If you are still unsure as to whether particular techniques, procedures or ideas are relevant, then pay special attention to the 'Focus on student research', 'Focus on management research' and 'Focus on research in the news' boxes. 'Focus on student research' boxes are based on actual students' experiences and illustrate how an issue has been addressed or a technique or procedure used in a student's research project. 'Focus on management research' boxes discuss recent research articles in established refereed academic journals, allowing you to see how research is undertaken successfully. These articles are easily accessible via the main online business and management databases. 'Focus on research in the news' boxes provide topical news stories of how particular research techniques, procedures and ideas are used in the business world. You can also look in the 'Further reading' for other examples of research where these have been used. If you need further information on an idea, technique or procedure then, again, start with the references in the further reading section.

Material in some of the chapters is likely to prove less relevant to some research topics than others. However, you should beware of choosing techniques because you are happy with them, if they are inappropriate. Completion of the tasks in the section headed 'Progressing your research project' at the end of Chapters 2–13 will enable you to generate all the material that you will need to include in your research project, dissertation or consultancy report. This will also help you to focus on the techniques and ideas that are most appropriate to your research. When you have completed these tasks for Chapter 14 you will have written your research project, dissertation or consultancy report and also prepared a presentation using slides or a poster.

As a reference source

It may be that you wish to use this book now or subsequently as a reference source. If this is the case, an extensive index will point you to the appropriate page or pages. Often you will find a 'checklist' box within these pages. 'Checklist' boxes are designed to provide you with further guidance on the particular topic. You will also find the contents pages and the glossary useful reference sources, the latter defining over 700 research terms. In addition, we have tried to help you to use the book in this way by including cross-references between sections in chapters as appropriate. Do follow these up as necessary. If you need further information on an idea or a technique then begin by consulting the references in the further reading section. Wherever possible we have tried to reference books that are in print and readily available in university libraries and journal articles that are in the major business and management online databases.

Preface

In writing the eighth edition of *Research Methods for Business Students* we have responded to the many comments we have received regarding previous editions. In particular, this has led us to fully incorporate the use of visual research methods when both collecting and analysing data (Chapters 8 to 13). In addition: Chapter 3 now includes new sections on what it means to be 'critical', and the drafting of the critical literature review; Chapter 4 contains a more developed discussion of research paradigms; the section in Chapter 6 on data protection and management has been fully revised to take account of the main elements of the European Union's General Data Protection Regulation; Chapter 7 now contains more detailed discussion about sample sizes and a new section on multi-stage sampling; Chapter 9 contains an enlarged section on ways to conduct observation using audio recordings and visual images as well as videography; Chapter 10 has a new section on the use of research diaries to collect data; Chapter 11 reflects the latest development use of online survey tools; Chapter 12 incorporates material on content analysis; Chapter 13 includes a new section on visual analysis; Chapter 14 includes advice for preparing and presenting a poster; and we have developed further the Glossary, which now includes over 700 research-related terms. New case studies at the end of each chapter have been developed with colleagues, providing up-to-date scenarios through which to illustrate issues associated with undertaking research. Alongside this we have also taken the opportunity to update examples and revise the tables of Internet addresses.

As in previous editions, we have taken a predominantly non-software-specific approach in our discussion of methods. By doing this, we have been able to focus on the general principles needed to utilise a range of analysis software and the Internet effectively for research. However, recognising that many students have access to sophisticated data collection and analysis software and may need help in developing these skills, we provide access to up-to-date 'teach yourself' guides to Qualtrics™, IBM SPSS Statistics™, Excel™ and Internet searching via the book's website (**www.pearsoned.co.uk/saunders**). Where appropriate, these guides are provided with data sets. In the preparation of the eighth edition we were fortunate to receive considerable feedback from colleagues and students in universities throughout the world. We are extremely grateful to all the reviewers who gave their time and shared their ideas.

Inevitably, the body of knowledge of research methods has developed further since 2016, and we have revised all chapters accordingly. Our experiences of teaching and supervising students and working through the methods in classes have suggested alternative approaches and the need to provide alternative material. Consequently, we have taken the opportunity to update and refine existing worked examples, remove those that were becoming dated, and develop new ones where appropriate. However, the basic structure remains much the same as the previous seven editions.

Other minor changes and updating have been made throughout. Needless to say, any errors of omission and commission continue to remain our responsibility.

As with previous editions, much of our updating has been guided by comments from students and colleagues, to whom we are most grateful. We should like particularly to thank students from University of Birmingham, and on the Research Methods Summer Schools and Doctoral Symposiums for their comments on all of the chapters. Colleagues in both our own and other universities have continued to provide helpful comments, advice and ideas. We are particularly grateful to Heather Cairns-Lee (University of Surrey), Fariba Darabi (Sheffield Hallam University), Andy Hodder (University of Birmingham), Emily Morrison (George Washington University) Phil Renshaw (Cranfield University), Jenny Robinson (Cranfield University), Céline Rojon (ITB Consulting, Bonn) and Andrew Thornhill (Shaw + Scott Ltd). Colleagues and friends again deserve thanks for their assistance in providing examples of research across the spectrum of business and management, co-authoring chapters, writing case studies and in reviewing parts of this book: Deborah Anderson (Kingston University, London), Frank Bezzina (University of Malta), Alexandra Bristow (The Open University), Vincent Cassar (University of Malta), Catherine Cassell (University of Birmingham), Zeineb Djebali (University of Surrey), Simon Grima (University of Malta), Will Harvey (University of Exeter), David Houghton (University of Birmingham), Colin Hughes (Dublin Institute of Technology), Neve Isaeva (University of Birmingham), Finola Kerrigan (University of Birmingham), Amanda Lee (University of Derby), Bill Lee (University of Sheffield), Alumuth McDowall (Birkbeck, University of London), Katherin Schwark, Andreas Paul Spee (University of Queensland), Matina Terzidou (Middlesex University, London), Catherine Wang (Brunel University), and Des Williamson (University of York).

We would also like to thank all of the staff at Pearson (both past and present) who supported us through the process of writing the eighth edition. Our thanks go, in particular, to Vicky Tubb, our commissioning editor, and Kay Richardson our online content developer for their support and enthusiasm throughout the process. We would also like to express our thanks to Andrew Muller as desk editor and Annette Abel as copy-editor.

MNKS
PL
AT
January 2019

Contributors

Mark N.K. Saunders, BA, MSc, PGCE, PhD, Chartered FCIPD, is Professor of Business Research Methods and Director of the PhD Programme at the Birmingham Business School, University of Birmingham. He is a Fellow of the British Academy of Management and member of the Fellows' College and, in 2017, was awarded the Academy's medal for Leadership in recognition of his contribution to research capacity building. He currently holds visiting professorships at the Birkbeck, University of London, University of Surrey and the University of Worcester. Mark teaches research methods to master's and doctoral students as well as supervising master's dissertations and research degrees. He has published articles on research methods and human resource aspects of the management of change, including trust and organisational learning, in a range of journals such as *Annals of Tourism Research, British Journal of Management, Field Methods, Human Relations, Journal of Small Business Management, Management Learning* and *Social Science and Medicine.* Mark is book series editor of the *Handbooks of Research Methods* (Edward Elgar) and a co-series book editor of *Understanding Research Methods for Business and Management Students* (Sage). He is co-author with Phil and Adrian of three further books, all published by Pearson. He is lead editor of *Organizational Trust: A Cultural Perspective* (Cambridge University Press) and co-editor of the *Keeping your Research on Project on Track, Handbook of Research Methods on Human Resource Development* and the *Handbook of Research Methods on Trust* (all published by Edward Elgar). Mark has also written two books on business statistics, the most recent being *Statistics: What You Need to Know* (Open University Press), co-authored with Reva Berman-Brown. He continues to undertake consultancy in the public, private and not-for-profit sectors. Prior to becoming an academic, he had a variety of research jobs in the public sector. Mark also enjoys hill walking, dinghy sailing and riding his motor-trike.

Philip Lewis, BA, PhD, MSc, Chartered MCIPD, PGDipM, Cert Ed, began his career in HR as a training adviser with the Distributive Industry Training Board. He then taught HRM and research methods in three UK universities. He studied part-time for degrees with the Open University and the University of Bath, from which he gained an MSc in industrial relations and a PhD for his research on performance pay in retail financial services. He is co-author with Adrian and Mark of *Employee Relations: Understanding the Employment Relationship* and with Mark, Adrian, Mike Millmore and Trevor Morrow of *Strategic Human Resource Management* and with Adrian, Mark and Mike Millmore of *Managing Change: A Human Resource Strategy Approach,* all published by Pearson. He has undertaken consultancy in both public and private sectors.

Adrian Thornhill, BA, PhD, PGCE, Chartered FCIPD. Prior to his career as a university lecturer and Head of Department, he worked as an industrial relations researcher and in training and vocational education. He has also undertaken consultancy and training for a range of private and public-sector organisations. He has taught a range of subjects, including HRM, the management of change and research methods, to undergraduate, postgraduate and professional students. He has experience of supervising undergraduate and postgraduate dissertations, professional management projects and research degrees.

Adrian has published a number of articles principally associated with employee and justice perspectives related to managing change and the management of organisational downsizing and redundancy. He is co-author with Phil and Mark of *Employee Relations: Understanding the Employment Relationship,* with Phil, Mark, Mike Millmore and Trevor Morrow of *Strategic Human Resource Management* and with Phil, Mark and Mike Millmore of *Managing Change: A Human Resource Strategy Approach,* all published by Pearson. He has also co-authored a book on downsizing and redundancy.

Dr Deborah Anderson is a National Teaching Fellow and an Associate Professor in Strategy, Marketing and Innovation and Kingston Business School, Kingston University, London.

Dr Alexandra Bristow is a Lecturer in People and Organisations at the Open University Business School.

Dr Frank Bezzina is Associate Professor in Applied Business Statistics and Dean of the Faculty of Economics, Management and Accountancy, University of Malta.

Dr Vincent Cassar is Associate Professor in Organisational Behaviour and Deputy Dean of the Faculty of Economics, Management and Accountancy, University of Malta.

Professor Catherine Cassell is Dean of the Birmingham Business School, University of Birmingham.

Dr Zeineb Djebali is a Teaching Fellow in Management at the Surrey Business School, University of Surrey.

Dr Simon Grima is Senior Lecturer in Risk Management and Head of the Department of Insurance, University of Malta.

Professor William S. Harvey is Professor of Management and Co-Director of the Centre for Leadership Studies at the University of Exeter Business School.

Dr David Houghton is Assistant Head of School in Marketing at the Birmingham Business School, University of Birmingham.

Colin Hughes is Assistant Head of School and Head of Department at the College of Business, Dublin Institute of Technology, Dublin, Ireland.

Dr Neve Isaeva is a teaching fellow in Organisational Behaviour at Birmingham Business School, University of Birmingham.

Dr Finola Kerrigan is Reader in Marketing and Consumption at Birmingham Business School, University of Birmingham.

Dr Amanda Lee is a Senior Lecturer in Human Resource Management at Derby Business School, University of Derby.

Professor Bill Lee is Professor of Accounting at The Management School University of Sheffield.

Professor Almuth McDowall is Professor of Organizational Psychology and Head of the Department of Organizational Psychology at Birkbeck, University of London.

Kathrin Schwark is a Junior Product Manager within the cosmetics industry and is based in Germany.

Dr Andreas Paul Spee is an Associate Professor in Strategy at the University of Queensland Business School.

Dr Matina Terzidou is a Lecturer in Tourism at Middlesex University, London.

Professor Catherine L. Wang is Professor of Strategy and Entrepreneurship at Brunel Business School, Brunel University.

Dr Des Williamson is a Lecturer in Business Strategy at the York Management School, University of York.

Publisher's acknowledgements

Text

Inc 101 Google LLC: Google LLC 103 Emerald Group Publishing: Saunders et al. (2014). Copyright © 2014 Emerald Group Publishing (https://www.emeraldinsight.com.ezproxyd. bham.ac.uk/doi/abs/10.1108/EJTD-07-2013-0073). Reproduced by permission of the publisher; p.104 SAGE Publications: Wallace, M. and Wray, A. (2016) *Critical Reading and Writing for Postgraduates* (3rd edn). London: Sage; p.104 SAGE Publications: Wallace, M. and Wray, A. (2016) *Critical Reading and Writing for Postgraduates* (3rd edn). London: Sage; p.132 Alexandra Bristow: © 2018 Alexandra Bristow and Mark N.K. Saunders; p.138 The Financial Times Ltd: Why do entrepreneurs get such a bad rap? Janan Ganesh (2017) *Financial Times* 25 August. Copyright © 2017 The Financial Times Ltd; p.140 Taylor & Francis Group: Burrell, G. and Morgan, G. (2016) *Sociological Paradigms and Organisational Analysis.* Abingdon: Routledge (originally published by Heinemann 1979); p.148 Developed from Bhaskar: Bhaskar, R. (2008) *A Realist Theory of Science.* London: Verso (originally published by Harvester Press 1978); p.151 Emerald Publishing Limited: Rutherford, B.A. (2016). 'Articulating accounting principles', *Journal of Applied Accounting Research.*, Vol.17, No. 2, pp. 118–135; p.158 Taylor & Francis: Hakim, C. (2000) *Research Design: Successful Designs for Social and Economic Research* (2nd edn). London: Routledge; p.158 Taylor & Francis Group: Buchanan, D., Boddy, D. and McAlman, J. (2013) 'Getting in, getting on, getting out and getting back', in A. Bryman (ed.) *Doing Research in Organisations.* London: Routledge, pp. 53–67 (originally published by Routledge 1988); p.161 Alexandra Bristow: HARP and all materials relating to HARP are copyright © 2014 A. Bristow and M.N.K. Saunders; p.176 SAGE Publications: Walsh, I., Holton, J.A., Bailyn, L., Fernandez, Levina, N. and Glaser, B. (2015b) 'Rejoinder: Moving the management field forward', *Organizational Research Methods,* Vol. 18, No. 4, pp. 620–628; p.186 SAGE Publications: Molina-Azorin, J.F., Bergh, D.D., Corley, K.G. and Ketchen, Jr., D.J. (2017) 'Mixed methods in the organizational sciences: Taking stock and moving forward', *Organizational Research Methods,* Vol. 20, No. 2, pp. 179–192; p.187 Penguin Random House: Naipaul, V.S. (1989) *A Turn in the South.* London: Penguin; p.194 The Financial Times Ltd: Source of extract: Warwick-Ching, L. (2017) 'Young people rely on parents and credit cards to cover costs', *Financial Times,* 20 October. Copyright The Financial Times Limited; p.195 SAGE Publications: Lee, B. (2012) 'Using documents in organizational research', in G. Symon and C. Cassell (eds) *Qualitative Organisational Research Core Methods and Current Challenges.* London: Sage, pp. 389–407; p.197 Elsevier: Dubois, A. and Gadde, L-E. (2002) 'Systematic combining: An abductive approach to case research', *Journal of Business Research,* Vol. 55, pp. 553–560; p.203 SAGE Publications: Coghlan, D. and Brannick, T. (2014). *Doing Action Research in Your Own Organisation* (4th edn). London: Sage. Useful for Action Research strategy; p.203 SAGE Publications: Reason, P. (2006) 'Choice and quality in action research practice', *Journal of Management Inquiry,* Vol. 15, No. 2, pp. 187–202; p.204 John Wiley & Sons, Inc: Eden, C. and Huxham, C. (1996) 'Action research for management research', *British Journal of Management,* Vol. 7, No. 1, pp. 75–86; p.207 SAGE Publications: Isabelle Walsh et al. (2015) 'What grounded theory is … a critically reflective conversation among scholars', *Organizational Research Methods* 1–19; p.207 SAGE Publications: Locke, K. (2015) 'Pragmatic reflections on a conversation about grounded theory in management and organization studies', *Organizational Research Methods,* Vol. 18, No. 4, pp. 612–619; p.210 SAGE Publications: Gabriel, Y. and Griffiths, D.S. (2004) 'Stories in organizational research', in C. Cassell and G. Symon (eds) *Essential Guide to Qualitative Methods in Organizational Research.* London: Sage, pp. 114–126; p.211 SAGE Publications: Musson, G. (2004) 'Life histories', in C. Cassell and G. Symon (eds) *Essential Guide to Qualitative Methods in Organizational Research.* London: Sage, pp. 34–46; p.213 Taylor & Francis: Raimond, P. (1993) *Management Projects.* London: Chapman & Hall; p.213 Hachette UK: Rogers, C.R. (1961) *On Becoming a Person.* London: Constable; p.219 Taylor & Francis: Raimond, P. (1993) *Management Projects.* London: Chapman & Hall; p.220 SAGE Publications: Tietze, S. (2012) 'Researching your own organization', in G. Symon and

C. Cassell (eds) *Qualitative Organisational Research Core Methods and Current Challenges.* London: Sage, pp. 53–71; p.238 Taylor & Francis: Buchanan, D., Boddy, D. and McCalman, J. (2013) 'Getting in, getting on, getting out and getting back', in A. Bryman (ed.) *Doing Research in Organisations.* London: Routledge Library Edition, pp. 53–67; p.242 JISC: Call for Participants (2017) Researchers page. Available at https://www.callforparticipants. com/ [Accessed 11 December 2017]; p.245 John Wiley & Sons, Inc: Saunders, M.N.K., Gray, D.E. and Bristow, A. (2017) 'Beyond the single organization: Inside insights from gaining access for large multiorganization survey HRD research', *Human Resource Development Quarterly,* Vol. 28, No. 3, pp. 401–425; p.245 Taylor & Francis: Buchanan, D., Boddy, D. and McCalman, J. (2013) 'Getting in, getting on, getting out and getting back', in A. Bryman (ed.) *Doing Research in Organisations.* London: Routledge Library Edition, pp. 53–67; p.248 Taylor & Francis: Buchanan, D., Boddy, D. and McCalman, J. (2013) 'Getting in, getting on, getting out and getting back', in A. Bryman (ed.) *Doing Research in Organisations.* London: Routledge Library Edition, pp. 53–67; p.257 Health Research Authority: Health Research Authority (2017) *Is my study research? Decision Tool.* Available at: http://www.hra-decisiontools.org.uk/research/ [Accessed 12 December 2017]; p.262 Association of Internet Researchers: Markham, A. and Buchanan, E. (2012) *Ethical Decision-Making and Internet Research: Recommendations from the AoIR Ethics Working Committee* (Version 2.0). Available at: http://aoir.org/reports/ethics2.pdf [Accessed 14 December 2017]; p.262 Association of Internet Researchers: Markham, A. and Buchanan, E. (2012) *Ethical Decision-Making and Internet Research: Recommendations from the AoIR Ethics Working Committee* (Version 2.0). Available at: http://aoir.org/ reports/ethics2.pdf [Accessed 14 December 2017]; p.262 The British Psychological Society: British Psychological Society (2017) *Ethics Guidelines for Intermediated Research.* INF206/04.2017 Leicester: British Psychological Society. Available at: https://www.bps. org.uk/sites/beta.bps.org.uk/files/Policy-Files/Ethics-Guidelines-Internet-mediated-Research-2017.pdf [Accessed 14 December 2017]; p.265 Cambridge University Press: Rowlinson, K., Appleyard, L. and Gardner, J. (2016) 'Payday lending in the UK: the regul(aris)ation of a necessary evil?', *Journal of Social Policy,* Vol. 45, No. 3, pp. 527–523; p.259 Social Research Association: Social Research Association (2001) *A Code of Practice for the Safety of Social Researchers.* Available at: http://the-sra.org.uk/wp-content/ uploads/safety_code_of_practice.pdf [Accessed 12 December 2017]; p.276 European Union: Official Journal of the European Union (2016) *Regulation (EU) 2016/679 of The European Parliament and of The Council of 27 April 2016 on the protection of natural persons with regard to the processing of personal data and on the free movement of such data, and repealing Directive 95/46/EC.* Vol 59, L119, pp. 1–88. Available at: https://eur-lex.europa.eu/legal-content/EN/TXT/PDF/?uri = OJ:L:2016:119:FULL&from = EN [Accessed 06 May 2018]; p.277 European Union: Official Journal of the European Union (2016) *Regulation (EU) 2016/679 of The European Parliament and of The Council of 27 April 2016 on the protection of natural per-sons with regard to the processing of personal data and on the free movement of such data, and repealing Directive 95/46/EC.* Vol 59, L119, pp. 1–88. Available at: https://eur-lex.europa.eu/legal-content/EN/TXT/PDF/?uri = OJ:L:2016:119:FULL&from = EN [Accessed 06 May 2018]; p.279 The Financial Times Ltd: Extracts from 'Companies need to embrace data laws regardless of burden. The General Data Protection Regulation will next year protect EU citizens' data', Sarah Gordon (2017) *Financial Times,* 14 June. Copyright © 2018 The Financial Times Limited; p.278 European Union: Official Journal of the European Union (2016) *Regulation (EU) 2016/679 of The European Parliament and of The Council of 27 April 2016 on the protection of natural per-sons with regard to the processing of personal data and on the free movement of such data, and repealing Directive 95/46/EC.* Vol 59, L119, pp. 1–88. Available at: https://eur-lex.europa.eu/legal-content/EN/TXT/PDF/?uri = OJ:L:2016:119:FULL&from = EN [Accessed 06 May 2018]; p.301 The Financial Times Ltd: Source: Extract from O'Connor, S (2017) 'Britain's gig economy is a man's world, FT.com, 27 April. Available at https://www.ft.com/content/5b74dd26-2a96-11e7-bc4b-5528796fe35c [Accessed 10 May 2017] Copyright © 2017 *The Financial Times;* p.317 British Journal of Management: Saunders, M.N.K. and Townsend, K. (2016). 'Reporting and justifying the number of participants in organisation and workplace research'. *British Journal of Management.* Vol. 27, pp. 837–852; p.346 Kingston Smith LLP: Gray, D.E., Saunders, M.N.K. and Farrant, K. (2016) *SME Success: Winning New Business.* London: Kingston Smith LLP; p.350 SAGE Publications: Carton, A.M. (2018) '"I'm not mopping floors, I'm putting a man on the moon" : How NASA Leaders enhanced the meaningfulness of work by changing the meaning of work', *Administrative Science Quarterly,* Vol. 63, No. 2, pp. 323–369; p.350 SAGE Publications: Carton, A.M. (2018) '"I'm not mopping floors, I'm putting a man on the moon": How NASA Leaders enhanced the meaningfulness of work by changing the meaning of work', *Administrative Science Quarterly,* Vol. 63, No. 2, pp. 323–369; p.352 Cambridge University Press: Kanji, S. (2017) 'Grandparent care: A key factor in mothers' labour force participation in the UK', *Journal of Social Policy,* pp. 1–20. Available at: doi:10.1017/S004727941700071X; p.354 Crown Copyright: Office for National Statistics 2014c; p.354 University of Chicago Press: Becker, H.S. (1998) *Tricks of the Trade.* Chicago, IL: Chicago University Press; p.356 The Financial Times Ltd: Source: 'EU presses tech groups to do more to tackle 'fake news' Rochelle Toplensky, FT.Com, 26 April 2018. *The Financial Times;* p.357 The Financial Times Ltd: Source: Abridged from 'Lawyers trump listeners in China's online music world', Duan Yan, *FT Confidential Research,* 3 May 2018. Copyright © 2018 The Financial Times Ltd; p.359 SAGE Publications: Tinati, R., Halford, S., Carr, L. and Pope, C. (2014) 'Big Data: Methodological challenges and approaches for sociological analysis', *Sociology,* Vol. 48. No. 4, pp. 663–681; p.362 Morgan Motor Company: © Morgan Motor Company, 2018. Reproduced with permission; p.365 European Communities: Eurostat (2018) Copyright © European Communities 2018. Reproduced with Permission; p.365 European Communities: Eurostat (2018) Copyright © European Communities 2018. Reproduced with Permission; p.366 Taylor & Francis: Hair, J.F., Celsi, M., Money, A.H., Samouel, P. and Page, M.J. (2016) *Essentials of Business Research Methods* (3rd edn). New York: Routledge; p.400 Taylor & Francis Group: Clark, A., Holland, C., Katz, J. and Peace, S. (2009) 'Learning to see: lessons from a participatory observation research project in public spaces', *International Journal of Social Research Methodology,* Vol. 12, No. 4, pp. 345–360; p.401 The Financial Times Ltd: Extract from 'Opinion FT Magazine How Facebook is changing democracy', Simon Kuper (2017) *Financial Times,* 15 June. Copyright © 2017 The Financial Times Ltd; p.408 SAGE Publications: Kozinets, R.V. (2015) *Netnography: Redefined* (2nd edn). London: Sage; p.416 SAGE Publications: Jarzabkowski, P., LeBaron, C., Phillips, K. and Pratt, M. (2014) 'Call for papers; Feature topic: Video-based research methods', *Organizational Research Methods,* Vol. 17, No. 1, pp. 3–4; p.422 The Financial Times Ltd: 'Encryption is out of sight for camera makers', Kana Inagaki (2017) *Financial Times,* 25 May. Copyright © 2017 The Financial Times Ltd; p.471 SAGE Publications: David-Barrett, E., Yakis-Douglas, B., Moss-Cowan, A. and Nguyen, Y. (2017) 'A Bitter Pill? Institutional Corruption and the Challenge of Antibribery Compliance in the Pharmaceutical Sector', *Journal of Management Inquiry,* Vol. 26, No. 3, pp. 326–347; p.475 SAGE Publications: Irvine, A. (2011) 'Duration, Dominance and Depth in Telephone and Face-to-Face Interviews: A Comparative Exploration', *International Journal of Qualitative Methods,* Vol. 10, No. 3, pp. 202–220; p.475 Academy of Management: Banks, G.C., Pollack, J.M., Bochantin, J.E., Kirkman, B.L., Whelpley, C.E. and O'Boyle, E.H. (2016) 'Management's Science-Practice Gap: A Grand Challenge for All Stakeholders', *Academy of Management Journal,* Vol. 59, No. 6, pp. 2205–2231; p.477 The Financial Times Ltd: How AI helps recruiters track job-seekers' emotions', Patricia Nilsson, *Financial Times,* 28 February 2018. Copyright © 2018 The Financial Times Ltd; p.479 Oxford University Press: Vermaak, M. and de Klerk, H.M. (2017) 'Fitting room or selling room? Millennial female consumers' dressing room experiences', *International Journal of Consumer Studies,* Vol. 41, pp. 11–18; p.485 Qualitative

Research in Psychology: Day. M and Thatcher, J. (2009) '"I'm Really Embarrassed That You're Going to Read This …": Reflections on Using Diaries in Qualitative Research', *Qualitative Research in Psychology*, Vol. 6, No. 4, pp. 249–259; p.511 Qualtrics: This screenshot was generated using Qualtrics software, of the Qualtrics Research Suite. Copyright © 2018 Qualtrics. Qualtrics and all other Qualtrics product or service names are registered trademarks or trademarks of Qualtrics, Provo, UT, USA. http://www.qualtrics.com. The authors are not affiliated to Qualtrics; p.521 The Financial Times Ltd: Adapted from 'Piety gives way to secularism and heavy metal worship', Matthew Engel, *Financial Times*, 15 Dec. 2012. Copyright © 2012 The Financial Times Ltd; p.523 Qualtrics: This question was generated using Qualtrics software, of the Qualtrics Research Suite. Copyright © 2018 Qualtrics. Qualtrics and all other Qualtrics product or service names are registered trademarks or trademarks of Qualtrics, Provo, UT, USA. http://www.qualtrics.com. The authors are not affiliated to Qualtrics; p.524 Yu and Zellmer: Yu and Zellmer-Bruhn, 2018: 347; p.525 SurveyMonkey Inc: Question created by SurveyMonkey Inc. (2018) San Mateo, Reproduced with permission; p.528 SurveyMonkey Inc: Question created by SurveyMonkey Inc. (2018) San Mateo, Reproduced with permission; p.523 Qualtrics: This question was generated using Qualtrics software, of the Qualtrics Research Suite. Copyright © 2018 Qualtrics. Qualtrics and all other Qualtrics product or service names are registered trademarks or trademarks of Qualtrics, Provo, UT, USA. http://www.qualtrics.com. The authors are not affiliated to Qualtrics; p.528 SurveyMonkey Inc: Question created by SurveyMonkey Inc. (2018) San Mateo, Reproduced with permission; p.530 The Financial Times Ltd: The tale of the Brexit referendum question', David Allen Green, *Financial Times*, 3 Aug 2017; p.540 McGraw-Hill Education: Bell, J. and Waters, S. (2014) *Doing Your Research Project* (6th edn). Maidenhead: Open University Press; p.545 Qualtrics: This question was generated using Qualtrics software, of the Qualtrics Research Suite. Copyright © 2018 Qualtrics. Qualtrics and all other Qualtrics product or service names are registered trademarks or trademarks of Qualtrics, Provo, UT, USA. http://www.qualtrics.com. The authors are not affiliated to Qualtrics; p.557 American Psychological Association: The PsycINFO® Database screenshot is reproduced with permission of the American Psychological Association, publisher of the PsycINFO database, all rights reserved. No further reproduction or distribution is permitted without written permission from the American Psychological Association; p.557 The International Journal of Human Resource Management: Brough, P., Timms, C., O'Driscoll, M. P., Kalliath, T., Siu, O.-L., Sit, C., & Lo, D. (2014). 'Work-Life balance: a longitudinal evaluation of a new measure across Australia and New Zealand workers', *The International Journal of Human Resource Management*, Vol. 25, No. 19, pp. 2724–2744; p.565 The Economist: The Economist (2017) The Big Mac Index: global exchange rates, to go. Available at http://www.economist.com/content/big-mac-index; p.583 Adapted from Eurostat (2017) © European Communities 2017: Eurostat (2017) Environment and energy statistics – primary production of renewable energies; p.586 Adapted from Eurostat (2017) © European Communities 2017: Eurostat (2017) Environment and energy statistics – primary production of renewable energies; p.587 Adapted from Harley-Davidson Inc. (2017): Harley-Davidson Inc. (2017) Harley-Davidson Inc. Investor Relations: Motorcycle Shipments; p.588 Adapted from Harley-Davidson Inc. (2017): Harley-Davidson Inc. (2017) Harley-Davidson Inc. Investor Relations: Motorcycle Shipments; p.589 Adapted from Harley-Davidson Inc. (2017): Harley-Davidson Inc. (2017) Harley-Davidson Inc. Investor Relations: Motorcycle Shipments; p.632 Developed form Bezzina and Grima (2012): Bezzina, F.H. & Grima, S. (2012). "Exploring factors affecting the proper use of derivatives: An empirical study with active users and controllers of derivatives", *Managerial Finance*, Vol. 38, No. 4, pp. 414–435; p.716 SAGE Publications: Carole Doherty, Charitini Stavropoulou, Mark N.K. Saunders and Tracey Brown (2017) 'The consent process: Enabling or disabling patients' active participation?', *Health*, Vol. 21, No. 2, p. 205. Reproduced with permission; p.719 The Financial Times Ltd: Extract from 'Staff bonuses:

there is no right way to reward employees', Dylan Minor (2018) *Financial Times*, 4 April. Copyright © 2018 The Financial Times Ltd; p.726 John Wiley & Sons, Inc: Watson, T.J. (2011) 'Ethnography, reality, and truth: The vital need for studies of "how things work" in organizations and management', *Journal of Management Studies*, Vol. 48, No. 1, pp. 202–217; p.734 Penguin Random House: Wright Mills, C. (1970) 'On intellectual craftsmanship', in C. Wright Mills, *The Sociological Imagination*. London: Pelican; p.736 Oryx Press: Day, R.A. (1998) *How to Write and Publish a Scientific Paper* (5th edn). Phoenix, AZ: Oryx Press; p.744 Emap Healthcare Ltd: Rawlins, K. (1999) *Presentation and Communication Skills: A Handbook for Practitioners*. London: Emap Healthcare Ltd; p.791 Pearson Education: Morris, C. (2012) *Quantitative Approaches in Business Studies* (8th edn). Harlow: Pearson; p.565 © The Economist (2017): © The Economist (2017), reproduced with permission; p.573 Simon & Schuster: Berelson, B. (1952) *Content Analysis in Communication Research*. Glencoe, IL: Free Press; p.578 Microsoft Corporation: Screenshot of Microsoft Excel; p.581 Oxford University Press: Kosslyn, S.M. (2006) *Graph Design for the Eye and Mind*. New York: Oxford University Press; p.595 The Financial Times Ltd: *The three ages of tax and welfare* by Vanessa Houlder OCTOBER 5, 2017; p.614 Oxford University Press: Wang, Z., Mao, H., Li, Y.J. and Liu, F. (2017) Smile big or not?, Effects of smile intensity on perceptions of warmth and competence. *Journal of Consumer Research*. Vol. 43, pp.787–805; p.624 The Financial Times Ltd: 'United Utilities hit three-year low after HSBC downgrade', Bryce Elderr (2017) *Financial Times*, 17 November. Copyright © The Financial Times Ltd; p.651 Taylor & Francis Group: Braun, V. and Clarke, V. (2006) 'Using thematic analysis in psychology', Qualitative *Research in Psychology*, Vol. 3, No. 2, pp. 77–101; p.656 John Wiley & Sons, Inc: McConville, D., Arnold, J. and Smith, A. (2016) 'Employees share ownership, psychological ownership and work attitudes and behaviours: a phenomenological analysis. *Journal of Occupational and Organizational Psychology*, Vol. 89, No. 3, pp. 634–651; p.659 Taylor & Francis Group: Dey, I. (1993) *Qualitative Data Analysis*. London: Routledge; p.664 SAGE Publications: Johnson, P. (2004) 'Analytic induction', in G. Symon and C. Cassell (eds) *Essential Guide to Qualitative Methods and Analysis in Organizational Research*. London: Sage, pp. 165–179; p.676 John Wiley & Sons, Inc: Heikkinen, S. and Lämsä, A-M. (2017) 'Narratives of Spousal Support for the Careers of Men in Managerial Posts', *Gender, Work and Organization*, Vol. 24, No. 2, pp. 171–193; p.679 The Financial Times Ltd: East Coast rail line failure leaves Chris Grayling with stark choices', Tanya Powley and Jim Pickard (2018) *Financial Times*, 6 February. Copyright © The Financial Times Ltd; p.680 SAGE Publications: Holstein, J.A. and Gubrium, J.F. (2011) 'The constructionist analytics of interpretive practice', in N.K. Denzin and Y.S. Lincoln (eds) *The Sage Handbook of Qualitative Research*. London: Sage; p.680 Pearson Education: Fairclough, N. (2010) *Critical Discourse Analysis: The Critical Study of Language* (2nd edn). Harlow: Pearson Education; p.681 Developed From Fairclough (1992): Fairclough, N. (1992) *Discourse and Social Change*. Cambridge: Polity Press; p.686 Elsevier: Clarke, J. and Holt, R. (2017) 'Imagery of adventure: Understanding entrepreneurial identity through metaphor and drawing'. *Journal of Business Venturing*, Vol. 32, pp. 476–497; p.686 SAGE Publications: Rose, G. (2016) *Visual Methodologies: An Introduction to Researching with Visual Materials* (4th edn.). London: Sage; p.686 SAGE Publications: Rose, G. (2016) *Visual Methodologies: An Introduction to Researching with Visual Materials* (4th edn.). London: Sage; p.690 SAGE Publications: Miles, M.B., Huberman, A.M. and Saldana, J. (2014) *Qualitative Data Analysis: A Methods Sourcebook* (3rd edn). London: Sage; p.694 CAQDAS: Developed from QUIC Working Paper software reviews available from the CAQDAS Networking Project and Qualitative Innovations in CAQDAS Project (QUIC) website hosted by the University of Surrey and/or software producers' websites; p.715 Emerald Group Publishing: Emerald Group Publishing (2018) Developed from advice on the Emerald website, www.emeraldgrouppublishing.com/authors/guides/write/abstracts.htm. Reproduced with permission; p.728 SAGE Publications: Charmaz, K. (2014) *Constructing Grounded Theory*

(2nd edn). London: Sage; p.746 Chaiyatorn Limapornvanich: © Chaiyatorn Limapornvanich 2018; p.791 Pearson Education: Morris, C. (2012) *Quantitative Approaches in Business Studies* (8th edn). Harlow: Pearson.

Photographs

p.3 Mark N.K. Saunders: Post-it® notes in use © Mark N.K. Saunders 2018; p.23 Shutterstock: Jaochainoi/Shutterstock; p.28 Shutterstock: Kaspars Grinvalds/Shutterstock; p.65 123RF: Jennifer Barrow/123RF; p.122 Shutterstock: michaeljung/Shutterstock; p.129 Shutterstock: John Gomez/Shutterstock; p.167 Shutterstock: Monkey Business Images/Shutterstock; p.227 Shutterstock: Scott Prokop/Shutterstock; p.233 Shutterstock: 9nong/Shutterstock; p.286 123RF: Pressmaster/123rf.com; p.294 Shutterstock: Ollyy/Shutterstock; p.332 Shutterstock: Westend61/Shutterstock; p.339 Mark N.K. Saunders: © Mark N.K. Saunders 2018; p.339 Mark N.K. Saunders: © Mark N.K. Saunders 2018; p.428 Matina Terzidou: © 2018 Matina Terzidou; p.435 Shutterstock: drserg/Shutterstock; p.496 Finola Kerrigan: © Finola Kerrigan 2017; p.497 Finola Kerrigan: © Finola Kerrigan 2017; p.503 Shutterstock: Matej Kastelic/Shutterstock; p.522 Mark N.K. Saunders: © 2018 Mark N.K. Saunders; p.555 Shutterstock: Dusit/Shutterstock; p.587 Mark N.K. Saunders: © Mark N.K. Saunders; p.624 Alamy: PA Images/Alamy Stock Photo; p.631 Shutterstock: Tobias Steinert/Shutterstock; p.637 Mark N.K. Saunders: © Mark N.K. Saunders 2018; p.684 Getty Images: designalldone/ DigitalVision Vectors/Getty Images; p.689 Mark N.K. Saunders: © Mark N.K. Saunders; p.689 Mark N.K. Saunders: © Mark N.K. Saunders; p.689 Mark N.K. Saunders: © Mark N.K. Saunders; p.700 Shutterstock: Oliver Jackson/Shutterstock; p.707 Shutterstock: Vladislav Gajic/Shutterstock; p.743 Mark N.K. Saunders: Mark N.K. Saunders; p.750 Shutterstock: Andresr/Shutterstock.

Chapter **1**

Business and management research, reflective diaries and the purpose of this book

---

Learning outcomes

By the end of this chapter you should:

- be able to explain the nature of research;
- be able to outline the features of business and management research;
- be able to place your research project on a basic–applied research continuum according to its purpose and context;
- understand the usefulness and importance of keeping a reflective diary;
- understand the stages you will need to complete (and revisit) as part of your research process;
- have an overview of this book's purpose, structure and features;
- be aware of some of the ways you can use this book.

1.1 Introduction

This book is designed to help you to undertake your research project, whether you are an undergraduate or postgraduate student of business and management or a practising manager. It provides a clear guide on how to undertake research as well as highlighting the realities of under-taking research, including the more common pitfalls. The book is written to provide you with a guide to the research process and with the necessary knowledge and skills to undertake a piece of research from first thoughts about a potential research topic to writing your project report. As such, you will find it useful as a manual or handbook on how to tackle your research project.

After reading the book you will have been introduced to research philosophies and approaches to reasoning; explored a range of strategies, techniques and procedures with which you could collect and analyse data; and considered how to report and present your research. Of equal importance, you will know that there is no one best way for undertaking all research. Rather you will be aware of the choices you will have to make and how these will impact upon what you can find out. This means you will be able to make a series of informed choices including your research philosophy, approaches to reasoning, strategies, techniques and procedures that are most suitable to your own research project and be able to justify them. In reading the book

you will have been introduced to the wealth of data that are available via the Internet, techniques for collecting your own data and procedures for analysing different types of data, have had a chance to practise them, and be able to select and justify which to use. When selecting and using these techniques and procedures you will be aware of the contribution that the appropriate use of information technology can make to your research.

The invention of Post-it® notes

The Post-it® note is one of the best-known and most widely used office products in the world. Yet, despite the discovery of the repositionable adhesive that made the Post-it® note possible in 1968, it was not until 1980 that the product was introduced to the market (Post-it® 2018). In the 1960s, 3M research scientist Spencer Silver was looking for ways to improve the adhesive used in tapes. However, he discovered something quite different from what he was looking for, an adhesive that did not stick strongly when coated onto the back of tapes! What was unclear was how it might be used. Over the next five years he struggled to find a use for his new adhesive, talking about it and its merits to colleagues whenever possible. He became known as 'Mr Persistent' because he would not give up!

Most people working for 3M know the story of what happened next and how the Post-it® note concept came about. A new product development researcher working for 3M, Art Fry, was frustrated by how the scraps of paper he used as bookmarks kept falling out of his church choir hymn book. He realised that Silver's adhesive would mean his bookmarks would not fall out. Soon afterwards the Post-it® note concept was developed and market research undertaken. This was extremely difficult as the product was

Post-it® notes in use
Source: © Mark Sanders 2018

revolutionary and was, in effect, designed to replace pieces of torn scrap paper! However, despite some initial scepticism within the company, Post-it® notes were launched in 1980. One year after their launch, they were named 3M's outstanding new product.

While your research project will be within the business and management discipline rather than natural science (such as developing a new adhesive), our introductory example still offers a number of insights into the nature of research and in particular the business and management research you will be undertaking. In particular, it highlights that when undertaking research we should be open to finding the unexpected and how sometimes the applicability of our research findings may not be immediately obvious. It also emphasises the importance of discussing your ideas with other people.

However, a word of caution before you continue. In your study, you will inevitably read a wide range of books and articles. In many of these the terms 'research method' and 'research methodology' will be used interchangeably, perhaps just using methodology as a more verbose way of saying method. In this book we have been more precise in our use of these terms. Throughout the book we use the term **method** to refer to a technique or procedure used to obtain and analyse data. This, therefore, includes questionnaires, observation and interviews as well as both quantitative (statistical) and qualitative (non-statistical) analysis techniques and, as you have probably gathered from the title, is the main focus of this book. In contrast, the term **methodology** refers to the theory of how research should be undertaken. We believe it is important that you have some understanding of this so that you can make informed choices about your research. For this reason, we also discuss a range of philosophical assumptions upon which research can be based and the implications of these for the method or methods adopted.

1.2 The nature of research

When listening to the radio, watching the television or reading a daily newspaper it is difficult to avoid the term 'research'. The results of 'research' are all around us. A debate about the findings of a recent poll of people's opinions inevitably includes a discussion of 'research', normally referring to the way in which the data were collected. Politicians often justify their policy decisions on the basis of 'research'. Newspapers report the research findings of academics' and organisations (Box 1.1). Documentary programmes tell us about 'research findings' and advertisers may highlight the 'results of research' to encourage you to buy a particular product or brand. However, we believe that what these examples really emphasise is the wide range of meanings given to the term 'research' in everyday speech.

Walliman (2011) argues that many of these everyday uses of the term 'research' are not research in the true meaning of the word. As part of this, he highlights ways in which the term is used wrongly:

- just collecting facts or information with no clear purpose;
- reassembling and reordering facts or information without interpretation;
- as an activity with no or little relevance to everyday life;
- as a term to get your product or idea noticed and respected.

The first of these highlights the fact that, although research often involves the collection of information, it is more than just reading a few books or articles, talking to a few people or asking people questions. While collecting data may be part of the research process, if it is not undertaken in a systematic way and without a clear purpose, it will not be seen as research. The second of these is commonplace in many reports. Data are collected, perhaps from a variety of different sources, and then assembled in a single document with the sources of these data listed without any explanation of what the data means. In other words, there is no interpretation of the data collected. Again, while the assembly of data from a variety of sources may be part of the research process, without interpretation it is not research. The third emphasises, as shown in the opening vignette, how despite research often appearing abstract, it influences our daily lives and creates our understanding of the world. Finally, the term 'research' can be used to get an idea or product noticed by people and to suggest that people should have confidence in it. In such instances, when you ask for details of the research process, these are either unclear or not forthcoming.

Box 1.1 Focus on research in the news

Buy-to-let investors target university cities

By James Pickford

Southampton, Liverpool and Leicester are among the English cities to have seen the biggest growth in student housing owned by private landlords, according to research that suggests buy-to-let investors are increasingly looking to university cities for better yields.

Between 2011 and 2016 the number of homes lived in wholly by students — excluding halls of residence or big blocks of student accommodation — has risen by 11,000, according to research by estate agency network Countrywide.

Southampton saw the biggest growth, with a rise of 3,428, compared with 2,560 in Liverpool, 2,163 in Tower Hamlets and 2,075 in Leicester. Other places to feature include Exeter, Brighton and Hove, Birmingham and Newcastle upon Tyne. Some cities saw a drop in student housing numbers, bringing the balance to 11,000.

The figures suggest buy-to-let investors are increasingly focusing on providing accommodation in places with swelling student populations. With student housing, landlords can typically achieve a yield that is two or three per cent higher than when renting a similar-sized home to a family…

The research identified student-occupied homes by identifying HMOs [houses in multiple occupation] which paid no council tax. Properties fully occupied by university or college students are exempt from paying the levy for local services. Average monthly room rents varied from £280 in Sunderland and £414 in Southampton, to £559 in Brighton and £752 in Tower Hamlets. There was anecdotal evidence that buyers in high-priced areas were purchasing outside their usual stamping grounds in search of higher yields. 'As the London market has slowed there's been a shift of landlords considering buying further away and considering the best yields rather than just capital growth,' Mr Morris said.

 Source: Abridged article by James Pickford, *FT.com,* 30 June 2017. Copyright © 2017 The Financial Times

Based upon this brief discussion we can already see that research has a number of characteristics:

- The purpose, to find out things, is stated clearly.
- The data are collected systematically.
- The data are interpreted systematically.

We can therefore define **research** as a process that is undertaken in a systematic way with a clear purpose, to find things out. Two phrases are important in this definition: 'systematic way' and 'to find out things'. 'Systematic way' suggests that research is based on logical relationships and not just beliefs (Ghauri and Grønhaug 2010). As part of this, your research will involve an explanation of the method or methods used to collect the data, will argue why the results obtained are meaningful and will explain any limitations that are associated with them. 'To find out things' suggests there are a multiplicity of possible purposes for your research. It is therefore an activity that has to be finished at some time to be of use. This will undoubtedly be true for your research project, which will have a specific deadline. Purposes are often stated as describing, explaining, understanding, criticising and analysing (Ghauri and Grønhaug 2010). Crucially, it also emphasises you have a clear purpose or set of 'things' that you want to find out, such as the answer to a question or number of questions.

1.3 Business and management research

Using our earlier definition of research we can define business and management research as undertaking systematic research to find out things about business and management.

Ongoing debate within journals has explored the nature and purpose of business and management research, its relevance and utility, as well as the purpose and future status of business schools where much of this research is located (Cassell and Lee 2011b). Two features, which have gained considerable support, are the transdisciplinary nature of such research and its relevance to or impact on business and management practice. The former of these emphasise that management research also draws on knowledge from other disciplines such as sociology, psychology and economics which have differing underlying assumptions. It also emphasises that the research 'cannot be reduced to any sum of parts framed in terms of contributions to associated disciplines' (Tranfield and Starkey 1998: 352). In other words, using knowledge from a range of disciplines enables management research to gain new insights that cannot be obtained through using these disciplines separately. The second 'relevance' or 'impact' feature of management research highlighted in the debate is a belief that it should have the potential for some form of practical consequences. In other words it should be relevant to and have the potential to impact upon business and management practice. Here it has been argued that such research should complete a virtuous circle of theory and practice (Tranfield and Starkey 1998) through which research on managerial practice informs practically derived theory. This in turn becomes a blueprint for managerial practice, thereby increasing the stock of relevant and practical management knowledge. Thus, business and management research needs to engage with both the world of theory and the world of practice. Consequently, the problems addressed should grow out of interaction between these two worlds rather than either on their own. This means that managers are unlikely to allow research access unless they can see the utility for their organisations or themselves.

An article by Hodgkinson et al. (2001) offers a useful four-fold taxonomy for considering rigour and relevance in relation to managerial knowledge. Using the dimensions of theoretical and methodological rigour, and of practical relevance (as discussed earlier) they identify four quadrants (see Table 1.1). Within this, **theoretical rigour** refers to the

Table 1.1 A taxonomy for considering the 'relevance gap' in relation to managerial knowledge

Theoretical and methodological rigour	Practical relevance	Quadrant
Higher	Lower	Pedantic science
Lower	Higher	Popularist science
Lower	Lower	Puerile science
Higher	Higher	Pragmatic science

Source: Developed from Hodgkinson et al. (2001)

clarity and thoroughness with which the research as reported is grounded in existing explanations of how things work. Although part of the same dimension, **methodological rigour** refers to the strength and quality of the research method used in terms of the planning, data collection, data analysis, and subsequent reporting; and therefore the confidence that can be placed in the conclusions drawn. Hodgkinson et al. argue that pedantic science is characterised by a focus on increasing methodological rigour at the expense of results that are relevant. This can sometimes be found in refereed academic journals. In contrast, popularist science is characterised by a focus on relevance and usefulness while neglecting theoretical and methodological rigour, examples being found in some books targeted at practising managers. Consequently, while findings might be useful to managers, the research upon which they are based is unlikely to be valid or reliable. Puerile science both lacks methodological rigour and is of limited practical relevance and, although unlikely to be found in refereed academic journals, can be found in other media. Finally, pragmatic science is both theoretically and methodologically rigorous and relevant.

In the past two decades, debate about the nature of management research has focused on how it can meet the double hurdle of being both theoretically and methodologically rigorous, while at the same time embracing the world of practice and being of practical relevance (Hodgkinson et al. 2001; Wensley 2011); practice being reframed recently more broadly than just the world of practice to being socially useful (Hodgkinson and Starkey 2011) and impactful (MacIntosh et al. 2017). Much of this debate centred initially around the work by Gibbons et al. (1994) on the production of knowledge and, in particular, the concepts of Mode 1 and Mode 2 knowledge creation. **Mode 1** knowledge creation emphasises research in which the questions are set and solved by academic interests, emphasising a basic rather than applied nature, where there is little, if any, focus on utilisation of the research by practitioners. In contrast, **Mode 2** emphasises a context for research governed by the world of practice, highlighting the importance of collaboration both with and between practitioners (Starkey and Madan 2001) and the need for the production of practical relevant knowledge. Based upon this, Starkey and Madan (2001) observe that research within the Mode 2 approach offers a way of bringing the knowledge created in universities together with the needs of businesses, thereby overcoming the double hurdle. Bresnen and Burrell (2012: 25) suggest a further alternative, which they consider is a 'more insidious' form of knowledge production. This form, termed **Mode 0** knowledge creation, they argue has been around since the seventeenth century. It refers to knowledge production based on power and patronage, being particularly visible in the close relationships between sponsor and researcher, for example pharmaceutical industry sponsorship of medical research.

Drawing upon these debates, it could be argued that business and management research not only needs to provide findings that advance knowledge and understanding in this subject area, it also needs to address business issues and practical managerial problems. However, this would negate the observation that Mode 2 practices develop from Mode 1. It might also result in business and management research that appears to have little obvious commercial benefit being ignored. This, Huff and Huff (2001) argue, could jeopardise future knowledge creation, because as highlighted in the opening vignette, research that is initially not of commercial value can have value in the future. Building upon these ideas, Huff and Huff highlight a further form of knowledge production: Mode 3. **Mode 3** knowledge production focuses on an appreciation of the human condition as it is and as it might become, its purpose being to 'assure survival and promote the common good at various levels of social aggregation' (Huff and Huff 2001: 53); in other words the research is of benefit to humankind rather than business. This emphasises the importance of broader issues of the wider implications of research and, we consider, links to the idea of research being of benefit to society in general rather than just business. Consequently, in addition to research that satisfies your intellectual curiosity for its own sake, the findings of business and management research might also contain practical implications, which may be far broader and complex than perhaps envisaged by Mode 2.

Tranfield and Denyer (2004) draw attention to concerns resulting from the separation of knowledge producers from knowledge users. This has introduced a schism, or what Starkey and Madan (2001) call the 'relevance gap', which has been the subject of considerable debate for more than a decade. Rousseau (2006) has drawn attention to ways of closing what she terms the prevailing 'research–practice gap' – the failure of organisations and managers to base practices on the best available evidence. She extols the virtues of 'evidence-based management', which derives principles from research evidence and translates them into practices that solve organisational problems. Research findings do not appear to have transferred well to the workplace. Instead of a scientific understanding of human behaviour and organisations, managers, including those with MBAs, continue to rely largely on personal experience, to the exclusion of more systematic knowledge. This has been discussed in articles and entire special issues of journals, including the *Journal of Management Studies* (2009, volume 46, number 3) and the *British Journal of Management* (2010, volume 21, supplement; volume 28, number 1), as well as in volumes such as Cassell and Lee's (2011a) *Challenges and Controversies in Management Research*. Within these debates some maintain that the gap between academic research and practice is fundamentally unbridgeable because management researchers and the researched inhabit different worlds, are engaged in different activities and have different research orientations, while others disagree. Hodgkinson and Rousseau (2009), for example, argue that the research–practice gap is due to more than differences in style and language, and that management researchers can generate knowledge that is both useful to society and academically rigorous.

Not surprisingly, many managers and academics perceive the gap between research undertaken by academics and management as practiced as problematic. Saunders (2011) categorises these as differences between academics' and practitioners' orientations in relation to their foci of interest, methodological imperatives, the key outcomes and how each views the other. These we summarise in Table 1.2, the contrasting orientations indicating where tensions may occur.

Table 1.2 Practitioner and management researcher orientations

Management researcher		Practitioner
Basic understanding General enlightenment Theoretical explanation 'Why' knowledge Substantive theory building	**Focus of interest**	Usable knowledge Instrumental Practical problem solutions 'How to' knowledge Local theory-in-use
Theoretical and methodological rigour	**Methodological imperative**	Timeliness
Academic publication	**Key outcome**	Actionable results with practice impact
Disdain of practitioner Desire to make a difference to practice	**Views of other**	Deprecate or ignore Belief research can provide relevant (socially useful) fresh insights to managers' problems

Source: Developed from Saunders (2011)

However, perhaps the most telling comment on the so-called 'relevance gap' is from Tranfield and Denyer (2004: 13), who assert that ignoring such a gap would be 'unthinkable in other professional fields, such as medicine or engineering, where a national scandal would ensue if science base and practice were not inextricably and necessarily interlinked'. This relates to the idea of conceptualising management as a design science rather than a social science. From the design science perspective, the main purpose of academic management research is therefore only to develop valid knowledge to support organisational problem solving. Many researchers would probably agree that the purpose of management research, like other social sciences, can be undertaken from a wide variety of perspectives involving exploration, description, evaluation, explanation and prediction. However, taking a design science mission therefore focuses upon solution-orientated research to develop valid knowledge which supports practitioners in solving business problems (Van Aken 2005). The counter argument proposes that management practice is characterised by a wide variety of organisational phenomena that are often ambiguous, and may not be suited to rule-like explanations offered by design science, and that there needs to be a balance between the different purposes of research and a need for application (Pandza and Thorpe 2010).

More recently, debate has focussed on the impact of management research and, in particular, for whom, how and when this is created. MacIntosh et al. (2017) have argued that research's impact is about the influence that it exerts on practice on both those engaged with academia (students, academics, practitioners) and those engaged in policy and practice communities such as professional bodies. New knowledge from research will result in, for example, new theories, models and frameworks, research agendas, methodologies and new curricula. This MacIntosh et al. consider is likely to act over time in one or more of four interrelated realms: changing ideas, influencing others, changing practice and changing self. The last of these highlights how you are likely to be shaped by your own research experiences.

Consequently, although increasing knowledge in a systematic way, the purpose and the context of your research project can differ considerably. For some research projects your purpose may be to understand and explain the impact of something, such as a particular policy. You may undertake this research within an individual organisation and suggest appropriate action on the basis of your findings. For other research projects you may wish to explore the ways in which various organisations do things differently. In such projects your purpose may be to discover and understand better the underlying processes in a wider context, thereby providing greater understanding for practitioners. For yet other research projects you may wish to place an in-depth investigation of an organisation within the context of a wider understanding of the processes that are operating.

Despite this variety, we believe that all business and management research projects can be placed on a continuum (Figure 1.1) according to their purpose and context. At one extreme of the continuum is research that is undertaken purely to understand the processes of business and management and their outcomes. Such research is undertaken largely in universities and largely as the result of an academic agenda. Its key impact is within the academic community, with relatively little attention being given to relevance to or impact on practice. This is often termed **basic, fundamental** or **pure research** and, although the focus may not have been on practical or commercial value, as illustrated in Box 1.2, the resultant model may be of considerable utility having impact in both academic and practitioner communities. Given our earlier discussion, it is unlikely that Mode 2 and Mode 3 business and management research would fulfil the criterion of being undertaken 'purely to understand' due to at least some consideration being given to the practical consequences of what has been found out. Through considering the practical consequences, the research would start to move towards the other end of the continuum (Figure 1.1). At this end is research that is impactful for practitioner communities being of direct and

Basic research ←————————————————————→ Applied research

Purpose:
- expand knowledge of processes of business and management
- results in universal principles relating to the process and its relationship to outcomes
- findings of significance and value to society in general

Context:
- undertaken by people based in academia
- choice of topic and objectives determined by the researcher
- flexible time scales

Impact:
- initially academic community and researcher
- may also impact policy and practice

Purpose:
- improve understanding of particular business or management problem
- results in solution to problem
- new knowledge limited to problem
- findings of practical relevance and value to manager(s) in organisation(s)

Context:
- undertaken by people based in a variety of settings including organisations and academia
- objectives negotiated with originator
- tight time scales

Impact:
- initially policy and practice community and researcher
- may also impact academia

Figure 1.1 Basic and applied research
Sources: Authors' experience; Easterby-Smith et al. (2012); Hedrick et al. (1993), MacIntosh et al. (2017)

immediate use to managers, addresses issues that they see as important, and is presented in ways that they understand and can act on. This is termed **applied research**. In our view, applied research can be very similar to consultancy, particularly when the latter is conducted in a thorough manner.

Box 1.2 Focus on management research

The value of research

As part of an article in the *Journal of Management Inquiry*, Hitt and Greer (2012) consider the value of basic research as opposed to applied research.

Within this they refer to Barney's (1991) article explaining the resource-based view of the firm published in the *Journal of Management*. They argue that Barney's article provides an example of how basic research can have considerable practical value. They note how Barney's article made the ideas of the resource-based view of the firm clear and usable to many management scholars; offering evidence of its utility in terms of the thousands of citations (the citation count according to Google Scholar was over 60,000 at the time we were writing this chapter!), its wide use in textbooks, its wide use in applied research and publications as well as in the development and delivery of management development programmes.

Building upon this, Hitt and Greer contend that such basic research both enhances the value of subsequent applied research and provides content for curricula.

Wherever your research project lies on this basic–applied continuum, and for each of the orientations in Table 1.2, we believe that you should undertake your research with rigour. To do this you will need to pay careful attention to the entire research process.

Inevitably, your own beliefs and feelings will impact upon your research. Although you might feel that your research will be value neutral (we will discuss this in greater detail later, particularly in Chapter 4), it is unlikely that you will stop your own beliefs and feelings influencing your research. Your choice of what to research is also likely to be influenced by topics that excite you, the way you collect and analyse your data and by the skills you have or are able to develop. (Similarly, as hinted by 'timeliness' in Table 1.2, in Chapter 2 we discuss practical considerations such as access to data and the time and resources you have available, which will also impact upon your research process.)

1.4 The research process

Most research textbooks represent research as a multi-stage process that you must follow in order to undertake and complete your research project. The precise number of stages varies, but they usually include formulating and clarifying a topic, reviewing the literature, designing the research, collecting data, analysing data and writing up. In the majority of these the research process, although presented with rationalised examples, is described as a series of stages through which you must pass. Articles you have read may also suggest that the research process is rational and straightforward. Unfortunately this is very rarely true, and the reality is considerably messier, with what initially appear as great ideas sometimes having little or no relevance. While research is often depicted as moving through each of the stages just outlined, one after the other, this is unlikely to be the case. In reality some stages will overlap and you will probably revisit each stage more than once. Each time you revisit a stage you will need to reflect on the associated issues and refine your ideas. In addition, as highlighted by some books, you will need to consider ethical and access issues during the process.

This book also presents the research process as a series of linked stages and gives the appearance of being organised in a linear manner. However, as you use the book you will see that we recognise the concurrent and iterative nature of the research process you will follow in the examples of research by well-known academic researchers, student research, how research is reported in the news and case studies, as well as our extensive use of cross-referencing. As part of this process we believe it is vital that you spend time formulating and clarifying your research topic. This we believe should be expressed as one or more research questions that your research must answer, accompanied by a set of objectives that your research must address. However, we would also stress the need to reflect on your ideas continually and revise both these and the way in which you intend to progress your research.

We believe that writing is an intrinsic part of developing your ideas and understanding your research. Indeed we, and our students, have found that it is not until we write our ideas that we discover where our arguments need further clarification. Often this will involve revisiting stages (including research question(s) and objectives) and working through them again. There is also a need to plan ahead, thereby ensuring that the necessary preliminary work for later stages has been undertaken. This is emphasised by Figure 1.2, which also provides a schematic index to the remaining chapters of the book. Within this flow chart (Figure 1.2) the stages you will need to complete as part of your research project are emphasised in the centre of the chart. However, be warned: the process is far messier than a brief glance at Figure 1.2 suggests!

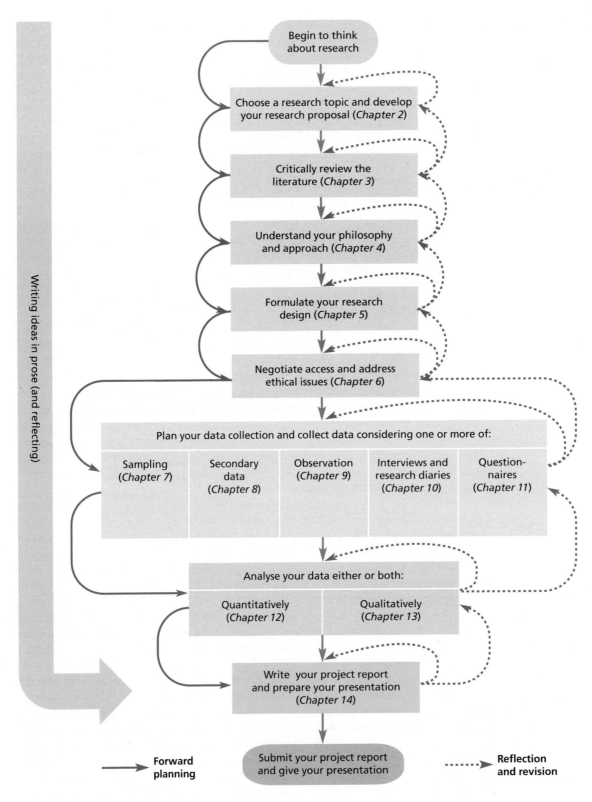

Figure 1.2 The research process
Source: © Mark Saunders, Philip Lewis and Adrian Thornhill 2018

1.5 Keeping a reflective diary or research notebook

You will notice in Figure 1.2 (page 12) that we include a series of arrows labelled 'reflection and revision'. During your research project you will find it helpful to keep a separate **reflective diary** in which you note down what has happened and the lessons you have learnt both from things that have gone well and things that have not gone so well during the research process, on a regular basis. Others keep a **learning journal** which uses a more free-flowing structure to describe, analyse and evaluate what has happened. Some researchers incorporate their reflective diary or journal into a **research notebook** in which they record chronologically other aspects of their research project such as useful articles they have read, notes of discussions with their project supervisor and other interesting conversations alongside their emergent thoughts about all aspects of their research. We have also found this helpful. The process of observing your own research practice and examining the way you do things is termed **reflection**. However, there is a more complex process incorporating interpretation as well as reflection and involving you in thinking about your experiences and questioning the way you have done things. This process, known as **reflexivity**, involves you being constantly aware of your effects on your research. You should therefore be thinking about and interpreting your role in the research and the way in which this is influenced by the object of the research; and acknowledging the way you affect both the processes of the research and the outcomes and how they have affected you (Haynes 2011; Box 1.3). (This is discussed further in Section 13.5.)

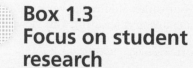

Box 1.3
Focus on student research

Keeping a reflective diary as part of a research notebook

As part of her master's research project, Amanda's project tutor had encouraged her to incorporate her reflective diary into a research notebook. Over time she began to realise that her diary entries were providing her with a useful way of not only recording her experiences, but also questioning her research practice. An extract from her reflective diary follows.

Monday 6th April 7:30 p.m.

I did my first observation today in a shop, watching and recording what people did when they came in, browsed the shoes and then, perhaps, made a purchase and left. Following what the textbook had told me, I sat as unobtrusively as possible in the corner on one of the sofas and used my tablet to make notes about the customer's and the sales assistant's behaviours. I'd prepared a checklist of what I was looking for. It all seemed to go well and, using the checklist, I

made some interesting observations about the sorts of interactions customers were having with the sales assistants when they purchased shoes. Also I feel my position was unobtrusive and I was not really noticed. What went less well was the fact I could not hear precisely what was being said. I was too far away from the sales assistant and the customer. I need to make adjustments and be closer next time, while still being unobtrusive.

10:00 p.m.

I have just watched a television documentary on retail shopping and the changing nature of such shops. I'm feeling worried that I might not have really observed all of what was happening. The programme makers had filmed the same purchase in a shop from three different views, presumably using different cameras. One camera filmed the purchase from low down and appeared to be quite a distance from the purchase. It seemed as if the camera operator was sitting on a sofa, rather like my observation. Another had filmed it more closely from behind the sales assistant so you could see the expressions on the customer's face and easily hear the conversation. The final camera had filmed from behind the customer and this time you could see the

Box 1.3
Focus on student research (*continued*)

Keeping a reflective diary as part of a research notebook

sales assistant's face; she looked really disinterested. I had never really thought about the impact of my position in the shop on what I would see and the data I would be able to collect until I saw that programme. I definitely need to think this through.

Tuesday 7th April, 7:30 a.m.

On reflection I really need to think more carefully about where would be the best place from which to observe and collect my data. I have already thought about the data I need, but given my emphasis on the interaction with customers, I think I was not in the right place to collect it for my first observation. I need to be able to see both the customer and the sales assistant and to hear what is being said and the tones of the voices. But, at the same time, I need to be unobtrusive as well so my presence does not influence the interaction. Also, there is also only one of me, so I cannot be in three places at once! However, if I remember correctly, there was a place to sit and try on shoes next to the sales desk. Perhaps that would be a better place to observe. I cannot use videography to record what is happening as, if I ask for permission to do this, it will completely change the way the people react with each other. However, I could note down what I saw and heard immediately afterwards. I'll talk to my project tutor.

You will almost certainly remember from your earlier studies the work of Kolb and of Honey and Mumford on the learning cycle (Marchington et al. 2016). This views the learning process as going through a four-stage cycle of:

1 concrete experience;
2 observation and reflection in relation to the experience;
3 forming abstract concepts and generalisations from these observations and reflections;
4 testing these concepts and generalisations in new situations.

The learning cycle emphasises that for learning to happen you need to pass through the complete cycle, as without reflection there will be no learning from experience. Such reflection is the process of stopping and thinking about a concrete experience that has happened or is happening, and the subsequent forming of concepts and generalisations, so you can apply what you have learnt from your experiences to new situations. In other words, you need to have an inquiring imagination and persistently ask yourself 'why?', 'what if?' and 'so what?' (Gabriel 2015).

Given the benefits to learning, it is not surprising that many universities require students to write a reflective essay or a reflective practice statement as part of the assessment for their research project. In order to do this well, and more importantly to enhance your learning during the research process, we recommend that you keep a reflective diary research notebook or learning journal. You should write in this frequently regarding what has gone well, what has gone less well, what you have learnt from each experience and how you will apply this learning in the future (Box 1.3). Indeed, as you read on you will find that we ask you to do this at the end of each chapter in the section 'Progressing your research project'! Questions our students have found helpful to guide them when writing their diary entries are listed as a checklist in Box 1.4. Be warned, many students forget to write in their reflective diaries regularly; this makes writing a good reflective essay difficult as much of the learning will have been forgotten!

Box 1.4
Checklist of questions to ask yourself when making reflective diary entries

In relation to each experience...

✔ What has gone well?
  • Why has it gone well?
  • So what does this mean in relation to my research?

✔ What has not gone so well?
  • Why has it not gone so well?
  • So what does this mean in relation to my research?

✔ What adjustments will/did I make to my research following my reflection?

Looking back...

✔ How could I have improved on the adjustments made?
  • Why?

✔ What key themes have emerged over a number of entries?

✔ How will I apply what I have learnt from each experience to new situations?

1.6 The purpose and structure of this book

The purpose

As we stated earlier (Section 1.1), the overriding purpose of this book is to help you to undertake research. This means that early on in your research project you will need to be clear about what you are doing, why you are doing it and the associated implications of what you are seeking to do. You will also need to ensure that you can show how your ideas relate to research that has already been undertaken in your topic area and that you have a clear research design and have thought about how you will collect and analyse your data. As part of this you will need to consider the validity and reliability (or credibility and dependability) of the data you intend to use, along with associated ethical and access issues. The appropriateness and suitability of the analytical techniques you choose to use will be of equal importance. Finally, you will need to write and present your research project report as clearly and precisely as possible, making sure you meet all your university's assessment criteria.

The structure of each chapter

Each of the subsequent chapters deals with part of the research process outlined in Figure 1.2. The ideas, methods and techniques are discussed using appropriate terms, but as little jargon as possible. Where appropriate you will find summaries of these, using tables, checklists or diagrams. When new terms are introduced for the first time they are shown in **bold** and a definition or explanation follows shortly afterwards. They are also listed with a brief definition in the glossary. The use of appropriate information technology is considered in most instances as an integral part of the book. Discussion of information technology is not software specific but is concerned with general principles. However, we recognise that you may wish to find out more about how to use data analysis software packages and so have included tutorials for the quantitative data analysis software IBM SPSS Statistics and the spreadsheet Excel™ (with practice data sets) on this book's companion website. These will enable you to utilise whatever software you have available most effectively. We have also included the Smarter Online Searching Guide to help you with your Internet searches. Chapters have been cross-referenced as appropriate, and an index is provided to help you to find your way around the book.

Included within each chapter are one or more boxes titled *Focus on student research.* These, like Box 1.3, reflect actual research projects, undertaken by students, in which points made in the book are illustrated. In many instances these examples illustrate possible pitfalls you may come across while undertaking your research. Further illustrations are provided by *Focus on management research* and *Focus on research in the news* boxes. *Focus on management research* boxes (such as Box 1.2) discuss recent research in business and management. These are normally derived from refereed academic journal articles and you are likely to be able to download the actual articles from online databases at your university. *Focus on research in the news* boxes, one of which you will have already read (Box 1.1), offer abridged versions of topical newspaper articles that illustrate pertinent research-related issues. All these will help you to understand the technique or idea and to assess its suitability or appropriateness for your research. Where a pitfall has been illustrated, it will, it is hoped, help you to avoid making the same mistake. There is also a series of boxed *Checklists* (such as Box 1.4) to provide you with further focused guidance for your own research. At the end of each chapter there is a *Summary* of key points, which you may look at before and after reading the chapter to ensure you digest the main points.

To enable you to check that you have understood the chapter, a series of *Self-check questions* is included at the end. These can be answered without recourse to other (external) resources. *Answers* are provided to all these self-check questions at the end of each chapter. Self-check questions are followed by *Review and discussion questions.* These suggest a variety of activities you can undertake to help you further develop your knowledge and understanding of the material in the chapter, often involving discussion with a friend. Self-test multiple choice questions with feedback are available on this book's companion website. Each chapter also includes a section towards the end headed *Progressing your research project.* This contains a series of questions that will help you to consider the implications of the material covered by the chapter for your research project. Answering the questions in the section *Progressing your research project* for each chapter will enable you to generate all the material that you will need to include in your project report and, where required, your reflective statement. These questions involve you in undertaking activities that are more complex than self-check questions, such as a library-based literature search or designing and piloting a questionnaire. They are designed to help you to focus on the aspects that are most appropriate to your research project. However, as emphasised by Figure 1.2, you will almost certainly need to revisit and revise your answers as your research progresses.

Each chapter is also accompanied by *References, Further reading* and a *Case study.* Further reading is included for two distinct reasons:

- to direct you to other work on the ideas and concepts contained within the chapter;
- to direct you to further examples of research where the ideas contained in the chapter have been used.

The main reasons for our choice of further reading are therefore indicated.

The new case studies towards the end of every chapter are drawn from a variety of business and management research scenarios and have been based on the case study's authors' and students' experiences when undertaking a research project. All case studies have been written to highlight real issues that occur when undertaking business and management research. To help to focus your thoughts or discussion on some of the pertinent issues, each case is followed by evaluative questions. Further case studies relating to each chapter are available from the book's companion website. This provides hyperlinks to over 75 additional case studies.

An outline of the chapters

The book is organised in the following way.

Chapter 2 is written to assist you in the generation of ideas, which will help you to choose a suitable research topic, and offers advice on what makes a good research topic. If you have already been given a research topic, perhaps by an organisation or tutor, you will need to refine it into one that is feasible, and should still therefore read this chapter. After your idea has been generated and refined, the chapter discusses how to turn this idea into a clear research question(s), aim and objectives. (Research questions and objectives are referred to throughout the book.) Finally, the chapter provides advice on how to write your research proposal.

The importance of critically reviewing the literature for your research is discussed in Chapter 3. This chapter commences by explaining what is meant by 'critical', when reviewing literature. The chapter explains the purpose of reviewing the literature, highlighting the content and possible structures. The range of secondary and grey (also known as primary) literature sources are outlined, and a range of search strategies discussed. We also offer advice on how to plan your search strategy and undertake your searches using online databases and search engines, and how to record (reference) items, evaluate their relevance and subsequently draft your critical review, acknowledging the work of others to avoid plagiarism.

Chapter 4 addresses the issue of understanding different research philosophies, including positivism, critical realism, interpretivism, post modernism and pragmatism. Within this the functionalist, interpretive, radical humanist and radical structuralist paradigms are discussed. Deductive, inductive, abductive and retroductive approaches to theory development are also considered. In this chapter we challenge you to think about your own values and beliefs reflexively and the impact this will have on the way you undertake your research.

These ideas are developed further in Chapter 5, which explores formulating your research design. Your methodological choice of quantitative, qualitative or mixed methods is considered and, within this, whether the research is exploratory, descriptive, explanatory or evaluative. A variety of research strategies are explored and longitudinal and cross-sectional time horizons discussed. Consideration is given to the implications of research design for the quality of your research findings and conclusions.

Chapter 6 explores issues related to gaining access and to research ethics. It offers advice on how to gain physical and cognitive access both to organisations and to individuals using both traditional and Internet-mediated strategies. Potential ethical issues are discussed in relation to each stage of the research process and different data collection methods, stressing the need to research ethically. Issues of data protection are also introduced.

A range of the probability and non-probability sampling techniques available for use in your research is explained in Chapter 7. The chapter considers why sampling may be necessary, and looks at issues of sample size and likely response rates for both probability and non-probability samples. Advice on how to relate your choice of sampling techniques to your research topic is given, and techniques for assessing the representativeness of those who respond are discussed. The extent to which it is reasonable to generalise from a sample is also assessed.

Chapters 8, 9, 10 and 11 are concerned with different methods of obtaining data. The use of secondary data is discussed in Chapter 8. This chapter introduces the variety of survey, document (text, audio and visual) and multiple source data that are likely to be available, suggesting ways in which they can be used. Advantages and disadvantages of secondary data are discussed, and a range of techniques for locating these data is suggested. Chapter 8 provides an indication of the myriad of sources available via the Internet and also offers advice on how to evaluate the suitability of secondary data for your research.

In contrast, Chapter 9 is concerned with collecting data through observation. The chapter examines three types of observation: participant observation, structured observation and Internet-mediated observation, as well as the use of videography, audio recordings and static visual images in the collection of observational data. Practical advice on using each is offered, and particular attention is given to ensuring that data are obtained ethically and are both reliable and valid.

Chapter 10 is also concerned with collecting primary data, this time using interviews and diaries. The appropriateness of using different forms of interview and diary in relation to your research strategy is discussed. Advice on how to undertake semi structured, in-depth and group interviews is offered, including the conduct of focus groups, telephone, Internet-mediated (including online) interviews and visual interviews. We also consider the use of both quantitative and qualitative research diaries.

Chapter 11 is the final chapter concerned with collecting data. It introduces you to the use of both self-completed and interviewer-completed questionnaires, and explores their advantages and disadvantages. Practical advice is offered on the process of designing, piloting and delivering Internet, SMS (text), postal, delivery and collection, telephone and face-to-face questionnaires to enhance their response rates. Within this we consider the use of images in questionnaires.

Analysis of data is covered in Chapters 12 and 13. Chapter 12 outlines and illustrates the main issues that you need to consider when preparing and analysing data quantitatively. Different types of data are defined and advice is given on how to categorise and code text and visual data (including using content analysis) and create a data matrix and to code data. Practical advice is also offered on the analysis of these data using statistical analysis software. The most appropriate diagrams to explore and illustrate data are discussed and suggestions are made about the most appropriate statistics to use to describe data, to explore relationships and to examine trends.

Chapter 13 outlines and discusses the main approaches available to you to analyse data qualitatively both manually and using computer-aided qualitative data analysis software (**CAQDAS**). The diverse nature of qualitative data and issues associated with transcription are considered. The use of deductively based and inductively based analytical approaches is discussed and different techniques are outlined to analyse text, audio and visual qualitative data. A number of analytical aids that will help you analyse data and record your ideas as you progress your research are also discussed.

Chapter 14 helps you with the structure, content and style of your final project report and any associated oral and poster presentations. Above all, and as illustrated by Figure 1.2, it encourages you to see writing as an intrinsic part of the research process that should not be left until everything else is completed.

Appendices and glossary

This book contains four appendices designed to support you at different stages of your research project. In the early stages, as you begin to read, you will need to keep a reference of what you have read using a recognised system, the most frequently used of which are detailed in Appendix 1. When selecting your sample you may need to calculate the minimum sample size required and use random sampling numbers (Appendices 2 and 3). Finally, when designing your data collection tools and writing your project report you will need to ensure that the language you use is non-discriminatory. Guidelines for this are given in Appendix 4. A separate glossary of over 700 research-methods-related terms is also included for quick reference.

1.7 Summary

- This book is designed to help you to undertake a research project whether you are an undergraduate or postgraduate student of business and management or a practising manager. It is designed as an introductory textbook and to support you through the entire research process.
- Business and management research involves undertaking systematic research to find out things. It is transdisciplinary and engages with both theory and practice.
- All business and management research projects can be placed on a basic–applied continuum according to their purpose and context.
- Wherever your research project lies on this continuum, you should undertake your research with rigour. To do this you will need to pay careful attention to the entire research process.
- In order to enhance your learning during your research we recommend you keep a reflective diary or notebook.
- In this book, research is represented as a multi-stage process; however, this process is rarely straightforward and will involve both reflecting on and revising stages already undertaken as well as forward planning.
- The text of each chapter is supported through a series of boxed examples. These include focus on student research, focus on management research and focus on research in the news. In addition, there are checklists, self-check questions and review and discussion questions, an assignment and a case study with questions. Answers to all self-check questions are at the end of the appropriate chapter.
- Answering the questions in the section 'Progressing your research project' for Chapters 1–13 will enable you to generate all the material that you will need to include in your project report and reflect on what you have learnt. When you have also answered the questions in this section for Chapter 14, you will have written your research report.

Self-check questions

Help with these questions is available at the end of the chapter.

1.1 Outline the features that can make business and management research distinctive from research in other disciplines.
1.2 What are the key differences between basic and applied research (and consultancy)?
1.3 Examine Figure 1.2. What does this suggest about the need to plan and to reflect on and revise your ideas?

Review and discussion questions

1.4 Agree with a friend to each read a different quality newspaper. Make a note of at least 10 articles in your newspaper that mention the word 'research'. Now examine the articles one at a time. As you examine each article, does the reference to research:
- refer to the collection of facts or information with no clear purpose?
- refer to the reassembling and reordering of facts or information without interpretation?

- provide a means of getting the reader to respect what is being written?
- refer to the systematic collection and interpretation of data with a clear purpose?
  Discuss your answers with your friend.

1.5 Revisit Table 1.2 and look at the differences in management researcher and practitioner orientations for foci of interest, methodological imperatives, key outcomes and how each views the other. For each of the continua implied by this table, where would you place yourself? To what extent do you believe that business and management research should meet the practitioner requirements? Give reasons for your answer.

Progressing your research project

Starting your reflective diary or notebook

- Find out if your university requires you to write a reflective practice statement, learning journal or keep a reflective diary or research notebook as part of your research project or research methods module.
- If the answer is 'yes', look carefully at precisely what is required by the assessment criteria and ensure

that your reflective diary or research notebook entries will enable you to meet fully the assessment criteria. In particular be sure to ascertain whether you are expected to be reflective or reflexive.

- When doing this, amend the questions in Box 1.4 to guide your diary or notebook entries as necessary.
- If the answer is 'no', we still believe it will be beneficial to your learning for your research project or research methods module if you keep a reflective diary or research notebook on a regular basis. Please use the questions in Box 1.4 to guide your reflective entries at the end of each chapter.

References

Barney, J.B. (1991) 'Firm resources and sustained competitive advantage', *Journal of Management,* Vol. 17, pp. 99–120.

Bresnen, M. and Burrell, G. (2012) 'Journals à la mode? Twenty years of living alongside Mode 2 and the new production of knowledge', *Organization,* Vol. 20, No. 1, pp. 25–37.

Cassell, C. and Lee, B. (eds) (2011a) *Challenges and Controversies in Management Research.* New York: Routledge.

Cassell, C. and Lee, B. (2011b) 'Introduction: Key debates, challenges and controversies in management research', in C. Cassell and B. Lee (eds) *Challenges and Controversies in Management Research.* New York: Routledge, pp. 1–16.

Easterby-Smith, M., Thorpe, R., Jackson, P. and Lowe, A. (2012) *Management Research* (4th edn). London: Sage.

Gabriel, Y. (2015) 'Reflexivity and beyond – a plea for imagination in qualitative research methodology', *Qualitative Research in Organizations and Management: An International Journal,* Vol. 10, No. 4, pp. 332–36.

Ghauri, P. and Grønhaug, K. (2010) *Research Methods in Business Studies: A Practical Guide* (4th edn). Harlow: FT Prentice Hall.

Gibbons, M.L., Limoges, H., Nowotny, S., Schwartman, P., Scott, P. and Trow, M. (1994) *The New Production of Knowledge: The Dynamics of Science and Research in Contemporary Societies.* London: Sage.

Haynes, K. (2011) 'Reflexivity in qualitative research', in C. Cassell and B. Lee (eds) *Challenges and Controversies in Management Research.* New York: Routledge, pp. 72–89.

Hedrick, T.E., Bickmann, L. and Rog, D.J. (1993) *Applied Research Design.* Newbury Park, CA: Sage.

Hitt, M.A.S. and Greer, C.R. (2012) 'The value of research and its evaluation in business schools: Killing the goose that laid the golden egg?', *Journal of Management Inquiry,* Vol. 21, No. 2, pp. 236–40.

Hodgkinson, G.P., Herriot, P. and Anderson, N. (2001) 'Re-aligning the stakeholders in management research: Lessons from industrial, work and organizational psychology', *British Journal of Management,* Vol. 12, Special Issue, pp. 41–8.

Hodgkinson, G.P. and Rousseau, D. (2009) 'Bridging the rigour–relevance gap in management research. It's already happening!', *Journal of Management Studies,* Vol. 46, No. 3, pp. 534–46.

Hodgkinson, G.P. and Starkey, K. (2011) 'Not simply returning to the same answer over and over again: Reframing relevance', *British Journal of Management,* Vol. 22, pp. 355–69.

Huff, A.S. and Huff, J.O. (2001) 'Refocusing the business school agenda', *British Journal of Management,* Vol. 12, Special Issue, pp. 49–54.

MacIntosh, R. Beech, N., Bartunek, J., Mason, K. Cooke, B. and Denyer, D. (2017) 'Impact and management research: Exploring relationships between temporality, dialogue, reflexivity and praxis', *British Journal of Management,* Vol. 28, N0.1, pp. 3–13.

Marchington, M., Wilkinson, A., Donnelly, R. and Kynighou, A. (2016) *Human Resource Management at Work* (6th edn). London: Chartered Institute of Personnel and Development, Kogan Page.

Pandza, K. and Thorpe, R. (2010) 'Management as design, but what kind of design? An appraisal of the design science analogy for management', *British Journal of Management,* Vol. 21, No. 2, pp. 171–86.

Post-it (2018) *About Post-it® Brand.* Available at https://www.3m.co.uk/3M/en_GB/post-it-notes/contact-us/about-us/ [Accessed 7 June 2018].

Rousseau, D. (2006) 'Is there such a thing as "Evidence-Based Management"?', *Academy of Management Review,* Vol. 31, No. 2, pp. 256–69.

Saunders, M.N.K. (2011) 'The management researcher as practitioner', in B. Lee and C. Cassell (eds) *Challenges and Controversies in Management Research.* New York: Routledge, pp. 243–57.

Starkey, K. and Madan, P. (2001) 'Bridging the relevance gap: Aligning stakeholders in the future of management research', *British Journal of Management,* Vol. 12, Special Issue, pp. 3–26.

Tranfield, D. and Denyer, D. (2004) 'Linking theory to practice: A grand challenge for management research in the 21st century?', *Organization Management Journal,* Vol. 1, No. 1, pp. 10–14.

Tranfield, D. and Starkey, K. (1998) 'The nature, social organization and promotion of management research: Towards policy', *British Journal of Management,* Vol. 9, pp. 341–53.

Van Aken, J.E. (2005) 'Management research as a design science: Articulating the research products of Mode 2 knowledge production in management', *British Journal of Management,* Vol. 16, No. 1, pp. 19–36.

Walliman, N. (2011) *Your Research Project: A Step by Step Guide for the First-Time Researcher* (3rd edn). London: Sage.

Wensley, R. (2011) 'Seeking relevance in management research', in C. Cassell and B. Lee (eds) *Challenges and Controversies in Management Research.* New York: Routledge, pp. 258–74.

Further reading

Bresnen, M. and Burrell, G. (2012) 'Journals à la mode? Twenty years of living alongside Mode 2 and the new production of knowledge', *Organization,* Vol. 20, No. 1, pp. 25–37. A clear explanation of the differences between Modes, 1, 2 and 3, as well as the proposal of a new mode, 0.

Cassell, C. and Lee, B. (eds) (2011) *Challenges and Controversies in Management Research.* New York: Routledge. This edited volume consists of a series of chapters looking at the key challenges and controversies facing business and management research at the start of the twenty-first century. The opening chapter includes a useful overview of the rest of the book and will enable you to easily follow up those aspects that you feel are most pertinent.

Davis, G.F. (2015) 'What is management research actually good for?', *Harvard Business Review,* 28 May, pp. 2–6. This adaption of Davis' 2015 editorial in *Administrative Science Quarterly* discusses the purpose of management research emphasising the importance of knowing the constituency served by the research.

Salmon, P. (2003) 'How do we recognise good research?', *The Psychologist,* Vol. 16, No. 1, pp. 24–7. This short article looks at how we can evaluate research in general looking at rigour of method and 'fit' with what is being studied, clarity and coherence of what has been undertaken and its utility.

Case 1
Investigating diversity and inclusion at OilCo

Caitlin is studying for a Master's degree in Organisational Psychology at her local Business School. Her project tutor is conducting research about diversity and organisational change with a major international oil company (OilCo.) and has asked Caitlin whether she would like to use the company as the focus of her research project. There is the opportunity to do an additional but discrete piece of research about diversity in the company. Specifically, the company would like to run focus groups with some female staff at their large London headquarters site. A focus group is like an interview but it takes place in a group format with a number of people participating. It is a well-used method within market research and also popular with management researchers because a variety of views on the same topic can be accessed at the same time. Oilco are aware that minority groups within the organisation feel somewhat excluded from career development opportunities and their new Head of Diversity and Inclusion is interested in finding out why this may be the case. Caitlin's project tutor has suggested that she can set up and run the focus groups and use the data gathered for her Master's research project. Her project tutor will offer advice on the design of the focus groups and how to analyse the data.

Caitlin is very enthused by this prospect. When her project tutor first mentioned it to her she wrote in her research diary that evening *'I am so excited about this. It was my favourite topic during the course, it is really hard to get people to take part in diversity research and here it seems to all be in place. Plus I will actually get the chance to make some real change in an actual organisation. I just hope I can make the most of it.'*

At the first meeting between the Head of Diversity for OilCo and Caitlin, the Head of Diversity set out her expectations of the work. The company will take responsibility for inviting people to be part of the focus groups and will organise the sessions at their headquarters. This will include making sure that staff have time off work to attend and sort out refreshments. Caitlin and her project tutor will be responsible for designing the content of the focus groups and Caitlin for running the sessions. Caitlin and her project tutor will retain exclusive publishing rights to the data, as long as the name of the company is kept confidential in all potential outputs, including Caitlin's project.

Once back at the University, Caitlin and her project tutor discuss how she will run the focus groups and what the interesting theoretical issues are that they would like to address. They are both interested in intersectionality theory and hope to capture some of that through the data analysis. Intersectionality theory suggests that there are a number of different characteristics upon which individuals can be discriminated against, for example race, gender and sexuality. Hence rather than focus upon one characteristic, intersectionality researchers focus upon the impact of the intersections between the different characteristics (Crenshaw 1989). Caitlin and her tutor also talk about Caitlin ensuring that she has University ethical approval for the project research, as her project tutor warns her that this can sometimes take a few weeks to come through.

When Caitlin gets home she looks at her research methods textbooks. Following advice, she decides that in choosing the participants the ideal would be to have mixed groups of staff of different ages from different parts of the country and ideally have some Black and Minority Ethnic (BAME) women as part of the sample. This will enable her to look for any interesting intersectionalities in diversity experiences. She also decides that the optimal number of focus groups would be three, and that there should be about six people in each group. She plans to audio-record the focus groups and analyse the qualitative data using template analysis, a form of qualitative data analysis strategy that she wrote an assignment on in her research methodology course. She notes all this down to discuss with her project tutor the next time she sees her.

Over the next week Caitlin spends more time familiarising herself with the literature on intersectionality. A week after the meeting at OilCo, Caitlin receives an email from the Head of Diversity. In it she says *'We are very much looking forward to the focus groups discussions. We have organised for five one-hour long focus groups to take place next Tuesday. There will be 15 people in each group. We have also organised for your findings to be presented to the Company HR Director at our regular catch-up meeting on the Monday after. I look forward to seeing you on Tuesday.'*

Caitlin is horrified by the email. She writes in her research diary, *'How could this have happened? How am I going to do five groups in a day, it will be exhausting. How will I be able to analyse all that qualitative data analysis in a week? And I haven't even filled in my ethics form yet. I might not have ethical clearance by then. What am I going to do? How can I explain to them that I can't do it? I can't see how I can do this but the worst thing would be to lose such a great opportunity. What is going to happen to my project now?'* Caitlin decides that she will see her project tutor as soon as she can to try and work out what to do next.

References

Crenshaw, K. (1991) 'Mapping the Margins: Intersectionality, Identity Politics, and Violence against Women of Color'. *Stanford Law Review,* Vol. 43, No. 6, pp. 1241–99.

Questions

1 How does Caitlin's experience illustrate the differences in approaches to research taken by academics and practitioners?
2 What, if anything, do you think Caitlin did wrong here? Give reasons for your answer.
3 What advice do you think Caitlin's project tutor will offer her about what to do next?

Additional case studies relating to material covered in this chapter are available via the book's companion website: **www.pearsoned.co.uk/saunders**.
  They are:

- Isabelle's research dilemma;
- Reporting evidence from business and management research;
- Researching buyer–supplier relationships.

Self-check answers

1.1 The features you outline are likely to include:
- the transdisciplinary nature of business and management research;
- the development of ideas that are related to practice and in particular the requirement for the research to have some practical consequence;
- the need for research to complete the virtuous circle of theory and practice;
- addressing problems that grow out of the interaction between the worlds of theory and practice.

1.2 The key differences between basic and applied research relate to both the purpose and the context in which it is undertaken. They are summarised in Figure 1.1.

1.3 Figure 1.2 emphasises the importance of planning during your research project. Forward planning needs to occur at all stages up to submission. In addition, you will need to reflect on and to revise your work throughout the life of the research project. This reflection needs to have a wide focus. You should both consider the stage you have reached and revisit earlier stages and work through them again. Reflection may also lead you to amend your research plan. This should be expected, although large amendments in the later stages of your research project are unlikely.

Get ahead using resources on the companion website at:
www.pearsoned.co.uk/saunders.

- Improve your IBM SPSS Statistics analysis with practice tutorials.
- Save time researching on the Internet with the Smarter Online Searching Guide.
- Test your progress using self-assessment questions.
- Follow live links to useful websites.

Chapter 2

Choosing a research topic and developing your research proposal

---

Learning outcomes

By the end of this chapter you should be able to:

- identify the characteristics of a good research topic;
- generate and refine ideas to choose a suitable research topic;
- express your research topic as a clear research question(s), and as an aim and objectives;
- understand the relationship between the research question(s), research aim and research objectives;
- recognise the role of theory in developing the research question(s), research aim and research objectives;
- develop a written research proposal that outlines your proposed research project.

2.1 Introduction

Many students think that choosing their research topic is the most exciting part of their course. After all, this is something that they get to decide for themselves rather than having to complete a task decided by their tutors. We will stress in this chapter that it is important to choose something that will sustain your interest throughout the months that you will need to complete it. You may even decide to do some research on something that forms part of your leisure activities!

We live in a world where we are exposed to a wide range of mainstream, online and social media. Such sources of news and information may present partial interpretations of and personal assertions about events. Media associated with a particular viewpoint are likely to attract people who are sympathetic to the views being expressed while repelling others who take a contrary view (the opening vignette outlines cross-national evidence on this issue). Rather than accepting any such interpretations and assertions at face value, as researchers we need to ask, 'What evidence do they have for saying this, or claiming that?' We may also ask, 'Why are they making such statements or claims?' Research involves obtaining, analysing and interpreting data.

Your interpretation flows from your analysis of data, taking into account its strengths and limitations. 'Research' should never be based on partial interpretations, personal assertions or pre-judged conclusions. Recognising this will be important in choosing a research topic and developing your research proposal.

Before you start your research, you need to have at least some idea of what you want to do. This is probably the most difficult, and yet the most important, part of your research project.

Digital news media, existing beliefs and bias

The *Reuters Institute Digital News Report 2017* examines a number of themes related to the use of digital news. These include how people source their news, by choosing between established news brands that have gone online, social media or other, aggregative news platforms; how people use different news media, such as polarisation (where people favour particular news channels they believe are sympathetic to their existing beliefs, such as their political orientation, and personal biases) or avoidance (news users who nevertheless avoid some news); and how people feel about the news media, such as their levels of trust or distrust about the news they use.

Based on a survey conducted in 36 countries of over 70,000 participants completing an online questionnaire, and follow-up focus group interviews held in four countries, the report highlights a number of changes including the polarisation of how different groups source their news. The younger the age group, the more likely they are to source news online and from social media; often using mobile phones. Printed newspapers are in decline generally, and television news is more likely to be watched by older age groups. Messaging apps are a growing source for finding, sharing and discussing news. Online newsfeeds from social media, searches and aggregative news platforms are now more important than going directly to a news brand website or receiving an email or mobile alert from one in many countries.

The report highlights a number of concerns. These include news source polarisation, news avoidance, fake news and trust and distrust of sources. The level of polarisation appears to be increasing in some countries although there are also large national differences. Almost 30 per cent of the Reuters sample reported that they sometimes or often avoided news. Concerns about fake news appeared to be particularly pronounced in relation to use of social media, although there are also concerns about mainstream news media. Low to moderate levels of overall trust in news media were prevalent, exacerbated by social media, the Internet and perceptions of bias in the mainstream media.

Up until now most of your studies will probably have been concerned with answering questions that other people have set. The start of this chapter is intended to help you think about choosing a research topic. If you are not clear about what you are going to research, it will be difficult to plan how you are going to research it. This reminds us of a favourite quote in *Alice's Adventures in Wonderland*. This is part of Alice's conversation with the Cheshire Cat. In this Alice asks the Cat (Carroll 1989: 63–4):

> 'Would you tell me, please, which way I ought to walk from here?'
> 'That depends a good deal on where you want to get to', said the Cat.
> 'I don't much care where', said Alice.
> 'Then it doesn't matter which way you walk', said the Cat.

Choosing a research topic is unlikely to involve you in a single moment of inspiration. Even if it does, arriving at a clearly defined research topic is still likely to be iterative, involving you in a process of formulating, clarifying and re-formulating your research idea(s) until it becomes an acceptable and practical topic. Part of this process will involve you devising one or more research questions, a related aim and set of research objectives. Once you are clear about your research topic, and the research question(s), aim and objectives that operationalise it, you will be better able to choose the most appropriate research strategy and data collection and analysis techniques. The processes involved in choosing your research topic and developing your research proposal will be time consuming and will probably take you up blind alleys (Saunders and Lewis 1997). However, without spending time on this you are far less likely to achieve a successful project. This is likely to be the case even when you have been given an embryonic research topic, perhaps by an organisation or a tutor. Whether you start with such a research topic or formulate one for yourself, it is also important to work on something that will sustain your interest throughout the months that you will need to complete it.

We commence this chapter by looking briefly and generally at the characteristics of a good research topic (Section 2.2). Choosing a research topic starts with the generation of ideas and we discuss ways in which to generate and refine research ideas in Section 2.3. Taking your research idea(s) and chosen topic and developing a research proposal will involve a number of tasks. You will need to formulate a research question(s), a research aim and a set of research objectives. You will also need to consider how your research topic fits into existing theory. Using theory may help you to clarify your research topic. It will also inform your research question, aim and objectives, and your research proposal more generally. We discuss these aspects in Section 2.4. The process of developing your research proposal will result in a written document. We discuss the rationale for and structure of a written research proposal in Section 2.5. Once approved, your research proposal will act as the guide for the rest of your research project.

Choosing your research project is a developmental exercise; not just in terms of generating and refining possible ideas and developing your research proposal, but also in terms of your self-development. Undertaking a research project will involve engaging in personal reflectivity and reflexivity. In Section 1.5 we referred to the experiential learning cycle, where personal reflection is vital to learning from experience. Choosing your research topic and developing your research proposal will involve you in a period of intense intellectual activity that will provide you with many opportunities to learn from this experience. You will be able to make a number of entries in your reflective diary or learning journal to record your actions in choosing your research topic and developing your research proposal, and the learning points that emerge for you from this process. Related to this will be personal reflexivity.

Lincoln et al. (2011: 124) define **reflexivity** as 'the process of reflecting critically on the self as researcher'. As we say elsewhere in this book, research is like going on a journey.

It is a journey that involves you making a number of decisions. Being reflexive will ensure you reflect on why you choose a research topic, why you prefer one research strategy over another, how you engage with those whom you wish to take part in your research, how you use the data they reveal to you, how you deal with any problems that confront you during your project, and so on. It will allow you to surface any preconceived ideas that you may have about your topic and what you expect to find, and help you to be aware of your own biases. Through doing this you will recognise your role or 'self' within the process of the research, remaining critically reflective and being open to new learning. This chapter is intended to encourage a reflective and reflexive approach and we would encourage you to retain these qualities as your research progresses.

Critical reflectivity may be approached not just through an introspective examination of the ways your attitudes and actions affect your role as researcher, but also in relation to the way broader social assumptions and context may influence it (see, for example: Charmaz 2017; Mortari 2015). Many preconceived ideas and personal biases have a social basis. The following vignette illustrates how recent changes in the way people use digital news media may reflect and reinforce such existing beliefs and bias. This may have consequences for the research environment in terms of the need for researchers not only to reflect on their own predilections, preconceived ideas and bias, but also on those of potential participants in a research project. Such reflections may be appropriate as you choose and refine your research topic and develop your research proposal.

2.2 Characteristics of a good research topic

The attributes of a business and management research topic do not vary a great deal between universities, although there will be differences in the emphasis placed on these attributes. Some of these characteristics reflect the need to fulfil the specification set for the research project and meet the assessment criteria. We outline these under the heading, 'Appropriateness'. Other characteristics of a good research topic will reflect the feasibility of it being undertaken and the associated developmental opportunities. We consider some of these briefly under the headings of 'Capability' and 'Fulfilment'. There may be other characteristics of a good research topic that become evident to you in relation to your own research project. Identifying these should be helpful in terms of choosing a research topic and developing your research project. You may also find it useful to discuss them with your project tutor.

Appropriateness

The scope of the research topic that you choose and the nature of the research proposal that you produce will need to meet the requirements of your examining body (such as your university, professional body or other accredited organisation). This means that you must choose a research topic and develop your research proposal with care. For example, some universities require students to collect their own data as part of their research project, whereas others allow them to base their project on data that have already been collected. Alternatively, some ask you to undertake an organisation-based piece of applied research, while others simply say that it must be within the subject matter of your course or programme. You therefore need to check the assessment criteria for your research project and ensure that your choice of topic and the specification of your proposal will enable you to meet these criteria. If you are unsure, you should discuss any uncertainties with your project tutor.

It will be important to use existing theory from the academic literature to inform your choice of research topic and in the development of your research proposal. As part of your assessment criteria you are almost certain to be asked to consider the theoretical context of your research topic in your research proposal. As we discussed earlier, using existing theory should help you to clarify your research topic and to inform your research question, aim and objectives. Using theory should also help you to develop clear definitions of the concepts that you use in your research (Podsakoff et al. 2016). We consider the role of theory further in Section 2.4 and the critical review of the literature that discusses it in Section 3.3.

Most project tutors will argue that one of the characteristics of a good topic is a clearly defined research question(s), aim and set of objectives (Section 2.4). These will, along with a good knowledge of the literature (Chapter 3), enable you to assess the extent to which your research is likely to provide new insights into the topic. Many students believe this is going to be difficult. Fortunately there are numerous ways in which such insight can be defined as new (Sections 2.3 and 2.4).

It is also important that your topic will have **symmetry of potential outcomes**: that is, your results will be of similar value whatever you find out (Gill and Johnson 2010). Without this symmetry you may spend a considerable amount of time researching your topic, only to find an answer of little importance. Whatever the outcome, you need to ensure you have the scope to write an interesting project report.

Capability

Your research topic must also be something you are capable of undertaking. Capability can be considered in a variety of ways. At the personal level you need to feel comfortable that you have, or can develop, the skills that will be required to research the topic. We hope that you will develop your research skills as part of undertaking your project, such as those related to data analysis. However, some skills, for example, learning a new foreign language, may be impossible to acquire in the time you have available.

Your ability to find the financial and time resources to undertake research on the topic will also affect your capability. This relates, in part, to the concept of feasibility (which we return to in Section 2.5 and also discuss in Section 6.2). Some topics are unlikely to be possible to complete in the time allowed by your course of study. This may be because they require you to measure the impact of an intervention over a long time period or because of their complexity. Similarly, topics that are likely to require you to travel widely or use expensive equipment or specialist software not available at your university should also be disregarded unless financial resources permit.

Capability also means you must be reasonably certain of gaining access to any data you might need to collect. Many people start with ideas where access to data will prove difficult. Certain, more sensitive topics, such as financial performance or decision making by senior managers, are potentially fascinating. However, they may present considerable access problems. You should, therefore, discuss this with your project tutor after reading Sections 6.2–6.4.

Fulfilment

Your research topic needs to be one that excites your imagination and in which you have or will develop a genuine interest. Most research projects are undertaken over at least a four-month period. A topic in which you are only vaguely interested at the start is likely to become one in which you have no interest and with which you will fail to produce your

Box 2.1
Checklist

Characteristics of a good research topic

Appropriateness

✔ Does the research topic fit the specifications and meet the standards set by the examining institution?

✔ Does the research topic contain issues that have a clear link to theory?

✔ Are you able to state your research question(s), aim and objectives clearly?

✔ Will the proposed research be able to provide fresh insights into this topic?

✔ Are the findings for this research topic likely to be symmetrical: that is, of similar value whatever the outcome?

Capability

✔ Do you have, or can you develop within the project time frame, the necessary research skills to undertake the research topic?

✔ Is the research topic achievable within the available time?

✔ Is the research topic achievable within the financial resources that are likely to be available?

✔ Are you reasonably certain of being able to gain access to data you are likely to require for this research topic?

Fulfilment

✔ Does the research topic really interest and motivate you?

✔ Will the research topic help towards the achievement of your future aspirations or career goals?

best work. It may also be important to consider your future aspirations. If you wish to obtain employment or pursue a career in a particular subject area, it is sensible to use this opportunity to start to develop some expertise in it.

It is almost inevitable that the extent to which these characteristics apply to you will depend on your research topic and the reasons why you are undertaking the research. However, most are likely to apply. For this reason it is important that you check and continue to check any potential research topic against the summary checklist contained in Box 2.1.

2.3 Generating and refining research topic ideas

Many business and management students are expected to generate and refine their own research ideas, whereas some others, particularly those on professional and post-experience courses, are provided with an embryonic research idea by their employing or sponsoring organisation. In the initial stages of their research they are expected to refine this to a clear and feasible idea that meets the requirements of the examining organisation. If you have already been given a research idea we believe you will still find it useful to read the next sub-section, which deals with generating research ideas. Many of the techniques that can be used for generating research ideas can also be used for subsequent refining.

If you have not been given a **research idea** there is a range of techniques that can be used to find and select a topic that you would like to research. These can be divided into two groups: those that predominantly involve **rational thinking** and those that involve more **creative thinking** (Table 2.1).

The precise techniques that you choose to use and the order in which you use them are entirely up to you. However, we believe you should choose those that you believe are going to be of most use to you and which you will enjoy using. By using one or more creative techniques you are more likely to ensure that your heart as well as your head is in

Table 2.1 More frequently used techniques for generating and refining research ideas

Rational thinking	Creative thinking
Examining your own strengths and interests	Keeping a notebook of your ideas
Examining academic staff research interests	Exploring personal preferences using past projects
Looking at past project titles	Exploring relevance to business using the literature
Discussion	
Searching existing literature	Relevance trees
Scanning the media	Brainstorming

your research project. In our experience, it is usually better to use both rational and creative techniques. In order to do this you will need to have some understanding of the techniques and the ways in which they work. We therefore list the techniques in Table 2.1 and then discuss possible ways they might be used to generate research ideas. These techniques will generate one of two outcomes:

- one or more possible project ideas that you might undertake;
- few ideas that relate to your interests. In this case you may want to revise the area in which you are interested, either by choosing another area or by refining and perhaps narrowing or widening your original area of interest.

In either instance we suggest that you make some notes and arrange to talk to your project tutor.

Rational thinking techniques for generating research ideas

Examining your own strengths and interests

It is important that you choose a topic in which you are likely to do well and, if possible, already have some academic knowledge. One way of doing this is to look at completed assignments for which you have received good grades (Box 2.4). Many, if not most, of these assignments are likely to be in subject areas in which you have an interest. These assignments will provide you with subject areas in which to search and find a research idea. In addition, you may, as part of your reading, be able to focus more precisely on the sort of ideas about which you wish to conduct your research.

As noted in Section 2.2, there is the need to think about your future. If you plan to work in financial management it would be sensible to choose a research project in the financial management field. One part of your course that will inevitably be discussed at any job interview is your research project. A project in the same field will provide you with the opportunity to display clearly your depth of knowledge and your enthusiasm.

Examining academic staff research interests

Your university's website will have profile pages of academic staff, which may be helpful in exploring and generating research ideas that could be of interest for your own project. These pages usually outline the subject area or areas taught by each member of staff (e.g. accounting, international management, marketing, strategic management) and are also likely to list their particular research interests (e.g. regulation of accounting standards, transnational management, pricing and price promotions, organisational learning). In many cases, academic staff provide short commentaries on their research interests offering more detail. Lists of publications and conference papers with hyperlinks to online copies may also be included. These provide even more detail about the exact nature of their research interests. Working through this information may allow you to generate ideas for your own research and guide you to some initial reading to test this interest.

Looking at past project titles

Many of our students have found looking at past projects a useful way of generating research ideas. For undergraduate and taught master's degrees these are often called **dissertations**. For research degrees they are termed **theses**. A common way of doing this is to scan a list of past project titles for anything that captures your imagination. Titles that look interesting or which grab your attention should be noted, as should any thoughts you have about the title in relation to your own research idea. In this process the fact that the title is poorly worded or the project report received a low mark is immaterial. What matters is the fact that you have found a topic that interests you. Based on this you can think of new ideas in the same general area that will enable you to provide fresh insights.

Scanning actual research projects may also produce research ideas. However, you need to beware. The fact that a project is in your library is no guarantee of the quality of the arguments and observations it contains. In some universities all projects are placed in the library whether they are bare passes or distinctions.

Discussion

Colleagues, friends and university tutors are all potentially good sources of possible research ideas. Often project tutors will have ideas for possible student projects, which they will be pleased to discuss with you.

Ideas can also be obtained by talking to people who work in, or have direct experience of, the topic area in which you are interested to develop a research idea. People who have experience of a topic area may include managers and other practitioners such as accountants, business analysts, marketing executives, human resource administrators, purchasing or sales staff as well as others. Self-employed people and small business owners may be useful to talk to depending on your proposed topic area. Members of professional groups or workplace representatives may also provide you with insights that help to generate research ideas. Your contact with such people at this early stage may be fortuitous, relying on being able to talk to someone you already know such as those in an organisation in which you have undertaken a work placement. If such people are willing to spare some time to talk to you, it may be worthwhile to help you towards generating a research idea. It is important that as well as discussing possible ideas you also make a note of them. What seemed like a good idea in the coffee shop may not be remembered quite so clearly after the following lecture!

Searching existing literature

As part of your discussions, relevant literature may also be suggested. There are various types of literature that are of particular use for generating research ideas. These include:

- articles in academic journals;
- articles in professional journals;
- reports;
- books.

Academic journal articles nearly always contain a section that reviews literature relevant to the article's topic area. Given the nature of published research, such articles are generally highly specialised, focusing on a particular aspect of a management subject. You will need to be prepared to undertake an extensive search lasting some hours (or even days) to find articles that might be helpful in generating research ideas related to your broader topic of interest. The (advanced) search facilities available to you within the online research databases that you have access to through your university or professional association will be very helpful here (Sections 3.5 and 3.6). You may also consider signing up to and using one or more of the online platforms used by academics to share their research papers. Millions of academics share pre-publication copies of their academic journal articles, research reports and conference papers on platforms such as acadmia.edu and ResearchGate. Although these copies are unlikely to be the final version for copyright reasons, they can provide access to those articles, reports and conference papers that are not available through those online databases for which your university's library has subscriptions.

Browsing journals online and using available search facilities should help you to identify possible research ideas and potential topics. The advent of the feature known as 'online publication ahead of print' or 'advance online publication' may also mean that you can gain early online access to articles in journals before they are formally published. These 'early view articles' are the final version (except for their volume numbering and pagination) and are usually made available through the specific journal's website some months ahead of being included in a specific volume/issue.

Of particular use, where you can find suitable ones, are academic **review articles**. Some journals such as the *International Journal of Management Reviews* only publish review articles – so look out for these! These articles contain a considered review of the state of knowledge in a particular topic area and are therefore likely to contain a wealth of ideas about that area (Box 2.2). These ideas will act as pointers towards aspects where further research needs to be undertaken.

For many subject areas your project tutor will be able to suggest recent review articles, or articles that contain recommendations for further research. Reports may also be of use. The most recently published are usually up to date and, again, often contain recommendations that may form the basis of your research idea. Books by contrast may be less up to

Box 2.2
Focus on management research

Corporate social responsibility

An article published in an issue of the *Academy of Management Journal (AMJ)* in 2016 reviews the development of, and literature relating to, corporate social responsibility. The aim of corporate social responsibility is defined as, 'businesses bearing a responsibility to society and a broader set of stakeholders beyond its shareholders' (Wang et al. 2016: 534). The authors of this review undertook a content analysis (see also Section 12.2) of 87 articles that had been published in

AMJ over nearly 60 years to determine trends in corporate social responsibility research on a decade-by-decade basis. They present and discuss these in this review article.

This review article also serves as an introduction to seven articles that make up this thematic issue of *AMJ*. The authors of the review article also include a discussion of possible directions for corporate social responsibility research. Referencing many of the articles from *AMJ* that they included in their content analysis, plus several others related to this topic area, this review article has an extensive list of references relating to corporate social responsibility. Any researcher setting out to explore and generate research ideas relating to corporate social responsibility would therefore need to include this review article in their first batch of reading, after conducting a preliminary search of the existing literature on this topic.

date than other written sources. They often, however, contain a good overview of research that has been undertaken, which may suggest ideas to you.

Alvesson and Sandberg (2011) report that articles published in academic management journals are predominantly based on research that finds new ways to investigate existing theoretical perspectives. They call this approach 'gap spotting', suggesting it results in incremental changes in theory. They identify a more critical and reflexive but rarer approach to research that challenges the assumptions underpinning existing theoretical perspectives and which has the potential to lead to more interesting and high-impact theories. Given the difficulties associated with designing an assumption-challenging study, it is much more likely that you will adopt the 'gap spotting' approach. We discuss this further when we consider the importance of theory in writing research questions and objectives in Section 2.4.

Searching for publications is only possible when you have at least some idea of the area in which you wish to undertake your research. One way of obtaining this is to re-examine your lecture notes and course textbooks and to note those subjects that appear most interesting (discussed earlier in this section) and the names of relevant authors. This will give you a basis on which to undertake a **preliminary search** (using techniques outlined in Sections 3.5 and 3.6). When you have located a series of articles, reports and other relevant items it is often helpful to look for statements on the absence of research and possibly unfounded assertions in some types of publication, as these are likely to contain or suggest ideas that may help you to choose a research topic.

Scanning the media

Keeping up to date with items in the news can be a very rich source of ideas. The stories which occur every day in the 'broadsheet' or 'compact' newspapers, in both online and traditional print versions, may provide ideas which relate directly to the item (e.g. the extent to which items sold by supermarkets contravene the principles of 'green consumerism' by involving excessive 'food miles' in order to import them). Please note, however, that some of these online media are only available by subscription. The stories in these media may also suggest other ideas which flow from the central story (e.g. the degree to which a company uses its claimed environmental credentials as part of its marketing campaign).

Creative thinking techniques for generating research ideas

Keeping a notebook of your ideas

One of the more creative techniques that we all use is to keep a **notebook of ideas**. This involves simply noting down any interesting research ideas as you think of them and, of equal importance, what sparked off your thought. You can then pursue the idea using more rational thinking techniques later. Mark keeps a notebook by his bed so he can jot down any flashes of inspiration that occur to him in the middle of the night!

Exploring personal preferences using past projects

One way to generate and evaluate possible project ideas is to explore your personal preferences by reading through a number of past project reports from your university. To get started you need to search through these and select a number that you like and a number that you do not like.

For each project that you like, note down your first thoughts in response to each of the following questions:

1 What do you like in general about the project?
2 Why do you like the project?
3 Which ideas in the project appeal to you?

For each project that you do not like, note down your first thoughts in response to each of the following questions:

1 What do you dislike in general about the project?
2 Why do you dislike the project?
3 Which ideas in the project do not appeal to you?

When you have completed this task, you may find it helpful to spend some time reflecting on each set of notes – for the projects you like and those you do not. By reflecting on and thinking about each list you should begin to understand those project characteristics that are important to you and with which you feel comfortable. Of equal importance, you will have identified those with which you are uncomfortable and should avoid.

This process has two benefits. Firstly, it may help you to generate possible research ideas. Secondly, you may use the project characteristics that emerge from exploring your personal preferences as parameters against which to evaluate possible research ideas.

Exploring relevance to business using the literature

There is an enormous amount of research published in business and management journals. The nature of these journals varies considerably, ranging from those with a more applied focus to those that are more esoteric. As a result, there will be many ways in which you may explore the relevance to business of ideas published in the literature. The relevance to business practice of academic business research and education remains a key issue (Box 2.3). Even more esoteric journal articles contain a wealth of ideas that may be explored for their relevance to business. Such articles can contain ideas that you may be able to translate, make operational and test in practice in a given setting, such as a particular organisation, albeit using a simpler methodology than that in the published study. The 'Discussion' section in many business and management journals routinely includes an 'Implications for practice' sub-section, which may guide you towards developing a research idea to explore the relevance of the theory in the article to a particular business setting, such as your employing organisation.

Articles based on empirical studies may also provide you with research ideas. A published empirical study may have been undertaken as a case study. It may have been based in a particular sector or industry, and it may have been based in a particular organisation or type of organisation. Reading it may lead you to think that you could undertake a similar study, albeit possibly scaled down, in a different type of organisation, in a different industry or sector.

There may be scope for you to undertake a case study that seeks to apply the findings from a large sample statistical study to a particular organisational context or type of organisation. This will allow you to test the applicability of these previous findings and to convert them into a relevant and accessible form for a particular context.

Creatively approaching the literature to convert existing work into a relevant and specifically applied study, in the ways we have described, may provide you with a rich and valuable research idea.

Box 2.3 Focus on research in the news

Where real-life crises provide valuable lessons

By Sarah Murray

It is not unusual for the opening sessions of executive finance courses to focus on markets and the role of banks as intermediaries. However, real events helped to underpin dramatically what was being taught to students during one Master of Science in Global Finance programme when it was launched 10 years ago.

"It was clear that the role of the intermediary was not what it used to be, not just taking deposits and lending," says Charmaine Cheuk, a real estate investment executive who was a student on the first MSc in Global Finance course run jointly by New York University's Stern School of Business and the Hong Kong University of Science and Technology (HKUST) Business School in 2007.

Hong Kong-born Ms Cheuk says she realised that she was watching a revolution take place as the 2008 financial crisis developed and the role of complex products such as subprime loans and collateralised debt obligations – which played a big part in the meltdown – became more obvious.

For Menachem Brenner, co-academic director of the programme, the crisis sharpened his ambitions for the programme. "It had so many lessons for us worldwide," he says. "And one of the things I saw as a mission was to bring into the programme those lessons drawn from the crisis."

Ms Cheuk remembers how the daily events added an unexpected dimension to her studies. "It was exciting. It was not just textbook in terms of what you were studying, it was literally in front of you every day."

The constant flux in the financial world has meant the content needs to be regularly updated. For example, two courses have recently been added, one in fintech and the other in behavioural finance, which combines behavioural and cognitive psychological theory with conventional economics and finance. The latter course has been able to draw on recent Chinese stock volatility to examine financial markets through a psychological lens.

"The financial market experience in China, with the recent crash in stock prices, is a great illustration of where we have a hard time as economists describing market behaviour using rational modelling," says Prof Nielsen.

 Source of extract: Murray, Sarah (2017) 'Where real-life crises provide valuable lessons', *Financial Times*, 19 June. Copyright 2017 The Financial Times Limited

Relevance trees

Relevance trees may also prove useful in generating research topics. In this instance, their use is similar to that of mind mapping (Buzan 2011) in which you start with a broad concept from which you generate further (usually more specific) topics. Each of these topics forms a separate branch from which you can generate further, more detailed sub-branches. As you proceed down the sub-branches more ideas are generated and recorded. These can then be examined and a number selected and combined to provide a research idea. This technique is discussed in more detail in Section 3.5 (and illustrated in Box 3.6).

Brainstorming

The technique of **brainstorming** (Box 2.4), taught as a problem-solving technique on many business and management courses, can also be used to generate and refine research ideas. It is best undertaken with a group of people, although you can brainstorm on your own. Brainstorming involves a number of stages:

1 *Defining the problem.* This will focus on the sorts of ideas you are interested in – as precisely as possible. In the early stages of formulating a topic this may be as vague as, 'I am interested in marketing but don't know what to do for my research topic'.
2 *Asking for suggestions.* These will relate to the problem.
3 *Recording suggestions.* As you record these you will need to observe the following rules:
   - No suggestion should be criticised or evaluated in any way before all ideas have been considered.
   - All suggestions, however wild, should be recorded and considered.
   - As many suggestions as possible should be recorded.
4 *Reviewing suggestions.* You will seek to explore what is meant by each as you review these.
5 *Analysing suggestions.* Work through the list of ideas and decide which appeal to you most as research ideas and why.

Box 2.4
Focus on student research

Brainstorming

George's main interest was football. In his university city he worked part-time in the retail store of the local football club and thought he would like to carry out his research project in this setting.

When he finished university he wanted to work in marketing, preferably for a sports goods manufacturer or retailer. He had examined his own strengths and discovered that his highest marks were in marketing. He wanted to do his research project on some aspect of marketing, preferably linked to the football club, but had no real research idea. He asked three friends, all taking business management degrees, to help him brainstorm the problem.

George began by explaining the problem in some detail. At first the suggestions emerged slowly. He noted them down on some flipchart sheets. Soon a number of sheets of paper were covered with suggestions and pinned up around the room. George counted these and discovered there were over 100.

Reviewing individual suggestions produced nothing that any of the group felt to be of sufficient merit for a research project. However, George recalled an article they had been asked to read based on a case study of an English Premier League football club (Ogbonna and Harris 2014). He had found this interesting because of its subject. He recalled that it was about organisational culture being perpetuated within organisations that have a long history of success, and stakeholder groups such as football fans who have a strong sense of identity.

George's recollections of this article encouraged the group to discuss their suggestions further. Combining a number of suggestions from the flipchart sheets with their discussion about organisational cultural perpetuation, George noted a possible research idea as: 'The impact of factors that perpetuate organisational culture on the development of marketing strategies – help or hindrance?'

George thought this idea could be based on his local football club.

George arranged to see his project tutor to discuss how to refine the idea they had just generated.

Refining research topic ideas

The Delphi technique

An approach that our students have found useful to refine their research ideas is the **Delphi technique** (Box 2.5). The standard Delphi method involves a researcher using a purposive sample of participants who are knowledgeable about the topic to be discussed; asking these participants to write down their answers anonymously to some initial questions to gather their opinions and perceptions; analysing these answers thematically; using this to generate a second round of questions to gain participants' feedback to the initial responses; repeating this process until a consensus is reached about the topic in order to inform decision-making, policy or practice. The initial round of questions is likely to be 'open' or 'semi-open', while subsequent rounds of questions are likely to be more focussed and structured. (Brady 2015).

One use of this technique, known as 'Policy Delphi', draws on these characteristics albeit in an informal and face-to-face way. Its intention is to encourage the identification of refinements or alternatives to an initial research idea. You use a small purposive sample (Section 7.3) of your classmates or colleagues who have some subject knowledge about and interest in your initial research idea, to generate related ideas, evaluate these and perhaps to arrive at a consensus around a specific research idea (Paraskevas and Saunders 2012). To use this technique you need:

1 to brief the members of the group about the initial research idea (they can make notes if they wish);
2 to encourage group members to seek clarification and more information as appropriate at the end of the briefing;

Box 2.5
Focus on student research

Using a Delphi Group

Tim explained to the group that his research idea was concerned with understanding the decision-making processes associated with mortgage applications and loan advances. His briefing to the three other group members, and the questions that they asked him, considered aspects such as:

- the particular situation of potential first-time house buyers;
- the way in which the nature of contact between potential borrowers and financial institutions might influence decision making.

The group then moved on to generate a number of more specific research ideas, among which were the following:

- the effect of being a first-time house purchaser on mortgage application decision making;
- the effect of websites and mobile apps that facilitate property searching and links to mortgage specialists on decision making;
- the effect of interpersonal contact on mortgage decisions;
- the attributes that potential applicants look for in financial institutions operating in the mortgage market.

These ideas were considered and commented on by all the group members. At the end of the second cycle Tim had, with the other students' agreement, refined his research idea to:

- an evaluation of the factors that influence potential first-time buyers' choice of lending institution.

Tim now needed to pursue this idea by undertaking a preliminary search of the literature.

3 to ask each member of the group, including the originator of the research idea, to generate independently up to three alternative research ideas based on the initial idea (they
can also be asked to provide a justification for their specific ideas);

4 to collect the research ideas in an unedited and non-attributable form and to distribute
them to all members of the group to reflect on;

5 to encourage group members to comment on each research idea, including giving reasons for their opinions;

6 a second cycle of steps 2 to 5 to encourage further refinements or new options in light
of what others have said during the first cycle;

7 subsequent cycles of the process until an outcome is reached. This may be a consensus
around a particular research idea. It may occur when saturation occurs – no further ideas
are forthcoming. It may also occur when participants become tired and less productive.
In practice, three cycles of this technique are likely to produce an effective outcome.

This process works well, not least because people enjoy trying to help one another. In
addition, it is very useful in forming cohesive groups.

The preliminary inquiry

Having generated a research idea you will need to refine it to choose a suitable topic and
express it as a clear research question(s), an aim and objectives. This will involve searching for and evaluating literature and other related sources. Even if you searched the literature to generate your initial research idea, it is likely to be necessary to conduct another
search of it in order to refine this idea into a workable research question. Once you have
your initial research idea you can re-visit the literature with a much clearer focus to understand how this helps you to refine your research idea, choose your topic and to develop
the research question(s), aim and set of objectives (Section 2.4).

This search activity to refine, focus and operationalise your initial research idea into a
suitable research topic and then into a research question(s), aim and objectives involves
a **preliminary inquiry** or initial inquiry. This may lead to the first iteration of your critical
literature review, or help to inform it (Figure 3.1). It is instructive to see how researchers
make the transition from initial ideas to actual research questions, and how their preliminary inquiry facilitates this. Unfortunately, because journal articles are word limited and
the 'methods' section of an article only describes the research methodology and techniques
used in the actual study, research is often presented as an unproblematic (and not a
'messy') process. While it is therefore helpful to locate articles that show how a preliminary inquiry was conducted to refine research ideas and develop research questions it is
not easy to find these!

For some researchers the preliminary inquiry may include informal discussions with
people who have personal experience of and knowledge about your research ideas. It may
also involve **shadowing** employees who are likely to be important in your research and
who may therefore be able to provide some initial insights. If you are planning on undertaking your research within an organisation, it is also important to gain a good understanding of your host organisation (McDonald 2005).

At this stage you should test your ideas using the checklist in Box 2.1 and, where necessary, amend them. It may be that after a preliminary inquiry, or discussing your ideas with
colleagues, you decide that the research idea is no longer feasible in the form in which
you first envisaged it. If this is the case, do not be too downhearted. It is far better to revise
your research ideas at this stage than to have to do it later, when you have undertaken far
more work.

Integrating ideas

Another, or complementary, way to refine, focus and operationalise your initial research idea into a suitable topic and then into a research question(s), aim and objectives is to integrate ideas generated using a number of different techniques. Integrating ideas will help your research to have a clear purpose and direction. Jankowicz (2005: 34–6) offers an integrative process that our students have found most useful. This he terms 'working up and narrowing down'. It involves classifying each research idea first into its area, then its field, and finally the precise aspect in which you are interested. These represent an increasingly detailed description of the research idea. For example, your initial area, based on examining your coursework, might be accountancy. After searching through relevant journal articles and holding a discussion with colleagues this might become more focused on the field of financial accounting methods. After a further literature search and reading, the use of a Delphi technique and discussion with your project tutor you decide to focus on the aspect of activity-based costing.

Refining topics given by your employing organisation

As a part-time student, your manager may provide you with an embryonic research topic. This may be something that affects your work and in which you have an interest. You may have discussed this with your manager and relish the opportunity to tackle this topic.

It may, however, be a topic in which you are not particularly interested. In this case you will have to weigh the advantage of doing something useful to the organisation against the disadvantage of a potential lack of personal motivation. You therefore need to achieve a balance. Often the research project your manager wishes you to undertake is larger than is appropriate for your course. In such cases, it may be possible to complete both by isolating an element of the larger organisational project that you find interesting and treating this as the project for your course.

One of our students was asked to do a preliminary investigation of the strengths and weaknesses of her organisation's pay system and then to recommend consultants to design and implement a new system. She was not particularly interested in this project. However, she was considering becoming a freelance personnel consultant. Therefore, for her research project she decided to study the decision-making process in relation to the appointment of personnel consultants. Her organisation's decision on which consultant to appoint, and why this decision was taken, proved to be a useful case study against which to compare management decision-making theory.

In this event you would write a larger report for your organisation and a part of it for your project report. Section 14.4 offers some guidance on writing two separate reports for different audiences.

Other problems may involve your political relationships in the organisation. For example, there will be those keen to commission a project which justifies their particular policy position and see you as a useful pawn in advancing their political interests. It is important to have a clear stance with regard to what you want to do, and your personal objectives, and to stick to this.

A further potential problem may be one of your own making: to promise to deliver research outcomes to your employer and not do so.

Conducting research in your own organisation is also likely to be problematic because of your role as an internal researcher (Tietze 2012). We return to discuss a range of issues related to this role in Section 5.12.

2.4 Developing your research proposal

You will know when the process of generating and refining ideas is complete as you will be able to say, 'I'd like to do some research on ...'. At this point, you will have chosen your research topic based on a clearly defined research idea! Obviously there is still a big gap between this and being able to start serious work on your research project. You will, however, be in position to develop your research proposal, commencing with expressing your research topic as a research question(s), related research aim and set of research objectives. We now discuss writing research questions, research aims and research objectives, the relationship between these, and the role of theory in their development.

Expressing your topic as a research question(s)

It will be important for you to express your research topic as a clearly defined **research question** before commencing the research process. As a student, you are likely to be required to include a research question in your written research proposal (Section 2.5). The importance of creating a clearly defined research question cannot be overemphasised. A research question will allow you to say what the issue or problem is that you wish to study and what your research project will seek to find out, explain and answer. One of the key criteria of your research success will be whether you have developed a set of clear conclusions from the data you have collected. The extent to which you can do that will be determined largely by the clarity with which you have posed your research question (Box 2.6).

This research question will be at the centre of your research project. It will influence your choice of literature to review, your research design, the access you need to negotiate, your approach to sampling, your choice of data collection and analysis methods, and help to shape the way in which you write your project report. This overarching research question is sometimes referred to as a 'general research question', 'general focus research question' or 'central research question'. It will also be used to generate a set of more detailed research objectives or investigative questions to guide your research, discussed later.

However, it is also important to recognise that some research approaches and research strategies start off in a more exploratory and emergent direction (Chapter 5). For a researcher undertaking this type of research, her or his finalised research question may only emerge during the process of data collection and analysis as she or he discovers the

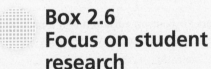

Box 2.6
Focus on student research

Defining the research question

Imran was studying for a BSc in Business Management and undertaking his placement year in an advanced consumer electronics company. When he first joined the company he was surprised to note that the company's business strategy, which was announced in the company newsletter, seemed to be inconsistent with what Imran knew of the product market.

Imran had become particularly interested in corporate strategy in his degree. He was familiar with some of the literature which suggested that corporate strategy should be linked to the general external environment in which the organisation operated. He wanted to do some research on corporate strategy in his organisation for his research project.

After talking this over with his project tutor, Imran decided on the following research question: 'Why does [organisation's name]'s corporate strategy not seem to reflect the major factors in the external operating environment?'

exact focus of her or his research project and refines its direction. Such an approach is open ended and time consuming and may not be practical where you are undertaking a time-limited research project. Despite this, some of the mainly qualitative strategies (discussed in Chapter 5), including Ethnographic Studies and Grounded Theory, are exploratory and emergent and will often lead you, where you use one of these, to refine your initial research question and project as you progress. Most tutors will say here that it is part of the process to refine your original research question as your project progresses to reflect the direction of your emerging research. It is always advisable to discuss such developments with your project tutor! The key point is that if you use such a research approach it is still important to define a clear research question at the outset of your project to focus your research, even if you then refine your research question accordingly.

Defining research questions, rather like generating research ideas (Section 2.3), is not a straightforward matter. It is important that the question is sufficiently involved to generate the sort of project that is consistent with the standards expected of you (Box 2.1). A question that only prompts a descriptive answer – for example, 'What is the proportion of graduates entering the UK civil service who attended top universities?' – is far easier to answer than: 'Why are graduates from top universities more likely to enter the UK civil service than graduates from other universities?' However, answering the first question is unlikely to satisfy your examining body's requirements as it only needs description.

Questions may be divided into ones that are exploratory, descriptive, explanatory or evaluative (Section 5.7). Any research question you ask is likely to begin with or include either 'What', 'When', 'Where', 'Who', 'Why', or 'How'. Each of these will lead to an answer that is partly descriptive and sometimes entirely descriptive, such as: 'How much did the marketing campaign for the new range of products cost?' Exploratory questions are likely to begin with 'How' or 'What'. For example, 'How has the corporate rebranding strategy affected consumer attitudes?' Questions that seek explanations will either commence with 'Why' or contain this word within the question. For example, a question may ask customers what they think about a new product and why they like or dislike it. Questions that are evaluative are also likely to begin with 'How' or 'What' but unlike the 'How much...?' or 'How has...?' questions, an evaluative question might ask, 'How effective was the marketing campaign for the new range of products?' Another way of wording this type of question might be, 'To what extent was the marketing campaign effective and why?' We discuss further the relationship between 'How', 'What' and 'Why' questions later in this section.

While some questions may be too simple, it is perhaps more likely that you might fall into the trap of asking research questions that are too difficult. The question cited earlier, 'Why are graduates from top universities more likely to enter the UK civil service than graduates from other universities?', is a case in point. It would probably be very difficult to gain sufficient access to the inner portals of the civil service to get a good grasp of the subtle 'unofficial' processes that go on at staff selection which may favour one type of candidate over another. Over-reaching yourself in the definition of research questions is a danger.

Clough and Nutbrown (2012) use what they call the '**Goldilocks test**' to decide if research questions are either 'too big', 'too small', 'too hot' or 'just right'. Those that are too big probably need significant research funding because they demand too many resources. Questions that are too small are likely to be of insufficient substance, while those that are too 'hot' may be so because of sensitivities that might be aroused as a result of doing the research. This may be because of the timing of the research or the many other reasons that could upset key people who have a role to play, either directly or indirectly, in the research context. Research questions that have been written to take into account

Table 2.2 Examples of research ideas and resulting general focus research questions

Research idea	Research question
Media campaign following product recalls	How effective is a media campaign designed to increase consumer trust in [company name] following a series of product recalls?
Graduate recruitment via the Internet	To what extent and in what type of context is Internet-based recruitment and selection of graduates effective and why?
Supermarket coupons as a promotional device	In what ways does the issue of coupons at supermarket checkouts affect buyer behaviour?
Challenger banks and small businesses	How has the emergence of challenger banks impacted upon small businesses' financing and why?

the researcher's capabilities and the availability of resources, including time and the research setting, are more likely to be about right.

The pitfall you must avoid at all costs is asking a research question that will not generate new insights (Box 2.1). This raises the question of the extent to which you have consulted the relevant literature. It is perfectly legitimate to replicate research because you have a genuine concern about its applicability to your research setting (for example, your organisation). However, it certainly is not legitimate to display your ignorance of the literature.

In order to clarify a research question, Clough and Nutbrown (2012) talk of the Russian doll principle. This means refining a draft research question until it reflects the essence of your research idea without including any unnecessary words or intentions. By stripping away any unnecessary layers (the larger outer dolls), the clearly defined research question (the smallest doll) that you reveal should provide you with an appropriately focused starting point for your research project.

Writing your research questions will be, in most cases, your task but it is useful to get other people to help. An obvious source of guidance is your project tutor. Consulting your project tutor will avoid the pitfalls of the questions that are too easy or too difficult or have been answered before. Discussing your area of interest with your project tutor will lead to your research questions becoming much clearer.

Prior to discussion with your project tutor you may wish to conduct a brainstorming session with your peers or use the Delphi technique (Section 2.3). Your research questions may flow from your initial examination of the relevant literature. As outlined in Section 2.3, journal articles reporting primary research will often end with a conclusion that includes the consideration by the author of the implications for future research of the work in the article. This may be phrased in the form of research questions. However, even if it is not, it may suggest possible research questions to you.

Table 2.2 provides some examples of general focus research questions.

Writing a research aim and set of research objectives

As well as your research question, you may also be required to formulate a **research aim**. A research aim is a brief statement of the purpose of the research project. It is often written as a sentence stating what you intend to achieve through your research. To illustrate this, the examples of research questions in Table 2.2 have been matched to their research aims in Table 2.3. You will see the close relationship between these – one stated as a question, the other as an aim.

Table 2.3 Examples of research questions and related research aims

Research question	Research aim
How effective is a media campaign designed to increase consumer trust in [company name] following a series of product recalls?	The aim of this research is to assess the effectiveness of a media campaign by [company name] designed to increase consumer trust following a series of recalls of its products.
In which situations and to what extent is Internet-based recruitment and selection of graduates effective and why?	The aim of this research is to understand situations within which Internet-based recruitment and selection of graduates is effective and why.
In what ways does the issue of coupons at supermarket checkouts affect buyer behaviour?	The aim of this research is to explore how the issue of coupons at supermarket checkouts affects buyer behaviour.
How has the emergence of challenger banks impacted upon small businesses' financing and why?	The aim of this research is to explore how the emergence of challenger banks has impacted upon small businesses' financing and why.

Your research question and research aim are complementary ways of saying what your research is about. However, neither gives sufficient detail about the steps you will need to take to answer your question and achieve your aim.

To do this you will need to devise a set of investigative questions or research objectives. Your research question may be used to generate more detailed investigative questions, or you may use it as a base from which to write a set of **research objectives**. Objectives are more generally acceptable to the research community as evidence of the researcher's clear sense of purpose and direction. Once you have devised your research question and research aim, we believe that research objectives are likely to lead to greater specificity than using investigative questions. It may be that either is satisfactory. Do check whether your examining body has a preference.

Research objectives allow you to **operationalise** your question – that is, to state the steps you intend to take to answer it. A similar way of thinking about the difference between questions, aims and objectives is related to 'what' and 'how'. Research questions and aims express 'what' your research is about. Research objectives express 'how' you intend to structure the research process to answer your question and achieve your aim. In this way, research objectives can be seen to complement a research question and aim, through providing the means to operationalise them. They provide a key step to transform your research question and aim into your research project.

Writing useful research objectives requires you to fulfil a number of fit-for-purpose criteria. Table 2.4 sets out criteria to help you devise research objectives to operationalise your research question and aim. Each of these criteria is also rephrased as a short question, which you can use as a checklist to evaluate your own draft research objectives.

Box 2.7 provides an example set of objectives at the stage when a student's research question and aim were developed into a sequence of research objectives.

The importance of theory in writing research questions and objectives

Section 4.4 outlines the role of theory in helping you to decide your approach to research design. However, your consideration of theory should begin earlier than this. It should inform your research questions and research objectives.

Table 2.4 Criteria to devise useful research objectives

Criterion	Purpose
Transparency (What does it mean?)	The meaning of the research objective is clear and unambiguous
Specificity (What I am going to do?)	The purpose of the research objective is clear and easily understood, as are the actions required to fulfil it
Relevance (Why I am going to do this?)	The research objective's link to the research question and wider research project is clear
Interconnectivity (How will it help to complete the research project?)	Taken together as a set, the research objectives illustrate the steps in the research process from its start to its conclusion, without leaving any gaps. In this way, the research objectives form a coherent whole
Answerability (Will this be possible?) (Where shall I obtain data?)	The intended outcome of the research objective is achievable. Where this relates to data, the nature of the data required will be clear or at least implied
Measurability (When will it be done?)	The intended product of the research objective will be evident when it has been achieved

Box 2.7
Focus on student research

Writing a set of research objectives

Diane worked for a medium-sized technology company that had been taken over by a much larger, multi-divisional firm. This company was gradually being integrated into its larger parent. Originally, the company had been incorporated as one division of the parent firm, although recently one of its most successful product areas had been reallocated into a different division. This had adverse consequences for many employees because it narrowed their scope to work across the company and to seek development opportunities. Many of the original employees had already left the company's employment. However, a significant number of the original employees remained and others who had joined since the take-over had been assimilated into the organisational culture that still prevailed from before the merger.

Diane was undertaking a management course as a part-time student. This course included a substantial research project and Diane thought that it would be fascinating to explore how employees felt about the changes at this company and how these affected their perceptions of working there. She searched literature related to organisational change, the impact of organisational structures on those who work within them, organisational culture and climate and then selected those that she felt were most relevant to read. She brainstormed some ideas related to this topic and spent time evaluating these. She then decided to discuss her research idea with two people whose advice she valued.

First she spoke to one of her tutors. Her tutor felt that this idea had merit but took time to discuss two possible concerns that focused around access and ethical issues. One focused on the likely sensitive nature of this research topic for both the company and those employees from whom Diane would need to collect data. The other focused on the fact that, as Diane worked for the company and alongside those from whom she would need to collect data, there were concerns about confidentiality and anonymity. However as they discussed this research idea they agreed that, if addressed in a sensitive way that absolutely ensured confidentially and anonymity, it could be possible to use her ideas to develop a suitable research project.

Second she spoke to one of the senior managers in the company. This manager knew that Diane was a part-time student on a management course and needed to undertake an organisationally-based research project.

She explained her research idea to this manager carefully and her justification for wishing to undertake it. This manager had been employed in the company for several months, having been recruited from outside both the company and the parent firm. This manager had experience of organisational change and integration and had been recruited in part because of this background. The manager was aware that some employees had spoken of their concerns about the ways in which the nature of work and scope for development had changed as a result of the take-over and structural changes.

This manager told Diane that there were significant concerns associated with her research idea. In particular, the manager thought there would be a risk of generating greater negativity with real consequences for the company. However, the manager also said that if conducted with sensitivity, her project might prove to be helpful. This the manager felt might be achieved by promoting a positive outcome from the research project by asking research participants to indicate how they could become re-engaged with and more committed to the company in spite of the changes that had occurred.

This manager also recognised that if employees felt the company was seen as being behind this research idea, they might be suspicious of Diane and refuse to share meaningful data with her. They discussed this and agreed that if she was going to proceed with this research idea, she should let potential participants know that the data produced would only be used for the purpose of her dissertation; she would separately produce a short summary document for senior managers that would only focus on recommendations for improvement based on an aggregated level of analysis to ensure confidentiality and anonymity.

These two discussions gave Diane a great deal to think about. She decided to undertake a preliminary inquiry to help refine her ideas about her research topic. Without referring to the discussion she had held with the manager to ensure confidentiality, she also held a Delphi group with a small trusted group of colleagues to refine her ideas and to build in scope for a positive focus. She also sought to integrate her ideas by working them up and narrowing them down. After this, she made an appointment to see her tutor. She took a draft research question, aim and set of objectives to this meeting.

The research question read, 'How have employee engagement, commitment and development been affected in [company name] and how may these be promoted following recent organisational change.' The research aim was, 'The aim of this research is to evaluate employee engagement, commitment and development in [company name] and explore how these may be promoted following recent organisational change.' The set of objectives were:

1 To describe the nature and cause of recent organisational changes in the company;
2 To define clearly the concepts used (employee engagement, employee commitment and employee development) to evaluate the impact of organisational change;
3 To evaluate the impact of recent organisational change on employee engagement and commitment;
4 To evaluate the impact of recent organisational change on employees' perceptions about their scope for development and future progression;
5 To explore ways to promote employee engagement, commitment, development and progression following recent organisational change in the company;
6 To make recommendations to promote employee engagement, commitment, development and progression in [company name].

To help you to think about this, we ask four questions that relate to the role of theory. What is theory? Why is theory important? How is theory developed? What types of theoretical contribution might be made? These questions lead into the discussion in Section 4.4.

What is theory?

The term **theory** is used to refer to 'a systematic body of knowledge grounded in empirical evidence which can be used for explanatory or predictive purposes' (Saunders et al. 2015: 37). Theories are therefore based upon the development and examination of concepts, the clear definition of concepts being essential for testing and developing theory (Box 2.7). A theory uses related facts and concepts to provide an explanation or predict an outcome. The explanatory power of a theory is based on its ability to explain relationships between concepts. These explanations need to be capable of being confirmed, refined or contradicted as understandings develop and change based on further research.

To explore the question 'what is theory?' in more detail we use the influential work of Whetten (1989). Whetten identified that theory is composed of four elements, related to 'what', 'how', 'why' and a fourth group of 'who', 'where' and 'when'. The first of these may be summarised as: what are the concepts or variables that the theory examines? For example, in Box 2.7, the concepts in Diane's research question are organisational change, employee engagement, employee commitment and employee development.

The second element may be summarised as: how are these concepts or variables related? Diane's research question was designed to examine the relationships between organisational change, on the one hand, and employee engagement, commitment and development, on the other hand. A key aspect here is **causality**. Theory is concerned with cause and effect. In her research, Diane was interested to explore how organisational change affected employee engagement, employee commitment and employee development. In other words, how did change have an effect on each one of these?

The third element may be summarised as: why are these concepts or variables related? This is the critical element in a theory because it explains the reasons for relationships between the concepts or variables. According to Whetten, 'what' and 'how' are descriptive; it is 'why' that explains the relationship. This point is worth developing, as you may be asking, 'what is the difference between "how" and "why" in this context?' In the case of Diane's research, she found that organisational change had affected employee engagement, commitment and development respectively. Diane's data allowed her to recognise a number of relationships that she could describe. However, this description did not explain why these outcomes had occurred and in fact the reasons for them were complex. For example, different categories of employee provided different explanations for the impact of organisational change upon themselves. Diane needed to analyse her data further (and where necessary to extend its collection) to answer the question, 'why do these relationships exist in my data?'

Once a good theory has been developed it may be used not only to explain why any relationship exists, but also to predict outcomes in a similar situation or where one or more of these theoretical variables are manipulated (changed). In the case of Diane's research, her theory may be used to predict a similar impact on employee engagement and commitment where change in another albeit similar organisation is implemented in the same way. Her theory may also be used to predict different outcomes for employee engagement and commitment where organisational change is managed differently.

While good theory has the power to explain and predict, it may also be subject to limitations. The scope of many theories will be limited by one or more constraints. The fourth group of elements that Whetten identified may therefore be summarised as: who does this theory apply to; where does this theory apply; when does this theory apply? In the case of Diane's research, she recognised that some of her theoretical conclusions applied more to professional-grade staff but less so to administrative staff. She also recognised that with the introduction of new policies to re-engage employees and offer development opportunities, the applicability of some of her conclusions would need to be re-evaluated in the future.

In this way, the explanations of the cause-and-effect relationships between variables in a theory may be contextual and time limited, indicating constraints to their generalisability. Another important contribution that addresses the question 'what is theory?' starts from the opposite perspective by discussing 'What theory is not' (Sutton and Staw 1995). This is a helpful contribution to our understanding and provides a complementary approach to that of Whetten (1989) (Box 2.8).

Box 2.8 Focus on management research

Clarifying what theory is not

Sutton and Staw (1995) make a helpful contribution to the question 'What is theory?' by defining what it is not. In their view theory is not:

1 *References.* Listing references to existing theories and mentioning the names of such theories may look impressive. However, alluding to the theory developed by other researchers may only provide a smokescreen. Instead researchers need to identify the concepts, causal relationships and logical explanations that they are using from previous theoretical work in relation to their own work.

2 *Data.* Data are important to be able to confirm, revise or overturn existing theory and to be able to develop new theory. However, data are used to describe the relationships or patterns that are revealed from their collection and analysis. Description by itself does not equal theory. Theory also requires logical explanations to discuss why such relationships or patterns were revealed, or why they might be expected to be revealed when testing existing theory (Section 4.3).

3 *Lists of variables.* Variables are important in the process of theory development but simply presenting or listing these by themselves does not represent a theory.

4 *Diagrams.* Diagrams are often helpful to show observed or expected causal relationships and how different relationships are related or how they are expected to be related. However, by themselves diagrams or figures are not theory. Sutton and Staw (1995: 376) state: 'Good theory is often representational and verbal.' They say that clear explanations can be represented graphically but that, to be able to develop a rich theoretical understanding, these will also require written discussion to explain why these relationships exist.

5 *Hypotheses or predictions.* In a similar manner to point 3, hypotheses are an important part of the process of developing and testing theory, in particular theoretical approaches (Experiment in Section 5.8), but they do not constitute a theory by themselves.

You are likely to use research questions rather than hypotheses in your research design and we would add to point 5 that the propositions or concepts that inform your research questions are also not theory by themselves.

Why is theory important?

There is probably no word that is more misused and misunderstood in education than the word 'theory'. It is thought that material included in textbooks is 'theory', whereas what is happening in the 'real world' is practice. Students who saw earlier editions of this book remarked that they were pleased that the book was not too 'theoretical'. What they meant was that the book concentrated on giving lots of practical advice. Yet the book is full of theory. Advising you to carry out research in a particular way (variable A) is based on the theory that this will yield effective results (variable B). This is the cause-and-effect relationship referred to in the definition of theory developed earlier and is very much the view of Kelly (1955). Kelly argues that the individual who attempts to solve the daily problems which we all face goes about this activity in much the same way as the scientist. Both continuously make and test hypotheses and revise their concepts accordingly. Both organise their results into what are called schemata and then into a system of broader schemata which are called theories. Kelly asserts that we need such schemata and theories in order to make sense of the complexity of the world in which we live. Without these organising frameworks we would be overwhelmed by the unconnected detail we would have to recall.

Implicitly each of us uses theory in our lives and in the jobs that we undertake. For example, the marketing manager who believes that issuing coupons in the supermarket chain for which he or she works makes customers less likely to shop regularly at a competitor supermarket (Table 2.2). This is a theory even though the marketing manager would probably not recognise it as such. He or she is less likely to refer to it as a theory, particularly in the company of fellow managers. Many managers are very dismissive of any talk that smacks of 'theory'. It is thought of as something that is all very well to learn about at business school but which bears little relation to what goes on in everyday organisational life. Yet the coupons example shows that it has everything to do with what goes on in everyday organisational life. By issuing coupons (variable A), the supermarket is attempting to influence the behaviour of customers (variable B). As every supermarket chain issues their own coupons, the marketing manager's personal theory that this encourages loyalty may begin to seem inadequate when confronted by a range of other complementary and innovative strategies to encourage customers to switch where they shop.

The use of coupons may become just one variable among many as supermarkets compete by offering extra loyalty card bonus points on particular goods, double or treble points if customers spend over a certain amount, the opportunity to redeem the value from accumulated bonus points against a range of discounted offers, and so on. In this case, research will provide the marketing manager with a much greater understanding of the effectiveness of the strategies used within her or his supermarket chain. The data collected will allow theoretical explanations to be developed, based on causal relationships that may then be used to predict which of these strategies is more effective. It may also indicate that different strategies will be effective in different locations and perhaps that specific strategies are more effective at particular times of the year, or that specific strategies should be targeted at particular socioeconomic groups. The ability to make these predictions potentially allows the supermarket chain to compete more effectively against its rivals. Valid theoretical explanations may lead to predictions that offer the supermarket chain increased opportunities for influence and control and the possibility of increasing market share.

If theory is so rooted in our everyday lives, it is something that we need not be apprehensive about. If it is implicit in all of our decisions and actions then recognising its importance means making it explicit. In research, the importance of theory must be recognised: therefore it must be made explicit.

How is theory developed and how does theory inform your research question and research objectives?

So far we have defined the elements of theory and discussed the need to recognise it in your research, even as you start to plan this. At this point, you may be asking, 'why is it important for me to recognise theory at this early stage, when writing my research question and research objectives?' Apart from its capacity to inform your research ideas (discussed earlier), the answer to this relates to the ways in which theory may also inform your research question and how theory is developed.

Theory published in the literature may inform your proposed research question in several ways. It will help you to formulate a research question that should lead to a theoretical explanation, rather than just a descriptive answer. It will allow you to find out whether others have asked similar questions to the question you propose. Where you find that a similar research question to yours has been addressed in the literature, you will be able to learn about the context within which it was explored and how the research was conducted. This may help to focus your question to provide you with a set of variables to test, or concepts to explore, to determine whether, how and why they are related in the context of your own research project (Box 2.9).

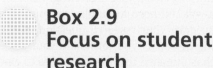

Box 2.9
Focus on student research

Writing a research question based on theory

Justine was a final-year marketing undergraduate who was interested in the theory of cognitive dissonance (Festinger 1957). She wanted to apply this to consumer-purchasing decision making in the snack foods industry (e.g. buying potato crisps) in the light of the adverse publicity that the consumption of such foods has as a result of 'healthy eating' campaigns.

Justine applied Festinger's theory by arguing in her research project proposal that a consumer who learns that eating too many snacks is bad for her health will experience dissonance, because the knowledge that eating too much snack food is bad for her health will be dissonant with the cognition that she continues to eat too many snacks. She can reduce the dissonance by changing her behaviour, i.e. she could stop eating so many snacks. (This would be consonant with the cognition that eating too many snacks is bad for her health.) Alternatively, she could reduce dissonance by changing her cognition about the effect of snack overeating on health and persuade herself that it does not have a harmful effect on health. She would look for positive effects of eating snacks, for example by believing that it is an important source of enjoyment which outweighs any harmful effects. Alternatively, she might persuade herself that the risk to health from snack overeating is negligible compared with the danger of car accidents (reducing the importance of the dissonant cognition).

Justine's research question was, 'To what extent does adverse "healthy eating" campaign publicity affect the consumer's decision to purchase snack foods and why?'

Using relevant theory to inform your research question will also sensitise you to the nature and level of importance of the research topic surrounding your question. You may find that a considerable body of relevant work exists, either in business and management or in another subject domain, for example in psychology, economics or sociology. Discovering this may help you to focus your research question so that later on you can firmly connect your findings and conclusions to this existing theory. It is unlikely that you will fail to find any literature that relates to your proposed question, although where you find that you are working in a more specialised topic area, this discovery may also help to focus your research question to relate to the theory that you locate. It will be important to discuss how the results of your research relate to theory, to be able to assess that theory in the context of your work and to demonstrate the theoretical contribution, no matter how limited, of your research.

Where you simply find it difficult to formulate a research question from your research idea, using existing theory may also help you to achieve this.

How theory is developed also provides a crucial reason for recognising relevant theory when writing your research question and objectives. Your research project will be designed to test a theory or to develop a theory. Where you wish to adopt a clear theoretical position that you will test through the collection of data, your research project will be theory driven and you will be using a **deductive approach**. Where you wish to explore a topic and develop a theoretical explanation as the data are collected and analysed, your research project will be data driven and you will be adopting an **inductive approach**.

We discuss approaches to theory development, also introducing the abductive approach, in much greater detail later (Section 4.5). However, it is useful to introduce this fundamental difference in the way theory is developed to be able to show why you need to think about this when drafting your research question and research objectives. A deductive approach will require you to identify a clear theoretical position when you draft the research question that you will then test. This is the approach we outlined earlier (Box 2.9).

An inductive approach does not rely on identifying an existing theoretical position, but it is likely that if you adopt this approach you will still need to familiarise yourself with theory in your chosen subject area before you draft your research question. Using an inductive approach does not mean disregarding theory as you formulate your research question and objectives. An inductive approach is intended to allow meanings to emerge from data as you collect them in order to identify patterns and relationships to build a theory, but it does not prevent you from using existing theory to formulate your research question and even to identify concepts that you wish to explore in the research process (Section 4.4). In this way, all researchers are likely to commence their research with knowledge of relevant literature and the theory it contains.

There is a further relationship between theory and your research question that is important to recognise when drafting your research question. In our discussion of theory we recognised that it is crucial to be able to explain how variables or concepts are related and why they are related. Research questions may therefore play a crucial role in encouraging research that is designed to produce theoretical explanations, no matter how limited these explanations might be (see the following sub-section). A question that only encourages a descriptive outcome will not lead to a theoretical explanation. For example, compare the following questions. 'How satisfied are employees with recent changes in the department's business strategy?' 'What are the implications of recent changes in the department's business strategy for employee satisfaction and why?' The first question is written to produce a descriptive outcome. The second question has the potential to explore and test relationships and to arrive at theoretical explanations to explain why these might exist.

What types of theoretical contribution might be made?

This discussion of theory has probably left you asking, 'what does this mean for me?' While you will be expected to produce a theoretical explanation, you will not be expected to develop a momentous theory that leads to a new way of thinking about management! Not all theoretical contributions are the same and it is reassuring to look at the threefold typology of theories shown in Figure 2.1.

'Grand theories' are usually thought to be the province of the natural scientists (e.g. Newton's theory of gravity, Darwin's theory of evolution or Einstein's theory of relativity). These may be contrasted with 'middle-range theories', which lack the capacity to change the way in which we think about the world but are nonetheless of significance. Some theories such as Maslow's (1943) hierarchy of needs and Herzberg et al.'s (1959) two-factor theory of motivation are well known to managers and would be in this category. However, most of us are concerned with 'substantive theories' that are restricted to a particular time, research setting, group or population or problem.

For example, studying the implications of a cost-saving strategy in a particular organisation would be an example of a substantive theory. Although they may be restricted, a host

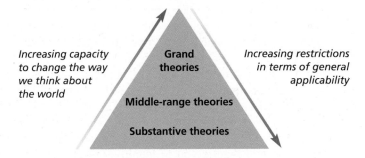

Increasing capacity to change the way we think about the world

Grand theories

Increasing restrictions in terms of general applicability

Middle-range theories

Substantive theories

Figure 2.1 Grand, middle range and substantive theories

Box 2.10
Focus on management research

What makes a theoretical contribution?

Corley and Gioia's (2011) study found that the theoretical contribution of management research can be measured along two dimensions. One of these relates to what they call the 'originality' of the contribution. This they divide into a contribution that is either 'incremental' or 'revelatory'. An incremental theoretical contribution is one that adds to or builds on a theory, perhaps by applying it in a new context. A revelatory theoretical contribution is more profound, offering a new theory to make sense of a problem or explain a phenomenon. The other dimension relates to what they call the 'utility' or 'usefulness' of a contribution. This they divide into a contribution that has 'scientific usefulness' or 'practical usefulness'. A scientifically useful contribution is one that emphasises methodological rigour and usefulness to an academic audience. A practically useful contribution emphasises organisational application and usefulness to organisational practitioners.

However, while theoretical contributions on the first dimension are likely to be exclusively either 'incremental' or 'revelatory' (it's unlikely that a contribution could be both!), this does not have to be the case on the second dimension. Corley and Gioia focus much of their article on discussing how to achieve research that is capable of being both academically and practically useful. They refer to designing research that has scope to be theoretically relevant to both academics and organisational practitioners. They consider ways in which this type of theoretical contribution may be achieved. This includes a continuing emphasis on examining the links between theoretical abstractions and practice implications. In interpreting their results, researchers also need to go beyond narrow generalisations and look for insights that can inform organisational practice. In a similar way, when developing theory, researchers need to look not only at the validity of their theories, but also their usefulness and applicability. Researchers also need to exercise some foresight when choosing their research topics so they pursue research that has, and will have, relevance to the problems and issues faced by organisations and organisational practitioners.

of 'substantive theories' that present similar propositions may lead to 'middle-range theories'. By developing 'substantive theories', however modest, we are doing our bit as researchers to enhance our understanding of the world about us. A grand claim, but a valid one!

Another way to examine the theoretical contributions of research into business and management is to assess its practical usefulness for organisations and those who work in them (Box 2.10).

2.5 Writing your research proposal

The **research proposal**, occasionally referred to as a protocol or outline, is a structured plan of your proposed research project. In this section we discuss why it is necessary and how it may be structured, but it is important to recognise that a competent research proposal needs to draw on material discussed in subsequent chapters. Before you can write your research proposal you will need to be aware of available literature and appropriate theory (Section 2.4 and Chapter 3), the research philosophy and approach that you wish to use (Chapter 4), your research design including methodological choice, research strategy and time frame (Chapter 5), access and ethical issues (Chapter 6), sample selection (Chapter 7), data collection methods and data analysis techniques (Chapters 8–13).

Why is a research proposal necessary?

Creating a clear specification to guide your research project

Your research project is likely to be a large element in your course. It is also yours! You will be responsible for conceiving, conducting and concluding this project and creating the report, dissertation or thesis. Apart from applying your research methods training and the advice you receive from your project tutor, it will be your piece of work. From this perspective, developing a research proposal offers you the opportunity to think carefully about your research project (Box 2.11).

We do not suggest that you use these questions to provide headings under which you write responses, but we feel that they should be helpful as a guide and as a checklist against which to evaluate your research proposal before submitting it to your tutor. A well-thought-out and well-written research proposal has the potential to provide you with a clear specification of the what, why, how, when and where of your research project.

Producing a research proposal is demanding: thinking through what you wish to do and why, identifying and synthesising literature and then envisaging all of the stages of your research will be time consuming, as will the necessary revisions to create a coherent and clearly written proposal. However, the effort is likely to prove to be very worthwhile. As you juggle several activities during the period of your research project, there may be occasions when you pick up your research proposal and feel glad that you spent so much time producing a clear specification to guide your project through its various stages.

Meeting the requirements of those who approve and assess your project

It is likely that your research proposal will be assessed before you are allowed to carry on with your research project. A proportion of the overall marks available for your project report may be given for the research proposal. Alternatively, a research proposal may be subject to approval before you are permitted to proceed with your research project. In either case, it will be necessary to reach a certain standard before being allowed to

Box 2.11
Checklist to guide and evaluate your research proposal

✔ Have I explained what am I going to do?
✔ Have I explained why I am doing this?
✔ Have I said why it is worth doing?
✔ Have I explained how it relates to what has been done before in my subject area?
✔ Have I stated which theory or theories will inform what I am doing and how I will use it or them?
✔ Have I stated my research question(s), research aim and my research objectives?
✔ Have I outlined how I will conduct my research?

✔ Have I outlined my research design?
✔ Have I outlined what data I need?
✔ Have I stated who and where my intended participants are?
✔ Have I explained how I will select my participants?
✔ Have I explained how I will gain access?
✔ Have I outlined how I will collect my data?
✔ Have I outlined how I will analyse my data and use this to develop theoretical explanations?
✔ Have I outlined what data quality issues I might encounter?
✔ Have I outlined how I will seek to overcome these data quality issues?
✔ Have I considered the ethical issues I might encounter at each stage of my research?
✔ Have I outlined how I will address these?

progress. There are potentially a number of different criteria that may be used to assess a research proposal. These may include criteria that are specific to each of the components of the proposal, which we describe later in this section. Part of the assessment and approval process may also centre on criteria that focus on more general concerns. We first consider three such criteria that are likely to be used to assess your research proposal: coherence, ethical considerations and feasibility.

Coherence

A research project is a complex and time-consuming activity. As we indicated earlier, you are likely to benefit from creating a clear specification to guide your research project. Your project tutor and any other assessor will be looking for evidence of coherence and lucidity in the way you have written your research proposal, to demonstrate that it will be fit for purpose and able to direct your research activity.

Ethical considerations

Part of the approval process for your research proposal may involve it being considered and approved by a research ethics committee. Your university's code of ethical practice is likely to require all research involving human participants to be considered and approved, especially where research involves young or vulnerable participants. It may also be necessary to state how data will be stored, whether they will be kept after the research is completed and under what conditions, in order to ensure the continuing anonymity of the participants and confidentiality of their data. Section 6.5 discusses ethical issues related to the design stage of a research project. You will need to be aware of and abide by the ethical requirements of your university. These requirements will add to the time that you will need to allow for the planning stage of your research project. As a professional student you may also need to be aware of and abide by the ethical requirements of your professional institute.

Feasibility

You may have devised a coherent and well-structured research proposal that would create much interest but it may not be possible to achieve, or sensible to contemplate. Feasibility is a multifaceted criterion that your assessors will be concerned about. Your proposal may not be possible to achieve in the time available to undertake the research project and produce your dissertation or management report. It may be that data collection would not be possible because you would not be able to gain access to participants, or it might not be practical and your tutor will tell you so! The proposal may require resources that are not available, finance commitments that are unaffordable or skills that you have not developed and would not be able to acquire in the timescale of the project.

It is always helpful to discuss your research proposal with a tutor. Where there are concerns about any of the issues just considered, it will be possible to discuss these to work out how the proposed research may be amended. For example, in relation to feasibility something more modest in scope may be discussed. Your task will then be to amend initial ideas and convince your tutor that the proposed research is achievable within the time and other resources available.

Ensuring that your research project isn't based on preconceived ideas

Your research project offers a valuable way to learn the skills involved in this activity. These skills are transferable to many other situations, including the world of work. It is about process as well as outcome. Concerns about feasibility (related to overenthusiasm) lie at one end of a continuum, at other end of which lies a very occasional concern about sincerity. Do not be like the student who came to Phil to talk over a research proposal and said, 'Of course, I know what the answer will be'. When asked to explain the purpose of doing the research if he already knew the answer, he became rather defensive and eventually looked for another supervisor and, probably, another topic.

Approval of your research proposal implies that it is satisfactory. While this is no guarantee of subsequent success, it will reassure you to know that you have started your research journey with an appropriate destination and journey plan. It will be for you to ensure that you do not get lost!

How can your research proposal be structured?

There are potentially different ways to structure your research proposal. Different research traditions (Chapter 5) may lead to different ways of structuring your proposal and, later on, your project report (Chapter 14). We describe what many think of as the standard approach to structuring your research proposal. You will therefore need to check if your university or faculty requires a different structure. Whichever structure you are required to adopt, this will need to be driven by and focused on your research question, aim and research objectives, and you will need to ensure that you produce a coherent proposal.

Title

The title should simply and concisely summarise the research question. It should avoid unnecessary phrases such as, 'A study to explore … ' Instead it should reflect the concepts or variables in your research question (Box 2.12). If your research question changes, this will naturally lead to a change to your title.

Background

This section has a number of related functions. It needs to introduce the reader to the research issue or problem. This addresses the question, 'what am I going to do?' You also need to provide a rationale for your proposed research and to justify this. This may be composed of two elements, one relating to you and the other relating to the value of the work. Your reader will be looking for some evidence that this is a topic in which you have sufficient interest to sustain the effort that will be required from you over the period of the research project. This may relate to the need to tackle a problem, to your intellectual curiosity, or to your intended career direction. It relates to the question, 'why am I going

---

Box 2.12
Focus on student research

Devising research proposal titles

Imran (Box 2.6) reworded his research question into the following title for his research proposal:

'The reasons for mismatch between corporate strategy and the external environment.'

Diane (Box 2.7) devised this title for her research proposal by rewording her research question:

'An evaluation of employee engagement, commitment and development, and scope for their promotion, following organisational change.'

Justine (Box 2.9) used her research question to develop this title for her proposal:

'The effect of "healthy eating" publicity on snack foods purchasing decisions.'

to do this?' The rationale will also need to address the question, 'why is it worth doing?' This will relate to one of the following types of justification: the application of a theory to a particular context (such as within an organisation); the development of a theory within a research setting; testing a theory within a given context. Your research may propose other such justifications depending on its nature.

This leads to another function of this section: to demonstrate 'how my research relates to what has been done before in this subject area'. In achieving this you will show your knowledge of relevant literature and clarify where your proposal fits into the debate in this literature (Section 3.3). You will also be able to begin to show 'which theory or theories will inform what I am doing and how I will use it or them'. The intention will be not to write a detailed review of the literature but rather to provide an overview of key literature sources from which you will draw and the theory or theories within them. This will not be the same as the critical literature review (Sections 3.2 and 3.3) that you will present in your final project report but the start of the process that leads to it.

Research question(s), aim and objectives

The Background section should lead logically into a statement of your research question(s), aim and research objectives. These should leave the reader in no doubt about what your research seeks to achieve. Be careful here to ensure that your objectives are precisely written and will lead to observable outcomes (Box 2.7).

Method

The Background and Method will be the longest sections of your proposal. The Method is designed to answer the question, 'how shall I conduct my research?' The Method may be divided into sub-sections that deal with research design, participants, techniques and procedures and ethical considerations. This final element may need to be dealt with in a discrete section of your research proposal.

Research design is discussed in Chapter 5. It involves you making a number of decisions about, 'what is my research design?' You will need to make a methodological choice between a quantitative, qualitative or mixed methods design. You will also need to select one or more research strategies (e.g. an experiment, a case study, a survey, a Grounded Theory strategy) and determine an appropriate time frame for your project depending on the nature of your research. You will need to describe each of these and justify your choice by the way these elements fit together to form a coherent whole.

How you design your research will affect the type of data you require, where you intend to locate them and from whom you will collect them. Your data may be collected from human participants, or they may be secondary data (Chapter 8) such as from archival research (Section 5.8) or a combination of these. You will therefore need to address the question, 'what type of data do I need?' If you are using secondary data you will need to explain what these are, where they are located, any issues related to access and justify this choice. If you intend to collect data from human participants, you will need to answer, 'who and where are my intended participants?' You may be intending to conduct research in a single organisation or across a number of organisations. You will need to explain and justify the nature of the organisation or organisations and possibly the sector or sectors within which it, or they, operate. Your intended participants may be located within a specific part of an organisation or be drawn from across it. You will need to explain and justify this.

You will also need to explain the nature of your research population and why you chose it. For example, they may be entrepreneurs, managerial employees, non-managerial employees, a particular occupational group, trade union officials or some combination of these. Where you need to select a sample from within a research population you will need to address the question, 'how shall I select them?' Chapter 7 discusses types of probability and non-probability sampling and you will need to describe and justify your sampling H technique(s) and sample size.

You will also need to describe the data collection and analysis techniques you intend to use by answering the questions, 'how will I collect my data?' and 'how will I analyse it and use this to develop theoretical explanations?' Data collection techniques include examination of secondary data, questionnaires, interviews and observation (Chapters 8–11). You will not need to explain the precise details of each technique you intend to use, such as including a copy of your questionnaire, interview questions or the content of an observation schedule, but you will need to describe how you will use it. For example, if you are using interviews, what type will you use, how many will you conduct, with what type of participant, their intended duration, how will you record the data (e.g. note taking and/or audio-recording)? You will also need to describe, albeit briefly, how you intend to analyse each type of data that you collect.

It will also be important to discuss ethical considerations so that you anticipate these and demonstrate to your tutor and ethics committee that your research design and proposal has been formulated to minimise ethical concerns and avoid unethical practice. This will be essential where you are dealing with human participants, and sometimes even if using secondary data already collected from human participants. There may be a reduced need for some of you undertaking certain types of research (e.g. where this is based on macro-level, completely anonymised data) but in nearly all cases this requirement is very likely to mean that you need to be sensitive to ethical concerns.

Timescale

It is very useful to divide your research project into its constituent stages or tasks. You may estimate the amount of time that each stage or task should take to complete. Allocating each stage or task so much time should help you and your tutor decide on the feasibility of the research project, by giving you a clear idea as to what needs to be achieved during the time allowed. Experience shows that however well the researcher's time is organised, the whole process seems to take longer than anticipated. Devising a timescale allows you to monitor your progress and indicates where you need to allocate more working hours to keep up with your intended schedule (Box 2.13).

Many researchers use a **Gantt chart** to produce a schedule for their research project. Developed by Henry Gantt in 1917, this provides a simple visual representation of the stages or tasks that make up your research project, the timings to be allocated to each of these and the relationship between them. It is a simple but effective tool used in various types of project management. In a grid of columns and rows, tasks are listed under each other in the first column. Each row therefore starts with a short description of a task and the remainder of the row indicates a timescale (Figure 2.2).

The time estimated that each task will take is represented by the length of its associated horizontal bar, while each task's start time and finish time is indicated by the beginning and end of the bar. As we can see from the first bar of the chart in Figure 2.2, the student has decided to schedule in two weeks of holiday. The first of these occurs over the Christmas and New Year period, and the second occurs while her tutor is reading a draft copy of the completed project in April. We can also see from the second and fourth bar that, like many of our students, she intends to begin to draft her critical literature review while she is still reading new articles and books. However, she has also recognised that some activities must be undertaken sequentially. For example, bars 9 and 10 highlight that

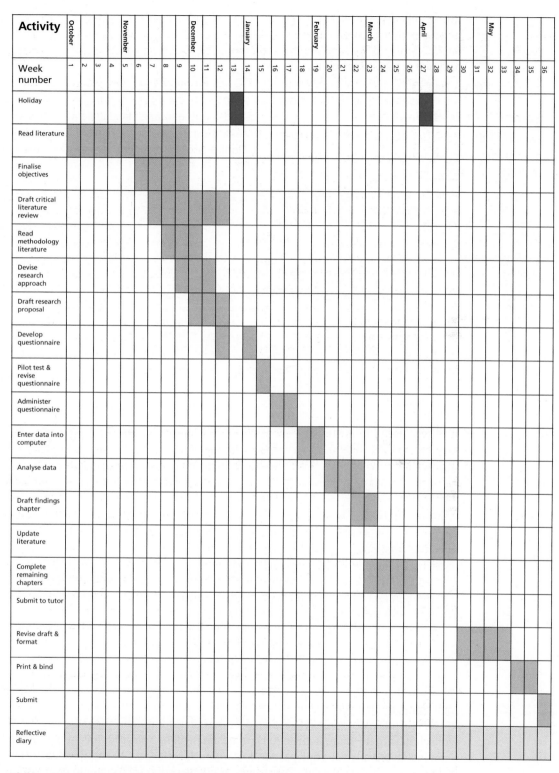

Figure 2.2 Gantt chart for a student's research project

Box 2.13
Focus on student research

Louisa's research timescale

As part of the final year of her undergraduate business studies degree, Louisa had to undertake an 8000–10,000-word research project. In order to assist her with her time management, she discussed the following 'To-Do List', developed using Microsoft Outlook's project planning tool 'Tasks', with her tutor.

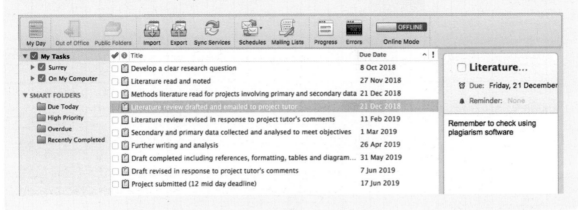

before she can administer her questionnaire (bar 10) she must complete all the revisions highlighted as necessary by the pilot testing (bar 9). Finally, this student has noted that her project assessment criteria include a reflective essay and has decided to keep a reflective diary throughout the research project (bar 20).

Resources

This is another facet of feasibility (Box 2.1 and also our earlier discussion in this section). Including this discussion in your research proposal will allow you and your tutor to assess whether what you are proposing can be resourced. Resource considerations may be categorised as finance, data access and equipment.

Conducting research costs money. This may include for example: travel, subsistence, help with transcription or, perhaps, postage for questionnaires. Think through the expenses involved and ensure that you can meet them.

Assessors of your proposal will need to be convinced that you have access to the data you need to conduct your research (Sections 6.2 and 6.3). This may be unproblematic if you are carrying out research in your own organisation. Many project tutors wish to see written approval from host organisations in which researchers are planning to conduct research. You will also need to convince your reader of the likely response rate to any questionnaire that you send.

It is surprising how many research proposals have ambitious plans for large-scale data collection with no thought given to how the data will be analysed. It is important that you convince the reader of your proposal that you have access to the necessary computer software to analyse your data. Moreover, it will be necessary for you to demonstrate that you have either the necessary skills to perform the analysis or can learn the skills in an appropriate time, or you have access to help.

References

It is not necessary to try to impress your proposal reader with an enormous list of references. A few key literature sources to which you have referred in the background section and which relate to the previous work and theory that directly informs your own proposal, as well as references to the methods literature, should be all that is necessary. We provide more detail on how to reference in Appendix 2.

Case 2 at the end of this chapter provides an example of an outline of a student's initial research proposal.

2.6 Summary

- Choosing a research topic and developing your research proposal are key parts of your research project.
- Characteristics of a good research topic include appropriateness, capability and fulfilment. However, the most important is that it will meet the requirements of the examining body.
- Generating and refining research ideas makes use of a variety of techniques. It is important that you use a variety of techniques, including those involving rational thinking and those involving creative thinking.
- Further refinement of research ideas may be achieved through using a Delphi technique, conducting a preliminary inquiry and integrating ideas by working these up and narrowing them down.
- A clearly defined research question expresses what your research is about and will become the focal point of your research project.
- A research aim is a brief statement of the purpose of the research project. It is often written as a sentence stating what you intend to achieve through your research.
- Well-formulated research objectives operationalise how you intend to conduct your research by providing a set of coherent and connected steps to answer your research question.
- It will be important to use academic theory to inform your research topic irrespective of the approach you will use to conduct your research project.
- A research proposal is a structured plan of your proposed research project.
- A well-thought-out and well-written research proposal has the potential to provide you with a clear specification of the what, why, how, when and where of your research project.

Self-check questions

Help with these questions is available at the end of the chapter.

2.1 You have decided to search the literature to 'try to come up with some research ideas in the area of operations management'. How will you go about this?

2.2 A colleague of yours wishes to generate a research idea in the area of accounting. He has examined his own strengths and interests on the basis of his assignments and has read some review articles, but has failed to find an idea about which he is excited. He comes and asks you for advice. Suggest two techniques that your colleague could use, and justify your choices.

2.3 You are interested in doing some research on the interface between business organisations and schools. Write three research questions that may be appropriate.

2.4 For the workplace project for her professional course, Karen had decided to undertake a study of the effectiveness of the joint negotiating and consultative committee in her NHS Trust. Her title was 'An evaluation of the effectiveness of the Joint Negotiating and Consultative Committee in Anyshire's Hospitals NHS Foundation Trust'. Draft some objectives which Karen may adopt to complement her title.

2.5 How may the formulation of an initial substantive theory help in the development of a research proposal?

2.6 How would you demonstrate the influence of relevant theory in your research proposal?

Review and discussion questions

2.7 Together with a few colleagues discuss the extent to which a number of research ideas would each constitute a 'good research topic' using the checklist in Box 2.1. The set of ideas you use may be past ones obtained from your tutor that relate to your course. Alternatively, they may be those which have been written by you and your colleagues as preparation for your project(s).

2.8 Look through several of the academic journals that relate to your subject area. Choose an article which is based upon primary research. Assuming that the research question and objectives are not made explicit, infer from the content of the article what the research question and objectives may have been.

2.9 Watch the news on television or access a news website. Look for a news item based on research which has been carried out to report a current issue related to business. Spend some time investigating other news websites (e.g. http://www.news.google.com) to learn more about the research which relates to this business news story. Study the story carefully and decide what further questions the report raises. Use this as the basis to draft an outline proposal to seek answers to one (or more) of these questions.

 ## Progressing your research project

Choosing a research topic and developing your research proposal

- If you have not been given a research idea, consider the techniques available for generating and refining research ideas. Choose a selection of those with which you feel most comfortable, making sure to include both rational and creative thinking techniques. Use these to try to generate a research idea or ideas. Once you have got a research idea(s), or if you have been unable to find an idea, talk to your project tutor.

- Evaluate your research idea(s) against the characteristics of a good research project (Box 2.1).

- Refine your research idea(s) using a selection of the techniques available for generating and refining research idea(s). Re-evaluate your research ideas against the characteristics of a good research project (Box 2.1). Remember that it is better to revise (and in some situations to discard) ideas that do not appear to be feasible at this stage. Integrate your ideas using the process of working up and narrowing down to form one research idea.

- Use your research idea to write a research question. Where possible this should be a 'how?' or a 'why?' rather than a 'what?' question.

- Use this research question to write a research aim and a set of connected research objectives.

- Write your research proposal making sure it includes a clear title and sections on:

- the background to your research;
- your research question(s), related aim and research objectives;
- the method you intend to use including research design, participants (data), techniques and procedures, and ethical considerations;
- the timescale for your research;
- the resources you require;
- references to any literature to which you have referred.
- Use the questions in Box 1.4 to guide your reflective diary entry.

References

Alvesson, M. and Sandberg, J. (2011) 'Generating research questions through problematization', *Academy of Management Review,* Vol. 36, No. 2, pp. 247–71.

Brady, S.R. (2015) 'Utilizing and adapting the Delphi method for use in qualitative research', *International Journal of Qualitative Methods,* pp. 1–6.

Buzan, T. (2011) *Buzan's Study Skills: Mind Maps, Memory Techniques, Speed Reading and More.* London: BBC.

Carroll, L. (1989) *Alice's Adventures in Wonderland.* London: Hutchinson.

Charmaz, K. (2017) 'The power of constructivist grounded theory for critical inquiry', *Qualitative Inquiry,* Vol. 23, No. 1, pp. 34–45.

Clough, P. and Nutbrown, C. (2012) *A Student's Guide to Methodology* (3rd edn). London: Sage.

Corley, K.G. and Gioia, D.A. (2011) 'Building theory about theory building: What constitutes a theoretical contribution?', *Academy of Management Review,* Vol. 36, No. 1, pp. 12–32.

Festinger, L. (1957) *A Theory of Cognitive Dissonance.* Stanford, CA: Stanford University Press.

Gill, J. and Johnson, P. (2010) *Research Methods for Managers* (4th edn). London: Sage.

Herzberg, F., Mausener, B., & Snyderman, B.B. (1959) *The Motivation to Work.* New York: John Wiley.

Jankowicz, A.D. (2005) *Business Research Projects* (4th edn). London: Thomson Learning.

Kelly, G.A. (1955) *The Psychology of Personal Constructs.* New York: Norton.

Lincoln. Y.S., Lynham S.A. and Guba, E.G. (2018). 'Paradigmatic controversies, contradictions and emerging confluences revisited', in N.K. Denzin and Y.S. Lincoln (eds) *The Sage Handbook of Qualitative Research* (5th edn). Los Angeles, CA: Sage, pp. 108–150.

Maslow, A.H. (1943) 'A theory of human motivation', *Psychological Review, 50* (4), pp. 370–396.

McDonald, S. (2005) 'Studying actions in context: A qualitative shadowing method for organisational research', *Qualitative Research,* Vol. 5, No. 4, pp. 455–73.

Mortari, L. (2015) 'Reflectivity in research practice: An overview of different perspectives', *International Journal of Qualitative Methods,* pp. 1–9.

Murray, S. (2017) 'Where real-life crises provide valuable lessons', *Financial Times,* 19 June.

Ogbonna, E. and Harris, L.C. (2014) 'Organizational cultural perpetuation: A case study of an English Premier League football club', *British Journal of Management,* Vol. 25, No. 4, pp. 667–86.

Paraskevas, A. and Saunders, M.N.K. (2012) 'Beyond consensus: an alternative use of Delphi enquiry in hospitality research', *International Journal of Contemporary Hospitality Management,* Vol. 24, No. 6, pp. 907–924.

Podsakoff, P.M., MacKenzie, S.B. and Podsakoff, N.P. (2016) 'Recommendations for creating better concept definitions in the organizational, behavioral and social sciences', *Organizational Research Methods,* Vol. 19, No. 2., pp. 159–203.

Reuters Institute (2017) *Reuters Institute Digital News Report 2017.* Reuters Institute and University of Oxford.

Saunders, M.N.K., Gray, D.E, Tosey, P. and Sadler-Smith, E (2015) 'Concepts and theory building', in Anderson, L., Gold, J., Stewart, J. and Thorpe, R. (eds.) *Professional Doctorates in Business and Management.* London: Sage. pp. 35–56.

Saunders, M.N.K. and Lewis, P. (1997) 'Great ideas and blind alleys? A review of the literature on starting research', *Management Learning,* Vol. 28, No. 3, pp. 283–99.

Sutton, R. and Staw, B. (1995) 'What theory is not', *Administrative Science Quarterly,* Vol. 40, No. 3, pp. 371–84.

Tietze, S. (2012) 'Researching your own organisation', in G. Symon and C. Cassell (eds) *Qualitative Organizational Research,* London, Sage.

Wang, H., Tong, L., Takeuchi, R. and George, G. (2016) 'Corporate Social Responsibility: An overview and new research directions', *Academy of Management Journal,* Vol. 59, No. 2, pp. 534–544.

Whetten, D. (1989) 'What constitutes a theoretical contribution?', *Academy of Management Review,* Vol. 14, No. 4, pp. 490–5.

Further reading

Alvesson, M. and Sandberg, J. (2011) 'Generating research questions through problematization', *Academy of Management Review,* Vol. 36, No. 2, pp. 247–71. This article discusses the established way in which research questions are generated by researchers and how this approach can be challenged. While the way in which you generate your research question is likely to be related to the established way they discuss, reading this will provide you with a deeper understanding of research questions and their relationship to theory.

Corley, K.G. and Gioia, D.A. (2011) 'Building theory about theory building: what constitutes a theoretical contribution?', *Academy of Management Review,* Vol. 36, No. 1, pp. 12–32. We featured this article in Box 2.10. You may wish to read it for yourself to explore their thought-provoking and useful discussion about making a theoretical contribution.

Podsakoff, P.M., MacKenzie, S.B. and Podsakoff, N.P. (2016) 'Recommendations for creating better concept definitions in the organizational, behavioral and social sciences', *Organizational Research Methods,* Vol. 19, No. 2., pp. 159–203. This is a significant paper that discusses the importance of concepts and conceptual clarity in undertaking research and their role in theory. It is well worth reading this paper and considering its guidance as you develop your research proposal.

Sutton, R. and Staw, B. (1995) 'What theory is not', *Administrative Science Quarterly,* Vol. 40, No. 3, pp. 371–84. This is a helpful article to read to gain some insights into the role of theory if you find this aspect daunting. In telling us what theory is not, they provide a very helpful discussion about what it is by referring to their own experiences. They also go further than this and evaluate the role of theory.

Case 2
Kristina's first draft research proposal

Kristina is studying for a master's degree in international business, Although she has chosen to study overseas, she wishes to undertake her research project in her home country. She is interested in the relationship between marketing strategy and international business and has prepared her research proposal for an applied research project. This states that the aim of her research project is 'to establish how the case study organisation ("Healthy-FoodCo") can market a dietary supplement ("DietSupp") successfully in another country ("OverSeasCountry").' She emails the first draft of her research proposal to her project tutor and is surprised that he emails back, requesting a meeting to 'talk through some concerns about the proposal'. Below we present an abbreviated version of the first draft of her research proposal. Please note the proposal intentionally includes methodological, as well as spelling and grammatical, errors to allow you to evaluate and improve it by working through the case study questions.

Title

The impact of national cultures and the marketing mix on consumer buying behaviour: A case study of HealthyFoodCo's marketing of a new diet supplement internationally.

Background (abridged)

The marketing mix is the central concept of marketing (Khan, 2014). Scholars argue that the concept originated in the 1940s with Neil Borden (e.g. Schultz and Dev, 2012). At this point, the concept of marketing mix was not formally defined and it was Jerome McCarthy who adapted this concept in the 1950s into what is known as the 4Ps: product, price, place and promotion (Schultze and Dev, 2012). Phillip Kotler then popularized the 4Ps (Schultz and Dev, 2012), which continue to be the most enduring marketing mixer framework. Each of the 4Ps may be seen to be a controllable element that an organisation may use to formulate and implement a marketing strategy that is adapted to the environment within which their target market exists (Dadzie et alia 2017). The intention here is to influence customer buying behaviour favourably towards the product being marketed.

However, as main critique surrounding the 4Ps is its internal orientation, referring to claims that it lacks customer orientation and interactivity (see criticism in Constantinides, 2006), consumer buying behavior will also need to be investigated further. Kotler et alia (2009) argue that it is difficult to understand consumer behavior as different factors influence it. Thus, several perspectives on consumer behavior can studied, ranging from a behaviorist perspective, to an information processing perspective, an emotional perspective, a cultural perspective and a multiple approach. As it can be argued that consumer behavior is greatly influenced by culture (e.g. Kacen and Lee, 2002; Kotler et alia, 2009), this research will examine the cultural perspective on consumer behavior. Within this perspective, marketing is seen as the means for transmitting value, which shapes culture, but at the same time is shaped by it (Kotler et alia 2009), hence marketing can further be taken as "a channel through which cultural meanings are transferred to consumer goods" (Kotler et alia, 2009: 245). Thus, culture serves as a kind of prism through which products are viewed. This further leads to the assumption, that a product should not merely be viewed as such, but also as a symbol, representing beliefs, norms and values (Kotler et alia, 2009). The purpose here will be to examine how culture in the new national target market may affect consumer purchasing behavior of dietary supplements and how this may be related to the elements of the marketing mix.

Drawing on this and other literature a research model will be established, establishing the dependent, independent and moderating variables for the research.

Research question and research objectives

The research question is:

How can 'HealthyFoodCo' market 'DietSupp' in 'OverSeasCountry' with regard to price, place and promotion and why?
The research objectives are:

1 To understand consumers' dietary supplements purchasing behaviour in 'OverSeasCountry'.
2 To examine the relationships between 'DietSupp' and the marketing mix elements of price, promotion and place in the context of 'OverSeasCountry'.
3 To develop a marketing strategy to 'HealthyFoodCo' for the promotion of 'DietSupp' in 'OverSeasCountry'.

Method

Research design

The research design is based on a mono-method, quantitative methodology that uses a survey strategy to collect data through an Internet questionnaire. This purpose of the research is to conduct an explanatory study that will to an action-oriented solution for the case study organisation. This will result in the collection of standardized data. The time horizon will be cross-sectional, as the primary data collection occurs at a single point of time (Saunders et alia, 2016; Malhotra et alia, 2012).

Design of the questionnaire

The primary data collection will take form in a structured self-completion questionnaire, which is in line with the research approach (Saunders et alia 2019), making use of fixed-response alternative questions (Malhotra et alia, 2012). This technique allows for standardized questions to be collected from a large number of respondents, which can be analysed statistically (Saunders et alia, 2019). This technique aids simplicity in regards to administration and it offers consistent data, hence reducing variability in the results (Malhotra et alia, 2012). The questions incorporated will be a mixture of open and closed questions, while focusing upon closed questions to ease the analysis of the data, (Saunders et alia, 2019), utilizing existing measurement scales. Further advantages of closed questions are, that they are easy to compare, less-time consuming to answer for the respondent and they possess a higher enforcement- and evaluation objectivity.

The choice of this method is further substantiated in that it is the most common method used in marketing research, accounting for about 72% of all spending for marketing research (Malhotra et alia, 2012).

Sampling strategy and sample size

A non-probability sample will be selected using volunteer sampling, each participant being able to determine whether to participate in the research (Saunders et alia, 2019). However, it is noted that a non-probability sampling can have a negative impact on the representativeness of the research.

As the target population is unknown, this research draws upon Tennent's (2013) advice of a sample size of 30 in regards to the sample size. Working with a 95% certainty level, a minimum of 32 people for each group have to be obtained to reach the minimum sample size of 30.

Distribution of the questionnaire

The questionnaire will be designed and distributed using the Qualtrics online software. The main advantages of this are that it enables the research to be conducted in a timely manner (Malhotra et alia, 2012), eliminating for example data entry by the researcher (Saunders et alia, 2019) and costs can be reduced to a minimum (Malhotra et alia, 2012), which is desirable due to the scope of the research and the financial and time limitations. The quality of the data will be enhanced through incorporating logic and validity checks, hence allowing the movement towards a more personalised questionnaire design (Malhotra et alia, 2012). Yet, the response rate will be lower compared to other modes of distributing questionnaires (Saunders et alia, 2019). To enhance the latter, incentives will be given.

The online distribution will be done via posting a link to the questionnaire in relevant online forums, concerned with dietary supplements and general nutrition, as this is in line with the nature of the product, making it available for a week. In addition to that, a link to the questionnaire will also be published on websites that frequently sell dietary supplements. The reason for choosing this channel is that even though storey-based channels remain the main channel for distribution for the category, looking at the technological dimension of the macro environment, it becomes evident that a trend towards online purchases is prevailing in 'OverSeasCountry' (Biesdorf & Niedermann, 2014). Furthermore, the selection of these specific channels for the survey distribution increase the likelihood that the audience is already a user of dietary supplements, to gain further insights into their perceptions. The questionnaire will be designed in 'OverSeasCountry's' language to ensure that the respondents will understand all questions.

Prior to launching the questionnaire, a pilot test will be conducted among 10-15 participants to ensure that the questionnaire works, the questions posed are generally understandable and that the respondents are able to answer the questions asked and follow the instructions given (Saunders et alia, 2019). This will aid finding unintentional mistakes in the questionnaire and estimating the duration for completing the questionnaire. Ultimately, this enhances the reliability level of the research.

Research ethics

The means for obtaining primary data is the Internet, which results in certain issues and dilemmas for ethnical principles (Saunders et alia, 2019). To ensure that the primary data collection will be conducted ethically, potential respondents will need to be able to make an informed decision about participation (Saunders et alia, 2019). Participant information about the research will be provided in the introduction to the questionnaire, highlighting the nature of the research, assurances about participation, including anonymity, rights of the respondents as well as how the data will be analysed, reported and saved (Saunders et alia, 2019). Lastly, information of the person to be contacted in regards to concerns will be provided (Saunders et alia, 2019).

Timescale

I anticipate it will take me a week to collect my data. Once all the data have been collected, I will finish my literature review over the next month and write up the project. The research will be completed in time for me to submit the project by the deadline.

Resources

The University has a subscription to Qualtrics. With regard to resources, at this point of the research it is not evident that any further resources will be required.

References

Biesdorf, S. and Niedermann, F. (2014). *Healthcare's digital future,* [Internet]. Available at: http://www.mckinsey.com/industries/healthcare-systems-and-services/our-insights/healthcares-digital-future.

Constantinides, E. (2006). The Marketing Mix Revisited: Towards the 21st Century of Marketing. *Journal of Marketing Management,* 22, 3–4, 407–438.

Dadzie, K.Q., Amponsah, D.K., Dadzie, C.A. and Winston, E.M. (2017). 'How Firms Implement Marketing Stratgies In Emerging Markets: An Empirical Assessment Of The 4A Marketing Mix Framework.' *Journal of Marketing Theory and Practice,* 25, 3, pp. 234–256.

Kacen, J. J. and Lee, J. A. (2002). 'The Influence of Culture on Consumer Impulse Buying Behaviour'. *Journal of Consumer Psychology,* 12, 2, pp- 163–176.

Khan, M. T. (2014). 'The Concept of "Marketing Mix" and its Elements (A Conceptual Review Paper)'. *International Journal of Information, Business and Management,* Vol. 6, No. 2, pp. 95–107.

Kotler, P., Keller, K. L., Brady, M., et alia. (2009). *Marketing Management.* 1st ed. Essex: Pearson Education Limited.

Malhotra, N. K., Birks, D. and Wills, P. (2012). *Marketing Research – an applied approach.* 4th ed. Harlow: Pearson Education Limited.

Saunders, M., Lewis, P. and Thornhill, A. (2019). *Research Methods for Business Students.* 8th edn. Essex: Pearson Education Limited.

Schultz, D. E. and Dev, C. S. (2012). '*Revisiting the Marketing Mix – The Apple Store experience typifies a new vision for Marketing*'. American Marketing Association – Marketing Management, 21, 2, pp 45–48.

Questions

1 To what extent do you consider the title adequately represents the research question and research objectives?
2 To what extent do you consider the literature discussed in the 'Background' section supports the research question and objectives? Give reasons for your answer.
3 In relation to the title, research question and research objectives, what key points would you wish to outline in a revised 'Background' section?
4 What are the strengths and weaknesses of the information provided in the 'Method', 'Timescale' and 'Resources' sections?
5 What key points would you wish to emphasise in revised 'Method', 'Timescale' and 'Resources' sections?
6 Proofread Katrina's draft proposal and make a list of all the spelling, typographical and referencing errors you can find.

Additional case studies relating to material covered in this chapter are available via the book's companion website: **www.pearsoned.co.uk/saunders**.
They are:

- The use of internal and word-of-mouth recruitment methods.
- Strategic issues in the brewing industry.
- Catherine Chang and women in management.
- Media climate change reporting and environmental disclosure patterns in the low-cost airline industry in the twenty-first century.
- Self-service technology: Does co-production harm value co-creation?
- Helpful but not required: A student research proposal.

Self-check answers

2.1 One starting point would be to ask your project tutor for suggestions of possible recent review articles or articles containing recommendations for further work that he or she has read. Another would be to browse recent editions of operations management journals such as the *International Journal of Operations and Production Management* for possible research ideas. These would include both statements of the absence of research and unfounded assertions. Recent reports held in your library or on the Internet may also be of use here. You could also scan one or two recently published operations management textbooks for overviews of research that has been undertaken.

2.2 From the description given, it would appear that your colleague has considered only rational thinking techniques. It would therefore seem sensible to suggest two creative thinking techniques, as these would hopefully generate an idea that would appeal to him. One technique that you could suggest is brainstorming, perhaps emphasising the need to do it with other colleagues. Exploring past projects in the accountancy area would be another possibility. You might also suggest that he keeps a notebook of ideas.

2.3 Your answer will probably differ from the points that follow. However, the sorts of things you could be considering include:

- How do business organisations benefit from their liaison with schools?
- Why do business organisations undertake school liaison activities?
- To what extent do business organisations receive value for money in their school liaison activities?

2.4 These may include:

- To identify the management and trade union objectives for the Joint Negotiating and Consultative Committee and use this to establish suitable effectiveness criteria.
- To review key literature on the use of joint negotiating and consultative committees.
- To carry out primary research in the organisation to measure the effectiveness of the Joint Negotiating and Consultative Committee.
- To identify the strengths and weaknesses of the Joint Negotiating and Consultative Committee.
- To make recommendations for action to ensure the effective function of the Joint Negotiating and Consultative Committee.

2.5   Let us go back to the example used in the chapter of the supermarket marketing manager who theorises that the introduction of a loyalty card will mean that regular customers are less likely to shop at competitor supermarkets. This could be the research proposal's starting point, i.e. a hypothesis that the introduction of a loyalty card will mean that regular customers are less likely to shop at competitor supermarkets. This prompts thoughts about the possible use of literature in the proposal and the research project itself. This literature could have at least two strands. First, a practical strand which looks at the research evidence which lends credence to the hypothesis. Second, a more abstract strand that studies human consumer behaviour and looks at the cognitive processes which affect consumer purchasing decisions.

  This ensures that the proposal and resultant research project are both theory driven and also ensures that relevant theory is covered in the literature.

2.6   Try including a sub-section in the background section that is headed 'How the previous published research has informed my research question, aim and objectives'. Then show how, say, a gap in the previous research that is there because nobody has pursued a particular approach before has led to you to fill that gap.

Get ahead using resources on the companion website at:
www.pearsoned.co.uk/saunders.

- Improve your IBM SPSS Statistics research analysis with practice tutorials.
- Save time researching on the Internet with the Smarter Online Searching Guide.
- Test your progress using self-assessment questions.

Chapter **3**

Critically reviewing the literature

Learning outcomes

By the end of this chapter you should:

- understand what is meant by being critical when reviewing the literature;
- understand the purpose of the critical literature review and its different forms;
- be clear about the content of a critical literature review and possible ways to structure it;
- be aware of types of literature available;
- be able to plan your literature search strategy and undertake searches;
- be able to evaluate the relevance, value and sufficiency of potentially relevant literature;
- be able to reference the literature accurately;
- understand the process of systematic review;
- be able to draft a critical literature review;
- understand why you must acknowledge others' work or ideas and avoid plagiarism;
- be able to apply the knowledge, skills and understanding gained to your own research project.

3.1 Introduction

As part of your studies, you have almost certainly been asked by your tutors to 'review the literature', 'produce a literature review' or 'critically review the literature' on a given topic. You may be like many students and have grown to fear the literature review, not because of the process of searching for and obtaining and reading the literature, but because of the requirement both to make reasoned judgements about the value of each piece of work and to organise ideas and findings of value into a written product known as the critical review. It is the processes of

making reasoned judgements and organising your thoughts into the written review that many find difficult and time consuming.

There are three ways in which you are likely to use literature in your research project (Creswell and Poth 2017). The first, the preliminary search that helps you to generate and refine your research ideas and draft your research proposal, has already been discussed in Sections 2.3 and 2.5. The second, often referred to as the **critical review** or **critical literature review**,

The critical review is more than a retailer's web page …

Recently, we were discussing the difficulties students have when writing their literature reviews for their research projects. Mark summarised what he felt we and fellow project tutors were saying:

> So, what happens sometimes is … a student comes to see their project tutor having obviously done a great deal of work. The student presents the tutor with what they say is the finished critical literature review. Yet the purpose of their review is unclear. It is little more than a summary of the articles and books read, each article or book being given one or two paragraphs. Some students have arranged these paragraphs alphabetically in author order, others have arranged them in chronological order. None have linked or juxtaposed the ideas. Their literature reviews look more like an online retailer's web pages than a critical review. Just like the items on these pages, each article or book has some similarities in terms of subject matter and so are grouped together. However, unlike the retailer's web pages, the reasons for these groupings are not made explicit. In addition, while it makes sense to provide similar length

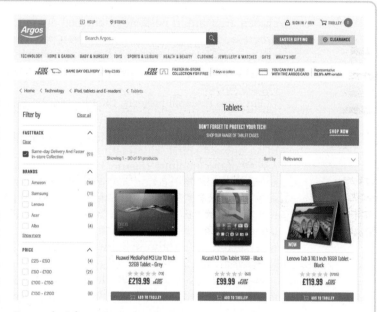

Screenshot from Argos.co.uk
Source: ©2018 Sainsbury's Argos. Reproduced with permission

summary descriptions of items on the retailer's web pages to help the prospective purchaser come to a decision about whether or not to purchase, this is not the case in a literature review. For each article or book in a literature review, the amount written should reflect its value to the student's research project.

Mark concluded: 'While such an approach obviously makes good sense for retailers and prospective purchasers, it does not work for the critical review of the literature. We obviously need to explain better what we mean by a critical review of the literature to our students.'

provides the context and theoretical framework for your research and is the focus of this chapter. The third is to place your research findings within the wider body of knowledge and forms part of your discussion chapter. We discuss this in Section 14.3. Most research textbooks, as well as your project tutor, will argue that a critical review of the literature is necessary. Although you may feel that you already have a reasonable knowledge of your research area, we believe that the process of critically reviewing and writing this review is essential. Project assessment criteria usually require you to demonstrate awareness of the current state of knowledge in your subject, its limitations and how your research fits in this wider context. As Colquitt (2013: 1211) reiterates, you need to connect your work with what has already been said and acknowledge your 'intellectual indebtedness'. This means you have to discuss what has been published and is relevant to your research topic critically.

The significance of your research and what you find out will inevitably be judged in relation to other people's research and their findings. Your written review needs to show you understand your field and its key theories, concepts and ideas, as well as the major issues and debates about your topic (Denyer and Tranfield 2009). It therefore needs to show you have established what research has been published in your chosen area and, if possible, identified any other research that might currently be in progress. Although the literature you read as part of the reviewing process will enhance your subject knowledge and help you to clarify your research question(s) further, only that which is relevant to your research will be included in your finished critical review.

For most research projects, the process of reviewing the literature and starting to draft your review will be an early activity. Despite this early start, it is usually necessary to continue refining your review throughout your project's life. The process can be likened to an upward spiral, culminating in the finished product, a written critical literature review of the literature (Figure 3.1). Once you have a good knowledge of the literature sources available (Section 3.4) you can start the process by planning your literature search (Section 3.5) and conducting your search (Section 3.6). Potentially relevant literature obtained can then be read and evaluated (Section 3.7), those which are relevant being noted and referenced (Section 3.8). You are then ready to start drafting your review (Section 3.10), fully acknowledging your sources and avoiding plagiarism (Section 3.11).

Alternatively, you may decide that rather than undertaking a traditional literature review, yours will be a self-contained research project to explore a clearly defined research question. In such situations, particularly where questions are derived from organisational practice or policy problems, business and management researchers often adopt the Systematic Review methodology to critically review the literature. We discuss this in more detail in Section 3.9.

Unlike some academic disciplines, business and management research makes use of a wide range of literature. While your review is likely to include specific business disciplines such as accounting, finance, operations, strategy, marketing and human resource management, it is also likely to include other disciplines. Those frequently consulted by our students include economics, psychology, sociology, education and geography. Given this, and the importance of the review to your research, it is vital for you to be aware of what a critical literature review is and the range of literature available before you start the reviewing process. We therefore start this chapter by outlining what is meant by being critical, and the various purposes and forms a critical review of the literature can have (Section 3.2). Subsequently we consider the structure of the literature review (Section 3.3). By doing this we hope you will understand what a critical literature review is, prior to looking at the process of creating one.

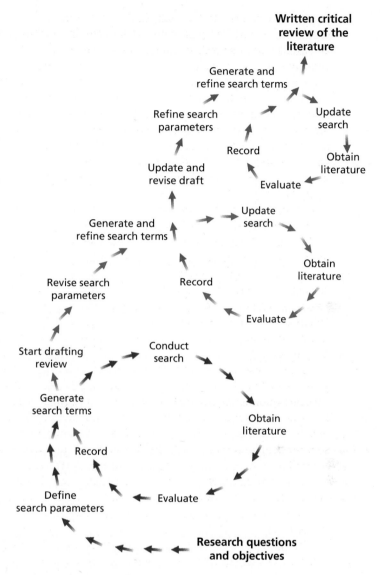

Figure 3.1 The literature review process

3.2 Being 'critical' and the purposes and forms of review

Your critical literature review should be a constructively critical analysis that develops a clear argument about what the published literature indicates is known and not known about your research question (Wallace and Wray 2016). This means, as highlighted in the opening vignette, your literature review is not just a series of paragraphs, each describing and summarising a book or journal article. Rather, you will need to assess what is significant to your research and, on this basis, decide whether or not to include it. If you think the concepts, theories, arguments or empirical research findings reported and discussed in an article are unclear, biased or inconsistent with other work and need to be researched further, you will need to justify why. This is not easy and requires careful thought.

However, by doing this you will be able to produce a reasonably detailed, constructively critical analysis of the key literature that relates to your research question. Within this you will need to discuss both theories and research findings that support and oppose your ideas.

Being 'critical'

Within your degree programme you have probably already been asked to take a critical approach for previous assignments. However, it is worth considering what we mean by critical within the context of your literature review. Mingers (2000: 225–6) argues that there are four aspects of a critical approach that should be fostered by management education:

- critique of rhetoric;
- critique of tradition;
- critique of authority;
- critique of objectivity.

The first of these, the 'critique of rhetoric', means appraising or evaluating a problem with effective use of language. In the context of your critical literature review, this emphasises the need for you, as the reviewer, to use your skills to make reasoned judgements and to argue effectively in writing. The other three aspects Mingers identifies also have implications for being critical when reading and writing about the work of others. This includes using other literature sources to question, where justification exists to do so, the conventional wisdom, the 'critique of tradition' and the dominant view portrayed in the literature you are reading, the 'critique of authority'. Finally, it is likely also to include recognising in your review that the knowledge and information you are discussing are not value-free, the 'critique of objectivity'.

Being critical in reviewing the literature is, therefore, a combination of your skills and the attitude with which you read and your ability to write cogently. In critically reviewing the literature, you need to read the literature about your research topic with some scepticism and be willing to question what you read; the term critical referring to the judgement you exercise. This means as you write your review you need to be constantly considering and justifying your own critical stance with clear arguments and references to the literature rather than just giving your own opinion. As you review the literature, your existing views and opinions are likely to be challenged by what you read. You should welcome these challenges and recognise that through thinking critically about what you are reading, your views and opinions may alter. Critically reviewing the literature for your research project, therefore, requires you to have gained topic-based background knowledge, understanding, the ability to reflect upon and to analyse the literature and, based on this, to make reasoned judgements that are argued effectively in writing. Your written review provides a detailed and justified analysis of, and commentary on, the merits and faults of the key literature within your chosen area.

Part of your critical judgement will involve you in identifying those theories and research findings that are most relevant to your research aims and objectives. This is not as easy as it seems and will invariably involve you in reading and evaluating literature that you sub-sequently judge is not relevant to your review. For some research topics, as you begin to review the literature you will observe that a certain theory and set of ideas provide the theoretical base for much of the research reported. This theory is likely to be considered by researchers as **seminal**, in other words it has been of great importance or had great influence. Seminal theories will often also be discussed in textbooks on your research area, the associated articles being frequently cited. At the same time, you will begin to recognise those researchers whose work is seminal and has been most influential in relation to your topic. The work of these researchers' is likely to be discussed more widely in journal arti-cles and they may also be referred to by name in textbooks. These researchers are likely to be recognised as the experts in your research area. However, although others consider a particular theory seminal and recognise particular researchers as experts for your topic, this does not mean that you should ignore alternative theories and other researchers. These will also need to be considered in relation to your own research in your critical review.

For other research topics you will need to integrate a number of different theoretical strands to develop your understanding. You may through your reading discover that there are contrasting theoretical perspectives on the same topic, or it may be that your research needs to integrate two or more theories from different subject areas. Dees (2003) suggests that this means you should:

- refer to and assess research by those recognised as experts in your chosen area accurately;
- consider, discuss and evaluate research that offers both similar and differing perspectives on your chosen area;
- explain your evaluation regarding the value of this research, showing clearly how it relates to your research and acknowledging key work;
- justify your arguments clearly in a logical manner;
- distinguish clearly between research findings and researchers' opinions;
- ensure your references are completely accurate.

When you draft your critical review (Section 3.10), the extent to which your literature review is critical can be evaluated using the checklist in Box 3.1. The more questions which you can answer 'yes', the more likely your review is critical.

Purposes of a critical review

Reviewing the literature critically will provide the foundation on which your research is built. As you will have gathered from the introduction, a critical review will help you to develop a good understanding and insight into relevant previous research and the trends

---

 **Box 3.1 Checklist**

Evaluating whether your literature review is critical

✔ Have you contextualised your own research showing how your research question relates to previous research reviewed, acknowledging seminal work?

✔ Have you assessed the strengths and weaknesses of the previous research reviewed in relation to your research topic?

✔ Have you been rigorous in your discussion and assessment of previous research?

✔ Have you referred to research that is counter to, as well as supports, your views and opinions, having now reviewed the literature?

✔ Have you distinguished clearly between research findings and researcher's opinions?

✔ Have you made reasoned judgements about the value and relevance of others' research to your own?

✔ Have you justified clearly your own ideas?

✔ Have you highlighted those areas where new research (yours!) is needed to provide fresh insights and taken these into account in your arguments? In particular where:
  - there are inconsistencies in current knowledge and understanding
  - you have identified potential bias in previous research
  - there are omissions in published research
  - research findings need to be tested in alternative contexts
  - evidence is lacking, inconclusive, contradictory or limited.

✔ Have you justified your arguments by accurately referencing published research?

that have emerged. Likewise, you should not expect to start your research without first reading what other researchers in your area have already found out.

Most critical reviews fulfil a series of related purposes. These can be summarised as providing: (Ridley 2018, University of Southern California 2018):

- the historical background to your research;
- an overview of your research's context by locating it in the associated contemporary debates, issues and questions provided by existing literature;
- resolution to conflicts amongst apparently contradictory previous research;
- a discussion of the relevant theories and concepts that underpin your research;
- definitions and clarifications regarding how relevant terms are being used in your research;
- insights into related research that your own work is designed to extend or challenge;
- supporting evidence that your research questions and aims are worth researching, in other words their significance.

Your literature review therefore contextualises your research in relation to previous research. You are, in effect, providing the background to and justification for your own research project. However, the way you do this in your critical review will depend on the approach you are intending to use in your research. For some research projects you will use the literature to help you to identify theories and ideas that you will subsequently test with data. This is known as a **deductive approach** (Section 4.5) in which you use the literature to develop a theoretical or conceptual framework for subsequent testing. For other research projects, the literature review, whilst outlining what is known, will reveal an aspect about which very little is known or for which there is no clear theoretical explanation. This can be likened to the literature revealing a black box within which you do not know what is happening. In such instances, the literature review will provide the context and justification for finding out what is going on inside the black box. You will then use data to explore what is going on inside the black box and from these insights develop a theory or conceptual framework. These will subsequently be related to the literature in your following discussion. This is known as an **inductive approach** (Section 4.5) and, although your research still has a clearly defined aim with research question(s) and objectives, you need to first use data to either get a clearer feeling of what is going on, or better understand the nature of the problem in order to create a conceptual framework or develop a theory. It may also be that you wish to explore the phenomenon in a particular context without being over sensitised to existing theoretical constructs. We believe such an approach cannot be taken without a competent knowledge of the literature in your subject area.

Forms of critical review

The form of critical review you undertake will depend on your research question and aim. The most widely used forms of review, along with their overall function, are summarised by the University of Southern California (2018) and include the:

> *Integrative review,* which critiques and synthesises representative literature on a topic in an integrative way to either generate new frameworks and perspectives on a topic for testing or, alternatively, reveal an area where it is unclear what is happening (a black box).

> *Theoretical review,* which examines the body of theory that has accumulated in regard to an issue, concept, theory or phenomenon. Theoretical reviews are often used to establish what theories exist and the relationships between them. They are also used

to reveal a lack of appropriate theories or that current theories are inadequate for explaining new or emerging research problems. They can therefore be used as the basis for developing new theory to be tested, or revealing an area where it is unclear what is happening (a black box).

Historical review, which examines the evolution of research on a particular topic over a period of time to place it in an historical context.

Methodological review, which focuses on research approaches (Section 4.5), strategies (Section 5.8), data collection techniques or analysis procedures, rather than the research findings. Methodological reviews are often used to provide a framework for understanding a method or methodology and to enable researchers to draw on a wide body of methodological knowledge.

Systematic Review, which uses a comprehensive pre-planned strategy for locating, critically appraising, analysing and synthesising existing research that is pertinent to a clearly formulated research question to allow conclusions to be reached about what is known (Section 3.9).

The most common of these forms for student research projects is the integrative review, although it should be noted that theoretical and systematic reviews are gaining in popularity. It is also worth noting that, depending upon the precise focus of your research project, your review may be a combination of these types. For example, a theoretical review may be supplemented with an integrative review, or a historical review may focus on the development of a particular body of theory. Alternatively, following an integrative or theoretical review, a methodological review may be incorporated into the methodology.

It is impossible to review every single piece of the literature before collecting your data. Consequently, your literature review should review the most relevant and significant research on your topic. If your review is effective, new findings and theories may emerge that neither you nor anyone else has thought about (Corbin and Strauss 2015). When you write your critical review, you will need to show how your findings and the theories you have developed, or are using, relate to the research that has gone before. This will help you demonstrate that you are familiar with what is already known about your research topic.

3.3 The content and structure of a critical review

The content of a critical review

As you begin to find, read and evaluate the literature, you will need to think how to combine the academic theories and ideas about which you are reading to form the critical review that will appear in your project report. Your review will need to evaluate the research that has already been undertaken in the area of your research project, show and explain the relationships between published research findings and reference the literature in which they were reported (Appendix 1). It will draw out the key points and trends (recognising any omissions and bias) and present them in a logical way which also shows the relationship to your own research. In doing this, you will provide readers of your project report with the necessary background knowledge to your research question(s) and objectives, and establish the boundaries of your own research. Your review will also enable the readers to see your ideas against the background of previous published research in the area. This does not necessarily mean that your ideas must extend, follow or approve those set out in the literature. You may be highly critical of the earlier research reported in the literature and seek to question or revise it through your own research. However, if

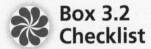

**Box 3.2
Checklist**

**Evaluating the content of your
critical literature review**

✔ Have you ensured that the literature covered
relates clearly to your research question and
objectives?

✔ Have you covered the most relevant and
significant theories of recognised experts in the
area?

✔ Have you covered the most relevant and
significant literature or at least a representative
sample?

✔ Have you included up-to-date relevant literature?

✔ Have you referenced all the literature used in the
format prescribed in the assessment criteria?

you wish to do this you must still review this literature, explain clearly why you consider
it may require revision and justify your own ideas through clear argument and with reference to the literature.

In considering the content of your critical review, you will therefore need:

- to include the key academic theories within your chosen area of research that are pertinent to, or contextualise, your research question;
- to demonstrate that your knowledge of your chosen area is up to date;
- to enable those reading your project report to find the original publications which you
cite through clear complete referencing.

When you draft your critical review (Section 3.10) its content can be evaluated using
the checklist in Box 3.2.

Possible structures for a critical review

The precise structure of the critical review is usually your choice, although you should
check, as it may be specified in the assessment criteria. Three common structures are:

- a single chapter;
- a series of chapters (for example in a larger research project);
- occurring throughout the project report as you tackle various issues (for example where
your research project is conducted inductively).

In all project reports, you should return to the key issues you raise in your literature
review in your discussion and conclusions (Section 14.3).

In the opening vignette we highlighted a common problem with literature reviews: they
just describe what each author has written, one author after another (horizontal arrows in
Figure 3.2), each item being selected subjectively by the researcher (Hart 2018). It is much
easier to be critical (and more interesting to read) if you take a thematic approach comparing and, where necessary, contrasting those authors who discuss each theme (vertical
arrows in Figure 3.2). Although there is no single structure that your critical review should
take, our students have found it useful to think of the review as a funnel in which you:

1 start at a more general level before narrowing down to your specific research question(s)
and objectives;

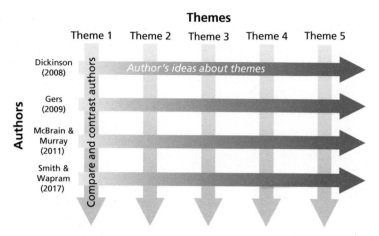

Figure 3.2 Literature review structure

2 provide a brief overview of key ideas and themes;

3 summarise, compare and contrast the research of the key authors;

4 narrow down to highlight previous research work most relevant to your own research;

5 provide a detailed account of the findings of this research and show how they are related;

6 highlight those aspects where your own research will provide fresh insights;

7 lead the reader into subsequent sections of your project report, which explore these issues.

Whichever way you structure your review, it must demonstrate that you have read, understood and evaluated the items you have located and know those which are key to your own research. The key to structuring a critical literature review is therefore to link the different ideas you find in the literature to form a coherent and cohesive argument, which sets in context and justifies your research. Obviously, it should relate to your research question and objectives. It should show a clear link from these as well as a clear link to the empirical work that will follow. Subsequent parts of your project report (Section 14.3) must follow on from this. Box 3.3 provides an extract from the literature review in a recently published paper.

Box 3.3
Focus on management research

Structure of the literature review

A refereed academic journal article by Matina Terzidou, Caroline Scarles and Mark Saunders, published in *Annals of Tourism Research* (Terzidou et al.

2017), includes a review of the literature on religious tourism. The following extract is taken from the first three paragraphs of the introduction to their article; although your review will be longer than this extract (pp. 16–117). It illustrates a structure which:

- in the first paragraph, starts at a more general level looking at the relationship between tourism and religion;
- then, in the second paragraph, narrows down to of the focus presenting an argument which

highlights that current research on religious tourism is limited to providing typologies, rather than looking at complexities that go beyond strict categories;

- and, in the third paragraph, builds on these arguments to justify clearly stated research aims.

Subsequent paragraphs in the article define and justify the particular use of the term 'pilgrimage' throughout the paper and detail the contribution of the research.

Historically, authors have reflected upon the relationship between religion and tourism as linked through the institution of pilgrimage (Vukonic, 1996), this being understood generally as a religiously motivated journey to a sacred place that has been sanctified by the present or past action of divinity (Coleman & Eade, 2004). Almost all religions encourage travel to religious sites (Cohen, 1998; Kaufman, 2005; Reader, 2014), some of which have become popular contemporary pilgrimage destinations, such as the Church of the Nativity in Bethlehem or Santiago de Compostela in Spain. Such travel is more pronounced in some non-western societies where religion and politics are strongly interrelated (Albera & Eade, 2017). In Saudi Arabia, for example, church and state are based on the Islamic law; all Muslims are expected to perform the hajj to Makkah as part of the fifth pillar of Islam, this being supported by government investment in infrastructure to control and reduce effects of crowding (Henderson, 2011; Jafari & Scott, 2014). The universality and puissance of such social movements (Albera & Eade, 2015; Boissevain, 2017; Eade and Albera, 2017), even in post-Marxist countries such as China (Bingenheimer, 2017), has triggered researchers to investigate them from a tourism perspective. Several studies discuss the 'theology of tourism' (Cohen, 1998); that is understanding travellers' behaviour based on their affiliation (Boissevain, 2017; Collins-Kreiner & Kliot, 2000), motivation, attachment and visitation patterns (Buzinde, Kalavar, Kohli, & Manuel-Navarrete, 2014; Poria, Reichel, & Biran, 2006). Others focus on the phenomenological (Andriotis, 2009), or explore the authenticity in the pilgrim experience (Andriotis, 2011; Belhassen, Caton, & Steward, 2008), the human geographical patterns in sacred spaces (Bhardwaj, 1973; Gartell & Collins-Kreiner, 2006), the impacts on hosts (Terzidou, Stylidis, & Szivas, 2008), management of sacred sites (Olsen, 2012; Shackley, 2001) or representation of religious heritage (Bandyopadhya, Morais, & Chick, 2008).

Where researchers address issues of experience and in-depth understanding of the religious tourism phenomenon, they tend to juxtapose tourism and religion; these being considered separate entities within the framework of meaning, constituting culturally erected divisions (Collins-Kreiner, 2010). Either comparisons are made between pilgrims and tourists based on their particular motivations and sociological functional perspectives (Boorstin, 1964; Nyaupane, Timothy, & Poudel, 2015; Smith, 1992), or they are linked based on mutual experiences in terms of existential and post-modern approaches highlighting spiritual elements (Eade & Albera, 2015; Gibson, 2005) that often propose the end of the sacred/ secular binary. In particular, postmodern studies consider alternative forms of religious tourism; namely secular pilgrimages, such as dark tourism (Collins-Kreiner, 2016; Hyde & Harman, 2011), nature-based tourism (Dunlap, 2006; Sharpley & Jepson, 2011), migration (Liebelt, 2010), literary tourism (Brown, 2016) and sport tourism (Gibson, 2005). These accumulate similar elements to religious journeys, such as feelings of communitas (Turner & Turner, 1978) that group members share. Such approaches allow scholars, such as Collins-Kreiner (2016) in her 'Lifecycle of Concepts', to assert that pilgrimage tourism in its traditional way has reached a stagnation point. Moreover, they limit research on religious tourism to providing typologies (Andriotis, 2009; Smith, 1992), categorizing tourists based on their motivations and experiences rather than extrapolating the complexities of a phenomenon that goes beyond strict categories (Olsen, 2017; Timothy & Olsen, 2006).

Departing from such notions, and accepting that tourism and religion co-exist in the pilgrimage experience (Timothy & Olsen, 2006), this paper aims to decipher ways of experiencing religiousness through tourist performances, intersecting textual approaches with the essential embodiment and materiality of the tourist world. Defining tourist performances as practices that occur away from home, it is argued that believers can enliven their institutionalised belief (religiousness); the trip providing the stage upon which believers can perform (Edensor, 2001). For example, while there are no specific references to tourism in the Bible, it can be inferred that a believer's behaviour and experience during leisure time could lead to a greater appreciation of God (Vukonic, 1996). More explicitly, the Qur'an often refers to travel as a means to contemplate the creation of God (Jafari & Scott, 2014). Attribution theory plays a key role within this respect as religious experience is any happening that an individual attributes at least in part to the action of supernatural forces (Proudfoot & Shaver, 1975). Through the process of sanctification (Pargament & Mahoney, 2005), believers as active performers may attribute godly intervention to activities other than the religious institutional ones, creating individualised spaces of religious experience. As part of an unfolding of cognitive and affective processes within the tourists' experience (Scarles, 2010), God may be experienced through effects of the events to which people's body parts respond (Barsalou, Barbey, Simmons, & Santos, 2005) and in which they participate, like emotional states of happiness arising through helping others. While this resembles post-modern ways of belief (Collins-Kreiner, 2016; Dunlap, 2006; Gibson, 2005), individual spaces of religious tourism experience are created within the understanding of one's religious belief system. Thus, no matter how unusual the emotional or the physical sensations are, if the individual does not consciously connect them to godly intervention, then the individual has not had a religious experience.

Source: Terzidou, M., Scarles, C. and Saunders, M.N.K. (2017). Copyright © Elsevier, Reproduced by permission of the publisher

3.4 Literature sources

The amount of literature available to help you to develop a good understanding of, and insight into, previous research is expanding rapidly as new resources are developed and made available online. The literature sources you are likely to make most use of are often referred to as:

- **secondary literature** sources, these being formally published items such as journals and books;
- **grey** (or **primary**) **literature** sources, these being items produced by all levels of government, academics, business and industry in print and electronic formats, but which are not controlled by commercial publishers; including materials such as reports and conference proceedings.

Your university's librarians are likely to be aware of a wide range of business and management literature sources that can be accessed, principally from your library's web pages, and will keep themselves up to date with new resources. In addition, you may wish to visit your country's national library or your local public library.

The main secondary and primary literature sources that you are likely to use are outlined in Table 3.1. When placing your ideas in the context of earlier research the most important sources are likely to be refereed academic journals. Books (many of which will be available as e-books) are, however, likely to be more important than professional and trade journals in this context.

Journals

Journals are also known as 'periodicals', 'serials' and 'magazines', and are published on a regular basis. Journals are a vital literature source for any research. The articles are accessed using full-text databases, this usually being restricted to members of the university (Table 3.1). Subject to copyright restrictions, many academics also make pre-publication versions of their articles available at no charge on social networking platforms such as Academia.edu and ResearchGate. Whilst the articles uploaded are not facsimiles of published versions, usually being an earlier draft, they are still extremely useful. In addition, a growing number of national governments, including the UK, are implementing 'access to research' initiatives to provide free, walk-in access to academic articles and research in public libraries (Access to Research 2018). Trade and some professional journals may be covered only partially by online databases (Table 3.2). You may therefore need to browse these journals regularly to be sure of finding useful items. Although these are increasingly available online, they are often only available to subscribers. For many academic journals you can receive email 'alerts' of the table of contents (TOC). TOCs can also be browsed online and downloaded through tertiary literature sources such as JournalTOCs and the British Library's ZETOC database (Table 3.2).

Articles in **refereed academic journals** (such as the *Journal of Management Studies* and the *Academy of Management Review*) are evaluated by academic peers prior to publication to assess their quality and suitability. They are usually written by those considered to be experts in the field. There will usually be detailed footnotes; an extensive list of references; rigorous attention to detail and verification of information. Such articles are written for a narrower audience of scholars with a particular interest in the field. The language used may be technical or highly specialised as a prior knowledge of the topic will be assumed. Prior to being accepted for publication, articles usually undergo several serious revisions, based on the referees' comments, before they are published.

These are usually the most useful for research projects as they will contain detailed reviews of relevant earlier research. Not all academic journals are refereed. Most **non-refereed academic journals** will have an editor and possibly an editorial board with subject knowledge to select articles. The relevance and usefulness of such journals varies considerably, and occasionally you may need to be wary of possible bias.

Professional journals (such as *People Management*) are produced for their members by organisations such as the Chartered Institute of Personnel and Development (CIPD), the Association of Chartered Certified Accountants (ACCA) and the American Marketing Association (AMA). They contain a mix of news-related items and articles that are more detailed. However, you need to exercise caution, as articles can be biased towards their author's or the organisation's views. Articles are often of a more practical nature and more closely related to professional needs than those in academic journals. Some organisations will also produce newsletters or current awareness publications that you may find useful for up-to-date information. Some professional organisations now give access to selected articles in their journals via their web pages, although these may be only accessible to members. **Trade journals** fulfil a similar function to professional journals. They are published by trade organisations or aimed at particular industries or trades such as catering or mining. Often they focus on new products or services and news items. They rarely contain articles based on empirical research, although some provide summaries of research. You should therefore use these with considerable caution for your research project, although they may be helpful to obtain contextual information about organisations within which you wish to conduct research.

Table 3.1 Main literature sources

Source	Content	Use for the literature review	Coverage by online databases	Likely availability
Refereed (peer-reviewed) academic journal	Detailed reports of research. Written by experts and evaluated by other experts to assess quality and suitability for publication. Rigorous attention paid to detail and verification.	Most useful of all.	Well covered. In addition, content pages often available for searching via publishers' websites.	Accessible online through various subscription services. Increasingly available via institutional repositories, national 'access to research' initiatives or social networking platforms. Those not available can usually be obtained using inter-library loans.
Non-refereed academic journal	May contain detailed reports of research. Selected by editor or editorial board with subject knowledge.	Varies considerably. Beware of bias.	Reasonably well covered. In addition, content pages often available for searching via publishers' websites.	Majority accessible online through various subscription services. Increasingly available via institutional repositories, national 'access to research' initiatives or social networking platforms. Those not available can usually be obtained using inter-library loans.
Professional journals	Mix of news items and practical detailed accounts. Sometimes include summaries of research.	Insights into practice but use with caution.	Reasonably well covered by online databases. In addition, content pages often available for searching via professional associations' websites.	Majority accessible online through various subscription services. Those not available can usually be obtained using inter-library loans. Professional associations may also provide access to their journals via their own web pages.
Trade journals/ magazines	Mix of news items and practical detailed accounts.	Insights into practice but use with caution.	Content pages often available for searching via professional associations' websites.	Not as widely available in university libraries as academic and refereed journals. Most trade associations will have an associated website.
Books and e-books	Written for specific audiences. Usually in an ordered and relatively accessible format. Often draw on wide range of sources.	Particularly useful for an overview and to find recognised experts.	Well covered by abstracts and indexes. Searches can be undertaken on remote university OPACs* via the Internet.	Widely available. Those not available locally can be obtained using inter-library loans.

(continued)

Table 3.1 (*Continued*)

Source	Content	Use for the literature review	Coverage by online databases	Likely availability
Newspapers	Written for a particular market segment. Filtered dependent on events. May be written from particular viewpoint.	Good for topical developments. Beware of possible bias in reporting and coverage.	National newspapers reasonably well covered by specialised databases.	Recent paper copies of home nation 'quality' newspapers may be kept as reference in university libraries. Online access to stories, often with additional information on the websites, for most national and international 'quality' newspapers via subscription services.
Conference proceedings	Selected papers presented at a conference.	Can be very useful if on same theme as research.	Depends on conference, although often limited. Specialist indexes sometimes available, such as 'Index to conference proceedings'.	Not widely held by university libraries. Can be difficult to find unless online. Increasingly only contain abstracts.
Reports	Topic specific. Written by academics and organisations. Those from established organisations often of high quality.	Very useful, when matches your topic.	Poor, although some specialised indexes exist.	Not widely held by university libraries. Often available online. May be possible to obtain others using inter-library loans.
Theses	Often most up-to-date research but very specific.	Good for doctorate level (and to a lesser extent MPhil) research degrees, otherwise less useful.	Covered by indices of theses.	Increasingly available online, although can also be obtained using inter-library loans. May still only be one hard (paper) copy.

*OPAC, Online Public Access Catalogue.

Source: © Mark Saunders, Philip Lewis and Adrian Thornhill 2018

Books

Books and monographs are written for specific audiences. Some are aimed at the academic market, with a theoretical slant. Others, aimed at practising professionals, may be more applied in their content. The material in books is usually presented in a more ordered and accessible manner than in journals, pulling together a wider range of topics. They are,

Table 3.2 Online databases, portals and their coverage

Name	Coverage
Access to Research	Online database for locating walk-in access to over 15 million research articles (including Business and Management) via participating UK public libraries
Blackwell Reference Online	Blackwell Encyclopaedia of Management, Blackwell 'handbooks' and 'Companions' in Management
British National Bibliography (BNB)	Bibliographic information for books and serials (journals) deposited at the British Library by UK and Irish publishers since 1950
British Library Integrated Catalogue	Online catalogue of print and electronic resources held by the British Library. Includes reference collections and document supply collections
British Library Management and Business Studies Portal	Online interface to digital full-text research reports, summaries, working papers, videos and articles as well as details of journal articles, sound recordings, video and other resources relevant to business and management
British Newspapers 1600–1900	Cross-searchable interface to full-text British Newspapers
Business Source Complete (also referred to as EBSCO)	Database including full-text articles from over 3,500 management, business, economics and information technology journals. Contains a wide range of trade and professional titles. Gives access to *Datamonitor*
Conference Index	British Library database containing proceedings of all significant conferences held worldwide (over 400,000 at time of writing)
Emerald Management eJournals (also known as Emerald Insight)	Database providing access to over 170,000 articles from over 300 journals in management and complementary subjects
EThOS (E Thesis Online Service)	Aggregated record of all doctoral theses awarded by UK HEIs dating back to 1800. Approximately 475,000 records with free access to c. 160,000 digitised theses.
Hospitality and Tourism Index	Access to hospitality and tourism journals and trade magazines since 1924
IngentaConnect	Details of articles from over 13,000 publications, some of which are available on subscription. Pay-per-view access available. Updated daily
ISI Web of Knowledge	Includes access to a wide range of services, including citation indexes for social sciences and for arts and humanities
JournalTOCs	Tables of contents (TOCs) for over 12,500 journals. Can specify journals for which there is a wish to receive future TOCs
JSTOR	Database containing full-text journals, most going back to first issue (in some cases going back to the eighteenth or nineteenth century). Covers sciences, social sciences and arts and humanities. Most recent years usually not available
Key Note	Database containing detailed market reports covering a range of sectors

(continued)

Table 3.2 (*Continued*)

Name	Coverage
Mintel Reports	Database containing detailed market research reports on wide range of sectors
Nexis	Database of full text of UK national and regional newspapers. Increasing international coverage and company profiles and industry reports
Orbis	Information on companies from around the world
ProQuest Business Premium Collection	Database covering over 5,400 journals, covering all areas of business, over 80 per cent in full text. Includes wide range of trade and professional titles and working papers
Regional Business News	Database of full text regional business publications for USA and Canada. Updated daily
Sage Premier	Database of full text for over 1,000 peer reviewed journals including business, humanities, social sciences and research methods since 1999
Science Direct	Database of full text of Elsevier journals including social sciences
Social Science Citation Index	Access to current and retrospective bibliographic information, author abstracts, and cited references found in over 1,700 social sciences journals covering more than 50 disciplines. Also covers items from approximately 3,300 of the world's leading science and technology journals
Times Digital Archive 1785–2010	Database containing complete digital editions (including photographs, illustrations and advertisements) from *The Times* national newspaper (UK)
Web of Knowledge	Single access point to Web of Science, Journal Citation Reports, Current Contents and many others
Wiley Online	Database of 1,100 full-text journals including business and law
ZETOC	British Library's index of journals and conference proceedings tables of contents (TOCs). Allows setting up of email alerts of selected journal contents pages

therefore, particularly useful as introductory sources to help clarify your research question(s) and objectives or the research methods you intend to use. Most academic textbooks, like this one, are supported by websites providing additional information. However, books may contain out-of-date material even by the time they are published.

Newspapers

Newspapers are a good source of topical events, developments within business and government, as well as recent statistical information such as share prices. They also sometimes review recent research reports (Box 3.4). Back copies starting in the early 1990s are

Box 3.4 Focus on research in the news

Accounting watchdogs find 'serious problems' at 40% of audits

By Madison Marriage

World's top accounting firms face fresh concerns about quality of their work. 47 Global accounting watchdogs identified serious problems at 40 per cent of the audits they inspected last year, raising fresh concerns about the quality of work being carried out by the world's largest accounting firms.

According to the International Forum of Independent Audit Regulators, accounting lapses were identified at two-fifths of the 918 audits of listed public interest entities they inspected last year. The audit inspections focused on organisations in riskier or complex situations such as mergers or acquisitions, according to the IFIAR, whose members include 52 audit regulators around the world. The most common issue identified by these regulators was a failure among auditors to "assess the reasonableness of assumptions". The second biggest problem was a failure among auditors to "sufficiently test the accuracy and completeness of data or reports produced by management" . . .

Prem Sikka, an accounting expert and emeritus professor at Essex University, said the frequency of problems identified by the IFIAR was "terrible". "There are a whole range of issues and there is no simple fix. There is a huge knowledge failure in the audit industry which is not being looked at. The whole industry is ripe for reform. The question is where is the political will for this?"

The report showed that 41 per cent of the problems identified by audit regulators last year related to independence and ethics. These included accounting firms failing to maintain their independence due to financial relationships with clients, and failing to evaluate the extent of non-audit and audit services provided to clients. Many firms also failed "to implement a reliable system for tracking business relationships, audit firm financial interests, and corporate family trees", the IFIAR said. Its research was based on feedback from 33 audit regulators who inspected the work done by 120 audit firms.

 Source of abridged extract: Marriage, M. (2018) 'Accounting watchdogs find 'serious problems' at 40% of audits', FT.com, 11 March. Available at https://www.ft.com/content/b9dbd1cc-23a5-11e8-ae48-60d3531b7d11 [Accessed 16 March 2018]. Copyright ©2018 Financial Times Limited

available online via a full-text subscription service, such as *Nexis* (Table 3.2). Current editions of newspapers are available in print form and online, although there is often a charge for full online access. Items in earlier issues are more difficult to access and often only include text. An exception is the *Times Digital Archive 1785–2010* (Table 3.2) of *The Times* newspaper. You need to be careful, as newspapers may contain bias in their coverage, be it political, geographical or personal. Reporting can also be inaccurate, and you may not pick up any subsequent amendments. In addition, the news presented is filtered depending on events at the time, with priority given to more headline-grabbing stories (Stewart and Kamins 1993).

Reports

Reports include market research reports such as those produced by Mintel and Key Note, government reports and academic reports. Even if you are able to locate these, you may find it difficult to gain access to them because they are often not available free of charge (Section 8.3). Reports are not well indexed in the databases, and you will need to rely on specific search tools such as the *British Library Integrated Catalogue* (Table 3.2).

Freedom of information legislation by many governments now means a vast number of reports are now available online; for example, through the European Union's EUROPA website and the Commission's Statistics website Eurostat. These and other governmental websites are listed in Table 8.1.

Conference proceedings

Conference proceedings, sometimes referred to as symposia, are often published as unique titles within journals or as books. Most conferences will have a theme that is very specific, but some have a wide-ranging overview. Proceedings are not well indexed by tertiary literature, so, as with reports, you may have to rely on specific search tools such as the *British Library Integrated Catalogue* (Table 3.2) as well as general search engines such as Google. If you do locate and are able to obtain the proceedings for a conference on the theme of your research, you will have a wealth of relevant information. Many conferences have associated web pages providing abstracts and occasionally the full papers presented at the conference.

Theses

Theses are unique and so for a major research project can be a good source of detailed information; they will also be a good source of further references. Unfortunately, they can be difficult to locate and, when found, difficult to access as there may be only one copy at the awarding institution. Specific search tools are available, such as *E Thesis Online Service* (Table 3.2). Only research degrees, in particular PhDs, are covered well by these tertiary resources. Research undertaken as part of a taught master's degree (usually called a dissertation) is not covered as systematically.

3.5 Planning your literature search

It is important that you plan this search carefully to ensure that you locate relevant and up-to-date literature. This will enable you to establish what research has previously been published in your area and to relate your own research to it. All our students have found their literature search a time-consuming process, which takes far longer than expected. Fortunately, time spent planning will be repaid in time saved when searching for relevant literature. As you start to plan your search, you need to beware of information overload! One of the easiest ways to avoid this is to start the main search for your critical review with clearly defined research question(s), objectives and outline proposal (Sections 2.4 and 2.5). Before commencing your literature search, we suggest that you undertake further planning by writing down your search strategy and, if possible, discussing it with your project tutor. This should include:

- the parameters of your search;
- the search terms and phrases you intend to use;
- the online databases and search engines you intend to use;
- the criteria you intend to use to select the relevant and useful studies from all the items you find.

While it is inevitable that your search strategy will be refined as your literature search progresses, we believe that such a planned approach is important as it forces you to think carefully about your research strategy and justify, at least to yourself, why you are doing what you are doing.

Defining the parameters of your search

For most research questions and objectives, you will have a good idea of which subject matter is going to be relevant. You will, however, be less clear about the parameters within which you need to search. In particular, you need to be clear about the following (derived from Bell and Waters 2014):

- language of publication (e.g. English);
- subject area (e.g. accounting);
- business sector (e.g. manufacturing);
- geographical area (e.g. Europe);
- publication period (e.g. the last 10 years);
- literature type (e.g. refereed journals and books).

One way of starting to firm up these parameters is to re-examine your lecture notes and course textbooks in the area of your research question. While re-examining these, we suggest you make a note of subjects that appear most pertinent to your research question and the names of relevant authors. These will be helpful when generating possible search terms and phrases later.

For example, if your research was on the benefits of cause-related marketing to charities you might identify the subject area as marketing and charities. Implicit in this is the need to think broadly. A frequent comment we hear from students who have attempted a literature search is 'there's nothing written on my research topic'. This is usually because they have identified one or more of their parameters too narrowly or chosen their search terms poorly. We therefore recommend that if you encounter this problem you broaden one or more of your parameters to include material that your narrower search would not have located (see Box 3.7).

Generating your search terms

It is important at this stage to read both articles by key authors and recent review articles in the area of your research. This will help you to define your subject matter and to suggest appropriate search terms and phrases. Recent review articles in your research area are often helpful here, as they discuss the current state of research for a particular topic and can help you to refine your search terms. In addition, they will probably contain references to other work that is pertinent to your research question(s) and objectives (Box 3.5). If you are unsure about review articles, your project tutor should be able to point you in the right direction. Another potentially useful source of references are dissertations and theses in your university's library.

Box 3.5
Focus on student research

Generating search terms

Han's research question was, 'How do the actual management requirements of a school pupil record administration system differ from those suggested by the literature?' She brainstormed this question with her peer group, all of whom were teachers in Hong Kong. The resulting list included the following search terms and phrases:

schools, pupil records, administration, user requirements, computer, management information system, access, legislation, information, database, security, UK, Hong Kong, theories

The group evaluated these and others. As a result, the following search terms (and phrases) were selected:

pupil records, management information system, computer, database, user requirement

Online dictionaries and encyclopaedias were used subsequently to add to the choice of search terms:

student record, MIS, security

Han made a note of these prior to using them in combination to search the tertiary literature sources.

After re-reading your lecture notes and textbooks and undertaking this limited reading, you will have a list of subjects that appear relevant to your research project. You now need to define precisely what is relevant to your research in terms of search terms.

The identification of search terms is the most important part of planning your search for relevant literature (Bell and Waters 2014). **Search terms** are the basic terms that describe your research question(s) and objectives, and will be used to search the tertiary literature. Search terms (which can include authors' family names identified in the examination of your lecture notes and course textbooks) can be identified using one or a number of different techniques in combination. Those found most useful by our students include:

Discussion

We believe you should be taking every opportunity to discuss your research. In discussing your work with others, whether face-to-face or online, you will be sharing your ideas, getting feedback and obtaining new ideas and approaches. This process will help you to refine and clarify your topic.

Brainstorming

Brainstorming has already been outlined as a technique for helping you to develop your research question (Section 2.3). However, it is also helpful for generating search terms. Either individually or as part of a group, you write down all the words and short phrases that come to mind on your research topic (Box 3.5). These are then evaluated and search terms (and phrases) selected.

Initial reading, dictionaries, encyclopaedias, handbooks and thesauruses

To produce the most relevant search terms you may need to build on your brainstorming session with support materials such as dictionaries, encyclopaedias, handbooks and thesauruses, both general and subject specific. These are also good starting points for new topics with which you may be unfamiliar and for related subject areas. Initial reading, particularly of recent review articles, may also be of help here. Project tutors, colleagues and librarians can also be useful sources of ideas.

It is also possible to obtain definitions via the Internet. Google offers a 'define' search option (by typing 'Define:[enter term]') that provides links to websites providing definitions. Definitions are also offered in online encyclopaedias such as Wikipedia. These are often available in multiple languages and, although registered users are allowed to edit the entries, inappropriate changes are usually removed quickly. While entries tend to become more comprehensive and balanced as contributors add to and revise them, Wikipedia (2018) 'makes no guarantee of validity'. However, while online encyclopaedias such as Wikipedia may be useful for a quick reference or in helping to define keywords, your university will almost certainly expect you to justify the definitions in your research project using refereed journal articles or textbooks.

Relevance trees

Relevance trees provide a useful method of bringing some form of structure to your literature search and of guiding your search process (Sharp et al. 2002). They look similar to an organisation chart and are a hierarchical 'graph-like' arrangement of headings and subheadings (Box 3.6). These headings and subheadings describe your research question(s) and objectives and may be terms (including authors' names) with which you can search. Relevance trees are often constructed after brainstorming and can help you decide:

- those search terms that are most relevant to your research question(s) and objectives;

Box 3.6
Focus on student research

Using a relevance tree

Simone's research question was 'How does power facilitate knowledge integration in supply chains?'

After brainstorming her question, she decided to construct a relevance tree on her tablet using the search terms and phrases that had been generated.

Using her relevance tree, Simone identified those areas that she needed to search immediately (in blue) and those that she particularly needed to focus on (starred*).

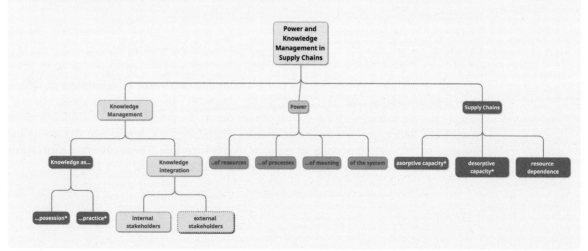

- those areas you will search first and which your search will use later;
- the areas that are more important – these tend to have more branches.

  To construct a relevance tree:

1 Start with your research question or an objective at the top level.
2 Identify two or more subject areas that you think are important.
3 Further subdivide each major subject area into sub-areas that you think are of relevance.
4 Further divide the sub-areas into more precise sub-areas that you think are of relevance.
5 Identify those areas that you need to search immediately and those that you particularly need to focus on. Your project tutor will be of particular help here.
6 As your reading and reviewing progress, add new areas to your relevance tree.

Apps such as SimpleMind (2018) and software such as Webspiration Pro (2018) and MindGenius (2018) can be used to help generate relevance trees. Many apps or software also allow you to attach notes to your relevance tree and can help generate an initial structure for your literature review.

3.6 Conducting your literature search

Your literature search will probably be conducted using a variety of approaches:

- searching using online databases;
- obtaining relevant literature referenced in books and journal articles you have already read;
- browsing and scanning secondary literature in your library;
- general online searching.

Eventually it is likely you will be using a variety of these in combination. However, we suggest that you start your search by obtaining relevant literature that has been referenced in books and articles you have already read. Although books are unlikely to give adequate up-to-date coverage of your research question, they provide a useful starting point and usually contain some references to further reading. Reading these will enable you to refine your research question(s), objectives and the associated search terms prior to searching using tertiary literature sources. It will also help you to see more clearly how your research relates to previous research, and will provide fresh insights.

Searching using databases

It is very tempting with easy access to the Internet to start your literature search with a general search engine such as Bing or Google. While this can retrieve some useful information, it must be treated with care. Your project report is expected to be an academic piece of work and hence must use academic sources. Therefore it is essential that you use online literature sources which provide access to academic literature. These consist of three types of online databases and are listed in order of likely importance to your search:

1 **Full-text (online) databases** that index and provide abstracts and full-text of articles from a range of journals (and sometimes books, chapters from books, reports, theses and conferences), as well as the full text of articles.

2 **Abstracts** that only include an index of the abstracts of articles from a range of journals (and sometimes books, chapters from books, reports, theses and conferences), hence the name abstract.

3 **Indexes** that, as the name suggests, only index articles from a range of journals (and sometimes books, chapters from books, reports, theses and conferences).

Within all of these, the information provided will be sufficient to locate the item – for example, for journal articles:

- author or authors of the article;
- date of publication;
- title of the article;
- title of the journal;
- volume (and part number) of the journal issue;
- page numbers of the article.

Most searches will be undertaken to find articles using user defined search terms or an author's name. Occasionally you may wish to search by finding those authors who have referenced (cited) an article after it has been published. A citation index enables you to do this as it lists by author the other authors who have cited that author's works subsequent to their publication. Alternatively, if you are using the specialised search engine Google Scholar you can find out who has cited a particular article by clicking on 'cited by'. The article's abstract will be useful in helping you to assess the content and relevance of an article to your research before obtaining a copy. You should beware of using abstracts as a substitute for the full article, as a source of information for your research. They contain only a summary of the article and are likely to exclude much of relevance. Full-text databases usually allow both the searching and retrieval of the full text, principally for journal articles; the articles being retrieved in portable document file (PDF) format. These are read using software such as Adobe Reader, which can be downloaded free of charge.

Your access to the majority of full-text databases will be paid for by a subscription from your university (Table 3.2). There are, however, some pay-as-you-use databases, where the cost of the search is passed on to the user. Specialist search engines (such as Google Scholar) are often free, but offer only limited access to the full text (Table 3.4). While many databases are intuitive to use, it is still advisable to obtain a librarian's help or to attend a training session prior to your search to find out about the specific features available. It is also vital that you plan and prepare your search in advance so your time is not wasted.

Virtually all universities' library OPACs (online public access catalogues) are accessible online. These provide a very useful means of locating resources. If you identify useful collections of books and journals, it is possible to make use of other university libraries in the vacations. Within the UK, the SCONUL Vacation Access Scheme allows students to use books and journals at the 170 institutions who participate in the scheme.[1] In addition over 70 research libraries in the UK and Ireland (including the British Library, Oxford and Cambridge Universities and the National Libraries of Scotland and Wales) have also made their catalogues available online. These can be accessed through COPAC, the National Academic and Specialist Library Catalogue.[2]

---

[1]Details of these can be found at: https://www.sconul.ac.uk/

[2]The Internet address for COPAC is https://copac.ac.uk/

To ensure maximum coverage in your search, you need to use all appropriate online databases. One mistake many people make is to restrict their searches to one or two business and management online databases rather than use a variety. The coverage of each online database differs both geographically and in type of journal. In addition, a database may state that it indexes a particular journal yet may do so only selectively. This emphasises the importance of using a range of databases to ensure a wide coverage of available literature. Some of those more frequently used are outlined in Table 3.2. However, new databases and portals are being developed all the time, so it is worth asking a librarian for advice.

Once your search terms have been identified, searching using databases is a relatively straightforward process. You need to:

1 make a list of the search terms that describe your research question(s) and objectives;
2 search appropriate online databases;
3 note precise details, including the search strings used, of the actual searches you have undertaken for each database;
4 note the full reference of each item found; this can normally be done by importing the references into software for managing bibliographies, such as Endnote™ or Reference Manager™ or research tools such as 'Mendeley' or 'Zotero'.
5 Wherever possible import the article into your bibliography or research tool or, alternatively, download it in PDF format and save it on your USB mass storage device using the author, date and a brief description as a filename. This will help you locate it later. For example, an article by Mark on the use of web questionnaires might be saved using the filename: Saunders[2012]web_questionnaire.pdf.

Tranfield et al. (2003) emphasise the importance of reporting your literature search strategy in sufficient detail to ensure that your search could be replicated (see Box 3.8). Your review will be based on the subset of those items found which you consider are relevant.

Most databases now allow full-text searches using natural language where you decide on the word or phrase combinations for search terms. This means, for example, you can search the complete text of an article using your search terms. All relevant results are returned, usually after applying a process of **lemmatization** to you search query. This removes all inflectional endings and takes categories and inflections into account to reduce

Box 3.7
Checklist

Minimising problems with your database search

✔ Is the spelling incorrect? Behaviour is spelt with a 'u' in the UK but without in the USA.
✔ Is the language incorrect? Chemists in the UK but drug stores in the USA.
✔ Are you using incorrect terminology? In recent years some terms have been replaced by others, such as 'redundancy' being replaced by 'downsizing'.

✔ Are you using recognised acronyms and abbreviations? For example, UK for United Kingdom or BA instead of British Airways.
✔ Are you avoiding jargon and using accepted terminology? For example, downsizing rather than redundancy.
✔ Are you searching over a sensible publication period? For example, the last 15 years rather than the last five years.
✔ Are you searching the most suitable type of literature for your research project? For example, peer-reviewed (refereed) journal articles rather than all articles.

Box 3.8
Focus on management research

Systematically analysing the strategic flexibility literature to produce a new conceptual framework

In his recent article in the *International Journal of Management Reviews,* Brozovic (2018) systematically analysed the literature on strategic flexibility to link different aspects together. His review of 156 contributions resulted in a comprehensive analytic model offering a novel perspective to understanding strategic flexibility.

The first step in the review process was to identify the relevant literature on strategic flexibility. Five databases were identified for the search, Business Source Premier, Elsevier, Emerald, Google Scholar and Wiley. These were searched in the title, keyword and abstract fields using the search term 'strategic flexibility'.

All articles which mentioned, but did not focus on, strategic flexibility were excluded. The reference lists of those that remained were scanned to identify other relevant publications. Brozovic's final list of 156 contributions on which he based his review comprised 141 articles, eight book chapters and seven books. Three of the articles were available online in advance of publication.

each word used as a search term to its base or 'lemma'. However, some databases rely on or also offer the option to search using **stemming**. This cuts off a word's ending in order to determine the word stem. Despite using these tools, your searches may still be unsuccessful. The most frequent causes of failure are summarised in Box 3.7 as a checklist.

Searches normally use a combination of search terms linked using **Boolean logic**. These are known as **search strings** and enable you to combine, limit or widen the variety of items found using 'link terms' (Table 3.3). Initially, it may be useful also to limit your search to peer-reviewed journal articles for which the full text is available. It may also be valuable to narrow your search to specific years, especially if you are finding a wealth of items and need to concentrate on the most up-to-date. By contrast, searching by author allows you to broaden your search to find other work by known researchers in your area.

There are, however, problems with searching the full text. In particular, the context of a search term may be inappropriate, leading to retrieval of numerous irrelevant articles and information overload. Fortunately, you can also search one or more specified fields in the database such as the abstract, author or title. Usually, searching the abstract results in fewer irrelevant articles although, inevitably, you may not find some relevant ones either! Specifying other fields, for example the abstract, will be useful if you wish to find articles by a key author in your subject area.

Table 3.3 Search connectors

Connector	Purpose	Example	Outcome
AND	Narrows search	Recruitment AND interviewing AND skills	Only articles containing all three search terms selected
OR	Widens search	Recruitment OR selection	Articles with at least one search term selected
NOT	Excludes terms from search	Recruitment NOT selection	Selects articles containing the search term 'recruitment' that do not contain the search term 'selection'

Browsing and scanning

Any search will find only some of the relevant literature. You will therefore also need to browse and scan the literature. New publications such as journal articles are unlikely to be indexed immediately in databases, so you will need to browse the relevant journals to gain an idea of their most recent and 'advance online' content. In contrast, scanning will involve you going through individual items such as a journal article to pick out points and references to additional relevant articles, which you have not found elsewhere (Box 3.8). It is particularly important that you browse and scan trade and professional journals, as these are less likely to be covered by the online databases.

To make browsing and scanning easier you should:

- identify when those journals that are the most relevant are published and, where possible, ensure you receive email 'alerts' of their tables of contents (TOCs);
- identify those professional journals that are most relevant and regularly browse them;
- scan new book reviews in journals and newspapers;
- scan publishers' new book catalogues where available;
- discuss your research with your project tutor and librarians, who may be aware of other relevant literature.

Websites of bookshops such as Amazon and Blackwell provide access to catalogues of books in print. These can usually be searched by author, title and subject, and may have reviews attached. Some bookseller websites (and Google Books) have a facility whereby you can view selected pages from the book. However, as when using electronic indexes and abstracts, it is important that you keep full details of the literature you have scanned and browsed (Box 3.9). As well as enabling you to outline the method you used for your literature review, it will also help prevent you repeating searches you have already undertaken.

Other search tools

When using other search tools, we recommend you keep full details of the searches you have undertaken, making a note of:

- the search tool used;
- the precise search undertaken;
- the date when the search was undertaken;
- the total number of items retrieved.

Search tools, often referred to as **search engines**, are probably the most important method of online searching for your literature review as they will enable you to locate most current and up-to-date items. Although normally accessed through home pages, each search tool will have its own address (Table 3.4). Search tools can be divided into four distinct categories (Table 3.4):

- general search engines;
- metasearch engines;
- specialised search engines and information gateways;
- subject directories.

Most search engines index every separate document. In contrast, subject directories index only the 'most important' online documents. Therefore, if you are using a clear term to search for an unknown vaguely described document, use a search engine. If you are looking for a document about a particular topic, use a subject directory.

Box 3.9
Focus on student research

Searching using databases

Matthew described his research project using the search terms 'marketing' and 'non profit'. Unfortunately, he encountered problems when carrying out his search using one of the online databases of full text and abstracts for business, management and economics journals to which his university subscribed.

When he entered the search term 'marketing', he retrieved references to over 1,156,000 items, many of which were in trade magazines. Entering the term 'non profit' on its own retrieved fewer references, only 40,000! He was unsure how to combine his search terms into search strings to make his search more specific. Full-text versions were not available for many of the most recent items retrieved.

After discussing the problem, the librarian showed Matthew how to use the advanced search option of the online database. Using this, Matthew first searched using the terms 'marketing' AND 'non profit combined as a search string. This still resulted in over 3,200 items

being highlighted. He then refined his search further by limiting it to the collection of scholarly (peer-reviewed) journals. This resulted in over 1,100 items being retrieved. He therefore decided to limit his search to the abstract field rather than the full text. This resulted in 222 items being retrieved.

He then copied the references for these items (articles) onto his MP3 player. As Matthew scrolled through these, he noted that some of them had direct links to copies of the full text stored as a PDF file. For many of the others, the librarian informed him that he could access the full text using different online databases. However, he still needed to assess each article's relevance to his research before obtaining full copies.

Matthew made a note of the details of his search:

Database:	Business Source Complete
Collection:	Scholarly (peer-reviewed) journals
Dates:	1951 to 2018
Search:	marketing AND non profit
Fields searched:	Abstract
Date of search:	16 May 2018
Total items retrieved	222

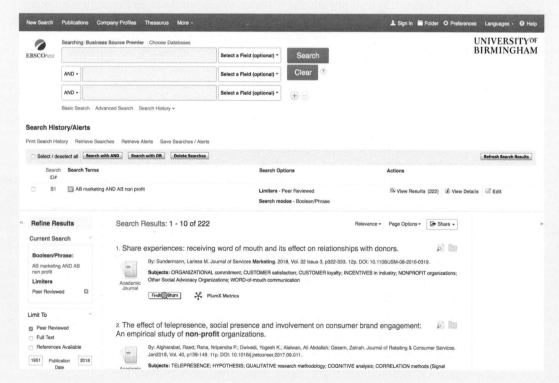

Table 3.4 Selected online search tools and their coverage

Name	Internet address	Comment
General search engines		
Bing	www.bing.com	Access to billions of web pages, can link to Facebook
Google	www.google.com	Access to billions of web pages
Google UK	www.google.co.uk	Country-based Google – optimised to show country results
Specialised search engines		
Google Scholar	www.scholar.google.com	Searches scholarly literature allowing you to locate and sometimes download the complete document, often from an institutional repository
UK government	www.gov.uk	Searches central and local government websites and government agencies
Information gateways		
Publishers' catalogues homepage	www.lights.ca/publisher/	Searchable links to major publishers' websites, listed alphabetically by country
Subject directories		
Dotdash	www.dotdash.com	Organised by subjects, offers numerous guides
ipl2	www.ipl.org	High-quality site only providing 'information you can trust'

General search engines such as Google and Bing normally use search terms and Boolean logic (Table 3.3) or a phrase. Each search engine indexes and searches automatically, usually finding a very large number of sites (Box 3.10). As people have not evaluated these sites, many are inappropriate or unreliable. As no two general search engines search in precisely the same way, it is advisable (and often necessary) to use more than one. In contrast, metasearch engines allow you to search using a selection of search engines at the same time, using the same interface. This makes searching easier, and the search can be faster. Unfortunately, it is less easy to control the sites that are retrieved. Consequently, metasearch engines often generate more inappropriate or unreliable sites than general search engines.

Specialised search engines cater for specific subject areas. For example, Google Scholar searches scholarly literature across many disciplines using sources such as articles, theses, books and abstracts from academic publishers, professional bodies, universities and websites, allowing you to locate the complete document. Documents are subsequently ranked on a combination of factors including how often it has been cited, where it was published and by whom it was written. Of particular use is the direct link to open access articles stored on institutional repositories and on social networking sites (discussed next). To use specialised search engines it is necessary to define your general subject area prior to your search. Information gateways also require you to define your subject area. Information gateways are often compiled by staff from departments in academic institutions. Although the number of websites obtained is fewer, they can be far more relevant, as each site is evaluated prior to being added to the gateway.

Subject directories are searchable catalogues of sites collected and organised by humans. The sites are categorised into subject areas and are useful for searching for broad topics. As people normally compile them, their content has been partly censored and

Box 3.10
Focus on student research

Undertaking an online search using a specialist search engine

Kay's research question was reasonably defined, if somewhat broad. She wanted to look at dark tourism and the impact of place on visitors to sites of genocide. As part of her search strategy she decided, alongside the academic databases of business and management journals, to search the Internet using a specialised search engine - Google Scholar. Her first search term 'dark tourism' revealed that there were over 213,000 scholarly publications and displayed the first few. Of these, the second appeared to be potentially useful as it focussed on the consumption of dark tourist sites.

Kay clicked on the pdf link and downloaded the paper from the author's university's institutional repository. She then returned to Google Scholar and clicked on 'Cited by 569'. The first screen revealed a few of the 569 publications that had cited that paper since it had been published. As many could be downloaded as PDF files, she downloaded, and saved those publications that seemed relevant on her MP3 player. Kay then made a note of the authors listed on the page, so she could search for them, using her university's online databases.

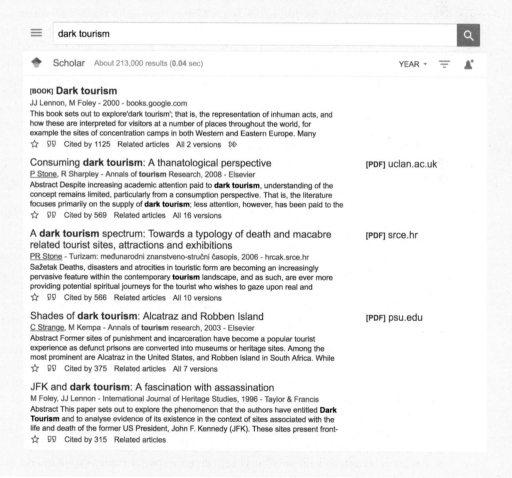

evaluated. Consequently, the number of sites retrieved is fewer but they usually provide material that is more appropriate (Table 3.4).

Search tools are becoming more sophisticated all the time. Be careful, their use can be extremely time consuming. Your search will probably locate a mass of resources, many of which will be irrelevant to you. It is also easy to become side tracked to more interesting and glossy websites not relevant to your research needs! There are numerous web-based tutorials to help you learn to search the web. One of these, Marketing Insights' *Smarter Online Searching Guide*, is available via this book's web page. This outlines how to use a range of search tools, including Advanced search in Google and online e-business resources.

Institutional repositories and social networking platforms

Many universities now expect their academics to deposit digital full-text copies of their publications, particularly journal articles, in their **institutional repository.** This is an open access collection of the university staff's research outputs from which full-text items can be downloaded. Increasingly academics (including Mark!) are also uploading pre-publication copies of their journal articles, book chapters and conference papers to social networking platforms such as Academia.edu and ResearchGate. Providing you know the author's name (and their university), you can often access their publications through these resources free of charge. Such institutional repositories and social networking sites are useful if your university does not subscribe to the online database of full-text articles in which their publications are stored, particularly as uploaded copies can often be found using specialised search engines such as Google Scholar (Table 3.4, Box 3.10).

Obtaining the literature

As outlined earlier, searches using online databases (Table 3.2) and search tools (Table 3.4) will provide you with details of what literature is available and where to locate it, in many cases providing a hyperlink to an electronic copy. We emphasise again, you should, whenever possible, download the electronic copy in PDF format and save it on your USB mass storage device. However, where there is no hyperlink, the next stage (Figure 3.1) is to obtain the remaining items. To do this you need to:

1 Check your library online catalogue to find out whether your library holds the appropriate publications.

2 For those publications that are held by your library or available online, note their location and:

   i find the publication and scan it to discover whether it is likely to be worth reading thoroughly – for articles it is often possible to make a reasonable assessment of their utility using the abstract (Box 3.11); or

   ii browse other books and journals with similar classmarks to see whether they may also be of use.

3 For those items not held by your library either as paper copies or via online subscriptions, it may still be possible to obtain them online, either through institutional repositories or, for books which are no longer copyright, through Google Books.

Box 3.11
Focus on student research

Assessing the utility of an article using the abstract

Jana's research project was about how small- and medium-sized enterprises' (SMEs) use of formal and informal learning differed between Eastern and Western European countries. In a search using the Emerald Insight online database she had found a peer-reviewed article in the *European Journal of Training and Development* by Saunders, Gray and Goregaokar (2014) that she considered might be useful. She decided to read the abstract online to check.

The abstract confirmed that the **Purpose** of the article was to explore how SMEs learn and innovate using both formal and informal learning. More details regarding this were given in the **findings** section of the abstract. The **design/methodology/approach** indicated that the research had been undertaken with over 1,000 SMEs, data being collected using both questionnaires and focus groups. The **research limitations/implications** section indicated the need for further research to understand the interrelationships between informal learning, crisis events and SME innovation. Jana wondered if this might be a good aspect to focus on in her research.

Based on this information, Jana decided the article was likely to be useful for her research project, so she downloaded it and saved an electronic copy in PDF format.

Source: Saunders et al. (2014). Copyright © 2014 Emerald Group Publishing (https://www-emeraldinsight-com .ezproxyd.bham.ac.uk/doi/abs/10.1108/EJTD-07-2013-0073/). Reproduced by permission of the publisher

4 Alternatively you may be able:

i to borrow the item from another library using the **inter-library loan** service. This is not a free service so make sure you really need it first. Our students have found that, in general, it is only worthwhile to use inter-library loans for articles from refereed journals and books; or

ii visit a library where they are held as 'reference only' copies. The British Library in London, for example, has one of the most extensive collection of books, journals, market research reports, trade literature, company annual reports, research reports, doctoral theses and conference proceedings in the world.[3]

3.7 Reading critically and evaluating the literature

Adopting a critical perspective in your reading

Harvard College Library (2018) provides its students with a useful checklist of skills to be practised for effective reading. These skills include:

Previewing: which is considering the precise purpose of the text before you start reading in detail to establish how it may inform your literature search.

Annotating: that is, conducting a dialogue with yourself, the author and the issues and ideas at stake.

Outlining, summarising and analysing: the best way to determine that you've really got the point is to be able to state it in your own words. Outlining the argument of a text is a version of annotating, and can be done quite informally in the margins of the text. Summarising does the same thing, making the connections between ideas explicit; analysing incorporates an evaluation to your summary.

Looking for repetitions and patterns: these, alongside the way authors use language, indicate what is important.

Contextualising: which is looking at what you have read and acknowledging how it is framed by other work.

Comparing and contrasting: which involves you asking yourself how your thinking has been altered by this reading and how it has affected your response to the issues and themes you have already considered.

Wallace and Wray (2016) recommend the use of **review questions**. These are specific questions you ask of the reading, which will be linked either directly or indirectly to your research question. So you may, for example, address a piece of reading with the view to it answering the question: 'What does research suggest are the main reasons why customers are likely to change car insurance provider?'

The word 'critical' has appeared in this chapter a number of times so far. It is vital in your reading of the literature that a critical stance should be taken. So what is meant by critical reading? Wallace and Wray (2016: 8) sum this up rather succinctly by saying that critical skills 'can be boiled down to the capacity to evaluate what you read and the capacity to relate what you read to other information'.

---

[3]Further details of the business and management collection can be found at www.bl.uk/managementbusiness.

More specifically, Wallace and Wray (2016) advocate the use of five critical questions to employ in critical reading. These are:

1 Why am I reading this? (The authors argue that this is where the review question is particularly valuable. It acts as a focusing device and ensures that you stick to the purpose of the reading and do not get side tracked too much by the author's agenda.)
2 What is the author trying to do in writing this? (The answer to this may assist you in deciding how valuable the writing may be for your purposes.)
3 What is the writer saying that is relevant to what I want to find out?
4 How convincing is what the author is saying? (In particular, is the argument based on a conclusion which is justified by the evidence?)
5 What use can I make of the reading?

Evaluating the literature

Although the Internet has revolutionised searching for literature, you should beware as the quantity of material is enormous and the quality highly variable. Not surprisingly, a question frequently asked by our students is, 'How do I know what I'm reading is relevant?' Two further questions often asked by our students are, 'How do I assess the value of what I read?' and 'How do I know when I've read enough?' All of these are concerned with the process of evaluation. They involve defining the scope of your review and assessing the value of the items that you have obtained in helping you to answer your research question(s) and meet your objectives. Although there are no set ways of approaching these questions, our students have found the following advice helpful.

Assessing relevance

Assessing the relevance of the literature you have collected to your research depends on your research question(s) and objectives. Remember that you are looking for relevance, not critically assessing the ideas contained within. When doing this, it helps to have thought about and made a note of the criteria for inclusion and exclusion prior to assessing each item of literature. Box 3.11 also provides some help here.

You should, of course, try to read all the literature that is most closely related to your research question(s) and objectives. For some research questions, particularly for new research areas, there is unlikely to be much closely related literature and so you will have to review more broadly. For research questions where research has been going on for some years, you may be able to focus on more closely related literature.

Remember to make notes about the relevance (and value) of each item as you read it and the reasons why you came to your conclusion. You may need to include your evaluation as part of your critical review.

Assessing value

Assessing the value of the literature you have collected is concerned with the quality of the research that has been undertaken. As such it is concerned with issues such as methodological rigour, theory robustness and the quality of the reasoning or arguments. For example, you need to beware of managerial autobiographies, where a successful entrepreneur's or managing director's work experiences are presented as the way to achieve business success (Fisher 2010), and articles in trade magazines. The knowledge presented in such books and articles may well be subjective rather than based upon systematic research.

For refereed journal articles (and some book chapters), the review process means that peers have assessed the quality of research and suggested amendments before they are published. This means the research is likely to have been undertaken with methodological rigour, have used theory appropriately and been argued cogently. However, it is still important to assess the value yourself in terms of possible bias, methodological omissions and precision (Box 3.12).

It is worth noting that, within business and management and other subjects, lists exist that rank peer-reviewed journals according to their quality; higher rankings indicating better quality journals. The fortunes of academics and their business schools depend on publishing in such highly ranked journals. Harzing (2018) provides a regularly updated Journal Quality List for business and management, which includes lists from over 20 different sources. While there is little doubt that journals ranked highly on lists are quality journals and are more likely to contain quality articles, this does not mean that every single paper within them will be of the same high quality. It also does not mean that articles in lower ranked journals are of little value. As pointed out by MacDonald and Kam (2007), there is a circularity in the argument that quality journals contain quality papers which

 **Box 3.12**
Checklist

Evaluating the relevance, value and sufficiency of literature to your research

Relevance

✔ How recent is the item?
✔ Is the item likely to have been superseded?
✔ Are the research questions or objectives sufficiently close to your own to make it relevant to your own research (in other words, does the item meet your relevance criteria for inclusion)?
✔ Is the context sufficiently different to make it marginal to your research question(s) and objectives (in other words, is the item excluded by your relevance criteria)?
✔ Have you seen references to this item (or its author) in other items that were useful?
✔ Does the item support or contradict your arguments? For either it will probably be worth reading!

Value

✔ Has the item been subject to a reviewing process prior to publication?

✔ Does the item appear to be biased? For example, does it use an illogical argument, emotionally toned words or appear to choose only those cases that support the point being made? Even if it is, it may still be relevant to your critical review.
✔ What are the methodological omissions within the work (e.g. sample selection, data collection, data analysis)? Even if there are many it still may be of relevance.
✔ Is the precision sufficient? Even if it is imprecise it may be the only item you can find and so still of relevance!
✔ Does the item provide guidance for future research?

Sufficiency

✔ As I read new items, do I recognise the authors and the ideas from other items I have already read?
✔ Have I read the work by those acknowledged by others as key researchers in my research area?
✔ Can I critically discuss the academic context of my research with confidence?
✔ Have I read sufficient items to satisfy the assessment criteria for my project report?

Sources: Authors' experience; Bell and Waters (2014); Colquitt (2013); Fisher (2010); Jankowicz (2005)

are known to be quality papers because they appear in quality journals! Consequently, although journal ranking lists can provide a broad indicator of the quality of research, they are not a substitute for reading the article and making your own assessment. You should not just rely on these lists but should make your own assessment of the quality of the research in relation to your research question(s) and objectives. The checklist in Box 3.12 will help in this assessment.

Assessing sufficiency

Your assessment of whether you have read a sufficient amount is even more complex. It is impossible to read everything, as you would never start to write your critical review, let alone your project report. Yet you need to be sure that your critical review discusses what research has already been undertaken and that you have positioned your research project in the wider context, citing the main writers in the field (Section 3.2). One clue that you have achieved this is when further searches provide mainly references to items you have already read (Box 3.12). You also need to check what constitutes an acceptable amount of reading, in terms of both quality and quantity, with your project tutor.

3.8 Note taking and referencing

The literature search, as you will now be aware, is a vital part of your research project, in which you will invest a great deal of time and effort. As you read each item, you need to ask yourself how it contributes to your research question(s) and objectives and to make notes with this focus (Bell and Waters 2014). When doing this, many students download and save copies of articles or photocopy or scan pages from books to ensure that they have all the material. We believe that, even if you save, print or photocopy, you still need to make notes.

The process of note making will help you to think through the ideas in the literature in relation to your research. When making your notes, make sure you always use quotation marks and note the page number if you are copying the text exactly. This will ensure you know it is a direct quotation when you begin to write your project report and so help you avoid committing plagiarism (Section 3.11). The Harvard College Library (2018) suggests that you should get into the habit of hearing yourself ask questions of your reading and makes notes as you read. Their advice is summarised in Box 3.13.

In addition to making notes, it is helpful to record the:

- bibliographic details;
- brief summary of content;
- supplementary information.

Bibliographic software such as Reference Manager™, EndNote™ or research tools such as 'Mendeley' or 'Zotero' provide a powerful and flexible method for recording the literature and automatically generating references in the required style. In addition, there are online bibliography generators such as or 'Cite This For Me' which can help you create a bibliography or reference list in the prescribed format. Many specialist search engines, such as Google Scholar, allow references (and in some case full text) to be exported directly into such software and tools. Where this is not the case, recording can seem very tedious, but it must be done. We have seen many students frantically repeating searches for items that are crucial to their research because they failed to record all the necessary details in their database of references.

Box 3.13
Checklist

Advice on how to make notes when reading

✔ First of all, throw away the highlighter in favour of a pen or pencil. Highlighting can actually distract from the business of learning and dilute your comprehension. It only seems like an active reading strategy; in actual fact, it can lull you into a dangerous passivity.

✔ Mark up the margins of your text with words: ideas that occur to you, notes about things that seem important to you, reminders of how issues in a text may connect with your research questions and objectives. If you are reading a PDF copy on screen, use the 'sticky notes' feature of Adobe Reader®. This kind of interaction keeps you conscious of the

reason you are reading. Throughout your research these annotations will be useful memory triggers.

✔ Develop your own symbol system: asterisk a key idea, for example, or use an exclamation mark for anything that is surprising, absurd, bizarre etc. Like your margin words, your hieroglyphs can help your thoughts when you first read it. They will be indispensable when you return to a text later in the term, in search of a particular passage that you may want to refer to in your project report.

✔ Get in the habit of hearing yourself ask questions – 'what does this mean?'; 'why is she or he drawing that conclusion?' Write the questions down (in your margins, at the beginning or end of the reading, in a notebook or elsewhere). They are reminders of the unfinished business you still have with a text: to come to terms with on your own, once you've had a chance to digest the material further or have done further reading.

Bibliographic details

For some project reports you will be required to include a **bibliography**. Convention dictates that this should include all the relevant items you consulted for your project, including those not directly referred to in the text. For the majority, you will be asked to include only a list of **references** for those items referred to directly in the text. The **bibliographic details** contained in both need to be sufficient to enable readers to find the original items. These details are summarised in Table 3.5.

If you located the item online, you need to record the full Internet address of the resource and the date you accessed the information (Appendix 1). This address is the URL,

Table 3.5 Bibliographic details required

Journal	Book	Chapter in an edited book
• Author(s) – family name, first name, initials • Year of publication (in parentheses) • Title of article • Title of journal (italicised) • Volume • Part/issue • Page numbers (preceded by 'p'. for page or 'pp'. for pages)	• Author(s) – family name, first name initials • Year of publication (in parentheses) • Title and subtitle of book (italicised) • Edition (unless first) • Place of publication • Publisher	• Author(s) – family name, first name initials • Year of publication (in parentheses) • Title of chapter • Author(s) of book – family name, first name initials • Title and subtitle of book (italicised) • Edition (unless first) • Place of publication • Publisher • Page numbers of chapter (preceded by 'pp'. for pages)

the unique resource location or universal/uniform resource locator. For a journal article accessed online, and some other electronic documents, it is becoming more usual to also include that document's **digital object identifier** (DOI). The DOI provides a permanent and unique two-part identifier for the electronic document.

Most universities have a preferred referencing style that you must use in your project report. This will normally be prescribed in your assessment criteria. Three of the most common styles are the Harvard system (a version of which we have used in this book), the American Psychological Association (APA) system and the Vancouver or footnotes system. Guidelines on using each of these are given in Appendix 1.

Brief summary of content

A brief summary of the content of each item in your reference database will help you to locate the relevant items and facilitate reference to your notes and photocopies. This can be done by annotating each record with the search terms used, to help locate the item and the abstract. It will also help you to maintain consistency in your searches.

Supplementary information

As well as recording the details discussed earlier, other information may also be worth recording. These items can be anything you feel will be of value. In Table 3.6 we outline those that we have found most useful.

Table 3.6 Supplementary information

Information	Reason
ISBN	The identifier for any book, and useful if the book has to be requested on inter-library loan
DOI	The digital object identifier is both permanent and unique, meaning an electronic document can be found more easily
Class number (e.g. Dewey decimal)	Useful to locate books in your university's library and as a pointer to finding other books on the same subject
Quotations	Always note useful quotations in full and with the page number of the quote; if possible also save entire document as a PDF file
Where it was found	Noting where you found the item is useful, especially if it is not in your university library and you could only take notes
The search engine, database or other resource used to locate it	Useful to help identify possible resources for follow-up searches
Evaluative comments	Your personal notes on the value of the item to your research in relation to your relevance and value criteria
When the item was consulted	Especially important for items found via the Internet as these may disappear without trace
Filename	Useful if you have saved the document as a PDF file

3.9   Using systematic review

Systematic Review is a process for reviewing the literature using a comprehensive pre-planned strategy to locate existing literature, evaluate the contribution, analyse and synthesise the findings and report the evidence to allow conclusions to be reached about what is known and, also, what is not known (Denyer and Tranfield 2009). Originating in the medical sciences, Systematic Review has been used widely to evaluate specific medical treatments; in the past two decades its importance has been recognised in other disciplines. Within business and management, Denyer and Tranfield (2009) have adapted the medical sciences guidance, ensuring that the process is transparent, inclusive, explanatory and enables learning. Systematic Reviews usually, although not exclusively, focus on policy or practice questions such as the effectiveness of a particular intervention and the associated mechanisms with an emphasis on informing action. It is therefore not surprising that Petticrew and Roberts (2006) argue that Systematic Review is only suitable for some research projects (Box 3.14), emphasising that it is time-consuming and the need to involve others in the process.

Prior to conducting your Systematic Review, most writers suggest you undertake an exploratory **scoping study** to assess whether or not other Systematic Reviews have already been published and determine the focus of the literature search. Subsequent to this, a five-step process in which each stage is noted precisely is suggested (Denyer and Tranfield 2009).

1   Formulate the review question(s), for example 'What are marketing professionals' understanding and definition of viral marketing?', involving a broad range of expert stakeholders such as potential academic and practitioner users of the review as an advisory group. Resulting review questions can be developed using the CIMO acronym. This emphasises the need to include review questions which relate to the:

   Context – the individuals, relationships or wider settings being researched;

   Intervention – the effects of the events, actions or activities being researched;

   Mechanisms – the mechanisms that explain how the intervention (within the context) results in the outcome;

   Outcome – the effects of the intervention and how they are measured (Jones and Gatrell 2014).

2   Locate and generate a comprehensive list of potentially relevant research studies using online database searches, specialist bibliographies, tables of contents and other sources and attempt to track down unpublished research (Section 3.3).

Box 3.14
Checklist

Establishing whether a project may be suitable for Systematic Review

✔ Is there uncertainty about the effectiveness of the policy/service/intervention?

✔ Is there a need for evidence about the likely effects of a policy/service/intervention?

✔ Despite a large amount of research on the topic, do key questions remain unanswered?

✔ Is there a need for a general overall picture of the research evidence on the topic to direct future research?

✔ Is an accurate picture of past research and associated methods needed to help develop new methods?

(If the answer to one or more of these is 'yes' then the project may be suitable for Systematic Review.)

Source: Developed from Petticrew and Roberts (2006)

3 Select and evaluate relevant research studies using predetermined explicit inclusion and exclusion (selection) checklists of criteria to assess the relevance of each in relation to the review question(s). These checklists can be developed by undertaking a small number of pilot searches and making a list for reasons for inclusion or exclusion of each article or adapting checklists developed for previous Systematic Reviews, by journals to assess general quality of research or to assess issues of relevance and value (Box 3.14). Common criteria include adequate methods, clear data analysis and conclusions derived from findings. Selection and evaluation are usually undertaken:

  a initially by title and abstract;

  b for those not excluded by title and abstract, by reading the full text.

4 Analyse and synthesise the relevant research studies by:

  a breaking down each study into its constituent parts and recording the key points (research question/aim; study context – country, industry sector, organisational setting etc.; method(s) of data collection; sample size, frame and demographics; key findings; relevance to review questions) on a data extraction form;

  b using the data extraction forms to explore and integrate the studies and answer the specific review questions.

5 Report the results providing:

  a an introductory section that states the problem and review questions;

  b a methodology section that provides precise details of how the review was conducted (search strategy, selection criteria, key points used for the analysis and synthesis) (Sections 3.3 and 3.4);

  c findings and discussion sections that review all the studies (Section 3.2), specifying precisely what is known and what is not known in relation to the review questions.

Many researchers who use Systematic Review are adopting the PRISMA (Preferred Reporting Items for Systematic Reviews and Meta Analyses) checklist (Moher et al. 2009) and flow diagram for reporting and presenting their Systematic Reviews. Using their checklist when presenting your Systematic Review will help ensure the report of your review is clear, allowing others to assess the strengths and weaknesses of the studies you have reviewed. Using a flow diagram (Figure 3.3) allows the number of studies reviewed in stages two and three in the Systematic Review process to be reported clearly.

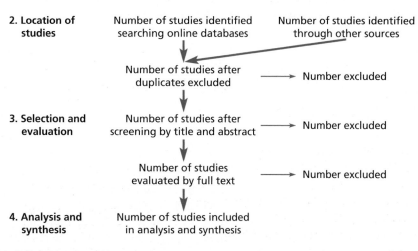

Figure 3.3 Reporting a Systematic Review
Source: Developed from Moher et al. 2009

3.10 Drafting your critical review

As we saw in Sections 3.2 and 3.3 the literature review that you write for your project report should be a description and critical analysis of what other authors have written, providing the background for your own research. When drafting your review, you therefore need to focus on using the literature to contextualise and justify your research question(s) and objectives. One way of helping you to focus is to think of your literature review as discussing how far existing published research goes in answering your research question(s). The shortfall in the literature will be addressed, at least partially, in the remainder of your project report – unless your entire research project is a literature review! Another way of helping you to focus is to ask yourself how your review relates to your objectives. If it does not, or does so only partially, there is a need for a clearer focus on your objectives.

In drafting your critical review, you will need to juxtapose different authors' ideas and form your own opinions and conclusions, comparing and contrasting these to form an evidence-based evaluation of the literature you have used. In doing this you will need to ensure the key themes are presented logically and that you highlight explicitly those areas where your own research will provide fresh insights, restating the research questions you will answer (Section 14.3). Subsequently, as part of your method, you will explain how you obtained the data to enable these questions to be answered before outlining and discussing your findings (Section 14.3). Although you will not be able to start writing until you have undertaken some reading, we recommend in addition to notetaking you start summarising your literature thematically early on. A way of doing this, which our students have found helpful, is to create a Thematic Analysis Grid (Anderson et al. 2015). This structures your note-taking for each article in a matrix with articles listed in rows in date order and each column represented a separate theme (Box 3.15). Notes for each article pertaining to a specific theme are then inserted in the appropriate cell.

To construct a Thematic Analysis Grid, you:

1 Identify potential themes from your initial annotated reading of the literature; these will form the grid's columns.
2 As you re-read each journal article, book or book chapter, insert a new row (keeping the date order) and make brief notes under the appropriate potential themes (columns); these should be in your own words, the page number being noted for quotations.
3 In a final column, 'methodology', note briefly the methodology used.
4 As your grid develops be prepared to:
   a add new themes;
   b remove themes that are no longer relevant to your research question;
   c introduce sub themes.
5 As your grid develops further look for patterns emerging across the themes; look for where:
   a there is consensus;
   b there are contradictions;
   c the literature you have reviewed is most convincing (the methodology column will help here).

As your Thematic Analysis Grid develops you will be able to identify those themes that have been widely researched and those that are less well developed, in other words those that are most relevant and significant to your research and the associated recognised experts. You will also be able to see how themes have developed over time due to the articles being in date order. The Grid's final column will also allow you to see easily which methodologies have been used in the research. Because your reading is brought together in one place, you will have a clear overview about what is known about your research topic from which to begin drafting and re-drafting your review.

Box 3.15
Focus on student research

Developing a thematic analysis grid

Fariba was interested in university-SME (small and medium sized enterprise) partnerships and, in particular, the factors influencing how academics and practitioners worked together. Having undertaken her literature search and made brief notes on all those items she considered likely to be relevant, she began to compile her Thematic Analysis Grid. An extract of Fariba's grid follows:

	Barriers to academia-practice partnership	Rigour and relevance debate	Engaged scholarship
Bartunek JM (2007) Academic–practitioner collaboration need not require joint or relevant research: Toward a relational scholarship of integration. *Academy of Management Journal* 50(6): 1323–1333.			Both sides need to value collaborative working.
Bartunek JM and Rynes SL (2014) Academics and Practitioners are alike and unlike: The paradoxes of Academic-Practitioner relationships. *Journal of Management* 40(5):1181–1201.	Important to break down barriers. Need to address existing constraints.		Academics need to take the initiative. Responsibility lies with university researchers.
Boyer EL (1990) *Scholarship Reconsidered: Priorities of the Professoriate.* San Francisco, CA: Jossey-Bass	Professoriate place disproportionate value on scholarship of research. Scholarship as practiced has little relevance to wider society.	Recognises universities need to preserve intellectual and political independence.	Scholarship of engagement – connecting and communities to enrich quality of life. Acknowledges groups of stakeholders working together to identify problem and solve collectively.
Boyer EL (1996) The Scholarship of Engagement. Bulletin of the American *Academy of Arts and Sciences* 49(7): 18–33.	Barriers could be addressed by universities valuing four scholarships equally.		(see above)
Hodgkinson GP, Herriot P and Anderson N (2001) Re-aligning the Stakeholders in Management Research: Lessons from Industrial, Work and Organizational Psychology. *British Journal of Management* 12 Special Issue S41–S54.		Management research should satisfy double hurdle of rigour and relevance.	

Box 3.15
Focus on student
research (*continued*)

Developing a thematic analysis grid

	Barriers to academia-practice partnership	Rigour and relevance debate	Engaged scholarship
Rynes SL (2007) Editor's afterword. Let's create a tipping point: what academics and practitioners can do, alone and together. *Academy of Management Journal* 50(5): 1046–1054.	Academics career need is for papers in journals practitioners rarely contribute to/read.		
Saunders MNK (2011) The management researcher as practitioner – issues from the interface in C. Cassell and B. Lee (eds) *Challenges and Controversies in Management Research*. New York: Routledge. 243–57.	Need to address practical tensions and constraints. Some managers deprecate management research, some academics disdain practitioners.	Summarises these as differences in focus of interest and measured outcomes, methodological cynosure.	Only likely to occur when academics take initiative to engage.

Remember to be critical as you draft your review (Box 3.1) and ensure that what you write relates clearly to your research question(s) and objectives (Box 3.2). In order to improve the transparency of your review process, you should also explain precisely how you selected the literature you have included in your review, outlining your choice of search terms and of databases used. This is usually done at the start of the review and is essential if you are using the Systematic Review methodology (Section 3.9). This can be thought of as 'Step 0' of the literature funnel we outlined in Section 3.3. When you have completed your first draft you can use Box 3.16 to evaluate its suitability for your project report.

Box 3.16
Checklist

Evaluating your draft literature review

✔ Does your literature review have a clear title, which describes the focus of your research rather than just saying 'literature review'?

✔ Have you explained precisely how you searched the literature and the criteria used to select those studies included?

✔ Does your review start at a more general level before narrowing down?

✔ Is your literature review organised thematically around the ideas contained in the research being reviewed rather than the researchers?

✔ Are your arguments coherent and cohesive – do your ideas link in a way that will be logical to your reader?

✔ Have you used subheadings within the literature review to help guide your reader?

✔ Does the way you have structured your literature review draw your reader's attention to those issues that are the focus of your research, in particular your objectives?

✔ Does your literature review lead your reader into subsequent sections of your project report?

3.11 A note about plagiarism

There is no doubt that plagiarism has become an enormous concern in academic institutions in recent years, largely as a result of the ease with which material can be copied from the Internet and passed off as the work of the individual student. It is a serious topic because it is a breach of academic integrity when a person passes off another's work as their own. The consequences of being found guilty of plagiarism can be severe, including not being awarded your degree.

Neville (2016) argues that plagiarism is an issue that runs parallel to a debate with recurring questions about the purpose of higher education in the twenty-first century. He notes that, on the one hand, there is the argument that an insistence on 'correct' referencing is supporting a system and a process of learning that is a legacy of a different time and society. This argument holds that universities are enforcing upon you an arcane practice of referencing that you will probably never use again outside higher education. On the other hand, there is the argument that plagiarism is an attack upon values of ethical, proper, decent behaviour – values consistent with a respect for others. These are ageless societal values that universities should try to maintain.

So what precisely is plagiarism? Quite simply, it is presenting someone else's work or ideas as if they are your own, with or without their consent and failing to fully acknowledge the original source. The University of Oxford (2018) lists eight forms of plagiarism which are commonly found in universities. These are:

1 *Quoting* someone else's work, word for word, without acknowledgement.
2 *Cutting and pasting* text, diagrams or any other material from the Internet without acknowledgement.
3 *Paraphrasing* someone else's work by altering a few words or changing their order or closely following the structure of their argument without acknowledgement.
4 *Collaborating* with others (unless expressly asked to do so such as in group work) and not attributing the assistance received.
5 *Inaccurately referencing,* within the text and list of references, the source of a quoted passage. This often occurs when students pretend to have read an original source, when their knowledge is derived from a secondary source.
6 *Failing to acknowledge assistance* that leads to substantive changes in the content or approach.
7 *Using materials written by others* such as professional essay writing services, or friends, even with the consent of those who have written it.
8 *Auto or self-plagiarising,* that is submitting work that you have already submitted (either in part or fully) for another assessment. However, it usually acceptable to cite earlier work you have had published.

It is tempting to think that all cases of plagiarism are a consequence of students either being too idle to pursue their research and write diligently or wishing to appear cleverer than they really are. But the fact is that plagiarism is an extremely complex issue and the reasons for it may owe as much to student confusion as wilful negligence. That said, there is little excuse for confusion. All universities have ample guidance for students on the topic of plagiarism and will emphasise that it is the responsibility of the individual student to become aware of the university's regulations surrounding its conduct. In addition, an increasing number of universities ask students to check their own work using plagiarism detection software such as Turnitin and submit the report alongside the electronic copy of their work.

3.12 Summary

- Critically reviewing the literature is necessary to help you to develop a thorough understanding of, and insight into, previous work that relates to your research question(s) and objectives.
- Your written review will set your research in context by critically discussing and referencing work that has already been undertaken, drawing out key points and presenting them in a logically argued way, and highlighting those areas where you will provide fresh insights. It will lead the reader into subsequent sections of your project report.
- There is no one correct structure for a critical review, although it is helpful to think of it as a funnel in which you start at a more general level prior to narrowing down to your specific research question(s) and objectives.
- You are most likely to make use of formally published items (secondary literature) and those not controlled by commercial publishers (grey literature). Your use of these resources will depend on your research question(s) and objectives. Some may use only secondary literature. For others, you may need to locate grey literature as well.
- When planning your literature search you need to:
  - have a clearly defined research question(s) and research objectives;
  - define the parameters of your search;
  - generate search terms and phrases;
  - discuss your ideas as widely as possible.
- Techniques to help you in this include brainstorming and relevance trees.
- Your literature search is likely to be undertaken using a variety of approaches in tandem. These will include:
  - searching using online databases and search engines;
  - following up references in articles you have already read;
  - scanning and browsing books and journals in your university library.
- Don't forget to make precise notes of the search processes you have used and their results.
- Once obtained, the literature must be evaluated for its relevance and value to your research question(s) and objectives. Each item must be read and noted. Bibliographic details, a brief description of the content and appropriate supplementary information should also be recorded.
- For literature reviews focusing on policy or practice questions in particular, you may decide to a use a Systematic Review.
- Care should be taken when drafting and redrafting your literature review not to plagiarise the work of others.

Self-check questions

Help with these questions is available at the end of the chapter.

3.1 The following extract and associated references are taken from the first draft of a critical literature review. The research project was concerned with the impact of changes to UK legal aid legislation on motor insurance pricing policies.

List the problems with this extract in terms of its:
a content;
b structure.

The primary function of motor insurance is to provide financial protection against damage to vehicles and bodies resulting from traffic conditions and the liabilities that can arise (Wikipedia 2018). O'Brian (2014) suggests that motor insurers have been too eager to reap the benefits of legal aid. Papra-Servano (2013) notes that the average car insurance premium has reduced since changes in legislation brought about by the UK Legal Aid, Sentencing and Punishment of Offenders Act. This Act prohibits the payment and receipt of referral fees in relation to personal injury claims by solicitors, claims companies and other authorised persons (Norton Ross Fulbright 2012). Motor insurance is particularly price sensitive because of its compulsory nature and its perception by many to have no real 'value' to themselves.

O'Brien, S. (2013). 'Motor insurance: Jumping the gun'. *Post*. 29 October. Available at: https://www.postonline.co.uk/post/analysis/2301953/motor-insurance-jumping-the-gun. [Accessed 18 March 2018]

Norton Ross Fulbright. (2012). *The regulation of the motor industry*. Available at: http://www.nortonrosefulbright.com/knowledge/publications/63780/the-regulation-of-the-motor-insurance-industry [Accessed 18 March 2018].

Papra-Servano, C. (2013). 'Rates drop as motor insurers anticipate legal reform windfall'. *Post*. 17 July. Available at: https://www.postonline.co.uk/post/news/2282883/rates-drop-as-motor-insurers-anticipate-legal-reform-windfall [Accessed 18 March 2018]

Wikipedia (2018) *Vehicle Insurance*. Available at: http://en.wikipedia.org/wiki/Vehicle_insurance. [Accessed 18 March 2018].

3.2 Outline the advice you would give a colleague on:

a how to plan her search;

b which literature to search first.

3.3 Brainstorm at least one of the following research questions, either on your own or with a colleague, and list the search terms that you have generated.

a How effective are share options as a motivator?

b How do the opportunities available to a first-time house buyer through interpersonal discussion influence the process of selecting a financial institution for the purposes of applying for a house purchase loan?

c To what extent do new methods of direct selling of financial services pose a threat to existing providers?

[1]Hanson, S. and Blake, M. (2009) 'Gender and entrepreneurial networks', *Regional Studies,* Vol. 43, pp. 135–49.
[2]Watson, J. (2012) 'Networking: Gender differences and the association with firm performance', *International Small Business Journal,* Vol. 30, pp. 536–58.
[3]Cromie, S. and Birley, S. (1992) 'Networking by female business owners in Northern Ireland', *Journal of Business Venturing,* Vol. 7, pp. 237–51.
[1]Hanson, S. and Blake, M. (2009) 'Gender and entrepreneurial networks', *Regional Studies,* Vol. 43, pp. 135–49.
[4]Ardrich, H. (1989) 'Networking among women entrepreneurs', in O. Hagan, C.S. Rivchun and D. Sexton (eds) *Women-Owned Businesses*. New York: Praeger, pp. 103–32.
[5]Moore, G. (1990) 'Structural determinants of men's and women's personal networks', *American Sociological Review,* Vol. 55, pp. 726–35.
[6]Munch A., McPherson J.M. and Smith-Lovin L. (1997) 'Gender, children, and social contact: The effects of childrearing for men and women', *American Sociological Review,* Vol. 62, pp. 509–20.
[7]Orhan, M. (2001) 'Women business owners in France: The issue of financing discrimination', *Journal of Small Business Management,* Vol. 39, pp. 95–102.
[8]Watson, J. (2012) 'Networking: Gender differences and the association with firm performance', *International Small Business Journal,* Vol. 30, pp. 536–58.

3.4 You are having considerable problems with finding relevant material for your research when searching databases. Suggest possible reasons why this might be so.

3.5 Rewrite the following passage as part of a critical literature review using the Harvard system of referencing:

> Past research indicates important gender differences in the use of networks[1], and suggests that male SME owners are more likely to successfully network and benefit from networks-driven performance in contrast to female SME owners[2]. In particular, as many women come to self-employment from domestic or non-management background[3], and thus are likely to have previously engaged in the relatively isolating domestic and childrearing work or lower-status support work, they can be expected to possess fewer, more personal, less formal and less powerful contacts, as well as less time for networking[1,4,5,6,7]. However, recent empirical studies of SME owners challenge such expectations. For example, according to a 2012 survey of 2919 male- and 181 female-controlled SMEs, there is little gender difference, after controlling for education, experience, industry, age and size, in the SME owners' use of networking and its impact on business performance – in other words, SMEs owned by women and men enjoy similar performance benefits of networking [8].

Review and discussion questions

3.6 Go to the website of the general search engine Google (www.google.com). Use the specialised search services such as 'Google Scholar' and 'Google Finance' to search for articles on a topic which you are currently studying as part of your course.
  a Make notes regarding the types of items that each of these services finds.
  b How do these services differ?
  c Which service do you think is likely to prove most useful to your research project?

3.7 Agree with a friend to each review the same article from a refereed academic journal which contains a clear literature review section. Evaluate independently the literature review in your chosen article with regard to its content, critical nature and structure using the checklists in Boxes 3.2 and 3.15 respectively. Do not forget to make notes regarding your answers to each of the points raised in the checklists. Discuss your answers with your friend.

3.8 Visit an online database or your university library and obtain a copy of an article that you think will be of use to an assignment you are both currently working on. Use the checklist in Box 3.13 to assess the relevance and value of the article to your assignment.

Progressing your research project

Critically reviewing the literature

- Consider your research question(s) and objectives. Use your lecture notes, course textbooks and relevant review articles to define both narrow and broader parameters of your literature search, considering language, subject area, business sector, geographical area, publication period and literature type.
- Generate search terms using one or a variety of techniques such as reading, brainstorming and relevance trees. Discuss your ideas widely, including with your project tutor and colleagues.
- Start your search using databases, available via your university library's web pages, to identify relevant secondary literature. Begin with those databases that abstract and index academic journal articles and books. At the same time, obtain relevant literature that has been referenced in articles you have already read. Do not forget to record your searches systematically and in detail.
- Obtain copies of items, evaluate them systematically and make notes. Remember also to record bibliographic details, a brief description of the content and supplementary information in your bibliographic software.
- Construct a Thematic Analysis Grid and start drafting your critical review as early as possible, keeping in mind its purpose and taking care to reference properly and avoid plagiarism.
- Continue to search the literature throughout your research project and redraft your review to ensure that your review remains up to date.
- Use the questions in Box 1.4 to guide your reflective diary entry.

References

Access to Research (2018) *Access to research.* Available at http://www.accesstoresearch.org.uk/ [Accessed 20 March 2018].

Anderson, D., Lees, R. and Avery, B. (2015) 'Reviewing the literature using the Thematic Analysis Grid', *Poster presented at the European Conference on Research Methodology for Business and Management Studies,* Malta, June, 2015.

Bell, J. and Waters, S. (2014) *Doing Your Research Project* (6th edn). Maidenhead: Open University Press.

Brozovic, D. (2018) 'Strategic Flexibility: A Review of the Literature', *International Journal of Management Reviews,* Vol. 20, No. 1, pp. 3–31.

Colquitt, J.A. (2013) 'Crafting references in AMJ submissions', *Academy of Management Journal,* Vol. 56, No. 5, pp. 1221–4.

Corbin, J. and Strauss, A. (2015) *Basics of Qualitative Research* (4th edn). Thousand Oaks, CA: Sage.

Creswell, J.W. and Poth, C.N. (2017) *Qualitative Inquiry and Research Design: Choosing Among Five Approaches* (4th edn). Thousand Oaks, CA: Sage.

Dees, R. (2003) *Writing the Modern Research Paper* (4th edn). Boston, MA: Allyn and Bacon.

Denyer, D. and Tranfield, D. (2009) 'Producing a Systematic Review', in D.A. Buchanan and A. Bryman (eds) *The Sage Handbook of Organisational Research Methods.* London: Sage, pp. 671–89.

Fisher, C. (2010) *Researching and Writing a Dissertation for Business Students* (3rd edn). Harlow: Financial Times Prentice Hall.

Hart, C. (2018) *Doing a Literature Review* (2nd edn). London: Sage.

Harvard College Library (2018) *Interrogating texts: 6 reading habits to develop in your first year at Harvard.* Available at: https://guides.library.harvard.edu/sixreadinghabits [Accessed 17 March 2018].

Harzing, A. W. (2018) *Journal Quality List.* Available at: https://harzing.com/resources/journal-quality-list [Accessed 17 March 2018].

Jankowicz, A.D. (2005) *Business Research Projects* (4th edn). London: Thomson Learning.

Jones, O. and Gatrell, C. (2014) 'Editorial: The Future of Writing and Reviewing for IJMR', *International Journal of Management Reviews,* Vol. 16, pp. 249–264.

Macdonald, S. and Kam, J. (2007) 'Ring a Ring o' Roses: Quality journals and gamesmanship in management studies', *Journal of Management Studies,* Vol. 44, pp. 640–55.

MindGenius (2018) *MindGenius.* Available at https://www.mindgenius.com/default.aspx [Accessed 1 April 2018].

Mingers, J. (2000) 'What is it to be critical? Teaching a critical approach to management undergraduates', *Management Learning,* Vol. 31, No. 2, pp. 219–37.

Moher, D., Liberati, A., Tetzlaff, J. and Altman, D.G. (2009) 'Preferred reporting for systematic reviews and meta-analyses: The PRISMA statement', *British Medical Journal (BMJ),* No. 338, b2535. Available at: www.bmj.com/content/339/bmj.b2535.full?view=long&pmid=19622551 [Accessed 27 March 2011].

Neville, C. (2016) *The Complete Guide to Referencing and Plagiarism* (3rd edn). Maidenhead: Open University Press.

Petticrew, M. and Roberts, H. (2006) *Systematic Review in the Social Sciences: A Practical Guide.* Malden, MA: Blackwell.

Ridley, D. (2018) *The Literature Review: a step-by-step guide for students* (2nd edn). London: Sage.

Saunders, M.N.K., Gray, D. and Goregaokor, H. (2014) 'SME innovation and learning: the role of networks and crisis event', *European Journal of Training and Development,* Vol. 38, No. ½, pp. 136–149.

Sharp, J.A., Peters, J. and Howard, K. (2002) *The Management of a Student Research Project* (3rd edn). Aldershot: Gower.

SimpleMind (2018) *SimpleMind.* Available at: https://www.simpleapps.eu/ [Accessed 1 April 2018].

Stewart, D.W. and Kamins, M.A. (1993) *Secondary Research: Information Sources and Methods* (2nd edn). Newbury Park: CA, Sage.

Terzidou, M., Scarles, C. and Saunders, M.N.K. (2017) 'Religiousness as tourist performances: A case study of Greek Orthodox pilgrimage', *Annals of Tourism Research,* Vol. 66, pp. 116–129.

Tranfield, D., Denyer, D. and Smart, P. (2003) 'Towards a methodology for developing evidence-informed management knowledge by means of systematic review', *British Journal of Management,* Vol. 14, No. 3, pp. 207–22.

University of Oxford (2018) *Study Skills and Training: Plagiarism.* Available at https://www.ox.ac.uk/students/academic/guidance/skills/plagiarism?wssl=1 [Accessed 20 March 2018].

University of Southern California (2018) *Organising your Social Sciences Research Paper: 5. The Literature Review.* Available at http://libguides.usc.edu/writingguide/literaturereview [Accessed 7 March 2018].

Wallace, M. and Wray, A. (2016) *Critical Reading and Writing for Postgraduates* (3rd edn). London: Sage.

Webspiration Pro (2018) *Webspiration Pro.* Available at https://www.webspirationpro.com/ [Accessed 1 April 2018].

Wikipedia (2018) *Wikipedia.* Available at http://en.wikipedia.org/wiki/ Wikipedia [Accessed 20 March 2018].

Further reading

Colquitt, J.A. (2013) 'Crafting references in AMJ submissions', *Academy of Management Journal,* Vol. 56, No. 5, pp. 1221–4. This short editorial provides extremely useful insights regarding citations and references in academic writing.

Denyer, D. and Tranfield, D. (2009) 'Producing a Systematic Review', in D.A. Buchanan and A. Bryman (eds) *The Sage Handbook of Organizational Research Methods.* London: Sage, pp. 671–89. This chapter provides an excellent introduction to the process of Systematic Review. Although a full Systematic Review as outlined in this chapter may be too time consuming for your research project, there are many useful points made regarding how to plan your search strategy and explain in your project report how your review was undertaken.

Neville, C. (2016) *The Complete Guide to Referencing and Plagiarism* (3rd edn). Maidenhead: Open University Press. Chapter 6 is a very helpful guide on what constitutes plagiarism and how it can be avoided. The chapter ends with some useful exercises designed to ensure that the reader does not fall into some common traps.

Ridley, D. (2018) *The Literature Review: a step-by-step guide for students* (2nd edn). London: Sage. This has numerous examples and offers a wealth of practical advice with practice tasks. The sections on being critical and on foregrounding writers voice are particularly helpful.

Case 3
Using a Thematic Analysis Grid to help critically review the literature

Sam's undergraduate research project required him to draw together academic research on data privacy in marketing to develop practical recommendations for a company: an "industry briefing paper". At the heart of the project was a review of academic literature.

Like many students at this stage in the project, Sam initially felt overwhelmed by the scale of the project. Where should he start? Should he read each paper then make notes? Should he use high-lighters or index cards? Once his tutor had outlined how to use the Thematic Analysis Grid (TAG), he felt much more relaxed. He realised he could address the daunting literature review as a series of more easily managed inter-linked tasks. This suited his busy lifestyle. It also reassured him that he would not repeat the mistake from a previous assignment that had been criticised for being too descriptive by simply summarising each article and not drawing them together as a whole. He started by sorting the articles and book chapters he had found from his literature search into date order.

As Sam began to read the first article he soon identified a potential theme: 'data usage outcomes", which became the first column of his grid. He marked a number 1 on his printed version of the paper and in the cell on his matrix, where he also wrote a very brief summary of the point being made. He then carried on reading and identified several additional themes. By using a numbering system on the grid and on his papers, he could easily return to the relevant section of the paper in the future. In the last column of the grid he noted the methodology used. It should be noted here that although Sam preferred to work with paper and pen, many of his colleagues prefer to use Excel or a table in Word to store their work. After about 90 minutes, Sam had five themes identified, each heading up a column of his TAG. In the next two articles, some of the themes were also discussed, in which case Sam simply documented them on the next row of his TAG in the same way. However, he also identified an additional three themes, so started three new columns.

At the end of the afternoon, Sam had recorded all his reading to date in one place, cross-referenced to exactly where he had found the original discussion (Fig C3.1).

The next three days were busy for Sam; he had an in-class test, a football final and a quick trip home for his sister's 21st birthday celebration. It was a week before Sam could continue, but then the TAG's value really became apparent. By reviewing his work so far, he was reminded about what he had read. He also began to see patterns emerging; for example, he

Figure C3.1 Extract from a Thematic Analysis Grid on Data Privacy in Marketing showing four themes identified from first three papers (NB Bold numbers correspond to numbers marked by Sam on the paper for easy referral)

	Theme 1: Data usage outcomes	Theme 2: Privacy	Theme 3: Why do consumers share information in practice?	Theme 4: How to mitigate concerns	Comments on Methodology/Context
Aguirre, E., Roggeveen, A., Grewal, D. and Wetzels, M. (2016) The personalization-privacy paradox: implications for new media. *Journal of Consumer Marketing*, 33(2), pp. 98–110.	1. Leveraging data can: a. create deep connections; b. increase attention to the ad; c. improve response rates 5. Data can be collected overtly (e.g., fill in form) or covertly (click stream history) 6. When firm uses covertly collected data, concerns raised re manipulative intentions and loss of control 7. Leads to decrease in trust and willingness to engage and 8. Increases scepticism and ad avoidance 9. Negative consumer reactions – providing false information, negative word of mouth, seeking stricter regulatory controls	11. Privacy is a commodity with a quantifiable value 12. Authors identified conflict: one study shows consumers pay higher prices from sites offering more privacy 13. Another study: 2 gift cards – more valuable if permission given to track BUT preferences reflected which card was offered first 14. NB Difficult for consumers to know cost-benefit trade-off if info collected covertly 15. Privacy concerns are situational e.g. appearance of web site; no. of others who have given info	10. Consumers weigh up risks re loss of privacy against relevant offers and discounts	20. Grant consumers some control over privacy 21. NB This is difficult to exert and time-consuming 22. Increase consumer trust strategically e.g., explicit privacy policies 23. Offer third party privacy seals 24. Transform the firm into a social entity	Literature review – paper seeks to identify factors that determine how consumers respond to personalised communications. No detailed methodology of how literature search conducted. Useful summary table in appendix showing summary findings from c 50 articles from 2003–2015 (NB given the topic, early papers could be out of date)

(continued)

Figure C3.1 (*Continued*)

	Theme 1: Data usage outcomes	Theme 2: Privacy	Theme 3: Why do consumers share information in practice?	Theme 4: How to mitigate concerns	Comments on Methodology/Context
Zhu, Y. and Chang, J. (2016) The key role of relevance in personalized advertisement: Examining its impact on perceptions of privacy invasion, self-awareness, and continuous use intentions. *Computers in Human Behavior*, 65, pp. 442–447.		3. Note that 'privacy' is investigated from a number of perspectives e.g., perceived control, financial compensation, regulation, monetary rewards, convenience 9. Privacy invasion perception is negatively related to continuous use intention 11. Claim: privacy is a commodity that can be exchanged for perceived benefits	7. If better service, compensation or discounts are larger than perceived risks then consumers more willing to disclose personal information	4. Relevance of ad influences reaction 'Relevant personalised advertising reduces privacy invasion perceptions and increases continuous use intentions' (P443) 12. 'By accurately providing content that fits into users' interests and tastes, privacy invasion concerns are alleviated by the privacy calculus' p446 13. Relevant ads save time and resources	On-line survey in Taiwan. 386 responses from 1,000 (incentivised) questionnaires. Investigated relevance, perceptions of privacy, self-awareness and usage intentions. Drew on rational-choice theory and self-awareness theory. Used factor analysis and Structural Equation Modelling. Used fake web-site (NB real world?)
Martin, K. and Murphy, P. (2016) The role of data privacy in marketing. *Journal of the Academy of Marketing Science*, 45(2), pp. 135–155.	1. Negative: fraud, privacy invasion, unwanted marketing communications 2. Benefits: personalised offers, discounts, free services, more relevant communications 9. Key to personalised value/information trade-off is the way data collected i.e. overtly or covertly	3. No widely agreed definition– authors present a number 4. Agree with notion that it is 'fuzzy' 5. Privacy as a 'right' 6. Very disparate theories presented re psychology of privacy		10. Consumers more receptive when have some control	Extensive literature review to 'capture current state of privacy scholarship in marketing and related disciplines'. Recommend a multi-dimensional approach to span issues beyond marketing. No detailed methodology of how literature search conducted but several useful tables detailing different theoretical perspectives of privacy. Draws on over 150 articles

saw that Aguirre et al. (2016) and Zhu and Chang (2016) both identified that privacy could be regarded as a commodity with a quantifiable value. However, Martin and Murphy (2017) suggested that there is no widely agreed definition. So who was correct? By reviewing his methodology column, Sam could see that the reason for this discrepancy could be the scope of the studies: whilst Aguirre et al. (2016) and Zhu and Chang (2016) had focused on marketing and specifically marketing communications, the papers reviewed by Martin and Murphy (2017) covered a much wider range of disciplines including psychology. Without realising it, Sam was engaging in critical evaluation. On the grid, he subsequently added a series of arrows and linking lines to show where contradictions and consensus appeared.

Sam continued constructing his TAG over four sessions, each separated by a gap of 2–5 days. Each time he reviewed his developing TAG, Sam felt more and more confident that he was seeing patterns emerge which would ensure that his project was based on themes rather than just summaries of each article or book chapter he had read. He was also able to use the literature he had read to justify why he believed one view was more credible than another. In other words, he had moved to proper critical evaluation of academic literature. Once Sam had completed all his reading he found the writing of the literature review was made straightforward by using the themes as his sub-headings. Whilst he did not include every point on his TAG in his final work, he was confident that he had made informed decisions about the issues to include.

Questions

1 Do you think that Sam was being 'critical' in his approach to the academic literature on data privacy in marketing? Provide reasons for your answer.
2 How can Sam claim originality for a piece of work that relies so heavily on others' studies?
3 Why was it insufficient for Sam to simply present the results of a series of studies for this project?

References

Aguirre, E., Roggeveen, A., Grewal, D. and Wetzels, M. (2016) The personalization-privacy paradox: implications for new media. *Journal of Consumer Marketing,* 33(2), pp. 98-110.

Martin, K. and Murphy, P. (2016) The role of data privacy in marketing. *Journal of the Academy of Marketing Science,* 45(2), pp. 135–155.

Zhu, Y. and Chang, J. (2016) The key role of relevance in personalized advertisement: Examining its impact on perceptions of privacy invasion, self-awareness, and continuous use intentions. *Computers in Human Behavior,* 65, pp. 442–447.

Additional case studies relating to material covered in this chapter are available via the book's companion website: **www.pearsoned.co.uk/saunders**.

They are:

- The development of discount warehouse clubs.
- The problems of valuing intellectual capital.
- National cultures and management styles.
- Complexity theory and emergent change.
- Individual workplace performance: systematically reviewed.
- After the crisis: A systematic review.

Self-check answers

3.1 There are numerous problems with the content and structure of this extract. Some of the more obvious include:

- The content consists of Wikipedia, a company website and an online trade magazine, *Post*, and there are no references of academic substance.
- You would not expect to see Wikipedia referenced in a research project for reasons outlined earlier in this chapter.
- Some of the references to individual authors have discrepancies: for example, was the article by O'Brien (or is it O'Brian?) published in 2014 or 2013?
- The UK Government Act is not referenced directly (it should be!) and you would expect the actual Act to be referred to rather than a company's (Norton Ross Fulbright 2012) comments on the preceding draft bill.
- There is no real structure or argument in the extract. The extract is a list of what people have written, with no attempt to critically evaluate or juxtapose the ideas.

3.2 This is a difficult one without knowing her research question! However, you could still advise her on the general principles. Your advice will probably include:

- Define the parameters of the research, considering language, subject area, business sector, geographical area, publication period and literature type. Generate search terms using one or a variety of techniques such as reading, brainstorming or relevance trees. Discuss her ideas as widely as possible, including with her tutor, librarians and you.
- Start the search using online databases in the university library to identify relevant literature. She should commence with those online databases that abstract and index academic journal articles. At the same time she should obtain relevant literature that has been referenced in articles that she has already read.

3.3 There are no incorrect answers with brainstorming! However, you might like to check your search terms for suitability prior to using them to search an appropriate database. We suggest that you follow the approach outlined in Section 3.6 under 'searching using online databases'.

3.4 There are a variety of possible reasons, including:

- One or more of the parameters of your search are defined too narrowly.
- The keywords you have chosen do not appear in the controlled index language.
- Your spelling of the search term is incorrect.
- The terminology you are using is incorrect.
- The acronyms you have chosen are not used by databases.
- You are using jargon rather than accepted terminology.

3.5 There are two parts to this answer: rewriting the text and using the Harvard system of referencing. Your text will inevitably differ from the answer given below owing to your personal writing style. Don't worry about this too much as it is discussed in far more detail in Section 14.6. The references should follow the same format.

Past research indicates important gender differences in the use of networks (Hanson and Blake 2009) and suggests that male SME owners are more likely to successfully network and benefit from networks-driven performance in contrast to female SME owners (Watson 2012). In particular, as many women come to self-employment from domestic or non-management background (Cromie and Birley 1992), and thus are likely to have previously engaged in the relatively isolating domestic and childrearing work or lower-status support work, they can be expected to possess fewer, more personal, less formal and less powerful contacts, as well as less time for networking (Ardrich 1989; Hanson and Blake

2009; Moore 1990; Munch et al. 1997; Orhan 2001). However, recent empirical studies of SME owners challenge such expectations. For example, according to Watson's (2012) survey of 2919 male- and 181 female-controlled SMEs, there is little gender difference, after controlling for education, experience, industry, age and size, in the SME owners' use of networking and its impact on business performance – in other words, SMEs owned by women and men enjoy similar performance benefits of networking.

Ardrich, H. (1989) 'Networking among women entrepreneurs', in O. Hagan, C.S. Rivchun and D. Sexton (eds) *Women-Owned Businesses.* New York: Praeger, pp. 103–32.

Cromie, S. and Birley, S. (1992) 'Networking by female business owners in Northern Ireland', *Journal of Business Venturing,* Vol. 7, pp. 237–51.

Hanson, S. and Blake, M. (2009) 'Gender and entrepreneurial networks', *Regional Studies,* Vol. 43, pp. 135–49.

Moore, G. (1990) 'Structural determinants of men's and women's personal networks', *American Sociological Review,* Vol. 55, pp. 726–35.

Munch, A., McPherson, J.M. and Smith-Lovin, L. (1997) 'Gender, children, and social contact: The effects of childrearing for men and women', *American Sociological Review,* Vol. 62, pp. 509–20.

Orhan, M. (2001) 'Women business owners in France: The issue of financing discrimination', *Journal of Small Business Management,* Vol. 39, pp. 95–102.

Watson, J. (2012) 'Networking: Gender differences and the association with firm performance', *International Small Business Journal,* Vol. 30, pp. 536–58.

Get ahead using resources on the Companion Website at:
www.pearsoned .co.uk/saunders.

- Improve your SPSS research analysis with practice tutorials.
- Save time researching on the Internet with the Smarter Online Searching Guide.
- Test your progress using self-assessment questions.
- Follow live links to useful websites.

Chapter **4**

Understanding research philosophy and approaches to theory development

Learning outcomes

By the end of this chapter you should be able to:

- define ontology, epistemology and axiology, and explain their relevance to business research;
- reflect on your own epistemological, ontological and axiological stance;
- understand the main research paradigms that are significant for business research;
- explain the relevance for business research of philosophical positions such as positivism, critical realism, interpretivism, postmodernism and pragmatism;
- reflect on and articulate your own philosophical position in relation to your research;
- distinguish between deductive, inductive, abductive and retroductive approaches to theory development.

4.1 Introduction

Much of this book is concerned with the way in which you collect data to answer your research question(s). Many people plan their research in relation to a question that needs to be answered or a problem that needs to be solved. They then think about what data they need and the techniques they use to collect them. You are not therefore unusual if early on in your research you consider whether you should, for example, use a questionnaire or undertake interviews. However, how you collect your data belongs in the centre of the research 'onion', the diagram we use to depict the issues underlying the choice of data collection techniques and analysis procedures in Figure 4.1. (You may find that there is much terminology that is new to you in this diagram – do not worry about it for now, we will take you through it all as you progress through the book.) In coming to this central core, you need to explain why you made the choice you did so that others can see that your research should be taken seriously (Crotty 1998). Consequently there are important outer layers of the onion that you need to understand and explain rather than just peel and throw away!

This chapter is concerned principally with the outer two of the onion's layers: philosophy (Sections 4.2, 4.3 and 4.4) and approach to theory development (Section 4.5). In Chapter 5 we examine the layers we call methodological choice, strategy and time horizon. The sixth layer (data collection and analysis) is dealt with in Chapters 7–13.

Brexit: beliefs, assumptions and life-changing decisions

Our own beliefs and assumptions about what is important affect the decisions we make throughout our lives. Some of our decisions and the research we undertake to inform them can prove life-changing, not only for ourselves, but also for the wider society in which we live.

On the 23rd of June 2016 the British electorate voted by a majority to leave the European Union, setting the course for what is now known as 'Brexit'. Brexit is set to dramatically reshape the laws, norms and practices of UK-based individuals and organisations.

In the media and academic commentary on Brexit, much has been made of the different values and assumptions of voters, non-voters and politicians on both sides of the EU Referendum campaign and how they may have affected the outcome. For example, many 'Leavers' and 'Remainers' understood the reality of the EU and its membership in very different ways – some perceiving the EU as an overly-bureaucratic and expensive institution that limited UK sovereignty, with others seeing the EU as offering legal protections for

workplace rights and the environment, and the freedom of trade and movement throughout Member States. These assumptions informed each side's campaigns prior to the referendum vote with regards to the ways in which 'facts' and 'knowledge' about Brexit were used, some of which were challenged as unwarranted or even misleading in its aftermath. Additionally, some parts of the electorate felt that they and their values had been ignored by mainstream politicians and so used their votes to protest, while others assumed their individual votes (and values) did not matter so chose not to vote.

Just as our beliefs and assumptions affect our decisions in everyday life, they can also have an important impact on the business and management research we decide to pursue and the methodology and methods we use.

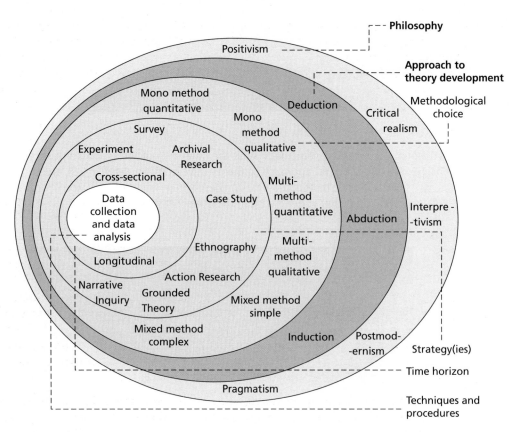

Figure 4.1 The 'research onion'
Source: ©2018 Mark Saunders, Philip Lewis and Adrian Thornhill

4.2 The philosophical underpinnings of business and management

What is research philosophy?

The term **research philosophy** refers to a system of beliefs and assumptions about the development of knowledge. Although this sounds rather profound, it is precisely what you are doing when embarking on research: developing knowledge in a particular field. The knowledge development you are embarking upon may not be as dramatic as a new theory of human motivation, but even addressing a specific problem in a particular organisation you are, nonetheless, developing new knowledge.

Whether you are consciously aware of them or not, at every stage in your research you will make a number of types of assumptions (Burrell and Morgan 2016). These include (but are not limited to) assumptions about the realities you encounter in your research (ontological assumptions), about human knowledge (epistemological assumptions), and about the extent and ways your own values influence your research process (axiological assumptions). These assumptions inevitably shape how you understand your research questions, the methods you use and how you interpret your findings (Crotty 1998). A well-thought-out and consistent set of assumptions will constitute a credible research philosophy, which will underpin your methodological choice, research strategy and data collection techniques and analysis procedures. This will allow you to design a coherent research project, in which all elements of research fit together. Johnson and Clark (2006) note that, as business and management researchers, we need to be aware of the philosophical commitments we make through our choice of research strategy, since this will have a significant impact on what we do and how we understand what it is we are investigating.

Prior to undertaking a research methods module, few of our students have thought about their own beliefs about the nature of the world around them, what constitutes acceptable and desirable knowledge, or the extent to which they believe it necessary to remain detached from their research data. The process of exploring and understanding your own research philosophy requires you to hone the skill of reflexivity, that is to question your own thinking and actions, and learn to examine your own beliefs with the same scrutiny as you would apply to the beliefs of others (Haynes 2012). This may sound daunting, but we all do this in our day-to-day lives when we learn from our mistakes. As a researcher, you need to develop reflexivity, to become aware of and actively shape the relationship between your philosophical position and how you undertake your research (Alvesson and Sköldberg 2009).

You may be wondering about the best way to start this reflexive process. In part, your exploration of your philosophical position and how to translate it into a coherent research practice will be influenced by practical considerations, such as your own and your project tutor's subject area, the time and finances available for your research project, and what access you can negotiate to data. However, there are two things that you can do to start making a more active and informed philosophical choice:

- begin asking yourself questions about your research beliefs and assumptions;
- familiarise yourself with major research philosophies within business and management.

This section introduces you to the philosophical underpinnings of business and management, and Section 4.4 to five research philosophies commonly adopted by its researchers. We will encourage you to reflect on your own beliefs and assumptions in relation to these five philosophies and the research design you will use to undertake your research (Figure 4.2). The chapter will also help you to outline your philosophy and justify it in relation to the alternatives you could have adopted (Johnson and Clark 2006). Through this you will be better equipped to explain and justify your methodological choice, research strategy and data collection procedures and analysis techniques.

At the end of the chapter in the section 'Progressing your research project', you will find a reflexive tool (HARP) designed by Bristow and Saunders to help you start thinking about your values and beliefs in relation to research. This will help you to make your values and assumptions more explicit, explain them using the language of research philosophy, and consider the potential fit between your own beliefs and those of major philosophies used in business and management research.

Is there a best philosophy for business and management research?

You may be wondering at this stage whether you could take a shortcut, and simply adopt 'the best' philosophy for business and management research. One problem with such a shortcut would be the possibility of discovering a clash between 'the best' philosophy and your own beliefs and assumptions. Another problem would be that business and management researchers do not agree about one best philosophy (Tsoukas and Knudsen 2003).

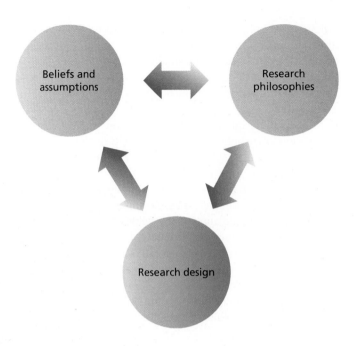

Figure 4.2
Source: ©2018 Alexandra Bristow and Mark Saunders

In terms of developing your own philosophy and designing your research project, it is important to recognise that philosophical disagreements are an intrinsic part of business and management research. When business and management emerged as an academic discipline in the twentieth century, it drew its theoretical base from a mixture of disciplines in the social sciences (e.g. sociology, psychology, economics), natural sciences (e.g. chemistry, biology), applied sciences (e.g. engineering, statistics), humanities (e.g. literary theory, linguistics, history, philosophy) and the domain of organisational practice (Starbuck 2003). In drawing on these disciplines it absorbed the various associated philosophies, dividing and defining them, and resulting in the coexistence of multiple research philosophies and methodologies we see today.

Business and management scholars have spent long decades debating whether this multiplicity of research philosophies, paradigms and methodologies is desirable, and have reached no agreement. Instead, two opposing perspectives have emerged: pluralism and unificationism. Unificationists see business and management as fragmented, and argue that this fragmentation prevents it from becoming more like a true scientific discipline. They advocate unification of management research under one strong research philosophy, paradigm and methodology (Pfeffer 1993). Pluralists see the diversity of the field as helpful, arguing that it enriches business and management (Knudsen 2003).

In this chapter, we take a pluralist approach and suggest that each research philosophy and paradigm contribute something unique and valuable to business and management research, representing a different and distinctive 'way of seeing' organisational realities (Morgan 2006). However, we believe that you need to be aware of the depth of difference and disagreements between these distinct philosophies. This will help you to both outline and justify your own philosophical choices in relation to your chosen research method.

Ontological, epistemological and axiological assumptions

Before we discuss individual research philosophies in Section 4.4, we need to be able to distinguish between them. We do this by considering the differences in the assumptions typically made by scholars working within each philosophy. To keep things relatively simple, we look at three types of research assumptions to distinguish research philosophies: ontology, epistemology and axiology. There are, of course, other types of assumptions that are relevant to research design and research philosophies – when you use the HARP tool at the end of this chapter, you will spot some of them. For example, researchers differ in terms of how free they believe individuals are to change their lives and the world around them, and conversely how constraining the societal structures are on the lives and actions of individuals. These are known as structure and agency assumptions.

Ontology refers to assumptions about the nature of reality. In this chapter's opening vignette we saw how voters made different assumptions regarding the realities of the UK's European Union membership, some perceiving it as over-bureaucratic whilst others saw it as providing legal protections for workplace rights and the environment. Although this may seem abstract and far removed from your intended research project, your ontological assumptions shape the way in which you see and study your research objects. In business and management these objects include organisations, management, individuals' working lives and organisational events and artefacts. Your ontology therefore determines how you see the world of business and management and, therefore, your choice of what to research for your research project.

Imagine you wanted to research resistance to organisational change. For a long time, business and management scholars made the ontological assumption that resistance to change was highly damaging to organisations. They argued it was a kind of organisational misbehaviour, and happened when change programmes went wrong. Consequently, they focused their research on how this phenomenon could be eliminated, looking for types of employee that were most likely to resist change and the management actions that could prevent or stop resistance. More recently, some researchers have started to view the concept of resistance to change differently, resulting in a new strand of research. These researchers see resistance as a phenomenon that happens all the time whenever organisational change takes place, and that benefits organisations by addressing problematic aspects of change programmes. Their different ontological assumptions mean that they focus on how resistance to change can best be harnessed to benefit organisations, rather than looking for ways to eliminate resistance (Thomas and Hardy 2011).

Epistemology refers to assumptions about knowledge, what constitutes acceptable, valid and legitimate knowledge, and how we can communicate knowledge to others (Burrell and Morgan 2016). In the opening vignette we saw that voters made assumptions about the acceptability and legitimacy of data presented by both the campaign for the UK to leave and the campaign for the UK to remain in the European Union. Whereas ontology may initially seem rather abstract, the relevance of epistemology is more obvious. The multidisciplinary context of business and management means that different types of knowledge – ranging from numerical data to textual and visual data, from facts to opinions, and including narratives and stories – can all be considered legitimate. Consequently, different business and management researchers adopt different epistemologies in their research, including projects based on archival research and autobiographical accounts (Martí and Fernández 2013), narratives (Gabriel et al. 2013) and fictional literature (De Cock and Land 2006).

This variety of epistemologies gives you a large choice of methods. However, it is important to understand the implications of different epistemological assumptions in relation to your choice of method(s) and the strengths and limitations of subsequent research findings. For example, the (positivist) assumption that objective facts offer the best scientific evidence is likely, but not exclusively, to result in the choice of quantitative research methods. Within this, the subsequent research findings are likely to be considered objective and generalisable. However, they will also be less likely to offer a rich and complex view of organisational realities, account for the differences in individual contexts and experiences or, perhaps, propose a radically new understanding of the world than if you based your research on a different view of knowledge. In other words, despite this diversity, it is your own epistemological assumptions (and arguably those of your project tutor) that will govern what you consider legitimate for your research.

Axiology refers to the role of values and ethics. We see this in the opening vignette where parts of the electorate felt their values have been ignored by mainstream politicians. One of the key axiological choices that you will face as a researcher is the extent to which you wish to view the impact of your own values and beliefs on your research as a positive thing. Consequently, you will need to decide how you deal with both your own values and those of the people you are researching. For example, you may believe, as Heron (1996) argues, that our values are the guiding reason for all human action, and that while it is inevitable that you will incorporate your values during the process, it is crucially important that you explicitly recognise and reflect on these as you conduct and write up your research. Choosing one topic rather than another suggests that you think one of the topics is more important. Your research philosophy is a reflection of your values, as is your choice of data collection techniques. For example, conducting a study where you place greatest importance on data collected using face-to-face interviews (Sections 10.5 to 10.8) or ethnography as a research strategy (Section 5.6) suggests you value data collected through personal interaction with your participants more highly than views expressed through responses to an anonymous questionnaire (Chapter 11). Whatever your view, it is important, as Heron (1996) argues, to demonstrate your axiological skill by being able to articulate your values as a basis for making judgements about what research you are conducting and how you go about doing it.

Some of our students have found it helpful to write their own statement of personal values in relation to the topic they are studying. For example, for the topic of career development, your personal values may dictate that you believe developing their career is an individual's responsibility. In finance, a researcher may believe (hold the value) that as much information as possible should be available to as many stakeholders as possible. Writing a statement of personal values can help heighten your awareness of value judgements you are making in drawing conclusions from your data. Being clear about your own value position can also help you in deciding what is appropriate ethically and explaining this in the event of queries about decisions you have made (Sections 6.5–6.7).

Objectivism and subjectivism

Now you are familiar with some types of assumptions that research philosophies make, you need to be able to distinguish between them. Earlier in this chapter we discussed the emergence of business and management as a discipline and how it absorbed a range of philosophies from natural sciences, social sciences and arts and humanities. Although this offers philosophical and methodological choice, it also means that business and management research philosophies are scattered along a multidimensional set of continua (Niglas 2010) between two opposing extremes. Table 4.1 summarises the continua and their objectivist and subjectivist extremes in relation to the three types of philosophical assumptions that we have just discussed.

Objectivism incorporates the assumptions of the natural sciences, arguing that the social reality that we research is external to us and others (referred to as **social actors**) (Table 4.1). This means that, ontologically, objectivism embraces **realism**, which, in its most extreme form, considers social entities to be like physical entities of the natural world, in so far as they exist independently of how we think of them, label them, or even of our awareness of them. Because the interpretations and experiences of social actors do not influence the existence of the social world according to this view, an objectivist in the most extreme form believes that there is only one true social reality experienced by all social actors. This social world is made up of solid, granular and relatively unchanging 'things', including major social structures such as family, religion and the economy into which individuals are born (Burrell and Morgan 2016).

From an objectivist viewpoint, social and physical phenomena exist independently of individuals' views of them and tend to be universal and enduring in character.

Table 4.1 Philosophical assumptions as a multidimensional set of continua

Assumption type	Questions	Continua with two sets of extremes		
		Objectivism	⇔	**Subjectivism**

Ontology	• What is the nature of reality?
	• What is the world like?
	• For example:
	  – What are organisations like?
	  – What is it like being in organisations?
	  – What is it like being a manager or being managed?
		Real
		
		External
		One true reality (universalism)
		Granular (things)
		Order
			⇔
			
			⇔
			⇔
			
			⇔
			⇔
				Nominal/decided by convention
				Socially constructed
				Multiple realities (relativism)
				Flowing (processes)
				Chaos

Epistemology	• How can we know what we know? • What is considered acceptable knowledge? • What constitutes good-quality data? • What kinds of contribution to knowledge can be made?	Adopt assumptions of the natural scientist Facts Numbers Observable phenomena Law-like generalisations	⇔ ⇔ ⇔ ⇔ ⇔	Adopt the assumptions of the arts and humanities Opinions Written, spoken and visual accounts Attributed meanings Individuals and contexts, specifics
Axiology	• What is the role of values in research? Should we try to be morally-neutral when we do research, or should we let our values shape research? • How should we deal with the values of research participants?	Value-free Detachment	⇔ ⇔	Value-bound Integral and reflexive

Consequently, it makes sense to study them in the same way as a natural scientist would study nature. Epistemologically, objectivists seek to discover 'the truth' about the social world, through the medium of observable, measurable facts, from which law-like generalisations can be drawn about the universal social reality. Axiologically, since the social entities and social actors exist independently of each other, objectivists strive to keep their research free of values, which they believe could bias their findings. They therefore also try to remain detached from their own values and beliefs throughout a rigorous scientific research process.

The social phenomenon of management can be researched in an objectivist way (Box 4.1). You may argue that management is an objective entity and decide to adopt an objectivist stance to the study of particular aspects of management in a specific organisation. In order to justify this, you would say that the managers in your organisation have job descriptions which prescribe their duties, there are operating procedures to which they are supposed to adhere, they are part of a formal structure which locates them in a hierarchy with people reporting to them and they in turn report to more senior managers. This view emphasises the structural aspects of management and assumes that management is similar in all organisations. Aspects of the structure in which management operates may differ, but the essence of the function is very much the same in all organisations. If you took this ontological stance, the aim of your research would be to discover the laws that govern management behaviour to predict how management would act in the future. You would also attempt to lay aside any beliefs you may have developed from interacting with

Box 4.1
Focus on student research

A management exodus at ChemCo

As part of a major organisational change, all the managers in the marketing department of the chemical manufacturer ChemCo left the organisation. They were replaced by new managers who were thought to be more in tune with the more commercially aggressive new culture that the organisation was trying to create. The new managers entering the organisation filled the roles of the managers who had left and had essentially the same formal job duties and procedures as their predecessors.

John wanted to study the role of management in ChemCo and in particular the way in which managers liaised with external stakeholders. He decided to use the new managers in the marketing department as his research 'subjects'.

In his research proposal he outlined briefly his research philosophy. He defined his ontological position as that of the objectivist. His reasoning was that management in ChemCo had a reality that was separate from the managers who inhabited that reality. He pointed to the fact that the formal management structure at ChemCo was largely unchanged from that which was practised by the managers who had left the organisation. The process of management would continue in largely the same way in spite of the change in personnel.

Emma also wanted to study the role of management in ChemCo; however, she wanted to approach her research from a subjectivist perspective. In her research proposal, Emma pointed out that even though the formal management structure at ChemCo remained the same, the demographics of the new management workforce were very different. Whereas the managers who had left the company had been mostly close to retirement age, male and white, the new managers were typically young and much more gender- and ethnically-diverse. Taken together with the ChemCo's emphasis on the new organisational culture, this led Emma to question whether the formal job descriptions and processes were still interpreted by the new managers in the same way. Emma therefore decided to focus her research on the old and new managers' interpretations of organisational and managerial practices.

individual managers in the past, in order to avoid these experiences colouring your conclusions about management in general.

Alternatively, you may prefer to consider the objective aspects of management as less important than the way in which managers attach their own individual meanings to their jobs and the way they think that those jobs should be performed. This approach would be much more subjectivist.

Subjectivism incorporates assumptions of the arts and humanities (Table 4.1), asserting that social reality is made from the perceptions and consequent actions of social actors (people). Ontologically, subjectivism embraces nominalism (also sometimes called conventionalism). **Nominalism**, in its most extreme form, considers that the order and structures of social phenomena we study (and the phenomena themselves) are created by us as researchers and by other social actors through use of language, conceptual categories, perceptions and consequent actions. For nominalists, there is no underlying reality to the social world beyond what people (social actors) attribute to it, and, because each person experiences and perceives reality differently, it makes more sense to talk about multiple realities rather than a single reality that is the same for everyone (Burrell and Morgan 2016). A less extreme version of this is **social constructionism**. This puts forward that reality is constructed through social interaction in which social actors create partially shared meanings and realities, in other words reality is constructed intersubjectively.

As social interactions between actors are a continual process, social phenomena are in a constant state of flux and revision. This means it is necessary as a researcher to study a situation in detail, including historical, geographical and socio-cultural contexts in order to understand what is happening or how realities are being experienced. Unlike an objectivist researcher who seeks to discover universal facts and laws governing social behaviour, the subjectivist researcher is interested in different opinions and narratives that can help to account for different social realities of different social actors. Subjectivists believe that as they actively use these data they cannot detach themselves from their own values. They therefore openly acknowledge and actively reflect on and question their own values (Cunliffe (2003) calls this 'radical reflexivity') and incorporate these within their research.

Let us suppose that you have decided to research the portrayal of entrepreneurs by the media. Media producers, like other social actors, may interpret the situations which they are filming differently as a consequence of their own view of the world. Their different interpretations are likely to affect their actions and the nature of the films and television programmes they produce. From a subjectivist view, the media producers' portrayals you are studying are a product of these producers' interaction with their environments and their seeking to make sense of it through their interpretation of events and the meanings that they draw from these events. As a subjectivist researcher, it is your role to seek to understand the different realities of the media producers in order to be able to make sense of and understand their portrayals of entrepreneurs in a way that is meaningful (Box 4.2). All this is some way from the objectivist position that being an entrepreneur has a reality that is separate from the media producers who perceive that reality. The subjectivist view is that the portrayal of entrepreneurship is constructed through the social interactions between media producers and entrepreneurs and is continually being revised as a result of this. In other words, at no time is there a definitive entity called 'entrepreneur'. Entrepreneurs are experienced differently by different media producers and, as an aggregate, the resultant portrayal is likely to be constantly changing.

Box 4.2 Focus on research in the news

Why do entrepreneurs get such a bad rap?

By Janan Ganesh

Nothing brings on early mid-life ennui* like watching friends set up their own businesses. When one describes his new venture to me, all forms of salaried life seem bloodless all of a sudden. It is not the prospect of riches (you can marry into that stuff) or even the freedom – I am less answerable to legal duties, bureaucratic wrangles, early mornings, late-night panics and the ordeal of managing people than he will ever be.

It is the blend of fun and high stakes. Every decision matters (above all recruitment) and is his to make. To imagine a product into being, to work in a field of personal interest, to influence the way people live: not all entrepreneurs do these things, but the ones who do need only break even to end up somewhere near the top of Maslow's hierarchy of needs.

And then they turn on the television and see a crew of spivs vying to impress a jaded martinet flanked by two stern-faced lieutenants. Criticism of The Apprentice, with its desolate picture of entrepreneurial life, is neither new nor effective. If there is something medieval about the show's idiots-in-a-cage concept, then viewers do not seem to mind. The new series of the UK version that starts this autumn is the 17th. An alumnus of the American version now governs the US.

As entertainment, it dazzles. As a portrait of business, it is poison. All commerce is shown as a racket spuriously dignified with mortifying TED-speak. "Don't tell me the sky's the limit," one boardroom Voltaire said, "when there are footprints on the Moon." The content of each "task" matters less than the distribution of blame after the fact. To the artful bluffer, the spoils. Real-life business is full of ineloquent but impressive people. The Apprentice rewards the opposite. Its corporate veneer is such a sham: it is a superb show about politics.

By itself, though, The Apprentice is not the problem. The problem is that The Apprentice is all there is. You can watch TV from January to December without seeing a heroic or even benign account of money being made – one that does not involve a plagiarised product, a betrayed friend, a hoodwinked customer or a corner flagrantly cut.

 Abridged from: 'Why do entrepreneurs get such a bad rap?', Janan Ganesh (2017) *Financial Times* 25 August. Copyright © 2017 The Financial Times Ltd

4.3 Research paradigms

Another dimension that can help you to differentiate between research philosophies relates to the political or ideological orientation of researchers towards the social world they investigate. Like the objectivism–subjectivism dimension, this ideological dimension has two opposing poles or extremes. Burrell and Morgan (2016) call these extremes 'sociology of regulation' (for short, regulation) and 'sociology of radical change' (simply, radical change).

---

*Feeling of dissatisfaction arising from having nothing interesting or exciting to do. The word is often used in relation to a person's job.

Regulation and radical change perspectives

Researchers working within the **regulation perspective** are concerned primarily with the need for the regulation of societies and human behaviour. They assume an underlying unity and cohesiveness of societal systems and structures. Much of business and management research can be classed as regulation research that seeks to suggest how organisational affairs may be improved within the framework of how things are done at present, rather than radically challenging the current position. However, you may wish to do research precisely because you want to fundamentally question the way things are done in organisations, and, through your research, offer insights that would help to change the organisational and social worlds. In this case, you would be researching within the **radical change perspective**. Radical change research approaches organisational problems from the viewpoint of overturning the existing state of affairs (Box 4.3). Such research is often visionary and utopian, being concerned with what is possible and alternatives to the accepted current position (Burrell and Morgan 2016). Table 4.2 summarises the differences between the regulation and radical change perspectives.

Much of business and management research undertaken from within the radical change perspective would fall within the area of management known as **Critical Management, Studies (CMS)**. CMS researchers question not only the behaviour of individual managers but also the very societal systems within which that behaviour is situated. CMS research therefore challenges their taken-for-granted acceptance of 'the best' or 'the only available' ways of organising societies and organisations (Fournier and Grey 2000). It therefore attempts to expose the problems and weaknesses, as well as the damaging effects, of these dominant ideas and practices.

CMS researchers also challenge dominant organisational ideas and practices, including 'management' itself. In his book *Against Management: Organization in the Age of Managerialism,* Martin Parker (2002) challenges the acceptance of management.

Parker starts by acknowledging just how difficult and almost unthinkable is it to be against something like management, which shapes so completely our everyday lives in today's world. It is one thing, he writes, to question some aspects of management, or some of its effects, so that we can learn how to do management better. It is a completely different and much harder thing to be against management itself, as a whole and categorically – it is a bit like opposing buildings, society or air. Nevertheless, Parker insists, it is the latter, radical questioning of management that is the purpose of his book. Just because management is everywhere, he writes, does not mean that management is necessary or good, or that it is not worthwhile being against it.

Table 4.2 The regulation–radical change dimension

The regulation perspective . . .	⇔	The radical change perspective . . .
. . . *advocates the* status quo	⇔	. . . *advocates* radical change
. . . *looks for* order	⇔	. . . *looks for* conflict
. . . *looks for* consensus	⇔	. . . *questions* domination
. . . *looks for* integration and cohesion	⇔	. . . *looks for* contradiction
. . . *seeks* solidarity	⇔	. . . *seeks* emancipation
. . . *sees the* satisfaction of needs	⇔	. . . *sees* deprivation
. . . *sees the* actual	⇔	. . . *sees the* potential

Source: Developed from Burrell and Morgan (2016)

Parker builds his radical critique by questioning three key assumptions typically made about management:

- management is part of scientific thought that allows human beings increasing control over their environment;
- management increases control over people;
- management is the best way to control people.

Questioning these assumptions might suggest that management is damaging to organisations and societies. For example, it might emphasise that the environment does not always benefit from being controlled by people, and that controlling employees in managerial ways is not necessarily good for organisations. Once fundamental assumptions about management are questioned, researchers are freer to think about proposing alternative ideas and practices, paving the way for radical societal change.

Sociological paradigms for organisational analysis

In their book *Sociological Paradigms and Organisational Analysis* (2016), Burrell and Morgan combine the objectivist–subjectivist continuum with a regulation–radical change continuum to create a 2 × 2 matrix of four distinct and rival 'paradigms' of organisational analysis (Figure 4.3). In their interpretation (and also as we use the term here) a **paradigm** is a set of basic and taken-for-granted assumptions which underwrite the frame of reference, mode of theorising and ways of working in which a group operates. The matrix's four paradigms represent four different ways of viewing the social and organisational world.

In the bottom right corner of the matrix is the **functionalist paradigm**. This is located on the objectivist and regulation dimensions and is the paradigm within which most business and management research operates. Research in this paradigm is concerned with rational explanations and developing sets of recommendations within the current structures. Functionalist theories and models of management, such as business process re-engineering, are often generalised to other contexts, the idea being that they can be used universally providing they are correctly implemented and monitored (Kelemen and Rumens 2008). A key assumption you would be making here as a researcher is that

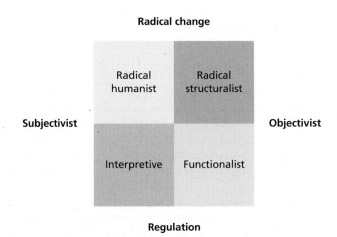

Figure 4.3 Four paradigms for organisational analysis
Source: Developed from Burrell and Morgan (2016) *Social Paradigms and Organisational Analysis*

Box 4.3
Focus on student research

Researching the employees' understandings of psychological contract violation

Working within an interpretive paradigm, Robyn believed that reality is socially constructed, subjective and could be perceived in different ways by different people. While reading for her master's programme she had been surprised by how many of the research papers she read on the psychological contract (an individual's belief regarding the terms and conditions of a reciprocal agreement between themselves and another) focused on aggregate findings rather than the specific context of each individual situation. She considered that these researchers often ignored the individualistic and subjective nature of contracts as well as individuals' interpretations and responses. Robyn therefore decided her research would be concerned with what individual employees interpreted as employers' psychological contract violations, and how they understood the impact of violations on their own attitudes and behaviours. Based on a thorough review of the literature she developed three objectives:

- to provide a new understanding of how individuals interpreted their psychological contracts as being violated;
- to ascertain the ways in which individuals felt their attitudes towards their employer changed as a result of these violations;
- to explore attitudinal and behavioural consequences of this violation from the employees' perspective.

Robyn argued in her methodology chapter that, as a subjectivist, she was concerned with understanding what her research participants perceived to be the reality of their psychological contract violation as they constructed it. She stated her assumption that every action and reaction was based in a context that was interpreted by the participant as she or he made sense of what had happened. It was her participants' perceptions and their emotional reactions to these perceptions that would then inform their actions. Robyn also made clear in the methodology chapter that her research was concerned primarily with finding the meaning and emotions that each participant attached to their psychological contract violation and their reactions, rather than changing what happened in organisations. This she equated with the regulatory perspective.

organisations are rational entities, in which rational explanations offer solutions to rational problems. Research projects could include an evaluation study of a communication strategy to assess its effectiveness and to make recommendations for improvement. Research carried out within the functionalist paradigm is most likely to be underpinned by the positivist research philosophy (Section 4.3), this type of research often being referred to as 'positivist-functionalist'.

The bottom left corner of the matrix represents the **interpretive paradigm**. The primary focus of research undertaken within this paradigm is the way we as humans attempt to make sense of the world around us (Box 4.4). The concern you would have working within this paradigm would be to understand the fundamental meanings attached to organisational life. Far from emphasising rationality, it may be that the principal focus you have here is discovering multiple subjectivities. Concern with studying an organisation's communication strategy may focus on understanding the ways in which it fails due to unforeseen reasons, maybe reasons which are not apparent even to those involved with the strategy. This is likely to take you into the realm of the organisation's politics and the way in which power is used. Your concern here would be to become involved in the organisation's everyday activities in order to understand and explain what is going on, rather than change things (Kelemen and Rumens 2008).

Box 4.4
Focus on management research

Engaged research as a new form of participatory action research: developing socially useful knowledge

In their 2017 *British Journal of Management* article, Cunliffe and Scaratti aim to reimagine the relevance of management scholarship by exploring a new form of participatory action research they call 'engaged research'. This form of research, they say, is focused on being 'socially useful' by enabling a dialogue between conceptual and practical forms of knowledge, and ensuring that an exchange of ideas between practitioners and academic researchers shapes the whole research process (they call this 'dialogical sensemaking').

Cunliffe and Scaratti explain that, methodologically, engaged research means continuously crossing many traditional research boundaries, involving much movement between researchers, participants and many types of data: conversational, artefactual, textual, visual etc., depending on how various research participants negotiate, reinterpret and reconfigure their practical knowledge.

Cunliffe and Scaratti illustrate this with reference to their research into the problems faced by a non-profit social work centre in Milan, as the centre attempted to balance their work of hosting Romanian families with their commitment to working with other community groups. This research was problem-oriented (academic researchers were asked by the social work centre to help resolve a particular issue) and aimed at producing social change. Instead of acting as detached 'experts', researchers worked as dialogue facilitators in a series of meetings held over the course of a year, and involving themselves, social workers dealing with Romanian families, and representatives of other community groups.

Cunliffe and Scaratti argue that their study highlights the need for the development of specific researcher skills and identities relevant to the shift in researcher roles that engaged research entails.

In the top right corner of the matrix, combining objectivist and radical change, is the **radical structuralist paradigm**. Here your concern would be to approach your research with a view to achieving fundamental change based upon an analysis of organisational phenomena such as structural power relationships and patterns of conflict. You would be involved in understanding structural patterns within work organisations such as hierarchies and reporting relationships and the extent to which these may produce structural domination and oppression. You would adopt an objectivist perspective due to your concern with objective entities. Research undertaken within the radical structuralist paradigm is often underpinned by a critical realist philosophy (Section 4.3), although such researchers differentiate themselves from extreme objectivists.

Finally, the **radical humanist paradigm** is located within the subjectivist and radical change dimensions. As we noted earlier, the radical change dimension adopts a critical perspective on organisational life. It emphasises both its political nature and the consequences that one's words and deeds have upon others (Kelemen and Rumens 2008). Working within this paradigm you would be concerned with changing the status quo. As with the radical structuralist paradigm, your primary focus would concern the issues of power and politics, domination and oppression. However, you would approach these concerns from within a subjectivist ontology, which would lead you to emphasise the importance of social construction, language, processes, and instability of structures and meanings in organisational realities.

Burrell and Morgan's (2016) book, although contentious, has been highly influential in terms of how organisational scholarship is seen. One of the most strongly disputed aspects of their work is the idea of **incommensurability**: the assertion that the four paradigms contain mutually incompatible assumptions and therefore cannot be combined. This debate is often referred to as 'paradigm wars' and has implications for thinking about the relationship between paradigms and research philosophies.

Paradigms and research philosophies

Whether or not you think that different research paradigms can be combined will depend to some extent on your own research philosophy and, going back to our discussion of philosophies as a set of assumptions, the extremity of your views on these continua (Table 4.1) and within paradigms (Figure 4.3). You will see later (Section 4.4) that pragmatists seek to overcome dichotomies such as objectivism–subjectivism in their research, and as such are quite likely to engage in multi-paradigmatic research. Critical realists, who are less objectivist than positivists, embrace 'epistemological relativism', which may include more subjectivist as well as objectivist research, ranging from radical structuralism to radical humanism. Burrell and Morgan's four paradigms for organisational analysis can therefore act as a helpful tool for mapping different research philosophies and understanding their relationships to different research paradigms. This highlights the fact that the connections between paradigms and research philosophies need to be seen in terms of philosophical affinity rather than equivocality, and should be treated with some caution and reflexivity. You will find such reflexivity easier as you become familiar with individual research philosophies.

There are good reasons to find the relationship between research paradigms and research philosophies confusing. In management research there tends to be little agreement about labels in general, and the labels 'paradigms' and 'philosophies' (and often others like 'approaches' and 'schools of thought') are sometimes used interchangeably to describe assumptions researchers make in their work. Alongside the substantial body of literature in which Burrell and Morgan's (2016) four sociological research paradigms are taken as the more-or-less enduring foundation of the management field, and in which a 'research paradigm' is taken to be specifically one of the four paradigms described by Burrell and Morgan, there is other research in which the term 'paradigm' is treated much more loosely. As a result, you may find yourself reading about, for example, the 'paradigm' (rather than 'philosophy') of positivism (see e.g. Lincoln et al. 2018).

In a similar way, you may find yourself reading about ideas that seem to cross the boundary between a 'paradigm' and a 'philosophy' (and also perhaps cross over into a 'methodology'). One example of this is the participatory inquiry – an intellectual position that emphasises experiential and practical learning and knowing, and the active involvement of research participants in the making of knowledge throughout the research process. Heron and Reason (1997) call the participatory inquiry a 'paradigm', and use it to critique Guba and Lincoln's earlier (1994) work on competing paradigms. Heron and Reason also describe the ontological, epistemological and axiological foundations of the participatory inquiry (as well as its methodological implications), as we do with five management philosophies in this chapter.

You may wonder how you should deal with this confusion of labels and philosophical ideas. As you develop as a researcher, you will continue to further your knowledge through reading and experience, and will begin to form your own opinions about which labels and debates matter to you personally. For now, if you are just starting out on your research journey, putting some of this complexity on hold (but being aware that it exists) whilst you come to understand the basic principles would be a good starting point. Being more familiar with the basics can also help you interpret more complex issues. For example, being familiar with the pragmatist research philosophy can help you spot how pragmatism tends to underpin and inform participatory action research.

4.4   Five management philosophies

In this section, we discuss five major philosophies in business and management: positivism, critical realism, interpretivism, postmodernism and pragmatism (Figure 4.1).

Positivism

We introduced the research philosophy of positivism briefly in the discussion of objectivism and functionalism earlier in this chapter. **Positivism** relates to the philosophical stance of the natural scientist and entails working with an observable social reality to produce law-like generalisations. It promises unambiguous and accurate knowledge and originates in the works of Francis Bacon, Auguste Comte and the early twentieth-century group of philosophers and scientists known as the Vienna Circle. The label positivism refers to the importance of what is 'posited' –i.e. 'given'. This emphasises the positivist focus on strictly scientific empiricist method designed to yield pure data and facts uninfluenced by human interpretation or bias (Table 4.3). Today there is a 'bewildering array of positivisms', some counting as many as 12 varieties (Crotty 1998).

Table 4.3 Comparison of five research philosophical positions in business and management research

Ontology (nature of reality or being)	Epistemology (what constitutes acceptable knowledge)	Axiology (role of values)	Typical methods
Positivism			
Real, external, independent One true reality (universalism) Granular (things) Ordered	Scientific method Observable and measurable facts Law-like generalisations Numbers Causal explanation and prediction as contribution	Value-free research Researcher is detached, neutral and independent of what is researched Researcher maintains objective stance	Typically deductive, highly structured, large samples, measurement, typically quantitative methods of analysis, but a range of data can be analysed
Critical realism			
Stratified/layered (the empirical, the actual and the real) External, independent Intransient Objective structures Causal mechanisms	Epistemological relativism Knowledge historically situated and transient Facts are social constructions Historical causal explanation as contribution	Value-laden research Researcher acknowledges bias by world views, cultural experience and upbringing Researcher tries to minimise bias and errors Researcher is as objective as possible	Retroductive, in-depth historically situated analysis of pre-existing structures and emerging agency Range of methods and data types to fit subject matter

Ontology (nature of reality or being)	Epistemology (what constitutes acceptable knowledge)	Axiology (role of values)	Typical methods
Interpretivism			
Complex, rich Socially constructed through culture and language Multiple meanings, interpretations, realities Flux of processes, experiences, practices	Theories and concepts too simplistic Focus on narratives, stories, perceptions and interpretations New understandings and worldviews as contribution	Value-bound research Researchers are part of what is researched, subjective Researcher interpretations key to contribution Researcher reflexive	Typically inductive. Small samples, in-depth investigations, qualitative methods of analysis, but a range of data can be interpreted
Postmodernism			
Nominal Complex, rich Socially constructed through power relations Some meanings, interpretations, realities are dominated and silenced by others Flux of processes, experiences, practices	What counts as 'truth' and 'knowledge' is decided by dominant ideologies Focus on absences, silences and oppressed/ repressed meanings, interpretations and voices Exposure of power relations and challenge of dominant views as contribution	Value-constituted research Researcher and research embedded in power relations Some research narratives are repressed and silenced at the expense of others Researcher radically reflexive	Typically deconstructive – reading texts and realities against themselves In-depth investigations of anomalies, silences and absences Range of data types, typically qualitative methods of analysis
Pragmatism			
Complex, rich, external 'Reality' is the practical consequences of ideas Flux of processes, experiences and practices	Practical meaning of knowledge in specific contexts 'True' theories and knowledge are those that enable successful action Focus on problems, practices and relevance Problem solving and informed future practice as contribution	Value-driven research Research initiated and sustained by researcher's doubts and beliefs Researcher reflexive	Following research problem and research question Range of methods: mixed, multiple, qualitative, quantitative, action research Emphasis on practical solutions and outcomes

If you were to adopt an extreme positivist position, you would see organisations and other social entities as real in the same way as physical objects and natural phenomena are real. Epistemologically you would focus on discovering observable and measurable facts and regularities, and only phenomena that you can observe and measure would lead to the production of credible and meaningful data (Crotty 1998). You would look for causal relationships in your data to create law-like generalisations like those produced by scientists. You would use these universal rules and laws to help you to explain and predict behaviour and events in organisations.

As a positivist researcher you might use existing theory to develop hypotheses. These statements provide hypothetical explanations that can be tested and confirmed, in whole or part, or refuted, leading to the further development of theory which then may be tested by further research. However, this does not mean that, as a positivist, you necessarily have to start with existing theory. All natural sciences have developed from an engagement with the world in which data were collected and observations made prior to hypotheses being formulated and tested. In fact, the original positivists emphasised the importance of inductive research due to the importance of empirical data, even though nowadays positivist research tends to be deductive (see Section 4.5). The hypotheses developed, as in Box 4.5, would lead to the gathering of facts (rather than impressions) that would provide the basis for subsequent hypothesis testing.

As a positivist you would also try to remain neutral and detached from your research and data in order to avoid influencing your findings. This means that you would undertake research, as far as possible, in a value-free way. For positivists, this is a plausible position, because of the measurable, quantifiable data that they collect. They claim to be external to the process of data collection as there is little that can be done to alter the substance of the data collected. Consider, for example, the differences between data collected using an Internet questionnaire (Chapter 11) in which the respondent self-selects from responses predetermined by the researcher, and in-depth interviews (Chapter 10). In the Internet questionnaire, the researcher determines the list of possible responses as part of the design process. Subsequent to this she or he can claim that her or his values do not influence the answers given by the respondent. In contrast, an in-depth interview necessitates the researcher framing the questions in relation to each participant and interpreting their answers. Unlike in a questionnaire, these questions are unlikely to be asked in exactly the same way. Rather the interviewer exercises her or his judgment in what to ask to collect participant-led accounts that are as rich as possible.

You may believe that excluding our own values as researchers is impossible. Even a researcher adopting a positivist stance exercises choice in the issue to study, the research

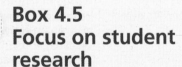

Box 4.5
Focus on student research

The development of hypotheses

Brett was conducting a piece of research for his project on the economic benefits of working from home for software developers. He studied the literature on home working and read two dissertations in his university's library that dealt with the same phenomenon, albeit that they did not relate specifically to software developers. As a result of his reading, Brett developed a number of theoretical propositions, each of which contained specific hypotheses. One of his propositions related to the potential increased costs associated with home working.

THEORETICAL PROPOSITION: Increased costs may negate the productivity gains from home working. From this he developed four SPECIFIC HYPOTHESES:

1 Increased costs for computer hardware, software and telecommunications equipment will negate the productivity gains from home working.

2 Home workers will require additional support from on-site employees, for example technicians, which will negate the productivity gains from home working.

3 Work displaced to other employees and/or increased supervisory requirements will negate the productivity gains from home working.

4 Reduced face-to-face access by home workers to colleagues will result in lost opportunities to increase efficiencies, which will negate the productivity gains from home working.

objectives to pursue and the data to collect. Indeed, it could be argued that the decision to try to adopt a value-free perspective suggests the existence of a certain value position!

Positivist researchers are likely to use a highly structured methodology in order to facilitate replication. Furthermore, the emphasis will be on quantifiable observations that lend themselves to statistical analysis (Box 4.5). However, as you will read in later chapters, sometimes positivist research extends itself to other data collection methods and seeks to quantify qualitative data, for example by applying hypothesis testing to data originally collected in in-depth interviews.

Critical realism

It is important not to confuse the philosophy of critical realism with the more extreme form of realism underpinning the positivist philosophy. The latter, sometimes known as **direct realism** (or naïve empirical scientific realism), says that what you see is what you get: what we experience through our senses portrays the world accurately. By contrast, the philosophy of **critical realism** focuses on explaining what we see and experience, in terms of the underlying structures of reality that shape the observable events. Critical realism originated in the late twentieth century in the work of Roy Bhaskar, as a response to both positivist direct realism and postmodernist nominalism (discussed later), and occupies a middle ground between these two positions (Reed 2005).

For critical realists, reality is the most important philosophical consideration, a structured and layered ontology being crucial (Fleetwood 2005). Critical realists see reality as external and independent, but not directly accessible through our observation and knowledge of it (Table 4.3). Rather, what we experience is 'the empirical', in other words sensations, which are some of the manifestations of the things in the real world, rather than the actual things. Critical realists highlight how often our senses deceive us. When you next watch a cricket or rugby match on television you are likely to see an advertisement for the sponsor on the actual playing surface. This advertisement appears to be standing upright on the pitch. However, this is an illusion. It is, in fact, painted on the grass. So what we see are sensations, which are representations of what is real.

Critical realism claims there are two steps to understanding the world. First, there are the sensations and events we experience. Second, there is the mental processing that goes on sometime after the experience, when we 'reason backwards' from our experiences to the underlying reality that might have caused them (this reasoning backwards is essentially abductive, but is often called 'retroduction' by critical realists (Reed 2005) – see Section 4.5). Direct realism says that the first step is enough. To pursue our cricket (or rugby) example, the umpire who is a direct realist would say about her or his umpiring decisions: 'I give them as they are!' The umpire who is a critical realist would say: 'I give them as I see them!' Critical realists would point out that what the umpire has observed (the 'Empirical') is only a small part of everything that he or she could have seen; a small fraction of the sum total of the 'Actual' events that are occurring at any one point in time (Figure 4.4). A player may, perhaps, have obscured the umpire's view of another player committing a foul. Critical realists would emphasise that what the umpire has not seen are the underlying causes (the 'Real') of a situation (Figure 4.4). For example, was a head-butt a real, intentional foul, or an accident? The umpire cannot experience the real significance of the situation directly. Rather, she or he has to use her/his sensory data of the 'Empirical' as observed and use reasoning to work it out.

If you believe that, as researchers, we need to look for the bigger picture of which we see only a small part, you may be leaning towards the critical realist philosophy. Bhaskar

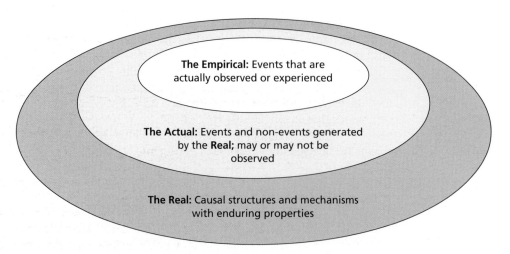

Figure 4.4 Critical realist stratified ontology
Source: Developed from Bhaskar (2008)

(2011) argues that we will only be able to understand what is going on in the social world if we understand the social structures that have given rise to the phenomena that we are trying to understand. He writes that we can identify what we do not see through the practical and theoretical processes of the social sciences. Critical realist research therefore focuses on providing an explanation for observable organisational events by looking for the underlying causes and mechanisms through which deep social structures shape everyday organisational life. Due to this focus, much of critical realist research takes the form of in-depth historical analysis of social and organisational structures, and how they have changed over time (Reed 2005).

Within their focus on the historical analysis of structures, critical realists embrace epistemological relativism (Reed 2005), a (mildly) subjectivist approach to knowledge. **Epistemological relativism** recognises that knowledge is historically situated (in other words, it is a product of its time and is specific to it), and that social facts are social constructions agreed on by people rather than existing independently (Bhaskar 2008). This implies that critical realist notions of causality cannot be reduced to statistical correlations and quantitative methods, and that a range of methods is acceptable (Reed 2005). A critical realist's axiological position follows from the recognition that our knowledge of reality is a result of social conditioning (e.g. we know that if the rugby player runs into an advertisement that is actually standing up he or she will fall over!) and cannot be understood independently of the social actors involved. This means that, as a critical realist researcher, you would strive to be aware of the ways in which your socio-cultural background and experiences might influence your research, and would seek to minimise such biases and be as objective as possible.

Interpretivism

Interpretivism, like critical realism, developed as a critique of positivism but from a subjectivist perspective. **Interpretivism** emphasises that humans are different from physical phenomena because they create meanings. Interpretivists study these meanings. Interpretivism emerged in early- and mid-twentieth-century Europe, in the work of German, French and occasionally English thinkers, and is formed of several strands, most notably hermeneutics, phenomenology and symbolic interactionism (Crotty 1998). Interpretivism argues that human beings and their social worlds cannot be studied in the same way as physical phenomena, and that therefore social sciences research needs to be different from natural sciences research rather than trying to emulate the latter (Table 4.3). As different people of different cultural backgrounds, under different circumstances and at different times make different meanings, and so create and experience different social realities, interpretivists are critical of the positivist attempts to discover definite, universal 'laws' that apply to everybody. Rather they believe that rich insights into humanity are lost if such complexity is reduced entirely to a series of law-like generalisations.

The purpose of interpretivist research is to create new, richer understandings and interpretations of social worlds and contexts. For business and management researchers, this means looking at organisations from the perspectives of different groups of people. They would argue, for example, that the ways in which the CEO, board directors, managers, shop assistants, cleaners and customers see and experience a large retail company are different, so much so that they could arguably be seen as experiencing different workplace realities. If research focuses on the experiences that are common to all at all times, much of the richness of the differences between them and their individual circumstances will be lost, and the understanding of the organisation that the research delivers will reflect this. Furthermore, differences that make organisations complex are not simply contained to different organisational roles. Male or female employees or customers, or those from different ethnic/cultural backgrounds, may experience workplaces, services or events in different ways. Interpretations of what on the surface appears to be the same thing (such as a luxury product) can differ between historical or geographical contexts.

Interpretivist researchers try to take account of this complexity by collecting what is meaningful to their research participants. Different strands of interpretivism place slightly different emphasis on how to do this in practice, so **phenomenologists**, who study existence, focus on participants' lived experience; that is, the participants' recollections and interpretations of those experiences. **Hermeneuticists** focus on the study of cultural artefacts such as texts, symbols, stories, and images. **Symbolic interactionists**, whose tradition derives from pragmatist thinking (discussed later in this section) and who see meaning as something that emerges out of interactions between people, focus on the observation and analysis of social interaction such as conversations, meetings, and teamwork. In general, interpretivists emphasise the importance of language, culture and history (Crotty 1998) in the shaping of our interpretations and experiences of organisational and social worlds.

With its focus on complexity, richness, multiple interpretations and meaning-making, interpretivism is explicitly subjectivist. An axiological implication of this is that interpretivists recognise that their interpretation of research materials and data, and thus their own values and beliefs, play an important role in the research process. Crucial to the interpretivist philosophy is that the researcher has to adopt an empathetic stance. The challenge for the interpretivist is to enter the social world of the research participants and understand that world from their point of view. Some would argue the interpretivist perspective is highly appropriate in the case of business and management research. Not only are business situations complex, they are often unique, at least in terms of context. They reflect a particular set of circumstances and interactions involving individuals coming together at a specific time.

Postmodernism

Postmodernism (not to be confused with postmodernity, which denotes a particular historical era) emphasises the role of language and of power relations, seeking to question accepted ways of thinking and give voice to alternative marginalised views (Table 4.3). It emerged in the late twentieth century and has been most closely associated with the work of French philosophers Jean-François Lyotard, Jacques Derrida, Michel Foucault, Gilles Deleuze, Félix Guattari and Jean Baudrillard. Postmodernism is historically entangled with the intellectual movement of poststructuralism. As the differences in focus between post-modernism and poststructuralism are subtle and have become less discernible over time, in this chapter we will focus on one label, postmodernism.

Postmodernists go even further than interpretivists in their critique of positivism and objectivism, attributing even more importance to the role of language (Table 4.3). They reject the modern objectivist, realist ontology of things, and instead emphasise the chaotic primacy of flux, movement, fluidity and change. They believe that any sense of order is provisional and foundationless, and can only be brought about through our language with its categories and classifications (Chia 2003). At the same time they recognise that language is always partial and inadequate. In particular, it always marginalises, suppresses and excludes aspects of what it claims to describe, while privileging and emphasising other aspects. As there is no order to the social world beyond that which we give to it through language, there is no abstract way of determining the 'right' or the 'true' way to describe the world. Instead, what is generally considered to be 'right' and 'true' is decided collectively. These collective 'choices', in turn, are shaped by the power relations and by the ideologies that dominate particular contexts (Foucault 1991). This does not mean that the dominant ways of thinking are necessarily the 'best' – only that they are seen as such at a particular point in time by particular groups of people. Other perspectives that are suppressed are potentially just as valuable and have the power to create alternative worlds and truths.

Postmodernist researchers seek to expose and question the power relations that sustain dominant realities (Calás and Smircich 1997). This takes the form of 'deconstructing' (taking apart) these realities, as if they were texts, to search for instabilities within their widely accepted truths, and for what has not been discussed – absences and silences created in the shadow of such truths (Derrida 2016). Postmodernists strive to make what has been left out or excluded more visible by the deconstruction of what counts as 'reality' into ideologies and power relations that underpin it, as you would dismantle an old building into the bricks and mortar that make it up. The goal of postmodern research is therefore to challenge radically the established ways of thinking and knowing (Kilduff and Mehra 1997) and to give voice and legitimacy to the suppressed and marginalised ways of seeing and knowing that have been previously excluded (Chia 2003).

As a postmodernist researcher, you would, instead of approaching the organisational world as constituted by things and entities such as 'management', 'performance' and 'resources', focus on the ongoing processes of organising, managing and ordering that constitute such entities. You would challenge organisational concepts and theories, and seek to demonstrate what perspectives and realities they exclude and leave silent and whose interests they serve. You would be open to the deconstruction of any forms of data – texts, images, conversations, voices and numbers. Like interpretivists, you would be undertaking in-depth investigations of phenomena. Fundamental to postmodernist research is the recognition that power relations between the researcher and research subjects shape the knowledge created as part of the research process. As power relations cannot be avoided, it is crucial for researchers to be open about their moral and ethical positions (Calás and Smircich 1997), and thus you would strive to be radically reflexive about your own thinking and writing (Cunliffe 2003).

Pragmatism

By now you may be thinking: do these differences in assumptions really matter? The proponents of the philosophies discussed above would say that they do, as they delineate fundamentally different ways of seeing the world and carrying out research. However, you may be feeling differently. If you are becoming impatient with the battle of ontological, epistemological and axiological assumptions between the different philosophies, if you are questioning their relevance, and if you would rather get on with research that would focus on making a difference to organisational practice, you may be leaning towards the philosophy of pragmatism. However, you need to be sure that you are not treating pragmatism as an escape route from the challenge of understanding other philosophies!

Pragmatism asserts that concepts are only relevant where they support action (Kelemen and Rumens 2008). Pragmatism originated in the late-nineteenth–early-twentieth-century USA in the work of philosophers Charles Pierce, William James and John Dewey. It strives to reconcile both objectivism and subjectivism, facts and values, accurate and rigorous knowledge and different contextualised experiences (Table 4.3). It does this by considering theories, concepts, ideas, hypotheses and research findings not in an abstract form, but in terms of the roles they play as instruments of thought and action, and in terms of their practical consequences in specific contexts (Table 4.3; Box 4.6). Reality matters to pragmatists as practical effects of ideas, and knowledge is valued for enabling actions to be carried out successfully.

For a pragmatist, research starts with a problem, and aims to contribute practical solutions that inform future practice. Researcher values drive the reflexive process of inquiry, which is initiated by doubt and a sense that something is wrong or out of place, and which recreates belief when the problem has been resolved (Elkjaer and Simpson 2011). As pragmatists are more interested in practical outcomes than abstract distinctions, their research may have considerable variation in terms of how 'objectivist' or 'subjectivist' it turns out to be. If you were to undertake pragmatist research, this would mean that the most important determinant for your research design and strategy would be the research problem that you would try to address, and your research question. Your research question, in turn, would be likely to incorporate the pragmatist emphasis of practical outcomes.

If a research problem does not suggest unambiguously that one particular type of knowledge or method should be adopted, this only confirms the pragmatist's view that it is perfectly possible to work with different types of knowledge and methods. This reflects a recurring theme in this book – that multiple methods are often possible, and possibly highly appropriate, within one study (see Section 5.3). Pragmatists recognise that there are many different ways of interpreting the world and undertaking research, that no single point of view can ever give the entire picture and that there may be multiple realities. This does not mean that pragmatists always use multiple methods; rather they use the method or methods that enable credible, well-founded, reliable and relevant data to be collected that advance the research (Kelemen and Rumens 2008).

 **Box 4.6
Focus on
management
research**

Researching accounting practices

In an article in the *Journal of Applied Accounting*, Rutherford (2016) highlights the schism between accounting practices and accounting research. Within this he comments that for over four decades academics have undertaken relatively little "classical accounting research" (page 119), that is research on practices of accounting such as financial reporting. Rutherford notes that one barrier to academics undertaking such research is the lack of a theoretical base. This he argues can be overcome by using pragmatism as the underpinning for theorisation, thereby providing a clear philosophical justification research to improve practice. Resumption of such research would, he considers, contribute positively to future accounting standard-setting.

4.5 Approaches to theory development

We emphasised that your research project will involve the use of theory (Chapter 2). That theory may or may not be made explicit in the design of the research (Chapter 5), although it will usually be made explicit in your presentation of the findings and conclusions. The extent to which your research is concerned with theory testing or theory building raises an important question regarding the design of your research project. This is often portrayed as two contrasting approaches to the reasoning you adopt: deductive or inductive; although as we highlight in Table 4.4 reasoning can, alternatively, be abductive. Deductive reasoning occurs when the conclusion is derived logically from a set of theory-derived premises, the conclusion being true when all the premises are true (Ketokivi and Mantere 2010). For example, our research may concern likely online retail sales of a soon-to-be-launched new mobile phone. We form three premises:

- that online retailers have been allocated limited stock of the new mobile phones by the manufacturer;
- that customers' demand for the phones exceeds supply;
- that online retailers allow customers to pre-order the phones.

If these premises are true we can deduce that the conclusion that online retailers will have 'sold' their entire allocation of the new mobile phone by the release day will also be true.

In contrast, in inductive reasoning there is a gap in the logic argument between the conclusion and the premises observed, the conclusion being 'judged' to be supported by the observations made (Ketokivi and Mantere 2010). Returning to our example of the likely online retail sales of a soon-to-be-launched mobile phone, we would start with observations about the forthcoming launch. Our observed premises would be:

- that news media are reporting that online retailers are complaining about only being allocated limited stock of the new mobile phone by manufacturers;
- that news media are reporting that demand for the phones will exceed supply;
- that online retailers are allowing customers to pre-order the phones.

Based on these observations, we have good reason to believe online retailers will have 'sold' their entire allocation of the new mobile phone by the release day. However, although our conclusion is supported by our observations, it is not guaranteed. In the past, manufacturers have launched new phones which have had underwhelming sales (Mangalindan 2014).

There is also a third approach to theory development that is just as common in research, abductive reasoning, which begins with a 'surprising fact' being observed (Ketokivi and Mantere 2010). This surprising fact is the conclusion rather than a premise. Based on this conclusion, a set of possible premises is determined that is considered sufficient or nearly sufficient to explain the conclusion. It is reasoned that, if this set of premises were true, then the conclusion would be true as a matter of course. Because the set of premises is sufficient (or nearly sufficient) to generate the conclusion, this provides reason to believe that it is also true. Returning once again to our example of the likely online retail sales of a soon-to-be-launched new mobile phone, a surprising fact (conclusion) might be that online retailers are reported in the news media as stating they will have no remaining stock of the new mobile phone for sale on the day of its release. However, if the online retailers are allowing customers to pre-order the mobile phone prior to its release then it would not be surprising if these retailers had already sold their allocation of phones. Therefore, using abductive reasoning, the possibility that online retailers have no remaining stock on the day of release is reasonable.

Building on these three approaches to theory development (Figure 4.1), if your research starts with theory, often developed from your reading of the academic literature, and you design a research strategy to test the theory, you are using a **deductive approach** (Table 4.4). Conversely, if your research starts by collecting data to explore a phenomenon and you generate or build theory (often in the form of a conceptual framework), then you are using an **inductive approach** (Table 4.4). Where you are collecting data to explore a phenomenon, identify themes and explain patterns, to generate a new or modify an existing theory which you subsequently test through additional data collection, you are using an **abductive approach** (Table 4.4).

The next three sub-sections explore the differences and similarities between these three approaches and their implications for your research.

Deduction

As noted earlier, deduction owes much to what we would think of as scientific research. It involves the development of a theory that is then subjected to a rigorous test through a series of propositions. As such, it is the dominant research approach in the natural sciences, where laws present the basis of explanation, allow the anticipation of phenomena, predict their occurrence and therefore permit them to be controlled.

Blaikie (2010) lists six sequential steps through which a deductive approach will progress:

1 Put forward a tentative idea, a premise, a hypothesis (a testable proposition about the relationship between two or more concepts or variables) or set of hypotheses to form a theory.

Table 4.4 Deduction, induction and abduction: from reason to research

	Deduction	Induction	Abduction
Logic	In a deductive inference, when the premises are true, the conclusion must also be true	In an inductive inference, known premises are used to generate untested conclusions	In an abductive inference, known premises are used to generate testable conclusions
Generalisability	Generalising from the general to the specific	Generalising from the specific to the general	Generalising from the interactions between the specific and the general
Use of data	Data collection is used to evaluate propositions or hypotheses related to an existing theory	Data collection is used to explore a phenomenon, identify themes and patterns and create a conceptual framework	Data collection is used to explore a phenomenon, identify themes and patterns, locate these in a conceptual framework and test this through subsequent data collection and so forth
Theory	Theory falsification or verification	Theory generation and building	Theory generation or modification; incorporating existing theory where appropriate, to build new theory or modify existing theory

2 By using existing literature, or by specifying the conditions under which the theory is expected to hold, deduce a testable proposition or number of propositions.

3 Examine the premises and the logic of the argument that produced them, comparing this argument with existing theories to see if it offers an advance in understanding. If it does, then continue.

4 Test the premises by collecting appropriate data to measure the concepts or variables and analysing them.

5 If the results of the analysis are not consistent with the premises (the tests fail!), the theory is false and must either be rejected or modified and the process restarted.

6 If the results of the analysis are consistent with the premises then the theory is corroborated.

Deduction possesses several important characteristics. First, there is the search to explain causal relationships between concepts and variables. It may be that you wish to establish the reasons for high employee absenteeism in a retail store. After reading about absence patterns in the academic literature you develop a theory that there is a relationship between absence, the age of workers and length of service. Consequently, you develop a number of hypotheses, including one which states that absenteeism is significantly more likely to be prevalent among younger workers and another which states that absenteeism is significantly more likely to be prevalent among workers who have been employed by the organisation for a relatively short period of time. To test this proposition you collect quantitative data. (This is not to say that a deductive approach may not use qualitative data.) It may be that there are important differences in the way work is arranged in different stores: therefore you would need to specify precisely the conditions under which your theory is likely to hold and collect appropriate data within these conditions. By doing this you would help to ensure that any change in absenteeism was a function of worker age and length of service rather than any other aspect of the store, for example the way in which people were managed. Your research would use a highly **structured methodology** to facilitate replication, an important issue to ensure reliability, as we emphasise in Section 5.11.

An additional important characteristic of deduction is that concepts need to be **operationalised** in a way that enables facts to be measured, often quantitatively. In our example, one variable that needs to be measured is absenteeism. Just what constitutes absenteeism would have to be strictly defined: an absence for a complete day would probably count, but what about absence for two hours? In addition, what would constitute a 'short period of employment' and 'younger' employees? What is happening here is that the principle of **reductionism** is being followed. This holds that problems as a whole are better understood if they are reduced to the simplest possible elements.

The final characteristic of deduction is **generalisation.** In order to be able to generalise it is necessary to select our sample carefully and for it to be of sufficient size (Sections 7.2 and 7.3). In our example above, research at a particular store would allow us only to make inferences about that store; it would be dangerous to predict that worker youth and short length of service lead to absenteeism in all cases. This is discussed in more detail in Section 5.11.

As a scientific approach that emphasises structure, quantification, generalisability and testable hypotheses, the deductive approach is most likely to be underpinned by the positivist research philosophy.

Induction

An alternative approach to developing theory on retail store employee absenteeism would be to start by interviewing a sample of the employees and their line managers about the experience of working at the store. The purpose here would be to get a feel of what was going on, so as to understand better the nature of the problem. Your task then would be to make sense of the interview data you collected through your analysis. The result of this analysis would be the formulation of a theory, often expressed as a conceptual framework. This may be that there is a relationship between absence and the length of time a person has worked for the retail store. Alternatively, you may discover that there are other competing reasons for absence that may or may not be related to worker age or length of service. You may end up with the same theory, but your reasoning to produce that theory is using an inductive approach: theory follows data rather than vice versa, as with deduction.

We noted earlier that deduction has its origins in research in the natural sciences. However, the emergence of the social sciences in the twentieth century led social science researchers to be wary of deduction. They were critical of a reasoning approach that enabled a cause–effect link to be made between particular variables without an understanding of the way in which humans interpreted their social world. Developing such an understanding is, of course, the strength of an inductive approach. In our absenteeism example, if you were adopting an inductive approach you would argue that it is more realistic to treat workers as humans whose attendance behaviour is a consequence of the way in which they perceive their work experience, rather than as if they were unthinking research objects who respond in a mechanistic way to certain circumstances.

Followers of induction would also criticise deduction because of its tendency to construct a rigid methodology that does not permit alternative explanations of what is going on. In that sense, there is an air of finality about the choice of theory and definition of the hypothesis. Alternative theories may be suggested by deduction. However, these would be within the limits set by the highly structured research design. In this respect, a significant characteristic of the absenteeism research design noted above is that of the operationalisation of concepts. As we saw in the absenteeism example, age was precisely defined. However, a less structured approach might reveal alternative explanations of the absenteeism–age relationship denied by a stricter definition of age.

Research using an inductive approach to reasoning is likely to be particularly concerned with the context in which such events take place. Therefore, the study of a small sample of subjects might be more appropriate than a large number as with the deductive approach. Researchers in this tradition are more likely to work with qualitative data and to use a variety of methods to collect these data in order to establish different views of phenomena (as will be seen in Chapter 10).

Due to its connection to humanities and its emphasis on the importance of subjective interpretations, the inductive approach is most likely to be informed by the interpretivist philosophy.

Abduction

Instead of moving from theory to data (as in deduction) or data to theory (as in induction), an abductive approach moves back and forth, in effect combining deduction and induction (Suddaby 2006). This, as we have noted earlier, matches what many business and management researchers actually do. Abduction begins with the observation of a 'surprising fact'; it then works out a plausible theory of how this could have occurred. Van Maanen et al. (2007) note that some plausible theories can account for what is observed better than others and it is these theories that will help uncover more 'surprising facts'. These surprises, they argue, can occur at any stage in the research process, including when writing your project report! Van Maanen et al. also stress that deduction and induction complement abduction as logics for testing plausible theories.

Box 4.7
Focus on management research

Developing empirical knowledge and theory abductively

In their paper on the working lives of Critical Management Studies (CMS), early-career academics, Bristow and colleagues (2017) analyse 24 semi-structured interviews with participants working in UK business schools. The dual purpose of their research is to, firstly, add to the empirical understanding of their participants' predicament as they navigate the tensions between business schools' pressures and their personal CMS commitments, and, secondly, to contribute to the dialectical theory of organisational resistance and compliance. As this dual purpose required repeated oscillation between theory and data, their approach is abductive, combining both inductive and deductive elements.

The authors' starting point was a surprising fact – their own and their participants' experiences of starting their first academic jobs, which were different from what was described in the existing literature on early career academics. Bristow et al. believed that the dialectical approach to resistance and compliance could help to better explore the complexities of the early-career experiences, so they used the theory to design broad interview questions. However, they also wanted to capture their participants' own understandings of themselves as resisters and compliers, so in the interviews the pre-prepared questions were used as a loose guide rather than a rigid structure, and interviewees were encouraged to talk at length about each subject. In this way, themes and issues were enabled to emerge in the interviews inductively.

Following the interviews, the authors collectively negotiated the inductively derived themes and issues, and mapped them against the pre-prepared theoretical framework, changing and modifying the latter in the process. This enabled them to make a theoretical as well as an empirical contribution.

Applying an abductive approach to our research on the reasons for high employee absenteeism in a retail store would mean obtaining data that were sufficiently detailed and rich to allow us to explore the phenomenon and identify and explain themes and patterns regarding employee absenteeism. We would then try to integrate these explanations in an overall conceptual framework, thereby building up a theory of employee absenteeism in a retail store. This we would test using evidence provided by existing data and new data and revise as necessary (Box 4.7).

Due to the flexibility of the abductive approach, it can be used by researchers from within a number of different research philosophies. In fact, some would argue that because pure deduction or pure induction are so difficult (or even impossible) to achieve, most management researchers in practice use at least some element of abduction. However, a well-developed abductive approach is most likely to be underpinned by pragmatism or postmodernism, and can also be underpinned by critical realism.

The abductive approach is sometimes called 'retroduction'. In fact, **retroduction** is believed to be the original label for what has become known as abduction through corrupt translation and misunderstanding of older philosophical texts (Peirce 1896). Apart from this trivia, the notion 'retroduction' may be important to you as a researcher if your chosen research philosophy is critical realism. Critical realists often choose to describe their approach as retroductive in order to emphasise the historical aspect of their research, where they would start with a surprising phenomenon in the present and move backwards in time in order to identify the underlying mechanisms and structures that might have produced it (Reed 2005).

Choosing an approach to theory development

At this stage you may be asking yourself: So what? Why is the choice that I make about my approach to theory development so important? Easterby-Smith et al. (2012) suggest three reasons. First, it enables you to take a more informed decision about your research design (Chapter 5), which is more than just the techniques by which data are collected and procedures by which they are analysed. It is the overall configuration of a piece of research involving questions about what kind of evidence is gathered and from where, and how such evidence is interpreted in order to provide good answers to your initial research question.

Second, it will help you to think about those research strategies and methodological choice that will work for you and, crucially, those that will not. For example, if you are particularly interested in understanding why something is happening, rather than being able to describe what is happening, it may be more appropriate to undertake your research inductively rather than deductively.

Third, Easterby-Smith et al. (2012) argue that knowledge of the different research traditions enables you to adapt your research design to cater for constraints. These may be practical, involving, say, limited access to data, or they may arise from a lack of prior knowledge of the subject. You simply may not be in a position to frame a hypothesis because you have insufficient understanding of the topic to do this.

So far, when discussing induction and deduction we have conveyed the impression that there are rigid divisions between deduction and induction. This would be misleading. As we have seen in our discussion of abduction, it is possible to combine deduction and induction within the same piece of research. It is also, in our experience, often advantageous to do so, although often one approach or another is dominant.

At this point you may be wondering whether your reasoning will be predominantly deductive, inductive or abductive. The honest answer is, 'it depends'. In particular, it depends on your research philosophy, the emphasis of the research (Box 4.8) and the nature of the research topic. Different philosophies tend to lead researchers to different approaches: so positivists tend to deduction, interpretivists to induction, and postmodernists, pragmatists and critical realists to abduction (although critical realists would often call their approach 'retroduction'). A topic on which there is a wealth of literature from which you can define a theoretical framework and a hypothesis lends itself more readily to deduction. With research into a topic that is new, is exciting much debate and on which there is little existing literature, it may be more appropriate to work inductively by generating data and analysing and reflecting upon what theoretical themes the data are suggesting. Alternatively, a topic about which there is a wealth of information in one context but far less in the context in which you are researching may lend itself to an abductive approach, enabling you to modify an existing theory.

The time you have available will be an issue. Deductive research can be quicker to complete, albeit that time must be devoted to setting up the study prior to data collection and analysis. Data collection is often based on 'one take'. It is normally possible to predict the time schedules accurately. On the other hand, abductive and, particularly, inductive research can be much more protracted. Often the ideas, based on a much longer period of data collection and analysis, have to emerge gradually. This leads to another important consideration, the extent to which you are prepared to indulge in risk. Deduction can be a lower-risk strategy, although there are risks, such as the non-return of questionnaires. With induction and abduction you have to live with the fear that no useful data patterns and theory will emerge. Finally, there is the question of audience. In our experience, most managers are familiar with deduction and much more likely to put faith in the conclusions

Box 4.8
Focus on student research

Deductive, inductive and abductive research

Sadie decided to conduct a research project on violence at work and its effects on the stress levels of staff. She considered the different ways she would approach the work were she to adopt:

- the deductive approach;
- the inductive approach;
- the abductive approach.

If she adopted a deductive approach to her reasoning, she would have to:

1 start with the hypothesis that staff working directly with the public are more likely to experience the threat or reality of violence and resultant stress;
2 decide to research a population in which she would have expected to find evidence of violence, for example, a sizeable social security office;
3 administer a questionnaire to a large sample of staff in order to establish the extent of violence (either actually experienced or threatened) and the levels of stress experienced by them;
4 be particularly careful about how she defined violence;
5 standardise the stress responses of the staff, for example, days off sick or sessions with a counsellor.

If she adopted an inductive approach then she might have decided to interview some staff who had been subjected to violence at work. She might have been interested in their feelings about the events that they had experienced, how they coped with the problems they experienced and their views about the possible causes of the violence.

If she adopted an abductive approach, she might have developed a conceptual model on the basis of her interview. She might then have used this model to develop a series of hypotheses and designed a questionnaire to collect data with which to test these hypotheses. Based on analyses of these data she might then have refined her conceptual model.

All approaches would have yielded valuable data about this problem (indeed, within this abductive approach, both inductive and deductive approaches were used at different stages). No approach should be thought of as better than the others. They are better at different things. It depends where her research emphasis lies.

emanating from this approach. You may also wish to consider the preferences of the person marking your research report. We all have our preferences about the approach to adopt.

This last point suggests that not all your decisions about the approach to reasoning should always be practically based. Hakim (2000) uses an architectural metaphor to illustrate this. She introduces the notion of the researcher's preferred style, which, rather like the architect's, may reflect 'the architect's own preferences and ideas . . . and the stylistic preferences of those who pay for the work and have to live with the final result' (Hakim 2000: 1). This echoes the feelings of Buchanan et al. (2013: 59), who argue that 'needs, interests and preferences (of the researcher) . . . are typically overlooked but are central to the progress of fieldwork'. However, a note of caution. Whilst researchers often refine their research questions as the research progresses, it is important that your preferences do not lead to you changing completely the essence of the research question, if only because you only have a limited amount of time to complete your research project. Ensuring that the essence of the research question does not change is particularly important if it has been defined by an organisation, for example, as a consultancy project they wish you to undertake.

4.6 Summary

- The term 'research philosophies' refers to systems of beliefs and assumptions about the development of knowledge. This means that your research philosophy contains important assumptions about the way in which you view the world. These assumptions shape all aspects of your research projects.
- To understand your research philosophy, you need to develop the skill of reflexivity, which means asking yourself questions about your beliefs and assumptions, and treating these with the same scrutiny as you would apply to the beliefs of others.
- From the pluralist perspective adopted in this book, there is no single 'best' business and management research philosophy. Each philosophy contributes a unique and valuable way of seeing the organisational world.
- All research philosophies make at least three major types of assumption: ontological, epistemological and axiological. We can distinguish different philosophies by the differences and similarities in their ontological, epistemological and axiological assumptions.
  - Ontology concerns researchers' assumptions about the nature of the world and reality. Ontological assumptions you make determine what research objects and phenomena you focus on, and how you see and approach them.
  - Epistemology concerns assumptions about knowledge – how we know what we say we know, what constitutes acceptable, valid and legitimate knowledge, and how we can communicate knowledge to fellow human beings. Epistemological assumptions you make determines what sort of contribution to knowledge you can make as a result of your research.
  - Axiology refers to the role of values and ethics within the research process, which incorporates questions about how we, as researchers, deal with our own values and also with those of our research participants.
- Research philosophies can be differentiated in terms of where their assumptions fall on the objectivism–subjectivism continua.
  - Objectivism incorporates assumptions of the natural sciences. It entails realist ontology (which holds that social entities exist in reality external to and independent from social actors), epistemology focused on the discovery of truth by means of observable, measurable facts, and claims to have a value-free, detached axiology.
  - Subjectivism incorporates assumptions of the arts and humanities. It entails nominalist ontology (which holds that social phenomena are created through the language, perceptions and consequent actions of social actors), epistemology focused on the social actors' opinions, narratives, interpretations, perceptions that convey these social realities, and claims to have a value-bound, reflexive axiology.
- Management and business research can be understood in terms of Burrell and Morgan's (2016) four social research paradigms: functionalist, interpretive, radical structuralist and radical humanist. These paradigms add the dimension of the political rationale for research to the objectivism–subjectivism continua.
- We have discussed five major philosophies: positivism, critical realism, interpretivism, postmodernism and pragmatism.
  - Positivism relates to the philosophical stance of the natural scientist. This entails working with an observable social reality and the end product can be law-like generalisations similar to those in the physical and natural sciences.
  - Critical realism focuses on explaining what we see and experience in terms of the underlying structures of reality that shape the observable events. Critical realists tend to undertake historical analyses of changing or enduring societal and organisational structures, using a variety of methods.

- Interpretivism is a subjectivist philosophy, which emphasises that human beings are different from physical phenomena because they create meanings. Interpretivists study meanings to create new, richer understandings of organisational realities. Empirically, interpretivists focus on individuals' lived experiences and cultural artefacts, and seek to include their participants' as well as their own interpretations into their research.
- Postmodernism emphasises the world-making role of language and power relations. Postmodernists seek to question the accepted ways of thinking and give voice to alternative worldviews that have been marginalised and silenced by dominant perspectives. Postmodernists deconstruct data to expose the instabilities and absences within them. Postmodernist axiology is radically reflexive.
- Pragmatist ontology, epistemology and axiology are focused on improving practice. Pragmatists adopt a wide range of research strategies, the choice of which is driven by the specific nature of their research problems.
- There are three main approaches to theory development: deduction, induction and abduction.
  - With deduction, a theory and hypothesis (or hypotheses) are developed and a research strategy designed to test the hypothesis.
  - With induction, data are collected and a theory developed as a result of the data analysis.
  - With abduction, (sometimes referred to as retroduction by critical realists) data are used to explore a phenomenon, identify themes and explain patterns, to generate a new or modify an existing theory which is subsequently tested, often through additional data collection.

Self-check questions

Help with these questions is available at the end of the chapter.

4.1   You have decided to undertake a project and have defined the main research question as 'What are the opinions of consumers on a 10 per cent reduction in weight, with the price remaining the same, of "Snackers" chocolate bars?' Write a hypothesis that you could test in your project.

4.2   Why may it be argued that the concept of 'the manager' is socially constructed rather than 'real'?

4.3   Why are the radical research paradigms relevant in business and management research, given that most managers would say that the purpose of organisational investigation is to develop recommendations for action to solve problems without radical change?

4.4   You have chosen to undertake your research project following a deductive approach. What factors may cause you to work inductively, although working deductively is your preferred choice?

Review and discussion questions

4.5   Visit an online database or your university library and obtain a copy of a research-based refereed journal article that you think will be of use to an assignment you are currently working on. Read this article carefully. From within which philosophical perspective do you think this article is written? Use Section 4.2 to help you develop a clear justification for your answer.

4.6 Think about the last assignment you undertook for your course. In undertaking this assignment, were you predominantly inductive, deductive or abductive? Discuss your thoughts with a friend who also undertook this assignment.

4.7 Agree with a friend to watch the same television documentary.

a To what extent is the documentary inductive, deductive or abductive in its use of data?

b Is the documentary based on positivist, critical realist, interpretivist, postmodernist or pragmatist assumptions?

c Do not forget to make notes regarding your reasons for your answers to each of these questions and to discuss your answers with your friend.

Progressing your research project

Heightening your Awareness of your Research Philosophy (HARP)*

HARP is a reflexive tool that has been designed by Bristow and Saunders to help you explore your research philosophy. It is just a starting point for enabling you to ask yourself more refined questions about how you see research. It will not provide you with a definitive answer to the question 'What is my research philosophy?' Rather it will give you an indication as to where your views are similar to and different from those of five major philosophical traditions discussed in this chapter. Do not be surprised if your views are similar to more than one tradition. Such potential tensions are an ideal opportunity to inquire into and examine your beliefs further.

HARP consists of six sections each comprising five statements (a total of 30 statements). Each section considers one aspect of philosophical beliefs (ontology, epistemology, axiology, purpose of research, meaningfulness of data and structure/agency). Each statement epitomises a particular research philosophy's position in relation to that particular aspect. By indicating your agreement or disagreement with each statement you can discover your similarities and differences with different aspects of each research philosophy. Following the completion of HARP, refer to the scoring key to calculate your score and interpret your answer.

HARP Statements	Strongly Agree	Agree	Slightly Agree	Slightly Disagree	Disagree	Strongly Disagree
Please indicate your agreement or disagreement with the statements below. There are no wrong answers.						
Your views on the nature of reality (ontology)						
1 Organisations are real, just like physical objects.	❑	❑	❑	❑	❑	❑
2 Events in organisations are caused by deeper, underlying mechanisms.	❑	❑	❑	❑	❑	❑
3 The social world we inhabit is a world of multiple meanings, interpretations and realities.	❑	❑	❑	❑	❑	❑
4 'Organisation' is not a solid and static thing but a flux of collective processes and practices.	❑	❑	❑	❑	❑	❑
5 'Real' aspects of organisations are those that impact on organisational practices.	❑	❑	❑	❑	❑	❑

Progressing your research project *(continued)*

Heightening your Awareness of your Research Philosophy (HARP)

HARP Statements						
Please indicate your agreement or disagreement with the statements below. There are no wrong answers.	Strongly Agree	Agree	Slightly Agree	Slightly Disagree	Disagree	Strongly Disagree
Your views on knowledge and what constitutes acceptable knowledge (epistemology)						
6 Organisational research should provide scientific, objective, accurate and valid explanations of how the organisational world really works.	❑	❑	❑	❑	❑	❑
7 Theories and concepts never offer completely certain knowledge, but researchers can use rational thought to decide which theories and concepts are better than others.	❑	❑	❑	❑	❑	❑
8 Concepts and theories are too simplistic to capture the full richness of the world.	❑	❑	❑	❑	❑	❑
9 What generally counts as 'real', 'true' and 'valid' is determined by politically dominant points of view.	❑	❑	❑	❑	❑	❑
10 Acceptable knowledge is that which enables things to be done successfully.	❑	❑	❑	❑	❑	❑
Your views on the role of values in research (axiology)						
11 Researchers' values and beliefs must be excluded from the research.	❑	❑	❑	❑	❑	❑
12 Researchers must try to be as objective and realistic as they can.	❑	❑	❑	❑	❑	❑
13 Researchers' values and beliefs are key to their interpretations of the social world.	❑	❑	❑	❑	❑	❑
14 Researchers should openly and critically discuss their own values and beliefs.	❑	❑	❑	❑	❑	❑
15 Research shapes and is shaped by what the researcher believes and doubts.	❑	❑	❑	❑	❑	❑
Your views on the purpose of research						
16 The purpose of research is to discover facts and regularities, and predict future events.	❑	❑	❑	❑	❑	❑
17 The purpose of organisational research is to offer an explanation of how and why organisations and societies are structured.	❑	❑	❑	❑	❑	❑
18 The purpose of research is to create new understandings that allow people to see the world in new ways.	❑	❑	❑	❑	❑	❑
19 The purpose of research is to examine and question the power relations that sustain conventional thinking and practices.	❑	❑	❑	❑	❑	❑
20 The purpose of research is to solve problems and improve future practice.	❑	❑	❑	❑	❑	❑

HARP Statements		Strongly Agree	Agree	Slightly Agree	Slightly Disagree	Disagree	Strongly Disagree
Please indicate your agreement or disagreement with the statements below. There are no wrong answers.							
Your views on what constitutes meaningful data							
21	Things that cannot be measured have no meaning for the purposes of research.	❑	❑	❑	❑	❑	❑
22	Organisational theories and findings should be evaluated in terms of their explanatory power of the causes of organisational behaviour.	❑	❑	❑	❑	❑	❑
23	To be meaningful, research must include participants' own interpretations of their experiences, as well as researchers' interpretations.	❑	❑	❑	❑	❑	❑
24	Absences and silences in the world around us are at least as important as what is prominent and obvious.	❑	❑	❑	❑	❑	❑
25	Meaning emerges out of our practical, experimental and critical engagement with the world.	❑	❑	❑	❑	❑	❑
Your views on the nature of structure and agency							
26	Human behaviour is determined by natural forces.	❑	❑	❑	❑	❑	❑
27	People's choices and actions are always limited by the social norms, rules and traditions in which they are located.	❑	❑	❑	❑	❑	❑
28	Individuals' meaning-making is always specific to their experiences, culture and history.	❑	❑	❑	❑	❑	❑
29	Structure, order and form are human constructions.	❑	❑	❑	❑	❑	❑
30	People can use routines and customs creatively to instigate innovation and change.	❑	❑	❑	❑	❑	❑

Now please complete the scoring key below.

Your answer scores

Give yourself the points as indicated below for each answer within each philosophical tradition. The different philosophies are represented by specific questions in the HARP as indicated below. Fill each philosophy table with your answer scores, then total up the numbers for each philosophy. (For your reference, in the tables below, the letters in brackets indicate whether the question tests your agreement with the ontological, epistemological, axiological, purpose of research, meaningfulness of data and structure and agency aspects of research philosophy.)

Each answer you gave is given a number of points as shown in the table below:

Strongly agree	Agree	Slightly agree	Slightly disagree	Disagree	Strongly disagree
3	2	1	−1	−2	−3

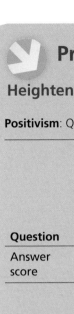

Progressing your research project *(continued)*

Heightening your Awareness of your Research Philosophy (HARP)

Positivism: Questions 1, 6, 11, 16, 21, 26

Question	1 (ontology)	6 (epistemology)	11 (axiology)	16 (purpose)	21 (data)	26 (structure/agency)	Total
Answer score							

Critical Realism: Questions 2, 7, 12, 17, 22, 27

Question	2 (ontology)	7 (epistemology)	12 (axiology)	17 (purpose)	22 (data)	27 (structure/agency)	Total
Answer score							

Interpretivism: Questions 3, 8, 13, 18, 23, 28

Question	3 (ontology)	8 (epistemology)	13 (axiology)	18 (purpose)	23 (data)	28 (structure/agency)	Total
Answer score							

Postmodernism: Questions 4, 9, 14, 19, 24, 29

Question	4 (ontology)	9 (epistemology)	14 (axiology)	19 (purpose)	24 (data)	29 (structure/agency)	Total
Answer score							

Pragmatism: Questions 5, 10, 15, 20, 25, 30

Question	5 (ontology)	10 (epistemology)	15 (axiology)	20 (purpose)	25 (data)	30 (structure/agency)	Total
Answer score							

Reflection

Now, for the first of what will almost certainly be many philosophical reflections, consider the following questions regarding how you scored yourself.

1 Do you have an outright philosophical winner? Or do you have a close contention between two or more philosophies?
2 Why do you think this is?
3 Which philosophy do you disagree with the most?
4 Why do you think this is?

References

Alvesson, M. and Sköldberg, K. (2009) *Reflexive Methodology: New Vistas for Qualitative Research* (2nd edn). London: Sage.

Bhaskar, R. (2008) *A Realist Theory of Science.* London: Verso (originally published by Harvester Press 1978).

Bhaskar, R. (2011) *Reclaiming Reality: A Critical Introduction to Contemporary Philosophy.* Abingdon: Routledge (originally published by Verso 1989).

Blaikie, N. (2010) *Designing Social Research* (2nd edn). Cambridge: Polity.

Bristow, A., Robinson, S.K. and Ratle, O. (2017) 'Being an Early-Career CMS Academic in the Context of Insecurity and "Excellence": The Dialectics of Resistance and Compliance', *Organization Studies,* Vol 38(9), pp. 1185–1207.

Buchanan, D., Boddy, D. and McCalman, J. (2013) 'Getting in, getting on, getting out and getting back', in A. Bryman (ed.) *Doing Research in Organisations.* London: Routledge, pp. 53–67 (originally published by Routledge 1988).

Burrell, G. and Morgan, G. (2016) *Sociological Paradigms and Organisational Analysis.* Abingdon: Routledge (originally published by Heinemann 1979).

Calás, M. and Smircich, L. (1997) *Postmodern Management Theory.* Aldershot: Ashgate/Dartmouth.

Chia, R. (2003) 'Organization theory as a postmodern science', in H. Tsoukas and C. Knudsen (eds) *The Oxford Handbook of Organization Theory: Meta-Theoretical Perspectives.* Oxford: Oxford University Press, pp. 113–40.

Crotty, M. (1998) *The Foundations of Social Research.* London: Sage.

Cunliffe. A.L. (2003) 'Reflexive inquiry in organizational research: Questions and possibilities', *Human Relations,* Vol. 56, pp. 983–1003.

Cunliffe. A.L. and Scaratti. G. (2017) 'Embedding Impact in Engaged Research: Developing Socially Useful Knowledge through Dialogical Sensemaking', *British Journal of Management,* Vol 28(1), pp. 29–44.

De Cock, C. and Land, C. (2006) 'Organization/Literature: Exploring the seam', *Organization Studies,* Vol. 27, pp. 517–35.

Derrida J. (2016) *Of Grammatology (40th Anniversary Edition).* Baltimore: Johns Hopkins University Press (originally published 1976).

Easterby-Smith, M., Thorpe, R., Jackson, P. and Lowe, A. (2012) *Management Research* (4th edn). London: Sage.

Elkjaer, B. and Simpson, B. (2011) 'Pragmatism: A lived and living philosophy. What can it offer to contemporary organization theory?' in H. Tsoukas and R. Chia (eds) *Philosophy and Organization Theory.* Bradford: Emerald Publishing, pp. 55–84.

Fleetwood, S. (2005) 'Ontology in organization and management studies: A critical realist perspective', *Organization,* Vol. 12, pp. 197–222.

Foucault, M. (1991) *Discipline and Punish: The Birth of Prison.* London: Penguin Books.

Fournier, V. and Grey, C. (2000) 'At the critical moment: Conditions and prospects for critical management studies', *Human Relations,* Vol. 53, pp. 7–32.

Gabriel, Y., Gray, D.E. and Goregaokar, H. (2013) 'Job loss and its aftermath among managers and professionals: Wounded, fragmented and flexible', *Work, Employment & Society,* Vol. 27, pp. 56–72.

Guba, E. G., & Lincoln, Y. S. (1994) 'Competing paradigms in qualitative research', in N. K. Denzin & Y S. Lincoln (Eds.), *Handbook of qualitative research.* Thousand Oaks, CA: Sage, pp. 105–116.

Hakim, C. (2000) *Research Design: Successful Designs for Social and Economic Research* (2nd edn). London: Routledge.

Haynes, K. (2012) 'Reflexivity in qualitative research', in C. Cassell and B. Lee (eds) *Challenges and Controversies in Management Research*. New York: Routledge.

Heron, J. (1996) *Co-operative Inquiry: Research into the Human Condition*. London: Sage.

Heron, J. and Reason, P. (1997) 'A Participatory Inquiry Paradigm', *Qualitative Inquiry,* Vol 3, Issue 3, pp. 274–294.

Johnson, P. and Clark, M. (2006) 'Editors' introduction: Mapping the terrain: An overview of business and management research methodologies', in P. Johnson and M. Clark (eds) *Business and Management Research Methodologies*. London: Sage, pp. xxv–iv.

Kelemen, M. and Rumens, N. (2008) *An Introduction to Critical Management Research*. London: Sage.

Ketokivi, M. and Mantere, S. (2010) 'Two strategies for inductive reasoning in organizational research', *Academy of Management Review,* Vol. 35, No. 2, pp. 315–33.

Kilduff, M. and Mehra, A. (1997) 'Postmodernism and organizational research', *The Academy of Management Review,* Vol. 22, pp. 453–81.

Knudsen, C. (2003) 'Pluralism, scientific progress, and the structure of organization theory', in H. Tsoukas and C. Knudsen (eds) *The Oxford Handbook of Organization Theory: Meta-Theoretical Perspectives*. Oxford: Oxford University Press, pp. 262–86.

Lincoln. Y.S., Lynham S.A. and Guba, E.G. (2018) 'Paradigmatic controversies, contradictions and emerging confluences revisited', in N.K. Denzin and Y.S. Lincoln (eds) *The Sage Handbook of Qualitative Research* (5th edn). Los Angeles, CA: Sage, pp. 108–150.

Mangalindan, J.P. (2014) 'Why Amazon's fire phone failed', *Fortune*. Available at http://fortune.com/2014/09/29/why-amazons-fire-phone-failed [Accessed 24 January 2018].

Martí, I. and Fernández, P. (2013) 'The institutional work of oppression and resistance: Learning from the Holocaust', *Organization Studies,* Vol. 34, pp. 1195–223.

Morgan, G. (2006) *Images of Organization*. Thousand Oaks, CA: Sage (originally published in 1986).

Niglas, K. (2010) 'The multidimensional model of research methodology: An integrated set of continua', in A. Tashakkori and C. Teddlie (eds) *The Sage Handbook of Mixed Methods in Social and Behavioural Research*. Thousand Oaks, CA: Sage, pp. 215–36.

Parker, M. (2002) *Against Management*. Cambridge: Polity Press.

Peirce, C. S. (1896 [c.]) *Lessons of the History of Science*. MS [R] 1288. Commens: Digital Companion to C.S. Peirce, available at http://www.commens.org/dictionary/term/retroduction [Accessed 11 Sept. 2018].

Pfeffer, J. (1993) 'Barriers to the advance of organizational science: paradigm development as a dependent variable', *Academy of Management Review,* Vol. 18, pp. 599–620.

Reed, M. (2005) 'Reflections on the 'realist turn' in organization and management studies', *Journal of Management Studies,* Vol. 42, pp. 1621–44.

Rutherford, B.A. (2016) 'Articulating accounting principles', *Journal of Applied Accounting Research.,* Vol.17, No. 2, pp. 118–135.

Starbuck, W. (2003) 'The origins of organization theory', in H. Tsoukas and C. Knudsen (eds) *The Oxford Handbook of Organization Theory: Meta-Theoretical Perspectives*. Oxford: Oxford University Press.

Suddaby, R. (2006) 'From the editors: What grounded theory is not', *Academy of Management Journal,* Vol. 49, No. 4, pp. 633–43.

Thomas, R. and Hardy, C. (2011) 'Reframing resistance to organizational change', *Scandinavian Journal of Management,* Vol. 27, pp. 322–31.

Van Maanen, J., Sørensen, J.B. and Mitchell, T.R. (2007) 'The interplay between theory and method', *Academy of Management Review,* Vol. 32, No. 4, pp. 1145–54.

Further reading

Brinkmann, S. and Kvale, S. (2015) *InterViews* (3rd edn). Los Angeles, CA: Sage. Chapter 3 provides an accessible discussion of the epistemological issues associated with interviewing.

Burrell, G. and Morgan, G. (2016) *Sociological Paradigms and Organisational Analysis.* Abingdon: Routledge. This is an excellent facsimile of the original 1979 book on paradigms which goes into far more detail than space has allowed in this chapter.

Hatch, M.J. and Yanow, D. (2008) 'Methodology by metaphor: Ways of seeing in painting and research', *Organization Studies,* Vol. 29, No. 1, pp. 23–44. A really enjoyable paper which uses the metaphor of paintings by Rembrandt and Pollock to explain differences between realism and interpretivism.

Kelemen, M. and Rumens, N. (2008) *An Introduction to Critical Management Research.* London: Sage. This contains an excellent chapter on pragmatism as well as going into considerable detail on other theoretical perspectives not covered in this chapter, including postmodernism, feminism and queer theory.

Tsoukas, H. and Chia, R. (2011) *Research in the Sociology of Organizations,* Vol. 32: *Philosophy and Organization Theory.* Bradford: Emerald Publishing. This book offers excellent in-depth reading about the role of philosophy in management research, and about individual philosophies, including pragmatism, interpretivism (hermeneutics and phenomenology) and postmodernism. There is also a chapter about combining (triangulating) philosophies.

Tsoukas, H. and Knudsen, C. (2003) *The Oxford Handbook of Organization Theory: Meta-Theoretical Perspectives.* Oxford: Oxford University Press. This book has in-depth chapters on positivism, interpretivism and postmodernism. It also has a chapter about pluralism in the field of management.

Case 4
In search of a research philosophy

After working for a decade in industry, returning to university to study for a Masters degree was not as easy as Janet had anticipated. Whilst she was being awarded good marks on the assignments for a number of her taught Modules, she found the research methods module quite challenging. Furthermore, she felt daunted at the prospect of completing the module assignment, which required her, as part of her research proposal, to outline and justify her research philosophy.

To begin with, Janet reread the research philosophy chapter in her module textbook. At the beginning of the module, she had found the descriptions of such terms as ontology, epistemology, axiology and methodology, confusing and difficult to understand. Now, after rereading the chapter, attending a seminar with her lecturer and discussing the concepts with other students in the coffee bar, she felt she was slowly making sense of such terms in her own mind.

However, despite this, Janet was still not clear as to how she might write about her research philosophy. The more Janet read around the subject and reflected on both the characteristics of different research philosophies discussed within the textbooks and her own values and beliefs, the more confused and frustrated she became. It seemed to Janet that each of the research philosophies outlined in the research methods textbooks had aspects that matched her values and how she viewed research and yet also had aspects with which she disagreed. The possibility of outlining and justifying her research philosophy seemed to be receding rather than becoming more obvious.

About this time Janet was encouraged by her lecturer to complete the HARP (Heightening Awareness of Research Philosophy) quiz to help her reflect on her research assumptions and research philosophy (you can find a copy in the section 'Progressing your research project' towards the end of Chapter 4). Whilst she was at first sceptical, Janet was intrigued and completed the quiz, which asked her to think about her assumptions and beliefs. Working out her scores, she found that she scored 10 for pragmatism, 9 for critical realism, 6 for positivism, 5 for postmodernism and 4 for interpretivism. She plotted these on a radar graph (Figure C4.1).

Janet was surprised at the results. For example, she had expected a higher score for positivism and was similarly amazed that her score for postmodernism and interpretivism were higher than zero. She was further surprised and to an extent confused that she did not have a clear philosophical preference, having high scores for both pragmatism and critical realism. This puzzled Janet. Having gained some awareness of the concept of research philosophies building on particular assumptions and beliefs, she questioned the possibility of holding more than one philosophical position at the same time. She decided to ask her lecturer whether it might be considered possible to have multiple philosophical research positions.

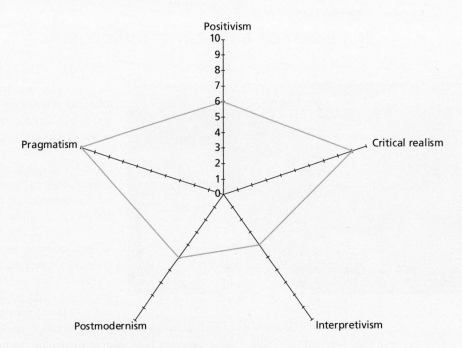

Figure C4.1 Radar Graph of HARP Scores

As she contemplated these complex and challenging issues, Janet felt that she was becoming increasingly aware of the impact of her own research philosophy on her research design. Moreover, Janet felt that she was beginning to understand that not only should her research design and data collection and analysis methods be consistent with her research philosophy, but also that the method or methods used by researchers are indicative of their research philosophy. Janet was enthused and encouraged as she now recognized why her lecturer had emphasised the need to identify her own research philosophy.

Janet realised that she still had a lot of work to do to ensure the research design for her project was consistent with her research philosophy. However, she now felt more confident of her ability to undertake this task and that she had taken a major step forward in her long research journey. Having been prompted to reflect on her own values, beliefs and assumptions – and the HARP quiz, Janet felt that she had begun to gain some awareness of how a research-er's perspective influences their choice of research topic and research question, their approach to theory development, methodological choice, data collection and analysis methods, as well as research outcomes (Alvesson and Sköldberg, 2009; Mir et al., 2016). Moreover, Janet's increasing awareness of her own values and research philosophy, and her ability to be reflex-ive, meant she felt more empowered to assess other researchers' work and their claimed con-tributions to knowledge (Cunliffe, 2003; Mir et al. 2016).

Later, over coffee, Janet had a thought-provoking discussion about research philosophies with her friend Brad, a doctoral research student. This, she felt, contributed significantly toward her developing capacity for reflexivity. After some debate about how certain research methods tended to be associated with particular research philosophies (Westwood and Clegg, 2003; Alvesson and Sköldberg, 2009; Mir et al., 2016), she began to wonder whether the way in which HARP had been framed, designed and intended to be used represented a particular philosophical perspective. Enthused and intrigued, Janet decided to undertake further reading and discuss her ideas with Brad. She recognised that although she had only just begun to understand her own assumptions and research philosophy, she could now complete her research proposal.

References

Alvesson, M. and Sköldberg, K. (2009) *Reflexive Methodology: New Vistas for Qualitative Research* (2nd edn.). London: SAGE.

Cunliffe, A. L. (2003) 'Reflexive Inquiry in Organizational Research: Questions and Possibilities', *Human Relations,* 56 (8): 983–1003.

Mir, R., H. Willmott, H. and Greenwood, M. (Eds.) (2016) *The Routledge Companion to Philosophy in Organization Studies.* Abingdon, Oxon.: Routledge.

Westwood, R. and Clegg, S. (Eds.) (2003) *Debating Organizations: Point-Counterpoint in Organiza-tion Studies.* Oxford: Blackwell Publishing.

Questions

1 If you have not done so already, complete HARP for yourself. Use the questions at the end of the Chapter 4's 'Progressing your research project' to reflect on your research philosophy. Discuss your answers with a colleague.

2 Why was it important for Janet to identify her research assumptions? Why is it important for you to reflect on your own assumptions?

3 Imagine you are Janet's tutor and answer her question, 'Is it possible to have more than one philosophical position?'

Case study extension question:

4   To what extent do you consider the way HARP is framed and designed and is intended to be used represents a particular philosophical perspective? Give reasons for your answer.

Additional case studies relating to material covered in this chapter are available via this book's companion website: **www.pearsoned.co.uk/saunders.**
   They are:

- Marketing music products alongside emerging digital music channels.
- Consultancy research for a not-for-profit organisation.
- Organisational learning in an English regional theatre.
- Chinese tourists and their duty-free shopping in Guam.

Self-check answers

4.1   Probably the most realistic hypothesis here would be 'consumers of "Snackers" chocolate bars did not notice the difference between the current bar and its reduced weight successor'. Doubtless that is what the Snackers' manufacturer would want confirmed!

4.2   Although you can see and touch a manager, you are only seeing and touching another human being. The point is that the role of the manager is a socially constructed concept. What counts as 'a manager' will differ between different national and organisational cultures and will differ over time. Indeed, the concept of the manager as we generally understand it is a relatively recent human invention, arriving at the same time as the formal organisation in the past couple of hundred years.

4.3   The researcher working in the radical humanist or structuralist paradigms may argue that they expect managers to prefer recommendations that do not involve radical change because radical change may involve changing managers! Radicalism implies root-and-branch investigation and possible change, and most of us prefer 'fine-tuning' within the framework of what exists already, particularly if change threatens our vested interests.

4.4   The question implies an either/or choice. But as you work through this chapter (and, in particular, the next one on deciding your research design), you will see that life is rarely so clear-cut! Perhaps the main factor that would cause you to review the appropriateness of the deductive approach would be that the data you collected might suggest an important hypothesis, which you did not envisage when you framed your research objectives and hypotheses. This may entail going further with the data collection, perhaps by engaging in some qualitative work, which would yield further data to answer the new hypothesis.

Get ahead using resources on the companion website at:
www.pearsoned.co.uk/saunders.

- Improve your IBM SPSS Statistics and research analysis with practice tutorials.
- Save time researching on the Internet with the Smarter Online Searching Guide.
- Test your progress using self-assessment questions.
- Follow live links to useful websites.

Chapter **5**

Formulating the research design

Learning outcomes

By the end of this chapter you should be able to:

- appreciate the importance of your decisions when designing research and the need to achieve methodological coherence throughout your research design;
- understand the differences between quantitative, qualitative and mixed methods research designs and choose between these;
- understand the differences between exploratory, descriptive, explanatory and evaluative research and recognise the purpose(s) of your research design;
- identify the main research strategies and choose from among these to achieve coherence throughout your research design;
- consider the implications of the time frames required for different research designs;
- consider some of the main ethical issues implied by your research design;
- understand criteria to evaluate research quality and consider these when designing your research;
- take into account the constraints of your role as researcher when designing your research.

5.1 Introduction

In Chapter 4 we introduced the research onion as a way of depicting the issues underlying your choice of data collection method or methods and peeled away the outer two layers – research philosophy and approach to theory development. In this chapter we uncover the next three layers: methodological choice, research strategy or strategies and choosing the time horizon for your research. As we saw in Chapter 4, the way you answer your research question will be

influenced by your research philosophy and approach to theory development. Your research philosophy and approach to theory development, whether this is deliberate or by default, will subsequently influence your selections shown in the next three layers of the research onion (Figure 5.1). These three layers can be thought of as focusing on the process of research design, which is the way you turn your research question into a research project. The key to these selections will be to achieve coherence all the way through your research design.

5.2 Choice and coherence in research design

Your **research design** is the general plan of how you will go about answering your research question(s) (the importance of clearly defining the research question cannot be overemphasised). It will contain clear objectives derived from your research question(s), specify the source or sources from which you intend to collect data, how you propose to collect and analyse these,

The research process is like a journey

The cover photographs of recent editions of this book have indicated that the research process is like a journey – a journey along a road with you as the driver of the vehicle. Like many such journeys, there is generally a choice of roads to travel along. When you are thinking about setting out on a new journey of some distance, you will probably enter the destination into your Sat-Nav and look at the possible route options to get to your destination. A

number of criteria will influence your decision about which route to take, including time, fuel economy and your preferences for avoiding motorways, ferries and toll roads. The route you choose will be calculated by the SatNav to meet your given preferences and ensure you reach your destination. As you actually undertake your journey you will find yourself interacting with the reality of your planned route. Some parts of the journey will go according to plan; other parts may not and you may need to amend your route, perhaps because of traffic congestion or a road being closed due to roadworks. In many ways, designing research is like planning a journey. Formulating the most appropriate way to address your research question is similar to planning the route to your destination. The research aim is your destination and the research objectives are your route criteria. These need to be coherent to ensure the research (journey) can be completed. Like your route, your research design may need to be amended due to unforeseen circumstances. Both will be interactive experiences.

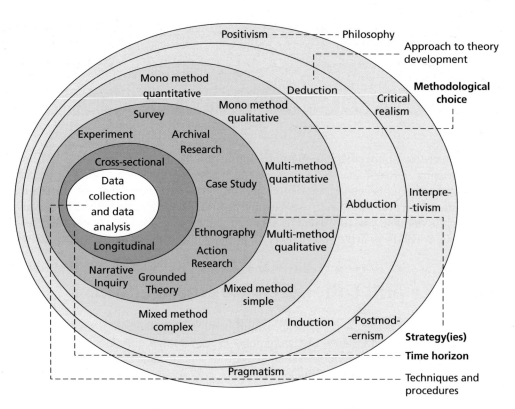

Figure 5.1 The research onion
Source: © 2018 Mark Saunders, Philip Lewis and Adrian Thornhill

and discuss ethical issues and the constraints you will inevitably encounter (e.g. access to data, time, location and money). Crucially, it should demonstrate that you have thought through the elements of your particular research design.

The first methodological choice is whether you follow a quantitative, qualitative or mixed methods research design. Each of these options is likely to call for a different mix of elements to achieve coherence in your research design. We introduce basic ways of understanding differences between quantitative, qualitative and mixed methods research designs in Section 5.3 before developing this discussion in Section 5.4 (which looks at quantitative research design), Section 5.5 (qualitative research design) and Section 5.6 (mixed methods research design). The nature of your research project will also be either exploratory, descriptive, explanatory, evaluative or a combination of these, and we discuss the role of these in your research design in Section 5.7. Within your research design you will need to use one or more research strategies, to carry out and ensure coherence within your research project. We discuss research strategies, their fit to research philosophy and to your choice of either a quantitative, qualitative or mixed methods methodology in Section 5.8. Your methodological choice and related strategies will also influence the selection of an appropriate time horizon, and we consider this in Section 5.9. Each research design will lead to potential ethical concerns and it will be important to consider these, in order to minimise or overcome them. We briefly consider ethical issues related to research designs in Section 5.10, before discussing these in greater detail in Sections 6.5 and 6.6. It is also important to establish the quality of your research design, and we discuss the ways in which this may be considered in Section 5.11. Finally, we recognise that practical constraints will affect research design, especially the nature of your own role as researcher, and briefly consider this in Section 5.12.

Each of these aspects is vital to research design. You are likely to be assessed at this stage of your research project by your university or examining institution and your research design, as set out in your research proposal, will need to achieve a pass standard before you are allowed to proceed. You therefore need to produce a clear and coherent design with valid reasons for each of your research design decisions, even if your design changes subsequently. Your justification for each element in your research design should be based on your research question(s) and objectives, and show consistency with your research philosophy.

It is useful at this point to recognise a distinction between design and tactics. Design is concerned with the overall plan for your research project; tactics are about the finer details of data collection and analysis – the centre of the research onion. Decisions about tactics will involve you being clear about the different quantitative and qualitative data collection techniques (e.g. questionnaires, interviews, focus groups and secondary data) and subsequent quantitative and qualitative data analysis procedures, which are discussed in later chapters.

We first outline and differentiate between the nature of quantitative, qualitative and mixed methods research in the following four sections.

5.3 Methodological choice: the use of a quantitative, qualitative or mixed methods research design

One way of differentiating quantitative research from qualitative research is to distinguish between numeric data (numbers) and non-numeric data (words, images, audio recordings, video clips and other similar material). In this way, 'quantitative' is often used as a synonym for any data collection technique (such as a questionnaire) or data analysis procedure (such as graphs or statistics) that generates or uses numerical data. In contrast, 'qualitative' is often used as a synonym for any data collection technique (such as an interview) or data analysis procedure (such as categorising data) that generates or uses non-numerical data. This is an important way to differentiate this methodological choice; however, this distinction is both problematic and narrow.

It is problematic because, in reality, many business and management research designs are likely to combine quantitative and qualitative elements. This may be for a number of reasons. For example, a research design may use a questionnaire but it may be necessary to ask respondents to answer some 'open' questions in their own words rather than ticking the appropriate box, or it may be necessary to conduct follow-up interviews to seek to explain findings from the questionnaire. Equally, some qualitative research data may be analysed quantitatively, or be used to inform the design of a subsequent questionnaire. In this way, quantitative and qualitative research may be viewed as two ends of a continuum, which in practice are often mixed. A research design may therefore mix methods in a number of ways, which we discuss in Section 5.6.

The distinction drawn earlier between quantitative research and qualitative research is also narrow. The purpose of Chapter 4 was to ask you to consider your research question through a philosophical lens. Given the way in which philosophical assumptions inform methodological choice, the initial distinction drawn earlier between numeric and non-numeric data appears insufficient for the purpose of choosing between quantitative and qualitative research. From this broader perspective, we can reinterpret quantitative, qualitative and mixed methodologies through their associations to philosophical assumptions

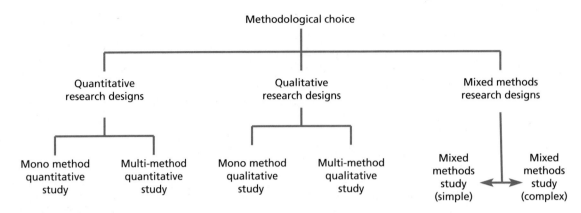

Figure 5.2 Methodological choice

and also to approaches to theory development and strategies. This will help you to decide how you might use these in a coherent way to address your research question. In the next three sections we consider some of these key associations in relation to the methodological choice between quantitative research designs, qualitative research designs and mixed methods research designs (Figure 5.2).

5.4 Quantitative research designs

Philosophical assumptions

Quantitative research designs are generally associated with positivism, especially when used with predetermined and highly structured data collection techniques. However, it is increasingly seen as a philosophical caricature to suggest that there is an exclusive link between positivism, deduction and a quantitative research design (Bryman 1998, Walsh et al 2015a). Rather, a distinction needs to be drawn between data about the attributes of people, organisations or other things and data based on opinions (Box 5.1). In this way, some survey research, whilst conducted quantitatively, may be seen to fit partly within an interpretivist philosophy. Quantitative research designs may also be undertaken within the realist and pragmatist philosophies (Section 5.6).

Approach to theory development

Quantitative research is usually associated with a deductive approach, where data are collected and analysed to test theory. However, it may also incorporate an inductive approach, where data are used to develop theory (Section 4.5). For example, a researcher may analyse quantitative data to determine hypotheses to test in a subsequent round of data collection and analysis. It may also be that original hypotheses are poorly framed, or even absent, and initial analysis of quantitative data is needed to clarify these inductively prior to further analysis. Walsh et al. (2015b: 621) refer to this generally undeclared approach as '"**Harking**" – hypothesising after the results are known.' We suggest you do not use this approach without first discussing it with your project tutor. However, you may find it necessary to refine original hypotheses.

Box 5.1 Focus on research in the news

Data and public opinion – How well do you know your country?

By Alan Smith, David Blood and Ændrew Rininsland

This month, Ipsos Mori published the latest in its annual Perils of Perception series, a 40-country survey of public perceptions about "key global issues and features of the population". The survey found widespread social misperceptions, with Bobby Duffy, managing director of Ipsos Mori's Social Research Institute, writing in the *Guardian* that this latest set of results reflected that "objective facts are less influential in shaping public opinion than appeals to emotion and personal belief".

A cocktail of personal experience, circumstances and external influences - from social networks to media and advertising - mean that everyone will have their own perception of reality. Fascinated by the Ipsos findings, David Blood and Ændrew Rininsland at the Financial Times devised the "How well do you really know your country?" quiz, challenging FT readers to compare their own perceptions of their country with both the public's perceptions (as provided by the Ipsos Mori survey) and the "actual" figures used by Ipsos Mori.

Some two weeks after the quiz was published, and with thousands of results from FT readers across the world, we decided to take a look at some of the emerging patterns. We extracted FT reader responses for each country/question combination for comparison with Ipsos's figures, excluding those countries with a low level of reader responses. We then used the median figure for each question for comparison, as this is more resistant to extreme individual guesses influencing the average.

In many ways, that FT readers have a different view of the world from the general public should not be a surprise: the Ipsos Mori survey uses stratified samples to try and provide a "representative" view of each country's population.

FT readers are not likely to be as representative of the broader population. And the results of the quiz should not be considered as statistically robust as a well-designed survey.

Nevertheless, the quiz does provide a fascinating glimpse into how different groups of people can have distinct and, at times, diverging views of the same reality. Failure to acknowledge this - or the fact that our own social interactions may not reflect the diversity of perception - may contribute to the "filter bubble" effect, or "echo chamber" of similar views.

As many become worried about the rise of fake news, the need for informed debate based on reality, and the various perceptions of it, has never been greater. So this is a good time to ask, "How well do you really know your country?"

 Source of extract: Smith, A., Blood, D. and Rininsland, Æ. (2016) 'Data and Public Opinion – How well do you know your country?', *Financial Times,* 31 December. Copyright © 2016 The Financial Times Limited

Characteristics

Quantitative research examines relationships between variables, which are measured numerically and analysed using a range of statistical and graphical techniques. It often incorporates controls to ensure the validity of data, as in an experimental design. Because data are collected in a standardised manner, it is important to ensure that questions are expressed clearly so they are understood in the same way by each participant. This methodology generally uses probability sampling techniques to ensure generalisability (Section 7.2). The researcher is seen as independent from those being researched, who are usually called respondents. The characteristics of quantitative research are summarised in Table 5.1.

A quantitative research design may use a single data collection technique, such as a questionnaire, and corresponding quantitative analytical procedure. This is known as a **mono method quantitative study** (Figure 5.2). A quantitative research design may also use more than one quantitative data collection technique and corresponding analytical procedure. This is known as a **multi-method quantitative study** (Figure 5.2). You might, for example, decide to collect quantitative data using both questionnaires and structured observation, analysing these data statistically. **Multi-method** is the branch of **multiple methods** research that uses more than one quantitative or qualitative method but does not mix them (Figure 5.2).

Use of multiple methods has been advocated within business and management research (Bryman 2006) because it is likely to overcome weaknesses associated with using only a single or mono method, as well as providing scope for a richer approach to data collection, analysis and interpretation.

Research strategies

Quantitative research is principally associated with experimental and survey research strategies, which we discuss in Section 5.8. In quantitative research, a survey strategy is normally conducted through the use of questionnaires or structured interviews or, possibly, structured observation. However, it is important to note that quantitative data and analysis techniques can be and are used in research strategies that are often thought of as being qualitative, such as action research, case study research and grounded theory (Section 5.8).

Techniques

Techniques associated with the use of these particular methods are considered in Chapters 9, 11 and 12. Structured observation is discussed in Section 9.4; Chapter 11 discusses the use of questionnaires including structured interviewing; and Chapter 12 is devoted to analysing data quantitatively.

Table 5.1 Characteristics of quantitative research

- Researcher is generally seen as independent from those being researched.
- Those taking part are usually referred to as respondents.
- Designed to examine relationships between variables.
- Often uses probability sampling techniques to ensure generalisability.
- Method(s) used to collect data are rigorously defined and highly structured.
- Collection results in numerical and standardised data.
- Analysis conducted through the use of statistics and diagrams.
- Resulting meanings derived from numbers.

5.5   Qualitative research designs

Philosophical assumptions

Qualitative research is often associated with an interpretive philosophy (Denzin and Lincoln 2018). It is interpretive because researchers need to make sense of the subjective and socially constructed meanings expressed about the phenomenon being studied. Such research is sometimes referred to as naturalistic since researchers need to operate within a natural setting, or research context, in order to establish trust, participation, access to meanings and in-depth understanding. Like quantitative research, qualitative research may also be undertaken within realist and pragmatist philosophies (see 'Mixed methods research design' later).

Approach to theory development

Many varieties of qualitative research commence with an inductive approach to theory development, where a naturalistic and emergent research design is used to build theory or to develop a richer theoretical perspective than already exists in the literature. However, some qualitative research strategies start with a deductive approach, to test an existing theory using qualitative procedures (Yin 2018). In practice, much qualitative research also uses an abductive approach to theory development where inductive inferences are developed and deductive ones are tested iteratively throughout the research (Section 4.5).

Characteristics

Qualitative research studies participants' meanings and the relationships between them, using a variety of data collection techniques and analytical procedures, to develop a conceptual framework and theoretical contribution. The success of the qualitative researcher's role is dependent not only on gaining physical access to those who take part, but also building rapport and demonstrating sensitivity to gain cognitive access to their data (Section 6.2). Those who consent to take part in qualitative research are therefore not seen as mere respondents but as participants in the collection of data.

In qualitative research, meanings are derived from words and images, not numbers. Since words and images may have multiple meanings as well as unclear meanings, it is often necessary to explore and clarify these with participants. Methods used are unstructured or semi-structured (Sections 9.3 and 10.3), so that questions, procedures and focus may alter or emerge during a research process that is both naturalistic and interactive. Qualitative research is likely to use non-probability sampling techniques (Section 7.3). The qualitative data that are collected will be non-standardised and generally require being classified into categories for analysis. The characteristics of qualitative research are summarised in Table 5.2.

A qualitative research design may use a single data collection technique, such as semi-structured interviews, and corresponding qualitative analytical procedure. This is known as a **mono method qualitative study** (Figure 5.2). A qualitative research design may also use more than one qualitative data collection technique and corresponding analytical procedure. This is known as a **multi-method qualitative study** (Figure 5.2). You might, for example, decide to collect qualitative data using in-depth interviews and diary accounts, analysing these data using qualitative procedures. Box 5.2 provides an example of a multi-method qualitative study.

Table 5.2 Characteristics of qualitative research

- Researcher is generally recognised as not being independent from those researched.
- Those taking part are referred to as participants or informants.
- Designed to study participants' attributed meanings and associated relationships.
- Generally uses non-probability sampling techniques.
- Based on meanings expressed through words (spoken and textual) and images.
- Method(s) used to collect data are unstructured or semi-structured.
- Collection results in non-standardised data generally requiring classification into categories.
- Analysis conducted through the use of conceptualisation.
- Resulting meaning derived from words (spoken or text) and images.

Research strategies

Qualitative research is associated with a variety of strategies. Some of the principal strategies used with qualitative research are: Action Research, Case Study research, Ethnography, Grounded Theory and Narrative Inquiry. These are discussed in Section 5.8. Some of these strategies can also be used in a quantitative research design, such as a case study strategy, or be used in a mixed methods research design as we discuss in Section 5.6.

Techniques

Techniques associated with the use of particular methods are considered in Chapters 9, 10 and 13. Collecting qualitative data through observation is considered in Chapter 9; this includes Internet-mediated observation (Section 9.5) and observation using videography (Section 9.6). Collecting qualitative data using semi-structured and in-depth interviews is considered in Chapter 10; this includes group interviews (Section 10.8), telephone interviews (Section 10.9) and Internet-mediated interviews (Section 10.10). Techniques to analyse data qualitatively are considered in Chapter 13.

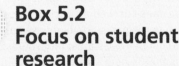

Box 5.2
Focus on student research

Multi-method qualitative study

Harry wanted to establish how new supervisors learned to do their job. In order to do this he thought it essential that he should have the clearest possible grasp of what the supervisor's job entailed.

This involved him in:

- shadowing a new supervisor for a week (qualitative data);

- interviewing a day and a night shift supervisor to establish any differences in approach (qualitative data);
- interviewing the managers to whom these two supervisors reported (qualitative data).

This gave Harry a much better grasp of the content of the supervisor's job. It also did much to enhance his credibility in the eyes of the supervisors. He was then able to draw on the valuable data he had collected to complete his main research task: interviewing new supervisors to discover how they learned to do the job. This provided further qualitative data.

5.6 Mixed methods research designs

Philosophical assumptions

Mixed methods research is the branch of multiple methods research that integrates the use of quantitative and qualitative data collection techniques and analytical procedures in the same research project (Figure 5.2). It is therefore based on philosophical assumptions that guide the collection and analysis of data and the mixing of quantitative and qualitative collection techniques and analysis procedures (Molina-Azorin et al. 2017). We consider two philosophical positions that are often associated with mixed methods designs: pragmatism and critical realism.

As we noted in Section 4.4, pragmatists assert that there are many different ways of interpreting the world and that different methods are often appropriate within one research study. This does not mean pragmatists will always use mixed methods, rather that the methods pragmatists use are chosen because they will enable credible reliable and relevant data to be collected to address the research problem. For pragmatists, the nature of the research question, the research context and likely research consequences are driving forces determining the most appropriate methodological choice (Nastasi et al. 2010). Both quantitative and qualitative research are valued by pragmatists and their choice will be contingent on the particular nature of the research. Pragmatism can therefore be seen as informing qualitative and quantitative, as well as mixed methods, research.

Critical realism, like pragmatism, has implications for research design that may support the use of mixed methods research. To accommodate this realist ontology and subjectivist epistemology, researchers may, for example, use initially qualitative research methods to explore perceptions. This could be followed by quantitative analysis of officially published data (Section 8.2) or documentary sources (Section 5.8) to conduct a retroductive analysis (Section 4.5) to seek to understand the relationship between socially constructed knowledge and possible underlying casual structures, processes and forces. It is also possible to undertake qualitative research within a critical realist philosophy.

Researchers using mixed methods approaches have a **pluralist** view of research methodology. This means they believe that flexibility in the selection and use of methods (both quantitative and qualitative) is legitimate and that researchers should be tolerant of others' preferred methods even when they differ from their own. These views can be contrasted with those who believe there is, or should be, one legitimate method that should be followed. Researchers with this **unitarist** methodological view are unlikely to be tolerant of others' preferred methods if they differ from their own.

Approach to theory development

A mixed methods research design may use a deductive, inductive or abductive approach to theory development. For example, quantitative or qualitative research may be used to test a theoretical proposition or propositions, followed by further quantitative or qualitative research to develop a richer theoretical understanding. Theory may also be used to provide direction for the research. In this way a particular theory may be used to provide a focus for the research and to provide boundaries to its scope (Tashakkori and Teddlie 2010).

Characteristics

Mixed methods research draws from the characteristics of both quantitative research (Table 5.1) and qualitative research (Table 5.2). In mixed methods research, quantitative and qualitative techniques are combined in a variety of ways that range from simple, concurrent forms to more complex and sequential forms (Figure 5.2). The ways in which quantitative and qualitative research may be combined, as well as the extent to which this may occur, have led to the identification of a number of variations of mixed methods research (Creswell and Plano Clark 2011; Nastasi et al. 2010). We now consider these briefly.

Concurrent mixed methods research involves the separate use of quantitative and qualitative methods within a single phase of data collection and analysis (a **single-phase research design**) (Figure 5.3). This allows both sets of results to be interpreted together to provide a richer and more comprehensive response to the research question in comparison to the use of a mono method design. Where you collect qualitative and quantitative data in the same phase of research in order to compare how these data sets support one another, you will be using a **concurrent triangulation design**.

Using a concurrent mixed methods design should provide richer data than a mono method design and be shorter in timescale, as well as more practical to undertake, than a sequential mixed methods design.

Sequential mixed methods research involves more than one phase of data collection and analysis (Figure 5.3). In this design, the researcher will follow the use of one method with another in order to expand or elaborate on the initial set of findings. In a **double-phase research design** this leads to two alternative mixed methods research strategies, either a **sequential exploratory research design** (qualitative followed by quantitative) or a **sequential explanatory research design** (quantitative followed by qualitative). In a more complex, sequential, **multi-phase design**, mixed methods research will involve multiple phases of data collection and analysis (e.g. qualitative followed by quantitative, then by a further phase of qualitative) (Box 5.3).

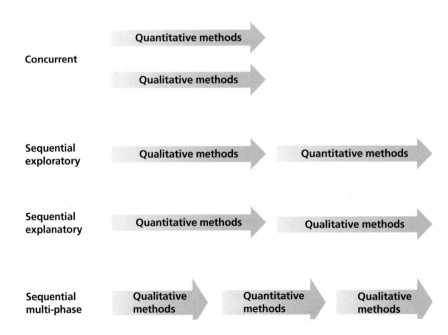

Figure 5.3 Mixed methods research designs

Box 5.3
Focus on student research

Mixed methods research

Andreas conducted research into organisational change in an IT company, using a mixed methods research design. This was designed as a sequential mixed methods research project and consisted of four stages:

1 *Initial exploratory discussions* were held with key senior managers, which combined the purpose of helping to negotiate access, agree the scope of the project and gain essential contextual data. These data were analysed qualitatively in order to get a picture of important internal and external organisational issues.

2 *Individual in-depth interviews* were held with 28 directly employed staff (excluding contractor staff), who formed a sample representing the organisation across its departments and throughout its grade structure. These data were also analysed qualitatively. This was to establish the issues that were important to staff, to help to inform the content of the questionnaire.

3 *A questionnaire* was designed, pilot-tested, amended and then administered to a representative sample of directly employed staff, producing a 42 per cent response rate. The quantitative data produced were analysed statistically to allow the views of employee groups to be compared for differences by age, gender, length of service, occupation and grade. The subsequent production of summary data based on these findings was particularly important to the IT company.

4 A fourth stage consisted of *presentations to groups of employees*. This allowed employees' questions to be answered with care, while continuing to ensure anonymity. It also allowed discussion to occur to clarify the content of some of the questionnaire results. Notes from these presentations were analysed qualitatively.

Using a double-phase or multi-phase research design suggests a dynamic approach to the research process which recognises that mixed methods research is both interactive and iterative, where one phase subsequently informs and directs the next phase of data collection and analysis. The exact nature of this interaction and iteration in a particular research project may shape the way in which qualitative and quantitative methods are chosen and integrated at each phase of the research (Greene 2007; Nastasi et al. 2010; Ridenour and Newman 2008; Teddlie and Tashakkori 2009).

Where you mix quantitative and qualitative methods at every stage of your research (design, data collection and analysis, interpretation and presentation of the research), you will be using a **fully integrated mixed methods research** design. Where you use quantitative and qualitative methods at only one stage or particular stages of your research, you will be using a **partially integrated mixed methods research** approach (Nastasi et al. 2010; Teddlie and Tashakkori 2009, 2011).

Quantitative and qualitative methods may also be 'merged' so that qualitative data are '**quantitised**' (e.g. specific events in the data are counted as frequencies and numerically coded for statistical analysis) and quantitative data are '**qualitised**' (e.g. frequencies are turned into text, although this is extremely rare in practice). Both types of data may also be presented together on a matrix, qualitative data may be presented diagrammatically (Box 12.9) and quantitative data presented using categorisation. This approach to mixing methods may be risky, since there is a danger that the respective value of each form of data may be diluted; for example, excessively 'quantitising' qualitative data may lead to loss of its exploratory or explanatory richness.

Mixed methods research may use quantitative research and qualitative research equally or unequally (Creswell and Plano Clark 2011). In this way, the priority or weight given to either quantitative or qualitative research may vary, so that one methodology has a dominant role, while the other plays a supporting role, depending on the purpose of the research project. This prioritisation may also reflect the preferences of the researcher or the expectations of those who commission the research (such as your project tutor or the managers in an organisation).

The purpose of the research may emphasise the initial use and prioritisation of qualitative research (as in an exploratory study, where qualitative precedes quantitative) or the initial use and prioritisation of quantitative research (as in a descriptive study, before the possible use of supporting qualitative research to explain particular findings further). The overall purpose of the research may also emphasise the dominance of either quantitative or qualitative research (e.g. as in a sequential project which commences with a qualitative, exploratory phase, followed by a quantitative, descriptive phase and which is completed by a further qualitative, explanatory phase). The purpose of other research projects may lead to the more equal use of quantitative and qualitative research methods. The research approach may also lead to the relative prioritisation of either quantitative or qualitative methods. In this way, an inductive approach designed to generate theoretical concepts and to build theory may lead to a greater emphasis on the use of qualitative methods.

Embedded mixed methods research is the term given to the situation where one methodology supports the other (Creswell and Plano Clark 2011). During data collection, this may occur in a number of ways. One methodology may be embedded within the other during a single means to collect data (e.g. some quantitative questions are included in an interview schedule, or some questions within a questionnaire require a qualitative response). This is known as a **concurrent embedded design**. Alternatively, a single-phase research design may use both quantitative and qualitative methods concurrently but collect these separately, one of which will be analysed to support the other. Within a double-phase, sequential research design, both quantitative and qualitative methods will be collected and analysed, one after the other, with one being used in a supporting role.

The characteristics that help to define mixed methods research highlight how quantitative and qualitative methods may be combined in a number of ways to provide you with better opportunities to answer your research question (Tashakkori and Teddlie 2010). Table 5.3 outlines a number of reasons for and advantages of using a mixed methods design. The specific nature of your mixed methods design will be related to particular reasons and advantages.

Box 5.4 summarises how mixed methods have been used in strategic management research.

Research designs

As we have just discussed, different combinations of mixed methods research characteristics lead to various research designs. The principal mixed methods research designs summarised earlier in this section are: concurrent triangulation design, concurrent embedded design, sequential exploratory design, sequential explanatory design (Creswell 2009; Creswell and Plano Clark 2011) and sequential, multi-phase design.

Techniques

Quantitative data collection techniques and analytical procedures that may be used as part of mixed methods research are considered in Chapters 9, 11 and 12. Structured observation

Table 5.3 Reasons for using a mixed methods design

Reason	Explanation
Initiation	Initial use of a qualitative or quantitative methodology may be used to define the nature and scope of sequential quantitative or qualitative research. May also be used to provide contextual background and to better understand the research problem (e.g. Box 5.3). May also help in the formulation or redrafting of research questions, interview questions and questionnaire items and the selection of samples, cases and participants
Facilitation	During the course of the research, one method may lead to the discovery of new insights which inform and are followed up through the use of the other method
Complementarity	Use of mixed methods may allow meanings and findings to be elaborated, enhanced, clarified, confirmed, illustrated or linked
Interpretation	One method (e.g. qualitative) may be used to help to explain relationships between variables emerging from the other (e.g. quantitative)
Generalisability	Use of mixed methods may help to establish the generalisability of a study or its relative importance. In a similar way the use of mixed methods may help to establish the credibility of a study or to produce more complete knowledge (Section 5.11)
Diversity	Use of mixed methods may allow for a greater diversity of views to inform and be reflected in the study
Problem solving	Use of an alternative method may help when the initial method reveals unexplainable results or insufficient data
Focus	One method may be used to focus on one attribute (e.g. quantitative on macro aspects), while the other method may be used to focus on another attribute (e.g. qualitative on micro aspects)
Triangulation	Mixed methods may be used in order to combine data to ascertain if the findings from one method mutually corroborate the findings from the other method (Section 5.11)
Confidence	Findings may be affected by the method used. Use of a single method will make it impossible to ascertain the nature of that effect. To seek to cancel out this 'method effect', it is advisable to use mixed methods. This should lead to greater confidence in your conclusions

Source: Developed from Bryman (2006), Greene et al. (1989), Molina-Azorin (2011) and authors' experience

is discussed in Section 9.4; Chapter 11 discusses the use of questionnaires, including structured interviewing; and Chapter 12 is devoted to the analysis of quantitative data.

Qualitative data collection techniques and analytical procedures that may be used as part of mixed methods research are considered in Chapters 9, 10 and 13. Collecting qualitative data through observation is considered in Chapter 9; this includes Internet-mediated observation (Section 9.5) and observation using videography (Section 9.6). Collecting qualitative data using semi-structured and in-depth interviews is considered in Chapter 10; this includes group interviews (Section 10.8), telephone interviews (Section 10.9) and

**Box 5.4
Focus on
management
research**

Recognition and use of mixed methods in organisational research

Molina-Azorin et al. (2017) note in an article published in *Organizational Research Methods* that while mixed methods research has been recognised and developed as a distinct methodological approach over recent decades in many social sciences fields such as education and health, this does not appear to be the case in organisational research to the same degree. They point out, however, that some caution is required in relation to this apparent difference.

They argue that organisational and management researchers have used quantitative and qualitative methods in an integrated way for a long time without referring to this as mixed methods research. This they consider is understandable before the identification of the term 'mixed methods research' in the latter part of the twentieth century and its subsequent development as a distinct methodological approach. However, Molina-Azorin et al. (2017: 181) also state that, "in the past few years, organizational researchers are also integrating quantitative and qualitative methods without using the 'mixed methods' approach to refer to their studies."

They comment that although the term 'mixed methods research' is not always used, many journals welcome research that integrates quantitative and qualitative approaches. Consequently, searching for such research using the search term 'mixed methods' is likely to reveal only a relatively small number of articles in business and management journals. For greater success, a wider variety of search terms incorporating both qualitative and quantitative research methods is likely to be required.

Internet-mediated interviews (Section 10.10). Techniques to analyse qualitative data are considered in Chapter 13.

5.7 Recognising the purpose of your research design

Earlier we referred to your research following an exploratory or explanatory purpose. Research can be designed to fulfil either an exploratory, descriptive, explanatory or evaluative purpose, or some combination of these. In Chapter 2 we encouraged you to think about your research project in terms of the question you wish to answer and your research objectives. The way in which you ask your research question will inevitably involve you in exploratory, descriptive, explanatory or evaluative research. The purpose of your research may also change over time.

In this section we discuss each purpose in more detail to help you to choose which of these is appropriate to the nature of your research project.

Exploratory studies

An **exploratory study** is a valuable means to ask open questions to discover what is happening and gain insights about a topic of interest. As we noted in Section 2.4, research questions that are exploratory are likely to begin with 'What' or 'How'. Questions that you ask during data collection to explore an issue, problem or phenomenon will also be likely to start with 'What' or 'How' (Chapter 10). An exploratory study is particularly useful if you wish to clarify your understanding of an issue, problem or phenomenon, such as if you are unsure of its precise nature. It may be that time is well spent on exploratory research, as it might show that the research is not worth pursuing!

There are a number of ways to conduct exploratory research. These include a search of the literature; interviewing 'experts' in the subject; conducting in-depth individual interviews or conducting focus group interviews. Because of their exploratory nature, these interviews are likely to be relatively unstructured and to rely on the quality of the contributions from those who participate to help guide the subsequent stage of your research (Sections 10.2 and 10.3).

Exploratory research has the advantage that it is flexible and adaptable to change. If you are conducting exploratory research, you must be willing to change your direction as a result of new data that appear and new insights that occur to you. A quotation from the travel writer V.S. Naipaul (1989: 222) illustrates this point beautifully:

> I had been concerned, at the start of my own journey, to establish some lines of enquiry, to define a theme. The approach had its difficulties. At the back of my mind was always a worry that I would come to a place and all contacts would break down . . . If you travel on a theme the theme has to develop with the travel. At the beginning your interests can be broad and scattered. But then they must be more focused; the different stages of a journey cannot simply be versions of one another. And . . . this kind of travel depended on luck. It depended on the people you met, the little illuminations you had. As with the next day's issue of fast-moving daily newspapers, the shape of the character in hand was continually being changed by accidents along the way.

Exploratory research may commence with a broad focus but this will become narrower as the research progresses.

Descriptive studies

The purpose of **descriptive research** is to gain an accurate profile of events, persons or situations. As we noted in Section 2.4, research questions that are descriptive are likely to begin with, or include, either 'Who', 'What', 'Where', 'When' or 'How'. Questions that you ask during data collection to gain a description of events, persons or situations will also be likely to start with, or include, 'Who', 'What', 'Where', 'When' or 'How' (Chapters 10 and 11). Descriptive research may be an extension of a piece of exploratory research or a forerunner to a piece of explanatory research. It is necessary to have a clear picture of the phenomenon on which you wish to collect data prior to the collection of the data. One of the earliest well-known examples of a descriptive survey is the *Domesday Book*, which described the population of England in 1085.

Often project tutors are rather wary of work that is too descriptive. There is a danger of their saying 'That's very interesting . . . but so what?' They will want you to go further and draw conclusions from the data you are describing. They will encourage you to develop the skills of evaluating data and synthesising ideas. These are higher-order skills than those of accurate description. Description in business and management research has a very clear place. However, it should be thought of as a means to an end rather than an end in itself. This means that if your research project utilises description it is likely to be a precursor to explanation. Such studies are known as **descripto-explanatory** studies.

Explanatory studies

Studies that establish causal relationships between variables may be termed **explanatory research**. As we noted in Section 2.4, research questions that seek explanatory answers are likely to begin with, or include, 'Why' or 'How'. Questions that you ask during data collection to gain an explanatory response will also be likely to start with, or include, 'Why' or 'How' (Chapters 10 and 11).

The emphasis in explanatory research is to study a situation or a problem in order to explain the relationships between variables. You may find, for example, that a cursory analysis of quantitative data on manufacturing scrap rates shows a relationship between scrap rates and the age of the machine being operated. You could analyse these data using a statistical test such as correlation (discussed in Section 12.6) in order to get a clearer view of the relationship. Alternatively, you might collect qualitative data to explain the reasons why customers of your company rarely pay their bills according to the prescribed payment terms.

Evaluative studies

The purpose of **evaluative research** is to find out how well something works. As we noted in Section 2.4, research questions that seek to evaluate answers are likely to begin with 'How', or include 'What', in the form of 'To what extent'. Evaluative research in business and management is likely to be concerned with assessing the effectiveness of an organisational or business strategy, policy, programme, initiative or process. This may relate to any area of the organisation or business: for example, evaluating a marketing campaign, a personnel policy, a costing strategy, the delivery of a support service.

Questions that you ask during data collection to seek an evaluative understanding will be likely to start with, or include, 'What', 'How' or 'Why'. As part of your evaluative study you may also make comparisons between events, situations, groups, places or periods, so that you ask questions that include 'Which', 'When', 'Who' or 'Where' (Chapters 10 and 11). Asking such questions would help you to compare the effectiveness of, say, an advertising campaign in different locations or between different groups of consumers. In this way, evaluative research allows you to assess performance and to compare this. An evaluative study may produce a theoretical contribution where emphasis is placed on understanding not only 'how effective' something is, but also 'why', and then comparing this explanation to existing theory.

Combined studies

A research study may combine more than one purpose in its design. This may be achieved by the use of multiple methods in the research design (Sections 5.4 to 5.6), to facilitate some combination of exploratory, descriptive, explanatory or evaluative research. Alternatively, a single method research design may be used in a way that provides scope to facilitate more than one purpose. Box 5.5 provides two examples of multiple methods studies that combine research purposes.

Box 5.5
Focus on management research

Multiple methods studies that combine research purposes

It is useful to look at business and management research published in journals to see whether they are based on a single method or multiple methods, and to recognise the research purpose(s) of each method. While these articles outline the research method(s) their authors used, the purpose of each method is often implied rather than being explicitly categorised as exploratory, descriptive, explanatory or evaluative. Some journals tend to publish articles based on multiple methods studies and it is helpful to examine this type of article to work out how the methods used are related to research purpose. The *Journal of Marketing* publishes many articles based on multiple methods studies, which help to show the relationship between research method and research purpose. Here are two examples.

Dion and Borraz (2017) undertook research whose aim was to examine how stores dedicated to selling luxury brands manage status during service encounters. Their qualitative multi-method study involved the collection of four sets of data based on three research methods: (i) interviews conducted with a sample of luxury brand customers; (ii) interviews conducted with a range of luxury store employees; (iii) a series of semi-structured observations of service encounters in luxury stores in the city of Paris; and (iv) Internet-mediated observation of websites, online stores and blogs to access consumer and employee accounts of their experiences of shopping or working in luxury stores. The exploratory, descriptive and explanatory nature of this research emerges through the description of its design and especially through the presentation of the results of this research project.

Böttger et al. (2017) undertook research whose aim was to conceive of, develop and validate a scale to measure customer inspiration. Some 93 initial possible scale items were generated by the authors using existing literature and the results of interviews with 918 customers, which were then evaluated by an expert panel of marketing academics and organisational managers to form a list of 37 potential items. Subsequently, five distinct studies were undertaken to develop and validate the scale. These studies included the use of laboratory and field experiments and the administration of questionnaires. This research collected both qualitative and quantitative data, which were primarily analysed quantitatively. The various stages of this mixed-methods study illustrate the exploratory, descriptive, explanatory and evaluative nature of this research.

5.8 Choosing a research strategy or strategies

The different research strategies

In this section we turn our attention to your choice of **research strategy** (Figure 5.1). In general terms, a strategy is a plan of action to achieve a goal. A research strategy may therefore be defined as a plan of how a researcher will go about answering her or his research question. It is the methodological link between your philosophy and subsequent choice of methods to collect and analyse data (Denzin and Lincoln 2018).

Different research traditions have led to the development of a range of research strategies, as we outlined earlier. In Sections 5.4 to 5.6 we outlined the research strategies that are principally linked with quantitative, qualitative and mixed methods research designs, respectively. Particular research strategies may be associated with a particular research philosophy and also a deductive, inductive or abductive approach; however, we also recognised in Sections 5.4 to 5.6 that there are often open boundaries between research philosophies, research approaches and research strategies.

In a similar way, a particular research strategy should not be seen as inherently superior or inferior to any other. Consequently, we believe that what is most important is not attaching labels for their own sake or linking research elements to try to be methodologically aloof. For us, the key to your choice of research strategy or strategies is that you achieve a reasonable level of coherence throughout your research design which will enable you to answer your particular research question(s) and meet your objectives.

Your choice of research strategy will therefore be guided by your research question(s) and objectives, the coherence with which these link to your philosophy, research approach and purpose, and also to more pragmatic concerns including the extent of existing knowledge, the amount of time and other resources you have available and access to potential participants and to other sources of data. Finally, it must be remembered that these strategies should not be thought of as being mutually exclusive. For example, it is quite possible to use the survey strategy within a case study or combine a number of different strategies within mixed methods.

The first two research strategies in the list below that we consider in this section are principally or exclusively linked to a quantitative research design. The next two may involve quantitative or qualitative research, or a mixed design combining both. The final four strategies are principally or exclusively linked to a qualitative research design.

In our experience it is the choice between qualitative research strategies that is likely to cause the greatest confusion. Such confusion is often justified given the diversity of qualitative strategies (many more than those we consider), with their conflicting tensions and 'blurred genres' (Denzin and Lincoln 2018: 10). In our discussion we draw out the distinctions between these strategies to allow you to make an informed methodological choice between qualitative designs (as between or across quantitative and qualitative designs). This is intended to help you avoid the vague assertion that you are 'doing qualitative research', without any further qualification! The strategies we discuss are:

- Experiment;
- Survey;
- Archival and documentary research;
- Case study;
- Ethnography;
- Action Research;
- Grounded Theory;
- Narrative Inquiry.

Experiment

We start with discussion of the experiment strategy because its roots in natural science, laboratory-based research and the precision required to conduct it mean that the 'experiment' is often seen as the 'gold standard' against which the rigour of other strategies is assessed. **Experiment** is a form of research that owes much to the natural sciences, although it features strongly in psychological and social science research. The purpose of an experiment is to study the probability of a change in an **independent variable** causing a change in another, **dependent variable**. Table 5.4 provides a description of types of variable. An experiment uses hypothetical explanations, known as hypotheses, rather than research questions. This is because the researcher hypothesises whether or not a relationship will exist between the variables. Two types of (opposing) hypotheses are formulated

Table 5.4 Types of variable

Variable	Meaning
Independent (IV)	Variable that is being manipulated or changed to measure its impact on a dependent variable
Dependent (DV)	Variable that may change in response to changes in other variables; observed outcome or result from manipulation of another variable
Mediating (MV)	A variable located between the independent and dependent variables, which transmits the effect between them (IV → MV → DV)
Moderator	A new variable that is introduced which will affect the nature of the relationship between the IV and DV
Control	Additional observable and measurable variables that need to be kept constant to avoid them influencing the effect of the IV on the DV
Confounding	Extraneous but difficult to observe or measure variables that can potentially undermine the inferences drawn between the IV and DV. Need to be considered when discussing results, to avoid spurious conclusions

in a standard experiment: the **null hypothesis** and the **hypothesis** (also referred to as the alternative **hypothesis**). The null hypothesis is the explanation that there is no difference or relationship between the variables. An example of a null hypothesis is:

User satisfaction of online customer support is not related to the amount of training support staff have received.

The hypothesis is the explanation that there is a difference or relationship between the variables. An example of a (directional) hypothesis is:

User satisfaction of online customer support is related to the amount of training support staff have received.

In an experiment, the compatibility of the data with the null hypothesis is tested statistically. The statistical test is based on the probability of these data or data more extreme occurring by chance (Wassenstein and Lazer, 2016) and in effect measures the probability that the data are compatible with the null hypothesis. The smaller the probability (termed the p-value), the greater the statistical incompatibility of the data with the null hypothesis. This 'incompatibility' is interpreted as casting doubt on or providing evidence against the null hypothesis and its associated underlying assumptions. Where this probability is greater than a prescribed value (usually $p = 0.05$), the null hypothesis is usually accepted and the hypothesis is rejected. Where the probability is less than or equal to the prescribed value (usually p = 0.05), this indicates that the hypothesis can be accepted. The simplest experiments are concerned with whether there is a link between two variables. More complex experiments also consider the size of the change and the relative importance of two or more independent variables. Experiments therefore tend to be used in exploratory and explanatory research to answer 'what', 'how' and 'why' questions.

Different experimental designs may be used, each with different advantages and disadvantages, particularly in relation to **control variables** and **confounding variables** (Table 5.2). Experimental designs include classical experiments, quasi-experiments and within-subject designs. In a **classical experiment,** a sample of participants is selected and then randomly assigned to either an experimental group or to the control group. In the **experimental group**, some form of planned intervention or manipulation will be tested. In the **control group**, no such intervention is made. Random assignment means each group should be similar in all aspects relevant to the research other than whether or not they are exposed to the planned intervention or manipulation. In assigning the members to the control and experimental groups at random and using a control group, you try to control (that is, remove) the possible effects of an alternative explanation to the planned intervention (manipulation) and eliminate threats to internal validity. This is because the control group is subject to exactly the same external influences as the experimental group other than the planned intervention and, consequently, this intervention is the only explanation for any changes to the dependent variable.

A **quasi-experiment** will still use an experimental group(s) and a control group, but the researcher will not randomly assign participants to each group, perhaps because participants are only available in pre-formed groups (e.g. existing work groups). Differences in participants between groups may be minimised by the use of matched pairs. **Matched pair analysis** leads to a participant in an experimental group being paired with a participant in the control group based on matching factors such as age, gender, occupation, length of service, grade etc., to try to minimise the effect of extraneous variables on the experiment's outcomes. Those factors relevant to the nature of the experiment will need to be matched.

The basic experimental procedure in classical and quasi-experiments is the same (Figure 5.4), with the exception of random assignment, and we illustrate this procedure with an example related to the introduction of a sales promotion. The dependent variable in this example, purchasing behaviour, is measured for members of both the experimental group and control group before any intervention occurs. This provides a **pre-test** measure of purchasing behaviour. A planned intervention is then made to members of the experimental group in the form of a 'buy two, get one free' promotion. In the control group, no such intervention is made. The dependent variable, purchasing behaviour, is measured after the manipulation of the independent variable (the use of the 'buy two, get one free' promotion) for both the experimental group and the control group, so that a pre-test and **post-test** comparison can be made. On the basis of this comparison, any difference between the experimental and control groups for the dependent variable (purchasing behaviour) is attributed to the intervention of the 'buy two, get one free' promotion. This experimental approach is known as a **between-subjects design**, where participants belong to either the experimental group or control group but not both. In a between-subjects design, if more than one intervention or manipulation is to be tested, a separate experimental group will be required for each test (known as **independent measures**). For example, if the experiment was designed to compare two separate interventions, such as

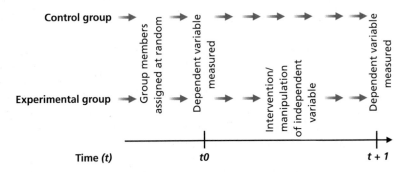

Figure 5.4 A classical experiment strategy

a 'buy one, get one free' as well as the 'buy two, get one free' manipulation, two experimental groups would be required alongside the control group.

In a **within-subjects design**, or within-group design, there will be only a single group, rather than a separation into an experimental group and a control group. In this approach every participant is exposed to the planned intervention or series of interventions. For this reason, this approach is known as **repeated measures**. The procedure involves a pre-intervention observation or measurement, to establish a baseline (or control for the dependent variable). This is followed by a planned intervention (manipulation of the independent variable) and subsequent observation and measurement (related to the dependent variable). Following the withdrawal of the intervention and a period of 'reversal', to allow a return to the baseline, a further planned intervention may be attempted followed by subsequent observation and measurement. A within-subject design may be more practical than a between-subjects design because it requires fewer participants, but it may lead to carryover effects where familiarity or fatigue with the process distorts the validity of the findings. This may lead to a counterbalanced design, where some of the participants undertake tasks in a different order to see if familiarity or fatigue affects the outcomes.

Often experiments, including those in disciplines closely associated with business and management such as organisational psychology, are conducted in laboratories rather than in the field (for example in an organisation). This means that you have greater control over aspects of the research process such as sample selection and the context within which the experiment occurs. However, while this improves the **internal validity** of the experiment, that is, the extent to which the findings can be attributed to the interventions rather than any flaws in your research design, **external validity** is likely to be more difficult to establish (we discuss issues of validity in Section 5.11). Laboratory settings, by their very nature, are unlikely to be related to the real world of organisations. As a consequence, the extent to which the findings from a laboratory experiment are able to be generalised to all organisations is likely to be lower than for a field-based experiment.

The feasibility of using an experimental strategy will depend on the nature of your research question. As we noted, an experiment uses predictive hypotheses rather than open research questions. It may be appropriate to turn your question into hypotheses where you wish to test for expected relationships between variables. However, most business and management research questions will be designed to inquire into the relationships between variables, rather than to test a predicted relationship. This indicates the difference between experiments and other research strategies. Within quantitative research designs, it highlights a key difference between an experimental strategy and a survey strategy.

Survey

The **survey** strategy is usually associated with a deductive research approach. It is a popular strategy in business and management research and is most frequently used to answer 'what', 'who', 'where', 'how much' and 'how many' questions. It therefore tends to be used for exploratory and descriptive research. Survey strategies using questionnaires are popular as they allow the collection of standardised data from a large number of respondents economically, allowing easy comparison. In addition, the survey strategy is perceived as authoritative by people in general and is comparatively easy both to explain and to understand. Every day a news bulletin, news website or newspaper reports the results of a new survey that is designed to find out how a group of people thinks or behaves in relation to a particular issue (Box 5.6).

The survey strategy allows you to collect data which you can analyse quantitatively using descriptive and inferential statistics (Sections 12.5 and 12.6). In addition, data

Box 5.6 Focus on research in the news

Young people rely on parents and credit cards to cover costs

By Lucy Warwick-Ching

In a report published this week, the Financial Conduct Authority (FCA) said half of UK adults – over 25m people – were potentially "financially vulnerable" for reasons including a reliance on high-cost credit, or their inability to cope with a small rise in their monthly bills.

The report, based on a survey of 13,000 adults conducted between January and April of this year, identified 4.1m people, typically between the ages of 25 and 34, who are already in "serious financial difficulty" having failed to pay bills in three or more of the past six months.

A shift in the generational pattern of earnings and income is creating a growing "wealth gap" between the young and the old in Britain, which the FCA said is resulting in more young people experiencing debt problems.

The report highlights just how precarious the financial lives of many under-35s are.

The report found that 25-34-year-olds have above-average holdings of credit or loan products. Despite making up only 18 per cent of all UK adults, this age group accounts for around one quarter of those who hold a personal loan, regularly switch a credit card balance and have a car finance loan. They also account for 22 per cent of those borrowing on store cards, catalogue credit or other retail credit.

 Source of extract: Warwick-Ching, L. (2017) 'Young people rely on parents and credit cards to cover costs', *Financial Times,* 20 October. Copyright © 2017 The Financial Times Limited

collected using a survey strategy can be used to suggest possible reasons for particular relationships between variables and to produce models of these relationships. Using a survey strategy should give you more control over the research process and, when probability sampling is used, it is possible to generate findings that are statistically representative of the whole population at a lower cost than collecting the data for the whole population (Section 7.2). You will need to spend time ensuring that your sample is representative, designing and piloting your data collection instrument and trying to ensure a good response rate. Preparing and analysing the data will also be time consuming, even with readily available cloud-based data collection and analysis software. However, it will be your time and, once you have collected your data, you will be independent. Many researchers complain that their progress is delayed by their dependence on others for data.

Data collected using a survey strategy is unlikely to be as wide ranging as those collected by other research strategies. For example, there is a limit to the number of questions that any questionnaire can contain if the goodwill of the respondent is not to be presumed on too much. Despite this, perhaps the biggest drawback with using a questionnaire as part of a survey strategy is (as emphasised in Section 11.2) the capacity to do it badly!

The questionnaire, however, is not the only data collection technique that belongs to the survey strategy. Structured observation, of the type most frequently associated with organisation and methods (O&M) research, and structured interviews, where standardised questions are asked of all interviewees, also often fall into this strategy. Structured observation techniques are discussed in Section 9.4 and structured interviews in Section 11.2.

Archival and documentary research

The digitalisation of data and the creation of online archives, along with open data initiatives by governments and businesses, have increased the scope for you to use an archival or documentary research strategy. This means it is now possible to access such sources online from around the world. These potentially provide you with considerable scope to design a research project that capitalises on the wide range of secondary data sources (Chapter 8). There are limitations in attempting to use this strategy and we briefly consider these after outlining types of documentary sources and discussing their attributes.

It is difficult to describe adequately the range of archival and documentary materials potentially available. Lee (2012: 391) suggests that 'a document is a durable repository for textual, visual and audio representations'. This illustrates the wide range of materials encompassed by this definition. Categories of textual documents include:

- communications between individuals or within groups such as email, letters, social media and blog postings;
- individual records such as diaries, electronic calendars and notes;
- organisational documents such as administrative records, agendas and minutes of meetings, agreements, contracts, memos, personnel records, plans, policy statements, press releases, reports and strategy statements;
- government documents such as publications, reports and national statistics data sets;
- media documents including printed and online articles and other data.

Visual and audio documents include advertising posters, artefacts, audio recordings, audio-visual corporate communications, digital recordings, DVDs, films, photographs, products, promotional advertisements and recordings, television and radio programmes and web images.

Many types of archival and documentary materials may be accessed online. Section 8.4 and in particular Table 8.1 provide examples of online data archives and gateways to governmental websites. Organisations' websites may provide access to certain types of documentary sources such as annual reports, company results, financial highlights, press releases and regulatory news. Media websites also provide facilities to search for articles about organisations and business and management topics. As we discuss in Sections 6.2 to 6.4, other internal organisational documents are less likely to be available online and you would need to contact an organisation to seek access, providing these were not considered to be commercially sensitive. Some documents created by individuals may be accessible through data archives (e.g. a collection of papers of a notable business person) but use of recently created materials will probably require you to contact a potential participant to negotiate access, where these are not considered to be private or commercially sensitive (Sections 6.2– 6.4).

Documents used for research are considered secondary sources because they were originally created for a different purpose (see the earlier bullet-point list). Researchers using an archival or documentary research strategy therefore need to be sensitive to the fact that the documents they use were not originally created for a research purpose. We discuss the advantages and disadvantages of using secondary source material in Section 8.3. However, we would like to stress the difference between a secondary data analysis that re-analyses data originally collected for a research purpose and using secondary sources in an archival or documentary research strategy. Where original research data are re-analysed for a different purpose in a secondary data analysis, you should assess the quality of the original research data – i.e. were these data drawn from a representative sample; was the original research designed to overcome threats to reliability and validity (Section 5.11). In contrast, where documents are used as secondary sources in an archival or documentary research strategy, their original purpose had nothing to do with research and so as a researcher using this strategy, you will need to be sensitive to the nature and original purpose of the documents you select, the way in which you analyse them and the generalisations that you can draw (Hakim 2000).

While great care needs to be taken when using documents for research purposes, they potentially offer a rich source of data for you to analyse. The data they provide may be analysed quantitatively, qualitatively or both. Analysing qualitative documents quantitatively may allow you to generate a rich or 'thick' description of key events, the context within which these events occurred, the roles of the actors involved, the influence of external influences such as economic or commercial pressures, as well as outcomes. Your scope to achieve such an outcome will of course depend on the nature of your research question and whether you find suitable documents. Documents may, for example, allow you to analyse critical incidents or decision-making processes, or evaluate different policy positions or strategies. Using quantitative data in documents such as annual or financial reports will provide you with access to actual data that may, for example, facilitate comparisons between organisations or across reporting periods. Prior (2007) points out that documents can also be analysed to reveal:

- not only what they contain but what is omitted;
- which facts are used and why these might be emphasised while others are not used;
- how they are used in an organisation and how they are circulated and to whom.

Archival or documentary research may be an effective and efficient strategy to use but this will depend on its appropriateness to your research question and being able to gain access to sufficient numbers of suitable documents. You may be refused access to documents or find that some data are restricted for confidentiality reasons. You may also find that the documents you locate vary in quality, especially where they come from different sources. Some data may be missing or not presented in a consistent way, making comparison difficult or potentially leaving gaps in your analysis. Using an archival research strategy may therefore necessitate you establishing what documents are available and designing your research to make the most of these. This may mean combining this research strategy with another. This could be undertaken in a number of ways, so that, for example, you conduct documentary research alongside a Grounded Theory strategy based on qualitative interviews and use a similar procedure to analyse both sets of data. Another example could involve using documentary research within a case study strategy.

Case study

A **case study** is an in-depth inquiry into a topic or phenomenon within its real-life setting (Yin 2018). The 'case' in case study research may refer to a person (e.g. a manager), a group (e.g. a work team), an organisation (e.g. a business), an association (e.g. a joint venture), a change process (e.g. restructuring a company), an event (e.g. an annual general meeting) as well as many other types of case subject. Choosing the case to be studied and determining the boundaries of the study is a key factor in defining a case study (Flyvberg 2011). Once defined, case study research sets out to understand the dynamics of the topic being studied within its setting or context (Eisenhardt 1989; Eisenhardt and Graebner 2007). 'Understanding the dynamics of the topic' refers to the interactions between the subject of the case and its context.

The study of a case within its real-life setting or context helps to distinguish this research strategy from others. In an experimental strategy, outlined earlier, contextual variables are highly controlled as they are seen as a potential threat to the validity of the results. In a survey strategy, research is undertaken in a real-life setting, but the ability to understand the impact of this context is limited by the number of variables for which data can be collected. In contrast, case study research is often used when the boundaries between the phenomenon being studied and the context within which it is being studied are not always apparent (Yin 2018). Understanding context is fundamental to case study research.

A case study strategy has the capacity to generate insights from intensive and in-depth research into the study of a phenomenon in its real-life context, leading to rich, empirical descriptions and the development of theory (Dubois and Gadde 2002; Eisenhardt 1989; Eisenhardt and Graebner 2007; Ridder et al. 2014; Yin 2018). Dubois and Gadde (2002: 554) make the point that, 'the interaction between a phenomenon and its context is best understood through in-depth case studies'. These can be designed to identify what is happening and why, and perhaps to understand the effects of the situation and implications for action. To achieve such insights, case study research draws on data, often both qualitative and quantitative, from a range of sources to understand fully the dynamics of the case.

Flyvberg (2011) refers to the paradox of case study research: case studies have been widely used over a long period, including in business and management, but have been criticised by some as a research strategy because of 'misunderstandings' about their ability to produce generalisable, reliable and theoretical contributions to knowledge. This is largely based on positivist criticisms of using small samples and more generally about using interpretive, qualitative research. This type of criticism has been countered in many works (e.g. Buchanan 2012; Flyvberg 2011) and is generally losing favour as the value of qualitative and mixed methods research is recognised more widely (e.g. Bansal and Corley 2011; Denzin and Lincoln 2018). We return to consider how the quality of both quantitative and qualitative research may be recognised in Section 5.11.

The long and widespread use of case studies has resulted in them being designed in different ways and for different purposes. They have been used by 'positivist' as well as 'interpretivist' researchers; deductively as well as inductively; and for descriptive, exploratory or explanatory purposes. Some positivist researchers have also advocated using case studies inductively to build theory and to develop theoretical hypotheses, which can be tested subsequently. In this way, the use of the case study is advocated in the early, exploratory stage of research as a complement to deductive research (Eisenhardt 1989; Eisenhardt and Graebner 2007). This approach has been called 'indicative case study research', designed to reveal 'specific attributes' rather than rich description (Ridder et al. 2014: 374).

Yin (2018) recognises that case studies may be used not only for exploratory but also descriptive and explanatory purposes. An explanatory case study is likely to use a deductive approach, using theoretical propositions to test their applicability in the case study, to build and verify an explanation (Chapter 13). Interpretivist researchers are more interested, at least initially, to develop richly detailed and nuanced descriptions of their case study research (Ridder et al. 2014). For some interpretivists, making comparisons with existing theory is unnecessary. Stake (2005) says that many interpretivist researchers prefer to describe their case study in ample detail, allowing readers to make their own links to existing theory. Other interpretivist researchers will work inductively, analysing their data, identifying themes and patterns in these data, and at some point locating this in existing literature in order to refine, extend or generate theory (Ridder et al. 2014; Chapter 13). Where you work as an interpretivist, it is highly likely that you will need to follow this second route and provide a clear link to theory!

Lee and Saunders (2017) differentiate between research designs for 'orthodox cases' and 'emergent cases'. An **orthodox case study** strategy involves an approach that is rigorously defined and highly structured before the research commences, with the intention that it will proceed in a linear way. This reflects the rational approach to conducting research where literature is reviewed first, the research question is defined, the research project is designed, preparation for the conduct of the research undertaken, and data are collected, analysed, interpreted and then reported. This approach to case study strategy is likely to be underpinned by realist philosophical assumptions (Sections 5.4 to 5.6). An **emergent case study** strategy involves a researcher strategically choosing a case study environment within which research will be conducted but allowing the focus of the research to emerge through his or her engagement in this setting (involving different stages of data collection and analysis) and with relevant literature. This approach allows the core focus to emerge and is likely to be underpinned by interpretivist-constructivist philosophical assumptions. In this way it is similar to the constructivist grounded theory strategy that we discuss later in this section.

The existence of these various approaches to case study research potentially provides you with opportunities to use this strategy, as well as challenges when using it. Where you are considering using a case study strategy, you may be able to find earlier work in the social sciences if not specifically in business and management, which provides guidance in an approach that fits logically with your research idea and question (deductive or inductive, exploratory or explanatory etc.). To achieve an in-depth inquiry and a rich, detailed flow of analytical data, a case study strategy can offer you the opportunity to use a mixed methods research design (although case studies may rely on a multi-method choice). Case study research often uses a combination of archival records and documentation (discussed earlier and in Chapter 8), different forms of observation (Chapter 9), ethnography (discussed later in this section), interviews and focus groups (Chapter 10), questionnaires (Chapter 11), reflection and the use of research diaries and other research aids (Chapters 1 and 13). Case study research is likely to prove to be challenging because of its intensive and in-depth nature and your need to be able to identify, define and gain access to a case study setting.

You will also need to identify the nature of your case study strategy and we conclude our discussion of this by considering ways in which your case study research may be structured. Yin (2018) distinguishes between four case study strategies based upon two discrete dimensions:

- single case versus multiple cases;
- holistic case versus embedded case.

A single case is often used where it represents a critical case or, alternatively, an extreme or unique case. Conversely, a single case may be selected purposively because it is typical or because it provides you with an opportunity to observe and analyse a phenomenon that few have considered before (Section 7.3). Inevitably, an important aspect of using a single case is defining the actual case. For many part-time students this is the organisation for which they work (Box 5.7). The key here will be to ensure that this approach is suitable for the nature of your research question and objectives.

A case study strategy can also incorporate multiple cases, that is, more than one case. The rationale for using multiple cases focuses on whether findings can be replicated across cases. Cases will be carefully chosen on the basis that similar results are predicted to be produced from each one. Where this is realised, Yin (2018) terms this **literal replication**. Another set of cases may be chosen where a contextual factor is deliberately different. The impact of this difference on the anticipated findings is predicted by the researcher. Where this predicted variation is realised, Yin terms this **theoretical replication**.

Box 5.7
Focus on student research

Using a single organisation as a case study

Simon was interested in discovering how colleagues within his organisation were using a recently introduced financial costing model in their day-to-day work. In discussion with his project tutor, he highlighted that he was interested in finding out how it was actually being used in his organisation as a whole, as well as seeing if the use of the financial costing model differed between senior managers, departmental managers and front-line operatives. Simon's project tutor suggested that he adopt a case study strategy, using his organisation as a single case within which the senior managers', departmental managers' and front-line operatives' groups were embedded cases. He also highlighted that, given the different numbers of people in each of the embedded cases, Simon would be likely to need to use different data collection techniques with each.

Yin (2018) proposes that a multiple case study strategy may combine a small number of cases chosen to predict literal replication and a second small number chosen to predict theoretical replication. Where all of the findings from these cases are as predicted, this would clearly produce very strong support for the theoretical propositions on which these predictions were based. This particular approach to case study strategy therefore commences deductively, based on theoretical propositions and theory testing, before possibly incorporating an inductive or abductive approach (Section 4.5). Where the findings are in some way contrary to the predictions in the theoretical propositions being tested, it would be necessary to reframe these propositions and choose another set of cases to test them.

Yin's second dimension, holistic versus embedded, refers to the unit of analysis. For example, you may have chosen to use an organisation in which you have been employed or are currently employed as your case. If your research is concerned only with the organisation as a whole, then you are treating the organisation as a holistic case study. Conversely, even if you are only researching within a single organisation, you may wish to examine a number of logical sub-units within the organisation, such as departments or work groups. Your case will inevitably involve more than one unit of analysis and, whichever way you select these units, would be called an embedded case study (Box 5.7).

As a student you are likely to find a single case study strategy to be more manageable. Alternatively, you may be able to develop a research design based on two to three cases, where you seek to achieve a literal replication. However, as we have indicated earlier, choosing between a single or multiple case study is not simply related to producing more evidence. While a multiple case study is likely to produce more evidence, the purpose of each approach is different. A single case study approach is chosen because of the nature of the case (i.e. because it is a critical, unique or typical case etc.). A multiple case study approach is chosen to allow replication. Where you are interested in using this strategy, you will therefore need to ensure that the approach chosen is suitable for the nature of your research question and objectives.

Ethnography

Ethnography is used to study the culture or social world of a group. Ethnography literally means a written account of a people or ethnic group. It is the earliest qualitative research strategy, with its origins in colonial anthropology. From the 1700s to the early 1900s, ethnography was developed to study cultures in so-called 'primitive' societies that had been brought under the rule of a colonial power, to facilitate imperialist control and administration. Early anthropologists treated those among whom they lived and conducted their fieldwork as subjects and approached their ethnography in a detached way, believing that they were using a scientific approach, reminiscent of a positivism, to produce monographs that were meant to be accurate and timeless accounts of different cultures (Denzin and Lincoln 2005; Tedlock 2005). From the 1920s the use of ethnography changed through the work of the Chicago School (University of Chicago), which used ethnographic methods to study social and urban problems within cultural groups in the USA. A seminal example of this work is Whyte's (1993) 'Street Corner Society' originally published in 1943, which examined the lives of street gangs in Boston. This approach to ethnography involved researchers living among those whom they studied, to observe and talk to them in order to produce detailed cultural accounts of their shared beliefs, behaviours, interactions, language, rituals and the events that shaped their lives (Cunliffe 2010). This use of ethnography adopted a more interpretive and naturalistic focus by using the language of those being studied in writing up cultural accounts. However, the researcher remained the arbiter of how to tell the story and what to include, leading many to question how the socialisation and values of this person might affect the account being written (Geertz 1988).

This problem of 'representation' (Denzin and Lincoln 2018) meant that ethnography, as well as qualitative research more generally, was still in a fluid developmental state. Researchers developed a 'bewildering array' (Cunliffe 2010: 230) of qualitative research strategies in the second half of the twentieth century, associated with a great deal of 'blurring' across these strategies (Denzin and Lincoln 2018). We discuss some of these new strategies (action research, grounded theory and narrative inquiry) later in this section. As we shall see, these other strategies were designed for a different research focus to that of ethnography. Ethnographers study people in groups, who interact with one another and share the same space, whether this is at street level, within a work group, in an organisation or within a society. Conflict about how best to achieve this focus led to a range of ethnographic strategies of which Cunliffe (2010) outlines three: Realist Ethnography, Impressionist or Interpretive Ethnography and Critical Ethnography.

Realist ethnography is the closest to the ethnographic strategy described earlier. The realist ethnographer believes in objectivity, factual reporting and identifying 'true' meanings. She or he will report the situation observed through 'facts' or data about structures and processes, practices and customs, routines and norms, artefacts and symbols. Such reporting is likely to use standardised categories that produce quantitative data from observations. The realist ethnographer will write up her or his account in the third person, portraying their role as the impersonal reporter of 'facts'. This account will present a detailed contextual background and the nature of the cultural interactions observed, and identify patterns of behaviour and social processes. It will use edited quotations in a dispassionate way without personal bias or seeking to act as an agent for change. The realist ethnographer's final written account is his or her representation of what he or she has observed and heard.

In contrast, **interpretive ethnography** places much greater stress on subjective impressions than on perceived objectivity. The interpretive ethnographer believes in the likelihood of multiple meanings rather than being able to identify a single, true meaning. Multiple meanings will be located in the socially constructed interpretations of the different participants. This suggests a more pluralistic approach, in which the interpretive ethnographer focuses on understanding meanings, with those being observed treated as participants rather than subjects. This requires an ethnographic researcher to engage in continuous reflexivity to try to ensure reliability/dependability and validity/credibility/transferability in this research process (Delamont 2007) (Section 5.11). The research report will reflect the participation of both the ethnographer (writing in the first person, editing herself into the text, rather than out of it) and those being observed, through devices such as personalisation, use of dialogue and quotations, dramatisation and presentation of different perspectives as well as contextualisation, orderly and progressive description, factual reporting, analysis and evaluation.

Critical ethnography has a radical purpose, designed to explore and explain the impact of power, privilege and authority on those who are subject to these influences or marginalised by them (Section 5.5). You may therefore ask if it can have any appeal to business and management research that is dependent on achieving organisational access. Critical ethnographers often adopt an advocacy role in their work to try to bring about change. You may be able to adopt a constrained or bounded version of critical ethnography to explore the impact of a problematic issue within an organisation or work group, with a view to advocating internal or external change. Such issue might be concerned with strategy, decision-making procedures, regulation, governance, organisational treatment, reward and promotion, communication and involvement and so forth.

We have partly presented our discussion of ethnography as a developmental account because it would be misleading to suggest that ideas about this strategy are unified. While ethnography is a demanding strategy to use, because you would need to develop some grounding in this approach and because of the time scale and intensity involved, it may be relevant to you. If you are currently working in an organisation, there may be scope to undertake participant observation of your workgroup or another group in the organisation (Chapter 9). Alternatively, where you have recently undertaken a work placement, you will be familiar with the context and complexity of this workplace and you may be able to negotiate access based on your credibility to undertake an ethnographic study related to a work group.

Ethnography is relevant for modern organisations. For example, in market research ethnography is a useful technique when companies wish to gain an in-depth understanding of their markets and the experiences of their consumers (Arnould and Cayla 2015; Cayla and Arnould 2013; IJMR 2007) (Box 5.8). If you are interested in undertaking your research in the field of marketing, the use of an ethnographic research strategy may be relevant to you. Likewise, use of this research strategy may well be relevant in other business and management subject areas.

Being successful with this strategy is likely to include making sure that the scale or scope of your proposed ethnographic research project is achievable. This will relate to your research question and objectives, which you should discuss with your project tutor. When undertaking 'fieldwork' you will need to make detailed notes of everything you observe and spend as much time as you can reflecting on what you have observed. You will also need to make additional notes to elaborate on these and supplement the process of observation, by conducting informal discussions and interviews to explore what you have observed and collect any documentation that supports your data collection (Delamont 2007). This should help you to collect a sufficient set of data to analyse to answer your research question and fulfil your objectives.

Where an ethnographic strategy is appropriate to you and proves to be feasible (Sections 6.2– 6.4), you will need to consider which ethnographic approach relates to the nature of your research question. You should then be in position to build trust and commence fieldwork to be able to undertake this approach successfully.

Action Research

Lewin first used the term **Action Research** in 1946. It has been interpreted subsequently by management researchers in a variety of ways, but a number of common and related themes have been identified within the literature. In essence, Action Research is an

Box 5.8
Focus on management research

How commercial organisations use ethnography and videography to undertake market research

Arnould and Cayla (2015) examine how commercial organisations use ethnography and videography to undertake market research in an article published in *Organization Studies.* They state that market research is the most important way in which organisations gain information about their consumers and that commercial ethnography is increasingly being used by companies to allow them to learn about their customers.

Arnould and Cayla conducted semi-structured interviews with 35 participants. The average time to undertake each of these interviews was about one and a half hours. These participants worked either as managers in companies who commissioned ethnographic market research (the commissioning client), or as commercial ethnographers providing this service. Some of these ethnographic researchers were directly employed by a commissioning company, whereas others were external consultants. Arnould and Cayla conducted multiple interviews in the same organisation, where feasible, to gain the perspectives of different stakeholders working together on a market research project involving commercial ethnography.

The aim of Arnould and Cayla's research was to understand how companies use ethnography in strategic marketing decision making. They developed four research questions and interview themes. (1) How do companies use ethnography in marketing decision making? (2) What is the scope of ethnography's application? (3) What are the benefits of using ethnography? (4) What are the challenges of using ethnography, including ethical ones?

This article focuses on the way in which commercial ethnography is used to research profiles of actual consumers, who are seen to represent a market segment, and the implications for organisations of using this approach. This approach involves accompanying a consumer and often video recording their actions and comments. This enables a commercial ethnographer and/or the commissioning client to get to know the consumer by spending time with them, observing them, and talking and listening to them to understand how they feel about and use the product(s) being researched. Using video as part of this process of observing and recording is seen as important and powerful. The use of video recording is widespread because it provides a powerful means to present 'real consumers' and to bring these 'to life' in the edited accounts that are produced from these recorded observations (Arnould and Cayla 2015: 1367).

Arnould and Cayla discuss how the consumer profiles that are constructed as a result of using commercial ethnography can become very influential within organisations. The use of commercial ethnography allows members of organisations to construct representations and images of their customers that are otherwise difficult to imagine. These can lead to the creation of consumer personas, to represent the characteristics of an organisation's typical customer. Such fictionalised personas may be represented in the organisation by images, cardboard cut-outs and narrative descriptions that are used to guide organisational efforts including product development, marketing and sales.

emergent and iterative process of inquiry that is designed to develop solutions to real organisational problems through a participative and collaborative approach, which uses different forms of knowledge, and which will have implications for participants and the organisation beyond the research project (Coghlan 2011; Coghlan and Brannick 2014) (Section 5.5). Our definition identifies five themes, which we briefly consider in the following order: purpose, process, participation, knowledge and implications.

The purpose of an Action Research strategy is to promote organisational learning to produce practical outcomes through identifying issues, planning action, taking action and evaluating action. Coghlan and Brannick (2014: 4) state that Action Research is about 'research in action rather than research about action'. This is because Action Research focuses on 'addressing worthwhile practical purposes' (Reason 2006: 188) and resolving real organisational issues (Shani and Pasmore 1985).

The process of Action Research is both emergent and iterative. An Action Research strategy commences within a specific context and with a research question but because it works through several stages or iterations the focus of the question may change as the research develops. Each stage of the research involves a process of diagnosing or constructing issues, planning action, taking action and evaluating action (Figure 5.5). Diagnosing or constructing issues, sometimes referred to as fact finding and analysis, is undertaken to enable action planning and a decision about the actions to be taken. These are then taken and the actions evaluated (cycle 1). This evaluation provides a direction and focus for the next stage of diagnosing or constructing issues, planning action, taking action and evaluating action (cycle 2), demonstrating the iterative nature of the process. Subsequent cycles (cycle 3 and possibly beyond) involve further diagnosing or constructing of issues, taking into account previous evaluations, planning further actions, taking these actions and evaluating them. In this way, Action Research differs from other research strategies because of its explicit focus on action related to multiple stages, to explore and evaluate solutions to organisational issues and to promote change within the organisation.

Participation is a critical component of Action Research. Greenwood and Levin (2007) emphasise that Action Research is a social process in which an action researcher works with members in an organisation, as a facilitator and teacher, to improve the situation for these participants and their organisation. For Greenwood and Levin, a process can only

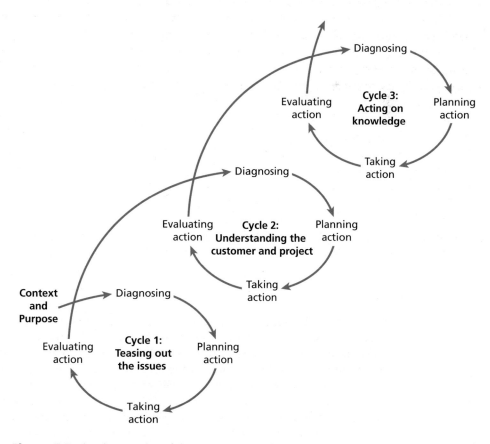

Figure 5.5 The three cycles of the Action Research spiral

be called Action Research if research, action and participation are all present. Participation by organisational members may take a number of forms. Firstly, organisational members need to cooperate with the researcher to allow their existing work practices to be studied. The process of Action Research then requires participation in the form of collaboration through its iterative cycles (as we described earlier) to facilitate the improvement of organisational practices. Collaboration means building a democratic approach to communication and decision making when constructing, planning, taking and evaluating each Action Research stage or cycle. The researcher passes on her or his skills and capabilities to participants so that they effectively become co-researchers in the Action Research process. Without such participation, this approach simply would not be viable, although creating such participation is likely to be difficult in practice and to meet with resistance at various levels (Reason 2006).

How then may this form of participation be developed? Eden and Huxham (1996: 75) argue that the participation of organisational members results from their involvement in 'a matter which is of genuine concern to them'. Schein (1999) emphasises that members of an organisation are more likely to implement change they have helped to create. Once the members of an organisation have identified a need for change and have widely shared this need, it becomes difficult to ignore, and the pressure for change comes from within the organisation. In this way, an Action Research strategy combines both data gathering and the facilitation of change.

The nature of Action Research means that it will also be able to incorporate different forms of knowledge. Action Research will not only be informed by abstract theoretical knowledge, known as propositional knowledge, but also by participants' everyday lived experiences (their experiential knowledge) and knowing-in-action (knowledge that comes from practical application) (Reason 2006). These forms of knowledge will inform and be incorporated into each stage or cycle of the Action Research process, encouraged by the collaborative approach that underpins this strategy. Incorporating these forms leads to 'actionable knowledge' that has the potential to be useful to organisational practitioners as well as being academically robust (Coghlan 2011: 79). Coghlan believes that Action Research not only affects 'what we know' but emphasises understanding of 'how we know'.

Action Research also has implications beyond the research project. Participants in an organisation where action research takes place are likely to have their expectations about future treatment and involvement in decision making raised (Greenwood and Levin 2007). There are also likely to be consequences for organisational development and culture change. Implications from the process may be used to inform other contexts. Academics will use the results from undertaking Action Research to develop theory that can be applied more widely. Consultants will transfer knowledge gained to inform their work in other contexts. Such use of knowledge to inform, we believe, also applies to others undertaking Action Research, such as students undertaking research in their own organisations.

Where you think about using Action Research there will be a number of practical concerns to consider. Identifying an accommodating context, the emergent nature of this strategy, the need to engender participation and collaboration, the researcher's role as facilitator, and the stages or iterations involved are some of the reasons that make Action Research a demanding strategy in terms of the intensity involved and the resources and time required. As we have indicated, Action Research can be suited to part-time students who undertake research in their own organisation. The longitudinal nature of this strategy means that it is more appropriate for medium- or long-term research projects rather than short-term ones. There is the related issue of deciding how many Action Research cycles are sufficient. Where these practical as well as political concerns have been properly anticipated and evaluated in terms of a feasible design, Action Research has the potential to offer a worthwhile and rich experience for those involved.

Grounded Theory

'**Grounded theory**' can be used to refer to a methodology, a method of inquiry and the result of a research process (Bryant and Charmaz 2007; Charmaz 2011; Corbin and Strauss 2008; Walsh et al 2015a). 'Grounded theory methodology' refers to the researcher's choice of this strategy as a way to conduct research. '**Grounded theory method**' refers to the data collection techniques and analytic procedures that it uses (discussed in Chapter 13). 'Grounded theory' may be used loosely to incorporate methodology and method but more specifically it refers to a theory that is grounded in or developed inductively from a set of data. In this section we refer to 'Grounded Theory' (i.e. as a proper noun), to indicate its use as a research strategy and to distinguish this from 'a grounded theory' (no capital letters).

Grounded Theory was developed by Glaser and Strauss (1967) as a response to the 'extreme positivism' of much social research at that time (Suddaby 2006: 633). They disputed the view that social research should use a paradigm based on a premise that theory will reveal a pre-existing reality. In positivism, reality is seen as existing independently and externally (to human cognition). While positivism is suited to research in the natural sciences, they believed that social research should use a different philosophy. By adopting an interpretive approach in social research to explore human experience, 'reality' is seen as being socially constructed through the meanings that social actors ascribe to their experiences and actions. Grounded Theory was therefore developed as a process to analyse, interpret and explain the meanings that social actors construct to make sense of their everyday experiences in specific situations (Charmaz 2014; Glaser and Strauss 1967; Suddaby 2006). We return later in this sub-section to see how this approach has been developed further.

Grounded Theory is used to develop theoretical explanations of social interactions and processes in a wide range of contexts, including business and management. As many aspects of business and management are about people's behaviours, for example consumers' or employees', a Grounded Theory strategy can be used to explore a wide range of business and management issues. As the title of Glaser and Strauss's (1967) book *The Discovery of Grounded Theory* indicates, the aim is to 'discover' or generate theory grounded in the data produced from the accounts of social actors. This inductive, theory-building approach of Grounded Theory illustrates an important difference from the theory-testing approach associated with much previous social research, where hypotheses were deduced from existing theory and tested to confirm, modify or falsify this theory.

Not only did Glaser and Strauss (1967) challenge traditional philosophical assumptions about conducting social research at that time, they also developed a set of principles and guidelines to conduct Grounded Theory. We now outline the key elements of Grounded Theory that date back to *Discovery* to enable you to assess whether it may be appropriate for the nature of your proposed research project, before evaluating its use in practice. Grounded Theory provides you with a systematic and emergent approach to collect and analyse qualitative data. Whereas in quantitative research it is usual to collect a complete set of data and then analyse these, in qualitative data it is often useful to analyse data as you collect them (e.g. you conduct an interview or observation and analyse it before conducting the next one). Grounded Theory is designed to allow you to do this.

Grounded Theory is usually thought of as using an inductive approach, although, as we discuss later, it may be more appropriate to think of it as abductive, moving between induction and deduction (Charmaz 2011; Strauss and Corbin 1998; Suddaby 2006). The researcher starts research by collecting data from an initial interview or observation and then analysing this as close in time to the act of conducting it as is possible and before collecting more data. This is usually referred to as collecting and analysing data simultaneously. The researcher commences analysis by identifying analytical codes that emerge from the data in the interview or observation transcript. Each code will be used to label pieces of data with the same or similar meaning. Coding is therefore the process of labelling related bits of data (such as a line, sentence or paragraph in an interview transcript) using a code that symbolises or summarises the meaning of that data. Coding allows related fragments of data from different interviews or observations to be linked together to facilitate the on-going process of analysis by identifying the properties of the data contained in such a data category (Section 13.9).

In the Grounded Theory strategy of Strauss and Corbin (1998) there are three coding stages: the reorganisation of data into categories is called **open coding**, the process of recognising relationships between categories is referred to as **axial coding** and the integration of categories to produce a theory is labelled **selective coding**. Charmaz's (2014) approach is more flexible, involving two principal coding stages known as **initial coding** and **focused coding**. More recently, Corbin has altered the approach in Corbin and Strauss (2008), with axial coding being combined within open coding and selective coding simply becoming 'integration'. We expand on analytical coding in some detail in Section 13.9; needless to say here that coding is a key element of Grounded Theory. Theory-building during the use of either of these coding approaches requires the sufficient use of the other key elements of Grounded Theory that we now outline (constant comparison, memo writing, theoretical sampling, theoretical sensitivity and theoretical saturation).

Underpinning coding is the process of **constant comparison**. Each item of data collected is compared with others, as well as against the codes being used to categorise data. This is to check for similarities and differences, to promote consistency when coding data and to aid the process of analysis. Where appropriate, new codes are created and existing codes reanalysed as new data are collected. Constant comparison promotes the higher levels of analytical coding we referred to earlier because it involves moving between inductive and deductive thinking. As the researcher codes data into categories, a relationship may begin to suggest itself between specific codes (here, the researcher is using inductive thinking because she or he will be linking specific codes to form a general proposition). This emerging interpretation will need to be 'tested' through collecting data from new cases (here, the researcher will use deductive thinking to 'test' this abstract generalisation back to a new set of specific cases, to see if it stands up as an explanatory relationship to form a higher-level code) (Strauss and Corbin 1998). The process of gaining insights to create new conceptual possibilities which are then examined is termed abduction (Charmaz 2011; Reichertz 2007; Suddaby 2006) (Section 4.4).

Another key element that aids the development of grounded theory is **memo writing** (Section 13.5). Memos are created throughout a research project to define or make notes about:

- the codes being used;
- how codes change through the research process;
- how codes might be related, leading to the identification of theoretical relationships and the emergence of higher-level codes and categories;
- any other ideas that occur to the researcher that help him or her to develop the research process and analyse the data.

Where you use a Grounded Theory strategy, your collection of self-memos will provide you with a chronological record of the development of your ideas and your project, and show how you arrived at your grounded theory.

When using Grounded Theory you will also need to decide how to select cases for your research. As you analyse data, the categories being developed will indicate the type of new cases (e.g. new participants) to select for further data collection. The purpose of sampling is therefore to pursue theoretical lines of enquiry rather than to achieve population representativeness. As you identify a core theme, relationship or process around which to focus the research, a particular focus will be provided from which to select new cases to collect and analyse further data. This is a form of purposive sampling, known as theoretical sampling (Section 7.3), which continues until **theoretical saturation** is reached. This occurs when data collection ceases to reveal any new properties that are relevant to a category, where categories have become well developed and understood and relationships between categories have been verified (Strauss and Corbin 1998). This is also referred to as achieving conceptual density (Glaser 1992) or conceptual saturation (Strauss and Corbin 2008). Using these elements of Grounded Theory means that the process of data collection and analysis becomes increasingly focused, leading to the generation of a contextually based theoretical explanation (Bryant and Charmaz 2007).

Grounded Theory is a useful and widely recognised research strategy and yet it has been the subject of much evaluation, criticism and even misunderstanding (Box 5.9). This is partly due to the development of different approaches to grounded theory method.

Box 5.9
Focus on management research

What is Grounded Theory?

A symposium held to debate the question, "What is Grounded Theory?" is reported in a dedicated section of an issue of *Organizational Research Methods*. Following an Introduction, this section is composed of five related articles that seek to address and debate this question. The first article contains the edited comments of the six panel members who contributed to this symposium (Walsh et al. 2015a). These contributors include Barney Glaser, one of the originators of Grounded Theory. Three further articles form commentaries on the symposium (Corley 2015; Dougherty 2015; Locke 2015). The final article is a rejoinder by the panel members to the three commentaries (Walsh et al. 2015b). Walsh's introductory comments in Walsh et al. (2015a) provide the rationale for this symposium, "In 2006, Suddaby wrote a very interesting piece detailing what Grounded Theory 'is not'. . . . It has now become even more essential and urgent to understand the full reach and scope of Grounded Theory and to clarify what GT 'is' as different applications of GT have led to a rather blurred picture of it."

Walsh says that approaches to Grounded Theory vary from the way in which it was originally conceived, some using all of its methodological elements and

others only using particular elements such as a coding procedure. Variations to Grounded Theory are referred to as remodelling. The original, orthodox version is referred to as 'Classic' Grounded Theory, defined in Holton's comments in Walsh et al. (2015a) as the grounded theory methodology outlined in Glaser and Strauss (1967) and then developed in the subsequent work of Glaser (e.g. 1978, 1992). The scope of this approach is seen to be:

- philosophically flexible; it can be used by either positivist or interpretive researchers;
- a general methodology: it can be used with qualitative or quantitative data, or both, providing that theoretical sampling occurs in its collection;
- one that emphasises the study of a phenomenon in its context over the use of prior existing theory;
- a theory-building method that implies use of an exploratory and inductive data-driven process that may incorporate deduction to build theory.

The debate between the six panel members of this symposium and the authors of the three articles who offered their comments provides further insight into the question, 'What is Grounded Theory.' In seeking to address this question, Locke (2015: 615) points readers interested in developing "a fuller picture of the grounded theory arena [to] consult *Developing Grounded Theory: The Second Generation* (Morse et al 2009) complied by six grounded theory practitioners. . . who apprenticed with Glaser and Strauss. . . and embody the distinctions and tussles that have evolved in the domain."

Glaser and Strauss, who developed Grounded Theory, each went on to develop different approaches to its use. Strauss has become associated with the development of a particularly prescriptive approach to grounded theory method (e.g. Corbin and Strauss 2008; Strauss and Corbin 1998).

A further difference has been revealed by Charmaz (2014), who makes a distinction between 'objectivist grounded theory' and 'constructivist grounded theory'. Charmaz views the approach of Glaser, Strauss and Corbin to grounded theory as being 'objectivist', which assumes that data indicate an external reality, just waiting to be 'discovered'. She considers that 'objectivist grounded theory' has positivist leanings. According to this view, it is only 'constructivist' grounded theory that is truly based on an interpretive approach, because it recognises that the researcher's role in interpreting the data will affect the development of a grounded theory. In this approach, grounded theories are 'constructed', not discovered. This might seem a rather abstract difference, but because Charmaz advocates a 'constructivist' approach she also promotes a more flexible approach to grounded theory method (Section 13.9).

Adopting a Grounded Theory strategy leads to other issues and implications. These concern the collection of data; the use of existing theory; identifying a core category or categories around which to focus the research; the emergence of theory; and the time required to undertake this strategy. We briefly consider each of these.

In Grounded Theory, data collection may start as soon as the research idea has been developed and the initial research participants have agreed to take part (or the first set of documents have been identified). Using this strategy places an obligation on you to make sure you are interested in and committed to your research idea.

There is sometimes confusion about the role of published theory in a Grounded Theory research project (Suddaby 2006; Locke 2015). Grounded Theorists may use published theory before and during their research project. The idea for such a research project may come from existing theory and your understanding of the theoretical background to your research topic may help to inform the project in general terms. Where existing theory should not be allowed to influence the conduct of your Grounded Theory project is in relation to the way you code your data, decide on new cases and conduct your analysis, as we have discussed in this section. Grounded Theory is an emergent strategy and researchers wish to be guided by concepts emerging from the data they collect rather than being sensitised by concepts in existing theory. Using this strategy will mean you should avoid being overly sensitised to pre-existing theoretical concepts, to allow yourself to make sense of participants' meanings in the data to guide your research. This is known as **theoretical sensitivity**, where you focus on interpreting meanings by using *in vivo* and researcher-generated rather than *a priori* codes (explained in Section 13.6) to analyse your data and construct a grounded theory (Glaser 1978). Theoretical sensitivity means that you must be sensitive to meanings in your data and orientated towards generating a grounded theory from these data. You will, however, need to allow yourself sufficient time later on to link your grounded theory to published theories as you write your research report!

Because Grounded Theory is emergent, you will need at some point to identify a core category or categories around which to focus your research and develop a grounded theory to explain the relationships you identify. This will require rigorous use of coding, constant comparison, theoretical sampling, theoretical saturation and theoretical sensitivity to develop a theoretical explanation. Use of this strategy is also associated with a concern that either little of significance will emerge at the end of the research process, or that what emerges is simply descriptive.

Using Grounded Theory is time consuming, intensive and reflective. Before committing yourself to this strategy, you need to consider the time that you have to conduct your research, the level of competence you will need, your access to data, and the logistical implications of immersing yourself in an intensive approach to research. Kenealy (2012) advises novice Grounded Theory researchers to identify one approach to grounded theory method and follow it without too much adaptation. He also advises researchers to focus on identifying 'ideas that fit and work' from their data to develop a grounded theory (Kenealy 2012: 423). Kenealy recognises that using Grounded Theory requires experience but says that the only way to build this is to practise the use of grounded theory method!

In summary, while some Grounded Theory authors produce prescriptive accounts of grounded theory method and others offer more flexible accounts, all appear to be agreed on the key elements we discussed earlier:

- early commencement of data collection;
- concurrent collection and analysis of data;
- developing codes and categories from the data as these are collected and analysed;
- use of constant comparison and writing of self-memos to develop conceptualisation and build a theory;
- use of theoretical sampling and theoretical saturation aimed at building theory rather than achieving (population) representativeness;
- use of an abductive approach that seeks to gain insights to create new conceptual possibilities which are then examined;
- initial use of literature as a complementary source to the categories and concepts emerging in the data, rather than as the source to categorise these data. Later use to review the place of the grounded theory in relation to existing, published theories;
- development of a theory that is grounded in the data.

Narrative Inquiry

A narrative is a story; a personal account which interprets an event or sequence of events (Box 5.8). Using the term 'narrative' requires a distinction to be drawn between its general meaning and the specific meaning used here. A qualitative research interview inevitably involves a participant in storytelling. In this way, the term 'narrative' can be applied generally to describe the nature or outcome of a qualitative interview. As a research strategy, however, **Narrative Inquiry** has a more specific meaning and purpose. There will be research contexts where the researcher believes that the experiences of her or his participants can best be accessed by collecting and analysing these as complete stories, rather than collecting them as bits of data that flow from specific interview questions and which are then fragmented during data analysis. Chase (2011) distinguishes between asking participants to generalise when answering questions in more structured types of qualitative research and being invited to provide a complete narrative of their experience. This contrasts with the approach to Grounded Theory which we discussed earlier.

Narrative Inquiry seeks to preserve chronological connections and the sequencing of events as told by the narrator (participant) to enrich understanding and aid analysis. Chase (2011: 421) refers to this strategy as providing the opportunity to connect events, actions and their consequences over time into a 'meaningful whole'. Through storytelling the narrator will also provide his or her interpretation of these events, allowing the narrative researcher to analyse the meanings which the narrator places on events. Where there is more than one participant providing a personal account of a given context, the narrative researcher will also be able to compare and to triangulate or contrast these narratives.

The depth of this process is also likely to produce 'thick descriptions' of contextual detail and social relations. Gabriel and Griffiths (2004: 114) believe that using this strategy may allow researchers to 'gain access to deeper organisational realities, closely linked to their members' experiences'. A **narrative** may therefore be defined as an account of an experience that is told in a sequenced way, indicating a flow of related events that, taken together, are significant for the narrator and which convey meaning to the researcher (Coffey and Atkinson 1996).

In Narrative Inquiry, the participant is the narrator, with the researcher adopting the role of a listener facilitating the process of narration (Box 5.10). The narrative provided may be a short story about a specific event; a more extended story (for example, about a work project, managing or setting up a business, or an organisational change programme); or a complete life history (e.g. Chase 2011; Maitlis 2012). While in-depth interviews are the primary method to collect stories, other methods may be used by the narrative researcher to record stories as they occur naturally, such as participant observation in the research setting (Coffey and Atkinson 1996; Gabriel and Griffiths 2004). Other sources of narratives include autobiographies, authored biographies, diaries, documentation (see our earlier discussion of this strategy) and informal discussions (Chase 2011; Maitlis 2012). This raises the issue of the Narrative Researcher adopting the role of narrator in particular

Box 5.10
Focus on student research

Using Narrative Inquiry to explore a marketing strategy

Kasia was undertaking a marketing degree and, because of her longstanding interest in fashion and textiles, she hoped to find a job in that sector. Kasia's interests led her to focus her research project on factors that affected the success of marketing strategies in a small sample of fashion companies. After considering her choice of research strategy and discussing this with her project tutor, she decided to adopt a narrative inquiry strategy, using in-depth interviews with senior managers in a sample of carefully selected companies. She negotiated access to conduct interviews with the marketing directors or managers of three medium-sized fashion companies. Kasia realised that the outcome of her research would very much depend on the quality of these three in-depth interviews and the ways in which her interviewees responded to her request to participate in this narrative approach. She decided to send each of these three managers a letter very briefly outlining this approach and a list of the structural elements of narrative inquiry she had read about.

She was nervous going to the first interview and realised that her participant, Hetal, sensed this. Hetal had read Kasia's letter and knew a little about Narrative Inquiry from her own degree studies. Hetal provided Kasia with a full and useful narrative of the factors affecting the outcomes of her employer's marketing strategy over the past year. However, after the interview Kasia realised that she had interrupted Hetal unnecessarily with interview questions on several occasions, interrupting the flow of Hetal's narrative account. Kasia wrote and thanked Hetal for her very useful narrative account and resolved to read more about conducting this type of in-depth interview before conducting the second one. She read Czarniawska's (1997) book, *Narrating the Organization,* and learnt that she would need to move from the interviewer's standard role of asking questions and instead allow her interviewees to act as narrators, using their own voices to tell their stories.

Kasia contacted her next participant and went to the interview with a list of elements and themes in which she was interested but resolved that her second participant, Jorg, should be allowed to use his own voice. Jorg provided Kasia with another full and useful narrative, with Kasia acting as listener rather than traditional interviewer, only seeking clarification occasionally, after explaining the nature and purpose of the process as they started. Kasia left this second interview feeling very pleased and looked forward to the next one.

circumstances, which we will consider further later. It is also important to note that Narrative Inquiry may be used as the sole research strategy, or it may be used in conjunction with another strategy as a complementary approach (Musson 2004).

Narrative Inquiry may be used in different ways. It may be used with a very small number of participants (one, two or three), where these are selected because they are judged as being typical of a much larger culture-sharing population (Chase 2011). As an example, you may decide to interview a small number of accountants or marketing managers who are typical of their occupational population (Box 5.10). It may also be used with a very small sample because those selected are judged as being critical cases or extreme cases, from whom much may be learnt. In this context, in-depth narrative interviews with a small sample of company founders or entrepreneurs may prove to be valuable (Musson 2004). Narrative Inquiry may also be used with slightly larger samples, where, for example, narrative interviews are conducted with, or observations made of, participants from across an organisation, to be able to analyse how narratives are constructed around an event or series of events and to be able to compare how accounts differ, such as between departments, occupational groups, genders and/or grades.

This strategy is generally associated with small, purposive samples (Section 7.3) because of its intensive and time-consuming nature. It is likely to generate large amounts of data in the form of the narrative account, or of interview transcripts or observational notes. The narratives that emerge may not do so in an easy-to-use structural and coherent form (Gabriel and Griffiths 2004). Coffey and Atkinson (1996) recognise this, drawing on previous research to outline the structural elements that are useful to facilitate analysis of narratives:

- What is the story about?
- What happened, to whom, whereabouts and why?
- What consequences arose from this?
- What is the significance of these events?
- What was the final outcome?

To achieve such analytical coherence in a narrative account may involve the narrative researcher in (re)constructing the story from the strands that emerge from conducting one or more in-depth interviews with one participant, or a number of interviews with different participants (Box 5.8). As we recognised earlier, this action places the narrative researcher in a central role in telling the story. Decisions will need to be taken about what to include and what to leave out, and how to connect parts of the account. We consider issues of narrative analysis further in Section 13.10.

Where your research question and objectives suggest the use of an interpretive and qualitative strategy, Narrative Inquiry may be suitable for you to use. Narrative Inquiry will allow you to analyse the linkages, relationships and socially constructed explanations that occur naturally within narrative accounts in order 'to understand the complex processes which people use in making sense of their organisational realities' (Musson 2004: 42). The purpose of Narrative Inquiry is to derive theoretical explanations from narrative accounts while maintaining their integrity. While analysis in Narrative Inquiry does not use the analytical fragmentation of Grounded Theory, neither does it offer a well-developed set of analytical procedures comparable to those used by grounded theorists. Despite this, analytical rigour is still important in order to derive constructs and concepts to develop theoretical explanations. While narrative researchers may believe that predefined analytical procedures are neither advisable nor desirable, this may make the task of analysis more demanding for you. We return in Section 13.10 to consider some of the approaches that narrative researchers have used to analyse their data.

5.9 Choosing a time horizon

An important question to be asked in designing your research is, 'Do I want my research to be a "snapshot" taken at a particular time or do I want it to be more akin to a diary or a series of snapshots and be a representation of events over a given period?' This will, of course, depend on your research question. The 'snapshot' time horizon we call **cross-sectional**, while the 'diary' perspective we call **longitudinal**.

Cross-sectional studies

It is probable that your research will be cross-sectional, involving the study of a particular phenomenon (or phenomena) at a particular time. We say this because we recognise that most research projects undertaken for academic courses are necessarily time constrained. However, the time horizons on many courses do allow sufficient time for a longitudinal study, provided, of course, that you start your research early!

Cross-sectional studies often employ the survey strategy. They may be seeking to describe the incidence of a phenomenon (for example, the IT skills possessed by managers in one organisation at a given point in time) or to explain how factors are related in different organisations (e.g. the relationship between expenditure on customer care training for sales assistants and sales revenue). However, they may also use qualitative or mixed methods research strategies. For example, many case studies are based on interviews conducted over a short period of time.

Longitudinal studies

The main strength of longitudinal research is its capacity to study change and development. This type of study may also provide you with a measure of control over some of the variables being studied. One of the best-known examples of this type of research comes from outside the world of business. It is the long-running UK television series, 'Seven Up'. This has charted the progress of a cohort of people every seven years of their life since 1964 (56 Up, 2012). Not only is this fascinating television, it has also provided the social scientist with a rich source of data on which to test and develop theories of human development.

Even with time constraints it is possible to introduce a longitudinal element to your research. There is a massive amount of published data collected over time just waiting to be reanalysed (as Section 8.2 indicates)! An example is the Edelman Trust Barometer, an annual trust and credibility survey undertaken every year since 2001 (Edelman, 2017). From these surveys you would be able to gain valuable secondary data, which would give you a global measurement of trust across the world and how it is changing with regard to government, businesses, media and non-governmental organisations (NGOs).

5.10 Establishing the ethics of the research design

Research ethics are a critical part of formulating your research design. This is discussed in detail in Chapter 6, which focuses on issues associated with negotiating access and research ethics. In particular, Section 6.5 defines research ethics and discusses why it is crucial to act ethically, and Section 6.6 highlights ethical issues at specific stages, including when designing research and gaining access. Here we introduce two ethical issues that you need to consider when starting to design your research.

Your choice of topic will be governed by ethical considerations. You may be particularly interested to study the consumer decision to buy flower bouquets. Although this may provide some interesting data collection challenges (who buys, for whom and why), there are not the same ethical difficulties as will be involved in studying, say, the funeral purchasing decision. Your research design in this case may have to concentrate on data collection from the undertaker and, possibly, the purchaser at a time as close to the death as delicacy permits. The ideal population, of course, may be the purchaser at a time as near as possible to the death. It is a matter of judgement as to whether the strategy and data collection method(s) suggested by ethical considerations will yield data that are valid. The general ethical issue here is that the research design should not subject those you are researching to the risk of embarrassment, pain, harm or any other material disadvantage.

You may also need to consider whether you should collect data covertly, in other words where those you are researching are unaware they are the subject of research and so have not consented. Beware, although covert research such as undertaking observation in a public place is usually considered acceptable, many university research ethics procedures preclude the use of covert research. Circumstances related to the use of covert observation and issues related to privacy are considered further in Chapters 6 and 9.

5.11 Establishing the quality of the research design

Underpinning our discussion of research design is the issue of the quality of the research and its findings. This is neatly expressed by Raimond (1993: 55) when he subjects findings to the 'how do I know?' test, 'Will the evidence and my conclusions stand up to the closest scrutiny?' For example, how do you know that the advertising campaign for a new product has resulted in enhanced sales? How do you know that manual employees in an electronics factory have more negative feelings towards their employer than their clerical counterparts? The answer, of course, is that, in the literal sense of the question, you cannot know. All you can do is reduce the possibility of getting the answer wrong. This is why good research design is important.

This is aptly summarised by Rogers (1961; cited by Raimond 1993: 55): 'scientific methodology needs to be seen for what it truly is, a way of preventing me from deceiving myself in regard to my creatively formed subjective hunches which have developed out of the relationship between me and my material'.

A split often occurs at this point between positivist and interpretivist researchers. The former will use the 'canons of scientific inquiry' related to reliability and validity to assess the quality of their research or, perhaps more pertinently, that of others. The latter either seek to adapt the terms 'reliability' and 'validity' to assess their research or reject them as inappropriate to interpretivist studies (Guba and Lincoln 1989; Lincoln and Guba 1985; Lincoln et al. 2011). We briefly discuss each of these approaches to establish and assess research quality.

Scientific canons of inquiry: reliability and validity

Reliability and validity are central to judgements about the quality of research in the natural sciences and quantitative research in the social sciences. Their role in relation to qualitative research is contested, as we discuss later. **Reliability** refers to replication and consistency. If a researcher is able to replicate an earlier research design and achieve the same findings, then that research would be seen as being reliable. In essence, **validity** refers to the appropriateness of the measures used, accuracy of the analysis of the results and generalisability of the findings:

1 Do the measures being used in the research to assess the phenomenon being studied actually measure what they are intended to – are they appropriate for their intended purpose?
2 Are the analysis of the results and the relationships being advanced accurate?
3 What do the research findings represent: does the claim about how generalisable they are stand up?

This first aspect of validity is sometimes termed **measurement validity** and is associated with different types of validity designed to assess this intention. These include face validity, construct validity, content validity and predictive validity (which are discussed in Section 11.4). The second aspect of validity refers to internal validity and the third aspect to external validity, both discussed later in this section.

When considering reliability, sometimes a distinction is made between internal reliability and external reliability. Internal reliability refers to ensuring consistency during a research project. This may be achieved, where possible, by using more than one researcher within a research project to conduct interviews or observations and to analyse data to be able to evaluate the extent to which they agree about the data and its analysis. You may seek to ensure consistency through the stages of your research project by writing memos to promote stability in the way you code your data and analyse and interpret it. External reliability refers to whether your data collection techniques and analytic procedures would produce consistent findings if they were repeated by you on another occasion or if they were replicated by a different researcher. Ensuring reliability is not necessarily easy and a number of threats to reliability are described in Table 5.5. Research that is unreliable will also prove to be invalid since any error or bias will affect the results and subsequent interpretation, and possibly cast doubt on the means to measure the phenomenon being studied.

These threats imply that you will need to be methodologically rigorous in the way you devise and carry out your research to seek to avoid threatening the reliability of your

Table 5.5 Threats to reliability

Threat	Definition and explanation
Participant error	Any factor which adversely alters the way in which a participant performs. For example, asking a participant to complete a questionnaire just before a lunch break may affect the way they respond compared to choosing a less sensitive time (i.e. they may not take care and hurry to complete it)
Participant bias	Any factor which induces a false response. For example, conducting an interview in an open space may lead participants to provide falsely positive answers where they fear they are being overheard, rather than retaining their anonymity
Researcher error	Any factor which alters the researcher's interpretation. For example, a researcher may be tired or not sufficiently prepared and misunderstand some of the more subtle meanings of his or her interviewees
Researcher bias	Any factor which induces bias in the researcher's recording of responses. For example, a researcher may allow her or his own subjective view or disposition to get in the way of fairly and accurately recording and interpreting participants' responses

findings and conclusions. More specific advice appears in other chapters but one key aspect is to ensure that your research process is clearly thought through and evaluated and does not contain 'logic leaps and false assumptions'. You will need to report each part of your work in a fully transparent way to allow others to judge for themselves and to replicate your study if they wished to do so.

Reliability is a key characteristic of research quality; however, while it is necessary, it is not sufficient by itself to ensure good-quality research. As indicated earlier, the quality of research depends not only on its reliability but also its validity. Forms of measurement validity are discussed in Section 11.4. **Internal validity** refers to the extent your findings can be attributed to the intervention you are researching rather than to flaws in your research design. For example, in an experiment, internal validity would be established where an intervention can be shown statistically to lead to an outcome rather than this having been caused by some other confounding variable acting at the same time. In a questionnaire-based survey, we usually talk about **criterion validity**, that is whether the questions are actually measuring what they are intended to measure, thereby allowing accurate statistical predictions to be made. (Section 11.3). These concepts are associated with positivist and quantitative research and can be applied to causal or explanatory studies, but not to exploratory or purely descriptive studies.

Your research findings would be seen as invalid when a finding has been arrived at falsely or when a reported relationship is inaccurate. There are a number of reasons that might threaten the internal validity of your research (Cook and Campbell 1979). We offer definitions and examples of the most frequent in Table 5.6. Research that produces

Table 5.6 Threats to internal validity

Threat	Definition and explanation
Past or recent events	An event which changes participants' perceptions. For example, a vehicle maker recalling its cars for safety modifications may affect its customers' views about product quality and have an unforeseen effect on a planned study (unless the objective of the research is to find out about post-product recall opinions)
Testing	The impact of testing on participants' views or actions. For example, informing participants about a research project may alter their work behaviour or responses during the research if they believe it might lead to future consequences for them
Instrumentation	The impact of a change in a research instrument between different stages of a research project affecting the comparability of results. For example, in structured observational research on call centre operations, the definitions of behaviours being observed may be changed between stages of the research, making comparison difficult
Mortality	The impact of participants withdrawing from studies. Often participants leave their job or gain a promotion during a study
Maturation	The impact of a change in participants outside of the influence of the study that affects their attitudes or behaviours etc. For example, management training may make participants revise their responses during a subsequent research stage
Ambiguity about causal direction	Lack of clarity about cause and effect. For example, during a study, it was difficult to say if poor performance ratings were caused by negative attitudes to appraisal or if negative attitudes to appraisal were caused by poor performance ratings

invalid results and conclusions will also adversely affect its reliability since it will be highly unlikely for a subsequent study to find the same false results and statistical relationships.

External validity is concerned with the question: can a study's research findings be generalised to other relevant contexts? For example, a corporate manager may ask, 'Can the findings from the research study in one organisation in our corporation also be used to inform policy and practice in other organisations in the group?' The chief executive of a multinational organisation may ask, 'Are the findings from the survey in the Finance and Resources Department applicable to other departments in the organisation?' Just as researchers take great care when selecting a sample from within a population to make sure that it represents that population, researchers and their clients are often concerned to establish the generalisability of their findings to other contexts. Even in such cases, however, it will be necessary to replicate the study in that other context, or contexts, to be able to establish such statistical generalisability.

Alternative criteria to assess the quality of research design

All researchers take issues of research quality seriously if they wish others to accept their research as credible. However, while types of measurement validity (Section 11.4) are appropriate to assess quantitative research based on positivist assumptions, they are often considered as philosophically and technically inappropriate in relation to qualitative research based on interpretive assumptions, where reality is regarded as being socially constructed and multifaceted. If good-quality research is judged against the criteria of reliability and validity, but these concepts are applied in a rigid way that is inappropriate to qualitative research, it becomes difficult for qualitative researchers to demonstrate that their research is of high quality and credible.

Three types of response to this are evident. Firstly, there are those who continue to use the concepts of reliability and validity, adapting them to qualitative research. Those who adopt this response generally believe that since all research needs to be reliable and valid, using these terms is important to be able to demonstrate the quality and comparable status of qualitative research. As we recognise in Section 10.4, qualitative research is not necessarily intended to be replicated because it will reflect the socially constructed interpretations of participants in a particular setting at the time it is conducted. However, rigorous description of the research design, context and methods may help others to undertake similar studies. Where possible, use of more than one interviewer, observer and data analyst will also improve the quality of the research, referred to as its internal reliability. As we note in Section 10.4, the adaptation of the concept of internal validity to qualitative research is generally not seen as a problem since the in-depth nature of qualitative methods means that the theoretical relationships that are proposed can be shown to be well grounded in a rich collection of data. The adaptation of external validity to qualitative research has been questioned because small samples limit the generalisability of such studies. However, qualitative researchers have pointed to other forms of generalisability that demonstrate the quality and value of qualitative research. For example, findings from one qualitative research setting may lead to generalisations across other settings, where, for example, characteristics of the research setting are similar, or where learning from the research setting can be applied in other settings (Buchanan 2012).

Secondly, there are those who have developed parallel versions of reliability, internal validity and external validity, with distinct names, that recognise the nature of qualitative research. In this regard, Lincoln and Guba (1985) formulated 'dependability' for 'reliability', 'credibility' for 'internal validity' and 'transferability' for 'external validity' (Table 5.7). Thirdly, there are those who have moved further away from the concepts of reliability and validity and have sought to develop new concepts through which to ensure and judge the quality of qualitative research. In this regard, Guba and Lincoln (1989) and Lincoln et al. (2011) have developed 'authenticity criteria' as an alternative to validity (Table 5.7).

A key concern in designing your research will be to familiarise yourself with the criteria to be used to assess your research project. These assessment criteria might state that your research design and report has to consider issues of reliability/dependability and validity/

Table 5.7 Alternative quality criteria

Criterion	Definition and techniques to achieve each criterion
Dependability	This is the parallel criterion to reliability. In interpretivist research, the research focus is likely to be modified as the research progresses. Dependability in this context means recording all of the changes to produce a reliable/dependable account of the emerging research focus that may be understood and evaluated by others
Credibility	This is the parallel criterion to internal validity. Emphasis is placed on ensuring that the representations of the research participants' socially constructed realities actually match what the participants intended. A range of techniques to ensure this match include: • lengthy research involvement to build trust and rapport and to collect sufficient data; • use of reflection using a different person to discuss ideas and test out findings etc.; • developing a thorough analysis that accounts for negative cases by refining the analysis in order to produce the best possible explanation of the phenomenon being studied; • checking data, analysis and interpretations with participants; • making sure that the researchers' preconceived expectations about what the research will reveal are not privileged over the social constructions of the participant by regularly recording these and challenging them during analysis of the data
Transferability	This is the parallel criterion to external validity or generalisability. By providing a full description of the research questions, design, context, findings and interpretations, the researcher provides the reader with the opportunity to judge the transferability of the study to another setting in which the reader is interested to research
Authenticity criteria	These were not conceived as parallel criteria but as criteria that are specifically designed for the nature of constructivist/interpretivist research. Guba and Lincoln (1989) devised 'fairness', 'ontological', 'educative', 'catalytic' and 'tactical' authenticity criteria. These are designed to promote fairness by representing all views in the research; raise awareness and generate learning; and bring about change

Sources: Developed from Guba and Lincoln 1989; Lincoln and Guba 1985; Lincoln et al. 2011

credibility/authenticity. Other assessment criteria will be generic, related to analytical and evaluative abilities, only implicitly recognising the need for reliable/dependable and valid/credible/authentic research in assessing your research design and outcomes. Familiarising yourself with the assessment criteria to be used will help you to decide how you should approach the way you describe and discuss the quality of your research.

Validation

In our discussion about assessing quality and alternative criteria to evaluate it (i.e. reliability/dependability and validity/credibility/authenticity) we have already referred to techniques of validation (e.g. measurement validity, checking data with participants), without using this term. **Validation** is the process of verifying research data, analysis and interpretation to establish their validity/credibility/authenticity. We now discuss two validation techniques which may help you to establish the quality of your research:

- triangulation;
- participant or member validation.

Triangulation involves using more than one source of data and method of collection to confirm the validity/credibility/authenticity of research data, analysis and interpretation. This will necessitate you using a multi-method quantitative study, multi-method qualitative study or a mixed methods study (Sections 5.4 to 5.6). The purpose is to use two or more independent sources of data and methods of collection within one study to ensure that the data are telling you what you think they are telling you. In a research study based on positivist assumptions, this will help to reveal the 'reality' in the data. Interpretivist researchers challenge this outcome as they consider that in relation to studies involving people's beliefs, attitudes and interpretations, 'reality' is socially constructed and multifaceted. For interpretivists, the value of using triangulation is that it adds depth, breadth, complexity and richness to their research (Denzin 2012; Denzin and Lincoln 2018).

Participant or **member validation** involves taking or sending research data back to participants to allow them to confirm its accuracy, by permitting them to comment on and correct it to validate it. This may take the form of showing them interview transcripts, observation or other notes, storied accounts as well as researcher interpretations of participants' data (e.g. Cayla and Arnould 2013). Participant collaboration is essential in some qualitative research strategies such as Action Research, while forms of collaboration such as member validation will be important in other qualitative research strategies and in mixed methods research. While the nature of quantitative data may preclude member validation, where you use a survey strategy you may still find it useful to discuss the results from your quantitative analysis with a sample of your respondents to help you to explain and interpret these data. Member validation may be problematic when a participant wishes to withdraw some of the data shared with you. You will need to differentiate between cases where participants correct your interpretation of the data they shared with you and cases where they simply change their attitude. The latter scenario may relate to an ethical concern and you will need to reflect on the extent to which you should alter the original data (Sections 6.5 and 6.6).

Logic leaps and false assumptions

So far in this chapter we have shown that there are a host of research design decisions to be made in order that your research project can yield sufficient good-quality data. These decisions will necessitate careful thought. Your research design will need to be logical and, along with any assumptions you make, to stand up to careful scrutiny. Raimond (1993: 128) advises you to 'stand back from your research [design] and take a critical, objective view of it, as though you were a detached observer'. This will allow you to see your design as others might, so that you can examine the logic of the research steps you propose to take to see if they will stand up to rigorous scrutiny.

We also considered the issue of false assumptions and claims in the Introduction to Chapter 2 as you think about choosing your research topic and developing your research proposal. Concern about false assumptions and claims will continue to be a major issue as you design your research and then conduct it. Looked at this way, establishing the quality of your research is not an abstract idea but a tangible one that you need to be concerned about throughout your research project.

5.12   Taking into account your role as researcher

This chapter has discussed the decisions you will need to take to formulate your research design. You need to choose between quantitative, qualitative or mixed methods; between research strategies; and between time frames. Each decision will have implications for the nature of your design (between an exploratory, descriptive, explanatory or evaluative purpose, or some combination of these). Each decision also has implications for the ways in which you seek to establish a quality research design that is ethical. As you have read through this chapter, you have probably been evaluating each of these decisions in relation to practical constraints as well as personal preferences. We have alluded to practical constraints in a number of places in the chapter in terms of the way they may affect each choice. An important practical consideration in deciding how to formulate a research design is related to your role as researcher.

The role of the external researcher

If you are a full-time student, you are likely to adopt the role of an **external researcher**. Where you intend to undertake research in one or a few organisations you will need to negotiate access to the organisation(s) and to those from whom you would like to collect data. Having achieved this you will need to gain their trust so that they will participate meaningfully to allow you to collect these data. You will need to take these practical factors into account when formulating your research question and your research design. Sections 6.2 to 6.4 provide more detail about issues of access that you need to take into account as an external researcher before finalising your research design.

The role of the internal researcher or practitioner researcher

If you are currently working in an organisation, you may choose to undertake your research project within that organisation, adopting the role of an **internal researcher** or **practitioner researcher**. As a part-time student, you will be surrounded by numerous opportunities to pursue business and management research. You are unlikely to encounter one of the most difficult hurdles that an external researcher has to overcome: that of negotiating research access. Indeed, like many people in such a position, you may be asked to research a particular problem by your employer.

As an internal researcher, another advantage for you will be your knowledge of the organisation and all this implies about understanding the complexity of what goes on in that organisation. It will not be necessary to spend a great deal of time 'learning the context' in the same way as an external researcher will need to do. However, this advantage carries with it a significant disadvantage. You need to become conscious of the assumptions and preconceptions that you normally take-for-granted in your workplace. This is an inevitable consequence of knowing the organisation well and can prevent you from exploring issues that would enrich the research.

Familiarity may create other problems for the internal researcher. When we were doing case study work in a manufacturing company, we found it very useful to ask 'basic' questions revealing our ignorance about the industry and the organisation. These 'basic' questions are ones that as a practitioner researcher you would be less likely to ask because you, and your respondents, would feel that you should know the answers already. There is also the problem of status. If you are a junior employee, you may feel that working with more senior colleagues inhibits your interactions as researcher practitioner. The same may be true if you are more senior than your colleagues.

A more practical problem is that of time. Combining two roles at work is obviously very demanding, particularly as it may involve you in much data recording 'after hours'. This activity is hidden from those who determine your workload. They may not appreciate the demands that your researcher role is making on you. For this reason, practitioner researchers may need to negotiate a proportion of their 'work time' to devote to their research. There are no easy answers to these problems. All you can do is be aware of the possible impact on your research of being too close to your research setting.

Tietze (2012) offers some guidance for internal researchers. These include reflecting on your role as internal researcher so that you may recognise how this affects the way you design and conduct your research (where you have scope to influence what you are going to research). The research you undertake and the report you produce of it may have implications for those you work with and you will therefore need to consider the implications of how you research and what you report (Section 6.6). You will need to consider your emotions and to manage these during this process of being an internal researcher. The process of analysing, interpreting and theorising about the research data you collect may have the effect of making 'strange the all-too-familiar' (Tietze 2012: 68) and you will need to cope with the degree of detachment that this may produce as you re-evaluate the way in which you view the organisation.

5.13 Summary

- Research design is the way a research question and objectives are operationalised into a research project. The research design process involves a series of decisions that need to combine into a coherent research project.
- A methodological choice has to be made to use quantitative or qualitative methods, or both, to create a mono method, multi-method or mixed methods research design.
- Methodological choice will be underpinned by your research philosophy and it is important to recognise the associated assumptions and implications of these.
- The focus of your research will be exploratory, descriptive, explanatory, evaluative or a combination of these.
- A decision has to be made to use one or more research strategies, related to the nature of the research question and objectives and to ensure coherence with the other elements of your research design.

- Possible research strategies include: Experiment; Survey; Archival and documentary research; Case study; Ethnography; Action Research; Grounded Theory and Narrative Inquiry.
- Choice of research strategy or strategies will be related to use of an appropriate time horizon.
- Research ethics play a critical part in formulating a research design.
- Establishing the quality of research is also a critical part of formulating a research design. Researchers from different research traditions have developed different criteria to judge and ensure the quality of research.
- Practical considerations will also affect research design, including the role of the researcher.

Self-check questions

Answers to these questions are available at the end of the chapter.

5.1 You wish to study the reasons why car owners join manufacturer-sponsored owners' clubs. You choose to use a qualitative methodology and narrative inquiry research strategy involving unstructured 'discussions' with some members of these owners' clubs. You are asked by a small group of marketing managers to explain why your chosen research design is as valid as using a quantitative methodology and survey strategy that uses a questionnaire. What would be your answer?

5.2 You are working in an organisation that has branches throughout the country. The managing director is mindful of the fact that managers of the branches need to talk over common problems on a regular basis. That is why there have always been monthly meetings. However, she is becoming increasingly concerned that these meetings are not cost-effective. Too many managers see them as an unwelcome intrusion. They feel that their time would be better spent pursuing their principal job objectives. Other managers see it as a 'day off': an opportunity to recharge the batteries.

She has asked you to carry out some research on the cost effectiveness of the monthly meetings. You have defined the research question you are seeking to answer as 'What are the managers' opinions of the value of their monthly meetings?'

Your principal research strategy will be a survey using a questionnaire to all managers who attend the monthly meetings. However, you are keen to triangulate your findings. How might you do this?

5.3 You have started conducting interviews in a university with the non-academic employees (such as administrative and other support staff). The research objective is to establish the extent to which those employees feel a sense of 'belonging' to the university. You have negotiated access to your interviewees through the head of each of the appropriate departments. In each case you have been presented with a list of interviewees.

It soon becomes apparent to you that you are getting a rather rosier picture than you expected. The interviewees are all very positive about their jobs, their managers and the university. This makes you suspicious. Are all the non-academic staff as positive as this? Are you being given only the employees who can be relied on to tell the 'good news'? Have they been 'got at' by their manager?

There is a great risk that your results will not be valid. What can you do?

5.4 You are about to embark on a year-long study of customer service training for sales assistants in two national supermarket companies. The purpose of the research is to compare the way in which the training develops and its effectiveness. What measures would you need to take in the research design stage to ensure that your results were valid?

Review and discussion questions

5.5   Agree with a friend to watch the same television documentary.

    a Does the documentary use quantitative, qualitative or mixed methods?

    b To what extent is the nature of the documentary exploratory, descriptive, explanatory, evaluative or a combination of these?

    c What other observations can you make about the research strategy or strategies the documentary makers have used in their programme?

    Do not forget to make notes regarding your reasons for your answers to each of these questions and to discuss these answers with your friend.

5.6   Use the search facilities of an online database to search for scholarly (peer-reviewed) articles which have used firstly a case study, secondly Action Research and thirdly Experiment research strategy in an area of interest to you. Download a copy of each article. What reasons do the articles' authors give for the choice of strategy?

5.7   Visit the Internet gateway to the European Union website (http://europa.eu/) and click on the link in your own language. Discuss with a friend how you might use the data available via links from this web page in archival research. In particular, you should concentrate on the research questions you might be able to answer using these data to represent part of the reality you would be researching.

Progressing your research project

Deciding on your research design

- Review your research question, research aim and research objectives.
- Based on this review, do your research question, aim, objectives and philosophy support using a mono method (qualitative or quantitative) multi-method (qualitative or quantitative) or mixed methods approach? Make notes as you undertake this evaluation. Reflect on your options and decide which methodological approach is most appropriate in relation to your research question, aim and objectives.
- Based on the decision(s) you have made so far, either (a) choose the research strategy that is suitable for your research, or (b), where you possibly have a choice, including using a combination of strategies, create a shortlist of research strategies which may be appropriate to conduct your research, together with the advantages and disadvantages of each.

- *If you have chosen (a),* search for studies in the literature that are based on the use of your chosen research strategy. Evaluate how the authors of these studies have used this research strategy. Compare this to your proposed use of this research strategy. Identify learning points from these studies for your proposed research. Reflect on your choice of this strategy: confirm and justify that it is an appropriate choice for your research, or re-appraise your choice of research strategy.
- *If you have chosen (b),* set this shortlist aside and search for studies in the literature that are similar to your own. Use these to note which strategies have been used. What explanations do the researchers give for their choice of strategy? Evaluate your shortlist against the notes from your search of studies in the literature. Use this evaluation to decide which strategy or combination of strategies would be most appropriate for your own research.
- Decide on the time frame to conduct your proposed research.
- Ask yourself, 'What practical constraints may affect my choice of proposed research design?'

Use this question to review your decisions above and if necessary make changes. Repeat this step until you are satisfied that your proposed research design is practical.
- Use your draft research design to list (a) potential threats to research quality and (b) ethical issues in your design and make notes about how you propose

to deal with each. Where necessary, make further changes to the decisions in the steps above until you are satisfied with your proposed research design.
- You should now be ready to discuss your proposed research design with your project tutor.
- Use the questions in Box 1.4 to guide your reflective diary entry.

References

56 Up (2012) [DVD] London: Network.

Arnould, E.J. and Cayla, J. (2015) 'Consumer Fetish: Commercial Ethnography and the Sovereign Consumer', *Organization Studies,* Vol. 36, No. 10, pp. 1361–1386.

Bansal, P. and Corley, K. G. (2011) 'The coming of age for qualitative research: Embracing the diversity of qualitative methods', *Academy of Management Review,* Vol. 54, No. 2, pp. 233–237.

Böttger, T., Rudolph, T., Evanschitzky, H. and Pfrang, T. (2017) 'Customer Inspiration: Conceptualization, Scale Development, and Validation', *Journal of Marketing,* Vol. 81, November, pp.116–131.

Bryant, A. and Charmaz, K. (2007) *The Sage Handbook of Grounded Theory.* London: Sage.

Bryman, A. (1998) 'Quantitative and qualitative research strategies in knowing the social world', in T. May and M. Williams (eds), *Knowing the Social World.* Buckingham: Open University Press, pp. 138–157.

Bryman, A. (2006) 'Integrating quantitative and qualitative research: How is it done?', *Qualitative Research,* Vol. 6, No. 1, pp. 97–113.

Buchanan, D.A. (2012) 'Case studies in organizational research', in G. Symon and C. Cassell (eds) *Qualitative Organisational Research Core Methods and Current Challenges.* London: Sage, pp. 351–370.

Cayla, J. and Arnould, E. (2013) 'Ethnographic stories for market learning', *Journal of Marketing,* Vol. 77, July, pp. 1–16.

Charmaz, K. (2011) 'Grounded theory methods in social justice research', in N.K. Denzin and Y.S. Lincoln (eds) *The Sage Handbook of Qualitative Research* (4th edn). London: Sage, pp. 359–380.

Charmaz, K. (2014) *Constructing Grounded Theory* (2nd edn). London: Sage.

Chase, S.E. (2011) 'Narrative Inquiry: Still a field in the making', in N.K. Denzin and Y.S. Lincoln (eds) *The Sage Handbook of Qualitative Research* (4th edn). London: Sage, pp. 421–434.

Coffey, A. and Atkinson, P. (1996) *Making Sense of Qualitative Data.* London: Sage.

Coghlan, D. (2011) 'Action Research: Exploring perspectives on a philosophy of practical knowing', *The Academy of Management Annals,* Vol. 5, No. 1, pp. 53–87.

Coghlan, D. and Brannick, T. (2014) *Doing Action Research in Your Own Organisation* (4th edn). London: Sage.

Cook, T.D. and Campbell, D.T. (1979) *Quasi-experimentation: Design and Analysis Issues for Field Settings.* Chicago: Rand McNally.

Corbin, J. and Strauss, A. (2008) *Basics of Qualitative Research* (3rd edn). London: Sage.

Corley, K.G. (2015) 'A Commentary on "What Grounded Theory Is." Engaging a Phenomenon from the Perspective of Those Living it', *Organizational Research Methods,* Vol. 18, No. 4, pp. 600–605.

Creswell, J.W. (2009) 'Mapping the field of mixed methods research', *Journal of Mixed Methods Research,* Vol. 3, No. 2, pp. 95–108.

Creswell, J.W. and Plano Clark, V.L. (2011) *Designing and Conducting Mixed Methods Research* (2nd edn). Thousand Oaks, CA: Sage.

Cunliffe, A.L. (2010) 'Retelling tales of the field: In search of organisational ethnography 20 years on', *Organizational Research Methods,* Vol. 13, No. 2, pp. 224–239.

Czarniawska, B. (1997) *Narrating the Organization: Dramas of Institutional Identity.* Chicago: University of Chicago Press.

Delamont, S. (2007) 'Ethnography and participant observation', in C. Seale, G. Gobo, J.F. Gubrium and D. Silverman (eds) *Qualitative Research Practice.* London: Sage, pp. 205–217.

Denzin, N.K. (2012) 'Triangulation 2.0', *Journal of Mixed Methods Research,* Vol. 6, No. 2, pp. 80–88.

Denzin, N.K. and Lincoln, Y.S. (2005) *The Sage Handbook of Qualitative Research* (3rd edn). London: Sage.

Denzin, N.K. and Lincoln, Y.S. (2018) *The Sage Handbook of Qualitative Research* (5th edn). London: Sage.

Dion, D. and Borraz, S. (2017) 'Managing Status: How Luxury Brands Shape Class subjectivities in the Service Encounter', *Journal of Marketing,* Vol. 81, September, pp. 67–85.

Dougherty, D. (2015) 'Reflecting on the Reflective Conversation', *Organizational Research Methods,* Vol. 18, No. 4, pp. 606–611.

Dubois, A. and Gadde, L E. (2002) 'Systematic combining: An abductive approach to case research', *Journal of Business Research,* Vol. 55, pp. 553–560.

Edelman (2017) *Edelman Trust Barometer ™ Archive.* Available at https://www.edelman.com/insights/intellectual-property/edelman-trust-barometer-archive/ [Accessed 8 Nov. 2017].

Eden, C. and Huxham, C. (1996) 'Action research for management research', *British Journal of Management,* Vol. 7, No. 1, pp. 75–86.

Eisenhardt, K.M. (1989) 'Building theories from case study research', *Academy of Management Review,* Vol. 14, No. 4, pp. 532–550.

Eisenhardt, K.M. and Graebner, M.E. (2007) 'Theory building from cases: Opportunities and challenges', *Academy of Management Journal,* Vol. 50, No. 1, pp. 25–32.

Flyvberg, B. (2011) 'Case study', in N.K. Denzin and Y.S. Lincoln (eds) *The Sage Handbook of Qualitative Research* (4th edn). London: Sage, pp. 301–316.

Gabriel, Y. and Griffiths, D.S. (2004) 'Stories in organizational research', in C. Cassell and G. Symon (eds) *Essential Guide to Qualitative Methods in Organizational Research.* London: Sage, pp. 114–126.

Geertz, C. (1988) *Works and Lives: The Anthropologist as Author.* Stanford, CA: Stanford University Press.

Glaser, B. and Strauss, A. (1967) *The Discovery of Grounded Theory.* Chicago, IL: Aldine.

Glaser, B.G. (1978) *Theoretical Sensitivity: Advances in the Methodology of Grounded Theory.* Mill Valley, CA: Sociology Press.

Glaser, B.G. (1992) *Basics of Grounded Theory.* Mill Valley, CA: Sociology Press.

Greene, J.C. (2007) *Mixed Methods in Social Inquiry.* San Francisco, CA: Jossey-Bass.

Greene, J.C., Caracelli, V.J. and Graham, W.F. (1989) 'Towards a conceptual framework for mixed-method evaluation designs', *Educational Evaluation and Policy Analysis,* Vol. 11, No. 3, pp. 255–274.

Greenwood, D.J. and Levin. M. (2007) *Introduction to Action Research* (2nd edn). London: Sage.

Guba, E.G. and Lincoln, Y.S. (1989) *Fourth Generation Evaluation.* Newbury Park, CA: Sage.

Hakim, C. (2000) *Research Design: Successful Designs for Social and Economic Research* (2nd edn). London: Routledge.

IJMR (2007) 'Special Issue on Ethnography', *International Journal of Market Research,* Vol. 49, No. 6, pp. 681–778.

Kenealy, G.J.J. (2012) 'Grounded Theory: A theory building approach', in G. Symon and C. Cassell (eds) *Qualitative Organisational Research Core Methods and Current Challenges.* London: Sage, pp. 408–425.

Lee, B. (2012) 'Using documents in organizational research', in G. Symon and C. Cassell (eds) *Qualitative Organisational Research Core Methods and Current Challenges.* London: Sage, pp. 389–407.

Lee, B. and Saunders M. (2017) *Doing Case Study Research for Business and Management Students.* London: Sage.

Lewin, K. (1946) 'Action Research and Minority Problems', *Journal of Social Issues,* Vol. 24, No. 1, pp. 34–46.

Lincoln, Y.S. and Guba, E.G. (1985) *Naturalistic Inquiry.* Beverly Hills, CA: Sage.

Lincoln. Y.S., Lynham S.A. and Guba, E.G. (2018). 'Paradigmatic controversies, contradictions and emerging confluences revisited', in N.K. Denzin and Y.S. Lincoln (eds) *The Sage Handbook of Qualitative Research* (5th edn.). Los Angeles, CA: Sage, pp. 108–150.

Locke, K. (2015) 'Pragmatic Reflections on a Conversation about Grounded Theory in Management and Organization Studies', *Organizational Research Methods,* Vol. 18, No. 4, pp. 612–619.

Maitlis, S. (2012) 'Narrative analysis', in G. Symon and C. Cassell (eds) *Qualitative Organisational Research Core Methods and Current Challenges.* London: Sage, pp. 492–511.

Molina-Azorin, J.F. (2011) 'The use and added value of mixed methods in management research', *Journal of Mixed Methods Research,* Vol. 5, No. 1, pp. 7–24.

Molina-Azorin, J.F., Bergh, D.D., Corley, K.G. and Ketchen, Jr., D.J. (2017) 'Mixed Methods in the Organizational Sciences: Taking Stock and Moving Forward', *Organizational Research Methods,* Vol. 20, No. 2, pp. 179–192.

Morse, J.M., Stern, P.N., Corbin, J., Bowers, B., Charmaz, K. and Clarke, A.E. (2009) *Developing Grounded Theory: The Second Generation,* Walnut Creek, CA: Left Coast Press.

Musson, G. (2004) 'Life histories', in C. Cassell and G. Symon (eds) *Essential Guide to Qualitative Methods in Organizational Research.* London: Sage, pp. 34–46.

Naipaul, V.S. (1989) *A Turn in the South.* London: Penguin.

Nastasi, B.K., Hitchcock, J.H. and Brown, L.M. (2010) 'An inclusive framework for conceptualising mixed methods typologies', in A. Tashakkori and C. Teddlie (eds) *The Sage Handbook of Mixed Methods in Social and Behavioural Research* (2nd edn). Thousand Oaks, CA: Sage.

Prior, L. (2007) 'Documents', in C. Seale, G. Gobo, J.F. Gubrium and D. Silverman (eds) *Qualitative Research Practice.* London: Sage, 345–360.

Raimond, P. (1993) *Management Projects.* London: Chapman & Hall.

Reason, P. (2006) 'Choice and quality in action research practice', *Journal of Management Inquiry,* Vol. 15, No. 2, pp. 187–202.

Reichertz, J. (2007) 'Abduction: The logic of discovery of grounded theory', in A. Bryant and K. Charmaz (eds) *The Sage Handbook of Grounded Theory.* London: Sage.

Ridder, H-G., Hoon, C. and McCandless Baluch, A. (2014) 'Entering a dialogue: Positioning case study findings towards theory', *British Journal of Management,* Vol. 25, No. 2, pp. 373–387.

Ridenour, C.S. and Newman, I. (2008) *Mixed Methods Research: Exploring the Interactive Continuum.* Carbondale, IL: South Illinois University Press.

Rogers, C.R. (1961) *On Becoming a Person.* London: Constable.

Schein, E. (1999) *Process Consultation Revisited: Building the Helping Relationship.* Reading, MA: Addison-Wesley.

Shani, A.B. and Pasmore, W.A. (1985) 'Organization inquiry: Towards a new model of the action research process', in D.D. Warrick (ed.) *Contemporary Organization Development.* Glenview, IL: Scott Foresman, pp. 438–448.

Stake, R.E. (2005) 'Qualitative case studies', in N.K. Denzin and Y.S. Lincoln (eds) *The Sage Handbook of Qualitative Research* (3rd edn). London: Sage, pp. 443–465.

Strauss, A. and Corbin, J. (1998) *Basics of Qualitative Research* (2nd edn). London: Sage.

Suddaby, R. (2006) 'From the editors: What grounded theory is not', *Academy of Management Journal,* Vol. 49, No. 4, pp. 633–642.

Tashakkori, A. and Teddlie, C. (eds) (2010) *The Sage Handbook of Mixed Methods in Social and Behavioural Research* (2nd edn). Thousand Oaks, CA: Sage.

Teddlie, C. and Tashakkori, A. (2009) *Foundations of Mixed Methods Research: Integrating Quantitative and Qualitative Approaches in the Social and Behavioral Sciences.* Thousand Oaks, CA: Sage.

Teddlie, C. and Tashakkori, A. (2011) 'Mixed methods research: Contemporary issues in an emerging field', in N.K. Denzin and Y.S. Lincoln (eds) *The Sage Handbook of Qualitative Research* (4th edn). London: Sage, pp. 285–299.

Tedlock, B. (2005) 'The observation of participation and the emergence of public ethnography', in N.K. Denzin and Y.S. Lincoln (eds) *The Sage Handbook of Qualitative Research* (3rd edn). London: Sage.

Tietze, S. (2012) 'Researching your own organization', in G. Symon and C. Cassell (eds) *Qualitative Organisational Research Core Methods and Current Challenges.* London: Sage, pp. 53–71.

Walsh, I., Holton, J.A., Bailyn, L., Fernandez, Levina, N. and Glaser, B. (2015a) 'What Grounded Theory Is . . . A Critically Reflective Conversation Among Scholars', *Organizational Research Methods,* Vol. 18, No. 4, pp. 581–599.

Walsh, I., Holton, J.A., Bailyn, L., Fernandez, Levina, N. and Glaser, B. (2015b) 'Rejoinder: Moving the Management Field Forward', *Organizational Research Methods,* Vol. 18, No. 4, pp. 620–628.

Wasserstein R.L. and Lazar, N.A. (2016) 'The ASA's statement on p-values: context, process and purpose', *The American Statistician,* Vol. 70, No. 2, pp. 129–133.

Whyte, W.F. (1993) *Street Corner Society: The Social Structure of an Italian Slum* (4th edn). Chicago, IL: University of Chicago Press.

Yin, R.K. (2018) *Case Study Research and Applications: Design and Methods* (6th edn). London: Sage.

Further reading

Charmaz, K. (2014) *Constructing Grounded Theory* (2nd edn). London: Sage. Useful for Grounded Theory strategy.

Coghlan, D. and Brannick, T. (2014) *Doing Action Research in Your Own Organisation* (4th edn). London: Sage. Useful for Action Research strategy.

Cunliffe, A.L. (2010) 'Retelling tales of the field: In search of organisational ethnography 20 years on', *Organizational Research Methods,* Vol. 13, No. 2, pp. 224–239. Useful for organisational ethnography.

deVaus, D.A. (2014) *Surveys in Social Research* (6th edn). Abingdon: Routledge. Useful for survey strategy.

Hakim, C. (2000) *Research Design: Successful Designs for Social and Economic Research* (2nd edn). London: Routledge. Chapter 9 is useful for experiment strategy.

Symon, G. and Cassell, C. (eds) (2012) *Qualitative Organisational Research Core Methods and Current Challenges.* London: Sage. Useful for several research strategies including Action Research, Case study, Documentary Research, Ethnography, Grounded Theory and Narrative Inquiry.

Yin, R.K. (2018) *Case Study Research and Applications: Design and Methods* (6th edn). London: Sage. Useful for case study strategy.

Case 5
The relationship between risk and return in loan decisions at credit unions

Josef is entering the final year of a four-year sandwich programme, reading for a BSc in Banking and Finance. He spent his third year in an internship, gaining work experience in a small credit union (CU) in Wales near to his parents' home. The CU has agreed to Josef volunteering to help in administration when he visits his parents' home during university holidays. Josef has to conduct a research project and chooses the topic of "Risk and return in loan decisions at credit unions". Josef intends to use the small CU as a case study.

Josef has learned about the relationship between risk and return that commercial, high street, retail banks assume when making personal loan decisions, so they vary interest rates according to (i) size of loan vis-à-vis borrower's income, (ii) the security – and concomitant reduction in risk – against which the loan is borrowed such as equity in a house and (iii) the number of defaults on borrowers' previous loans that may indicate increased risk on non-payment of a subsequent loan. Josef knows that as commercial organisations, getting loan decisions right affects banks' ability to attract investors and savers to generate additional funds.

Josef knows that CUs are different from banks as they are mutual organisations that promote self-help within communities through an ethos of thrift by encouraging members to save before borrowing. Josef also knows that the CU where he spent his internship provided financial services to people who were too poor to obtain accounts with high street banks. However, he does not know how those differences affect risk and return policies. Josef applies to his university for ethical approval for his study using the title "Risk and Return in Loan Decisions at Credit Unions: A Case Study". He received permission to collect information through observations, documents and interviewing the CU's paid worker and volunteers.

Josef starts his preparations by writing what he learned about risk and return during his internship. He noted that one way of managing risk is by making people save by purchasing shares in the CU for eight weeks before borrowing. He also recalls a tiered policy of only lending £500 more than savings for first loans, twice the savings for a second loan and a maximum of three multiples of savings for third and subsequent loans. However, he did not see how these policies were linked to dividend payments or to a tale he heard about when someone had defrauded the credit union of £10,000 and disappeared.

Josef surveys the literature on CUs and finds that while Ferguson and McKillop (1997) class all CUs in Britain as broadly identical, Lee and Brierley (2017) propose a three tier classification. Using that classification, Josef decides that the CU that he knows is neither a Version 2 CU with legal authority to offer many financial products, nor a large Version 1 CU, but instead a small

Version 1 CU. He changes the title of his project to "Risk and Return in Loan Decisions at a Small Version 1 credit union".

During his Christmas holiday, Josef returns to Wales. While volunteering, he collects a range of documents including manuals on loan decisions, he observes how people advise members who enquire about loans and he interviews both the paid manager and other volunteers. He starts every interview by asking the interviewee to confirm what Josef thinks he already knows about the CU's policies. He finds the interview with the paid manager both interesting and frustrating. The manager confirms that the CU does not vary its interest rate according to notions of risk and that the dividends paid to members depends on the surplus at the year end, but members are not worried about dividends because the more affluent save with the CU to help others. When Josef asks about the risk of fraud of £10,000, the manager says that will not happen again because the CU now recognises suspicious characters. When Josef prompts the manager about how, he receives only vague answers such as "you just know", or information not in the CU's manuals such as whether someone's relatives lived locally and were CU members, or whether it was the first time of applying for the maximum loan, or whether the reason for the loan could be verified.

Josef shares a house with Briony, a Sociology undergraduate student. Josef tells Briony about the problem of no clear relationship between risk and returns at the small CU and that the manager only seemed to say "you just know whether someone is suspicious" when discussing risk-management. Briony introduces Josef to Polanyi's (1966) concept of tacit knowledge. Josef reads Polanyi's work and understands that while some knowledge may be formalised into codes and explained to others, people possess types of knowledge that entail knowing more than they can tell, so although knowledge is not codified, people may go through a rational, implicit question and answer process to surface concerns based on past experiences.

Josef decides to use template analysis (see Chapter 13 for more details) to interpret the interviews. Josef uses two primary headings in the template; criteria for loan decisions in formal manuals; and informal criteria affecting loan decisions. He finds the latter most interesting. When writing up, he changes his project's title to "The Tacit Knowledge of Credit Union Workers when making loan decisions". He submits his project to his supervisor for initial review. The supervisor thinks that the methodology chapter needs strengthening. He recommends that Josef reads Lee and Saunders' (2017) discussion of emergent case studies. Josef re-writes his methodology chapter to state how he conducted an emergent case study in an iterative way, by continually moving between the research and literature to develop and refine his argument.

References

Ferguson, C. and McKillop, D. (1997) *The Strategic Development of Credit Unions,* Chichester: Wiley.

Lee, B. and Brierley, J.A. (2017) 'UK government policy, credit unions and payday loans', *International Journal of Public Administration,* Volume 40, Issue 4, pp. 348–360.

Lee, B. & Saunders, M.N.K. (2017) *Conducting Case Study Research,* London: Sage.

Polanyi, M. (1966) *The Tacit Dimension,* Chicago: University of Chicago Press.

Questions

1 What methods of data collection did Josef employ?
2 How was Josef's approach to a case study different from a conventional or orthodox approach?
3 Will Josef be able to 'generalise' his findings to other credit unions? Does it matter whether he can or cannot do so?
4 Did Josef apply for ethical approval for his study at the correct point and what should he have done when changing his research question?

Additional case studies relating to material covered in this chapter are available via the book's companion website: **www.pearsoned.co.uk/saunders**.
They are:

- The effectiveness of computer-based training at Falcon Insurance Company.
- Embedded quality at Zarlink Semi-conductor.
- The international marketing management decisions of UK ski tour operators.
- Managing the acquisition from the middle.
- Sangita's career.
- Managers' challenges when dealing with change.

Self-check answers

5.1 You would need to stress here that your principal interest would be in getting a deep understanding of why car owners join manufacturer-sponsored owners' clubs. You would discover why the owners joined these clubs and what they thought of them. In other words, you would establish what you set out to establish and, no doubt, a good deal besides. There is no reason why your discussions with owners should not be as valid as a survey questionnaire. Your initial briefing should be skilful enough to elicit rich responses from your interviewees (Chapter 10) and you may also use prompts to focus on themes that emerge in the narratives of your participants.

Of course, you may alleviate any fears about 'validity' by using a mixed methods research methodology and delivering a questionnaire as well, so that your findings may be triangulated!

5.2 The questionnaire will undoubtedly perform a valuable function in obtaining a comprehensive amount of data that can be compared easily, say, by district or age and gender. However, you would add to the understanding of the problem if you observed managers' meetings. Who does most of the talking? What are the non-verbal behaviour patterns displayed by managers? Who turns up late, or does not turn up at all? You could also consider talking to managers in groups or individually. Your decision here would be whether to talk to them before or after the questionnaire, or both. In addition, you could study the minutes of the meetings to discover who contributed the most. Who initiated the most discussions? What were the attendance patterns?

5.3 There is no easy answer to this question! You have to remember that access to organisations for research is an act of goodwill on the part of managers, and they do like to retain a certain amount of control. Selecting whom researchers may interview is a classic way of managers doing this. If this is the motive of the managers concerned then they are unlikely to let you have free access to their employees.

What you could do is ask to see all the employees in a particular department rather than a sample of employees. Alternatively, you could explain that your research was still uncovering new patterns of information and more interviews were necessary. This way you would penetrate deeper into the core of the employee group and might start seeing those who were rather less positive. All this assumes that you have the time to do this!

You could also be perfectly honest with the managers and confess your concern. If you did a sound job at the start of the research in convincing them that you are purely interested in academic research, and that all data will be anonymous, then you may have less of a problem.

Of course, there is always the possibility that the employees generally are positive and feel as if they really do 'belong'!

5.4 This would be a longitudinal study. Therefore, the potential of some of the threats to internal validity explained in Section 5.8 is greater simply because they have longer to develop. You would need to make sure that most of these threats were controlled as much as possible. For example, you would need to:

- account for the possibility of a major event during the period of the research (wide-scale redundancies, which might affect employee attitudes) in one of the companies but not the other;
- ensure that you used the same data collection devices in both companies;
- be aware of the 'mortality' problem. Some of the sales assistants will leave. You would be advised to replace them with assistants with similar characteristics, as far as possible.

Get ahead using resources on the companion website at:
www.pearsoned.co.uk/saunders.

- Improve your IBM SPSS for Windows research analysis with practice tutorials.
- Save time researching on the Internet with the Smarter Online Searching Guide.
- Test your progress using self-assessment questions.
- Follow live links to useful websites.

Chapter 6

Negotiating access and research ethics

> ## Learning outcomes
>
> By the end of this chapter you should be:
>
> - aware of issues associated with gaining traditional and Internet-mediated access;
> - able to evaluate a range of strategies to help you to gain access to organisations and to individual participants;
> - aware of the importance of research ethics and the need to act ethically;
> - able to anticipate ethical issues at each stage of your research and in relation to particular techniques, and aware of approaches to help you deal with these;
> - aware of the principles of data protection and data management.

6.1 Introduction

Many students want to start their research as soon as they have identified a topic area, forgetting that access and ethics are critical aspects for the success of any research project. Such considerations are equally important whether you are using secondary data (Chapter 8) or collecting primary data through person-to-person, Internet-mediated or questionnaire-based methods (Chapters 9–11). Over the recent past, concerns about the ethics of research practice have grown substantially. Consequently, you need to think carefully about how access can be gained to collect your data, and about possible ethical concerns that could arise through the conduct of your research project. Without paying careful attention to both of these aspects, what seems like a good idea for your research may flounder and prove impractical or problematic once you attempt to undertake it.

Business and management research almost inevitably involves human participants. Ethical concerns are greatest where research involves human participants, irrespective of whether the research is conducted person-to-person. In thinking about undertaking business and management research you need to be aware that universities, as well as an increasing number of organisations, require researchers to obtain formal Research Ethics Committee approval (or a favourable ethical opinion) for their proposed research prior to granting permission to

commence a project. Universities and other organisations help facilitate the process of ethical scrutiny and approval by providing ethical guidelines for researchers to use in developing their research projects. We consider ethical guidelines later but it is worth noting that ethical concerns are crucial throughout your research project, requiring continuous reflection and evaluation, as our opening vignette illustrates.

In this chapter we start by considering types and levels of traditional access and the issues associated with these (Section 6.2). In this section we also explore issues of feasibility and

Judging the ethics of our own behaviour requires careful reflection

We all need to be sensitive about the ethics of our own behaviour. This appears to be the message from the work of Maryam Kouchaki and Francesca Gino (CIPD 2017). Kouchaki and Gino asked the question, why do some individuals repeatedly engage in unethical behaviour, not seeing themselves as behaving badly?

A key finding from their work points to the idea that people may develop what they call 'unethical amnesia'. In this state, people forget their unethical actions in order to continue to feel good about their behaviour. This appears to be related to the psychological state where people may deny their actions or seek to distance themselves from the implications of their behaviour.

Individuals may use a number of strategies to distance themselves from their unethical actions. They may seek to blame others for their behaviour, so that the fault is somehow shifted onto these others. They may seek to minimise the wrong-doing involved in their actions, so that unethical behaviour is somehow trivialised. They may seek to justify the actions they took, so that they re-evaluate their behaviour leading

to a belief that in the circumstances it was okay to do what they did.

Judging the ethical nature of our own behaviour is therefore difficult. What we may find unacceptable in others we may seek to excuse in ourselves. Our quest to achieve our goals, such as undertaking our research, may lead us to act first and only then, if at all, to consider the nature of our actions. The pressures and constraints on researchers mean that they need to reflect carefully on their practices to ensure that the principles of ethical research are upheld, including maintaining integrity, respecting others, avoiding harm, not pressuring participants, adhering to informed consent, ensuring confidentially and anonymity, and practising responsibility in analysing data and reporting findings.

sufficiency in relation to gaining access and the impact of these on the nature and content of your research question and objectives. Section 6.3 examines Internet-mediated access and the issues associated with this. Section 6.4 discusses a number of established strategies to help you gain access to organisations and to your intended participants within these organisations. Section 6.5 provides an overview of research ethics and outlines why it is essential to act ethically. Section 6.6 anticipates the scope for ethical issues to occur during the various stages of your research project and in relation to the use of particular techniques. Section 6.7 introduces principles of data protection and data management, which you will need to consider in order to manage your data ethically.

6.2   Issues associated with gaining traditional access

Your ability to collect your own primary, or obtain secondary, data will depend on gaining access to an appropriate source, or sources where there is a choice. The appropriateness of a source will, of course, depend on your research question, related objectives and research design (Chapter 5). In this discussion about gaining access, it is useful to differentiate between types and levels of access and we now discuss each of these.

We commence by considering types of access. The first type is **traditional access**, which involves face-to-face interactions (to conduct experiments, interviews, focus groups, observations or to deliver questionnaires), telephone conversations (for telephone interviews), correspondence (for postal questionnaires) or visiting data archives (such as record offices or organisational archives, where data are not available online). The second type is **Internet-mediated access**, which involves the use of different computing technologies (e.g. the Web, email, instant messaging, webcams), to gain virtual access to deliver questionnaires, conduct archival research, discussions, experiments or interviews, or to gather secondary data. A variant of this is **intranet-mediated access**, where you seek to gain virtual access (usually as an employee or worker) to an organisation using its intranet.

Even where you attempt to gain Internet-mediated access to conduct your research you may still need to use an element or some elements of traditional access (Box 6.6). We therefore define a further type, **hybrid access**, which combines traditional and Internet-mediated approaches. We focus on traditional access in this section and on Internet, intranet and hybrid types of access in Section 6.3.

Another useful way to differentiate types of access (and therefore to recognise the approach you need) relates to whether you wish to conduct your research in a single organisation or across multiple organisations. For many research projects it will be sufficient to gain access to one organisation to conduct research and collect data. We refer to this as **single-organisation access**. For other research projects, it will be necessary to gain access to a number of organisations in order to be able to conduct research and collect data. We refer to this as **multi-organisation access**. For example, a researcher using a case study strategy may decide to focus their research project in a particular organisation, hoping to be able to negotiate access to intended participants within this single case (Box 5.7). Another researcher also using a case study strategy may decide that her or his research question and objectives requires research to be conducted in multiple case organisations (Section 5.8).

Other research projects will not involve you seeking organisational access. You may wish to collect data directly from individuals with the same role from a large number of organisations, or from people who do not have an organisational affiliation. This may, for example, be the case where you wish to conduct research with small business entrepreneurs, who self-manage and run their own businesses. In some specific research projects you may also wish to gain access to individuals who are notable in their field (such as a retired CEO or business expert) but who do not necessarily have an organisational affiliation. Due to their notability, we refer to this as **elite person access**, distinguishing it from **individual person access** where the individual is not affiliated to an organisation and is not considered to be elite.

Gaining research access to one organisation can be difficult. Gaining access to multiple organisations may be even more difficult, as it will be necessary to repeat the process of negotiating access for each intended organisation where you would like to conduct research. This will obviously also be more time-consuming. Box 6.6 outlines management research that examines issues in gaining access to individuals in multiple organisations to conduct surveys. We discuss strategies to gain access that apply to both single-organisation and multi-organisation research in Section 6.4.

Even where you wish to conduct your research within a single organisation, gaining access to intended participants is still likely to involve you in a multi-faceted process of negotiation across different **levels of access** (physical, continuing and cognitive). The level(s) you require will depend on your research objectives and the depth of access you need to achieve. For example, in some research projects the person you approach to negotiate access to conduct research in an organisation will also be the person you wish to ask to participate in your research. This would be the case where you approach a financial manager in an organisation to ask him or her to take part in a research interview conducted by yourself. However, one of your research objectives may require you to ask members of staff in this finance department to participate in an online survey. In this case you would need to negotiate access not only with the finance manager, but also with the members of staff in this department whom you wish to participate.

Gaining initial entry to an organisation is therefore the first level of traditional access, referred to as **physical access** (Gummesson 2000). However, gaining physical access can be difficult for three important reasons. First, organisations, groups or individuals may not be prepared to engage in additional, voluntary activities because of the time and resources required. Many organisations receive frequent student requests for access and cooperation and would find it impossible to agree to all or even some of these. Second, the request for access and cooperation may fail to interest the **gatekeeper** or **broker** who receives it, and who makes the final decision whether or not to allow the researcher to undertake the research. This may be for a number of reasons, related to:

- a lack of perceived value in relation to the work of the organisation, group or the individual;
- the nature of the topic because of its potential sensitivity, or because of concerns about the confidentiality of the information that would be required;
- perceptions about your credibility and doubts about your competence.

Third, the organisation or group may find itself in a difficult situation owing to external events totally unrelated to any perceptions about the nature of the request or the person making it, so that they have no choice but to refuse access. There may be other, internal reasons for refusing access, known to the organisation, group or individuals concerned. For example, an organisation may be undertaking a strategic review or considering whether to restructure its functions, and therefore be unwilling to allow access to any researcher at such a sensitive time. Even when someone is prepared to offer access, this may be overruled at a higher level in the organisation. For example, there may be issues related to some aspect of organisational politics that lead to a higher level refusal to allow access to any researcher. This may result in a 'false start' and an associated feeling of disappointment (Johnson 1975). Where you are unable to gain this type of access, you will need to find another organisation or group, or to modify your research question and objectives.

However, even when you are able to negotiate physical access or entry there are other levels of access that you will need to consider and plan for if your research strategy is to be realised. Many writers see access as a **continuing** process and not just a single event (Gummesson 2000; Marshall and Rossman 2016; Okumus et al. 2007). This may take two forms. First, access may be an iterative and incremental process, so that you gain entry to carry out the initial part of your research and then seek further access in order to conduct another part (see Box 6.1).

Second, those from whom you wish to collect data may be a different set of people to those who agreed to your request for access. Physical access to an organisation will be granted formally through its management. Because of this, it will also be necessary for you to gain the acceptance and trust of, as well as consent from, intended participants within the organisation or group in order to gain actual access to the data that they are able to provide. This type of access is referred to as **cognitive access**. Where you achieve this, you will have gained access to the data that you need your intended participants to share with you in order to be able to address your research question and objectives. Simply obtaining physical access to an organisation is highly unlikely to be adequate unless you are also able to negotiate yourself into a position where you can collect data that provide you with participants' accounts (such as from completed questionnaires or interview transcripts) related to your research question and objectives.

Gaining cognitive access to intended participants will ultimately be determined by whether they decide to take part in your research following a request to do so. Whether or not potential research participants agree to a request, for example, to complete a questionnaire or take part in a research interview is the subject of **Leverage-Saliency Theory**, proposed by Groves et al. (2000). This recognises that different people will respond to different levers such as a request to participate in research in different ways, and that the impact of different levers is dependent on this being made salient to them. The key is to understand what encourages people to agree to participate and what discourages them, leading in the latter case to the problem of non-response rates for researchers.

The theory recognises that there are a number of different attributes associated with any request to participate in research, to which intended participants respond in terms of making a decision about whether to take part or not. For example, the topic of the research may be more or less interesting to different potential participants (Groves et al. 2004). The way in which the request to participate in the research is presented is also likely to affect how intended participants respond to this. Other attributes that may affect

Box 6.1
Focus on student research

Negotiating access incrementally

Luc wished to undertake a series of interviews in the departments and sections of a data management company. He initially managed to negotiate access to commence his research in the management systems support department, where he was granted permission to interview a sample of information systems support workers. As a result of conducting these interviews, he was then granted access within the same department to interview a sample of staff in the information technology section. Following the conduct of these interviews, the department's management team agreed to support his attempt to negotiate further access to interview staff in the company's accounting, human resources, marketing and sales departments.

response rates include the offer of incentives to participate, the purpose and use of the research, and the requirements of participating in the research (Groves et al, 2000; Groves et al. 2004; Trussell and Lavrakas 2004).

The importance of this theory is that it does not just focus on being aware of the attributes that affect how different people respond to a request to participate in research. It also helps us to understand the dangers of appealing only to those who are interested in the research topic leading to the possibility of **non-response error**, where non-respondents in the intended sample differ in important ways from those who participate in the research. In this way, non-respondents will represent different characteristics and viewpoints in relation to those who do respond and participate. This is likely to lead to non-response bias, where the research results in biased and therefore unreliable data, even where you are using non-probability sampling (Sections 7.2 and 7.3).

The nature of the access you manage to negotiate will therefore impact on your ability to select a suitable sample of participants, or of secondary data, affecting your attempt to produce reliable and valid data to fulfil your objectives and answer your research question in an unbiased way (Box 6.2). In order to select a suitable sample of, for example, customers, clients or employees you will require access to organisational data, either directly or indirectly, through a request that outlines precisely how you require the sample to be selected (see Chapter 7 for a full discussion of sampling techniques). Where you wish to undertake a longitudinal study using primary data, you will require access to the organisation and your research participants on more than one occasion. The difficulty of obtaining access in relation to these more **intrusive methods** and approaches has been recognised many times in the literature (e.g. Buchanan et al. 2013; Johnson 1975).

Negotiating physical access is therefore likely to be important to gain **personal entry** to one or more organisations (or, in the case of Internet-mediated research, virtual access), being a precursor to developing cognitive access to allow you to collect the necessary data. In this context, there are two general concepts that you may consider, which will help you to evaluate the nature of the access that you will require. These concepts are feasibility and sufficiency. **Feasibility** is concerned with whether it is practicable to negotiate access for your proposed research project. A research proposal may be grand and elegant, but if it is not possible to gain access to data then it will be necessary to revise what is being proposed. Once you have a proposal that you believe will be feasible in general terms, the next point to consider is whether you will be able to gain sufficient access to fulfil all of your research objectives. **Sufficiency** is therefore concerned with the extent to which the access you negotiate will enable your proposed research project to be achieved. You do

Box 6.2
Focus on student research

Gaining access to a suitable sample

Maria wished to discover how component suppliers viewed the just-in-time delivery requirements of large manufacturing organisations that they supplied. Two large manufacturing organisations agreed to introduce her to a sample of their component suppliers, whom Maria could then interview. While undertaking the interviews Maria noted that all of the interviewees' responses were extremely positive about the just-in-time delivery requirements of both large manufacturing organisations. As both manufacturing organisations had selected who would be interviewed, Maria wondered whether these extremely positive responses were typical of all the component suppliers used by these organisations, or whether they were providing an unreliable and untypical picture.

not want to have to say, 'I could achieve research objectives a, b and c but not x, y and z!' Or, perhaps more likely, 'I can achieve research objectives a and b, but now I think about this carefully, I'm going to find it difficult to collect much data for c and x, which will then mean I can't do y and z!' You therefore need to consider fully the nature of the access that you will require and whether you will able to gain sufficient access in practice to fulfil all of your objectives, to answer your research question. These issues of feasibility and sufficiency will be related in practice but it is useful to consider them separately as you formulate your research proposal. Your clarity of thought, which should result from having considered the nature and extent of the access that you require, may also be helpful in persuading organisations or groups to grant entry since they are more likely to be convinced about your credibility and competence.

The issues of feasibility and sufficiency will determine the construction or refinement of your research question and objectives and may sometimes lead to a clash with the hallmarks of good research (e.g. Marshall and Rossman 2016; Sekaran and Bougie 2013). The ways in which these issues may clash with the hallmarks of good research and also affect the practice of research has been recognised by Buchanan et al. (2013: 53–4):

> Fieldwork is permeated with the conflict between what is theoretically desirable on the one hand and what is practically possible on the other. It is desirable to ensure representativeness in the sample, uniformity of interview procedures, adequate data collection across the range of topics to be explored, and so on. But the members of organisations block access to information, constrain the time allowed for interviews, lose your questionnaires, go on holiday, and join other organisations in the middle of your unfinished study. In the conflict between the desirable and the possible, the possible always wins.

This quotation reveals how, even when you consider feasibility and sufficiency carefully, access is still unlikely to be straightforward, requiring persistence and emotional resilience (Peticcia-Harris et al. 2016). However, with careful planning you will be able to anticipate and, hopefully, overcome problems that occur in practice. The extent to which a careful consideration of feasibility will affect the approach that you adopt is made clear by Johnson (1975). He recognises that the reality of undertaking a research project may be to consider where you are likely to be able to gain access and to develop a topic to fit the nature of that access.

Problems of access may also vary with regard to your status relative to the organisations, groups or people you wish to research. We therefore consider further your role as either an external researcher or as an internal researcher. This latter role may involve you adopting the role of participant researcher.

Access issues as an external researcher

If you are approaching one or more organisations or groups where you have little or no prior contact, you will be seeking to act as an **external researcher**. You will need to negotiate access at each level discussed earlier (physical, continuing and cognitive). Operating as an external researcher is likely to pose problems, although it may have some benefits. Your lack of status in relation to an organisation or group in which you wish to conduct research will mean not only that gaining physical access is a major issue to overcome, but also that this concern will remain in relation to negotiating continued and cognitive access (Box 6.3). Goodwill on the part of the organisation or group and its members is something that external researchers have to rely on at each level of access. In this role, you need to remain

Box 6.3
Focus on student research

The impact of a researcher's organisational status

David recalls a case of mistaken identity. His research involved gaining access to several employers' and trade union organisations. Having gained access to the regional office of one such organisation, David read and noted various organisational documents kept there over a period of a few days. During the first day David was located in a large, comfortable room and frequently brought refreshments by the caretaker of the building.

This appeared to David to be very kind treatment. However, David did not know that a rumour had spread among some staff that he was from 'head office' and was there to 'monitor' in some way the work of the office. On attending the second day, David was met by the caretaker and taken to a small, plain room and no more refreshments appeared for the duration of the research visit. The rumour had been corrected!

Of course, this example of the effect of the researcher's (lack of) organisational status is most unfair on the large number of people who treat those who undertake research within their organisation very well in full knowledge of their status. However, it illustrates the way in which some people may react to perceptions about status.

sensitive to the issue of goodwill and seek to foster it at each level. Your ability to demonstrate clearly your research competence and integrity, and in particular your ability to explain your research project clearly and concisely, will also be critical at each level of access. These are key issues of access faced by all external researchers.

Where you are able to demonstrate competence (see Chapters 9–11) and integrity, your role as an external researcher may prove to be beneficial. This is because participants are usually willing to accept you as being objective and without a covert, often organisationally focused agenda. Your gatekeeper can also play an important role by creating awareness of your research, adding credibility by her or his intervention, and introducing you and your research project to the relevant people.

Access issues as an internal researcher or participant researcher

As an organisational employee or group member operating in the role of an **internal researcher** or a **participant researcher**, you are still likely to face problems of access to data, although these may differ compared to those faced by external researchers. As an internal researcher you may still face the problems associated with negotiating physical or continuing access, and may still need to obtain formal approval to undertake research in your organisation or group. In addition, your status in the organisation or group may pose particular problems in relation to cognitive access. This may be related to suspicions about why you are undertaking your research project and the use that will be made of the data, perceptions about the part of the organisation for which you work and your status in relation to those whom you wish to be your research participants. Any such problems may be exacerbated if you are given a project to research, perhaps by your line manager or mentor, where others are aware that this is an issue about which management would like to implement change. This is particularly likely to be the case where resulting change is perceived as being harmful to those whom you would wish to be your research participants. This will not only provide a problem for you in terms of gaining cognitive access but may also suggest ethical concerns as well (which we discuss in Section 6.5). As an internal researcher, you will need to consider these issues and, where appropriate, discuss them with those who provide you with the research project.

6.3   Issues associated with Internet-mediated access

The Internet enables access to research participants and provides a means to conduct research online, although in practice its use may be challenging. It will be challenging where you find it difficult to achieve access to participants online who are suitable for your research and who match the characteristics of your intended sample. This may in turn lead to data quality issues. Use of the Internet to conduct research will also be associated with ethical issues. In this section, we first briefly outline types of research that may be conducted using the Internet and then consider issues associated with Internet-mediated access. We consider ethical issues later in this chapter.

Both quantitative and qualitative data can be collected using the Internet. Web and mobile questionnaires can be accessed through a hyperlink displayed in an email or on a Web page (Section 11.5). Some experiments may be conducted via the Internet. Internet-mediated observation can be conducted, especially in relation to the use of an online ethnographic research strategy (Section 9.5). Interviews or discussion groups may also take place online. These may be text based using instant messaging applications, social networks or emails. They may also be conducted using video-chat and voice call applications such as Skype™ helping to overcome the impersonal nature of a text-based Internet interview (Section 10.10). In addition to data that are created through such online methods, the Internet also provides gateways to existing data sets that are available for secondary analysis (Chapter 8).

Online communities have generated extremely large amounts of material, especially qualitative but also quantitative, which may be accessible to researchers. As these communities organise around an interest or a particular product, service, place or lifestyle, forums and bulletin (message) boards can be used to post messages and create a discussion over time among members. These differ from chat rooms as messages are often longer than one line of text and likely to be archived, at least temporarily. Email lists also allow groups to converse around a subject or subjects of mutual interest. Linked web pages provide online community resources organised by interest, such as for consumer-to-consumer discussion. **Blogs** (web logs) and limited character blogs or tweets are also popular. As a form of online journal or diary, where an individual provides for public consumption a narrative about his or her everyday life, or some aspect of it, blogs provide a commentary on events at an individual, group, organisational or societal level. For example, numerous bloggers comment on political events, often from the perspective of their political beliefs. Others comment on their shopping experiences and offer consumer advice, or on their employment (Schoneboom 2011). Many blogs and bulletin boards are organised through content management systems and, although these can be accessed through specialised blog search engines, the most useful search engines are Google and YouTube (Kozinets 2015).

Internet-mediated access is subject to the same issues that affect traditional access. In some circumstances, issues associated with access may even be exacerbated using Internet-based approaches. While the Internet, and more specifically the use of web links, messaging apps, email, social networks, webcam and web conferencing, may facilitate communication between you and your participants, it will first still be necessary to determine the most suitable way to conduct your research and negotiate access. This will, of course, depend on the nature of your research question and research objectives. In some

Box 6.4
Focus on student research

Where sensitivity and context determined type of access

Sab had a keen interest in IT and thought that he would conduct his research using Internet-mediated access and data collection methods. His research focused on the ways in which senior managers influence board-level strategic decision making. His interest in this topic had developed after a fortuitous conversation with a senior personnel policy manager who worked for a large organisation, who had explained how in some cases strategy formation was influenced by promoting incremental changes rather than trying to bring about a radical change in one movement. This idea interested Sab and he formulated a research project to explore it in a range of organisational contexts. However, the more he thought about it and discussed it with his project tutor the more he realised that he would have to research it using traditional methods.

After negotiating physical access to interview six senior managers who worked in different functional areas in different organisations, he conducted an in-depth, exploratory interview with each one. While conducting these interviews he realised that the value and depth of the data he collected would have been much less if he had tried to conduct these using the Internet. His questioning was shaped by the data each participant shared with him during the interview. Because of the sensitive nature of the topic most of the interviews took the form of discussions, allowing Sab to clarify points and ask for illustrative examples. As each interview progressed, he found that some of his participants were willing to show him quite sensitive documents in the privacy of the interview room (which was the manager's own office). He found that rapport and trust were vital to the conduct of each interview. He also found that conducting an interview at the organisation helped to focus his mind and enhance his understanding of the organisational context. This in turn helped him to make sense of the data his participants shared with him.

Sab concluded that first negotiating physical access and then cognitive access on a person-to-person basis had been the most appropriate strategy to adopt and also the most effective. However, as he had met with each participant and established some rapport and trust, he asked each one if he would be able to email any further questions for clarification. Some agreed but others said that they would prefer to undertake this either by telephone or another face-to-face discussion.

circumstances you may conclude that it is more effective to use traditional access and methods to conduct your research rather than Internet-mediated access and techniques (Box 6.4).

Where you decide to use Internet-mediated techniques, there may be circumstances where it would still be advantageous to negotiate initial, physical access. This is likely to be the case where you require access to an organisation and need to obtain the permission of a broker or gatekeeper to gain access to a sample of organisational members (Box 6.6). Where you are able to negotiate this initial level of access, you may then be able to get the organisation to allow you to advertise your research by email or letter prior to any attempt to conduct research online. Subsequently, you may be able to send an email containing a hyperlink to your questionnaire to an organisation email list which composes your sample (Section 11.5). In this case you will need to ensure that your intended participants are aware of your research, its purpose, how it will be used, its nature and what will be required if they decide to participate in it. Part of the purpose of the email or letter you send to them prior to the attempt to collect data will be to influence their decision positively about whether to take part. This decision is likely to be related to how well you construct this email or letter to explain the purpose, use and nature of your research and the requirements of taking part.

This example highlights how gaining access to an organisation and intended participants within it may involve a hybrid strategy. The value of using a hybrid access strategy may be even greater in circumstances where you wish to:

- achieve multi-organisation access, and need to negotiate access to intended participants within several organisations;
- negotiate continuing access and meet with your organisational broker or gatekeeper and intended participants to develop rapport and demonstrate your competence and establish trust to achieve this.

Where you plan to conduct your research with individuals (individual person access or elite person access) it may be more efficient to use Internet-mediated access than traditional access. You will need to identify an appropriate sample and then to negotiate **virtual access** (the equivalent of physical access) and cognitive access with these intended participants. The ability to identify your sample will be a key determinant of the feasibility of this approach. The choice of this access strategy will also depend on the nature of your research question and research objectives (Box 6.5). Where you find it challenging to identify an appropriate sample yourself (see Section 6.4 and especially the sub-section entitled, Using existing contacts and developing new ones), you may wish to consider using the resources of websites such as 'Call for Participants'. This allows researchers including undergraduate, postgraduate and doctoral students to, "Easily advertise your surveys, interviews, and other research studies to thousands of potential participants around the world for free" (Call for

Box 6.5
Focus on student research

Where topic and strategy determined type of access

Elina's research focused on consumers' purchasing decisions. She was interested in assessing the relative importance of information obtained from online shopping sites and from high street shops in informing purchasing decisions for different product categories. These categories covered all of the products purchased by her age group, such as people on her marketing course.

Elina had formulated a mixed methods research design. She had designed a Web questionnaire that asked respondents to identify actual recent purchasing decisions related to the categories in which she was interested. For each of these, where applicable, she asked questions about the product, the sources of information used to inform the purchase decision and the way in which these sources determined the purchasing decision. Following ethical approval from her university, an email was sent to each person on her course asking for their help and containing a hyperlink to the questionnaire. The questionnaire included a question asking each respondent if they were willing to help further by completing an electronic diary. Those who answered yes were asked to provide their email address so Elina could send them the diary.

Elina emailed the template of the electronic diary to all those willing to help further. She had designed this to allow respondents to record purchasing decisions related to her list of product categories, the sources of information used to inform these purchases and the way in which these sources determined the decision. Respondents returned the diary as an email attachment.

Elina was aware that her request to maintain an electronic diary of influences on purchasing decisions would sensitise respondents to their use of different information sources, so had distributed the questionnaire first. This she felt would help her judge the extent the participant had been sensitised as well as about the relative impact of these different sources.

Her use of an Internet-mediated access strategy proved successful in gaining access to both questionnaire respondents and a group of people who would keep a diary.

Participants 2017). You will need to evaluate whether using this or any other such online platform would enable access to appropriate potential participants.

6.4 Strategies to gain access

This section considers strategies that may help you to obtain physical, virtual, continuing and cognitive access to appropriate data. The applicability of the strategies discussed here to gain access will depend on the nature of your research design and research strategy (Chapter 5). It will also depend on your data collection methods (Chapters 8–11) and your use of traditional or Internet-mediated means to gain access. However, where you wish to gain access to one or more organisations or groups, irrespective of whether you intend to use traditional or Internet-mediated means, or where your research involves human participants, irrespective of whether you wish to observe or interview them or ask them to complete a postal or Internet questionnaire, the strategies discussed here should be applicable. In addition, some of the points that follow will apply to the way in which you construct the pre-survey contact and the written request to complete the questionnaire (Sections 11.5 to 11.6). The applicability of these strategies will also vary in relation to your status as either an internal researcher or an external researcher. Table 6.1 presents the list of strategies that may help you to gain access.

Ensuring familiarity with the organisation or group

Before attempting to gain physical access it is essential that you familiarise yourself fully with the characteristics of the organisation or group. The knowledge you gain will enable you to signal to the gatekeeper that you have thought carefully about your research, as you will be able to provide a credible case to justify your request to grant access to the organisation or group.

Allowing yourself sufficient time

Physical access may take weeks or even months to arrange, and in many cases the time invested will not result in access being granted (Buchanan et al. 2013). An approach to an organisation or group will result in either a reply or no response at all. A politely worded but clearly reasoned refusal at least informs you that access will not be granted. The non-reply situation means that if you wish to pursue the possibility of gaining access you will

Table 6.1 Strategies that may help you to gain access

- Ensuring you are familiar with the organisation or group before making contact
- Allowing yourself sufficient time
- Using existing contacts and developing new ones
- Providing a clear account of the purpose of your research and the type and level of access required
- Overcoming organisational concerns about granting access
- Identifying possible benefits to the organisation of granting you access
- Using suitable language
- Facilitating replies when requesting access
- Developing access incrementally
- Establishing your credibility

need to allow sufficient time before sending further correspondence, emailing or making a follow-up telephone call. Great care must be taken in relation to this type of activity so that no grounds for offence are given. Seeking access to a large, complex organisation, where you do not have existing contacts, may also necessitate several telephone calls to contact the most appropriate person to consider your request for access, or to establish who this will be. You may also consider using email as a way of making contact, although great care needs to be taken given the ease with which emails may be sent 'in all directions'. Care also needs to taken in the composition of any email, as with any phone call or letter.

Gaining physical access to people across a large number of organisations offers additional challenges. Where data will be collected using questionnaires, researchers usually either purchase a list of potential respondents or, alternatively, select them from a volunteer panel (Saunders et al. 2017). However, access in such cases is dependent upon the willingness of potential respondents to take part and, as highlighted in Box 6.6, the accuracy of the purchased list. Consequently, the process of gaining access may well be problematic and involve several stages, for which you need to allow sufficient time.

If you can contact a participant directly, such as a manager, an exchange of correspondence may be sufficient to gain access. Here you should clearly set out what you require from this person and persuade them of the value of your work and your credibility. Even so, you will still need to allow time for your request to be received and considered and an interview meeting to be arranged at a convenient time for your research participant. This may take a number of weeks, and you may have to wait for longer to schedule the actual interview.

Where you are seeking access to conduct a number of interviews, to undertake a questionnaire, to engage in observation or to use secondary data, your request may be passed 'up' the organisation or group for approval and is likely be considered by a number of people. Where you are able to use a known contact in the organisation or group this may help, especially where they are willing to act as a sponsor for your research. Even so, you will still need to allow for this process to take weeks rather than days. Where the organisation or group is prepared to consider granting access, it is likely that you will be asked to attend a meeting to discuss your research. There may also be a period of delay after this stage while the case that you have made for access is evaluated in terms of its implications for the organisation or group, and it may be necessary to make a number of telephone calls or emails to pursue your request politely.

In the situation where your intended participants or respondents are not the same people who grant you physical access, you will need to allow further time to gain their acceptance. This may involve you making **pre-survey contact** by telephoning these people (Section 11.8), engaging in correspondence or holding an explanatory meeting with them (discussed later and Box 6.6). You may well need to allow a couple of weeks or more to establish contact and to secure cooperation, especially given any operational constraints that restrict individuals' availability.

Once you have gained physical access to the organisation or group and to your participants or respondents, you will be concerned with gaining cognitive access. Whichever method you are using to gather data will involve you in a time-consuming process, although some methods will require that more of your time be spent within the organisation or group to understand what is happening. The use of a questionnaire will mean less time spent in the organisation compared with the use of non-standardised interviews, whereas the use of some observation techniques can result in even more time being spent gathering data (Chapter 9). Where you are involved in a situation of continuing access, as outlined in this section, there will also be an issue related to the time that is required to negotiate, or renegotiate, access at each stage. You will need to consider how careful planning may help to minimise the possibility of any 'stop–go' approach to your research activity.

Box 6.6
Focus on management research

Process of gaining access to participants in multiple organisations

In an article in *Human Resource Development Quarterly,* Saunders et al. (2017) examine the problem of gaining access to appropriate, potential participants in multiple organisations. This article focuses on their experiences of conducting large-scale, survey research using Internet questionnaires in two different projects. In each project, criteria were established to define the required characteristics to be a research participant. The client who commissioned these research projects also stipulated that it would be necessary to obtain completed questionnaires from at least one thousand respondents.

Here we focus on their account of undertaking the first of these two research projects. This involved using "a compiled list of contact details for named SME owner/managers purchased from a reputable data list broker" (Saunders et al. 2017: 414).

In this research project, Saunders et al. assumed a response rate of ten percent so they purchased a list of contact details, including names and email addresses, for over ten thousand potential respondents. However, having distributed the link to their questionnaire in emails to these intended respondents, they report that almost five thousand emails were bounced back. In addition, despite having sent two follow-up emails to contactable non-respondents, they had still only received just over five hundred completed questionnaires after one month. They then decided to employ four assistants to telephone non-respondents to invite them to participate. This was not particularly successful and these assistants "quit due to the difficulty in obtaining respondents" (Saunders et al. 2017: 415). Their next strategy to gain access to appropriate respondents was to approach local business networks (Chambers of Commerce). Using this strategy involved traditional, physical access to gain the support of the Chambers of Commerce who agreed to help. They used the researchers' introductory letter to email their members and explain the research purpose and invite them to participate. The letter included assurances about confidentiality and provided a hyperlink to the online questionnaire. Together with a further strategy that involved emailing other appropriate, potential respondents identified from small business directories, they eventually reached their target of one thousand returned questionnaires.

Saunders et al. go on to make recommendations with regard to gaining physical access when undertaking large-scale survey research in multiple organisations. These include:

1 Always check third-party compiled lists and volunteer panels for accuracy, even if purchased from a reputable source.

2 Use pilot testing to establish the likely response rate and likely representativeness of respondents.

3 Log actual and complete returns regularly against sample requirements so that it becomes clear at an early stage that response targets or representativeness are unlikely to be met.

4 Be persistent and follow-up non-respondents and organisations that help in distributing the questionnaire with polite but regular reminders to maximise returns.

5 Have a contingency plan to activate if response rates are lower than expected.

Using existing contacts and developing new ones

Most management and organisational researchers suggest that you are more likely to gain access where you are able to use **existing contacts** (Buchanan et al. 2013; Johnson 1975). Buchanan et al. (2013: 56) say that, 'we have been most successful where we have a friend, relative or student working in the organisation'. We have also found this to be the case. In order to request access we have approached colleagues, present or past students, course advisors, LinkedIn connections or those who are otherwise known to us through our networks. Their knowledge of us means that they can trust our stated intentions and the assurances we give about the use of any data provided. It can also be useful to start a research project by utilising these existing contacts in order to establish a track record that you can refer to in approaches you make to other organisations or groups where you do not have such contacts. This should help your credibility with these new contacts.

Use of known contacts will depend largely on your choice of research strategy, approach to selecting a sample, research question and objectives. It is likely to be easier to use appropriate known contacts in an in-depth study that focuses on a small, purposively selected sample, such as a case study strategy. However, use of known contacts may also be possible in relation to a survey strategy where you have a large number of appropriate connections through your professional and online networks. There will clearly be a high level of convenience in terms of gaining access through contacts that are familiar; however, these contacts may also be cases in other non-probability samples (Section 7.3).

It may be possible for you to use a previous employer or your work placement organisation as the context for your research project. In such cases, you will undoubtedly have made a number of contacts who may be able to be very helpful in terms of cooperating with you and granting access. You may have become interested in a particular topic because of the time that you spent in the organisation. Where this is so, you can spend time reading theoretical work that may be relevant to this topic, then identify a research question and objectives, and plan a research project to pursue your interest within the context of your placement organisation. The combination of genuine interest in the topic and relatively easy access to organisational participants should help towards the production of a good-quality and useful piece of work.

Where you need to develop **new contacts**, there may be several ways of finding these, depending on your research topic. You may consider asking the local branch of an appropriate professional association for the names and contact details of key employees to contact in organisations where it would be suitable for you to conduct research. You could also contact this professional association at national level, where this is more appropriate to your research question and objectives. It might also be appropriate to contact either an employers' association for a particular industry, or a trade union, at local or national level. Alternatively, it might be appropriate for you to contact one or more chambers of commerce (Box 6.6), skills training organisation or other business network. However, you need to be mindful that such associations and organisations are likely to receive literally hundreds of requests from students every year and so may have insufficient time or resources to respond.

You may also consider making a direct approach to an organisation or group in an attempt to identify the appropriate person to contact in relation to a particular research project. This has the advantage of potentially providing access to organisations or groups that you would like to include in your research project; however, great care needs to be exercised at each stage of the process (Box 6.7).

Using the approach outlined in Box 6.7 may result in you obtaining the email addresses of possible organisational 'leads'. In this case you will need to send an email request to each person (Box 6.8). Where you consider this to be appropriate you will, of course, still need to follow the standards of care that you should use for a formal letter. The ease of using email may tempt some to use a lower level of care about the way their written communication is constructed. It may also lead to a temptation to send repeated messages. Use of email is considered later in our discussion about 'netiquette'. From a practical point of view, using this means to make contact may result in a greater danger that the recipient of your email request simply deletes the message! People who receive large numbers of email may cope by deleting any that are not essential. Sending a letter to a potential gatekeeper may result in that person considering your request more carefully.

Box 6.7
Focus on student research

Identifying possible contacts through whom to request access

Andrew identified a number of specific organisations that matched the criteria established for the types of business he wished to include in his research project. Many of these were organisations where he did not have an appropriate contact, or indeed any contact at all. The different types of organisational structure in these organisations added to his difficulties in tracking down the most appropriate employee to contact in order to request access.

Organisations' websites were used to identify the corporate headquarters of each organisation, which was then contacted by telephone. When talking to each organisation, Andrew explained that he was a student and gave the title of his course and the name of his university. He also gave a very brief explanation of his research to the person who answered the telephone. This resulted in him being provided with a telephone number or email address for that part of the organisation the person who answered the telephone thought was appropriate, or being connected directly. Andrew always ended this initial telephone conversation by thanking the person for the help that they had provided.

At the next stage, Andrew again explained that he was a student and gave the title of his course and the name of his university. The purpose of the research was also explained briefly to the personal assistant who inevitably answered the telephone. Andrew asked for the name and email address of the person whom the personal assistant thought would be the most appropriate person to email. In most cases the people to whom he spoke at this stage were helpful and provided some excellent leads.

Sometimes, particularly in relation to complex organisations, Andrew found that he was not talking to someone in the appropriate part of the organisation. He therefore asked the person to help by transferring the telephone call. Sometimes this led to a series of calls to identify the right person. Andrew always remained polite, thanking the person to whom he spoke for her or his help. He always gave his name and that of his university to reduce the risk of appearing to be threatening in any way. It was most important to create a positive attitude in what could be perceived as a tiresome enquiry.

Andrew chose to ask for the name and email address of a hoped-for organisational 'lead'. Using this he could send a written request to this person, which could be considered when it was convenient, rather than attempt to talk to them then, when it might well have not been a good time to make such a request. This process resulted in many successes, and Andrew added a number of good contacts to his previous list. However, the key point to note is the great care that was exercised when using this approach.

Using the type of contact outlined in Box 6.7 may result in identifying the person whom you wish to participate in your research. Alternatively, your reason for making contact with this person may be to ask them to grant you access to others in the organisation or group whom you wish to be your participants, or to secondary data. This type of contact may be the functional manager or director of those staff to whom you would like access. Having identified a gatekeeper you will have to persuade that person about your credibility, overcome any issues that exist about the sensitivity of your research project and demonstrate the potential value of this for the organisation.

Providing a clear account of the purpose and type of access required

Providing a clear account of your requirements will allow your intended participants to be aware of what will be required from them. Asking for access and cooperation without

Box 6.8
Focus on student research

Email requesting access

Annette was undertaking her research project on the use of lean production systems. Having made telephone contact with the Production Controller's personal assistant, she was asked to send an email requesting access (see below).

Unfortunately, Annette relied on her email software's spellcheck to proofread her email. This resulted in the Production Controller receiving an email containing four mistakes:

- the addition of the word 'I' at the end of the first paragraph;
- the phrase 'between 30 minutes and half an hour' instead of 'between 30 minutes and an hour' at the end of the second paragraph;
- two digits being transposed in the mobile telephone number at the end of the last paragraph, resulting in it being incorrect;
- the second sentence of the final paragraph being poorly worded.

Not surprisingly, Annette was denied access.

Research Project: The Use of Lean Production Systems

Dear Mr Kolowski

Further to my telephone conversation with your personal assistant, Tom Penny, I would like to meet with you and discuss the use of lean production systems at Manufac PLC. The interview is part of a series I am arranging with a carefully selected sample of production managers for my degree in Business Management at the University of Anytown. I

An outline of my proposed interview structure is attached, although it is not my intention to follow it slavishly. I am hoping to conduct these interviews in January and February and envisage that they will last between 30 minutes and half an hour.

I am fully aware of the need to treat the data you give me with the utmost confidentiality. No source, individual or organisational, will be identified or comment attributed without written permission of the originator.

One of my intended outputs will be a report summarising the findings and I will be sending a copy of this to each of the participants in the study.

I hope that you are able to help me and would be extremely grateful if you could let me know by replying to this email. As discussed with Tom Penny, I can then contact them to arrange a suitable time and venue at your convenience. If you prefer to talk to me to agree a suitable time and venue, please telephone me on 07987-6543210. If you require further information, please do not hesitate to get in touch.

Yours sincerely,

---

being specific about your requirements will probably lead to a cautious attitude on their part, since the amount of time that could be required might prove to be disruptive. It is also likely to be considered unethical (Section 6.5). Even where the initial contact or request for access involves a telephone call, it is still probably advisable to send an email or letter that outlines your proposed research and requirements (Box 6.8). Your request for access should outline in brief the purpose of your research, how the person being contacted might be able to help, and what is likely to be involved in participating. The success of this request will be helped by the use of short and clear sentences. Its tone should be polite, and it should seek to generate interest on the part of intended respondents. You will need to evaluate whether to send this as an email, email attachment or by post. This may depend on the preference expressed by the person you spoke to during any initial telephone conversation.

Establishing your credibility will be vital in order to gain access. The use of known contacts will mean that you can seek to trade on your existing level of credibility.

However, when you are making contact with a potential participant for the first time, the nature of your approach will be highly significant in terms of beginning to establish credibility – or not doing so! Any request will need to be well presented and demonstrate your clarity of thought and purpose. Any lack of preparation at this stage will be apparent and is likely to reduce the possibility of gaining access. These issues are discussed in more detail in Section 10.4.

Overcoming organisational concerns about granting access

Organisational concerns may be placed into one of three categories. First, concerns about the amount of time or resources that will be involved in the request for access. Your request for access is more likely to be accepted if the amount of time and resources you ask for are kept to a minimum. As a complementary point, Healey (1991) reports earlier work which found that introductory letters (or emails) containing multiple requests are also less likely to be successful. However, while the achievement of access may be more likely to be realised where your demands are kept to a minimum, there is still a need to maintain honesty. For example, where you wish to conduct an interview you may be more likely to gain access if the time requested is kept within reason. Remember, stating falsely that it will last for only a short time and then deliberately exceeding this is very likely to annoy your participant and may prevent you gaining further access.

The second area of concern is related to **sensitivity** about the topic. We have found that organisations are less likely to cooperate where the topic of the research has negative implications. Organisations do not normally wish to present themselves as not performing well in any aspect of their business. In such cases you may be able to highlight a positive approach to the issue by, for example, emphasising that your work will be designed to identify individual and organisational learning in relation to the topic (a positive inference). You should avoid sending any request that appears to concentrate on aspects associated with non-achievement or failure if you are to gain access. Your request for access is more likely to be favourably considered where you are able to outline a research topic that does not appear to be sensitive to the organisation.

The third area of concern is related to the **confidentiality** of the data that would have to be provided and the **anonymity** of the organisation or individual participants. To overcome this concern, you will need to provide clear assurances about these aspects (Box 6.8). When offering these you must be sure that you will be able to keep to your agreement. Strictly, if you have promised confidentiality you should not share your raw data with anyone, not even your project tutor, or present this as it may be recognised or identified. Data remain confidential and you will need to present the analysed results at a sufficient level of generalisation so that identification is not possible. Anonymity ensures that no one will know who participated in your research and that no one is able to identify the source of any response. One advantage of using an introductory email or letter is to give this guarantee in writing at the time of making the request for access, when this issue may be uppermost in the minds of those who will consider your approach. Once initial access has been granted you will need to repeat any assurances about anonymity and confidentiality to your participants as you seek their consent (Section 6.6). You will also need to consider how to maintain these assurances when you write your project report to ensure participants cannot be indirectly identified (Section 14.6). Illustrations of how not to do this are provided in Box 6.18.

Possible benefits to the organisation of granting access

Apart from any general interest that is generated by the subject of your proposed research, you may find that it will be useful to the jobs undertaken by those whom you approach for access. Practitioners often wrestle with the same subjects as researchers and may therefore welcome the opportunity to discuss their own analysis and course of action related to an issue, in a non-threatening, non-judgemental environment. A discussion may allow them to think through an issue and to reflect on the action that they have adopted to manage it. For this reason, in our own interviews with practitioners we are pleased when told that the discussion has been of value to them.

For those who work in organisations where they are perhaps the only subject practitioner, this may be the first time they have had this type of opportunity. You therefore need to consider whether your proposed research topic may provide some advantage to those from whom you wish to gain access, although this does not mean that you should attempt to 'buy' your way in based on some promise about the potential value of your work. Where it is unlikely that your proposed research may assist those whose cooperation you seek, you will need to consider what alternative course of action to take.

Such decisions to participate may be related to **social exchange theory**, where the potential participant evaluates the benefits and costs of taking part. Where the potential benefits are judged to outweigh the costs, potential participants are more likely to take part. This notion of exchange does, however, have consequences. You will need to be well prepared for any research interview that you undertake, for example, as your research participant may otherwise feel 'let down' and regret their decision to take part (Section 10.5).

It may help to offer a summary report of your findings to those who grant access. The intention here would be to provide something of value and to fulfil any expectations about exchange between the provider and receiver of the research data, thereby prompting some of those whom you approach to grant access (Johnson 1975). We believe it is essential that this summary report is designed specifically for those who granted access rather than, say, a copy of the research project you submit to your university. It is also possible that feedback from the organisation about this summary report may help you further with your research.

Where access is granted in return for supplying a report of your findings it may be important to devise a simple 'contract' to make clear what has been agreed. This should state the broad form of the report and the nature and depth of the analysis that you agree to include in it, and how you intend to deal with issues of confidentiality and anonymity. This may vary from a summary report of key findings to a much more in-depth analysis. For this reason it will be important to determine what will be realistic to supply to those who grant you access.

Using suitable language

Some researchers advise against using certain research terms when making an approach to an organisation for access, because these may be perceived as threatening or not interesting to the potential participant. Buchanan et al. (2013: 57) suggest using the phrase 'learn from your experience' in place of research, 'conversation' instead of interview and 'write an account' rather than publish.

Use of language will depend largely on the nature of the people you are contacting. Your language should be appropriate to the person being contacted, without any hint of being patronising, threatening or just boring. Given the vital role of initial telephone conversations, introductory emails or letters, we would suggest allowing adequate time to consider and draft these and using someone to check through your message. (You may find Section 11.7, and in particular Box 11.15, helpful in this process.) Do not forget that you need to engender interest in your research project, and the initial point of contact needs to convey this.

Facilitating replies when requesting access

We have found that the inclusion of a number of different contact methods (telephone, mobile phone, email) in our written requests for access helps to ensure a reply. These may not be suitable in all cases and should be selected to fit the data collection technique you intend to use. Inclusion of a stamped or postage pre-paid (freepost) addressed envelope may also facilitate a reply.

Developing access incrementally

We have already referred to the strategy of achieving access by stages, as a means of overcoming organisational concerns about time-consuming, multiple requests. Johnson (1975) provides an example of developing access on an incremental basis. He used a three-stage strategy to achieve his desired depth of access. The first stage involved a request to conduct interviews. This was the minimum requirement in order to commence his research. The next stage involved negotiating access to undertake observation. The final stage was in effect an extension to the second stage and involved gaining permission to audio-record the interactions being observed.

There are potentially a number of advantages related to the use of this strategy. As suggested earlier, a request to an organisation for multiple access may be sufficient to cause them to decline entry. Using an incremental strategy at least gains you access to a certain level of data. This strategy will also allow you the opportunity to develop a positive relationship with those who are prepared to grant initial access of a restricted nature. As you establish your credibility, you can develop the possibility of achieving a fuller level of access. A further advantage may follow from the opportunity that you have to design your request for further access specifically to the situation and in relation to opportunities that may become apparent from your initial level of access. On the other hand, this incremental process will be time consuming, and you need to consider the amount of time that you will have for your research project before embarking on such a strategy. In addition, it can be argued that it is unethical not to explain your access requirements fully.

Establishing your credibility

In Section 6.2 we differentiated between physical and cognitive access. Just because you have been granted entry into an organisation you will not be able to assume that those whom you wish to interview, observe or answer a questionnaire will be prepared to provide their cooperation. Indeed, assuming that this is going to happen raises an ethical issue that is considered in the next section. Gaining cooperation from intended participants is a matter of developing relationships. This will mean repeating much of the process that you will have used to gain entry into the organisation. You will need to explain the purpose of your research project, state how you believe that they will be able to help your study and provide assurances about confidentiality and anonymity. This may involve emailing or writing to your intended participants, or talking to them individually or in a group. Which of these means you use will depend on your opportunity to make contact with participants, the number of potential participants involved, the nature of the setting and your intended data collection techniques. However, your credibility and the probability of

Box 6.9
Focus on student research

Email request to participate in a focus group

Sara's research project involved her in undertaking a communication audit for an organisation near her university. As part of her research design she had chosen to use mixed method research using focus groups followed by a questionnaire. Those selected to attend the focus groups were invited by individual emails sent jointly from herself and a senior manager within the organisation.

Invitation to Join an Employee Discussion Group

Dear <forename> <family name>

As you have read in the latest edition of *Staff News*, we are undertaking a communications audit. This work is being undertaken on our behalf by Sara Smith from the University of Anytown Business School. In order to explore attitudes held by members of staff we will be holding a series of five discussion groups. Your views are important in order for us to be able to build up a clear picture of employee attitudes about internal communication. The attitudes revealed at these discussion groups will be used to help design a questionnaire emailed to all members of staff.

Each discussion group should last no longer than one hour. Comments made during the discussion group will not be attributable to any individual or that group and will only be used to help designing the questionnaire. The discussion group will be chaired by Sara Smith from the University. On completion of the audit, key results will be communicated to all members of staff in *Staff News*.

The discussion group to which you have been invited will be held on <day> <date> of <month> at <time> in room <number>. Whilst you are under no obligation to attend, we hope you will. If you are unable to attend, please can you click on the reply button. Alternatively you can contact Sara at the University on 01234-567891. This will allow us to invite an appropriate alternative person in your place.

We very much hope that you can attend. If you have any queries or are unable to attend, please let Sara or myself know.

Michaela Munroe   Sara Smith
Director of Personnel   University of Anytown
Ext. 12345   01234-567891

---

individuals' participation are likely to be enhanced if the request for participation is made jointly with a senior person from the organisation (Box 6.9). Where your intended data collection technique may be considered intrusive, you may need to exercise even greater care and take longer to gain acceptance. This might be the case, for example, where you wish to undertake observation (Chapter 9). The extent to which you succeed in gaining cognitive access will depend on this effort.

The strategies that we have outlined to help you to gain access to organisations and to those whom you wish to participate in your research project are summarised as a checklist in Box 6.10.

6.5   Research ethics and why you should act ethically

Defining research ethics

Ethical concerns will emerge as you design and plan your research, seek access to organisations and to individuals, collect, analyse, manage and report your data. In the context of research, **ethics** refer to the standards of behaviour that guide your conduct in relation

Box 6.10
Checklist

To help to gain access

✔ Have you allowed yourself plenty of time for the entire process?

✔ Are you clear about the purpose of your research project?

✔ Are you clear about your requirements when requesting access (at least your initial requirements)?

✔ Can you use existing contacts, at least at the start of your research project, in order to gain access and gather data?

✔ (If you have been employed or on a work placement) Is the organisation an appropriate setting for your research project?

✔ Have you approached appropriate local and/or national employers, or employees, professional or trade bodies to see if they can suggest contacts through whom you might gain access?

✔ Have you considered making a direct approach to an organisation to identify the most appropriate person to contact for access?

✔ Have you identified the most appropriate person and been willing to keep on trying to make contact?

✔ Have you drafted a list of the points you wish to make, including your thanks to those to whom you speak?

✔ Have you considered and thought through how you will address likely organisational concerns such as:
- the amount of time or resources that would be involved on the part of the organisation;
- the sensitivity of your research topic;
- the need for confidentiality and anonymity?

✔ Have you considered the possible benefits for the organisation should access be granted to you, and the offer of a report summarising your findings to enhance your chance of achieving access?

✔ Are you willing to attend a meeting to present and discuss your request for access?

✔ Where your initial request for access involves a telephone conversation, have you followed this with an introductory email or letter to confirm your requirements?

✔ Is the construction, tone and presentation of your introductory email or letter likely to support your request to gain access?

✔ Have you ensured that your use of language is appropriate to the person who receives it without any hint of being patronising, threatening or boring?

✔ Have you considered including a range of contact methods for recipients to use to reply?

✔ Are you prepared to work through organisational gatekeepers in order to gain access to intended participants?

✔ Have you allowed sufficient time to contact intended participants and gain their acceptance once physical access has been granted?

✔ Have you allowed sufficient time within your data collection to gain 'cognitive access' to data?

to the rights of those who become the subject of your work or are affected by it. Standards of behaviour will be guided by a number of influences. The appropriateness or acceptability of a researcher's conduct will be influenced by broader social norms of behaviour. A **social norm** indicates the type of behaviour that a person ought to adopt in a particular situation; however, the norms of behaviour that prevail will in reality allow for a range of ethical positions.

The philosophical foundations of research ethics also illustrate that a researcher's conduct may be open to competing and conflicting ethical positions. Two dominant and conflicting philosophical positions have been identified: deontological and teleological. A **deontological view** is based on following rules to guide researchers' conduct. According to this view, acting outside the rules can never be justified. Where the rules are inadequate or contested, it would be necessary to reappraise and if required amend them. In contrast, the **teleological view** argues that deciding whether an act of conduct is justified or not should be determined by its consequences, not by a set of predetermined rules. This would involve deciding whether the benefits of undertaking an act outweigh the negative consequences from this action. However, it is unlikely that a simple comparison between the benefits to one group and costs to another would provide you with a clear answer to such an ethical dilemma.

Attempts to overcome ethical dilemmas arising from different social norms and conflicting philosophical approaches have resulted in the widespread development of **codes of ethics**. These generally contain a list of principles outlining the nature of ethical research and a statement of ethical standards to accompany these principles that are intended to guide your research conduct. As a member of a university (and where appropriate a professional association) you will be required to abide by such an ethical code or adhere to its ethical guidelines for research. Codes of ethics (Table 6.2) explicitly or implicitly recognise that ethical dilemmas exist and that it will often be necessary to exercise some choice about conduct. For example, the Statement of Ethical Practice produced by British Sociological Association expressly recognises that it is not possible to produce 'a set of recipes' to deal with all ethical dilemmas but that researchers need to exercise choice based on ethical principles and standards (British Sociological Association 2017: 2). The key point is that by producing such ethical principles and standards, researchers and ethical reviewers (discussed shortly) have an ethical basis against which to anticipate issues and risk, and exercise choice to avoid conflict and harm.

The conduct of your research will therefore be guided by your university's code of ethics or ethical guidelines, highlighting what is and what is not considered ethical. This will be helpful and should be followed to ensure that you do not transgress the behavioural norms established by your university or professional association. However, as Bell and Bryman (2007) point out, such codes tend to be written in abstract terms and are designed to prevent misconduct. This means you will need to interpret the principles and standards contained in the code of ethics with care and apply them to the context of your own proposed research project. Table 6.2 provides Internet addresses for a selection of codes of ethics and ethical guidelines, which may be useful for your research.

Table 6.2 Internet addresses for ethical codes, guidelines and statements of research practice

Name	Internet address
Academy of Management's Code of Ethics	http://aom.org/uploadedfiles/about_aom/governance/aom_code_of_ethics.pdf
Academy of Social Sciences' Generic Ethics Principles for Social Science Research	https://www.acss.org.uk/developing-generic-ethics-principles-social-science/
All European Academies (ALLEA) The European Code of Conduct for Research Integrity	https://ec.europa.eu/research/participants/data/ref/h2020/other/hi/h2020-ethics_code-of-conduct_en.pdf
American Psychological Association's Ethical Principles of Psychologists and Code of Conduct	http://www.apa.org/ethics/code/ethics-code-2017.pdf
British Academy of Management's Code of Ethics and Best Practice	https://www.bam.ac.uk/sites/bam.ac.uk/files/The%20British%20Academy%20of%20Management%27s%20Code%20of%20Ethics%20and%20Best%20Practice%20for%20Members.pdf

Name	Internet address
British Psychological Society's Code of Ethics and Conduct	https://www.bps.org.uk/sites/beta.bps.org.uk/files/Policy%20-%20Files/Code%20of%20Ethics%20and%20Conduct%20(2009).pdf
British Psychological Society's Code of Human Research Ethics	https://www.bps.org.uk/sites/beta.bps.org.uk/files/Policy%20-%20Files/Code%20of%20Human%20Research%20Ethics%20(2014).pdf
British Sociological Association's Statement of Ethical Practice	https://www.britsoc.co.uk/media/24310/bsa_statement_of_ethical_practice.pdf
Chartered Association of Business Schools' Ethics Guide Advice and Guidance	https://charteredabs.org/wp-content/uploads/2015/06/Ethics-Guide-2015-Advice-and-Guidance.pdf
Economic and Social Research Council's (ESRC) Framework for Research Ethics (FRE)	http://www.esrc.ac.uk/files/funding/guidance-for-applicants/esrc-framework-for-research-ethics-2015/
European Union's Respect Code of Practice for Socio-Economic Research (The Respect Project)	http://www.respectproject.org/code/respect_code.pdf
Market Research Society's Code of Conduct	https://www.mrs.org.uk/pdf/mrs%20code%20of%20conduct%202014.pdf
Research Councils UK Policy and Guidelines on Governance of Good Research Conduct	http://www.rcuk.ac.uk/documents/reviews/grc/rcukpolicyguidelinesgovernancegoodresearch-conduct-pdf/
Researcher Development Initiative's Research Ethics Guidebook	www.ethicsguidebook.ac.uk
Social Research Association's Ethical Guidelines	http://the-sra.org.uk/wp-content/uploads/ethics03.pdf
UK Data Archive Managing and Sharing Data Best Practice for Researchers	http://www.data-archive.ac.uk/media/2894/managingsharing.pdf
UK Department for Innovation, Universities and Skills' Universal Ethical Code for Scientists	https://www.gov.uk/government/uploads/system/uploads/attachment_data/file/283157/universal-ethical-code-scientists.pdf
UK Research Integrity Office's Code of Practice for Research	http://ukrio.org/wp-content/uploads/UKRIO-Code-of-Practice-for-Research.pdf
Universities UK's The Concordat to Support Research Integrity	http://www.universitiesuk.ac.uk/policy-and-analysis/reports/Documents/2012/the-concordat-to-support-research-integrity.pdf

You should expect to submit your research proposal for ethical review. All students' research will need to comply with a university's code of ethics or ethical guidelines and the principles and standards that it contains. The form of ethical review will depend on the nature of the research being proposed. Ethical review may be conducted by your project tutor or by two or more academic staff using an ethics protocol. You may also be asked to complete an ethical review form. This 'light touch' or 'fast track' review, overseen by your school or faculty ethics committee, is likely to allow non-controversial research proposals that pose minimal risk to participants and others to be considered without too much delay. A full ethical review conducted by your school or faculty ethics committee will be required where proposals raise ethical concerns or are considered to have higher levels of risk. You will need to be aware of potential ethical concerns and risks to those involved as you design your research proposal so that you can seek to avoid them. You should not assume that using particular techniques will reduce the possibility of ethical concerns or risk. While the use of observation or interviews may appear to be more intrusive than designing a questionnaire, it is possible that the latter may raise ethical concerns and risk to participants. It is the nature of the questions that you wish to ask and the nature of your intended participants that may raise ethical concerns rather than the research method that you intend to use.

Research ethics committees fulfil a number of objectives. These may include a proactive role, such as developing an ethical code, and an educational one, such as disseminating advice about conducting research ethically. The primary role of a research ethics committee will be to review all research conducted by those in the institution that involves human participants and personal data. The research ethics committee will be responsible for examining aspects of research quality that relate to ethics; protecting the rights, dignity and welfare of those who participate in this research as well as others who may be affected by it; and considering the safety of researchers. A research ethics committee is therefore responsible for all aspects of ethical review and approval. It is likely to be composed of experienced researchers from a variety of backgrounds, who are able to draw on their range of experience and knowledge of different ethical perspectives to provide advice. It will be expected to act in an impartial and independent way and its independence is likely to be supported by the inclusion of at least one external member, who otherwise has no connection to the institution.

In some cases you may also have to satisfy the requirements of an ethics committee established in your host organisation as well as your university. This may apply where your research is based in the health service. For example, many of our students undertaking research within the UK's National Health Service (NHS) have had to meet the requirements established by their local NHS Trust's ethics committee (Box 6.11). Such a requirement is often time consuming to meet.

Approval of your research proposal should not be interpreted as the end of your consideration of ethical issues (McAreavey and Muir 2011). Consideration of ethical issues should remain at the forefront of your thinking throughout the course of your research project and even beyond it. In Section 6.6 we consider ethical issues that arise at specific stages in the research process. In preparation for this consideration we firstly consider a range of general ethical issues that permeate research and which therefore form the focus of codes of ethical conduct. We also consider a range of general issues that are associated with Internet-mediated research.

General categories of ethical issues and the formulation of principles to recognise and overcome or minimise these

General categories of ethical issues are recognised in codes of ethics. These are ethical issues that occur across many approaches to research. Rather than write highly detailed and prescriptive regulations to anticipate and deal with these for each research approach, codes of ethics instead contain a set of principles that allow researchers to apply these principles to the context of their own research and to that of others. We now consider a number of principles that have been developed to recognise ethical issues that occur across many different approaches to research. These are outlined in Table 6.3.

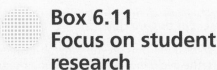

Box 6.11
Focus on student research

Establishing whether research warrants ethical review

Rachel worked for a local hospital. At her first meeting with her project tutor, he had reminded her to check whether she would need to submit her research project to the hospital's research ethics committee (REC) for review. Subsequently, she discussed this with her line manager who suggested she use the UK NHS Health Research Authority's Decision Tool, available online to address this question (Health Research Authority 2017).

The initial webpage of this tool told her that its aim is to help users decide whether their "study is research as defined by the UK Policy Framework for Health and Social Care Research" (Health Research Authority 2017: 1). This tool also allowed Rachel to click through to a webpage that provides clear definitions of what is meant by the terms 'research', 'service evaluation', 'clinical audit' and 'usual practice' in the context of the NHS.

Research is 'the attempt to derive generalisable or transferable new knowledge to answer questions with scientifically sound methods including studies that aim to generate hypotheses as well as studies that aim to test them, in addition to simply descriptive studies'.

Service evaluation is 'designed and conducted solely to define or judge current care'.

Clinical Audit is 'designed and conducted to produce information to inform delivery of best care'.

Usual Practice is 'designed to investigate the health issues in a population in order to improve population health'

(Health Research Authority 2017)

Rachel used the decision-making tool by answering the questions on consecutive web pages. After clicking through these it became evident that her proposed project would be defined as a 'service evaluation'. The policy framework stated that service evaluation "does not require REC review" (Health Research Authority 2017). After using the online tool she returned to discuss this decision with her line manager and later with her project tutor.

Table 6.3 Ethical principles and the ethical rationale for and development of each principle

Ethical principle	Ethical rationale for and development of this principle
Integrity, fairness and open-mindedness of the researcher	The quality of research depends in part on the integrity, fairness and open-mindedness of the researcher. This means acting openly, being truthful and promoting accuracy. Conversely it also means avoiding deception, dishonesty, misrepresentation (of data and findings etc.), partiality, reckless commitments or disingenuous promises. Where appropriate, any conflict of interest or commercial association should be declared
Respect for others	A researcher's position is based on the development of trust and respect. The conduct of research entails social responsibility and obligations to those who participate in or are affected by it. The rights of all persons should be recognised and their dignity respected
Avoidance of harm (non-maleficence)	Any harm to participants must be avoided. Harm may occur through risks to emotional well-being, mental or physical health, or social or group cohesion. It may take a number of forms including embarrassment, stress, discomfort, pain or conflict. It may be caused by using a research method in an intrusive or zealous way that involves mental or social pressure causing anxiety or stress. It may also be caused by violating assurances about confidentiality and anonymity, or through harassment or discrimination

(continued)

Table 6.3 (*Continued*)

Ethical principle	Ethical rationale for and development of this principle
Privacy of those taking part	Privacy is a key principle that links to or underpins several other principles considered here. Respect for others, the avoidance of harm, the voluntary nature of participation, informed consent, ensuring confidentiality and maintaining anonymity, responsibility in the analysis of data and reporting of findings, and compliance in the management of data are all linked to or motivated by the principle of ensuring the privacy of those taking part
Voluntary nature of participation and right to withdraw	The right not to participate in a research project is unchallengeable. This is accompanied by the right not to be harassed to participate. It is also unacceptable to attempt to extend the scope of participation beyond that freely given. Those taking part continue to exercise the right to determine how they will participate in the data collection process, including rights: not to answer any question, or set of questions; not to provide any data requested; to modify the nature of their consent; to withdraw from participation and possibly to withdraw data they have provided
Informed consent of those taking part	The principle of informed consent involves researchers providing sufficient information and assurances about taking part to allow individuals to understand the implications of participation and to reach a fully informed, considered and freely given decision about whether or not to do so, without the exercise of any pressure or coercion. This leads to the right of those taking part to expect the researcher to abide by the extent of the consent given and not to find that the researcher wishes to prolong the duration of an interview or observation, or to widen the scope of the research without first seeking and obtaining permission, or to commit any subsequent breach of the consent given
Ensuring confidentiality of data and maintenance of anonymity of those taking part	Research is designed to answer 'who', 'what', 'when', 'where', 'how' and 'why' questions, not to focus on those who provided the data to answer these. Individuals and organisations should therefore remain anonymous and the data they provide should be processed to make it non-attributable, unless there is an explicit agreement to attribute comments. Harm may result from unauthorised attribution or identification. Reliability of data is also likely to be enhanced where confidentiality and anonymity are assured. This principle leads to the right to expect assurances about anonymity and confidentiality to be observed strictly
Responsibility in the analysis of data and reporting of findings	Assurances about privacy, anonymity and confidentiality must be upheld when analysing and reporting data. Primary data should not be made up or altered and results should not be falsified. Findings should be reported fully and accurately, irrespective of whether they contradict expected outcomes. The same conditions apply to secondary data, the source or sources of which should also be clearly acknowledged. Analyses and the interpretations that follow from these should be checked carefully and corrections made to ensure the accuracy of the research report and any other outcome
Compliance in the management of data	Research is likely to involve the collection of personal data. Many governments have passed legislation to regulate the processing, security and possible sharing of personal data. There is therefore a statutory requirement to comply with such legislation. In the European Union, Directive 95/46/CE and subsequently the General Data Protection Regulation EU2016/679 required member states to pass data protection legislation. Other laws may exist in particular countries relating to the processing, security and possible sharing of data. It will therefore be essential for researchers to understand and comply with the legal restrictions and regulations that relate to the management of research data within the country or countries within which they conduct research

Ethical principle	Ethical rationale for and development of this principle
Ensuring the safety of the researcher	The safety of researchers is a very important consideration when planning and conducting a research project. The Social Research Association's Code of Practice for the Safety of Social Researchers identifies possible risks from social interactions including 'risk of physical threat or abuse; risk of psychological trauma . . . ; risk of being in a compromising situation . . . ; increased exposure to risks of everyday life' (Social Research Association 2001: 1). Research design therefore needs to consider risks to researchers as well as to participants

Notes and Sources: The ethical codes and guidelines listed in Table 6.2 were helpful in informing the contents of this table. Table 6.3 seeks to synthesise key points from many different approaches to writing ethical principles. It should not be interpreted as providing completely comprehensive guidance. You are advised to consult the code of ethics defined as being appropriate for your research project. References to legislation in Table 6.3 and elsewhere provide only general indications and should not be interpreted as providing legal advice, or the existence of such types of law in all countries.

Codes of ethics are intended to avoid poor practice, malpractice and harm (**non-maleficence**) as well as to promote ethical practice and private or public good (**beneficence**). To avoid harm, or at the very least to minimise it, it is necessary to evaluate risk. Evaluating risk involves thinking about the likelihood of harm occurring and the extent or severity of the harm that would be caused. As we indicated in Table 6.3, harm may take a number of forms and lead to a range of consequences. Estimating risk is not straightforward and it may be affected by a number of contextual or cultural factors. However, it is important to anticipate risk in each research situation to attempt to avoid the likelihood of causing harm. Box 6.12 suggests a number of questions that you may ask to seek to assess risk, although others may suggest themselves related to the research context within which you are operating (Section 6.6).

Research may result in benefits for the researcher, research participants, the group or organisation being researched, or for the community or society within which it occurs. As we discussed in Section 6.4, it is important and ethical to be realistic about the benefits you claim for your research project and to honour any promises made about sharing findings, such as promising to send a summary report to an organisation that provides access to host your research. Adopting ethical behaviour means more than just using a code of ethics as a way to get your research proposal approved. Acting ethically means thinking about each aspect and each stage of your research from an ethical perspective. Where you do this, you will have internalised the values of acting ethically and this should help you to anticipate concerns at each stage of your research.

General ethical issues associated with Internet-mediated research

While the Internet may help to facilitate access to some categories of participants and certain types of data, its use raises a number of issues and even dilemmas about the applicability of the ethical principles referred to in Table 6.3 to Internet-mediated research. The ethical issues and dilemmas raised by the use of blogs, bulletin boards, chat rooms, discussion groups, email lists, social media and web pages include the following points:

- *Scope for deception.* Researchers joining online communities with the intention of collecting data rather than participating and seeking consent (known as 'passive analysis' or 'lurking') may be seen as committing a form of deception. Declaring your real intention after a period of 'lurking' is seen by many moderators of online groups as unethical and may increase the chance of you, as a researcher, being asked to leave (Madge 2010).

Box 6.12
Checklist

Assessing risk in research

✔ Is your proposed research likely to harm the well-being of those participating?

✔ Will others be harmed by the process or outcomes of your proposed research?

✔ How may this harm occur and what characteristics may make this more likely?

✔ How likely it is that harm might result?

✔ How severe would be any resulting harm?

✔ Which features or what aspects of your research may cause harm?

✔ How intrusive is your proposed research method or methods?

✔ How sensitive are your proposed questions, observations, searches or requests for data?

✔ Can you justify your choice of research method or methods and tactics; in particular, can you explain why alternatives that involve fewer potential risks cannot be used?

✔ Where anticipated risk cannot be reduced any further during the design of the research and ethical review is favourable, how will the implementation of your research seek to avoid the occurrence of risk in practice, or at the very least seek to minimise it?

✔ Does the information you provide to intended participants to facilitate informed consent also allow them to contact you to discuss potential concerns? How have you facilitated this while maintaining your own privacy (e.g. using a university email address, not your personal email or home address)?

✔ How will you commence a data collection activity to allow potential concerns to be raised first? How will you make yourself aware of themes that may be sensitive for particular participants?

✔ How will you reinforce the voluntary nature of participation to allow participants not to answer a particular question, set of questions, or to decline any request for data?

✔ Other potential risks are likely to be evident within the context of your particular research project. What might these be and how will you manage them?

- *Lacking respect and causing harm.* 'Harvesting' data from online communities without the knowledge and permission of those who create it may be seen as disrespectful and opposed to the principle of gaining trust. Deception and the development of mistrust may cause damage to online communities and to their members.

- *Respecting privacy.* While it may be technically possible to access online communities because they operate in a publicly accessible virtual space, it can be argued that content on these websites should be treated as private conversations, albeit 'publicly private' ones.

- *Nature of participation and scope to withdraw.* 'Harvesting' data may be seen as violating the principle of the voluntary nature of participation. Lack of consent while using accessible material also negates the right to limit the nature of data used or to withdraw.

- *Informed consent.* Is it ethical to waive the need to obtain consent because material is seen as being in the public domain and because it may be difficult to achieve this? Informed consent in a virtual setting may be obtained by contacting an online community's moderator or administrator; or by specifically asking participants in the case of a web questionnaire or online interview, for example. Informed consent for online research may include agreed limits about the scope of participation. It may also include procedures to allow concerns to be raised or for withdrawal to take place. Such procedures will be important in Internet-mediated research because the issue of distance and lack of face-to-face contact makes it difficult to anticipate participants' concerns and attitudes. Signed consent may be facilitated by issuing a consent form by email or online using electronic checkboxes.

- *Confidentiality of data and anonymity of participants.* Even though members of an online community may produce discussions that are publicly accessible and which create a permanent record, they may do this in the belief that no one will be 'harvesting' or analysing this material, or using it subsequently. Bakardjieva and Feenberg (2000) found that members of an online community expected to be asked for consent before access was achieved in practice; and that access was then only granted for subsequently generated online discussions, not to archived discussions that took place before community members knew they were to be the subject of research. This approach enables members of online communities to control data that is available to researchers. Bakardjieva and Feenberg (2000) provide an example of how members of an online community went further to exercise control and to protect the confidentiality of their discussions and their anonymity. The researchers were not permitted to save these online discussions or to use quotations from them. Instead they were allowed to read these discussions and then ask members questions about what they had read. The researchers were allowed to use these answers and to take suitably anonymised quotations from them for their research. This effectively separated the private nature of members' online discussions from public access to research data, enabling members of the online community to control their participation and to ensure the confidentiality of their discussions as well as maintaining their anonymity.
- *Analysis of data and reporting of findings.* Issues of confidentiality, anonymity, privacy and copyright are raised when Internet data are analysed and reported. Where data are 'harvested' the researcher is confronted with the dilemma of whether to use these data openly or anonymously. Since 'harvesting' occurs without obtaining consent, at least initially, should the researcher use pseudonyms and other changes to disguise the identities of those who created the material? Where the researcher wishes to quote from this material, there is the possibility that others could use Internet search engines to identify the author of a quotation. This raises issues about the confidentiality of the data and researchers should avoid using quotations that would be traceable without first obtaining consent, particularly where harm may result (British Psychological Society 2017). These issues are compounded by copyright. Blogs are protected by copyright laws and those who create them have exclusive rights in relation to their reproduction (Hookway 2008). Web pages and content on social network sites are also protected by copyright laws (British Psychological Society 2017). Those who author or create web materials may wish their work to be properly attributed; conversely they may wish to protect its use, or for any permitted use to be anonymised. Seeking informed consent should help to overcome the dilemmas associated with using materials from the Internet as data.
- *Management of data.* Data protection legislation has (or is likely to have, depending on country) implications for Internet-mediated research, including in the UK the need for notification and consent if personal data are to be processed. Researchers using the Internet need to comply with current data protection legislation as well as with any other legal requirements. A further set of issues concerns the potential insecurity of data transmission and storage. This may be because of errors. For example, emails containing personal data may be sent to the wrong address. Questionnaire software may contain errors. Insecurity may also occur because others have access to a website and are able to alter data or to copy and direct it elsewhere. As researchers do not control websites or networks, risks associated with data transmission and storage need to be recognised and participants told about these in relation to confidentiality, anonymity and possible 'data hacking' or misuse as part of seeking informed consent.

- *Safety of the researcher.* The researcher may help to ensure her or his safety when conducting Internet-mediated research by using a university email address, not a personal email address; nor should a researcher provide details of his or her home address. Researchers also need to be diligent when setting up access rights to their own personal information on social media sites to protect their privacy.

This review has highlighted several issues and dilemmas associated with the use of Internet-mediated research, although others will exist in practice. In addition, many aspects associated with these issues will need to be considered during the use of Internet-mediated research. The guidelines from the Association of Internet Researchers advocate, "a process approach to ethical decision making in Internet research . . . [where]. . . At each juncture of a research project different ethical issues become relevant" (Markham and Buchanan 2012: 5). This approach is also recommended by Whiting and Pritchard (2018), who see ethical considerations as a process that need to be anticipated and revisited at each stage of research. This is an approach to ethical concerns that we have advocated through the editions of this book and which is outlined and discussed in Section 6.6. The use of the Internet to conduct research may, however, place an even greater emphasis on the need to approach ethical considerations as an on-going process through the stages of the research, and with this a related commitment by the Internet researcher to engage in ethical reflexivity to anticipate and respond to the issues related to the use of this particular approach.

Table 6.4 refers to sets of guidelines for Internet-mediated research. Markham and Buchanan state, "We advocate guidelines rather than a code of practice so that ethical research can remain flexible, be responsive to diverse contexts, and be adaptable to continually changing technologies" (2012: 5). The British Psychological Society's Ethics Guidelines for Internet-mediated Research state, "It should be recognised that technologies, their social uses and the associated implications for research may change rapidly over time and new considerations become salient" (2017: 2). Where you consider using Internet-mediated research, you will therefore need to refer very carefully to your university's guidelines about using this approach (or those that they recommend you to use).

A further aspect of Internet use concerns **netiquette**, which refers to user standards to encourage courtesy. The principal focus of netiquette is the use of email and messaging. The ease of creating these may lead to issues that impair your attempt to use Internet-mediated research. Emails and messages may be poorly worded (Box 6.8), and they may appear unfriendly or unclear so that they fail to interest those whom you approach. Emails and messages need to be worded appropriately for their intended audience and to be clearly structured, relevant and succinct. The ease of sending emails and messages may

Table 6.4 Internet addresses for ethical guidelines for the conduct of online research

Name	Internet address
Association of Internet Researchers Ess, C. and AoIR ethics working committee (2002)	http://aoir.org/reports/ethics.pdf
Markham. A., Buchanan, E. and AoIR Ethics Working Committee (2012) Ethical Decision-Making and Internet Research	http://aoir.org/reports/ethics2.pdf
British Psychological Society Ethics Guidelines for Internet-mediated Research (2017)	https://www.bps.org.uk/sites/beta.bps.org.uk/files/Policy-Files/Ethics-Guidelines-Internet-mediated-Research-2017.pdf

lead to 'spamming' potential and actual participants. 'Spamming' involves sending large numbers of unwanted mail and should be avoided. Another netiquette custom involves respecting the intentions of other users, so that private messages should not subsequently be made public. We consider netiquette further in Sections 6.6, 10.10 (Internet-mediated interviews) and 11.8 (Internet questionnaires).

6.6 Ethical issues at specific stages of the research process

As can be seen in Figure 6.1, ethical issues are likely to be important throughout your research. This will require ethical integrity from you in relation to your role as the researcher, any organisational gatekeeper(s) involved and, where appropriate, your research sponsor. Where you are undertaking research for an organisation, you will need to find the middle ground between the organisation's expectation of useful research and your right not to be coerced into researching a topic in which you are not interested, or that does not satisfy the assessment requirements of your university.

Ethical issues during choice of topic, research design and gaining access

Ethical issues need to be anticipated and considered from the very start of your research project. This will be from the time you start to think about the choice of your research topic. Each potential research topic will be associated with a number of possible ethical concerns. Anticipating these will be an important way to help you to decide which of your potential topics you chose as the topic to research. As you focus more attention on your chosen topic you will start to formulate the research question and objectives that will give direction to the conduct of your research. Devising your research question and objectives should also lead you to evaluate these in relation to potential ethical concerns. For example:

- what is the purpose of asking this question?
- what will be the implications of asking it?
- what type(s) of data will you need to collect to answer it?
- how will you collect these data?
- what are the implications for those whom you ask to participate in this research?
- how might the research be used and with what consequences?

These and other possible ethical considerations will be important to anticipate as you choose your research topic and formulate your research question and objectives, before you embark on designing your research.

Most ethical issues can be anticipated and considered (at least initially) during the design stage of any research project. You should plan to conduct the research project in line with the ethical principle of not causing harm (discussed earlier) and by adapting your research strategy or choice of methods where appropriate. Evidence that ethical issues have been considered and evaluated at this stage is likely to be one of the criteria against which your research proposal is judged.

One of the key stages at which you need to consider the potential for ethical issues to arise is when you seek access. As noted earlier, you should not attempt to apply any pressure on intended participants to grant access. This is unlikely to be the case where you

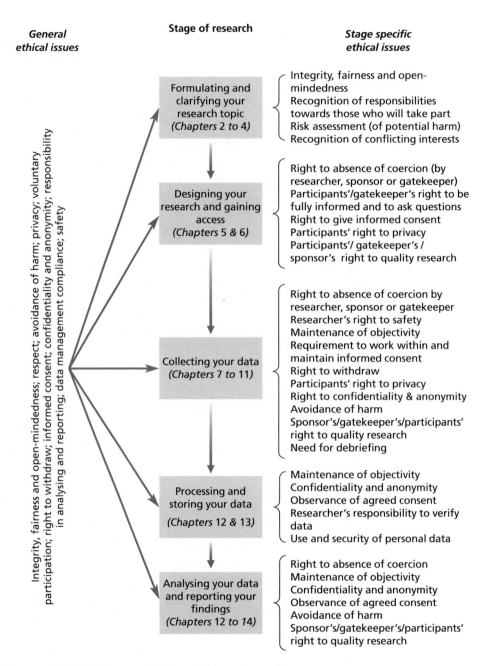

General
ethical issues

Stage of research

Stage specific
ethical issues

Integrity, fairness and open-mindedness; respect; avoidance of harm; privacy; voluntary participation; right to withdraw; informed consent; confidentiality and anonymity; responsibility in analysing and reporting; data management compliance; safety

Formulating and clarifying your research topic
(Chapters 2 to 4)

Integrity, fairness and open-mindedness
Recognition of responsibilities towards those who will take part
Risk assessment (of potential harm)
Recognition of conflicting interests

Designing your research and gaining access
(Chapters 5 & 6)

Right to absence of coercion (by researcher, sponsor or gatekeeper)
Participants'/gatekeeper's right to be fully informed and to ask questions
Right to give informed consent
Participants' right to privacy
Participants'/ gatekeeper's / sponsor's right to quality research

Collecting your data
(Chapters 7 to 11)

Right to absence of coercion by researcher, sponsor or gatekeeper
Researcher's right to safety
Maintenance of objectivity
Requirement to work within and maintain informed consent
Right to withdraw
Participants' right to privacy
Right to confidentiality & anonymity
Avoidance of harm
Sponsor's/gatekeeper's/participants' right to quality research
Need for debriefing

Processing and storing your data
(Chapters 12 & 13)

Maintenance of objectivity
Confidentiality and anonymity
Observance of agreed consent
Researcher's responsibility to verify data
Use and security of personal data

Analysing your data and reporting your findings
(Chapters 12 to 14)

Right to absence of coercion
Maintenance of objectivity
Confidentiality and anonymity
Observance of agreed consent
Avoidance of harm
Sponsor's/gatekeeper's/participants' right to quality research

Figure 6.1 Ethical issues at different stages of research

are approaching a member of an organisation's management to request access. However, where you are undertaking a research project as an internal researcher within your employing organisation (Section 6.2), in relation to a part-time qualification, there may be a temptation to apply pressure on others (colleagues or subordinates) to cooperate. Individuals have a right to privacy and should not feel pressurised or coerced into participating. By not respecting this, you may well be causing harm.

Consequently, you will have to accept any refusal to take part. Box 6.13 contains a checklist to help you ensure that you are not putting pressure on individuals to participate.

Box 6.13
Checklist

Assessing your research in relation to not pressurising individuals to participate

✔ Have you ensured that participants have not been coerced into participating?

✔ Have you made sure that no inducements (e.g. financial payments), other than reimbursement for travel expenses or in some cases time, are offered?

✔ Have you checked that the risks involved in participation are likely to be acceptable to those participating?

✔ Are participants free to withdraw from your study at any time and have you informed them of this?

You may also cause harm by the nature and timing of any approach that you make to intended participants – perhaps by telephoning at 'unsociable' times, or by 'confronting' those from whom you would like to collect data. Access to secondary data may also raise ethical issues in relation to harm. Where you happen to obtain access to personal data about individuals who have not consented to let you have this (through personnel or client records), you will be obliged to anonymise these or to seek informed consent from those involved.

Consent to participate in a research project is not a straightforward matter (Box 6.14). In general terms, an approach to a potential participant or respondent is an attempt to gain consent. However, this raises a question about the scope of any consent given. Where someone agrees to participate in a particular data collection method, this does not necessarily imply consent about the way in which the data provided may be used. Clearly, any assurances that you provide about anonymity or confidentiality will help to develop an

Box 6.14
Focus on management research

Gaining informed consent

Rowlinson et al. (2016) undertook research that explored experiences of using what is called 'payday lending' in the UK. This is a type of short-term but high-cost loan provided by private companies to people who are employed but who have low incomes, so that they can survive financially until their next payday, when the loan is due to be repaid.

Twenty-one in-depth, exploratory interviews were undertaken with participants who had taken loans from payday lending companies over the previous year.

These participants had originally completed a questionnaire administered by a specialist research company in town centres and shopping areas and were recruited to participate in the researchers' interviews.

The researchers state they, "took ethical concerns seriously", including gaining informed consent (Rowlinson et al. 2016: 533). At the start of each interview they explained the nature of the research they were undertaking and how the data that participants provided would be used. They assured participants that data and reporting would be anonymised and provided them with a research information sheet.

Rawlinson and colleagues acknowledged their research was intrusive, reporting that each interviewer was trained and experienced in conducting interviews which intruded into sensitive issues. Researcher safety as well as data quality were given as reasons for conducting interviews in pairs.

understanding of the nature of the consent being entered into, but even these may be inadequate in terms of clarifying the nature of that consent.

This suggests a continuum that ranges from a lack of consent, involving some form of deception, through **inferred consent**, where agreement to take part leads the researcher to presume that data may be analysed, used, stored and reported as he or she wishes without clarifying this with the participant, to informed consent. **Informed consent** involves ensuring those involved in the research are given sufficient information (discussed next), the opportunity to ask questions, and time to consider without any pressure or coercion, to be able to reach a fully informed, considered and freely given decision about whether or not to take part (see Table 6.3). This continuum is shown in Figure 6.2.

Three points are outlined in Figure 6.2, although in reality this is likely to operate as a continuum because a multitude of positions are possible around the points described. For example, research that is conducted with those who have agreed to participate can still involve an attempt to deceive them in some way. This **deception** may be related to deceit over the real purpose of the research, or in relation to some undeclared sponsorship, or related to an association with another organisation that will use any data gained for commercial advantage. Where this is the case, it could cause embarrassment or harm to those who promote your request for access within their employing organisation, as well as to yourself.

The information that is required for prospective participants or respondents to reach a fully informed decision about whether or not to participate should be produced formally as a **participant information sheet** or **information sheet.** This may be given or sent to intended participants or respondents or emailed or made available online in the case of Internet-mediated research. It should include information about the nature of the research, the requirements and implications of taking part, participants' or respondents' rights, how their data will be analysed, reported and stored and whom to contact in the case of concerns. These points are developed in Box 6.15, where they are presented as a checklist.

The nature of information required for informed consent may vary according to your research strategy, as will the way in which you seek to establish consent. If you are intending to use a questionnaire where personal data are not collected or where data are completely anonymised, the return of a completed questionnaire by a respondent is often taken to imply consent. Yet, as illustrated in Box 11.16, including a question in a questionnaire explicitly to request consent is straightforward. Either approach will require you to include an information sheet detailing how these data will be analysed and reported, for what purpose, and what will then happen to them, as well as your identity (UK Data Archive 2011). If you are intending to interview a senior manager, correspondence may be

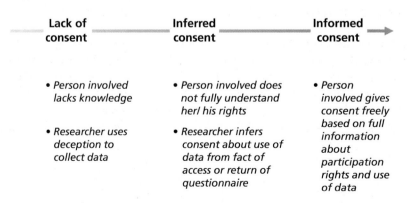

Lack of consent	Inferred consent	Informed consent
• Person involved lacks knowledge	• Person involved does not fully understand her/ his rights	• Person involved gives consent freely based on full information about participation rights and use of data
• Researcher uses deception to collect data	• Researcher infers consent about use of data from fact of access or return of questionnaire	

Figure 6.2 The nature of consent

Box 6.15
Checklist

Requirements for an information sheet

Organisational 'gatekeepers' (discussed earlier in Section 6.4) and intended participants need to be informed about the following aspects of a research project. This can be drawn together in a research information sheet or participant information sheet.

About the nature of the research
✔ What is the title of the research project?
✔ What is the purpose of the research?
✔ Who is or will be undertaking it – the name(s) of the researcher(s)?
✔ Where does the research originate from – the name of the researcher's university or employing organisation?
✔ Is the research being funded or sponsored – if so, by whom and why?
✔ Who is being asked to participate – i.e. broad details about the sampling frame, sample determination and size?
✔ How far has the research project progressed?

About the requirements of taking part
✔ What type of data will be required from those who agree to take part?
✔ How will these data be collected (e.g. interview, observation or questionnaire)?
✔ How much time will be required and on how many occasions?
✔ What are the target dates to undertake the research and for participation?

About the implications of taking part
✔ What assurances will be provided about anonymity and data confidentiality?
✔ What will be the consequences of participating – possible risks, depending on the nature of the approach, and expected benefits?

✔ When will any expected benefit, such as the promise of a summary report of the findings, be made available?
✔ Depending on the nature of the research, when and how will any debriefing be conducted?

About the rights of those taking part
✔ Recognition that participation is voluntary.
✔ Recognition that those taking part have the right to decline to answer a question or set of questions; or to be observed in particular circumstances.
✔ Recognition that those taking part have control over the recording of any of their responses where it is agreed that any type of photographic, video or voice recording may be made.
✔ Recognition that those taking part may withdraw at any time.

About the use of the data collected and the way in which it will be reported
✔ Who will have access to the data collected?
✔ How will the results of the research project be disseminated?
✔ How will assurances about anonymity and confidentiality be observed at this stage?
✔ What will happen to the data collected after the project is completed?
✔ Where data are to be destroyed, what is the date by which this will happen?
✔ Where data are to be preserved, where and how will these be stored securely, who might be given access to them, and what safeguards will be established to ensure the continuing future confidentiality of these data and anonymity of those taking part?

Whom to contact to raise any concerns and questions about the research
✔ Have you established how you will provide those taking part with a person to contact about the research, including name, work address, email and contact phone number?

exchanged to establish informed consent (Section 6.4). When interviewing individuals, informed consent should be supplemented by a more detailed written agreement, such as a **consent form** (Box 6.16), which is signed by both parties. Use of a written consent form helps to clarify the boundaries of consent and should help you to comply with data protection legislation where your research involves the collection of confidential, personal or sensitive personal data (see Section 6.7) (UK Data Archive 2011). Depending on the nature of your research project you may need to seek consent to collect photographic or video-recorded data. As with audio-recording, consent needs to be obtained before the event, given potential reluctance or sensitivity about using these types of recording media. Your consent form enabling this needs to be recorded formally.

You will also need to operate on the basis that informed consent is a continuing requirement for your research. This, of course, will be particularly significant where you seek to gain access on an incremental basis (Section 6.4). Although you may have established informed consent through prior written correspondence, it is still worthwhile re-establishing this with each intended participant immediately prior to collecting data. (An example of this is provided in Box 10.9, in relation to opening a semi-structured interview.)

Earlier (Section 6.4) we discussed possible strategies to help you to gain access. One of these was related to possible benefits to an organisation of granting you access. You should be realistic about this. Where you are anxious to gain access, you may be tempted to offer more than is feasible. Alternatively, you may offer to supply information arising from your work without intending to do this. Such behaviour would be unethical and, to make this worse, the effect of such action (or inaction) may result in a refusal to grant access to others who come after you.

Ethical issues during data collection

As highlighted in Figure 6.1, the data collection stage is associated with a range of ethical issues. Some of these are general issues that will apply to whichever technique is being used to collect data. Others are more specifically related to a particular data collection technique. Finally, and of paramount importance, there are issues associated with ensuring your own safety while collecting your data.

Irrespective of data collection technique, there are a number of ethical principles to which you need to adhere. In the previous subsection we referred to the importance of not causing harm or intruding on privacy. This was in relation to the right not to take part. Once individuals or organisations have consented to take part in your research, they still maintain their rights. This means that they have the right to withdraw, and that they may decline to take part in a particular aspect of your research. You should not ask them to participate in anything that will cause harm or intrude on their privacy. We have also referred to rights in relation to deceit. Once access has been granted, you should keep to the aims of your research project that you agreed. To do otherwise, without raising this with those taking part and renegotiating access, would be, in effect, another type of deceit. This will be likely to cause upset and could result in the premature termination of your data collection. There are perhaps some situations where deception may be accepted in relation to 'covert' research, and we shall discuss this later in this subsection.

Another general ethical principle is related to the maintenance of your objectivity. During the data collection stage this means making sure that you collect your data accurately and fully – that you avoid exercising subjective selectivity in what you record. The importance of this action also relates to the validity and reliability of your work, which is discussed in Chapters 5 and 7–11. Without objectively collected data, your ability to analyse and report your work accurately will be impaired. We return to this as an ethical issue in

Box 6.16
Focus on student research

Consent form

Anna's research involved interviewing a number of franchisees who had expanded their franchises to run multiple outlets, to understand the competence required to achieve this expansion successfully and how they had developed this. Prior to commencing each interview, Anna gave each participant an information sheet that summarised her research project, including the possible benefits and disadvantages of taking part. After carefully explaining her research, the reasons why (with the participant's permission) she wished to audio-record or video the interview and emphasising that individuals were not obliged to participate unless they wished, Anna asked them if they wished to participate. Those who did were asked to complete and sign the following consent form:

Anytown Business School

CONSENT FORM

Title of research project:
The greening of automotive advertising

Name and position of researcher:
Anna Verhoeven, Final year student, Anytown Business School, University of Anytown

please initial box

1. I confirm that I have read and understand the information sheet for the above study and have had the opportunity to ask questions.

2. I understand that my participation is voluntary and that I am free to withdraw at any time without giving reason.

3. I agree to take part in the study.

please tick box
Yes   No

4. I agree to the interview being audio recorded.

1. I agree to the interview being video recorded.

2. I agree to the use of anonymised quotes in publications.

Name of participant: Date: Signature:

Anna Verhoeven (researcher)   Date: Signature:

the next subsection. Obviously, **falsification** (distorting or misrepresenting) and **fabrication** (inventing) of any data are also totally unacceptable and unethical courses of action.

Confidentiality and anonymity may be important in gaining access to organisations and individuals (Section 6.4). Once such promises have been given, it is essential to make sure that these are maintained. Where confidentiality has been promised you must ensure the data collected remain confidential. This is particularly important in relation to personal and sensitive personal data (see Section 6.7). Ways of ensuring anonymity are inevitably research-method specific. While the main concern is likely to be individuals or organisations being able to be identified, it is worth recognising that permission may be given for data to be attributed directly to them.

Anonymising quantitative data by aggregating or removing key variables is relatively straightforward. However, where qualitative data are being reported it may be less straightforward. New points of significance will emerge as the research progresses which you will wish to explore with others. Your key concern is to ensure that you do not cause harm. For example, within interviews, participants can often infer what earlier interviewees might have said from the questions being asked. This may lead to participants indirectly identifying which person was responsible for making the earlier point that you now wish to explore with them, with repercussions for the person whose openness allowed you to identify this point for exploration. Where you wish to get others to discuss a potentially sensitive point you may attempt to steer the discussion to see if they will raise it without in any way making clear that one of the other participants has already referred to it.

Use of the Internet and email during data collection can lead to the possibility of serious ethical and netiquette issues, related to confidentiality and anonymity. For example, it would be technically possible to forward the email (or interview notes) of one research participant to another participant in order to ask this second person to comment on the issues being raised. Such an action would infringe the right to confidentiality and anonymity, perhaps causing harm. It should definitely be avoided. It may also lead to data protection issues related to the use of personal data (discussed in Section 6.7).

The ability to explore data or to seek explanations through interview-based techniques means that there will be greater scope for ethical and other issues to arise in relation to this approach to research. The resulting personal contact, scope to use non-standardised questions or to observe on a 'face-to-face' basis, and capacity to develop your knowledge on an incremental basis, mean that you will be able to exercise a greater level of control (Chapter 10). This contrasts with the use of a quantitative approach based on structured interviews or self-completed questionnaires (Chapter 11).

The relatively greater level of research control associated with interview-based techniques should be exercised with care so that your behaviour remains within appropriate and acceptable parameters. In face-to-face interviews, you should avoid overzealous questioning and pressing your participant for a response. Doing so may make the situation stressful for your participant. You should also make clear to your interview participants that they have the right to decline to respond to any question. The nature of questions to be asked also requires consideration. For example, you should avoid asking questions that are in any way demeaning to your participant (Sections 10.5–10.11). In face-to-face interviews it will clearly be necessary to arrange a time that is convenient for your participant; however, where you wish to conduct an interview by telephone (Sections 10.9, 11.2 and 11.8) you should not attempt to do this at an unreasonable time of the day. In interviews, whether face-to-face or by telephone, it would also be unethical to attempt to prolong the discussion when it is apparent that your participant has other commitments.

The use of observation techniques raises its own ethical concerns (Chapter 9). The boundaries of what is permissible to observe need to be drawn clearly. Without this type of agreement those being observed may feel that their actions are constrained. You should also avoid attempting to observe behaviour related to private life, such as personal telephone calls and so forth. Without this, the relationship between observer and observed will break down, with the latter finding the process to be an intrusion on their right to privacy. There is, however, a second problem related to the use of this method. This is the issue of '**reactivity**' – the reaction on the part of those being investigated to the researcher and their research instruments (Bryman 1988: 112). This issue applies to a number of strategies and methods but is clearly a particular problem in observation.

One solution to this problem could be to undertake a **covert** study so that those being observed are not aware of this fact. In a situation of likely 'reactivity' to the presence of an observer you might use this approach in a deceitful yet benign way, since to declare your purpose at the outset of your work might lead to non-participation or to problems related to validity and reliability if those being observed altered their behaviour. The rationale for this choice of approach would thus be related to a question of whether 'the ends justify the means', provided that other ethical aspects are considered (Wells 1994: 284). However, the ethical concern with deceiving those being observed may prevail over any pragmatic view. Indeed, the problem of reactivity may be a diminishing one where those being observed adapt to your presence as declared observer. Their adaptation is known as **habituation** (Section 9.2).

Where access is denied after being requested you may consider that you have no other choice but to carry out covert observation – where this would be practical. We strongly advise against this. Covert observation after access has been denied will prove to be a considerable source of irritation. Indeed, many universities' ethical codes prohibit any form of research being carried out if access has been denied. In such situations, you will need to re-evaluate your research where any denial of access is critical to your intended project.

One group of students who sometimes consider using a covert approach are internal researchers or practitioner–researchers. There are recognised advantages and disadvantages associated with being an internal researcher (see Sections 6.2 and 9.4) One of the possible disadvantages is related to your relationship with those from whom you will need to gain cooperation in order to acquire cognitive access to their data. This may be related to the fact that your status is relatively junior to these colleagues, or that you are more senior to them. Any status difference can impact negatively on your intended data collection. One solution would be to adopt a covert approach in order to seek to gain data. You may therefore decide to interview subordinate colleagues, organise focus groups through your managerial status or observe interactions during meetings without declaring your research interest. The key question to consider is: will this approach be more likely to yield trustworthy data than declaring your real purpose and acting overtly? The answer will depend on a number of factors:

- the existing nature of your relationships with those whom you wish to be your participants;
- the prevailing managerial style within the organisation or that part of it where these people work;
- the time and opportunity that you have to attempt to develop the trust and confidence of these intended participants in order to gain their cooperation.

Irrespective of the reason why a deception occurred, it is widely accepted that after covert observation has taken place you should inform those affected about what has occurred and why. This process is known as **debriefing**. Debriefing also occurs after agreed participation in strategies such as a research experiment. The purpose of debriefing is to inform participants about the nature of the research, its outcomes and to ascertain if there have been any adverse consequences from taking part; if so, to talk to the participant affected and arrange for assistance as required (British Psychological Society 2009).

Absolute assurances about the use of the data collected may also be critical to gain trust, and the time you invest in achieving this may be very worthwhile. You will also need to consider the impact on yourself of adopting a covert approach when others learn of it.

In comparison with the issues discussed in the preceding paragraphs, Dale et al. (1988) believe that the ethical problems associated with questionnaires and other research using the survey strategy are likely to be less onerous. This is due to the nature of structured questions, which are rarely designed to explore responses, and the avoidance of the in-depth interview situation, where the ability to use probing questions can lead to more revealing information. However, where questionnaires are designed to ask questions of a personal or sensitive nature, respondents may be reluctant to answer these or to partici-pate in the research. One method to overcome this issue is the use of computer-assisted self-interviewing. This involves the interviewer handing a tablet or laptop to respondents for them to enter their own responses to questions, thereby ensuring confidentiality. Using this method may lead to data quality and data processing advantages, but is likely to be suitable only for a large-scale survey and where the researcher has access to specialist software.

When thinking about avoiding harm, many researchers forget about themselves! The possibility of harm to you as the researcher is an important ethical issue that you should not ignore. You should not reveal personal information about yourself such as your home address or telephone number. Careful consideration needs to be given to a range of risk factors including the nature of the research, the location and timing of data collection activities and health and safety considerations. Researchers need to consider risks to their safety and to seek to avoid these through strategies such as meeting participants in safe spaces, conducting data collection during the daytime and letting other people know your arrangements, including where you will be.

In discussing the safety of researchers with our students, we have found the guidance sheets provided by the Suzy Lamplugh Trust (http://www.suzylamplugh.org/) to be extremely helpful. As the Trust's guidance sheets emphasise, you should never allow your working practices (research design and conduct) to put your own safety in danger. You will need to take into account the nature of your research, your participants, data collec-tion methods and the locations to collect data to assess potential risks associated with undertaking this activity. We advise you to consult the 'Code of Practice for the Safety of Social Researchers' (Social Research Association 2001) and guidance leaflets on working alone and dealing with aggression available from the Suzy Lamplugh Trust (http://www.suzylamplugh.org/), as these may contain other items of helpful advice that are relevant to the context of your research, including a range of strategies to promote safety (Box 6.17).

Ethical issues related to analysis and reporting

The maintenance of your research objectivity will be vital during the analysis stage to make sure that you do not misrepresent the data collected. This will include not being selective about which data to report or, where appropriate, misrepresenting its statistical accuracy. A great deal of trust is placed in each researcher's integrity, and it would clearly be a major ethical issue were this to be open to question. This duty to represent your data honestly extends to the analysis and reporting stage of your research. Lack of objectivity at this stage will clearly distort your conclusions and any associated recommendations. Distorting or misrepresenting data, findings and conclusions are all examples of falsifica-tion, which we noted earlier as being a totally unacceptable and unethical course of action.

The ethical issues of confidentiality and anonymity also come to the fore during the reporting stage of your research. Wells (1994) recognises that it may be difficult to

Box 6.17
Checklist

Personal safety when collecting primary data

✔ Plan your meeting with a person in a busy public place or office where other people work nearby if at all possible.

✔ Carefully consider the location you are travelling to and your travel plans: what risks might you encounter; note your route and carry a map; consider whether you will use public transport, a reputable taxi firm or a private car (if you use a private car ensure there is a safe place to leave it).

✔ Carry sufficient money to cover your expenses and any unexpected ones; in some cities where you have a local transport travel card make sure it has sufficient credit.

✔ Carry a mobile phone and make sure it is switched on.

✔ Make a mental note of a safe way to leave the building or place where you meet.

✔ Make a telephone call to a friend before a particular meeting to tell them who you are meeting, where and how long you expect the meeting to last; call them again to tell them you have left and about your subsequent meeting plans and/or travel arrangements.

✔ Set up a system where you contact someone each day with a full list of whom you are meeting, where and at what times.

✔ In a meeting be aware of the use of body language, appearance, cultural norms, social distance and the gender dynamics of interactions.

✔ The considerable majority of meetings are helpful and non-threatening but in very rare cases someone may become aggressive or angry: be aware of any changes in behaviour; consider what questions you are asking and how you are asking them; remain calm; where necessary be assertive but not aggressive; if necessary end the meeting politely and leave quickly.

✔ Carry a screech (rape) alarm in case of an emergency.

✔ Carefully consider your safety if the location of your research means that you will be in a lone working situation; some researchers work in pairs in such situations to reduce safety risks.

✔ Always consider your safety and any risks to yourself, and avoid any situation that might be difficult or dangerous.

maintain the assurances that have been given. However, allowing a participating organisation to be identified by those who can 'piece together' the characteristics that you reveal may result in embarrassment and also in access being refused to those who seek this after you. Great care therefore needs to be exercised to avoid this situation. You also have the option of requesting permission from the organisation to use their name. To gain this permission you will almost certainly need to let them read your work to understand the context within which they would be named.

This level of care also needs to be exercised in making sure that the anonymity of individuals is maintained (Box 6.18). Embarrassment and even harm could result from reporting data that are clearly attributable to a particular individual. Care therefore needs to be taken to protect those who participate in your research. Do not collect data that identify individuals where it is not necessary to do so, e.g. full names where you do not need this type of data. Always seek to anonymise the identities of those who take part by using a level of generalisation which ensures that others are not able to identify them. For example, do not refer to specific ages, dates, locations, names of countries, real names, actual organisational names or job positions or include photographs that will make it easy to identify participants or respondents, participating organisations, groups or communities (UK Data Archive 2017), unless there is express permission to identify any of these.

Box 6.18
Focus on student research

Inadvertently revealing participants' identities

Over the years we have been fortunate to read a large number of student research projects. The following examples, drawn from some of these, highlight how easy it is to inadvertently reveal the identities of research participants when presenting your findings:

- reporting a comment made by a female accounts manager when in fact there is only one such person;
- referring to a comment made by a member of the sales team, when only one salesperson would

have had access to the information referred to in the comment;
- reporting data and comments related to a small section of staff, where you state the name or job title of the one person interviewed from that section elsewhere in your research report;
- referring to an 'anonymous' organisation by name on the copy of the questionnaire placed in an appendix;
- attributing comments to named employees;
- thanking those who participated in the research by name;
- using pseudonyms where the initials of the pseudonym are the same as those of the actual person interviewed, or where the name is similar, e.g. using Tim Jennings for Tom Jenkins;
- including a photograph of the interview site or interviewee in your project report.

A further ethical concern stems from the use made by others of the conclusions that you reach and any course of action that is explicitly referred to or implicitly suggested, based on your research data. How ethical would it be to use the data collected from a group of people effectively to disadvantage them because of the decisions that are then made in the light of your research? On the other hand, there is a view which says that while the identity of those taking part should not be revealed, they cannot be exempt from the way in which research conclusions are then used to make decisions. This is clearly an ethical issue, requiring very careful evaluation.

Where you are aware that your findings may be used to make a decision that could adversely affect the collective interests of those who took part, it would be ethical to refer to this possibility even if it reduces the level of access you achieve. An alternative position is to construct your research question and objectives to avoid this possibility, or so that decisions taken as a result of your research should have only positive consequences for the collective interests of those who participate. You may find that this alternative is not open to you, perhaps because you are a part-time student in employment and your employing organisation directs your choice of research topic. If so, it will be more honest to concede to your participants that you are in effect acting as an internal consultant rather than in a (dispassionate) researcher's role.

This discussion about the impact of research on the collective interests of those who participate brings us back to the reference made earlier to the particular ethical issues that arise in relation to the analysis of secondary data derived from questionnaires. Dale et al. (1988) point out that where questionnaire data are subsequently used as secondary data, the original assurances provided to those who participated in the research may be set aside, with the result that the collective interests of participants may be disadvantaged through this use of data. The use of data for secondary purposes therefore also leads to ethical concerns of potentially significant proportions, and you will need to consider these in the way in which you make use of this type of data.

More recent work by Bishop and Kuula-Luumi (2017) indicates that researchers are concerned about ethical issues when using secondary data. They estimate that approximately half of articles based on re-use of qualitative research consider ethical concerns related to the use of these secondary data. They also say that where primary data may be re-used later as secondary data, the ethical concerns associated with this can be anticipated during collection. These concerns can be reduced by anonymising these data as they are collected and recorded, so that real names and organisations do not enter any enduring set of data.

A final checklist to help you anticipate and deal with ethical issues is given in Box 6.19.

Box 6.19
Checklist

To help anticipate and deal with ethical issues

✔ Attempt to recognise potential ethical issues that will affect your proposed research.

✔ Treat the consideration of ethical issues as an active, continuous and reflexive process that occurs throughout the stages of your research, from conception to completion, rather than just something you consider at the start of your project.

✔ Utilise your university's code on research ethics to guide the choice, design and conduct of your research.

✔ Anticipate potential ethical issues at the stage of thinking about which research topic to choose and anticipate how you would seek to control these. Use this consideration to help you evaluate your choice of potential topics and to decide which topic to research.

✔ Anticipate ethical issues at the design stage of your research and discuss how you will seek to control these in your research proposal.

✔ Seek informed consent through the use of openness and honesty, rather than using deception.

✔ Do not exaggerate the likely benefits of your research for participating organisations or individuals.

✔ Respect others' rights to privacy at all stages of your research project.

✔ Maintain integrity and quality in relation to the processes you use to collect data.

✔ Recognise that more intrusive approaches to research will be associated with greater scope for ethical issues to arise and seek to avoid the particular problems related to interviews and observation.

✔ Avoid referring to data gained from a particular participant when talking to others, where this would allow the individual to be identified with potentially harmful consequences to that person.

✔ Only consider covert research where reactivity is likely to be a significant issue and a covert presence is practical. However, other ethical aspects of your research should still be respected when using this approach and where possible debriefing should occur after the collection of data.

✔ Maintain your objectivity during the stages of analysing and reporting your research.

✔ Maintain the assurances that you gave to participating organisations with regard to confidentiality of the data obtained and their organisational anonymity.

✔ Recognise that use of the Internet may raise particular ethical issues and dilemmas. Anticipate these in relation to your project to determine how you will conduct your Internet-mediated research ethically. You should be able to justify your approach to those who review and assess it.

✔ Where you use Internet-mediated research, seek informed consent and agreement from those taking part; maintain confidentiality of data and anonymity of participants, unless they expressly wish to be acknowledged; consider issues related to copyright of Internet sources.

✔ Avoid using the Internet or email to share data with others taking part.

Box 6.19
Checklist (*continued*)

To help anticipate and deal with ethical issues

✔ Protect those involved by taking great care to ensure their anonymity in relation to anything that you refer to in your project report unless you have their explicit permission to do otherwise.

✔ Consider how the collective interests of those involved may be adversely affected by the nature of the data that you are proposing to collect, and alter the nature of your research question and objectives where this possibility is likely. Alternatively, declare this possibility to those whom you wish to participate in your proposed research.

✔ Consider how you will use secondary data in order to protect the identities of those who contributed to its collection or who are named within it.

✔ Unless necessary, base your research on genuinely anonymised data. Where it is necessary to process personal data, ensure that you comply carefully with all current data protection legal requirements.

6.7 An introduction to the principles of data protection and data management

This section outlines principles of data protection and data management, which you will need to consider in order to manage your data ethically and even lawfully. In this section we first consider the use and protection of personal data, followed by the use of anonymised data, and finally data management.

Use and protection of personal data

When reference is made to data protection, this specifically refers to protecting personal data. **Personal data** either directly identify individuals (by, for example, naming them or showing their image), or make individuals identifiable when used in combination. Both types are subject to data protection. In this way, personal data are different to **anonymised data**, which if effective mean individuals cannot be identified. We return to consider anonymised data later in this section.

Data protection in the European Union (EU) has assumed even greater importance since the implementation of the General Data Protection Regulation EU 2016/679 (GDPR). This Regulation repealed and replaced Directive 95/46/EC on 25 May 2018 (Box 6.20). As a Regulation of the European Parliament and European Council, it is directly applicable and legally binding in all EU Member States. The GDPR provides protection for living individuals in relation to the processing of personal data.

Article 1 of the GDPR establishes, "rules relating to the protection of natural persons with regard to the processing of personal data and rules relating to the free movement of personal data" (Official Journal of the European Union 2016: L119/32 EN). Article 2 outlines the material scope of the GDPR, and Article 3 its territorial scope. Article 4 provides a number of definitions related to the purpose of the GDPR. These include the following. 'Personal data' are defined as data that allow an individual, known as a 'data subject', to be identified, perhaps in combination with other information known to the controller of the data. These data include a person's name, identification number, location, online presence, or some other attribute. 'Processing' is defined as any action or actions performed on personal data, by automated or manual means, including collecting, recording, organising and storing these. 'Controller' refers to the person who (or legal entity which) determines the processing of personal data; while the 'processor' processes these data on behalf of the controller.

Article 5 establishes principles for processing personal data so that it must be:

1 processed lawfully, fairly and transparently;
2 obtained for specified, explicit and lawful purposes and not processed further in a manner incompatible with those purposes, while allowing data to be processed further for scientific, historical and statistical research purposes where this is in accordance with Article 89 (1) (we outline Article 89 later in this section);
3 adequate, relevant and limited to the purpose for which they are processed;
4 accurate and, where necessary, kept up to date;
5 kept in a form that allows identification of data subjects for no longer than is necessary in relation to the purpose for which they are processed, while allowing personal data to be stored for longer periods where this is solely for scientific, historical and statistical research purposes in accordance with Article 89 (1) and subject to measures to safeguard the rights and freedoms of data subjects;
6 kept securely and protected from wrongful processing and accidental loss or damage;
7 held responsibly by the person who controls them and compliantly with the points listed above.

Article 6 discusses the lawfulness of processing personal data, providing a number of conditions for this, of which the first is a data subject has consented to the processing of his or her personal data for a specific purpose. Article 7 outlines conditions for consent and states that where data processing is based on consent, the data 'controller' will be able to demonstrate that this has been given by 'data subjects'. The definition of consent given by data subjects in Article 4 states that this, "means any freely given, specific, informed and unambiguous indication of the data subject's wishes by which he or she . . . signifies agreement to the processing of personal data relating to him or her" (Official Journal of the European Union 2016: L119/34 EN). Article 8 concerns consent relating to children.

Article 9 considers the processing of special categories of personal data, generally referred to as sensitive personal data. The processing of data that reveal racial or ethnic origin, political opinions, religious or philosophical beliefs, or trade union membership, or which concern an individual person's genetic or biometric data, health or sex life is prohibited, unless one of a number of conditions applies of which the first is explicit consent given by a data subject to process such personal data. Effective explicit consent is likely to mean clear and unambiguous written consent in this context.

Articles 12–23 deal with the rights of data subjects. In particular, Article 13 deals with information to be provided to data subjects where personal data are collected from them. Article 14 deals with information to be provided to data subjects where personal data are obtained from another source. Article 15 deals with the rights of data subjects to access data held about them, Article 16 with the right to rectification and Article 17 the right to be forgotten (the erasure of personal data). Article 18 deals with the data subject's right to restrict processing under certain conditions and Article 19 the need for a data controller to notify those to whom personal data have been disclosed where this is subsequently rectified, erased or its processing restricted. Subsequent articles regulate: the role of data controllers and processors; transfers of personal data to third countries or international organisations; mechanisms to supervise the implementation of this Regulation; remedies, liabilities and penalties; and provision relating to specific processing situations. In relation to specific processing situations, Article 89 deals with safeguards and derogations (exemptions) relating to scientific, historical and statistical research purposes. These safeguards are designed to protect data subjects during the processing of personal data. Safeguarding measures include the use of pseudonyms where appropriate, and other ways to process personal data which prevent the identification of data subjects. This Article also permits Member States to legislate for exemptions in relation to various Articles including 15, 16 and 18 where scientific or statistical research would otherwise be made impossible or seriously impaired.

While the GDPR is directly applicable and legally binding in all EU Member States, it also allows Member States scope to introduce legislation to specify some aspects more precisely. In the UK, for example, this has led to a third generation of data protection legislation. The latest Data Protection Act to be passed in the UK makes provisions for the processing of personal data by supplementing the GDPR, applying a similar regime to areas of data processing not covered by the GDPR, and making provisions for the UK Information Commissioner and for the enforcement of this legislation.

Our brief summary of selected aspects of this legislation should only be treated as an introductory outline and not as providing any type of advice or guidance. Neither should this brief summary be interpreted as suggesting whether or not this or any other legislation is applicable to your work. The nature of your status as researcher may help to determine whether or not your research is covered by the scope of this or other legislation, where you intend to process personal data. Where your research is covered by the scope of this or other legislation, you should seek advice that is appropriate to the particular circumstances of your research project where this involves the processing of personal data. Data protection legislation is likely to exist in countries outside the European Union, and you will need to be familiar with legislative requirements where you undertake your research project to understand how these may affect your research and the legal obligations that this places on you. Whether or not your research is affected by data protection legislation, you will also be aware of the need to conduct your research ethically, and your university will have ethical requirements for researchers and the conduct of their research projects (Sections 6.5 and 6.6).

Use of anonymised data

This discussion of legally based data protection concerns has hopefully focused your mind on the implications of processing personal data. Unless there is a clear reason for processing these data, the best course of action is likely to be to ensure that your data are completely and genuinely anonymised and that any 'key' to identify data subjects is not retained by those who control these data. Data protection legislation does not apply to data that have been effectively anonymised although there may be other legal requirements that still need to be taken into account. Recital 26 of the GDPR states that, "The principles of data protection should therefore not apply to anonymous information, namely information which does not relate to an identified or identifiable natural person or to personal data rendered anonymous in such a manner that the data subject is not or no longer identifiable. This Regulation does not therefore concern the processing of such anonymous information, including for statistical or research purposes" (Official Journal of the European Union 2016: L119/5 EN).

There are various techniques to anonymise personal data. In relation to qualitative data these include removing data subjects' names and other personal identifiers from

Box 6.20 Focus on research in the news

Companies need to embrace data laws regardless of burden

By Sarah Gordon

The General Data Protection Regulation aims to protect EU citizens' data, regardless of borders or where the data are processed. The rules will affect any company collecting and utilising data – which in practice means almost all groups will need to get much better at good data protection practices, and quickly. For individuals, it is good news. WannaCry was just the latest example of how vulnerable our data are, with the cyber attack hitting organisations in 150 countries, from the UK's National Health Service to Spain's Telefónica and FedEx, the US logistics company. And WannaCry followed a litany of other breaches at companies entrusted with our information.

We will have the right to see our information in an easily read format – so-called "data portability" – as well as to have it erased – the "right to be forgotten". The transfer of our data outside the EU will be further restricted. For the first time there will be specific rules protecting children.

GDPR will transform how all organisations store and manage personal data. Companies which do not yet have an organised data protection programme will need to establish one. All data activities will have to be accurately recorded – and the obligation extends to anybody working with a company, such as third-party contractors. The regulation applies to companies both big and small. But for organisations with more than 250 employees, there are significant new obligations to maintain records of data processing activities. Even those with less than 250 employees will have to maintain records of activities related to "higher risk" processing such as Criminal Records Bureau checks.

This – non-exhaustive – list gives some sense of the mountain of preparation many companies will have to climb to comply with GDPR. Those that know it is coming are already fretting about the work involved. More worryingly, many appear unaware of what looms on the horizon. But the risks, both financial and reputational, of not complying are substantial, involving fines of up to €20m or 4 per cent of annual global turnover, whichever is the higher.

Advisers suggest such uncertainty should not stop any company in the EU getting its act together. The list of what this involves is long but it includes: appointing a data protection officer; revising customer terms and privacy policies; checking that record-keeping is up to scratch; reviewing contracts with outside parties; and making sure the board is aware of the risks if the company does not comply.

 Source: Extracts from 'Companies need to embrace data laws regardless of burden. The General Data Protection Regulation will next year protect EU citizens' data', Sarah Gordon (2017) *Financial Times,* 14 June. Copyright © 2018 The Financial Times Limited

documents and records; using pseudonyms, especially in reporting; obscuring faces and other identifiers in visual images; blurring facial images and other identifiers in video recordings; and electronically altering voices in audio recordings. In relation to quantitative data these include data masking, where personal identifiers are removed; using pseudonyms, especially in reporting; and data aggregation. One source that we have found to be particularly useful when considering the various aspects involved in data anonymisation is, '*Anonymisation: managing data protection risk code of practice*' (UK Information Commissioner's Office 2012).

Data management

The requirement to manage your data in an ethical and legally compliant way can be formalised in a **data management plan**, which outlines how data will be collected, organised, managed, stored securely and backed up.

Files containing confidential or personal data will need to be properly labelled and securely kept. This refers not only to your original notes or recordings, but also to any subsequent drafts, transcriptions, re-recordings, backup and anonymised versions. Original notes or recordings are likely to include personal identifiers such as names, job titles, workplace locations that clearly identify the person being interviewed or observed. Personal identifiers may also exist on completed questionnaire forms. Anonymised versions of data will have used tactics such as aggregating data, pseudonyms and higher levels of generalisation to remove personal identifiers. Nevertheless, where these personal identifiers still exist in another document, there remains the possibility they may be used to reveal the identities of participants or respondents. Particular care needs to be exercised when storing original versions of data that include personal identifiers, or when storing personal identifiers that relate to anonymised versions of data where these identifiers hold the key to revealing the identities of individuals in these anonymised versions. Data that contain personal identifiers therefore need to be held securely and separately to anonymised versions of data to which they relate (UK Data Archive 2011) to protect them from unauthorised access.

Security will take a number of forms. Paper copies of interview or observation notes, signed consent forms, structured observation forms, questionnaires, transcriptions and other documents that contain confidential or personal data need to be kept in a restricted, secure and safe place. Data held externally, such as on USB mass storage devices, will also need to be stored under the same conditions and password protected. Data held on a computer hard drive will also need to be protected through the use of a password as well as by firewall and network protection software. Online file sharing and storage services will also allow you to keep an online copy of your data files, although it is advisable not to store confidential or sensitive data in a cloud service without first using additional security. Indeed many universities explicitly prohibit the use of third party cloud services.

When data are to be destroyed this needs to be carried out with due care so that paper documents are shredded, not just placed in a bin, and computer files and other digital material are permanently deleted (UK Data Archive 2011). The management of your data in these ways illustrates how ethical concerns are likely to remain beyond the end of your research project in order to continue to maintain the confidentiality of the data that was collected, the anonymity of participants, their privacy and to ensure that harm is not caused to those who helped you.

6.8 Summary

- Access and ethics are critical aspects for the conduct of research.
- Different types of access exist: traditional access, Internet-mediated access, intranet-mediated access and hybrid access.

- In addition, it is helpful to differentiate between organisational access (sub-divided into either multi-organisation access or single-organisation access) and access to individuals (individual person access and elite person access).
- Each type of access is associated with issues that may affect your ability to collect suitable, high-quality data.
- Different levels of access have been identified: physical access, virtual access, continuing access and cognitive access.
- Feasibility and sufficiency are important determinants of what you choose to research and how you will conduct it.
- Issues related to gaining access will depend to some extent on your role as either an external researcher or a participant researcher.
- Your approach to research may combine traditional access with Internet- or intranet-mediated access leading to the use of a hybrid access strategy.
- There are a range of strategies to help you to gain access to organisations and to intended participants or respondents within them.
- Research ethics refers to the standards of behaviour that guide your conduct in relation to the rights of those who become the subject of your work or are affected by it.
- Potential ethical issues should be recognised and considered from the outset of your research and are one of the criteria against which your research is judged. Issues may be anticipated by using codes of ethics, ethical guidelines and ethical principles.
- The Internet has facilitated access for particular types of research strategy; however, its use is associated with a range of ethical concerns and even dilemmas in certain types of research, notably related to respecting rights of privacy and copyright.
- Ethical concerns can occur at all stages of your research project: during choice of research topic and research design, when seeking access, during data collection, as you analyse data, when you report your findings and subsequently as you manage data.
- Qualitative research is likely to lead to a greater range of ethical concerns in comparison with quantitative research, although all research methods have specific ethical issues associated with them.
- Ethical concerns are also associated with the 'power relationship' between the researcher and those who grant access, and the researcher's role (as external researcher, internal researcher or internal consultant).
- Researchers also need to consider their own safety very carefully when planning and conducting research.
- Further ethical and legal concerns are associated with data protection and data management, affecting the collection, processing, storage and use of personal and confidential data. Researchers need to comply carefully with data protection legislation when using personal data, to protect the privacy of their data subjects and to avoid the risk of any harm occurring.

Self-check questions

Help with these questions is available at the end of the chapter.

6.1 How can you differentiate between types of access and why is it important to do this?

6.2 What do you understand by the use of the terms 'feasibility' and 'sufficiency' when applied to the question of access?

6.3 Which strategies to help to gain access are likely to apply to the following scenarios:

a an 'external' researcher seeking direct access to managers who will be the research participants;

b an 'external' researcher seeking access through an organisational gatekeeper/broker to their intended participants or respondents;

c an internal researcher planning to undertake a research project within their employing organisation?

6.4 What are the principal ethical issues you will need to consider irrespective of the particular research methods that you use?

6.5 What problems might you encounter in attempting to protect the interests of participating organisations and individuals despite the assurances that you provide?

Review and discussion questions

6.6 In relation to your proposed research project, evaluate your scope to use:

a a traditional approach;

b an Internet- or intranet-mediated approach;

c a hybrid access strategy to gain access to those you wish to take part. Make notes about the advantages and disadvantages of each access strategy.

6.7 With a friend, discuss the outcomes of the evaluation you carried out for Question 6.6. From this, discuss how you intend to gain access to the data you need for your research project. In your discussion make a list of possible barriers to your gaining access and how these might be overcome. Make sure that the ways you consider for overcoming these barriers are ethical!

6.8 Agree with a friend to each obtain a copy of your university's or your own professional association's ethical code. Each of you should make a set of notes regarding those aspects in the ethical code that you feel are relevant to your own research proposal and a second set of notes of those aspects you feel are relevant to your friend's research proposal. Discuss your findings.

6.9 Visit the Suzy Lamplugh Trust website at http://www.suzylamplugh.org and the Social Research Association at http://the-sra.org.uk/sra_resources/safety-code/. Browse the guidance leaflets/web pages and safety code located at these websites. Make a list of the actions you should take to help ensure your own personal safety when undertaking your research project. Make sure you actually put these into practice.

6.10 Visit the Research Ethics Guidebook at www.ethicsguidebook.ac.uk and browse through the sections of this guide. In relation to the context of your proposed research project, make a note of points that provide additional guidance to help you to anticipate and deal with potential ethical concerns.

 ## Progressing your research project

Negotiating access and addressing ethical issues

Consider the following aspects:

• Which types of data will you require in order to be able to answer your proposed research question and address your research objectives sufficiently?

• Which research methods do you intend to use to obtain these data (including secondary data as appropriate)?

• What type(s) of access will you require in order to be able to collect data?

• What problems are you likely to encounter in gaining access?

• Which strategies to gain access will be useful to help you to overcome these problems?

- Depending on the type of access envisaged and your research status (i.e. as an external researcher or internal/practitioner researcher), produce appropriate requests for organisational access and/or requests to individuals for their cooperation along with associated information sheets.
- Describe the ethical issues that are likely to affect your proposed research project, including your own personal safety. Discuss how you will seek to overcome or control these. This should be undertaken in relation to the various stages of your research project.
- Note down your answers. Use the questions in Box 1.4 to guide your reflective diary entry.

References

Bakardjieva, M. and Feenberg, A. (2000) 'Involving the virtual subject', *Ethics and Information Technology,* Vol. 2, pp. 233–240.

Bell, E. and Bryman, A. (2007) 'The ethics of management research: An exploratory content analysis', *British Journal of Management,* Vol. 18, No. 1, pp. 63–77.

Bishop, L. and Kuula-Luumi, A. (2017) 'Revisiting Qualitative Data Reuse: A Decade On', *Sage Open,* January–March, pp. 1–15.

British Psychological Society (2009) *Code of Ethics and Conduct.* Leicester: British Psychological Society. Available at: https://www.bps.org.uk/sites/bps.org.uk/files/Policy%20-%20Files/Code%20 of%20Ethics%20and%20Conduct%20(2009).pdf [Accessed 12 December 2017].

British Psychological Society (2017) *Ethics Guidelines for Internet mediated Research.* INF206/04.2017 Leicester: British Psychological Society. Available at: https://www.bps.org.uk/ news-and-policy/ethics-guidelines-internet-mediated-research-2017 [Accessed 14 December 2017].

British Sociological Association (2017) *Statement of Ethical Practice.* Available at: https://www.britsoc. co.uk/media/24310/bsa_statement_of_ethical_practice.pdf [Accessed 12 December 2017].

Bryman, A. (1988) *Quantity and Quality in Social Research.* London: Unwin Hyman.

Buchanan, D., Boddy, D. and McCalman, J. (2013) 'Getting in, getting on, getting out and getting back', in A. Bryman (ed.) *Doing Research in Organisations.* London: Routledge Library Edition, pp. 53–67.

Call for Participants (2017) *Researchers page.* Available at https://www.callforparticipants.com/ [Accessed 11 December 2017].

Chartered Institute of Personnel and Development (2017) 'Unethical amnesia in repeat offenders', *Work,* Summer, p. 6.

Dale, A., Arber, S. and Procter, M. (1988) *Doing Secondary Research.* London: Unwin Hyman.

Forbes (2017) *The Big (Unstructured) Data Problem* Available at https://www.forbes.com/sites/ forbestechcouncil/2017/06/05/the-big-unstructured-data-problem/#7ca6f54e493a [Accessed 2 May 2018].

Groves, R.M., Presser, S. and Dipko, S. (2004) 'The Role of Topic Interest in Survey Participation Decisions', *Public Opinion Quarterly,* Vol. 68, No. 1, pp. 2–31.

Groves, R.M., Singer, E. and Corning, A. (2000) 'Leverage-Saliency Theory of Survey Participation', *Public Opinion Quarterly,* Vol. 64, No. 3, pp. 299–308.

Gummesson, E. (2000) *Qualitative Methods in Management Research* (2nd edn). Thousand Oaks, CA: Sage.

Healey, M.J. (1991) 'Obtaining information from businesses', in M.J. Healey (ed.) *Economic Activity and Land Use.* Harlow: Longman, pp. 193–251.

Health Research Authority (2017) *Is my study research? Decision Tool.* Available at http://www.hra-decisiontools.org.uk/research/ [Accessed 12 December 2017].

Hookway, N. (2008) 'Entering the blogosphere: Some strategies for using blogs in social research', *Qualitative Research,* Vol. 8, No. 1, pp. 91–113.

Information Commissioner's Office (2012) *Anonymisation: managing data protection risk code of practice.* Wilmslow: Information Commissioner's Office. Available at https://ico.org.uk/media/for-organisations/documents/1061/anonymisation-code.pdf [Accessed 6 May 2018].

Johnson, J.M. (1975) *Doing Field Research.* New York: Free Press.

Kozinets, R.V. (2015) *Netnography Redefined* (2nd edn). London: Sage.

Madge, C. (2010) *Online research ethics.* Available at http://www.restore.ac.uk/orm/ethics/ethprint3.pdf [Accessed 14 December 2017].

Markham, A. and Buchanan, E. (2012) *Ethical Decision-Making and Internet Research: Recommendations from the AoIR Ethics Working Committee (Version 2.0).* Available at http://aoir.org/reports/ethics2.pdf [Accessed 14 December 2017].

Marshall, C. and Rossman, G.B. (2016) *Designing Qualitative Research* (6th edn). London: Sage Publications.

McAreavey, R. and Muir, J. (2011) 'Research ethics committees: Values and power in higher education', *International Journal of Social Research Methodology,* Vol. 14, No. 5, pp. 391–405.

Official Journal of the European Union (2016) *Regulation (EU) 2016/679 of The European Parliament and of The Council of 27 April 2016 on the protection of natural persons with regard to the processing of personal data and on the free movement of such data, and repealing Directive 95/46/EC.* Vol 59, L119, pp. 1–88. Available at https://eur-lex.europa.eu/legal-content/EN/TXT/PDF/?uri=OJ:L:2016:119:FULL&from=EN [Accessed 06 May 2018].

Okumus, F., Altinay, L. and Roper, A. (2007) 'Gaining access for research: Reflections from experience', *Annals of Tourism Research,* Vol. 34, No. 1, pp. 7–26.

Peticca-Harris, A., deGama, N, and Elias, S.R.S.T.A. (2016) 'A dynamic process model for finding informants and gaining access in qualitative research', *Organizational Research Methods,* Vol. 19, No. 3, pp. 376–401.

Rowlinson, K., Appleyard, L. and Gardner, J. (2016) 'Payday lending in the UK: the regul(aris)ation of a necessary evil?', *Journal of Social Policy,* Vol. 45, No. 3, pp. 527–523.

Saunders, M.N.K., Gray, D.E. and Bristow, A. (2017) 'Beyond the Single Organization: Inside Insights From Gaining Access for Large Multiorganization Survey HRD Research', *Human Resource Development Quarterly,* Vol. 28, No. 3, pp. 401–425.

Schoneboom, A. (2011) 'Workblogging in a Facebook age', *Work, Employment and Society,* Vol. 25, No. 1, pp. 132–40.

Sekaran, U. and Bougie, R. (2013) *Research Methods for Business: A Skill-Building Approach* (6th edn). Chichester: John Wiley.

Social Research Association (2001) *A Code of Practice for the Safety of Social Researchers.* Available at http://the-sra.org.uk/wp-content/uploads/safety_code_of_practice.pdf [Accessed 12 December 2017].

Stationery Office, The (1998) *Data Protection Act 1998.* London: The Stationery Office.

Trussell, N. and Lavrakas, P. J. (2004) 'The Influence of Incremental Increases in Token Cash Incentives on Mail Survey Response', *Public Opinion Quarterly,* Vol. 68, No. 3, pp. 349–367.

UK Data Archive (2011) *Managing and Sharing Data: Best Practice for Researchers* (3rd edn). Available at www.data-archive.ac.uk/media/2894/managingsharing.pdf [Accessed 14 December 2017].

UK Data Archive (2017) *Create and Manage Data – Anonymisation.* Available at https://www.ukdata-service.ac.uk/manage-data/legal-ethical/anonymisation [Accessed 15 December 2017].

Wells, P. (1994) 'Ethics in business and management research', in V.J. Wass and P.E. Wells (eds) *Principles and Practice in Business and Management Research.* Aldershot: Dartmouth, pp. 277–297.

Whiting, R. and Pritchard, K. (2018) 'Digital Ethics', in C. Cassell, A.L. Cunliffe and G. Grandy (eds) *The Sage Handbook of Qualitative Business and Management Research Methods.* Sage: London, pp. 562–579.

Further reading

Buchanan, D., Boddy, D. and McCalman, J. (2013) 'Getting in, getting on, getting out and getting back', in A. Bryman (ed.) *Doing Research in Organisations.* London: Routledge Library Edition, pp. 53–67. This continues to provide a highly readable, relevant and very useful account of the negotiation of access.

Hookway, N. (2008) 'Entering the blogosphere: Some strategies for using blogs in social research', *Qualitative Research,* Vol. 8, No. 1, pp. 91–113. This provides an interesting and useful account of the author's experience of using blogs in social research. Hookway provides a practical account of the steps that he took along with discussion of the data quality and ethical issues associated in attempting to use this approach.

Kozinets, R.V. (2015) *Netnography Redefined* (2nd edn). London: Sage. Chapter 6 provides a useful insight into the notions of ethical territory, research ethics and when data and people can be considered public or private. Issues of informed consent and harm are also discussed, along with concealment and fabrication.

Suzy Lamplugh Trust website at http://www.suzylamplugh.org and the Social Research Association website at http://the-sra.org.uk/sra_resources/safety-code/ to give you useful tips and information to help improve your personal safety.

Case 6
Gaining and maintaining fieldwork access with management consultants

Jean-Pierre (known to everyone as JP) is a Master's student studying for an MSc in International Management. He has previously worked for two different management consulting firms, which has led to his interest in conducting a research project on the sector. One of things that JP noticed when working for both firms is the importance that clients place on the firm's reputation when deciding which management consulting firm to work with. Yet, despite its importance, JP was not clear how clients were making judgements about the reputation of management consulting firms. This motivated him to research the question:

'How do clients form judgments about the reputation of management consulting firms?'

Since JP's research question was exploratory, he decided to conduct semi-structured interviews with both partners and clients of management consulting firms to gain a rich explanatory insight into judgements of reputation from the perspective of employees and clients. When he was previously employed in two different management consulting firms, JP worked with many employees and clients. Since he was planning to interview a senior group of people, he decided to read more about strategies for conducting elite interviews from the perspective of a junior researcher (Harvey, 2011).

JP had read in his research methods textbook that it was good practice to pilot his interview questions first, so he decided to draw on some of his existing contacts to help set up these interviews. He very quickly arranged two telephone interviews: one with a partner of an American management consulting firm and one with a chief operating officer of a major aerospace company based in France. He was fortunate to speak to both interviewees for approximately 45 minutes and felt that he gained some interesting insights about how clients evaluate reputation. However, one interviewee asked about the ethical code of conduct for his research project, a question he felt he did not answer particularly well. JP also asked both interviewees whether they could recommend other people for him to speak to, which both said they would think about, although neither ever got back to him.

Having completed two pilot interviews with senior professionals, JP felt that he was ready to embark on the main interviews for his fieldwork. He planned to interview a further seven employees and seven clients of different management consulting firms. Unfortunately, he struggled to gain access to other interviewees, despite following-up with former professional contacts and the two interviewees that he interviewed for the pilot study.

As a final resort, JP decided to contact Claire, a junior Board member of a professional association representing management consultants, to see if she was willing to be interviewed as part of his research. Fortunately, Claire agreed to be interviewed and the conversation lasted for over two hours, providing what JP considered was excellent data. Claire gave suggestions of how JP's interview questions could be phrased more clearly and outlined some possible areas related to how clients judged reputation which she felt JP might pursue with other interviewees.

Following JP's request, Claire agreed to refer several partners and clients for him to interview. JP made good initial progress with his interviews and he felt that he had a better command over his questions. However, several weeks later, JP received a rather terse e-mail from Claire saying that she had spoken to a few of his interviewees that she had referred him to. They were not happy with some of his questions and none of them had received an email, letter or telephone call from him to say thank you or explain how they could learn more about the outcomes of the project. Claire said that she was extremely reluctant to encourage other members of her professional network to be interviewed by JP unless he revised his questions. It transpired that JP had not taken the time to rephrase his questions or include the possible areas Claire had suggested. Claire also wanted reassurance about JP's professional conduct and dissemination plan for participants.

JP reflected critically on his conduct and realised that he needed to take on board the feedback and incorporate this into his interview conduct. He also realised that he needed to be as focused on the context and needs of the interviewees as he was about his own concerns around completing his fieldwork in a timely manner. He started doing some further reading about gaining access to, conducting interviews on and following-up with interviewees (Irvine and Gaffikin 2006; Dundon and Ryan 2010; Berger 2015; Lancaster 2017). He also apologised to Claire and contacted all the interviewees to thank them for their time and to explain when he would be in touch with an executive summary of his findings.

Having learned a hard lesson and read further, JP was better able to continue his fieldwork to a significantly higher standard. Fortunately, Claire and some of the other interviewees helped him to gain access to further interviewees. As a result, JP completed all 14 additional interviews within his timeframe. The quality of the data were sufficiently high for him to identify important themes related to his research question which subsequently enabled him to make an important contribution to the extant literature in his research project. He also learned some valuable lessons about gaining and maintaining access, which he wished he had known about before embarking on the fieldwork.

References

Berger, R. (2015). 'Now I see it, now I don't: Researcher's position and reflexivity in qualitative research'. *Qualitative Research,* 15(2), 219–234.

Dundon, T., & Ryan, P. (2010). 'Interviewing reluctant respondents: Strikes, henchmen, and Gaelic games', *Organizational Research Methods,* 13(3), 562–581.

ESRC (2017). Research Ethics. Url: http://www.esrc.ac.uk/funding/guidance-for-applicants/research-ethics/

Harvey, W.S. (2011). 'Strategies for conducting elite interviews', *Qualitative Research,* 11(4), 431–441.

Irvine, H., & Gaffikin, M. (2006) 'Getting in, getting on and getting out: reflections on a qualitative research project', *Accounting, Auditing & Accountability Journal,* 19(1), 115–145.

Lancaster, K. (2017). 'Confidentiality, anonymity and power relations in elite interviewing: conducting qualitative policy research in a politicised domain', *International Journal of Social Research Methodology,* 20(1), 93–103.

Questions

1 What are some ethical and procedural steps that JP could have adopted in his research design?
2 What are some of the ways that JP could have considered gaining access?
3 How might JP have piloted more effectively?

Additional case studies relating to material covered in this chapter are available via the book's companion website: **www.pearsoned.co.uk/saunders.**
    They are:

- The effects of a merger in a major UK building society.
- The quality of service provided by the accounts department.
- Misreading issues related to access and ethics in a small-scale enterprise.
- Mystery customer research in restaurant chains.
- Gaining access to business angels' networks.
- The impact of colour on children's brand choice.
- Chinese students' interpretations of trust.

Self-check answers

6.1   The initial types of access we referred to in this chapter are traditional, Internet- and intranet-mediated and hybrid. Traditional access is divided into a number of levels. These are: physical entry or initial access to an organisational setting; continuing access, which recognises that researchers often need to develop their access on an incremental basis; and cognitive access, where you will be concerned to gain the cooperation of individuals once you have achieved access to the organisation in which they work. We also referred to personal access, which allows you to consider whether you actually need to meet with participants in order to carry out an aspect of your research as opposed to corresponding with them or sending them a self-completed, postal questionnaire. Internet- and intranet-mediated access involves using one or more computing technologies to gain access to participants. Hybrid access involves using a combination of traditional and Internet-mediated forms of access. Access is strategically related to the success of your research project and needs to be carefully planned. In relation to many research designs, it will need to be thought of as a multifaceted aspect and not a single event.

6.2   Gaining access can be problematic for researchers for a number of reasons. The concept of feasibility recognises this and suggests that in order to be able to conduct your research it will be necessary to design it with access clearly in mind. Sufficiency refers to another issue related to access. There are two aspects to the issue of sufficiency. The first of these relates to whether you have sufficiently considered and therefore fully realised the extent and nature of the access that you will require in order to be able to answer your research question and objectives. The second aspect relates to whether you are able to gain sufficient access in practice in order to be able to answer your research question and objectives.

6.3   We may consider the three particular scenarios outlined in the question in Table 6.5.

6.4   The principal ethical issues you will need to consider irrespective of which research method you use are:

- maintaining your integrity and objectivity during the data collection, analysis and reporting stages;
- avoiding deception about why you are undertaking the research, its purpose and how the data collected will be used;
- respecting rights to privacy and not to be exposed to the risk of harm;

Table 6.5 Considering access

	Scenario A	Scenario B	Scenario C
Allowing yourself sufficient time to gain access	Universally true in all cases. The practitioner–researcher will be going through a very similar process to those who wish to gain access from the outside in terms of contacting individuals and organisations, meeting with them to explain the research, providing assurances, etc. The only exception will be related to a covert approach, although sufficient time for planning, etc. will of course still be required		
Using any existing contacts	Where possible		Yes
Developing new contacts	Probably necessary		This may still apply within large, complex organisations, depending on the nature of the research
Providing a clear account of the purpose of your research and what type of access you require, with the intention of establishing your credibility	Definitely necessary		Still necessary, although easier to achieve (verbally or internal memo) with familiar colleagues. Less easy with unfamiliar colleagues, which suggests just as much care as for external researchers
Overcoming organisational concerns in relation to the granting of access	Definitely necessary	Absolutely necessary. This may be the major problem to overcome since you are asking for access to a range of employees	Should not be a problem unless you propose to undertake a topic that is highly sensitive to the organisation! We know of students whose proposal has been refused within their organisation
Outlining possible benefits of granting access to you and any tangible outcome from doing so	Probably useful		Work-based research projects contain material of value to the organisation, although they may largely be theoretically based
Using suitable language	Definitely necessary		Still necessary at the level of individuals in the organisation
Facilitating ease of reply when requesting access	Definitely useful		Might be useful to consider in relation to certain internal individuals
Developing your access on an incremental basis	Should not be necessary, although you may wish to undertake subsequent work	Definitely worth considering	Might be a useful strategy depending on the nature of the research and the work setting
Establishing your credibility	Access is not being sought at 'lower' levels within the organisation: however, there is still a need to achieve credibility in relation to those to whom you are applying directly	Definitely necessary	May still be necessary with unfamiliar individuals in the organisation

- emphasising that participation is voluntary and that participants retain the right not to answer any questions that they do not wish to, or to provide any data requested. Those involved also retain the right to withdraw;
- achieving consent that is fully informed, considered and freely given. Research without prior fully informed consent should only be acceptable in very specific and previously approved circumstances;
- respecting assurances provided to organisations about the confidentiality of data and their anonymity;
- respecting assurances given to individuals about the confidentiality of the data they provide and their anonymity;
- considering the collective interests of individuals and organisations in the way you analyse, use and report the data which they provide;
- complying with legislation and other legal requirements relating to the processing and management of personal and confidential data;
- considering your own personal safety and that of other researchers.

6.5 A number of ethical problems might emerge. These are considered in turn. You may wish to explore a point made by one of your participants but to do so might lead to harmful consequences for this person where the point was attributed to him or her. It may be possible for some people who read your work to identify a participating organisation, although you do not actually name it. This may cause embarrassment to the organisation. Individual participants may also be identified by the nature of the comments that you report, again leading to harmful consequences for them. Your report may also lead to action being taken within an organisation that adversely affects those who were kind enough to take part in your research. Finally, others may seek to reuse any survey data that you collect, and this might be used to disadvantage those who provided the data by responding to your questionnaire or other data collection method. You may have thought of other problems that might also emerge.

Get ahead using resources on the companion website at: **www.pearsoned.co. uk/saunders.**

- Improve your IBM SPSS Statistics research analysis with practice tutorials.
- Save time researching on the Internet with the Smarter Online Searching Guide.
- Test your progress using self-assessment questions.

Chapter **7**

Selecting samples

Learning outcomes

By the end of this chapter you should:

- understand the need to select samples in business and management research;
- be aware of a range of probability and non-probability sampling techniques and the possible need to combine techniques within a research project;
- be able to choose appropriate sampling techniques for a variety of research scenarios and justify your choices;
- be able to use a range of sampling techniques;
- be able (where appropriate) to assess the representativeness of the sample selected;
- be able to assess the extent to which it is reasonable to generalise from a sample;
- be able to apply the knowledge, skills and understanding gained to your own research project.

7.1 Introduction

Whatever your research question(s) and objectives, you will need to consider whether you need to select one or more samples. Occasionally, it may be possible to collect and analyse data from every possible case or group member; this is termed a **census**. However, for many research questions and objectives it will be impossible for you either to collect or to analyse all the potential data available to you, owing to restrictions of time, money and often access. This means you will need to select data for a subgroup or **sample** of all possible cases. Sampling techniques enable you to reduce the amount of data you need to collect by considering only data from a subgroup rather than all possible cases or **elements**. Some research questions will require sample data that can allow you to generalise statistically about all the cases from

Interpreting advertisers' claims

In our daily lives we constantly see claims made by advertisers in news media and on television about products and services such as "87 per cent of women who used . . . said . . ." or "76 per cent of shoppers who liked . . . also liked . . .". Often these claims are based on data collected from a sample of consumers using some form of question-naire. When interpreting these claims, like most consumers, we usually assume the claim made from the sample is applicable to all consumers of that product or service. Not surprising advertisers are expected, often through self-regulation, to ensure there is a reasonable basis for these claims and that they are made on the basis of objective evidence. To support such self-regulation the associated industry bodies have developed codes of practice. These set out what is considered a reasonable basis and what is objective evidence, some offering guidance about sample requirements.

The *Canadian Code of Advertising Standards,* produced and administered by the self-regulating industry body Advertising Standards Canada (2016), requires that advertisers and advertisement agencies in that country are able to substantiate all objective claims that an advertisement conveys to consumers. In their associated guidance (Advertising Standards Canada, 2012) they recommend an overall sample size of not less than 300 when selected from large populations, and that the sample must produce a margin of error of no more than plus or minus 6 per cent at the 95 per cent level of certainty. This means that if an advertisement for skin cream in Canada makes the claim "87 per cent say it reduces wrinkles", then it can be inferred that somewhere between 81 per cent and 93 per cent of the target consumers will respond in this particular way (the margin of error) with 95 per cent certainty that the sample represented the characteristics of the target population of consumers.

In contrast, the UK's advertising self-regularity system is set out in two advertising codes: the *BCAP Code* for broadcast advertising and the *CAP Code* for non-broadcasting advertising (Committee of Advertising Practice, 2010; 2014). These are administered by the Advertising Standards Authority and referred to as rules or regulations. Like the Canadian code these two sets of 'rules' require that advertisers' claims, which are likely to be regarded by consumers as objective, can be substantiated. However, although there is no easily accessible advice on sample size or associated margin of error and level of certainty, a subsequent 'quick guide' (Committee of Advertising Practice, 2016) offers useful advice regarding sample size. If the sample size is relatively small so that the findings may not be statistically significant, the guide suggests it is best to include details about the sample in the advertisement. As a consequence advertisements in the UK containing claims based on a small sample size such as "87 per cent of consumers say it reduces wrinkles*" usually include a 'small print' statement such as "*59 out of 67 consumers surveyed, May 2018".

which your sample has been selected. In the opening vignette you will see how advertisers are expected to substantiate claims made about consumers' views by selecting a robust representative sample of consumers. For example, if an advertiser claims 87 per cent of a sample of users of a skin cream said it reduced wrinkles you might infer that 87 per cent of all that skin cream's users thought the same. Yet, whether this claim was sufficiently robust and representative to allow you to make this (statistical) generalisation would depend on the number of consumers from whom data were collected and how that sample of consumers had been selected. Other research questions may not involve such generalisations. To gain an understanding of how people manage their careers, you may select a small sample of company chief executives. For such research your sample selection would be based on the premise that, as these people have reached executive level they have been very successful in managing their own careers, and so will be most likely to be able to offer insights from which you can build understanding. Alternatively you may adopt a case study strategy using one large organisation and collect your data from a number of employees and managers using unstructured interviews. For this research you will still need to select your case study (sample) organisation and a group (sample) of employees and managers to interview. Consequently, whatever your research question, an understanding of techniques for selecting samples is likely to be very important.

The full set of cases or elements from which a sample is taken is called the **population**. In sampling, the term 'population' is not used in its normal sense, as the full set of cases need not necessarily be people. For research to discover the level of service at Indian restaurants throughout a country, the population from which you would select your sample would be all Indian restaurants in that country. Alternatively, you might need to establish the normal 'range' in miles that can be travelled by electric cars in everyday use produced by a particular manufacturer. Here the population would be all the electric cars in everyday use produced by that manufacturer.

When selecting a sample to study, it should represent the population from which it is taken in a way that is meaningful and which we can justify in relation to answering our research question and meeting our objectives (Becker 1998). If we are using our sample data to infer statistically something about a population, it is important that our sample is sufficiently large to allow such statistical inferences to be made with an acceptable margin of error. In the opening vignette we see how the requirement for advertisers to ensure the claims conveyed in their advertisements are reasonable and can be substantiated, necessitates careful consideration of sample size. We also see (in the UK) the expectation that qualifying text is included in the advertisements to allow claims made to be assessed where the findings may not be statistically significant due to the small sample size.

The need to sample

For some research questions it is possible to collect data from an entire population as it is of a manageable size. However, you should not assume that a census would necessarily provide more useful results than collecting data from a sample. Sampling provides a valid alternative to a census when:

- it would be impracticable for you to survey the entire population;
- your budget constraints prevent you from surveying the entire population;
- your time constraints prevent you from surveying the entire population.

For all research questions where it would be impracticable for you to collect data from the entire population, you need to select a sample. This is equally important whether you are planning to use interviews, questionnaires, observation or some other data collection technique. You might be able to obtain permission to collect data from only two or three organisations. Alternatively, testing an entire population of products to destruction, such as to establish the actual duration of long-life batteries, would be impractical for any manufacturer.

With other research questions it might be theoretically possible for you to collect data from the entire population, but the overall cost would prevent it. It is obviously cheaper for you to collect, prepare for analysis and check data from 250 customers than from 2,500, even though the cost per case for your study (in this example, customer) is likely to be higher than with a census. Your costs will be made up of new costs such as sample selection, and the fact that overhead costs such as the questionnaire, interview or observation schedule design and general preparation of data for analysis are spread over a smaller number of cases. Sampling also saves time, an important consideration when you have tight deadlines. The organisation of data collection is more manageable as fewer cases are involved. As you have less data to prepare for analysis and then to analyse, the results will be available more quickly.

Many researchers, for example Barnett (2002), argue that using sampling makes possible a higher overall accuracy than a census. The smaller number of cases for which you need to collect data means that more time can be spent designing and piloting the means of collecting these data. Collecting data from fewer cases also means that you can collect information that is more detailed. If you are employing people to collect the data (perhaps as interviewers) you can afford higher-quality staff. You can also devote more time to trying to obtain data from more difficult to reach cases. Once your data have been collected, proportionally more time can be devoted to checking and testing the data for accuracy prior to analysis. However, one point remains crucial when selecting a sample: it must enable you to answer your research question!

The importance of defining the research population clearly

The sample selected should be related to the population that is highlighted in the research question and objectives. This means that if a research question is about all owners of a particular brand of tablet, then the population is all owners of a particular brand of tablet computer, and the sample selected should be a subset of all those owners. This sample, providing it is selected carefully, will allow conclusions to be drawn about all owners of that brand of tablet. However, such a population may be difficult to research as not all elements or cases may be known to the researcher or easy to access. Consequently, the researcher may redefine the population as something more manageable. This is often a subset of the population and is called the **target population** (Figure 7.1) and is the actual focus or target of the research inquiry. For example, rather than defining your population as all owners of a particular brand of tablet computer, you may redefine your target population as all owners of a particular brand of tablet who are studying for a business and management degree at one university. However, business and management students at one university are unlikely to be the same as all tablet owners, and even students from other universities may differ! Consequently, using a sample drawn from this target population of students to find out about all owners of a brand of tablet computer may result in biased or incorrect conclusions. In selecting your sample from this target population, you have narrowed the focus of your research to business and management students at

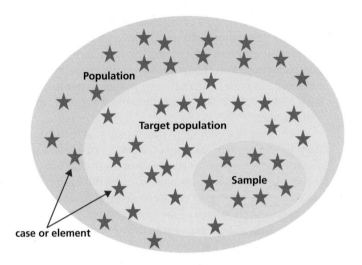

Figure 7.1 Population, target population, sample and individual cases

a particular university who own that brand of tablet computer. We discuss this further in Sections 7.2 and 7.3.

An overview of sampling techniques

Sampling techniques available to you can be divided into two types:

- probability or representative sampling;
- non-probability sampling.

Those discussed in this chapter are highlighted in Figure 7.2. With **probability samples** the chance, or probability, of each case being selected from the target population is known and is usually equal for all cases. This means it is possible to answer research questions and to achieve objectives that require you to estimate statistically the characteristics of the target population from the sample. Consequently, probability sampling is often associated with survey and experiment research strategies (Sections 5.4 and 5.8). For **non-probability samples**, the probability of each case being selected from the target population is not known and it is impossible to answer research questions or to address objectives that require you to make statistical inferences about the characteristics of the population. You may still be able to generalise from non-probability samples about the target population, but not on statistical grounds. However, with both types of sample you can answer other forms of research question, such as 'What job attributes attract people to jobs?' or 'How are financial services institutions adapting their services in response to the post-2009 crash liquidity rules?'

Subsequent sections of this chapter outline the most frequently used probability (Section 7.2) and non-probability (Section 7.3) sampling techniques, discuss their advantages and disadvantages and give examples of how and when you might use them. Although each technique is discussed separately, for many research projects you will need to use a combination of sampling techniques, some projects involving both probability and non-probability sampling techniques. Sampling designs that have two or more successive stages using either probability, non-probability, or both types of sample selection techniques are known as **multi-stage sampling** and are discussed in Section 7.4.

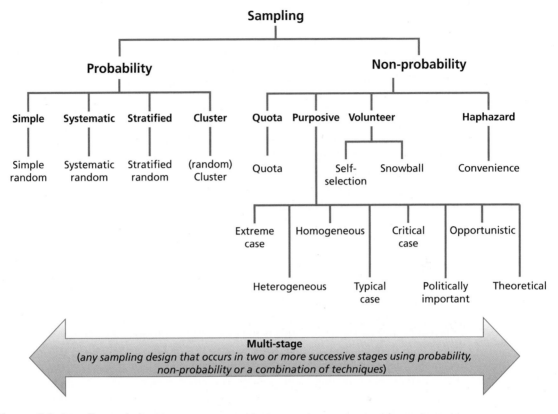

Figure 7.2 Sampling techniques

7.2 Probability sampling

Probability sampling (or **representative sampling**) is associated most commonly with survey research strategies where you need to make statistical inferences from your sample about a population to answer your research question(s) and to meet your objectives. The process of probability sampling can be divided into four stages:

1 Identify a suitable sampling frame based on your research question(s) and objectives.
2 Decide on a suitable sample size.
3 Select the most appropriate sampling technique and select the sample.
4 Check that the sample is representative of the target population.

Each of these stages will be considered in turn. However, for target populations of fewer than 50 cases, Henry (1990) advises against probability sampling. He argues that you should collect data on the entire target population, as the influence of a single extreme case on subsequent statistical analyses is more pronounced than for larger samples.

Identifying a suitable sampling frame and the implications for generalisability

The **sampling frame** for any probability sample is a complete list of all the cases in the target population from which your sample will be drawn. Without a sampling frame, you will not be able to select a probability sample and so will have to consider using non-probability sampling. If your research question or objective is concerned with members of a student society, your sampling frame will be the complete member-ship list for that society. If your research question or objective is concerned with registered child-minders in a local area, your sampling frame will be the directory of all registered child-minders in this area. Alternatively, if your research question is concerned with organisations in a particular sector, you may be thinking of creating a sampling frame from an existing database of companies available at your university, such as Fame or Amadeus. You then select your sample from your list.

Obtaining a sampling frame is therefore essential if you are going to use probability sampling. However, as highlighted in research by Edwards et al. (2007), you need to be aware of the possible problems of using existing databases for your sampling frame. In their work on multinationals in Britain, they found that:

- individual databases are often incomplete;
- the information held about organisations in databases is sometimes inaccurate;
- the information held in databases soon becomes out of date.

This emphasises the importance of ensuring your sampling frame is as complete, accu-rate and up to date as possible. An incomplete or inaccurate list means that some cases will have been excluded and so it will be impossible for every case in the target population to have a chance of selection. If this is the case you need to state it clearly.

Where no suitable list exists, and you wish to use probability sampling, you will have to compile your own sampling frame (perhaps drawing upon existing lists). It is important to ensure that your sampling frame is valid. You might decide to use a business directory as the sampling frame from which to select a sample of typical businesses. However, the business directory covers only subscribers who pay to be listed, often in one geographi-cal area. Your sample will therefore be biased towards businesses that have chosen to subscribe. If the directory is only updated annually, the sampling frame will be out of date ('non-current'). As some businesses choose not to subscribe, it will not be a valid repre-sentation of all businesses as it does not include these businesses. This means that you will be selecting a sample of businesses that choose to subscribe at the date the directory was compiled by a particular company!

The way you define your sampling frame also has implications regarding the extent to which you can generalise from your sample. As we have already discussed, sampling is used when it is impracticable or unnecessary to collect data from the entire population. Within probability sampling, by defining the sampling frame you are defining the target population about which you want to generalise. This means that if your sampling frame is a list of all customers of an organisation, strictly speaking you can only generalise, that is, apply statistically the findings based upon your sample, to that target population. Similarly, if your sampling frame is all employees of an organisation (the list being the organisation's payroll) you can only generalise statistically to employees of that organisa-tion. This can create problems, as often we hope that our findings have wider applica-bility than the target population from which our sample was selected. However, even if your probability sample has been selected from one large multinational organisation, you should not claim that what you have found would also occur in similar organisations. In other words, you should not generalise statistically beyond your sampling frame. Despite this, researchers often do make such claims, rather than placing clear limits on the gen-eralisability of the findings.

An increasing number of organisations specialise in selling electronic lists of names, addresses and email addresses. These lists include a wide range of people such as com-pany directors, chief executives, marketing managers, production managers and human

Box 7.1
Checklist

Selecting your sampling frame

✔ Are cases listed in the sampling frame relevant to your research topic, in other words does your target population enable you to answer your research question and meet your objectives?

✔ How recently was the sampling frame compiled; is it up to date?

✔ Does the sampling frame include all cases in the target population; is it complete?

✔ Does the sampling frame contain the correct information; is it accurate?

✔ Does the sampling frame exclude irrelevant cases; is it precise?

✔ For purchased lists, can you establish and control precisely how the sample will be selected?

resource managers, for public, private and non-profit-making organisations, and can be merged into standard email letters such as those requesting completion of online questionnaires (Section 11.4). Because you pay for the list or completed questionnaire by the case (named individual), the organisations that provide them usually select your sample. It is therefore important to establish precisely how they will select your sample as well as obtaining an indication of the database's completeness, accuracy and currency. For example, when obtaining a list of email addresses don't forget that some people change their Internet service provider and their email address regularly. This means the sampling frame is likely to under-represent this group. More generally, you need to ensure your intended sampling frame is relevant to your target population. Box 7.1 provides a checklist against which to check your sampling frame.

Deciding on a suitable sample size

Generalisations about target populations from data collected using any probability samples are based on statistical probability. The larger your sample's size the lower the likely error in generalising to the target population. Probability sampling is therefore a compromise between the accuracy of your findings and the amount of time and money you invest in collecting, checking and analysing the data. Your choice of sample size within this compromise is governed by:

- the confidence you need to have in your data – that is, the level of certainty that the characteristics of the data collected will represent the characteristics of the target population;
- the margin of error that you can tolerate – that is, the accuracy you require for any estimates made from your sample;
- the types of analyses you are going to undertake – in particular, the number of categories into which you wish to subdivide your data, as many statistical techniques have a minimum threshold of data cases (e.g. chi square, Section 12.5); and, to a lesser extent,
- the size of the target population from which your sample is being drawn.

Given these competing influences, it is not surprising that the final sample size is almost always a matter of judgement as well as of calculation. However, as we discuss in Section 12.5, if your sample is extremely large you may find that while relationships are statistically significant, the practical implications (effect size) of this difference are small (Ellis 2010). For many research questions and objectives, the specific statistical analyses (Section 12.5) you need to undertake will determine the threshold sample size for individual categories. In particular, an examination of virtually any statistics textbook (or Sections 12.3 and 12.5) will highlight that, in order to ensure spurious results do not occur, the data analysed must be normally distributed. While the normal distribution is discussed in Chapter 12, its implications for sample size need to be considered here. Statisticians have proved that the larger the absolute size of a sample, the closer its distribution will be to the normal distribution and thus the more robust it will be. This relationship, known as the **central limit theorem**, occurs even if the population from which the sample is drawn is not normally distributed. Statisticians have also shown that a sample size of 30 or more will usually result in a sampling distribution for the mean that is very close to a normal distribution. For this reason, Stutely's (2014) advice of a minimum number of 30 for statistical analyses provides a useful rule of thumb for the smallest number of cases in each category within your overall sample. Where the population in the category is less than 30, and you wish to undertake your analysis at this level of detail, you should normally collect data from all cases in that category.

It is likely that, if you are undertaking statistical analyses on your sample, you will be drawing conclusions from these analyses about the target population from which your sample was selected. This process of coming up with conclusions about a population on the basis of data describing the sample is called **statistical inference** and allows you to calculate how probable it is that your result, given your sample size, could have been obtained by chance. Such probabilities are usually calculated automatically by statistical analysis software. However, it is worth remembering that, providing they are not biased, samples of larger absolute size are more likely to be representative of the target population from which they are drawn than smaller samples and, in particular, the mean (average) calculated for the sample is more likely to equal the mean for the target population. This is known as the **law of large numbers**.

Researchers normally work to a 95 per cent level of certainty. This means that if your sample was selected 100 times, at least 95 of these samples would be certain to represent the characteristics of the target population. The confidence level states the precision of your estimates of the target population as the percentage that is within a certain range or margin of error (Box 7.2). Table 7.1 provides a guide to the different minimum sample sizes required from different sizes of target population given a 95 per cent confidence level for different margins of error. It assumes that data are collected from all cases in the sample (details of the calculation for minimum sample size and adjusted minimum sample size are given in Appendix 2). For most business and management research, researchers are content to estimate the target population's characteristics at 95 per cent certainty to within plus or minus 3 to 5 per cent of its true values. This means that if 45 per cent of your sample are in a particular category then you will be 95 per cent certain that your estimate for the target population, within the same category, will be 45 per cent plus or minus the margin of error – somewhere between 42 and 48 per cent for a 3 per cent margin of error.

As you can see from Table 7.1, the smaller the absolute size of the sample and, to a far lesser extent, the smaller the relative proportion of the target population sampled, the greater the margin of error. Within this, the impact of absolute sample size on the margin of error decreases for larger sample sizes. De Vaus (2014) argues that it is for this reason that many market research companies limit their samples' sizes to approximately 2,000.

Box 7.2 Focus on research in the news

Britain's gig economy 'is a man's world'

By Sarah O'Connor

Gig economy companies vaunt the flexibility of their online labour platforms, which often allow people to log on to work whenever they want. Yet, while part-time or flexible work is often assumed to appeal more to women, data suggest the gig economy is powered by men.

Men account for 95 per cent of Uber taxi drivers and 94 per cent of Deliveroo couriers, the most visible gig workers in Britain. But the gender imbalance appears to extend beyond these traditionally male-dominated sectors to other parts of the gig economy too.

Roughly 1.1m people work in Britain's gig economy and 69 per cent of them are male, according to a face-to-face survey of 8,000 people by Ipsos Mori and the RSA (the Royal Society for the encouragement of Arts, Manufactures and Commerce). The survey found that 59 per cent of all UK gig workers were doing professional, creative or administrative tasks, while only 16 per cent were providing driving or delivery services.

The RSA defined gig workers as people who completed tasks via online platforms. This includes online white-collar work platforms such as Upwork and Talmix, but excludes those such as AirBnB, where people rent their assets rather than their labour. Roughly half of the gig workers surveyed by the RSA dabbled less than once a month, but men were particularly dominant among those who used the platforms weekly, accounting for about three-quarters of these committed giggers.

"We find no evidence of the gig economy being more appealing to women than men – in fact, gig workers in the UK are more than twice as likely to be men than women," said Brhmie Balaram, a senior researcher at the RSA. "Although this mostly reflects the types of occupations in the gig economy, there is still some under-representation of women."

The RSA's survey should be treated with some caution since it is based on a relatively small sample of 243 people who reported they had been involved in gig economy work. But the think-tank said all the comparisons in its report were statistically significant. Because the sample size is small, the proportion of gig workers who are men could be within a 62–76 per cent range. It is not clear why women should be under-represented in the gig economy. It is true that men are more likely to be self-employed in general – they account for about two-thirds of the 4.8m people in Britain who work for themselves – but most "gig economy" work is part-time and part-time self-employment in Britain tends to skew towards women. Official data show that almost 60 per cent of the part-time self-employed workforce is female.

 Source: Extract from O'Connor, S (2017) 'Britain's gig economy is a man's world', FT.com, 27 April. Copyright © 2017 The Financial Times.

Unfortunately, from many samples, a 100 per cent response rate is unlikely and so your sample will need to be larger to ensure sufficient responses for the margin of error you require.

Table 7.1 Sample sizes for different sizes of target population at a 95 per cent confidence level (assuming data are collected from all cases in the sample)

Target population	Margin of error			
	5%	3%	2%	1%
50	44	48	49	50
100	79	91	96	99
150	108	132	141	148
200	132	168	185	196
250	151	203	226	244
300	168	234	267	291
400	196	291	343	384
500	217	340	414	475
750	254	440	571	696
1 000	278	516	706	906
2 000	322	696	1091	1655
5 000	357	879	1622	3288
10 000	370	964	1936	4899
100 000	383	1056	2345	8762
1 000 000	384	1066	2395	9513
10 000 000	384	1067	2400	9595

The importance of a high response rate

The most important aspect of a probability sample is that it represents the target population. A perfect **representative sample** is one that exactly represents the target population from which it is taken. If 60 per cent of your sample were small service sector companies then, provided the sample was representative, you would expect 60 per cent of the target population to be small service sector companies. You therefore need to obtain as high a response rate as possible to reduce the risk of non-response bias and ensure your sample is representative (Groves and Peytcheva 2008). This is not to say that a low response rate will necessarily result in your sample being biased, just that it is more likely!

In reality, you are likely to have non-responses. Non-respondents are different from the rest of the target population because they are unable or unwilling to be involved in your research for whatever reason. Consequently, your respondents will not be representative of the target population and the data you collect may be biased. Bias resulting from respondents differing in meaningful ways from non-respondents is known as **non-response bias**. In addition, each non-response will necessitate an extra respondent being found to reach the required sample size, increasing the cost of your data collection.

You should therefore collect data on refusals to respond to both individual questions and entire questionnaires or interview schedules to check for non-response bias (Section 12.2) and report this briefly in your project report. For returned questionnaires or structured interviews, the American Association for Public Opinion Research (2016) suggests four levels of non-response that can be reported with regard to the proportion of applicable questions that have been answered:

- **complete refusal**: none of the questions answered;
- **break-off**: less than 50 per cent of all questions answered other than by a refusal or no answer (this therefore includes complete refusal);
- **partial response**: 50 per cent to 80 per cent of all questions answered other than by a refusal or no answer;

- **complete response**: over 80 per cent of all questions answered other than by a refusal or no answer.

Non-response is due to four interrelated problems:

- refusal to respond;
- ineligibility to respond;
- inability to locate respondent;
- respondent located but unable to make contact.

The most common reason for non-response is that your respondent refuses to answer all the questions or be involved in your research but does not give a reason. Such non-response can be minimised by paying careful attention to the methods used to collect your data (Chapters 9, 10 and 11). Alternatively, some of your selected respondents may not meet your research requirements and so will be **ineligible** to respond. Non-location and non-contact create further problems; the fact that these respondents are **unreachable** means they will not be represented in the data you collect.

As part of your research report, you will need to include your **response rate**. Neuman (2014) suggests that when you calculate this you should include all eligible respondents:

$$\text{total response rate} = \frac{\text{total number of responses}}{\text{total number in sample} - \text{ineligible}}$$

This he calls the **total response rate**. A more common way of doing this excludes ineligible respondents and those who, despite repeated attempts (Sections 10.7 and 11.8), were unreachable. This is known as the **active response rate**:

$$\text{active response rate} = \frac{\text{total number of responses}}{\text{total number in sample} - (\text{ineligible} + \text{unreachable})}$$

An example of the calculation of both the total response rate and the active response rate is given in Box 7.3.

Even after ineligible and unreachable respondents have been excluded, it is probable that you will still have some non-responses. You therefore need to be able to assess how representative your data are and to allow for the impact of non-response in your calculations of sample size. These issues are explored in subsequent sections.

Box 7.3
Focus on student research

Calculation of total and active response rates

Ming had decided to collect data from people who had left his company's employment over the past five years by using a telephone questionnaire. He obtained a list of the 1,034 people who had left over this period (the total population) and selected a 50 per cent sample. Unfortunately, he could obtain current telephone numbers for only 311 of the 517 ex-employees who made up his total sample. Of these 311 people who were potentially reachable, he obtained a response from 147. In addition, his list of people who had left his company was inaccurate, and nine of those he contacted were ineligible to respond, having left the company over five years earlier.

$$\text{His total response rate} = \frac{147}{517 - 9} = \frac{147}{508} = 28.9\%$$

$$\text{His active response rate} = \frac{147}{311 - 9} = \frac{147}{302} = 48.7\%$$

Estimating response rates and actual sample size required

With all probability samples, it is important that your sample size is large enough to provide you with the necessary confidence in your data. The margin of error must be within acceptable limits, and you must ensure that you will be able to undertake your analysis at the level of detail required. You therefore need to estimate the likely response rate – that is, the proportion of cases from your sample who will respond or from which data will be collected – and increase the sample size accordingly. Once you have an estimate of the likely response rate and the minimum or the adjusted minimum sample size, the actual sample size you require can be calculated using the following formula:

$$n^a = \frac{n \times 100}{re\%}$$

where n^a is the actual sample size required,

n is the minimum (or adjusted minimum) sample size (see Table 7.1 or Appendix 2),

$re\%$ is the estimated response rate expressed as a percentage.

This calculation is shown in Box 7.4.

If you are collecting your sample data from a secondary source (Section 8.2) within an organisation that has already granted you access, for example a database recording customer complaints, your response rate should be virtually 100 per cent. Your actual sample size will therefore be the same as your minimum sample size.

In contrast, estimating the likely response rate from a sample to which you will be sending a questionnaire or interviewing is more difficult. One way of obtaining this estimate is to consider the response rates achieved for similar surveys that have already been undertaken and base your estimate on these. Alternatively, you can err on the side of caution. For most academic studies involving individuals or organisations' representatives, response rates of approximately 50 per cent and 35 to 40 per cent respectively are reasonable (Baruch and Holtom 2008).

However, beware: response rates can vary considerably when collecting primary data. Reviewing literature on response rates for questionnaires Mellahi and Harris (2016) noted wide variation and no consensus as to what was acceptable. Noting response rates of

---

Box 7.4
Focus on student research

Calculation of actual sample size

Jan was a part-time student employed by a large manufacturing company. He had decided to send a questionnaire to the company's customers and calculated that an adjusted minimum sample size of 439 was required. From previous questionnaires that his company had used to collect data from customers, Jan knew the likely response rate would be

approximately 30 per cent. Using these data he could calculate his actual sample size:

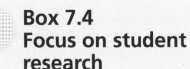

$$n^a = \frac{439 \times 100}{30}$$

$$= \frac{43900}{30}$$

$$= 1463$$

Jan's actual sample, therefore, needed to be 1,463 customers. The likelihood of 70 per cent non-response meant that Jan needed to include a means of checking that his sample was representative when he designed his questionnaire.

Box 7.5
Focus on management research

Reporting questionnaire response rates

In their 2008 *Human Relations* paper 'Survey responses rates: Levels and trends in organizational research', Baruch and Holtom offer useful advice regarding reporting responses rates from questionnaires. Within this they stress that authors should make it clear whether their questionnaire was administered (in other words respondents filled it in as part of their job, role or studies) or truly voluntary. They

also offer a checklist for authors (and editors), which covers information that should be included about the sample and the questionnaires returned. In particular:

- number of respondents to whom the questionnaire was sent;
- how the questionnaire was distributed;
- whether prior consent was obtained from respondents;
- the number of questionnaires returned;
- of those returned, the numbers that were useable;
- reasons (if known) for questionnaires not being useable;
- where different populations received a questionnaire, differences (if any) in response rates;
- techniques (if any) used to increase response rates;
- where response rates differ from likely norms, possible reasons for this.

between 1 per cent and 100 per cent in published Business and Management research they offer general guidelines dependent upon discipline suggesting mean response rates of 35 per cent for International Business and Marketing, while Human Resource Management and General Management typically achieve 50 per cent. Looking at mode of questionnaire delivery, Neuman (2014) suggests response rates of between 10 and 50 per cent for postal questionnaire surveys and up to 90 per cent for face-to-face interviews. Our examination of response rates to recent business surveys reveals rates as low as 10–20 per cent for Web and postal questionnaires, an implication being that respondents' questionnaire fatigue was a contributory factor! With regard to telephone questionnaires, response rates have fallen from 36 per cent to less than 9 per cent, due in part to people using answering services to screen calls (Dillman et al. 2014). Fortunately a number of different techniques, depending on your data collection method, can be used to enhance your response rate. These are discussed with the data collection method in the appropriate sections (Sections 10.3 and 11.5).

Selecting the most appropriate sampling technique and the sample

Having chosen a suitable sampling frame and establishing the actual sample size required, you need to select the most appropriate sampling technique to obtain a representative sample. Four main techniques can be used when selecting a probability sample (Figure 7.3):

- simple random;
- systematic random;
- stratified random;
- cluster.

Your choice of probability sampling technique depends on your research question(s) and your objectives. Subsequently, your need for face-to-face contact with respondents, and the geographical area over which the population is spread, further influence your choice of probability sampling technique (Figure 7.3). The structure of the sampling frame,

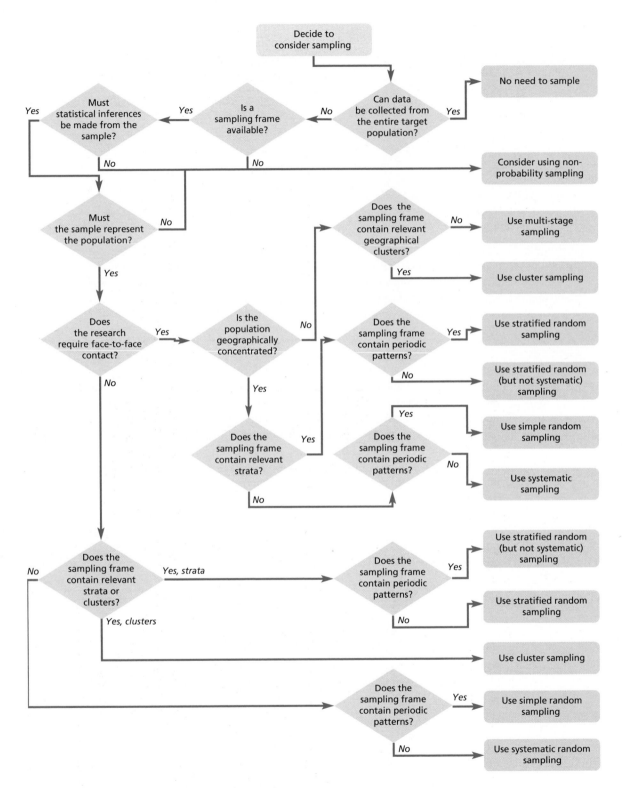

Figure 7.3 Choosing a probability sampling technique
Note: Simple random sampling ideally requires a sample size of over a few hundred

Table 7.2 Impact of various factors on choice of probability sampling techniques

Sample technique	Sampling frame required	Size of sample needed	Geographical area to which suited	Relative cost	Easy to explain to support workers?	Advantages compared with simple random
Simple random	Accurate and easily accessible	Better with over a few hundred	Concentrated if face-to-face contact required, otherwise does not matter	High if large sample size or sampling frame not computerised	Relatively difficult to explain	
Systematic random	Accurate, easily accessible and not containing periodic patterns. Actual list not always needed	Suitable for all sizes	Concentrated if face-to-face contact required, otherwise does not matter	Low	Relatively easy to explain	Normally no difference
Stratified random	Accurate, easily accessible, divisible into relevant strata (see comments for simple random and systematic random as appropriate)	See comments for simple random and systematic random as appropriate	Concentrated if face-to-face contact required, otherwise does not matter	Low, provided that lists of relevant strata available	Relatively difficult to explain (once strata decided, see comments for simple random and systematic random as appropriate)	Better comparison and hence representation across strata. Differential response rates may necessitate reweighting
Cluster	Accurate, easily accessible, relates to relevant clusters, not individual population members	As large as practicable	Dispersed if face-to-face contact required and geographically based clusters used	Low, provided that lists of relevant clusters available	Relatively difficult to explain until clusters selected	Quick but reduced precision

Source: © Mark Saunders, Philip Lewis and Adrian Thornhill 2018

the size of sample you need and, if you are using a research assistant, the ease with which the technique may be explained will also influence your decision. The impact of each of these is summarised in Table 7.2.

Simple random sampling

Simple random sampling (sometimes called just **random sampling**) involves you selecting the sample at random from the sampling frame using a spreadsheet's random number generator function or random number tables. To do this you:

1 Number each of the cases in your sampling frame with a unique number. The first case is numbered 1, the second 2 and so on.
2 Select cases using random numbers such as those generated by a spreadsheet (Table 7.3) until your actual sample size is reached.

Starting with your first random number, you use this and subsequent random numbers in the order they were generated to select the cases (elements) until your sample size is

Table 7.3 Extract of spreadsheet generated random numbers between 1 and 5011

4306	1966	1878	4428	3571	62	838	4881	3045	4192
4582	4543	457	4151	1208	2014	3891	111	4197	1455
1303	2463	151	1236	2822	4539	1970	3788	3070	967
1547	139	3175	3773	3883	2161	209	2364	2324	3849
2009	4352	4685	4820	1386	4990	786	4516	2851	2571
3589	539	2809	2065	1548	661	4506	788	4082	1450
4311	4827	3137	3000	69	1925	393	42	1032	3450
1605	1105	4949	1791	2761	879	709	221	2894	3232

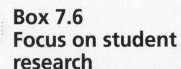

Box 7.6
Focus on student research

Simple random sampling

Jemma was undertaking her work placement at a large supermarket, where 5011 of the supermarket's customers used the supermarket's online shopping and home delivery scheme. She was asked to interview customers and find out what aspects they liked and disliked. As there was insufficient time to interview all of them she decided to interview a sample using the telephone. Her calculations revealed that to obtain acceptable levels of confidence and accuracy she needed an actual sample size of approximately 360 customers. She decided to select them using simple random sampling.

Having obtained a list of Internet customers and their telephone numbers, Jemma gave each of the cases (customers) in this sampling frame a unique number starting with 1 through to 5011.

Using her spreadsheet's random number generator function, Jemma generated a series of random numbers between 1 and 5011. The first random number generated was 4306 (shown in bold and shaded in Table 7.3). Starting with this number she used the random numbers in the order they were generated (in this example continuing along the line) to select her cases:

4306 1966 1878 4428 3571 62 838 4881 3045 . . .

She continued in this manner until 360 different cases had been selected, ensuring that where a random number was repeated, the associated case was disregarded and the cases selected therefore all different. These 360 cases selected formed her random sample.

reached. If the same random number is generated more than once it must be disregarded as you need different cases. This means that you are not putting each case's number back into the sampling frame after it has been selected and is termed 'sampling without replacement'. If a number is selected that is outside the range of those in your sampling frame, you simply ignore it and continue reading off numbers until your sample size is reached (Box 7.6).

Random numbers allow you to select your sample without bias. The sample selected, therefore, can be said to be representative of the target population. However, it is not a perfect miniature replica of this population, since it still possesses sampling error. In addition, the selection that simple random sampling provides is more evenly dispersed throughout the target population for samples of more than a few hundred cases. The first few hundred cases selected using simple random sampling normally consist of groups of cases whose numbers are close together followed by a gap and then a further grouping. For more than a few hundred cases, this pattern occurs far less frequently. Because of the technique's random nature it is possible that a chance occurrence of such patterns will result in certain parts of a population being over- or under-represented.

Simple random sampling is best used when you have an accurate and easily accessible sampling frame that lists the target population, preferably in electronic format. While you can often obtain these for employees within organisations or members of clubs or societies, adequate lists are less likely to be available for organisations. If your population covers a large geographical area, random selection means that selected cases are likely to be dispersed throughout the area. Consequently, this form of sampling is not suitable if collecting data over a large geographical area using a method that requires face-to-face contact, owing to the associated high travel costs. Simple random sampling would still be suitable for a geographically dispersed area if you used an alternative technique of collecting data such as Internet or postal questionnaires or telephone interviewing (Chapter 11).

Sampling frames used for computer aided telephone interviewing (CATI) have, in the main, been replaced by random digital dialling. Although selecting particular within-country area dialling codes for land-line telephone numbers provides a chance to reach any household within that area represented by that code which has a landline telephone, regardless of whether or not the number is ex-directory, care must be taken. Such a sample excludes households who use only mobile telephones as their dialling codes are network operator rather than geographical area specific (Tucker and Lepkowski 2008).

Systematic random sampling

Systematic random sampling (often called just **systematic sampling**) involves you selecting the sample at regular intervals from the sampling frame. To do this you:

1 Number each of the cases in your sampling frame with a unique number. The first case is numbered 1, the second 2 and so on.
2 Select the first case using a random number.
3 Calculate the sampling fraction.
4 Select subsequent cases systematically using the sampling fraction to determine the frequency of selection.

To calculate the **sampling fraction** – that is, the proportion of the target population that you need to select – you use the formula:

$$\text{Sampling fraction} = \frac{\text{actual sample size}}{\text{total population}}$$

If your sampling fraction is 1/3 you need to select one in every three cases – that is, every third case from the sampling frame. Unfortunately, your calculation will usually result in a more complicated fraction. In these instances it is normally acceptable to round your population down to the nearest 10 (or 100) and to increase your minimum sample size until a simpler sampling fraction can be calculated.

On its own, selecting one in every three would not be random as every third case would be bound to be selected, whereas those between would have no chance of selection. To overcome this, a random number is used to decide where to start on the sampling frame. If your sampling fraction is 1/3 the starting point must be one of the first three cases. You therefore generate a random number (in this example a one-digit random number between 1 and 3) as described earlier and use this as the starting point. Once you have selected your first case at random you then select, in this example, every third case until you have gone right through your sampling frame (Box 7.7).

In some instances it is not necessary to actually construct a list for your sampling frame. For Internet questionnaires, such as pop-up questionnaires that appear in a window on the computer screen, there is no need to create an actual list if an invitation to participate is triggered at random. For systematic random sampling, a random selection could be triggered by a mechanism such as every tenth visitor to the website over a specified time period (Bradley 1999).

Despite the advantages, you must be careful when using existing lists as sampling frames. You need to ensure that the lists do not contain periodic patterns. Let us assume a high street bank needs you to administer a questionnaire to a sample of individual customers with joint bank accounts. A sampling fraction of 1/2 means that you will need to select every second customer on the list. The names on the customer lists, which you intend to use as the sampling frame, are arranged alphabetically by joint account, with predominantly males followed by females (Table 7.4). If you start with a male customer, the majority of those in your sample will be male. Conversely, if you start with a female

---

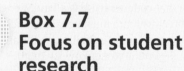

Box 7.7
Focus on student research

Systematic random sampling

Stefan worked as a receptionist in a dental surgery with approximately 1,500 patients. He wished to find out their attitudes to the new automated appointments scheme. As there was insufficient time and money to collect data from all patients using a questionnaire he decided to send the questionnaire to a sample. The calculation of sample size revealed that to obtain acceptable levels of confidence and accuracy he needed an actual sample size of approximately 300 patients. Having obtained ethical approval he generated an alphabetical list of all registered patients from the patient record system for his sampling frame and selected his sample systematically.

First, he calculated the sampling fraction:

$$\frac{300}{1500} = \frac{1}{5}$$

This meant that he needed to select every fifth patient from the sampling frame. Next, he used a random number to decide where to start on his sampling frame. As the sampling fraction was 1/5, the starting point had to be one of the first five patients. He therefore selected a one-digit random number between 1 and 5.

Once he had selected his first patient at random he continued to select every fifth patient until he had gone right through his sampling frame (the list of patients). If the random number Stefan had selected was 2, then he would have selected the following patient numbers:

2 7 12 17 22 27 32 37 . . .

and so on until 300 patients had been selected.

Table 7.4 The impact of periodic patterns on systematic random sampling

Number	Customer	Sample	Number	Customer	Sample
1	Mr J. Lewis	✓	7	Mr J. Smith	✓
2	Mrs P. Lewis	*	8	Mrs K. Smith	*
3	Mr T. Penny	✓	9	Mr R. Thompson	✓
4	Mrs J. Penny	*	10	Ms M. Wroot	*
5	Mr A. Saunders	✓	11	Mr J. Whalley	✓
6	Mrs C. Saunders	*	12	Mr C. Simon	*

✓ Sample selected if you start with 1. * Sample selected if you start with 2.

customer, the majority of those in your sample will be female. Consequently, your sample will be biased (Table 7.4). Systematic random sampling is therefore not suitable without reordering or stratifying the sampling frame (discussed later).

Unlike simple random sampling, systematic random sampling works equally well with a small or large number of cases. However, if your target population covers a large geographical area, the random selection means that the sample cases are likely to be dispersed throughout the area. Consequently, systematic random sampling is suitable for geographically dispersed cases only if you do not require face-to-face contact when collecting your data.

Stratified random sampling

Stratified random sampling is a modification of random sampling in which you divide the target population into two or more relevant and significant strata based on one or a number of attributes. In effect, your sampling frame is divided into a number of subsets. A random sample (simple or systematic) is then drawn from each of the strata. Consequently, stratified random sampling shares many of the advantages and disadvantages of simple random or systematic random sampling.

Dividing the population into a series of relevant strata means that the sample is more likely to be representative, as you can ensure that each of the strata is represented proportionally within your sample. However, it is only possible to do this if you are aware of, and can easily distinguish, significant strata in your sampling frame. In addition, the extra stage in the sampling procedure means that it is likely to take longer, to be more expensive, and to be more difficult to explain than simple random or systematic random sampling.

In some instances, as pointed out by De Vaus (2014), your sampling frame will already be divided into strata. A sampling frame of employee names that is in alphabetical order will automatically ensure that, if systematic random sampling is used (discussed earlier), employees will be sampled in the correct proportion to the letter with which their name begins. Similarly, membership lists that are ordered by date of joining will automatically result in stratification by length of membership if systematic random sampling is used. However, if you are using simple random sampling or your sampling frame contains periodic patterns, you will need to stratify it. To do this you:

1 Choose the stratification variable or variables.
2 Divide the sampling frame into the discrete strata.
3 Number each of the cases within each stratum with a unique number, as discussed earlier.
4 Select your sample using either simple random or systematic random sampling, as discussed earlier.

Box 7.8
Focus on student research

Stratified random sampling

Dilek worked for a major supplier of office supplies to public and private organisations. As part of her research into her organisation's customers, she needed to ensure that both public- and private-sector organisations were represented correctly. An important

stratum was, therefore, the sector of the organisation. Her sampling frame was therefore divided into two discrete strata: public sector and private sector. Within each stratum, the individual cases were then numbered (see below).

She decided to select a systematic random sample. A sampling fraction of 1/4 meant that she needed to select every fourth customer on the list. As indicated by the ticks (✓), random numbers were generated to select the first case in the public sector (2) and private sector (4) strata. Subsequently, every fourth customer in each stratum was selected.

Public sector stratum			Private sector stratum		
Number	**Customer**	**Selected**	**Number**	**Customer**	**Selected**
1	Anyshire County Council		1	ABC Automotive manufacturer	
2	Anyshire Hospital Trust	✓	2	Anytown printers and bookbinders	
3	Newshire Army Training Barracks		3	Benjamin Toy Company	
4	Newshire Police Force		4	Jane's Internet Flower shop	✓
5	Newshire Housing		5	Multimedia productions	
6	St Peter's Secondary School	✓	6	Roger's Consulting	
7	University of Anytown		7	The Paperless Office	
8	West Anyshire Council		8	U-need-us Ltd	✓

The stratification variable (or variables) chosen should represent the discrete characteristic (or characteristics) for which you want to ensure correct representation within the sample (Box 7.8).

Samples can be stratified using more than one characteristic. You may wish to stratify a sample of an organisation's employees by both department and salary grade. To do this you would:

1 Divide the sampling frame into the discrete departments.
2 Within each department divide the sampling frame into discrete salary grades.
3 Number each of the cases within each salary grade within each department with a unique number, as discussed earlier.
4 Select your sample using either simple random or systematic random sampling, as discussed earlier.

In some instances the relative sizes of different strata mean that, in order to have sufficient data for analysis, you need to select larger samples from the strata with smaller target populations. Here the different sample sizes must be taken into account when aggregating data from each of the strata to obtain an overall picture. More sophisticated statistical analysis software packages enable you to do this by differentially weighting the responses for each stratum (Section 12.2).

Cluster sampling

Cluster sampling (sometimes known as **one-stage cluster sampling**) is, on the surface, similar to stratified random sampling as you need to divide the target population into discrete groups prior to sampling (Barnett 2002). The groups are termed clusters in this form of sampling and can be based on any naturally occurring grouping. For example, you could group your data by type of manufacturing firm or geographical area (Box 7.9).

For cluster sampling, your sampling frame is the complete list of clusters rather than a complete list of individual cases within the population. You then select a few clusters, normally using simple random sampling. Data are then collected from every case within the selected clusters. The technique has three main stages:

1 Choose the cluster grouping for your sampling frame.
2 Number each of the clusters with a unique number. The first cluster is numbered 1, the second 2 and so on.
3 Select your sample of clusters using some form of random sampling, as discussed earlier.

Selecting clusters randomly makes cluster sampling a probability sampling technique. Despite this, the technique normally results in a sample that represents the target population less accurately than stratified random sampling. Restricting the sample to a few relatively compact geographical sub-areas (clusters) maximises the amount of data you can collect using face-to-face methods within the resources available. However, it may also reduce the representativeness of your sample. For this reason you need to maximise the number of sub-areas to allow for variations in the target population within the available resources. Your choice is between a large sample from a few discrete subgroups and a smaller sample distributed over the whole group. It is a trade-off between the amount of precision lost by using a few subgroups and the amount gained from a larger sample size.

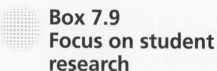

Box 7.9
Focus on student research

Cluster sampling

Ceri needed to select a sample of firms from which to collect data using an interviewer completed face-to-face questionnaire about the use of large multi-purpose digital printer copiers. As she had limited resources with which to pay for travel and other associated data collection costs, she decided to collect data from firms in four geographical areas selected from a cluster grouping of local administrative areas. A list of all local administrative areas formed her sampling frame. Each of the local administrative areas (clusters) was given a unique number, the first being 1, the second 2 and so on. The four sample clusters were selected from this sampling frame of local administrative areas using simple random sampling.

Ceri's sample was all firms within the selected clusters. She decided that the appropriate directories could probably provide a suitable list of all firms in each cluster.

Checking that the sample is representative

Often it is possible to compare data you collect from your sample with data from another source for the population, such as data contained in an 'archival' database. For example, you can compare data on the age and socioeconomic characteristics of respondents in a marketing survey with these characteristics for the population in that country as recorded by the latest national census of population. If there is no statistically significant difference, then the sample is representative with respect to these characteristics.

When working within an organisation, comparisons can also be made. In a questionnaire Mark sent to a sample of employees in a large UK organisation, he asked closed questions about salary grade, gender, length of service and place of work. Possible responses to each question were designed to provide sufficient detail to compare the characteristics of the sample with the characteristics of the entire population of employees as recorded by the organisation's Human Resources (HR) database. At the same time he kept the categories sufficiently broad to preserve, and to be seen to preserve, the confidentiality of individual respondents. The two questions on length of service and salary grade from a questionnaire he developed illustrate this:

37 How long have you worked for **organisation's name?**

less than 1 year ❏   1 year to less than 3 years ❏   3 or more years ❏

38 Which one of the following best describes your job?

Clerical (grades 1–3)	❏	Management (grades 9–11)	❏
Supervisory (grades 4–5)	❏	Senior management (grades 12–14)	❏
Professional (grades 6–8)	❏	Other (please say)	❏

Using the Kolmogorov test (Section 12.5), Mark found there was no statistically significant difference between the proportions of respondents in each of the length of service groups and the data obtained from the organisation's HR database for all employees. This meant that the sample of respondents was representative of all employees with respect to length of service. However, those responding were (statistically) significantly more likely to be in professional and managerial grades than in technical, administrative or supervisory grades. He therefore added a note of caution about the representativeness of his findings.

You can also assess the representativeness of samples in a variety of other ways (Rogelberg and Stanton 2007). Those our students have used most often, in order of quality of assessment of possible bias, include:

- replicating your findings using a new sample selected using different sampling techniques, referred to as 'demonstrate generalisability';
- resurveying non-respondents, the 'follow-up approach';
- analysing whether non-response was due to refusal, ineligibility or some other reason through interviews with non-respondents, known as 'active non-response analysis';
- comparing late respondents' responses with those from early respondents, known as 'wave analysis'.

In relation to this list, the quality of the assessment of bias provided by archival analysis, as outlined earlier, is similar to that provided by the follow-up approach and active non-response analysis.

7.3 Non-probability sampling

The techniques for selecting samples discussed earlier have all been based on the assumption that your sample will be chosen at random from a sampling frame. Consequently, it is possible to specify the probability that any case will be included in the sample. However, within business and management research, this may either not be possible (where you do not have a sampling frame) or not be appropriate to answering your research question. This means your sample must be selected some other way. Non-probability sampling (or **non-random sampling**) provides a range of alternative techniques to select samples, the majority of which include an element of subjective judgement. In the exploratory stages of some research projects, such as a pilot testing a questionnaire, a non-probability sample may be the most practical, although it will not allow the extent of the problem to be determined. Subsequent to this, probability sampling techniques may be used. In addition, non-probability samples have become far more prevalent with the rapid growth of online questionnaires. For these a likely source of potential respondents is an online panel (discussed later in relation to quota sampling) recruited in advance of the research (Baker et al. 2013). For other research projects your research question(s), objectives and choice of research strategy (Sections 2.4 and 5.5) may dictate non-probability sampling. To answer your research question(s) and to meet your objectives you may need to undertake an in-depth study that focuses on a small number of cases, perhaps one, selected for a particular purpose. This sample would provide you with an information-rich case study in which you explore your research question and gain particular or theoretical insights.

Deciding on a suitable sample size

For all non-probability sampling techniques, other than for quota samples (which we discuss later), the issue of sample size is ambiguous and, unlike probability sampling, there are no rules. Rather the logical relationship between your sample selection technique and the purpose and focus of your research is important (Figure 7.4); the sample selected being used, for example, to illustrate a particular aspect or to make generalisations to theory rather than about a population. Often case study research selects one or two case studies to explore a particular phenomenon or institution in depth (Lee and Saunders 2017). Data are then collected from all participants or from some form of sample of participants for the selected case studies. Your sample size is therefore dependent on your research question(s) and objectives – in particular, what you need to find out, what will be useful, what will have credibility and what can be done within your available resources (Patton, 2015). This is particularly so where you are intending to collect qualitative data using participant observation, semi-structured or unstructured interviews (Chapters 9 and 10). Although the validity, understanding and insights that you will gain from your data will be more to do with your data collection and analysis skills than with the size of your sample (Patton 2015), it is possible to offer guidance as to the sample size to ensure you have undertaken sufficient observations or conducted sufficient interviews.

In addressing this issue, many research textbooks simply recommend continuing to collect qualitative data, such as by conducting additional interviews, until **data saturation** is reached: in other words until the additional data collected provide little, if any, new information or suggest new themes. However, while some consider saturation to be crucial (Guest et al. 2006) to establishing how many interviews or observations are required; others note that not reaching saturation only means the phenomenon has still to be fully explored and that the findings are still valid (O'Reilly and Parker 2013). Saturation is also inappropriate for some research questions such as, for example, where research is to

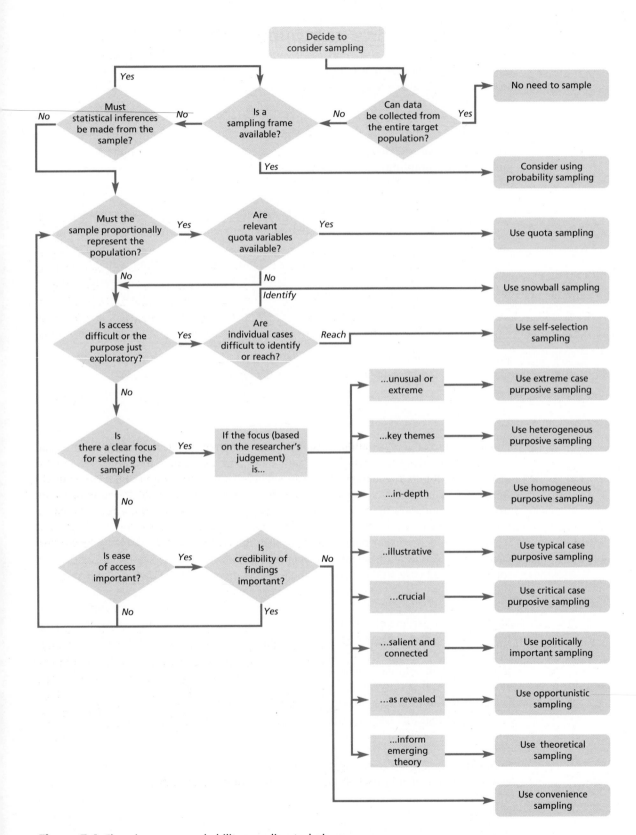

Figure 7.4 Choosing a non-probability sampling technique

Table 7.5 Non-probability sample size norms when using qualitative interviews

Purpose	Sample size norm
Planning research where participants are from a single organisation or will be analysed as a single group	30
Planning research where participants are from multiple organisations or will be analysed in multiple groups	50
Overall number likely to be considered sufficient	15–60

Source: Developed from Saunders and Townsend (2016)

establish whether something is possible. Consequently, while saturation may be helpful, it does not answer the question of how many participants you will need to select. Mark (Saunders 2012) summarises the limited guidance available as between four and 12 participants for a homogenous and 12 and 30 participants for a heterogeneous group. This he notes differs between groups, research strategies and complexities and is dependent upon the research question. His more recent research on practices in published organisation and workplace research (Saunders and Townsend 2016), whilst recognising that for some research purposes a sample of one can be sufficient, offers guidance on credible sample sizes for qualitative interviews. This is summarised in Table 7.5.

Selecting the most appropriate sampling technique and the sample

Having decided the likely suitable sample size, you need to select the most appropriate sampling technique to enable you to answer your research question from the range of non-probability sampling techniques available (Figure 7.4). At one end of this range is quota sampling, which, like probability samples, tries to represent the total population. At the other end of this range is haphazard sampling, based on the need to obtain a sample as quickly as possible. With this technique you have virtually no control over the cases that will be included in your sample. Purposive sampling and volunteer sampling techniques lie between these extremes (Table 7.6).

Quota sampling

Quota sampling is entirely non-random and is often used as an alternative to probability sampling for Internet and interviewer completed questionnaires as part of a survey strategy. It is based on the premise that your sample will represent the target population as the variability in your sample for various quota variables is the same as that in the target population. However, this depends on the appropriateness of the assumptions on which the quota are based and having high quality data (Baker et al. 2013). Quota sampling has similar requirements for sample size as probabilistic sampling techniques (Section 7.2). To select a quota sample you:

1 Divide the population into specific groups.
2 Calculate a quota for each group based on relevant and available data.
3 Either:

Table 7.6 Impact of various factors on choice of non-probability sampling techniques

Group	Technique	Likelihood of sample being representative	Types of research in which useful	Relative costs	Control over sample contents
Quota	Quota	Reasonable to high, although dependent on selection of quota variables	Where costs constrained or data needed very quickly so an alternative to probability sampling needed	Moderately high to reasonable	Specifies quota criteria
Purposive	Extreme case	Low	Unusual or special to offer more revealing insights to explain the more typical	Reasonable	Specifies what is unusual or extreme
	Heterogeneous	Low, although dependent on researcher's choices	Reveal/illuminate key themes	Reasonable	Specifies criteria for maximum diversity
	Homogeneous	Low	In-depth exploration and reveal minor differences	Reasonable	Specifies criteria to identify particular group
	Typical case	Low, although dependent on researcher's choices	Illustrative	Reasonable	Specifies what is 'normal'
	Critical case	Low	Where focus is on importance	Reasonable	Specifies criteria as to what is important
	Politically important	Low	Where focus is on salience and connections	Reasonable	Specifies criteria re political importance
	Opportunistic	Low	Where unexpected occurs during research	Reasonable	Recognises and decides whether to take opportunity
	Theoretical	Low	Inform emerging theory	Reasonable	Specifies where to select initial participants and subsequent choice to inform emerging theory
Volunteer	Snowball	Low, but cases likely to have characteristics desired	Where cases difficult to identify	Reasonable	Selects only initial participant
	Self-selection	Low, as cases self-selected	Where access difficult, research exploratory	Reasonable	Offers general invitation
Haphazard	Convenience	Very low (often lacks credibility)	Ease of access	Low	Haphazard

Sources: Developed from Patton (2015); Saunders (2012)

a (for Internet questionnaires) contract an online panel company specifying the number of cases in each quota from which completed questionnaires must be obtained; or

b (for interviewer completed questionnaires) ensure that where multiple interviewers are used each interviewer has an 'assignment', which states the number of cases in each quota from which they must collect data.

4 Where necessary, combine the data collected to provide the full sample.

Quota sampling has a number of advantages over the probability sampling techniques. In particular, it is less costly and can be set up very quickly. If, as with television audience research surveys, your data collection needs to be undertaken very quickly then quota sampling may be the only possibility. In addition, it does not require a sampling frame and therefore may be the only technique you can use if one is not available. Quota sampling is normally used for large target populations. Decisions on sample size are governed by the need to have sufficient responses in each quota to enable subsequent statistical analyses to be undertaken. This often necessitates a sample size of between 2,000 and 5,000.

Calculations of quotas are based on relevant and available data and are usually relative to the proportions in which they occur in the population (Box 7.10). Without sensible and relevant quotas, data collected may be biased. For many market research projects, quotas are derived from census data. Your choice of quota is dependent on two main factors:

- usefulness as a means of stratifying the data;
- ability to overcome likely variations between groups in their availability for interview.

Where people who are retired are likely to have different opinions from those in work, a quota that does not ensure that these differences are captured may result in the data being biased as it would probably be easier to collect the data from those people who are retired. Quotas used in market research surveys and political opinion polls usually include

---

Box 7.10
Focus on student research

Devising a quota sample

Paolo was undertaking the data collection for his dissertation as part of his full-time employment. For his research his employer had agreed to pay an online panel company to distribute his questionnaire to a sample of people representing those aged 16–74 who were either economically active or inactive. No sampling frame was available. Once the data had been collected, he was going to disaggregate his findings into subgroups dependent on gender and whether they were economically active or economically inactive. Previous research had suggested that whether or not people were retired would also have an impact

on responses and so he needed to make sure that those interviewed in each group also reflected these people. Fortunately, his country's national census of population contained a breakdown of the number of people who were economically active and inactive, their employment status and gender. These formed the basis of the categories for his quotas:

Gender ×	economic activity ×	employment status
male, female	active, inactive	part-time employee, full-time employee, self-employed, unemployed, full-time student, retired, student, looking after home or family, long-term sick or disabled, other

Box 7.10
Focus on student
research (*continued*)

As he was going to analyse the data for economic activity and gender, it was important that each of these four groups (male and economically active, male and economically inactive, female and economically active, female and economically inactive) had sufficient respondents (at least 30) to enable meaningful statistical analyses. Paolo calculated that a 0.00001 per cent quota (1 in 100,000) would provide sufficient numbers in each of these four groups. This gave him the following quotas:

Gender	Economic activity	Employment status	Population	Quota
Male	Active	Part-time employee	1 175 518	12
		Full-time employee	9 013 615	90
		Self-employed	2 670 662	27
		Unemployed	1 015 551	10
		Full-time student	619 267	6
	Inactive	Retired	2 270 916	22
		Student	1 148 356	11
		Looking after home or family	156 757	2
		Long-term sick or disabled	823 553	8
		Other	385 357	4
Female	Active	Part-time employee	4 158 750	42
		Full-time employee	6 002 949	60
		Self-employed	1 122 970	11
		Unemployed	687 296	7
		Full-time student	717 556	7
	Inactive	Retired	3 049 775	30
		Student	1 107 475	11
		Looking after home or family	1 538 377	15
		Long-term sick or disabled	750 581	8
		Other	467 093	5
Total			38 882 374	388

These were specified to the online panel company who were paid for each completed questionnaire received up to the number in each quota group.

measures of age, gender and economic activity or social class. These may be supplemented by additional quotas, dictated by the research question(s) and objectives (Box 7.10).

When you provide an online panel company the quota specification, they deliver your questionnaire to a 'volunteer panel' of potential respondents they have selected to meet your quota criteria. For online panel company data it is important to establish whether or not the online panel company offers panel members an incentive to encourage response and the likely implications of this for the characteristics of the respondents and, consequently, their responses (Section 11.2). Despite this being a non-probability sample, the number invited to complete a particular questionnaire and the number who do so are both known. It is therefore possible to calculate a **participation rate** (American Association for Public Opinion Research, 2016):

$$\text{Participation rate} = \frac{\text{Number of respondents providing a usable response}}{\text{Number of respondents invited to participate}}$$

For interviewer collected data, assignments from each interviewer are combined to provide the full sample. Because the interviewer can choose within quota boundaries whom they interview, your quota sample may be subject to bias. Interviewers tend to choose respondents who are easily accessible and who appear willing to answer the questions. Clear controls may therefore be needed. In addition, it has been known for interviewers to fill in quotas incorrectly. This is not to say that your quota sample will not produce good results; they can and often do! However, you cannot measure the level of certainty or margins of error as the sample is not probability based.

Purposive sampling

With **purposive sampling** you need to use your judgement to select cases that will best enable you to answer your research question(s) and to meet your objectives. For this reason it is sometimes known as **judgemental sampling**. You therefore need to think carefully about the impact of your decision to include or exclude cases on the research when selecting a sample in this way. Purposive sampling is often used when working with very small samples such as in case study research and when you wish to select cases that are particularly informative. A particular form of purposive sampling, theoretical sampling, is used by researchers adopting the Grounded Theory strategy (Section 13.9).

Purposive samples cannot be considered to be statistically representative of the target population. The logic on which you base your strategy for selecting cases for a purposive sample should be dependent on your research question(s) and objectives (Box 7.12). Patton (2015) emphasises this point by contrasting the need to select information-rich cases in purposive sampling with the need to be statistically representative in probability sampling. The more common purposive sampling strategies were outlined in Table 7.6.

Extreme case or **deviant sampling** focuses on unusual or special cases on the basis that the data collected about these unusual or extreme outcomes will enable you to learn the most and to answer your research question(s) and meet your objectives most effectively (Box 7.11). This is often based on the premise that findings from extreme cases will be relevant in understanding or explaining more typical cases (Patton 2015).

Heterogeneous or **maximum variation sampling** uses your judgement to choose participants with sufficiently diverse characteristics to provide the maximum variation possible in the data collected. It enables you to collect data to describe and explain the key themes that can be observed. Although this might appear a contradiction, as a small sample may contain cases that are completely different, Patton (2015) argues that this is in fact a strength. Any patterns that do emerge are likely to be of particular interest and value and represent the key themes. In addition, the data collected should enable you to document uniqueness. To ensure maximum variation within a sample, Patton (2015) suggests you identify your diverse characteristics (sample selection criteria) prior to selecting your sample.

In direct contrast to heterogeneous sampling, **homogeneous sampling** focuses on one particular subgroup in which all the sample members are similar, such as a particular occupation or level in an organisation's hierarchy. Characteristics of the selected

Box 7.11
Focus on management research

Extreme case sampling

In their 2014 *Academy of Management Journal* article 'It's not easy being green: The role of self evaluations in explaining the support of environmental issues', Sonenshein, DeCelles and Dutton outline their mixed methods approach comprising an initial inductive qualitative study followed by a quantitative observational study. In the first study they develop theory regarding how environmental supporters evaluate themselves both positively and negatively and how these evaluations are shaped on an ongoing basis by work, home and other contexts. In the second study, using observational data, they derive three distinct profiles of environmental supporters and relate these profiles to environmental issue supportive behaviours.

The sample for the first qualitative study was drawn from a degree programme at a North American university called the 'Environment and Business Program'. This programme was designed to develop sustainability-orientated leaders who could also act as change agents. Sonnenshein et al. (2014) argue that although these people were clearly different from the population, this sample was important for developing theory as it allowed the researchers to learn from a non-typical group of people who had taken steps to learn about how to address climate change.

Using contact details provided by the degree programme for 25 current and 25 past students selected at random, individuals specifically interested in climate change were asked if they would be willing to take part in the research. Twenty-nine (14 current students and 15 past students) agreed to participate, identifying themselves as climate change issue supporters. Each of these people were interviewed for approximately an hour, each interview being transcribed in full.

Following analysis of data from the qualitative study, the second quantitative study collected data from two independent samples of environmental issues supporters in a large North American city. Participants were recruited by contacting the leaders of 21 groups that described themselves as active in environmental issues. Nineteen of these groups' leaders agreed to forward information about the research to their members with a link to a secure website through which they could sign up to take part in the research. In all, 91 people who were active members of environmental groups agreed to take part, comprising a second extreme case sample.

participants are similar, allowing them to be explored in greater depth and minor differences to be more apparent.

Typical case sampling is usually used as part of a research project to provide an illustrative profile using a representative case. Such a sample enables you to provide an illustration of what is 'typical' to those who will be reading your research report and may be unfamiliar with the subject matter. It is not intended to be definitive.

In contrast, **critical case sampling** selects critical cases on the basis that they can make a point dramatically or because they are important. The focus of data collection is to understand what is happening in each critical case so that logical generalisations can be made. Patton (2015) outlines a number of clues that suggest critical cases. These can be summarised by the questions such as:

- If it happens there, will it happen everywhere?
- If they are having problems, can you be sure that everyone will have problems?
- If they cannot understand the process, is it likely that no one will be able to understand the process?

Politically important sampling relies on your judgement regarding anticipated politically sensitive issues and associated outcomes when deciding whether to include one or a number of prominent potential participants. Consequently you choose to include (or exclude) participants on the basis of their connections with politically sensitive issues (Miles et al. 2014).

Opportunistic sampling acknowledges how, particularly within qualitative research involving inductive theory building, unforeseen opportunities can occur. For example, new potential research participants may emerge requiring an on-the-spot decision about their fit with the research and their inclusion. As such it relies on you using your judgment as to recognise such opportunities and assess whether or not to take them (Miles et al. 2014).

Theoretical sampling is a special case of purposive sampling, being particularly associated with Grounded Theory and analytic induction (Sections 13.9 and 13.8). Initially, you need to have some idea of where to sample, although not necessarily what to sample for, participants being chosen as they are needed. Subsequent sample selection is dictated by the needs of the emerging theory and the evolving storyline, your participants being chosen purposively to inform this. A theoretical sample is therefore cumulatively chosen according to developing categories and emerging theory based upon your simultaneous collecting, coding and analysis of the data.

Volunteer sampling

Snowball sampling is the first of two techniques we look at where participants volunteer to be part of the research rather than being chosen. It is used commonly when it is difficult to identify members of the desired population; for example, people who are working while claiming unemployment benefit. You, therefore, need to:

1 Make contact with one or two cases.
2 Ask these cases to identify further cases.
3 Ask these new cases to identify further new cases (and so on).
4 Stop when either no new cases are given or the sample is as large as is manageable or data saturation has been reached.

The main problem is making initial contact. Once you have done this, these cases identify further members of the population, who then identify further members, and so the sample grows like a snowball being rolled in snow. For such samples the problems of bias are huge, as respondents are most likely to identify other potential respondents who are similar to themselves, resulting in a homogeneous sample (Lee 2000). The next problem is to find these new cases. However, for populations that are difficult to identify, snowball sampling may provide the only possibility.

A development of snowball sampling is **respondent driven sampling (RDS)**. This combines snowball sampling with the use of coupons or some other method to track the identification of further cases and statistical modelling to compensate for the sample being collected in a non-random way. This can enable researchers to make unbiased estimates of their target population (Baker et al. 2013).

Self-selection sampling is the second of the volunteer sampling techniques we look at. It occurs when you allow each case, usually individuals, to identify their desire to take part in the research. You therefore:

1 Publicise your need for cases, either by advertising through appropriate media or by asking them to take part.
2 Collect data from those who respond.

Publicity for volunteer samples can take many forms. These include articles and advertisements in magazines that the population are likely to read, postings on appropriate online newsgroups and discussion groups, hyperlinks from other websites as well as

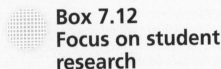

Box 7.12
Focus on student research

Self-selection sampling

Siân's research was concerned with the impact of student loans on studying habits. She had decided to distribute her questionnaire using the Internet. She publicised her research on Facebook in a number of groups' pages, using the associated description to invite people to self-select and click on the link to the questionnaire. Those who self-selected by clicking on the hyperlink were automatically taken to the Web questionnaire she had developed using the SurveyMonkey.com online survey software.

letters, emails or tweets of invitation to colleagues and friends (Box 7.12). Cases that self-select often do so because of their strong feelings or opinions about the research question(s) or stated objectives. In some instances, this is exactly what the researcher requires to answer her or his research question and meet the objectives.

Haphazard sampling

Haphazard sampling occurs when sample cases are selected without any obvious principles of organisation in relation to your research question, the most common form being **convenience sampling** (also known as **availability sampling**). This involves selecting cases haphazardly only because they are easily available (or most convenient) to obtain for your sample, such as the person interviewed at random in a shopping centre for a television programme 'vox pop'. Although convenience sampling is used widely (for example, Facebook polls or questions), it is prone to many sources of bias and influences that are beyond your control. Cases appear in the sample only because of the ease of obtaining them; consequently all you can do is make some statement about the people who felt strongly enough about the subject of your question to answer it (and were using Facebook) during the period your poll was available! Not surprisingly, as emphasised in Table 7.6, findings from convenience samples may be given very little credibility. Despite this, samples ostensibly chosen for convenience often meet purposive sample selection criteria that are relevant to the research aim (Saunders and Townsend 2017). It may be that an organisation you intend to use as a case study is 'convenient' because you have been able to negotiate access through existing contacts. Where this organisation also represents an 'extreme' case, it can also offer insights about the unusual or extreme, providing justification regarding its purpose when addressing the research aim. Alternatively, whilst a sample of operatives in another division of an organisation for which you work might be easy to obtain and consequently 'convenient', the fact that such participants allow you to address a research aim necessitating an in-depth focus on a particular homogenous group is more crucial.

Where the reasons for using a convenience sample have little, if any, relevance to the research aim, participants appear in the sample only because of the ease of obtaining them. Whilst this may not be problematic if there is little variation in the target population, where the target population is more varied it can result in participants that are of limited use in relation to the research question. Often a sample is intended to represent more than the target population, for example, managers taking a part-time MBA course as a surrogate for all managers. In such instances the selection of individual cases may introduce bias to the sample, meaning that subsequent interpretations must be treated with caution.

7.4 Multi-stage sampling

Multi-stage sampling refers to any sampling design that occurs in two or more successive stages using either probability, non-probability, or both types of sample selection techniques. For example, in the first stage you might select two organisations using critical case purposive sampling. Subsequently, in the second stage, you might select a sample of employees from each organisation using stratified random sampling, thereby combining non-probability with probability sampling. Alternatively, you may first select a large sample of customers or organisations using quota sampling. Subsequently, based on analysis of the data collected from these customers or organisations, you may select a smaller heterogeneous purposive sample to illustrate the key themes. Multi-stage sampling can also use cluster sampling to overcome problems associated with a geographically dispersed population when face-to-face contact is needed, or when it is expensive and time consuming to construct a sampling frame for a large geographical area (Box 7.13).

Where multi-stage sampling uses one or more probability sampling techniques, you need to ensure that the sampling frames are appropriate and available. In order to minimise the impact of selecting smaller and smaller subgroups on the representativeness of your sample, you can apply stratified random sampling techniques (Section 7.2). This technique can be further refined to take account of the relative size of the subgroups by adjusting the sample size for each subgroup. As you have selected your sub-areas using different sampling frames, you only need a sampling frame that lists all the members of the population for those subgroups you finally select (Box 7.13). This provides considerable savings in time and money.

Box 7.13
Focus on student research

Multi-stage sampling

Laura worked for a market research organisation that needed her to interview a sample of 400 households in England and Wales. She decided to use the electoral register as a sampling frame. Laura knew that selecting 400 households using either systematic or simple random sampling was likely to result in these 400 households being dispersed throughout England and Wales, resulting in considerable amounts of time spent travelling between interviewees as well as high travel costs. By using multi-stage sampling Laura felt these problems could be overcome.

In her first stage the geographical area (England and Wales) was split into discrete sub-areas (counties). These formed her sampling frame. After numbering all the counties, Laura selected a small number of counties at random using cluster sampling. Since each case (household) was located in a county, each had an equal chance of being selected for the final sample.

As the counties selected were still too geographically large, each was subdivided into smaller geographically discrete areas (electoral wards). These formed the next sampling frame (stage 2). Laura selected another sample at random. This time she selected a larger number of wards using simple random sampling to allow for likely important variations in the nature of households between wards.

A sampling frame of the households in each of these wards was then generated. Laura purchased copies of the edited electoral register from the relevant local authorities. These contained the names and addresses of people who had registered to vote and had not 'opted out' of allowing their details to be made widely available for others to use. Laura finally selected the actual cases (households) that she would interview using systematic random sampling.

7.5 Summary

- Your choice of sampling techniques is dependent on the feasibility and sensibility of collecting data to answer your research question(s) and to address your objectives from the target population. When using probability sampling it is usually more sensible to collect data from the entire population where the target population is 50 or fewer.
- Choice of sampling technique or techniques is dependent on your research question(s) and objectives:
    - Research question(s) and objectives that need you to estimate statistically the characteristics of the target population from a sample nearly always require probability samples.
    - Research question(s) and objectives that do not require such statistical generalisations can, alternatively, make use of non-probability sampling techniques.
- Probability sampling techniques all necessitate some form of sampling frame.
- Where it is not possible to construct a sampling frame you will need to use non-probability sampling techniques.
- The size of probability samples selected to address research questions that require statistical estimation should be calculated. It is dependent upon the target population, and the margin of error and confidence level required. Statistical analyses usually require a minimum sample size of 30.
- The size for non-probability samples selected to address research questions that do not require statistical estimation is dependent upon the research question and objectives, what will be credible and what can be done within available resources. Whilst guidance suggests between 15 and 60 interviews is likely to be sufficient, for some research purposes a sample of one can be sufficient and credible.
- Sample size and the technique used are also influenced by the availability of resources, in particular financial support and time available to select the sample and to collect, input and analyse the data.
- Non-probability sampling techniques provide the opportunity to select your sample purposively and to reach difficult-to-identify members of the target population.
- For many research projects you will need to use a combination of different sampling techniques.
- Your sampling choices will be dependent on your ability to gain access to organisations. The considerations summarised earlier must therefore be tempered with an understanding of what is practically possible.

Self-check questions

Help with these questions is available at the end of the chapter.

7.1 Identify a suitable sampling frame for each of the following research questions.
  a How do company directors of manufacturing firms of over 500 employees think a specified piece of legislation will affect their companies?
  b Which factors are important in accountants' decisions regarding working in mainland Europe?
  c How do employees at Cheltenham Gardens Ltd think the proposed introduction of compulsory Sunday working will affect their working lives?

7.2 Lisa has emailed her tutor with the following query regarding sampling and dealing with non-response. Imagine you are Lisa's tutor. Draft a reply to answer her query.

HELP!!!! Sampling non-response

Hi,

I hope you are well.

I interviewed someone yesterday and I (almost) failed to get him to say anything useful for my research project. This was strange as he had appeared to have really useful background. I was unable to get him to reflect on the issue of inhibitors of spin out companies in the *light of his own experiences* or *provide actual examples.* He clearly wanted to talk about what he wanted to and had decided this before the interview and I asked my questions 😔 He obviously though there were right and wrong answers and he was telling me what he thought he should say rather than giving me the actual examples I asked for. This meant he did not talk about feedback loops, linkages or ideas, which you know is what my research is about. My attempts to get the conversation onto my research were gently, but firmly, put aside.

My question is: **Can I just exclude this interview from my sample?** He was a great person and I really enjoyed meeting him. However, because I could not get him to answer my questions, the interview did not yield any insights. What should I do?

With best wishes

Lisa

---

^A_A $A^{\cdot}$ B I U A A ≔ ≔ ⇥ ⇤ ☰ ☰ ☰ ☰ ☰ ⌘ ⌘ x² x₂ abe ⌄

7.3 You have been asked to select a sample of manufacturing firms using the sampling frame below. This also lists the value of their annual output in tens of thousands of pounds over the past year. To help you in selecting your sample the firms have been numbered from 1 to 100.

a Select two simple random samples, each of 20 firms, and mark those firms selected for each sample on the sampling frame.

b Describe and compare the pattern on the sampling frame of each of the samples selected.

c Calculate the average (mean) annual output in tens of thousands of pounds over the past year for each of the samples selected.

d Given that the true average annual output is £6,608,900, is there any bias in either of the samples selected?

	Output		Output		Output		Output		Output
1	10	21	7	41	29	61	39	81	55
2	57	22	92	42	84	62	73	82	66
3	149	23	105	43	97	63	161	83	165
4	205	24	157	44	265	64	275	84	301
5	163	25	214	45	187	65	170	85	161
6	1359	26	1440	46	1872	66	1598	86	1341
7	330	27	390	47	454	67	378	87	431

(*continued*)

	Output		Output		Output		Output		Output
8	2097	28	1935	48	1822	68	1634	88	1756
9	1059	29	998	49	1091	69	1101	89	907
10	1037	30	1298	50	1251	70	1070	90	1158
11	59	31	10	51	9	71	37	91	27
12	68	32	70	52	93	72	88	92	66
13	166	33	159	53	103	73	102	93	147
14	302	34	276	54	264	74	157	94	203
15	161	35	215	55	189	75	168	95	163
16	1298	36	1450	56	1862	76	1602	96	1339
17	329	37	387	57	449	77	381	97	429
18	2103	38	1934	58	1799	78	1598	98	1760
19	1061	39	1000	59	1089	79	1099	99	898
20	1163	40	1072	60	1257	80	1300	100	1034

7.4 You have been asked to select a 10 per cent sample of firms from the sampling frame used for self-check question 7.3.

a Select a 10 per cent systematic random sample and mark those firms selected for the sample on the sampling frame.

b Calculate the average (mean) annual output in tens of thousands of pounds over the past year for your sample.

c Given that the true average annual output is £6,608,900, why does systematic random provide such a poor estimate of the annual output in this case?

7.5 You need to undertake a series of face-to-face interviews with managing directors of small- to medium-sized organisations. From the data you collect you need to be able to generalise about the attitude of such managing directors to recent changes in government policy towards these firms. Your generalisations need to be accurate to within plus or minus 5 per cent. Unfortunately, you have limited resources to pay for interviewers, travelling and other associated costs.

a How many managing directors will you need to interview?

b You have been given the choice between cluster and multi-stage sampling. Which technique would you choose for this research? You should give reasons for your choice.

7.6 You have been asked to use face-to-face questionnaires to collect data from local residents about their opinions regarding the siting of a new supermarket in an inner city suburb (estimated catchment population 111,376 at the last census). The age and gender distribution of the catchment population at the last census is listed below.

	Age group							
Gender	0–4	5–15	16–19	20–29	30–44	45–59 /64[*]	60/65[#]–74	75+
Males	3498	7106	4884	7656	9812	12892	4972	2684
Females	3461	6923	6952	9460	8152	9152	9284	4488

[*]59 females, 64 males; 60 females, 65 males.

    a Devise a quota for a quota sample using these data.

    b What other data would you like to include to overcome likely variations between groups in their availability for interview and replicate the target population more precisely? Give reasons for your answer.

    c What problems might you encounter in using interviewers?

7.7 For each of the following research questions it has not been possible for you to obtain a sampling frame. Suggest the most suitable non-probability sampling technique to obtain the necessary data, giving reasons for your choice.

    a What support do people sleeping rough believe they require from social services?

    b Which television advertisements do people remember watching last weekend?

    c How do employers' opinions vary regarding the impact of Government legislation on age discrimination?

    d How are manufacturing companies planning to respond to the introduction of road tolls?

    e Would users of the squash club be prepared to pay a 10 per cent increase in subscriptions to help fund two extra courts (answer needed by tomorrow morning!)?

Review and discussion questions

7.8 With a friend or colleague choose one of the following research questions (or one of your own) in which you are interested.

- What attributes attract people to jobs?
- How are financial institutions adapting the services they provide to meet recent legislation?

Use the flow charts for both probability sampling (Figure 7.3) and non-probability sampling (Figure 7.4) to decide how you could use each type of sampling independently to answer the research question.

7.9 Agree with a colleague to watch a particular documentary or consumer rights programme on the television. If possible, choose a documentary with a business or management focus. During the documentary, pay special attention to the samples from which the data for the documentary are drawn. Where possible, note down details of the sample such as who were interviewed or who responded to questionnaires, and the reasons why these people were chosen. Where this is not possible, make a note of the information you would have liked to have been given. Discuss your findings with your colleague and come to a conclusion regarding the nature of the sample used, its representativeness and the extent to which it was possible for the programme maker to generalise from that sample.

7.10 Obtain or access online a copy of a quality daily newspaper and, within the newspaper, find an article that discusses a 'survey' or 'poll'. Share the article with a friend. Make notes of the process used to select the sample for the 'survey' or 'poll'. As you make your notes, note down any areas where you feel there is insufficient information to fully understand the sampling process. Aspects for which information may be lacking include the target population, size of sample, how the sample was selected, representativeness and so on. Discuss your findings with your friend.

Progressing your research project

Using sampling as part of your research

- Consider your research question(s) and objectives. You need to decide whether you will be able to collect data on the entire population or will need to collect data from a sample.
- If you decide that you need to sample, you must establish whether your research question(s) and objectives require probability sampling. If they do, make sure that a suitable sampling frame is available or can be devised, and calculate the actual sample size required, taking into account likely response rates.
- If your research question(s) and objectives do not require probability sampling, or you are unable to obtain a suitable sampling frame, you will need to use non-probability sampling. Estimate the sample size you will require.
- Select the most appropriate sampling technique or techniques after considering the advantages and disadvantages of all suitable techniques and undertaking further reading as necessary.
- Select your sample or samples following the technique or techniques as outlined in this chapter.
- Remember to note down the reasons for your choices when you make them, as you will need to justify your choices when you write about your research method.
- Use the questions in Box 1.4 to guide your reflective diary entry.

References

Advertising Standards Canada (2012) *Guidelines for the Use of Comparative Advertising. Guidelines for the Use of Research and Survey Data to Support Comparative Advertising Claims.* Available at http://www.adstandards.com/en/ASCLibrary/guidelinesCompAdvertising-en.pdf [Accessed 9 May 2017].

Advertising Standards Canada (2016) *The Canadian Code of Advertising Standards.* Available at http://www.adstandards.com/en/standards/canCodeOfAdStandards.pdf [Accessed 9 May 2017].

American Association for Public Opinion Research (2016) *Standard Definitions: Final Dispositions of Case Codes and Outcome Rates for Surveys 9th edition.* Lenexa, KA: AAPOR. Available at http://www.aapor.org/AAPOR_Main/media/publications/Standard-Definitions20169theditionfinal.pdf [Accessed 11 May 2017].

Baker, R., Brick. J.M., Bates, N.A., Battaglia, M., Couper, M.P., Dever, J.A., Gile, K.J. and Tourangeau, R. (2013) 'Summary of the AAPOR task force on non-probability sampling', *Journal of Survey Statistics and Computing.* Vol. 1, pp. 90–143.

Barnett, V. (2002) *Sample Survey Principles and Methods* (3rd edn). Chichester: Wiley.

Baruch, Y. and Holtom, B.C. (2008) 'Survey response rate levels and trends in organizational research', *Human Relations*, Vol. 61, pp. 1139–1160.

Becker, H.S. (1998) *Tricks of the Trade: How to Think About Your Research While You're Doing It.* Chicago: Chicago University Press.

Bradley, N. (1999) 'Sampling for Internet surveys: An examination of respondent selection for Internet research', *Journal of the Market Research Society*, Vol. 41, No. 4, pp. 387–395.

Committee of Advertising Practice (2010) *The BCAP Code: The UK Code of broadcast Advertising (Edition 1).* London: Committee of Advertising Practice. Available at https://www.asa.org.uk/asset/846F25EB-F474-47C1-AB3FF571E3DB5910/ [Accessed 9 May 2017].

Committee of Advertising Practice (2014) *The CAP Code: The UK Code of Non-broadcast Advertising and Direct & Promotional Marketing (Edition 12).* London: Committee of Advertising Practice.

Available at https://www.asa.org.uk/asset/47EB51E7-028D-4509-AB3C0F4822C9A3C4/ [Accessed 9 May 2017].

Committee of Advertising Practice (2016) 'A quick guide to advertising consumer surveys' CAP News. Available at https://www.asa.org.uk/news/a-quick-guide-to-advertising-consumer-surveys.html [Accessed 9 May 2017].

De Vaus, D.A. (2014) *Surveys in Social Research* (6th edn). Abingdon: Routledge.

Dillman, D.A., Smyth, J.D. and Christian, J.M. (2014) *Internet, Phone, Mail and Mixed Mode Surveys: The Tailored Design Method* (4th edn). Hoboken, NJ: Wiley.

Edwards, T., Tregaskis, O., Edwards, P., Ferner, A., Marginson, A. with Arrowsmith, J., Adam, D., Meyer, M. and Budjanovcanin, A. (2007) 'Charting the contours of multinationals in Britain: Methodological challenges arising in survey-based research', *Warwick Papers in Industrial Relations*, No. 86. Available at http://www.cbs.dk/files/cbs.dk/charting_the_contours_of_multinationals_in_britain.pdf [Accessed 14 May 2017].

Ellis, P.D. (2010) *The Essential Guide to Effect Sizes*. Cambridge: Cambridge University Press.

Farey-Jones, D. (2011) '"Hello Boys" voted greatest poster ever created', *Campaign*, 31 March. Available at http://www.campaignlive.co.uk/news/1063405/Hello-Boys-voted-greatest-poster-ever-created/ [Accessed 14 April 2014].

Groves, R.M. and Peytcheva, E. (2008) 'The impact of nonresponse rates on nonresponse bias', *Public Opinion Quarterly*, Vol. 72, No. 2, pp. 167–189.

Guest, G., Bunce, A. and Johnson, L. (2006) 'How many interviews are enough? An experiment with data saturation and validity', *Field Methods*, Vol. 18, No. 1, pp. 59–82.

Henry, G.T. (1990) *Practical Sampling*. Newbury Park, CA: Sage.

Lee, B. and Saunders, M.N.K (2017) *Doing Case Study Research for Business and Management Students*. London: Sage.

Lee, R.M. (2000) *Doing Research on Sensitive Topics*. London: Sage.

Mellahi, K. and Harris, L.C. (2016) 'Response rates in business and management research: An overview of current practice and suggestions for future direction', *British Journal of Management*, Vol. 27, No. 2, pp. 426–437.

Miles, M.B, Huberman, A.M. and Saldaña, J (2014) *Qualitative Data Analysis: A Methods Sourcebook.* (3rd edn) Thousand Oaks, CA: Sage.

Neuman, W.L. (2014) *Social Research Methods* (7th edn). Harlow: Pearson.

O'Reilly, M. and Parker, N. (2013) 'Unsatisfactory saturation: a critical exploration of the notion of the notion of saturated sample sizes in qualitative research', *Qualitative Research*. 13, pp. 190–197.

Patton, M.Q. (2015) *Qualitative Research and Evaluation Methods: Integrating Theory and Practice* (4th edn). Thousand Oaks, CA: Sage.

Rogelberg, S.G. and Stanton, J.M. (2007) 'Introduction: Understanding and dealing with organizational survey non-response', *Organizational Research Methods*, Vol. 10, No. 2, pp. 195–209.

Saunders, M.N.K. (2012) 'Choosing research participants', in G. Symons and C. Cassell (eds) *The Practice of Qualitative Organizational Research: Core Methods and Current Challenges*. London: Sage, pp. 37–55.

Saunders, M.N.K. and Townsend, K. (2016) 'Reporting and justifying the number of participants in organisation and workplace research', *British Journal of Management*. Vol. 27, pp. 837–852.

Saunders M.N.K and Townsend, K (2017) 'Choosing participants' in Cassell, C, Cunliffe, A, and Grandy, G (eds) *Sage Handbook of Qualitative Business and Management Research Methods*. London: Sage. Chapter 30.

Sonenshein, S., DeCelles, K. and Dutton, J.E. (2014) 'It's not easy being green: The role of self evaluations in explaining the support of environmental issues', *Academy of Management Journal*, Vol. 57, No. 1, pp. 7–37.

Stutely, R. (2014) *The Economist Numbers Guide: The Essentials of Business Numeracy* (6th edn). London: Profile Books.

Tucker, C. and Lepkowski, J.M. (2008) 'Telephone survey methods: Adapting to change', in J.M. Lepkowski, C. Tucker, J.M. Brick, E.D. De Leeuw, L. Japec, P.J. Lavrakas, M.W. Link and R.L. Sangster (eds), *Advances in Telephone Survey Methodology*. Hoboken, NJ: Wiley, pp. 3–28.

Further reading

Baruch, Y. and Holtom, B.C. (2008) 'Survey response rate levels and trends in organizational research', *Human Relations*, Vol. 61, pp. 1139–1160. This examines 490 academic studies using surveys published in 2000 and 2005 covering 100,000 organisations and over 400,000 individual respondents. The paper suggests likely response rates for different types of study and offers useful advice for reporting response rates.

De Vaus, D.A. (2014) *Surveys in Social Research* (6th edn). Abingdon: Routledge. Chapter 6 provides a useful overview of both probability and non-probability sampling techniques.

Patton, M.Q. (2015) *Qualitative Research and Evaluation Methods: Integrating Theory and Practice* (4th edn). Thousand Oaks, CA: Sage. Chapter 5, 'Qualitative designs and data collection', contains a useful discussion of non-probability sampling techniques, with examples.

Saunders, M.N.K. and Townsend, K. (2016) 'Reporting and justifying the number of participants in organisation and workplace research', *British Journal of Management.* Vol. 27, pp. 837–852. In addition to summarising the literature on sample size for interviewing, this examines sample selection practice and reporting for 248 academic studies using interviews published in 2003 and 2013. The paper suggests likely sample sizes for different types of interview study and offers useful advice for justifying sample size.

Case 7
Starting-up, not slowing down: social entrepreneurs in an ageing society

Nabila, a Master's student, wanted to investigate the motivations of social entrepreneurs for her research project. In reviewing relevant academic and practitioner literature, she had found there was limited research that considered social entrepreneurs in 'later life' (Hatak, et al. 2015; Singh and De Noble 2003). 'Later life social entrepreneurs' is a term used to refer to individuals aged 50 and over who set up a social enterprise to address a specific social, environmental or a cultural need. On investigating further, she also discovered that there was an interest from the UK government to extend the economic and social participation of individuals aged 50 and over (Department for Work and Pensions 2014). This was driven by the increase in the number of people aged 50 and over who are reaching the retirement age compared to the working age population (persons aged between 15 and 64 years who are in employment).

Based on this review of the literature, Nabila decided to conduct a study of social entrepreneurs aged 50 and over for her research project. More specifically, she wanted to find out what motivated these individuals to become social entrepreneurs. In particular she was interested in their social orientations, the influence of prior professional experiences on their decision to set up a social enterprise, and the challenges they faced in their everyday lives as social entrepreneurs. She phrased this as four interrelated investigative questions:

1 Why have people aged 50 and over become social entrepreneurs?
2 What is the relationship between their previous career background and their decision to set up a social enterprise?
3 How do they view their everyday experiences as social entrepreneurs?
4 What challenges do social entrepreneurs aged 50 and over face?

Nabila decided to undertake a qualitative study collecting data through semi-structured interviews as these would provide opportunities for open conversation to take place, enabling her and the participants to talk about ideas they saw as significant. However, Nabila had to think carefully about how many interviews she needed to undertake, how to gain access to potential participants and how to select her sample. Fortunately, a friend who worked for a charity that supports social entrepreneurs agreed to act as her gatekeeper, brokering access to social entrepreneurs who had been supported by the charity. The charity agreed to provide her with an anonymised list of over 200 social entrepreneurs from whom she could select those she wanted to interview. The charity would then make the request for the interview on Nabila's behalf and, if the social entrepreneur agreed, provide Nabila with their contact details. She now faced the challenges of how many participants would be needed and how to select them.

Nabila decided she would plan to interview 30 participants as she felt this was a reasonable number. All potential participants would have to satisfy two criteria to be selected. Firstly, they would have to be social entrepreneurs with real-life experience of running a social enterprise, in other words the participants' enterprises needed to have explicit social, environment, and cultural aims. Secondly participants would have to be aged 50 and over at the time of the interview. Fortunately, the charity could provide such data for all the social entrepreneurs they had supported.

At her next meeting with her project tutor Nabila outlined the criteria for selecting her sample and her intended sample size. The project tutor appeared concerned by what Nabila was saying and asked a number of questions, which Nabila was unable to answer. These included:

1 Provide me with the reason why your plan is to interview 30 rather than 15 or even 50 entrepreneurs who meet your criteria.
2 You have explained how you intend to select your sample without making any reference to the type of sampling or the technique you intend to use. Can you state whether you intend to use either probability or non-probability sampling and explain why?
3 It is likely that the anonymised list of over 200 social entrepreneurs provided by the charity will contain more than 30 who meet your criteria fully. If this is the case how will you select those you actually want to interview? You need to name the sampling technique or techniques you intend to use and provide me with a clear justified exposition.
4 Outline the concept of data saturation and explain how you could usefully apply this to the research you are planning to undertake.

References

Department for Work and Pensions (2014) *Fuller Working Lives: A Framework for Action*. Available at: https://www.gov.uk/government/publications/fuller-working-lives-a-framework-for-action [Accessed 16 May 2017].

Hatak, I., Harms, R., and Fink, M. (2015) 'Age, Job Identification, and Entrepreneurial Intention', *Journal of Managerial Psychology*, 30(1), pp.38–53.

Singh, G. and De Noble, A. (2003) 'Early Retirees as the Next Generations of Entrepreneurs', *Entrepreneurship Theory and Practice*, 27(3), pp. 207–225.

Question

1 Develop clear fully justified answers to each of the four questions asked by Nabila's project tutor.

Additional case studies relating to material covered in this chapter are available via the book's companion website: **www.pearsoned.co.uk/saunders**.
   They are:

- Change management at Hattersley Electronics.
- Employment networking in the Hollywood film industry.
- Auditor independence and integrity in accounting firms.
- Implementing strategic change initiatives.
- Comparing UK and French perceptions and expectations of online supermarket shopping.
- Understanding and assessing economic inactivity among Maltese female homemakers.

Self-check answers

7.1 **a** A complete list of all directors of large manufacturing firms could be purchased from an organisation that specialised in selling such lists to use as the sampling frame. Alternatively, a list that contained only those selected for the sample could be purchased to reduce costs. These electronic data could be merged into standard letters such as those included with questionnaires.

b A complete list of accountants, or one that contained only those selected for the sample, could be purchased from an organisation that specialised in selling such lists. Care would need to be taken regarding the precise composition of the list to ensure that it included those in private practice as well as those working for organisations. Alternatively, if the research was interested only in qualified accountants then the professional accountancy bodies' yearbooks, which list all their members and their addresses, could be used as the sampling frame.

c Subject to ethical approval, the personnel records or payroll of Cheltenham Gardens Ltd could be used. Either would provide an up-to-date list of all employees with their addresses.

7.2 Your draft of Lisa's tutor's reply is unlikely to be worded the same way as the one below. However, it should contain the same key points:

"tutor's name" <lisas.tutor@anytown.ac.uk>
To: <lisa@anytown.ac.uk>
Sent: today's date 7:06
Subject: Re: Help!!! Sampling non-response?

Hi Lisa
Many thanks for the email. This is not in the least unusual. I reckon to get about 1 in 20 interviews which go this way and you just have to say 'c'est la vie'. This is not a problem from a methods perspective as, in sampling terms, it can be treated as a non-response due to the person refusing to respond to your questions. This would mean you could not use the material. However, if he answered some other questions then you should treat this respondent as a partial non-response and just not use those answers.
Hope this helps.
'Tutor's name'

7.3 a Your answer will depend on the random numbers you selected. However, the process you follow to select the samples is likely to be similar to that outlined. You will need to generate two separate sets of 20 random numbers between 1 and 100 using a spreadsheet. If a random number is generated two or more times it can only be used once. Two possible sets are:

Sample 1: 38 41 14 59 53 03 52 86 21 88 55 87 85 90 74 18 89 40 84 71
Sample 2: 28 100 06 70 81 76 36 65 30 27 92 73 20 87 58 15 69 22 77 31

These are then marked on the sampling frame (sample 1 is shaded in blue, sample 2 is shaded in orange) as shown below:

1	10	21	7	41	29	61	39	81	55
2	57	22	92	42	84	62	73	82	66
3	149	23	105	43	97	63	161	83	165
4	205	24	157	44	265	64	275	84	301
5	163	25	214	45	187	65	170	85	161
6	1359	26	1440	46	1872	66	1598	86	1341
7	330	27	390	47	454	67	378	87	431
8	2097	28	1935	48	1822	68	1634	88	1756
9	1059	29	998	49	1091	69	1101	89	907
10	1037	30	1298	50	1251	70	1070	90	1158
11	59	31	10	51	9	71	37	91	27
12	68	32	70	52	93	72	88	92	66
13	166	33	159	53	103	73	102	93	147
14	302	34	276	54	264	74	157	94	203
15	161	35	215	55	189	75	168	95	163
16	1298	36	1450	56	1862	76	1602	96	1339
17	329	37	387	57	449	77	381	97	429
18	2103	38	1934	58	1799	78	1598	98	1760
19	1061	39	1000	59	1089	79	1099	99	898
20	1163	40	1072	60	1257	80	1300	100	1034

b Your samples will probably produce patterns that cluster around certain numbers in the sampling frame, although the amount of clustering may differ, as illustrated by samples 1 and 2 above.

c The average (mean) annual output in tens of thousands of pounds will depend entirely upon your sample. For the two samples selected the averages are:

Sample 1 (blue): £6,659,500
Sample 2 (orange): £7,834,500

d There is no bias in either of the samples, as both have been selected at random. However, the average annual output calculated from sample 1 represents the target population more closely than that calculated from sample 2, although this has occurred entirely at random.

7.4 a Your answer will depend on the random number you select as the starting point for your systematic sample. However, the process you followed to select your sample is likely to be similar to that outlined. As a 10 per cent sample has been requested, the sampling fraction is 1/10. Your starting point is selected using a random number between 1 and 10, in this case 2. Once the firm numbered 2 has been selected, every tenth firm is selected:

2 12 22 32 42 52 62 72 82 92

These are marked with orange shading on the sampling frame and will result in a regular pattern whatever the starting point:

1	10	21	7	41	29	61	39	81	55
2	57	22	92	42	84	62	73	82	66
3	149	23	105	43	97	63	161	83	165
4	205	24	157	44	265	64	275	84	301
5	163	25	214	45	187	65	170	85	161
6	1359	26	1440	46	1872	66	1598	86	1341
7	330	27	390	47	454	67	378	87	431
8	2097	28	1935	48	1822	68	1634	88	1756
9	1059	29	998	49	1091	69	1101	89	907
10	1037	30	1298	50	1251	70	1070	90	1158
11	59	31	10	51	9	71	37	91	27
12	68	32	70	52	93	72	88	92	66
13	166	33	159	53	103	73	102	93	147
14	302	34	276	54	264	74	157	94	203
15	161	35	215	55	189	75	168	95	163
16	1298	36	1450	56	1862	76	1602	96	1339
17	329	37	387	57	449	77	381	97	429
18	2103	38	1934	58	1799	78	1598	98	1760
19	1061	39	1000	59	1089	79	1099	99	898
20	1163	40	1072	60	1257	80	1300	100	1034

b The average (mean) annual output of firms for your sample will depend upon where you started your systematic sample. For the sample selected above it is £757,000.

c Systematic sampling has provided a poor estimate of the annual output because there is an underlying pattern in the data, which has resulted in firms with similar levels of output being selected.

7.5 **a** If you assume that there are at least 100,000 managing directors of small- to medium-sized organisations from which to select your sample, you will need to interview approximately 380 to make generalisations that are accurate to within plus or minus 5 per cent (Table 7.1).

b Either cluster or multi-stage sampling could be suitable; what is important is the reasoning behind your choice. This choice between cluster and multi-stage sampling is dependent on the amount of limited resources and time you have available. Using multi-stage sampling will take longer than cluster sampling as more sampling stages will need to be undertaken. However, the results are more likely to be representative of the target population owing to the possibility of stratifying the samples from the sub-areas.

7.6 **a** Prior to deciding on your quota you will need to consider the possible inclusion of residents who are aged under 16 in your quota. Often in such research projects residents aged under 5 (and those aged 5–15) are excluded. You would need a quota of between 2,000 and 5,000 residents to obtain a reasonable accuracy. These should be divided proportionally between the groupings as illustrated in the possible quota below:

Gender	Age group					
	16–19	20–29	30–44	45–59/64	60/65–74	75+
Males	108	169	217	285	110	59
Females	154	209	180	203	205	99

b Data on social class, employment status, socioeconomic status or car ownership could also be used as further quotas. These data are often available from your national Census and are likely to affect shopping habits.

c Interviewers might choose respondents who were easily accessible or appeared willing to answer the questions. In addition, they might fill in their quota incorrectly or make up the data.

7.7 **a** Either snowball sampling as it would be difficult to identify members of the target population or, possibly, convenience sampling because of initial difficulties in finding members of the target population.

b Quota sampling to ensure that the variability in the target population as a whole is represented.

c Heterogeneous purposive sampling to ensure that the full variety of responses are obtained from a range of respondents from the target population.

d Self-selection sampling as it requires people who are interested in the topic.

e Convenience sampling owing to the very short timescales available and the need to have at least some idea of members' opinions.

Chapter **8**

Utilising secondary data

Learning outcomes

By the end of this chapter you should be able to:

- identify the variety of types of secondary data that are available;
- appreciate ways in which secondary data can be used to help to answer your research question(s) and to meet your objectives;
- understand the advantages and disadvantages of using secondary data in research projects;
- use a range of techniques to search for secondary data;
- evaluate the suitability of secondary data for answering your research question(s) and meeting your objectives in terms of measurement validity, coverage, precise suitability, measurement bias, costs and benefits;
- apply the knowledge, skills and understanding gained to your own research project.

8.1 Introduction

When thinking about how to obtain data to answer their research question(s) or meet their objectives, students are increasingly expected to consider undertaking further analyses of data that were collected initially for some other purpose. Such data are known as **secondary data** and include both raw data and published summaries. Once obtained, these data can be further analysed to provide additional or different knowledge, interpretations or conclusions (Bishop and Kuula-Luumi 2017; Bulmer et al. 2009). Despite this, many students automatically think in terms of collecting new **(primary) data** specifically for that purpose. Yet, unlike national governments, non-governmental agencies and other organisations, they do not have the time, money or access to collect detailed large data sets themselves. Fortunately, over the past decade the numbers of sources of potential secondary data have, alongside the ease of gaining access, grown rapidly. Such secondary data may enable you to answer, or partially answer, your research question(s).

Most organisations collect and store a wide variety and large volume of data to support their day-to-day operations: for example, payroll details, organisation charts, copies of letters, minutes of meetings and business transactions including sales queries and purchases. Quality daily newspapers contain a wealth of data, such as reports about takeover bids, interviews with business leaders, photographs of events, graphs and infographics and listings of companies' share prices. Government departments undertake surveys and publish official statistics covering social, demographic and economic topics alongside reports summarising these. Consumer research organisations collect data that are used subsequently by different clients. Trade organisations collect data from their members on topics such as sales that are subsequently aggregated, presented and published. Search engines such as Google collect data on the billions of searches undertaken daily, and social networking sites (such as Facebook) host web pages for particular interest groups, including those set up by organisations, storing them alongside other data including group members' posts and photographs and demographic and geographic location data.

Your digital data trail

When you awoke this morning you probably checked your emails and skimmed the news using an app on your mobile phone or tablet. The sites you visited would have probably recorded your IP (Internet Protocol) address, identifying your Internet service provider and your approximate geographic location. If you used a search engine, your search history may well have been saved; as would any material you intentionally submitted online. You will have already started to leave your digital data trail for the day.

For the rest of the day, you will continue to be traced and tracked through the apps you access and the technology you used. As you view your emails, any responses you send will be saved. When you use your University ID card to swipe into the Library the card informs security who you are and later your exit will be recorded.

Source: © Mark Saunders 2018

Your University's Virtual Learning Environment (VLE) will record when you log in, the amount of time you spend on different pages for different modules and when you log out, extending your trail still further. When you withdraw cash from an ATM, your digital trail will be extended and your location logged and time and date stamped, allowing you to be placed in the vicinity of specific events. This tracking occurs wherever you are in the world allowing you to be located in the vicinity of events taking place such as Sydney's Mardi Gras.

Every day each of us creates vast amounts of digital data. When we search online our searches are recorded. When we tweet, comment on or reply to other tweets, these are stored by Twitter. When updating our status, commenting or liking on Facebook or other social media platforms we are generating data about ourselves which is stored. Each time we pay by bank card, we give the retailer, and our bank, information about where we are and how much we have just spent. When we post feedback or consumer reviews we are, again, generating data that are stored

Our digital data trail or digital footprint is a set of traceable digital activities, actions and communications. Such data, although often collected for an immediate purpose (for example, stock control, payment, enabling access) can, and are, re-used by companies such as Facebook, Amazon and Google for, for example, target advertising. Others including researchers increasingly re-use these data, often in combination with other data such as official statistics. Re-using such 'secondary' data can reveal new insights into trends and patterns as well as infer personal information such as demographic traits, religious and political views and purchasing preferences.

Some of these data, in particular documents such as company minutes, are available only from the organisations that produce them, and so access will need to be negotiated (Sections 6.2 to 6.4). Others, particularly historical documents, such as photographs, illustrations and the like, may be only available from archives or museums either in their original form or, increasingly, digitally. Web pages on social networking sites can range from being 'open' for everyone using the site to view, to being 'restricted' only to group members. Governments' survey data, such as censuses of population, are widely available to download in aggregated form via the Internet as governments allow open access to data they have collected. Such survey data are also often deposited in, and available from, data archives. Online computer databases containing company information, such as Amadeus and Datamonitor, can often be accessed via your university library web pages (Table 8.1). In addition, companies and professional organisations usually have their own websites, which may contain a wide variety of data that are useful to your research project.

For certain types of research project, such as those requiring national or international comparisons, data from a large number of people, or a historical or longitudinal study, secondary data will probably provide the main source to answer your research question(s) and to address your objectives. However, if you are undertaking your research project as part of a course of study, we recommend that you check your course's assessment regulations before deciding whether you are going to use primary or secondary or a combination of both types of data. Some universities explicitly require students to collect primary data for their research projects. Most research questions are answered using some combination of secondary and primary data. Invariably where limited appropriate secondary data are available, you will have to rely mainly on data you collect yourself.

In this chapter we examine the different types of secondary data that are likely to be available to help you to answer your research question(s) and meet your objectives, how you might use them (Section 8.2) and outline the advantages and disadvantages of using secondary data (Section 8.3). We then consider a range of methods for locating these data (Section 8.4) and discuss ways of evaluating their suitability for your specific research question (Section 8.5). We do not attempt to provide a comprehensive list of secondary data sources because, as these continue to grow exponentially, it would be an impossible task.

Table 8.1 Selected online databases with potential secondary data

Name	Secondary data
Amadeus	Financial, descriptive and ownership information for companies in Europe
British Newspapers Archive	Full text and images of British newspapers since c. 1700
Datamonitor	Company profiles for world's 10,000 largest companies, industry profiles for various industries
Datastream	Company, financial and economic information
Euromonitor International	Global market information database searchable by industry, product, country etc.
Key Note Reports	1,600 market reports covering a range of sectors
Mintel Reports	Market research reports on wide range of sectors
Nexis	Full text of UK national and regional newspapers. Some international coverage and company data
QIN	Company accounts, ratios and activities for over 300,000 companies in mainland China
Regional Business News	Full text of US business journals, newspapers and newswires. Updated daily
Times Digital Archive 1785–2012	Digital editions (including photographs, illustrations and advertisements) from *The Times* national newspaper (UK)

8.2 Types of secondary data and uses in research

Secondary data include both quantitative (numeric) and qualitative (non-numeric) data (Section 5.3), and are used principally in both descriptive and explanatory research. The secondary data you analyse further may be **raw data**, where there has been little if any processing, or **compiled data** that have received some form of selection or summarising. They may be **structured data**, that is organised into a format that is easy to process, such as in a database or spreadsheet; or **unstructured data**, which are not easy to search or process as, in their current form, they do not follow a predefined structure. Structured data often comprise numerical data and now account for less than 20 per cent of all stored data (Forbes 2017). In contrast, unstructured data usually comprise text, audio and visual/audio visual data, although they may also include dates and other numerical data. Many secondary data sets currently available comprise data that have been re-combined with other data to create larger multiple-source data sets. Some, as highlighted in the opening vignette, comprise continually updated data from a range of sources. Where such data sets are massive in volume, complex in variety (often comprising both structured and unstructured data) and the velocity to which they are being added to is high, they are referred to as **big data**. Within business and management research projects secondary data are used most frequently in case study and survey research strategies. However, there is no reason not to use secondary data in other research strategies, including archival, action and experimental research.

We find it useful to group the different forms of secondary data into three broad types:

- survey, including census, continuous, regular and ad-hoc surveys;
- document, be they text, audio or visual media;
- compiled from multiple sources to create a snapshot, time series or continually updated dataset.

These are summarised along with examples in Figure 8.1.

Survey secondary data

Survey secondary data refers to existing data originally collected for some other purpose using a survey strategy, usually questionnaires (Chapter 11). Such data normally refer to organisations, people or households. They are made available either as compiled data tables or, increasingly frequently, in structured form as a downloadable matrix of data (Section 12.3, Box 8.11) for secondary analysis.

Survey secondary data will have been collected through one of three distinct subtypes of survey strategy: census, continuous or regular survey or ad hoc survey (Figure 8.1). Censuses are usually carried out by governments and are unique because, unlike other surveys, participation is obligatory. Consequently, they provide very good coverage of the population from who data are collected. They include censuses of populations, which have been carried out in many countries since the eighteenth century and in the UK since 1801 (Office for National Statistics n.d., a). Published tabulations are available via the Internet for more recent UK censuses, and the raw data 100 years after the census was conducted can also be accessed via the Internet. Data from censuses conducted by many governments are intended to meet the needs of government departments as well as of local government. As a consequence they are usually clearly defined, well documented and of a high quality. Such data are easily accessible in compiled form and are widely used by other organisations and individual researchers.

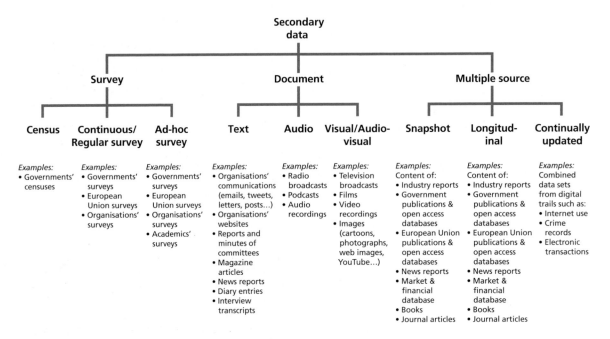

Figure 8.1 Types and examples of secondary data

Continuous and regular surveys are those, excluding censuses, which are repeated over time (Hakim 1982). They include surveys where data are collected throughout the year, such as the UK's *Living Costs and Food Survey* (Office for National Statistics 2017) and those repeated at regular intervals. The latter include the EU Labour Force Survey, which since 1998 has been undertaken quarterly using a core set of questions by member states throughout the European Union. This means that some comparative data are available for member states, although access to these data is limited by European and individual countries' legislation (Eurostat 2017). Non-governmental bodies also carry out regular surveys. These include general-purpose market research surveys such as Kantar Media's Target Group Index. Because of the commercial nature of such market research surveys, the data are likely to be costly to obtain. Many large organisations also undertake regular surveys, a common example being the employee attitude survey. However, because of the sensitive nature of such information, it is often difficult to gain access to such survey data, especially in its raw form.

Census and continuous and regular survey data provide a useful resource with which to compare or set in context your own research findings from primary data. Aggregate data are usually available via the Internet (Section 8.4), in particular for government surveys. When using these data you need to check when they were collected, as there can be over a year between collection and publication! If you are undertaking research in one UK organisation, you could use these data to place your case study organisation within the context of its industry group or division using the *Annual Business Survey* (Office for National Statistics n.d. c). Aggregated results of the Annual Business Survey can be found via the UK government's statistics information gateway, the *Office for National Statistics* (Table 8.2).

Table 8.2 Selected Internet secondary data gateways and archives

Name	Internet address	Comment
General focus		
RBA Business Information Sources	rba.co.uk/sources	Gateway with links to business, statistical, government and country sites
UK Data Archive	data-archive.ac.uk	Archive of UK social and economic digital data
UK Data Service (UKDS)	ukdataservice.ac.uk	Gateway to and support for social, economic and population data, both quantitative and qualitative for both the UK and other countries
Wharton Research Data Service (WRDS)	whartonwrds.com	Gateway to databases in finance, accounting, banking, finance, economics, management, marketing and public policy
Morningstar	morningstar.co.uk	Financial information, guide to companies and investment trusts, report service and market activity analysis
Country focus		
Australia: Australian Data Archive	ada.edu.au/	Archive of Australian digital research data including census. Includes data from other Asia-Pacific countries. Links to other secondary data sites
Canada: Statistics Canada	statcan.gc.ca/start-debut-eng.html	Gateway to statistics on economy, society and culture (including census) of Canada

(*continued*)

Table 8.2 (*Continued*)

Name	Internet address	Comment
China: Universities Service Centre Databank for China Studies	usc.cuhk.edu. hk/?lang=en	Archive of social science data about People's Republic of China
Czech Republic: Czech Social Science Data Archive	archiv.soc.cas.cz/en	Archive of social science data about the Czech Republic
European Union: Europa	europa.eu/	Gateway to information (including press releases, legislation, fact sheets) published by the European Union
Eurostat	ec.europa/eurostat	EU statistics information gateway
France: National Institute for Statistics	insee.fr/en/accueil	France's National Institute for Statistics gateway for both statistics and government publications. Much of this website is available in English
Germany: Federal Statistics Office	destatis.de/EN/ Homepage.html	Germany's Federal Statistical Office providing a gateway to data. Much of this website is available in English
Ireland (Eire): Central Statistics Office	cso.ie	Irish Central Statistical Office (CSO), the government body providing a gateway to Irish official statistics
Japan: Social Science Japan Data Archive	scsrda.iss.u-tokyo. ac.jp/en	Archive of social science datasets available providing details in both Japanese and English. Datasets in Japanese only
Korea: Korean Social Science Data Archive	kossda.or.kr/eng	Archive of social science statistical data including census available in Korean, English and Japanese
The Netherlands: Statistics Netherlands	cbs.nl/en-gb	Site of the Netherlands' Central Bureau of Statistics (CBS). Much of this website is available in English. Provides gateway to StatLine, which contains statistical data that can be downloaded free of charge
North America: Compustat	spglobal.com/mar-ketintelligence/en/	Financial data and supplementary items for North American Companies
Norway: Norwegian Social Science Data Services	nsd.uib.no/nsd/ english/	Archive of social science data on Norway
South Africa: South African Data Archive	sada.nrf.ac.za	Archive of social science data such as the census on South Africa
United Kingdom: GOV.UK	gov.uk	UK government information service providing a gateway to government departments, official statistics, etc.
United Kingdom: Office for National Statistics	ons.gov.uk/ons	The official UK statistics gateway containing official UK statistics and information about statistics, which can be accessed and downloaded free of charge
United States: Census Bureau	www.census.gov	US Government data about the economy and people living in the United States

Alternatively, you might explore issues already highlighted by undertaking further analysis of data provided by an earlier organisation survey through in-depth interviews.

Survey secondary data may be available in sufficient detail to provide the main data set from which to answer your research question(s) and to meet your objectives. They may be the only way in which you can obtain the required data. If your research question is concerned with national variations in consumer spending it is unlikely that you will be able to collect sufficient data of your own. You will therefore need to rely on secondary data such as those contained in the report *Family Spending* (Office for National Statistics 2018). For some research questions and objectives, suitable data will be available in published form. For others, you may need more disaggregated data. This is most likely to be available via the Internet, often from data archives (Section 8.4). We have found that for most business and management research requiring secondary data you are unlikely to find all the data you require from one source. Rather, your research project is likely to involve detective work in which you build your own multiple-source data set using different data items from a variety of secondary data sources (Box 8.1). Like all detective work, finding data that help to answer a research question or meet an objective is immensely satisfying but also time consuming.

Ad hoc surveys are usually one-off surveys and are far more specific in their subject matter. They include data from questionnaires that have been undertaken by independent researchers as well as interviews undertaken by organisations and governments. Because of their ad hoc nature, you will probably find it more difficult to discover relevant surveys. However, it may be that an organisation in which you are undertaking research has conducted its own questionnaire or interview-based survey on an issue related to your research. Some organisations will provide you with a report containing aggregated data; others may be willing to let you undertake further analyses using the raw data from their ad hoc survey. Alternatively, you may be able to gain access to and use raw data from an ad hoc survey that has been deposited in a data archive (Section 8.4).

Document secondary data

Document secondary data are often used in research projects that also collect primary data. However, you can also use them on their own or with other sources of secondary data, for example, for business history research within an archival research strategy. **Document secondary data** are defined as data that, unlike the spoken word, endure physically (including digitally) as evidence, allowing data to be transposed across both time and space and reanalysed for a purpose different to that for which they were originally collected (Lee 2012). They therefore include text, audio and visual media.

Text media include notices, correspondence (including emails), minutes of meetings, reports to shareholders, diaries, transcripts of speeches and conversations, administrative and public records as well as text of web pages (Box 8.2). Text media can also include books, journal and magazine articles and newspapers. Although books, articles, journals and reports are a common storage medium for compiled secondary data, the text can be important raw secondary data in its own right. You could analyse the text of companies' annual reports to establish the espoused attitude of companies in different sectors to environmental issues. Using Content Analysis (Section 12.2) such text, secondary data could also be used to generate statistical measures such as the frequency with which environmental issues are mentioned.

Audio media, such as archived recordings of radio programmes, speeches, audio blogs and podcasts can, like other forms of document secondary data, be analysed both quantitatively and qualitatively by transcribing the spoken words (Section 10.7) and treating

Box 8.1
Focus on student research

SME Success: Winning New Business

Using secondary data to contextualise research findings

Prisha's research project was focussed on how Asian ethnic minority small businesses develop their customer bases. Working with the Asian Business Chamber of Commerce in the City where her University was located, she was planning to meet and interview a sample of at least 30 of these small business owners in a variety of sectors.

Prisha was also keen to contextualise her findings. She searched online using the phrases "SME customer base developing" and "SME winning new business". The second of these phrases displayed a list of links to pages including two titled 'SME Success:

Winning New Business Kingston Smith'. Prisha clicked on these and discovered a link to a research report *SME Success: Winning New Business* (Gray et al. 2016). She downloaded the 20 page 'highlights and executive summary' report. This outlined the key findings of research using data from a questionnaire completed by over 1,000 UK SMEs and included a number of useful graphs including one showing the importance and effectiveness of different ways of generating new sales, and another the importance and effectiveness of different enablers for winning new business.

Prisha felt that, ideally, she would like to use the precise data from which the graph was drawn for her research project. She therefore decided to search for the report's title and its three authors. This revealed that a full copy of the report, including tables containing the data she needed could be downloaded from the platform academia.edu as well as the authors' universities' research repositories.

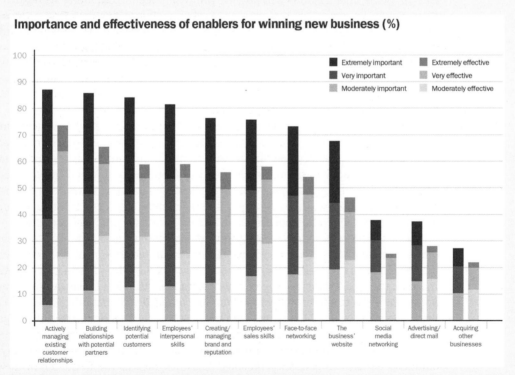

Importance and effectiveness of enablers for winning new business (%)

Source: Gray et al. (2016). © Kingston Smith LLP, reproduced with permission

Box 8.2
Focus on student research

Using organisation-based document secondary data

Sasha's work placement company had a problem. They felt customers' initial complaints were often not addressed, with minor issues often developing into major problems. Sasha was asked by her mentor to investigate how the company dealt with complaints by customers. Her mentor arranged for her to have access to the electronic copies of customers' emails and letters of complaint and the replies sent by the organisation's customer relations team (text document secondary data) over the past 12 months. Reading through these customers' letters, Sasha soon realised that many of these customers complained in writing because they

had not received a satisfactory response when they had complained earlier by telephone. She therefore asked her mentor if audio-recordings were kept of customers' telephone complaints. Her mentor said that audio-recordings of all telephone conversations, including complaints (text document secondary data), were stored in the customer relations database, each being given a unique reference number which could be matched to the customers' written complaints.

On receiving details of the audio-data stored in the customer relations' database, Sasha realised that the next stage would be to match the complaints letters and emails with the audio recordings. The latter, she hoped, would enable her to understand the context of the written complaints and, hopefully, establish why the customer had written. However, she realised this would be an extremely time-consuming task, so decided to select a purposive sample of the audio recordings.

---

them as text (Sections 12.2 and 13.4) However, this ignores other aspects of these data that may be important such as the tone of voice. Document visual data can be classified into three media groups: two-dimensional static, two-dimensional moving and three-dimensional lived (Bell and Davison 2013). **Two-dimensional static media** include photographs, pictures, cartoons, maps, graphs, logos and diagrams, whereas **two-dimensional moving media** include films, videos, interactive web pages and other multi-media, often being combined with audio (Box 8.6). In contrast, **three-dimensional and lived media** includes architecture and clothing. As a consequence visual documentary secondary data may be found, for example, in organisations annual reports, or other documents such as web pages and research reports (Box 8.1). Alternatively, it may be found in news reports and television programmes as well as pay on demand and subscription-based online streaming services such as Netflix and Amazon Prime.

Business and management researchers are making greater use of visual and to a lesser extent audio documents as data. Much of these are web-based materials generated by organisations and online communities. While data stored in the majority of web pages, such as blogs and those set up by social networking sites' user groups, were never intended to be used in this way, they can still provide secondary data for research projects. There are, however, a number of issues related to using such data, including locating it, evaluating its usefulness in relation to your research question and objectives ensuring any associated ethical concerns are met (Sections 6.5, 6.6 and 9.6).

Records stored in public, private and not-for-profit organisations' databases, as part of their day-to-day business operations are another source of document data that, when reanalysed for a different purpose, are secondary data. These include structured text-based data such as details of employees, members and customers and, as illustrated by the opening vignette, their interactions, such as customer transactions and mobile telephone calls, as well as unstructured audio and visual media data (Box 8.2). Where you are able to gain access and satisfy ethical concerns, it may be possible to link and reanalyse such data to answer your research question (Box 8.2).

For your research project, the document sources you have available can depend on whether you have been granted access to an organisation's records as well as on your success in locating data archives, and other Internet, commercial and library sources (Section 8.4). Access to an organisation's data will be dependent on gatekeepers within that organisation (Sections 6.2–6.4). In our experience, those research projects that make use of document secondary data often do so as part of a within-company action research project or a case study of a particular organisation (Box 8.2).

When you analyse text and non-text materials, such as a web page, a television news report or a newspaper article directly as part of your research, you are using those materials as secondary data. However, often such materials are just the source of your secondary data, rather than the actual secondary data you are analysing (Box 8.3).

Multiple-source secondary data

Multiple-source secondary data can be compiled entirely from document or survey secondary data, or can be an amalgam of the two. It can include data that are being added to continually such as records of transactions, as well as data that are added to less frequently on an ad-hoc basis or collected only once. The key factor is that different data sets have been combined to form another data set prior to your accessing the data. One of the more common types of multiple-source data that you are likely to come across are already undertaken online compilations of company information stored in databases such as *Amadeus* (Table 8.1). This contains comparable financial data about over 21 million public and private European companies, often for a specified date to provide a 'snapshot'. Other multiple-source secondary data snapshots include the various share price listings for different stock markets reported in the financial pages of quality newspapers. While newspapers are available online, there may be a charge to view their web pages. Fortunately university libraries usually have recent paper copies, while national and regional newspapers can also be accessed using online databases such as *Nexis* and, for older newspapers, the *British Newspapers Archive* (Table 8.1).

Secondary data from different sources can also be combined, if they have the same geographical basis, to form area-based data sets (Hakim 1982). Such data sets usually draw together quantifiable information and statistics. They are commonly compiled by national governments for their country and their component standard economic planning regions and by regional and local administrations for their own region. Such area-based multiple-source data sets are increasingly only available online through national governments' information gateways, regional administration's information gateways or data archives (Table 8.1). Widely used European examples of such snapshot data include the European Union's annual online publication *Eurostat Regional Yearbook* (Eurostat 2017) and collections such as Eurostat's (2018) statistical data for member countries (Box 8.8).

The way in which a multiple-source data set has been compiled will dictate the sorts of research question(s) or objectives for which you can use it. One method of compilation is for you to extract and combine one or more comparable variables from a number of surveys or from the same snapshot survey that has been repeated over time to provide **longitudinal** data. For many undergraduate and taught master's courses' research projects, this is one of the few ways in which you will be able to obtain data over a long period. Other ways of obtaining longitudinal data include using a series of company documents, such as appointment letters or public and administrative records, as sources from which to create your own longitudinal secondary data set (Box 8.4). Other examples of such data sets include the UK Employment Department's stoppages at work data held by the UK Data Archive (Table 8.2) and those derived by researchers from nineteenth- and

Box 8.3
Focus on student research

When are the reports in newspapers and on YouTube secondary data?

Jana's research question was, 'To what extent is the media's reporting of United States Government's policies on climate change and their impact on business change biased?' She had downloaded and read journal articles about the case for climate change as well as a number of the United States' Center for Climate and Energy Solutions briefs, factsheets and library papers. The latter included the Center's (2018) document "Comments on State Guidelines for Greenhouse Gas Emissions" which she used to establish the role of the state and federal governments in implementing clean energy policies. She had also obtained copies of reports in quality newspapers about climate change reform in the United States for the past two years and found YouTube clips of television news reports uploaded by media companies such as the NBC News, Fox Business Networks and CNN.

As she began to write the methodology chapter of her research project, Jana became confused. She knew that the journal articles about the case for climate change and its impact on business were literature rather than secondary data. However, she was unclear whether the Center's library paper, the media reports and the YouTube clips were secondary data. She emailed her tutor who responded:

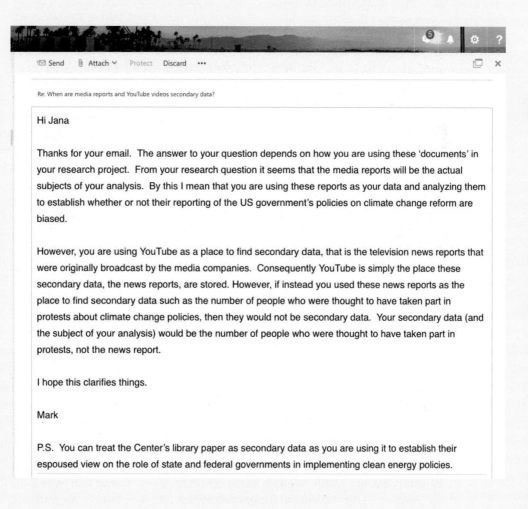

✉ Send   📎 Attach ∨   Protect   Discard   •••

Re: When are media reports and YouTube videos secondary data?

Hi Jana

Thanks for your email. The answer to your question depends on how you are using these 'documents' in your research project. From your research question it seems that the media reports will be the actual subjects of your analysis. By this I mean that you are using these reports as your data and analyzing them to establish whether or not their reporting of the US government's policies on climate change reform are biased.

However, you are using YouTube as a place to find secondary data, that is the television news reports that were originally broadcast by the media companies. Consequently YouTube is simply the place these secondary data, the news reports, are stored. However, if instead you used these news reports as the place to find secondary data such as the number of people who were thought to have taken part in protests about climate change policies, then they would not be secondary data. Your secondary data (and the subject of your analysis) would be the number of people who were thought to have taken part in protests, not the news report.

I hope this clarifies things.

Mark

P.S. You can treat the Center's library paper as secondary data as you are using it to establish their espoused view on the role of state and federal governments in implementing clean energy policies.

Box 8.4
Focus on management research

"I'm not mopping floors, I'm putting a man on the moon"

Using document secondary data

It is often assumed that leaders can boost employees' motivation by communicating their organisations' ultimate aspirations. Yet, evidence suggests a more paradoxical position where the breadth and timelessness of a goal such as 'to put a man on the moon' makes it difficult for employees to see how this relates to their daily responsibilities. To understand how leaders can help employees resolve this paradox, Andrew Carton (2018) used a range of secondary archival data from different sources to explore the actions of John F Kennedy when he was leading NASA (National Aeronautics and Space Administration) in the 1960s. His research is reported in the journal *Administrative Science Quarterly.*

Realising there were hundreds of thousands of pages of archived records, video clips and books covering leaders' communications about NASA's ultimate aspirations and employees' perceptions of their day-to-day work over the period 1959–69, Carton narrowed his focus to four themes derived from the literature:

- Day to day work and individual's daily routine;
- Organisational objectives and ultimate aspirations;
- Perceived connections between day-to-day work and ultimate aspirations;

- Meaningfulness and perceived significance of work.

Given that the moon landing was in 1969, it is not surprising that the vast majority of the data Carton used originated before 1970. His key data sources were 60 documents, each comprising 150 to 300 pages, in which NASA's Public Information Office had provided a synthesis of news releases, transcripts of discussions and internal memos. He also sampled a range of online sources containing almost entirely original spoken dialogue. These included five transcripts of onboard communication, 23 web pages, five audio recordings featuring John F. Kennedy and NASA lower level employees, 4.5 hours of documentary film, 95 published interviews and 800 pages in books containing information on employees' perceptions for the period 1959–69. These were supplemented by data from further documents held at the NASA archives, which could only be accessed in person. Finally Carton visited NASA headquarters to help establish the layout of mission control in the 1960s.

Carton searched these data using search terms that reflected each of his four themes to generate insights about how employees with different backgrounds and responsibilities saw the connections between the aspiration to put a man on the moon and their daily work. He found that through four sense-giving steps Kennedy was able to help employees to see a stronger connection between their work and the ultimate goal. In doing this he argues his findings ". . . redirect research by conceptualizing leaders as architects who motivate employees most effectively when they provide a structural blueprint that maps the connections between employees' everyday work and the organization's ultimate aspirations" (Carton 1918: 323).

early twentieth-century population census returns, the raw data for which can often be accessed through national governments' information gateways such as the UK's Office for National Statistics (Table 8.1). Longitudinal multiple source data can also be audio or visual; for example, a series of interviews with a business person, photographs of the same retail park over a number of years, or advertisements for a particular product for a specified time period.

Data can also be compiled for the same population over time using a series of 'snapshots' to form **cohort studies**. Such studies are relatively rare, owing to the difficulty of maintaining contact with members of the cohort from year to year. An example is the UK television series 'Seven Up', which has followed a cohort since they were schoolchildren at seven-year intervals since 1964 (Section 5.9).

The final form of multiple-source secondary data is compiled from digital sources that are being updated continually (as highlighted in our opening vignette). These are usually data that are being collected on a very large scale and are referred to as big data. In general terms, big data is about collecting and managing large varied data sets that have three core elements, often referred to as the three Vs (McAfee and Brynjolfsson 2012; George et al. 2016):

- volume – the enormous size of the data set due to the aggregation of large numbers of variables and the even larger number of observations for each of them;
- velocity – the speed in which data are being constantly added in real time or near real time from a wide variety of (digital) sources;
- variety – the multiplicity of unstructured and structured data being added.

Big data comprise both structured and unstructured data, being more comprehensive in terms of both the number of variables and the number of observations and offering greater granularity, that is a deeper level of detail, than traditional data sources (George et al. 2016). With big data, rather than collecting data from, for example, a sample of employees' using a survey strategy, researchers, subject to ethical approval, focus on the entire population of employees using digital data collected in real time.

Big data can therefore be thought typically as being massive and complex multiple source secondary data sets and can be drawn from a wide variety of online sources, public records or transactions that are continuously updated in large quantities being difficult to process using traditional computing techniques. The combinations of volume, velocity and speed result in data sets that often run into millions of observations, meaning that data science applications are required for analysis. Whilst big data and the associated data science applications for their analysis are becoming more widely used in business and management research (George et al. 2016), even if such data are available, they are at present unlikely to be practicable for an undergraduate or masters' research project due to the amount of computing power required for their analysis.

8.3 Advantages and disadvantages of secondary data

Advantages

May have fewer resource requirements

For many research questions and objectives the main advantage of using secondary data is the enormous saving in resources, in particular your time and money (Vartanian 2011). In general, it is much less expensive and time consuming to use secondary data than to collect the data yourself, especially where the data can be downloaded as a file that is compatible with your analysis software. You will also have more time to think about theoretical aims and substantive issues, and subsequently you will be able to spend more time and effort analysing and interpreting the data. If you need your data quickly, secondary data may be the only viable alternative. In addition, they are often higher-quality data than could be obtained by collecting your own (Box 8.5; Smith 2006).

Unobtrusive

Using secondary data within organisations may also have the advantage that, because they have already been collected, they provide an unobtrusive measure. Cowton (1998) refers to this advantage as eavesdropping, emphasising its benefits for sensitive situations.

Box 8.5
Focus on
management
research

Grandparent care and mothers' participation in the labour force – using cohort study secondary data

Kanji's (2017) research looks at the relationship between mothers being in paid work and the informal care of their children by grandparents. Using the UK's Millennium Cohort Study she was able to download a large dataset of 12,013 partnered mothers and 2,938 lone parent mothers whose children had just entered primary school at around the age of five. Of these, 522 mothers were excluded due to missing data.

Data variables downloaded for the remaining 14,429 mothers included their paid work status, use of grandparent childcare, grandmother's age, distance from grandparents, education, urban/rural area, number of children, number of younger children, and each mother's agreement/disagreement with the statement 'A child is likely to suffer if his or her mother works before he/she starts school'.

Statistical modelling using these data revealed that grandparents' care of their grandchildren significantly raises the labour force participation and the extent of participation of both lone and partnered mothers with a child of school entry age.

Longitudinal studies may be feasible

For many research projects time constraints mean that secondary data provide the only possibility of undertaking longitudinal studies. This is possible either by creating your own (Box 8.4) or by using an existing multiple-source data set (Section 8.2). Comparative research can also be undertaken where such data are available. You may find this to be of particular use for research questions and objectives that require regional or international comparisons (Box 8.11). However, you need to ensure that the data you are comparing were collected and recorded using methods that are comparable. Comparisons relying on unpublished data or data that are currently unavailable in the required format, such as the creation of new tables from existing census data, are likely to be expensive, as such tabulations will have to be specially prepared. Although your research is dependent on access being granted by the owners of the data, principally governments, many countries are enshrining increased rights of access to information held by public authorities through freedom of information legislation such as the UK's Freedom of Information Act 2005. This gives a general right to access to recorded information held by public authorities, although a charge may be payable. However, this is dependent upon your request not being contrary to relevant data protection legislation or agreements (Section 6.7).

Can provide comparative and contextual data

Often it can be useful to compare data that you have collected with secondary data. This means that you can place your own findings within a more general context (Box 8.1) or, alternatively, triangulate your findings (Section 5.3). If you have used a questionnaire, perhaps to collect data from a sample of potential customers, secondary data such as a national census can be used to assess the generalisability of findings, in other words how representative these data are of the total population (Section 7.2).

Can result in unforeseen discoveries and new insights

Reanalysing secondary data can also lead to unforeseen or unexpected new discoveries and new insights (Box 8.6). Dale et al. (1988) cite establishing the link between smoking

Box 8.6
Focus on management research

Whistle while you work?

Using two-dimensional moving media to provide new insights into puzzles

In their 2017 *Organisation Studies* paper, Griffin and colleagues use secondary data to explore socio-cultural expectations about working that prepare young people for their future lives in organisations, a concept they term "organizational readiness" (Griffin et al., 2017, pp. 869). The secondary data for their research were the 54 animations considered by the Disney Corporation to be their best and most well-known animations, all of which were available in DVD format.

The 54 DVDs comprised both traditional animations such as *Snow White and the Seven Dwarfs* (released 1937) and *The Jungle Book* (released 1967); and contemporary animations such as *Frozen* (released 2013) and *Big Hero 6* (released 2014). Each was watched by all authors who took extensive notes on work related events, recording aspects such as gender, the types of work portrayed and how the work was characterised. Subsequently the researchers undertook an in-depth analysis of the issues relating to work that had been identified.

Their analysis revealed that in Disney's traditional animations work is represented as no place for women and especially not strong women. Within this norm, females were depicted as rejecting organisations in favour of the home. Griffin et al. comment that, in terms of organisational readiness, where girls were portrayed as workers they were not acting as women. In contrast in contemporary animations, although story-lines are similar, passivity and favouring the home is replaced by females being active and strong, or helping others to face up to their responsibilities. This they argue highlights that strength rather than weakness is now desirable and encapsulates the expectation that women should perform actively in the workplace.

Griffin and colleagues consider that while early animations may arouse fear and the desire for rescue in viewers, the more recent may offer these viewers a sense of their own strength and refusal to be passive. This they argue offers new insights into women's organisational readiness. Young viewers watching both traditional and contemporary animations are presented with a paradox: Girls must be both weak and strong and must work and not work.

and lung cancer as an example of such a serendipitous discovery. In this example the link was established through secondary analysis of medical records that had not been collected with the intention of exploring any such relationship.

Permanence of data

Unlike data that you collect yourself, secondary data generally provide a source of data that is often permanent and available in a form that may be checked relatively easily by others (Denscombe 2007). This means that the data and your research findings are more open to public scrutiny.

Disadvantages

May be collected for a purpose that does not match your need

Data that you collect yourself will be collected with a specific purpose in mind: to answer your research question(s) and to meet your objectives. Unfortunately, secondary data will have been collected for a specific purpose that differs, at least to some extent, from your research question(s) or objectives (Denscombe 2007). Consequently, the data you are considering may be inappropriate to your research question. If this is the case then you need to find an alternative source, or collect the data yourself. More probably, you will be able to answer your research question(s) or address your objectives only partially. Common reasons for this include the data being collected a few years earlier and so not being current, or the methods of collection differing between the original data sources which have been amalgamated subsequently to form the secondary data set you intend to use. For example, the 2011 UK National Census question on marital status asked 'What is your legal marital or same-sex civil partnership status?' while the 2001 question on marital status asked 'What is your marital status?' (Office for National Statistics 2014c), reflecting changes in social norms and legislation. Where the data are non-current and you have access to primary data, such as in a research project that is examining an issue within an organisation, you are likely to have to combine secondary and primary data. Alternatively, the secondary data you rely on may 'leave things out because the people whose information we are using don't think it's important, even if we do' (Becker 1998: 101).

Access may be difficult or costly

Where data have been collected for commercial reasons, gaining access may be difficult or costly. Market research reports, such as those produced by Mintel or Key Note (Table 8.2), may cost a great deal if the report(s) that you require are not available online via your university's library.

Aggregations and definitions may be unsuitable

The fact that secondary data were collected for a different purpose may result in other, including ethical (Section 6.6), problems. Much of the secondary data you use is likely to be in published reports. As part of the compilation process, data will have been aggregated in some way. These aggregations, while meeting the requirements of the original research, may not be quite so suitable for your research. The definitions of data variables may not be the most appropriate for your research question(s) or objectives. In addition, where you are intending to combine data sets, definitions may differ markedly or have been revised over time (Box 8.7). Alternatively, the documents you are using may represent the interpretations of those who produced them, rather than offer an objective picture of reality.

No real control over data quality

Although many of the secondary data sets available from governments and data archives are likely to be of a higher quality than you could ever collect yourself, there is still a need to assess the quality of these data. Wernicke (2014) notes that although many national statistical agencies are obliged by national law to provide data of high quality, this may not be the case. Looking at official economic data, he argues that these are distorted by the informal economy, hidden money and false and non-responses. For this reason care must be taken and all data sources must be evaluated carefully, as outlined in Section 8.5.

Initial purpose may affect how data are presented

When using data that are presented as part of a report you also need to be aware of the purpose of that report and the impact that this will have on the way the data are presented. This is most likely for internal organisational documents and external documents such as published company reports and newspaper reports. Reichman (1962; cited by Stewart and Kamins 1993) emphasises this point referring to newspapers, although the sentiments apply to many documents. He argues that newspapers select what they consider to be the

Box 8.7
Focus on student research

Changing definitions

As part of his research, Jeremy wished to use longitudinal data on the numbers of males and females disaggregated by some form of social grouping. Using the UK Office for National Statistics website (Table 8.1), he quickly found and downloaded data which classified males and females using the National Statistics Socio-economic Classification (NS-SEC). However, this classification appeared to have been used only from 2001. Prior to this date, two separate classifications had been used: social class (SC) and socio-economic group (SEG), for which much longer time series of data were available. Before arranging an appointment with his project tutor to discuss this potential problem, Jeremy made a note of the two classifications:

NS-SEC	SC
1 Higher managerial and professional occupations	I Professional
2 Lower managerial and professional occupations	II Managerial and technical
3 Intermediate occupations	IIIa Skilled non-manual
4 Small employers and own account workers	IIIb Skilled manual
5 Lower supervisory and technical occupations	IV Semi-skilled
6 Semi-routine occupations	V Unskilled
7 Routine occupations	

During their meeting later that week, Jeremy's tutor referred him to research on the NS-SEC which compared this with the old measures of SC and SEG and made suggestions regarding the continuity of the measures. Jeremy noted down the reference: Heath, A., Martin, J. and Beerten, R. (2003) 'Old and new social class measures – a comparison', in D. Rose and D.J. Pevalin (eds) *A Researcher's Guide to the National Statistics Socio-economic Classification*. London: Sage, pp. 226–42.

most significant points and emphasise these at the expense of supporting data. This, Reichman states, is not a criticism as the purpose of the reporting is to bring these points to the attention of readers rather than to provide a full and detailed account. However, if we generalise from these ideas, we can see that the culture, predispositions and ideals of those who originally collected and collated the secondary data will have influenced the nature of these data at least to some extent. This is especially the case for online sources where there is increasing concern regarding the possibility of fake news stories being posted (Box 8.8). For these reasons you must evaluate carefully any secondary data you intend to use. Possible ways of doing this are discussed in Section 8.5.

8.4 Searching for and locating secondary data

Unless you are approaching your research project with the intention of analysing one specific secondary data set that you already know well, your first step will be to ascertain whether the data you need are likely to be available. Your research question(s), objectives and the literature you have already reviewed will guide this. For many research projects you are likely to be unsure as to whether the data you require are available as secondary data. Fortunately, there are a number of clues to the sorts of data that are likely to be available.

Box 8.8 Research in the news

EU presses tech groups to do more to tackle 'fake news'

By Rochelle Toplensky

The European Union is giving Facebook and other platforms until the end of the year to tackle "fake-news" online before officials begin to consider further regulation.

European officials expect online platforms to inform users where the information came from but Mariya Gabriel, digital commissioner, said they do not want to "create a ministry of truth". Online platforms are asked to agree a "code of practice on disinformation" that flags sponsored content; helps to quickly identify and close fake accounts or bots; explains to users how their news feeds are built; and assists independent fact-checking organisations.

Officials want to see results by the end of the year, so that they can have an action plan in place ahead of the European elections in 2019. Julian King, security commissioner, said deliberate disinformation online seeks to "influence and manipulate behavior, to sow doubt and division [which] is a real threat to the cohesion and stability of our society and to our democratic institutions." Fake-news is a "new kind of combat with no rules of engagement" according to Mr King, who cautioned that "Russian military doctrine explicitly recognises information warfare as one of its domains".

Disinformation is "far from new, but digital tools enable it to spread with a scale and at a speed not seen before and with an unprecedented degree of intrusion," added Mr King. He said the commission's initiative aims to enable people to make informed decisions about what they are reading by creating transparency, traceability and accountability online.

 Source: 'EU presses tech groups to do more to tackle "fake news"' Rochelle Toplensky, FT.Com, 26 April 2018. ©The Financial Times

The breadth of data discussed in the previous section serves only to emphasise that, despite the increasing importance of the Internet, potential secondary data are still stored in a variety of locations. Finding relevant secondary data requires detective work, which has two interlinked stages:

1 establishing whether the sort of data you require are likely to be available as secondary data;
2 locating the precise data you require.

Establishing the likely availability of secondary data

There are a number of clues to whether the secondary data you require are likely to be available. As part of your literature review you will have already read journal articles and books on your chosen topic. Where these have made use of secondary data (as in Box 8.4), they will provide you with an idea of the sort of data that are available. In addition, these articles and books should contain full references to the sources of the data. Where these refer to published secondary data such as those stored in online databases or multiple-source or survey reports, it is usually relatively easy to find the original source. Your university library will have subscriptions to a number of these online databases (Table 8.1) and is well worth browsing to establish the secondary data that are available. Quality national newspapers are also often a good source as they often report summary findings of recent reports (Box 8.9) and can be searched online. Your tutors have probably already suggested that you read a quality national newspaper on a regular basis, advice we would fully endorse, as it is an excellent way of keeping up to date with recent events in the business world. In addition, there are many online news services, although some charge a subscription.

Box 8.9 Focus on research in the news

Lawyers trump listeners in China's online music world

FTCR survey finds surge in paying users amid legal battles over exclusive licence deals

By Duan Yan

The development of streaming services in China has been good for music fans but arguably better for lawyers, as the leading platforms slug it out over exclusive licensing. Just ask Jay Chou fans on Netease Cloud Music: last month they lost access to songs by the popular Taiwanese singer following complaints from rival Tencent Music about violation of a sharing agreement.

This was the latest in a string of legal rows among China's music-streaming platforms, which see exclusive content rights as their path to dominance in a small but rapidly growing sector. FT Confidential Research has tracked a sharp increase in the willingness of Chinese consumers to pay to listen to music online, unthinkable just a few years ago. Our latest survey of 1,000 urban consumers nationwide found 43.3 per cent saying they had paid over the past year, up from 29 per cent when we last asked in 2016 and marking the biggest jump among the content categories we track.

There is lots of room for growth. We estimate 30m subscribers paid an average Rmb123 ($19.40) to listen to online music over the past 12 months, equating to total annual sales of Rmb3.7bn. In contrast, Spotify alone reported subscriber revenues last year of $4.5bn. Chinese market leader Tencent Music is now reportedly planning an initial public offering that would value the company at more than $25bn, versus Spotify's $28.7bn market capitalization . . .

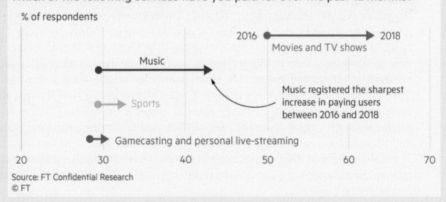

Paying for online content

Which of the following services have you paid for over the past 12 months?

% of respondents

2016 — 2018 Movies and TV shows

Music

Sports

Music registered the sharpest increase in paying users between 2016 and 2018

Gamecasting and personal live-streaming

20   30   40   50   60   70

Source: FT Confidential Research
© FT

 Source: Abridged from 'Lawyers trump listeners in China's online music world', Duan Yan, *FT Confidential Research,* 3 May 2018. Copyright © 2018 The Financial Times Ltd

References for unpublished and document secondary data are often less specific, referring to 'unpublished survey results' or an 'in-house company survey'. Although these may be insufficient to locate or access the actual secondary data, they still provide useful clues about the sort of data that might be found within organisations and which might prove useful. Subject-specific textbooks such as Malhortra et al.'s (2017) *Marketing Research: An Applied Approach* can provide a clear indication of secondary data sources available in your research area, in this instance marketing. Other textbooks, such as Kavanagh and Johnson's (2018) *Human Resource Information Systems: Basics, Applications and Future Directions,* can provide you with valuable clues about the sort of documentary secondary data that are likely to exist within organisations' management information systems.

Tertiary literature such as indexes and catalogues can also help you to locate secondary data (Section 3.4). Online searchable data archive catalogues, such as for the UK Data Archive, may prove a useful source of the sorts of secondary data available (Table 8.1). This archive holds the UK's largest collection of qualitative and quantitative digital social science and humanities data sets for use by the research community (UK Data Archive 2018). These data have been acquired from academic, commercial and government sources, and relate mainly to post-war Britain. However, it should be remembered that the supply of data and documentation for all of the UK Data Archive's data sets is charged at cost, and there may be additional administrative and royalty charges.

Online indexes and catalogues often contain direct linkages to downloadable files, often in spreadsheet format. Government websites (Table 8.1) such as the UK government's *Direct.gov* and the European Union's *Europa* provide useful gateways to a wide range of reports, legislative documents and statistical data as well as links to other sites. However, although data from such government sources are usually of good quality, those from other sources may be neither valid nor reliable. It is important, therefore, that you evaluate the suitability of such secondary data for your research (Section 8.5).

Establishing the availability of relevant web-based materials generated by online communities which can be used as secondary data such as blogs and pages set up by social networking sites' user groups can be even more difficult. With the number of Wikis (collaborative content sharing pages), blogs (including online diaries) and discussion forums growing rapidly and over two million blog posts being published every day (Web Hosting Rating 2018), there are almost certainly going to be blogs about your research topic. However, as we discuss later in this section, actually finding them is more difficult! In contrast, although estimates suggest similar rapid growth for organisation web pages, with more than 143 million .com and .net domain names in existence (Web Hosting Rating 2018), finding these organisations or their Facebook pages is far easier. This can be done using a general search engine or, in the case of UK-based companies, the links provided by the Yell UK business search engine. However, you will still need to assess their relevance.

Finally, informal discussions are also often a useful source. Acknowledged experts, colleagues, librarians or your project tutor may well have knowledge of the sorts of data that might be available.

Locating secondary data

Once you have ascertained that secondary data are likely to exist, you need to find their precise location. For secondary data held in online databases to which your university subscribes, published by governments or held by data archives this will be relatively easy, especially where other researchers have made use of them and a full reference exists. All you will need to do is search the appropriate online database (Table 8.2) data archive or gateway (Table 8.1), find and download your data. Locating published secondary data held by specialist libraries is also relatively straightforward. Within the UK, specialist libraries with specific subject collections can usually be located using the most recent Chartered Institute of Library and Information Professional's (2015) publication *Libraries and Information Services in the United Kingdom and Republic of Ireland.* If you are unsure where to start, confess your ignorance and ask a librarian. This will usually result in a great deal of helpful advice, as well as saving you time. Once the appropriate abstracting tool or catalogue has been located and its use demonstrated, it can be searched using similar techniques to those employed in your literature search (Section 3.6).

Data that are held by companies, professional organisations or trade associations are more difficult to locate or gain access to. For within-organisation data we have found that the information or data manager within the appropriate department is most likely to know the precise secondary data that are held. This is the person who will also help or hinder your eventual access to the data and can be thought of as the gatekeeper to the information (Section 6.2).

One way to locate relevant web-based materials generated by online communities is to use Blog Content Management Systems such as Blogster, which contain their own search engines, to identify potentially relevant blogs. Others content management systems such as WordPress can be searched using a general search engine such as Google or Bing. However, working through blogs composed of indeterminate numbers of postings to locate those that are potentially useful can be extremely time consuming!

Micro blogging sites such as Twitter offer another potential source of secondary data. Tweets are (almost entirely) visible to anyone who chooses to search and follow a particular username such as a brand, trade union or person and their posts can be copied retrospectively. Another way, providing you have reasonable programming skills, is to use Twitter's own application program interface (API) to actively gather and export (a process known as scraping) up to 3,200 tweets. You can do this in three ways:

- via their search or streaming service;
- as a 10 per cent random sample;
- or, via the 'firehose' of all tweets made (Tinati et al. 2014).

However, these all require data to be collected as it is generated, so this may take some time.

Alternatively, you could use a specialist data scraping tool to gather such data. There are increasing numbers of such tools available, some of which are free, with most having free trial periods to allow you to establish whether it will be suitable. One, which our students have used, is Tweet Archivist Desktop (Tweet Archivist 2018). This tracks searches, archives, analyses, saves and can export tweets in real time. Another, CrowdTangle (CrowdTangle 2018), which can be used to scrape date from Twitter, Facebook, Instagram and Reddit, both tracks accounts and associated posts and comments and provides access to historical data. However, it is crucial to remember that, although these data are publicly available, it is worth anonymising them by removing the hashtag or usernames.

Additional guidance regarding how to use general search engines such as Google is given in Marketing Insights' *Smarter Internet Searching Guide,* which is available via this book's web page. However, searching for relevant data is often very time consuming. Although the amount of data on the Internet is increasing rapidly, much of it is, in our experience, of dubious quality. Consequently the evaluation of secondary data sources is crucial (Section 8.5).

Once you have located a possible secondary data set, you need to be certain that it will meet your needs. For most forms of secondary data the easiest way is to obtain and evaluate a sample copy of the data and a detailed description of how they were collected. For survey-derived data this may involve some cost. One alternative is to download and evaluate detailed definitions for the data set variables (which include how they are coded; Section 12.2) and the documentation that describes how the data were collected. This evaluation process is discussed in the next section.

8.5 Evaluating secondary data sources

Secondary data must be viewed with the same caution as any primary data that you collect. You need to be sure that:

- they will enable you to answer your research question(s) and to meet your objectives;
- the benefits associated with their use will be greater than the costs;
- you will be allowed access to the data (Sections 6.2–6.4).

Secondary sources that appear relevant at first may not on closer examination be appropriate to your research question(s) or objectives. It is therefore important to evaluate the suitability of secondary data sources for your research. Invariably this can be problematic where insufficient information is provided by the data source to allow this.

Stewart and Kamins (1993) argue that, if you are using secondary data, you are at an advantage compared with researchers using primary data. Because the data already exist you can evaluate them prior to use. The time you spend evaluating any potential secondary data source is time well spent, as rejecting unsuitable data earlier can save much wasted time later! Such investigations are even more important when you have a number of possible secondary data sources you could use. Most authors suggest a range of validity and reliability (Section 5.11) criteria against which you can evaluate potential secondary data. These, we believe, can be incorporated into a three-stage process (Figure 8.2). However, this is not always a straightforward process, as sources of the secondary data do not always contain all the information you require to undertake your evaluation.

Alongside this process you need also to consider the accessibility of the secondary data. For some secondary data sources, in particular those available via the Internet or in your university library, this will not be a problem. It may, however, still necessitate long hours working in the library if the sources are paper based and 'for reference only'. For other data sources, such as those within organisations and online forums requiring membership, you need to obtain permission prior to gaining access and may well also need to consider potential ethical implications where personal data are involved. This will be necessary even if you are working for the organisation or a member of the forum. These issues are discussed in Chapter 6, so we can now consider the evaluation process in more detail.

Overall suitability of data to research question(s) and objectives
Measurement validity
Coverage including unmeasured variables
(If not suitable, then do not proceed)

Precise suitability of data for analysis
Reliability and validity
Measurement bias
(If not suitable, then do not proceed)

**Assessment of costs
and benefits**
(If costs outweigh benefits
or unethical, do not proceed)

Figure 8.2 Evaluating potential secondary data sources

Overall suitability

Measurement validity

One of the most important criteria for the suitability of any data set is **measurement validity**. Secondary data that fail to provide you with the information that you need to answer your research question(s) or meet your objectives will result in invalid answers (Smith 2008). Often when you are using secondary survey data you will find that the measures used do not quite match those that you need. For example, a manufacturing organisation may record monthly sales whereas you are interested in monthly orders, hence the measure is invalid.

This may cause you a problem when you undertake your analyses believing that you have found a relationship with sales whereas in fact your relationship is with the number of orders. Alternatively, you may be using minutes of company meetings as a proxy for what actually happened in those meetings. Although these provide a record of what happened, they may be subtly edited to exclude aspects the chairperson did not wish recorded as well as comments that were made 'off the record'. You therefore need to be cautious before accepting such records at face value (Denscombe 2017).

Unfortunately, there are no clear solutions to problems of measurement invalidity. All you can do is try to evaluate the extent of the data's validity and make your own decision (Box 8.10). A common way of doing this is to examine how other researchers have coped with this problem for a similar secondary data set in a similar context. If they found that the measures, while not exact, were suitable, then you can be more certain that they will be suitable for your research question(s) and objectives. If they had problems, then you may be able to incorporate their suggestions as to how to overcome them. Your literature search (Sections 3.5 and 3.6) will probably have identified other such studies already.

Coverage and unmeasured variables

The other important overall suitability criterion is **coverage**. You need to be sure that the secondary data cover the population about which you need data, for the time period you need, and contain data variables that will enable you to answer your research question(s) and to meet your objectives. For all secondary data sets coverage will be concerned with two issues:

- ensuring that unwanted data are or can be excluded;
- ensuring that sufficient data remain for analyses to be undertaken once unwanted data have been excluded.

When analysing secondary survey data, you will need to exclude those data that are not relevant to your research question(s) or objectives. Service companies, for example, need to be excluded if you are concerned only with manufacturing companies. However, in doing this it may be that insufficient data remain for you to undertake the quantitative analyses you require (Sections 12.4 to 12.6). For document sources, you will need to ensure that the data contained in them relate to the population identified in your research. For example, check that the social media content on an organisation's social media pages actually relate to the organisation. Where you are intending to undertake a longitudinal study, you also need to ensure that the data are available for the entire period in which you are interested.

Some secondary data sets, in particular those collected using a survey strategy, may not include variables you have identified as necessary for your analysis. These are termed unmeasured variables. Their absence may not be particularly important if you are undertaking descriptive research. However, it could drastically affect the outcome of explanatory research as a potentially important variable has been excluded.

Box 8.10
Focus on student research

Using a social networking site as a source of secondary data

Mike's research project was concerned with the impact of social media on brand awareness and brand loyalty. He was particularly interested in how small automobile manufacturers used social networking sites in their marketing. His research question was: 'How effectively do small automotive manufacturers use social networking sites in their marketing?'

Mike was aware from the academic and trade literature that social media was of major importance in marketing and could influence various aspects of consumer behaviour, such as product awareness, information acquisition and purchase behaviour. Based on the academic literature on branding and social media, Mike argued that, to use social media most effectively, organisations needed to follow a three-stage process of providing material of interest, engaging people and using them as advocates for their products.

Mike was also aware from Internet searches and his own interest in cars that automotive manufacturers had each created their own Facebook presence, providing content, and using their pages to interact with their fans (customers). Mike was already a fan of the Morgan Motor Company's Facebook page which was 'liked' by over 53,000 Facebook members. Morgan's wall contained company posts about their products and comments and other posts from fans. Although the data in these posts were not originally intended to answer Mike's research question, after careful evaluation he considered that further analysis of the posts and comments would enable him to do this.

Because Morgan's Facebook page was open to everyone, Mike considered that the information was in the public domain and so he could use it for his research project without seeking consent provided he anonymised individuals who posted, including blurring their faces. He now needed to analyse the posts (data) available on Morgan's Facebook wall to establish the extent to which this form of social media was being used by the organisation to provide consumers with material of interest, engage them and allow them to become advocates for the product.

Source: © Morgan Motor Company, 2018. Reproduced with permission

Precise suitability

Reliability and validity

The reliability and validity (Section 5.11) you ascribe to secondary data are functions of the method by which the data were collected and the source. You can make a quick assessment of these by looking at the source of the data. Dochartaigh (2007) and others refer to this as assessing the authority or reputation of the source. Survey data from large, well-known organisations such as those found in Mintel and Key Note market research reports (Table 8.1) are likely to be reliable and trustworthy. The continued existence of such organisations is dependent on the credibility of their data. Consequently, their procedures for collecting and compiling the data are likely to be well thought through and accurate. Survey data from government organisations are also likely to be reliable, although they may not always be perceived as such. However, you will probably find the validity of documentary data such as organisations' records more difficult to assess. While organisations may argue their records are reliable, there are often inconsistencies and inaccuracies. You therefore need also to examine the method by which the data were collected and try to ascertain the precision needed by the original (primary) user.

Dochartaigh (2012) suggests a number of areas for initial assessment of the authority of documents available via the Internet. These, we believe, can be adapted to assess the authority of all types of secondary data. First, as suggested in the previous paragraph, it is important to discover the person or organisation responsible for the data and to be able to obtain additional information through which you can evaluate the reliability of the source. For data in printed publications this is usually reasonably straightforward (Section 3.7).

However, for secondary data obtained via the Internet it may be more difficult. Although organisation names, such as the 'Center for Research into . . . ' or 'Institute for the Study of . . . ', may appear initially to be credible, publication via the Internet is not controlled, and such names are sometimes used to suggest pseudo-academic credibility. Dochartaigh (2012) therefore suggests that you look also for a copyright statement and the existence of published documents relating to the data to help validation. The former of these, when it exists, can provide an indication of who is responsible for the data. The latter, he argues, reinforces the data's authority, as printed publications are regarded as more reliable. In addition, Internet sources often contain an email address or other means of contacting the author for comments and questions about the Internet site and its contents. However, beware of applying these criteria too rigidly as sometimes the most authoritative web pages do not include the information outlined above. Dochartaigh (2012) suggests that this is because those with most authority often feel the least need to proclaim it!

For all secondary data, a detailed assessment of the validity and reliability will involve you in an assessment of the method or methods used to collect the data (Dale et al. 1988). These may be provided as hyperlinks for Internet-based data sets, although they may not be sufficiently detailed to enable you to make a full assessment. Alternatively, they may be discussed in the method section of an associated report. Your assessment will involve looking at who were responsible for collecting or recording the information and examining the context in which the data were collected. From this you should gain some feeling regarding the likelihood of potential errors or biases. In addition, you need to look at the process by which the data were selected and collected or recorded. Where sampling has been used to select cases, the sampling procedure adopted and for surveys, the associated sampling error and response rates (Section 7.2) will give clues to validity. Secondary data collected using a questionnaire with a high response rate are also likely to be more reliable than those from one with a low response rate. However, commercial providers of high-quality, reliable data sets may be unwilling to disclose details about how data were collected. This is particularly the case where these organisations see the methodology as important to their competitive advantage.

For some documentary sources, such as blogs, social media pages and transcripts of interviews or meetings, it is unlikely that there will be a formal methodology describing how the data were collected. The reliability of these data will therefore be difficult to assess, although you may be able to discover the context in which the data were collected. For example, blogs, emails and memos contain no formal obligation for the writer to give a full and accurate portrayal of events. Rather they are written from a personal point of view and expect the recipient to be aware of the context. This means that these data are more likely to be useful as a source of the writer's perceptions and views than as an objective account of reality. The fact that you did not collect and were not present when these data were collected will also affect your analyses. Dale et al. (1988) argue that full analyses of in-depth interview data require an understanding derived from participating in social interactions that cannot be fully captured from audio-recordings or transcripts.

The validity and reliability of collection methods for survey data will be easier to assess where you have a clear explanation of the techniques used to collect the data (Box 8.11).

Box 8.11
Focus on student research

Assessing the suitability of online multiple-source longitudinal data

As part of her research project on changing consumer spending patterns in Europe, Jocelyn wished to establish how the cost of living had altered in the European Union since the accession of the 10 new member states in 2004. Other research that she had read as part of her literature review had utilised the European Union's Harmonized Index of Consumer Prices (HICPs). She therefore decided to see whether this information was available via the Internet from the European Union's *Europa* information gateway. She clicked on the link to the *Eurostat Official EU Statistics* home page and searched for 'Harmonized Indices of Consumer Prices'. This revealed that there were publications, monthly data and indices data of consumer prices. Jocelyn then clicked on the link to the Harmonized Indices of Consumer Prices (HCIP) Metadata and read the data description. As the data were relevant to her research she clicked on the filters to ensure she searched only for dataset that had been published in the current year and scrolled through the results, eventually finding the dataset she wanted "HICP – all items – annual average indices".

She clicked on the link to look at the data table and examined it briefly. It appeared to be suitable in terms of coverage for her research so she downloaded and saved it as an Excel spreadsheet on her MP3 player.

Jocelyn was happy with the data's overall suitability and the credibility of the source; the data having been compiled for the European Union using data collected each year by each of the member states. She also discovered that the actual data collected were governed by a series of European Union regulations.

In order to be certain about the precise suitability of the HICP, Jocelyn needed to find out exactly how the index had been calculated and how the data on which it was based had been collected. Hyperlinks from the data description web page provided an overview of how the index was calculated, summarising the nature of goods and services that were included. The data for the HICP were collected in each member state using a combination of visits to local retailers and service providers and central collection (via mail, telephone, email and the Internet), over one million price observations being used each month! One potential problem was also highlighted: there was no uniform basket of goods and services applying to all member states. Rather, the precise nature of some goods and services included in the HICP varied from country to country, reflecting the reality of expenditure in each of the countries. Jocelyn decided that this would not present too great a problem as she was going to use these data only to contextualise her research.

The Eurostat web pages emphasised that the HICP was a price rather than a cost of living index. However, it also emphasised that, despite conceptual differences between price and the cost of living, there were unlikely to be substantial differences in practice. Jocelyn therefore decided to use the HICP as a surrogate for the cost of living.

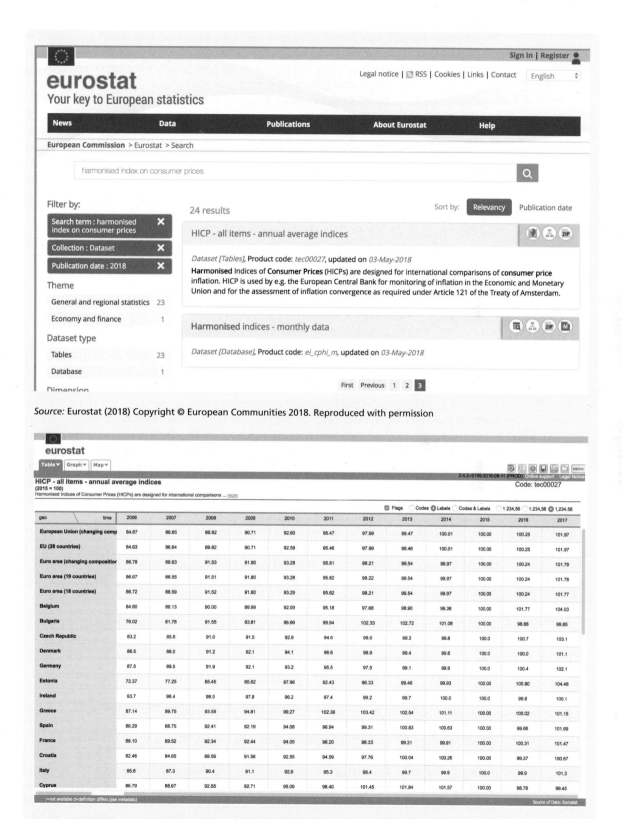

Source: Eurostat (2018) Copyright © European Communities 2018. Reproduced with permission

Source: Eurostat (2018) Copyright © European Communities 2018. Reproduced with permission

This needs to include a clear explanation of any sampling techniques used and response rates (discussed earlier) as well as a copy of the data collection instrument, which is usually a questionnaire. By examining the questions by which data were collected, you will gain a further indication of the validity.

Where data have been compiled, as in a report, you need to pay careful attention to how these data were analysed and how the results are reported. Where percentages (or proportions) are used without actually giving the totals on which these figures are based, you need to examine the data very carefully. For example, a 50 per cent increase in the number of clients from two to three for a small company may be of less relevance than the 20 per cent increase in the number of clients from 1,000 to 1,200 for a larger company in the same market! Similarly, where quotations appear to be used selectively without other supporting evidence you should beware, as the data may be unreliable.

Measurement bias

Measurement bias can occur for three reasons (Hair et al. 2016):

- deliberate distortion of data;
- changes in the way data are collected;
- when the data collection technique did not truly measure the topic of interest.

Deliberate distortion occurs when data are recorded inaccurately on purpose and is most common for secondary data sources such as organisational records. Managers may deliberately fail to record minor accidents to improve safety reports for their departments. Data that have been collected to further a particular cause or the interests of a particular group are more likely to be suspect as the purpose of the study may be to reach a predetermined conclusion (Smith 2008). Reports of consumer satisfaction surveys may deliberately play down negative comments to make the service appear better to their target audience of senior managers and shareholders, and graphs may deliberately be distorted to show an organisation in a more favourable light. In addition, online news reports may contain 'fake news' or misrepresent the truth, providing disinformation to influence and manipulate readers' behaviours (Box 8.8).

Other distortions may be deliberate but not intended for any advantage. Employees keeping time diaries might record only the approximate time spent on their main duties rather than accounting precisely for every minute. People responding to a structured interview (questionnaire) might adjust their responses to please the interviewer (Section 11.2).

Unfortunately, measurement bias resulting from deliberate distortion is difficult to detect. While we believe that you should adopt a neutral stance about the possibility of bias, you still need to look for pressures on the original source that might have biased the data. For written documents such as minutes, reports and memos the intended target audience may suggest possible bias, as indicated earlier in this section. Therefore, where possible you will need to triangulate the findings with other independent data sources. Where data from two or more independent sources suggest similar conclusions, you can have more confidence that the data on which they are based are not distorted. Conversely, where data suggest different conclusions you need to be more wary of the results.

Changes in the way in which data were collected can also introduce changes in measurement bias. Provided that the method of collecting data remains constant in terms of the people collecting it and the procedures used, the measurement biases should remain constant. Once the method is altered, perhaps through a new procedure for taking minutes or a new data collection form, then the bias also changes. This is very important for longitudinal data sets where you are interested in trends rather than actual numbers. Your detection of biases is dependent on discovering that the way data are recorded has changed. Within-company sources are less likely to have documented these changes than government-sponsored sources.

Measurement bias also occurs where the data collected does not truly represent the topic of interest. For example, minimum income standards need to take account of what people need for a minimum acceptable standard of living, something that both differs between countries and has altered over time. In establishing their 2017 minimum income standard for the UK, the Joseph Rowntree Foundation (Padley and Hirsh 2017) included in the basket of minimum requirements the necessity for pensioner households to have a computer and the Internet, something that would not be normal in all countries.

Costs and benefits

Hair et al. (2016) argue an assessment of secondary data also needs to consider the costs of acquiring them with the benefits they will bring. Costs include both time and financial resources that you will need to devote to locating and obtaining the data. Some data will be available online at no charge (Box 8.11). Other data will require lengthy negotiations to gain access, the outcome of which may be a polite 'no' (Sections 6.2–6.4). Data from market research companies or special tabulations from government surveys will have to be ordered specially and will normally be charged for: consequently, these will be relatively costly.

Benefits from data can be assessed in terms of the extent to which they will enable you to answer your research question(s) and meet your objectives. You will be able to form a judgement on the benefits from your assessment of the data set's overall and precise suitability (discussed earlier in this section). This assessment is summarised as a checklist of questions in Box 8.12. An important additional benefit is the form in which you receive the data. If the data are already in spreadsheet readable format (often referred to as csv, comma separated values), this will save you considerable time as you will not need to re-enter the data prior to analysis (Sections 12.3 and 13.4). However, when assessing the costs and benefits you must remember that data that are not completely reliable and contain some bias are better than no data at all, if they enable you to start to answer your research question(s) and achieve your objectives.

Box 8.12
Checklist

Evaluating your secondary data sources

Overall suitability

✔ Does the data set contain the information you require to answer your research question(s) and meet your objectives?
✔ Do the measures used match those you require?
✔ Is the data set a proxy for the data you really need?

✔ Does the data set cover the population that is the subject of your research?
✔ Does the data set cover the geographical area that is the subject of your research?
✔ Can data about the population that is the subject of your research be separated from unwanted data?
✔ Are the data for the right time period or sufficiently up to date?
✔ Are all the data you require to answer your research question(s) and meet your objectives available?
✔ Are the variables defined clearly?

Box 8.12
Checklist
(continued)

Evaluating your secondary data sources

Precise suitability

✔ How reliable is the data set you are thinking of using?
✔ Is it clear what the source of the data is?
✔ How credible is the data source?
✔ Do the credentials of the source of the data (author, institution or organisation sponsoring the data) suggest it is likely to be reliable?
✔ Do the data have an associated copyright statement?
✔ Do associated published documents exist?
✔ Does the source contain contact details for obtaining further information about the data?
✔ Is the method of data collection described clearly?
✔ If sampling was used, what was the procedure and what were the associated sampling errors and response rates?
✔ Who was responsible for collecting or recording the data?
✔ (For surveys) Is a copy of the questionnaire or interview checklist included?
✔ (For compiled data) Are you clear how the data were analysed and compiled?
✔ Are the data likely to contain measurement bias?

✔ What was the original purpose for which the data were collected?
✔ Who was the target audience and what was its relationship to the data collector or compiler (were there any vested interests)?
✔ Have there been any documented changes in the way the data are measured or recorded including definition changes?
✔ How consistent are the data obtained from this source when compared with data from other sources?
✔ Have the data been recorded accurately?
✔ Are there any ethical concerns with using the data?

Costs and benefits

✔ What are the financial and time costs of obtaining these data?
✔ Can the data be downloaded into a spreadsheet, statistical analysis software or word processor?
✔ Do the overall benefits of using these secondary data sources outweigh the associated costs?

And finally

✔ Were the data obtained ethically?
✔ Is permission required to use these data and, if 'yes', can you obtain it?
✔ Have you ensured, wherever appropriate, personal data are anonymised?

Source: Authors' experience; Dale et al. (1988); Dochartaigh (2012); Hair et al. (2016); Smith (2006); Stewart and Kamins (1993); Vartanian (2011)

8.6 Summary

- Secondary data are data that you analyse which were originally collected for some other purpose, perhaps processed and subsequently stored. There are three main types of secondary data:
  - Survey;
  - document (including text, audio and visual);
  - multiple source.
- Most research projects require some combination of secondary and primary data to answer your research question(s) and to meet your objectives. You can use secondary data in a variety of ways. These include:
  - to provide your main data set;
  - to provide longitudinal (time-series) data;

- to provide area-based data;
- to compare with, or set in context, your own research findings.
- Any secondary data you use will have been collected for a specific purpose. This purpose may not match that of your research. Other than where continuously updated, secondary data are often less current than any data you collect yourself.
- Finding the secondary data you require is a matter of detective work. This will involve you in:
  - establishing whether the sort of data that you require are likely to be available;
  - searching for and locating the precise data.
- Once located, you must assess secondary data sources to ensure their overall suitability for your research question(s) and objectives. In particular, you need to pay attention to the measurement validity and coverage of the data.
- You must also evaluate the precise suitability of the secondary data. Your evaluation should include reliability and any likely measurement bias. You can then make a judgement on the basis of the costs and benefits of using the data in comparison with alternative sources.
- When assessing costs and benefits, you need to be mindful that secondary data that are not completely reliable and contain some bias are better than no data at all if they enable you partially to answer your research question(s) and to meet your objectives.

Self-check questions

Help with these questions is available at the end of the chapter.

8.1 Give three examples of different situations where you might use secondary data as part of your research.

8.2 You are undertaking a research project as part of your course. Your initial research question is 'How has the UK's import and export trade with other countries altered in the past 30 years?' List the arguments that you would use to convince someone of the suitability of using secondary data to answer this research question.

8.3 Suggest possible secondary data that would help you answer the following research questions. How would you locate these secondary data?

a To what extent do organisations' employee relocation policies meet the needs of employees?

b How have consumer spending patterns in your home country changed in the last 10 years?

c How have governments' attitudes to the public sector altered in the twenty-first century?

d To what extent does baby product advertising reflect changes in societal gender norms?

8.4 As part of case study research based in a manufacturing company with over 500 customers, you have been given access to an internal market research report. This was undertaken by the company's marketing department. The report presents the results of a recent customer survey as percentages. The section in the report that describes how the data were collected and analysed is reproduced below:

> Data were collected from a sample of current customers selected from our customer database. The data were collected using an Internet questionnaire designed and administered via the online software tool Qualtrics™. Twenty-five customers responded, resulting in a 12.5 per cent response rate. These data were analysed using IBM SPSS Statistics. Additional qualitative data based on in-depth interviews with customers were also included.

a Do you consider these data are likely to be reliable?

b Give reasons for your answer.

Review and discussion questions

8.5 With a friend revisit Figure 8.1, types of secondary data, and re-read the accompanying text in Section 8.2. Agree to find and, where possible, make copies (either electronic or photocopy) of at least two examples of secondary data for each of the nine subheadings:

a censuses;

b continuous and regular surveys;

c ad hoc surveys;

d text documents;

e audio documents;

f visual/audio-visual documents;

g multiple-source snapshots;

h multiple source longitudinal data;

i multiple source continually updated data.

Compare and contrast the different examples of secondary data you have found.

8.6 Choose an appropriate information gateway from Table 8.2 to search the Internet for secondary data on a topic which you are currently studying as part of your course.

a 'Add to favourites' (bookmark) those sites which you think appear most relevant.

b Make notes regarding any secondary data that are likely to prove useful to either seminars for which you have to prepare, or coursework you have still to undertake.

8.7 Agree with a friend to each evaluate the same secondary data set obtained via the Internet. This could be one of the data sets you found when undertaking Question 8.6. Evaluate independently your secondary data set with regard to its overall and precise suitability using the checklist in Box 8.12. Do not forget to make notes regarding your answers to each of the points raised in the checklist. Discuss your answers with your friend.

Progressing your research project

Assessing the suitability of secondary data for your research

- Consider your research question(s) and objectives. Decide whether you need to use secondary data or a combination of primary and secondary data to answer your research question. (If you decide that you need only use secondary data and you are undertaking this research as part of a course of study, check your course's assessment regulations to ensure that this is permissible.)
- If you decide that you need to use secondary data, make sure that you are clear why and how you intend to use these data.

- Assess whether suitable secondary data are available and accessible.
- Locate the secondary data that you require and make sure that, where necessary, permission for them to be used for your research is likely to be granted. Evaluate the suitability of the data for answering your research question(s) and make your judgement based on assessment of its suitability, other benefits and the associated costs.
- Note down the reasons for your choice(s), including the possibilities and limitations of the data. You will need to justify your choice(s) when you write about your research methods.
- Use the questions in Box 1.4 to guide your reflective diary entry.

References

Becker, H.S. (1998) *Tricks of the Trade: How to Think About Your Research While You're Doing It.* Chicago, IL: Chicago University Press.

Bell, E. And Davison, J. (2013) 'Visual Management Studies: Empirical and Theoretical Approaches', *International Journal of Management Reviews,* Vol. 15, pp. 167–184.

Bishop, L. and Kuula-Luumi, A. (2017) 'Revisiting qualitative data reuse: A decade on', *SAGE Open,* Vol. 7, No. 1, pp. 1–15.

Bulmer, M., Sturgis, P.J. and Allum, N. (2009) 'Editors' introduction', in M. Bulmer, P.J. Sturgis and N. Allum (eds) *Secondary Analysis of Survey Data.* Los Angeles: Sage, pp. xviii–xxvi.

Carton, A.M. (2018) '"I'm not mopping floors, I'm putting a man on the moon": How NASA Leaders enhanced the meaningfulness of work by changing the meaning of work', *Administrative Science Quarterly,* Vol. 63, No. 2, pp. 323–369.

Center for Climate and Energy Solutions (2018) *Comments of the Center For Climate And Energy Solutions on State Guidelines for Greenhouse Gas Emissions from Existing Electric Utility Generating Units; Advance Notice Of Proposed Rulemaking. Docket Id No. EPA–HQ–OAR–2017–0545.* Available at https://www.c2es.org/site/assets/uploads/2018/01/policy-options-for-resilient-infra-structure-01-2018.pdf [Accessed 1 May 2018]

Chartered Institute of Library and Information Professionals (2015) *Libraries and Information Services in the United Kingdom and Republic of Ireland 2015* (38th edn). London: Facet Publishing.

Cowton, C.J. (1998) 'The use of secondary data in business ethics research', *Journal of Business Ethics,* Vol. 17, No. 4, pp. 423–434.

CrowdTangle (2018) *CrowdTangle,* Available at http://www.crowdtangle.com/ [Accessed 9 May 2018]

Dale, A., Arber, S. and Proctor, M. (1988) *Doing Secondary Analysis.* London: Unwin Hyman.

Denscombe, M. (2017) *The Good Research Guide for small-scale social research projects* (5th edn). Maidenhead: Open University Press.

Dochartaigh, N.O. (2012) *Internet Research Skills: How to Do Your Literature Search and Find Research Information Online.* (3rd edn). London: Sage.

European Commission (2017) *EU Labour Force Survey - data and publication.* Available at http://ec.europa.eu/eurostat/statistics-explained/index.php/EU_labour_force_survey_%E2%80%93_data_and_publication [Accessed 9 May 2018].

Eurostat (2017) *Eurostat Regional Yearbook 2017.* Available at http://ec.europa.eu/eurostat/en/web/products-statistical-books/-/KS-HA-17-001 [Accessed 4 May 2018].

Eurostat (2018) *Eurostat: Your Key to European Statistics.* Available at http://ec.europa.eu/eurostat/data/statistics-a-z/abc [Accessed 4 May 2018].

George, G, Osinga, E.C., Lavie, D. and Scott, B.A. (2016) 'Big data and data science methods for management research: From the Editors', *Academy of Management Journal,* Vol. 59, No. 5, pp. 1493–1507.

Gray, D.E., Saunders, M.N.K. and Farrant, K. (2016) *SME Success: Winning New Business.* London: Kingston Smith LLP.

Griffin, M., Harding, N. and Learmonth, M. (2017) 'Whistle while you work: Disney animation, organizational readiness and gendered subjugation', *Organization Studies,* Vol. 38, No. 7, pp. 869–894.

Hair, J.F., Celsi, M., Money, A.H., Samouel, P. and Page, M.J. (2016) *Essentials of Business Research Methods* (3rd edn). New York: Routledge.

Hakim, C. (1982) *Secondary Analysis in Social Research.* London: Allen & Unwin.

Kanji, S. (2017) 'Grandparent care: A key factor in mothers' labour force participation in the UK', *Journal of Social Policy,* 1–20. Available at doi:10.1017/S004727941700071X.

Kavanagh, M.J. and Johnson, R.D. (eds) (2018) *Human Resource Information Systems: Basics, Applications, and Future Directions* (4th edn). Thousand Oaks, CA: Sage.

Lee, W.J. (2012) 'Using documents in organizational research', in G. Symon and C. Cassell (eds) *Qualitative Organizational Research: Core Methods and Current Challenges.* London: Sage, pp. 389–407.

Malhotra, N.K. Nunan, D. and Birks, D.F. (2017), *Marketing Research: An Applied Approach* (5th edn). Harlow: Pearson.

McAfee, A., and Brynjolfsson, E. (2012) 'Big data: The management revolution', *Harvard Business Review,* Vol. 90, No. 10, pp. 61–67.

Office for National Statistics (n.d., a) *Census history*. Available at https://www.ons.gov.uk/census/2011census/howourcensusworks/aboutcensuses/censushistory [Accessed 2 May 2018].

Office for National Statistics (n.d., b) *200 years of the Census*. Available at https://www.ons.gov.uk/census/2011census/howourcensusworks/aboutcensuses/censushistory/200yearsofthecensus [Accessed 5 May 2018].

Office for National Statistics (n.d., c) *Annual Business Survey*. Available at https://www.ons.gov.uk/surveys/informationforbusinesses/businesssurveys/annualbusinesssurvey [Accessed 7 May 2018].

Office for National Statistics (2017) *Living Costs and Food Survey*. Available at https://www.ons.gov.uk/peoplepopulationandcommunity/personalandhouseholdfinances/incomeandwealth/methodologies/livingcostsandfoodsurvey [Accessed 9 May 2018].

Office for National Statistics (2018) *Family Spending*. Available at https://www.ons.gov.uk/peoplepopulationandcommunity/personalandhouseholdfinances/expenditure/bulletins/familyspendingintheuk/financialyearending2017 [Accessed 9 May 2018]

Padley, M. and Hirsch, D. (2017) *A Minimum Income Standard for the UK in 2017*. Available at file:///Users/saundmnk/Downloads/mis_2017_final_report_0.pdf [Accessed 9 May 2018].

Reichman, C.S. (1962) *Use and Abuse of Statistics.* New York: Oxford University Press.

Smith, E. (2008) *Using Secondary Data in Educational and Social Research.* Maidenhead: Open University Press.

Stewart, D.W. and Kamins, M.A. (1993) *Secondary Research: Information Sources and Methods* (2nd edn). Newbury Park, CA: Sage.

Tinati, R., Halford, S., Carr, L. and Pope, C. (2014) 'Big Data: Methodological challenges and approaches for sociological analysis', *Sociology,* Vol. 48. No. 4, pp. 663–681.

Tweet Archivist (2018) *Tweet Archivist,* Available at http://www.tweetarchivist.com/ [Accessed 5 May 2018].

UK Data Archive (2018) *UK Data Archive.* Available at www.data-archive.ac.uk/ [Accessed 9 May 2018].

Vartanian, T.P. (2011) *Secondary Data Analysis.* Oxford: Oxford University Press.

Web Hosting Rating (2018) *100+ Internet Stats and Facts for 2018,* Available at https://www.websitehostingrating.com/internet-statistics-facts-2018/ [Accessed 5 May 2018].

Wernicke, I.H. (2014) 'Quality of official statistics data on the economy', *Journal of Finance, Accounting and Management*, Vol. 5, No. 2, pp. 77–93.

Further reading

Lee, W.J. (2012) 'Using documents in organizational research', in G. Symon and C. Cassell (eds) *Qualitative Organizational Research: Core Methods and Current Challenges.* London: Sage, pp. 389–407. A really useful chapter on the use of document secondary data looking at how research questions may be formulated, the gathering of documents and how to analyse these data dependent upon your epistemology.

Levitas, R. and Guy, W. (eds) (1996) *Interpreting Official Statistics*. London: Routledge. Although published nearly two decades ago, this book still provides a fascinating insight into UK published statistics. Of particular interest are Chapter 1, which outlines the changes in UK statistics since the 1980 Raynor review, Chapter 3, which looks at the measurement of unemployment, the discussion in Chapter 6 of the measurement of industrial injuries and their limitations, and Chapter 7, which examines gender segregation in the labour force, utilising data from the Labour Force Survey.

Wernicke, I.H. (2014) 'Quality of official statistics data on the economy', *Journal of Finance, Accounting and Management,* Vol. 5, No. 2, pp. 77–93. This paper outlines the quality principles adopted by governments and organisations such as the National Statistics Offices, United Nations, World Bank and Eurostat and offers insights into why these data are often distorted.

Case 8
Using social media for research

Alice is an undergraduate student studying business at a UK university. Approaching final year, and her research project, Alice was unsure as to which topic she would investigate. Deciding to play to her strengths, Alice noticed how much time she spent using social media, and in particular, the interaction she was having with her favourite brands via Twitter. She observed that brands were being promoted informally using such media, the interactions with consumers being wider than just responding to requests and complaints. Noting from her research methods class that she needed a robust justification for carrying out the research, Alice conducted a review of the marketing literature that examined Twitter data. Seeing the technique used in Business-to-Business research (e.g. Leek et al., 2016), and work on consumer complaint behaviour on Twitter and social media more generally (e.g. Ma et al. 2015; Istanbulluoglu 2017; Istanbulluoglu, Leek and Szmigin 2017), Alice decided to set her project somewhere within this broad research area. After a further examination of the existing literature, she ultimately chose to investigate the messages and sentiments that were being used to engage with consumers via Twitter.

Finding evidence of the validity of using Twitter data for monitoring brand perceptions (see Culotta & Cutler 2016), Alice decided to collect the tweets and retweets from three of her favourite brands, one in the fast-moving consumer goods category, a fitness brand and a telecoms service provider. Recognising that the tweets were accessible and in the public domain without needing a Twitter account, Alice felt the tweets were a viable, rich data source. Considering the tweets to be public, Alice did not discuss the ethical issues surrounding this decision with her supervisor, and started thinking about her data collection.

Alice spent some time looking for suitable, easy access software that she could use to collect the tweets, but did not find any free software that provided the data she wanted. However, Alice found *Tweet Archivist Desktop,* which allowed her to actively gather and store tweets from Twitter (a process known as 'scraping'), but this required data to be collected in real time. This meant that if she wanted six months' worth of data, Alice would need to have the software running and collecting tweets for that period. Given the time limitations of her dissertation, she decided that a retrospective examination of tweets would be sufficient for her purpose. Alice went to the Twitter profile pages for the three brands and copied every tweet posted by the brand in the last six months. This approach allowed her to collect a sufficient sample of tweets in a matter of minutes, rather than months. She pasted the content into a word processor to save the data for later analysis.

Table C8.1 Number of tweets and consumer tweets for each of Alice's three chosen brands

	FMCG Brand	Fitness Brand	Telecoms Service Provider	Total
Original tweets (from the brand account)	623	697	300	1,620
Consumer tweets (from other Twitter users)	236	753	998	1,987
			Total	3,607

Alice counted all the tweets from the three brands for that period and realised that she had a large sample of 1,620 tweets. In addition, there were 1,987 tweets from other Twitter users interacting with the brand, making a total of 3,607 tweets in her sample. Alice tabulated these descriptive statistics (Table C8.1).

After discussing several options for data analysis with her project tutor, Alice decided to first identify tweets that were general, informal engagement with other users, and those that were complaints and responses, and thus of interest to her research objectives. Next, Alice decided to conduct content analysis on all the tweets to code them for the number of times a positive or negative interaction was mentioned, and the number of times this interaction then had a visible successful outcome for the consumer (for an example of similar research, see Einwiller & Steilen, 2015).

The analysis took Alice three months, as she needed to read each of the 3,607 tweets, make an interpretation as to its meaning and code it as either positive or negative, and whether there was a successful outcome. Alice wrote the following conclusion about her data analysis:

Of the 3,607 tweets collected in this sample, 65.01% were positive interactions, of which 33.33% had a visible successful outcome for the consumer; and 34.99% were negative, of which 50.00% had a visible successful outcome for the consumer. Therefore, brands should use social media for engaging with consumers, as the majority of interactions are positive, and when brand-consumer interactions start off negatively, they often had a successful outcome for the consumer.

References

Culotta, A., and Cutler, J. (2016) 'Mining brand perceptions from Twitter social networks', *Marketing Science*, 35 (3), pp. 343–362.

Einwiller, S. A., and Steilen, S. (2015) 'Handling complaints on social network sites – An analysis of complaints and complaint responses on Facebook and Twitter pages of large US companies', *Public Relations Review*, 41, pp. 195–204.

Istanbulluoglu, D. (2017) 'Complaint handling on social media: The impact of multiple response times on consumer satisfaction', *Computers in Human Behavior*, 74, pp. 72–82.

Istanbulluoglu, D., Leek, S., and Szmigin, I. T. (2017) 'Beyond exit and voice: Developing an integrated taxonomy of consumer complaining behaviour', *European Journal of Marketing*, 51 (5/6), pp. 1109–1128.

Leek, S., Canning, L., and Houghton, D. J. (2016) 'Revisiting the task media fit model in the era of web 2.0: Twitter use and interaction in the healthcare sector', *Industrial Marketing Management*, 54, pp. 25–32.

Ma, L. Sun, B., and Kekre, S. (2015) 'The squeaky wheel gets the grease – An empirical analysis of customer voice and firm intervention on Twitter', *Marketing Science*, 34 (5), pp. 627–645.

Questions

1 What issues can you see with Alice's steps from idea generation to research design?

2 Consider the advantages and disadvantages of Alice's sample selection technique.

3 When Alice's research supervisor found that she had collected so many tweets in this way, she was concerned that Alice may have violated ethical procedures. Are Tweets (and similarly open social media data) really considered to be public, and does this mean it is acceptable to use these data for research?

4 By using tweets from Twitter, what legal concerns may exist over the ownership of the data?

5 Alice collected her data before considering or discussing her analysis techniques. What issues may arise here?

6 Given the richness of social media data, Alice's project tutor felt the conclusions are somewhat basic, and perhaps not even suitable. What other techniques could Alice adopt to better utilise the source of data she has?

Additional case studies relating to material covered in this chapter are available via the book's companion website: **www.pearsoned.co.uk/saunders.**
They are:

- The involvement of auditors in preliminary profit announcements.
- Research and development in the UK pharmaceutical industry.
- Small firms' internationalisation.
- Patent grants and the implications for business.
- Trust repair in a major finance company.
- Values and behaviours for sustainable tourism.

Self-check answers

8.1   Although it would be impossible to list all possible situations, the key features that should appear in your examples are listed below:
- to compare findings from your primary data;
- to place findings from your primary data in a wider context;
- to triangulate findings from other data sources;
- to provide the main data set where you wish to undertake research over a long period, to undertake historical research or to undertake comparative research on a national or international scale with limited resources.

8.2   The arguments you have listed should focus on the following issues:
- The study suggested by the research question requires historical data so that changes that have already happened can be explored. These data will, by definition, have already been collected.
- The timescale of the research (if part of a course) will be relatively short. One solution for longitudinal studies in a short time frame is to use secondary data.
- The research question suggests an international comparative study. Given your likely limited resources, secondary data will provide the only feasible data sources.

8.3   a   The secondary data required for this research question relate to organisations' employee relocation policies. The research question assumes that these sorts of data are likely to be available from organisations. Textbooks, research papers and informal discussions would enable you to confirm that these data were likely to be available.

Informal discussions with individuals responsible for the personnel function in organisations would also confirm the existence and availability for research of such data.

b The secondary data required for this research question relate to consumer spending patterns in your home country. As these appear to be the sort of data in which the government would be interested, they may well be available via the Internet or in published form. For the UK, examination of the Office for National Statistics and gov.uk information gateways (Table 8.2) would reveal that these data were collected by the annual Expenditure and Food Survey providing hyperlinks to a series of reports including *Living Costs and Food Survey* (Office for National Statistics 2017). Summary data could also be downloaded. In addition, reports could be borrowed either from your university library or by using inter-library loan.

c The secondary data required for this research question are less clear. What you require is some source from which you can infer past and present government attitudes. Relative changes in spending data, such as appears in quality newspapers, might be useful; although this would need to be examined within each department budget. Transcripts of ministers' speeches and newspaper reports might prove useful. However, to establish suitable secondary sources for this research question you would need to pay careful attention to those used by other researchers. These would be outlined in research papers and textbooks. Informal discussions could also prove useful.

d You are likely to require document visual secondary data to answer this research question. This is likely to comprise both two-dimensional static and two-dimensional moving advertisements. An Internet image search would reveal if these forms of data were available online. Two other possible sources would be the archives of London's Museum of Brands, Packaging and Advertising, and New York's Museum of Advertising.

8.4 a The data are unlikely to be reliable.

b Your judgement should be based on a combination of the following reasons:

- Initial examination of the report reveals that it is an internally conducted survey. As this has been undertaken by the marketing department of a large manufacturing company, you might assume that those undertaking the research had considerable expertise. Consequently, you might conclude the report contains credible data. However:
- The methodology is not clearly described. In particular:
  - The sampling procedure and associated sampling errors are not given.
  - It does not appear to contain a copy of the questionnaire. This means that it is impossible to check for bias in the way that questions were worded.
  - The methodology for the qualitative in-depth interviews is not described.
- In addition, the information provided in the methodology suggests that the data may be unreliable:
  - The reported response rate of 12.5 per cent is very low for a telephone survey (Section 7.2).
  - Responses from 25 people means that all tables and statistical analyses in the report are based on a maximum of 25 people. This may be too few for reliable results (Sections 7.2 and 12.5).

Get ahead using resources on the companion website at:
www.pearsoned.co.uk/saunders.

- Improve your IBM SPSS Statistics research analysis with practice tutorials.
- Save time researching on the Internet with the Smarter Online Searching Guide.
- Test your progress using self-assessment questions.
- Follow live links to useful websites.

Chapter **9**

Collecting data through observation

Learning outcomes

By the end of this chapter you should be able to:

- appreciate the scope of observation as a data collection method;
- understand the dimensions of observation and the choices to be made when using observational research;
- develop an understanding of participant observation, structured observation and Internet-mediated observation and appreciate how these methods may overlap in practice;
- develop an understanding of the use of videography, audio-recording and static visual images in the collection of observational data;
- identify ethical concerns and quality issues related to the collection of observation data and consider how to avoid or reduce these.

9.1 Introduction

Observation has traditionally been a somewhat neglected method for business and management research. Yet it can be rewarding and enlightening to pursue and, what is more, add considerably to the richness of your research data. Technological changes have helped to facilitate new forms of observation, helping it to become a more popular research method. The opening vignette shows how Internet-mediated structured observation is being used to conduct market research. If your research question(s) and objectives are concerned with what people do and how they interact, an obvious way in which to discover this is to watch and listen to them do it. This is essentially what observation involves: the systematic viewing, recording, description, analysis and interpretation of people's behaviour in a given setting.

Three observation methods are presented and discussed in this chapter: participant observation (Section 9.3); structured observation (Section 9.4) and Internet-mediated observation (Section 9.5). Participant observation is qualitative and derives from the work of social anthropology early in the twentieth century. Its emphasis is on discovering the meanings that people attach

Observing online behaviour and digital marketing

Over recent years, digital marketing platforms have been developed that gather various types of data in order to retarget specific groups of customers with relevant and timely messages that may help to inform their purchasing decisions. These data are divided into three types. 'First party data' are composed of any data directly collected by an organisation from its own customers. These include data collected using tracking pixels technology incorporated into web content (such as user behaviour on a website), call centres, point of sale systems and customer relationship management systems. 'Second party data' are composed of another organisation's first party data, which have been purchased directly from them. For example, an online travel company may purchase data from an online advertisement network, because it is interested in the destinations searched and browsed on partner websites. 'Third party data' are collected by an organisation that does not have a direct relationship to the organisation which purchases these data. These data are often anonymised and aggregated, and can be used to enhance and profile first party data.

Digital marketing platforms vary according to their purpose but generally use the same methods of data collection. These data may be analysed in various ways such as by audience criteria and market segment. Traditionally this analysis was undertaken by people but computational learning models are beginning to automate some of the process. Appropriate digital channels are then identified to deliver targeted messages to customers. These include display advertising, email, push and SMS messaging. The success of campaigns can also be tracked via pixels. For example, when a marketing message is sent it often contains metadata indicating the source from which it came. A 'conversion' pixel can be placed on a thank you page once an order has been placed which can be linked back to the campaign source. Marketers can then use statistical modelling to understand which campaigns are successful at an aggregated level, i.e. comparing the relative open, click and conversion rates for two similar campaigns. This information can be fed back to refine and improve further audience targeting. This process is shown in the flow diagram.

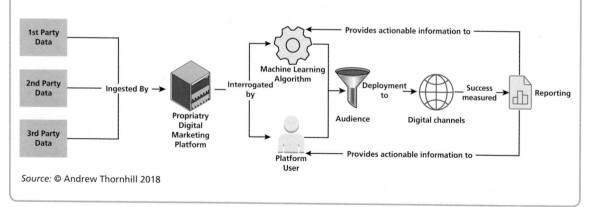

Source: © Andrew Thornhill 2018

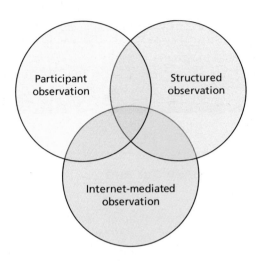

Figure 9.1 Overlap between types of observation

to their actions and social interactions. In contrast, structured observation is quantitative and is more concerned with the frequency of actions ('what' rather than 'why'). Internet-mediated observation involves the collection of data from online communities. This approach adapts traditional observation by changing its mode of observing from oral/visual/near to textual/digital/virtual to allow researchers purely to observe or to participate with members of an online community to collect data.

In practice, there can be overlap between these methods (Figure 9.1) and you will begin to see this as you read Sections 9.3 to 9.5. Before you reach these sections, we provide an overview of observation by discussing its core dimensions in Section 9.2. In this section you will see how the use of observation will involve you as researcher making a number of choices.

It is interesting to note that Internet-mediated observation can alter the nature of data collection. Participant observation and structured observation have traditionally involved researchers collecting primary data. Internet-mediated observation makes it possible for researchers to apply observational techniques to both primary and secondary data (Chapter 8). This is reflected in the discussion in Section 9.5.

In other approaches to research, those who take part are called either respondents or participants. Those who complete a questionnaire are usually called respondents. Those who agree to take part in most forms of qualitative research are usually called participants. These labels don't work for observation since it is the researcher who is participating in the environment of other people, responding to the ways in which they carry out their usual activities. In observational research, those who agree to be observed are usually called **informants** (Monahan and Fisher 2010). This is the term that we will use throughout this chapter.

A common theme in this book is our effort to discourage you from thinking that you should only use one research method in your study. This also applies to observation research, which is often combined with data collected from interviews, documents and visual images.

9.2   Dimensions of observation

A researcher who wants to use observation will need to make a number of choices. He or she will need to choose whether to enter an observational setting with an open mind about what to observe, or, alternatively, with a pre-determined and specific list of aspects on which to focus observation. She or he will need to choose whether to participate in the event to be observed, or observe it without taking an active part. Related to this, he or she will need to choose whether or not to tell those involved in an observation setting that they are being observed. He or she will also need to choose whether to conduct observation in a naturalistic setting, taking advantage of the opportunity to observe an event or activity that occurs irrespective of the researcher's interest, or whether to set up some activity in which the specified event can be observed.

These choices relate to the following dimensions of observation:

- the structure and formality that the researcher uses in designing observation, ranging from unstructured and informal to structured and formal;
- the role of the researcher during observation comprising:
  - their participation in the observation setting, ranging from full participation in the activity or event being observed, through passive observation at the margin of this activity or event, to observation in a detached location as a non-participant;
  - their decision to reveal they wish to observe the event or activity for a research purpose; or to conceal this from those being observed, involving ethical issues that focus on informed consent;
- the nature of the observational setting, involving conducting observation in either a naturalistic setting or in a contrived situation.

The ways in which these dimensions are combined in practice therefore define different types of observation. For example, a researcher may choose to conduct unstructured, exploratory observation whilst taking part in a workplace departmental meeting without telling her colleagues. A different researcher may design a laboratory based experiment in order to measure the responses of those who agree to take part using a pre-determined and structured observation instrument. These are of course only illustrative examples and in practice many other observational combinations are possible.

In the literature on observation two principal types of observation are generally identified. These are referred to as participant observation and structured observation. We discuss these in Sections 9.3 to 9.4, although as you will see these two principal types are not entirely distinct along each dimension. In brief, **participant observation** is a qualitative approach to observation research but incorporates different levels of structure. **Structured observation** is highly structured and quantitative, although a researcher using this type may also make use of unstructured, qualitative observation in an initial exploratory stage. Researchers using either of these types will also need to exercise choice in relation to each of the other dimensions of observation. For example, in participant observation it is recognised that the researcher may choose whether to reveal or conceal his or her research purpose, while also taking part or just observing the event or activity being observed. Similarly, in structured observation the researcher may reveal or conceal her or his purpose, and while she or he is more likely to act as a pure observer, it may be possible to participate in an activity and undertake structured observation.

A different distinction is sometimes drawn between participant observation and non-participant observation, and we also define and discuss non-participant observation later in this section. As we recognise elsewhere in this book, the choice of a research method and the particular type to be used will depend on the nature of the research question and research objectives. Before we discuss the different types of observation that we have just introduced here, we consider in more detail the dimensions of observation. We do this under the following headings: structure and formality in observation; role of the researcher during observation; nature of the observational setting.

Structure and formality in observation

Rather like types of interview that we discuss in Section 10.2, types of observation range from unstructured to structured. Observation may be structured and highly formalised based on the use of a pre-determined and standardised observation instrument that is generally referred to as a coding schedule. As we describe later, this may be designed to observe the activities or behaviour of an individual person, such as a consumer or a worker, or the interactions between members of a group, such as in a workplace meeting, or the prevalence of particular events, such as in a production study. Standardisation is of course important where structured observation is to be repeated and a researcher wishes to produce data that are comparable between individuals or groups, and across events or different times. An example of a structured coding schedule is shown later in Box 9.6 and we discuss this type of observation in greater detail later. This type of observation produces numerical data which are analysed quantitatively (Chapter 12).

Observation may also be unstructured and informal. In this way, the researcher does not start with a predetermined list of attributes, behaviours or responses to observe. Instead the focus of the observation is broadly flexible and open, with the observer recording the flow of events or behaviours being observed. The use of such an unstructured and informal approach to observation is likely to be exploratory in nature to understand the setting within which it occurs, and to describe who is involved, what they each do, how they interact together, the sequence of events, their aim in undertaking this activity and how they respond to one another emotionally (Spradley 2016). Observation studies that commence with an unstructured and informal approach are likely to become more structured as they progress.

Where observation is conducted sequentially in the same setting, it is therefore likely to become more structured. As subsequent observations are undertaken, the researcher will move through stages from descriptive observation, to focused observation, finally reaching selective observation (we describe these stages in more detail later). These stages in observation illustrate points along a continuum between unstructured and structured observation, which are still a long way from the use of a highly structured coding schedule that we introduced earlier.

While structured observation produces numerical data, unstructured and semi-structured observation generally produce qualitative data. The nature of these qualitative data varies from field notes to highly detailed transcripts, with the latter often being produced from video or audio (voice) recordings. The scope to collect one form of data or the other will depend on the level of access negotiated with informants and the intended qualitative analysis (Chapter 13).

Role of the researcher during observation

The role of the researcher comprises two dimensions. One of these relates to the researcher's level of participation in the activity or event being observed. In the classic approach to observation roles, Gold (1958) described this as a continuum ranging from complete participation at one extreme to complete observation at the other. In between these two extremes he reported two further possible roles: nearer to the complete participant is the participant-as-observer and closer to the complete observer is the observer-as-participant (Figure 9.2).

The other dimension relates to whether the act of observation is revealed to or concealed from those being observed. The four classic observation roles described by Gold (1958) also incorporate this dimension. Where the researcher reveals her or his research

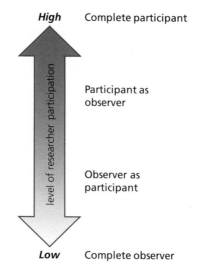

Figure 9.2 Level of participation in classic observation

purpose to those she or he wishes to observe, this will lead to **overt observation**, where these intended informants agree to being observed. Where the researcher conceals his or her research purpose from those he or she observes, this will lead to **covert observation**, where observation is conducted without those being observed becoming aware of this.

Figure 9.3 shows the relationship between the four observation roles along these two dimensions.

We now discuss these observation roles and consider ethical issues related to their use. This is followed by the introduction of two further observation roles: nonparticipant observer and collaborative observer. The nonparticipant role refers to observation that takes place in a detached location to that of the activity or event being observed, and after it has occurred, so that there is no physical or virtual proximity between its occurrence and the observation. This, along with the four participant roles already outlined, comprises the **classic approach to observational research**. These claim to be objective and to rely solely on the researcher's perspective and interpretation to make sense of what is observed (Section 4.2). The **collaborative observer** role questions the idea of objective observation and reliance on the single

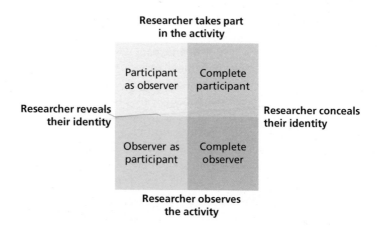

Figure 9.3 Classic observation roles

perspective of the researcher's interpretation. This is designed not only to encourage open and critically reflective participation by the researcher but also the collaborative involvement of informants in the conduct of observation research and interpretation of data.

Complete participant

The **complete participant** role sees you deciding to conduct observation in an organisational or social setting in which you already fully participate. Your position as an 'insider' will allow you to select a particular situation to observe related to your membership of the organisation or group. Since you are already accepted as a member of the group or organisation in which you chose to conduct observational research you do not reveal this purpose to other members.

You may be able to justify this role on pure research grounds in the light of your research questions and objectives. For example, you may be interested to know the extent of lunchtime drinking in a particular work setting. You would probably be keen to discover which groups of employees drink at lunchtimes, what they drink, how much they drink and how they explain their drinking. Were you to explain your research objectives to the group you wished to study, it is rather unlikely that they would cooperate since employers would usually discourage lunchtime drinking. In addition, they might see your research activity as prying.

This example raises questions of ethics. These ethical concerns relate to several aspects discussed in Section 6.5 and in particular to concern about lack of informed consent and use of data. You would be in a position where you were 'spying' on people who have probably become your friends as well as colleagues. They may have learnt to trust you with information that they would not share were they to know your true purpose. This example suggests the researcher should not adopt this role where the focus of the research may result in risk to individuals with the potential to cause embarrassment or even harm (Section 6.5). However, there may be other foci where you might consider adopting the role of complete participant, where there would not be any risks of breaching trust or creating harm. An example might be where you were researching working practices in an organisation, to evaluate the relationship between theory and practice, where it would be possible to maintain the anonymity of both the organisation and informants as you participated as a co-worker.

Participant-as-observer

In the role of **participant-as-observer** you would both take part and reveal your research purpose. You may adopt this role as an 'insider' related to your existing membership of a group or organisation, but unlike the complete participant role decide to reveal your intention to use this setting to conduct observation if you can gain the consent of other members to do so. Alternatively, you may join a group or enter an organisation as an employee to become a fully accredited participant while making your research purpose known to those you wish to observe (e.g. Brannan and Oultram 2012; Plankey-Videla 2012). As a part-time business or management student you may be able to use your existing employment status to adopt the role of participant-as-observer.

You may also be able to participate in a group in the role of participant-as-observer without taking on all of the attributes of being a full member. In this regard Spradley (2016) recognises 'active participation' which he differentiates from full participation. In **active participation** you would enter a research setting as an 'outsider' to observe but with the intention of learning how to participate in it in order to be able to achieve an understanding that is similar to being an 'insider'. For example, Waddington (2004) describes his experiences of being a participant-as-observer, in which he participated in a strike, spending long hours on the picket line and socialising with those on strike, without being an employee of the company involved. To achieve this, it was necessary to gain the support and trust of those involved. Waddington describes how he immersed himself in this context, how he experienced the emotional involvement of participating in this event and how he experienced the same feelings as the defeated strikers at the end of the strike.

Observer-as-participant

Acting in the role of **observer-as-participant** will primarily involve you in observing, although your purpose will be known to those whom you are studying (Box 9.1). Participation in this role will only be low level and will mostly be restricted to being present at an event or activity in order to be able to observe it. 'Being present' means that you might sit in a meeting while it takes place, act as a spectator or onlooker while some event occurs, or watch an activity from the margins. In some cases in this role it may become necessary to engage in a slightly greater but still limited level of participation in order to be able to continue observation. In this case it will become necessary to have some limited interaction with informants. For example, adopting the role of observer-as-participant in an outward-bound course to assist team building would mean that you were there as a spectator, but it may be necessary to interact with informants and take part in some activities to be able to conduct your observation.

Spradley (2016) refers to this limited level of involvement as **moderate participation**. In this you take on some of the attributes of being an 'insider' where necessary while maintaining other characteristics of being an 'outsider'. This would allow you to participate in an event or activity to a sufficient level to be able to conduct your role as observer.

Box 9.1 Focus on management research

Observation to explore the impact of communication practices on hedge fund decision making

Kellard, Millo, Simon and Engel (2017) undertook research to evaluate whether communication and working practices in the hedge fund industry leads to 'herding', or group, behaviour. 'Herding' involves a group of participants deciding to do the same thing at the same time. In the case of hedge funds, herding may lead participants to make the same investment decisions, with potential consequences for trading risk and market prices (unduly pushing these up or down).

Their study, published in the *British Journal of Management,* involved qualitative interviews with and observations of those who work in the hedge fund industry in Europe, Asia and the United States of America. In their research they used purposive and snowball sampling to generate a sample of sixty informants to undertake this study. This sample was partly made up of those who work for hedge funds and partly of those who work for brokerage firms. The research focused on the nature of working practices between those involved in the hedge fund industry to understand its possible implications.

Observational fieldwork was undertaken in eight hedge fund firms and two brokerage firms. Observation was conducted in each firm over a number of days. A number of different professionals in each firm was observed by a researcher, with each being observed for between half of a day and two days. They refer to this as observational 'rotation'. Observations were also conducted at different times through the working day. These observations allowed them to gain an in-depth understanding of the context they were researching; to observe the working practices of and communications between participants in this industry; and to triangulate their understanding. To follow up questions raised during observations, some informants agreed to meet the observer informally after the observation session to discuss what had been observed. Overall, 60 informants were interviewed and observed across the firms involved in this research.

As an observer-as-participant, your identity as a researcher would be clear to all concerned and they would know your purpose. This would present the advantage of you being able to focus on your researcher role. For example, you would be able to jot down insights as they occurred to you. You may also be able to undertake discussions with the informants to clarify and improve your understanding. What you would lose, of course, would be the emotional involvement: really knowing what it feels like to be on the receiving end of the experience.

Complete observer

In the role of **complete observer** you would not reveal the purpose of your activity to those you were observing, nor take part in the activity or event being observed. Like the role of observer-as-participant you would be present at the activity or event in order to observe it, either by being able to sit in, acting as a spectator or onlooker, or watching from the margins.

For example, the complete observer role may be used to study consumer behaviour in supermarkets. Your research question may concern your wish to observe consumers at the checkout. Which checkouts do they choose? How much interaction is there with fellow shoppers and the cashier? How do they appear to be influenced by the attitude of the cashier? What level of impatience is displayed when delays are experienced? This behaviour may be observed by the researcher being located near the checkout in an unobtrusive way. The patterns of behaviour displayed may be the precursor to further observational research, involving a higher level of participation by the researcher, in which case this would be the exploratory stage of such a research project.

Like the other covert role of complete participant, use of this role also raises questions of ethics. These ethical concerns relate to several aspects discussed in Section 6.5 and in particular to concern about privacy, lack of informed consent and use of the data that are collected. The complete observer, in seeking to undertake research in an unobtrusive way, at worst ignores concerns about the privacy of those who are observed and at best acts as his or her own judge in deciding what is appropriate to observe in this way. This is particularly pertinent in relation to observation involving children, those who are vulnerable and power relationships, where authority is being exercised over others. Related to this concern will be the lack of informed consent from those who are observed and a further concern about the nature of the data produced through this type of observation, how it is to be used and what will happen to it at the end of the research project. In complete observation, the researcher treats those who are observed as research subjects rather than informants. In this role, it is the subjective judgement of the researcher which will be used to interpret data, rather than any involvement from those being observed.

Nonparticipant observer

In addition to the four roles we have discussed in which the researcher attends the setting being observed, even if this is only passively where she or he merely sits in or watches from the margin, or if online lurks, there is a further role possible in which the act of observation is detached from the event being observed. This is the **nonparticipant observer** role as defined by Spradley (2016), in which the researcher does not share any physical or virtual proximity to those whom they observe. This role is made possible by technology allowing the researcher not to be present in the place where, or at the time when, the event or activity occurs.

This may involve the use of the Internet where a researcher observes material online in order to conduct observation. Such material would have been produced and uploaded for another reason, without considering that it may subsequently be used for a research purpose. Using this type of observation is likely to raise a number of ethical issues (Section 6.5) including those related to consent and use of the data observed, not least because this may involve observing 'informants' in distant locations, whom it would be impossible to contact to negotiate any level of consent.

The nonparticipant observer may also use content available from public or subscription service broadcasters, such as television or radio programmes, in order to conduct observation. For example, you may be interested in observing the reporting of company results. Observing the business-related output from a number of different broadcast companies over a defined period of time may provide you with a sufficient amount of data to analyse and compare, without needing to attend these events in real time. You may instead be interested in analysing advertising strategies and decide to observe a range of commercial advertisements that are broadcast over a period of time as part of your research.

Collaborative observer

Collaborative observation seeks to overcome potential ethical concerns, data quality issues and epistemological questions associated with the classic approach to observation. We noted earlier that covert observation leads to ethical concerns because of lack of informed consent and use of data gathered without this. Even overt observation that is not collaborative may lead to similar ethical concerns; as we recognise in Chapter 6, research ethics should not be treated as a one-off, initial concern but need to be considered throughout a research project (Section 6.6). Likewise, data quality issues and epistemological questions may result from the dominant role of the researcher in the classic approach to observation. Claims about the objectivity of the researcher have been challenged by the need to recognise how her or his background (social, cultural, political, gender and so forth) may affect data collection, analysis and interpretation. This raises an important question about relying on the single perspective of the researcher's interpretation to make sense of what is observed and casts doubt on the idea that the researcher is able to reveal an objective reality or absolute truth in the account produced of these observations (Angrosino and Rosenberg 2011; Van Maanen 2011).

As a collaborative observer you would not assume a dominant role and those being observed would not be treated as mere informants from whom the researcher gathers data. Instead you would treat them as collaborators and involve them in many aspects of the research process. Collaboration may commence from the outset of the research design through their involvement in the formulation of the research plan based on their understanding of the research question, aim and objectives. As active collaborators throughout the research process they may engage with the researcher in discussions, interviews, providing feedback, offering their interpretations of the data and informant accounts. In analysing and interpreting data you will not try to reconcile different accounts to produce a single unified account. Instead you will accept the presence of multiple interpretations and conflicting accounts to portray the range of perspectives represented in the research.

In this way you will enter the observational setting and seek to develop a high level of participation. You should also try to recognise how your own position may affect the nature of the observations that occur and interactions with those who collaborate. This stresses the importance of you being critically reflective and engaging in reflexivity throughout the research process (Sections 1.5 and 2.1). The adoption of this stance recognises that the presence of the researcher in this setting, no matter how well accepted, is likely to affect others' behaviour and therefore what may be observed.

In this light, collaborative observation may appear as an ideal observational role to use. In practice though, attempting to negotiate and use collaborative observation is likely to be demanding and time-consuming, and may be beyond the resources of many researchers

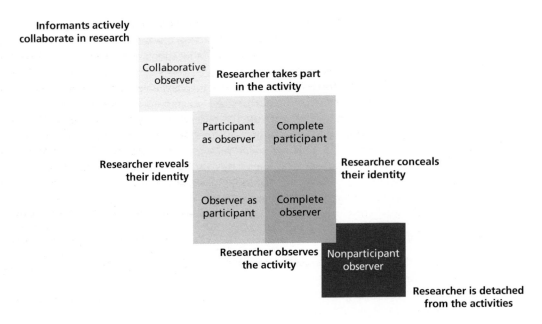

Figure 9.4 Observer roles
Source: © 2018 Mark Saunders, Philip Lewis and Adrian Thornhill

except those who undertake longitudinal and deep observational research projects. There may, however, be scope to achieve as many aspects of collaborative observation as is possible within a time-constrained research project. For example, you may not be able to involve informants in the design of your research project, but you may be able to involve them in discussions about what has been observed to seek their interpretations. You may also reflect critically about your role as observer. This suggests a continuum between the classic role of participant-as-observer and that of the collaborative observer, with increasing scope to involve informants as active collaborators (Figure 9.4).

The relationship between the six observer roles we have discussed is shown in Figure 9.4.

Where you are planning to undertake observation research you may still be unsure which observer role will be most appropriate for your research project. Table 9.1 outlines some of the aspects you need to consider in making this choice. There may be other aspects that are relevant to your choice of observer role in relation to the context of your proposed observation research. You will also need to identify and consider these in making your choice.

We now consider the final dimension of observation that we identified earlier, related to the nature of the observational setting.

Nature of the observational setting

Choosing an appropriate observational setting is crucial to the success of this research method. The nature of any observational setting will need to enable you to answer your research question and meet your research objectives. For example, your research question and objectives may require you to observe a particular activity in a single location. Alternatively, your research question may require you to observe multiple events across a range of settings. As the former scenario is likely to be easier to accomplish than the latter, you will need to consider this implication and choose a research question that is feasible in relation to finding an appropriate observational setting or settings.

Table 9.1 Aspects to consider in choosing an observer role

Aspect	Consideration
Ethical concerns	You will need to: • ensure that your observer role does not produce any risk of embarrassment or harm to those you wish to observe; • negotiate informed consent with intended informants and ensure compliance with ethical principles such as those outlined in Table 6.3 (Section 6.5); • ensure that ethical principles are upheld through the stages of your research project including the management of data afterwards (Section 6.6).
The purpose of your research	Your observer role should be appropriate to the nature of your research question and scope of your research objectives.
Your status in relation to informants in the observational setting	You will need to consider how your status as either an 'insider' or 'outsider' might affect your ability to carry out your observer role. Where you are an 'insider', you will need to consider how your status in relation to other members of the group or organisation will affect your proposed observation of them. Where you are an 'outsider' you will need to consider how your status might affect what you are able to observe.
The level of participation you need to demonstrate in the observational setting	You will need to consider whether you need particular attributes or skills to participate in the observational setting. Where you do not possess these you will need to consider whether it is feasible to acquire them in the time available and how you might achieve this.
The depth of understanding you will need to develop in the observational setting and how much time you have to devote to your research	All observation research is time consuming but the amount of time required will vary depending on the scope of the research objectives and the nature of the observer role. If you are to develop a rich and deep understanding of an organisational phenomenon, it will need much careful study. A period of attachment to the organisation will often be necessary. Many full-time courses have placement opportunities that may be used for this purpose. In addition, many full-time students have part-time jobs and many part-time students have full-time jobs, each of which potentially provides wonderful opportunities to undertake observation research.
Observer role preference	Not everybody feels suited to observational research. Much of it relies on the building of relationships with others. Some may have a personal preference for an observer role with high levels of researcher participation and informant involvement while others may prefer a role with a low level of, or no, participation. Since your observer role should be appropriate to your research question and objectives, your observer role preference is likely to influence the nature of your research project.
Organisational access	This may present a problem for some researchers as it is obviously a key issue. The level of access that is gained may influence your choice of observer role. More is said about gaining access to organisations for research in Sections 6.2 to 6.4.

Observational settings may be broadly placed into a small number of categories. Observation may be conducted in a real world setting. **Naturalistic observation** is conducted in a 'real world' location where the intention is to conduct observation without influencing the setting being observed. In a traditional ethnographic research strategy (Section 5.8) this involves the researcher physically going to the place where intended informants live, work or otherwise socially interact, to conduct observation. This is referred to as going into the field and is known as doing **fieldwork**. Alternatively, observation may be conducted in a contrived or artificially created setting, such as where the researcher sets up a laboratory-based experiment, in order to observe those taking part in this research activity. Observation may also be conducted in a virtual setting, involving

Internet-mediated observation, which we discuss later in this chapter. Non-participatory observation also leads to the possibility of a researcher conducting observation in a detached setting, as we noted earlier.

9.3 Participant observation

What is participant observation?

Earlier we referred to fieldwork, where an ethnographer physically goes to the location where intended informants live or work to study them; the research process she or her engages in during field work is participant observation. In participant observation, the researcher enters into the social world of those to be observed and attempts to participate in their activities by becoming a member of their workgroup, organisation or community. This term sums up the dual purpose of this research method: to take part in the activity or event being studied and to observe those whose lives shape and are shaped by this social world. Spradley (2016) identifies six aspects that characterise participant observation. These are shown in Table 9.2.

Participant observation has its roots in social anthropology, but it was the Chicago School (at the University of Chicago) that changed its focus by using ethnographic methods to study social and urban problems within cultural groups in the USA. A seminal example of this work is Whyte's (1993) *Street Corner Society*, which examined the lives of street gangs in Boston. This approach involved researchers living among those whom they studied, to observe and talk to them to produce detailed cultural accounts of their shared beliefs, behaviours, interactions, language, rituals and the events that shaped their lives (Cunliffe 2010; Van Maanen 2011). Participant observation is a key data collection technique used within an ethnographic study, although the two concepts should not be used interchangeably as ethnography refers to a research strategy and to a particular type of research output (Section 5.8).

The high level of immersion achieved by the researcher in the research setting is a key strength of using participant observation, especially when compared with other data collection techniques. In a co-authored chapter (Brannan and Oultram 2012), Brannan reports

Table 9.2 Characteristics of participant observation

Characteristic	The participant observer . . .
Engaging in a dual purpose	. . . participates in the observational setting as well as observing those within it
Experiencing as both 'insider' and 'outsider'	. . . experiences the observational setting from the perspective of both insider as participant and outsider as observer
Developing an explicit awareness	. . . needs to develop an explicit awareness of all aspects of the observational setting including the people within it
Using a wide angle lens to observe	. . . needs to see, hear and record everything that may be relevant in the observational setting
Being reflective	. . . engages in reflection to learn from the experiences gained in the observational setting
Carefully recording all observations	. . . needs to record carefully what is observed and how this has been experienced

Source: Developed from Spradley (2016)

that when he returned to interview his former call centre co-workers some four to six months after working alongside them, their willingness to share their thoughts with him had diminished. The resulting interviews were more formal than expected and his informants were reluctant for their answers to his questions to be audio-recorded.

Because the researcher becomes a member of the group within which participant observation is conducted, she or he comes to understand the symbolic world of the informants and their perceptions about their social situation. This allows the participant observer to develop a deep and nuanced understanding of the meanings of informants' interactions, and how they respond to their social situation and changes to it. This is quite different from using a questionnaire to collect data, where ability to understand individual interactions and relationship to social context is likely to be less (Section 11.2). Brannan's reflections on returning to interview his former co-workers illustrates that even using interviews may not reveal the same level of depth in comparison to engaging in participant observation to understand informants' symbolic world.

The symbolic frame of reference is located within the school of sociology known as symbolic interactionism. In symbolic interactionism the individual derives a sense of identity from interaction and communication with others. Through this process of interaction and communication the individual responds to others and adjusts his or her understandings and behaviour as a shared sense of order and reality is 'negotiated' with others. Central to this process is the notion that people continually change in the light of the social circumstances in which they find themselves. The transition from full-time student to career employee is one example of this. (How often have you heard people say, 'She's so different since she's worked at that new place'?) The individual's sense of identity is constantly being constructed and reconstructed as he or she moves through differing social contexts and encounters different situations and different people.

Where your research question is intended to explore the dynamics of a social situation, this may point you to the use of participant observation where this technique is practical (Box 9.2).

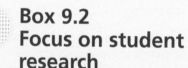

Box 9.2
Focus on student research

Managers and their use of power: a cross-cultural approach

Mong was a young Chinese business graduate who had recently been working in a Chinese/German joint venture in the automotive industry. She was located in the supply chain department. As part of her MBA she had to submit a research project on a management topic of her choice.

Mong was interested in the international management part of her course that dealt with cross-cultural matters. This was particularly significant in her case as she worked at a company site that comprised both Chinese and German managers.

Mong felt that a body of theory, which she could usefully link to the issue of cross-cultural integration, was that of power. With help from her project tutor she developed a research question that allowed her to explore the way in which Chinese and German managers used power to 'negotiate' their relationships in a situation which was unfamiliar to both sets of managers. Mong's question was: 'What strategies are used by different groups of national managers collaborating in an international joint venture to negotiate their transnational relationships and how effective are these?'

Mong was fortunate that one of her duties was to take minutes at the twice-weekly management meetings in the department. She obtained permission to observe these meetings to collect her data. She developed a semi-structured observation schedule, which related to her research objectives, and used this during each meeting.

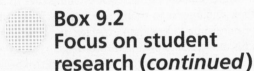

Box 9.2
Focus on student research (*continued*)

Managers and their use of power: a cross-cultural approach

Data collection was not easy for Mong as she had to take minutes in addition to noting the type and frequency of responses of managers. However, as time progressed she became skilled at fulfilling both her minute-taking and data collection roles. She also obtained permission to audio-record the meetings. At the end of four months, when she had attended over 30 meetings, she had collected a considerable amount of data and was in a good position to analyse these and draw some insightful conclusions.

Mong's observation role raised ethical questions as she did not reveal her researcher role to the meeting delegates. She discussed these questions with her senior manager in the company and project tutor and completed the necessary university ethics committee documentation. It was agreed by all concerned that Mong's research objectives justified the data collection approach chosen and met the university's ethical code.

Observer roles

If you wish to engage in participant observation you will need to enter a setting in order to participate, ideally immersing yourself in its routines, rituals, use of language and social relations to gain insights as an insider, as well as to observe (Van Maanen 2011). However, in participant observation the level of participation varies considerably. It varies from full participation in the way we have just outlined to passive participation where the researcher merely observes from the margin. Participant observation also recognises that participation and observation may be undertaken overtly or covertly. In relation to our discussion of observational roles earlier, this means that participant observation may use any role except that of the nonparticipant (Section 9.2).

Nature of the observational setting

In Section 9.2 we discussed the nature of observational settings and recognised that these may be broadly placed into a small number of categories. We also recognised earlier that participant observation involves gaining entry to a setting where intended informants live, work or otherwise socially interact. Participant observation will therefore occur in a naturalistic setting, where social relations occur in their natural context. Participant observation may also be conducted in a virtual setting, involving Internet-mediated observation, which we discuss in Section 9.5.

Structure and data collection

As we have discussed, in participant observation the researcher immerses himself or herself in the research setting and directly experiences this through participation in, and observation of, its activities and social interactions. This has a number of implications for the way participant observation research is conducted and nature of the data that are collected.

Participant observation, as an immersive and experience-based approach, is capable of producing data that are substantial in terms of their quantity, rich in terms of their meanings, complex in terms of their variety, and grounded in terms of being based in their setting. These data will primarily be qualitative but may also include some that are quantitative. Achieving such a substantial, rich, complex and grounded set of data will not only involve being present in the research setting to participate and observe, but also using supplementary techniques to collect data. As participant observation progresses, the researcher's focus is also likely to become more defined leading to a more structured approach to research. We now consider each of these aspects, starting with focus and structure before considering data collection techniques and data recording.

Focus and structure

Spradley (2016) describes participant observation as a process where research focus, research structure, data collection and data analysis are interrelated and emergent. At the commencement of participant observation, the focus of research is likely to be loose and the researcher's approach relatively unstructured and informal. At this stage, the focus of observation is broadly flexible and open, with the researcher recording the flow of events, behaviours or social interactions being observed. The purpose of this approach is likely to be exploratory, and the job of the researcher will be to describe the setting, those within it and what it is like to take part in it (Section 9.2). This initial stage, known as **descriptive observation**, will lead to the production of a considerable amount of data. As these data are collected and recorded the researcher also needs to analyse them to make sense of what is happening and why, and to understand what appears to be interesting and important; this interactive process of data collection and analysis is described in much greater detail in Chapter 13.

During the process of undertaking descriptive observation, the participant observer will be likely to choose a narrower focus on which to concentrate her or his on-going observations. Spradley (2016) advises that all observational settings, even seemingly simple and straightforward ones, are characterised by cultural complexity. During descriptive observation the participant observer begins to understand this complexity, which allows him or her to identity an aspect on which to focus. Being a participant observer means faithfully recording what is observed during each observation session even if this involves noting down events or activities that appear to be the same as, or similar to, those previously recorded. It is only by following this repetitious procedure that the participant observer is able to develop analytical insight and to understand the cultural complexity of the setting being observed. Where it would not be possible to analyse the entirety of this cultural complexity within a single study, the participant observer will choose a narrower focus on which to concentrate. This will be important in a time-constrained study.

Spradley suggests criteria to choose a narrower focus. These include choosing a focus related to personal interest, informant suggestions, theoretical interest, strategic importance or the recognition of a core aspect that would help to explain other aspects and bring these together conceptually. This second stage in participant observation is known as **focused observation**. During this stage, observation concentrates on the aspect or those aspects that relate to this more defined focus. This narrower focus is also likely to lead to a more structured approach as the participant observer defines questions on which to focus.

This interactive process of collecting data, analysing them, narrowing the focus of the research and increasing the structure of the questions you ask to concentrate observation on a particular theme or aspect leads to a third stage in participant observation, known as **selective observation**. This stage continues until the participant observer answers the questions that define this selective focus. This will be evident when continued data collection and analysis produces theoretical saturation (Section 5.8) and leads to the development of a well-grounded explanation, or theory that is grounded in the data.

The research process described here is similar to the Grounded Theory approach discussed in Section 5.8. Where you follow this research process to conduct participant observation you may consider analysing your data using the Grounded Theory Method approach described in Section 13.9.

Data collection techniques

Immersion in the research setting is the central technique to collect data during use of participant observation – referred to as **direct participation and observation**. This is, however, likely to be supplemented by use of other data collection techniques. These include interviewing informants, discussing findings with them, seeking informant accounts and interpretations, using documentary evidence, asking informants to keep diaries, arranging for informants to video their activity or to take photographic images, and engaging in reflection.

Your scope to use any of these supplementary data collection techniques will depend in part on your choice of observer role. For example, where you adopt the role of collaborative observer, you may be able to use a wide range of supplementary data collection techniques including involving your informants through discussing findings with them and seeking informant accounts and interpretations from them. Alternatively, where you adopt the role of complete observer, your scope to involve those who unknowingly act as informants will be severely limited unless in a particular setting you are able to talk to them individually without them knowing your true purpose for doing so. This might be the case if you were acting as complete observer in a public meeting and sat amongst other people in the audience. In between these two extremes there is likely to be varied scope to use supplementary data collection techniques.

Where you adopt an overt observer role – as collaborative observer, participant-as-observer or observer-as-participant – you may be able to arrange to interview some of your informants. This may be a formal interview where you arrange a time and place with an informant to conduct it. This may be the case where you have observed an activity and in order to allow you to make sense of it you arrange one or more subsequent, formal interviews with willing informants to discuss what happened and how they interpret this. Many of the interviews you conduct in this type of situation may, however, be more opportunistic and informal. You may be able to have a lunchtime chat or corridor conversation which helps you to make sense of something you have taken part in or observed. This will produce what Van Maanen (2011: 56) refers to as 'conversational data'.

Where you adopt an overt observer role you may also be able to arrange for your informants to video their activity or to take digital images; we discuss these visual techniques later in this chapter. You may also ask them to keep diaries and we discuss this technique in Chapter 10. You may also be able to use documentary evidence such as the minutes of meetings or material available on a company website (Section 5.8). Depending on the context where you use participant observation there may be other supplementary data collection techniques which you can use.

In addition, you will be able to engage in reflection to think through your experiences of participating in and observing a setting. This will involve you reflecting about how you have interpreted your observations in order to understand the assumptions you have used to reach these interpretations, and to evaluate other ways of making sense of your observations, especially from the perspectives of those involved. Such reflections may be recorded in self-memos, a research notebook or a reflective diary (Section 13.5). These reflections will subsequently form another important source of data related to your observational research as you continue to conduct your analysis.

Data recording

Data recording is also a crucial part of participant observation. Observational fieldwork will produce a considerable amount of data that need to be recorded. Where you use this method there is a danger of feeling overwhelmed by the amount of data to be recorded. As an immersive approach you need to be willing to devote your time and energy to participant observation to use this method successfully.

As we discussed earlier, the initial stage of participant observation involves a great deal of observational description (Section 9.2); but even as you move through the stages of focused observation and selective observation, you will still need to record observations that describe the research setting and the activities and social interactions that occur in it in order to understand what is happening and to be able to contextualise your focused and selective observational data. You will also need to record all of the data from the supplementary data collection techniques you use and your reflections.

Recording data needs to occur as close to its observation as is possible. Your scope to record data while you undertake observation will depend in part on the observer role you adopt. Where you have revealed your research purpose you may be able to make notes to record observations as you perceive these (e.g. in the role of observer-as-participant). However, this may not be the case in some settings where your role as participant makes this difficult (e.g. sometimes in the role of collaborative observer or participant-as-observer). In such situations your role as participant may mean that taking part and observing is as much as you can manage. For example if you are working in a factory on a production line it would be very difficult to stop taking part for a few minutes every hour to makes notes! In such a circumstance you would have to use your 'break times' to make some 'scratch notes', which you could then write up more fully after you have finished your time at work.

Where you do not reveal your research purpose to your intended informants and undertake observation in a covert role you may be able to make brief notes right away. However, this will not be the case in some settings where it would be evident to your informants that you were observing them. Here you need to wait until the activity or event has finished to record your observations. However, the longer you leave between observing activities or events and recording these observations as data, the more likely you are to forget details about the setting and the social interactions that define and make sense of what you have observed.

The usual way to optimise the data you wish to record is first of all to create a written, typed or voice recorded outline of key points as close to the time of observation as is possible. These are often called **scratch notes**. This outline of key points serves as an immediate and condensed version of what you have observed. Then as soon as you are able you will need to work this up into a fuller, expanded account of your observation session. Using the key points that you noted down, you should be able to produce an expanded account that fills in the details of what you observed. You will also be able to produce a separate but linked account that records your personal perceptions and feelings about what you experienced. You may then start to analyse these data and produce a further account that records your initial thoughts to make sense of them. Analysis will involve coding and categorising data (Chapter 13), while thinking about these to make sense of them involves the start of interpretation and reflection. Of course where you are able to video or audio record an observation session, you will have a visual and/or audio recording to watch or listen to again, although you are still advised where possible to follow the process just outlined!

When undertaking an observation you will produce and record several different categories of data, related to the original observation, your thoughts and feelings about taking part in and observing it, interpretation and reflection, as well as from any supplementary methods used. These are summarised in Table 9.3. Some types of data – those that are

Table 9.3 Types of data generated by participant observation

Data type	Explanation
Observational data	Data created by the participant observer from undertaking observations-in-person or using video or audio recordings, or visual images. These data record observations about the setting and the events and social interactions observed within it and may be recorded in a fieldwork/research notebook. Recordings and visual images may be created either by the participant observer or the informants
Experiential data	Data created by the participant observer based on her or his experience of undertaking observations, interviews or informal discussions. These personal perceptions and feelings may be recorded as self-memos, or in a research journal or diary
Supplementary data	Data created by the participant observer from conducting interviews, informal discussions with informants, or using documentary sources. These data may be recorded in a research notebook
Interpretive data	Data created by the participant observer from interpreting observational, experiential or supplementary data, or from informants' interpretations. These may be recorded as self-memos, or in a research journal or diary
Reflective data	Data created by the participant observer following periods of introspection or reflection about any or all of the other types of data, leading to the creation of further interpretive data that are recorded as self-memos, or in a research journal or diary

directly observed – may be recorded in a fieldwork or research notebook. Other types – personal thoughts or interpretive and reflective – may be recorded separately in self-memos or in a research journal or diary (Section 13.5). In relation to the analysis of data you may also find it helpful to classify your data by date of observation as well as by analytical category (Chapter 13).

Data quality issues

As participant observation involves studying social actors and social phenomena (i.e. informants and their activities) in their natural setting, research findings usually exhibit high **ecological validity** because of their relevance to the situation. However, using participant observation may lead to a number of threats to reliability/dependability and validity/credibility (Section 5.11 and in particular Table 5.7). This is because the setting is unknown to the observer and he or she needs to understand the cultural and interpersonal nuances that characterise it in order to interpret it. Alternatively, where the observer is an insider and therefore very familiar with the setting, she or he may take some things for granted instead of 'standing back' and analysing these through an outsider's viewpoint. In relation to participant observation, we discuss four such issues: observer error, observer drift, observer bias and observer effect.

Observer error

Your lack of understanding about, or over-familiarity with, the setting in which you are trying to operate as a participant observer may lead you unintentionally to misinterpret what is happening. This would be **observer error**. This error would not be deliberate but because you need to understand the setting better before you seek to interpret it. Interpretation arises from understanding and the insights that follow from this. This illustrates that observation is a process requiring immersion in a context in order to produce valid and reliable results.

Observer drift

Related to observer error is the idea of **observer drift**. This occurs when the observer unintentionally redefines the way in which similar observations are interpreted. Spending a long time in the field combined with unthinking familiarity may lead to inconsistencies when interpreting similar events across time. As data collection and data analysis are part of an ongoing iterative process, observers need to revisit their earlier observations and analysis as they continue to collect and analyse data in order to maintain consistency of interpretation.

Observer bias

Conversely, an observer may not allow herself or himself the time necessary to develop the depth of understanding required in order to interpret the setting objectively. This would lead to **observer bias**, where the observer uses her or his own subjective view or disposition to interpret events in the setting being observed. The observer may be unaware that she or he is doing this.

When you are using observation, you will need to be aware that every observation you record may be open to more than one interpretation. This may appear to be a daunting thought! However, it shouldn't be read as such. Instead it should encourage you to give yourself enough time in the setting to begin to understand it and then to develop a rigorous analytical approach to the way you make interpretations.

Your attempts to make interpretations will depend on whether you are using covert or overt observation. As a covert researcher, you will not be able to check your interpretations with informants. You will therefore need to think about the possible ways that a particular type of observation may be interpreted and then as you continue to make observations to reflect on how each interpretation helps to explain what you observe. You also need to be open to the idea that multiple interpretations may help to explain what is observed and to record these.

Where you are using overt observation, you have the possibility of asking your informants to meet and discuss with you, or to read, some of the observational data that relate to them. This would provide you with the opportunity to check some of your interpretations with your informants and perhaps to benefit from the insights that they are able to add to your own views (see Box 9.3). This process is known as **informant verification** and is similar to participant or member validation discussed in Section 5.11.

Observer effect

A more tricky threat to the reliability and validity of data collected through observation relates to the presence of the observer. By simply being present, the researcher may affect the behaviour of those being observed, potentially resulting in unreliable and invalid data (LeCompte and Goetz 1982; Spano 2005). This is referred to as the **observer effect**. The implication of this effect is that informants will work harder or act more ethically when they know they are being observed (Monahan and Fisher 2010). Conversely, those being observed may decide to slow their work if they feel that any measurements of this will lead to them being given more demanding targets. Either way, observations will not be reliable.

Box 9.3
Focus on student research

Informant verification

Susanna undertook participant observation in the customer services call centre of a retail company. Her research focused on the training and quality assurance of call centre staff. One of the aspects of her research project focused on the training needed to be able to deal with complex customer issues. For this aspect of her research project, Susanna negotiated access to spend a period in the call centre, in the role of observer-as-participant. This gave her access to observe call centre staff dealing with complex customer issues, to understand how they used their discretion to deal with customers sensitively while seeking to adhere to their training and to any scripted parts of their telephone conservations with callers. To achieve cognitive access (Chapter 6), she gained the consent of individual informants to observe each for a day or part of a day. This provided her with the opportunity to observe a number of informants during the period of her agreed access.

Susanna negotiated to meet each informant during part of his or her main rest break on the following day. This provided Susanna with the opportunity to describe and discuss her observations about a particular call that the informant had taken. Most of these informants were interested to help and provided Susanna with their own interpretations and insights, often recalling what they had been thinking as they had dealt with the call being discussed. These additional interpretations, directly from the informants, were very helpful to Susanna as she continued to observe and interpret and later when she wrote up her research project.

One solution to this is for the observer to act covertly. This solution assumes that it would be appropriate for the researcher to adopt the role of complete participant or of complete observer (Figure 9.3). However, this may not be appropriate, even if it were ethically acceptable. Another solution to this is for the observer to achieve **minimal interaction**, where the observer tries as much as possible to 'melt into the background' – having as little interaction as possible with informants. This may involve sitting in an unobtrusive position in the room and avoiding eye contact with those being observed. In relation to Figure 9.3, this would mean adopting a purely observing role, rather than a participatory one – acting in the role of observer-as-participant. However, as we discussed earlier, adopting this role may not be appropriate to the nature of the research.

A further solution where the observation is overtly conducted is related to familiarisation. As you operate in the role of collaborative observer, participant-as-observer or observer-as-participant your informants will become familiar with you and take less notice of your presence, where they feel they can trust you. This is known as **habituation**, where the informants being observed become familiar with the process of observation so that they take it for granted and behave normally. To achieve habituation it will probably be necessary for you to undertake several observation sessions in the same research setting with the same informants before you begin to achieve reliable and valid data. In fact, it will probably be necessary for you to undertake several sessions in order to begin to understand the dynamics of this setting, so this would be time well spent.

Not all researchers agree that observer effects inevitably lead to unreliable results. In addition, other strategies have been proposed to recognise and manage observer effects. Monahan and Fisher (2010) challenge some of the assumptions about observer effects. They argue that all research methods can have researcher effects that may lead to bias. In this way qualitative research including participant observation may be no more prone to bias than quantitative approaches to research, which are often held up as being more objective.

They also cast doubt on the idea that observer effects will always be negative and negate the value of the observer's results. Instead they believe that while the presence of an observer may have an effect on those whom they observe, the result of this effect may actually lead to the collection of valuable data. For them, observer effects may prove to be positive rather than being negative. They refer to the possibilities that informants may either 'stage' a performance for an observer or 'self-censor' their activities.

Monahan and Fisher suggest that staged performances may be welcomed because informants demonstrate an idealised set of behaviours to observers. They show what the informants think the observer ought to know and see. This idealised performance may then be compared to other observations where the performance cannot be staged or managed so easily. This may occur when the observer is watching a more pressured or stressful situation, or perhaps where other organisational participants are involved and the ability to manage a staged performance is not possible. Observations made of other informants in the same or a similar setting may also be compared to those that are being staged. Such situations offer the possibility of gaining rich and multi-layered data that would be very valuable to the observer in understanding the setting and when undertaking data analysis and interpretation.

Another way in which informants may try to manage their performance is through self-censorship. This may be designed to hide any behaviour that informants feel would be undesirable for the observer to see. Monahan and Fisher suggest that informants may behave worse when not being observed but are unlikely to behave better. Habituation may result in such cloaking behaviour being dropped. Apart from habituation, observers may try to check the validity of their observations by looking for inconsistencies in the data they observe and also by identifying differences between informants, to identify any facade of self-censorship.

Monahan and Fisher conclude that irrespective of whether a performance is being staged, or whether self-censorship is occurring, or whether neither of these is affecting what is being observed, the process of observation allows researchers to get close to and interact with informants. This may be seen as providing observation with an advantage over other research methods where distance and separation mean that data cannot be as intricate and rich. Rather than only focusing on observer effects, there is scope to focus on these other attributes of observation in assessing its value as a research method.

The advantages and disadvantages of participant observation are summarised in Table 9.4.

Table 9.4 Advantages and disadvantages of participant observation

Advantages	Disadvantages
• It is good at explaining 'what is going on' in particular social situations • It heightens the researcher's awareness of significant social processes • It is particularly useful for researchers working within their own organisations • Some participant observation affords the opportunity for the researcher to experience 'for real' the emotions of those who are being researched • Virtually all data collected are useful	• It can be very time consuming • It can pose difficult ethical dilemmas for the researcher • There can be high levels of role conflict for the researcher (e.g. 'colleague' versus researcher) • The closeness of the researcher to the situation being observed can lead to significant observer bias • The participant observer role is a very demanding one, to which not all researchers will be suited • Access to organisations may be difficult • Data recording is often very difficult for the researcher

9.4 Structured observation

In this section we first ask the question, 'What is structured observation?' We then discuss observer roles that may be used in structured observation, followed by the nature of observational settings where structured observation may take place. Data collection in structured observation involves the use of a coding schedule and we discuss how you might make use of one of these to record relevant data. We finish this section by looking at data quality issues that may arise from using structured observation.

What is structured observation?

Structured observation uses a high level of predetermined structure. If you use this method your purpose will be to observe the incidence of particular behaviours, interactions or events and record these systematically. Structured observation is particularly effective at revealing "the mundane, routine activities that collectively make up those practices of everyday life" (Clarke et al 2009: 348). As such, structured observation may form only a part of your data collection approach because its function is to tell you which things happen, how often and possibly when and in what sequence rather than why they happen. Once again, we see that all research methods may have a place in an overall research strategy. What is important is choosing methods that are suitable for your research question and objectives.

Structured observation as a method of collecting and analysing data in business may be more prevalent than you think. It has a long history that extends into the present and was used over many decades to analyse how factory workers carried out their tasks and to measure the times that it took to complete these. This is known as a 'time-and-motion' study and was used by employers to increase their control over the way work was conducted. It has been used to 'speed up' work by reducing the time required to undertake different tasks. This approach has been facilitated more recently by computer technologies. Software may be used to record the work activities of those who work in call centres and on checkouts in shops, for example. Most of us participate in forms of structured observation without really thinking about it or consciously giving our consent. You may have a 'loyalty' card from a retailer that allows them to record what you have purchased when you present the card at the checkout.

Digital or video-recording adds another layer of observation to monitor those in particular types of workplace as well as within areas covered by CCTV, such as in city and town centres, shopping centres and within retail outlets. We live in a world where in many situations our movements are routinely observed while we go about our daily lives, often without being aware that this is happening. Adrian uses an independent retail outlet which makes light of this situation: at various places in the store there are signs which state, 'Smile, you're on camera!'

The Internet has widened the scope to conduct forms of structured observation. The Internet may be used in 'real time' to make virtual structured observations. These range from simple to more complex structured observations. Every time you 'visit' a website this will be recorded electronically. This allows organisations to count the number of visits to their websites and how much time is spent on each page. Internet behaviour may also be tracked and analysed, including analysing the links between online behaviour. As we saw in the opening vignette in this chapter, digital marketing platforms gather various types of online data in order to retarget specific groups of customers. Recently we have become more aware of the ways in which the data that we create online may be used to target and retarget our behaviours. Box 9.4 provides an example related to targeting voting behaviour. However, the use of these approaches is subject to legal regulation in different countries related to data protection and online privacy, including the provision of consent such as for the use of 'cookies' (Section 6.7).

Box 9.4 Focus on research in the news

Targeting voters online

During the election campaign held in 2017, national newspapers in the UK ran stories about targeting voters using social media channels. In the *Financial Times*, Simon Kuper provided an imagined example to show how this works.

"Let's say that, in the UK election, you wanted to sway forty-something women in a particular Kensington street who own homes abroad. You a make video of Theresa May saying, 'Brexit means Brexit' and you experiment with formats. One might be a question: 'Is hard Brexit risky?' Another is a statement: 'Hard Brexit: Insane.' You vary colours. You pay Facebook to send out the videos, and see which gets the most clicks. Then you retarget those who clicked it. Only they, and friends with whom they share it, will see your ad. So you can send an entirely different ad, maybe even a pro-Brexit one, to voters elsewhere. It's practically a secret campaign. And it's cheap."

 Source: Extract from 'Opinion FT Magazine How Facebook is changing democracy', Simon Kuper (2017) *Financial Times,* 15 June. Copyright © 2017 The Financial Times Ltd

Structured observation by itself may be little more than surveillance or fact finding. It is the ways in which such data are analysed that can transform this activity into valuable research findings. One of the best-known examples of managerial research that used structured observation as part of its data collection approach was the study of the work of senior managers by Mintzberg (1973). This led Mintzberg to cast doubt on the long-held theory that managerial work was a rational process of planning, controlling and directing. Mintzberg studied what five chief executives actually did during one of each of the executives' working weeks. He did this by direct observation and the recording of events on three predetermined coding schedules. This followed a period of 'unstructured' observation in which the categories of activity that formed the basis of the coding schedules he used were developed. In this way Mintzberg 'grounded' his structured observation on data collected in an initial period of participant observation (Grounded Theory is explained in Sections 5.8 and 13.9).

Modern uses of structured observation do not have to rely on computer technologies. Structured observation is still used as a tool to assess the way in which workers in modern workplaces carry out their tasks, as Box 9.5 indicates. The advantages and disadvantages of structured observation are summarised in Table 9.5.

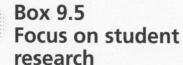 **Box 9.5 Focus on student research**

Observing staff behaviours at Fastfoodchain

Sangeeta worked at Fastfoodchain for her holiday job. She became interested in measuring service quality in her course and decided to do a preliminary study of customer interaction at Fastfoodchain.

Fastfoodchain has restaurants all over the world. Central to its marketing strategy is that the customer experience should be the same in every restaurant in every country of the world. An important part of this strategy is ensuring that customer-facing staff observe the same behavioural standards in every restaurant. This is achieved by defining precise standards of

Box 9.5
Focus on student research (*continued*)

Observing staff behaviours at Fastfoodchain

behaviour that customers should experience in every transaction undertaken. These standards are used in the training of staff and assessment of their performance. Reproduced below is part of the section of the standards schedule concerned with dealing with the customer. (There are also sections which deal with the behaviours needed to prepare for work, e.g. till readiness, and general issues, e.g. hygiene.)

The standards schedule is an observation document used by trainers in order to evaluate the degree to which their training is effective with individual employees. It is also used by managers in their assessment of the performance of employees. Sangeeta was very impressed with the level of precision contained in this schedule and wondered whether it could form the basis of her research project.

Section 2: Delighting the customer

Staff member:		
Behaviour	**Was the behaviour observed?**	**Comments**
Smiles and makes eye contact with the customer		
Greets the customer in a friendly manner		
Gives the customer undivided attention throughout the transaction		
Suggests extra items that have not been ordered by the customer		
Places items on clean tray with tray liner facing customer		
Ensures that customer is told where all relevant extras (e.g. cream, sugar) are located		
Explains to customer reasons for any delays and indicates likely duration of delay		
Neatly double-folds bags containing items with the Fastfoodchain logo facing the customer		
Price of order is stated and customer offered choice of payment method		
For card payments, customer offered POS terminal for chip and pin or contactless payment. Completes payment and presents receipt		
For cash payments, lays all money notes across till drawer until change is given and clearly states the appropriate amount of change. Completes payment and presents receipt		
Customer is finally thanked for transaction, hope expressed that the meal will be enjoyed, and an invitation to return to the restaurant issued		

Observer roles

Structured observation requires the observer to use a passive or detached observational role. Martinko and Gardner (1985) recognise that structured observation cannot be conducted by an active participant. In other words you cannot conduct structured observation in a setting in which you are taking an active part. If you did attempt this it would mean that you were interacting with people whose behaviour, interactions or activities you were

Table 9.5 Advantages and disadvantages of structured observation

Advantages	Disadvantages
• It can be used by anyone after suitable training in the use of the measuring instrument. Therefore, you could delegate this extremely time-consuming task. In addition, structured observation may be carried out simultaneously in different locations. This would present the opportunity of comparison between locations	• Unless virtual observation is used, the observer must be in the research setting when the phenomena under study are taking place
• It should yield reliable results by virtue of its replicability. The easier the observation instrument is to use and understand, the more reliable the results will be	• Behaviours, interactions and events being observed may occur simultaneously or in complex ways, making coding difficult and potentially unreliable (discussed later in 'Data quality issues arising from structured observation')
• Structured observation is capable of more than simply observing the frequency of events. It is also possible to record the relationship between events. For example, does a visit to a website lead to the exploration of related pages and video-recordings; does this lead to a decision to purchase?	• While structured observation is helpful in recording the incidence of behaviours, interactions or events, these observations are limited to overt actions or surface indicators. This may be inadequate to explore the impact or effectiveness of the behaviours, interactions or events being observed, leaving the observer to make inferences
• The method allows the collection of data at the time they occur in their natural setting. Therefore, there is no need to depend on 'second-hand' accounts of phenomena from informants who put their own interpretation on events	• Without the prior specification or development of theory, structured observations will be of only limited value for research. Analysis needs to look for patterns of behaviours, interactions or events to explain the data collected and to understand their impact in the observed situation. Such analysis may show how behaviours are linked, which are effective or ineffective and how they affect outcomes
• Structured observation secures data that most informants would ignore because to them these are too mundane or irrelevant	• Not recognising environmental variability within a research setting may invalidate conclusions drawn from structured observation. Behaviours, interactions and events are likely to be contingent on (shaped by) the environment and ignoring this variable is likely to cast doubt on the conclusions. Conversely, controlling for or taking environmental variables into account is likely to enhance the validity of the conclusions drawn
	• Data may be slow (and expensive) to collect, although this is not always the case

also trying to categorise. The problem with this is that your interventions in the setting would affect, or contaminate, what you observe. You would therefore not be able to conduct structured observation in the role of collaborative observer, participant-as-observer or complete participant.

Where you commence your observational research using an active participant role and then decide that you also wish to undertake some structured observations, you will need to switch roles to either observer-as-participant or complete observer to use the method. In either of these roles your participation will only be passive – you will be present at the observational setting but only as a pure observer.

You may also be able to undertake structured observation in the role of nonparticipant observer. In this role your observation is conducted in a completely detached location to the original setting (Section 9.2). As part of your research you may wish to conduct structured observation using video recordings of interviews conducted with a number of business leaders. In this case you will not have been present when these interviews occurred. Instead you will observe recordings of them in a different location. In this situation you would have the advantage of being able to replay and observe these interviews as many times as you wished to be able to conduct a thorough set of structured observations.

Nature of the observational setting

Structured observation may take place in a naturalistic setting (Section 9.2). For example, Mueller et al. (2012) observed several entrepreneurs by following each over a number of days to record their workplace activities using what they called a structured observation template. Structured observation may be conducted in a contrived or artificially created setting. You may set up a laboratory-based experiment, in order to observe those taking part in this research activity using a structured observation coding schedule. It can also be conducted in a virtual setting, involving Internet-mediated observation, using a coding schedule. As we have also noted, structured observation may be conducted in a detached setting by the nonparticipant observer.

This indicates that structured observation may be used in different types of observational setting. However, in each observation setting there is likely to be a limit to the number of informants whose behaviours, interactions or activity a single observer may reliably observe at any one time.

Data collection

Data collection in structured observation will involve you using a **coding schedule**. A structured observation coding schedule records categories of behaviours, interactions or events that have been predetermined and defined before observation takes place (Box 9.6).

Using coding schedules to collect data

A quick comparison of the two examples of coding schedules in Boxes 9.5 and 9.6 shows how their purpose can vary. The example in Box 9.5 records whether a category of behaviour has occurred. It forms a checklist of numerous items that need to be recorded as having been observed or not. The example in Box 9.6 focuses on a smaller number of more general categories that provide a predetermined basis to record the frequencies of each category of behaviour or interaction.

Further variations of coding schedules are possible. For example, behaviours, interactions or events may be recorded as a sequence rather than as frequencies. They may also be recorded by time intervals, such as recording behaviours or interactions evident at the beginning of a meeting, those evident in the middle of a meeting and those at the end of the meeting. You may also be interested to observe the occurrence of particular behaviours. For example, if you were conducting the research project described in Box 9.6, you might focus on recording behaviours that follow from cases of disagreement. In this case, you would wait for disagreement to occur and code the following sequence of behaviour. Structured observation potentially provides you with a number of options to collect data depending on your research question and objectives.

Deciding on a coding schedule to collect data

A key decision you will need to make before undertaking structured observation is whether to use an existing coding schedule or to design your own. We now discuss these options.

Using an existing coding schedule is associated with key disadvantages and advantages. The first task you will face is finding an existing coding schedule which is suitable to answer your research question and address your objectives, or part of them. This may not prove to be possible. We would go further and say that for most business and management research projects using structured observation, you will not find an existing coding schedule that is suitable and available for you to use. For some research projects

Box 9.6
Focus on student research

Structured observation schedule of categories and codes

Adam undertook a project examining the effectiveness of team meetings in his employing organisation. As part of this he planned to undertake structured observation of a number of team meetings in different parts of the organisation. He developed a schedule of categories and codes for his structured observation that included the following extract.

Adam produced an observation sheet from the full schedule to record the frequencies of these behaviours at each team meeting he observed. He attended the equivalent meeting held by three different teams and produced a summary sheet of his structured observations from these meetings.

Category	Definition	Observable action	Code
Providing Information	Provision of facts or information to others	Team Leader provides information to team members	TLPI
		Team member provides information to others	TMPI
Seeking Information	Seeking facts or clarification of information from another person	Team Leader seeks information from team members	TLSI
		Team member seeks information from Team Leader	TMSI
Checking understanding of others	Seeking to establish whether earlier facts or information has been understood by others	Team Leader checks understanding of team members	TLCU
		Team member checks understanding of others	TMCU
Offering clarification	Offer of clarification of earlier information to others	Team Leader offers clarification to team members	TLOC
		Team member offers clarification to others	TMOC
Giving viewpoint	Expression of opinions on facts and information provided or on a point of discussion	Team Leader expresses viewpoint to team members	TLGV
		Team member expresses viewpoint to others	TMGV
Summarising	Sum up or go over the main points of earlier information or a recent discussion	Team Leader summarises information for team members	TLSUM
		Team member summarises information for others	TMSUM

Meeting	Summary of structured observations from team meetings in Week 6											
	Providing Information		Seeking Information		Checking Understanding		Offering Clarification		Giving Viewpoint		Summarising	
	TLPI	TMPI	TLSI	TMSI	TLCU	TMCU	TLOC	TMOC	TLGV	TMGV	TLSUM	TMSUM
1	15	2	5	4	4	1	5	0	7	1	5	0
2	11	4	3	7	6	1	6	2	4	5	7	3
3	7	6	4	6	4	4	3	4	3	8	2	4
TOTALS	33	12	12	17	14	6	14	6	14	14	14	7

> **Box 9.6**
> **Focus on student research (*continued*)**
>
> He arranged to conduct a semi-structured interview with each team leader and with a sample of the members from each team. He also undertook a theoretical review of the literature (Chapter 3) to help to analyse and interpret his data to explain it and to evaluate the effectiveness of team meetings in his employing organisation.

you may be fortunate and locate previous research that provides you with an existing coding schedule (e.g. Mueller et al. 2012).

Where you are fortunate to locate an existing coding schedule you will need to evaluate its suitability for your research question and objectives. It is unlikely that this coding schedule was designed to address the same research question and objectives as yours; but even if it does, you will still need to evaluate if it is designed to address all of the behaviours, interactions or events in which you are interested. If it is designed to address these, you will still need to evaluate whether the observation schedule is well designed to overcome concerns about reliability and validity. Here, you may be asking, 'How can I do this?' Box 9.7 offers advice on evaluating and developing a coding schedule.

Where you manage to locate an existing coding schedule that is suitable for your research question and objectives and which is adequately designed to overcome concerns about its reliability and validity, you will be able to enjoy two important advantages. Firstly, its use will save you the need to develop a new coding schedule. Secondly, it will be tried and tested, which may help to make your results and conclusions more reliable and valid as well as comparable to those from its earlier use.

However, where existing coding schedules are unsuitable for your purposes, or where none exist, you will need to develop your own schedule. Box 9.7 contains a checklist to guide this activity, to help to ensure the reliability and ease of use of the codes you devise. There are a number of sources that may help you to devise categories, definitions and codes for your own coding schedule. Your research question and objectives will help to focus your efforts to devise your own coding schedule as it must be suitable to answer this question and address your research objectives. In addition, your research design may be sequential so that you initially undertake some in-depth or semi-structured interviews, or a period of participant observation, to determine categories for structured observation and develop a coding schedule. You may also identify categories for structured observation from existing research or theories, through reading journal articles and other published literature. Your experience as a participant or inside researcher, or work placement student, may also help you to develop categories for structured observation and a coding schedule. Always evaluate your own coding schedule (Box 9.7) and pilot test it before using it to collect data (Section 11.7).

Another alternative approach may be to incorporate part or parts of an existing schedule into your own coding schedule. Existing coding schedules may be inappropriate for your own research but you may be able to model your own schedule on the design of one used for a different purpose, or to incorporate some part of it into yours. If this is the option that seems most appropriate in the light of your research question(s) and objectives, we recommend that you also use the checklist in Box 9.7 to ensure that your schedule is as valid and reliable as possible and to pilot test it.

Box 9.7
Checklist

To evaluate or develop a coding schedule

✔ Is the coding schedule suitable to answer your research question and address your objectives?
✔ Does the coding schedule cover all of the specific behaviours, interactions or events in which you are interested and exclude others outside the scope of your research?

✔ Are these categories of behaviour, interaction or events clearly defined and written down, observable in action and exclusive (not overlapping)?
✔ Are the categories in the coding schedule flexible enough to be applied across the different settings of your research?
✔ Are the codes being used indicated on the observation sheet, simple to understand and undemanding to apply so that you will not need to memorise or check their meanings?

Data quality issues

The main issues for structured observation relate to aspects of reliability (Section 5.11): observer error, informant error, time error and observer effects. We discussed observer error and observer effects earlier, in Section 9.3. Here we consider informant error and time error.

Informant error

Informant error may cause your data to be unreliable. You may be concerned with observing the normal output of sales administrators as measured by the amount of orders they process in a day. Informant error may be evident if you are observing administrators in a work group that was short-staffed owing to illness. This may mean that they were spending more time answering telephones and less time processing orders, as there were fewer people available to handle telephone calls. The message here is clear: select your sample of informants using the sampling technique that best enables you to answer your research question and meet your objectives (Chapter 7).

Time error

Closely related to the issue of informant error is that of **time error**. It is essential that the time at which you conduct an observation does not provide data that are untypical of the total time period in which you are interested. For example, the number of calls taken in a call centre is often higher in the hours surrounding lunchtime in comparison to any other two-hour period. Conversely, it may be lower in the hours just before the lines close than in any other two-hour period. It would therefore be necessary to conduct periods of observation at intervals throughout the day in order to gain a reliable set of data. Of course, electronic monitoring allows a researcher with access to use already collected data to establish which periods were busiest as well as other aspects such as average call times, the number of calls taken by particular members of staff and how many callers were waiting to be answered at particular times of the day!

9.5 Internet-mediated observation

The development of the Internet has created a subject to be researched and a wealth of data for research. Internet and social media researchers have studied a multitude of Internet related research topics in many fields including business and management and the sometimes relative ease of accessing Internet data is likely to maintain this trend. The Internet allows access to a huge amount of archived data, including primary data derived from past social interactions on social networks, discussion sites and Internet forums. This type of data is available in various forms including text, video, audio (sound) and visual files, the latter including images, photographs and drawings (Chapter 8). The Internet also allows access to social interactions currently taking place in social networks, Internet forums and virtual worlds. In seeking access to these types of primary data, the issue for the Internet researcher is to develop an appropriate research method and to apply this in an ethical way. In this section we outline how an ethnographic approach has been adapted to provide a suitable research approach to use these types of data and in particular how participant observation has been adapted for this purpose. As you will have already noted, we discuss this under the heading of 'Internet-mediated observation'.

During this outline, we first address the question, 'What is Internet-mediated observation?' We then discuss observer roles that may be used in Internet-mediated observation, followed by the nature of the observational setting where this takes place. We also discuss data collection during Internet-mediated observation before we finish this section by looking at data quality issues that may arise from using Internet-mediated observation. We refer to some ethical issues during this outline but discuss these more fully in Chapter 6.

What is Internet-mediated observation?

Internet researchers adopt an ethnographic approach and use participant observation to conduct research where data are derived from archived and current online social interactions. As we have noted, this approach involves some adaptation from traditional, 'offline' ethnographic research and emphasises its own ethical concerns (Chapter 6). This has led to various general and more specific terms to describe this research approach, including online ethnography, netnography, virtual ethnography, webethnography and mobile ethnography.

Online ethnography studies people in online or virtual communities, whose participation is motivated by their shared interest and/or some level of social attachment. Many online communities organise themselves around a shared interest or activity; for example in relation to a particular brand, product, service, business focus, occupation, lifestyle or set of beliefs. These online communities operate through bulletin boards, email lists, Internet forums, linked web pages, social networks and virtual worlds. Many other online communities organise themselves around interpersonal relationships, operating principally though social networking sites including major social media ones. These online communities produce large amounts of qualitative material, in the form of text and audio-visual material from the social interactions that occur between members over time.

The purpose of online ethnography or netnography is to obtain "cultural understandings of the experiences of people and groups from online social interaction and content" (Kozinets 2015: 76). However, studying online communities and culture is likely to be problematic and we return to consider this later.

This type of Internet-mediated observation will broadly follow the approach to participant observation that we outlined in Section 9.3 and is termed **Internet-mediated participant observation**. Such observation is likely to be exploratory as it commences and to become explanatory as it progresses (Section 5.7). It is also likely to work though the phases of participant observation that we outlined earlier, emphasising descriptive observation in its early phase, developing more focused observation in its middle phase and highlighting selective observation in its final phase (Section 9.3).

However, it is also important to recognise that online observation may commence as and focus on structured observation. Such **Internet-mediated structured observation** may use quantitative as well as qualitative data and analysis. The very nature of the Internet means that huge amounts of quantitative data are recorded every day from the billions of clicks and taps that we all collectively make on all of our Internet connected devices. The vast majority of these potential data are not accessible to researchers and will remain unanalysed unless subjected to advanced big data analytical techniques. However, some of these data will become available to researchers and in addition the huge amount of qualitative Internet data available may be analysed in part using quantitative techniques such as those discussed in Chapter 12. Box 9.8 provides an example of Internet-mediated structured observation that examined relationships between use of social networks and the incidence of online shopping.

Observer roles

Internet-mediated observation affects the nature of the researcher's participation. Earlier we outlined types of participant observation arranged across different dimensions (Figures 9.3 and 9.4). Depending on accessibility to an online community, it may be possible for a researcher to enter the website as a guest without revealing his or her identity or without participating other than reading or viewing available material. This is a form of

---

 **Box 9.8
Focus on
management
research**

Internet-mediated structured observation to examine relationships between use of social networks and online shopping

In an article published in the *Journal of Marketing*, Zhang, Trusov, Stephen and Jamal (2017) examine whether the use of social networks and the incidence of online shopping are related and, if so, how. They commenced their research by recognising two broad possibilities. One possibility is that time spent on social networks may expose participants to information about products, where this may come from social interactions with friends on social media or from online brand advertising. This possibility may be positively associated with purchasing decisions. Another possibility is that time spent on social networks may distract participants from using shopping websites and therefore be negatively associated with online shopping.

During their study to explore these possible relationships, the researchers were given access to structured observation data collected from over ten thousand Internet users whose online activities had been observed over one calendar year. These data were made available to the researchers by a global market data management company and consist of three types related to this panel of Internet users. The first type consists of detailed records of their online purchases. The second type consists of a detailed history of their web-browsing activities. The third type consists of their demographic details including age, gender, employment status, income, number of people and presence of children in the household. These highly structured data allowed the researchers to examine for associations between use of social networks and incidence of online shopping using empirical modelling and statistical analysis.

lurking (Section 6.5) and is similar to the role of 'complete observer'. A researcher may also become a member of an online community but remain 'silent' as a non-participant and only be interested in reading and observing what others have posted (although her or his presence may be detectable to others when online). This is also a form of lurking and still similar to the 'complete observer' role since the researcher is not participating and while his or her presence may be detectable, the researcher's purpose is not revealed. The alternative to lurking is to participate in an online community by adopting a different participant observation role.

Paechter (2013) discusses the relative merits of non-participation and participation when collecting data from an online community. She asks whether lurking is sufficient to collect data or whether more active participation is necessary to achieve a richer understanding. Full and open participation, based on either the collaborative observer or participant-as-observer role discussed earlier, potentially has a number of advantages. It should help to avoid missing important aspects of the interactions between members of the community and reduce misunderstanding. Full and open participation allows a researcher to check her or his interpretations (Section 5.11) and to explore these with members. Participation in the interactions of the online community is more likely to provide the deepest level of access to understand it. While non-participation may provide access to data, acting covertly and practising deception is fraught with ethical issues (see our discussion of issues relating to informed consent and privacy among others in Section 6.5) and may lead to researchers being asked to leave when they reveal their activity and request access to undertake research overtly (Madge 2010; Paechter 2013).

Nature of the observational setting

As we discussed earlier, use of the Internet in observation research may facilitate access to huge amounts of data. Most of this will be primary data while some may be secondary data (Chapter 8).

Most instances of Internet-mediated observation are likely to involve a form of participant observation transposed to an online setting, where the intention of this approach is to allow you to participate in and observe social interactions that naturalistically happen online. Where you wish to undertake Internet-mediated participant observation you will attempt to gain access to an online community to communicate with its members in real-time, using synchronous text or perhaps a live video link, and in delayed time, through asynchronous text. You may also wish to gain access to archived data, in the form of text, video, audio and visual material.

Where you consider undertaking Internet-mediated structured observation you will need to collect or gain access to data that are appropriate for your research question and objectives. This may well be difficult to achieve for both practical and data protection reasons (Section 6.7), unless you are able to gain informed consent from each member of your informant group or negotiate access to use a data set collected by an organisation (Box 9.8). In the latter case this indicates that you would be using secondary online data.

Data collection

Online ethnography shares many attributes of traditional ethnography, although its use affects the way data are collected. Participant observation, informal discussions and interviews are important means to collect data in traditional ethnography (Section 9.3). In online ethnography, the nature of observation is altered and the scope for informal discussions and interviews depends on the type of engagement a researcher has with a specific online community. The primary methods that participants in online communities use to communicate with one another are synchronous and asynchronous text. Paechter (2013: 73) refers to online textual exchanges as 'analogous to written speech', to which the researcher 'listens in' in a similar way to the traditional participant observer who listens to oral exchanges before writing these down. Online text provides a complete record of observed exchanges compared to the notes made from observing oral exchanges. While the traditional researcher is able to observe body language, facial expressions and tone of voice to assist in the interpretation of interactions she or he observes, the online researcher may be able to recognise nuances in the text, associated emojis and audio-visual material available to aid interpretation. Online observation may also take place in real time, like traditional observation. In these ways, Internet-mediated observation has the capacity to reveal plentiful amounts of rich data.

Paechter (2013) outlines the process of collecting data that she used when researching an online community. The first issue was to identify material available in the online community which would address the research question and objectives (we return to consider this further in the next sub-section). Having identified the source of data, she decided to use an approach which was analogous to participant observation. The appropriate and available postings in the online forum were treated as observational data. She read through each thread in a relevant topic domain and took notes. This allowed her to identify threads on which she wished to focus. Note making also commenced the process of data analysis by coding these data, which can then be sorted into categories (see 'Grounded Theory' in Sections 5.8 and 13.9). She also identified a number of key informants upon whom she wished to focus her data collection and analysis. She was able to track these informants through their community profiles in order to use their posts and blog entries to collect data and analyse these.

In more general terms, Kozinets (2015) provides advice about searching for online sites; choosing an appropriate site or sites to conduct your research; and which data to collect from the site or sites where you choose to conduct your research. His criteria to help you choose an appropriate site to conduct your research relate to:

- its relevance to your research question and objectives;
- how current and active are social interactions on the site;
- how substantial and rich are social interactions on the site; and
- the nature, scope and suitability of the site's participants and content for your research.

We discuss some of these points later in this section in relation to data quality. In relation to which data to collect from your chosen site, these need to be relevant, rich, representative, contextual and interesting. In addition, you should be open to data that reveal the unexpected, the anomalous and offer scope to explore these and develop insights.

Kozinets (2015) identifies three types of online ethnographic or netnographic data. The first type is the archival data that the researcher collects from the online site. These are data created by members of the online community without any interaction with or intervention by the researcher. These data are likely to be in the form of text but may include video, or purely visual or audio material (Section 9.6). The second type is 'co-created' data (Kozinets 2015: 165), which result from the researcher's social interactions in the online community and with its members. The third type is reflective data, produced by the researcher engaging in introspection or reflection.

Data quality issues

If you decide that Internet-mediated observation is an appropriate data collection method for your research, you will need to think through the issues that will arise from your approach. In evaluating the issues and risks associated with your approach, you will need to explain how you will seek to overcome or at least minimise these and be able to justify your approach in relation to any alternative course of action that might be open to you to adopt. A central issue that we have discussed is about adopting a covert approach rather than an overt one, and the ethical dilemmas that follow from this (Section 6.5).

A further set of issues for you to consider relates to evaluating the quality of the data produced from using Internet-mediated observation. Issues discussed earlier relating to data collected using participant observation and structured observation will be relevant. These include observer error, observer drift and observer bias, and may include observer effects where you collect data overtly. We now consider other issues related to data quality from using Internet-mediated observation. These are considered under the headings of: the nature of (online) communities . . . and the role of the researcher; the scope of online communities; the nature of data from Internet-mediated observation; the reliability/dependability and validity/credibility/transferability of Internet-mediated observation data.

The nature of (online) communities . . . and the role of the researcher

Ethnography developed as an approach to study the culture of a people, or community, hence the literal meaning of this term (Section 5.8). We recognised earlier that studying communities and culture is likely to be problematic, especially in relation to those online. Kozinets (2015) provides a useful critique of studying culture and community. While recognising that online ethnography or netnography has emphasised the study of online culture and community, he outlines how these concepts have been re-evaluated in a way that questions their status as solid, stable and straightforward constructs.

Cultural identity will vary between individuals and across time and therefore be difficult to categorise in a simple way. In a similar way, 'communities' are not simply composed of homogenous, like-minded beings. A shared interest or activity and/or some level of social attachment should not be equated with the idea of identically-minded people communicating with one another in an uncritical way. If studying the concepts of culture and community is problematic in traditional ethnographic settings these are likely to be even more difficult to study in virtual, online settings.

If culture and community are not solid, stable and straightforward constructs, how should we try to study and understand these concepts in online ethnography? The answer to this question will be related to the role of the researcher in online ethnographic research. The level of the researcher's participation and the extent of the collaboration between the researcher and informants are likely to be related to the opportunity to gain different perspectives and multiple interpretations to achieve some cultural understanding of those engaged in social interactions online. As we recognised in Section 9.3, understanding and insight are likely to be a function of careful and repetitive participant observation. Studying online communities and culture requires immersion and thoughtful reflection to achieve depth of understanding, to avoid superficiality and uncritical simplicity.

The scope of online communities

This issue relates to understanding the nature of the sample you have chosen to research. In a traditional ethnographic study, you should be able to observe all of the interactions in the setting to which you have gained access. Where access is denied to some aspect of the setting (e.g. you may be granted access to observe a workgroup but not to observe confidential meetings between the managers of that group), you will be aware of the limitations placed on your observation. Where you base your research on 'observing' an online community, you will need to determine whether the online exchanges you make use of represent all or nearly all of the interactions between its members, or whether those members also interact 'offline', through other forums such as physical meetings or conferences, or perhaps even through other, related Internet forums to discuss the same shared interest. It is likely that where your research is based on using Internet-mediated observation you will focus on using one online community, so you will need to evaluate whether this accounts for the majority of the interactions of the group you are researching.

The nature of data

Prior and Miller (2012) consider the characteristics of Internet-mediated observation data that affect its representativeness in comparison to traditionally derived observation data. They report that while some members of an online community will consistently post messages over time, others may be active for a period but then become less active or inactive, while many others will only lurk, reading the posts of others and perhaps making the occasional post. They note that these patterns will not be consistent with the 'offline' behaviours of these members. Members of an online community may also adopt an online pseudonym or persona, which can protect their identity but may also be used to project views that they would not voice in face-to-face communication. These characteristics may cast doubt on the representativeness of Internet-mediated observation data in two ways. Firstly, the views of more active members may not represent the opinions of the whole group. Secondly, views expressed may not represent those that are held more widely in the population where this is also composed of others who are not members of an online community.

Prior and Miller argue that because interactions between members in an online community rely on written text, this may mean that the language used does not adequately represent the complexity of the issue being discussed and may lack the type of contextual consideration that would facilitate a fuller evaluation. On the other hand, a range of posts by different members or contributors may produce a range of perspectives that does permit an adequate contextualisation and evaluation.

Where you use Internet-mediated observation you will need to consider the range of contributors to each discussion, the possible impact from using online pseudonyms, and the nature of the language used and contextualisation included in discussion to evaluate the data you collect. Internet-mediated observation may produce rich and valuable data and represent a range of views on a pertinent topic which help you to pursue your research, or it may produce data of variable quality.

The reliability/dependability and validity/credibility/transferability of data

The scope and nature of data collected from Internet-mediated observation are likely to affect its reliability/dependability as well as the research's internal validity/credibility and generalisability/transferability (Section 5.11 and in particular Table 5.7). Data that only represent the views of some members of an online community may be unreliable or undependable because 'observing' the views of other members may produce data with a different emphasis. Using data that does not adequately represent the views of all members of an online community or their behaviour in real life will also adversely affect the internal validity/credibility and generalisability/transferability of the research (Section 5.11).

This does not mean that data collected using Internet-mediated observation are of dubious quality but, rather, you will need to evaluate the suitability of this method in the context of your research project before embarking on its use.

9.6 Observation using videography, audio recordings and visual images

So far we have discussed three methods to conduct observational research: participant observation, structured observation and Internet-mediated observation, albeit that there is scope for, or actual overlap between these methods. We have also recognised that observational data may be collected not only by the researcher acting as observer-in-person but also through using video or audio recordings and visual images.

Observation, particularly in its traditional approach, is an audio-visual method: it involves listening and seeing. Use of video, audio recordings and visual images therefore provide us with ways to collect observational data in conjunction with any of the three methods we have discussed. Use of these techniques also means that observational research may become more collaborative, where informants participate in the collection of data and in analysing these through informant interpretations.

Participatory approaches in this context include the use of participatory video, participatory audio and participant photography. **Participatory video** involves providing informants with video cameras to let them record their experiences or perspectives, including the freedom to choose what to record. This approach may involve informants being given video cameras to use on an individual basis or it may involve a group activity within a community. The video produced is often referred to as a **video diary** and the informants involved are sometimes called **video diarists**. In a similar way, **participatory audio** involves providing informants with audio recorders to let them record their experiences or perspectives, again with the freedom to choose what to record. We outline an example of this approach later in this section. **Participant photography** involves providing informants with digital cameras or asking them to use their mobile phones as cameras to record their experiences or perspectives, including the freedom to choose the subject of each image they take.

Use of these participatory approaches varies in relation to their purpose and focus. For example, video diaries may be used in market research for the purpose of recording consumers' experiences and understanding their perspectives. In this case, the focus of participation will be closely defined by the organisation who commissions this market research, related to a particular brand or product for example. In critical ethnography and Critical Management Studies (Sections 5.8 and 4.3), where the intended purpose is to bring about change or to represent an informant perspective normally hidden from those in power, the focus of a participatory approach will be much broader and left in the control of participating informants. This second type of participatory approach will lead to a much greater level of informant involvement and collaboration throughout the research process, from design, through data collection, to analysis and interpretation. We return to discuss this in Chapter 13, when we consider the analysis of visual research related to photovoice and participatory video.

Our focus in the rest of this section is much narrower: here we discuss how each of these techniques (video, audio and visual images) may be used to collect observational data, although we recognise elsewhere in this book that visual and audio research is more than just a data collection method. We discuss video, audio and visual images separately as each has different attributes. To identify these attributes we briefly consider the potential advantages and possible data quality issues of each technique. We also consider how either the researcher or the informants (or both) may use any of these techniques to collect observational data.

Using videography

Videography has two distinct meanings. The first is technical and refers to the process of recording moving images onto electronic media. We use the term 'video' in the text here to refer to this meaning of videography to avoid confusion with the second, related to the ethnographic analysis of recorded sequences (Knoblauch 2012).

Video-recording may be used in several ways to aid the collection of data. A few of these ways relate to methods discussed in other chapters. For example, semi-structured or in-depth interviews may be recorded using video (Chapter 10). But it is in relation to observation that video offers the most ways to aid the collection of data. Some of these ways involve the researcher collecting primary data or arranging for this to be collected by informants, while others involve the use of secondary data.

Researcher created video

Researchers may be able to record video in a research setting to collect observational data with the fully informed and expressly given consent of their informants (Box 9.9). This may involve the researcher using standard video equipment or a body-worn camera to record informants' activities, or the use of a mobile phone camera in a research setting. High quality video may be created using any of these devices.

Concealed body-worn cameras are less obtrusive than other types, raising serious ethical and data protection concerns where any attempt is made to use one of these covertly. Ethical approval to use such an intrusive approach in a covert way is extremely unlikely to be granted. For most research projects, only observer roles in which the researcher's purpose is revealed to informants and where their informed and formally expressed consent to be videoed is given are likely to be acceptable.

Video recordings may also be directly available to the researcher to use in observational research as secondary data (Chapter 8). Jarzabkowski et al. (2014) report that some

Box 9.9
Focus on management research

Using video to collect observational data in market research

In Box 5.8 we describe a study by Arnould and Cayla (2015) published in *Organization Studies* that explores how companies use ethnography and videography in their market research. They state that market research is the most important way in which organisations gain information about their consumers and that commercial ethnography is increasingly being used by companies to allow them to learn about their customers.

This article focuses on the way in which commercial ethnography is used to research profiles of actual consumers, who are seen to represent a market segment. This approach involves accompanying a consumer and often video recording their actions and comments. This enables a commercial ethnographer to get to know the consumer by spending time with them, observing them, and talking and listening to them to understand how they feel about and use the product(s) being researched. Alternatively it may involve providing consumers with video cameras to allow them to record their own experiences.

Using video as part of this process of observing and recording is seen as important and powerful. The use of video recording is widespread because it provides a powerful means to present "real consumers" and to bring these "to life" in the edited accounts that are produced from these recorded observations (Arnould and Cayla 2015: 1367).

organisations are creating video archives that may provide a valuable resource for researchers where access can be negotiated. Suitable recorded material, in the form of archived video and film, may possibly be downloaded through the Internet, from media, sharing and social networking websites. Video-blogs, or vlogs, may also provide suitable sources from which to collect data for research.

Informant created video

Researchers may also ask informants to record video diaries related to the focus of their research. This approach may be particularly useful where considerable distances exist between researcher and informants, making face-to-face observation difficult or impossible to undertake. It may also be useful where the observational site is transient in the sense that the informant being observed needs to be mobile. This may be the case in relation to video recording a shopping experience or some types of work experience.

In such cases, a video diary or blog may be uploaded to the Internet by willing informants and downloaded for analysis by the researcher. Video and Internet technologies mean that an event may be recorded in its entirety and streamed to a different location, so that the researcher may view these data as an observer-as-participant, although this observational research is likely to involve a high level of informant collaboration (Figure 9.4). Mobile phones may also be used by informants engaged in observational research to record digital video (Hein et al. 2011; Jarzabkowski et al. 2014).

A researcher may also gain access to vlogs created by others for personal reasons and use these in observational research to collect data (Chapter 8). This may involve using personal vlogs that have been uploaded to sharing websites, subject to gaining consent from those who have created these. It may also involve gaining access to a live broadcasting vlog to act as an observer-as-participant, or possibly as a participant-as-observer where this vlog involves live textual social interaction.

Advantages of using video

A number of advantages from using video have been identified (Basil 2011; Jarzabkowski et al. 2014). Video-recording creates a permanent record, overcoming the transient nature of observation. This allows the researcher to achieve a number of outcomes that would not be possible where observation only involves watching and note taking. Because video provides a record in real time, a recording can be replayed many times to allow the researcher to reflect on the behaviours being shown, informants' interactions and the role of the environment or setting. This should enhance accuracy when coding data and permit verification of observational events.

Observation is demanding to undertake and you may miss important data when using this method, which a video-recording would subsequently allow you to notice. Video-recordings may be paused, slowed, rewound, fast forwarded, zoomed, copied and subsequently edited to help you code sequences of this record. Jarzabkowski et al. (2014: 3) point out that this helps to identify 'who did what, when, where and how'. In addition, the scope for reflection permitted by video-recording encourages a deeper understanding and allows alternative explanations to be evaluated by replaying this material (Basil 2011).

There are also particular advantages related to the use of body-worn cameras and the recording of video diaries for observational research. Starr and Fernandez (2007) believe that the use of a body-worn camera, as used in consumer marketing research, can help to convey the narrative of the research and create a richer understanding of a subject. Use of this recording device facilitates the capture of precise details and exact cognitions, helping to differentiate between perceptions/recollections and reality, and encourages expression of informants' thoughts and feelings about the processes portrayed. In a similar way, a video diary is capable of creating an influential narrative and shared understanding in observational research (Arnould and Cayla 2015).

Issues related to data quality

Using video to help you collect observational data is likely to be technically and practically challenging. While it may be relatively easy to use a camera, the act of doing so begins to limit what will be recorded for future analysis. Selecting a frame and focusing a camera has implications for the actual data collected. Luff and Heath (2012) discuss some of the technical challenges of using video to record and collect observational data. Recording sound is also likely to be necessary where you decide to use video to record an observation. Recording good-quality sound may be difficult depending on the nature of the research setting and the equipment being used. We briefly consider sound recording in the next subsection.

The practical difficulties of using audio-visual recording equipment are therefore likely to be much greater than simply being physically present in a research setting, watching what is occurring and using a pad to make notes. One of our colleagues who used video commented that the researcher tends to focus on using the recording equipment and capturing the event rather than trying to make sense of it at the time it occurs. Using video may also be problematic where the quality of the recording is poor in some way or where a technical issue occurs during recording. Using more than one researcher when using video to record observational data may help to overcome some of these issues.

Our discussion in this section indicates that the advantages to the researcher of directly using video to collect observational data need to be balanced against these technical and practical issues. Good-quality recorded data may help to overcome the likelihood of observer bias discussed in Section 9.2. Yet, poor-quality recorded data may make the process of analysis difficult and increase the likelihood of observer error and observer bias occurring.

There are other issues related to recording an observation that may also affect data quality. Recording an observation using video is much more intrusive than simply watching and making notes. This raises a number of ethical issues (discussed in Section 6.5), including respect for others, avoidance of harm, informed consent, privacy, confidentiality, use of the data and data management. Negotiating these issues with potential informants may be problematic given the intrusive nature of using video. However, even where access can be negotiated and agreed, there may be a continuing issue related to the willingness of informants to act as they would without the presence of the video. Informants may be concerned about the way in which the recording may be edited and the use to be made of this and other, raw data. We discussed the process where informants become familiar with being observed, known as habituation, in Section 9.3, so that they accept being observed and behave normally. We noted that to achieve habituation, it will probably be necessary for you to undertake several observation sessions in the same research setting with the same informants before you begin to achieve reliable and valid data. We also noted in Section 9.3 that informants may respond to being observed by using this as an opportunity to 'stage' a performance for the observer or to 'self-censor' their activities. Given the intrusive nature of video-recording observation, it is likely that you would need not only to spend time in the research setting to understand its dynamics. But also then to record several observation sessions to develop trust and for informants to behave normally. While this would be time well spent, it will be intensive and very time consuming.

Researchers can ask informants to keep video diaries. This approach also has implications for data quality and analysis. Data quality will partly be dependent on the willingness and competence of informants to undertake this task. In addition, while informants' video diaries provide a first-person perspective and encourage expression of informants' thoughts and feelings, a major disadvantage is the loss of external physical clues. Often, when a body-worn camera is used, the researcher will see what the informant sees, hear everything he or she may say and be able to watch much of what he or she does, but the frame of the recording is likely to be forward looking and narrow. The researcher will not be able to see what the informant looks like while she or he is holding the video-recorder or wearing the body-worn camera. In this way, this approach does not capture the informants' facial expressions or body language while they are engaging in the focal activity and may also not record the surrounding, situational context.

If body-worn cameras are used covertly, there will also be serious ethical issues to consider when using this technology (including a number of those discussed in Section 6.5), which will especially need to be considered in relation to non-informants who are inadvertently recorded.

Using secondary video data (Chapter 8) in observational research can lead to data quality issues. The key here is suitability. Such material may provide you with a source of data, but this will have been collected and edited for a different purpose to that of your research question and objectives and so may be of limited use. In evaluating the possible use of such secondary video data, you will need to consider the original intentions of the video maker or vlogger and evaluate how editing this material may have affected its properties and purpose (Jarzabkowski et al. 2014).

Using audio recordings

The development of relatively small and inexpensive digital video recorders has opened up many possibilities to use these for observational research, as we have indicated. This is especially the case in relation to high quality body-worn and mobile phone digital cameras. These devices are well-suited to observational studies that require continuous observations to be recorded in 'out-and-about' or 'on-the-move' situations. However, there may be situations where you wish to focus on audio-based observation. In such situations you may evaluate using a high quality, digital voice recorder that is small enough to be clipped onto a pocket or belt.

This technology is suited to record the occurrence of talk over long time periods. It is also particularly appropriate for observation research where a detailed record is required of the way language is used in social interactions. Depending on the nature of the research objectives and intended analysis, a recorder may be chosen to record continuously when switched on or it may be voice activated, where recording of background sounds, periods of silence and pauses are not considered relevant data. Observational audio recordings can be created by both the researcher and the informant.

Researcher created audio recordings

A researcher may technically make audio recordings in an observational setting in which he or she is present. However, the unobtrusive nature of some audio recorders means that it would be possible to record verbal interactions without those present being aware that this is happening: an action that would raise serious ethical concerns related to numerous aspects discussed in Section 6.5. Issues related to data protection may also be raised in relation to this action (Section 6.7). Ethical approval to use such an intrusive approach in a covert way is extremely unlikely to be granted. For most research projects, only observer roles in which the researcher's purpose is revealed to informants and where their informed and formally expressed consent to be audio recorded is given are likely to be acceptable.

Informant created audio recordings

Researchers may also ask informants to make audio recordings related to the focus of their research. This will involve providing willing informants with audio recorders to record their conversations with others who are relevant to the research topic. These may be thought of as primary informants, while those with whom they interact and record form another, secondary group of informants. Both groups need to be considered in relation to ethical concerns. Where you consider using this approach, you will need to ensure that this other group of informants are given the choice by your primary informants about whether or not to have their social interactions audio recorded.

Negrón (2012) arranged for a group of her informants to create audio recordings over a two week period. She accompanied these informants during the first week to observe their social interactions in a conventional manner using a field notebook to gain contextual data. This provided her with the opportunity to ensure that those with whom interactions occurred were made aware of the audio recording and agreed to this occurring. She achieved this by visually prompting any of the primary informants where necessary. The microphone used also had a flashing light which helped to make the recording equipment visible and avoid it being unobtrusive. This group of primary informants then agreed to conduct audio recording of their social interactions for a second week without her presence.

Advantages of using audio recordings

A number of advantages of using audio recording are already evident in our discussion. These include being able to record talk accurately and continuously in real time, and over long periods. This overcomes some of the physical demands that would be placed on the researcher to concentrate continuously to record the details of the social interactions being observed using pen and paper. It also potentially allows the researcher to make field notes to record contextual data about the observational setting, while the audio recording captures the voices engaged in the social interaction.

An audio recording potentially allows the researcher to transcribe all or part of each recorded social interaction. Such transcriptions may range from the fairly basic to the highly detailed. The first category is composed of verbatim transcripts, which exactly reproduce the actual words spoken in turn by each participant, using standard punctuation. The second category is composed of highly annotated accounts containing symbols inserted into a verbatim transcript to indicate interactional pauses, word cut-offs or extensions, emphases, intonation and so forth. This more detailed type of transcription will be necessary where you wish to undertake linguistic or conversation analysis. The level of transcription will therefore depend on the nature of your research objectives and analytical approach but the key point here is that a high quality audio recording will facilitate this, albeit that the production of any transcript will be very demanding in terms of time and effort (Section 10.7 and 13.4)!

An audio recording, depending on the quality of the recorder you use, may also allow you to capture something of the environment within which the observation occurs. This may include background noise and other social interactions that are occurring away from the focal interaction. Examples here might be audio recordings made inside a shopping centre, factory or an office. This contextual sound may be important for you to record depending on your research objectives.

Audio-recording also creates a permanent record, overcoming the transient nature of conventional observation. Like video-recording, this allows the researcher to achieve a number of outcomes that would not be possible where observation only involves watching and note taking. An audio recording can be replayed many times to allow the researcher to reflect on the nature and progression of the social interaction, the voices being heard, the intonation being used, spoken emphasis, pauses in speech, and the role of sound in the environment or setting where this is audible and relevant. This should also enhance accuracy when coding data and permit verification of observational events.

Observation is demanding to undertake and you may miss important data when using this method, which audio-recording could subsequently allow you to notice. Audio-recordings may be paused, rewound, fast forwarded, copied and subsequently edited to help you code sequences of this record. This will help you to identify who said what, to whom, in what sequence, when in the conversation, and with what effect or outcome, as well as allowing you to recognise critical incidents. Repeatedly listening to audio recordings may also increase your scope for reflection to encourage your depth of understanding and allow alternative explanations to be evaluated.

Issues related to data quality

Although audio recording offers potential advantages over conventional observation techniques, you need to recognise that the quality of your data will depend on the quality of the recordings you make. You will therefore need to think carefully about the nature of the data you require to be able to evaluate your choice of audio recorder. Negrón (2012) discusses a number of features of audio recorders. These include recording capabilities such as being able to record several voices at different distances from the audio recorder, use of a lavalier (small, clip-on) microphone, quality of a microphone for multidirectional recording and recording different sounds, portability and ease of use of the recorder, continuous recording capability and recording capacity. Poor-quality recorded data may make the process of analysis difficult and increase the likelihood of observer error and observer bias occurring (Section 9.3).

Audio recording does not necessarily involve the complete loss of 'visual' data where the researcher also uses a field notebook to record contextual data. Used in combination with field notes, high quality audio recording may help to reduce the likelihood of observer error and observer bias occurring (Section 9.3). Where informants collect observational data through audio recording, this can help to reduce the likelihood of observer effects occurring. This may be the case where informants independently record their social interactions once they and their co-informants who are also being recorded become used to the presence of the audio recorder, although this will mean the loss of other observational data where the researcher is not present. Negrón (2012) achieved a balance in this situation by spending one week with her primary informants to observe and collect contextual data, with these informants spending a second week collecting audio data independently. In comparison to the use of video recording, audio recording will of course mean the loss of visual data, but where audio data are important, especially the recording of talk, the creation of high quality audio recordings may produce helpful or even vital data.

We discussed covertly using audio recording earlier and the serious ethical concern posed by this. There are other ethical issues that you need to consider even after you have gained the informed consent of your informants to audio record their social interactions. Audio recording an observation is more intrusive than simply watching and making notes. Ethical issues related to privacy, confidentiality and use of the data, amongst others, may remain in the minds of informants leading to observer effects given the intrusive nature of this means to record data. For example, informants may remain concerned about the way in which a recording is to be edited and then used. Where you wish to use audio recording you will therefore need to consider the full range of ethical issues that may arise and to remain sensitive to informants' on-going concerns about these. You will also need to act ethically in relation to non-informants who are inadvertently recorded.

Using visual images

In this subsection we focus on static visual images, having already discussed the use of video. Digital images or photographs are most likely to be used to collect this type of observational data. However there are other types of static visual image that may be used to collect observational data. These range from formal representations, such as charts, diagrams, logos and maps, to freehand drawings and art works, such as sketches, schematic doodles and paintings. An early article on visual research in organisational studies by Meyer (1991) provides a helpful and interesting discussion about using these types of visual image. Visual images are also used in research interviews that incorporate a technique known as visual elicitation and we discuss more fully the use of various types of visual image in relation to this approach in Chapter 10.

Visual images may be created by the researcher or by informants, or they may be 'found'. **Found visual images** already exist, are accessible to the researcher and relevant to the research. A researcher may think about using a found image where permission is given by its copyright owner, although there may still be ethical issues to consider in relation to those shown in the image.

Researcher created images

Researchers may create various types of static visual image. A researcher may be able to take digital images or photographs in a research setting to collect observational data with the fully informed and expressly given consent of his or her informants. This may involve the researcher using a digital camera or possibly a mobile phone to take images (Box 9.10). Researchers may also create other types of visual image. For example, a researcher may find it helpful to create a map or drawing of an observational setting; or perhaps to create a chart or diagram showing the organisational relationships between those being observed in such a setting.

Informant created images

A researcher may ask informants to create digital images related to the research topic or some aspect of it. This is the technique called participant photography that we introduced earlier in this section, where informants take photographs to represent their experiences or perspectives (Box 9.10).

Use of informant created visual images may also be useful where considerable distance exists between researcher and informants, making face-to-face observation difficult or impossible to undertake. Where participatory photography takes place in a distant location, digital images may be uploaded to the Internet by willing informants and downloaded by the researcher. Participant photography may also be useful where an observational setting covers a large area and informants need to move around within it. For example, an observational setting may be a company campus, corporate headquarters, distribution centre, factory or warehouse. Participant photography would help informants capture their experiences of interacting with others in such a setting.

A researcher may also ask informants to create other types of visual image. These include informants' freehand drawings that form visual representations of their perceptions or experiences about some aspect of their work. This type of visual image taps into emotional states and may potentially create powerful images, raising ethical concerns that would need to be very carefully considered before deciding to use this technique. Any decision to adopt this approach is likely to include controls to avoid the risk of embarrassment and harm arising from its use. Researchers may also ask informants to create diagrams or charts that help to provide data in relation to observational research.

Box 9.10 Focus on research in the news

Use of cameras

The market, particularly for low-cost "point and shoot" cameras, has suffered a big downturn as consumers have turned to the convenience of smartphone cameras that allow them to take photos that can be instantly shared on social networking sites such as Facebook and Instagram.

In 2016, global shipments of digital cameras declined 32 per cent from a year earlier to 24.2m units, according to the Camera and Imaging Products Association, a Tokyo-based industry group. This compared with a peak of 121.5m units in 2010.

Companies have tried to adapt to shrinking sales and consumer trends by shifting their focus to more expensive products with internet connectivity through WiFi-equipped cameras.

 Source: Extract from 'Encryption is out of sight for camera makers', Kana Inagaki (2017) *Financial Times*, 25 May. Copyright © 2017 The Financial Times Ltd

Advantages of using visual images

Our discussion points to several advantages of using visual images to collect observational data. Observation is a visual research method and visual images may help to record the observational setting and social interactions within it. However, the way in which visual images are subsequently used may not fully take advantage of their potential.

In the three observational methods discussed in this chapter, emphasis is placed on using words or numbers to represent and record observations. Visual images that are created tend to be used to generate written or numerical data. This occurs in two ways. Visual images are 'directly' analysed using words or numbers, where the visual is transformed into written or numerical representations (Box 12.4; Chapter 13). Visual images are also used as an intermediary means to generate written data. This involves a researcher using a visual image as the basis for a discussion with an informant, to explore aspects of or objects in the image, to generate a verbal account and record this as written data. We consider visual elicitation in Chapter 10.

While both of these approaches show the value of using visual images to collect observational data, they do not represent their full potential nor fully integrate them in the analytical process; an important point that we consider further in Chapter 13. The wealth of visual images evident in an observational setting may lead us to ask, 'should we not recognise the nature of this type of data and use it in its natural, visual form rather than just seek to transform it by describing it using words?' If visual images are retained as visual data in their own right, there is scope to integrate these in your research report using them as visual representations. In this way, there is scope to use visual images as visual data in parallel with or as a complement to visually-generated written or numerical data.

By recording visual observations as visual data, we may record something more than just reducing these to written or numerical data. 'Something more' in this context means being able to recognise what would otherwise be lost or just taken for granted if observations are only recorded as written or numerical data (Rose 2014). Visual images potentially have the capacity to extend the ways in which we understand our data and conduct analysis, as well as generate new knowledge. By their nature, visual images are likely to be rich data sources, providing insights that written or numerical data alone are unlikely to produce. Even used as a complementary source, visual data may help to validate or triangulate findings from written or numerical data.

Using visual images in observational research is also associated with other advantages. These include appealing to groups who are normally reluctant to engage in research projects. One such group of potential informants are those who prefer to use, or excel at using, their visual skills rather than engaging in talking methods (Ozanne et al. 2013). More generally, by asking informants to create visual images, a researcher may generate larger numbers of those who are willing to take part in the research project. Informant created visual images implies at least some level of collaboration in the research project and this approach may help to produce well-grounded data. It may also be associated with other forms of researcher-informant collaboration that help to reduce threats to reliability (Section 5.11).

Issues related to data quality

Even though visual images may be viewed as just a way of making things visible, their use in practice is also likely to be problematic (Rose 2014). In a similar way to the use of video that we discussed earlier, the act of selecting a frame and focusing a digital camera has implications for the collection of data. While it may be relatively easy to use a digital camera, the act of doing so begins to limit what will be recorded for future analysis. In taking a digital image, the researcher or informant is selecting part of what may be seen in the setting. Exploring the reason why an informant took a particular image may be valuable in terms of producing wider data, but any visual analysis and interpretation will depend on and be limited by the scope of the image. Perhaps only by taking further images, by panning around or standing back with the camera to achieve a wider angle, can this limitation be overcome? An informant may also take visual images that represent an issue or act as a metaphor, requiring the researcher to explore the meaning of the image with the person who took it. An example here might be an image taken of a particular object, such as a computer or a desk, to symbolise some meaning, which needs to be decoded in discussion between the informant and the researcher. A digital image in observational research will also capture a scene at a point in time, in which case it may also be necessary to take further images at the same location at other times.

The nature of visual images is also very revealing. They show informants in a particular setting, revealing what they are doing and with whom they are interacting, allowing them to be identified. Gaining informants' informed consent to take such images is vital, but issues may still remain. For example, taking visual images in some settings may require every member of a group or team to consent to the use of this approach. However, it is possible for a group-effect to occur that initially encourages consent to be given by all members of the group or team, only for some of these to be uncomfortable with the use of this intrusive technique in practice. Such a possibility has implications for the way in which informed consent is negotiated as well as for data quality issues. It may be possible to blur faces on images or to avoid facial images being taken, but this may still not prevent informants from being identified.

Ozanne et al. (2013) suggest ways to avoid or minimise the risk of embarrassment or harm to those who consent to the taking of visual images during observation. These include:

- training those who take visual images about ethical concerns;
- explaining to informants how images will be used, controlled and stored and who owns them as part of a formal consent process;
- avoiding taking images that threaten an informant's privacy, or which exceed the consent given;

- allowing informants to see images relating to themselves and granting them the right to edit or destroy those that pose a risk; and
- allowing informants to be involved in deciding how images will be selected and edited for any type of display or publication.

Involvement in these aspects may help to alleviate data quality issues as well as avoid ethical issues.

Finally, analysis of visual images is problematic irrespective of the type of data produced, potentially leading to data quality issues. We consider this further in Chapter 13, where we discuss techniques to analyse visual images.

9.7 Summary

- Different dimensions of observation can be identified which have implications for a researcher intending to undertake observational research. These relate to the level of structure and formality to be used, the role of the researcher during observation, whether it is conducted overtly or covertly, and the nature of the observational setting.
- Participant observation allows the researcher to participate in or closely observe the lives and activities of those whom they are studying. It is used to attempt to get to the root of 'what is going on' in a wide range of social settings.
- Participant observation has high ecological validity but may be affected by observer error, observer drift, observer bias and observer effects. These issues may be minimised or overcome by observer familiarisation, interpretive rigour, informant verification, habituation and the observer using strategies to explore and validate interpretations. Using these strategies can allow the benefits of gaining intricate and rich data to prevail over concerns about unreliable data.
- Structured observation is used to observe the incidence of particular behaviours, interactions or events and record these systematically. It is characterised by a high level of predetermined structure and quantitative analysis.
- Structured observation will involve the use of a coding schedule, which you will probably need to develop and pilot test before using in your research setting.
- Structured observation may be affected by observer error, informant error, time error and observer effects. These issues may also be minimised or overcome by those strategies discussed in relation to participant observation and by designing a coding schedule that is free from interpretive ambiguity.
- Internet-mediated observation involves the collection of data from online communities, with the researcher purely observing or participating in an online community to collect data.
- Internet-mediated observation may be affected by observer error, observer drift, observer bias and observer effects. The reliability and validity of these data may also be affected by the scope of the online community and the nature of data from Internet-mediated observation.
- Video recordings, audio recordings and static visual images can be used in the collection of observational data.
- Researchers and informants can both create video recordings, audio recordings and visual images in observational research. The recordings or images produced will be transformed into written or numerical data although they may also be treated as visual or audio data in their own right to be used in analysis and as visual representations in the research report.
- There are potential advantages, ethical concerns and data quality issues associated with the use of video recordings, audio recordings and static visual images that need to be evaluated.

Self-check questions

Help with these questions is available at the end of the chapter.

9.1 You are a project manager responsible for the overall management of a large project to introduce your company's technology into the development of a new hospital. Most of the members of your team are from the UK, France and Germany. However, several of the newer engineers are from other EU member states. You notice at project meetings that these engineers tend to be far more reticent than the other team members in volunteering ideas for solving problems.

This issue has coincided with the arrival on the scene of a management student from the local university who is keen to study a real-life management problem for her final-year undergraduate dissertation. You have asked her to study the assimilation experience of these engineers into your company with a view to recommending any changes that may be necessary to change the programme designed to effect the assimilation process.

You ask her to start the research by sitting in on the project team meetings and, in particular, observing the behaviour of these newer engineers. What suggestions would you make to your student to help her structure her observation of the meetings?

9.2 You have been asked to give a presentation to a group of managers at the accountancy firm in which you are hoping to negotiate access for research. You wish to pursue the research question: 'What are the informal rules that govern the way in which trainee accountants work, and how do they learn these rules?'

You realise that talk of 'attempting to learn the trainee accountants' symbolic world' would do little to help your cause with this group of non-research-minded businesspeople. However, you wish to point out some of the benefits to the organisation that your research may yield. Outline what you believe these would be.

9.3 You are a bank branch manager. You feel your staff are too reluctant to generate interest from customers in relation to new accounts that the bank offers. You would like to understand the reasons for their reluctance.

a As the participant observer, how would you go about this?

b How would you record your observations?

9.4 You have been granted access to conduct observation in the department of an organisation where you previously undertook a work placement. You are considering seeking permission to video-record some periods of observation. What issues would be raised by this?

Review and discussion questions

9.5 Compile a behaviour observation sheet similar to that in Box 9.5 in respect of either your job or that of a friend. Use this to compile a record of the behaviours observed.

9.6 Choose an everyday example of social behaviour, such as the way that motorists park their cars in 'open' (not multi-storey) car parks. Observe this behaviour (for example, the distance from the entrance/exit that they park) and draw general conclusions about observed behaviour patterns.

9.7 Video-record a current affairs (or similar) discussion on TV. Initially watch the programme to identify the main categories of behaviour that occur. It may be appropriate to use some of the categories listed in the schedule in Box 9.6. Having developed a draft coding schedule, watch the programme again to record the interactions evident in the discussion and then assess these interaction patterns.

Progressing your research project

Deciding on the appropriateness of observation

- Return to your research question(s) and objectives. Decide how appropriate it would be to use observation as part of your research strategy.
- If you decide that this is appropriate, explain the relationship between your research question(s) and objectives and observation. If you decide that using observation is not appropriate, justify your decision. Respond for each form of observation discussed in this chapter.

- If you decide that one or more of these forms of observation is appropriate, address the following questions for each type of observation that you consider using:
  - What practical problems do you foresee?
  - Which ethical concerns may arise (see Chapter 6)?
  - What threats to data quality are you likely to encounter?
  - How will you attempt to overcome these issues?
- If you decide that structured observation is appropriate, attempt to develop a coding schedule that will be suitable for your research, conduct a pilot test if possible at this stage and amend it if appropriate.
- Use the questions in Box 1.4 to guide your reflective diary entry.

References

Angrosino, M. and Rosenberg, J. (2011) 'Observations on observation: Continuities and challenges', in N.K. Denzin and Y.S. Lincoln (eds) *The Sage Handbook of Qualitative Research* (4th edn). London: Sage, pp. 467–478.

Arnould, E.J. and Cayla, J. (2015) 'Consumer Fetish: Commercial Ethnography and the Sovereign Consumer', *Organization Studies,* Vol. 36, No. 10, pp. 1361–1386.

Basil, M. (2011) 'Use of photography and video in observational research', *Qualitative Market Research: An International Journal,* Vol. 14, No. 3, pp. 246–257.

Brannan, M.J. and Oultram, T. (2012) 'Participant observation', in G. Symon and C. Cassell (eds) *Qualitative Organisational Research Core Methods and Current Challenges.* London: Sage, pp. 296–313.

Clark, A., Holland, C., Katz, J. and Peace, S. (2009) 'Learning to see: lessons from a participatory observation research project in public spaces', *International Journal of Social Research Methodology,* Vol. 12, No. 4, pp. 345–360.

Cunliffe, A.L. (2010) 'Retelling tales of the field: In search of organisational ethnography 20 years on', *Organizational Research Methods,* Vol. 13, No. 2, pp. 224–239.

Gold, R.L. (1958) 'Roles in Sociological Field Observations', *Social Forces,* Vol. 36, No. 3, pp. 217–223.

Hein, W., O'Donohoe, S. and Ryan, A. (2011) 'Mobile phones as an extension of the participant observer's self', *Qualitative Market Research: An International Journal,* Vol. 14, No. 3, pp. 258–273.

Jarzabkowski, P., LeBaron, C., Phillips, K. and Pratt, M. (2014) 'Call for papers; Feature topic: Video-based research methods', *Organizational Research Methods,* Vol. 17, No. 1, pp. 3–4.

Kellard, N., Millo, Y., Simon, J. and Engel, O. (2017) 'Close Communications: Hedge Funds, Brokers and the Emergence of Herding', *British Journal of Management,* Vol. 28, No. 1, pp. 84–101.

Knoblauch, H. (2012) 'Introduction to the special issue of *Qualitative Research*: Video-analysis and videography', *Qualitative Research,* Vol. 12, No. 3, pp. 251–254.

Kozinets, R.V. (2015) *Netnography: Redefined* (2nd edn). London: Sage.

LeCompte, M.D. and Goetz, J.P. (1982) 'Problems of reliability and validity in ethnographic research', *Review of Educational Research,* Vol. 52, No. 1, pp. 31–60.

Luff, P. and Heath, C. (2012) 'Some "technical challenges" of video analysis: Social actions, objects, material realities and the problems of perspective', *Qualitative Research,* Vol. 12, No. 3, pp. 255–279.

Madge, C. (2010) *Online Research Ethics.* Available at http://www.restore.ac.uk/orm/ethics/ethprint3. pdf [Accessed 25 March 2018].

Martinko, M.J. and Gardner, W.L. (1985) 'Beyond Structured Observation: Methodological Issues and New Directions', *Academy of Management Review,* Vol. 10, No. 4, pp. 676–695.

Meyer, A. D. (1991) 'Visual Data in Organizational Research', *Organization Science,* Vol. 2, No. 2, pp. 218–236.

Mintzberg, H. (1973) *The Nature of Managerial Work.* New York: Harper & Row.

Monahan, T. and Fisher, J.A. (2010) 'Benefits of "observer effects": Lessons from the field', *Qualitative Research,* Vol. 10, No. 3, pp. 357–376.

Mueller, S., Volery, T. and von Siemens, B. (2012) 'What do entrepreneurs actually do? An observational study of entrepreneurs' everyday behavior in the start-up and growth stage', *Entrepreneurship Theory and Practice,* Vol. 36, No. 5, pp. 995–1017.

Negrón, R. (2012) 'Audio Recording Everyday Talk', *Field Methods,* Vol. 24, No. 3, pp. 292–309.

Ozanne, J.L., Moscato, E.M., Kunkel, D.R. (2013) 'Transformative Photography: Evaluation and Best Practices for Eliciting Social and Policy Changes', *Journal of Public Policy and Marketing,* Vol. 32, No. 1, pp. 45–65.

Paechter, C. (2013) 'Researching sensitive issues online: Implications of a hybrid insider/outsider position in a retrospective ethnographic study', *Qualitative Research,* Vol. 13, No. 1, pp. 71–86.

Plankey-Videla, N. (2012) 'Informed consent as process: Problematizing informed consent in organizational ethnographics', *Qualitative Sociology,* Vol. 35, pp. 1–21.

Prior, D.D. and Miller, L.M. (2012) 'Webethnography: Towards a typology for quality in research design', *International Journal of Market Research,* Vol. 54, No. 4, pp. 503–20.

Rose, G. (2014) 'On the relation between "visual research methods" and contemporary visual culture', *The Sociological Review,* Vol. 62, No. 1, pp. 24–46.

Spano, R. (2005) 'Potential sources of observer bias in police observational data', *Social Science Research,* Vol. 34, pp. 591–617.

Spradley, J.P. (2016) *Participant Observation.* Long Grove IL: Waveland Press.

Starr, R. and Fernandez, K. (2007) 'The mindcam methodology: Perceiving through the natives eye', *Qualitative Market Research,* Vol. 10, No. 2, pp. 168–82.

Van Maanen, J. (2011) *Tales of the Field: On Writing Ethnography* (2nd edn). Chicago and London: University of Chicago Press.

Waddington, D. (2004) 'Participant observation', in C. Cassell and G. Symon (eds) *Essential Guide to Qualitative Methods in Organizational Research.* London: Sage, pp. 154–164.

Whyte, W.F. (1993) *Street Corner Society: The Social Structure of an Italian Slum.* (4th edn) Chicago: University of Chicago Press.

Zhang, Y., Trusov, M. Stephen, A.T. and Jamal, Z. (2017) 'Online Shopping and Social Media: Friends or Foes?', *Journal of Marketing,* Vol. 81, No. 6, pp. 24–41.

Further reading

Spradley, J.P. (2016) *Participant Observation.* Long Grove IL: Waveland Press. The reissue of this classic text provides a clear and detailed account of the process of participant observation.

Mintzberg, H. (1973) *The Nature of Managerial Work.* New York: Harper & Row. Appendix C has a full account of the methodology that Mintzberg employed. You will be struck by how such a seemingly simple methodology can lead to such important conclusions.

Kozinets, R.V. (2015) Netnography: Redefined (2nd edn). London: Sage. This edition provides a valuable account if you are considering the use of online ethnography/netnography.

Luff, P. and Heath, C. (2012) 'Some "technical challenges" of video analysis: Social actions, objects, material realities and the problems of perspective', *Qualitative Research,* Vol. 12, No. 3, pp. 255–279. If you are thinking of using video in observational research, you should find this article helpful from a technical and methodological perspective.

Negrón, R. (2012) 'Audio Recording Everyday Talk', *Field Methods,* Vol. 24, No. 3, pp. 292–309. If you are thinking of using audio recording in observational research, you should find this article very helpful.

Ozanne, J.L., Moscato, E.M., Kunkel, D.R. (2013) 'Transformative Photography: Evaluation and Best Practices for Eliciting Social and Policy Changes', *Journal of Public Policy and Marketing,* Vol. 32, No. 1, pp. 45–65. This article discusses many aspects related to the use of digital images including the use of video.

Case 9
Observing Religious Tourists

Source: ©2018 Matina Terzidou

Maria has always been interested in the role religion plays in human life and behaviour. Being raised in a family with different religious backgrounds further cultivated this interest. When she was asked to propose a topic for her research project for her MSc programme in Tourism Management, Maria had no doubt that her ideal topic was to investigate how religion influenced people's behaviour whilst on holiday. Tourism and religion after all seemed to have several commonalities, with some tourism spaces allowing for people to express their religiousness, particularly those visited by people who were on pilgrimages. She was convinced that in order to understand the complexity of pilgrims' actions and the link to their religious beliefs, a qualitative method would be most appropriate. Specifically, participant observation would enable her to become aware of how the participants construct and interpret their worlds (Andriotis, 2009; Terzidou et al., 2017). Her closeness would allow her as a researcher to see through the participants' eyes, to understand their conversations as well as to record performances, such as crawling or buying particular religious souvenirs that participants are taking for granted.

Living near a well-known religious site made Maria's decision to select the setting of her study easy. She enthusiastically proposed this to her project tutor who was glad to approve this case. It was only after spending a few days on-site that Maria started realising how inconvenient the place and the particular type of pilgrimage actually was for her research. Most religious tourists to the site were transient and of different religious affiliations to her. In fact, the transient nature of tourism is a problem experienced widely by tourism ethnographers (Schmid, 2008). Pilgrims' intensive and exhausting programme diminishes the quality of the observations as participants are usually too tired and in a rush. After considering all the above issues, Maria decided that the best way to observe pilgrims was to actually travel with them rather than meet them at the destination. Moreover, she decided to travel with pilgrims of her own religious affiliation, arguing that being of similar background would make it easier to engage with them (Andriotis, 2009) and would allow a more thorough understanding of the particular group of believers. With the help of gatekeepers, such as the travel agency's manager and the tour guide, she finally managed to participate in a four-day bus tour to one of the most well-known pilgrimage sites in her country. This she considered would provide sufficient time for observation.

At a second stage Maria realised that gaining access to the group did not automatically mean she had access to the group members themselves. Building trust and rapport was indeed necessary as many pilgrims were initially very suspicious and reluctant with her presence there, especially when she revealed that one of her parents was of different religious affiliation. As she was told later by the tour guide, many pilgrims were afraid due to recent attempts by others to convert them. Maria knew that she had to clearly position herself in the group and, although taking part fully in the pilgrimage, decided to also let the members of the group know she was conducting research. Through such a role, she thought she would be able to minimise reactions due to her presence as an outsider by adjusting to their cultural norms and potentially gaining their trust. Using their language and her inherited knowledge of their religious belief system helped her improve rapport. Maria was able to react immediately to religious social situations, her actions showing marks of habituation, which demonstrated that she belonged to and was one of them. To strengthen this feeling she took part in acts of devotion using material elements such as a rosary that she wore around her hand. The rosary provided a sign of belief that triggered conversations with people as it was positively evaluated.

Maria was also concerned with the problem of reactivity, that is, of people changing their behaviour when they know they are studied. For instance, she noticed that every time she kept notes of events and behaviour and of her reflections on them, participants seemed to be distracted looking at her and somehow stopping their current activities. She knew, however, the importance of keeping a research diary in order to record her observations. After all, Maria was not focusing only on observing specific issues and features but rather had the freedom to note whatever she felt was correct and relevant to her study – her observations encompassing everything that occurred during the trip. She needed to look for suitable times and ways of writing down her observations. She decided not to take notes in front of the participants, even though they knew about her role as a researcher, as she did not want to appear disrespectful as well as wanting to avoid violation of the scene. As soon as she was alone, she made scratch notes in her hidden pocket notebook or on whatever convenient item she could find, such as receipts or postcards (Figure C9.1). She then wrote up observations in detail in her research diary as soon as she returned to her hotel room at the end of the day, making sure she used pseudonyms rather than participants' real names (Figure C9.2).

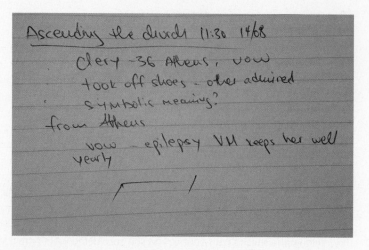

Figure C9. 1 Scratch notes

14 August, 2018, 11:30, upon arrival to the Church of the Annunciation, Tinos

"Upon ascending to the church, we came across Clery, a nice looking 36 year old woman, who joined our group. Once we arrived at the carpet that leads to the church, Clery took off her shoes and continued barefoot. Even though it wasn't so striking in my eyes, (as I compared her to other pilgrims ascending on their bleeding knees), it was for all others, who immediately admired her for this gesture. I assume that it was rather the symbolic meaning it denoted that touched them; the acting different as usual in order to express respect and thankfulness.

In response to their congratulations Clery explained that she came from Athens because of a vow to the Virgin Mary of Tinos. As she said, even though she suffers from epilepsy after an unsuccessful operation, the Virgin Mary keeps her well and she therefore thanks her every year by visiting her."

Figure C9.2 Diary notes

During all this process Maria knew that she had to abide by her university's ethical code. Accordingly, she revealed herself as a researcher to the group at the beginning of the tour, explaining her research intentions and the purpose and scope of her study, and assured the confidentiality of any data collected as well as anonymity, so as to allow the participants to decide whether they would participate or not. She also distributed leaflets with information about her research and her contact details to allow participants to ask questions as well as a consent form to sign, in order to observe only those who wished to participate in the study. To her surprise, while most wanted to participate no one wanted to sign the form. She therefore sought verbal consent and noted where this was given. She realised that while some cultures are familiar with practices like this one, writing one's name or putting a signature on a piece of paper may seem uncommon to some other cultures (Marshall and Rossman, 2006). Some people even felt afraid to participate because of the need to sign a piece of paper. A woman said: "Why should I sign this? For whom is it? What will they do with this form?" (Eleni).

References

Andriotis, K. (2009). Sacred site experience: A phenomenological study, Annals of Tourism Research. 36(1), 64–84.

Marshall, C. and Rossman, G. (2006). Designing Qualitative Research. London: Sage.

Schmid, K. A. (2008). Doing Ethnography of tourist enclaves: Boundaries, ironies, and insights, Tourist Studies. 8(1), 105–121.

Terzidou, M., Scarles, C. and Saunders, M.N.K. (2017). Religiousness as tourist performances: A case study of Greek Orthodox pilgrimage. Annals of Tourism Research, 66, 116–129.

Questions

1 a   What role has Maria adopted in her fieldwork?
   b   Why do you think she has done this?
2 a   What kind of problems did Maria face in gaining physical and subsequently cognitive access of her site/participants?
   b   How did she manage them?
3   What is reactivity and how did Maria minimise it?
4   What issues do Maria's experiences of obtaining consent highlight for researchers?

Additional case studies relating to material covered in this chapter are available via the book's companion website: **www.pearsoned.co.uk/saunders**.
They are:

- Manufacturing in a textile company.
- Customer satisfaction on a long-haul tour holiday.
- Exploring service quality in bank customers' face-to-face experience.
- Online images of tourist destinations.
- Strategy options in a mature market.
- Observing work–life balance in my own organisation.

Self-check answers

9.1   It may be as well to suggest to her that she start her attendance at meetings with an unstructured approach in order to simply get the 'feel' of what is happening. She should make notes of her general impressions of these newer team members' general participation in meetings. She could then analyse these data and develop an observational instrument which could be used in further meetings she attends. This instrument would be based on a coding schedule that allowed her to record, among other things, the amount of contribution by each person at the meeting and the content of that contribution.

Data collection at the meetings does, of course, raise questions of research ethics. In our view, you, as the project manager, should explain to the team the role that the researcher is playing at the meetings. It would be quite truthful to say that the meeting participation of all team members is being observed with the overall purpose of making the meetings more effective, although it need not be emphasised what gave rise to the project manager's initial concern.

9.2   The research question is very broad. It allows you plenty of scope to discover a host of interesting things about the world of the trainee accountant. Without doubt, one of the things you will emerge with a clear understanding of is what they like about their work and what they do not like. This has practical implications for the sort of people that the firm ought to recruit, and how they should be trained and rewarded. You may learn about some of the short cuts practised by all occupations that may not be in the interest of the client. By the same token you will probably discover aspects of good practice that managers can disseminate to other accountants. The list of practical implications is numerous.

All this assumes, of course, that you will supply the managers with some post-research feedback. This does raise issues of confidentiality, which you must have thought through beforehand.

9.3   This is a difficult one. The question of status may be a factor. However, this would depend on your relationship with the staff. If you are, say, of similar age and have an open, friendly, 'one of the team' relationship with them, then it may not be too difficult. The element of threat that would attend a less open relationship would not be present.

You could set aside a time each day to work on the counter in order really to get to know what life is like for them. Even if you have done their job, you may have forgotten what it is like! It may have changed since your day. Direct conversations about account generation would probably not feature in your research times. However, you would need to have a period of reflection after each 'research session' to think about the implications for your research question of what you have just experienced.

9.4   A number of issues may occur that you would need to consider and seek to overcome. You may have enjoyed your work placement and become an accepted member of your workgroup. However, you may find that you are viewed differently when you return as a researcher. As a member of the workgroup, you became an insider and aware of the views of your co-workers. As a researcher, you would be returning as an outsider, although with recollections of having been an insider. This may mean that your former colleagues are more distant than you might expect.

You now wish to return to observe your former colleagues and also to video-record some periods of observation. This will mean that you will need to explain your intentions to those who would be affected by your research and negotiate access at various levels (Chapter 6) in order to be able to collect reliable observational data. This may not be easy to achieve and will in any case be a time-consuming activity. It may be that your former colleagues are very willing to become informants in your observational research and for their work-related activities and interactions to be video-recorded; however, you would not be wise to expect this to be the case without needing to discuss and negotiate this with them.

Where you are able to negotiate access and gain informed consent, you will still need to remain vigilant of the ethical issues that we referred to earlier in this chapter. Observation is an intrusive research method. While there are many potential benefits to be gained from video-recording observations, the use of this method to collect data means that you would be using a very intrusive approach that may inhibit or alter the behaviours of your intended informants. This effect should not be underestimated. In addition, there are technical and practical challenges to video-recording observation. These challenges would require you to develop a sufficient level of competence before embarking on the use of this method to avoid the risk of ending up with poor-quality recorded data.

Get ahead using resources on the companion website at:
www.pearsoned.co.uk/saunders.

- Improve your IBM SPSS Statistics research analysis with practice tutorials.
- Save time researching on the Internet with the Smarter Online Searching Guide.
- Test your progress using self-assessment questions.
- Follow live links to useful websites.

Chapter 10

Collecting primary data using research interviews and research diaries

Learning outcomes

By the end of this chapter you should be:

- able to classify research interviews in order to help you understand the purpose of each type;
- aware of situations favouring the use of particular types of research interview, and the logistical and resource issues that affect their use;
- able to identify potential data quality issues related to the use of research interviews and evaluate how to overcome these;
- able to consider the development of your competence to undertake semi-structured and in-depth research interviews;
- aware of the advantages and disadvantages of using one-to-one and group research interviews, including focus groups, in particular contexts;
- aware of the advantages, disadvantages and mode implications of telephone interviews;
- aware of types of Internet-mediated research interview to be able to evaluate their use;
- aware of the nature of visual interviews and ways to use these;
- able to understand how quantitative and qualitative research diaries may be used to collect primary data;
- aware of the advantages, issues and strategies associated with using research diaries.

10.1 Introduction

The **research interview** is a purposeful conversation between two or more people, during which the interviewer asks concise and unambiguous questions and listens attentively to the interviewee talking. Such interviews rely on establishing some level of rapport between the interviewer and the interviewee. By listening carefully to an interviewee, an interviewer will be able to explore points of interest, and clarify and confirm meanings. The use of research interviews

can help you to gather valid and reliable data that are relevant to your research question(s) and objectives. Research interviews can also be used to help you refine your ideas where you have not yet fully formulated a research question and objectives.

We considered how objective and subjective perspectives inform opposing views about the nature of reality (Section 4.2). This distinction may be applied to approaches to research

Journalists' interviewing skills

Interviews occur constantly. Every day there is scope to watch and listen to interviews, or to read about them. Interviews of all sorts occur, such as those related to business, jobs, celebrities, the arts, current events and news stories. Interviews may be accessed online, in newspapers and on television and radio programmes. Every time an event happens, those who witness it, those who are involved in it and those

who have some expertise associated with it will be interviewed. However, despite the seeming ease with which interviews may be conducted, their conduct requires considerable skill.

One profession that relies on good-quality interviewing skills is journalism. The BBC Academy outlines a number of key interviewing skills on its website. Interviewers need to think clearly about the purpose of each interview and to be aware that their first question will set the direction of an interview and establish its style. Think of the interview style of a 'hard' interviewer you have seen or heard and contrast that with the style of a 'friendly, inviting' interviewer! Interviewers also need to be clear in the way they ask questions and not to be obscure or to use jargon. One key way to realise clarity is to achieve simplicity. This means finding ways to ask questions about complex issues that are simple

and direct. Interviewers should also ask questions that are appropriate. Open questions invite interviewees to describe or explain, or to develop a previous answer. Closed questions seek straightforward answers, like 'yes' or 'no'. In journalism, this type of question can be used to get to the heart of a particular matter and for this reason it is often called the 'killer' question. Where an interviewee wants to avoid directly answering such a question, its use will expose this reluctance to give a straightforward answer. The use of a 'killer' question isn't likely to be appropriate in business and management research interviewing, but the skills outlined on the BBC Academy website related to journalistic interviewing (2014) are likely to be helpful to business and management researchers. This website contains video guides that you can access to watch highly skilled journalists demonstrating a range of interviewing skills.

interviewing. An objective approach sees the research interview as a method to collect data from interviewees who are treated as witnesses to a reality that exists independently from them. This approach has historical roots in research which used interviews to obtain answers to questions that were largely treated as being factual. In this way, the research interview was seen as being fairly unproblematic and an effective means to gather data, providing that access to appropriate participants could be gained. The problem with this approach is that it only seeks answers rather than trying to understand the views and culture of interviewees, as social actors who interact with, interpret and create their social world as well as being shaped by it. A subjective approach is linked to the perspective that views about the social world are socially constructed. This approach sees interview data as being socially constructed; co-produced on the one hand by the views and interpretations of the participant and on the other hand by the interviewer, who asks questions, responds to the participant's views and interprets the resulting data during data analysis (Denzin 2001; Heyl 2005). It recognises the central role of the interviewer in the process of constructing meaning and the need for reflexivity, to reflect on and evaluate his or her approach to interviewing. These two approaches to interviewing indicate a distinct contrast in philosophy, purpose and style.

The research interview is a general term for several types of interview. This is important, since the nature of any interview should be consistent with your research question(s) and objectives, the purpose of your research and the research strategy that you have adopted. We provide an overview of types of research interview in the next section (Section 10.2) and show how each type is related to a research purpose. Our main focus in this chapter is on semi-structured and in-depth research interviews, with structured interviews (based on the use of researcher- or interviewer-completed questionnaires) also being discussed in Chapter 11. Section 10.3 considers situations favouring the use of semi-structured and in-depth interviews. Section 10.4 identifies data quality issues associated with their use and discusses how to overcome these. Section 10.5 discusses preparing for semi-structured and in-depth interviews and Section 10.6 their conduct. Section 10.7 considers logistical and resource issues and how to manage these.

Semi-structured and in-depth interviews can be conducted in different ways: face-to-face, by telephone and via the Internet. These interviews may also be conducted on a one-to-one or group basis. Interviews may rely on the use of talk or they may also involve visual images during their conduct. Sections 10.8 to 10.11 discuss these different ways or modes of conducting research interviews. These comprise group interviews and focus groups (Section 10.8), telephone interviews (Section 10.9), Internet-mediated (electronic) interviews (Section 10.10), and visual interviews (Section 10.11).

This chapter also considers the use of both quantitative and qualitative research diaries to collect primary data (Section 10.12).

10.2 Types of research interview and their link to the purpose of research and research strategy

Types of research interview

Research interviews may be classified into different types. These types are more than just labels as they help you to choose the most appropriate sort of interview for your research purpose. We discuss a number of interview typologies here. These relate to the:

- level of standardisation or structure in the research interview;
- number of participants and interview modes.

We consider these in turn.

Level of standardisation or structure in the research interview

One commonly used typology differentiates between standardised interviews and non-standardised interviews. Another commonly used typology differentiates between structured interviews, semi-structured interviews and unstructured interviews. These typologies overlap: standardised interviews and structured interviews refer to the same type; while non-standardised interviews may be divided into semi-structured and unstructured interviews (Figure 10.1). We use the three-fold typology of structured, semi-structured and unstructured to describe the nature of, and differences between, research interviews.

Structured interviews

Structured interviews are conducted using researcher-completed questionnaires. As we discuss in Section 11.2, questionnaires are 'standardised' because they are based on a predetermined set of identical questions. If you use a structured interview, you read out each question from the questionnaire exactly as it is written and in the same tone of voice so that you do not indicate any bias. Then you record the response on a standardised schedule, usually with pre-coded answers (Sections 11.4 and 12.2). As structured interviews are used to collect quantifiable data they are also referred to as 'quantitative research interviews'.

Semi-structured interviews

By comparison, semi-structured and unstructured interviews are 'non-standardised'. These are often referred to as 'qualitative research interviews'.

In **semi-structured interviews** you start with a predetermined list of themes, and possibly some key questions related to these themes, to guide the conduct of each interview. How you use this predetermined list of themes will depend on your philosophical assumptions. Where you adopt the stance of the realist you will believe that there is a truth waiting to be discovered that is external to the interpretations of your participants (Sections 4.2 and 4.4). In this case, you will use a more structured and consistent approach to conduct semi-structured interviews in which you systematically explore each theme with every participant. This will allow you to compare your participants' responses to each theme to identify the underpinning reality that you seek to reveal.

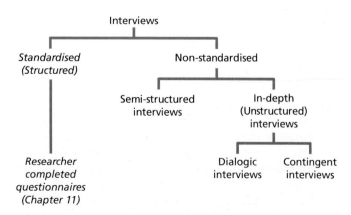

Figure 10.1 Interview structures

Where you adopt an interpretivist approach (Section 4.4), the way in which you deal with your list of predetermined themes is likely to be more flexible and contingent on what each participant says. In this case, the order in which you ask each participant to address these themes will vary depending on the flow of the conversation and the data shared with you. You may omit a theme or modify your questions about a theme in a particular interview, given the context or some other characteristic that you encounter. On the other hand, new themes to explore may emerge from participants' interpretations or the research setting.

The source of your interview themes will also be likely to affect the nature of the semi-structured interviews you conduct. These themes may be developed from the findings of previously conducted unstructured interviews (discussed later) and possibly from discussions with others such as your colleagues or project tutor. Either of these sources would suggest that you have commenced your research inductively (Section 4.5), possibly where you are using a grounded theory approach (Section 5.8 and Section 13.9) or an inductive (data driven) thematic analysis (Section 13.6), template analysis (Section 13.7) or explanation building approach (Section 13.8). Where you conduct semi-structured interviews based on an inductive approach, you will naturally follow an exploratory and emergent course of action and allow your interview themes to evolve depending on what emerges from the analysis of your data.

If the themes used in your semi-structured interviews are derived from existing theory you will be commencing your data collection deductively, and your intention will be to test this theory in the context of your own research (Section 4.4). In this case, these theoretically-deduced themes will need to be used consistently in each interview, in order to be able to produce comparable and valid data to test the applicability of this theory in your research context. Such theoretically-based semi-structured interviews may be used in conjunction with a theory testing approach to thematic analysis (Section 13.6), template analysis (Section 13.7) or deductive explanation building (Section 13.8).

Where your research commences inductively and you then wish to test a theory or explore a surprising fact that emerges from the data you have already collected and analysed, you will be switching to use a deductive approach. The use of both induction and deduction in your research is associated with an abductive approach (Section 4.5). In this case, you will also need to apply these theoretically-deduced themes in a consistent way in the semi-structured interviews that you subsequently conduct to be able to test the applicability of this emerging theory in the context of these interview settings.

Apart from containing the list of themes and questions to be covered, the interview guide for this type of interview will also be likely to contain some comments to open the discussion, a possible list of prompts to promote and further discussion, and some comments to close it. These are discussed in more detail later. Data from a semi-structured or in-depth interview may be audio-recorded with the consent of the participant or recorded by making notes (Section 10.5).

In-depth interviews

In-depth interviews are informal. They are used to explore in depth a general area in which you are interested. This means that they do not use predetermined and written down themes or questions to structure or guide the course of the interview. Instead, this type of interview is entirely exploratory and emergent. We therefore can also refer to these as **unstructured interviews**. Instead of commencing with predetermined themes or questions, you will be interested to find out which themes emerge from the data you collect from your participants. While you do not commence with predetermined themes or questions to ask in an in-depth interview, you will need to have at least some idea about the topic, event, experience or aspect that you want to explore with a participant. Where necessary you will need to ask questions and use prompts during the course of an in-depth interview but these should emerge from what your interviewee tells you rather than be determined beforehand. You need to ensure that any questions or prompts only emerge from what your interviewee tells you, in order to clarify, probe and explore meanings, not from your own pre-conceived ideas. Use of your pre-conceived ideas to formulate questions risks altering the course of this type of interview and therefore contaminating potential data.

In an in-depth interview, the interviewee is given the opportunity to talk freely about the topic or event being explored or about their experiences, behaviours and beliefs, so this type of interaction is sometimes called non-directive. An in-depth interview may be used for a number of different purposes. It may be used to explore a topic or event, to deconstruct and understand meanings, to generate stories as in a **narrative interview**, to record a life history as in a **biographical interview**, to focus on participants' perceptions by recording their experiences, or some combination of these. It has also been labelled as an **informant interview** since it is the interviewee's perceptions that guide the conduct of the interview and related discussion. In comparison, a **respondent interview** is one where the interviewer exercises greater direction over the interview while allowing the interviewee's opinions to emerge as he or she responds to the questions of the researcher (Powney and Watts 1987).

We have said that an in-depth interview is led by the participant. Despite this there is still scope for some variation during the conduct of these interviews. The conduct of an in-depth interview may be directed almost entirely by the interviewee talking, with the researcher needing to ask very few questions or provide hardly any prompts. Adrian undertook one such interview with the HR director of a large financial services organisation, which required few questions to be asked or prompts to be used but which produced a wealth of relevant and rich data over the course of more than one hour. Alternatively, an in-depth interview may take the form of a dialogue, albeit one in which the interviewee is the principal speaker and the interviewer focuses on asking spontaneous questions and using prompts that stem from what the interviewee says, to encourage her or him to talk further. While a semi-structured interview involves more predetermined structure before it commences, indicating a respondent interview, there is also scope for its direction by either the interviewer or interviewee to vary considerably. In practice then, in-depth and semi-structured interviews refer to two distinct but not entirely singular types, indicating some scope for variation within each type.

We consider two such variants now, which in some respects may be seen to contrast with one another. Both of these commence as in-depth interviews and seek to establish rapport, but their respective purpose is very different. These are dialogic interviews and convergent interviews. We start by outlining a dialogic interview (Way et al. 2015).

Dialogic interviews

The term 'dialogic' relates to dialogue. In our context a dialogue refers to discussion. In a **dialogic interview** the interviewer works to establish rapport with the interviewee and to gain her or his trust. If this is achieved the hope is that the interviewee will be willing to engage reflexively to allow a more open discussion to occur in which pre-conceived ideas and beliefs may be evaluated. At first glance this might read like another way to define a conventional in-depth interview – with its emphasis on achieving depth of understanding. However, the purpose of a dialogic interview may be philosophically different.

Many interviewers simply focus on what their interviewees are telling them. This stance assumes that there is a truth waiting to be discovered and reported (as we also noted earlier). This is the objective assumption of the positivist or realist (Section 4.2). Attention in this approach is likely to be focused on the empirical – what has been observed or experienced. The positivist or realist interviewer simply focuses on recording events and how these were experienced by participants. However, if you are interested in understanding how meanings are socially constructed, a dialogic interview possibly offers a more appropriate approach. Reflexive engagement by the interviewee may help you explore his or her underlying assumptions and beliefs. If achieved, this should help you explore how meanings are socially constructed and understood.

To try to achieve this approach, Way et al. say that it is important to devote time to research participants to develop their trust, and to show curiosity towards them within the context of the research topic. Dialogic interviewing may occur in a situation where the interviewer and participant engage with one another in an open dialogue in which the interviewer is non-critical and accepting and the participant freely reflects on and questions her or his own assumptions and beliefs. No attempt should be made to try to force or cajole participants to engage in this approach. Way et al. also say that researchers wishing to use dialogic interviewing must themselves be willing to engage reflexively and question their own assumptions.

Convergent interviews

In comparison, the purpose and process of a **convergent interview** is materially different. This commences as an unstructured, in-depth interview, with the interviewer also seeking to develop rapport. At this point, the interviewee is given the opportunity to talk freely in relation to the topic area being explored. This is an informant interview, where its conduct is directed by the interviewee talking, with the researcher asking few questions or providing hardly any prompts. However, later in the interview, or more likely, in a subsequent interview(s), more specific and focused probing questions are used. At this stage, the interview becomes more like a respondent one. These more specific and focused probing questions are used to test an emerging theory or refine a developing explanation that is grounded in the data generated through the initial exploratory interview stage (Dick 2013). This is the notion of convergence in this approach, where the interviewing process is used to converge on an explanation or grounded theory.

Dick (2013) refers to convergence interviewing as a package or a process. In this view, it is more than just a way to conduct an interview or series of interviews. Integral to this process of starting with unstructured interviewing and developing more specific and focused questions to converge on an explanation or theory, is the analysis of data. Analysis of data from an interview is used to develop and refine probing questions, and current data are also compared to previous data to develop questions and move towards an emergent explanation or theory. This may be seen as similar to a grounded theory approach, albeit that it does not suggest anything like the same level of procedural specificity (Sections 5.8 and 13.9). The process outlined by Dick also provides guidance for sampling when convergent interviewing is used, based on the idea of using maximum variation sampling (Section 7.3).

The process of convergence interviewing outlined here may be a quick method to converge on key aspects in an emergent research project; it stresses the importance of the interactive relationship between data collection and analysis and suggests an efficient way to do this; and it provides a means to reach a conclusion in the research process (Williams and Lewis 2005). However, a quick (or even premature) focus on particular issues may unduly limit the scope of the research project, lead to bias and affect the generalisability or transferability of the research findings (Williams and Lewis 2005). Convergence interviewing as outlined here may be appropriate to use in a specific organisational context, possibly as part of the approach used in an Action Research strategy (Section 5.8), but its capacity for theory building may be limited.

It is worth noting that many research designs that use interviews commence by using in-depth interviews during an exploratory and emergent stage and later use semi-structured interviews to examine possible relationships between themes that have emerged from the analysis of data from the first stage of in-depth interviews. Within these, convergence is used as part of a wider strategic goal to build well-grounded theories, or to test extant theories (Section 2.4).

Scope for informal and unstructured interviews in participatory research designs

While unstructured interviews are informal in the sense that questions emerge rather than being predetermined and written down beforehand, in most research designs these interviews will nevertheless be pre-arranged so that the interviewer and interviewee agree to meet in a particular place at the specific time for an agreed period. This suggests a formal arrangement to an informal process.

In other research designs, such as those where you participate in the research setting rather than just enter it to conduct a pre-arranged interview or number of interviews, your scope to conduct interviews more spontaneously will be increased. Such participatory research designs include using participant observation (Section 9.3) or action research (Section 5.8). Your scope to conduct interviews more spontaneously may also be related to your role as an internal or practitioner researcher (Section 5.12). In each of these situations you may have scope to conduct unstructured interviews more opportunistically and spontaneously as well as informally.

In this way, as participant researcher or practitioner researcher you can listen to talk, engage in talk and have informal conversations, as well as pre-arrange interviews. Where you engage in participant observation or use an action research strategy, you should also benefit from being immersed in the research setting to witness and participate in natural, authentic conversations. Each of these may be recalled and written down to create research data.

Number of participants and interview modes

We can also differentiate types of research interview by number of participants and the modes used to conduct them.

One-to-one interviews

Interviews may be conducted on a one-to-one basis, between you and a single participant. As we go on to outline, such one-to-one interviews may be conducted in person, through a face-to-face interview, over the telephone, or as an Internet-mediated interview (Figure 10.2).

One-to-many interviews

There may be other situations where you conduct a semi-structured or in-depth research interview with a small number of participants to explore an aspect of your research through a group discussion that you facilitate. As we will outline, such one-to-many interviews may be conducted in person, through a face-to-face interview, or as an Internet-mediated interview (Figure 10.2).

Two-to-many interviews

In some circumstances, two interviewers may conduct an interview, such as in the case of a group interview, where one interviewer leads the discussion and the other acts as principal note taker.

Face-to-face interviews

A frequently used way to conduct a research interview is to meet your participant in person, often referred to as a 'face-to-face' interview. An advantage of this mode is that you meet each of your research participants and have the opportunity to build rapport while allaying any concerns that participants may have about sharing data with you. A face-to-face interview may encourage open discussion, leading to data that are rich and free from bias, given the scope to explore and check understandings during this meeting.

Telephone and Internet-mediated interviews

There may be some situations where you conduct an interview by telephone or using the Internet. It may be more convenient or appropriate for interviews to be conducted through one of these means for some or all of your participants. Distances between you and your participants may mean that using one of these means is the only feasible way to conduct interviews. Use of the telephone is likely to be associated with a one-to-one interview; while Internet-mediated interviews may be conducted on a one-to-one or one-to-many basis (Figure 10.2). Section 10.9 considers telephone interviews and Section 10.10 discusses Internet-mediated interviews.

Group interviews

We have referred to situations where a number of participants take part in a group discussion (as in one-to-many or two-to-many). These are referred to as group interviews. In particular situations it will be advantageous to interview participants together. Two different types of group interview exist. One type is referred to as a group interview and the other as a focus group (Figure 10.2). These titles are sometimes used interchangeably, although this should be avoided as each have a distinct purpose. Section 10.8 considers the advantages and issues related to the use of group interviews and focus groups.

The number of participants and modes of interview are summarised in Figure 10.2.

Visual interviews

A further interview mode can be differentiated related to the use of visual images. In Section 9.6, we discussed the use of visual images in relation to observation research and noted that images may also be used in research interviews. Visual images may be used in face-to-face interviews and in some group interviews, including focus groups. Section 10.11 discusses the nature of visual interviews and introduces ways to use these.

Links to the purpose of research and research strategy

Each type of research interview outlined above has a distinct purpose. Structured, standardised interviews are normally used to gather data which will then be the subject of quantitative analysis (Chapter 12), for example as part of a survey strategy. Semi-structured and in-depth interviews are used to gather data which are normally analysed qualitatively (Chapter 13), for example as part of a case study or Grounded Theory strategy. These data are likely to be used not only to understand the 'what' and the 'how', but also to place more emphasis on 'why'.

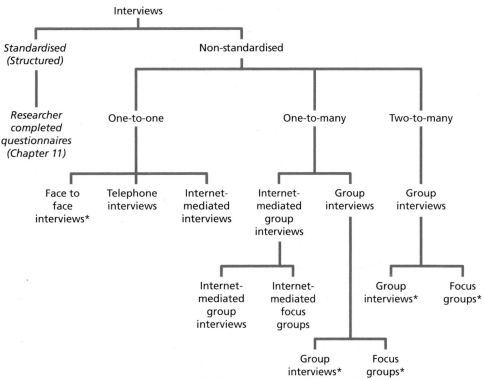

*Visual images may be used in these modes of interviewing, such interviews being known collectively as 'visual interviews

Figure 10.2 Number of participants and interview modes

In Chapter 5 we outlined how the purpose of your research may be classified as either exploratory, descriptive, explanatory or evaluative (Section 5.7). Different types of interview may be used to gather data for each kind of study.

- In an exploratory study, in-depth interviews can be very helpful to find out what is happening and to understand the context. Semi-structured interviews may also be used in an exploratory study. Both of these types of interview may provide important background or contextual material for your study. You will find it helpful to conduct exploratory, qualitative interviews where your research design adopts an inductive approach, such as in the development of grounded theory (Sections 4.3 and 5.8).
- In a descriptive study, structured interviews (Section 11.2) can be used to identify general patterns. You may find it helpful to conduct structured interviews where your research design uses a deductive approach to test a theory, as the standardised nature of the data will make it easier to test statistical propositions or hypotheses (Chapter 12).
- In an explanatory study, semi-structured interviews may be used to understand relationships between variables, such as those revealed from a descriptive study (Section 5.7). Structured interviews may also be used in relation to an explanatory study, in a statistical sense (Section 12.5). Research interviews used for an explanatory purpose may be useful in both inductive and deductive approaches because of the intention to explain why relationships exist (Section 2.4).
- In an evaluative study, you may find it useful to use one type of interview, or a combination of types, depending on the nature of your study. In many cases, semi-structured interviews may be used to understand the relationships between your evaluation or effectiveness criteria. Research interviews used for an evaluative purpose may be useful in either an inductive or deductive approach (Section 2.4).

Table 10.1 Uses of different types of interview for each research purpose

	Exploratory	Descriptive	Explanatory	Evaluative
Structured		✓✓	✓	✓
Semi-structured	✓		✓✓	✓✓
Unstructured	✓✓			✓

✓✓ = more frequent, ✓ = less frequent

This is summarised in Table 10.1.

Your research may incorporate more than one method of data collection, as in mixed methods (Section 5.6). As part of a survey strategy, for example, you may decide to use in-depth or semi-structured interviews initially to help identify the questions that should be asked in a researcher-completed questionnaire. The data that you gather from such exploratory interviews will be used in the design of your questionnaire. Alternatively, semi-structured interviews may be used as part of a mixed methods design to explore, explain or validate themes that have emerged from the use of a questionnaire (Teddlie and Tashakkori 2009). Different types of interview question may also be used within one interview. For example, one section of an interview may be composed of a set of questions with pre-specified responses, while another section may use semi-structured questions to explore responses.

We can therefore see that the various types of interview have a number of potentially valuable uses in terms of undertaking your research project. The key is to ensure consistency between your research question(s) and objectives, the strategy you will employ and the methods of data collection you will use.

10.3 When to use semi-structured and in-depth interviews

There are many situations in which collecting data using a semi-structured or in-depth research interview may be advantageous. These situations can be grouped into four categories:

- the purpose of the research;
- the importance of establishing personal contact;
- the nature of the data collection questions;
- length of time required and completeness of the process.

We examine each of these in turn.

The purpose of the research

Where you are undertaking an exploratory study, or a study that includes an exploratory element, it is likely that you will include in-depth or semi-structured interviews in your design. Similarly, an explanatory study is also likely to include interviews in order for the researcher to be able to infer causal relationships between variables (Sections 2.4 and 11.4). Where it is necessary for you to understand the reasons for the decisions that your participants have taken, or to understand the reasons for their attitudes and opinions, you are likely to need to conduct an in-depth or semi-structured interview.

Semi-structured and in-depth interviews also provide you with the opportunity to 'probe' a response, where you want your interviewees to explain, or build on, their previous answers. This is important if, for example, you are adopting an interpretivist philosophy, where you will be concerned to understand the meanings that participants ascribe to various phenomena (Section 4.4). Interviewees may use words or ideas in a particular way, and the opportunity to probe these meanings will add significance and depth to the data you obtain. They may also lead the discussion into areas that you had not previously considered but which are significant for your understanding, and which help you to address your research question and objectives, or indeed help you formulate such a question. Interviews also afford each interviewee an opportunity to hear herself or himself 'thinking aloud' about things she or he may not have previously thought about. The result should be that you are able to collect a rich and detailed set of data. However, you need to be aware that the manner in which you interact with your interviewees and ask questions will impact on the data you collect.

The importance of establishing personal contact

We have found that managers and employees are more likely to agree to be interviewed, rather than complete a questionnaire, especially where the interview topic is seen to be interesting and relevant to their current work. An interview provides them with an opportunity to reflect on events without needing to write anything down. This situation also provides the opportunity for interviewees to receive feedback and personal assurance about the way in which their data will be used (Sections 6.2 and 6.5).

Potential respondents who receive a questionnaire via the Internet or through the post may be reluctant to complete it for a number of reasons. They may feel that it is not appropriate to provide sensitive and confidential data to someone they have never met. They may also not completely trust the way in which the data are to be used. They may be reluctant to spend time providing written explanatory answers, where these are requested, especially if the meaning of any question is not entirely clear. The use of personal interviews, where appropriate, may therefore achieve a higher response rate than using questionnaires (Sections 7.2 and 7.3). Where a questionnaire is received by a manager who is not inclined to complete it, it may also be passed to another person to complete, which will adversely affect your control over those whom you wish to answer your questions and also possibly the reliability of the data that you receive.

The nature of the data collection questions

An in-depth or semi-structured interview is likely to be the most advantageous approach to attempt to obtain data in the following circumstances:

- where there are a large number of questions to be answered;
- where the questions are either complex or open ended;
- where the order and logic of questioning may need to be varied (Box 10.1).

Length of time required and completeness of the process

Often the complexity of issues to be covered or their number and variety mean that an interview is the best or only means of collecting data. In our experience, where expectations have been established clearly about the length of time required and participants understand and agree with the objectives of the research interview, they have generally been willing to agree to be interviewed. Some negotiation is, in any case, possible and the interview can be arranged at a time when the interviewee will be under least pressure.

We have found that our participants tend to be generous with their time, and sometimes when interviews have been organised to start at mid-morning they will arrange for lunch,

Box 10.1
Focus on student research

The need to vary the order and logic of questioning

Val undertook a series of semi-structured interviews into the approach used to manage public relations (PR) activities in 30 organisations. It soon became evident that it would not be meaningful to ask exactly the same questions in each organisation. For example, some organisations had centralised PR as part of the marketing function, whereas in other organisations it was devolved to individual business units. Another significant variable was associated with the public-relations styles adopted. Some organisations adopted a 'press agency' approach where the main focus was to get the organisation or product mentioned in the media as often as possible, the nature of the mention being of secondary importance. Others adopted a 'public information' approach where the main aim was to get media exposure for the organisation or product.

The impact of these and other variables meant that it was not sensible to ask exactly the same questions at each interview, even though many questions remained applicable in all cases and the underlying intention was to ensure consistency between interviews. It was not until each interview had started that Val was able to learn which of these different variables operated within the particular organisation. Fortunately, the flexibility offered by the use of semi-structured interviews enabled her to do this.

which can allow the discussion and exploration of issues to continue. However, for those of you who fancy a free lunch, we do not want to raise your expectations falsely, and the start time for an interview should not be set with this in mind!

Your aim will be to obtain data in relation to each question you ask, allowing for the right of a research participant not to answer any interview question which they wish to pass over. Where you conduct the interaction skilfully an interview is more likely to achieve this than the use of a self-completed or interviewer-completed questionnaire. Where your participant does not provide an answer to a particular question or questions in an in-depth or semi-structured interview, you are likely to have some idea why a response was not provided. This may even lead you to modify the question or to compose another where this would be appropriate. Section 6.6 considers the ethical issues associated with seeking to obtain answers.

Situations are likely to occur where you will consider the choice between using research interviews and other qualitative methods such as observation (Chapter 9). In this regard, a distinction has been made between contrived and natural data. **Natural** or naturally occurring **data** are those observed from real conversations that take place in everyday, authentic situations. **Contrived data** are those that result from a researcher organising an experiment, interview or survey (Speer 2008). One type of data is not necessarily superior to the other, but where it is possible, data collected naturally may be more authentic and reliable. Speer (2008) recognises that for some research topics there are reasons why it is not possible to collect observed, natural data. These reasons relate to the taken-for-granted assumptions, sensitivity and hidden nature of some social phenomena (such as in personal relationships) that mean it is difficult to gain access to and observe these in action. Using interviews to explore such phenomena means that you are able to gain access to authentic accounts that you would not be able to observe in action. As a result, the distinction between natural and contrived data may be too rigid (Speer 2008). It should, however, help you to think about the nature of your research topic and then to consider how best to attempt to gain access to your informants (Chapter 9), participants or respondents (Chapter 11).

Box 10.2 provides a checklist to help you in your deliberations about whether or not to use in-depth or semi-structured interviews.

Box 10.2
Checklist

To help you decide whether to use in-depth or semi-structured interviews

✔ Is your research exploratory or explanatory?
✔ Will it help to be able to probe interviewees' responses to build on or seek explanation of their answers and meanings?

✔ Will it help to seek personal contact in terms of gaining access to participants and their data?
✔ Are your data collection questions large in number, complex or open-ended?
✔ Will there be a need to vary the order and logic of questioning?
✔ Will the data collection process with each individual involve a relatively lengthy period?
✔ Will interviews allow you to reveal and explore social phenomena that you would not be able to observe in action?

10.4 Data quality issues associated with semi-structured and in-depth interviews

Data quality issues

Before discussing how to prepare for and conduct semi-structured or in-depth interviews we consider data quality issues associated with these types of research interview. This is because your preparation for and conduct of these interviews will be influenced by the need to ensure data quality. We introduced this in Section 5.11 and the issues we discuss here that impact on semi-structured and in-depth interviews are related to:

- reliability/dependability;
- forms of bias;
- cultural differences;
- generalisability/transferability;
- validity/credibility.

The lack of standardisation in semi-structured and in-depth interviews can lead to concerns about reliability/dependability (Section 5.11 and in particular Table 5.7). In relation to qualitative research, this is concerned with whether alternative researchers would reveal similar information. The concern about reliability/dependability in these types of interview is also related to issues of bias. There are three types of potential bias to consider. The first of these is related to **interviewer bias**. This is where the comments, tone or non-verbal behaviour of the interviewer creates bias in the way that interviewees respond to the questions being asked. This may be because you attempt to impose your own beliefs and frame of reference through the questions that you ask. It is also possible that you will demonstrate bias in the way you interpret responses. Where you are unable to gain interviewees' trust, or perhaps where your personal credibility is seen to be lacking, the value of the data given may also be limited, raising doubts about its validity and reliability.

Related to this is **interviewee** or **response bias**. This type of bias can be caused by interviewees' perceptions about the interviewer, or perceived interviewer bias. However, the cause of this type of bias may not be linked to perceptions of the interviewer. Taking part in an interview is an intrusive process. This is especially true in the case of in-depth or semi-structured interviews, where your aim will be to explore events or to seek explanations. An interviewee may, in principle, be willing to participate but still be sensitive to the unstructured exploration of certain themes. Interviewees may therefore choose not to reveal and discuss an aspect of a topic that you wish to explore, because this would lead to probing questions that would intrude on sensitive information that they do not wish, or are not empowered, to discuss with you. The outcome of this may be that the interviewee provides only a partial 'picture' of the situation that casts himself or herself in a 'socially desirable' role, or the organisation for which they work in a positive or even negative fashion.

Bias may also result from the nature of the individuals or organisational participants who agree to be interviewed (Box 10.3). This is called **participation bias**. The amount of time required for an interview may result in a reduction in willingness to take part by some. This may bias your sample from whom data are collected. This is an issue that you will need to consider carefully and attempt to overcome through the approach taken to sampling (Sections 7.2 and 7.3).

Further concerns may arise from cultural differences between the interviewer and intended interviewees. Gobo (2011) sees the research interview as the product of individualistic societies, which may not be so well suited to societies and participants with a different cultural orientation. He argues that the research interview makes certain assumptions:

- that it is acceptable to discuss issues with outsiders;
- that issues may be considered public and able to be discussed rather than being kept private and restricted;
- that it is permissible for a person to hold independent views and to speak as an individual.

Gobo also refers to societies where there may be a tendency to respond to an interviewer's questions by only being positive or by agreeing.

The cultural differences that an interviewer has to cope with may be more subtle. Court and Abbas (2013) provide an account of a cross-cultural interview they conducted with two Israeli Druze women. One of the researchers is a Canadian woman, living in Israel, who speaks English and Hebrew; the other researcher is an Israeli Druze woman, who speaks Hebrew and Arabic. The interview they conducted yielded valuable data for their research, but their reflections about it reveal issues related to language and cultural nuances. Because one of the researchers shared a similar cultural background to that of the participants, she was able to interact with them and develop a rapport that helped to facilitate the interview to a greater extent than the other researcher. Cultural differences

Box 10.3
Focus on student research

Willingness (or otherwise) to be interviewed

Saffron's research project involved her interviewing people about their perceptions of the real benefits of different hair products. She decided that the best way to conduct these interviews was, with the permission of the owner, to interview customers at her local hairdresser. Saffron discovered that although some of the customers were willing to be interviewed, others were not. A minority of customers, often smartly dressed in business suits, refused outright, saying that they had insufficient time. In contrast, others, particularly pensioners, were happy to answer her questions in considerable detail and appeared to wish to prolong the interview.

may affect what the interviewee is willing to say, how the researcher interprets the interviewee's words and meanings, or fails to understand these, and influence the questions that the interviewer asks. Although this research is not related to business and management, it emphasises how cultural differences can impact on the scope to collect data and the implications of operating as either a cultural insider or outsider.

An issue is often raised about the generalisability/transferability of findings from qualitative research interviews, although the validity/credibility of the data they produce is generally seen to be less of an issue (Section 5.11 and in particular Table 5.7). Generalisability/transferability refers to the extent to which the findings of a research study are applicable to other settings. This may be questioned in relation to the statistical generalisability of qualitative research studies where these are based on a small sample. However, this should not be interpreted as meaning that a qualitative study is intrinsically less valuable than a quantitative study. As we noted in Section 10.2, such studies are more likely to be used to explore and explain and provide insights that can be used to develop theory, rather than to provide statistical generalisations. Validity/credibility refers to the extent to which the researcher has gained access to a participant's knowledge and experience, and is able to infer meanings that the participant intends from the language used by that person. The scope to explore meanings during a semi-structured or in-depth interview may help to enhance the validity/credibility of the data collected, although forms of bias and cultural differences may impair this outcome.

Overcoming data quality issues

Reliability/dependability

One response to the issue of reliability/dependability (Section 5.11 and in particular Table 5.7) in relation to findings derived from using in-depth or semi-structured interviews is that these are not necessarily intended to be repeatable since they reflect reality at the time they were collected, in a situation which may be subject to change. The assumption behind this type of research is that the circumstances to be explored are complex and dynamic. The value of using in-depth or semi-structured interviews is derived from the flexibility that you may use to explore the complexity of the topic. Therefore, an attempt to ensure that qualitative, non-standardised research could be replicated by other researchers would not be realistic or feasible without undermining the strength of this type of research.

However, where you use this approach you should explain your research design, the reasons underpinning the choice of strategy and methods, and how the data were obtained. This will be needed by others to understand the processes you used and your research findings. The use of in-depth or semi-structured interviews should not lead to a lack of rigour in relation to the research process – rather there is a need to use a rigorous design and ensure your explanation of how the data were obtained and analysed provides sufficient detail to show your findings are dependable.

Interviewer and interviewee bias

Overcoming these forms of bias is related to the ways in which these types of interview are prepared for (Section 10.5 and Box 10.6) and conducted (Section 10.6 and Box 10.11).

Cultural reflexivity and participatory research

As we discussed earlier, where your research involves interviewing participants from a different culture, whether this is in a cross-national or multicultural setting, you will need to ensure that you minimise any form of bias or threat to reliability. Cultural reflexivity may be helpful in your preparation. As we noted in Section 2.1, the foundation of reflexivity involves reflecting critically on your role as researcher – for example, what motivates you to research a particular topic; why have you chosen your research strategy and methods to collect data; evaluating how you can conduct your research project in an unbiased and meaningful way; how you interact with your participants.

Cultural reflexivity will involve you reflecting on the nature of the relationship between you and your intended participants and how differing and similar cultural customs may affect your interactions (Court and Abbas 2013). Prior to interviewing, you may wish to visit a workplace and observe, listen or participate in informal conversations so that you become more familiar with the research setting. Such understandings will help you to develop rapport with those whom you wish to interview and to gain their acceptance.

Cultural reflexivity will also involve you considering how to engage your participants and involve them. This is likely to include evaluating how best to conduct interviews: whether to conduct these individually or on a group basis; choosing the most appropriate level of structure and formality to use; and whether to attempt to gather data in a single interview or in more than one to develop rapport and understanding. It may also be appropriate to use an informal conversational approach, rather than too many interviewer-led questions. A series of discussions may be helpful to develop rapport, understanding and to involve your participants in the process of interpreting, exploring, confirming and analysing data and meanings in a cultural context. Adopting a culturally reflexive approach may help to overcome cultural differences that affect what is discussed and not discussed, clarify what is important and what is not, and reveal what should be followed up and explored.

One way to achieve cultural contact is, where feasible, to engage in participatory forms of research. In Section 5.8 we outlined two such participatory strategies: ethnography and Action Research. Ethnography involves participation by a researcher in the research setting over time in order to begin to understand the context, develop rapport and be accepted into that community. Using this strategy to immerse yourself in a cultural context may help you to achieve greater acceptance and access to meanings, in comparison to the realist interviewer who seeks to rush in, collect some data and leave with whatever she or he expected to find, irrespective of the expectations of those being interviewed! Action Research is an emergent and iterative process of inquiry designed to develop solutions to real organisational problems through a participative and collaborative approach (Section 5.8). Neither of these research strategies may be appropriate to your research project, although both suggest that participation in the research setting may help to alleviate cultural differences.

Generalisability/transferability

Earlier we stated that a concern may be raised about the generalisability of findings from qualitative research using only one case or a small number of cases. A number of different responses can be made regarding this concern.

The first of these involves examining the nature of the single case or limited number of cases being used. Although you may be basing your research on a single case study, such as your employing organisation, within this case you may be planning to interview a wide cross-section of participants. This allows you to collect data from a representative sample of those who work in this setting. Alternatively, using a single case may also encompass a number of settings; where for example it involves a study in a large organisation with sites across the country, or even around the world. A well-planned and rigorous qualitative case study may therefore be just as likely to produce valuable findings.

A second response to questions of generalisability is based on the ability of qualitative research to be used to test existing theory, or for an emergent theory to be subsequently discussed in relation to a pre-existing theory. Where you are able to relate your research project to existing theory you will be in a position to demonstrate that your findings have a broader theoretical significance than the case or cases that form the basis of your work. It will be up to you to establish how the findings from your particular case or cases are related to existing theory in order to be able to demonstrate their broader significance. This should allow you to test the applicability of existing theory to the setting(s) that you are examining and where this is found wanting to suggest why. It will also allow theoretical propositions to be advanced that can then be tested in another context.

A third argument focuses on the transferability of a research design, using the definition we outlined of this concept in Table 5.7. In this table, transferability was defined as the need to provide a full description of the research questions, design, context, findings and resulting interpretations in the project report. This allows another researcher to design a similar research project to be used in a different, although suitable, research setting.

However, in seeking to counter arguments about the generalisability/transferability of qualitative research studies using semi-structured or in-depth interviews, it is important to recognise that such studies cannot be used to make statistical generalisations about an entire population (whatever this may be in the context of the research topic) where your data are from a small non-probability sample.

Validity/credibility

Semi-structured and in-depth interviews can achieve a high level of validity/credibility (Section 5.11 and in particular Table 5.7) where conducted carefully using clarifying questions, probing meanings and by exploring responses from a variety of angles or perspectives. The use of questioning in such interviews is discussed in detail in Section 10.6. In Table 5.7 in Section 5.11 we outlined further ways in which credibility may be achieved through using qualitative interviews. Their use should help you to build trust and rapport, collect sufficient data and provide you with the opportunity to ask participants to check these data. Credibility may also be achieved by accounting for negative cases (those that are counter to other cases) during analysis in the explanations you develop and being reflective and reflexive about your research.

10.5 Preparing for semi-structured or in-depth interviews

Like all research methods, the key to a successful interview is careful preparation. When using in-depth or semi-structured interviews, remember the 'five Ps': prior planning prevents poor performance. In particular, we believe it is crucial that you plan precisely how you are going to demonstrate your competence and credibility to obtain the confidence of your interviewees and collect quality data.

In order to ensure data quality, we now consider some key measures that your preparations will need to include. These are:

• your level of knowledge;
• developing interview themes and supplying information to the interviewee before the interview;
• the appropriateness of the intended interview location.

Your level of knowledge

You need to be knowledgeable about the research topic and the organisational or situational context in which the interview is to take place. There is likely to be helpful contextual information available online, which you can locate by visiting appropriate organisational websites, online national, local or specialist news sites and any relevant trade association's website. Organisational websites will often allow you to access company annual reports, other organisation-related and product information, market and financial data and press releases. Research databases providing further access to organisational information relevant to your research are likely to only be accessible through your university's or professional association's online learning resources. You may also find additional helpful contextual information located in your university's library and learning resources (Sections 3.4 to 3.6), such as articles or resources about the organisation that is participating in your research. These searches can reveal a wealth of background information about organisations that allow you to develop a good level of contextual knowledge. The ability to draw carefully on this type of information in the interview should help to demonstrate your credibility, and to allow you to assess the accuracy of responses and encourage the interviewee to offer a more detailed account of the topic under discussion. As you undertake later interviews, you will also be able to draw on the initial analysis that you make of data previously collected.

Successfully interviewing participants from different cultures requires some knowledge about those cultures. Without adequate preparation, there may be misinterpretation because of the cultural differences between the interviewee and the interviewer. An in-depth interview offers the opportunity to explore meanings, including those that may be culturally specific, but you will need to be aware of cultural differences and their implications (see our earlier discussion). Brinkmann and Kvale (2015) highlight some of the verbal and non-verbal cues that may have contrary or different meanings between cultures. For example, answering 'yes' to a question may indicate agreement in some cultures, but in others it may be a way of telling the interviewer that the question has been understood, or in others to recognise its importance. A nod of the head indicates agreement in some cultures but in others it may mean something else. Brinkmann and Kvale (2015) note the importance of being aware of social conventions in a culture in order to understand the way answers are constructed and also not to cause offence. Cultural differences exist not only between countries but between groups, social classes and organisations and some prior knowledge about those you wish to interview will invariably be helpful.

Developing interview themes and supplying information to the interviewee before the interview

Credibility may also be promoted through the supply of relevant information to participants before the interview. Providing participants with a list of the interview themes before the event, where this is appropriate, should help this. This list of themes (Box 10.4) may help to promote validity and reliability because it informs the interviewee about the information you are interested in and provides them with the opportunity to prepare for the interview by assembling supporting organisational documentation from their files. We can testify to this approach and the value of allowing participants to prepare themselves for the discussion in which they are to engage. Access to organisational documentation also allows for triangulation of the data provided (Sections 8.2 and 8.3). Our experience is that participants are generally willing to supply a photocopy or a PDF file of such material,

Box 10.4
Focus on student research

Developing interview themes

Karl was interested in understanding why some employees in his organisation used the IT Help Desk while others did not. This subject was felt to be important in relation to perceptions about service-level agreements, service relationships and service quality. He decided to provide his interviewees with a list of themes that he wished to explore during interviews. After some deliberation and reading of

the academic literature he came up with the following list of themes:

- the extent to which employees feel they know when and how to use the IT Help Desk;
- the nature of support employees feel they are receiving;
- the services employees feel the IT Help Desk should be providing;
- the nature of employees' knowledge of service-level agreements;
- the extent to which the IT Help Desk is meeting employees' needs.

He subsequently used this list of themes to develop his interview guide (Box 10.5).

---

although of course it will be necessary to conceal any confidential or personal details in the research report.

Interview themes may be derived from the literature that you read, the theories that you consider, your experience of a particular topic, common sense and discussions with co-workers, fellow students, tutors and research participants, or a combination of these approaches. You will need to have some idea of the theme or themes that you wish to discuss with your participants even if you intend to commence with exploratory, in-depth interviews as part of a Grounded Theory strategy to your research project (Section 5.8).

Without at least some focus, your interview will lack a sense of direction and purpose. You should therefore start with a set of themes that reflect the variables being studied, or at least one or more general questions related to your research topic that you could use to start your interview. These can be incorporated into your interview guide (Box 10.5).

Box 10.5
Focus on student research

Extract from an interview guide

Karl was interested in understanding why some employees in his organisation used the IT Help Desk while others did not. Using his interview themes (Box 10.4), he began to develop his guide:

Help Desk Support

1 To what extent does the IT Help Desk meet your needs?

a *Probe*: In what ways? [ask for real-life examples]
b *Probe*: Can you give me an example (if possible) of when you received good support from the IT Help Desk?
c *Probe*: Can you give me an example (if possible) of when you received insufficient support from the IT Help Desk?

2 Do you consider you have enough support from the IT Help Desk?

a *Probe*: How is this support provided (e.g. telephone, face-to-face)?
b *Probe*: What else (if anything) could usefully be done?

This lists topics that you intend to cover in the interview along with initial questions and probes that may be used to follow up initial responses and obtain greater detail from your participants. When creating your guide, you need to try to ensure that the order of questions is likely to be logical to your participants and that the language you use will be comprehensible. Using your guide, you will be able to develop and/or explore research themes through the in-depth or semi-structured interviews that you conduct to see whether you can identify and test relationships between them (Chapter 13).

Appropriateness of the intended interview location

It is possible that the location where you conduct your interviews will influence the data you collect. As we discussed in Section 6.6, you should choose the location for your interviews with regard to your own personal safety. You should also think about the impact that the location may have upon your participants and the way they respond (Box 10.6). The location should be convenient for your participants, where they will feel comfortable and where the interview is unlikely to be disturbed. Your research interviews may be hosted by an organisation which has granted you access to undertake your research and you will be able to discuss these requirements about safety, convenience, neutrality of the space and not being overheard when talking normally, with the person who makes the arrangements for your interviews (Box 10.6).

You also need to choose a place that is quiet so that outside noise will not reduce the quality of your audio-recording of the interview. Each of us has experienced situations when conducting interviews where noise from outside the building or even from within it has been disruptive. In particular, Mark recalls an interview in a room where noise from building work outside meant that although he was able to hear the participant's responses clearly while the interview was taking place, much of the audio-recording of this interview was unintelligible due to the sound of a very loud pneumatic drill!

In many cases, the interview location will be arranged by those whom you interview. When you interview organisational participants such as managers in their offices, this has the advantage that they are able to find documents which support points they are making.

Box 10.7 provides a checklist of the key points considered in this section to help you to prepare for semi-structured or in-depth interviews.

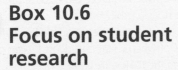

Box 10.6
Focus on student research

Choosing an appropriate location

Anne was pleased that the manufacturing company in which she was undertaking her research had arranged for her to use a room in the Human Resources Department. The room contained a low table and chairs, and she had been provided with bottled water and glasses as well. However, after her third interview she was beginning to doubt her own interviewing skills. Her participants, the company's production line workers, seemed unwilling to be open in their responses. She began to wonder if something was wrong with the interview location and decided to ask the next participant about this. At the end of that interview she had her answer. Her participants were unhappy with the interview location. Prior to being interviewed by Anne, the only time they or their colleagues had visited the Human Resources Department was to receive a reprimand. The location was, therefore, inappropriate!

Box 10.7
Checklist

To help you prepare for your semi-structured or in-depth interview

✔ What level of knowledge about your research topic will be required in order to demonstrate your competence and credibility to gain the confidence of your participants?

✔ What level of knowledge about the research context will be required in order to demonstrate your competence and credibility to gain the confidence of your participants?

✔ What level of knowledge about the culture of your participants will be required in order to gain their confidence before they are willing to share data?

✔ What will be the broad focus of your in-depth interview, or what are the themes that you wish to explore or seek explanations for during a semi-structured interview?

✔ What type of information, if any, will it be useful to send to each participant prior to the interview?

✔ What did you agree to supply to your participant when you arranged the interview? Has this been supplied?

✔ Have you considered the impact that your interview location may have on participants' responses and for your own personal safety (Box 6.17)?

10.6 Conducting semi-structured or in-depth interviews

This section is about actually conducting semi-structured or in-depth interviews. The aspects we discuss here are intended to avoid forms of bias that would affect the reliability/dependability and validity/credibility of the data produced. These aspects relate to the:

- appropriateness of your appearance at the interview;
- nature of your comments to open the interview;
- approach to questioning;
- appropriate use of different types of questions;
- nature and impact of your behaviour during the interview;
- demonstration of attentive listening skills;
- scope to summarise and test understanding;
- dealing with difficult participants;
- approach to recording data.

We discuss these in turn. Key points are summarised as a checklist at the end of this section (Box 10.12).

Appropriateness of your appearance at the interview

Your appearance may affect the perception of the interviewee. Where this has an adverse effect on your credibility in the view of interviewees, or results in a failure to gain their confidence, the resulting bias may affect the reliability of the information provided. Where appropriate you should consider wearing a similar style of clothing to those to be interviewed, although this may not always be appropriate. For example, your interviewees would not expect you to wear the same work wear that they need to put on to work on the production line. Essentially, this means that you will need to wear clothing that will be generally acceptable for the setting within which the interview is to occur (Box 10.8).

Box 10.8
Focus on student research

Checking out the dress code

Mal arranged to visit the administration centre of a large insurance company on a Friday to conduct a group interview with staff drawn from one of its telephone sales divisions and two one-to-one interviews with senior managers. He felt that it was appropriate to wear fairly 'formal' clothes to match what he thought would be the dress code of the organisation. Indeed, for four days of the working week this assumption would have been appropriate. However, the organisation had recently introduced the practice of not wearing such formal work clothes on Fridays. Thus he found himself the only one dressed formally in the organisation on the day of his visit. Taking lunch proved to be a memorable experience, as he mingled with everyone else dressed in jeans and tee shirts, etc. His 'mistake' proved to be an amusing opening at the start of each interview rather than a barrier to gaining access to participants' data. Indeed, it might not have been appropriate for him to match the 'dress-down' style of participants too closely. Nevertheless, it does provide a useful example of the way in which expectations about appearance are likely to be noticed.

Nature of your comments to open the interview

Where the interviewee has not met you before, the first few minutes of conversation will have a significant impact on the outcome of the interview – again related to the issue of your credibility and the level of the interviewee's confidence. Often such interviews occur in a setting that is unfamiliar to you. Despite this, it is your responsibility to shape the start of the conversation. You will need to explain your research to the participant and, hopefully, gain consent (Section 6.6). As part of this you will need to establish your credibility and gain the interviewee's confidence. During these initial discussions we have found that the interviewee often has some uncertainties about sharing information, and about the manner in which these data may be used. Alternatively, she or he may still need clarification about the exact nature of the data that you wish to obtain. We have found that a pre-prepared participant information sheet (Section 6.6, Box 6.15) and consent form (Section 6.6, Box 6.16) are both extremely helpful in reducing such anxieties. There may also be a degree of curiosity on the part of the interviewee and probably a genuine level of interest in the research, related to the reason why the request to participate was accepted. This curiosity and interest will offer an opening for both parties to start a conversation, probably before the 'intended discussion' commences. You may find it appropriate to follow the initial discussion by demonstrating interest in the interviewee by asking about her or his role within the host organisation. However, you need to make sure that these opening moves to demonstrate credibility and friendliness, and to relax and develop a positive relationship, are not overstated, so that too much time is used and the interviewee starts to become bored or restive.

The start of the interview needs to be shaped by you. It is your opportunity to allay, wherever possible, the interviewee's uncertainties about providing data, establish the participant's rights and, based upon this, hopefully, obtain informed consent. Box 10.9 provides a structure that you can adapt for starting your interviews.

An assurance from you that confidential information is not being sought should make interviewees more relaxed and open about the data that they are willing to provide you. Combined with assurances about anonymity, this should increase the level of confidence in your trustworthiness and reduce the possibility of interviewee or response bias. You can also demonstrate your commitment to confidentiality by not naming other individuals or organisations that have participated in your research, or by talking about the data you obtained from them.

Box 10.9
Focus on student research

Opening a semi-structured interview

As part of her research project, Beth undertook a series of semi-structured interviews with freelance consultants working for a range of organisations. She covered the following points at the start of each interview:

- The participant was thanked for considering the request for access and for agreeing to the meeting.
- The purpose of the research and its progress to date were outlined briefly. As part of this, the participant was given an information sheet to keep.
- The previously agreed right to confidentiality and anonymity was reiterated by stating that nothing said by the participant would be attributed to him/her without first seeking and obtaining permission.

- The participant's right not to answer any question was emphasised and that the interview would be stopped if the participant wished.
- The participant was told about the nature of the outputs to which the research was intended to lead and what would happen to the data collected during and after the project.
- The offer to provide a summary of the research findings to the interviewee was also restated and the participant was told when this would happen.
- The request to audio-record the interview was restated and, where agreed, this was used subsequently.
- Before the substantive discussion started, Beth again requested permission to undertake the interview, summarised the themes to be covered, confirmed the amount of time available and requested that the participant read and signed the informed consent form.

All of these points were dealt with within the first few minutes of the interview.

Approach to questioning

When conducted appropriately, your approach to questioning should reduce the scope for bias during the interview and increase the reliability of the information obtained. Your questions need to be phrased clearly, so that the interviewee can understand them, and you should ask them in a neutral voice tone. The use of open questions should help to avoid bias. These can then be followed up by the use of appropriately worded probing questions. The use of these types of question will help you to explore the topic and to produce a fuller account. These types of questions are discussed more fully in the following subsection.

Conversely, questions that seek to lead the interviewee or which indicate bias on your part should be avoided. Perceived interviewer bias may well lead to interviewee or response bias. Long questions or those that are really made up of two or more questions (known as double-barrel questions) should also be avoided if you are to obtain a response to each aspect that you are interested to explore.

Questions should also avoid too many theoretical concepts or jargon since your understanding of such terms may vary from that of your interviewees. Where theoretical concepts or specific terminology need to be used, you will have to ensure that both you and the interviewee have the same understanding (Box 10.10).

When asking questions it is important that, wherever possible, these are grounded in the real-life experiences of your participants rather than being discussed as abstract concepts. One approach to questioning which makes use of key participant experiences is the **critical incident technique**, in which participants are asked to describe in detail a critical incident or number of incidents that are relevant to the research question. A **critical**

Box 10.10
Focus on student research

(Mis)understanding terminology

Sven was conducting an interview with the European sales manager of a large multinational corporation. Throughout the interview the sales manager referred to the European Division. Sven assumed that the sales manager meant continental Europe. However, by chance, later questions revealed that, for this organisation, Europe extended into parts of Asia, including Turkey, the United Arab Emirates, Saudi Arabia, Kuwait and Israel. Until this point in the interview, Sven had assumed that these countries were the responsibility of another sales manager!

incident is defined as an activity or event where the consequences were so clear that the participant has a definite idea regarding the effects (Keaveney 1995).

It will also be important to consider when to ask sensitive questions. Leaving these until near the end of an interview will provide your participant with some time to build up trust and confidence in you and to allay any doubts about your intentions, as Box 10.11 illustrates. This will also affect the nature of the questions that you may ask during the early part of an interview, as you attempt to build trust and gain your participant's confidence.

Once this position of trust has been reached and you wish to ask potentially sensitive questions, the wording of these deserves very particular attention in order to avoid any negative inferences related to, for example, responsibility for failure or error. Care taken over the exploration of sensitive questions should help towards the compilation of a fuller and more reliable account.

Appropriate use of different types of questions

Formulating appropriate questions to explore areas in which you are interested is critical to achieving success in semi-structured or in-depth interviews. It is also important to word your questions in a factual way, avoiding emotional language. We now discuss the types of question that you can use during semi-structured and in-depth interviews.

Open questions

The use of **open questions** allows participants to define and describe a situation or event. An open question is designed to encourage the interviewee to provide an extensive and

Box 10.11
Focus on student research

Establishing trust and asking sensitive questions

Sam recalls an occasion when her treatment by her participants altered as her group interview progressed. For the first hour of a two-hour interview it appeared to her that the participants were convinced that she was really there to sell them a consultancy service. When they accepted that she was not going to try to sell them something, the mood of the interview changed and they became much more relaxed and responsive to the questions that Sam wished to ask. It was at this point that she was able to ask and pursue more sensitive questions that could have led to the interview being terminated during the period when the participants mistrusted her motives.

developmental answer, and can be used to reveal attitudes or obtain facts. It encourages the interviewee to reply as they wish. An open question is likely to start with, or include, one of the following words: 'what', 'how' or 'why'. Examples of open questions include:

'Why did the organisation introduce its marketing strategy?'
'How does the organisation use Internet recruitment?'
'How has corporate strategy changed over the past two years?'

Probing questions

Probing questions are used to explore responses that are of significance to the research topic. They may be worded like open questions but request a particular focus or direction. Examples of this type of question include:

'How would you evaluate the success of this new marketing strategy?'
'What were the drawbacks of using Internet recruitment in that region?'
'Why do you think the board of directors decided to shift the strategy to a partnered product development model?'

These questions may be prefaced with, for example, 'That's interesting . . . ' or 'Tell me more about. . . '.

Probing questions can also be used to seek an explanation where the response does not reveal the reasoning involved or where you do not understand the interviewee's meaning. Examples include:

'How do you plan to develop the use of digital marketing during the next two years?'
'That's interesting: do you mind telling me more about the relationship between the shift to the partnered product development model and the expansion of the established products division?'

The use of reflection may also help you to probe a theme. This is where you will 'reflect' a statement made by the interviewee by paraphrasing their words. For example:

'Why do you think that those employees do not understand the need for advertising?'

The intention will be to encourage exploration of the point made without offering a view or judgement on your part.

Where an open question does not reveal a relevant response, you may also probe further using a supplementary question that rephrases the original question.

Specific and closed questions

These types of question may be used as introductory questions when you commence questioning about a particular interview theme. Examples of this might be:

'Could you tell me about the change to the pricing policy'
'Can you describe the production process?'

They can also be used to obtain specific information or to confirm a fact or opinion (Section 11.4):

'How many people responded to the customer survey?'
'Has the old Central Region been merged with the Southern Region?'
'Do you prefer the new training programme?'

Other means to further your questioning

There are a number of ways of prompting further answers to a question you have asked. These include:

- follow-up expressions, such as: 'Ah', 'Oh' or 'Um';
- short follow-up statements, such as: 'That's interesting' or 'Really!';
- short follow-up questions, such as: 'Will you please tell me more?', 'When did that happen?' or 'What happened then?';
- short reflective questions where you rephrase what you have just been told to reflect it back, such as: 'So that was when . . . ?' or 'They felt the investment had been worthwhile?';
- interpretation and extension questions, where you seek to explore the implications of an answer, such as: 'Because they have diversified into Internet sales, does that mean that they are also going to build new distribution centres?';
- silence, where the participant is effectively invited to fill this by offering more information;
- using these devices in combination to explore a theme, but you will need to be very careful if you use this approach as it may be interpreted as being overbearing, stressful and confrontational. It will be more productive and ethical to maintain an even pace and respectful stance when asking questions.

Types of question to avoid

In phrasing questions, remember that you should avoid using leading or proposing types of question in order to control any bias that may result from their use (Section 11.4).

Nature and impact of your behaviour during the interview

Appropriate behaviour by the researcher should also reduce the scope for bias during the interview. Comments or non-verbal behaviour, such as gestures, which indicate any bias in your thinking, should be avoided. Rather, a neutral (but not an uninterested) response to the interviewee's answers should be used to ensure your own opinions do not bias responses. You should enjoy the interview opportunity, or at least appear to do so; any appearance of boredom on your part is hardly likely to encourage your interviewee!

Your posture and tone of voice may also encourage or inhibit the flow of the discussion. You should sit slightly inclined towards the interviewee and adopt an open posture, avoiding folded arms. This should provide a signal of attentiveness to your interviewee. Tone of voice can also provide a signal to the interviewee. You need to project interest and enthusiasm through your voice, avoiding any impression of anxiety, disbelief, astonishment or other negative signal.

Demonstration of attentive listening skills

The purpose of a semi-structured or in-depth interview will be to understand your participant's explanations and meanings. This type of interaction will not be typical of many of the conversations that you normally engage in, where those involved often compete to speak rather than concentrate on listening. You therefore need to recognise that different skills will be emphasised in this kind of interaction. Attentive listening will involve you attending to and being sensitive to your participants by spending the time needed to listen to them to build your understanding. You will need to hold back your own thoughts where these would compete with those of your participant(s), or stray from the theme being explored.

It will be necessary for you to explore and probe explanations and meanings, but you must also provide the interviewee with reasonable time to develop her or his responses, and you must avoid projecting your own views.

Scope to summarise and test understanding

You may test your understanding by summarising responses provided by the interviewee. This will allow your participant to tell you whether your summary is adequate and to add points to this to further or correct your understanding where appropriate. This can be a powerful tool for avoiding a biased or incomplete interpretation. It may also act as a means to explore and probe the interviewee's responses further.

In addition you may also ask the interviewee to read through the factual account that you produce of the interview (Section 5.11). Where the interviewee is prepared to undertake this, it will provide a further opportunity for you to test your understanding and for the interviewee to add any further points of relevance that may not previously have been apparent.

Dealing with difficult participants

Inevitably, during the course of your interviews you will meet some participants who are difficult to interview. In such circumstances it is imperative that you remain polite and do not show any irritation. Although it is impossible for us to highlight all the possible variations, the most common difficulties are summarised in Table 10.2, along with suggestions about how you might attempt to deal with them. However, while reading Table 10.2 will give you some ideas of what to do, the best advice we can give is to undertake practice interviews in which a colleague introduces one or more of these 'difficulties' and you have to deal with them!

Approach to recording data

Where possible we believe it is beneficial to audio-record an interview and also make notes as it progresses. Using both methods to record interview data has a number of advantages. Notes provide a backup if the audio-recording does not work. Making notes can help you to maintain your concentration, formulate points to summarise back to the interviewee to test your understanding and devise follow-up probing questions. Note taking demonstrates to your interviewee that her or his responses are important to you. It also allows you to record your own thoughts and any events that would not be evident from the audio-recording. For example, if you think there may be a relationship between two variables that you wish to explore later, if your interviewer uses a facial expression or provides another non-verbal cue, or if someone enters the room, you can make a note about each of these. Most people have their own means of making notes, which may range from an attempt to create a verbatim account to a diagrammatic style that records key words and phrases, perhaps using mind mapping (Section 2.3).

Table 10.2 Difficult interview participants and suggestions on how to address them

Recognised difficulty	Suggestion
Participant appears willing only to give monosyllabic answers, these being little more than 'yes' or 'no'	Reasons for this are varied If it is due to limited time, or worries about anonymity, then this can be minimised by careful opening of the interview (Box 10.9) If the participant gives these answers despite such precautions, try phrasing your questions in as open a way as possible; also use long pauses to signify that you want to hear more
Participant repeatedly provides long answers which digress from the focus of your interview	Although some digression should be tolerated, as it can lead to aspects in which you are interested, you will need to impose more direction This must be done subtly so as not to cause offence, such as by referring back to an earlier relevant point and asking them to tell you more, or requesting that they pause so you can note down what they have just said
Participant starts interviewing you	This can suggest that you have created rapport. However, you need to stress that you are interested in their opinions and that, if they wish, they can ask you questions at the end
Participant is proud of their status relative to you and wants to show off their knowledge, criticising what you do	This is extremely difficult and at times like this you will have to listen attentively and be respectful Remember that you are also likely to be knowledgeable about the research topic, so be confident and prepared to justify your research and the research design you have chosen
Participant becomes noticeably upset during the interview and, perhaps, starts to cry	Another difficult one for you You need to give your participant time to answer your question and, in particular, do not do anything to suggest that you are feeling impatient If your participant starts crying or is obviously very distressed, it is probably a good idea to explain that the question does not have to be answered Do not end the interview straight away as this is likely to make the participant even more upset

Source: King (2004); authors' experiences

The task of note making in this situation will be a demanding one. As you seek to test your understanding of what your interviewee has told you, this will allow some time to complete your notes concurrently in relation to the particular aspect being discussed. Most interviewees recognise the demands of the task and act accordingly. For example, Adrian recalls one particular interviewee who paused at the end of the main part of each of his answers to allow notes of this to be completed before adding some supplementary data which could also be noted down. However, the actual interview is not the occasion to perfect your interviewing skills, and we advise you to practise in a simulated situation: for example, by watching an interview on television and attempting to produce a set of notes.

To optimise the value from the interview you should compile a full record of the interview, including contextual data. If you cannot do this immediately after the interview, this should be done as soon as possible. Where you do not do this, the detailed understanding of what was said may be lost as well as general points of value. There is also the possibility that you may mix up data from different interviews, where you carry out several of these within a short period of time and you do not complete a record of each one at the time it takes place. Either situation will clearly lead to an issue about the trustworthiness of any data. You therefore need to allocate time to complete a full set of notes soon after the event. In addition to your notes from the actual interview, you should also record the following **contextual data**:

- the location of the interview (e.g. the organisation, the place);
- the date and time;
- the setting of the interview (e.g. was the room quiet or noisy, could you be overheard, were you interrupted?);
- background information about the participant (e.g. role, post title, gender);
- your immediate impression of how well (or badly) the interview went (e.g. was the participant reticent, were there aspects about which you felt you did not obtain answers in sufficient depth?).

You may be wondering how, if you are recording both of these types of data, you can still ensure the anonymity of your participants where this has been promised. As we outlined in Section 6.6, the best course of action is to ensure that your data are completely and genuinely anonymised. To help to achieve this you should store the contextual data separately from your interview transcripts. We suggest that you should only be able to link these two sets of data by using a 'key', such as an impersonal code number. Where it is absolutely necessary to retain a 'key' that allows participants to be linked to their data using their real name, this 'key' should be kept securely and separately, not by those who control the data.

Audio-recording your data where permission is given, making notes, compiling a full record of the interview immediately or soon after it has occurred and producing a set of contextual data and related memos (Chapter 13) are all means to control bias and produce reliable data. Most interviewers audio-record their interviews, where permission is given. Audio-recording interviews has both advantages and disadvantages and these are summarised in Table 10.3.

Permission should always be sought to audio-record an interview. You should also explain why you believe it would be beneficial to use an audio-recorder and to offer guarantees about your participant's rights over its use. Where it is likely to have a detrimental effect, it is better not to use a recorder. However, most interviewees adapt quickly to the use of the recorder. It is more ethical to allow your interviewee to maintain control over the recorder so that if you ask a question that they are prepared to respond to, but only if their words are not audio-recorded, they have the option to switch it off (Section 6.6). It will inevitably be necessary to make notes in this situation.

Table 10.3 Advantages and disadvantages of audio-recording the interview

Advantages	Disadvantages
Allows the interviewer to concentrate on questioning and listening	May adversely affect the relationship between interviewee and interviewer (possibility of 'focusing' on the audio-recorder rather than the interview process)
Allows questions formulated at an interview to be accurately recorded for use in later interviews where appropriate	
Can re-listen to the interview, especially during data analysis	May inhibit some interviewee responses and reduce reliability
Accurate and unbiased record provided	Possibility of a technical problem
Allows direct quotes to be used	Time required to transcribe the audio-recording (Section 13.4)
Permanent record for others to use	

Source: authors' experience

Box 10.12
Checklist

To help you conduct your semi-structured or in-depth interview

Appearance at the interview

✔ How will your appearance at the interview affect the willingness of the participant to share data?

Opening the interview

✔ How will you open the interview to gain the confidence of your participant?

✔ What will you tell your participant about yourself, the purpose of your research, its funding and your progress?

✔ What concerns, or need for clarification, may your participant have?

✔ How will you seek to overcome these concerns or provide this clarification?

✔ In particular, how do you intend to use the data to which you are given access, ensuring, where appropriate, its confidentiality and your participant's anonymity?

✔ What will you tell your participant about their right not to answer particular questions and to end the interview should they wish?

✔ How will you explain the structure of the interview?

Asking questions and behaviour during the interview

✔ How will you use appropriate language and tone of voice, and avoid jargon when asking questions or discussing themes?

✔ How will you word open questions appropriately to obtain relevant data?

✔ How will you word probing questions to build on, clarify or explain your participant's responses?

✔ How will you avoid asking leading questions that may introduce forms of bias?

✔ Have you devised an appropriate order for your questions to avoid asking sensitive questions too early where this may introduce participant bias?

✔ How will you maintain a check on the interview themes that you intend to cover and to steer the discussion where appropriate to raise and explore these aspects?

✔ How will you avoid overzealously asking questions and pressing your participant for a response where it should be clear that they do not wish to provide one?

✔ How will you avoid projecting your own views or feelings through your actions or comments?

✔ How might you identify actions and comments made by your participant that indicate an aspect of the discussion that should be explored in order to reveal the reason for the response?

✔ How will you listen attentively and demonstrate this to your participant?

✔ How will you summarise and test your understanding of the data that are shared with you in order to ensure accuracy in your interpretation?

✔ Where appropriate, how will you deal with difficult participants while remaining polite?

Recording data during the interview

✔ How will you record the data that are revealed to you during the interview? Where this involves using an audio-recorder, have you requested this and provided a reason why it would help you to use this technique?

✔ How will you allow your participant to maintain control over the use of an audio-recorder, where used, if they wish to do this?

✔ Have you practised to ensure you can carry out a number of tasks at the same time, including listening, note taking and identifying where you need to probe further?

Closing the interview

✔ How will you draw the interview to a close within the agreed time limit and thank the participant for their time and the data they have shared with you?

10.7 Managing logistical and resource issues

Issues

Time

Interviewing is a time-consuming process. Where the purpose of the interview is to explore themes or to explain findings, the process may call for a fairly lengthy discussion. In such cases the time required to obtain data is unlikely to be less than one hour and could easily exceed this, perhaps taking two hours or longer. This may have an adverse impact on the number and representativeness of those who are willing to be interview participants, as we discussed earlier. Where managers or other potential participants receive frequent requests to participate in research projects, they will clearly need to consider how much of their time they may be willing to devote to such activities. It will therefore be important for you to establish credibility with, and to engender the interest of, potential interviewees.

Cost and other resources

Your decision to collect data through interviewing will have particular resource issues. Conducting interviews may become a costly process where it is necessary to travel to the location of participants, although this can be kept to a minimum by cluster sampling (Section 7.2) or using the Internet (Section 10.10). Interviews are almost certainly likely to be more expensive than using self-completed or telephone questionnaires to collect data. Choice of method should be determined primarily by the nature of the research question and objectives rather than by cost considerations. This highlights the need to examine the feasibility of the proposed question and research strategy in relation to resource constraints, including time available and expense, before proceeding to the collection of data.

Logistics

Where your research question and objectives require you to undertake semi-structured or in-depth interviews, you need to consider the logistics of scheduling interviews. Thought needs to be given to the number of interviews to be arranged within a given period, and to the time required to compose notes and/or transcribe audio-recordings of each one, and undertake an initial analysis of the data collected (Section 13.4). More time and consideration will be required where you also need to translate a transcription from one language into another.

Management

Time management

In the preceding subsection, the issue of time required to collect data through interviewing was raised. You need to consider very carefully the amount of time that will be required to conduct an interview. In our experience, the time required to undertake qualitative research interviews is usually underestimated. The likely time required should be referred to clearly in any initial contact, and it may be better to suggest that interviews are envisaged to last up to, say, one, one and a half, or two hours, so that a willing participant sets aside sufficient time. Some negotiation is in any case possible with an interested participant who feels unable to agree to a request for, say, two hours but who is prepared to agree to a briefer meeting. The interview can also be arranged at a time when the interviewee will be under least pressure.

Interview scheduling

Another possible strategy is to arrange two or more shorter interviews in order to explore a topic thoroughly. This might have the added advantage of allowing participants to reflect on the themes raised and questions being asked, and therefore to provide a fuller account and more accurate set of data. In order to establish this option, it may be beneficial to arrange an initial meeting with a potential participant to discuss this request, where you will be able to establish your credibility. A series of exploratory interviews may then be agreed. Consideration also needs to be given to the number of interviews that may be undertaken in a given period. It is easy to overestimate what is practically possible (Box 10.13).

These are all factors that need to be considered in the scheduling of semi-structured and in-depth interviews. Where you are undertaking interviews at one establishment, it may be more practical to undertake a number of interviews in one day, although there is still a need to maintain concentration, make notes and write up information, and to conduct your initial analysis. Even in this situation, conducting more than three interviews per day is likely to be challenging.

Interview management

The nature of semi-structured or in-depth interviews also has implications for the management of the time available during the meeting. The use of open-ended questions and reliance on participant responses means that, while you must remain responsive to the objectives of the interview and the time constraint, interviewees need the opportunity to provide full answers. You should avoid making frequent interruptions but will need to cover the themes and questions indicated and probe responses in the time available. The intensive nature of the discussion and the need to be clear about your understanding of what has been revealed means that time must be found to write up notes as soon as possible after an interview.

Recording and transcription

Where an audio-recorder has been used (Section 10.6), you will need to decide whether to work directly from the recording or to produce a transcription of all or parts of the recording. This decision will depend on your research strategy and the way in which you

---

Box 10.13
Focus on student research

Calculating the number of in-depth interviews to be undertaken in one day

Feroz arranged two interviews in a capital city during the course of a day, which involved travelling some miles across the city during the lunch hour. Two interviews appeared to be a reasonable target. However, a number of logistical issues were experienced even in relation to the plan to undertake two such interviews in one day. These issues included the following: the total travelling time to and from the city; the time to find the appropriate buildings; the transfer time during a busy period; the time to conduct the interviews; the need to maintain concentration, to probe responses, to make initial notes and then to write these up without too much time elapsing. Because of his experience, Feroz took a decision not to conduct more than one interview per day where significant travel was involved, even though this necessitated more journeys and greater expense.

intend to analyse your qualitative data (Chapter 13). For example, using a Grounded Theory strategy (Sections 5.8 and 13.9) is likely to mean that you will need to transcribe the whole of each interview. Each hour of recording is likely to take at least seven hours to transcribe or to process ready for entry into computer-assisted qualitative data analysis software, unless you are a very competent audio-typist, or you know one who will undertake this task for you! Use of software to assist the transcription of audio-recordings may also be helpful.

Translation

In some cases it may not only be necessary to transcribe an audio-recording but also to translate it from the one language to another. Translations require care to ensure that the meanings contained in the original or source language are reproduced authentically in the translated language. However, translation may be more problematic than just technically producing language equivalence. Chidlow et al. (2014) discuss the need to go beyond translational equivalence and to use a contextualised approach in order to promote understanding. We consider potential problems associated with translations in Section 11.5 and outline different translation techniques in Table 11.4, together with their respective advantages and disadvantages.

10.8 Group interviews and focus groups

Semi-structured and in-depth interviews may also be conducted as group interviews, where one or more interviewers asks questions and records responses with a group of participants. Figure 10.2 summarised the number of participants and interview modes earlier in this chapter. A variety of terms are used interchangeably to describe group interviews, which are often wrongly assumed to have equivalent meanings (Boddy 2005). These include focus group, group interview, group discussion and various combinations of these words! In this section we use **group interview** as a general term to describe all semi-structured and in-depth interviews conducted with two or more interviewees. In contrast, the term **focus group** is used to refer to a specific type of group interview. In this, type, the topic to be explored is predetermined and precisely defined and the role of the researcher is to facilitate or enable discussion amongst participants rather than lead this, or be the focal point of interaction (Carson et al. 2001; Krueger and Casey 2015). In this way, a focus group is a type of group interview, but not all group interviews should be labelled as focus groups. We return to these definitions later as we discuss each of these approaches.

Typically group interviews (and focus groups) involve between 4 and 12 participants, the precise number depending upon the nature of the participants, the topic matter and the skill of the interviewer. Some suggest a narrower range of participants of between 6 and 8. Inevitably, the more complex the subject matter the smaller the number of interviewees. Participants are normally chosen using non-probability sampling, often with a specific purpose in mind (Section 7.3), such as they are typical of the group being researched or they represent those who are critical to a particular operation. For many group interviews the underlying reason is that you believe you will learn a great deal from these specific individuals. Krueger and Casey (2015: 43) refer to such participants as being 'information rich'.

If you are thinking about using group interviews, or specifically focus groups, consideration of the following issues may help.

- Where your research project (or part of it) occurs within an organisation, the request to participate in a group interview may be received by individuals as an instruction rather than allowing them a choice about whether to take part. This may be the case where an organisation is acting as a host for your research and the request is sent in the name of a manager, or because of your own position in the organisation. Where this is the case it is likely to lead to some level of non-attendance, or to unreliable data. In our experience, participants often welcome the chance to 'have their say'. However, where any request may be perceived as indicating lack of choice, to gain their confidence and participation you will need to exercise care over the wording to be used in the request that is sent to them to take part. You will also need to exercise similar care in your introduction to the group when the interview occurs in order to provide a clear assurance about confidentiality.

- Once your sample has been selected, participants should be grouped so as not to inhibit each individual's possible contribution. This may be related to lack of trust, to perceptions about status differences or because of the dominance of certain individuals. The nature and selection of each group will affect the first two elements. We would advise using a series of horizontal slices through an organisation so that, within each group, participants have a similar status and similar work experiences. (Using a vertical slice would introduce perceptions about status differences and variations in work experience.) In this way, group interviews can be conducted at a number of levels within an organisation. A reference may be made about the nature of the group to provide reassurance, and you may consider asking people to introduce themselves by their first name only without referring to their exact job.

- To realise the benefits of a group interview, it is important to encourage every person in a group to participate. This commences when you ask each person to introduce himself or herself. You may also need to encourage contributions by drawing group members into the discussion, particularly where some appear reluctant to take part. This needs to be managed sensitively and participation may increase naturally as group members become more familiar with each other. Occasions may occur during a group interview when participants talk over one another and you will need to manage the flow of contributions while ensuring that each participant has an opportunity to offer her or his contribution. Where one or two people dominate the discussion, you should seek to reduce their contributions by encouraging others. This may be attempted in a specific way:

> 'What do you think, Yuksel?'
> 'How does Emma's point relate to the one that you raised, Kristie?'

A question posed more generally to other group members should also have the effect of inhibiting the contribution of a dominant member:

> 'What do other people think about this?'
> 'What do you think about Johan's suggestion?'

The interviewer may also seek to manage the flow of the discussion through using non-verbal signals. You may try to reduce the contribution of a dominant member by temporarily minimising eye contact with him or her and draw others into the discussion by looking or gesturing in their direction. You will need to remain attentive throughout the interview, appearing friendly and relaxed in your approach but also purposeful and interested, encouraging each member to take part and providing opportunities to listen to and discuss contributions.

- You will need to ensure that participants understand each other's contributions and that you develop an accurate understanding of the points being made. Asking a participant to clarify the meaning of a particular contribution, where it has not been understood, and testing understanding through summarising should help to ensure this.
- You will need to consider the location and setting for a group interview. It is advisable to conduct the interview in a neutral setting rather than, say, in a manager's office, where participants may not feel relaxed. There should be no likelihood of interruption or being overheard. You should consider the layout of the seating in the room where the interview is to be held. Where possible, arrange the seating in a circular fashion so that everyone will be facing inward and so that they will be an equal distance from the central point of this circle.
- Finally, students often ask, 'When will I know that I have undertaken sufficient group interviews or focus groups?' Writing about focus groups, Krueger and Casey (2015) suggest that you should plan to undertake three or four group interviews with any one type of participant. If after the third or fourth group interview you are no longer receiving new information you will have reached **saturation**, in which case you will have heard the full range of ideas.

The demands of conducting all types of group interview, including focus groups, and the potential wealth of ideas that may flow from them mean that it is likely to be difficult to manage the process and note key points at the same time. We have managed to overcome this in two ways: by audio-recording group interviews or using two interviewers. To audio-record a group interview you will need the freely given and express consent of each participant. Where two interviewers are used, one person facilitates the discussion and the other person makes notes. We would recommend that you use two interviewers, even if you are audio-recording the group interview, as it will allow one interviewer to concentrate fully on managing the process while the other ensures the data are recorded. Where you cannot audio-record the group interview, you will need to write up any notes immediately afterwards. As with one-to-one interviews, your research will benefit from the making of notes about the nature of the interactions that occur in the group interviews that you conduct. We would not advise you to undertake more than one group interview in a day on your own because of the danger of forgetting or confusing data.

Group interviews

In a group interview your role will be to ensure that all participants have the opportunity to state their points of view in answer to your questions, and to record the resulting data. This type of interview can range from being structured to unstructured, although it tends to be relatively unstructured and fairly free-flowing in terms of both breadth and depth of topics. The onus will be placed firmly on you to explain the interview's purpose, to encourage participants to relax, and to initiate, encourage and direct the discussion. The use of this method is likely to necessitate a balance between encouraging participants to provide answers to a particular question or questions that you introduce, and allowing them to range more freely in discussion where this may reveal data that provide you with important insights. Thus once you have opened the interview (Box 10.9) and the discussion is established, it will need to be managed carefully.

Group interactions may lead to a highly productive discussion as participants respond to your questions and evaluate points made by the group. However, as the opportunity to develop an individual level of rapport with each participant is less (compared with a one-to-one interview), there may also emerge a group effect where certain participants effectively try to dominate the interview while others may feel inhibited. This may result in some participants publicly agreeing with the views of others, while privately disagreeing. As a consequence a reported consensus may, in reality, be a view that nobody wholly endorses and nobody disagrees with (Stokes and Bergin 2006). You will therefore need to test the validity of emergent views by trying to encourage involvement of all group members and pursuing the interview's exploratory purpose through the use of open and probing questions. A high level of skill will be required in order for you to be able to conduct this type of discussion successfully, as well as to try to record its outcomes.

Despite this reference to the potential difficulties of using group interviews, there are distinct advantages arising from their use. Because of the presence of several participants, this type of situation allows a breadth of points of view to emerge and for the group to respond to these views. A dynamic group can generate or respond to a number of ideas and evaluate them, thus helping you to explore or explain concepts. You are also likely to benefit from the opportunity that this method provides in terms of allowing your participants to consider points raised by other group members and to challenge one another's views. In one-to-one interviews, discussion is of course limited to the interviewer and participant. Stokes and Bergin (2006) highlight that while group interviews, and in particular focus groups, are able to identify principal issues accurately, they are not able to provide the depth and detail in relation to specific issues that can be obtained from individual interviews.

The use of group interviews may also provide an efficient way for you to interview a larger number of individuals than would be possible through the use of one-to-one interviews. Linked to this point, their use may allow you to adopt an interview-based strategy that can more easily be related to a representative sample, particularly where the research project is being conducted within a specific organisation or in relation to a clearly defined population. This may help to establish the credibility of this research where an attempt is made to overcome issues of bias associated with interviews in general and this type in particular.

Group interviews can also help to identify key themes that will be used to develop items that are included in a questionnaire. This particular use of group interviews may inform subsequent parts of your data collection, providing a clearer focus. For example, the initial use of group interviews can lead to a 'bottom-up' generation of concerns and issues, which subsequently inform a questionnaire's content.

Focus groups

Focus groups are well known because of the way they have been used by political parties to test voter reactions to particular policies and election strategies, and in market research to test reactions to products, as well as being used in academic research (Macnaghten and Myers 2007). A **focus group**, sometimes called a 'focus group interview', is a group interview that focuses upon a particular issue, product, service or topic by encouraging discussion among participants and the sharing of perceptions in an open and tolerant environment (Krueger and Casey 2015) (Box 10.14). Participant interaction is a key feature of focus group design, although this focus on enabling interactive discussion is used for two distinct purposes.

Positivist or critical realist researchers use the focus group to encourage interactions between participants as an effective means to articulate pre-held views about a particular issue or topic. The aim of using focus groups in this way is to reveal these pre-held views. Interpretivist researchers use focus groups as a means to construct meanings through social interactions and sense making about a topic. The aim of using focus groups for this purpose relates to the ability to analyse how participant interactions and group dynamics lead to the construction of shared meanings (Belzile and Oberg 2012).

If you are running a focus group, you will probably be referred to as the **moderator** or 'facilitator'. These two labels emphasise the dual purpose involved in running a focus group, namely to:

- keep the group within the boundaries of the topic being discussed;
- generate interest in the topic and encourage discussion, while at the same time not leading the group towards any particular opinion.

In some focus groups, the moderator's role may be less evident in comparison to the researcher's role in other group interviews. This is because the moderator's role is to facilitate and encourage group interaction. However, while some parts of a focus group may be largely non-directive, other parts may require greater direction from the moderator.

The purpose of a focus group is also likely to affect the level of interviewer-led structure and intervention that is required. Focus groups used to reveal participants' views are likely to be associated with greater structure; those used to study how participants interact are likely to be associated with less structure. Oates and Alevizou (2018) discuss the relationship between focus group purpose and structure, identifying the use of an unstructured approach for an exploratory purpose and the use of a semi-structured approach for either a theoretical, impression-gathering, diagnostic or explanatory purpose.

Participants are selected because they have certain characteristics in common that are relevant to the topic being discussed. Focus group discussions may be conducted several times, with similar participants, to enable trends and patterns to be identified. The size of a focus group may vary according to the nature of the topic. A focus group designed to obtain views about a product is likely to be larger than one that explores a topic related to a more emotionally involved or sensitive construct, such as attitudes to performance-related pay or the way in which employees rate their treatment by management. You may

Box 10.14
Focus on management research

Using a focus group in research about antibribery compliance

David-Barrett, Yakis-Douglas, Moss-Cowan and Nguyen (2017: 326) investigated "Why top-down directives aimed at eradicating corruption are ineffective at altering on-the-ground practices for organizations that have adopted industry-wide 'gold standards' to prevent bribery and corruption." This research, published in the *Journal of Management Inquiry,* is based on the use of in-depth, semi-structured and focus group interviews conducted over three phases with

senior managers and managers of companies in the pharmaceutical industry.

Following the conduct of the first phase of one-to-one, face-to-face research interviews and analysis of the data, a focus group composed of fifteen compliance directors from a range of pharmaceutical companies was held. The discussion at this focus group was defined by the initial presentation of the preliminary findings from the first phase of research interviews and by the perspective of these compliance directors who were responsible for the conduct of operations in emerging markets.

The focus group was moderated by the first named author following the presentation of the preliminary findings. This process resulted in the collection of detailed data from the perspectives expressed by these informed participants who were drawn from very similar and highly relevant backgrounds.

also choose to design smaller groups as you seek to develop your competence in relation to the use of this interviewing technique to collect qualitative data.

Lijadi et al. (2015) discuss the scope to use online focus groups. These follow the same general purpose as traditional focus groups and involve an online discussion within a consenting and interactive group to explore a predetermined and clearly defined topic facilitated by a moderator. Focus group interactions may occur in real time, using online conferencing or audio facilities, or text, or in delayed sequences using text. There are likely to be issues and advantages associated with the use of online focus groups. Where these are text based, online participants may only make relatively short contributions (related to this, see the discussion of data quality issues in Section 9.6). However, use of online focus groups may overcome constraints related to distance and cost, where it is possible to arrange these.

10.9 Telephone interviews

Most semi-structured or in-depth interviews occur on a face-to-face basis. However, these types of interview may also be conducted by telephone, using either a voice/listening-only mode or a video calling service. Mobile phones have significantly extended the scope to conduct research interviews by telephone, especially with regard to the use of video telephony services, such as Skype™ or Facetime™. In this section we first outline research that compares telephone interviews with face-to-face interviews. We then discuss possible disadvantages and advantages of using a phone to conduct research interviews. We conclude this section by discussing strategies that may be helpful when conducting phone interviews.

Interview mode effects: telephone versus face-to-face

The purpose of your interview will be broadly the same regardless of whether it is conducted by telephone or face-to-face. However, the way in which an interview is conducted is likely to affect its outcomes. This is referred to as a **mode effect** (Irvine 2011; Irvine et al. 2012; Vogl 2013). Irvine et al. (2012) compared the nature of spoken interactions in two sets of semi-structured interviews: six conducted by telephone and five carried out face-to-face. The aim of their study was to evaluate the impact of interview mode on the nature of spoken interactions, based on actual data that had been transcribed systematically to facilitate detailed analysis. Their analysis revealed five areas where interactional differences were evident between these interview modes.

Telephone interviews were on average shorter than face-to-face ones although there was a great deal of variation between these interviews. Possible explanations relate to less rapport developed and greater effort required, with the implication that telephone interviews may be less suitable for research studies that are designed to rely on richly detailed and in-depth accounts.

In telephone interviews, interviewees spoke for less time and generally gave shorter answers, being more likely to ask if their responses were adequate. This may be related to lack of visual cues, reduced scope to discuss the purpose of the research at the start of interviews, less rapport developed and greater task orientation in this interview mode. Conversely, while telephone interviewees spoke for less time, the researcher spoke for slightly more, markedly altering the balance between the two.

Telephone interviewees were slightly more likely to ask the researcher to clarify or repeat her questions. This did not mean that interviewees experienced difficulty in their understanding; instead this may be explained by the quality of the phone connection, the effort and concentration required in a listening-only mode of interview and resulting fatigue, and the need for interview questions to be phrased clearly and succinctly.

In face-to-face interviews, the researcher was more likely to interact with the interviewee during an answer, say by helping an interviewee find an appropriate word or by summarising the answer to show understanding. Possible explanations suggested may be because greater rapport was developed during face-to-face interviews, and because during telephone interviews the interviewer needed to concentrate more on listening given the absence of non-verbal prompts or signals.

Also in face-to-face interviews, the researcher used verbal acknowledgements (e.g. by saying 'Yeah', 'Ah', 'Oh', 'Um', etc.) to the interviewee more frequently than in telephone interviews. This appears surprising as use of verbal acknowledgements may be expected to be more frequently used in telephone interviews to compensate for the lack of visual contact. Possible explanations suggested may be because of the need to concentrate on listening during telephone interviews and also because the researcher used the lack of visual contact to concentrate on taking notes.

Disadvantages of using a telephone to conduct a research interview

Discussion of these mode effects suggests that telephone interviews are associated with a number of disadvantages. Vogl (2013) places these disadvantages into two broad categories: the limited scope for personal contact, and the reliance on verbal and paralinguistic signals during a telephone interview. We discuss each of these briefly.

Earlier we referred to the importance of establishing personal contact in semi-structured and in-depth interviews. Establishing rapport and trust will be particularly important in such interviews where you wish to ask your participants to be reflective and to provide you with richly detailed and in-depth accounts. However, personal contact during a telephone interview is limited, especially in relation to the use of a voice/listening-only mode. A telephone interview may be perceived as impersonal and relatively anonymous and it may be more difficult to establish rapport and trust as a result. Conducting a telephone interview will also be difficult if your participants are uncomfortable with this mode. This may lead to issues of (reduced) reliability where your participants are reluctant to engage in an exploratory discussion by telephone, or even a refusal to take part.

Telephone interviews place reliance on verbal and paralinguistic signals. Interviews conducted through the use of a voice/listening-only telephone mode obviously exclude the use of visual cues between interviewee and interviewer to aid understanding. Verbal signals refer to what is said by interviewer or interviewee, such as, 'that's interesting, may I ask you to say more about . . .'; or, 'I am not sure I understand your question, please can you rephrase it.' Paralinguistic signals refer to any vocal effects used by a speaker that affect the way words are spoken or sounds are used, and which often convey meaning in their own right. Such effects include voice quality, tone or pitch of voice, rhythm or rate of speech, stress placed on individual words, syllables or sounds and on groups of words known as prosodic or sentence stress, and sounds made using the breath such as a sigh or use of 'hmm' or 'mhm'. The focus here is on how things are said as opposed to just what is being said. Using the telephone to conduct an interview will mean that in the absence of visual signals, the interviewer will need to concentrate more on how something is being said as well as what is being said to be sensitive to any nuances in the language and paralanguage used by the interviewee. Listening only may help to provide focus in this interaction but without the scope to recognise, explore and understand visual signalling this will be demanding.

473

There are also practical issues that need to be managed when using telephone interviews. These include your ability to control the pace of a telephone interview and to record data. Conducting an interview by telephone and taking notes is a difficult and demanding process. The normal visual cues that allow your interviewee to control the flow of data that she or he shares with you will be absent in a voice-only telephone interview. As the interviewer, you will also lose the opportunity to witness the non-verbal behaviour of your participant, which may adversely affect your interpretation of how far to pursue a particular line of questioning. You may also encounter difficulties in developing more complex questions in comparison with a face-to-face interview situation. Finally, attempting to gain access by telephone may lead to ethical issues (Section 6.6).

Advantages of using a telephone to conduct a research interview

While telephone interviews are associated with disadvantages, their use may actually be advantageous in some circumstances. These circumstances also relate to practical issues, limited scope for personal contact, and reliance on verbal and paralinguistic signals, which we now consider.

Conducting semi-structured or in-depth interviews by telephone can offer advantages associated with access, speed and lower cost (Box 10.15). In particular you may be able to interview participants with whom it would otherwise be impractical to do so due to the distance and prohibitive costs involved and time required. Even where 'long-distance' access is not an issue, conducting interviews by telephone can still offer advantages associated with speed of data collection and lower cost. It may also be safer for the researcher to conduct interviews by telephone in some circumstances. In other words, this approach may be seen as easier and more convenient.

While the limited scope for personal contact and reliance on verbal and paralinguistic signals are usually considered a disadvantage, this may not be so. Both Holt (2010) and Trier-Bieniek (2012) report that not meeting their participants helped in terms of producing open and full accounts. There are a number of reasons for this outcome. The anonymity of a voice/listening-only mode of interviewing helped to reduce participants' inhibitions in providing accounts about very personal matters. This suggests that exploring sensitive issues by telephone interview may in some contexts be advantageous. The use of the telephone also facilitated participation, by allowing participants to choose a suitable time of day to be interviewed, to stop an interview in progress when this became unavoidable and to rearrange a time for it to continue, and to move around their environment when necessary to avoid being overheard. Participants also reported to Holt (2010) and Trier-Bieniek (2012) that they had enjoyed this mode of participation and many would not have found it so easy to take part in a face-to-face interview.

Telephone interview strategies

Telephone interview strategies relate to encouraging participation; establishing rapport, making preliminary contact and encouraging in-depth answers; recording data; and using video telephony.

Potential participants who express many concerns are more likely to refuse to take part; however, those expressing fewer concerns and who are more conversational during initial contact are more likely to agree to take part (Broome 2015). You therefore need to recognise the nature of the concerns expressed by those you ask to participate in a telephone interview. These range from disinterest, to concerns about taking part, including concern about the purpose of the interview or its content and concern about the length of time required to take part. Broome (2015: 78) refers to disinterest as a 'red flag', which needs to be addressed with care as this often leads to refusal. Concerns about purpose, content and time required may potentially be recognised as 'green lights' where a researcher is genuinely able to respond to these (Broome 2015: 79). In addition, an initial phone request to participate can be rescheduled where the potential participant says the present time is not appropriate to discuss this.

Establishment of rapport is also likely to be important to gain access and achieve in-depth answers in telephone interviews. Irvine notes that 'small talk' between a researcher and interviewee generally characterises the initial stage of their meeting to conduct a face-to-face interview. This is important to build some rapport. However, there may be less small talk in the initial stage of a telephone interview, which tend to "get down to business more quickly" (Irvine 2011: 211). This more task-oriented approach to a telephone interview may set the mood of what follows, leading to a quicker pace and less depth. It may be that in those telephone interviews where greater rapport is established, that more in-depth answers are likely and greater exploration of these is possible. In this regard, Irvine (2011: 215) suggests that telephone interviewers "consider ways of establishing a more relaxed conversational style prior to asking specific interview questions." You can audio-record a (voice-only) telephone interview with your participant's consent (Box 10.15). In this case you will find it helpful to reflect on the interview after it ends and make further notes about it. Your reflections and notes may help you to improve your approach to your next telephone interview.

As noted, developments in video telephony mean that it is possible to conduct interviews through a video calling service. Such interviews may overcome some of the potential disadvantages of using voice-only telephony. Using this technology may help to build

---

Box 10.15
focus on
management
research

Using telephone interviews in a mixed methods study

While a key aim of management research is to contribute to management practice, Banks et al. (2016: 2205) recognise that there is still a "widening gap between science and practice, [where] the relevance of research conducted in the management domain remains in question." Their research, published in the *Academy of Management Journal,* explores the challenges posed by this gap by applying stakeholder theory.

Using a mixed methods approach, they conducted 38 semi-structured interviews, of which 22 were with a range of practitioners and 16 with academics. They also established a focus group composed of 4 practitioners and 3 academics. During a subsequent stage, they undertook a survey of 828 academics and 939 practitioners. Using content analysis this led them to identify what they term "22 grand challenges", of which eight are relevant to both academics and practitioners, eight are focused on academics and six relate to practitioners (Banks et al. 2016: 2205).

The 38 in-depth interviews were conducted by telephone because of the geographical distances involved. Banks et al. report that these semi-structured interviews lasted between 20 minutes and one hour, with an average time of half-an-hour. An interview guide was prepared for these semi-structured telephone interviews based on the research questions devised for this project. They report that each telephone interviewee agreed to the interview being audio-recorded. From these recordings they produced single line spaced interview transcripts totalling over three hundred pages.

rapport and trust, while the ability for you and your participant to see each other and to interact visually should provide both of you with some contextual and visual cues, even if these are limited by the screen frame. Using a screen-recording application with your participant's consent will provide you with a recording of the interview. You will need to ensure that you and your participant both have access to a supported and compatible platform before considering using this technology.

Developments in technology therefore add to ways in which you may be able to conduct interviews. In addition to face-to-face interviews, you may consider using telephone interviews based on voice-only or video telephony. In the next sub-section we also consider choice of other types of electronic interview. In considering this, you will need to focus on the preferences of your intended participants and the need to be guided by ethical principles. You will need to be aware of any cultural norms related to the nature and conduct of telephone conversations.

10.10 Internet-mediated interviews

Interviews may also be conducted electronically via the Internet using mobile or computing technologies. These are collectively referred to as **electronic interviews**. A distinction is made between electronic interviews conducted in real time (**synchronous**) and those not conducted in real time (**asynchronous**). An **asynchronous electronic interview** will be conducted through exchanges of text. This will use email or text messaging but will involve gaps in time or delays between the interviewer asking a question and the participant providing an answer (Figure 10.3). In this way it is sometimes partly undertaken offline. A **synchronous electronic interview** will be conducted in real time using email, instant messaging or web conferencing (Figure 10.3).

In this section we briefly discuss asynchronous and synchronous electronic interviews and the advantages and disadvantages associated with each type. Technology is also intervening in interviews more generally in novel and as yet untested ways (Box 10.16).

Asynchronous electronic interviews

An email interview is generally described as an asynchronous form because of the nature of the technology used and because it is not necessary to ask questions and answer these sequentially without any time gaps. However, it may be possible to conduct an email interview in one period, where the interviewee responds immediately to each question and emails continue to be exchanged until the interviewer draws it to a close and thanks the interviewee for her/his participation. This may be after a pre-arranged period has been reached. We return to consider text-based synchronous interviewing later in this section.

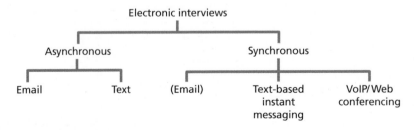

Figure 10.3 Forms of electronic interview

Box 10.16 Focus on research in the news

How AI helps recruiters track jobseekers' emotions

By Patricia Nilsson

Facial recognition technology allows us to pay for lunch, unlock a phone – it can even get us arrested. Now, that technology is moving on: algorithms are not only learning to recognise who we are, but also what we feel.

So-called emotion recognition technology is in its infancy. But artificial intelligence companies claim it has the power to transform recruitment.

Their algorithms, they say, can decipher how enthusiastic, bored or honest a job applicant may be – and help employers weed out candidates with undesirable characteristics.

London-based Human, founded in 2016, is a start-up that analyses video-based job applications. The company claims it can spot the emotional expressions of prospective candidates and match them with personality traits – information its algorithms collect by deciphering subliminal expressions when the applicant answers questions.

Human sends a report to the recruiter detailing candidates' emotional reactions to each interview question, with scores against characteristics that specify how 'honest' or 'passionate' an applicant is.

If [the recruiter] says, 'We are looking for the most curious candidate,' they can find that person by comparing the candidates' scores,' says Yi Xu, Human's founder and chief executive.

'An interviewer will have bias, but [with technology] they don't judge the face but the personality of the applicant,' she says. One aim, she claims, is to overcome ethnic and gender discrimination in recruitment.

Frederike Kaltheuner, policy adviser on data innovation at Privacy International, a global campaigning organisation, agrees that human interviewers can be biased. But she says, 'new systems bring new problems'.

The biggest problem is privacy, and what happens to the data after it is analysed. Ailidh Callander, a legal officer at Privacy International, says it is unclear whether data used to train emotion recognition algorithms – such as that collected during video-based job interviews – count as 'personal', and whether data privacy legislation applies.

Paul Ekman, who . . . now runs the Paul Ekman Group, which trains emotion recognition specialists, says reliable artificial emotional intelligence based on his methods is possible. But he adds, 'No one has ever published research that shows automated systems are accurate.'

Mr Ekman says even if artificial emotional intelligence were possible, the people interpreting the data – in this case employers – should also be trained to properly decipher the results. 'Faces can tell you someone is pressing their lips together, but this can mean different things depending on culture or context,' he says.

People differ in their ability to manipulate their emotions to trick the system, and Mr Ekamn says, 'If people know they are being observed they change their behaviour.' Those who are told their emotions will be analysed are self-conscious.

 Source: Extracts from 'How AI helps recruiters track jobseekers' emotions', Patricia Nilsson, *Financial Times*, 28 February 2018. Copyright © 2018 The Financial Times Ltd

An **email interview** therefore consists of a series of emails each containing a question or small number of questions and the replies to these. Although you can send one email containing a series of questions, this would really be an Internet questionnaire (Sections 11.2 and 11.5). After making contact and obtaining agreement to participate, you initially email a question or small number of questions, or introduce a topic to which the participant will (hopefully) reply. You then need to respond to each reply, asking further questions, raising points of clarification and pursuing ideas that are of further interest. Email interviews may last for some time where there is a delay between each question being asked and an answer being received. This may be advantageous in terms of allowing time for reflection on the part of the interviewer, in forming appropriate questions, and the participant, in terms of providing a considered response, but it may also mean that the interviewee may lose focus and interest so that the email interview ends without all questions being answered. Another advantage related to all forms of text-based electronic interview is that data are recorded as they are typed in, thereby removing problems associated with other forms of recording and transcription such as cost, accuracy and participants' apprehension.

Synchronous electronic interviews

An electronic interview conducted by text-based instant messaging is described as a synchronous form because the technology uses real-time transmission. However, there may be time gaps between the interviewer asking a question and the interviewee providing a response and this type of electronic interview may extend over several periods when both are online. While instant messaging originally developed as a synchronous text service, these technologies now also support aural and video services.

Pearce et al. (2014) evaluate the use of electronic interviews using synchronous text-based instant messaging. They intentionally chose this means to conduct electronic interviews because of the sensitive nature of their research topic. They conclude that for research topics where the researcher wishes to ask personal or sensitive questions, the anonymity offered by the interviewer and interviewee typing synchronously to each other is likely to produce reliable and useful data. For these types of research topic the lack of face-to-face contact may prove to be an advantage rather than a disadvantage.

Electronic interviews featuring vision and sound may be conducted using a Voice over Internet Protocol (VoIP) or web conferencing service. There are a multitude of these types of service, providing proprietary software. Services such as Skype™ allow users to conduct electronic interviews in real time. In addition to one-to-one video facilities, this technology facilitates video-conferencing between several users. Skype™ also provides other facilities through which to conduct electronic interviews such as instant messaging. This type of software also facilitates file transfers. As with video telephony discussed earlier, software can be used to produce an audio-visual recording of the interview, providing that the research participant consents to this. Hanna (2012) provides a favourable evaluation of using Skype for research interviewing, referring to advantages associated with access, ability to interact visually, and those discussed earlier in relation to telephone interviews. Hanna also makes the point that this interview mode allows both researcher and participant to remain in their own familiar and safe locations.

Using this technology has significant advantages where the population you wish to interview are geographically dispersed. Using this approach, you may be able to build up rapport with an interviewee during an Internet mediated interview where you have carefully prepared for this, including sending pre-interview information to your participant, taking into account any cultural differences and practising with this technology. However, as you will remember from Sections 6.5 and 6.6, electronic interviews have their own set of ethical issues that you will need to consider.

10.11   Visual interviews

Most interviews are based on people talking and listening, even though face-to-face interviews also contain a visual dimension, where visual cues are used to guide their conduct and aid understanding (Section 10.9). The subordinate status of this visual dimension in conventional interviews is altered when visual interviews are conducted. In a **visual interview**, visual images are used to elicit interviewee accounts and interpretations and stimulate dialogue. The use of images in these interviews means that the visual becomes fully integrated with the oral and aural in the production of participant meanings.

One approach used in visual interviews is **photo-elicitation**. In this technique a participant will be given one or more photographic or digital images to interpret. The participant will be likely to focus on the objects or activity in the image to explain these or this from her or his perspective, constructing meanings related to the image (Box 10.17). At its simplest, this means that a researcher provides a participant with an image to elicit a story about it from him or her. The settings shown in many images will be familiar to the participants and in this way the researcher will show an image of a setting to a participant to use this to elicit an insider's account from her or him. The image will be used to generate a verbal account which will then be transcribed to produce written data. These photographic or digital images may either be found or created by the researcher, or created by research participants (Box 10.17). Found images are those that already exist (Section 9.6)

Visual interviews may use other types of image to stimulate dialogue and elicit interviewee accounts and interpretations. We discuss different types of visual image in Section 9.6. These may also be found or created by the researcher, or created by the participant, before being used in a visual interview. We now discuss visual interviews based on researcher found or created images and visual interviews based on participant created images.

 Box 10.17
Focus on
management
research

Use of photo-elicitation based on participant photography

In a study published in the *International Journal of Consumer Studies,* Vermaak and de Klerk (2017) used a photo-elicitation technique in visual interviews based on participant photographs. The focus of their study was to explore millennial consumers' experiences of using retail dressing rooms. The researchers conducted two sets of research interviews with a purposive sample of female consumers aged between 18 and 25 years, who were given the task of shopping for clothes.

The first set of interviews explored consumer expectations about using retail dressing rooms. At the end of this first interview, each participant was provided with a digital camera to take photographs of any feature of a dressing room that positively or negatively impressed her in a retail store she visited.

Each participant's photographs were then used by the researchers during a second interview to elicit responses about this experience. Vermaak and de Klerk (2017: 13) report that they used questions to elicit responses from participants, like: "Why did you take this photo?" or "What did you think about this dressing room?" Responses to these questions were explored by using probing questions such as, "Why do you say so?"

Visual interviews based on researcher found or created images

In this type of visual interview, the interviewer introduces visual images during the interview and asks the participant to interpret what he or she sees in each image. This type of visual elicitation may occur during a one-to-one interview, a group interview or a focus group. One digital image may be introduced at a time or a number of images may be presented simultaneously. An individual image may show a particular situation or aspect related to the research topic. It may be an image of the research setting. Each image presented individually will be intended to elicit interpretation and stimulate discussion. Several images shown simultaneously will represent different attributes of a topic. An example here might relate to consumer research. Participants will be asked to discuss the relative merits of the attributes shown, possibly being requested to choose from amongst these or to rank them. This type of approach has a long history in some areas of business and management research. Meyer (1991) reports examples from accounting research where accountants were shown pictures of schematic faces representing a range from satisfactory to alarming, which were used to depict the financial health of organisations.

An interviewer may also introduce visual images to be able to gather contextual details or background information about the research setting. These may include photographic or digital images of the research setting which can be explored with interviewees. These images will allow contextual and mundane details to be seen, discussed and evaluated which would otherwise be missed in a conventional talking and listening interview. An interviewer may also introduce other types of visual image such as an organisation chart to be able to understand the broader context within which the research is being conducted.

One type of visual interview is based on images of research participants taken by the researcher. These images are explored using a particular photo-elicitation technique known as autodriving. This technique was developed and refined by Heisley and Levy (1991). The term **autodriving** refers to an interview that is 'self-driven' by the interviewee talking about visual images of her or him: from the definitions of types of research interview we introduced in Section 10.2, this is an informant interview. The researcher will initially enter the setting where a research participant lives, works or conducts their daily activities. The researcher will observe the participant in this setting and take visual images that capture aspects of the activity being observed. Particular images will be selected by the researcher from amongst those taken to represent key aspects of this activity. These images will then be used in an interview with the participant who features in them, to elicit this participant's interpretations of what is shown in each image. This technique is potentially powerful because it captures the participant's actions and interactions in the setting but then places the participant in the role of an outsider looking in on a scene in which she or he takes a part. The interviewer uses these visual images to elicit the participant's insider perspective of what is shown, producing insights that would be unlikely to be revealed using any other method.

While this technique is potentially powerful and insightful, it is the researcher who decides which visual images to take and which ones to select for use in the visual interview. While the visual interview used to explore these images is an informant one based on an interpretivist approach (Chapter 4), it is the researcher who elicits the interviewee's interpretation rather than the participant presenting images they have taken and explaining these. There is therefore scope for a range of more participative approaches to the use of visual images in visual interviews as we now consider.

Visual interviews based on participant created images

A more participatory approach will range from a researcher encouraging participants to create their own images which can then be explored in visual interviews (Box 10.17), through collaborative forms of visual research in which participants are involved in different aspects of the research process (see also Section 9.3), including taking, selecting, analysing and interpreting images, to the use of a participant-led approach known as photovoice. The level of participation increases over this range of possibilities from passive participation to active and fully engaged participation.

We discussed participatory approaches in Section 9.6, including the use of participatory video, participatory audio and participant photography. These approaches involve research participants using their mobile phone or being provided with a video camera, audio-recorder, or digital camera and given the freedom to choose what to record related to the focus of the research. A further participatory approach exists which may be used before or during the conduct of a visual interview. This is **participant drawing** where a participant is asked to create a drawing using paper and pencil to represent her or his feelings about an issue, or some aspect of his or her experience (Box 10.18). Techniques of participant photography or drawing are sometimes used to facilitate interaction with children or participants who are less articulate but may be used successfully with many types of participant.

In an approach where the researcher encourages participants to create their own images, a visual interview is still likely to be based on the interviewer eliciting interpretations from each participant. However, the interviewer will also need to explore the

Box 10.18
Focus on
student research

Using participant drawing in an interview

As part of her research Heather wanted her participants to reflect on what they saw as the essence of leadership. She decided to ask each of them to 'sketch' what they considered to be the essence of leadership at the start of their interview. Although some participants were initially reluctant to draw protesting that their drawings would not be 'any good', offering colour pens and paper to each participant resulted in 30 drawings. Most were relatively quickly sketched in 5 to 10 minutes. Despite the initial hesitation from some participants, most were pleased with their sketches. Heather used each participant's drawing as the basis for their subsequent interview. Drawings such as the one included in this box highlight aspects of leadership such

as taking followers on a journey (the path), through troubled times (the clouds and rain) and areas where it might be difficult to see what was going to happen next (the trees), to a successful finish (the chequered flag) where things were brighter (the sun shining).

participant's reason for creating each image. This will include asking why the participant chose to take the image, the significance of the objects, activity or interaction shown in the image, and how the image represents the experience or viewpoint of the participant. Some participant-created images will be literal visual representations while others may be abstract ones and it will be necessary to explore these with the participant to understand what an image represents and why it was chosen, in order to gain insight. Exploring images may encourage a participant to 'relive' an experience or reflect on its personal significance. The emphasis in this process will be to facilitate participant interpretation, to understand subjective perspectives using a non-judgemental approach.

A participatory approach may involve participants collaborating in various aspects of a research project, possibly through all of its stages from design to presentation. In this approach the role of the participant in a visual interview is more likely to be that of a collaborative discussant. One technique associated with greater participation is **reflexive photography**. This involves participants engaging in participant photography and reflective interviews to explore how their experiences are situated within social structures and attitudes related to class, gender, race, role and other social categories. This technique is likely to involve participants in several stages of participant photography and reflection, often involving group interviews in which participants meet together to present, discuss and analyse their photographic or digital images (Ozanne et al. 2013).

Related to reflexive photography and often led by participants, **photovoice** involves participants using participant photography centred on a research focus of social concern and meeting with other participants in group discussions to present, discuss and analyse images which they have created. Images are then selected by the participants to represent this issue of social concern. These will be presented in a public exhibition with the aim of generating wider public support and action, or to change public policy.

10.12   Use of research diaries to collect data

A **research diary** is a systematic, participant-centred research method. Participants who use this method will either complete daily questionnaires to produce quantitative data, or they will create written, typed or audio-recorded diary entries to produce qualitative data. A research diary is used in a longitudinal study in the sense that data are collected consecutively rather than at a single point in time, although this may range from a few days to three months (Section 5.9) (Box 10.19). The period over which the research diary will be completed or created will be agreed between the researcher and the participants, although extended use of research diaries is likely to lead to participant fatigue and attrition. Research diaries are designed to record data about participants' experiences. The focus of the research question will determine which aspect of these participants' experiences to record and how frequently. At this level, research diaries are a powerful means to collect data about participants' activities, social interactions, behaviours, attitudes, emotions or sense of well-being. More broadly, research diaries provide a means to understand complex processes in organisations. A research project based on the use of research diaries is often called a **diary study**. Research participants in a diary study may be referred to as diarists or diary-keepers.

Research diaries allow data to be collected at multiple points in time. This may involve you asking your participants to complete or create a diary entry on a daily basis, or at some other interval depending on the frequency of the activity or aspect that your research is designed to focus upon. This activity or aspect may occur more than once a day, or less often than daily. Box 10.19 provides examples of research participants being asked to complete timed diary entries more than once a day, for a pre-arranged number of days or weeks.

One aim of using a research diary is to encourage data to be recorded soon after an activity or event has occurred. In this way, diarists' perceptions about the activity or event can be recorded while their experience of it is still foremost in their minds. This should allow diarists accurately to recall what they experienced, when and where it occurred, how they were involved and how they feel about it. This is likely to be advantageous when compared to research methods which ask participants to recollect a past activity or event when their perceptions and feelings about it have been lessened by time. In this way, data from research diaries should have high internal validity/credibility/authenticity (Section 5.11). This will be the case where you gain access to a participant's directly expressed experience and are able to infer meanings that the participant intended from the language used by that person.

Repeatedly collecting data through the completion or creation of multiple diary entries is also likely to produce rich data sets. This should allow frequencies, patterns and themes to be recognised in these data. Use of research diaries also leads to the production of comparable data – within and between individuals (we return to discuss this point later). Research diary data are collected unobtrusively since diarists complete or create their own entries without the researcher being present.

As we noted earlier, diary entries may be recorded in writing, where participants complete paper-based questionnaires or create hand-written entries, they may be completed online where participants complete questionnaires or word process entries, and in qualitative studies they may be recorded as audio-diaries or video-diaries. These means to record diary entries will each have implications for participants. Your choice of method to record diary data will need to consider its suitability for the context of the research and for the circumstances of individual participants. We consider this further in the discussion which follows.

These characteristics may suggest that the use of research diaries could form part of your research strategy. To help you decide whether they might, we first look at types of research diary and then explore advantages, issues and strategies associated with their use.

Types of research diary

Like research interviews, research diaries may be highly structured and formalised, using pre-specified questions and responses, or less structured and informal, where participants are asked to write, type or audio record their responses to pre-determined open questions. The first type is used in a **quantitative diary study** and the second type is used in a **qualitative diary study**. In this sub-section we briefly describe each of these types.

Quantitative diary study

A **quantitative research diary** will be composed of a series of identical, reasonably short questionnaires that are designed to be self-completed by a participant (Section 11.2). The purpose of a quantitative research diary is to enable repeated measurements to be obtained from each participant at regular intervals through the course of the study. Participants may be asked to complete a questionnaire every day and to date this, while in some studies they will be asked to complete more than one questionnaire per day, which they will be asked to date and state the time at which it was completed. A quantitative diary study may last from a few days to a number of weeks, depending on the nature of the research objectives and the purpose of the research (Box 10.19).

Completing a quantitative research diary will demand both time and dedication from those who agree to participate. This will especially be the case where you ask your participants to complete more than one diary entry (questionnaire) per day (Box 10.19). We outlined the different modes of delivery, completion and return of questionnaires in

Section 11.2 (for example, online or by hand). These different modes will also be relevant for quantitative diary entries (daily questionnaires). However, where participants are being asked to complete diary entries at least once a day, the mode chosen needs to facilitate ease of completion and return. Uy et al. (2017) facilitated this by asking their participants to complete paper and pencil diary entries, which were issued every day in person by a researcher and once completed, were deposited in a drop box in the workplace. In some circumstances this approach will not be appropriate. Biron and Van Veldhoven (2016) produced booklets that contained an initial, longer questionnaire, the diary entries composed of shorter questionnaires and a set of instructions, which were either given out to participants, or posted to them. At the end of the study, these booklets were either collected in person or returned using a stamped addressed envelope that had been provided. In some circumstances, you will be able to ask your participants to access a daily diary entry through a web browser using a hyperlink, which they can then complete and return electronically.

Box 10.19
Focus on management research

Examples of quantitative diary studies

In a study published in the *Journal of Management,* Vogel and Mitchell (2017) undertook research on the ways employees respond to diminished self-esteem after suffering from abusive supervision. Based on a theoretical model that examined the effects of abusive supervision on affected employees' workplace behaviours, which was mediated by sense of self-esteem and moderated by intention to leave, they undertook three field studies. The third of these was based on a quantitative diary study, referred to as a 'daily diary design'. For this study, they used 85 participants. These participants were given a link to an initial questionnaire that was used to measure demographic data about each participant, traits related to their self-esteem, their intentions to remain in or leave their employment and scope for alternative employment. The 83 participants who completed the initial questionnaire within one week were then sent daily questionnaires to complete during the last hour of each working day for 21 days. The measures in this daily questionnaire included those to assess, 'daily abusive supervision', 'daily self-esteem', 'turnover intentions' and 'daily workplace deviance'.

In a quantitative diary study published in the *Journal of Organizational Behaviour,* Prem et al. (2017) focused on the within-individual effects of time pressure and learning demands on knowledge workers' scope to thrive at work. 124 participants took part in this 5 day diary study, in which each participant completed questionnaires three times each day: during the morning, afternoon and at the end of the working day. Prior to commencing this 5 day diary study, participants completed a general questionnaire. The daily questionnaires were based on abbreviated scales and measured time pressure and learning demands in the morning, appraisal of the challenges and hindrances related to work in the afternoon, and learning and sense of vitality in the final daily questionnaire.

In a quantitative diary study published in the *Academy of Management Journal,* Uy et al. (2017) examined the relationship between surface acting at work, resulting emotional exhaustion and next-day work engagement. They also examined the moderating effects of giving and receiving help at work. Their analytical focus in examining these relationships was at the within-individual level. After completing an online initial, background questionnaire, the 102 participants took part in this 5 day diary study, with each participant completing a questionnaire before commencing work, a second questionnaire at the end of the working day while still in the workplace and a third questionnaire at home before going to bed.

The completion of daily questionnaires in a quantitative diary study not only allows analysis to be conducted on variations between participants' responses (referred to as a **between persons analysis**) but also analyses at the level of each individual person (referred to as **within-individual level analysis**). This means that analysis may measure how each person's responses vary from day-to-day and whether any relationships are evident between the variables being measured at the level of the individual. In diary studies where participants complete more than one daily questionnaire, analysis may also be conducted to measure differences in a participant's responses at different times of the day. For example, a quantitative diary study may be designed to measure the levels of stress or exhaustion of individuals at different times of each working day. In such a study, analysis could measure differences between persons and within individuals in relation to different times of the day.

Qualitative diary study

A **qualitative research diary** will be created by participants writing or typing diary entries, or audio-recording their spoken thoughts. Recording a date and time in relation to either of these will be important. Qualitative diary entries will either be created at regular intervals, usually daily, or more randomly related to the occurrence of a particular event or activity. These options are referred to as an interval-contingent approach and event-contingent approach. This choice will depend on the focus of the research question and research objectives. Qualitative research diaries are used in longitudinal studies, ranging from a few days to three months, although extended use of this method may be associated with participant fatigue and attrition. A qualitative diary study is also likely to be conducted with a small numbers of participants, ranging from four to twelve (Box 10.20).

Qualitative research diaries are designed to produce accounts of participants' experiences, and their thoughts and feelings related to these (Box 10.20). The production of these accounts may be structured by providing participants with a diary template or prompt sheet containing a number of open questions to which you ask them to respond. In relation to the specific focus of your research question, this may ask diarists to respond along the lines of the approach we indicated earlier: to describe what was experienced, why it occurred, when and where, how they were involved, what were the outcomes, and how they feel about it. However, this type of semi-structured approach may be seen as making assumptions about the nature of participants' experiences and imposing a rational and structured approach to the entries you expect them to produce. This may be what you wish them to do! Alternatively, you may wish participants to reflect more on their subjective interpretations of their experiences, in which case you may wish to provide them with a less structured template that offers some guidance about their purpose in creating diary entries but without a framework of questions to which to respond. This is the difference between a semi-structured and unstructured approach to designing a qualitative research diary. In either case, the support that you offer to your diarists will be important in terms of the relevance, quality and quantity of the data that they produce in their research diaries (Day and Thatcher 2009). This is likely to include at least some guidance about creating diary entries to prevent participants dropping out of a diary study because of uncertainty about what to record (Crozier and Cassell 2016) (Box 10.20).

Well supported diarists can produce rich and plentiful data. Day and Thatcher (2009: 254) report that participants in a qualitative diary study which they conducted provided, "full length answers with a great deal of detail. . . . [and that] . . . the depth of answers remained consistent throughout each participant's diary." They say that participants often began each diary entry by describing and discussing events, before providing an account of their own thoughts and feelings. These entries were written using a conversational style in which diarists often engaged in an internal dialogue. Diarists sometimes chose to emphasise parts of what they wrote by using capital letters, exclamation marks and under-scoring; they also drew emotive symbols such as smiley or sad faces. All of these aspects could be incorporated in the analysis of these data.

Crozier and Cassell (2016) also recognise that qualitative research diaries are suitable to encourage participants to produce discursive and narrative accounts and, like the use of quantitative research diaries, can be used to understand how individuals react to particular events and cope with these (Box 10.20). Qualitative research diary entries can also be used to generate reflective accounts, where a diarist uses an entry to evaluate an earlier experience or set of experiences retrospectively.

While qualitative diary entries may be created unobtrusively by participants, some potential diarists may nevertheless find this process to be difficult or intrusive. Keeping a diary will be unfamiliar to many participants. Some may not feel that they have the skills to do this adequately and may struggle to express their thoughts and feelings. This sense of struggle may be related to the feeling that what they are being asked to do is intrusive; thoughts and feelings that they normally keep to themselves or only share with significant others will now be recorded and shared with people who they do not know or trust. Some participants may be uncertain about what will happen to the sensitive data which they create. While some participants will welcome and relish the opportunity to create a qualitative research diary, others may be reticent and self-conscious. You will therefore need to consider how you communicate with intended participants about issues related to informed consent, participant guidance and support, privacy, the avoidance of risk and harm, the voluntary nature of participation, anonymity and confidentiality, responsibility in the way data are handled, analysed and reported, and subsequently managed, if you wish to use this research method (Chapter 6).

Box 10.20
Focus on management research

Examples of qualitative diary studies

In a study published in *Qualitative Research in Psychology*, Day and Thatcher (2009) asked eight participants to keep hand-written qualitative research diaries. The pages in each diary were headed with a printed date to encourage completion of entries. Other support provided to participants included sending text message reminders to complete entries and the opportunity to discuss any issues about this task with one of the researchers. This study was conducted over a period of three months, and while participants were not expected to complete an entry every day because of the event-based nature of the research, some did by explaining why a particular day's activities were not relevant to the research focus.

In an audio diary study published in the *Journal of Occupational and Organizational Psychology,* Crozier and Cassell (2016) selected six participants to represent a small but diverse sample with regard to age and gender. Choice of this relatively small sample was related to the in-depth, individual level of the analysis, which was designed to focus on within-individual variability. Participants were asked to audio-record entries twice a week for four weeks. A message was sent to each participant by mobile phone on the day an audio diary entry was scheduled to be recorded. Participants were provided with a set of instructions for audio recording and a prompt sheet to provide some structure and guidance about what to comment and reflect on in their audio recordings. This list of ten prompts indicates the semi-structured nature of this approach, although in the spirit of a semi-structured approach (Section 10.2) participants were advised to be flexible in the way they used these prompts depending on their relevance to the situation. The individual recordings that participants produced varied from less than two minutes to twelve minutes each. In total the six participants produced 287 minutes of audio recordings.

Advantages and issues associated with using research diaries

In our discussion about research diaries we have discussed a number of advantages and issues associated with their use. Box 10.21 provides a checklist to summarise these. This checklist leads to a discussion of strategies you may consider using to help you design and conduct a diary study.

Box 10.21
Checklist

Advantages and issues associated with using research diaries

Research diaries:

✔ are a powerful means to collect data about participants' activities, social interactions, behaviours, attitudes, emotions and sense of well-being;

✔ provide a means to understand complex processes in organisations;

✔ allow data to be collected at multiple points in time;

✔ encourage data to be recorded soon after an activity or event has occurred while perceptions about it may be recalled easily;

✔ should have high internal validity/credibility/authenticity because of the nature of the data;

✔ used in qualitative diary studies are capable of producing data that are descriptive, discursive, evaluative, narrative and reflective;

✔ are likely to produce rich data sets through the completion or creation of multiple diary entries during the course of a study;

✔ are likely to allow frequencies, patterns and themes to be recognised in the data;

✔ lead to the production of comparable data – within and between individuals;

✔ allow data to be collected unobtrusively.

When using research diaries, you need to:

✔ recognise the importance of ensuring participants create or complete sufficient diary entries for your study to be viable;

✔ consider how often and when diary entries should be created or completed, related to the use of an interval-contingent or event-contingent approach;

✔ consider how many diary entries each participant should produce in total and over what period of time;

✔ recognise the scope for participant fatigue and attrition, leading to non-completion;

✔ consider the logistical difficulties participants may face in accessing, completing and returning individual diary entries or completed diaries;

✔ recognise the scope for participant uncertainty about what should be included in qualitative diary entries, in relation to both the relevance and sufficiency of this content;

✔ consider the amount of guidance and structure that should be provided to participants, especially in a qualitative diary study;

✔ recognise that too little guidance or support in an unstructured qualitative diary study may lead to uncertainty and adverse consequences for participation, and for the relevance, quality and quantity of data that are produced;

✔ recognise that the provision of a diary template or prompt sheet in a semi-structured qualitative diary study should be sufficient to facilitate relevant, high quality responses without being restrictive;

✔ recognise that some participants in a qualitative diary study may find it difficult to express themselves in the way envisaged in this approach, potentially affecting the quality of any data produced or leading to non-completion;

✔ recognise that some participants in qualitative diary studies may find the use of this method to be intrusive or risky, leading to non-participation, non-completion or adversely affected data quality.

Strategies to help you design and conduct a diary study

We noted earlier that a diary study is a systematic, participant-centred research method. The successful conduct of such a method will partly depend on factors considered during its design. You will therefore need to plan your diary study very carefully, attempting to anticipate all possible issues. Depending on the quantitative or qualitative nature of your diary study, this will include pilot testing your proposed instructions, guidance notes, questionnaires, template or prompt sheet in a suitable context to evaluate these, and making changes where necessary. You will need to consider your participants and discuss the nature of their participation carefully with them, to gain informed consent and provide assurances and information related to ethical, participatory and logistical issues. As a diary study will demand both time and dedication from participants, you will need to discuss the requirements of participation. Establishing informed and realistic expectations before commencement may help to reduce participant attrition. This will include clear expectations about what to include in a qualitative diary entry, how to complete a quantitative (daily questionnaire) diary, the frequency of diary entries, the likely time required to complete or create each entry, the way entries will be recorded and any logistical issues related to this, and the overall duration of the diary study.

Achieving positive outcomes when you conduct a diary study will depend on the instructions, research diary and support provided to participants. The instructions should include a short, clear statement that informs participants about what they need to do, when or how often and how to contact the researcher to ask for advice. In a qualitative diary study the instructions will also include a template or prompt sheet to guide participants as they compose diary entries. As we noted, this template or prompt sheet may be more or less structured, depending on the nature and purpose of the research. The research diary will be the means through which data are recorded. As we described earlier, the research diary may take a number of forms. Providing participants with a suitable means to complete regular questionnaires or create diary entries will be vital. This may involve use of paper-based documents, the Internet or, in some qualitative diary studies, audio-recording equipment. You will need to ensure that the means you use is appropriate for your participants and to the setting of your research. An inappropriate or difficult to use diary technique is likely to lead to a poor outcome.

The support you offer your participants in a diary study will also be very important. Contact during the early days of a diary study will enable you to find out whether participants are experiencing any issues in relation to completing diary entries. This will offer you the opportunity to resolve these and deal with any concerns or doubts. Assurances given at this stage may help to avoid participant attrition. As we noted earlier, you may also send each participant a message by mobile phone on the day a diary entry is scheduled to be recorded. After participants have become used to completing or creating diary entries, you may feel more confident about the conduct of the diary study. However there is still a risk that participants may stop completing entries at agreed intervals, or even stop participating. Keeping in contact may help to avoid these possibilities. In a longer diary study lasting several weeks you should consider contacting your participants on a reasonably regular basis to check if any issues have arisen in relation to their participation. Some participants may relish the task of completing or creating their diary and some of these may not welcome regular checking; you will therefore need to be sensitive to this type of participant, as well as to others who welcome reminders or need reassurance to keep participating.

Depending on the means you are using to conduct your diary study you will also need to consider the return of diary entries or complete diaries at the end of the study. You will need to recognise that participants will have invested a great deal of time and dedication to completing or creating their diaries. They will have become involved in the research project. You will need to consider offering them a debriefing at the time they complete their diaries and later when you have analysed the data and produced your report. Feedback from participants at the time you collect the completed diary, or final diary entry, may be very helpful to you in terms of making sense of the data you have gathered.

10.13 Summary

- The use of semi-structured and in-depth interviews allows you to collect rich and detailed data, although you will need to develop a sufficient level of competence to conduct these and to be able to gain access to the type of data associated with their use.
- Interviews can be differentiated according to the level of structure and modes adopted to conduct them.
- Semi-structured and in-depth research interviews can be used to explore topics and explain findings.
- There are situations favouring semi-structured and in-depth interviews that will lead you to use either or both of these to collect data. Apart from the purpose of your research, these are related to the significance of establishing personal contact, the nature of your data collection questions, and the length of time required from those who provide data.
- Your research design may incorporate more than one type of interview.
- Semi-structured and in-depth interviews can be used in a variety of research strategies.
- Data quality issues related to reliability/dependability, forms of bias, cultural differences and generalisability/transferability may be overcome by considering why you have chosen to use interviews, recognising that all research methods have limitations and through careful preparation to conduct interviews to avoid bias that would threaten the reliability/dependability and validity/credibility of your data.
- The conduct of semi-structured and in-depth interviews will be affected by the appropriateness of your appearance, opening comments when the interview commences, approach to questioning, appropriate use of different types of question, nature of the interviewer's behaviour during the interview, demonstration of attentive listening skills, scope to summarise and test understanding, ability to deal with difficult participants and ability to record data accurately and fully.
- Logistical and resource matters need to be considered and managed when you use in-depth and semi-structured interviews.
- Apart from one-to-one interviews conducted on a face-to-face basis, you may consider conducting such interviews by telephone or electronically.
- You may consider using group interviews or focus group interviews. There may be particular advantages associated with group interviews, but these are considerably more difficult to manage than one-to-one interviews.
- You may also consider using visual images during the conduct of interviews depending on the purpose of your research.
- Primary data may also be collected through the use of a quantitative or qualitative diary study.

Self-check questions

Help with these questions is available at the end of the chapter.

10.1 What type of interview would you use in each of the following situations:
  a a market research project?
  b a research project seeking to understand whether attitudes to working from home have changed?
  c following the analysis of a questionnaire?

10.2 What are the advantages of using semi-structured and in-depth interviews?

10.3 During a presentation of your proposal to undertake a research project, which will be based on semi-structured or in-depth interviews, you feel that you have dealt well with the relationship between the purpose of the research and the proposed methodology, when one of the panel leans forward and asks you to discuss the trustworthiness and usefulness of your work for other researchers. This is clearly a challenge to see whether you can defend such an approach. How do you respond?

10.4 Having quizzed you about the trustworthiness and usefulness of your work for other researchers, the panel member decides that one more testing question is in order. He explains that interviews are not an easy option. 'It is not an easier alternative for those who want to avoid statistics', he says. 'How can we be sure that you're competent to get involved in inter-view work, especially where the external credibility of this organisation may be affected by the impression that you create in the field?' How will you respond to this concern?

10.5 What are the key issues to consider when planning to use semi-structured or in-depth interviews?

10.6 What are the key areas of competence that you need to develop in order to conduct an interview successfully?

10.7 Which circumstances will suggest the use of visual interviews based on researcher-created images, even where the researcher favours using visual interviews based on participant-created images wherever possible?

10.8 You are designing a qualitative diary study but are not sure whether to ask your partici-pants to record their diary entries on paper, word process them, or to create an audio-diary. You decide to brain storm the merits of each approach. What points might be included in this consideration?

Review and discussion questions

10.9 Watch and, if possible, record a television interview such as one that is part of a chat show or a documentary. It does not matter if you record an interview of only 10 to 15 minutes' duration.
  a As you watch the interview, make notes about what the participant is telling the inter-viewer. After the interview, review your notes. How much of what was being said did you manage to record?
  b If you were able to record the television interview, watch it again and compare your notes with what was actually said. What other information would you like to add to your notes?
  c Either watch the interview again or another television interview that is part of a chat show or a documentary. This time pay careful attention to the questioning techniques used by the interviewer. How many of the different types of question discussed in Section 10.5 can you identify?

d How important are the non-verbal cues given by the interviewer and the interviewee in understanding the meaning of what is being said?

10.10 With a friend, each decide on a topic about which you think it would be interesting to interview the other person. Separately develop your interview themes and prepare an interview guide for a semi-structured interview. At the same time, decide which one of the 'difficult' participants in Table 10.2 you would like to role-play when being interviewed.

a Conduct both interviews and, if possible, make a recording. If this is not possible either audio-record or ensure the interviewer takes notes.

b Watch each of the recordings – what aspects of your interviewing technique do you each need to improve?

c If you were not able to record the interview, how good a record of each interview do you consider the notes to be? How could you improve your interviewing technique further?

d As an interviewer, ask your friend an open question about the topic. As your friend answers the question, note down her/his answer. Summarise this answer back to your friend. Then ask your friend to assess whether you have summarised their answer accurately and understood what s/he meant.

10.11 Obtain a transcript of an interview that has already been undertaken. If your university subscribes to online newspapers such as ft.com, these are a good source of business-related transcripts. Alternatively, typing 'interview transcript' into a search engine such as Google or Bing will generate numerous possibilities on a vast range of topics!

a Examine the transcript, paying careful attention to the questioning techniques used by the interviewer. To what extent do you think that certain questions have led the interviewee to certain answers?

b Now look at the responses given by the interviewer. To what extent do you think these are the actual verbatim responses given by the interviewee? Why do you think this?

Progressing your research project

Using research interviews

- Assess whether research interviews will help you to answer your research question and address your objectives. Where you do not think that they will be helpful, justify your decision. Where you think that they will be helpful, respond to the following points.
- Which type or types of research interview will be appropriate to use? Explain how you intend to use these and how they will fit into your chosen research strategy.
- Draft a topic focus to explore during in-depth interviews or list of themes to use in the conduct of semi-structured interviews and use your

research question(s) and objectives to assess this or these.

- What threats to the trustworthiness of the interview data you collect are you likely to encounter? How will you seek to overcome these?
- What practical problems do you foresee in using research interviews? How will you attempt to overcome these practical problems?
- Ask your project tutor to comment on your judgement about using research interviews, the relationship between these and your proposed research strategy, the fit between your topic focus or interview themes and your research question(s) and objectives, the issues and threats that you have identified, and your suggestions to overcome these.
- Use the questions in Box 1.4 to guide your reflective diary entry.

Progressing your research project *(continued)*

Using research diaries

- Assess whether the use of a research diary study will help you to answer your research question and address your objectives. Where you do not think that this will be helpful, justify your decision. Where you think that this will be helpful, respond to the following points.
- Which research strategy or strategies do you propose to use (Section 5.8)? What will be the implications of this strategy or strategies for the type of diary study that you use and the way in which you will analyse your data (Chapters 12 and 13)?
- Which issues are likely to arise in relation to using this diary study? Which strategies will you use to anticipate and seek to overcome these?
- Ask your project tutor to comment on your judgement about using a diary study and its relationship to your proposed research strategy, the issues you have identified that may affect its conduct and your strategies to anticipate and seek to overcome these.
- Use the questions in Box 1.4 to guide your reflective diary entry.

References

Banks, G.C., Pollack, J.M., Bochantin, J.E., Kirkman, B.L., Whelpley, C.E. and O'Boyle, E.H. (2016) 'Management's Science-Practice Gap: A Grand Challenge for All Stakeholders', *Academy of Management Journal,* Vol. 59, No. 6, pp. 2205–2231.

BBC Academy (2018) *Interviewing.* Available at http://www.bbc.co.uk/academy/journalism/skills/interviewing [Accessed 12 March 2018].

Belzile, J.A. and Oberg, G. (2012) 'Where to begin? Grappling with how to use participant interaction in focus group design', *Qualitative Research,* Vol. 12, No. 4, pp. 459–72.

Biron. M. and Van Veldhoven, M. (2016) 'When control becomes a liability rather than an asset: Comparing home and office days among part-time teleworkers', *Journal of Organizational Behaviour,* Vol. 37, pp. 1317–1337.

Boddy, C. (2005) 'A rose by any other name may smell as sweet but "group discussion" is not another name for "focus group" nor should it be', *Qualitative Market Research,* Vol. 8, No. 3, pp. 248–55.

Brinkmann, S. and Kvale, S. (2015) *InterViews: Learning the Craft of Qualitative Research Interviewing* (3rd edn). London: Sage.

Broome, J. (2015) 'How Telephone Interviewers' Responsiveness Impacts Their Success', *Field Methods,* Vol. 27, No. 1, pp. 66–81.

Carson, D., Gilmore, A., Perry, C. and Grønhaug, K. (2001) *Qualitative Marketing Research.* London: Sage.

Chidlow, A., Plakoyiannaki, E. and Welch, C. (2014) 'Translation in cross-language international business research: Beyond equivalence', *Journal of International Business Studies,* Vol. 45, pp. 562–582.

Court, D. and Abbas, R. (2013) 'Whose interview is it, anyway? Methodological and ethical challenges of insider-outsider research, multiple languages, and dual-researcher cooperation', *Qualitative Inquiry,* Vol. 19, No. 6, pp. 480–8.

Crozier, S.E. and Cassell, C.M. (2015) 'Methodological considerations in the use of audio diaries in work psychology: Adding to the Qualitative toolkit', *Journal of Occupational and Organizational Psychology,* Vol. 89, No. 2, pp. 396–419.

David-Barrett, E., Yakis-Douglas, B., Moss-Cowan, A. and Nguyen, Y. (2017) 'A Bitter Pill? Institutional Corruption and the Challenge of Antibribery Compliance in the Pharmaceutical Sector', *Journal of Management Inquiry,* Vol. 26, No. 3, pp. 326–347.

Day. M and Thatcher, J. (2009) '"I'm Really Embarrassed That You're Going to Read This . . . ": Reflections on Using Diaries in Qualitative Research', *Qualitative Research in Psychology,* Vol. 6, No. 4, pp. 249–259.

Denzin, N.K. (2001) 'The reflexive interview and a performative social science', *Qualitative Research,* Vol. 1, No. 1, pp. 23–46.

Dick, B. (2013) 'Convergent interviewing [Online]. Available at http://www.aral.com.au/resources/coin.pdf [Accessed 23 June 2018].

Gobo, G. (2011) 'Glocalizing methodology? The encounter between local methodologies', *International Journal of Social Research Methodology,* Vol. 14, No. 6, pp. 417–37.

Hanna, P. (2012) 'Using internet technologies (such as Skype) as a research medium: A research note', *Qualitative Research,* Vol. 12, No. 2, pp. 239–42.

Heisley, D.D. and Levy, S.J. (1991) 'Autodriving: A Photoelicitation Technique', *Journal of Consumer Research,* Vol. 18, No. 4, pp. 257–272.

Heyl, B.S. (2005) 'Ethnographic interviewing', in P. Atkinson, A. Coffey, S. Delamont, J. Lofland and L. Lofland (eds) *Handbook of Ethnography.* Thousand Oaks, CA: Sage, pp. 369–383.

Holt, A. (2010) 'Using the telephone for narrative interviewing: A research note', *Qualitative Research,* Vol. 10, No. 1, pp. 113–121.

Irvine, A. (2011) 'Duration, Dominance and Depth in Telephone and Face-to-Face Interviews: A Comparative Exploration', *International Journal of Qualitative Methods,* Vol. 10, No. 3, pp. 202–220.

Irvine, A., Drew, P. and Sainsbury, R. (2012) '"Am I not answering your questions properly?" Clarification, adequacy and responsiveness in semi-structured telephone and face-to-face interviews', *Qualitative Research,* Vol. 13, No. 1, pp. 87–106.

Keaveney, S.M. (1995) 'Customer switching behaviour in service industries: An exploratory study', *Journal of Marketing,* Vol. 59, No. 2, pp. 71–82.

King, N. (2004) 'Using interviews in qualitative research', in C. Cassell and G. Symon (eds) *Essential Guide to Qualitative Methods in Organizational Research.* London: Sage, pp. 11–22.

Krueger, R.A. and Casey, M.A. (2015) *Focus Groups: A Practical Guide for Applied Research* (5th edn). London: Sage.

Lijadi, A.A, and van Schalkwyk, G.J. (2015) 'Online Facebook Focus Group Research of Hard-to-Reach Participants', *International Journal of Qualitative Methods,* Vol. 14, No. 1, pp. 1–9.

Macnaghten, P. and Myers, G. (2007) 'Focus groups', in C. Seale, G. Gobo, J.F. Gubrium and D. Silverman (eds) *Qualitative Research Practice.* London: Sage, pp. 65–79.

Meyer, A. D. (1991) 'Visual Data in Organizational Research', *Organization Science,* Vol. 2, No. 2, pp. 218–236.

Oates, C. and Alevizou, P.J. (2018) *Conducting Focus Groups for Business and Management Students.* London: Sage.

Ozanne, J.L., Moscato, E.M., Kunkel, D.R. (2013) 'Transformative Photography: Evaluation and Best Practices for Eliciting Social and Policy Changes', *Journal of Public Policy and Marketing,* Vol. 32, No. 1, pp. 45–65.

Pearce, G., Thogersen-Ntoumani, C. and Duda, J.L. (2014) 'The development of synchronous text-based instant messaging as an online interviewing tool', *International Journal of Social Research Methodology,* Vol. 17, No. 6, pp. 677–92.

Powney, J. and Watts, M. (1987) *Interviewing in Educational Research.* London: Routledge & Kegan Paul.

Prem, R., Ohly, S., Kubicek, B. and Korunka. C. (2017) 'Thriving on challenge stressors? Exploring time pressure and learning demands as antecedents of thriving at work', *Journal of Organizational Behaviour,* Vol. 38, No. 1, pp. 108–123.

Speer, S.A. (2008) 'Natural and contrived data', in P. Alasuutari, L. Bickman, and J. Brannen (eds) *The Sage Handbook of Social Research Methods.* London: Sage, pp. 290–312.

Stokes, D. and Bergin, R. (2006) 'Methodology or "methodolatry"? An evaluation of focus groups and depth interviews', *Qualitative Market Research,* Vol. 9, No. 1, pp. 26–37.

Teddlie, C. and Tashakkori, A. (2009) *Foundations of Mixed Methods Research: Integrating Quantitative and Qualitative Approaches in the Social and Behavioural Sciences.* Thousand Oaks, CA: Sage.

Trier-Bieniek, A. (2012) 'Framing the telephone interview as a participant-centred tool for qualitative research: A methodological discussion', *Qualitative Research,* Vol. 12, No. 6, pp. 630–44.

Uy, M.A., Lin, K.J. and Ilies, R. (2017) 'Is It Better To Give Or Receive? The Role Of Help In Buffering The Depleting Effects Of Surface Acting', *Academy of Management Journal,* Vol. 60, No. 4, pp. 1442–1461.

Vermaak, M. and de Klerk, H.M. (2017) 'Fitting room or selling room? Millennial female consumers' dressing room experiences', *International Journal of Consumer Studies,* Vol. 41, pp. 11–18.

Vogel, R.M. and Mitchell, M.S. (2017) 'The Motivational Effects of Diminished Self-Esteem for Employees Who Experience Abusive Supervision', *Journal of Management,* Vol. 43, No. 7, pp. 2218–2251.

Vogl, S. (2013) 'Telephone Versus Face-to-Face Interviews: Mode Effect on Semistructured Interviews With Children', *Sociological Methodology,* Vol. 43, No. 1, pp. 133–177.

Way, A.K., Zwier, R.K. and Tracy, S.J. (2015) 'Dialogic Interviewing and Flickers of Transformation: An Examination and Delineation of Interactional Strategies That Promote Participant Self-Reflexivity', *Qualitative Inquiry,* Vol. 2, No. 8, pp. 720–731.

Williams, W. and Lewis, D. (2005) 'Convergent interviewing: a tool for strategic investigation', *Strategic Change,* Vol. 14, No. 4, pp. 219–229.

Further reading

Brinkmann, S. and Kvale, S. (2015) *InterViews: Learning the Craft of Qualitative Research Interviewing* (3rd edn). London: Sage. This provides a useful general guide to interviewing skills.

Court, D. and Abbas, R. (2013) 'Whose interview is it, anyway? Methodological and ethical challenges of insider-outsider research, multiple languages, and dual-researcher cooperation', *Qualitative Inquiry,* Vol. 19, No. 6, pp. 480–8. This is a helpful account to understand how cultural differences may impact on the scope to collect data and the implications of operating as either a cultural insider or outsider.

Krueger, R.A. and Casey, M.A. (2014) *Focus Groups: A Practical Guide for Applied Research* (5rd edn). Thousand Oaks, CA: Sage. This provides a useful source for those considering the use of this method of group interviewing.

Symon, G. and Cassell, C. (eds) (2012) *Qualitative Organizational Research: Core Methods and Current Challenges.* London: Sage. This edited work contains a helpful range of contributions related to qualitative data collection including interviews and focus groups.

Case 10
Visualising consumption

Benita wants to understand more about film consumption as she has made some short films in her spare time and is interested in a career in the film industry. She has read a lot about how films are promoted and what attracts consumers to specific types of film. She is aware that quite a few journal articles have looked at predicting success based on the film's characteristics, such as genre, actors, director and so on. But, she is particularly interested in motivations for non-theatrical consumption such as watching films at home, or on the move. In preparation for her meeting with her supervisor, she had looked at some of the research her supervisor had been involved in and wanted to discuss a recent paper (Hart et al. 2016) which took a very different approach to understanding how people select films to watch. This paper used Subjective Personal Introspection (SPI), pioneered by Morris Holbrook (1995) to examine how a consumer made sense of information about film and how this informed his selection of films to watch. Benita is very interested in the fact that films may be considered as suiting an outing to the cinema, or to being watched at home and that the viewing context really impacted on intention to watch (in general) and most particularly, to when, where and with whom. She is also fascinated by her supervisor's and colleagues' research findings in another study that reveal women appear to have broader taste in film than men (Cuadrado et al. 2013). This seems to run counter to industry wisdom where men are seen as heavier film consumers.

Benita agreed with her supervisor that she should think about how to develop the ideas in Hart et al.'s (2016) paper for her own research and she considered recruiting people to undertake their own SPIs, building on the findings of Hart et al. (2016) in relation to in-home consumption. She was surprised that there was little focus on film consumption 'on the move' in that study. In our next meeting, Benita raised doubts about doing this, based on Patterson's (2012) findings that in order for SPI to be undertaken, the researcher needs to train consumers in how to write introspective essays that can then be used as data. She doubted that she would be able to do this in the time available to her and also was not confident in her ability to coach her participants to produce meaningful work. However, inspired by Holbrook's (2005) use of photographs, Benita decided to ask her participants to photograph their film viewing contexts. She could then discuss these using a number of group and individual semi-structured interviews. As it is now possible to take and share digital photographs so easily, Benita thought this was a less intrusive way to gain insight into how, where and with whom consumers watched films.

As Benita was now going to ask her participants to take photos of their film viewing contexts, this would most likely include their homes and the images of their friends and families, so this required careful treatment in terms of gaining ethical approval as well as ensuring that the privacy of the participants would be protected. Benita intended for the photographs to be used as an elicitation technique, following Harper (2002) during the interview, therefore the ethical application was fairly straightforward. Benita was careful to design a participant information sheet which made it clear that the images were only to be used for the purpose of the interview and that participants should ask permission from anyone appearing in the photographs, confirming whether or not they agreed for their photographs to be shown to the interviewer and other participants in the focus group. Having received ethical approval from her University, Benita recruited her participants.

Figure C10.1 Watching a film alone
Source: © Finola Kerrigan 2017

Benita was unsure as to whether she should interview participants individually or as part of a focus group, having read up about both methods. She understood an advantage of a focus group was that agreement could be reached among participants regarding their attitudes to specific issues. On this basis, she recruited seven female participants to attend an initial focus group. She booked a room at the university, organised some drinks and snacks and nervously waited for her participants to turn up. The focus group was due to start at 6.30pm, and by 6.45, only three people had turned up. Benita had asked the participants to send through their images in advance so that she could print them to be used in the group. She had only received five sets of images, but one of the participants had promised to print them out herself to bring to the group. Having established whose images belonged to whom, Benita started the focus group by asking participants about their interest in films, how often they tend to watch films, where and with whom, before turning to the images. Participants had been briefed that they should (inspired by the Hart et al. 2016 paper) take a photo or photos of the context each time they watched a film over a period of three weeks.

In general, the focus group discussion went well, with participants picking up their photos and explaining the context. The images ranged from in-home shots such as a sofa with a blanket draped over it, to lying on a bed watching a film alone (Figure C10.1), a group of friends sitting around on a sofa and beanbag, to one of the participants snuggled up on the sofa with her daughter and son.

In addition, there were a series of out-of-home images; a shot of a mobile phone in a hotel room, a laptop (Figure C10.2) in a train carriage and a selfie of a date night at the cinema.

However, over the course of two hours, the focus group discussion often moved away from the research topic, with participants telling jokes and discussing their favourite films. Often the discussion was so interesting that Benita forgot that she was supposed to be the focus group moderator and joined in with the discussion, or forgot to remind participants to speak clearly and not speak over each other so that she could more easily transcribe the audio recording.

After the focus group, Benita felt a bit upset. She had not managed to get all seven participants to attend and at times she felt that the focus group discussion had deviated from her research topic.

When Benita started to transcribe the audio recording, she panicked. Parts of her audio-recording were inaudible, with participants speaking or laughing over each other. She was embarrassed at how enthusiastic and unprofessional she seemed to sound, and each time she heard herself say 'yes, yes, fantastic, I know' she cringed. She was very worried that she did not have a complete transcript to work with, and also realised that she had not conducted the focus group in a way that allowed her to always match the photographs to the discussion and contextualise what participants were saying.

Figure C10.2 Watching a film on a laptop Source: © Finola Kerrigan 2017

References

Cuadrado, M. Filimon, N., Kerrigan, F. and Rurale, A. (2013) Exploring cinema attendance facilitators and constraints, a marketing research approach, 5th Workshop on Cultural Economics and Management, Cádiz, Spain.

Hart, A., Kerrigan, F. and vom Lehn, D. (2016) Understanding Film Consumption, International Journal of Research in Marketing, 33(2): 375–391.

Harper, D. (2002) Talking about pictures: A case for photo elicitation, Visual Studies, 17(1): 13–26.

Holbrook, M.B., (2005) Customer Value and Autoethnography: Subjective Personal Introspection and the Meanings of a Photograph Collection. Journal of Business Research 58 (1): 45–61.

Holbrook, M.B., (1995) Consumer Research: Introspective Essays on the Study of Consumption. Sage, California.

Patterson, A. (2012). Social-networkers of the world, unite and take over: A meta-introspective perspective of the Facebook brand. Journal of Business Research 65 (4):, 527–34.

Questions

1 Should Benita be concerned about missing some of the dialogue in her transcript?
2 If Benita wants to use participants' photographs in her research project, what ethical issues does this raise and how should this be handled?
3 Other than ethical issues, what other considerations should be given to including the participants' images in reporting on this study?
4 Was Benita's decision to use focus groups, rather than interviews, appropriate? What are the advantages and disadvantages of using one-to-one interviews compared to the use of a focus group?

Additional case studies relating to material covered in this chapter are available via the book's companion website: **www.pearsoned.co.uk/saunders**.
They are:

- The practices and styles of public relations practitioners.
- Students' use of work-based learning in their studies.
- Equal opportunities in the publishing industry.
- Students' and former students' debt problems.
- Organisations in a flash?
- How do you network in your SME?

Self-check answers

10.1 The type of interview that is likely to be used in each of these situations is as follows:

   a A standardised and structured interview where the aim is to develop response patterns from the views of people. The interview schedule might be designed to combine styles so that comments made by interviewees in relation to specific questions could also be recorded.

   b The situation outlined suggests an exploratory approach to research, and therefore an in-depth interview would be most appropriate.

   c The situation outlined here suggests that an explanatory approach is required in relation to the data collected, and in this case a semi-structured interview is likely to be appropriate.

10.2 Reasons that suggest the use of interviews include:

- the exploratory or explanatory nature of your research;
- situations where it will be significant to establish personal contact, in relation to interviewee sensitivity about the nature of the information to be provided and the use to be made of this;
- situations where the researcher needs to exercise control over the nature of those who will supply data;
- situations where there are a large number of questions to be answered;
- situations where questions are complex or open-ended;
- situations where the order and logic of questioning may need to be varied.

10.3 Certainly politely! Your response needs to show that you are aware of the issues relating to reliability/dependability, bias and generalisability/transferability that might arise. It would be useful to discuss how these might be overcome through the following: the design of the research; the keeping of records or a diary in relation to the processes and key incidents of the research project as well as the recording of data collected; attempts to control bias through the process of collecting data; the relationship of the research to theory.

10.4 Perhaps it will be wise to say that you understand his position. You realise that any approach to research calls for particular types of competence. Your previous answer touching on interviewee bias has highlighted the need to establish credibility and to gain the interviewee's confidence. While competence will need to be developed over a period of time, allowing for any classroom simulations and dry runs with colleagues, probably the best approach will be your level of preparation before embarking on interview work. This relates first to the nature of the approach made to those whom you would like to participate in the research project and the information supplied to them, second to your intellectual preparation related to the topic to be explored and the particular context of the organisations participating in the research, and third to your ability to conduct an interview. You also recognise that piloting the interview themes will be a crucial element in building your competence.

10.5 Key issues to consider include the following:

- planning to minimise the occurrence of forms of bias where these are within your control, related to interviewer bias, interviewee bias and sampling bias;
- considering your aim in requesting the research interview and how you can seek to prepare yourself in order to gain access to the data that you hope your participants will be able to share with you;
- devising interview themes that you wish to explore or seek explanations for during the interview;
- sending a list of your interview themes to your interviewee prior to the interview, where this is considered appropriate;
- requesting permission and providing a reason where you would like to use an audio-recorder during the interview;
- making sure that your level of preparation and knowledge (in relation to the research context and your research question and objectives) is satisfactory in order to establish your credibility when you meet your interviewee;
- considering how your intended appearance during the interview will affect the willingness of the interviewee to share data.

10.6 There are several areas where you need to develop and demonstrate competence in relation to the conduct of semi-structured and in-depth research interviews. These areas are:

- opening the interview;
- using appropriate language;
- questioning;
- listening;
- testing and summarising understanding;
- behavioural cues;
- recording data.

10.7 An important circumstance in which a researcher chooses to use researcher-created images is where these images are taken of the research participants. These images will show participants engaged in some activity in the research setting, enabling the researcher to use them to elicit participants' insider accounts of what is shown. A researcher may also take images to explore with participants in visual interviews where this will help the researcher to understand aspects of the research setting. The researcher may be using a combination of research methods to collect data, such as a form of participant observation and in the process of conducting observation may take images which he or she wishes to explore with informants. Access may also be an issue prompting the use of researcher-created visual images, where the researcher is given permission to take images in a particular setting while research participants are not given this right.

10.8 One key point might be to see if your research question or one or more of your research objectives suggests an obvious choice. It might be the case, for example, that you require an audio diary because you are interested in analysing the performative way in which the diary is recorded – which would be lost in any written version of a research diary. The act of creating audio diaries may also lead to more spontaneous diary entries, in which participants speak with greater fluidity offering you a less edited version of their thoughts that captures emotions more easily and which may possibly lead to greater depth compared to written versions. Audio diaries may also be easier for some groups who have problems in writing or problems with sight (Crozier and Cassell 2015).

A hand-written or word processed diary may each lead to the creation of considered, full length entries with ample detail carefully woven into composed accounts. These forms of diary keeping may encourage a more structured approach, and be more suitable for particular types of participant. Written or word processed diaries may be more appropriate where you wish to encourage the use of a particular approach, such as a descriptive, discursive or evaluative style. Hand-written diaries may promote greater free style compared with word processed diaries, which may be helpful during analysis. Conversely, word processed diaries may provide you with a well-structured set of entries which are easy to use during data analysis. Use of word processed diaries may also be particularly suitable for some groups of participant.

These may only be some of the points you have included in considering the merits of using either hand-written diaries, word processed diaries, or audio diaries. In the context of a given research project there are likely to be many points that may be considered. By brain-storming these, an informed and appropriate choice may be made.

Get ahead using resources on the companion website at:
www.pearsoned.co.uk/saunders.

- Improve your IBM SPSS Statistics research analysis with practice tutorials.
- Save time researching on the Internet with the Smarter Online Searching Guide.
- Test your progress using self-assessment questions.
- Follow live links to useful websites.

Chapter 11

Collecting primary data using questionnaires

Learning outcomes

By the end of this chapter you should:

- understand the advantages and disadvantages of questionnaires as a data collection method;
- be aware of a range of self-completed (Internet, SMS, postal, delivery and collection) and researcher-completed (telephone, face-to-face) questionnaires;
- be aware of the possible need to combine data collection methods within a research project;
- be able to select and justify the use of appropriate questionnaire methods for a variety of research scenarios;
- be able to design, pilot and deliver a questionnaire to answer research questions and to meet objectives;
- be able to take appropriate action to enhance response rates and to ensure the validity and reliability of the data collected;
- be able to apply the knowledge, skills and understanding gained to your own research project.

11.1 Introduction

Within business and management research, the greatest use of questionnaires is made within the survey strategy (Section 5.8). However, both experiment and case study research strategies can make use of these methods. Although you probably have your own understanding of the term 'questionnaire', it is worth noting that there are a variety of definitions. Some people reserve it exclusively for questionnaires where the person answering the question actually records their own answers, when it is **self-completed**. Others use it as a more general term to include interviews in which precisely the same set of questions are asked and the respondent's answers recorded by the researcher.

In this book we use **questionnaire** as a general term to include all methods of data collection in which each person is asked to respond to the same set of questions in a predetermined order (De Vaus 2014). An alternative term, which is also widely used, is **instrument** (Ekinci 2015). It therefore includes both face-to-face and telephone questionnaires as well as those in which the questions are answered without a researcher being present, such as an airline passenger questionnaire accessed using the inflight entertainment system. The range of data collection modes that fall under this broad heading are outlined in the next section (11.2), along with their relative advantages and disadvantages.

Please rate your experience. . .

Questionnaires are a part of our everyday lives. For modules in your course, your lecturers have probably asked you and your fellow students to complete module evaluation questionnaires, thereby collecting data on students' views. Similarly, when we visit a tourist attraction, have a meal in a restaurant or travel by air there is often the opportunity to complete a visitor feedback form, comment card or passenger survey. Airlines are no exception, wanting to collect data from their passengers so they can enhance their customers' experiences. Whilst on a flight, and normally as the plane is nearing the destination, each passenger is asked via the aircraft's inflight entertainment system if they would be willing to answer a few questions about their experiences. If a passenger is willing, she or he then clicks on the "passenger survey" icon displayed on their seat back screen and the first of the questions appears. Subsequently they can comment on their experiences by answering a series of multiple choice questions using the plane's inflight entertainment

system. This starts with a brief introduction emphasising the importance of passengers' opinions in helping the Airline to improve:

Here at [Airline Name] we are dedicated to the continual improvement of our services and to the airline itself. To assist us in achieving this and to be in with a chance of winning 10,000 air miles we would be grateful if you could tell us what you thought of your experience flying with us today – thank you.

This is followed by series of multiple choice questions such as those given below.

Other topics about which questions are often asked include the service given by the cabin crew, the quality of the inflight entertainment system and the overall value for money of the airline. Personal details are also usually collected from each passenger, including their name, age, country of origin and email address; passengers being informed that this will enable the airline to contact them, if they win the prize.

How did you check-in for your flight?

Online ☐   Check-in counter ☐   Kiosk ✔

Please rate your check-in experience for each of the following:

	Excellent	Very good	Good	OK
Ease of finding the check-in area	☐	☐	☐	☐
Waiting time in queue	☐	☐	☐	☐
Politeness of check-in staff	☐	☐	☐	☐
Knowledge and helpfulness of check-in staff	☐	☐	☐	☐

The use of questionnaires is discussed in many research methods texts. These range from those that devote a few pages to it to those that specify precisely how you should construct and use them, such as Dillman et al.'s (2014) **tailored design method**. Perhaps not surprisingly, the questionnaire is one of the most widely used data collection methods within the survey strategy. Because each person (respondent) is asked to respond to the same set of questions, it provides an efficient way of collecting responses from a large sample prior to quantitative analysis (Chapter 12). However, before you decide to use a questionnaire we should like to include a note of caution. Many authors (for example, Bell and Waters 2014) argue that it is far harder to produce a good questionnaire than you might think. You need to ensure that it will collect the precise data that you require to answer your research question(s) and achieve your objectives. This is of paramount importance because, like an airline, you are unlikely to have more than one opportunity to collect the data. In particular, you will be unable to go back to those individuals who choose to remain anonymous and collect additional data using another questionnaire. These, and other issues, are discussed in Section 11.3.

The design of your questionnaire will affect the response rate and the reliability and validity of the data you collect (Section 11.4). These, along with response rates, can be maximised by:

- careful design of individual questions;
- clear and pleasing visual presentation;
- lucid explanation of the purpose;
- pilot testing;
- carefully and appropriately planned and executed delivery, and return of completed questionnaires.

Our discussion of these aspects forms Sections 11.5 through to 11.8. In Section 11.5 we discuss designing individual questions, translating them into other languages and question coding. Constructing the questionnaire is discussed in Section 11.6 and pilot testing it in Section 11.7. Delivery and return of the questionnaire is considered in Section 11.8 along with actions to help ensure high response rates.

11.2 An overview of questionnaires

When to use questionnaires

We have found that many people use a questionnaire to collect data without considering other methods such as examination of archive and secondary sources (Chapter 8), observation (Chapter 9) and semi-structured or unstructured interviews (Chapter 10). Our advice is to evaluate all possible data collection methods and to choose those most appropriate to your research question(s) and objectives. Questionnaires are usually not particularly good for exploratory or other research that requires large numbers of open-ended questions (Sections 10.2 and 10.3). They work best with standardised questions that you can be confident will be interpreted the same way by all respondents (Robson and McCartan 2016).

Questionnaires therefore tend to be used for descriptive or explanatory research. Descriptive research, such as that undertaken using attitude and opinion questionnaires and questionnaires of organisational practices, will enable you to identify and describe the variability in different phenomena. In contrast, explanatory or analytical research will enable you to examine and explain relationships between variables, in particular cause-and-effect relationships. Alternatively, research requiring respondents to complete a quantitative diary regularly may use a short questionnaire administered repeatedly. These purposes have different research design requirements, which we shall discuss later (Section 11.3).

Although questionnaires may be used as the only data collection method, it may be better to link them with other methods in a mixed or multiple method research design (Sections 5.3 and 5.6). For example, a questionnaire to discover customers' attitudes can be complemented by in-depth interviews to explore and understand these attitudes (Section 10.3).

Questionnaire modes

The design of a questionnaire differs according to whether it is completed by the respondent or a researcher and how it is delivered, returned or collected (Figure 11.1). **Self-completed questionnaires** are usually completed by the respondents and are often

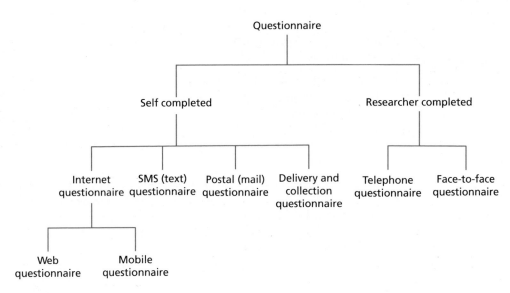

Figure 11.1 Questionnaire modes

referred to as surveys. Such questionnaires can be distributed to respondents electronically usually using the Internet (**Internet questionnaire**), respondents either accessing the questionnaire through a web browser using a hyperlink (**Web questionnaire**) on their computer, tablet or phone; or directly such as via a QR (quick response) code scanned into their mobile device (**mobile questionnaire**). However, it is worth noting that such devices are increasingly blurring into each other (Kozinets, 2015). Alternatively, the questionnaire can be delivered to each respondent's mobile device as a series of SMS (short message service) texts (**SMS questionnaires**), posted to respondents who return them by post after completion (**postal** or **mail questionnaires**) or delivered by hand to each respondent and collected later (**delivery and collection questionnaires**). Responses to **researcher-completed questionnaires** (also known as interviewer-completed questionnaires) are recorded by the researcher or a research assistant on the basis of each respondent's answers. Researcher completed questionnaires undertaken using the telephone are known as **telephone questionnaires**. The final category, **face-to-face questionnaires**, refers to those questionnaires where the researcher or a research assistant physically meet respondents and ask the questions face-to-face. These are also known as **structured interviews** but differ from semi-structured and unstructured (in-depth) interviews (Section 10.2), as there is a defined schedule of questions from which the researcher or research assistant should not deviate.

The choice of questionnaire mode

Your choice of questionnaire mode will be influenced by a variety of factors related to your research question(s) and objectives (Table 11.1), and in particular the:

- characteristics of the respondents from whom you wish to collect data;
- importance of reaching a particular person as respondent;
- importance of respondents' answers not being contaminated or distorted;
- size of sample you require for your analysis, taking into account the likely response rate;
- types of question you need to ask to collect your data;
- number of questions you need to ask to collect your data.

Table 11.1 Main attributes of questionnaires

Attribute	Web and mobile	SMS	Postal	Delivery and collection	Telephone	Face-to-face
Population's characteristics for which suitable	IT literate individuals with access to the Internet, often contacted by email	Individuals with a mobile telephone	Literate individuals who can be contacted by post; selected by name, household, organisation, etc.	Individuals who can be con-	Individuals who can be telephoned; selected by name, household, organisation, etc.	Any; selected by name, household, organisation, in the street etc.
Confidence that right person has responded	High with email	High as have mobile phone number	Low	Low but can be checked at collection	High	
Likelihood of contamination or distortion of respondent's answer	Low, except where relate to use of Web or associated technologies	Low	May be contaminated by consultation with others		Occasionally distorted or invented by researcher/ research assistant	Occasionally contaminated by consultation or distorted/invented by researcher/ research assistant
Size of sample	Large, can be geographically dispersed			Dependent on number of field workers	Dependent on number of researchers/research assistants	
Likely response rate[a]	Variable to low, 30–50% reasonable for web within organisations, otherwise 10% or even lower	Low, often 10% or even lower	Variable, 30–50% reasonable		High, 50–70% reasonable	
Feasible length of questionnaire	Equivalent of 6–8 A4 pages, minimise scrolling down	Short, as few questions as possible, preferably no more than 3	6–8 A4 pages		Up to half an hour	Variable depending on location
Suitable types of question	Closed questions but not too complex; complicated sequencing fine if uses software; must be of interest to respondent	Closed questions but not too complex; Questions need to be kept as succinct as possible	Closed questions but not too complex; simple sequencing only; must be of interest to respondent			Open and closed questions, including complicated questions; complicated sequencing feasible

(continued)

Table 11.1 Main attributes of questionnaires (*Continued*)

Attribute	Web and mobile	SMS	Postal	Delivery and collection	Telephone	Face-to-face
Time taken to complete collection	2–6 weeks from distribution (dependent on number of follow-ups)	Almost immediate	4–8 weeks from posting (dependent on number of follow-ups)	Dependent on sample size, number of research assistants, etc.	Dependent on sample size, number of researchers/research assistants, etc., but slower than self-completed for same sample size	
Main financial resource implications	Cost of software, purchase of list of respondents' email addresses or data panel participants	Cost of software, purchase of list of mobile phone numbers or data panel participants	Outward and return postage, photocopying, clerical support, data entry	Research assistants, travel, photocopying, clerical support, data entry	Research assistants, telephone calls, clerical support; photocopying and data entry if not using CATI[b]; survey tool if using CATI	Research assistants, travel, clerical support; photocopying and data entry if not using CAPI[c]; survey tool if using CAPI
Role of researcher/ research assistants in data collection	None			Delivery and collection of questionnaires; enhancing respondent participation	Enhancing respondent participation; guiding the respondent through the questionnaire and recording responses; answering respondents' questions	
Data input[d]	Automated through cloud-based software		Closed questions can be designed so that responses may be entered using optical mark readers after questionnaire has been returned		Response to all questions entered at time of collection using cloud-based software or CATI[c]	Response to all questions can be entered at time of collection using cloud-based software or CAPI[d]

[a]Discussed in Chapter 7.   [b]Computer-aided telephone interviewing.   [c]Computer-aided personal interviewing.   [d]Discussed in Section 12.2.

Sources: Authors' experience; Baruch and Holtom (2008); De Vaus (2014); Dillman et al. (2014); Saunders (2012); van de Heijden (2017)

These factors will not apply equally to your choice of questionnaire mode, and for some research questions or objectives may not apply at all. The mode of questionnaire you choose will dictate how certain you can be that the respondent is the person whom you wish to answer the questions and thus the reliability of responses (Table 11.1). Even if you address a postal questionnaire to a company manager by name, you have no way of ensuring that the manager will be the respondent. The manager's assistant or someone else could complete it! Internet questionnaires, delivered by an emailed hyperlink, offer greater control because most people read and respond to their own emails. Similarly, SMS questionnaires, although only suitable for short questionnaires, are likely to be answered by the actual respondent as most people read and reply to text messages sent to them. With delivery and collection questionnaires, you can sometimes check who has answered the questions at collection. By contrast, researcher-completed questionnaires enable you to ensure that the respondent is whom you want. This improves the reliability of your data. In addition, you can record some details about non-respondents, allowing you to give some assessment of the impact of bias caused by refusals.

Any contamination of respondents' answers will reduce your data's reliability (Table 11.1). Sometimes, if they have insufficient knowledge or experience, they may deliberately guess at the answer, a tendency known as **uninformed response**. This is particularly likely when the questionnaire has been incentivised (Section 11.5). Respondents to self-completed questionnaires are relatively unlikely to answer to please you or because they believe certain responses are more **socially desirable** (Dillman et al. 2014). They may, however, discuss their answers with others, thereby contaminating their response. Respondents to telephone and face-to-face questionnaires are more likely to answer to please due to their contact with you, although the impact of this can be minimised by good interviewing technique (Sections 10.5 and 10.6). Responses can also be contaminated or distorted when recorded. In extreme instances, research assistants may invent responses. For this reason, random checks of research assistants are often made by survey organisations. When writing your project report you will be expected to state your response rate (Section 7.2). When doing this you need to be careful not to make unsubstantiated claims if comparing with other questionnaires' response rates. While such comparisons place your response rate in context, a higher than normal response rate does not prove that your findings are unbiased (Rogelberg and Stanton 2007). Similarly, a lower than normal response rate does not necessarily mean that responses are biased.

The type of questionnaire you choose will affect the number of people who respond (Section 7.2). Researcher-completed questionnaires will usually have a higher response rate than self-completed questionnaires (Table 11.1). The size of your sample and the way in which it is selected will have implications for the confidence you can have in your data and the extent to which you can generalise (Section 7.2).

Longer questionnaires are best presented face-to-face. In addition, they can include more complicated questions than telephone questionnaires or self-completed questionnaires (Oppenheim 2000). The presence of a researcher (or the use of Cloud based survey design, data collection and analysis software such as Qualtrics Research core™ and SurveyMonkey™) means that it is also easier to route different subgroups of respondents to answer different questions using a filter question (Section 11.4). The suitability of different types of question also differs between methods.

Your choice of questionnaire will also be affected by the resources you have available (Table 11.1), and in particular the:

- time available to complete the data collection;
- financial implications of data collection and entry;
- availability of research assistants and field workers to assist;
- cloud based survey design, data collection and analysis software.

The time needed for data collection increases markedly for delivery and collection and researcher completed questionnaires where the samples are geographically dispersed (Table 11.1). One way you can overcome this constraint is to select your sample using cluster sampling (Section 7.2). Unless you are using an Internet questionnaire, **computer-aided personal interviewing (CAPI)** or **computer-aided telephone interviewing (CATI)**, you will need to consider the costs of reproducing the questionnaire, clerical support and entering the data for computer analysis. For Internet questionnaires you will need to consider the availability (and often the cost) of obtaining lists of email addresses/telephone numbers and for postal and telephone questionnaires the cost estimates for postage and telephone calls. If you are working for an organisation, postage costs may be reduced by using *Freepost* for questionnaire return. This means that you pay only postage and a small handling charge for those questionnaires that are returned by post. However, the use of Freepost rather than a stamp may adversely affect your response rates (see Table 11.5).

Virtually all data collected by questionnaires will be analysed by computer. Many cloud based survey design, data collection and analysis software such as Qualtrics Research CORE™ and SurveyMonkey™ go one stage further and allow you to design your questionnaire, capture and automatically save the data, and either analyse the data within the software or download it as a data file for external analysis (Box 11.1). For self- and researcher completed questionnaires, data capture is most straightforward for closed questions where respondents select their answer from a prescribed list. Such data will need subsequently to be coded, entered (typed) and saved in the analysis software for analysis (Section 12.2). Once this has been done and the data checked, you will be able to explore and analyse your data far more quickly and thoroughly than by hand (Sections 12.3–12.5). As a rough rule, you should analyse questionnaire data by computer if they have been collected from 30 or more respondents.

In reality, you are almost certain to have to make compromises in your choice of questionnaire. These will be unique to your research as the decision about which questionnaire is most suitable cannot be answered in isolation from your research question(s) and objectives and the population or sample from which you are collecting data.

11.3 Deciding what data need to be collected

Research design requirements

Unlike in-depth and semi-structured interviews (Chapter 10), the questions you ask in questionnaires need to be defined precisely prior to data collection. Whereas you can prompt and explore issues further with in-depth and semi-structured interviews, this will not be possible using questionnaires. In addition, the questionnaire offers only one chance to collect the data as it is often impossible to identify respondents or to return to collect additional information. This means that the time you spend planning precisely what data you need to collect, how you intend to analyse them (Chapter 12) and designing your questionnaire to meet these requirements is crucial if you are to answer your research question(s) and meet your objectives.

For most business and management research, the data you collect using questionnaires will be used for either descriptive or explanatory purposes. For questions where the main purpose is to describe the population's characteristics either at a fixed time or at a series of points over time to enable comparisons, you will normally need to deliver your questionnaire to a sample. The sample needs to be as representative and accurate as possible where it will be used to generalise about a population (Sections 7.1–7.3). You will also probably need to relate your findings to earlier research. It is therefore important that you

Box 11.1
Focus on student research

Using cloud based software to design a questionnaire

Ben's research project involved emailing a hyperlink to a Web questionnaire to small and medium-sized enterprise owners to discover how they defined small business success. He designed his questionnaire using the cloud-based software Qualtrics as this would either allow him to analyse his data within the software or download his data and use analysis software such as IBM SPSS Statistics, a spreadsheet or a database.

Source: This screenshot was generated using Qualtrics software, of the Qualtrics Research Suite. Copyright © 2018 Qualtrics. Qualtrics and all other Qualtrics product or service names are registered trademarks or trademarks of Qualtrics, Provo, UT, USA. http://www.qualtrics.com. The authors are not affiliated to Qualtrics

select the appropriate characteristics to answer your research question(s) and to address your objectives. You will need to have:

- reviewed the literature carefully;
- discussed your ideas with colleagues, your project tutor and other interested parties.

For research involving organisations, we have found it essential to understand the organisational context in which we are undertaking the research. Similarly, for international or cross-cultural research it is important to have an understanding of the countries and cultures in which you are undertaking the research. Without this it is easy to make mistakes, such as using the wrong terminology or language, and to collect useless data. For many research projects an understanding of relevant organisations can be achieved through browsing company websites (Section 8.2), observation (Chapter 9) and in-depth and semi-structured interviews (Chapter 10).

Explanatory research is usually deductive, using data to test a theory or theories. This means that, in addition to those issues raised for descriptive research, you need to define

Box 11.2
Focus on management research

Using questionnaire as diaries

Research by Breevaart and colleagues (2016) published in the *Journal of Organizational Behaviour* examined whether transformational leadership behaviours, employee self-leadership strategies, contributed to employee work engagement and job performance. Data were collected from a sample of 57 unique leader-employer dyads using separate short online quantitative diary questionnaires for leaders and employees. Respondents received an email including a hyperlink to their questionnaire at the end of each week over a five-week period. The questions Breevaart and colleagues used were adapted from existing questionnaires to allow variables to be measured on a weekly basis, the source of the questions being referenced in their article. Their results revealed that when leaders used more transformational leadership behaviours, and employees used more self-leadership strategies, employees were more engaged in their work and received higher performance ratings.

the theories you wish to test as relationships between variables prior to designing your questionnaire. You will need to have reviewed the literature carefully, discussed your ideas widely and conceptualised your own research clearly prior to designing your questionnaire (Ghauri and Grønhaug 2010). In particular, you need to be clear about which relationships you think are likely to exist between variables:

- a **dependent variable** that changes in response to changes in other variables;
- an **independent variable** that causes changes in a dependent variable;
- a **mediating variable** that transmits the effect of an independent variable to a dependent variable;
- a **moderating variable** that affects the relationship between an independent variable and a dependent variable (Table 5.4).

As these relationships are likely to be tested through statistical analysis (Sections 12.5 and 12.6) of the data collected by your questionnaire, you need to be clear about the detail in which they will be measured at the design stage. Where possible, you should ensure that measures are compatible with those used in other relevant research so that comparisons can be made (Section 12.2).

For research requiring respondents to provide regular reports of particular events or experiences repeatedly over a period of time, a short questionnaire can be distributed repeatedly for completion. In such time-based designs, you need to decide the questions to be asked and the rate and timing of the self reports (Box 11.2). For such research, Internet or SMS questionnaires allow responses to be collected immediately.

Types of data variable

Dillman et al. (2014) distinguishes between three types of data variable that can be collected through questionnaires:

- factual or demographic;
- attitudes and opinions;
- behaviours and events.

These distinctions are important as they relate to the ease of obtaining accurate data and influence the way your questions are worded (Box 11.3). **Factual** and **demographic variables** contain data that are readily available to the respondent and are likely, assuming

Box 11.3
Focus on student research

Opinion, behaviour and attribute questions

Emily was asked by her employer to undertake an anonymous survey of financial advisors' ethical values.

In particular, her employer was interested in the advice given to clients. After some deliberation she came up with three questions that addressed the issue of putting clients' interests before their own:

2 How do you feel about the following statement? 'Financial advisors should place their clients' interest before their own.'

(please tick the appropriate box)

strongly agree	❑
mildly agree	❑
neither agree or disagree	❑
mildly disagree	❑
strongly disagree	❑

3 In general, do financial advisors place their clients' interests before their own?

(please tick the appropriate box)

always yes	❑
usually yes	❑
sometimes yes	❑
seldom yes	❑
never yes	❑

4 How often do you place your clients' interests before your own?

(please tick the appropriate box)

81–100% of my time	❑
61–80% of my time	❑
41–60% of my time	❑
21–40% of my time	❑
0–20% of my time	❑

Emily's choice of question or questions to include in her questionnaire was dependent on whether she needed to collect data on financial advisors' attitudes, opinions or behaviours. She designed question 2 to collect data on respondents' opinions about financial advisors placing their clients' interest before their own. This question asks respondents how they feel. In contrast, question 3 asks respondents whether financial advisors in general place their clients' interests before their own. It is therefore concerned with their individual opinions regarding how financial advisors act.

Question 4 focuses on how often the respondents actually place their clients' interests before their own. Unlike the previous questions, it is concerned with their actual behaviour rather than their opinion.

To answer her research questions and to meet her objectives Emily also needed to collect data to explore how ethical values differed between subgroupings of financial advisors. One theory she had was that ethical values were related to age. To test this, she needed to collect demographic data on respondents' ages. After some deliberation she came up with question 5:

5 How old are you?

(please tick the appropriate box)

Less than 30 years	❑
30 to less than 40 years	❑
40 to less than 50 years	❑
50 to less than 60 years	❑
60 years or over	❑

the respondent is willing to disclose, to be accurate. These variables include characteristics such as age, gender, marital status, education, occupation and income. They are used to explore how attitudes and opinions, and behaviours and events, differ, as well as to check that the data collected are representative of the total population (Section 7.2). **Attitude** and **opinion variables** contain data that respondents may have needed to think about before answering. They are likely to be influenced by the context in which the question was asked; recording how respondents feel about something or what they think or believe is true or false. **Behaviour** and **event variables** are also likely to be influenced by context. They contain data about what people did (behaviours) or what happened (events) in the past, is happening now, or will happen in the future.

Ensuring that essential data are collected

A problem experienced by many students and organisations we work with is how to ensure that the data collected will enable the research question(s) to be answered and the objectives achieved. Although no method is infallible, one way is to create a **data require-ments table** (Table 11.2). This summarises the outcome of a six-step process:

1 Decide whether the main outcome of your research is descriptive or explanatory.
2 Use your aim, objectives or research question(s) to develop more specific investigative questions about which you need to gather data, noting how it relates to theory and key concepts in the literature.
3 Repeat the second stage if you feel that the investigative questions are not sufficiently precise.
4 Keeping in mind relevant theory and key concepts in the literature, identify the variables about which you must collect data to answer each investigative question.
5 Establish the level of detail required from the data for each variable.
6 Develop measurement questions to capture the data at the level required for each variable.

Investigative questions are the questions that you need to answer in order to address satisfactorily each research question and to meet each objective (Bloomberg et al. 2014). They need to be generated with regard to your research question(s) and objectives. For some investigative questions you will need to subdivide your first attempt into more detailed investigative questions. For each you need to be clear whether you are interested in facts/demographics, attitudes/opinions or behaviours/events (discussed earlier), as

Table 11.2 Data requirements table

Research aim/objectives/question(s):

Type of research:

Investigative questions	Variable(s) required	Detail in which data measured	Relation to theory and key concepts in the literature	Check measurement question included in questionnaire ✓

what appears to be a need to collect one sort of variable frequently turns out to be a need for another. We have found theory and key concepts from the literature, discussions with interested parties and pilot studies to be of help here.

You should then identify the variables about which you need to collect data to answer each investigative question and to decide the level of detail at which these are measured. Again, the review of the literature and associated research can suggest possibilities. However, if you are unsure about the detail needed you should measure at a more precise level. Although this is more time consuming, it will give you flexibility in your analyses. In these you will be able to use computer software to group or combine data (Section 12.2).

Once your table is complete (Box 11.4), it must be checked to make sure that all data necessary to answer your investigative questions are included. When checking, you need to ensure that only data which are essential to answering your research question(s) and meeting your objectives are included. The final column is to remind you to check that your questionnaire actually includes a measurement question that collects the precise data required!

Box 11.4
Focus on student research

Data requirements table

As part of his work placement Greg was asked to discover employees' attitudes to the outside smoking area at his organisation's restaurants and bars. Discussion with senior management and colleagues at the restaurant where he worked and reading relevant literature helped him to firm up his objective and investigative questions and the level of detail in which the data were measured. In addition, he wanted to be able to compare his findings with earlier research by Jackson and Taylor (2015) in the journal *Tourism and Hospitality Research* and Louka et al. (2006) in the *Journal of Health Psychology*.

One of his objectives is included in the extract from his table of data requirements:

• **Research objective:** To establish employees' attitudes to the outside smoking area at restaurants and bars.				
• **Type of research:** Predominantly descriptive, although wish to examine differences between restaurants and bars, and between different groups of employees.				
Investigative questions	Variable(s) required	Detail in which data measured	Relation to theory and key concepts in literature	Check included in questionnaire ✓
• Do employees feel that restaurants and bars should provide an outside smoking area for smokers? (opinion)	• Opinion of employee to the provision of an outside smoking area for smokers	• Feel . . . very strongly that it should, quite strongly that it should, no strong opinions, quite strongly that it should not, very strongly that it should not [N.B. will need separate questions for restaurants and for bars]		
• Do employees' opinions differ depending on. . .	• (Opinion of employee – outlined above)	• (Included above)		

○

(515)

Box 11.4
Focus on student
research (*continued*)

Investigative questions	Variable(s) required	Detail in which data measured	Relation to theory and key concepts in literature	Check included in questionnaire ✓
• . . . whether or not a smoker? (behaviour)	• Smoker	• Smoker, former smoker or non-smoker	• use these 3 groups from Jackson and Taylor (2015)	
• . . . nationality (factual)		• Country of origin	• Louka et al. (2006) high-lights differ-ences between nationalities	
• How representa-tive are the responses of employee? (demographic)	• Gender of employee • Job • number of hours worked	• Male, female • Will need to obtain a list of jobs from the organisation • Actual hours worked on week of questionnaire	• Note: UK government defines full time work as at least 35 hours a week	

11.4 Questionnaire validity and reliability

The internal validity and reliability of the data you collect and the response rate you achieve depend, to a large extent, on the design of your questions, the structure of your questionnaire and the rigour of your pilot testing (Sections 11.5, 11.6 and 11.7). A valid questionnaire will enable accurate data that actually measure the concepts you are interested in to be collected, while one that is reliable will mean that these data are collected consistently. Hardy and Ford (2014) argue that even if everyone understands a questionnaire they may interpret it in different ways due to three forms of miscomprehension:

- instructional, where instructions such as 'please rank the following in order of importance, ranking the most important 1, the next 2 and so on' are not followed; the respondent doing something else such as ranking all as 1;
- sentinel, where the respondent enriches or depletes the syntax of a question; for example, a respondent answers a question about 'management' as her or his 'line manager';
- lexical, where the respondent deploys a different meaning to a word to that intended by the researcher; for example, where the word 'satisfied' in a question is intended to refer to obligations being fulfilled, but is interpreted as gratification.

Building on these ideas it is therefore crucial that the instructions given and questions asked are acted on or understood by the respondent in the way intended by the researcher. Similarly the answers given by the respondent need to be understood by the researcher in the way intended by the respondent. This means the design stage is likely to involve you in substantial rewriting in order to ensure that the respondent follows instruction and decodes your questions in the way you intended. We incorporate guidance to help you achieve this in Section 11.4.

Establishing validity

Internal validity in relation to questionnaires refers to the ability of your questionnaire to measure what you intend it to measure. It is sometimes termed **measurement validity** as it refers to concerns that what you find with your questionnaire actually represents the reality of what you are measuring. This presents you with a problem as, if you actually knew the reality of what you were measuring, there would be no point in designing your questionnaire and using it to collect data! Researchers get around this problem by looking for other relevant evidence that supports the answers found using the questionnaire, relevance being determined by the nature of their research question and their own judgement.

Often, when discussing the validity of a questionnaire, researchers refer to content validity, criterion-related validity and construct validity. **Content validity** refers to the extent to which the measurement device, in our case the questions in the questionnaire, provides adequate coverage of the investigative questions. Judgement of what is 'adequate coverage' can be made in a number of ways. One involves careful definition of the research through the literature reviewed and, where appropriate, prior discussion with others. Another is to use a panel of individuals to assess whether each question in the questionnaire is 'essential', 'useful but not essential' or 'not necessary'.

Criterion-related validity, sometimes known as **predictive validity**, is concerned with the ability of the measures (questions) to make accurate predictions. This means that if you are using the data collected by questions within your questionnaire to predict customers' future buying behaviours then a test of these questions' criterion-related validity will be the extent to which the responses actually predict these customers' buying behaviours. In assessing criterion-related validity, you will be comparing the data from your questionnaire with that specified in the criterion in some way. Often this is undertaken using statistical analysis such as correlation (Section 12.6).

Construct validity refers to the extent to which a set of questions (known individually as scale items, and discussed later in this section) actually measures the presence of the construct you intended them to measure. It is therefore dependent upon lexical and sentinel miscomprehension for each scale item being minimised. The term is normally used when referring to constructs such as attitude scales, customer loyalty and the like (Section 11.4) and can be thought of as answering the question: 'How well can I generalise from this set of questions to the construct?' Because validation of such constructs against existing data is difficult, other methods are used. Where different scales are used to measure the same construct, the overlap (or correlation) between these scales is known as **convergent validity**. In contrast, where different scales are used to measure theoretically distinct constructs, an absence of overlap (or correlation) between the scales means they are distinctive and have **discriminant validity**. These are discussed in more detail in a range of texts, including Bloomberg et al. (2014).

Testing for reliability

As we outlined earlier, reliability refers to consistency. Although for a questionnaire to be valid it must be reliable, this is not sufficient on its own. Respondents may consistently interpret a question in your questionnaire in one way, when you mean something else! This might be because of lexical or sentinel miscomprehension for a specific question. Consequently, although the question is reliable, this does not really matter as it has no internal validity and so will not enable your research question to be answered. Reliability is therefore concerned with the robustness of your questionnaire and, in particular, whether or not it will produce consistent findings at different times and under different conditions, such as with different samples or, in the case of a researcher-completed questionnaire, with different research assistants or field workers. Alternatively, respondents may answer inconsistently due to instructional miscomprehension. Between five and nine per cent of respondents do not read instructions that accompany a questionnaire, this being due to familiarity with the task of completing questionnaires (Hard and Ford, 2014).

Mitchell (1996) outlines three common approaches to assessing reliability, in addition to comparing the data collected with other data from a variety of sources. Although the analysis for each of these is undertaken after data collection, they need to be considered at the questionnaire design stage. They are:

- test re-test;
- internal consistency;
- alternative form.

Test re-test estimates of reliability are obtained by correlating data collected with those from the same questionnaire collected under as near equivalent conditions as possible. The questionnaire therefore needs to be delivered and completed twice by respondents. This may create problems, as it is often difficult to persuade respondents to answer the same questionnaire twice. In addition, the longer the time interval between the two questionnaires, the lower the likelihood that respondents will answer the same way. We therefore recommend that you use this method only as a supplement to other methods.

Internal consistency involves correlating the responses to questions in the questionnaire with each other. However, it is nearly always only used to measure the consistency of responses across a subgroup of the questions. There are a variety of methods for calculating internal consistency, of which one of the most frequently used is **Cronbach's alpha**. This statistic is usually used to measure the consistency of responses to a sub-set of questions (scale items) that are combined as a scale (discussed in Section 11.5) to measure a particular concept. It consists of an alpha coefficient with a value between 0 and 1. Values of 0.7 or above indicate that the questions combined in the scale internally consistent in their measurement. Further details of this and other approaches can be found in Mitchell (1996) and in books discussing more advanced statistics and analysis software such as Field (2018).

The final approach to testing for reliability outlined by Mitchell (1996) is 'alternative form'. This offers some sense of the reliability within your questionnaire through comparing responses to alternative forms of the same question or groups of questions. Where questions are included for this purpose, usually in longer questionnaires, they are often called 'check questions'. However, it is often difficult to ensure that these questions are substantially equivalent. Respondents may suffer from fatigue owing to the need to increase the length of the questionnaire, and they may spot the similar question and just refer back to their previous answer! It is therefore advisable to use check questions sparingly.

11.5 Designing individual questions

The design of each question should be determined by the data you need to collect (Section 11.3). When designing individual questions researchers do one of three things (Bourque and Clark 1994):

- adopt questions used in other questionnaires;
- adapt questions used in other questionnaires;
- develop their own questions.

Adopting or adapting questions may be necessary if you wish to replicate, or to compare your findings with, another study. This can allow reliability to be assessed. It is also more efficient than developing your own questions, provided that you can still collect the data you need to answer your research question(s) and to meet your objectives. Some cloud-based survey software include questions that you may use. Alternatively, you may find questions and coding schemes that you feel will meet your needs in existing questionnaires, journal articles or in Internet-based question banks, such as the UK Data Service's Variable and Question Bank (2018). This provides searchable access to over half a million questions drawn from a range of UK and cross-national surveys since the mid-1990s.

However, whilst using existing questions is often sensible as it allows you to compare your findings with other research, you need to be careful. Questions designed by researchers have been designed with a specific purpose in mind, which may not meet your research aim and objectives. Unfortunately, there are a vast number of poorly worded or biased questions in circulation, so always assess each question carefully. In addition, you will need to check whether you require permission to use these questions because of copyright. Questions are usually subject to copyright unless there is an express indication that these may be used. Even where no formal copyright has been asserted you should, where possible, contact the author and obtain permission. In your project report you should always state where you obtained the questions and give credit to their author.

Types of question

Initially, you need only consider the type, wording and length of individual questions rather than the order in which they will appear on the form. Clear wording of questions using terms that will be familiar to, and understood by, respondents can improve the validity of the questionnaire. Shorter questions are easier to understand than longer ones and questions should, ideally, be no longer than 20 words, excluding possible answers (Sekeran and Bougie 2016). Most types of questionnaire include a combination of open and closed questions. **Open questions**, sometimes referred to as open-ended questions, allow respondents to give answers in their own way (Fink 2016). **Closed questions**, sometimes referred to as closed-ended questions (Fink 2016) or **forced-choice questions** (De Vaus 2014), provide two or more alternative answers from which the respondent is instructed to choose. Closed questions are usually quicker and easier to answer, as they require minimal writing. Responses are also easier to compare as they have been predetermined. However, if these predetermined responses are misunderstood by respondents then they will not be valid (Hardy and Ford 2014). Within this section we highlight six types of closed question that we discuss later:

- list, where the respondent is offered a list of items, any of which may be selected;
- category, where only one response can be selected from a given set of categories;
- ranking, where the respondent is asked to place something in order;
- rating, in which a rating device is used to record responses;
- quantity, to which the response is a number giving the amount;
- matrix, where responses to two or more questions can be recorded using the same grid.

As well as:

- creating scales to measure constructs by combining rating questions.

We also consider issues associated with translating questions into other languages and pre-coding responses.

Open questions

Open questions are used widely in in-depth and semi-structured interviews (Section 10.5). In questionnaires they are useful if you are unsure of the response, such as in exploratory research, when you require a detailed answer, when you want to find out what is uppermost in the respondent's mind or do not wish to list all possible answers. With such questions, the precise wording of the question and the amount of space partially determine the length and fullness of response. However, if you leave too much space the question becomes off-putting. Respondents tend to write more when answering open questions on Internet questionnaires than the paper based equivalent; although they are mainly just more verbose rather than offering more insights (Saunders 2012). An example of an open question (from a self-completed questionnaire) is:

6   Please list up to three things you like about your current employment:

    1 ....
    2 ....
    3 ....

This question collects data about each respondent's opinion of what they like about their current employment. Thus, if salary had been the reason uppermost in their mind this would probably have been recorded first. When questionnaires are returned by large numbers of respondents, responses to open questions are extremely time consuming to code (Section 12.2). This may be compounded by illegible handwriting. For this reason, it is usually advisable to keep their use to a minimum.

List questions

List questions offer the respondent a list of responses from which she or he can choose either one or more responses. Such questions are useful when you need to be sure that the respondent has considered all possible responses. However, the list of responses must be defined clearly and be meaningful to the respondent. For researcher-completed questionnaires, it is often helpful to present the respondent with a prompt card listing all responses. The response categories you can use vary widely and include 'yes/no', 'agree/disagree' and 'applies/does not apply' along with 'don't know' or 'not sure'. If you intend to use what you hope is a complete list, you may wish to add a catch-all category of 'other'. This has been included in question 7, which collects data on respondents' religion. However, as you can read in Box 11.5, the use of 'other' can result in unforeseen responses, especially where the question is considered intrusive!

7   What is your religion?

Please tick ✓ the appropriate box.

Buddhist	❏	No religion	❏
Christian	❏	Other	❏
Hindu	❏		
Jew	❏	(Please say:)	
Muslim	❏		
Sikh	❏		

Box 11.5 Research in the news

Piety gives way to secularism and heavy metal worship

By Matthew Engel

It is not really appropriate for someone who filled in their 2011 census form with my niggardly gracelessness to start taking an interest now. Nonetheless, the census results announced this week about religious belief are very striking. They tell us a good deal about Britain's progression towards becoming a post religious country. They also tell us something about the way the British fill in forms.

The headline figures were that almost a quarter of the population of England and Wales, 14.1m people, said they had no religion, compared with just under 15 per cent in 2001. This fits with a corresponding fall in the number of declared Christians, from 71 per cent to 59 per cent. The statistics also provided a platform for the right wing press to go off on an anti-immigration riff since they showed a near doubling in the number of Muslims, which ought not to have taken anyone by surprise.

There was much enlightenment in the deepest recesses, too. The number of those calling themselves Jedi knights has halved, the best joke of the 2001 census having run out of steam, but at 176,000 they still outnumbered the 56,000 pagans, 39,000 spiritualists, 30,000 atheists (is that all?), 6,000 heavy metal worshippers (many of them in Norwich) and 2,500 Scientologists, and were not that far behind the 263,000 Jews. . .

When I put my religion on the census form, I was being bad tempered, resenting the impertinent question. I put myself down as a Myobist. But actually I have adopted, by accident, the sanest religion in the world. I hope the census checkers grasped that Myob was an acronym and remembered what MYOB stands for.

FT *Source:* Adapted from 'Piety gives way to secularism and heavy metal worship', Matthew Engel, *Financial Times,* 15 Dec. 2012. Copyright © 2012 The Financial Times Ltd

Question 7 collects demographic data on religion, the respondent ticking (checking) the response that applies. In this list question, the common practice of not asking respondents to both check those that do apply and those which do not has been adopted. Consequently, respondents are not asked to indicate those religions to which they do not belong. If you choose to do this, beware: non-response could also indicate uncertainty, or for some questions that an item does not apply! It is also likely that respondents will not read the list from which they have to select appropriate responses so carefully (Dillman et al. 2014).

Category questions

In contrast, **category questions** are designed so that each respondent's answer can fit only one category. Such questions are particularly useful if you need to collect data about behaviour or attributes. The number of categories that you can include without affecting the accuracy of responses is dependent on the type of questionnaire. Self-completed questionnaires and telephone questionnaires should usually have no more than five response categories (Fink 2016). Researcher-completed questionnaires can have more categories provided that a prompt card is used (Box 11.6) or, as in question 8, the researcher categorises the responses.

Box 11.6
Focus on student research

Use of a prompt card as part of a face-to-face questionnaire

As part of her face-to-face questionnaire, Jemma asked the following question:

Which of the following tourist sites did you visit whilst staying in Cusco?

[Show respondent cards 1 and 2 with the pictures of tourist sites. Read out names of the tourist sites one at a time. Record their response with a ✓ in the appropriate box.]

	Visited	**Not visited**	**Not sure**
Maras	❏	❏	❏
Moray	❏	❏	❏
Misminay Andean Village	❏	❏	❏
Sacsaywaman	❏	❏	❏
Priory of Santa Domingo	❏	❏	❏
Ollantaytambo	❏	❏	❏
Inca Pachacutec Monument	❏	❏	❏
Qorikancha	❏	❏	❏
Pukapora (Red Fort)	❏	❏	❏
The Sacred Valley	❏	❏	❏

Jemma gave card 1 (below) and subsequently card 2, both of which were A4 size, to each respondent; reading out the name of each tourist site and pointing to the photograph. She collected both cards after the question had been completed.

1. Maras

2. Moray

3. Misminay Andean village

4. Sacsaywaman

5. Priory of Santa Domingo

6. Ollantaytambo

Source: Copyright © 2018 Mark NK Saunders

---

8 How often do you visit this retail park?

[Researcher: listen to the respondent's answer and tick ✓ as appropriate.]

❏ First visit

❏ Once a week

❏ Less than fortnightly to once a month

2 or more times a week ❏

Less than once a week to fortnightly ❏

Less often ❏

You should arrange responses in a logical order so that it is easy to locate the response category that corresponds to each respondent's answer. Your categories should be mutually exclusive (not overlapping), and should cover all possible responses. The layout of your questionnaire should make it clear which boxes refer to which response category by placing them close to the appropriate text.

Ranking questions

A **ranking question** asks the respondent to place things in rank order. This means that you can discover their relative importance to the respondent. In question 9, taken from an online questionnaire created in Qualtrics, the respondents are asked their opinions about the relative importance of a series of features when choosing a new car. The catch-all feature of 'other' is included to allow respondents to add one other feature, a subsequent question asking them to describe this.

9. Drag and drop the factors listed below so they are in order of importance to you in your choice of a new car.

Place the most important item at the top [1], the next second [2] and so on.

①	Driving enjoyment
②	Boot (trunk) size
③	Depreciation
④	Carbon dioxide (CO_2) emissions
⑤	Safety features
⑥	Fuel economy
⑦	Price
⑧	Other

Source: This question was generated using Qualtrics software, of the Qualtrics Research Suite. Copyright © 2018 Qualtrics. Qualtrics and all other Qualtrics product or service names are registered trademarks or trademarks of Qualtrics, Provo, UT, USA http://www.qualtrics.com. The authors are not affiliated to Qualtrics.

With such questions, you need to ensure that the instructions are clear and will be understood by the respondent. In general, respondents find that ranking more than seven items takes too much effort, reducing their motivation to complete the questionnaire, so you should keep your list to this length or shorter (Bloomberg et al. 2014). Respondents can rank accurately only when they can see or remember all items. This can be overcome with face-to-face questionnaires by using prompt cards on which you list all of the features to be ranked. However, telephone questionnaires should ask respondents to rank fewer items, as the respondent will need to rely on their memory.

Rating questions

Rating questions are often used to collect opinion data. They should not be confused with **scales** to measure concepts (discussed later in this section), which are a coherent set of questions or scale items that are regarded as indicators of a construct or concept (Bruner 2013). Rating questions most frequently use the **Likert-style rating** in which the respondent is asked how strongly she or he agrees or disagrees with a statement or series of statements, usually on a four-, five-, six- or seven-point rating scale (Box 11.7). Possible responses to rating questions should be presented in a straight line (such as in question 10) rather than in multiple lines or columns, as this is how respondents are most likely to process the data (Dillman et al. 2014). If you intend to use a series of statements, you should keep the same order of response categories to avoid confusing respondents (Dillman et al. 2014). You should include both positive and negative statements so as to ensure that the respondent reads each one carefully and thinks about which box to tick.

Question 10 (created using the cloud-based survey development software SurveyMonkey) has been taken from an Internet questionnaire to an organisation's employees and is designed to collect opinion data. In this rating question, an even number of points (four)

10. For the following statement please select the response that matches your view most closely
I feel employees' views have influenced the decisions taken by management

Strongly agree	Agree	Disagree	Strongly disagree
○	○	○	○

Source: Question created by SurveyMonkey Inc. (2018) San Mateo, reproduced with permission

Box 11.7
Focus on management research

Team mindfulness and conflict safeguarding

Lingtao Yu and Mary Zellmer-Bruhn (2018) published findings from a study examining team mindfulness as a safeguard for multi-level team conflict during transformational processes in the *Academy of Management Journal.*

Prior to designing their questionnaire, Yu and Zellmer-Bruhn reviewed the literature on team mindfulness, identifying statements that could be modified to be succinct and easily understood; and were consistent with their definition of team mindfulness as a shared perception of the typical group experience. Using these they developed and validated a scale for team mindfulness, comprising ten items (questions).

These comprised statements such as (Yu and Zellmer-Bruhn, 2018: 347):

"The team is friendly to members when things go wrong"

"The team experiences moments of peace and ease, even when things get hectic and stressful"

This scale was validated in their first study.

Following scale validation, data were collected in two further studies using a questionnaire comprising both the team mindfulness scale and scales to measure a number of other concepts including team trust and task conflict. These further studies comprised, firstly 198 MBA students at a large United States midwestern university and, secondly 318 employees in a Chinese healthcare organisation. In each study respondents recorded their reactions to each statement on mindfulness using a seven-point Likert scale where "1" equalled "strongly disagree" and "7" equalled "strongly agree". The results of both studies indicated that team mindfulness offers a safeguard against multi-level conflict processes.

has been used to force the respondent to express their feelings towards the statement by clicking on the 'radio button' under the response that matches their view most closely. By contrast, question 11, also from an Internet questionnaire created using SurveyMonkey, contains an odd number of points (five). This inclusion of a neutral point allows the respondent to 'sit on the fence' by selecting the middle 'not sure' category when considering an implicitly negative statement. The phrase 'not sure' is used here as it is less threatening to the respondent than admitting they do not know. This rating question is designed to collect data on employees' opinions of the current situation.

> 11. For the following statement please select the answer that matches your view most closely
> *I believe there are 'them and us' barriers to communication in the company now*
>
> | Strongly agree | Agree | Neither agree or disagree | Disagree | Strongly disagree |
> |:---:|:---:|:---:|:---:|:---:|
> | ○ | ○ | ○ | ○ | ○ |

Source: Question created by SurveyMonkey Inc. (2018) San Mateo, reproduced with permission

Both questions 10 and 11 are balanced rating scales as the possible answers are reflected around either an implicit (question 10) or an explicit (question 11) neutral point. The alternative is an unbalanced rating scale, such as question 12, which does not have a neutral point.

You can expand this form of rating question further to record finer shades of opinion, a variety of which are outlined in Table 11.3. However, respondents to telephone questionnaires find it difficult to distinguish between values when rating more than five points plus 'don't know'. In addition, there is little point in collecting data for seven or nine response categories, if these are subsequently combined in your analysis (Chapter 12). Colleagues and students often ask us how many points they should have on their rating scale. This is related to the likely measurement error. If you know that your respondents can only respond accurately to a three-point rating, then it is pointless to have a finer rating scale with more points!

In question 12 (created in Qualtrics and optimised in the software for completion on a mobile phone) a respondent's opinion – how hot they usually like their curry – is captured on a 10-point numeric rating scale. In such rating questions it is important that the numbers reflect the answer of the respondent. Thus, 1 reflects a mild curry (korma) and 10 an extremely hot curry (phal), the number increasing as the temperature increases. Only these end categories (and sometimes the middle) are labelled and these are known as self-anchoring rating scales. As in this question, a graphic that alters as the slider is moved can be used to reflect the rating scale visually and aid the respondent's interpretation. The use of a slider has been shown to have no impact on responses when compared to more traditional radio-button formats (Roster et al. 2015) as in question 11. An additional category of 'not sure' or 'don't know' can be added and should be separated slightly from the rating scale.

Another variation is the **semantic differential rating question**. These are often used in consumer research to determine underlying attitudes. The respondent is asked to rate a single object or idea on a series of bipolar rating scales. Each bipolar scale is described by a pair of opposite adjectives (question 13), designed to anchor respondents' attitudes. For these rating scales, you should vary the position of positive and negative adjectives from left to right to reduce the tendency to read only the adjective on the left (Bloomberg et al. 2014).

13   On each of the lines below, place an x to show how you feel about the service you received at our restaurant.

Fast	_|_|_|_|_|_|_|_|_	Slow
Unfriendly	_|_|_|_|_|_|_|_|_	Friendly
Value for money	_|_|_|_|_|_|_|_|_	Overpriced

12. On a scale of 10 to 1, where...

10 is a phal (**extremely hot**) curry,

and

1 is a korma (**mild**) curry.

How hot do you usually like your curry?

5

Source: This question was generated using Qualtrics software, of the Qualtrics Research Suite. Copyright © 2018 Qualtrics. Qualtrics and all other Qualtrics product or service names are registered trademarks or trademarks of Qualtrics, Provo, UT, USA. http://www.qualtrics.com. The authors are not affiliated to Qualtrics

Table 11.3 Response categories for different types of rating questions

Type of rating	Five categories	Seven categories
Agreement	Strongly agree	Strongly agree
	Agree	Agree/moderately agree/mostly agree*
	Neither agree nor disagree/not sure/uncertain*	Slightly agree
	Disagree	Neither agree nor disagree/not sure/uncertain*
	Strongly disagree	Slightly disagree
		Disagree/moderately disagree/mostly disagree*
		Strongly disagree
Amount	Far too much/nearly all/very large*	Far too much/nearly all/very large*
	Too much/more than half/large*	Too much/more than half/large*
	About right/about half/some*	Slightly too much/quite large*
	Too little/less than half/small*	About right/about half/some*
	Far too little/almost none/not at all*	Slightly too little/quite small*
		Too little/less than half/small*
		Far too little/almost none/not at all*
Frequency	All the time/always*	All the time/always*
	Frequently/very often/most of the time*	Almost all the time/almost always*
	Sometimes/about as often as not/about half the time*	Frequently/very often/most of the time*
	Rarely/seldom/less than half the time*	Sometimes/about as often as not/about half the time*
	Never/practically never*	Seldom
		Almost never/practically never*
		Never/not at all*
Likelihood	Very	Extremely
	Good	Very
	Reasonable	Moderately
	Slight/bit*	Quite/reasonable*
	None/not at all*	Somewhat
		Slight/bit*
		None/not at all*

*Response dependent on question.
Source: Developed from Tharenou et al. (2007) and authors' experience

Quantity questions

The response to a **quantity question** is a number, which gives a factual amount of a characteristic. For this reason, such questions tend to be used to collect behaviour or attribute data. A common quantity question, which collects attribute data, is:

14 What is your year of birth?

(for example, for 1997 write:)

1	9	9	7

Because the response to this question data is coded by the respondent, the question can also be termed a **self-coded** question.

Matrix questions

A **matrix** or grid of questions enables you to record the responses to two or more similar questions at the same time. As can be seen from question 15, created in SurveyMonkey, questions are listed down the left-hand side of the page, and responses listed across the top. The appropriate response to each question is then recorded in the cell where the row and column meet. Although using a matrix saves space, Dillman et al. (2014) suggests that respondents may have difficulties comprehending these designs and that they are a barrier to response.

15. The following items refer to your treatment by managers in general who are responsible for making decisions in Anytown Manufacturing Company that affect your work. *To what extent:*

	to a large extent	to a quite large extent	to some extent	to a quite small extent	to a small extent	not at all
do they treat you with dignity?	○	✓	○	○	○	○
do they treat you with respect?	○	○	✓	○	○	○
are they at least as honest with bad news as good news in their communication with you?	○	✓	○	○	○	○

Source: Question created by SurveyMonkey Inc. (2018) San Mateo. Reproduced with permission

Combining rating questions into scales

Rating questions have been combined into scales to measure a wide variety of concepts such as customer loyalty, service quality and job satisfaction. Referred to as **constructs**, these are attributes that can be inferred and assessed using a number of indicators but are not directly observable. Researchers infer the existence of a construct using a series of measures (rating questions), these being combined into a scale that measures the construct. For each construct the resultant **scale** is represented by a scale score created by combining the scores for each of the rating questions. Each rating question is often referred to as a **scale item**. In the case of a simple Likert-type scale, for example, the scale (or composite) score for each case would be calculated by adding together the scores of each of the rating questions (items) selected (De Vaus 2014). When doing this it is important to ensure that scores for any items worded negatively are reverse coded. Using **reverse coding**, also known as **reverse scoring**, means high values will indicate the same type of response on every item. A detailed discussion of creating scales, including those by Likert and Guttman, can be found in DeVellis (2012). However, rather than developing your own scales, it often

Box 11.8
Focus on student research

Using existing scales from the literature

When planning his questionnaire David, like most students, presumed he would need to design and develop his own measurement scale. However, after reading Schrauf and Navarro's (2005) paper on using existing scales, he realised that it would probably be possible to adopt an existing scale, which had been reported in the academic literature. As he pointed out to his project tutor, this was particularly fortunate because the process of scale development was hugely time consuming and could distract his attention from answering the actual research question.

In looking for a suitable published scale David asked himself a number of questions:

- Does the scale measure what I am interested in?
- Has the scale been empirically tested and validated?
- Was the scale designed for a similar group of respondents as my target population?

Fortunately, the answer to all these questions was 'yes'. David, therefore, emailed the scale's author to ask for formal permission.

---

makes sense to use or adapt existing scales (Schrauf and Navarro 2005). Since scaling techniques were first used in the 1930s, literally thousands of scales have been developed to measure attitudes and personality dimensions and to assess skills and abilities. Details of an individual scale can often be found by following up references in an article reporting research that uses that scale. In addition, there are a wide variety of handbooks that list these scales (e.g. American Psychological Association 2018; Bruner 2013). These scales can, as highlighted in Box 11.8, be used in your own research providing they:

- measure what you are interested in;
- have been empirically tested and validated;
- were designed for a reasonably similar group of respondents;
- are internally consistent when used with your respondents (Section 11.4).

It is worth remembering that you should only make amendments to the scale where absolutely necessary as significant changes could impact upon both the validity of the scale and, subsequently, your results! You also need to be aware that existing scales may be subject to copyright constraints. Even where there is no formal copyright, you should, where possible, contact the author and ask for permission. In your project report you should note where you obtained the scale and give credit to the author.

Question wording

The wording of each question will need careful consideration to ensure that the responses are valid – that is, measure what you think they do. Your questions will need to be checked within the context for which they were written rather than in abstract to ensure they are not misread and that they do not privilege a particular answer (Box 11.9). Given this, the checklist in Box 11.10 should help you to avoid the most obvious problems associated with wording that threatens the validity of responses.

Translating questions into other languages

Translating questions and associated instructions into another language requires care if your translated or target questionnaire is to be decoded and answered by respondents in the way you intended. For international research this is extremely important if the questions are to

Box 11.9 Focus on research in the news

The tale of the Brexit referendum question

By David Allen Green

The referendum question was: "Should the United Kingdom remain a member of the European Union or leave the European Union?" The question was originally planned to be: "Should the United Kingdom remain a member of the European Union?" The Electoral Commission assessed the original question and decided: "We have previously recommended the possibility of either a yes/no question for use at a referendum on European Union membership. However, in this assessment we have heard clearer views, particularly from potential campaigners to leave the European Union, about their concerns regarding the proposed yes/no question. Our assessment suggests that it is possible to ask a question which would not cause concerns about neutrality, whilst also being easily understood." The commission thereby recommended the wording used, and this was accepted by government and parliament.

Research had indicated there could be a difference. "It seemed to reveal there was 4 per cent in what the question was, whether it was a "yes/no" question or a "remain/leave" question."

The referendum produced a 51.89 per cent vote for Leave. On a narrow and strict reading of the question, it meant there was a small but clear majority for the whole of the UK to leave the EU. In other words, there was a mandate for the ultimate objective. However, the same question, but in another form, might have had a different result.

FT *Source:* Abridged from 'The tale of the Brexit referendum question', David Allen Green, *Financial Times*, 3 Aug 2017. Copyright © 2017 The Financial Times

 ## Box 11.10 Checklist

Your question wording

✔ Does your question collect data at the right level of detail to answer your investigative question as specified in your data requirements table?

✔ Will respondents have the necessary knowledge to answer your question? A question on the implications of a piece of legislation would yield meaningless answers from those who were unaware of that legislation.

✔ Does your question appear to talk down to respondents? It should not!

✔ Does your question challenge respondents' mental or technical abilities? Questions that do this are less likely to be answered.

✔ Are the words used in your question familiar to all respondents, and will all respondents comprehend them in the same way? In particular, you should use simple words and avoid jargon, abbreviations and colloquialisms.

✔ Are there any words that sound similar and might be confused with those used in your question? This is a particular problem with researcher-completed questionnaires.

✔ Are there any words that look similar and might be confused if your question is read quickly? This is particularly important for self-completed questionnaires.

✔ Are there any words in your question that might cause offence? These might result in biased responses or a lower response rate.

✔ Can your question be shortened? Long questions are often difficult to understand, especially in researcher-completed questionnaires, as the respondent needs to remember the whole question. Consequently, they often result in no response at all.

✔ Are you asking more than one question at the same time? The question 'How often do you visit your mother and father?' contains two separate questions, one about each parent, so responses would probably be impossible to interpret.

✔ Does your question include a negative or double negative? Questions that include the word 'not' are sometimes difficult to understand. The question 'Would you rather not use a non-medicated shampoo?' is far easier to understand when rephrased as: 'Would you rather use a medicated shampoo?'

✔ Is your question unambiguous? This can arise from poor sentence structure, using words with different lexical meanings or having an unclear investigative question. If you ask 'When did you leave school?' some respondents might state the year, others might give their age, while those still in education might give the time of day! Ambiguity can also occur in category questions. If you ask employers how many employees they have on their payroll and categorise their answers into three groups (up to 100, 100–250, 250 plus), they

will not be clear which group to choose if they have 100 or 250 employees.

✔ Does your question imply that a certain answer is correct? If it does, the question is biased and will need to be reworded, such as with the question 'Many people believe that too little money is spent on our public Health Service. Do you believe this to be the case?' For this question, respondents are more likely to answer 'yes' to agree with and please the researcher.

✔ Does your question prevent certain answers from being given? If it does, the question is biased and will need to be reworded. The question 'Is this the first time you have pretended to be sick?' implies that the respondent has pretended to be sick whether they answer yes or no!

✔ Is your question likely to embarrass the respondent? If it is, then you need either to reword it or to place it towards the end of the survey when you will, it is to be hoped, have gained the respondent's confidence. Questions on income can be asked as either precise amounts (more embarrassing), using a quantity question, or income bands (less embarrassing), using a category question. Questions on self-perceived shortcomings are unlikely to be answered.

✔ Have you incorporated advice appropriate for your type of questionnaire (such as the maximum number of categories) outlined in the earlier discussion of question types?

✔ Are answers to closed questions written so that at least one will apply to every respondent and so that each of the responses listed is mutually exclusive?

✔ Are the instructions on how to record each answer clear?

have the same meaning to all respondents. For this reason, Usunier et al. (2017) suggests that when translating the source questionnaire attention should be paid to:

- **lexical meaning** – the precise meaning of individual words (e.g. the French word *chaud* can be translated into two concepts in English and German, 'warm' and 'hot');
- **idiomatic meaning** – the meanings of a group of words that are natural to a native speaker and not deducible from those of the individual words (e.g. the English expression for informal communication, 'grapevine', has a similar idiomatic meaning as the German expression *Mundpropaganda*, meaning literally 'mouth propaganda');

- **experiential meaning** – the equivalence of meanings of words and sentences for people in their everyday experiences (e.g. terms that are familiar in the source questionnaire's context such as 'dual career household' may be unfamiliar in the target questionnaire's context);
- **grammar and syntax** – the correct use of language, including the ordering of words and phrases to create well-formed sentences (e.g. in Japanese the ordering is quite different from English or Dutch, as verbs are at the end of sentences).

Usunier et al. (2017) outline a number of techniques for translating your source questionnaire. These, along with their advantages and disadvantages, are summarised in Table 11.4. In this table, the **source questionnaire** is the questionnaire that is to be translated, and the **target questionnaire** is the translated questionnaire. When writing your final project report, remember to include a copy of both the source and the target questionnaire as appendices. This will allow readers familiar with both languages to check that equivalent questions in both questionnaires have the same meaning.

Coding question responses

As you will be analysing your data by computer, question responses will need to be coded prior to entry. If you are using a cloud-based survey tool, this will be done automatically. The selected response to each closed question will either be given a numeric code or the selected answer recorded. For open questions the text entered by the respondent should be recorded verbatim. Responses will be automatically saved and can subsequently be exported as a data file in a variety of formats such as Excel™, IBM SPSS Statistics compatible or a comma-delimited file (Box 11.1).

For paper-based questionnaires you will need to allocate the codes yourself. For numerical responses, actual numbers can be used as codes. For other responses, you will need to design a coding scheme. Whenever possible, you should establish the coding scheme

Table 11.4 Translation techniques for questionnaires

	Direct translation	Back-translation	Parallel translation
Approach	Source questionnaire to target questionnaire	Source questionnaire to target questionnaire; target questionnaire to source questionnaire; comparison of two new source questionnaires; creation of final version	Source questionnaire to target questionnaire by two or more independent translators; comparison of two target questionnaires; creation of final version
Advantages	Easy to implement, relatively inexpensive	Likely to discover most problems; easy to implement with translators at source country	Leads to good wording of target questionnaire
Disadvantages	Can lead to many errors (including those relating to meaning) between source and target questionnaire	Requires two translators, one a native speaker of the source language, the other a native speaker of the target language	Cannot ensure that lexical, idiomatic and experiential meanings are kept in target questionnaire

Source: Developed from Usunier et al. (2017) 'Translation techniques for questionnaires' in International and Cross-Cultural Management Research. Copyright © 2017 Sage Publications, reprinted with permission

prior to collecting data and incorporate it into your questionnaire. This should take account of relevant existing coding schemes to enable comparisons with other data sets (Section 12.2).

For most closed questions codes are given to each response category. If you are using a paper questionnaire, these can be printed on the questionnaire, thereby **pre-coding** the question and removing the need to code after data collection. Two ways of doing this are illustrated by questions 16 and 17, which collect data on the respondents' opinions.

16 Is the service you receive?	Excellent	Good	Reasonable	Poor	Awful
(Please circle O the number)	5	4	3	2	1
17 Is the service you receive?	Excellent	Good	Reasonable	Poor	Awful
(Please tick ✓ the box)	$\square_5$	$\square_4$	$\square_3$	$\square_2$	$\square_1$

The codes allocated to response categories will affect your analyses. In both questions 16 and 17 an ordered scale of numbers has been allocated to adjacent responses. This will make it far easier to aggregate responses using a computer (Section 12.2) to 'satisfactory' (5, 4 or 3) and 'unsatisfactory' (2 or 1). Consequently, we recommend that when responses to closed questions are recorded as text by a cloud-based survey tool records, these are re-coded to numerical values.

For open questions you will need to reserve space on your data collection form to code responses after data collection. Question 18 has been designed to collect attribute data in a sample survey of 5,000 people. Theoretically there could be hundreds of possible responses, and so sufficient spaces are left in the 'For office use only' box.

18 What is your full job title?

....

For Office use only
$\square$ $\square$ $\square$

Open questions, which generate lists of responses, are likely to require more complex coding using either the multiple-response or the multiple-dichotomy method. These are discussed in Section 12.2, and we recommend that you read this prior to designing your questions.

11.6 Constructing the questionnaire

The order and flow of questions

When constructing your questionnaire, it is a good idea to spend time considering the order and flow of your questions. These should be logical to the respondent (and researcher) rather than follow the order in your data requirements table (Table 11.2). They should take account of possible bias caused by the ordering of the questions. For example, a question asking a respondent to list the possible benefits of a new shopping centre could, if preceding a question about whether the respondent supports the proposed new shopping centre, bias respondents' answers in favour of the proposal.

To assist the flow of the questions it may be necessary to include **filter questions**. These identify those respondents for whom the following question or questions are not applicable, so they can skip those questions. You should beware of using more than two or three filter questions in paper-based self-completed questionnaires, as respondents tend to find having to skip questions annoying. More complex filter questions can be programmed using cloud-based software (and CAPI and CATI software) so that skipped questions are never displayed on the screen and as a consequence never asked (Dillman et al. 2014). In such situations the respondent is unlikely to be aware of the questions that have been skipped. The following example uses the answer to question 19 to determine whether questions 20 to 24 will be answered. (Questions 19 and 20 both collect factual data.)

19   Are you currently registered as unemployed?   Yes   ☐₁

  If 'no' go to question 25   No   ☐₂

20   How long have you been registered as unemployed?   ☐☐ years ☐☐ months

  (for example, for no years and six months write:)   0 years 6 months

Where you need to introduce new topics, phrases such as 'the following questions refer to . . .' or 'I am now going to ask you about . . .' are useful, although respondents may ignore or miscomprehend instructions (Section 11.4). For researcher-completed questionnaires, you will have to include instructions for the researcher or research assistant (Box 11.11). The checklist in Box 11.12 should help you to avoid the most obvious problems associated with question order and flow. For some questionnaires the advice contained may be contradictory. Where this is the case, you need to decide what is most important for your particular population.

The visual presentation of the questionnaire

Visual presentation is important for researcher-completed, Internet and other self-completed questionnaires. Researcher-completed questionnaires should be designed to make reading questions and filling in responses easy. The visual presentation of Internet and

---

Box 11.11
Focus on student research

Introducing a series of rating questions in a telephone questionnaire

As part of a telephone questionnaire, Stefan needed to collect data on respondents' opinions about motorway service stations. To do this he asked respondents to rate a series of statements using a Likert-type rating scale. These were recorded as a matrix. Because his survey was conducted by telephone, and he wanted respondents to express an opinion, the rating scale was restricted to four categories: strongly agree, agree, disagree, strongly disagree.

In order to make the questionnaire easy to follow, Stefan used italic script to highlight the instructions and the words that the research assistant needed to read in bold. An extract is given below:

Now I'm going to read you several statements. Please tell me whether you strongly agree, agree, disagree or strongly disagree with each.

Read out statements 21 to 30 one at a time and after each ask. . .

Do you strongly agree, agree, disagree or strongly disagree?

Record respondent's response with a tick ✓

	strongly agree	agree	disagree	strongly disagree
21 I think there should be a greater number of service stations on motorways	☐₄	☐₃	☐₂	☐₁

Box 11.12
Checklist

Your question order

✔ Are questions at the beginning of your question-naire more straightforward and ones the respondent will enjoy answering? Questions about attributes and behaviours are usually more straightforward to answer than those collecting data on opinions.

✔ Are questions at the beginning of your question-naire obviously relevant to the stated purpose of your questionnaire? For example, questions requesting contextual information may appear irrelevant.

✔ Are questions and topics that are more complex placed towards the middle of your questionnaire? By this stage most respondents should be

undertaking the survey with confidence but should not yet be bored or tired.

✔ Are personal and sensitive questions towards the end of your questionnaire, and is their purpose explained clearly? On being asked these a respondent may refuse to answer; however, if they are at the end of a researcher-completed questionnaire you will still have the rest of the data!

✔ Are filter questions and routing instructions easy to follow so that there is a clear route through the questionnaire?

✔ (For researcher-completed questionnaires) Are instructions to the researcher easy to follow?

✔ Are questions grouped into obvious sections that will make sense to the respondent?

✔ Have you re-examined the wording of each question and ensured it is consistent with its position in the questionnaire as well as with the data you require?

other self-completed questionnaires should, in addition, be attractive to encourage the respondent to fill it in and to return it, while not appearing too long. A two-column layout for a paper-based questionnaire can look attractive without decreasing legibility (Ekinci 2015). For Internet questionnaires a single column is preferable while, due to the screen size, only one question per page is often preferable for mobile questionnaires (Section 11.5, question 12) (Dillman et al. 2014). However, where the choice is between an extra page (or screen) and a cramped questionnaire the former is likely to be more acceptable to respondents (Dillman et al. 2014). Cloud based survey software contain a series of style templates for typefaces, colours and page layout, as well as optimisation routines for screen, tablet and mobile phone. These are all helpful in producing a professional-looking questionnaire more quickly. For paper-based surveys, the use of colour will increase the printing costs. However, it is worth noting that the best way of obtaining valid responses to questions is to keep both the visual presentation of the questionnaire and the wording of each question simple (Dillman 2014).

Research findings on the extent to which the length of your questionnaire will affect your response rate are mixed (De Vaus 2014). There is a widespread view that longer questionnaires will reduce response rates relative to shorter questionnaires (Edwards et al. 2002). However, a very short questionnaire may suggest that your research is insignificant and hence not worth bothering with. Conversely, a questionnaire that takes over an hour to complete might just be thrown away by the intended respondent. In general, we have found that a length of between four and eight A4 pages (or equivalent) has been acceptable for both Internet and paper-based within-organisation self-completed questionnaires. In contrast, SMS questionnaires need to have far fewer questions, preferably five or less. Telephone questionnaires of up to half an hour have caused few problems, although this is dependent upon the respondents' location and time of day. Similarly the acceptable length for face-to-face questionnaires can vary from only a few minutes in the

Box 11.13
Checklist

Avoiding common mistakes in questionnaire layout

✔ (For self-completed questionnaires) Do questions appear well spaced on the page or screen? A cramped design will put the respondent off reading it and reduce the response rate. Unfortunately, a thick questionnaire is equally off-putting!

✔ (For paper-based self-completed questionnaires) Is the questionnaire going to be printed on good-quality paper? Poor-quality paper implies that the survey is not important.

✔ (For self-completed questionnaires) Is the questionnaire going to be printed or displayed on a warm pastel colour? Warm pastel shades, such as yellow and pink, generate slightly more responses than white (Edwards et al. 2002) or cool colours, such as green or blue. White is a good neutral colour but bright or fluorescent colours should be avoided.

✔ (For researcher completed questionnaires) Will the questions and instructions be printed on one side of the paper only? A researcher will find it difficult to read the questions on the back of pages if you are using a questionnaire attached to a clipboard!

✔ Is your questionnaire easy to read? Questionnaires should be typed in 12 point or 10 point using a plain font. Excessively long and unduly short lines reduce legibility. Similarly, respondents find CAPITALS, *italics* and shaded backgrounds more difficult to read. However, if used consistently, they can make completing the questionnaire easier.

✔ Have you ensured that the use of shading, colour, font sizes, spacing and the formatting of questions is consistent throughout the questionnaire?

✔ Is your questionnaire laid out in a format that respondents are accustomed to reading? Research has shown that many people skim-read questionnaires (Dillman et al. 2014). Instructions that can be read one line at a time from left to right moving down the page are, therefore, more likely to be followed correctly.

✔ Is your questionnaire optimised for the distribution mode(s) you intend to use?

street to over two hours in a more comfortable environment (Section 10.6). Based on these experiences, we recommend you follow De Vaus' (2014) advice:

- Do not make the questionnaire longer than is really necessary to meet your research questions and objectives.
- Do not be too obsessed with the length of your questionnaire.

Remember you can reduce apparent length without reducing legibility by using matrix questions (discussed earlier) and, for paper questionnaires, presenting the questions in two columns. Box 11.13 summarises the most important layout issues as a checklist of common mistakes to avoid.

Explaining the purpose of the questionnaire

The covering letter or welcome screen

Most self-completed questionnaires are accompanied by a **covering letter**, email, text or SMS message, or have a welcome screen which explains the purpose of the research and offers instructions on how to complete the questionnaire. This is the first part of the questionnaire that a respondent should look at. Unfortunately, between four per cent and nine per cent of your sample will not read instructions (Hardy and Ford 2014), while others will use it to decide whether to answer the accompanying questionnaire.

Dillman et al. (2014) and others note the messages contained in a self-completed questionnaire's covering letter will affect the response rate. The results of Dillman et al.'s research, along with requirement of most ethics committees to stress that participation is voluntary, are summarised in the annotated letter (Figure 11.2).

For some research projects you may also send an email or letter prior to delivering your questionnaire. This will be used by the respondent to decide whether to grant you access. Consequently, it is often the only opportunity you have to convince the respondent to participate in your research. Ways of ensuring this are discussed in Sections 6.2 to 6.4.

Introducing the questionnaire

At the start of your questionnaire you need to explain clearly and concisely why you want the respondent to complete the survey. Dillman et al. (2014) argue that, to achieve as high a response rate as possible, this should be done on the first page of the questionnaire in addition to the covering email or letter. He suggests that in addition to a summary of the main messages in the covering email or letter (Figure 11.2) you include:

- a clear unbiased banner or title, which conveys the topic of the questionnaire and makes it sound interesting;
- a subtitle, which conveys the research nature of the topic (optional);
- a neutral graphic illustration or logo to add interest and to set the questionnaire apart (self-completed questionnaires).

Researcher-completed questionnaires will require this information to be phrased as a short introduction, given in the researcher's own words to each respondent. A template for this (developed from De Vaus 2014), which the researcher would paraphrase, is given in the next paragraph, while Box 11.14 provides an example from a self-completed questionnaire.

> **Good morning/afternoon/evening. My name is [your name] from [your organisation]. I am undertaking a research project to find out [brief description of purpose of the research]. Your telephone number was drawn from a random sample of [brief description of the total population]. The questions I should like to ask will take about [number] minutes. If you have any queries, I shall be happy to answer them. [Pause] Before I continue please can you confirm that this is [read out the telephone number] and that I am talking to [read out name/occupation/position in organisation to check that you have the right person]. Please can I confirm that you consent to answering the questions and ask you them now?**

You will also need to have prepared answers to the more obvious questions that the respondent might ask you. These include the purpose of the research, how you obtained the respondent's telephone number, who is conducting or sponsoring the research, and why someone else should not answer the questions instead

Closing the questionnaire

At the end of your questionnaire you need to explain clearly what you want the respondent to do with their completed questionnaire. It is usual to start this section by thanking the respondent for completing the questionnaire, and restating the contact name, email address and telephone number for any queries they may have from the covering letter

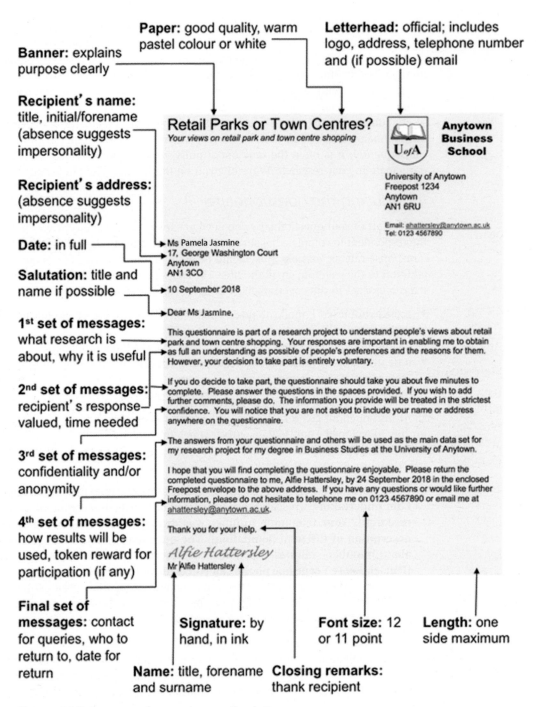

Paper: good quality, warm pastel colour or white

Letterhead: official; includes logo, address, telephone number and (if possible) email

Banner: explains purpose clearly

Recipient's name: title, initial/forename (absence suggests impersonality)

Recipient's address: (absence suggests impersonality)

Date: in full

Salutation: title and name if possible

1st set of messages: what research is about, why it is useful

2nd set of messages: recipient's response valued, time needed

3rd set of messages: confidentiality and/or anonymity

4th set of messages: how results will be used, token reward for participation (if any)

Final set of messages: contact for queries, who to return to, date for return

Signature: by hand, in ink

Name: title, forename and surname

Font size: 12 or 11 point

Closing remarks: thank recipient

Length: one side maximum

Retail Parks or Town Centres?
Your views on retail park and town centre shopping

Anytown Business School

University of Anytown
Freepost 1234
Anytown
AN1 6RU

Email: ahattersley@anytown.ac.uk
Tel: 0123 4567890

Ms Pamela Jasmine
17, George Washington Court
Anytown
AN1 3CO

10 September 2018

Dear Ms Jasmine,

This questionnaire is part of a research project to understand people's views about retail park and town centre shopping. Your responses are important in enabling me to obtain as full an understanding as possible of people's preferences and the reasons for them. However, your decision to take part is entirely voluntary.

If you do decide to take part, the questionnaire should take you about five minutes to complete. Please answer the questions in the spaces provided. If you wish to add further comments, please do. The information you provide will be treated in the strictest confidence. You will notice that you are not asked to include your name or address anywhere on the questionnaire.

The answers from your questionnaire and others will be used as the main data set for my research project for my degree in Business Studies at the University of Anytown.

I hope that you will find completing the questionnaire enjoyable. Please return the completed questionnaire to me, Alfie Hattersley, by 24 September 2018 in the enclosed Freepost envelope to the above address. If you have any questions or would like further information, please do not hesitate to telephone me on 0123 4567890 or email me at ahattersley@anytown.ac.uk.

Thank you for your help.

Alfie Hattersley
Mr Alfie Hattersley

Figure 11.2 Structure of a covering email or letter

Box 11.14
Focus on student research

Introducing a self-completed questionnaire

Lil asked her project tutor to comment on what she hoped was the final draft of her Internet questionnaire. This included the following introduction:

ANYTOWN PRIVATE HOSPITAL STAFF SURVEY

Dear Sir or Madam

I am undertaking research on behalf of Anytown Private Hospital and we are inviting some people to take part. The research will help us develop the future of the hospital. If you would like to take part in this research please answer the questionnaire.

Thank you for your time.

Not surprisingly, her project tutor suggested that she re-draft her introduction. Her revised introduction follows:

Anytown Private Hospital

Staff Survey 2018

This survey is being carried out to find out how you feel about the Hospital's policies to support colleagues like you in your work. Please answer the questions freely. You cannot be identified from the information you provide, and no information about individuals will be given to the Hospital.

Caring for All

ALL THE INFORMATION YOU PROVIDE WILL BE TREATED IN THE STRICTEST CONFIDENCE. YOUR DECISION TO PARTICIPATE IN THIS RESEARCH IS ENTIRELY VOLUNTARY.

If you do not wish to take part, just do not return the questionnaire to me. If you do decide to take part, the questionnaire should take you about five minutes to complete. Please answer the questions in the space provided. Try to complete the questions at a time when you are unlikely to be disturbed. Also, do not spend too long on any one question. Your first thoughts are usually your best! Even if you feel the items covered may not apply directly to your working life please do not ignore them. Your answers are essential in building an accurate picture of the issues that are important to improving our support for people working for this Hospital.

There are no costs associated with completing the questionnaire other than your time.

WHEN YOU HAVE COMPLETED THE QUESTIONNAIRE PLEASE RETURN IT TO US IN THE ENCLOSED FREEPOST ENVELOPE NO LATER THAN 6 APRIL.

I hope you will be willing to complete and return the questionnaire and thank you for your time. A summary of the findings will be published on the Hospital intranet. If you have any queries or would like further information about this project, please telephone me on 01234–5678910 or email me on l.woollons@anytown-healthcare.com.

Thank you for your help.
Lily Woollons
Lily Woollons
Human Resources Department
Anytown Private Hospital
Anytown AN99 9HS

(Figure 11.2). You should restate details of the date by which you would like the questionnaire returned and how and where to return it. A template for this is given in the next paragraph:

> **Thank you for taking the time to complete this questionnaire. If you have any queries please do not hesitate to contact [your name] by telephoning [contact work/university telephone number with answer machine/voice mail] or emailing [work/university email address].**
>
> **Please return the completed questionnaire by [date] in the envelope provided to:**
>
> **[your name]**
>
> **[your address]**

Sometimes, as in Box 11.14, you may wish to make a summary of your research findings available to respondents. If you do make this offer, don't forget to actually provide the summary!

11.7 Pilot testing

Prior to using your questionnaire to collect data it should be pilot tested with respondents who are similar to those who will actually complete it. The purpose of the **pilot test** is to refine the questionnaire so that respondents will have no problems in answering the questions and there will be no problems in recording the data. In addition, it will enable you to obtain some assessment of the questions' validity and the likely reliability of the data that will be collected both for individual questions and, where appropriate, scales comprising a number of questions. Preliminary analysis using the pilot test data can be undertaken to ensure that the data collected will enable your investigative questions to be answered.

Initially you should ask an expert or group of experts to comment on the suitability of your questions. As well as allowing suggestions to be made on the structure of your questionnaire, this will help establish content validity and enable you to make necessary amendments prior to pilot testing with a group as similar as possible to the final population in your sample. For any research project there is a temptation to skip the pilot testing. We would endorse Bell and Waters' (2014:167) advice, 'however pressed for time you are, do your best to give the questionnaire a trial run', as, without a trial run, you have no way of knowing whether your questionnaire will succeed.

The number of people with whom you pilot your questionnaire and the number of pilot tests you conduct will be dependent on your research question(s), your objectives, the size of your research project, the time and money resources you have available, and how well you have initially designed your questionnaire. Where surveys are particularly important, such as referenda and national censuses, there will be numerous field trials, starting with individual questions (Box 11.9) and working up to larger and more rigorous pilots of later drafts.

For smaller-scale surveys you are unlikely to have sufficient financial or time resources for large-scale field trials. However, it is still important that you pilot test your questionnaire. The number of people you choose should be sufficient to include any major variations in your population that you feel are likely to affect responses. For most student questionnaires this means that the minimum number for a pilot is 10 (Fink 2016), although for large surveys between 100 and 200 responses is usual (Dillman et al. 2014). Occasionally you may be extremely pushed for time. In such instances it is better to pilot test the questionnaire using friends or family than not at all! This will provide you with at least some idea of your questionnaire's **face validity**: that is, whether the questionnaire appears to make sense.

As part of your pilot you should check each completed pilot questionnaire to ensure that respondents have had no problems understanding or answering questions and have followed all instructions correctly (Fink 2016). Their responses will provide you with an idea of the reliability and suitability of the questions (Box 11.15). For self-completed questionnaires, additional information about problems can be obtained by giving respondents a further short questionnaire. Bell and Waters (2014) suggest you should use this to find out:

- how long the questionnaire took to complete;
- the clarity of instructions;
- which, if any, questions were unclear or ambiguous;
- which, if any, questions the respondents felt uneasy about answering;
- whether in their opinion there were any major topic omissions;
- whether the layout was clear and attractive;
- any other comments.

Researcher-completed questionnaires need to be tested with the respondents for all these points other than layout. One way of doing this is to form an assessment as each questionnaire progresses. Another is to interview any research assistants you are employing. However, you can also check by asking the respondent additional questions at the end of their questionnaire. In addition, you will need to pilot test the questionnaire with the research assistants to discover whether:

- there are any questions for which visual aids should have been provided;
- they have difficulty in finding their way through the questionnaire;
- they are recording answers correctly.

Box 11.15
Focus on student research

Pilot testing a questionnaire

Neve pilot tested her questionnaire with ten people who had similar characteristics to her potential respondents. When looking at the completed questionnaires she noticed that two of her respondents had amended question 22 on marital status.

On this basis, Neve added another possible response 'separated' to question 22.

22. How would you describe your current relationship status?

single, never married   ◉
married or domestic partnership   ◉
widowed   ◉
divorced   *None of these, I'm separated!*   ◉

Once you have completed pilot testing you should email or write to these respondents thanking them for their help.

11.8 Delivering and collecting the questionnaire

When your questionnaire is designed, pilot tested and amended and your sample selected, it can be used to collect data. Within business and management research reports, it is often not clear whether respondents felt compelled to respond to the questionnaire (Baruch and Holtom 2008). Respondents' feelings of compulsion are usually signified by stating the questionnaire was 'administered', whereas non-compulsion is signified by phrases such as 'invited to fill out a questionnaire voluntarily' or 'voluntary response'. In collecting data using your questionnaire it is important that you abide by your university's or professional body's code of ethics (Sections 6.5 and 6.6). Although, when a respondent answers questions and returns their questionnaire they are giving their implied consent, they have rights just like all research participants.

Inevitably you will need to gain access to your sample (Sections 6.2 to 6.4) and attempt to maximise the response rate. A large number of studies have been conducted to assess the impact of different strategies for increasing the response to postal questionnaires. Fortunately, the findings of these studies have been analysed and synthesised by Edwards et al. (2002), Anseel et al. (2010) and Mellahi and Harris (2016). As you can see from Table 11.5, response rates can be improved by careful attention to a range of factors, including visual presentation, length, content, delivery methods and associated communication as well as being clearly worded. In addition, it must be remembered that organisations and individuals are increasingly being bombarded with requests to respond to questionnaires and so may be unwilling to answer your questionnaire. Which of these techniques you use to help to maximise responses will inevitably be dependent, at least in part, on the way in which your questionnaire is delivered. It is the processes associated with delivering each of the five types of questionnaire that we now consider.

Internet questionnaires

For both Web and mobile questionnaires, it is important to have a clear timetable that identifies the tasks that need to be done and the resources that will be needed. A good response is dependent on the recipient being motivated to answer the questionnaire and to send it back. Although the covering email and visual appearance will help to ensure a high level of response, it must be remembered that, unlike paper questionnaires, the designer and respondent may see different images displayed on their screens. It is therefore crucial that your cloud based software can optimise the questionnaire for different displays, or alternatively, you ensure the questionnaire design is clear across all display media (Dillman et al. 2014).

Web and mobile questionnaires are usually delivered via a Web link. This normally uses email or a Web page to display the hyperlink (Web link) to the questionnaire and is dependent on having a list of addresses. If you are using the Internet for research, you should abide by the general operating guidelines or **netiquette**. This includes (Hewson et al. 2003):

- ensuring emails and postings to user groups are relevant and that you do not send junk emails (spam);

Table 11.5 Relative impact of strategies for raising postal questionnaire response rates

Strategy	Relative impact
Incentives	
Monetary incentive v. no incentive	Very high
Incentive sent with questionnaire v. incentive on questionnaire return	High
Non-monetary incentive (such as free report) v. no incentive	Low
Length	
Shorter questionnaire v. longer questionnaire	Very high
Appearance	
Brown envelope v. white envelope	High but variable
Coloured ink v. standard	Medium
Folder or booklet v. stapled pages	Low
More personalised (name, hand signature etc.) v. less personalised	Low
Coloured questionnaire v. white questionnaire	Very low
Identifying feature on the return v. none	Very low but variable
Delivery	
Recorded delivery v. standard delivery	Very high
Stamped return envelope v. business reply or franked	Medium
First class post outwards v. other class	Low
Sent to work address v. sent to home address	Low but variable
Pre-paid return v. not pre-paid	Low but variable
Commemorative stamp v. *ordinary stamp*	Low but variable
Stamped outward envelope v. franked	Negligible
email v. paper (within organisations and providing all are regular users)	Medium
Contact	
Pre-contact (advanced notice) v. no pre-contact	Medium
Follow-up v. no follow-up	Medium
Postal follow-up including questionnaire v. postal follow-up excluding questionnaire	Medium
Pre-contact by telephone v. *pre-contact by post*	Low
Mention of follow-up contact v. none	Negligible
Content	
More interesting/relevant v. less interesting/relevant topic	Very high
User-friendly language v. standard	Medium
Demographic and behaviour questions only v. demographic, behaviour and attitude questions	Medium
More relevant questions first v. other questions first	Low
Most general question first v. *last*	Low
Sensitive questions included v. *sensitive questions not included*	Very low
Demographic questions first v. other questions first	Negligible
'Don't know' boxes included v. not included	Negligible
Origin	
University sponsorship as a source v. other organisation	Medium
Sent by more senior or well-known person v. *less senior or less well-known*	Low but variable
Ethnically unidentifiable/white name v. other name	Low but variable

(*continued*)

Table 11.5 (Continued)

Strategy	Relative impact
Communication	
Explanation for not participating requested v. not requested	Medium
Confidentiality/anonymity stressed v. not mentioned	Medium
Choice to opt out from study offered v. *not given*	Low
Instructions given v. *not given*	Low but variable
Benefits to respondent stressed v. other benefits	Very low
Benefits to sponsor stressed v. other benefits	Negligible
Benefits to society stressed v. other benefits	Negligible
Response deadline given v. no deadline	Negligible

Note: Strategies in italics increase response rates relative to those in normal font
Source: Developed from Anseel et al. 2010; Edwards et al. 2002; Mellahi and Harris 2016

- remembering that invitations to participate sent to over 20 user groups at once are deemed as unacceptable by many net vigilantes and so you should not exceed this threshold;
- avoiding sending your email to multiple mailing lists as this is likely to result in individuals receiving multiple copies of your email (this is known as **cross-posting**);
- avoiding the use of email attachments as these can contain viruses.

For within-organisation research, questionnaires can be easily delivered as a hyperlink within an email to employees, provided all of the sample have access to it and use email. If you choose to use email with a direct hyperlink to the questionnaire, we suggest that you:

1 Contact recipients by email and advise them to expect a questionnaire – a pre-survey contact (Section 6.3).
2 Email the hyperlink to the questionnaire with a covering email. Where possible, the letter and questionnaire or hyperlink should be part of the email message rather than an attached file to avoid viruses. You should make sure that this will arrive when recipients are likely to be receptive. For most organisations Fridays and days surrounding major public holidays have been shown to be a poor time.
3 Summarise the purpose of the research and include an explicit request for the respondent's consent in the welcome screen at the start of the questionnaire (Box 11.16).
4 Email the first follow-up one week after emailing out the questionnaire to all recipients. This should thank early respondents and remind non-respondents to answer (a copy of the hyperlink should be included again).
5 Email the second follow-up to people who have not responded after three weeks. This should include another covering letter and the hyperlink. The covering letter should be reworded to further emphasise the importance of completing the questionnaire.
6 Also use a third follow-up if time allows or your response rate is low.
7 When the respondent completes the questionnaire, their responses will be saved automatically. However, you may need to select the online survey tool option that prevents multiple responses from one respondent.

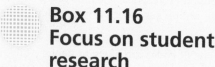

Box 11.16
Focus on student research

Request for respondent's consent in an Internet questionnaire

Ana had decided to collect her data using an Internet questionnaire. She emailed potential respondents explaining the purpose of her research and requesting their help. At the end of her email she included a hyperlink to the Internet questionnaire created in Qualtrics™.

The first page of Ana's Internet questionnaire included a summary of the main messages in her email. This was followed by a formal request to the respondent for their consent, which stressed that the decision to participate was entirely voluntary and that they could withdraw at any time.

Thank you for your interest in my research. Before you start the questionnaire, I need to make sure you know what my research is about, what your involvement will be, and confirm that you agree to take part.

By agreeing to take part in the research you are stating that you understand the following:

- I am participating in a research study;
- I have been given an explanation of the research I am about to participate in and I know what is involved in my participation;
- my participation in this research is voluntary and I am free to withdraw at any time without giving any reason;
- my identity cannot be linked to my data and that all information I give remains anonymous;
- if I have any questions about this research I can contact ana on ana123@anytown.edu.

Do you agree to take part?

Yes   No

Source: This question was generated using Qualtrics software, of the Qualtrics Research Suite. Copyright © 2018 Qualtrics. Qualtrics and all other Qualtrics product or service names are registered trademarks or trademarks of Qualtrics, Provo, UT, USA. http://www.qualtrics.com. The authors are not affiliated to Qualtrics

---

Alternatively, the questionnaire can be advertised online or in printed media and potential respondents invited to access the questionnaire by clicking on a hyperlink or scanning a QR (quick response) code using their tablet or mobile phone. Adopting either approach observes netiquette and means that respondents can remain anonymous. The stages involved are:

1 Ensure that a website has been set up that explains the purpose of the research and has the hyperlink to the questionnaire (this takes the place of the covering letter).
2 Advertise the research website widely using a range of media (for example, an email pre-survey contact or a banner advertisement on a page that is likely to be looked at by the target population) and highlight the closing date.

3 When respondents complete the questionnaire, their responses will be saved automatically. However, you may need to select the online survey tool option that prevents multiple responses from one respondent.

Response rates from web advertisements and QR codes are likely to be very low, and there are considerable problems of non-response bias as the respondent has to take extra steps to locate and complete the questionnaire. Consequently, it is likely to be very difficult to obtain a representative sample from which you might generalise. This is not to say that this approach should not be used as it can, for example, enable you to contact difficult-to-access groups. It all depends, as you would expect us to say, on your research question and objectives!

SMS questionnaires

SMS (text) questionnaires are used typically to obtain feedback immediately after an event such as a purchase delivery, meal at a restaurant or similar. For these questionnaires the introduction is invariably shorter as a maximum of 918 characters can be sent by text message. SMS questionnaires are usually sent using cloud-based survey software being delivered directly to recipients' mobile phones comprising very few questions (preferably three of less). Questions are delivered one question at a time, subsequent questions only being delivered if a question is answered. If you choose to use an SMS questionnaire we suggest that you:

1 Obtain and import a list of potential respondents' mobile phone numbers into the cloud-based software and schedule the distribution of the questionnaire at a time when you believe they will be able to take part.
2 For the first question, text recipients and ask if they would be willing to take part in the research.
3 Subsequent questions will be sent by text message immediately after the respondent answers the question.
4 On receipt of a response to the last question, ensure the software is set up to text the respondent and thank them for taking part.

Postal questionnaires

For postal questionnaires, it is important to have a concise and clear covering letter and good visual presentation to help to ensure a high level of response. As with Internet questionnaires, a clear timetable and well-executed administration process are important (Box 11.17).

Our advice for postal questionnaires (developed from De Vaus 2014) can be split into six stages:

1 Ensure that questionnaires and letters are printed and envelopes addressed.
2 Contact recipients by post, telephone or email and advise them to expect a questionnaire – a pre-survey contact (Section 6.3). This stage is often omitted for cost reasons.
3 Post the survey with a covering letter and a return envelope. You should make sure that this will arrive when recipients are likely to be receptive. For most organisations Fridays and days surrounding major public holidays have been shown to be a poor time.

Box 11.17
Focus on
management
research

Questionnaire administration

Mark undertook an attitude survey of employees in a large organisation using a questionnaire. Within the organisation, 50 per cent of employees received an Internet questionnaire by a hyperlink in an email, the remaining 50 per cent receiving a paper questionnaire by post.

General information regarding the forthcoming survey was provided to employees using the staff intranet, the normal method for such communications. Subsequently each employee received five personal contacts including the questionnaire:

- One week before the questionnaire was delivered a pre-survey notification letter, jointly from the organisation's Chief Executive and Mark, was delivered in the same manner as the potential respondent would receive their questionnaire.
- Covering letter/email and questionnaire/hyperlink to Internet questionnaire.
- Personal follow-up/reminder designed as an information sheet re-emphasising the deadline for returns at the end of that week.
- First general reminder (after the deadline for returns) posted on the staff intranet.
- Second general reminder (after the deadline for returns) posted on the staff intranet.

The following graph records the cumulative responses for both the Internet and postal questionnaire, emphasising both the impact of deadlines, follow-up/reminders and the length of time required (over 7 weeks) to collect all the completed questionnaires.

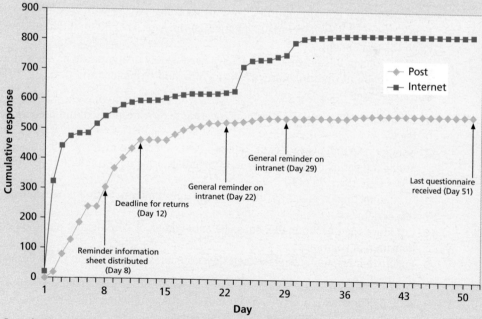

Cumulative questionnaires returned by Internet and post
Source: Unpublished data; details of research from Saunders (2012)

4 Post (or email) the first follow-up one week after posting out the survey to all recipients. For posted questionnaires this should take the form of a postcard designed to thank early respondents and to remind rather than to persuade non-respondents.

5 Post the second follow-up to people who have not responded after three weeks. This should contain another copy of the questionnaire, a new return envelope and a new covering letter. The covering letter should be reworded to emphasise further the importance of completing the questionnaire. For anonymous questionnaires a second follow-up will not be possible, as you should not be able to tell who has responded!

6 Also use a third follow-up if time allows or your response rate is low. For this it may be possible to use 'signed for' delivery (post), telephone calls or even call in person to emphasise the importance of responding.

Additionally, De Vaus (2014) advises placing a unique identification number on each questionnaire, which is recorded on your list of recipients. This makes it easy to check and follow up non-respondents and, according to Dillman et al. (2014) and Edwards et al. (2002), has little, if any, effect on response rates. However, identification numbers should not be used if you have assured respondents that their replies will be anonymous!

Delivery and collection questionnaires

For delivery and collection questionnaires either you or research assistants will deliver and call to collect the questionnaire. It is therefore important that your covering letter states when the questionnaire is likely to be collected. As with postal questionnaires, follow-ups can be used, calling at a variety of times of day and on different days to try to catch the respondent.

A variation of this process that we have used widely in organisations allows for delivery and collection of questionnaires the same day and eliminates the need for a follow-up. The stages are:

1 Ensure that all questionnaires and covering letters are printed and a collection box is ready.

2 Contact respondents by email, internal post, telephone or text/SMS advising them to attend a meeting or one of a series of meetings to be held (preferably) in the organisation's time (Section 6.3).

3 At the meeting or meetings, hand out the questionnaire with a covering letter to each respondent.

4 Introduce the questionnaire, stress its anonymous or confidential nature and that participation is voluntary.

5 Ensure that respondents place their questionnaires in a collection box before they leave the meeting.

Although this adds to costs, as employees are completing the questionnaire in work time, response rates as high as 98 per cent are achievable!

Telephone questionnaires

The quality of data collected using telephone questionnaires will be affected by the researcher's competence to conduct interviews. This is discussed in Section 10.5. Once your sample has been selected, you need to:

1 Ensure that all questionnaires are printed or, for CATI, that the survey tool has been programmed and tested.

2 Where possible and resources allow, contact respondents by email, post or telephone advising them to expect a telephone call (Section 6.3).

3 Telephone each respondent, recording the date and time of call and whether or not the questionnaire was completed. You should note any specific times that have been arranged for call-backs. For calls that were not successful you should note the reason, such as no reply or telephone disconnected.

4 For unsuccessful calls where there was no reply, try three more times, each at a different time and on a different day, and note the same information.

5 Make call-back calls at the time arranged.

Face-to-face questionnaires

Conducting face-to-face questionnaires uses many of the skills required for in-depth and semi-structured interviews (Section 10.5). Issues such as researcher appearance and preparedness are important and will affect the response rate (Section 10.4). However, once your sample has been selected you need to:

1 Ensure that all questionnaires are printed or, for CAPI, that the survey tool has been programmed and tested.

2 Contact respondents by email, post or telephone advising them to expect a researcher to call within the next week. This stage is often omitted for cost reasons.

3 (For large-scale surveys) Divide the sample into assignments that are of a manageable size (50–100) for one research assistant.

4 Contact each respondent or potential respondent in person, recording the date and time of contact and whether or not the questionnaire was completed. You should note down any specific times that have been arranged for return visits. For contacts that were not successful, you should note down the reason.

5 Try unsuccessful contacts at least twice more, each at a different time and on a different day, and note down the same information.

6 Visit respondents at the times arranged for return visits.

11.9 Summary

- Questionnaires collect data by asking people to respond to exactly the same set of questions. They are often used as part of a survey strategy to collect descriptive and explanatory data about facts/demographics, attitudes/opinions and behaviours/events. Data collected are normally analysed quantitatively.

- Your choice of questionnaire will be influenced by your research question(s) and objectives and the resources that you have available. The six main types are Internet, SMS, postal, delivery and collection, telephone and face-to-face.

- Prior to designing a questionnaire, you must know precisely what data you need to collect to answer your research question(s) and to meet your objectives. One way of helping to ensure that you collect these data is to use a data requirements table.

- The validity and reliability of the data you collect and the response rate you achieve depend largely on the design of your questions, the structure of your questionnaire and the rigour of your pilot testing.

- When designing your questionnaire, you should consider the wording of individual questions prior to the order in which they appear. Questions can be divided into open and closed. The six types of closed questions are list, category, ranking, rating, quantity and matrix.

- Responses for closed questions in Internet and SMS questionnaires are coded automatically within the cloud-based survey software. For other types of questionnaire closed questions should, wherever possible, be pre-coded on your questionnaire to facilitate data input and subsequent analyses.
- The order and flow of questions in the questionnaire should be logical to the respondent. This can be assisted by filter questions and linking phrases.
- The visual appearance of the questionnaire should be attractive, easy to read and the responses easy to fill in.
- Questionnaires must be introduced carefully to the respondent to ensure a high response rate. For self-completed questionnaires this should take the form of a covering letter or email or included in the welcome screen; for researcher-completed questions it will be done by the researcher or a research assistant.
- All questionnaires should be pilot tested prior to their delivery to assess the validity and likely reliability of the questions.
- Delivery of questionnaires needs to be appropriate to the type of questionnaire.

Self-check questions

11.1 In what circumstances would you choose to use a delivery and collection questionnaire rather than an Internet questionnaire? Give reasons for your answer.

11.2 The following questions have been taken from a questionnaire about flexibility of labour.

  i Do you agree or disagree with the use of zero hours contracts by employers? (Please tick appropriate box)

    Strongly agree $\square_4$
    Agree $\square_3$
    Disagree $\square_2$
    Strongly disagree $\square_1$

  ii Have you ever been employed on a zero hours contract? (Please tick appropriate box)

    Yes $\square_1$
    No $\square_2$
    Not sure $\square_3$

  iii What is your marital status? (Please tick appropriate box)

    Single $\square_1$
    Married or living in long-term relationship $\square_2$
    Widowed $\square_3$
    Divorced $\square_4$
    Other $\square_5$
    ($\square$ Please describe)

  iv Please describe what you think would be the main impact on employees of a zero hours contract.

For each question identify:
a the type of data variable for which data are being collected;
b the type of question.
You should give reasons for your answers.

11.3 You are undertaking research on the use of children's book clubs by householders within mainland Europe. As part of this, you have already undertaken in-depth interviews with households who belong and do not belong to children's book clubs. This, along with a literature review, has suggested a number of investigative questions from which you start to construct a table of data requirements.

a For each investigative question listed, decide whether you will need to collect factual/demographic, attitude/opinion or behaviour/event data.

b Complete the table of data requirements for each of the investigative questions already listed. (You may embellish the scenario to help in your choice of variables required and the detail in which the data will be measured as you feel necessary, but you do not have to explore the relation to theory and key concepts in the literature.)

Research objective: To establish mainland Europe's householders' opinions about children's book clubs.

Type of research: Predominantly descriptive, although wish to explain differences between householders.

Investigative questions	Variable(s) required	Detail in which data measured	Relation to theory and key concepts in literature	Check included in questionnaire ✓
A Do householders think that children's book clubs are a good or a bad idea?				
B What things do householders like most about children's book clubs?				
C Would householders be interested in an all-ages book club?				
D How much per year do households spend on children's books?				
E Do households' responses differ depending on (i) number of children? (ii) whether already members of a children's book club?				

11.4 Design pre-coded or self-coded questions to collect data for each of the investigative questions in Question 11.3. Note that you will need to answer self-check question 11.3 first (or use the answer at the end of this chapter).

11.5 What issues will you need to consider when translating the questions you designed in answer to question 11.4?

11.6 You work for a major consumer research bureau that has been commissioned by 11 major UK companies to design, deliver and analyse the data collected from a telephone questionnaire. The purpose of this questionnaire is to describe and explain relationships between adult consumers' lifestyles, opinions and purchasing intentions. Write the introduction to this telephone questionnaire, to be read by a research assistant to each respondent. You may embellish the scenario and include any other relevant information you wish.

11.7 You have been asked by a well-known national charity 'Work for All' to carry out research into the effects of long-term unemployment throughout the UK. The charity intends to use the findings of this research as part of a major campaign to highlight public awareness about the effects of long-term unemployment. The charity has drawn up a list of names and postal addresses of people who are or were long-term unemployed with whom they have had contact over the past six months. Write a covering letter to accompany the postal questionnaire. You may embellish the scenario and include any other relevant information you wish.

11.8 You have been asked to give a presentation to a group of managers at an oil exploration company to gain access to undertake your research. As part of the presentation you outline your methodology, which includes piloting the questionnaire. In the ensuing question and answer session, one of the managers asks you to justify the need for a pilot study, arguing that 'given the time constraints the pilot can be left out'. List the arguments that you would use to convince him that pilot testing is essential to your methodology.

Review and discussion questions

11.9 If you wish for more help with designing questionnaires, visit the website www.statpac.com/surveys/ and download and work through the 'Survey Design Tutorial'.

11.10 Obtain a copy of a 'customer questionnaire' from a department store or restaurant. For each question on the questionnaire establish whether it is collecting factual/demographic, attitude/opinion or behaviour/event data. Do you consider any of the questions are potentially misleading? If yes, how do you think the question could be improved? Discuss the answer to these questions in relation to your questionnaire with a friend.

11.11 Visit the website of a cloud-based survey design, data collection and analysis software provider. A selection of possible providers can be found by typing 'Internet questionnaire provider' or 'online survey provider' into the Google search engine. Use the online survey tool to design a simple questionnaire. To what extent does the questionnaire you have designed meet the requirements of the checklists in Boxes 11.10, 11.12 and 11.13?

11.12 Visit your university library or use the Internet to view a copy of a report for a recent national government survey in which you are interested. If you are using the Internet, the national government websites listed in Table 8.2 are a good place to start. Check the appendices in the report to see if a copy of the questionnaire used to collect the data is included. Of the types of question – open, list, category, ranking, rating, quantity and grid – which is most used and which is least frequently used? Note down any that may be of use to you in your research project.

Progressing your research project

Using questionnaires in your research

- Return to your research question(s) and objectives. Decide on how appropriate it would be to use questionnaires as part of your research strategy. If you do decide that this is appropriate, note down the reasons why you think it will be sensible to collect at least some of your data in this way. If

you decide that using a questionnaire is not appropriate, justify your decision.

- If you decide that using a questionnaire is appropriate, re-read Chapter 7 on sampling and, in conjunction with this chapter (Table 11.1 is a good place to start), decide which of the six main types of questionnaire will be most appropriate. Note down your choice of questionnaire and the reasons for this choice.

- Construct a data requirements table and work out precisely what data you need to answer your investigative questions. Remember that you will need to relate your investigative questions and data requirements to both theory and key concepts in the literature you have reviewed and any preliminary research you have already undertaken.

- Design the separate questions to collect the data specified in your data requirements table. Wherever possible, try to use closed questions and to adhere to the suggestions in the question wording checklist. If you are intending to analyse your questionnaire by computer, read Section 12.2 and pre-code questions on the questionnaire whenever possible.
- Order your questions to make reading the questions and filling in the responses as logical as possible to the respondent. Wherever possible, try to

adhere to the checklist for layout. Remember that researcher-completed questionnaires will need instructions for the researcher or research assistant.
- Write the introduction to your questionnaire and, where appropriate, a covering letter.
- Pilot test your questionnaire with as similar a group as possible to the final group in your sample. Pay special attention to issues of validity and reliability.
- Deliver your questionnaire and remember to send out a follow-up survey to non-respondents whenever possible.
- Use the questions in Box 1.4 to guide your reflective diary entry.

References

American Psychological Association (2018) *PsycTESTS* Available at http://www.apa.org/pubs/databases/psyctests/index.aspx [Accessed 3 Jan. 2018].

Anseel, F., Lievens, F., Schollaert, E. and Choragwicka, B. (2010) 'Response rates in organizational science, 1995–2008: A meta-analytic review and guidelines for survey researchers', *Journal of Business Psychology,* Vol. 25, pp. 335–49.

Baruch, Y. and Holtom, B.C. (2008) 'Survey response rate levels and trends in organizational research', *Human Relations,* Vol. 61, pp. 1139–60.

Bell, J. and Waters, S. (2014) *Doing Your Research Project* (6th edn). Maidenhead: Open University Press.

Bloomberg, B., Cooper, D.R. and Schindler, P.S. (2014) *Business Research Methods* (4th edn). Boston, MA and Burr Ridge, IL: McGraw-Hill.

Bourque, L.B. and Clark, V.A. (1994) 'Processing data: The survey example', in M.S. Lewis-Beck (ed.) *Research Practice.* London: Sage, pp. 1–88.

Breevaart, K., Baker, A.B., Demerouti, E. and Derks, D. (2016) 'Who takes the lead? A multi-source diary study on leadership, work engagement, and job performance', *Journal of Organizational Behavior,* Vol. 37, pp. 309–325.

Bruner, G.C. (2013) *Marketing Scales Handbook: The Top 20 Multi Item Measure Used in Consumer Research.* Fort Worth, TX: GBII Productions.

De Vaus, D.A. (2014) *Surveys in Social Research* (6th edn). Abingdon: Routledge.

DeVellis, R.F. (2012) *Scale Development: Theory and Applications* (3rd edn). Los Angeles: Sage.

Dillman, D.A., Smyth, J.D. and Christian, J.M. (2014) *Internet, Phone, Mail and Mixed Mode Surveys: The Tailored Design Method* (4th edn). Hoboken, NJ: Wiley.

Edwards, P., Roberts, I., Clarke, M., Di Giuseppe, C., Pratap, S., Wentz, R. and Kwan, I. (2002) 'Increasing response rates to postal questionnaires: Systematic review', *British Medical Journal,* No. 324, May, pp. 1183–91.

Ekinci, Y. (2015) *Designing Research Questionnaires for Business and Management Students.* London: Sage.

Field, A. (2018) *Discovering Statistics Using IBM SPSS Statistics* (5th edn). London: Sage.

Fink, A. (2016) *How to Conduct Surveys* (6th edn). Thousand Oaks, CA: Sage.

Ghauri, P. and Grønhaug, K. (2010) *Research Methods in Business Studies: A Practical Guide* (4th edn). Harlow: Financial Times Prentice Hall.

Hardy, B. and Ford, L.R. (2014) 'It's not me, it's you: Miscomprehension in surveys', *Organizational Research Methods,* Vol. 17, No. 2, pp. 138–162.

Hewson, C., Yule, P., Laurent, D. and Vogel, C. (2003) *Internet Research Methods: A Practical Guide for the Social and Behavioural Sciences.* London: Sage.

Jackson, L.A. and Taylor, M. (2015) 'Revisiting smoking bans in restaurants: Canadian employees' perspectives', *Tourism and Hospitality Research,* Vol. 15, No. 2, pp. 91–104.

Kozinets, R.V. (2015) *Netnography: Redefined* (2nd edn). London: Sage.

Louka, P., Maguire, M., Evans, P. and Worrell, M. (2006) '"I think that it's a pain in the ass that I have to stand outside in the cold and have a cigarette": Representations of smoking and experiences of disapproval in UK and Greek Smokers', *Journal of Health Psychology,* Vol. 11, No. 3, pp. 441–51.

Mellahi, K. and Harris, L.C. (2016) 'Response rates in Business and Management research: an overview of current practice and suggestions for future direction', *British Journal of Management,* Vol. 24, No. 2, pp. 426–37.

Mitchell, V. (1996) 'Assessing the reliability and validity of questionnaires: An empirical example', *Journal of Applied Management Studies,* Vol. 5, No. 2, pp. 199–207.

Qualtrics (2018). *Qualtrics.* Available at http://www.qualtrics.com/ [Accessed 20 March 2018].

Robson, C. and McCartan, K. (2016) *Real World Research: A Resource for Users of Social Research Methods in Applied Settings* (4th edn). Chichester: John Wiley.

Rogelberg, S.G. and Stanton, J.M. (2007) 'Introduction: Understanding and dealing with organizational survey non-response', *Organizational Research Methods,* Vol. 10, No. 2, pp. 195–209.

Roster, C.A., Lucianetti, L. and Albaum, G. (2015) 'Exploring slider vs. categorical response formats in web-based surveys', *Journal of Research Practice,* Vol 11, No. 1, Article D1, 15 pp.

Saunders, M.N.K. (2012) 'Web versus mail: The influence of survey distribution mode on employees' response', *Field Methods,* Vol. 24, No. 1, pp. 56–73.

Schrauf, R.W. and Navarro, E. (2005) 'Using existing tests and scales in the field', *Field Methods,* Vol. 17, No. 4, pp. 373–93.

Sekeran, U. and Bougie, R. (2016) *Research Methods for Business* (7th edn). Chichester: Wiley.

SurveyMonkey (2018) *SurveyMonkey.* Available at www.surveymonkey.com [Accessed 5 March 2018].

Tharenou, P., Donohue, R. and Cooper, B. (2007) *Management Research Methods.* Melbourne: Cambridge University Press.

UK Data Service (2018) *Variable and Question Bank.* Available at http://discover.ukdataservice.ac.uk/variables [Accessed 25 Feb 2018].

Usunier, J.-C., Van Herk, H. and Lee, J.A. (2017) *International and Cross-Cultural Management Research.* (2nd edn) London: Sage.

van de Heijden, P. (2017) 'The practicalities of SMS research', *Journal of Marketing Research,* Vol. 59, No. 2, pp. 157–72.

Yu, L. and Zellmer-Bruhn, M. (2018) 'Introducing team mindfulness and considering its safeguard role against transformation and social undermining', *Academy of Management Journal,* Vol. 61, No. 1, pp. 324–347.

Further reading

De Vaus, D.A. (2014) *Surveys in Social Research* (6th edn). Abingdon: Routledge. Chapters 7 and 8 provide a detailed guide to constructing and delivering questionnaires, respectively.

Dillman, D.A., Smyth, J.D. and Christian J.M. (2014) *Internet, Phone, Mail and Mixed Mode Surveys: The Tailored Design Method* (4th edn). Hoboken, NJ: Wiley. The fourth edition of this classic text contains an extremely detailed and well-researched discussion of how to design and deliver Internet, telephone amd postal-based questionnaires to maximise response rates.

Hall, J.F. (2018) *Journeys in Survey Research*. Available at http://surveyresearch.weebly.com/ [Accessed 12 March 2018]. This site contains a wealth of information about the use of questionnaires and has an informative section on survey research practice.

Case 11
Work-life balance – from the idea to the questionnaire

Malcom is a particularly enthusiastic mature student in the final stages of a masters in Organisational Psychology and Human Resource Management. He works in a large public-sector organisation and is passionate about doing his research project on health and wellbeing in the work-place. In our first supervision meeting, he makes it clear he wants to find out "how men can achieve work-life balance at work". To get Malcom started I send him off with some suggestions on further reading. At our next meeting, he comes in slightly dejected. "This is a lot harder than I had imagined, I don't know where to start – but it's all so interesting. . . .!" I start by asking Malcom what the most important thing is he has learned, he responds that writers find it hard to agree on how to define 'work-life balance'. We discuss that 'work-family conflict', a very prominent construct which looks at how work and family affect each other, is quite narrow as it looks mainly at what does not work, rather than what works, and many of the measures used in questionnaires are specific to 'families'. Plus, there is little evidence that men and women might differ (Shockley et al. 2017). My next question to Malcom is, 'What are the gaps in our knowledge'. He says that little is still known about potentially marginalised groups in organisational settings (Özbilgin et al. 2011) and in particular nothing is known about how employees who have special requirements and need reasonable adjustments (Doyle & McDowall, 2015) in the workplace manage work-life balance. To the best of my knowledge, there is little if any published research in this area so I ask Malcom to formulate a clear research aim and research questions.

In our next supervision, Malcom says his aim is to establish the extent to which work-life balance (WLB) requirements differ between employees with and without special requirements and the role of organisational support, using the following research questions:

1   To what extent does the WLB of employees with special requirements differ from the WLB of other employees?

2   Is workplace support which aims at WLB better for enhancing WLB than more general organisational support?

3   Do employees who have better WLB report better health?

Malcom has clearly done more reading, and now understands that WLB is not only a matter of perception that different areas in life are aligned, but also that organisational level factors such as the level of support offered make a difference. He recognises such support tends to be more effective if its targeted at WLB rather than support in general (Kossek et al. 2012).

The next step is for Malcom to begin to develop a 'data requirements table' for his questionnaire, noting which are the independent, dependent and control variables (Table C11.1).

Table C11.1 Data requirements table
Research aim: To establish the extent work-life balance (WLB) requirements differ between employees with and without special requirements and the role of organisational support within this.
Type of research: Exploratory and explanatory

Research questions	Variable(s) required	Detail in which data are measured	Relationship to theory and key concepts in the literature
To what extent does the work-life balance (WLB) of employees with special requirements differ from the WLB of other employees?	Groups of employees (Independent variable)	With special requirements/ without special requirements	Özbilgin et al. (2011), Doyle & McDowall (2015)
	Work-life balance (Dependent variable)	Measure needed for construct	
	Demographic data (Control variables)	Age (in years), gender (male/female), job role (broad), employment status (full-time/part-time)	Shockley et al. (2017)
What is the role of organisational support? What is the role of support which is specifically aimed at enhancing WLB?	Perceived general organisational support (Independent variable)	Measure needed for construct	
	Perceived WLB specific organisational support (Independent variable)	Measure needed for construct	
Do employees who have better WLB report better health?	Health (Dependent variable)	Measure needed for construct	Kossek et al. (2012)

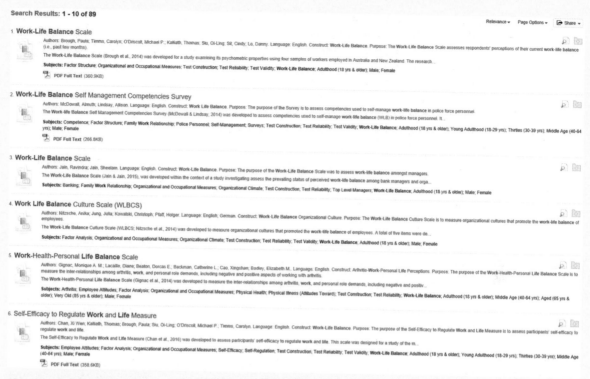

Figure C11.1 Search results for WLB scales from PsycTESTS

The next step is selecting the best measures for the constructs given empirical and pragmatic considerations. Malcom knows his own questionnaire has to be short to have any chance of getting a decent response rate, so measures have to be very succinct. It's up to Malcom to investigate. I suggest he uses the database 'PsycTESTS' (American Psychological Association 2018) which includes nearly 50,000 different tests and measures, although he could have also undertaken a literature search. Malcom's search for 'work-life balance' elicits 80 results (Figure C11.1)

Malcom downloads the original paper referring to the first measure listed (Brough et al. 2014). He considers it is suitable as it is inclusive, being applicable to all employees, and comprising only four items each. Each respondent is asked to reflect on their work and non-work activities over the past three months before scoring four items. These comprise (Brough et al. 2014: 2744):

1 "I currently have a good balance between the time I spend at work and the time I have available for non-work activities.

2 I have difficulty balancing my work and non-work activities.

3 I feel that the balance between my work demands and non-work activities is currently about right.

4 Overall, I believe that my work and non-work life are balanced."

Each item is scored on a five-point scale; 1 = strongly disagree, 2 = disagree, 3 = neutral, 4 = agree, and five =strongly agree. One item (number 2) needs reverse scoring (so Malcom will need to reverse the numbers for the agreement scales when he enters it into statistical analysis software).

Malcom's search for a health measure proves more challenging, the database finding nearly 6,000 results using 'health' as a keyword. I suggest to search for 'well being measure short' which reveals a relevant scale (Smith et al. 2017) which can be abbreviated to seven items.

We now agree the rest of the questionnaire. Malcom includes six items to measure workplace support (Cheng et al. 2017). As he cannot find an existing measure for WLB specific support, we agree he should include his own question "My organisation is supportive of employees' work-life balance" rated on a seven-point Likert-type agreement scale. He then develops his demographic questions using his table of data requirements.

Malcolm pilots the questionnaire with six friends who are in similar jobs. He is disappointed that some people only answered a few of the demographics questions on the front page, and then none of the subsequent questions. He asks these people why, and they say such personal questions are 'quite intrusive'. As a result, Malcom rewords them, and we also change the order of the questionnaire so that the demographics page came last, before a final thank you for participation.

References

American Psychological Association (2018) *PsycTESTS* Available at http://www.apa.org/pubs/databases/psyctests/index.aspx [Accessed 3 Jan. 2018].

Brough, P., Timms, C., O'Driscoll, M. P., Kalliath, T., Siu, O. L., Sit, C., & Lo, D. (2014). 'Work-Life balance: a longitudinal evaluation of a new measure across Australia and New Zealand workers', The *International Journal of Human Resource Management*, Vol. 25, No. 19, pp. 2724–2744.

Cheng, P. Y., Yang, J. T., Wan, C. S., & Chu, M. C. (2013). Perceived Organizational Support Measure [Database record]. Retrieved from PsycTESTS.

Doyle, N., & McDowall, A. (2015). Is coaching an effective adjustment for dyslexic adults? *Coaching: An International Journal of Theory, Research and Practice, 8*(2), 154–168.

Kossek, E.E., Ruderman, M.N., Braddy, P.W. and Hannum, K.M. (2012) 'Work-nonwork boundary management profiles: A person-centered approach', *Journal of Vocational Behavior,* Vol. 81, No. 1, pp. 112–128.

Özbilgin, M. F., Beauregard, T. A., Tatli, A., & Bell, M. P. (2011). Work–life, diversity and intersectionality: a critical review and research agenda. *International Journal of Management Reviews, 13*(2), 177–198.

Shockley, K. M., Shen, W., DeNunzio, M. M., Arvan, M. L., & Knudsen, E. A. (2017). Disentangling the relationship between gender and work–family conflict: An integration of theoretical perspectives using meta-analytic methods. *Journal of Applied Psychology, 102*(12), 1601.

Smith, O. R. F., Alves, D. E., Knapstad, M., Haug, E., & Aarø, L. E. (2017). Warwick-Edinburgh Mental Well-Being Scale -- Norwegian Version [Database record]. Retrieved from PsycTESTS.

Questions

1 What is the most important starting point for undertaking research using a questionnaire?
2 Malcom has identified the dependent, independent and control variables in his data requirements table. His project tutor asks him to justify this. Outline Malcom's response for each variable in Table C11.1.
3 How should Malcolm justify that the measure (scale) he has selected for the construct work-life balance is appropriate for his research?
4 Why was it important for Malcom to pilot his questionnaire?

Additional case studies relating to material covered in this chapter are available via the book's companion website: www.pearsoned.co.uk/saunders.

They are:

- The provision of leisure activities for younger people in rural areas.
- Job satisfaction in an Australian organisation.
- Service quality in health-care supply chains.
- Downsizing in the Middle East.
- A quantitative evaluation of students' desire for self-employment.
- Designing an attractive questionnaire for the Pegasus Memorial museum.

Self-check answers

11.1 When you:
- wanted to check that the person whom you wished to answer the questions had actually answered the questions;
- have sufficient resources to devote to delivery and collection and the geographical area over which the questionnaire is delivered is small;
- can use research assistants to enhance response rates. Delivery and collection questionnaires have a moderately high response rate of between 30 and 50 per cent compared with approximately 10 per cent offered on average by an Internet questionnaire;
- are delivering a questionnaire to an organisation's employees and require a very high response rate. By delivering the questionnaire to groups of employees in work time and collecting it on completion, response rates of up to 98 per cent can be achieved.

11.2 a i Opinion data: the question is asking how the respondent feels about the use of zero hours contracts by employees.

    ii Behaviour data: the question is asking about the concrete experience of being employed on a zero hours contract.

    iii Demographic data: the question is asking about the respondent's characteristics.

    iv Opinion data: the question is asking the respondent what they think or believe would be the impact on employees.

  b i Rating question using a Likert-type scale in which the respondent is asked how strongly they agree or disagree with the statement.

    ii Category question in which the respondent's answer can fit only one answer.

    iii Category question as before.

    iv Open question in which the respondent can answer in their own way.

11.3 Although your answer is unlikely to be precisely the same, the completed table of data requirements below should enable you to check you are on the right lines.

Research objective: To establish householders' opinions about children's book clubs.				
Type of research: Predominantly descriptive, although wish to explain differences between householders.				
Investigative questions	**Variable(s) required**	**Detail in which data measured**	**Relation to theory and key concepts in literature**	**Check included in questionnaire** ✓
Do householders think that children's book clubs are a good or a bad idea? (opinion – this is because you are really asking how householders feel)	Opinion about children's book clubs	Very good idea, good idea, neither a good nor a bad idea, bad idea, very bad idea		

(*continued*)

Investigative questions	Variable(s) required	Detail in which data measured	Relation to theory and key concepts in literature	Check included in questionnaire ✓
What things do householders like most about children's book clubs? (opinion)	What householders like about children's book clubs	Get them to rank the following things (generated from earlier in-depth interviews): monthly magazine, lower prices, credit, choice, special offers, shopping at home		
Would householders be interested in an all-ages book club? (behaviour)	Interest in a book club which was for both adults and children	Interested, not interested, may be interested		
How much per year do households spend on children's books? (behaviour)	Amount spent on children's books by adults and children per year by household	(Answers to the nearest €) €0 to €10, €11 to €20, €21 to €30, €31 to €50, €51 to €100, over €100		
Do households' responses differ depending on: Number of children? (demographic) Whether already members of a children's book club? (behaviour)	Number of children aged under 16 Children's book club member	Actual number yes, no		

11.4 a Please complete the following statement by ticking the phrase that matches your feelings most closely . . .

I feel children's book clubs are . . . . a very good idea   ❏5

  . . . a good idea   ❏4

  . . . neither a good nor a bad idea   ❏3

  . . . a bad idea   ❏2

  . . . a very bad idea   ❏1

b Please number each of the features of children's book clubs listed below in order of how much you like them. Number the most important 1, the next 2 and so on. The feature you like the least should be given the highest number.

Feature	How much liked
Monthly magazine	. . . .
Lower prices	. . . .
Credit	. . . .
Choice	. . . .
Special offers	. . . .
Shopping at home	. . . .

c Would you be interested in a book club that was for both adults and children?

(Please tick the appropriate box)

Yes	$\square_1$
No	$\square_2$
Not sure	$\square_3$

d How much money is spent in total each year on children's books by all the adults and children living in your household?

(Please tick the appropriate box)

€0 to €10	$\square_1$
€11 to €20	$\square_2$
€21 to €30	$\square_3$
€31 to €50	$\square_4$
€51 to €100	$\square_5$
Over €100	$\square_6$

e i How many children aged under 16 are living in your household?

children

(for example, for 3 write:)   3   children

ii Is any person living in your household a member of a children's book club?

(Please tick the appropriate box)

Yes	$\square_1$
No	$\square_2$

11.5 When translating your questionnaire, you will need to ensure that:
- the precise meaning of individual words is kept (lexical equivalence);
- the meanings of groups of words and phrases that are natural to a native speaker but cannot be translated literally are kept (idiomatic equivalence);
- the correct grammar and syntax are used.

In addition, you should, if possible, use back-translation or parallel translation techniques to ensure that there are no differences between the source and the target questionnaire.

11.6 Although the precise wording of your answer is likely to differ, it would probably be something like this:

Good morning/afternoon/evening. My name is _____ from JJ Consumer Research. We are doing an important national survey covering lifestyles, opinions and likely future purchases of adult consumers. Your telephone number has been selected at random. The questions I need to ask you will take about 15 minutes. If you have any queries I shall be happy to answer them [pause]. Before I continue please can you confirm that this is [read out telephone number including dialling code] and that I am talking to a person aged 18 or over. Please can I confirm that you are willing to take part and ask you the first question now?

11.7 Although the precise wording of your answer is likely to differ, it would probably be something like the letter below.

Work for All

B&J Market Research Ltd
St Richard's House
Malvern
Worcestershire WR14 12Z
Phone 01684–56789101
Fax 01684–56789102

Respondent's name

Email andy@b&jmarketresearch.co.uk

Respondent's address

Today's date

Dear *title name*

Work for All is conducting research into the effects of long-term unemployment. This is an issue of great importance within the UK and yet little is currently known about the consequences.

You are one of a small number of people who are being asked to give your opinion on this issue. You were selected at random from Work for All's list of contacts. In order that the results will truly represent people who have experienced long-term unemployment, it is important that your questionnaire is completed and returned.

All the information you give us will be totally confidential. You will notice that your name and address do not appear on the questionnaire and that there is no identification number. The results of this research will be passed to Work for All, who will be mounting a major campaign in the New Year to highlight public awareness about the effects of long-term unemployment.

If you have any questions you wish to ask or there is anything you wish to discuss please do not hesitate to telephone me, or my assistant Benjamin Marks, on 01684–56789101 during the day. You can call me at home on 01234–123456789 evenings and weekends. Thank you for your help.

Yours sincerely

Andy Nother

Mr Andy Nother

Project Manager

11.8 Despite the time constraints, pilot testing is essential to your methodology for the following reasons:
- to find out how long the questionnaire takes to complete;
- to check that respondents understand and can follow the instructions on the questionnaire (including filter questions);
- to ensure that all respondents understand the wording of individual questions in the same way and that there are no unclear or ambiguous questions;
- to ensure that you have the same understanding of the wording of individual questions as the respondents;
- to check that respondents have no problems in answering questions. For example:
  - all possible answers are covered in list questions;

- whether there are any questions that respondents feel uneasy about answering;
- to discover whether there are any major topic omissions;
- to provide an idea of the validity of the questions that are being asked;
- to provide an idea of the reliability of the questions by checking responses from individual respondents to similar questions;
- to check that the layout appears clear and attractive;
- to provide limited test data so you can check that the proposed analyses will work.

Get ahead using resources on the companion website at: **www.pearsoned.co.uk/ saunders**.

- Improve your IBM SPSS Statistics, Qualtrics and NVivo research analysis with practice tutorials.
- Save time researching on the Internet with the Smarter Online Searching Guide.
- Test your progress using self-assessment questions.
- Follow live links to useful websites.

Chapter 12

Analysing data quantitatively

Learning outcomes

By the end of this chapter, you should be able to:

- identify the main issues that you need to consider when preparing data for quantitative analysis and when analysing these data;
- recognise different types of data and understand the implications of data type for subsequent analyses;
- code data and create a data matrix using statistical analysis software;
- select the most appropriate tables and graphs to explore and illustrate different aspects of your data;
- select the most appropriate statistics to describe individual variables and to examine relationships between variables and trends in your data;
- interpret the tables, graphs and statistics that you use correctly.

12.1 Introduction

Virtually any business and management research you undertake is likely to involve some numerical data or contain data that has or could be quantified to help you answer your research question(s) and to meet your objectives. Quantitative data refer to all such primary and secondary data and can range from simple counts such as the frequency of occurrences of an advertising slogan to more complex data such as test scores, prices or rental costs. However, to be useful these data need to be analysed and interpreted. Quantitative analysis techniques assist you in this process. They range from creating simple tables or graphs that show the frequency of occurrence and using statistics such as indices to enable comparisons, through establishing statistical relationships between variables, to complex statistical modelling.

Before we begin to analyse data quantitatively we therefore need to ensure that our data are already quantified or that they are quantifiable and can be transformed into **quantitative data**, that is data which can be recorded as numbers and analysed quantitatively. This means that prior to undertaking our analysis, we may need to classify other forms of data (such as text, voice and visual) into sets or categories giving each category a numerical code.

Within quantitative analysis, calculations and diagram drawing are usually undertaken using analysis software ranging from spreadsheets such as Excel™ to more advanced data management and statistical analysis software such as SAS™, Stata™, IBM SPSS Statistics™. You might also use more specialised survey design and analysis online software such as Qualtrics Research CORE ™ and SurveyMonkey™, statistical shareware such as the R Project for Statistical Computing, or content analysis and text mining software such as

The Economist's Big Mac Index

The Big Mac Index is published biannually by *The Economist* (2017) to provide a light-hearted guide to differences in purchasing power between currencies. The index provides an idea of the extent to which currency exchange rates actually result in goods costing the same in different countries. Obviously the index does not take into account that Big Mac hamburgers are not precisely the same in every country; nutritional values, weights and sizes often differ. Similarly, it does not allow for prices within a country differing between McDonald's restaurants, McDonald's providing *The Economist* with a single price for each country. However, it does provide an indication of whether purchasing power parity exists between different currencies.

The Economist's "Raw" Big Mac Index for the US dollar
Source: ©The Economist (2017), reproduced with permission

In its "raw" form the Big Mac Index is calculated by first converting the country price of a Big Mac (in the local currency) to one of five other currencies (Chinese Yuan, Euro, Japanese Yen, UK Sterling or US dollars) using the current exchange rate. Using Big Mac Index figures available online (The Economist, 2017), the British price of a Big Mac was £3.19 in July 2017. Using the exchange rate at that time of £1 equals $1.28, this converts to $4.11. At this time, the price of a Big Mac in the USA was $5.30, $1.21 more than was charged in Britain. This means theoretically you could buy a Big Mac in Britain for $4.11 and sell it in the USA for $5.30, a profit of $1.21. Unlike most index numbers, which use the value 100 to express parity, the difference between a country's price and the chosen currency price (in our example US dollars) is expressed as a percentage in the Big Mac Index. Consequently, as the British price for a Big Mac was $1.21 less than the USA price, the value of the index was −22.8 per cent. This indicates that purchasing power of the British pound was approximately one fifth more than the US dollar, suggesting it was undervalued compared to the dollar.

According to the July 2017 index, one of the currencies with the greatest difference in purchasing power to the US dollar was the Ukrainian hryvnia; a Big Mac cost the equivalent of $1.70, less than a third of the price in the USA (with a Big Mac index value of −67.9 per cent). This suggests the currency was overvalued. In contrast, the Swiss franc can be considered overvalued; a Big Mac costing the equivalent of $6.74, over one and a quarter times the price in the USA (with a Big Mac Index value of +24.2 per cent). Where there is a parity of purchasing power, the index value is zero. This allows for easy comparisons between countries.

WordStat™. However, while this means you do not have to be able to draw charts by hand, undertake calculations using a calculator or count frequencies of occurrences of words and phrases by hand, if your analyses are to be straightforward and of any value you need to:

- have prepared your data with quantitative analyses in mind;
- be aware of and know when to use different graphing and statistical analysis techniques.

This is not to say that there is only one possible technique for any analysis situation. As we will see, a range of factors need to be taken into account when selecting the most appropriate graphs, tables, graphs and statistics. Consequently, if you are unsure about which of these to use, you need to seek advice.

This chapter builds on the ideas outlined in earlier chapters about secondary data and primary data collection, including issues of sample size. It assumes that you will use a spreadsheet or more advanced statistical analysis software to undertake all but the simplest quantitative analyses. Although it does not focus on one particular piece of analysis software, you will notice in the Focus on student research boxes that many of the analyses were undertaken using widely available software such as Excel and IBM SPSS Statistics. If you wish to develop your skills in either of these software packages, self-teach packages are available via our companion website. In addition, there are numerous statistics books already published that concentrate on specific software packages. These include Dancey and Reidy (2017), Field (2018) or Pallant (2016) on IBM SPSS Statistics, Swift and Piff (2014) on IBM SPSS Statistics and Excel, and Scherbaum and Shockley (2015) on Excel. Likewise, this chapter does not attempt to provide an in-depth discussion of the wide range of graphical and statistical techniques available or cover more complex statistical modelling, as these are already covered elsewhere (e.g. Dawson 2017; Hair et al. 2014; Hays 1994). Rather it discusses issues that need to be considered at the planning and analysis stages of your research project and outlines analytical techniques that our students have found of most use for analysing data quantitatively. In particular, the chapter is concerned with:

- preparing data for quantitative analysis (Section 12.2);
- data entry and checking (Section 12.3);
- selecting appropriate tables and graphs to explore and present data (Section 12.4);

- selecting appropriate statistics to describe data (Section 12.5);
- selecting appropriate statistics to examine relationships and trends in data (Section 12.6).

Ideally, all of these should be considered before obtaining your data. This is equally important for both primary and secondary data analysis, although you obviously have far greater control over the type, format and coding of primary data.

12.2 Preparing data for quantitative analysis

When preparing data for quantitative analysis you need to be clear about the:

- definition and selection of cases;
- data type or types (scale of measurement);
- numerical codes used to classify data to ensure they will enable your research questions to be answered.

We now consider each of these.

Definition and selection of cases

The definition, selection and number of cases required for quantitative analysis (sample size) have already been discussed in Section 7.2. In that section we defined a case as an individual unit for which data have been collected. For example, a case might be a respondent who had completed a questionnaire, an individual organisation or country for which secondary data had already been compiled, a magazine advertisement, a television commercial, or an organisation's tweets. The data set would comprise the data collected from the respondents, organisations or countries, magazine advertisements, television commercials or organisation's tweets you intend to analyse. Principles of probability sampling outlined in Chapter 7.2 apply when selecting such cases. However, for some research questions your data set might comprise one or only a few cases. A single case might be defined as the published report of a national inquiry, whereas if your data comprised main political parties' most recent general election manifestos, this would generate only a few cases, one for each political party. These cases would be most likely to be selected using non-probability sampling (Section 7.3). It is therefore crucial to ensure that the cases selected will be sufficient to enable you to analyse the data quantitatively, answer your research question and meet your objectives.

Data types

Many business statistics textbooks classify data for quantitative analysis into *data types* using a hierarchy of measurement, often in ascending order of numerical precision (Berman Brown and Saunders 2008; Dancey and Reidy 2017). These different levels of numerical precision dictate the range of techniques available to you for the presentation, summary and analysis of your data. They are discussed in more detail in subsequent sections of this chapter.

Data for quantitative analysis can be divided into two distinct groups: categorical and numerical (Figure 12.1). **Categorical data** refer to data whose values cannot be measured numerically but can be either classified into sets (categories) according to the characteristics that identify or describe the variable or placed in rank order (Berman Brown and Saunders

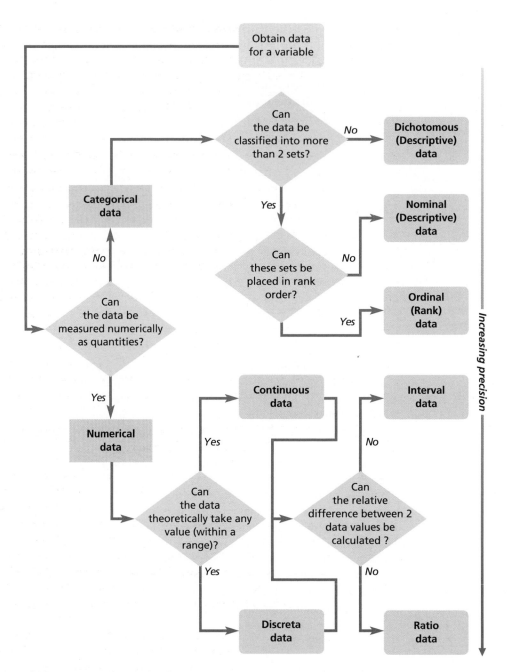

Figure 12.1 Defining the data type

2008). They can be further subdivided into descriptive and ranked. An auto manufacturer might categorise the types of vehicles it produces as hatchback, saloon, estate and SUV. You might classify aspects of an image in terms of the gender of the person depicted and whether or not she or he is smiling. The verbal responses to an open-ended interview question asking participants to describe their journey to work could, once transcribed into text, be used to generate data about their main mode of travel to work. These could be categorized as 'bicycle', 'bus', 'rail', 'car' or 'walk'. Alternatively, you may be looking at particular concepts in illustrations in annual reports such as whether the central figure in each is male or female.

Although the sources of these data differ, they are all known as **nominal data** or **descriptive data** as it is impossible to define such a category numerically or rank it. Rather, these data simply count the number of occurrences in each category of a variable. For virtually all analyses the categories should be unambiguous and discrete; in other words, having one particular feature, such as a vehicle being an SUV, excludes it from being in all other vehicle categories. This prevents questions arising regarding which category an individual case belongs to. Although these data are purely descriptive, you can count them to establish which category has the most and whether cases are spread evenly between categories. Some statisticians (and statistics) also separate descriptive data where there are only two categories. These are known as **dichotomous data**, as the variable is divided into two categories, such as the variable 'result' being divided into 'pass' and 'fail'.

Ordinal (or **rank**) **data** are a more precise form of categorical data. In such instances you know the relative position of each case within your data set, although the actual numerical measures (such as scores) on which the position is based are not recorded (Box 12.1). A researcher exploring an organisation's online communication may rank each of that organisation's tweets over a three-month period as positive, neutral or negative. You might rank individual festival goers' photographs uploaded to the festival website in terms of the prominence given to music related aspects; categorising this as high, medium, low or absent. Similarly, a questionnaire asking a rating or scale question, such as how strongly a respondent agrees with a statement, also collects ranked (ordinal) data. Despite this, some researchers argue that, where such data are likely to have similar size gaps between data values, they can be analysed as if they were numerical interval data (Blumberg et al. 2014).

Numerical data are those whose values are measured or counted numerically as quantities (Berman Brown and Saunders 2008). This means that numerical data are more precise than categorical as you can assign each data value a position on a numerical scale. It also means that you can analyse these data using a far wider range of statistics. There are two possible ways of subdividing numerical data: into interval or ratio data and, alternatively, into continuous or discrete data (Figure 12.1). If you have **interval data** you can state the difference or 'interval' between any two data values for a particular variable, but you cannot state the relative difference. This means that values on an interval scale can meaningfully be added and subtracted, but not multiplied and divided. The Celsius temperature scale is a good example of an interval scale. Although the difference between, say, 20°C and 30°C is 10°C it does not mean that 30°C is one and a half times as warm. This is because 0°C does not represent a true zero. When it is 0°C outside, there is still some warmth, rather than none at all! In contrast, for **ratio data**, you can also calculate the relative difference or ratio between any two data values for a variable. Consequently, if a multinational company makes a profit of $1,000,000,000 in one year and $2,000,000,000

Box 12.1
Focus on student research

Hierarchy of data measurement

As part of a marketing questionnaire, Rashid asked individual customers to rank up to five features of a new product in order of importance to them. Data collected were, therefore, categorical and ranked (ordinal). Initial analyses made use of these ranked data. Unfortunately, a substantial minority of customers had ticked, rather than ranked, those features of importance to them.

All responses that had been ranked originally were therefore re-coded to 'of some importance'. This reduced the precision of measurement from ranked (ordinal) to descriptive (nominal) but enabled Rashid to use all responses in the subsequent analyses.

the following year, we can say that profits have doubled. Similarly, if you are estimating the number of people attending events such as political rallies using aerial photographs you might estimate the number of people at one event is half as many as at another.

Continuous data are those whose values can theoretically take any value (sometimes within a restricted range) provided that you can measure them accurately enough (Dancey and Reidy 2017). Data such as furnace temperature, delivery distance and length of service are therefore continuous data. Similarly, data such as the amount of time a product is displayed in a television advertisement, or space (often referred to as 'column inches') devoted daily to reporting an industrial dispute in the print-based news media are also continuous data. **Discrete data** can, by contrast, be measured precisely. Each case takes one of a finite number of values from a scale that measures changes in discrete units. These data are often whole numbers (**integers**) such as the number of mobile phones manufactured, number of occurrences of a particular word or phrase in employer associations' communications, or number of illustrations containing non-white people in each issue of a fashion magazine over the last ten years. However, in some instances (e.g. UK shoe size) discrete data will include non-integer values. Definitions of discrete and continuous data are, in reality, dependent on how your data values are measured. The number of customers served by a large organisation is strictly a discrete datum as you are unlikely to get a part customer! However, for a large organisation with many customers you might treat this as a continuous datum, as the discrete measuring units are exceedingly small compared with the total number being measured.

Understanding differences between types of data is extremely important when analysing your data quantitatively, for two reasons. Firstly, it is extremely easy with analysis software to generate statistics from your data that are inappropriate for the data type and are consequently of little value (Box 12.2). Secondly, as we will see in Sections 12.5 and 12.6, the more precise the scale of measurement, the greater the range of analytical techniques available to you. Data that have been collected and coded using a precise numerical scale of measurement can also be regrouped to a less precise level where they can also be analysed (Box 12.1). For example, a student's score in a test could be recorded as the actual mark (discrete data) or as the position in their class (ranked data). By contrast, less precise data cannot be made more precise. Therefore, if you are not sure about the scale of measurement you require, it is usually better to collect data at the highest level of precision possible and to regroup them if necessary.

Data coding

All data for quantitative analysis should, with few exceptions, be recorded using numerical codes. This enables you to enter the data quickly and with fewer errors using the numeric keypad on your keyboard. It also makes subsequent analyses, in particular those that require re-coding of data to create new variables, more straightforward. Unfortunately, meaningless analyses are also easier, such as calculating a mean (average) gender from codes 1 and 2, or the mean hotel location (Box 12.2)! A common exception to using a numerical code for categorical data is where a postcode or zip code is used as the code for a geographical reference. If you are using a spreadsheet, you will need to keep a list of codes for each variable. Statistical analysis software can store these so that each code is automatically labelled.

Coding categorical data

For many secondary data sources (such as government surveys), a suitable coding scheme will have already been devised when the data were first collected. However, for other secondary sources such as documents (text, voice and visual) and all primary data you

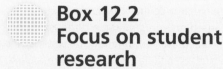

Box 12.2
Focus on student research

The implications of coding and data types for analysis

Pierre's research was concerned with customers' satisfaction for a small hotel group of six hotels. In collecting the data he had asked 760 customers to indicate the hotel at which they were staying when they completed their Internet questionnaires. When he downloaded his data, the survey design software had automatically allocated a numerical code to represent the hotel, named the variable and labelled each of the codes. The code labels for the six hotels were:

Hotel at which staying	Code
Amsterdam	1
Antwerp	2
Eindhoven	3
Nijmegen	4
Rotterdam	5
Tilburg	6

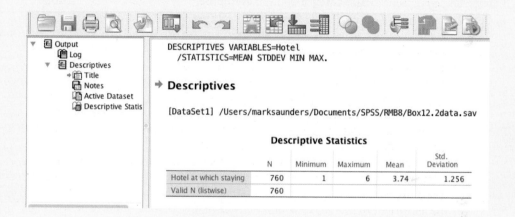

In his initial analysis, Pierre used the analysis software to calculate descriptive statistics for every data variable, including the variable 'Hotel'. These included the minimum value (the code for Amsterdam), the maximum value (the code for Tilburg), the mean and the standard deviation. Looking at his computer screen, Pierre noted that the mean (average) was 3.74 and the standard deviation was 1.256. He had forgotten that the data for this variable were categorical and, consequently, the descriptive statistics he had chosen were inappropriate.

will need to decide on a coding scheme. Prior to this, you need to establish the highest level of precision required by your analyses (Figure 12.1).

Existing coding schemes can be used for many variables. These include industrial classification (Prosser 2009), occupation (Office for National Statistics nd a), social class and socioeconomic classification (Office for National Statistics nd b) and ethnic group (Office for National Statistics nd c), social attitude variables (Harding 2017) as well as coding schemes devised and used by other researchers (Box 12.3). Wherever possible, we recommend you use these as they:

- save time;
- are normally well tested;
- allow comparisons of your findings with other research findings.

Box 12.3
Focus on student research

Developing a codebook for open questions with multiple responses

As part of his research project, Amil used a questionnaire to collect data from the customers of a local themed restaurant. The questionnaire included an open list question, which asked 'List up to three things you like about this restaurant'. Respondents could therefore provide more than one answer to the question, in other words multiple responses. Their answers included over 50 different 'things' that the 186 customers responding liked about the restaurant, the maximum number mentioned by any one customer being constrained to three by the phrasing of the question.

Once data had been collected, Amil devised a hierarchical coding scheme based on what the customers liked about the restaurant.

Extract from coding scheme used to classify responses:

Categories	Sub-categories	Response	Code
Physical surroundings			1–9
		Decoration	1
		Use of colour	2
		Comfort of seating	3
Dining experience			10–49
	Menu		10–19
		Choice	11
		Regularly changed	12
	Food		20–29
		Freshly prepared	21
		Organic	22
		Served at correct temperature	23
	Staff attitude		30–39
		Knowledgeable	31
		Greet by name	32
		Know what diners prefer	33
		Discreet	34
		Do not hassle	35
		Good service	36
		Friendly	37
		Have a sense of humour	38
	Drinks		40–49
		Value for money	41
		Good selection of wines	42
		Good selection of beers	43
		Served at correct temperature	44

The hierarchical coding scheme meant that individual responses could subsequently be re-coded into categories and sub categories to facilitate a range of different analyses. These were undertaken using statistical analysis software. Codes were allocated for each of up to three 'things' a customer liked, each of the three 'things' being represented by a separate variable.

Where possible these codes should be included on your data collection form or online survey software as **pre-set codes**, provided that there are a limited number of categories (Section 11.5). For such coding at data collection, the person filling in the form selects their response category and the associated code, this being added automatically when using survey design software (Section 11.5). Even if you decide not to use an existing coding scheme, perhaps because of a lack of detail, you should ensure that your codes are still compatible. This means that you will be able to compare your data with those already collected.

Coding of variables after data collection is necessary when you are unclear regarding the likely categories or there are a large number of possible categories in the coding scheme. To ensure that the coding scheme captures the variety in the data (and that it will work!) it is better to wait until data from the first 50 to 100 cases are available and then develop the coding scheme. This is called the **codebook** and can be used for both data from open questions' responses in questionnaires (Box 12.3) as well as visual and text data (Box 12.4). As when designing your data collection method(s) (Chapters 8–11), it is essential to be clear about the intended analyses, in particular the:

- level of precision required;
- coding schemes used by other research with which comparisons are to be made.

Content Analysis

Content Analysis is a specific analytical technique of categorising and coding text, voice and visual data using a systematic coding scheme to enable quantitative analysis. Although there are numerous definitions of Content Analysis, most draw on an early definition by Berelson (1952:18) as a "technique for the objective, systematic and quantitative description of the manifest content of communication." The technique is used to categorise and code (and subsequently analyse) both the manifest and latent content of the data. **Manifest content** refers to those components that are clearly visible in the data and can be counted. **Latent content** refers to the meaning that may lie behind the manifest content (Rose et al. 2015).

Within Berelson's definition, 'objective' emphasises that different researchers should be able to replicate a Content Analysis by using the explicit categories to code components and produce an identical outcome. A research project may focus, for example, on the attitude towards an organisational policy and who holds these views. Content Analysis of interview recordings (voice) or interview transcripts (text) may be used to code variables such as attitude towards the policy, views data being categorised as positive, neutral or negative. Terms denoting negative, neutral or positive attitudes will be identified, typically being pre-determined before analysis commences, the researcher categorising and coding specific instances of these in the text. The researcher will also identify the characteristics of the holders of each of these attitudes defining these categories using variables such as gender, age, occupation, work department and so forth.

'Systematic' in Berelson's definition emphasises that Content Analysis should be conducted in a consistent, transparent and replicable way with clear rules for defining and applying codes being detailed in a code book or coding manual. This coding scheme (Box 12.4) can draw on existing schemes developed by other researchers or developed inductively from the data using similar techniques to those outlined in Section 13.6). Holsti

(1969) advocates five general principles for the systematic development of variables' categories in Content Analysis. These should:

- link obviously to the scope and purpose of the research topic, not least so that the relationship of these categories to the research question and objectives is evident (Section 2.4);
- be exhaustive so that every relevant component of data may be placed into an analytical category;
- be mutually exclusive so that each component of data may only be placed into one analytical category, rather than possibly fitting into more than one;
- be independent so that components of data exhibiting related but not the same characteristics cannot be coded into the same category; and
- be developed from a single classification to avoid conceptual confusion.

Subsequent quantitative analysis ranges from calculating the frequency of different categories for a variable (Section 12.4) to examining relationships between variables created (Section 12.6). Using our earlier example about attitudes towards an organisational policy and who holds these views, the frequency for each category of the variable attitude towards the policy could be calculated and the relative importance of negative, neutral or positive attitudes established. It would also be possible to present these data graphically (Section 12.4) to, for example, show the relative amounts for each of the categories as well as testing statistically whether differences in attitudes were associated with or independent of variables such as gender (Section 12.6). Depending on the nature of the research question, research purpose and research strategy, Content Analysis may be used as either the main or secondary method to produce this type of data analysis.

Creating a codebook

To create your codebook for each variable you:

1 Examine the data and establish broad categories.
2 Subdivide the broad categories into increasingly specific subcategories dependent on your intended analyses.
3 Allocate codes to all categories at the most precise level of detail required.
4 Note the actual responses that are allocated to each category and produce a codebook.
5 Ensure that those categories that may need to be aggregated are given adjacent codes to facilitate re-coding.

Subsequently codes are attached to specific segments of data (Rose et al. 2015). Segments may be individual words, based on identifying and counting particular words in the content of your sample, as in our example about attitudes towards an organisational policy. Alternatively the segment may be larger than a word, being related to the occurrence of particular phrases or to sentences or paragraphs. Larger segments (sentences or paragraphs) are often used where it is important to contextualise content in order to be able to categorise its meaning. The distinction we highlighted earlier between manifest content and latent content is likely to be evident in the size of the segments used. Manifest content is likely to be reflected in the use of the word or phrase as a segment and latent content is likely to be reflected in the use of larger segments. The segment may also focus on the characteristics of those involved, as in our example where gender, age, occupation and work department were recorded. It may also focus on other characteristics of the content that are relevant to record and analyse in your research. The segment in visual materials varies from individual images to visual sequences.

Coding involves you working through your data to code segments of these data according to the categories you have devised. This will provide you with the opportunity to test your system of categories, where this is predetermined, on a sample of your data and to modify it if necessary before applying it across all of your data. An important way for you to assess

Box 12.4
Focus on management research

Developing a codebook for visual (and text) data

Lian and Yu (2017) conducted research into the online image of tourist destinations using photographic and textual information from official online media and online tourism marketers for the city of Huangshan in Japan. They published this in the *Asia Pacific Journal of Tourism Research*. In collecting data, they first selected a 10 per cent random sample of the 7,131 travel related pictures and 7,635 texts posted between January and June 2015. Building on previous research, this sample was used to establish categories of online images of tourist destinations and develop a codebook. Their final codebook comprised three categories, namely tourism facilities, tourism services and tourism resources. These were subdivided into 25 categories of photographic information and 31 sub categories of textual information. Those for the online photographic images are listed below:

Categories	Subcategories
Tourism facilities	Cable car
	Accommodation
	Camping
	Vantage point

Categories	Subcategories
	Safety fences
	Climbing stone steps
	Tour guide sign
Tourism services	Catering
	Order maintaining
Tourism resources	Guest-greeting Pine
	Pinus taiwanensis
	Canyon
	Thermal springs
	Sea of clouds
	Absurd stones
	Waterfall
	Winter snow
	"The Light of Buddha"
	Rime
	Night sky
	Ravine stream
	"Concentric lock"
	Pediment
	Carved stone

Subsequently all travel related pictures and texts were coded by both researchers and a content analysis undertaken. This revealed that the online image of Huangshan as a tourist destination comprised three elements: tourism resources, tourism facilities and tourism services, there being consistency across different media forms.

whether your system of categories is transparent and capable of being applied consistently by others is for you and a friend to code a sample of the same data separately using this system of categories and then to compare your results. This is known as inter-rater reliability and can be assessed by measuring the extent to which two coders agree. One way of doing this is to calculate the percentage agreement using the following formula:

$$PA = \frac{A}{n} \times 100$$

where:

PA = percentage agreement
A = number of agreements between the two coders
n = number of segments coded

Although there is no clear agreement regarding an acceptable percentage agreement, Rose et al. (2015) suggest that scores of 80 per cent or higher would normally be considered acceptable. A more sophisticated measure of inter-rater reliability is Cohen's Kappa (which can be calculated using IBM SPSS Statistics).

Coding numerical data

Actual numbers such as a respondent's age in years or the number of people visiting a theme park are often used as codes for numerical data, even though this level of precision may not be required. Once these data have been entered in a data matrix (Section 12.3), you can use analysis software to group or combine data to form additional variables with less detailed categories. This process is referred to as **re-coding**. For example, a Republic of Ireland employee's salary could be coded to the nearest euro and entered into the matrix as 53543 (numerical discrete data). Later, re-coding could be used to place it in a group of similar salaries, from €50,000 to €59,999 (categorical ranked data).

Coding missing data

Where you have been able to obtain at least some data for a case, rather than none at all, you should ensure that each variable for each case in your data set has a code. Where data have not been collected for some variables you therefore need a code to signify these data are missing. The choice of code to represent missing data is up to you, although some statistical analysis software have a code that is used by default. A missing data code can also be used to indicate why data are missing. Missing data are important as they may affect whether the data you have collected are representative of the population. If missing data follow some form of pattern, such as occurring for particular questions or for a subgroup of the population, then your results are unlikely to be representative of the population and so you should not ignore the fact they are missing. However, if data are missing at random, then it is unlikely that this will affect your results being representative of the population (Little and Rubin 2002). Four main reasons for missing data are identified by De Vaus (2014) in relation to questionnaires:

- the data were not required from the respondent, perhaps because of a skip generated by a filter question in a questionnaire;
- the respondent refused to answer the question (a **non-response**);
- the respondent did not know the answer or did not have an opinion. Sometimes this is treated as implying an answer; on other occasions it is treated as missing data;
- the respondent may have missed a question by mistake, or the respondent's answer may be unclear.

    In addition, it may be that:

- leaving part of a question in a survey blank implies an answer; in such cases the data are not classified as missing (Section 11.4).

12.3 Data entry and checking

When entering your data into analysis software you need to ensure the:

- data layout and format meet that required by the analysis software;
- data, once entered, have been saved and a back-up copy made;
- data have been checked for errors and any found corrected;
- need to weight cases has been considered.

Data layout

Some primary data collection methods, such as computer-aided personal interviewing (CAPI), computer-aided telephone interviewing (CATI) and Internet questionnaires, automatically enter and save data to a computer file at the time of collection, normally using numerical codes predefined by the researcher. These data can subsequently be exported in a range of formats to ensure they are compatible with different analysis software. Cloud based survey design, data collection and analysis software such as Qualtrics Research CORE™ and SurveyMonkey™ go one stage further and integrate the analysis in the same software as questionnaire design and data capture (Qualtrics 2017; SurveyMonkey 2017). Alternatively, secondary data (Section 8.3) downloaded from the Internet can be saved as a file, removing the need for re-entering. For such data, it is often possible to specify a data layout compatible with your analysis software. For other data collection methods, you will have to prepare and enter your data for computer analysis. You therefore need to be clear about the precise data layout requirements of your analysis software.

Virtually all analysis software will accept your data if they are entered in table format. This table is called a **data matrix** (Table 12.1). Once data have been entered into your analysis software, it is usually possible to save them in a format that can be read by other software. Within a data matrix, each column usually represents a separate **variable** for which you have obtained data. Each matrix row contains the variables for an individual **case**, that is, an individual unit for which data have been obtained. If your data have been collected using a questionnaire, each row will contain the coded data from one questionnaire; if your data are pictures tweeted by people attending a heavy metal music concert then each row will contain the coded data relating to a picture tweeted. Secondary data that have already been stored in a data file are almost always held as a data matrix. For such data sets you usually select the subset of variables and cases you require and save these as a separate matrix. If you enter your own data, these are input directly into your chosen analysis software one case (row) at a time using codes to record the data (Box 12.5). Larger data sets with more data variables and cases result in larger data matrices. Although data matrices store data using one column for each variable, this may not be the same as one column for each question for data collected using surveys (Box 12.6).

We strongly recommend that you save your data regularly as you are entering it, to minimise the chances of deleting it all by accident! In addition, you should save a backup or security copy on your MP3 player or other mass storage device, the cloud and making sure your data are secure, email it to yourself.

If you intend to enter data into a spreadsheet, the first variable is in Column A, the second in Column B and so on. Each cell in the first row (1) should contain a short variable name to enable you to identify each variable. Subsequent rows (2 onwards) will each contain the data for one case (Box 12.5). Statistical analysis software follows the same logic, although the variable names are usually displayed 'above' the first row (Box 12.6).

The **multiple-response method** of coding uses the same number of variables as the maximum number of different responses from any one case. For Question 2 these were named 'like1'through to 'like5' (Box 12.6). Each of these variables would use the same

Table 12.1 A simple data matrix

	Id	Variable 1	Variable 2	Variable 3	Variable 4
Case 1	1	27	1	2	1
Case 2	2	19	2	1	2
Case 3	3	24	2	3	1

Box 12.5
Focus on student research

A spreadsheet data matrix

Lucy was interested in what people videoed with their mobile phones when they attended a trade show. 30 trade show visitors who had used their mobile phones consented to allow her to use the video clips they had taken. In all she had 217 videos to analyse. Lucy decided to treat each video clip as a separate case. In her Excel spreadsheet, the first variable (*id*) was the video clip identifier. This meant that she could link data for each case (row) in her matrix to the video clip when checking for errors (discussed later). The second

variable (*age*) contained numerical (ratio) data, the age of each person who had taken the video clip (at the time the video had been taken). Subsequent variables contained further data: the third (*gender*) recorded this dichotomous (categorical) data using code 1 for a male and 2 for a female person taking the video clip. The fourth variable (*focus*) recorded the overall focus of the video clip. In developing her codebook for this nominal (categorical) variable Lucy had noted that the video clips focussed on three categories: products (code 1) services (code 2) and people (code 3). The codes used by Lucy, therefore, had different meanings for different variables. Subsequent variables related to different aspects of the content of the video clips, the codes being recorded in Lucy's codebook.

	A	B	C	D	E	
1	id	age	gender	focus	people	ir
2	1	27	1	2	3	
3	2	35	2	2	1	
4	3	41	2	3	1	

Box 12.6
Focus on student research

Data coding for more advanced statistical analysis software

As part of a market research project, Zack needed to discover which of four products (tomato ketchup, brown sauce, soy sauce, and mayonnaise) had been purchased within the last month by consumers. He therefore needed to collect four data items from each respondent:

- Tomato ketchup purchased within the last month?   Yes/No
- Brown sauce purchased within the last month?   Yes/No
- Soy sauce purchased within the last month?   Yes/No
- Mayonnaise purchased within the last month?   Yes/No

Each of these data items is a separate variable. However, the data were collected using one matrix question in an interviewer completed telephone questionnaire:

1 Which of the following items have you purchased within the last month?

Item	Purchased	Not purchased	Not sure
Tomato ketchup	$\square_1$	$\square_2$	$\square_3$
Brown sauce	$\square_1$	$\square_2$	$\square_3$
Soy sauce	$\square_1$	$\square_2$	$\square_3$
Mayonnaise	$\square_1$	$\square_2$	$\square_3$

The data Zack collected from each respondent formed four separate nominal (categorical) variables in the data matrix using numerical codes (1 = purchased, 2 = not purchased, 3 = not sure). This is known as multiple-dichotomy coding.

	tomato	brown	soy	mayonaise	like1	like2	like3	like4	like5
1	1	1	1	2	23	31	17.00	4.00	5.00
2	2	2	2	3	12	15	12.00	5.00	.
3	1	2	3	1	23	12	4.00	.	.

Zack also included a question (question 2 below) that could theoretically have millions of possible responses for each of the 'things'. For such questions, the number of 'things' that each respondent mentions may also vary. Our experience suggests that virtually all respondents will select five or fewer. Zack therefore left space to code up to five responses after data had been collected in the nominal (categorical) variables 'like1', 'like2', 'like3', 'like4' and 'like5'. This is known as multiple-response coding. When there were fewer than five responses given, the code '.' was entered automatically by the software into empty cells for the remaining 'like' variables, signifying missing data.

For office use only

2 List up to five things you like about tomato ketchup . . . . □ □ □ □

. . . . □ □ □ □

. . . . □ □ □ □

. . . . □ □ □ □

. . . . □ □ □ □

codes and could include any of the responses as a category. Statistical analysis software often contains special multiple-response procedures to analyse such data. The alternative, the **multiple-dichotomy method** of coding, uses a separate variable for each different answer (Box 12.5). For Question 2 (Box 12.6) a separate variable could have been used for each 'thing' listed: for example, flavour, consistency, bottle shape, smell, price and so on. You subsequently would code each variable as 'listed' or 'not listed' for each case. However, although the multiple dichotomy method makes it easy to calculate the number of responses for each 'thing' (De Vaus 2014), it means where there are a large number of different responses a large number of variables will be required. As entering data for a large number of variables is more time consuming, it is fortunate that more advanced statistical analysis software can calculate the number of responses for each 'thing' when the multiple response method of coding is used.

Entering and saving data

If you have downloaded secondary data as a file, or have used Internet questionnaire software, your data will already have been entered (input) and saved. However, often you will need to enter and save the data as a file yourself. Although some data analysis software contains algorithms that check the data for obvious errors as it is entered, it is essential that you take considerable care to ensure that your data are entered correctly and save the file regularly. When saving our data files we have found it helpful to include the word DATA in the filename. When entering data the well-known maxim 'rubbish in, rubbish out' certainly applies! More sophisticated analysis software allows you to attach individual labels to each variable and the codes associated with each of them. If this is feasible, we strongly recommend that you do this. By ensuring the labels replicate the exact words used in the data collection, you will reduce the number of opportunities for misinterpretation when analysing your data. Taking this advice for the variable 'like1' in Box 12.6 would result in the variable label 'List up to three things you like about this restaurant', each value being labelled with the actual response in the coding scheme.

Checking for errors

No matter how carefully you code and subsequently enter data there will always be some errors. The main methods to check data for errors are as follows:

- Look for illegitimate codes. In any coding scheme, only certain numbers are allocated. Other numbers are, therefore, errors. Common errors are the inclusion of letters O and o instead of zero, letters l or I instead of 1, and number 7 instead of 1.
- Look for illogical relationships. For example, if a person is coded to the 'higher managerial occupations' socioeconomic classification category and she describes her work as 'manual', it is likely an error has occurred.
- For questionnaire data check that rules in filter questions are followed. Certain responses to filter questions (Section 11.4) mean that other variables should be coded as missing values. If this has not happened, there has been an error.

For each possible error, you need to discover whether it occurred at coding or data entry and then correct it. By giving each case a unique identifier (normally a number; Box 12.5), it is possible to link the matrix to the original data. You must, however, remember to ensure the identifier is on the data collection form and entered along with the other data into the matrix.

Data checking is very time consuming and so is often not undertaken. Beware: not doing it is very dangerous and can result in incorrect results from which false conclusions are drawn!

Weighting cases

Most data you use will be collected from a sample. For some forms of probability sampling, such as stratified random sampling (Section 7.2), you may have used a different sampling fraction for each stratum. Alternatively, you may have obtained a different response rate for each of the strata. To obtain an accurate overall picture you will need to take account of these differences in response rates between strata. A common method of achieving this

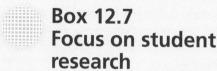

Box 12.7
Focus on student research

Weighting cases

Doris had used stratified random sampling to select her sample. The percentage of each stratum's population that responded is given below:

- Upper stratum: 90%
- Lower stratum: 65%

To account for the differences in the response rates between strata she decided to weight the cases prior to analysis.

The weight for the upper stratum was : $\dfrac{90}{90} = 1$

This meant that each case in the upper stratum counted as 1 case in her analysis.

The weight for the lower stratum was : $\dfrac{90}{65} = 1.38$

This meant that each case in the lower stratum counted for 1.38 cases in her analysis.

Doris entered these weights as a separate variable in her data set and used the statistical analysis software to apply them to the data.

---

is to use cases from those strata that have lower proportions of responses to represent more than one case in your analysis (Box 12.7). Most statistical analysis software allows you to do this by **weighting** cases.

To weight the cases you:

1 Calculate the percentage of the population responding for each stratum.
2 Establish which stratum had the highest percentage of the population responding.
3 Calculate the weight for each stratum using the following formula:

$$\text{Weight} = \frac{\text{highest proportion of population responding for any stratum}}{\text{proportion of population responding in stratum for which calculating weight}}$$

(Note: if your calculations are correct this will always result in the weight for the stratum with the highest proportion of the population responding being 1.)
4 Apply the appropriate weight to each case.

Beware: many authors (for example, Hays 1994) question the validity of using statistics to make inferences from your sample if you have weighted cases.

12.4 Exploring and presenting data

Once your data have been entered and checked for errors, you are ready to start your analysis. We have found Tukey's (1977) **Exploratory Data Analysis (EDA)** approach useful in these initial stages. This approach emphasises the use of graphs to explore and understand your data. Although within data analysis the term graph has a specific meaning: '. . . a visual display that illustrates one or more relationships among numbers' (Kosslyn 2006: 4), it is often used interchangeably with the term 'chart'. Consequently, while some authors (and data analysis software) use the term bar graphs, others use the term bar charts. Even more confusingly, what are referred to as 'pie charts' are actually graphs! Tukey (1977) also emphasises the importance of using your data to guide your choice of analysis techniques. As you would expect, we believe that it is important to keep your research question(s) and objectives in mind when exploring your data. However, the Exploratory

Data Analysis approach allows you flexibility to introduce previously unplanned analyses to respond to new findings. It therefore formalises the common practice of looking for other relationships in data which your research was not initially designed to test. This should not be discounted, as it may suggest other fruitful avenues for analysis. In addition, computers make this relatively easy and quick.

Even at this stage it is important that you structure and label clearly each graph and table to avoid possible misinterpretation. Box 12.8 provides a summary checklist of the points to remember when designing a graph or table.

We have found it best to begin exploring data by looking at individual variables and their components. The key aspects you may need to consider will be guided by your research question(s) and objectives, and are likely to include (Kosslyn 2006) for single variables:

- specific amounts represented by individual data values;
- relative amounts such as:

  - highest and lowest data values;
  - trends in data values;
  - proportions and percentages for data values;
  - distributions of data values.

Once you have explored these, you can then begin to compare variables and interdependences between variables, by (Kosslyn 2006):

- comparing intersections between the data values for two or more variables;
- comparing cumulative totals for data values and variables;
- looking for relationships between cases for variables.

These are summarised in Table 12.2. Most analysis software can create tables and graphs. Your choice will depend on those aspects of the data to which you wish to direct your readers' attention and the scale of measurement at which the data were recorded. This section is concerned only with tables and two-dimensional graphs, including pictograms, available with most spreadsheets (Table 12.2). Three-dimensional graphs are not discussed, as these can often mislead or hinder interpretation (Kosslyn 2006). Those tables and graphs most pertinent to your research question(s) and objectives will eventually appear in your research report to support your arguments. You should therefore save a copy of all tables and graphs you create.

Box 12.8
Checklist

Designing your graphs and tables

For both graphs and tables

✔ Does it have a brief but clear and descriptive title?
✔ Are the units of measurement used stated clearly?
✔ Are the sources of data used stated clearly?
✔ Are there notes to explain abbreviations and unusual terminology?
✔ Does it state the size of the sample on which the values in the graph/table are based?

For graphs

✔ Does it have clear axis labels?
✔ Are bars and their components in the same logical sequence?
✔ Is more dense shading used for smaller areas?
✔ Have you avoided misrepresenting or distorting the data?
✔ Is a key or legend included (where necessary)?

For tables

✔ Does it have clear column and row headings?
✔ Are columns and rows in a logical sequence?
✔ Are numbers in columns right justified?

Exploring and presenting individual variables

To show specific amounts

The simplest way of summarising data for individual variables so that specific amounts can be read is to use a **table (frequency distribution)**. For categorical data, the table summarises the number of cases (frequency) in each category. For variables where there are likely to be a large number of categories (or values for numerical data), you will need to group the data into categories that reflect your research question(s) and objectives.

To show highest and lowest values

Tables attach no visual significance to highest or lowest data values unless emphasised by alternative fonts. Graphs can provide visual clues, although both categorical and numerical data may need grouping. For categorical and discrete data, bar graphs and pictograms are both suitable. Generally, bar graphs provide a more accurate representation and should be used for research reports, whereas pictograms convey a general impression and can be used to gain an audience's attention. In a **bar graph**, also often known as **a bar chart**, the height or length of each bar represents the frequency of occurrence. Bars are separated by gaps, usually half the width of the bars. Bar graphs where the bars are vertical (as in Figure 12.2) are sometimes called bar or column charts. This bar graph emphasises that the European Union member state with the highest production of renewable energy in 2015 was Germany, while either Cyprus, Luxembourg or Malta had the lowest production of renewable energy.

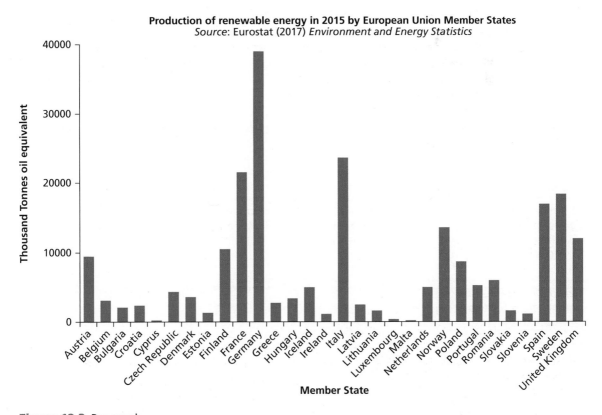

Production of renewable energy in 2015 by European Union Member States
Source: Eurostat (2017) *Environment and Energy Statistics*

Figure 12.2 Bar graph

Source: Adapted from Eurostat (2017) © European Communities 2017. Reproduced with permission

Table 12.2 Data presentation by data type: A summary

	Categorical		Numerical	
	Nominal (Descriptive)	**Ordinal (Ranked)**	**Continuous**	**Discrete**
To show one variable so that any *specific amount* can be read easily	Table/frequency distribution (data often grouped)			
To show the relative amount for categories or values for one variable so that *highest* and *lowest* are clear	Bar graph/chart, pictogram or data cloud (data may need grouping)		Histogram or frequency polygon (data must be grouped)	Bar graph/chart or pictogram (data may need grouping)
To show the *trend* for a variable		Line graph or bar graph/chart	Line graph or histogram	Line graph or bar graph/chart
To show the *proportion* or *percentage* of occurrences of categories or values for one variable	Pie chart or bar graph/chart (data may need grouping)		Histogram or pie chart (data must be grouped)	Pie chart or bar graph/chart (data may need grouping)
To show the *distribution* of values for one variable			Frequency polygon, histogram (data must be grouped) or box plot	Frequency polygon, bar graph/chart (data may need grouping) or box plot
To show the *interrelationship* between two or more variables so that any *specific* amount can be read easily	Contingency table/cross-tabulation (data often grouped)			
To compare the relative amount for categories or values for two or more variables so that *highest* and *lowest* are clear	Multiple bar graph/chart (continuous data must be grouped; other data may need grouping)			
To compare the *proportions* or *percentages* of occurrences of categories or values for two or more variables	Comparative pie charts or percentage component bar graph/chart (continuous data must be grouped; other data may need grouping)			
To compare the *distribution* of values for two or more variables			Multiple box plot	
To compare the *trends* for two or more variables so that *intersections* are clear		Multiple line graph or multiple bar graph/chart		

Table 12.2 Continued

	Categorical		Numerical	
	Nominal (Descriptive)	**Ordinal (Ranked)**	**Continuous**	**Discrete**
To compare the frequency of occurrences of categories or values for two or more variables so that *cumulative totals* are clear	Stacked bar graph/chart (continuous data must be grouped; other data may need grouping)			
To compare the *proportions* and *cumulative totals* of occurrences of categories or values for two or more variables	Comparative proportional pie charts (continuous data must be grouped; other data may need grouping)			
To show the *interrelationship* between cases for two variables			Scatter graph/scatter plot	

Source: © Mark Saunders, Philip Lewis and Adrian Thornhill 2018

To show relative amounts

To emphasise the relative values represented by each of the bars in a bar graph, the bars may be reordered in either descending or ascending order of the frequency of occurrence represented by each bar (Figure 12.3). It is now clear from the order of the bars that Malta has the lowest production of renewable energy.

For text data the relative proportions of key words and phrases can be shown using a **word cloud** (Box 12.9), there being numerous free word cloud generators such as Wordle™ available online. In a word cloud the frequency of occurrence of a particular word or phrase is represented by the font size of the word or occasionally the colour.

Most researchers use a histogram to show highest and lowest values for continuous data. Prior to being drawn, data will often need to be grouped into class intervals. In a **histogram**, the area of each bar represents the frequency of occurrence and the continuous nature of the data is emphasised by the absence of gaps between the bars. For equal width class intervals, the height of your bar still represents the frequency of occurrences (Figure 12.4) and so the highest and lowest values are easy to distinguish. For histograms with unequal class interval widths, this is not the case. In Figure 12.4 the histogram emphasises that the highest number of Harley-Davidson motorcycles shipped worldwide was in 2006, and the lowest number in 1986.

Analysis software treats histograms for data of equal width class intervals as a variation of a bar chart. Unfortunately, few spreadsheets will cope automatically with the calculations required to draw histograms for unequal class intervals. Consequently, you may have to use a bar chart owing to the limitations of your analysis software.

In a **pictogram**, each bar is replaced by a picture or series of pictures chosen to represent the data. To illustrate the impact of doing this, we have used data of worldwide Harley-Davidson motorcycle shipments to generate both a histogram (Figure 12.4) and a pictogram (Figure 12.5). In the pictogram each picture represents 20,000 motorcycles.

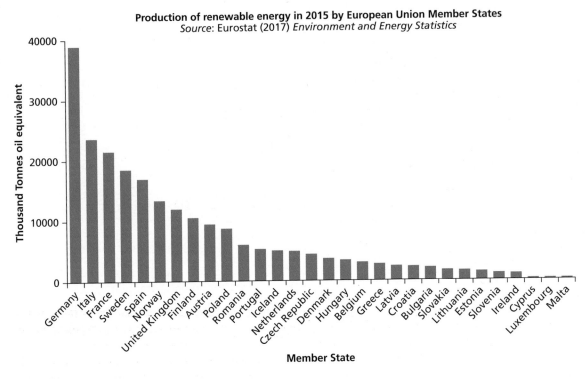

Figure 12.3 Bar graph (data reordered)

Source: Adapted from Eurostat (2017) © European Communities 2017, reproduced with permission

Pictures in pictograms can, like bars in bar graphs and histograms, be shown in columns or horizontally. The height of the column or length of the bar made up by the pictures represents the frequency of occurrence. In this case we felt it was more logical to group the pictures as a horizontal bar rather than vertically on top of each other. You will have probably also noticed that, in the pictogram, there are gaps between the 'bars'. While this normally signifies discrete categories of data, it is also acceptable to do this for continuous data (such as years) when drawing a pictogram, to aid clarity. Although analysis software allows you to convert a bar graph or histogram to a pictogram easily and accurately, it

Box 12.9
Focus on student research

Using a word cloud to display the frequency of key terms

Luca undertook a research project evaluating types of pay structure. This involved him conducting interviews in organisations that each used a different pay structure. Luca wanted to understand the reasons why each had decided to adopt a particular structure

and to evaluate perceptions about that structure's use in practice. To demonstrate the frequency of key terms used by his interview participants he thought it might be useful to produce a word cloud for each set of interviews exploring a particular pay structure. Since these data clouds would represent the actual terms used by his interview participants, they also helped Luca to demonstrate how he had derived his codes from his data. This data cloud represents the terms used by interview participants in an organisation that had implemented a Job Families pay structure.

is more difficult to establish the actual data values from a pictogram. This is because the number of units part of a picture represents is not immediately clear. For example, in Figure 12.5, how many motorcycles shipped would a rear wheel represent?

Pictograms have a further drawback, namely that it is very easy to misrepresent the data. Both Figures 12.4 and 12.5 show shipments of Harley-Davidson motorcycles declined between 2006 and 2010. Using our analysis software, this could have been represented using a picture of a motorcycle in 2006 that was nearly one and a half times as long as the picture in 2010. However, in order to keep the proportions of the motorcycle accurate, the

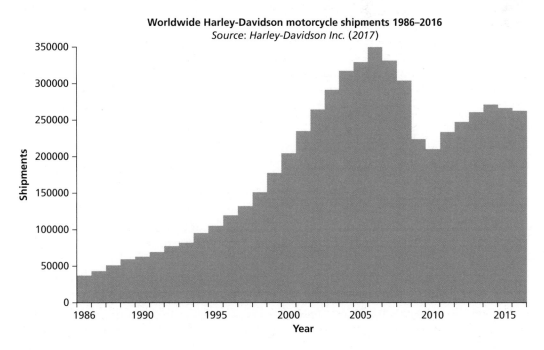

Figure 12.4 Histogram

Source: Adapted from Harley-Davidson Inc. (2017)

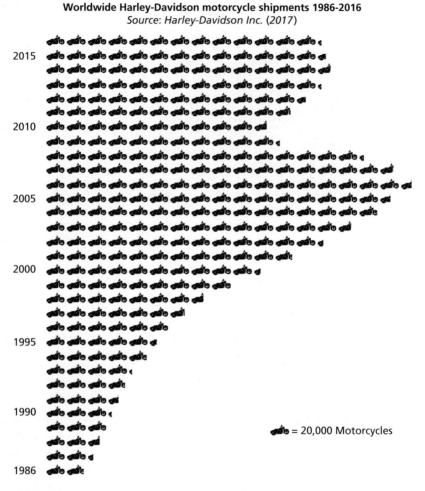

Figure 12.5 Pictogram
Source: Adapted from Harley-Davidson Inc. (2017)

picture would have needed to be nearly one and a half times as tall. Consequently, the actual area of the picture for 2006 would have been over twice as great and would have been interpreted as motorcycle shipments being twice as large in 2006 than 2010! Because of this we would recommend that, if you are using a pictogram, you decide on a standard value for each picture and do not alter its size. In addition, you should include a key or note to indicate the value each picture represents.

Frequency polygons are used less often to illustrate limits. Most analysis software treats them as a version of a line graph (Figure 12.6) in which the lines are extended to meet the horizontal axis, provided that class widths are equal.

To show a trend

Trends can only be presented for variables containing numerical (and occasionally ranked) longitudinal data. The most suitable diagram for exploring the trend is a **line graph** (Kosslyn 2006) in which the data values for each time period are joined with a line to represent the trend (Figure 12.6). In Figure 12.6 the line graph reveals the rise and decline in the number of Harley-Davidson motorcycles shipped worldwide between 1989 and 2016. You can also use histograms (Figure 12.4) to show trends over continuous time periods

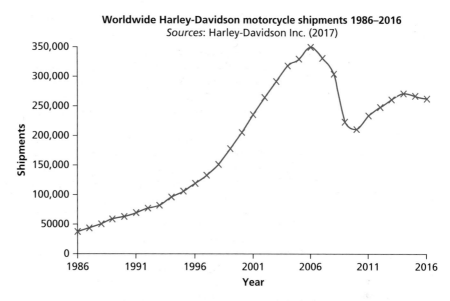

Figure 12.6 Line graph
Source: Adapted from Harley-Davidson Inc. (2017)

and bar graphs (Figure 12.2) to show trends between discrete time periods. The trend can also be calculated using time-series analysis (Section 12.6).

To show proportions or percentages

Research has shown that the most frequently used diagram to emphasise the proportion or share of occurrences is the pie chart, although bar charts have been shown to give equally good results (Anderson et al. 2017). A **pie chart** is divided into proportional segments according to the share each has of the total value and the total value represented by the pie is noted (Box 12.10). For numerical and some categorical data you will need to group data prior to drawing the pie chart, as it is difficult to interpret pie charts with more than six segments (Keen 2018).

Box 12.10
Focus on student research

Exploring and presenting data for individual variables

As part of audience research for his dissertation, Valentin asked people attending a play at a provincial theatre to complete a short questionnaire. This collected responses to 25 questions including:

3 How many plays (including this one) have you seen at this theatre in the past year?

11 This play is good value for money.

strongly disagree $\square_1$ disagree $\square_2$

agree $\square_3$ strongly agree $\square_4$

24 How old are you?

Under 18 $\square_1$ 18 to 34 $\square_2$

35 to 64 $\square_3$ 65 and over $\square_4$

Exploratory analyses were undertaken using analysis software and diagrams and tables generated. For Question 3, which collected discrete (numerical) data, the aspects that were most important were the distribution of values and the highest and lowest numbers of plays seen. A bar graph, therefore, was drawn:

Box 12.10
Focus on student
research (*continued*)

Exploring and presenting data for individual variables

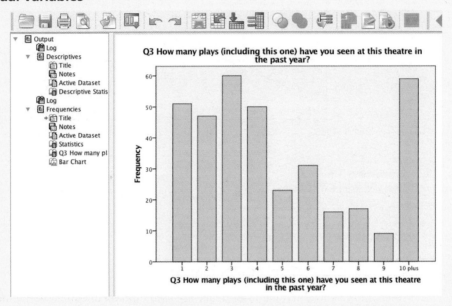

This emphasised that the most frequent number of plays seen by respondents was three and the least frequent number of plays seen by the respondents was either nine or probably some larger number. It also suggested that the distribution was positively skewed towards lower numbers of plays seen.

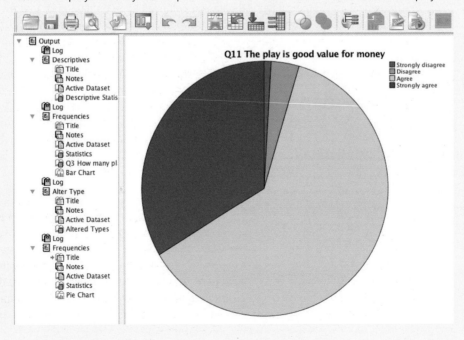

For Question 11 (ordinal categorical data), the most important aspect was the proportion of people agreeing and disagreeing with the statement. A pie chart was therefore drawn, although unfortunately the shadings were not similar for the two agree categories and for the two disagree categories.

This emphasised that the vast majority of respondents (95 per cent) agreed that the play was good value for money.

Question 24 collected data on each respondent's age. This question had grouped continuous (numerical) data into four unequal-width age groups meaning it was recorded as ordinal (categorical) data. For this analysis, the most important aspects were the specific number and percentage of respondents in each age category and so a table was constructed.

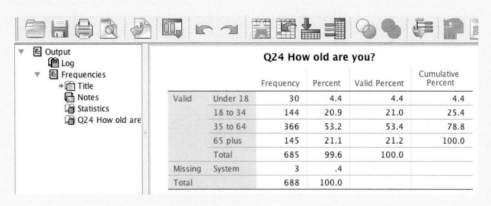

Q24 How old are you?

		Frequency	Percent	Valid Percent	Cumulative Percent
Valid	Under 18	30	4.4	4.4	4.4
	18 to 34	144	20.9	21.0	25.4
	35 to 64	366	53.2	53.4	78.8
	65 plus	145	21.1	21.2	100.0
	Total	685	99.6	100.0	
Missing	System	3	.4		
Total		688	100.0		

To show the distribution of values

Prior to using many statistical tests it is necessary to establish the distribution of values for variables containing numerical data (Sections 12.4, 12.5). For continuous data, this can be visualised by plotting a histogram or frequency polygon. For discrete data a bar graph or frequency polygon can be plotted. A **frequency polygon** is a line graph connecting the mid points of the bars of a histogram or bar graph (Figure 12.13). If your graph shows a bunching to the left and a long tail to the right, the data are **positively skewed** (Figure 12.7). If the converse is true, the data are **negatively skewed** (Figure 12.7). If your data are equally distributed either side of the highest frequency then they are **symmetrically distributed**. A special form of the symmetric distribution, in which the data can be plotted as a bell-shaped curve, is known as **normal distribution** (Figure 12.7).

The other indicator of the distribution's shape is **kurtosis** – the pointedness or flatness of the distribution compared with normal distribution. If a distribution is more pointed or peaked, it is said to be leptokurtic and the kurtosis value is positive. If a distribution is flatter, it is said to be platykurtic and the kurtosis value is negative. A distribution that is between the extremes of peakedness and flatness is said to be mesokurtic and has a kurtosis value of zero (Dancey and Reidy 2017).

An alternative, often included in more advanced statistical analysis software, is the **box plot** (Figure 12.8). This provides a pictorial representation of the distribution of the data for a variable. The plot shows where the middle value or median is, how this relates to the middle 50 per cent of the data or inter-quartile range, and highest and lowest values or *extremes* (Section 12.5). It also highlights outliers, those values that are very different from the data. In Figure 12.8 the two outliers might be due to mistakes in data entry. Alternatively, they may be correct and emphasise that sales for these two cases (93 and 88) are far higher. In this example we can see that the data values for the variable are positively skewed as there is a long tail to the right.

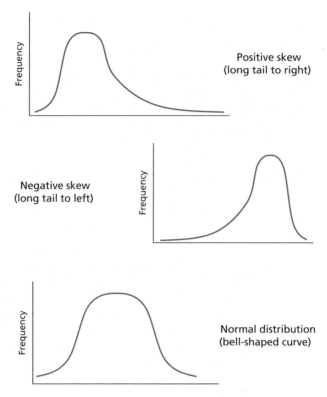

Figure 12.7 Frequency polygons showing distributions of values

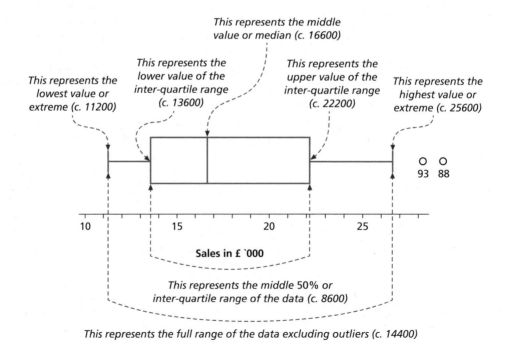

Figure 12.8 Annotated box plot

Comparing variables

To show interdependence and specific amounts

As with individual variables, the best method of showing interdependence between variables so that any specific amount can be discerned easily is a table. This is known as a **contingency table** or as a **cross-tabulation** (Table 12.3). For variables where there are likely to be a large number of categories (or values for numerical data), you may need to group the data to prevent the table from becoming too large.

Most statistical analysis software allows you to add totals and row and column percentages when designing your table. Statistical analyses such as chi square can also be undertaken at the same time (Section 12.6).

To compare the highest and lowest values

Comparisons of variables that emphasise the highest and lowest rather than precise values are best explored using a **multiple bar graph**, also known as a **multiple bar chart** (Kosslyn 2006), alternatively known as a **compound bar graph** or **compound bar chart**. As for a bar graph, continuous data – or data where there are many values or categories – need to be grouped. Within any multiple bar graph you are likely to find it easiest to compare between adjacent bars. The multiple bar graph (Figure 12.9) has therefore been drawn to emphasise comparisons between males and females rather than between numbers of claims.

To compare proportions or percentages

Comparison of proportions between variables uses either a **percentage component bar graph** (**percentage component bar chart** also known as a divided bar chart) or two or more pie charts. Either type of diagram can be used for all data types, provided that continuous data, and data where there are more than six values or categories, are grouped. Percentage component bar graphs are more straightforward to draw than comparative pie charts when using most spreadsheets. Within your percentage component bar graphs, comparisons will be easiest between adjacent bars. The chart in Figure 12.10 has been drawn to emphasise the proportions of males and females for each number of insurance claims in the year. Males and females, therefore, form a single bar.

Table 12.3 Contingency table: Number of insurance claims by gender, 2018

Number of claims*	Male	Female	Total
0	10032	13478	23510
1	2156	1430	3586
2	120	25	145
3	13	4	17
Total	12321	14937	27258

*No clients had more than three claims

Source: PJ Insurance Services

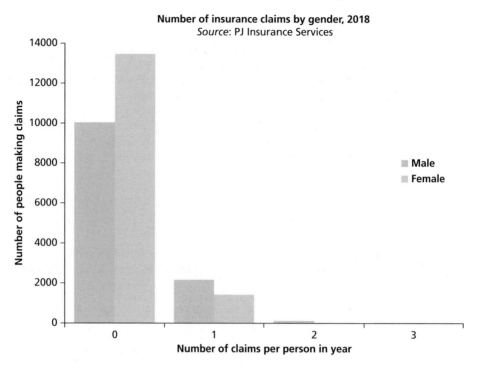

Figure 12.9 Multiple bar graph

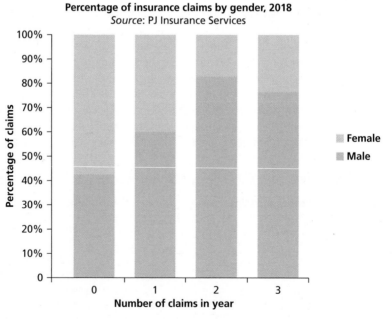

Figure 12.10 Percentage component bar graph

To compare trends so the intersections are clear

The most suitable diagram to compare trends for two or more numerical (or occasionally ranked) variables is a **multiple line graph** (Box 12.11) where one line represents each variable (Kosslyn 2006). You can also use multiple bar graphs in which bars for the same time period are placed adjacent to each other.

Conjunctions in trends – that is, where values for two or more variables intersect – are shown by the place where the lines on a multiple line graph cross.

 ## Box 12.11 Focus on research in the news

The three ages of tax and welfare

Representative profiles for UK tax, public services and welfare spending
Receipts/spending 2021-22 (£ '000)

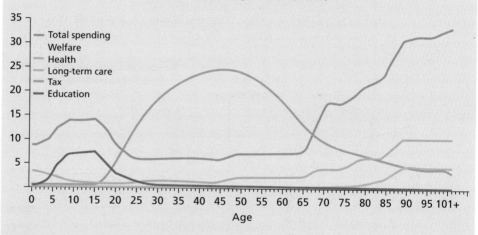

What does this chart show?

It reveals what an average Briton puts in and takes out of the welfare state at different ages. Unsurprisingly, it shows that children tend to be big beneficiaries. They typically consume a lot of healthcare and state-funded education, while parents can claim child benefit and child tax credits on their account. In their working years, people pay a lot of tax of all kinds — peaking, aged 45, at nearly £25,000 a year. At this stage of their lives, people tend to use relatively few public services. In later life, people pay less tax as their incomes and spending decline. At the same time, they make greater use of the health service and long-term care, while claiming state pension and other benefits. Spending shoots up from an average of £20,000 a year for a 78-year-old to £31,000 a year for a 90-year-old, according to figures from the Office for Budget Responsibility.

FT *Source:* Abridged from 'The three ages of tax and welfare', Vanessa Houlder (2017) *Financial Times,* 5 October. Copyright © The Financial Times Ltd.

To compare the cumulative totals

Comparison of cumulative totals between variables uses a variation of the bar chart. A **stacked bar graph**, also known as a **stacked bar chart**, can be used for all data types provided that continuous data and data where there are more than six possible values or categories are grouped. As with percentage component bar graphs, the design of the stacked bar graph is dictated by the totals you want to compare. For this reason, in Figure 12.11 males and females have been stacked to give totals which can be compared for zero, one, two and three claims in a year.

To compare the proportions and cumulative totals

To compare both proportions of each category or value and the cumulative totals for two or more variables it is best to use **comparative proportional pie charts** for all data types. For each comparative proportional pie chart the total area of the pie chart represents the total for that variable. By contrast, the angle of each segment represents the relative proportion of a category within the variable (Box 12.10). Because of the complexity of drawing comparative proportional pie charts, they are rarely used for Exploratory Data Analysis, although they can be used to good effect in research reports.

To compare the distribution of values

Often it is useful to compare the distribution of values for two or more variables. Plotting multiple frequency polygons (Box 12.11) or bar graphs (Figure 12.9) will enable you to

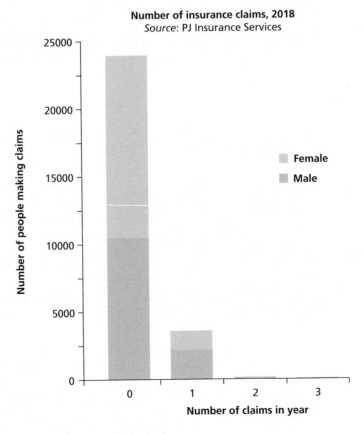

Figure 12.11 Stacked bar graph

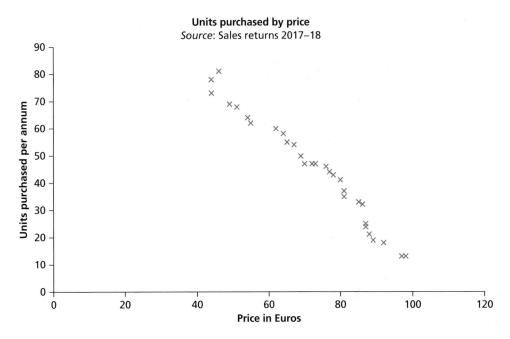

Figure 12.12 Scatter graph

compare distributions for up to three or four variables. After this your diagram is likely just to look a mess! An alternative is to use a diagram of multiple box plots, similar to the one in Figure 12.8. This provides a pictorial representation of the distribution of the data for the variables in which you are interested. These plots can be compared and are interpreted in the same way as the single box plot.

To show the interrelationships between cases for variables

You can explore possible interrelationships between ranked and numerical data variables by plotting one variable against another. This is called a **scatter graph** (also known as a **scatter plot**), and each cross (point) represents the values for one case (Figure 12.12). Convention dictates that you plot the **dependent variable** – that is, the variable that changes in response to changes in the other **(independent) variable** – against the vertical axis. The strength of the interdependence or relationship is indicated by the closeness of the points to an imaginary straight line. If as the values for one variable increase so do those for the other then you have a positive relationship. If as the values for one variable decrease those for the other variable increase then you have a negative relationship. Thus, in Figure 12.12 there is a negative relationship between the two variables. The strength of this relationship can be assessed statistically using techniques such as correlation or regression (Section 12.6).

12.5 Describing data using statistics

The Exploratory Data Analysis approach (Section 12.4) emphasised the use of diagrams to understand your data. **Descriptive statistics** enable you to describe (and compare) a variable's data values numerically. Your research question(s) and objectives, although limited by the type of data (Table 12.4), should guide your choice of statistics. Statistics to describe a variable focus on two aspects of the data values' distribution:

- the central tendency;
- the dispersion.

These are summarised in Table 12.4. Those most pertinent to your research question(s) and objectives will eventually be quoted in your project report as support for your arguments.

Table 12.4 Descriptive statistics by data type: a summary

To calculate a measure of:		Categorical		Numerical	
		Nominal (Descriptive)	Ordinal (Ranked)	Continuous	Discrete
Central tendency that . . .	. . . represents the value that occurs most frequently	Mode			
	. . . represents the middle value			Median	
	. . . includes all data values (average)			Mean	
	. . . includes all data values other than those at the extremes of the distribution			Trimmed mean	
Dispersion that . . .	. . . states the difference between the highest and lowest values			Range (data need not be normally distributed but must be placed in rank order)	
	. . . states the difference within the middle 50% of values			Inter-quartile range (data need not be normally distributed but must be placed in rank order)	
	. . . states the difference within another fraction of the values			Deciles or percentiles (data need not be normally distributed but must be placed in rank order)	
	. . . describes the extent to which data values differ from the mean			Variance, or more usually, the standard deviation (data should be normally distributed)	
	. . . compares the extent to which data values differ from the mean between variables			Coefficient of variation (data should be normally distributed)	
	. . . allows the relative extent that data values differ to be compared			Index numbers	

Source: © Mark Saunders, Philip Lewis and Adrian Thornhill 2018

Describing the central tendency

When describing data for both samples and populations quantitatively it is usual to provide some general impression of values that could be seen as common, middling or average. These are termed measures of **central tendency** and are discussed in virtually all statistics textbooks. The three main ways of measuring the central tendency most used in business research are the:

- value that occurs most frequently (mode);
- middle value or mid-point after the data have been ranked (median);
- value, often known as the average, that includes all data values in its calculation (mean).

However, as we saw in Box 12.2, beware: if you have used numerical codes, most analysis software can calculate all three measures whether or not they are appropriate!

To represent the value that occurs most frequently

The **mode** is the value that occurs most frequently. For descriptive data, the mode is the only measure of central tendency that can be interpreted sensibly. You might read in a report that the most common (modal) colour of motor cars sold last year was silver, or that the two equally most popular makes of motorcycle in response to a questionnaire were Honda and Yamaha. In such cases where two categories occur equally most frequently, this is termed bi-modal. The mode can be calculated for variables where there are likely to be a large number of categories (or values for numerical data), although it may be less useful. One solution is to group the data into suitable categories and to quote the most frequently occurring or **modal group**.

To represent the middle value

If you have quantitative data it is also possible to calculate the middle or **median** value by ranking all the values in ascending order and finding the mid-point (or **50th percentile**) in the distribution. For variables that have an even number of data values, the median will occur halfway between the two middle data values. The median has the advantage that it is not affected by extreme values in the distribution (Box 12.12).

To include all data values

The most frequently used measure of central tendency is the **mean** (average in everyday language), which includes all data values in its calculation. However, it is usually only possible to calculate a meaningful mean using numerical data.

The value of your mean is unduly influenced by extreme data values in skewed distributions (Section 12.4). In such distributions the mean tends to get drawn towards the long tail of extreme data values and may be less representative of the central tendency. For this and other reasons Anderson et al. (2017) suggest that the median may be a more useful descriptive statistic. Alternatively, where the mean is affected by extreme data values (outliers) these may be excluded and a **trimmed mean** calculated. This excludes a certain proportion (for example five per cent) of the data from both ends of the distribution, where the outliers are located. Because the mean is the building block for many of the statistical tests used to explore relationships (Section 12.6), it is usual to include it as at least one of the measures of central tendency for numerical data in your report. This is, of course, provided that it makes sense!

Box 12.12
Focus on student research

Describing the central tendency

As part of her research project, Kylie had obtained secondary data from the service department of her organisation on the length of time for which their customers had held service contracts.

Length of time held contract	Number of customers
< 3 months	50
3 to < 6 months	44
6 months to < 1 year	71
1 to < 2 years	105
2 to < 3 years	74
3 to < 4 years	35
4 to < 5 years	27
5+ years	11

Her exploratory analysis revealed a positively skewed distribution (long tail to the right).

From the table, the largest single group of customers were those who had contracts for 1 to 2 years. This was the modal time period (most commonly occurring). However, the usefulness of this statistic is limited owing to the variety of class widths. By definition, half of the organisation's customers will have held contracts below the median time period (approximately 1 year 5 months) and half above it. As there are 11 customers who have held service contracts for over 5 years, the mean time period (approximately 1 year 9 months) is pulled towards longer times. This is represented by the skewed shape of the distribution.

Kylie needed to decide which of these measures of central tendency to include in her research report. As the mode made little sense she quoted the median and mean when interpreting her data:

The length of time for which customers have held service contracts is positively skewed. Although mean length of time is approximately 1 year 9 months, half of customers have held service contracts for less than 1 year 5 months (median). Grouping of these data means that it is not possible to calculate a meaningful mode.

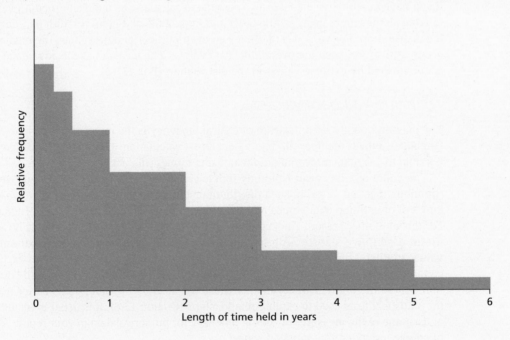

Describing the dispersion

As well as describing the central tendency for a variable, it is important to describe how the data values are dispersed around the central tendency. As you can see from Table 12.4, this is only possible for numerical data. Two of the most frequently used ways of describing the dispersion are the:

- difference within the middle 50 per cent of values (inter-quartile range);
- extent to which values differ from the mean (standard deviation).

Although these **dispersion measures** are suitable only for numerical data, most statistical analysis software will also calculate them for categorical data if you have used numerical codes.

To state the difference between values

In order to get a quick impression of the distribution of data values for a variable you could simply calculate the difference between the lowest and the highest values once they have been ranked in ascending order – that is, the **range**. However, this statistic is rarely used in research reports as it represents only the extreme values.

A more frequently used statistic is the **inter-quartile range**. As we discussed earlier, the median divides the range into two. The range can be further divided into four equal sections called **quartiles**. The **lower quartile** is the value below which a quarter of your data values will fall; the **upper quartile** is the value above which a quarter of your data values will fall. As you would expect, the remaining half of your data values will fall between the lower and upper quartiles. The difference between the upper and lower quartiles is the inter-quartile range (Anderson et al. 2017). As a consequence, it is concerned only with the middle 50 per cent of data values and ignores extreme values.

You can also calculate the range for other fractions of a variable's distribution. One alternative is to divide your distribution using **percentiles**. These split your ranked distribution into 100 equal parts. Obviously, the lower quartile is the 25th percentile and the upper quartile the 75th percentile. However, you could calculate a range between the 10th and 90th percentiles so as to include 80 per cent of your data values. Another alternative is to divide the range into 10 equal parts called **deciles**.

To describe and compare the extent by which values differ from the mean

Conceptually and statistically in research it is important to look at the extent to which the data values for a variable are spread around their mean, as this is what you need to know to assess its usefulness as a typical value for the distribution. If your data values are all close to the mean, then the mean is more typical than if they vary widely. To describe the extent of spread of numerical data you use the **standard deviation**. If your data are a sample (Section 7.1), this is calculated using a slightly different formula than if your data are a population, although if your sample is larger than about 30 cases there is little difference in the two statistics.

You may need to compare the relative spread of data between distributions of different magnitudes (e.g. one may be measured in hundreds of tonnes, the other in billions of tonnes). To make a meaningful comparison you will need to take account of these different magnitudes. A common way of doing this is:

1 to divide the standard deviation by the mean;
2 then to multiply your answer by 100.

Box 12.13
Focus on student research

Describing variables and comparing their dispersion

Cathy was interested in the total value of transactions at the main and sub-branches of a major bank. The mean value of total transactions at the main branches was approximately five times as high as that for the sub-branches. This made it difficult to compare the relative spread in total value of transactions between the two types of branches. By calculating the coefficients of variation, Cathy found that there was relatively more variation in the total value of transactions at the main branches than at the sub-branches. This is because the coefficient of variation for the main branches was larger (23.62) than the coefficient for the sub-branches (18.08).

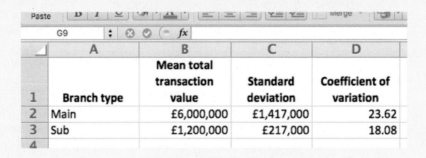

	Branch type	Mean total transaction value	Standard deviation	Coefficient of variation
1				
2	Main	£6,000,000	£1,417,000	23.62
3	Sub	£1,200,000	£217,000	18.08

This results in a statistic called the **coefficient of variation** (Black 2017). The values of this statistic can then be compared. The distribution with the largest coefficient of variation has the largest relative spread of data (Box 12.13).

Alternatively, as discussed at the start of the chapter in relation to the Economist's Big Mac Index, you may wish to compare the relative extent to which data values differ. One way of doing this is to use **index numbers** and consider the relative differences rather than actual data values. Such indices compare each data value against a base data value that is normally given the value of 100, differences being calculated relative to this value. An index number greater than 100 represents a larger or higher data value relative to the base value and an index less than 100, a smaller or lower data value.

To calculate an index number for each case for a data variable you use the following formula:

$$\text{Index number for case} = \frac{\text{data value for case}}{\text{base data value}} \times 100$$

We discuss index numbers further when we look at examining trends (Section 12.6).

12.6 Examining relationships, differences and trends using statistics

When analysing data quantitatively you are likely to ask questions such as: 'Are these variables related?', or 'Do these groups differ?' In statistical analysis you answer these questions by establishing the probability of the test statistic summarising the relationship or difference in your data, or one more extreme, occurring. This process of assessing the statistical significance of findings from a sample is known as **significance testing**, the classical approach to significance testing being **hypothesis testing**. Significance testing can therefore be thought of as assessing the possibility that your result could be due to random variation in your sample.

There are two main groups of statistical tests: non-parametric and parametric. **Non-parametric statistics** are designed primarily for use with categorical (dichotomous, nominal, ordinal) data where there is no distributional model and so we cannot use statistics to estimate parameters. In contrast, **parametric statistics** are used with numerical (interval and ratio) data. Although parametric statistics are considered more powerful because they use numerical data, a number of assumptions about the actual data being used need to be satisfied if they are not to produce spurious results (Blumberg et al. 2014). These include:

- the data cases selected for the sample should be independent – in other words the selection of any one case for your sample should not affect the probability of any other case being included in the same sample;
- the data cases should be drawn from normally distributed populations (Section 12.5 and later in Section 12.6);
- the populations from which the data cases are drawn should have equal variances (don't worry, the term variance is explained later in Section 12.6);
- the data used should be numerical.

In addition, as we will discuss later, you need to ensure that your sample size is sufficiently large to meet the requirements of the statistic you are using (see also Section 7.2). If the assumptions are not satisfied, it is often still possible to use non-parametric statistics.

The way in which statistical significance is assessed using both non-parametric and parametric statistics can be thought of as answering one from a series of questions, dependent on the data type:

- Is the independence or association statistically significant?
- Are the differences statistically significant?
- What is the strength of the relationship and is it statistically significant?
- Are the predicted values statistically significant?

When assessing significance each question will usually be phrased as a **hypothesis**; that is a tentative, usually testable, explanation that there is an association, difference or relationship between two or more variables. The questions and associated statistics are summarised in Table 12.5 along with statistics used to help examine trends.

Testing for normality

As we have already noted, parametric tests assume that the numerical data cases in your sample are drawn from normally distributed populations. This means that the data values for each quantitative variable should also be normally distributed, being clustered around the variable's mean in a symmetrical pattern forming a bell-shaped frequency distribution. Fortunately, it is relatively easy to check if data values for a particular variable are distributed normally, both using graphs and statistically.

In Section 12.3 we looked at a number of different types of graphs including histograms (Figure 12.4), box plots (Figure 12.8) and frequency polygons (Figure 12.13). All of these can be used to assess visually whether the data values for a particular numerical variable are clustered around the mean in a symmetrical pattern, and so normally distributed. For normally distributed data, the value of the mean, median and mode are also likely to be the same.

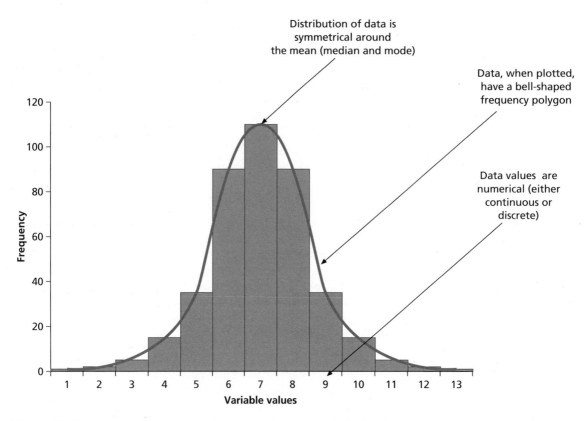

Figure 12.13 Annotated frequency polygon showing a normal distribution

Table 12.5 Statistics to examine relationships, differences and trends by data type: A summary

	Categorical		Numerical	
	Nominal (Descriptive)	**Ordinal (Ranked)**	**Continuous**	**Discrete**
To test *normality* of a distribution			Kolmogorov–Smirnov test, Shapiro–Wilk test	
To test whether two variables are *independent*	Chi square (data may need grouping)		Chi square if variable grouped into discrete classes	
To test whether two variables are *associated*	Cramer's V and Phi (both variables must be dichotomous)			
To test whether two groups (categories) are *different*		Kolmogorov–Smirnov (data may need grouping) or Mann–Whitney *U* test	Independent *t*-test or paired *t*-test (often used to test for changes over time) or Mann–Whitney *U* test (where data skewed or a small sample)	
To test whether three or more groups (categories) are *different*			Analysis of variance (ANOVA)	

Table 12.5 Continued

	Categorical		Numerical	
	Nominal (Descriptive)	Ordinal (Ranked)	Continuous	Discrete
To assess the *strength of relationship* between two variables		Spearman's rank correlation coefficient (Spearman's rho) or Kendall's rank order correlation coefficient (Kendall's tau)	Pearson's product moment correlation coefficient (PMCC)	
To assess the *strength of a relationship* between one dependent and one independent variable			Coefficient of determination	
To assess the *strength of a relationship* between one dependent and two or more independent variables			Coefficient of multiple determination	
To *predict* the value of a dependent variable from one or more independent variables			Regression equation	
To explore *relative change* (trend) over time			Index numbers	
To compare *relative changes* (trends) over time			Index numbers	
To *determine the trend* over time of a series of data			Time series: moving averages or regression equation (regression analysis)	

Source: © Mark Saunders, Philip Lewis and Adrian Thornhill 2018

Another way of testing for normality is to use statistics to establish whether the distribution as a whole for a variable differs significantly from a comparable normal distribution. Fortunately, this is relatively easy to do in statistical software such as IBM SPSS Statistics using the **Kolmogorov–Smirnov test** and the **Shapiro–Wilk test** (Box 12.14), as the software also calculates a comparable normal distribution automatically. For both these tests the calculation consists of the test statistic (labelled D and W respectively), the degrees of freedom[1] (df) and, based on this, the probability (p-value.). The p-value is the probability of the data for your variable, or data more extreme, occurring by chance alone from a comparable normal distribution for that variable if there really was no difference. For either statistic, a probability of 0.05 means there is a 5 per cent likelihood of the actual data distribution or one more extreme occurring by chance alone from a

---

[1]Degrees of freedom are the number of values free to vary when computing a statistic. The number of degrees of freedom for a contingency table of at least 2 rows and 2 columns of data is calculated from: (number of rows in the table – 1) × (number of columns in the table – 1).

Box 12.14
Focus on student research

Testing for normality

As part of his research project, Osama had collected quantitative data about music piracy and illegal downloading of music from a number of student respondents. Before undertaking his statistical analysis, Osama decided to test his quantitative variables for normality using the Kolmogorov–Smirnov test and the Shapiro–Wilk test. The output from IBM SPSS Statistics for one of his data variables, 'number of legal music downloads made in the past month', follows:

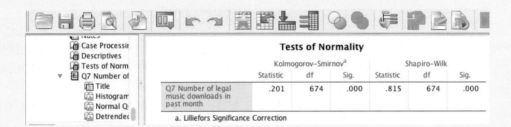

This calculated the significance (Sig.) for both the Kolmogorov–Smirnov test and the Shapiro–Wilk test as '000', meaning that for this variable the likelihood of the actual distribution or one more extreme differing from a normal distribution occurring by chance alone was less than 0.001. Consequently, the data values for variable 'Number of legal music downloads in past month' were not normally distributed, reducing his choice of statistics for subsequent analyses. This was confirmed by a bar chart showing the distribution of the data for the variable:

Osama reported the outcome of this analysis in his project report, quoting the test statistics 'D' and 'W' and their associated degrees of freedom 'df' and probabilities 'p' in brackets:

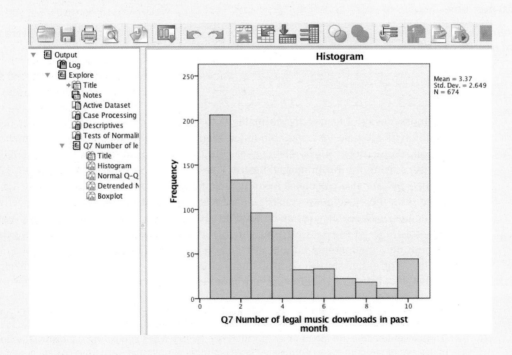

"Tests for normality revealed that data for the variable 'number of legal music downloads in the past month' cast considerable doubt on the data being normally distributed [$D = 0.201$, $df = 674$, $p < 0.001$; $W = 0.815$, $df = 674$, $p < 0.001$]."

comparable normal distribution if there was no real difference. Therefore a probability of 0.05 or lower[2] for either statistic means that these data are unlikely to be normally distributed. When interpreting probabilities from software packages, beware: owing to statistical rounding of numbers a probability of 0.000 does not mean zero, but that it is less than 0.001 (Box 12.14). If the probability is greater than 0.05, then this is interpreted as the data being likely to be normally distributed. However, you need to be careful. With very large samples it is easy to get significant differences between a sample variable and a comparable normal distribution when actual differences are quite small. For this reason it is often helpful to also use a graph to make an informed decision.

Assessing the statistical significance of relationships and differences

Assessing the statistical significance of relationships and differences between variables usually involves hypothesis testing. As part of your research project, you might have collected sample data to examine the association between two variables. You would have phrased this as a testable explanation that put forward the absence of that relationship (termed a **null hypothesis**) such as: 'there is no association between. . . ' Once you have entered data into the analysis software, chosen the statistic and clicked on the appropriate icon, an answer will appear as if by magic! With most statistical analysis software this consists of a test statistic, the degrees of freedom (*df*) and, based on these, the statistical significance (*p*-value). This is the probability that the value of the test statistic summarising a specific aspect of your data would be equal to or more extreme than its actual observed value, given the specified assumptions of that test (Wasserstein and Lazar 2016).

If the probability of your test statistic value or one more extreme having occurred is less than a prescribed significance value (usually $p < 0.05$ or lower[3]), this is usually interpreted as casting doubt on or providing evidence against your null hypothesis and the associated underlying assumptions. This means your data are more likely to support the explanation expressed in your hypothesis; in this example a testable statement such as: 'There is an association between. . . ' Statisticians refer to this as rejecting the null hypothesis and accepting the hypothesis, often abbreviating the terms null hypothesis to H_0 and hypothesis to H_1. Consequently, rejecting a null hypothesis could mean casting doubt on an explanation such as 'there is no difference between . . . ' or 'there is no relationship between. . . ' and accepting an explanation such as 'there is a difference between . . . ' or 'there is a relationship between. . . ' However, conclusions and policy decisions should not be based just on whether the *p*-value passes a specific threshold. Contextual factors such as the research

---

[2]A probability of 0.05 means that the probability of your test result or one more extreme occurring by chance alone, if there really was no difference, is 5 in 100, that is 1 in 20.

[3]A probability of 0.05 means that the probability of your test result or one more extreme occurring by chance alone, if there really was no difference in the population from which the sample was drawn (in other words if the null hypothesis was true), is 5 in 100, that is 1 in 20.

design, quality of data, and other external evidence are also important in interpreting the findings (Wasserstein and Lazar 2016). If the probability of obtaining the test statistic or one more extreme by chance alone is greater than or equal to a prescribed value (usually $p = 0.05$), this is normally interpreted as your data being compatible with the explanation expressed by your null hypothesis and its associated underlying assumptions. This indicates the null hypothesis can be accepted and is referred to by statisticians as failing to reject the null hypothesis. There may still be a relationship between the variables under such circumstances, but you cannot make the conclusion with any certainty. Remember, when interpreting probabilities from software packages, beware: owing to statistical rounding of numbers a probability of 0.000 does not mean zero, but that it is less than 0.001 (Box 12.15).

The hypothesis and null hypothesis we have just stated are often termed **non-directional**. This is because they refer to a difference rather than also including the nature of the difference. A **directional hypothesis** includes within the testable statement the direction of the difference, for example 'larger'. This is important when interpreting the probability of obtaining the test result, or one more extreme, by chance. Statistical software (Box 12.18) often states whether this probability is one-tailed or two-tailed. Where you have a directional hypothesis such as when the direction of the difference is larger, you should use the one-tailed probability. Where you have a non-directional hypothesis and are only interested in the difference, you should use the two-tailed probability.

Despite our discussion of hypothesis testing, albeit briefly, it is worth mentioning that a great deal of quantitative analysis, when written up, does not specify actual hypotheses. Rather, the theoretical underpinnings of the research and the research questions provide the context within which the probability of relationships between variables occurring by chance alone is tested. Thus, although hypothesis testing has taken place, statistical significance is often only discussed in terms of the probability (p-value) of the test statistic value or one more extreme occurring by chance.

The probability of a test statistic value or one more extreme occurring by chance is determined in part by your sample size (Section 7.2). One consequence of this is that it is very difficult to obtain a low p-value for a test statistic with a small sample. Conversely, by increasing your sample size, less obvious relationships and differences will be found to be statistically significant until, with extremely large samples, almost any relationship or difference will be significant (Anderson 2003). This is inevitable as your sample is becoming closer in size to the population from which it was selected. You therefore need to remember that small populations can make statistical tests insensitive, while very large samples can make statistical tests overly sensitive. There are two consequences to this.

- If you expect a difference, relationship or association will be small, you need to have a larger sample size.
- If you have a large sample and the difference, relationship or association has statistical significance, you need also to assess the practical significance of this relationship.

Both these points are crucial as it is not unusual for a test statistic to be statistically significant but trivial in the real world. Fortunately it is relatively straightforward to assess the practical significance of something that is statistically significant by calculating an appropriate **effect size index**. These indices measure the size of either differences between groups (the d family) or association between groups (the r family) and an excellent discussion can be found in Ellis (2010).

Type I and Type II errors

Inevitably, errors can occur when making inferences from samples. Statisticians refer to these as Type I and Type II errors. Blumberg et al. (2014) use the analogy of legal decisions

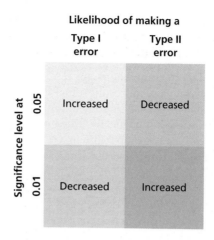

Figure 12.14 Type I and Type II errors

to explain Type I and Type II errors. In their analogy they equate a Type I error to a person who is innocent being unjustly convicted and a Type II error to a person who is guilty of a crime being unjustly acquitted. In business and management research we would say that an error made by wrongly rejecting a null hypothesis and therefore accepting the hypothesis is a **Type I error**. Type I errors might involve you concluding that two variables are related when they are not, or incorrectly concluding that a sample statistic exceeds the value that would be expected by chance alone. This means you are rejecting your null hypothesis when you should not. The term '**statistical significance**' discussed earlier therefore refers to the probability of making a Type I error. A **Type II error** involves the opposite occurring. In other words, you fail to reject your null hypothesis when it should be rejected. This means that Type II errors might involve you in concluding that two variables are not related when they are, or that a sample statistic does not exceed the value that would be expected by chance alone.

Given that a Type II error is the inverse of a Type I error, it follows that if we reduce our likelihood of making a Type I error by setting the significance level to 0.01 rather than 0.05, we increase our likelihood of making a Type II error by a corresponding amount. This is not an insurmountable problem, as researchers usually consider Type I errors more serious and prefer to take a small likelihood of saying something is true when it is not (Figure 12.14). It is therefore generally more important to minimise Type I than Type II errors.

To test whether two variables are independent or associated

Often descriptive or numerical data will be summarised as categorical data using a two-way contingency table (such as Table 12.3). The **chi square test** (χ^2) enables you to find out how likely it is that the two variables are independent. It is based on a comparison of the observed values in the table with what might be expected if the two distributions were entirely independent. Therefore you are assessing the likelihood of the data in your table, or data more extreme, occurring by chance alone by comparing it with what you would expect if the two variables were independent of each other. This could be phrased as the null hypothesis: 'there is no dependence . . . '.

The test relies on:

- the categories used in the contingency table being mutually exclusive, so that each observation falls into only one category or class interval;

- no more than 25 per cent of the cells in the table having expected values of less than 5. For contingency tables of two rows and two columns, no expected values of less than 10 are preferable (Dancey and Reidy 2017).

If the latter assumption is not met, the accepted solution is to combine rows and columns where this produces meaningful data.

Most statistical analysis software calculates the chi square statistic, degrees of freedom[4] and the *p*-value automatically. However, if you are using a spreadsheet you will usually need to look up the probability in a 'critical values of chi square' table using your calculated chi square value and the degrees of freedom. There are numerous copies of this table online. A probability of 0.05 means that there is only a 5 per cent likelihood of the data in your table or data more extreme occurring by chance alone and is usually considered statistically significant. Therefore, a probability of 0.05 or smaller means you can be at least 95 per cent certain that the dependence between your two variables represented by the data in the table could not have occurred by chance alone.

Some software packages, such as IBM SPSS Statistics, calculate the statistic **Cramer's V** alongside the chi square statistic (Box 12.15). If you include the value of Cramer's V in

Box 12.15
Focus on student research

Testing whether two variables are independent or associated

As part of his research project, John wanted to find out whether there was a significant dependence between salary grade of respondent and gender.

Earlier analysis using IBM SPSS Statistics had indicated that there were 385 respondents in his sample with no missing data for either variable. However, it had also highlighted there were only 14 respondents in the five highest salary grades (GC01 to GC05).

Bearing in mind the assumptions of the chi square test, John decided to combine salary grades GC01 through GC05 to create a combined grade GC01–5 using IBM SPSS Statistics:

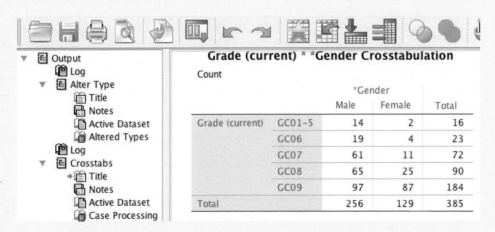

Grade (current) * *Gender Crosstabulation

Count

		*Gender Male	*Gender Female	Total
Grade (current)	GC01–5	14	2	16
	GC06	19	4	23
	GC07	61	11	72
	GC08	65	25	90
	GC09	97	87	184
Total		256	129	385

---

[4]Degrees of freedom are the number of values free to vary when computing a statistic. The number of degrees of freedom for a contingency table of at least two rows and two columns of data is calculated from (number of rows in the table – 1) × (number of columns in the table – 1).

He then used his analysis software to undertake a chi square test and calculate Cramer's V.

As can be seen, this resulted in an overall chi square value of 33.59 with 4 degrees of freedom (*df*).

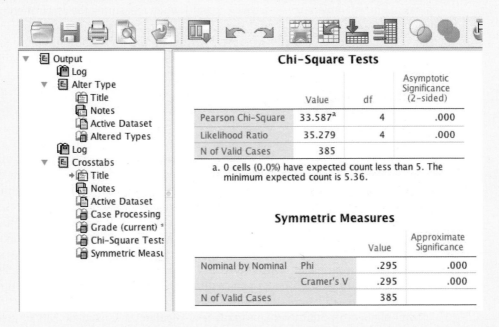

The significance of .000 (Asymp. Sig. – two sided) meant that the probability of the values in his table or values more extreme occurring by chance alone was less than 0.001. He therefore concluded that the gender and grade were extremely unlikely to be independent and quoted the statistic in his project report:

$$[x^2 = 33.59, df = 4, p < 0.001]^*$$

The Cramer's V value of .295, significant at the 0.001 level (Approx. Sig.), showed that the association between gender and salary grade, although weak, could be considered significant. This indicated that men (coded 1 whereas females were coded 2) were more likely to be employed at higher salary grades GC01–5 (coded using lower numbers). John also quoted this statistic in his project report:

$$[V_c = 0.295, p < 0.001]$$

To explore this association further, John examined the cell values in relation to the row and column totals. Of males, 5 per cent were in higher salary grades (GC01–5) compared to less than 2 per cent of females. In contrast, only 38 per cent of males were in the lowest salary grade (GC09) compared with 67 per cent of females.

*You will have noticed that the computer printout in this box does not have a zero before the decimal point. This is because most software packages follow the North American convention of not placing a zero before the decimal point.

your research report, it is usual to do so in addition to the chi square statistic. Whereas the chi square statistic gives the probability of data in a table, or data more extreme, occurring by chance alone, Cramer's V measures the association between the two variables within the table on a scale where 0 represents no association and 1 represents perfect association. Because the value of Cramer's V is always between 0 and 1, the relative strengths of associations between different pairs of variables that are considered statistically significant can be compared.

An alternative statistic used to measure the association between two variables is **Phi**. This statistic measures the association on a scale between − 1 (perfect negative association), through 0 (no association) to 1 (perfect association). However, unlike Cramer's V, using Phi to compare the relative strengths of associations between pairs of variables considered statistically significant can be problematic. This is because, although values of Phi will only range between − 1 and 1 when measuring the association between two dichotomous variables, they may exceed these extremes when measuring the association for categorical variables where at least one of these variables has more than two categories. For this reason, we recommend that you use Phi only when comparing pairs of dichotomous variables.

To test whether two groups are different

Ranked data

Sometimes it is necessary to see whether the distribution of an observed set of values for each category of a variable differs from a specified distribution other than the normal distribution, for example whether your sample differs from the population from which it was selected. The **Kolmogorov–Smirnov two-sample test** enables you to establish this for ranked data (Corder and Foreman 2014). It is based on a comparison of the cumulative proportions of the observed values in each category of your sample with the cumulative proportions in the same categories for a second 'sample' such as the population from which it was selected. Therefore you are testing the likelihood of the distribution of your observed values differing from that of the specified population by chance alone.

The Kolmogorov–Smirnov two-sample test calculates a *ks* statistic and an associated probability that the distribution in the first sample or one more extreme differs from the distribution in the second sample by chance (Corder and Foreman 2014). Although the two-sample test statistic is not often found in analysis software other than for comparisons with a normal distribution (discussed earlier), it is easily accessible online (Box 12.16). A test statistic with a *p*-value of 0.05 means that there is only a 5 per cent

---

Box 12.16
Focus on student research

Testing the representativeness of a sample

Jaimie's research question was: 'To what extent are my organisation's espoused customer service values evident in customer facing employees' views of the service they provide to customers?' As part of her research, she emailed a link to an Internet questionnaire to the 217 employees in the organisation where she worked and 94 of these responded. The responses from each category of employee in terms of their seniority within the organisation's hierarchy were as shown in the table below.

Using an online Kolmogrov-Smirnov two-sample test calculator (SciStatCalc 2013) Jaimie calculated a Kolmogorov-Smirnov test statistic (*ks*) of 0.632 with a *p*-value of 0.819. This meant that the probability of the distribution in her sample (or one more extreme) differing from that of the organisation's employees having occurred by chance alone was 0.819; in other words, more than 80 per cent. She concluded that those employees who responded were unlikely to differ significantly from the total population in terms of their seniority within the organisation's hierarchy. This was stated in her research report.

"Statistical analysis revealed the sample selected was very unlikely to differ significantly from all employees in terms of their seniority within the organisation's hierarchy [*ks* =.632, *p* =.819]."

○

		Shop floor workers	Technicians	Supervisors	Quality managers	Management team	Total
Respondents	Number	48	29	8	6	3	94
	Percentage	51.1	30.9	8.5	6.4	3.2	100
Total Employees	Number	112	68	22	14	1	217
	Percentage	51.6	31.3	10.1	6.5	0.5	100

likelihood that the distribution in the sample or one more extreme differs from that in the second sample by chance alone, and is usually considered statistically significant. Therefore a probability of 0.05 or smaller means you can be at least 95 per cent certain that the difference between your two distributions is unlikely to be explained by chance factors alone.

Numerical data

If a numerical variable can be divided into two distinct groups using a descriptive variable, you can assess the likelihood of these groups being different using an **independent groups *t*-test** (Box 12.17). This compares the difference in the means of the two groups using a measure of the spread of the scores. If the likelihood of an observed difference or one greater between these two groups occurring by chance alone is low, this is represented by a large *t* statistic with a low probability (*p*-value). A *p*-value of 0.05 or less is usually termed statistically significant.

Alternatively, you might have numerical data for two variables that measure the same feature but under different conditions. Your research could focus on the effects of an intervention such as employee counselling. As a consequence, you would have pairs of data that measure work performance before and after counselling for each case. To assess the likelihood of any difference or one greater between your two variables (each half of the pair) occurring by chance alone, you would use a **paired *t*-test**. Although the calculation of this is slightly different, your interpretation would be the same as for the independent groups *t*-test.

The ***t*-test** assumes that the data are normally distributed (discussed earlier and in Section 12.4) and this can be ignored without too many problems for sufficiently large samples, this often being defined as less than 100 (Lumley et al. 2002) and by some as less than 30 (Hays 1994). The assumption that the data for the two groups have the same variance (standard deviation squared) can also be ignored provided that the two samples are of similar size (Hays 1994). If the data are skewed or the sample size is small, the most appropriate statistical test is the Mann–Whitney *U* Test. This test is the non-parametric equivalent of the independent groups *t*-test (Dancey and Reidy 2017). Consequently, if the likelihood of a difference or one greater between these two groups occurring by chance alone is low, this will be represented by a large *U* statistic with a probability less than 0.05. This is termed statistically significant.

Box 12.17
Focus on management research

Testing whether groups are different

A vast body of research supports the benefits of smiling leading to the belief that the larger the smile the better for business. However, there is also evidence that, although broad smiles enhance warmth judgements of the person smiling, they also signal that the smiler is less competent than an individual who is smiling only slightly. Drawing on this, research by Wang et al. (2017) argue that whilst a broad as opposed to a slight smile conveys a marketer is friendly and sociable, the broad smile also suggests that a marketer may lack competence. In their paper titled, "Smile big or not? Effects of smile intensity on perceptions of warmth and competence" in the *Journal of Consumer Research* they expressed this as a hypothesis:

> "H[1]: Compared to a slight smile, a broad smile will lead to higher perceptions of the marketer's warmth, but lower perceptions of the marketer's competence." (Wang et al. 2017: 789).

To test this hypothesis they selected two images of the same person from a database of digital morphed photographs of facial expressions of different emotions at five different levels of intensity; one of a slight and one of a broad smile. These two photographs were consistence in other appearance cues such as head orientation, brow position and gaze orientation.

Next, they collected data from a sample of 123 adults from Amazon's Mechanical Turk (Mturk) who were each told that the purpose of the research was

to examine people's first impressions. Each respondent was shown one of the two photographs and asked to report their warmth and competence perceptions. Warmth was measured using a scale comprising four questions relating to whether the person in the photograph was (i) warm, (ii) kind, (iii) friendly, and (iv) sincere. Competence was measure using a scale comprising four questions relating to whether the person in the photograph was (i) competent, (ii) intelligent, (iii) capable, and (iv) skillful. All these questions were scored 1 = 'not at all', through to 7 = 'very much so'. To ensure that the manipulation of the smile had not affected the variables, respondents were also asked questions about the authenticity of the smile and the attractiveness of the person.

Independent sample *t*-tests revealed that the ratings of smile intensity were significantly higher when the person was smiling broadly ($t = 2.60$, $p = .01$). Ratings of the person's perceived authenticity and attractiveness did not appear to differ significantly between broad and slight smiles, the *t* statistic not being reported in the paper.

Subsequently Wang and colleagues tested their hypothesis regarding the differential effect of smile intensity on perceptions of warmth and competence by calculating ANOVA (analysis of variance) statistics. This revealed that judgements of warmth were significantly higher for a broad smile than for a slight smile ($F_{(1,121)} = 23.28$, $p < .001$). However, competence judgements were significantly lower for a broad smile than for a slight smile ($F_{(1,121)} = 6.29$, $p = .01$). This they noted provided support for their hypothesis arguing that individuals displaying broad smiles tend to be judged as warmer but less competent than those displaying slight smiles.

Subsequent research reported in the same paper investigated the impact on perceptions of smiles of different consumption contexts looking at the marketer's persuasive intent, perceived purchased risk and regulatory frameworks.

To test whether three or more groups are different

If a numerical variable is divided into three or more distinct groups using a descriptive variable, you can assess the likelihood of these groups being different occurring by chance alone by using **one-way analysis of variance** or one-way **ANOVA** (Table 12.5, Box 12.17). As you can gather from its name, ANOVA analyses the **variance**, that is, the spread of data values, within and between groups of data by comparing means. The F ratio or F statistic represents these differences. If the likelihood of the observed difference or one greater between groups occurring by chance alone is low, this will be represented by a large F ratio with a probability of less than 0.05. This is usually considered statistically significant.

The following assumptions need to be met before using one-way ANOVA. More detailed discussion is available in Hays (1994) and Dancey and Reidy (2017).

- Each data value is independent and does not relate to any of the other data values. This means that you should not use one-way ANOVA where data values are related in some way, such as the same case being tested repeatedly.
- The data for each group are normally distributed (discussed earlier and in Section 12.4). This assumption is not particularly important provided that the number of cases in each group is large (30 or more).
- The data for each group have the same variance (standard deviation squared). However, provided that the number of cases in the largest group is not more than 1.5 times that of the smallest group, this appears to have very little effect on the test results.

Assessing the strength of relationship

If your data set contains ranked or numerical data, it is likely that, as part of your Exploratory Data Analysis, you will already have plotted the relationship between cases for these ranked or numerical variables using a scatter graph (Figure 12.12). Such relationships might include those between weekly sales of a new product and those of a similar established product, or age of employees and their length of service with the company. These examples emphasise the fact that your data can contain two sorts of relationship:

- those where a change in one variable is accompanied by a change in another variable but it is not clear which variable caused the other to change, a **correlation**;
- those where a change in one or more (independent) variables causes a change in another (dependent) variable, a cause-and-effect relationship.

To assess the strength of relationship between pairs of variables

A **correlation coefficient** enables you to quantify the strength of the linear relationship between two ranked or numerical variables. This coefficient (usually represented by the letter r) can take on any value between $+ 1$ and $- 1$ (Figure 12.15). A value of $+ 1$ represents a perfect **positive correlation**. This means that the two variables are precisely related and that as values of one variable increase, values of the other variable will increase. By contrast, a value of $- 1$ represents a perfect **negative correlation**. Again, this means that the two variables are precisely related; however, as the values of one variable increase those of the other decrease. Correlation coefficients between $+ 1$ and $- 1$ represent weaker positive and negative correlations, a value of 0 meaning the variables are perfectly independent. Within business research it is extremely unusual to obtain perfect correlations.

For data collected from a sample you will need to know the probability of your correlation coefficient or one more extreme (larger) having occurred by chance alone. Most analysis software calculates this probability automatically (Box 12.18). As outlined earlier, if this probability is very low (usually less than 0.05) then the relationship is usually considered statistically significant. In effect you are rejecting the null hypothesis, that is a statement such as: "there is no correlation between. . . " and accepting a hypothesis such as: "there is a correlation between. . . " If the probability is greater than 0.05 then your relationship is usually considered not statistically significant.

If both your variables contain numerical data you should use **Pearson's product moment correlation coefficient** (PMCC) to assess the strength of relationship (Table 12.5). Where these data are from a sample then the sample should have been selected at random and the data should be normally distributed. However, if one or both of your variables contain ranked data you cannot use PMCC, but will need to use a correlation coefficient that is calculated using ranked data. Such rank correlation coefficients represent the degree of agreement between the two sets of rankings. Before calculating the rank correlation coefficient, you will need to ensure that the data for both variables are ranked. Where one of the variables is numerical this will necessitate converting these data to ranked data. Subsequently, you have a choice of rank correlation coefficients. The two used most widely in business and management research are **Spearman's rank correlation coefficient** (Spearman's ρ, the Greek letter rho) and **Kendall's rank correlation coefficient** (Kendall's τ, the Greek letter tau). Where data are being used from a sample, both these rank correlation coefficients assume that the sample is selected at random and the data are ranked (ordinal). Given this, it is not surprising that whenever you can use Spearman's rank correlation coefficient you can also use Kendall's rank correlation coefficient. However, if your data for a variable contain tied ranks, Kendall's rank correlation coefficient is generally considered to be the more appropriate of these coefficients to use. Although each of the correlation coefficients discussed uses a different formula in its calculation, the resulting coefficient is interpreted in the same way as PMCC.

To assess the strength of a cause-and-effect relationship between dependent and independent variables

In contrast to the correlation coefficient, the **coefficient of determination** enables you to assess the strength of relationship between a numerical dependent variable and one numerical independent variable and the **coefficient of multiple determination** enables you to assess the strength of relationship between a numerical dependent variable and two or more independent variables. Once again, where these data have been selected from a sample, the sample must have been selected at random. For a dependent variable and one (or perhaps two) independent variables you will have probably already plotted this relationship on a scatter graph. If you have more than two independent variables this is unlikely as it is very difficult to represent four or more scatter graph axes visually!

The coefficient of determination (represented by r^2) and the coefficient of multiple determination (represented by R^2) can both take on any value between 0 and $+1$. They measure the proportion of the variation in a dependent variable (amount of sales) that can be explained statistically by the independent variable (marketing expenditure) or variables (marketing expenditure, number of sales staff, etc.). This means that if all the variation in amount of sales can be explained by the marketing expenditure and the number of sales

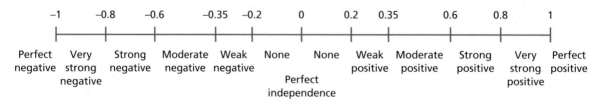

Figure 12.15 Interpreting the correlation coefficient
Source: Developed from earlier editions, Hair et al., (2014)

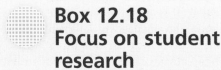

Box 12.18
Focus on student research

Assessing the strength of relationship between pairs of variables

As part of his research project, Hassan obtained data from a company on the number of television advertisements, number of enquiries and number of sales of their product. These data were entered into the statistical analysis software. He wished to discover whether there were any relationships between the following pairs of these variables:

- number of television advertisements and number of enquiries;
- number of television advertisements and number of sales;
- number of enquiries and number of sales.

As the data were numerical, he used the statistical analysis software to calculate Pearson's product moment correlation coefficients for all pairs of variables. The output was the correlation matrix below.

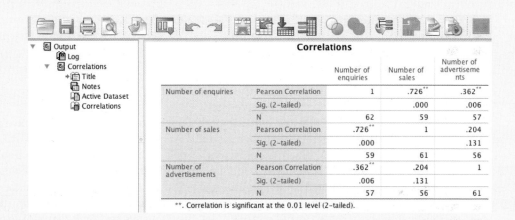

Hassan's matrix is symmetrical because correlation implies only a relationship rather than a cause-and-effect relationship. The value in each cell of the matrix is the correlation coefficient. Thus, the correlation between the number of advertisements and the number of enquiries is 0.362. This coefficient shows that there is a weak to moderate positive relationship between the number of television advertisements and the number of enquiries. The (**) highlights that the probability of this correlation coefficient or one more extreme occurring by chance alone is less than or equal to 0.01 (1 per cent). This correlation coefficient is therefore usually considered statistically significant. A two-tailed significance for each correlation, rather than a one-tailed significance, is used as correlation does not test the direction of a relationship, just whether they are related.

Using the data in this matrix Hassan concluded that:

There is a significant strong positive relationship between the number of enquiries and the number of sales (r (59) = .726, $p < 0.001$) and a significant but weak to moderate relationship between the number of television advertisements and the number of enquiries (r (57) = .362, $p = 0.006$). However, there appears to be no significant relationship between the number of television advertisements and the number of sales (r (56) = .204, $p = 0.131$).

Box 12.19
Focus on student research

Assessing a cause-and-effect relationship

As part of her research project, Arethea wanted to assess the relationship between all the employees' annual salaries and the number of years each had been employed by an organisation. She believed that an employee's annual salary would be dependent on the number of years for which she or he had been employed (the independent variable). Arethea entered these data into her analysis software and calculated a coefficient of determination (r^2) of 0.37.

As she was using data for all employees of the firm (the total population) rather than a sample, the probability of her coefficient occurring by chance alone was 0. She therefore concluded that 37 per cent of the variation in current employees' salary could be explained by the number of years they had been employed by the organisation.

---

staff, the coefficient of multiple determination will be 1. If 50 per cent of the variation can be explained, the coefficient of multiple determination will be 0.5, and if none of the variation can be explained, the coefficient will be 0 (Box 12.19). Within our research we have rarely obtained a coefficient above 0.8.

For a dependent variable and two or more independent variables you will have probably already plotted this relationship on a scatter graph.

The process of calculating the coefficient of determination and regression equation using one independent variable is normally termed **regression analysis**. Calculating a coefficient of multiple determination and regression equation using two or more independent variables is termed **multiple regression analysis**, and we advise you to use statistical analysis software and consult a detailed statistics textbook that also explains how to use the software, such as Field (2018). For sample data most statistical analysis software will automatically calculate the significance of the coefficient of multiple determination or one more extreme occurring by chance. A very low p-value (usually less than 0.05) means that your coefficient or one more extreme is unlikely to have occurred by chance alone.

To predict the value of a variable from one or more other variables

Regression analysis can also be used to predict the values of a dependent variable given the values of one or more independent variables by calculating a **regression equation** (Box 12.20). You may wish to predict the amount of sales for a specified marketing expenditure and number of sales staff. You would represent this as a regression equation:

$$AoS_i + \alpha + \beta_1 ME_i + \beta_2 NSS_i$$

where:

- *AoS* is the amount of sales (the dependent variable)
- *ME* is the marketing expenditure (an independent or predictor variable)
- *NSS* is the number of sales staff (an independent or predictor variable)
- α is the regression constant
- β_1 and β_2 are the beta coefficients

Box 12.20
Focus on student research

Forecasting the number of road injury accidents

As part of her research project, Nimmi had obtained data on the number of road injury accidents and the number of drivers breath tested for alcohol in 39 police force areas. In addition, she obtained data on the total population (in thousands) for each of these areas from the most recent census. Nimmi wished to find out if it was possible to predict the number of road injury accidents (*RIA*) in each police area (her dependent variable) using the number of drivers breath tested (*BT*) and the total population in thousands (*POP*) for each of the police force areas (independent variables). This she represented as an equation:

$$RIA_i + \alpha + \beta_1 BT_i + \beta_2 POP_i$$

Nimmi entered her data into the analysis software and undertook a multiple regression analysis. She scrolled down the output file and found the table headed 'Coefficients'. Nimmi substituted the 'unstandardised coefficients' into her regression equation (after rounding the values):

$$RIA_i = -30.689 + 0.011\ BT_i + 0.127\ POP_i$$

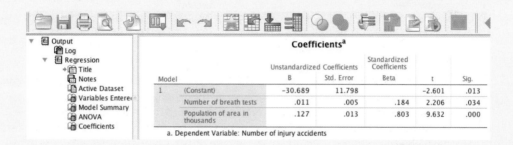

Coefficients[a]

Model		Unstandardized Coefficients B	Unstandardized Coefficients Std. Error	Standardized Coefficients Beta	t	Sig.
1	(Constant)	−30.689	11.798		−2.601	.013
	Number of breath tests	.011	.005	.184	2.206	.034
	Population of area in thousands	.127	.013	.803	9.632	.000

a. Dependent Variable: Number of injury accidents

This meant she could now predict the number of road injury accidents for a police area of different populations for different numbers of drivers breath tested for alcohol. For example, the number of road injury accidents for an area of 500,000 population in which 10,000 drivers were breath tested for alcohol can now be estimated:

$-30.689 + (0.011 \times 10000) + (0.127 \times 500)$
$= -30.689 + 110 + 49 + 63.5$
$= 81.8$

In order to check the usefulness of these estimates, Nimmi scrolled back up her output and looked at the results of R^2, *t*-test and *F*-test.

The R^2 and adjusted R^2 values of 0.965 and 0.931 respectively both indicated that there was a high degree of goodness of fit of her regression model. It also meant that over 90 per cent of variance in the dependent variable (the number of road injury accidents) could be explained by the regression model. The *F*-test result was 241.279 with a significance ('Sig.') of .000. This meant that the probability of these or more extreme results occurring by chance was less than 0.001. This she interpreted as a significant relationship between the number of road injury accidents in an area and the population of the area, and the number of drivers breath tested for alcohol.

The *t*-test results for the individual regression coefficients (shown in the first extract) for the two independent variables were 9.632 and 2.206. Once again, the probability of both these or more extreme results occurring by chance was less than 0.05, being less than 0.001 for the independent variable population of area in thousands and 0.034 for the independent variable number of breath tests. This means that the regression coefficients for these variables were both considered significant at the $p < 0.05$ level.

Box 12.20
Focus on student research (*continued*)

Forecasting the number of road injury accidents

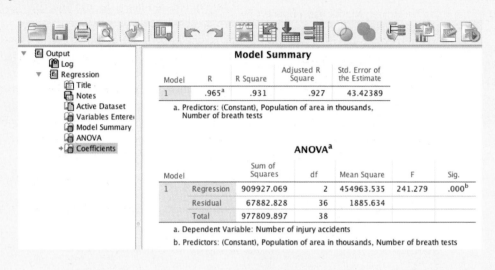

Model Summary

Model	R	R Square	Adjusted R Square	Std. Error of the Estimate
1	.965[a]	.931	.927	43.42389

a. Predictors: (Constant), Population of area in thousands, Number of breath tests

ANOVA[a]

Model		Sum of Squares	df	Mean Square	F	Sig.
1	Regression	909927.069	2	454963.535	241.279	.000[b]
	Residual	67882.828	36	1885.634		
	Total	977809.897	38			

a. Dependent Variable: Number of injury accidents
b. Predictors: (Constant), Population of area in thousands, Number of breath tests

This equation can be translated as stating:

Amount of sales$_i$ = value + (β_1* Marketing expenditure$_i$) + (β_2* Number of sales staff$_i$)

Using regression analysis you would calculate the values of the constant coefficient α and the slope coefficients β_1 and β_2 from data you had already collected on amount of sales, marketing expenditure and number of sales staff. A specified marketing expenditure and number of sales staff could then be substituted into the regression equation to predict the amount of sales that would be generated. When calculating a regression equation you need to ensure the following assumptions are met:

- The relationship between dependent and independent variables is linear. **Linearity** refers to the degree to which the change in the dependent variable is related to the change in the independent variables. Linearity can easily be examined through residual plots (these are usually drawn by the analysis software). Two things may influence the linearity. First, individual cases with extreme values on one or more variables (outliers) may violate the assumption of linearity. It is, therefore, important to identify these outliers and, if appropriate, exclude them from the analysis. Second, the values for one or more variables may violate the assumption of linearity. For these variables the data values may need to be transformed. Techniques for this can be found in other, more specialised books on multivariate data analysis, for example Hair et al. (2014).

- The extent to which the data values for the dependent and independent variables have equal variances (this term was explained earlier in Section 12.4), also known as **homoscedasticity**. Again, analysis software usually contains statistical tests for equal variance. For example, the Levene test for homogeneity of variance measures the equality of variances for a single pair of variables. If **heteroscedasticity** (that is, unequal variances) exists, it may still be possible to carry out your analysis. Further details of this can again be found in more specialised books on multivariate analysis, such as Hair et al. (2014).

- Absence of correlation between two or more independent variables (**collinearity** or **multicollinearity**), as this makes it difficult to determine the separate effects of individual variables. The simplest diagnostic is to use the correlation coefficients, extreme collinearity being represented by a correlation coefficient of 1. The rule of thumb is that the presence of high correlations (generally 0.90 and above) indicates substantial collinearity (Hair et al. 2014). Other common measures include the tolerance value and its inverse – the **variance inflation factor** (VIF). Hair et al. (2014) recommend that a very small tolerance value (0.10 or below) or a large VIF value (10 or above) indicates high collinearity.
- The data for the independent variables and dependent variable are normally distributed (discussed earlier in this section and Section 12.4).
- If your data are a sample, rather than a population, you also need to estimate the number of cases required in your sample. For regression analysis a widely used formula to estimate the number needed to satisfy the analysis' assumptions is:

Sample size = 50 + (8 × number of independent (predictor) variables)

Consequently for a regression analysis with two independent variables the sample size can be estimated as:

$$sample\ size = 50 + (8 \times 2)$$

$$= 50 + 16 = 66$$

However, this is an approximation and will overestimate the sample size required as the number of independent variables increases (Green 1991).

The coefficient of determination, r^2 (discussed earlier), can be used as a measure of how good a predictor your regression equation is likely to be. If your equation is a perfect predictor then the coefficient of determination will be 1. If the equation can predict only 50 per cent of the variation, then the coefficient of determination will be 0.5, and if the equation predicts none of the variation, the coefficient will be 0. The coefficient of multiple determination (R^2) indicates the degree of the goodness of fit for your estimated multiple regression equation. It can be interpreted as how good a predictor your multiple regression equation is likely to be. It represents the proportion of the variability in the dependent variable that can be explained by your multiple regression equation. This means that when multiplied by 100, the coefficient of multiple determination can be interpreted as the percentage of variation in the dependent variable that can be explained by the estimated regression equation. The adjusted R^2 statistic (which takes into account the number of independent variables in your regression equation) is preferred by some researchers as it helps avoid overestimating the impact of adding an independent variable on the amount of variability explained by the estimated regression equation.

The *t*-test and *F*-test are used to work out the probability of the relationship represented by your regression analysis or one more extreme having occurred by chance. In simple linear regression (with one independent and one dependent variable), the *t*-test and *F*-test will give you the same answer. However, in multiple regression, the *t*-test is used to find out the probability of the relationship between each of the individual independent variables and the dependent variable or one more extreme occurring by chance. In contrast, the *F*-test is used to find out the overall probability of the relationship or one more extreme between the dependent variable and all the independent variables occurring by chance. The *t* distribution table and the *F* distribution table are used to determine whether a *t*-test or an *F*-test is significant by comparing the results with the *t* distribution and *F* distribution respectively, given the degrees of freedom and the predefined significance level.

Examining trends

When examining longitudinal data the first thing we recommend you do is to draw a line graph to obtain a visual representation of the trend (Figure 12.6). Subsequent to this, statistical analyses can be undertaken. Three of the more common uses of such analyses are:

- to explore the trend or relative change for a single variable over time;
- to compare trends or the relative change for variables measured in different units or of different magnitudes;
- to determine the long-term trend and forecast future values for a variable.

These were summarised earlier in Table 12.5.

To explore the trend

To answer some research question(s) and meet some objectives you may need to explore the trend for one variable. One way of doing this is to use **index numbers** to compare the relative magnitude for each data value (case) over time rather than using the actual data value. Index numbers are also widely used in business publications and by organisations. Various share indices (Box 12.21), such as the *Financial Times* FTSE 100, and the UK's Consumer Prices Index are well-known examples.

Although such indices can involve quite complex calculations, they all compare change over time against a base period. The **base period** is normally given the value of 100 (or 1000 in the case of many share indices, including the FTSE 100) and change is calculated relative to this. Thus a value greater than 100 would represent an increase relative to the base period, and a value less than 100 a decrease.

To calculate simple index numbers for each case of a longitudinal variable you use the following formula:

$$\text{Index number for case} = \frac{\text{date value for case}}{\text{base period data value}} \times 100$$

Thus, if a company's sales were 125,000 units in 2018 (base period) and 150,000 units in 2019, the index number for 2018 would be 100 and for 2019 it would be 120.

To compare trends

To answer some other research question(s) and to meet the associated objectives you may need to compare trends between two or more variables measured in different units or at different magnitudes. For example, to compare changes in prices of fuel oil and coal over time is difficult as the prices are recorded for different units (litres and tonnes). One way of overcoming this is to use index numbers (as discussed in Section 12.5) and compare the relative changes in the value of the index rather than

Box 12.21 Focus on research in the news

United Utilities shares hit three-year low after HSBC downgrade

FTSE 100 down 6.26 points as Severn Trent and Centrica drift lower

United Utilities plumbed a three-year low on Friday as inflation and regulation worries kept pressure on the sector. Ahead of interim results next week, United dropped 4.4 per cent to 798p after HSBC downgraded to "hold" with a 900p target price. The recent strength of the retail price index means United's earnings are being eroded by its index-linked debt, which at more than half of total debt is a greater burden than for peers, HSBC said.

The broker also noted increased share price volatility because of "the political climate and fragility of the current government", as well as "tough talking" by regulator Ofwat ahead of a 2019 review of water price controls. Investors have limited visibility because United is relying on prudence and outperformance to get through the Ofwat review, yet the group seems to have no more financial headroom than its listed peers, HSBC added. A wider market drift pushed the FTSE 100 lower by 6.26 points, 0.1 per cent to 7,380.68 as Severn Trent lost 2.4 per cent to £20.92 and Centrica fell 1.6 per cent to 163.2p. Sky jumped 4.1 per cent to 940p in response to reports that both Comcast and Verizon have approached 21st Century Fox, its parent company, whose £10.75 per share bid to take full control is stuck in regulatory limbo.

actual figures. The index numbers for each variable are calculated in the same way as outlined earlier.

To determine the trend and forecasting

The trend can be estimated by drawing a freehand line through the data on a line graph. However, these data are often subject to variations such as seasonal fluctuations, and so this method is not very accurate. A straightforward way of overcoming this is to calculate a moving average for the time series of data values. Calculating a **moving average** involves replacing each value in the time series with the mean of that value and those values directly preceding and following it (Anderson et al. 2017). This smoothes out the variation in the data so that you can see the trend more clearly. The calculation of a moving average is relatively straightforward using either a spreadsheet or statistical analysis software.

Once the trend has been established, it is possible to forecast future values by continuing the trend forward for time periods for which data have not been collected. This involves calculating the **long-term trend** – that is, the amount by which values are changing in each time period after variations have been smoothed out. Once again, this is relatively straightforward to calculate using analysis software. Forecasting can also be undertaken using other statistical methods, including regression analysis.

If you are using regression for your time-series analysis, the **Durbin–Watson statistic** can be used to discover whether the value of your dependent variable at time t is related to its value at the previous time period, commonly referred to as $t-1$. This situation, known as **autocorrelation** or **serial correlation**, is important as it means that the results of your regression analysis are less likely to be reliable. The Durbin–Watson statistic ranges in value from zero to 4. A value of 2 indicates no autocorrelation. A value towards zero indicates positive autocorrelation. Conversely, a value towards 4 indicates negative autocorrelation. More detailed discussion of the Durbin–Watson test can be found in other, more specialised books on multivariate data analysis, for example Hair et al. (2014).

12.7 Summary

- For data to be analysed quantitatively it must either already be quantified or able to be transformed into quantitative data.
- Non-numerical data such as text, voice and visual data can be quantified by classifying into sets or categories.
- Data for quantitative analysis can be collected and subsequently coded at different scales of measurement. The data type (precision of measurement) will constrain the data presentation, summary and analysis techniques you can use.
- Data are prepared for analysis as a data matrix in which each column usually represents a variable and each row a case. Your first variable should be a unique identifier to facilitate error checking.
- All data should, with few exceptions, be recorded using numerical codes to facilitate analyses.
- Where possible, you should use existing coding schemes to enable comparisons.
- For primary data you should include pre-set codes on the data collection form to minimise coding after collection. For variables where responses are not known, you will need to develop a codebook after data have been collected for the first 50 to 100 cases.
- You should enter codes for all data values, including missing data.

- Your data matrix must be checked for errors.
- Your initial analysis should explore data using both tables and graphs. Your choice of table or graph will be influenced by your research question(s) and objectives, the aspects of the data you wish to emphasise, and the measurement precision with which the data were recorded.
- This may involve using:
  - tables to show specific amounts;
  - bar graphs, multiple bar graphs, histograms and, occasionally, pictograms and word clouds to show (and compare) highest and lowest amounts and relative distributions;
  - line graphs to show trends;
  - pie charts and percentage component bar graphs to show proportions or percentages;
  - box plots to show distributions;
  - multiple line graphs to compare trends and show intersections;
  - scatter graphs to show relationships between variables.
- Subsequent analyses will involve describing your data and exploring relationships using statistics and testing for significance. Your choice of statistics will be influenced by your research question(s) and objectives, your sample size, the measurement precision at which the data were recorded and whether the data are normally distributed. Your analysis may involve using statistics such as:
  - the mean, median and mode to describe the central tendency;
  - the inter-quartile range and the standard deviation to describe the dispersion;
  - chi square to test whether two variables are independent;
  - Cramer's V and Phi to test whether two variables are associated;
  - Kolmogorov–Smirnov to test whether the values differ from a specified population;
  - t-tests and ANOVA to test whether groups are different;
  - correlation and regression to assess the strength of relationships between variables;
  - regression analysis to predict values.
- Longitudinal data may necessitate selecting different statistical techniques such as:
  - index numbers to establish a trend or to compare trends between two or more variables measured in different units or at different magnitudes;
  - moving averages and regression analysis to determine the trend and forecast.

Self-check questions

Help with these questions is available at the end of the chapter.

12.1 The following secondary data have been obtained from the Park Trading Company's audited annual accounts:

Year end	Income	Expenditure
2010	11000000	9500000
2011	15200000	12900000
2012	17050000	14000000
2013	17900000	14900000
2014	19000000	16100000
2015	18700000	17200000
2016	17100000	18100000
2017	17700000	19500000
2018	19900000	20000000

a Which are the variables and which are the cases?

b Sketch a possible data matrix for these data for entering into a spreadsheet.

12.2 a How many variables will be generated from the following request?

Please tell me up to five things you like about this film.	**For office use**
. . . .	❏ ❏ ❏
. . . .	❏ ❏ ❏
. . . .	❏ ❏ ❏
. . . .	❏ ❏ ❏
. . . .	❏ ❏ ❏

b How would you go about devising a coding scheme for these variables from a survey of 500 cinema goers?

12.3 a Illustrate the data from the Park Trading Company's audited annual accounts (Question 12.1) to show trends in income and expenditure.

b What does your diagram emphasise?

c What diagram would you use to emphasise the years with the lowest and highest income?

12.4 As part of research into the impact of television advertising on donations by credit card to a major disaster appeal, data have been collected on the number of viewers reached and the number of donations each day for the past two weeks.

a Which diagram or diagrams would you use to explore these data?

b Give reasons for your choice.

12.5 a Which measures of central tendency and dispersion would you choose to describe the Park Trading Company's income (Question 12.1) over the period 2010–18?

b Give reasons for your choice.

12.6 a A colleague has collected data from a sample of 74 students. He presents you with the following output from the statistical analysis software:

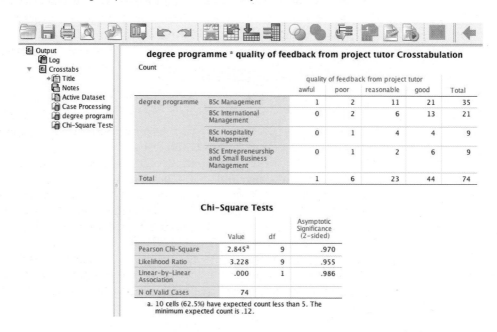

Explain what this tells you about students' opinions about feedback from their project tutor.

12.7 Briefly describe when you would use regression analysis and correlation analysis, using examples to illustrate your answer.

12.8 a Use an appropriate technique to compare the following data on share prices for two financial service companies over the past six months, using the period six months ago as the base period:

	EJ Investment Holdings	**AE Financial Services**
Price 6 months ago	€10	€587
Price 4 months ago	€12	€613
Price 2 months ago	€13	€658
Current price	€14	€690

b Which company's share prices have increased most in the last six months? (Note: you should quote relevant statistics to justify your answer.)

Review and discussion questions

12.9 Use a search engine to discover coding schemes that already exist for ethnic group, family expenditure, industry group, socio-economic class and the like. To do this you will probably find it best to type the phrase 'coding ethnic group' into the search box.

a Discuss how credible you think each coding scheme is with a friend. To come to an agreed answer pay particular attention to:
- the organisation (or person) that is responsible for the coding scheme;
- any explanations regarding the coding scheme's design;
- use of the coding scheme to date.

b Widen your search to include coding schemes that may be of use for your research project. Make a note of the web address of any that are of interest.

12.10 With a friend, choose a large company in which you are interested. Obtain a copy of the annual report for this company. Examine the use of tables, graphs and charts in your chosen company's report.

a To what extent does the use of graphs and charts in your chosen report follow the guidance summarised in Box 12.8 and Table 12.2?

b Why do you think this is?

12.11 With a group of friends, each choose a different share price index. Well-known indices you might choose include the Nasdaq Composite Index, France's CAC 40, Germany's Dax, Hong Kong's Hang Seng Index (HSI), Japan's Nikkei Index, the UK's FTSE 100 and the USA's Dow Jones Industrial Average Index.

a For each of the indices, find out how it is calculated and note down its daily values for a one-week period.

b Compare your findings regarding the calculation of your chosen index with those for the indices chosen by your friends, noting down similarities and differences.

c To what extent do the indices differ in the changes in share prices they show? Why do you think this is?

12.12 Find out whether your university provides you with access to IBM SPSS Statistics. If it does, visit this book's companion website and download the self-teach package and associated data sets. Work through this to explore the features of IBM SPSS Statistics.

Progressing your research project

Analysing your data quantitatively

- Examine the technique(s) you are proposing to use to collect data to answer your research question. You need to decide whether you are collecting any data that could usefully be analysed quantitatively.
- If you decide that your data should be analysed quantitatively, you must ensure that the data collection methods you intend to use have been designed to make analysis as straightforward as possible. In particular, you need to pay attention to the coding scheme for each variable and the layout of your data matrix.
- Once your data have been entered and the data set opened in your analysis software, you will

need to explore and present them. Bearing your research question in mind, you should select the most appropriate diagrams and tables after considering the suitability of all possible techniques. Remember to label your diagrams clearly and to keep a copy, as they may form part of your research report.
- Once you are familiar with your data, describe and explore relationships using those statistical techniques that best help you to answer your research questions and are suitable for the data type. Remember to keep an annotated copy of your analyses, as you will need to quote statistics to justify statements you make in the findings section of your research report.
- Use the questions in Box 1.4 to guide you in your reflective diary entry.

References

Anderson, D.R., Sweeney, D.J., Williams, T.A., Freeman, J. and Shoesmith E. (2017) *Statistics for Business and Economics* (4th edn). Andover: Cengage Learning.

Anderson, T.W. (2003) *An Introduction to Multivariate Statistical Analysis.* (3rd edn), New York: John Wiley.

Berelson, B. (1952) *Content Analysis in Communication Research.* Glencoe, IL: Free Press.

Berman Brown, R. and Saunders, M. (2008) *Dealing with Statistics: What You Need to Know.* Maidenhead: McGraw-Hill Open University Press.

Black, K. (2009) *Business Statistics* (6th edn). Hoboken, NJ: Wiley.

Blumberg, B., Cooper, D.R. and Schindler, D.S. (2014) *Business Research Methods* (4th edn). Maidenhead: McGraw-Hill.

Corder, G.W. and Foreman, D.I. (2014) *Nonparametric statistics* (2nd edn). Hoboken, NJ: Wiley.

Dancey, C.P. and Reidy, J. (2017) *Statistics Without Maths for Psychology: Using SPSS for Windows* (7th edn). Harlow: Prentice Hall.

Dawson, J. (2017) *Analysing Quantitative Survey Data for Business and Management Students.* London: Sage.

De Vaus, D.A. (2014) *Surveys in Social Research* (6th edn). Abingdon: Routledge.

Ellis, P.D. (2010) *The Essential Guide to Effect Sizes.* Cambridge: Cambridge University Press.

Eurostat (2017) Environment and energy statistics – primary production of renewable energies. Available at https://ec.europa.eu/eurostat/web/products-datasets/-/ten00081 [Accessed 17 November 2017].

Field, A. (2018) *Discovering Statistics Using SPSS* (5th edn). London: Sage.

Green, S.B. (1991) 'How many subjects does it take to do a regression analysis?', *Multivariate Behavioural Research,* Vol. 26, No. 3, pp. 499–510.

Hair, J.F., Black, B., Babin, B., Anderson, R.E. and Tatham, R.L. (2014) *Multivariate Data Analysis* (7th edn). Harlow: Pearson.

Harding, R. (2017) *British Social Attitudes 34.* London: NatCen Social Research. Available at http://www.bsa.natcen.ac.uk/latest-report/british-social-attitudes-34/key-findings/context.aspx [Accessed 27 November 2017]

Harley-Davidson Inc. (2017) *Harley-Davidson Inc. Investor Relations: Motorcycle Shipments* Available at http://investor.harley-davidson.com/phoenix.zhtml%3Fc%3D87981%26p%3Dirol-shipments [Accessed 12 October 2017].

Hays, W.L. (1994) *Statistics* (4th edn). London: Holt-Saunders.

Holsti, O.R. (1969) *Content Analysis for the Social Sciences and Humanities.* Reading, MA: Addison-Wesley.

Keen, K.J. (2018) *Graphics for Statistics and Data Analysis with R.* (2nd edn.) Boca Raton, FL: Chapman and Hall.

Kosslyn, S.M. (2006) *Graph Design for the Eye and Mind.* New York: Oxford University Press.

Lian, T. and Yu, C. (2017) 'Representation of online image of tourist destination: a content analysis of Huangshan', *Asia Pacific Journal of Tourism Research,* Vol. 22, No. 10, pp. 1063–1082.

Little, R. and Rubin, D. (2002) *Statistical Analysis with Missing Data* (2nd edn). New York: John Wiley.

Lumley. T., Diehr, P., Emerson, S. and Chen, L. (2002) 'The importance of the normality assumption in large public health data sets', *Annual Review of Public Health,* Vol. 23, pp. 151–169.

Office for National Statistics (2005) *The National Statistics Socio-Economic Classification User Manual.* Basingstoke: Palgrave Macmillan.

Office for National Statistics (no date a) *Standard Occupation Classification 2010 (SOC2010).* Available at https://www.ons.gov.uk/methodology/classificationsandstandards/standardoccupational-classificationsoc/soc2010 [Accessed 27 November 2017].

Office for National Statistics (no date b) *The National Statistics Socio-economic Classification (NS-SEC rebased on the SOC2010).* Available at https://www.ons.gov.uk/methodology/classificationsand-standards/otherclassifications/thenationalstatisticssocioeconomicclassificationnssecrebasedon-soc2010 [Accessed 27 November 2017].

Office for National Statistics (no date c) *Ethnic group, national identity and religion.* Available at https://www.ons.gov.uk/methodology/classificationsandstandards/measuringequality/ethnicgroup-nationalidentityandreligion [Accessed 27 November 2017].

Pallant, J. (2016) *SPSS Survival Manual: A Step-by-Step Guide to Data Analysis Using IBM SPSS* (6th edn). Maidenhead: Open University Press.

Prosser, L. (2009) *Office for National Statistics UK Standard Industrial Classification of Activities 2007 (SIC 2007).* Basingstoke: Palgrave Macmillan. Available at http://www.ons.gov.uk/ons/guide-method/classifications/current-standard-classifications/standard-industrial-classification/index.html [Accessed 27 November 2014].

Qualtrics (2017) *Qualtrics Research CORE: Sophisticated online surveys made simple.* Available at https://www.qualtrics.com/research-core/ [Accessed 27 November 2017]

Rose, S., Spinks, N. and Canhoto, I. (2015) *Management Research: Applying the Principles.* London: Routledge.

Sherbaum, C. and Shockley, K. (2015) *Analysing Quantitative Data for Business and Management Students.* London: Sage.

SciStatCalc (2013) *Two-sample Kolmogorov-Smirnov Test Calculator.* Available at http://scistatcalc.blogspot.co.uk/2013/11/kolmogorov-smirnov-test-calculator.html [Accessed 27 November 2017]

SurveyMonkey (2017) *What do you want to know?* Available at https://www.surveymonkey.com/ [Accessed 27 November 2017].

Swift, L. and Piff, S. (2014) *Quantitative Methods for Business, Management and Finance* (4th edn). Basingstoke: Palgrave Macmillan.

The Economist (2017) *The Big Mac Index: global exchange rates, to go.* Available at http://www.economist.com/content/big-mac-index [Accessed 12 November 2017].

Tukey, J.W. (1977) *Exploratory Data Analysis.* Reading, MA: Addison-Wesley.

Wang, Z., Mao, H., Li, Y.J. and Liu, F. (2017) 'Smile big or not?, Effects of smile intensity on perceptions of warmth and competence', *Journal of Consumer Research,* Vol. 43, pp.787–805.

Wasserstein R.L. and Lazar, N.A. (2016) 'The ASA's statement on p-values: context, process and pupose', *The American Statistician,* Vol. 70, No. 2, pp. 129–133.

Further reading

Berman Brown, R. and Saunders, M. (2008) *Dealing with Statistics: What You Need to Know.* Maidenhead: McGraw Hill Open University Press. This is a statistics book that assumes virtually no statistical knowledge, focusing upon which test or graph, when to use it and why. It is written for people who are fearful and anxious about statistics and do not think they can understand numbers!

De Vaus, D.A. (2014) *Surveys in Social Research* (6th edn). Abingdon: Routledge. Chapters 9 and 10 contain an excellent discussion about coding data and preparing data for analysis. Part IV (Chapters 12–18) provides a detailed discussion of how to analyse survey data.

Field, A. (2018) *Discovering Statistics Using SPSS* (5th edn). London: Sage. This book offers a clearly explained guide to statistics and using SPSS. It is divided into four levels, the lowest of which assumes no familiarity with the data analysis software and very little with statistics. It covers entering data and how to generate and interpret a wide range of tables, diagrams and statistics using SPSS.

Hair, J.F., Black, B., Babin, B., Anderson, R.E. and Tatham, R.L. (2014) *Multivariate Data Analysis* (7th edn). Harlow: Pearson. This book provides detailed information on statistical concepts and techniques. Issues pertinent to design, assumptions, estimation and interpretation are systematically explained for users of more advanced statistical techniques.

McCandless, D. (2014) *Knowledge is beautiful.* London: William Collins. This book of infographics shows a multitude of different ways for displaying data visually to make specific points. Every graphic in the book is paired with an online dataset and like the author's 2012 book *Information is beautiful,* it is best considered as a visual miscellenium of facts and ideas to explore.

Case 12
Giving proper attention to risk management controls when using derivatives

Derivatives are contracts that derive their value from the performance of other, more basic, underlying variables, which are generally but not limited to financial assets or rates (Hull, 2015). They are a category of financial instruments (like stocks and debt) and are used for speculating or hedging. Common derivatives include futures contracts, forward contracts, options, swaps and warrants. According to Swan (2000), the use of derivatives dates back to Venice in the 12th century.

Derivatives are used properly when they are neither misunderstood nor mishandled (Tavakoli, 2001). Various guidelines, rules and standards for risk management controls have been put forth by the Basel Committee as well as the Committee of Sponsoring Organisations of the Threadway Commission (COSO) among others. These have been translated into EU legislation such as the Capital Requirement Directive (CRD), Solvency II Directive (SII), and Markets in Financial Instruments Directive (MiFID). These require banks and other wealth management organisations to ensure that risks associated with derivatives are properly managed. The importance of giving proper attention and allocating sufficient resources towards risk management controls has increased following the 2008 financial crisis and ensuing recessions, and the massive financial losses by companies and government entities.

Alfred, an undergraduate student studying Insurance and Risk Management, is developing his research project. Following an internship at an international wealth management bank, he is intrigued to investigate the extent to which the users (consisting of managers, analysts, treasurers, brokers and investment bankers) and controllers (consisting of risk officers, auditors, compliance officers and regulators) of derivatives at the bank are giving proper attention towards risk management controls. Furthermore, he wants to test whether the overall scores across the two groups, on average, differed significantly from each other.

After obtaining the necessary ethical approval and agreement from the international wealth management bank, Alfred asks the HR manager to invite the users and controllers of derivatives at the bank to participate in a Web questionnaire he has developed using the SurveyMonkey cloud-based survey platform.

Alfred's questionnaire contains nine statements derived from Bezzina and Grima's (2012) 'proper derivative use inventory' that captures aspects related to the proper use of risk management controls. Respondents are asked to rate their level of agreement with each statement on an ordinal scale ranging from 1 = strongly disagree to 5 = strongly agree. These are listed in Table C12.1.

Table C12.1 Alfred's nine statements

Number	Statement
1	I evaluate both settlement and pre-settlement credit risk at the customer level across all products
2	I assess potential exposure through simulation analysis or other sophisticated techniques
3	In terms of market risk, I compare estimated market risk exposures with actual behaviour
4	I establish limits for market risk that relate to its risk measures and that are consistent with maximum exposures authorised by the senior management and board
5	In terms of liquidity risk, I establish guidelines when establishing limits
6	I assess the potential liquidity risks associated with the early termination of derivatives contracts
7	I allocate sufficient resources (financial and personnel) to support operations and systems development and maintenance
8	I have adequate support and operational capacity to accommodate the types of derivative activities in which our company engages
9	I evaluate systems needs for derivative activities during the strategic planning process

Source: Developed form Bezzina and Grima (2012)

A total of 420 employees complete the survey – 310 users and 110 controllers (a total response rate of 56.2%). The data are then exported as an SPSS statistics software data file comprising whether the respondent was a user or controller of derivatives ('Position') and the scores the respondent provided for each of the nine statements ('Q1' to 'Q9'). Although these data are entered using numeric codes, Alfred chooses to display the data as the responses represented by each code (Figure C12.1). The code '5' is therefore displayed as 'Strongly Agree', the code 4 as 'Agree', the code 3 as 'Neutral', the code 2 as 'Disagree' and the code 1 as 'Strongly Disagree'. Using SPSS Alfred calculates the factor score (the mean of the responses pertaining to the nine statements for each respondent) as a new variable ('RMC').

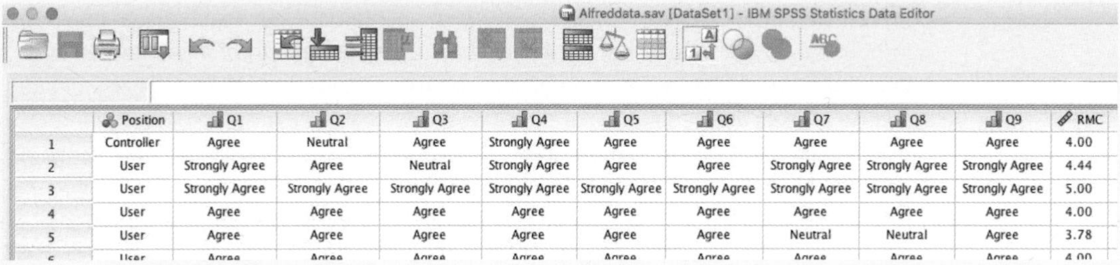

	Position	Q1	Q2	Q3	Q4	Q5	Q6	Q7	Q8	Q9	RMC
1	Controller	Agree	Neutral	Agree	Strongly Agree	Agree	Agree	Agree	Agree	Agree	4.00
2	User	Strongly Agree	Agree	Neutral	Strongly Agree	Agree	Agree	Strongly Agree	Strongly Agree	Strongly Agree	4.44
3	User	Strongly Agree	Strongly Agree	Strongly Agree	Strongly Agree	Strongly Agree	Strongly Agree	Strongly Agree	Strongly Agree	Strongly Agree	5.00
4	User	Agree	Agree	Agree	Agree	Agree	Agree	Agree	Agree	Agree	4.00
5	User	Agree	Agree	Agree	Agree	Agree	Agree	Neutral	Neutral	Agree	3.78
6	User	Agree	Agree	Agree	Agree	Agree	Agree	Agree	Agree	Agree	4.00

Figure C12.1 Alfred's data file using the SPSS

Questions

1 Alfred wants to describe the responses for each of the nine statements and for the factor score. Which statistic or statistics would you recommend and why?
2 Alfred wants to compare the factor score distributions for the users and controllers of derivatives separately. Which graph would you recommend and why?
3 Alfred wants to determine whether the factor scores of the users and controllers of derivatives differ significantly from each other. Which statistical test would you recommend and why?
4 Alfred has calculated that there is a significant statistical difference between the factor scores for the user and controllers. However, he is concerned that the difference may not be practically significant. Which statistical measure would you recommend he uses and why?

References

Bezzina, F.H. & Grima, S. (2012). 'Exploring factors affecting the proper use of derivatives: An empirical study with active users and controllers of derivatives', *Managerial Finance,* Vol. 38, No. 4, pp. 414–435.

Hull, J. C. (2015). *Options, Futures, and Other Derivatives,* 9th ed., Upper Saddle River, NJ: Pearson.

Swan, E. J. (2000). *Building the Global Market. A 4000 Year History of Derivatives.* The Hague, Netherlands: Kluwer Law International.

Tavakoli, J. (2001), *Credit Derivatives and Synthetic Structures: A Guide to Instruments and Applications,* 2nd ed., Wiley, New York, NY.

Additional case studies relating to material covered in this chapter are available via the book's companion website: **www.pearsoned.co.uk/saunders.**

They are:

- The marketing of arts festivals.
- Marketing a golf course.
- The impact of family ownership on financial performance.
- Small business owner-managers' skill sets.
- Food miles, carbon footprints and supply chains.
- Predicting work performance.

Self-check answers

12.1 a The variables are 'income', 'expenditure' and 'year'. There is no real need for a separate case identifier as the variable 'year' can also fulfil this function. Each case (year) is represented by one row of data.

b When the data are entered into a spreadsheet the first column will be the case identifier, for these data the year. Income and expenditure should not be entered with the £ sign as this can be formatted subsequently using the spreadsheet:

	A	B	C
1	**Year**	**Income (£)**	**Expenditure (£)**
2	2010	11000000	9500000
3	2011	15200000	12900000
4	2012	17050000	14000000
5	2013	17900000	14900000
6	2014	19000000	16100000
7	2015	18700000	17200000
8	2016	17100000	18100000
9	2017	17700000	19500000
10	2018	19900000	20000000
11			

12.2 a There is no one correct answer to this question as the number of variables will depend on the method used to code these descriptive data. If you choose the multiple-response method, five variables will be generated. If the multiple-dichotomy method is used, the number of variables will depend on the number of different responses.

b Your first priority is to decide on the level of detail of your intended analyses. Your coding scheme should, if possible, be based on an existing coding scheme. If this is of insufficient detail then it should be designed to be compatible to allow comparisons. To design the coding scheme you need to take the responses from the first 50–100 cases and establish broad groupings. These can be subdivided into increasingly specific subgroups until the detail is sufficient for the intended analysis. Codes can then be allocated to these subgroups. If you ensure that similar responses receive adjacent codes, this will make any subsequent grouping easier. The actual responses that correspond to each code should be noted in a codebook. Codes should be allocated to data on the data collection form in the 'For office use' box. These codes need to include missing data, such as when four or fewer 'things' have been mentioned.

12.3 a Park Trading Company – Income and Expenditure 2010–18.

   b Your diagram (it is hoped) emphasises the upward trends of expenditure and (to a lesser extent) income. It also highlights the conjunction where income falls below expenditure in 2016.

   c To emphasise the years with the lowest and highest income, you would probably use a histogram because the data are continuous. A frequency polygon would also be suitable.

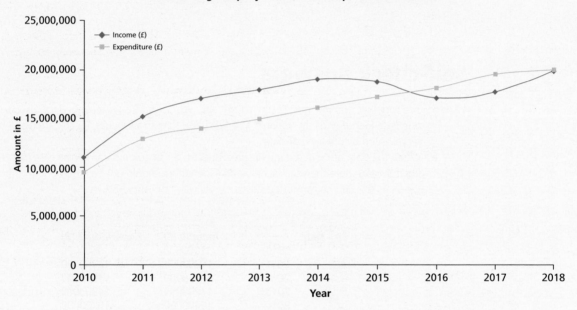

Park Trading Company – Income and Expenditure 2010-2018

12.4 a You would probably use a scatter graph in which number of donations would be the dependent variable and number of viewers reached by the advertisement the independent variable.

   b This would enable you to see whether there was any relationship between number of viewers reached and number of donations.

12.5 a The first thing you need to do is to establish the data type. As it is numerical, you could theoretically use all three measures of central tendency and both the standard deviation and inter-quartile range. However, you would probably calculate the mean and perhaps the median as measures of central tendency and the standard deviation and perhaps the inter-quartile range as measures of dispersion.

   b The mean would be chosen because it includes all data values. The median might be chosen to represent the middle income over the 2010–18 period. The mode would be of little use for these data as each year has different income values.

      If you had chosen the mean you would probably choose the standard deviation, as this describes the dispersion of data values around the mean. The inter-quartile range is normally chosen where there are extreme data values that need to be ignored. This is not the case for these data.

12.6 The probability of a chi square value of 2.845 with 9 degrees of freedom occurring by chance alone for these data is 0.970. This means that statistically the interdependence between students' degree programmes and their opinion of the quality of feedback from project tutors is extremely likely to be explained by chance alone. In addition, the assumption of the chi square test that no more than 20 per cent of expected values should be less than 5 has not been satisfied.

To explore this lack of interdependence further, you examine the cell values in relation to the row and column totals. For all programmes, over 80 per cent of respondents thought the quality of feedback from their project tutor was reasonable or good.

12.7 Your answer needs to emphasise that correlation analysis is used to establish whether a change in one variable is accompanied by a change in another. In contrast, regression analysis is used to establish whether a change in a dependent variable is caused by changes in one or more independent variables – in other words, a cause-and-effect relationship. Although it is impossible to list all the examples you might use to illustrate your answer, you should make sure that your examples for regression illustrate a dependent and one or more independent variables.

12.8 a These quantitative data are of different magnitudes. Therefore, the most appropriate technique to compare these data is index numbers. The index numbers for the two companies are:

	EJ Investment Holdings	AE Financial Services
Price 6 months ago	100	100.0
Price 4 months ago	120	104.4
Price 2 months ago	130	112.1
Current price	140	117.5

b The price of AE Financial Services' shares has increased by €103 compared with an increase of €4 for EJ Investment Holdings' share price. However, the proportional increase in prices has been greatest for EJ Investment Holdings. Using six months ago as the base period (with a base index number of 100), the index for EJ Investment Holdings' share price is now 140 while the index for AE Financial Services' share price is 117.5.

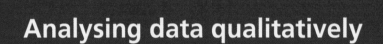

Chapter **13**

Analysing data qualitatively

Learning outcomes

By the end of this chapter you should be able to:

- understand the diversity of qualitative data and the interactive nature of qualitative analysis;
- identify the key aspects to consider when choosing a qualitative analysis technique and the main issues when preparing your qualitative data for analysis including using computer-aided qualitative data analysis software (CAQDAS);
- transcribe a recorded interview or notes of an interview or observation and create a data file for analysis by computer;
- choose from different analytical aids to help you to analyse your qualitative data, including keeping a reflective or reflexive journal;
- select an appropriate analytical technique or combination of techniques for your research project to undertake qualitative data analysis;
- identify the common functions of CAQDAS and describe the issues associated with its use.

13.1 Introduction

This chapter is about analysing your qualitative data. The diversity of such qualitative data and their implications for analysis are discussed in Section 13.2. This section also highlights the interactive nature of qualitative analysis. As you read through the sections of this chapter you will recognise the interrelated and interactive nature of qualitative data collection and analysis. Because of this it will be necessary to plan your qualitative research as an interconnected process where you collect and begin to analyse and interpret data as you undertake each interview or observation or collect visual images.

In Section 13.3 we discuss key aspects of different qualitative analysis techniques to help you to choose an appropriate technique, or combination of techniques. In Section 13.4 we discuss the preparation of your data for analysis and in Section 13.5 we outline a number of aids that will help you analyse these data and record your ideas about how to progress your research.

Sections 13.6–13.13 outline different qualitative analysis techniques. These are Thematic Analysis (Section 13.6), Template Analysis (Section 13.7), Explanation Building and Testing (Section 13.8), Grounded Theory Method (Section 13.9), Narrative Analysis (Section 13.10), Discourse Analysis (Section 13.11), Visual Analysis (Section 13.12) and Data Display and Analysis (Section 13.13).

Qualitative data analysis and completing a jigsaw puzzle

Nearly all of us have, at some time in our lives, completed a jigsaw puzzle. As children we may have played with jigsaw puzzles and, as we grew older, those we were able to complete became more complex. In some ways, qualitative data analysis can be likened to the process of completing a jigsaw puzzle in which the pieces represent data. These pieces of data and the relationships between them help us as researchers to create a picture of what we think the data are telling us!

When trying to complete a jigsaw puzzle, most of us begin by looking at the picture on the lid of our puzzle's box. A puzzle for which there is no picture is usually more challenging as we have no idea how the pieces fit together or what the picture will be! Similarly, we may not be clear about how, or even if, the data we have collected can form a clear picture.

Perhaps you haven't tried to complete a jigsaw puzzle for many years, but you might find the following useful as well as entertaining! Get a friend to give you the contents of a jigsaw in a bag without the box (since this normally shows the picture of what it is!). Turn all of the pieces picture side up. Think about how you will categorise these data that lie in front of you. What do they mean? You will be likely to group pieces with similar features such as those of a particular colour together. Normally you might then try to fit these similar pieces together to begin to reveal the picture

Source: © Mark Saunders 2018

that the fitted pieces are designed to show. Perhaps completing jigsaws reinforces a sense of there being an external reality 'out there', so all we need to do is reveal it! However, for many qualitative researchers, the picture that our pieces of data reveal will depend on the nature of our research question and the concepts we use to make sense of what we see!

A range of computer-aided qualitative data analysis software (CAQDAS) exists which we consider briefly in Section 13.14. Consequently, although you need to understand which analytical technique, or combination of techniques, is suitable for the nature of your qualitative or mixed methods research project to be able to make an informed choice about how to analyse your data, it may no longer be necessary for you to undertake routine qualitative data management tasks manually, such as coding your data and rearranging these into analytical categories. However, we do not assume that use of CAQDAS is automatic, for two reasons. Firstly, you may not have access to CAQDAS, or at least to software that is suitable for the nature of your research project. Secondly, qualitative data analysis is, as we noted, an interactive and iterative process, a gradual process and a thoughtful, reflective and reflexive rather than a mechanical process, so using CAQDAS isn't a quick fix. On the other hand, using CAQDAS helps the management and organisation of data, helping to facilitate analysis, where you are able to use a suitable program for your research project. Consequently, although we make reference to, and include screenshots of, different software packages in some worked examples, these are used to illustrate generic issues associated with analysis rather than imply that you must use such software.

13.2 The diversity of qualitative data, their implications for analysis and the interactive nature of this process

In Section 5.5 we discuss the characteristics of qualitative research, summarising these in Table 5.2. You may find it helpful to re-read this section and the points contained in this table. Our purpose here is to extend this earlier discussion to understand the diversity of qualitative data, their implications for analysis and the interactive nature of this process. Unlike quantitative research where analysis occurs after data collection, qualitative research often involves the concurrent collection, analysis and interpretation of data.

Diversity and analytical implications of qualitative data

We commence this discussion by considering the diversity and analytical implications of qualitative data, as this will help you to analyse these meaningfully. **Qualitative data** are derived from spoken words (verbal data), written, typed or printed words (textual data) and still or moving visual images (visual data). **Verbal data** are collected in the form of extended speech, which are passages of spoken words. These may be audio recorded or derived from existing audio or audio-visual sources. These data are likely to be transcribed and turned into text but may still be classified as verbal data if they maintain their structural integrity as a verbatim account (Chapters 8, 9 and 10). **Textual data** are collected as notes from interviews or observations, as written diaries and participant accounts (Chapters 9 and 10), or derived from documents (Section 5.8 and Chapter 8). **Visual data** may be created or found in many forms including drawings, digital images and video (Sections 9.6 and 8.2). These data are associated with particular analytical implications, which we consider in Section 13.12.

This diversity of qualitative data arises from the variety of ways used to obtain it. As we outline in Chapters 5, 8, 9 and 10, qualitative data are obtained through interviews, observations, naturally occurring conversations, research diaries, documents, images, and audio and video recordings. Many of these ways involve the collection of data in natural settings, where the researcher goes to the research setting to observe or interview participants, or to ask participants to collect data themselves from within this setting through audio or video recording, photography, or keeping a research diary. Such naturalistically collected data are often contrasted with contrived data collected through laboratory based experiments, or questionnaires that do not take into account the context within which these are used.

Qualitative data collected in natural settings are likely to be rich in contextual detail. The opportunity to explore issues in interviews, record mundane details during observations or read through participants' detailed accounts in research diaries is likely to produce descriptive and explanatory data that help to facilitate analysis and interpretation. Many of these data will come directly from participants, by recording the words they speak during interviews, detailing their actions during observations, using the words they write when keeping research diaries, transcribing the audio recordings they create, watching and making notes about the video recordings they make, or looking at the visual images they provide. Through these ways, the researcher is able to use the medium of collecting qualitative data to give participants a 'voice' through which to talk about and record their experiences and perceptions.

This production of highly contextualised data, emphasis on recording participants' interpretations and practice of using participants to collect data each have implications for qualitative analysis. Qualitative data sets characterised by their fullness and richness provide an opportunity for in-depth analysis, where context can be related to the themes that emerge from analysis, to produce well-grounded and contextualised explanations. In this way, a contrast is drawn between the 'thin' abstraction or description that principally results from quantitative data and the 'thick' or 'thorough' abstraction or description associated with qualitative data (Brekhus et al. 2005; Dey 1993).

The philosophical assumptions underpinning a research project will affect its design and conduct, including data collection and analysis. An interpretivist philosophy often informs qualitative research projects (Section 5.5). As we discuss in Section 4.4, interpretivism focuses on participants' interpretations of their social world, in opposition to the realist belief that reality exists independently of perceptions about it.

In interpretivism, reality is seen as being socially constructed. Social constructionism rests on the belief that social reality is subjectively constructed by social actors and that multiple social realities exist as a result of different interpretations (Section 4.2 and Table 4.3). Qualitative research conducted through the lenses of interpretivist philosophy will affect the nature of the data produced, with implications for their analysis. An interpretivist researcher will typically undertake research inductively, allowing the conduct of the research to follow the flow of the data collected. These data will reflect variations in participants' experiences and perspectives. Analysis of these data will need to recognise the breadth of these experiences and perspectives, welcoming this in the way these are reported rather than attempting to reconcile differences and write out this diversity of viewpoints. Analysis of data collected through an interpretivist approach therefore needs to be sensitive to their variability and complexity to be meaningful.

This inductive approach to qualitative analysis will involve deriving research-specific concepts from which a conceptual framework may be developed. This framework will initially be developed during data collection and then refined as your analysis progresses. Various techniques to develop this analytical approach are discussed in Sections 13.6 to 13.13.

A realist philosophy may also inform qualitative research projects (Section 5.5). The realist researcher believes that reality exists independently of participants' interpretations about it. In other words, 'reality' helps to shape participants' interpretations rather than being constructed by them (Sections 4.2 and 4.4). This idea of reality may be explained by the existence of political and economic societal structures and social attitudes, which affect the nature of social interactions and in turn social actors' interpretations about these. A researcher who commences from either a critical, cultural, environmental, feminist, gender or radical perspective will use her or his viewpoint to inform the design and conduct of her or his qualitative research (Section 13.11 offers further consideration of a critical approach).

As we outline in Section 10.2, qualitative research conducted through the lenses of a realist philosophy will affect the nature of the data produced, with implications for their analysis. A realist researcher will typically undertake research deductively with constructs to test in this context derived from existing theory, or with theoretical assumptions related to one or more of the perspectives we have just outlined. These constructs or assumptions will inform the questions asked of participants, which will need to be asked or applied consistently on each occasion data are collected to be able to produce comparable and valid data to test the applicability of this theory in this research context. Various techniques to develop this analytical approach are discussed in Sections 13.6 to 13.13 excluding 13.9.

Irrespective of whether qualitative data are collected through the lenses of an interpretivist or realist philosophy, their nature has implications for analysis. As we recognise in Table 5.2, meanings are principally derived from words and images, not numbers. Since words and images may have multiple meanings as well as unclear meanings, it is necessary to explore and clarify these with great care. This indicates that the quality of qualitative research partly depends on the interaction between data collection and data analysis to allow meanings to be explored and clarified. This aspect permeates much of the discussion in this chapter and we go on to discuss it in depth in the following sub-section.

Qualitative data collected by participants will also have analytical implications. These data will reflect the experiences and perspectives of those who collect them. They will be characterised by specific meanings that you will need to understand in order to interpret them. This may mean using multiple methods during data collection and analysis, often involving the use of a multi-method qualitative study (Figure 5.2), where, for example, you conduct interviews in conjunction with the use of either participant video, participant photography, participant drawing or participant research diaries, in order to explore meanings and produce participant-focused interpretations (Sections 9.6, 10.11 and 10.12).

The nature of qualitative data has further implications for their analysis. These non-standardised data will be likely to be large in volume and complex in nature. You will therefore be confronted by either a mass of paper, still images, audio and visual recordings or electronic files that you will need to explore, analyse, synthesise and transform in order to address your research objectives and answer your research question. Most of the analytical techniques discussed later in this chapter will involve you using processes where you summarise some parts of your data to condense them; code and categorise data in order to group them according to themes that begin to make sense of these data; and then to link these categories and themes in ways that provide you with a structure or structures to answer your research question. Without using such techniques, the most that may result is an impressionistic view of what these qualitative data mean.

The interactive nature of qualitative analysis

Data collection and data analysis are an interrelated and interactive set of processes in qualitative research. Analysis is undertaken during the collection of data as well as after it. This analysis helps to shape the direction of data collection, especially where you are following a more inductive or grounded approach. Research propositions that emerge from your data in an inductive approach or those you commenced with at the start of your data collection in a deductive approach will be tested as you compare them with the data in your study. The key point here is the relative flexibility that this type of process permits you.

The interactive nature of data collection and analysis allows you to recognise important themes, patterns and relationships during data collection: in other words, to allow these to emerge from the process of data collection and analysis. As part of this you are likely to have to re-categorise and re-code your existing data to see whether emergent themes, patterns and relationships are present in the cases where you have already collected data. You will also be able to adjust your future data collection to see whether related data exist in cases where you intend to conduct your research.

This concurrent process of data collection and analysis also has implications for the way in which you manage your time and organise your data and related documentation. It will be necessary to arrange interviews or observations with enough space between them to allow sufficient time to write up or word process a transcript or set of notes, and to analyse one before proceeding to the next (Section 10.6). Where you conduct a small number of interviews in one day, you will need time during the evening to undertake some initial analysis on these before carrying out further interviews. You may also be able to find a little time between interviews to carry out a cursory level of analysis. As part of this we have found it extremely helpful to listen to audio-recordings of interviews while travelling to and from the university.

There is a clear limit to the value of continuing to undertake interviews or observations without analysing these. There is also a danger of data overload where you just continue to collect data. This will be associated with a lost opportunity to understand what your data reveal in relation to your research question and the directions that might be worth pursuing for your research. Important ideas that occur to you as you undertake an interview, conduct an observation, read a document, listen to an audio-recording, or view a set of images or a visual-recording may be lost if you do not record these because you are focused only on collecting data.

13.3 Key aspects to consider when choosing a qualitative analysis technique

Choosing a qualitative analysis technique can be confusing. Choice in qualitative analysis is different to choice in quantitative analysis. Quantitative analysis necessitates specified statistical techniques dependent on the data type and what you are trying to illustrate, describe, examine or predict (Chapter 12). Choice in qualitative analysis is not necessarily between a 'right' and 'wrong' technique. Some forms of qualitative analysis are not exclusive; in other words, you may have to choose between alternative ways to analyse your qualitative data, making this choice uncertain and possibly confusing. Choice in qualitative analysis may also mean choosing two or more complementary ways to analyse your qualitative data, so that you gain more insights from your data than you would from using a single analytical technique. To achieve this you need to understand the nature of different techniques to be able to choose those which offer the possibility of complementary insights.

In this section we summarise some key aspects of different qualitative analysis techniques to help you to choose an appropriate technique, or combination of techniques that we introduce in Sections 13.6 to 13.13. These aspects relate to:

- the methodological and philosophical basis of the research;
- the approach to theory development used in the research;
- the analytical approach used in the technique.

We discuss each of these in turn.

The methodological and philosophical basis of the research

Some qualitative research strategies are associated with a specific or prescriptive methodology. In these the research philosophy, approach to theory development and research practices including analytical techniques are closely defined. Of the research strategies we consider (Section 5.8), Grounded Theory has a specific methodology. In order to use Grounded Theory Method you would need to follow each of the elements associated with this approach (Section 5.8 and 13.9). While the specific or prescriptive nature of this type of methodological approach may sometimes be portrayed as rigid, it provides you with a clear set of guidelines for your entire research project including the analytical technique.

Other qualitative research strategies discussed in this book are not so closely specified or prescriptive. This means you will need to choose an analytical technique that is appropriate for your research philosophy and strategy (Sections 4.4 and 5.8). In doing this you will also be choosing an analytical technique that is appropriate for the nature of the data you collect. Where, for example, you use an interpretivist philosophy, it will be important to ensure that your choice of analytical technique(s) is compatible with this research philosophy. In this example, you would need to allow the voices of your participants to emerge through your analysis, probably by including participant quotations. An analytical technique concentrating on condensing participants' data to display them in a highly reduced and summarised form would be unlikely to be suitable for interpretivist research. You therefore need to ensure that your choice of analytical technique is suitable for and sympathetic to your research philosophy as well as your methodology.

The approach to theory development used in the research

Theory is developed using either deductive, inductive or abductive reasoning (Section 4.5). Where you commence your research project using a deductive approach you will use existing theory to shape the qualitative research process and aspects of data analysis. Where you commence your research project using an inductive approach you will seek to build a theory that is grounded in your data. Subsequently if, based on a surprising fact, you collect additional data to revise or modify an existing theory you would be using an abductive approach. Some qualitative analysis techniques we discuss in Sections 13.6 to 13.13 are specifically associated with either a deductive or inductive approach, while others may be used more flexibly and pragmatically so that they are suitable for either approach. In this way, these theoretically flexible techniques work equally well regardless of your approach to theory development.

The analytical approach used in the technique

In this sub-section we consider two aspects of qualitative analysis that distinguish analytical techniques. These relate to:

- data fragmentation and reduction versus maintaining data integrity;
- analytical focus.

We discuss each of these in turn.

Data fragmentation and reduction versus maintaining data integrity

In qualitative data analysis, it is generally accepted that in order to analyse large amounts of non-standardised data it is necessary to fragment these data by coding and reorganising them into analytical categories. This process often involves simplifying or reducing qualitative data by summarising their meanings to be able to comprehend them and undertake further analysis. Later sections in this chapter outline analytical techniques that fragment and sometimes reduce data to analyse them. These include Thematic Analysis (Section 13.6), Template Analysis (Section 13.7), Grounded Theory Method (Section 13.9) and Data Display and Analysis (Section 13.13).

Where it is considered important to maintain the integrity of the data by analysing them without engaging in fragmentation and rearrangement other, alternative, approaches can be used. This is the case in Narrative Analysis, where the sequential and chronological nature of storied data is essential to and maintained during analysis (Section 13.10). It is also likely to be the case in relation to Discourse Analysis (Section 13.11), where analysis relies on the wholeness of data.

Analytical focus

The focus of analysis varies between qualitative analysis techniques. While a number of techniques focus on analysing themes or topics in the data, some focus more specifically on analysing actions or processes, and others on analysing the use of language.

This first analytical focus is referred to as thematic analysis. Some see thematic analysis as a generic approach rather than as a specific technique as it is used in various analytical approaches. In practice, there are a number of variants of thematic analysis, which can be used as standalone analytical techniques. We refer to one of these as Thematic Analysis, deliberately using capital letters to distinguish it from other variants (Section 13.6). Even if you use another variant we advise you to read this section on Thematic Analysis carefully as it should provide you with technical insights which are helpful in the application of whichever approach you use. Further standalone variants of thematic analysis include Template Analysis (outlined in Section 13.7) and Data Display and Analysis (considered in Section 13.13). Thematic analysis is also used in some approaches to Grounded Theory Method (Section 13.9), in Narrative Analysis (Section 13.10), and may be used in Analytical Induction (Section 13.8), Deductive Explanation Building (Section 13.8) and Visual Analysis (Section 13.12). As you read through these sections you will recognise similarities in analytical practice.

While some approaches in Grounded Theory Method code data for themes, indicating the use of thematic analysis, Charmaz (2014) advocates coding data for actions in order to be able to stay close to the meanings in the data and to understand these through the actions or interactions that take place in these data. We consider this further in Section 13.9.

Some qualitative analysis techniques focus on the use of language in the data collected. These techniques focus on structural elements to understand the implications of how language is used or how narratives are constructed. In this chapter, we introduce two analytical approaches that focus on the use of language. These are Structural Narrative Analysis (Section 13.10) and Discourse Analysis (Section 13.11).

We summarise these key aspects of different qualitative analysis techniques as a checklist in Box 13.1 to help you to choose an appropriate technique, or combination of techniques.

Box 13.1
Checklist

To help you to choose a qualitative analysis technique, or combination of techniques

✔ Are you using or do you wish to use an analytical technique linked to a specific or prescriptive methodology? In this chapter Grounded Theory Method is linked to such a methodology; all other analytical techniques discussed are not.

✔ Will your choice of analytical technique be appropriate for the research strategy you use and the research philosophy underpinning it? Your research philosophy has implications for all stages of your research including your research strategy and choice of analytical technique(s).

✔ Will your choice of analytical technique be appropriate for your approach to theory development?

Some qualitative analysis techniques are specifically associated with either a deductive or inductive approach, while others may be used more flexibly and pragmatically.

✔ Will it be beneficial to fragment your data during analysis to rearrange them, or to maintain the integrity of your data items during analysis? Most qualitative analysis techniques involve the fragmentation and reorganisation of data and sometimes their reduction, while some analytical techniques maintain the original form of the data during analysis.

✔ What will be the most appropriate analytical focus for the analysis of your data, or foci where you use a combination of approaches? The focus of analysis varies between qualitative analysis techniques, with most focusing on analysing themes or topics in the data, some more specifically on analysing actions or processes, and others on analysing the use of language.

13.4   Preparing your data for analysis

As we have seen in Chapters 5, 8, 9, 10 and 11, qualitative data can be generated in many forms. In Chapter 5, when we considered archival and documentary research, and Chapter 8, when we considered secondary data, we highlighted how documentary data are available in text, audio and visual forms. In Chapter 9 we considered how observational data may be generated through note-taking, a structured observation schedule, visual images, audio recordings and video recordings. In Chapter 10 we highlighted how research interview and research diary data may be generated through written notes, narrative accounts, visual images, audio recordings and video recordings. In Chapter 11 we recognised that while questionnaires principally produce quantitative data, they may also contain open questions which involve either the respondent or interviewer recording qualitative data. Finally, as we recognised in Section 5.6, in rare circumstances storied accounts may be generated from quantitative data to produce qualitative data.

It is important to emphasise the importance of copying any recordings you make and transcribing both these and your notes to ensure data are not lost. In this section we focus upon the conversion of qualitative data from oral or handwritten form to word-processed text, as this is the way that you are most likely to use these in your analysis. As part of this, we discuss the general requirements of CAQDAS packages (see Section 13.14).

Transcribing qualitative data

In Chapter 10 we emphasised that, in qualitative research interviews, the interview is often audio-recorded and subsequently **transcribed**, that is, reproduced verbatim as a word-processed account. We also emphasised that, as an interviewer, you would be interested not only in what participants said, but in the way they said it as well. This means that the task of transcribing audio-recorded interviews is likely to be time-consuming as you will need not only to record exactly what was said and by whom, but also try to give an indication of the tone in which it was said and the participants' non-verbal communications. Without this additional contextual information, important incidents that affect the conduct of your interview or observation may be missed (e.g. see Boxes 10.12 and 13.4). You also need to ensure it can be linked to the contextual information that locates the interview (Section 10.4).

Even if you are a touch-typist, you will find the task of transcribing an audio-recording extremely time-consuming. Most research methods texts suggest that it takes a touch-typist between 6 and 10 hours to transcribe every hour of audio-recording. Consequently, it is helpful if your interviews are transcribed as soon as possible after they are undertaken in order to avoid a build-up of audio-recordings and associated transcription work. Fortunately, there are a number of possible ways of reducing the vast amount of personal time needed to transcribe interviews verbatim. These are summarised in Table 13.1 along with some of the associated potential problems. As you will see in Table 13.1, one problem, however you choose to transcribe the data, is making sure that the transcription is accurate by correcting any transcription errors. This process is known as **data cleaning**. Once this has been done, some researchers send a copy of the transcript to the participant for final checking. While this can be helpful for ensuring factual accuracy, we have found that

Table 13.1 Alternative ways of reducing the time needed to transcribe audio-recordings

Alternative	Potential problems
Pay a touch-typist to transcribe your audio-recordings	• Expense of paying someone else • Important data such as pauses, coughs, sighs and the like may not be included • You will not be familiarising yourself with the data as you are not transcribing them yourself • The transcription will still require careful checking as errors can creep in
Borrow a transcription machine with a foot-operated play–pause–rewind–fast forward mechanism and software to control the audio speed	• Although this will allow you to control the audio-recorder more easily, the speed of transcription will still be dependent upon your typing ability • The transcription will still require careful checking • You may not be able to gain access to a transcription machine
'Dictate' your audio-recordings to your computer using voice-recognition software	• You will need to discover which voice-recognition software works best with your voice • You will also need to discover which voice-recognition software is suited to the needs of your research project • You will need to 'teach' the voice-recognition software to understand your voice • You will need to listen to and dictate the entire audio-recording • The transcription will still require careful checking as the software is not entirely accurate
Only transcribe those sections of each audio-recording that are pertinent to your research (**data sampling**)	• You will need to listen to the entire recording carefully first, at least twice • You may miss certain things, meaning you will have to go back to the audio-recording later • Those sections you transcribe will still require careful checking

interviewees often want to correct their own grammar and use of language as well! This is because spoken and written language are very different. For this reason, you need to think carefully before offering to provide a copy of a complete transcript to an interviewee.

Each interview you transcribe should be saved as a separate word-processed file. As part of this we recommend that you use a filename that maintains confidentiality and preserves anonymity but that you can easily recognise and which codifies important information. When doing this Mark always starts his transcription filenames with the interview number and saves the word-processed transcripts for each research project in a separate subdirectory. Subsequent parts of the filename provide more detail. Thus the file '26MPOrg1.docx' is the transcript of the **26**th interview, **M**ale, **P**rofessional, undertaken at **Org**anisation**1**. As some CAQDAS programs require filenames of eight or fewer characters, you may need to limit your filenames to this length.

When transcribing interviews and group interviews, you need to be able to distinguish between the interviewer and the participant or participants. This means you need to have clear speaker identifiers such as '17FA' for the 17th interviewee who is a female admin-istrator. This tends to be more visible in the transcript if they are in capitals (Box 13.2). Similarly, you need to be able to distinguish between any topic headings you use, ques-tions and responses. One way of doing this, dependent upon the precise requirements of your CAQDAS, is to put topic headings in CAPITALS, questions in *italics* and responses in normal font. The most important thing is to be consistent within and across all your transcriptions. Some authors also recommend the use of specific transcription symbols to record intakes of breath, overlapping talk and changes in intonation. A useful list of transcription symbols is provided as an appendix by Silverman (2013).

In a transcription of a more structured interview, you also need to include the question number and the question in your transcription. For example, by including the question number 'Q27' at the start of the question you will be able to search for and find question 27 quickly. In addition, by having the full question in your transcript you will be far less likely to misinterpret the question your respondent is answering.

When transcribing audio-recordings or your own notes you need to plan in advance how you intend to analyse your transcriptions. If you only have access to a black and white printer, there is little point in using different coloured fonts to distinguish between participants in a group interview or to distinguish non-verbal responses such as nervous

---

Box 13.2
Focus on student research

Extract from an interview transcript

Michael had decided to use the code IV to represent himself in the transcripts of his in-depth interviews and 01FS to represent his first interviewee, a female student. By using capital letters to identify both him-self and the interviewee Michael could identify clearly where questions and responses started. In addition, it reduced the chance of a mistype in the transcrip-tion as identifiers were always a combination of capi-tal letters and numbers. Michael used transcription

symbols such as '(.)' to represent a brief pause and '.hhh' to represent an in-breath. He also included brief comments relating to a respondent's actions in the interview transcript. These he enclosed with dou-ble parentheses (()). A brief extract from a transcript follows:

IV: So tell me, why do you use the Student Union Bar?

01FS: Well,.hhh (.), a lot of my friends go there for the final drink of the evening (.) there is an atmosphere and the drinks are cheap. I don't feel embarrassed to walk in on my own and there's always someone to talk to and scrounge a fag off ((laughs))

Box 13.3
Checklist

Transcribing your interviews

✔ Have you thought about how you intend to ana-lyse your data and made sure that your transcrip-tion will facilitate this?

✔ Have you chosen clear interviewer and respondent identifiers and used them consistently?

✔ Have you included the interview questions in full in your transcription?

✔ Have you saved your transcribed data using a separate file for each interview?

✔ Does your filename maintain confidentiality and preserve anonymity while still allowing you to rec-ognise important information easily?

✔ Have you ensured your data files maintain confi-dentiality and preserve anonymity?

✔ Have you checked your transcript for accuracy and, where necessary, 'cleaned up' the data?

✔ (If you intend to use CAQDAS) Will the package you are going to use help you to manage and analyse your data effectively? In other words, will it do what you need it to do?

✔ (If you intend to use CAQDAS) Are your saved transcriptions compatible with the CAQDAS package you intend to use, so you will not lose any features from your word-processed document when you import the data?

✔ (If you intend to use CAQDAS) Have you checked your transcript for accuracy and 'cleaned up' the data *prior* to importing into your chosen CAQDAS package?

✔ Have you stored a separate backup or security copy of each data file on your USB mass storage device?

laughter in your transcripts as these will be difficult to discern when working from the paper copies. You also need to be careful about using these and other word-processing software features if you are going to analyse the data using CAQDAS. These programs often have precise file formats which can mean that word-processing software features such as *bold* and *italics* generated by your word-processing software will disappear when your data file is imported (Silver and Lewins 2014). For example, although you may transcribe your interviews using a word processor such as Microsoft Word, your chosen CAQDAS package may require this textual data to be saved as a text-only file (.txt) or using rich text format (.rtf), resulting in the loss of some of these features. These are sum-marised as a checklist in Box 13.3.

Using electronic textual data including scanned documents

For some forms of textual data such as, for example, email interviews (Section 10.10) or electronic versions of documents (Section 8.2), including organisational emails, blogs and web-based reports, your data may already be in electronic format. Although these data have already been captured electronically, you are still likely to need to spend some time preparing them for analysis. This is likely to involve you in ensuring that, where neces-sary, the data are:

- suitably anonymised, such as by using separate codes for yourself and different participants;
- appropriately stored for analysis, for example one file for each interview, each meet-ing's minutes or each organisational policy;
- free of typographical errors that you may have introduced and, where these occurred, they have been 'cleaned up'.

Consequently, you are likely to find much of the checklist in Box 13.3 helpful. If you intend to use CAQDAS to help you to manage and analyse documents which are not available electronically, you will need to scan these into your word-processing software and ensure they are in a format compatible with your chosen CAQDAS.

13.5 Aids to help your analysis

In addition to transcribing your notes and audio or video recordings, it will also help your analysis if you record contextual information about the interviews or observations that you conduct (Section 10.4). This will help you to recall the context and content of each interview or observation as well as informing your interpretation as you will be more likely to remember the precise circumstances of your data collection. Various researchers have suggested ways of recording information and developing reflective ideas to supplement your written-up notes or transcripts and your categorised data (e.g. Brinkmann and Kvale 2015; Gerstl-Pepin and Patrizio 2009). These include:

- interim or progress summaries;
- transcript summaries;
- document summaries;
- self-memos;
- a research notebook;
- a reflective diary or journal.

The way in which you use these analytical aids will be dependent on your preferred approach to recording your ideas and reflections, and the context of your research. You may, for example, develop a preference for using either interim summaries or self-memos or a research notebook. You may decide to use more than one of these aids. Where you produce transcripts of interviews or observations, it will be helpful to write a transcript summary for each one; similarly where you use documents, it will be helpful to write document summaries. Your university may require you to keep a reflective diary, although you may also find it helpful to write interim summaries, self-memos or a research notebook to produce this. We recommend using these analytical aids to help you with your research project, although choice of which to use is partly a matter of personal preference.

Interim or progress summaries

As your analysis progresses you may wish to write an **interim summary** of your progress to date. You may decide to write an interim summary after each interview or observation, or after a set of related interviews or observations. Similarly, you may wish to write an interim summary after a period of using secondary data or conducting a search of the literature. In this way, you may write up a number of summaries that detail the development of your thoughts to aid your analysis and the direction of your data collection. Alternatively, your interim summary may become a unified working document that you modify and continue to refer to as your research project progresses. The way in which you use this analytical aid should suit your preferred approach. An interim summary may include:

- what you have found so far;
- how much confidence you have in your findings and explanations to date;

- what you need to do in order to improve the quality of your data and/or to seek to substantiate your apparent explanations, or to seek alternative explanations;
- how you will seek to achieve the needs identified by the interim analysis.

Transcript summaries

After you have written up your notes, or produced a transcript, of an interview or observation, you can also produce a summary of the key points that have emerged from undertaking this activity. A **transcript summary** compresses long statements into briefer ones in which the main sense of what has been said or observed is rephrased in fewer words. Through summarising you will become conversant with the principal themes that have emerged from each interview or observation. You may be able to identify apparent relationships between themes that you wish to note down so that you can return to these to seek to establish their validity. It will also be useful to make some comments about the person(s) you interviewed or observed, the setting in which this occurred and whether anything occurred during the interview or observation which might have affected the nature of the data that you collected (Box 13.4).

Once you have produced a summary of the key points that emerge from the interview or observation and its context, you should attach a copy to the file of your written-up notes or transcript for further reference.

Document summaries

Where you use any sort of documentation it is helpful to produce a **document summary**. A document summary can fulfil two purposes. It may be used to summarise and list the document's key points for your research. These points become part of your data set. Secondly, you may use it to describe the purpose of the document, how it relates to your work and why it is significant. You will be able to return to a document summary to look again at the data you drew from the document, to see how you coded and categorised these data, and to be able to re-read your notes about its relevance to your research. As a research project progresses, there is a likelihood that you will forget some of your thoughts about your previous data collection and analysis, so that a document summary, like other analytical aids discussed in this sub-section, will act as a reminder of your earlier ideas.

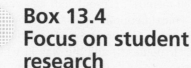

Box 13.4
Focus on student research

Noting an event that affected the nature of data collection

Birjit was facilitating a focus group whose participants were the customers of a large department store. Approximately halfway through the allotted time, an additional participant joined the group. This person almost immediately took control of the discussion, two other participants appearing to become reticent and withdrawing from the group's discussion. Despite this, all Birjit's questions were answered fully and she felt the data she had obtained was valuable. However, she recorded the point at which the new participant joined the group in a post-transcript summary in case any divergence was apparent between the nature of the data in the two parts of the focus group.

Self-memos

Self-memos allow you to record ideas that occur to you about any aspect of your research, as you think of them. Where you omit to record any idea as it occurs to you it may well be forgotten. The occasions when you are likely to want to write a memo include:

- when you are writing up interview or observation notes, or producing a transcript of this event;
- when you are coding and categorising data;
- as you continue to categorise, analyse and interpret these data;
- when you are constructing a narrative;
- when you engage in writing your research project.

Most CAQDAS programs include some form of writing tool that allows you to make notes, add comments or write self-memos as you are analysing your data (Silver and Lewins 2014). This facility is very helpful and, as your self-memos are automatically dated, you can also trace the development of your ideas.

Ideas may also occur as you engage in an interview or observation session. In this case you may record the idea very briefly as a margin note and write it as a memo to yourself after the event. Similarly, ideas may occur as you work through a documentary source or create a research diary entry. It may be useful to carry a reporter's notebook or an e-notebook in order to be able to record your ideas, whenever and wherever they occur. When you are undertaking the production of notes, or a transcript, or any aspect of qualitative analysis, we suggest you use the notebook to record your ideas.

Self-memos may vary in length from a few words to one or more pages. They can be written as simple notes – they do not need to be set out formally. It will be useful to date them and to provide cross-references to appropriate places in your written-up notes or transcripts, where appropriate. Alternatively, an idea that is not grounded in any data (which may nevertheless prove to be useful) should be recorded as such. Memos should be filed together and where appropriate they should be linked to specific data. Most CAQDAS software allows you to do this. Memos may also be categorised where this will help you to undertake later stages of your qualitative analysis. They may also be updated as your research progresses, so that your bank of ideas continues to have currency and relevance.

Research notebook

An alternative approach to recording your ideas about your research is to keep a **research notebook**. You may of course keep such a notebook alongside the creation of self-memos. Its purpose will be similar to the creation of self-memos: to record your ideas and reflections, and to act as an aide-mémoire about your intentions for the direction of your research. Using a chronological format may help you to identify the development of certain ideas (such as data categories, propositions or hypotheses) and the way in which your research has progressed, as well as providing an approach that suits the way in which you like to think.

Reflective diary or journal

In Chapter 1 we recommended you also keep a reflective diary or journal. This is devoted to reflections about your experiences of undertaking research, what you have learnt from these experiences, how you will seek to apply this learning as your research progresses and what you will need to do to develop your competence to further your research. Universities generally require students to reflect on their research as part of their project reports to be able to evaluate their learning from the research process. In Section 1.5 we talked about keeping a reflective diary and provided a checklist to help you to do this (Box 1.4).

Reflection may occur in a number of ways. It may occur during an event, so that you reflect on your approach while you are conducting an activity. This type of reflection may occur, for example, while you are interviewing or observing. Reflection may also occur after an activity has taken place so that you reflect on what occurred and how you might be able to do better next time. A more fundamental type of reflection, known as reflexivity, involves you in monitoring and reflecting on all aspects of the research project from initial ideas to submission of the project report (Section 2.1). It includes examining your reactions to what is being researched, the nature of your relationship with those who take part in the research and evaluating the way in which you interpret data to construct knowledge (Haynes 2012). Given its interpretivist nature, Finlay (2002: 211) says that reflexivity is 'now the defining feature of qualitative research'. Your reactions, your interactions with those taking part and your attitudes and beliefs may each impact on your interpretation of the data that are shared with you. Engaging in forms of reflexivity may enable you to develop greater insights as you explore and analyse these data. Developing a reflexive focus in your reflective diary may therefore prove to be a valuable aid to further your research (Section 1.5).

13.6 Thematic Analysis

Introduction

We start by outlining **Thematic Analysis** as this is often thought of as a general approach to analysing qualitative data. Braun and Clarke (2006: 78) refer to Thematic Analysis as a 'foundational method for qualitative analysis'. The process of thematic analysis is found in other approaches to qualitative analysis, albeit in more particularised ways, as we outline in the following sections. The essential purpose of this approach is to search for themes, or patterns, that occur across a data set (such as a series of interviews, observations, documents, diaries or websites being analysed). Thematic Analysis involves a researcher coding her or his qualitative data to identify themes or patterns for further analysis, related to his or her research question. We discuss procedures to undertake analysis in the next part of this section.

Thematic Analysis offers a systematic yet flexible and accessible approach to analyse qualitative data (Braun and Clarke 2006). It is systematic as it provides an orderly and logical way to analyse qualitative data. In this way, Thematic Analysis can be used to analyse large qualitative data sets, as well as smaller ones, leading to rich descriptions, explanations and theorising. Thematic Analysis can be used to help you:

1 comprehend often large and disparate amounts of qualitative data;
2 integrate related data drawn from different transcripts and notes;
3 identify key themes or patterns from a data set for further exploration;
4 produce a thematic description of these data; and/or
5 develop and test explanations and theories based on apparent thematic patterns or relationships;
6 draw and verify conclusions.

Thematic Analysis is flexible as it is not tied to a particular research philosophy. You may use Thematic Analysis irrespective of whether you are adopting an objectivist or subjectivist position (Chapter 4). Your assumptions will, however, affect how you use it to interpret your data (which is why you should be explicit about your philosophical assumptions and remain reflexive through your research project). As a realist you may use Thematic Analysis to seek to understand factors underpinning human attitudes and actions. Alternatively, as an interpretivist you may use it to explore different interpretations of a phenomenon. The reason why you may use Thematic Analysis irrespective of your philosophy relates to its development as a standalone analytical technique or process, rather than being part of a theoretically mounted methodological approach.

For the same reason, Thematic Analysis may be used irrespective of whether you adopt a deductive, inductive or abductive approach. In a deductive approach, the themes you wish to examine would be linked to existing theory. Your research question is also more likely to be firmly established and this and your research objectives may be used to derive themes to examine in your data. This may lead you to focus on parts of your data set rather than seek to analyse it all in an undiscriminating way. In an inductive approach, themes will be derived from the data. You will search for themes to explore related to your research interest but will not impose a framework of themes to examine your data set based on existing theory. Depending on which themes you decide to explore in an inductive approach, you may also modify your research question. Initially you will be likely to explore the whole data set looking for the occurrence and reoccurrence of themes. You may also use an abductive approach, commencing analysis with theoretically-derived themes which you then modify or add to as you explore your data set.

The nature and flexibility of Thematic Analysis mean that it is fairly straightforward to use in comparison to some of the techniques discussed later. Where you use Thematic Analysis, your energy can be invested in making sure your analysis is rigorous, rather than spending lots of time checking you are applying a more particularised approach to qualitative analysis according to strict rules advocated for its use. We now outline the procedure used in Thematic Analysis.

Procedure

The procedure outlined here provides a set of guidelines to undertake Thematic Analysis. In practice, this procedure does not occur in a simple linear progression. Instead it is likely to occur in a concurrent and recursive fashion, involving you analysing data as you collect them and going back over earlier data and analysis as you refine the way in which you code and categorise newly collected data and search for analytical themes.

The procedure outlined here involves four elements: becoming familiar with your data; coding your data; searching for themes and recognising relationships; refining themes and testing propositions. We now consider each of these.

Becoming familiar with your data

You will start to become familiar with your data as you produce transcripts of the interviews or observations you conduct, or as you read through documents or diaries or review visual images. The act of transcribing a data item yourself, although laborious, allows you to develop familiarity. This should also prompt you to generate summaries, self-memos or entries in your notebook that aid your analysis.

Familiarisation with your data involves a process of immersion that continues throughout your research project. You will need to read and re-read your data during your analysis. You will be interested to look for meanings, recurring themes and patterns in your data. Without familiarity, you will not be able to engage in the analytical procedures that follow. Producing transcripts and data familiarisation are therefore important elements in analysing data.

Coding your data

Coding is used to categorise data with similar meanings. **Coding** involves labelling each unit of data within a data item (such as a transcript or document) with a code that symbolises or summarises that extract's meaning. Your purpose in undertaking this process is to make each piece of data in which you are interested accessible for further analysis (Boxes 13.5 and 13.6). Qualitative data sets are frequently large and their content complex. A qualitative data set may include references to actions, behaviours, beliefs, conditions, events, ideas, interactions, outcomes, policies, relationships, strategies, etc. Without coding these data you may struggle to comprehend all of the meanings in your data in which you are interested. Coding is therefore an important means to manage your data so that you can rearrange and retrieve them under relevant codes. This process effectively involves fragmenting your original data items and regrouping units of data with similar meanings together to be able to examine them in relation to other groups of similar units of data. The act of coding your data is therefore a vital element in data analysis, as you will see.

A **code** is a single word or a short phrase, which may also be abbreviated in use (Boxes 13.5 and 13.6). A coded extract of data is referred to as a unit of data. A **unit of data** may be a number of words, a line of a transcript, a sentence, a number of sentences, a complete paragraph, other chunk of textual data, or visual image that is summed up by a particular code (Boxes 13.5 and 13.6). The exact size of a unit of data will be determined by its meaning. Some units of data will overlap and some will be coded using more than one code (Box 13.5).

If you think that a new piece of data has a similar meaning to a previously coded unit of data, it should be labelled with the same code. If you think that a new piece of data does not have a similar meaning to a previously coded unit of data, you will need to devise a new code for it. Throughout the process of coding it will be important to keep a list of codes you are using and a working definition for each, to ensure consistency.

At this point you may be asking two questions. How much of my data should I code – all or only some of it? Where should my codes come from? Both of these questions are related to your research approach and also to your research question – whether you are setting out to use an inductive or deductive approach and how well you have defined your research question. We now answer each of these questions in turn.

How much of your data you code will depend upon your research approach and research question. Where you use a purely inductive approach you will be likely to code all of it, as you explore all possible meanings in your data to guide the direction of your research. This search for meanings may also lead to finely detailed coding, where you find yourself coding smaller segments or units of data to capture every possible nuance. Where you use a purely deductive approach, you will commence with a framework of codes derived from prior conceptual or theoretical work. In this case you will commence coding by applying these prior codes to your data. Using a purely inductive or deductive approach may be problematic. A purely inductive approach may mean that you spend a great deal of time coding every possible unit of data before you decide on a particular research focus. Using a purely inductive approach is appropriate for a very exploratory study but you would need to ensure that you have ample time to conduct it, perhaps related to a major research project. Where you use an inductive approach and have defined a research question, you should be able to use this question to help select which data to code. In this case, while all of your data may be potentially interesting, your research question will help you focus on which data to code. Using a purely deductive approach may lead you to conclude that your list of prior codes is inadequate and that you need to devise other codes in order to be able to code your data adequately to begin to answer your research question and address your research objectives.

Box 13.5
Focus on student research

Interview extract with categories attached

Adrian's research project was concerned with how human resource management professionals managed a downsizing process in their own organisations. He derived initial codes from existing theory in the academic literature and attached them to appropriate units of data in each transcript. His initial categories were hierarchical; the codes he used being shown in brackets:

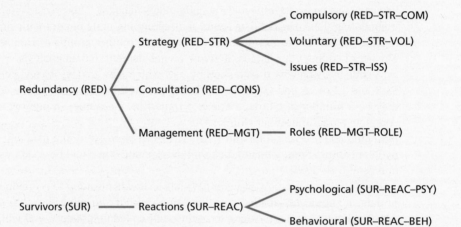

These were then attached to the interview transcript, using sentences as units of data. Like our jigsaw example at the start of this chapter, those units of data that were coded with more than one category suggested interrelationships:

RED–CONS	27MM The first stage is to find out what particular employees	1
	want for themselves and how they want this to happen. Staff are	2
	seen by their line manager and/or a member of personnel.	3
RED–MGT–ROLE	Employees might want to talk to someone from personnel rather	4
	than talk with their line manager – well, you know, for obvious	5
	reasons, at least as they see it – and this would be acceptable to the	6
RED–STR–VOL	organisation. This meeting provides them with the opportunity to	7
	opt for voluntary redundancy. We do not categorise employees	8
RED–STR–ISS	into anything like core or non-core, although we will tell a group	9
RED–CONS	of employees something like 'there are four of you in this	10
	particular function and we only need two of you, so you think	1
RED–CONS	about what should happen'. Sometimes when we attempt to give	2
	employees a choice about who might leave, they actually ask us to	3
	make the choice. This is one such situation where a compulsory	4
RED–STR–COM	selection will occur. We prefer to avoid this compulsory selection	5
SUR–REAC–PSY	because of the impact on those who survive – negative feelings,	6
	guilt and so on.	7

This discussion indicates where your codes may come from. There are three main sources of codes which, dependent on your approach to theory development can be used on their own or in combination. Codes may be:

- actual terms used by your participants, recorded in your data. These are often referred to as 'in vivo' codes;
- labels you develop from your data;
- derived from existing theory and the literature. These are often referred to as 'a priori' codes.

These sources of codes are shown in Figure 13.1 to illustrate their relationship.

Coding is a simple but versatile and valuable tool. The process of coding allows you to link units of data that refer to the same aspect or meaning, or to link aspects or meanings that you want to compare and contrast. It allows you to rearrange your original data into groupings for the next stage of analysis. Any unit of data may be coded with as many different codes as you think is appropriate, creating a web of connections to aid your analysis (Boxes 13.5 and 13.6). It is often important to understand the context of the data you are analysing. Where it is important to include some contextual background, you can code larger units of data such as whole paragraphs, as opposed to smaller units such as a few words or single sentences. You should also note that codes may be referred to as categories: these terms are sometimes used interchangeably and sometimes to refer to different aspects of the analytical process – see the next sub-section.

Your approach to coding will be guided by the purpose of your research as expressed through your research question and objectives. Another researcher with different objectives to you may derive different codes from the same data. You will be likely to develop new codes as you conduct more interviews or observations and expand your data set. You will also be likely to gain new insights from existing codes that suggest new ones during the process of analysis. This will require you to re-read all of your earlier data transcripts to re-code them according to your current list of codes. This process is termed constant comparison and is undertaken to ensure consistency in the way you code and analyse your data set.

Your codes will show the occurrence or non-occurrence of a phenomenon and the strength of opinion in some instances. Some codes may attract large numbers of units of data. Some of these may prove to be too broad for further analysis without being subdivided. For example, Adrian undertook a research project where some codes had large amounts of data attached to them, while others attracted relatively small amounts of data. This led to the large codes being subdivided into further codes, which was helpful in pursuing the analysis (Box 13.5). Codes attracting small numbers of units of data may be merged with similar ones or retained until later in the process of analysis in case they prove to be more important than they appear initially.

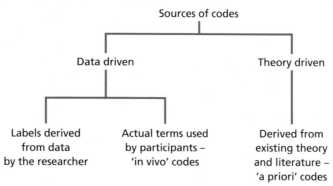

Figure 13.1 Sources and types of code

Box 13.6
Focus on management research

Developing, revising and applying codes to analyse data

In an article published in the *Journal of Occupational and Organizational Psychology* (2016: 634), McConville, Arnold and Smith analysed "qualitative data to explore how employees perceive the relationships between employee share ownership scheme participation, their attitudes and behaviours at work, and their feelings of psychological ownership." They used Thematic Analysis to analyse data collected from 37 semi-structured interviews which were conducted in nine companies with participants in employee share ownership schemes.

Initial codes to analyse these data were developed deductively from relevant theory and inductively during the process of data familiarisation following its collection. Interviews were audio-recorded and transcribed, aiding the process of data familiarisation. Following some revision to their initial set of codes, each data transcript was coded holistically using this revised set of codes. This led them to consider the units of data allocated to these codes in greater detail, which in turn led to some of these codes being revised further and new codes being added, with data being recoded as a consequence of these changes. Their introduction of new codes also suggests that these started to become more hierarchical since they refer to introducing sub-codes to recognise the relationship between an observed behaviour and reasons given for this by participants. They provide an example of these new codes and sub-codes.

They introduced a new code, 'CIT', to label incidents of organisational citizenship behaviours (OCB) which were evident in the data. The introduction of this new code led them to examine the reasons for incidents of OCB. One reason was linked to participations in the employee share ownership scheme. To recognise the relationship between incidents of OCB and employee share ownership participations they therefore developed a sub-code called 'CIT/ESO'.

These examples illustrate that as data analysis proceeded it became a recursive activity in its own right: codes were applied to data, leading to units of data being analysed further in relation to the application of these codes, leading to the revision of some codes and the development of others to refine analysis and recognise relationships between different codes and the units of data attached to these.

You may use CAQDAS to help you to code your data (Section 13.14) or you may use a manual approach. Where you use the second approach, you can label a unit of data with the appropriate code (or codes) in the margin of your transcript or set of notes (Box 13.6). This may then be copied, cut up and stuck onto a data card, or otherwise transferred and filed so that you end up with piles of related units of data. When doing this, it is essential to label each unit of data carefully so that you know its precise source (Section 13.4). An alternative is to index codes by recording precisely where they occur in your transcripts or notes (e.g. interview 7, page 2, line 16) on cards headed with particular codes. Undertaking this stage of the analytic process means that you are engaging in a selective process, guided by the aim of your research and your research objectives, which has the effect of reducing and rearranging your data into a more manageable and comprehensible form.

One way of achieving this reduction and rearrangement of your data, depending on its suitability, is to use one or more of the analytical techniques described by Miles et al. (2014). These are considered later in Section 13.13.

Searching for themes and recognising relationships

This is seen as a distinct stage of analysis that follows coding, although in practice you will be searching for themes, patterns and relationships in your data as you collect and code them. Producing progress summaries, transcript summaries, document summaries, self-memos and/or entries in your research notebook and reflective diary will help you to record your ideas about possible themes, patterns and relationships in your data.

The search for themes fully begins when you have coded all of your data set. At this point you will have a long list of codes that you have created to make sense of and draw meaning from your data. Advice about the number of codes you might be working with at this point varies considerably. Some advice refers to working with up to 30 codes. Other advice refers to creating as many codes as you require to interpret every relevant meaning in your data. This may mean creating up to a couple of hundred codes, or possibly more. Our view is that data should not be forced into a particular number of codes. The number of codes you create will be related to the meanings you wish to explore in your data set, the nature of your research approach and the focus of your research question. However, where you find yourself creating very large numbers of codes you will need to evaluate whether your coding is too detailed or whether you are trying to analyse too much data for your project. Always refer back to your research question, research aim and research objectives to focus your approach to data analysis.

This stage of analysis involves you searching for patterns and relationships in your long list of codes to create a short list of themes that relate to your research question. A **theme** is a broad category incorporating several codes that appear to be related to one another and which indicates an idea that is important to your research question. A theme may also be a single code which indicates an idea that assumes general importance to your research question and is therefore elevated to become a theme. Searching for themes is part of the overall process of condensing your raw data, firstly by coding them and then grouping these coded data into analytic categories.

In some discussions, terms like codes and themes are used interchangeably and this can lead to confusion (Ritchie et al. 2014). We are sometimes asked about the difference between a code and a theme. One way we have found it helpful to explain this is to say that data are organised by coding them while codes are organised by drawing them together as themes. This distinction reflects what we outline here. Sometimes you will also see the term 'thematic code': this is simply an alternative way to refer to the type of coding we describe here, where your coding leads to identification of themes as opposed to coding for actions as advocated by Charmaz (2014) in constructivist grounded theory, which we discuss in Section 13.9.

Searching for themes involves you making judgements about your data and immersing yourself in them. You will be looking to see how the codes you have created might fit together to allow you to further your analysis. As you search these codes, some initial questions you may ask include:

- What are the key concepts in these codes?
- What, if anything, seems to be recurring in these codes?
- What seems to be important, whether it recurs often or not?
- What patterns and/or trends are evident in the coded data?
- Which codes appear to be related?
- How do a particular set of codes appear to be related?

As you start to decide on themes to analyse your data further, some additional questions you may ask include:

- What is the essence of each apparent theme?
- How might themes be related to each other?
- Which themes appear to be main themes and which appear to be sub-themes (related to a main theme)? There may also be third level themes evident in your analysis.

- How may the relationship between themes be represented (as a hierarchy or a network) to produce a thematic map?
- Is there an overarching theme (or more than one) that unites your analysis?

You should not expect this process to be unproblematic. In attempting to achieve a thorough understanding of your data set, some further questions you may ask include:

- How well does this initial thematic map represent the relationships between themes?
- Which themes, if any, do not fit within this thematic representation?
- Does the way the data have been coded need to be revised; if so which data and how?
- Which themes need to be refined, discarded or newly introduced?
- How may the thematic representation be modified to represent my data better?

In the first set of questions, you begin to decide on themes to further your analysis. In the second set of questions, you begin to define your themes and the relationships between them (Box 13.5). Some themes will become main themes; some may become secondary-level themes, linked to a main theme; yet others may be tertiary-level themes, linked to a secondary-level theme. In the third set of questions, you evaluate your themes and the relationships between them. This will mean refining your themes and testing proposed relationships, as we discuss further in the next sub-section.

Refining themes and testing propositions

Refining themes and the relationships between them is likely to be an important part of your analytical process. The themes that you devise need to be part of a coherent set so that they provide you with a well-structured analytical framework to pursue your analysis. As you develop themes you should reorganise your coded data extracts under the relevant theme or sub-theme. This will help you to evaluate whether these coded data are meaningful to one another within their theme and whether (and how) themes are meaningful in relation to one another and in relation to your data set. This is likely to be a developmental process, as you re-read and reorganise your data. As you continue to examine your data set, the codes you have used and the themes you devise to organise your coded data to answer your research question, you will be likely to refine these themes.

You may decide that some of your initial themes should be combined to make a new theme while others should be separated into different themes. You may also decide that some of your initial themes should be discarded. Your decisions to make these changes will be based on re-reading the coded data that you have reorganised under each relevant theme. By reading the coded data attached to a possible theme, you will be able to evaluate whether these data support the continuation of the theme, or whether there is insufficient data to sustain it. This will allow you to decide whether these data are too dissimilar so that these should be separated into more than one theme. It will also allow you to decide whether two or more themes contain similar meanings and so should be collapsed into a single theme. As you refine your themes in this way you will also be able to revise the relationships between them.

As you seek to reveal patterns within your data and to recognise relationships between themes, you will be able to develop testable propositions (Box 13.7). The appearance of an apparent relationship or connection between themes will need to be tested if you are to be able to conclude that there is an actual relationship. However, while this is sometimes referred to as 'testing a hypothesis', it is not the same as the statistical hypothesis or significance testing we discuss in relation to quantitative analysis in Section 12.5.

It is important to test the propositions that emerge inductively from the data by seeking alternative explanations and negative examples that do not conform to the pattern or relationship being tested. Alternative explanations frequently exist, and only by testing

Box 13.7
Focus on student research

Research propositions

During the process of qualitative data analysis, a student evaluating the use of online retailing formulated the following proposition:

Customers' willingness to trust specific online retailers depends on their previous customers' reviews.

A student exploring mortgage borrowers' decision making drew up this proposition:

Potential mortgage borrowers' choice of lending institution is strongly affected by the level of customer service that they receive during the initial inquiry stage.

Another student investigating cause-related marketing formulated the following proposition:

Companies engaging in cause-related marketing are motivated principally by altruism.

A relationship is evident in each of these propositions. Each was tested using the data that had been collected.

---

the propositions that you identify will you be able to move towards formulating valid conclusions and an explanatory theory, even a simple one (Miles et al. 2014). Dey (1993: 48) points out that 'the association of one variable with another is not sufficient ground for inferring a causal or any other connection between them'. The existence of an intervening variable may offer a more valid explanation of an association that is apparent in your data (Box 13.8).

By rigorously testing your propositions against your data, looking for alternative explanations and seeking to explain why negative cases occur, you will be able to move towards the development of valid/credible and well-grounded conclusions. The validity/credibility of your conclusions needs to be verified by their ability to withstand alternative explanations and the nature of negative cases. **Negative cases** are those that do not support your

---

Box 13.8
Focus on student research

The impact of an intervening variable

Kevin's research project involved looking at the use of subcontractors by an organisation. A relationship appeared to emerge between the total value of contracts a particular subcontractor had been awarded and the size of that contractor in terms of number of employees; in particular, those contractors with larger numbers of employees had a larger total value of contracts. This could have led Kevin to conclude that the value of work undertaken by a particular subcontractor was related to that organisation's size

and that, in particular, the organisation tended to use subcontractors with large numbers of employees.

Reality was not so simple. The organisation had originally used over 2,500 subcontractors but had found this exceedingly difficult to manage. To address this issue the organisation had introduced a system of preferred contractors. All 2,500 subcontractors had been graded according to the quality of their work, with those whose work had been consistently of high quality being awarded preferred contractor status. This meant that they were invited by the organisation Kevin was researching to tender for all relevant contracts. The intervening variable was therefore the introduction of preferred contractor status dependent upon the quality of work previously undertaken. The fact that the majority of these subcontractors also had relatively large numbers of employees was not the reason why the organisation had awarded them contracts.

explanations and the induction of your grounded theory. Finding cases that do not fit with your analysis should be seen positively as these will help to refine your explanations and direct the selection of further cases to collect and analyse data.

This will help you to avoid interpretations that prove to be unreliable because you only notice evidence that supports your own opinions. It relates to our discussion of reflexivity in Section 13.5. As a researcher you need to recognise your own attitudes and beliefs about the topic being researched, perhaps by writing about these to make them explicit, in order to understand how this affects your judgement about what the research data might mean and to gain greater insights while analysing these data. Brinkmann and Kvale (2015: 278) refer to this process as seeking to achieve 'reflexive objectivity'.

Evaluation

Thematic Analysis offers a systematic approach to qualitative data analysis that is accessible and flexible. Compared to some qualitative approaches, it is not overly prescriptive about the application of its analytical procedures. As a generic approach to qualitative data analysis it is suitable to use with several qualitative research strategies, where you are not following a named version of a strategy that prescribes precise analytic procedures, as in Grounded Theory Method.

Thematic Analysis may be used to induce theory in a similar way to Grounded Theory Method, but without following its prescribed approach to coding (Section 13.9). It may also be used to produce descriptive or explanatory accounts that fall short of generating a grounded theory.

Thematic Analysis is more adaptable, so that if the research strategy you are using requires you to search for particular themes you may consider using it. The process of searching for themes is common to other analytical approaches, as we consider in the following sections of this chapter.

Thematic Analysis may also be used in relation to deductive and inductive research approaches. Using a purely deductive or inductive research approach may be problematic, affecting the scope of the analysis. Thematic Analysis allows the researcher to move between these approaches.

13.7 Template Analysis

Introduction

Template Analysis is a specific type of thematic analysis, with a few key differences to Thematic Analysis as outlined in Section 13.6. In Thematic Analysis all data items (transcripts or other text) are coded first before the search for interpretive themes fully begins (Section 13.6). This is to avoid early thematic interpretation prematurely shaping or skewing the direction of the research in this emergent approach. This concern is also recognised in Template Analysis, and while only a proportion of the data items are coded before developing an initial coding structure and interpretive themes, known as a coding template, these data items are chosen for their representativeness or heterogeneity to try to overcome it (King and Brookes 2017).

This **coding template** is a hierarchical representation of themes and codes (Section 13.6) and is used as the central analytical tool in Template Analysis. A researcher using Template Analysis will start by coding a sufficient part of their data to develop an initial coding template (Box 13.9). This may mean coding a small number of interview or observation transcripts to be able to develop an initial set of themes. These are then arranged and rearranged until a satisfactory initial template is developed, representing a hierarchy of higher order themes, subthemes and lower order thematic codes. Subsequent transcripts are then coded using the codes in this initial template, which is modified as new data suggests deficiencies in the codes being used, leading eventually to the development of a final coding template. We provide further information on the procedures involved in this approach in the next sub-section.

Like Thematic Analysis, Template Analysis is a standalone analytical technique, rather than being part of a wider methodological approach. As a consequence, it may be used irrespective of whether you are adopting an objectivist or subjectivist position or whether you adopt a deductive or inductive research approach (see Section 13.6, Introduction, for further explanation of this point). Template Analysis may commence with a number of a priori codes which are then supplemented by the use of in vivo codes, as we discussed earlier.

Procedure

King and Brookes (2017) describe a procedure for Template Analysis composed of six stages, involving familiarisation with data, preliminary coding, clustering codes, production of an initial coding template, development of this template and application of the final template. We follow these stages here. The first stage involving familiarisation with data is the same as the initial stage of Thematic Analysis. During this stage, you will need to become familiar with your data by transcribing these and carefully reading each transcript several times, to understand what is happening and why to gain insights into these data.

As you become familiar with your transcribed data, you can look for units of data that relate to your research question and begin to code these. To begin coding you may use a

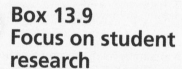

Box 13.9
Focus on student research

Part of an initial template to analyse an advertising campaign's impact

Joss was asked to gather and analyse perceptions from a range of professionals in an organisation about a recent advertising campaign it had commissioned. After conducting a number of interviews, transcribing the data and undertaking preliminary coding she embarked on the production of an initial template. She had used existing literature to inform her interview guide (Section 10.5) and also used this to commence her coding and the production of this initial template. This initial template reflected her use of a priori codes to commence analysis, with higher-order themes shown

in CAPITALS and lower-order ones in lower case and *italic script*. An extract of her initial template follows:

1 CONTEXTUAL FACTORS
    1.1 Reasons for campaign
    1.2 Environment
        1.2.1 *Political*
        1.2.2 *Economic*
        1.2.3 *Socio-cultural*
        1.2.4 *Technological*
        1.2.5 *Legal*
    1.3 Nature of the product
        1.3.1 *Cost*
        1.3.2 *Features*
        1.3.3 *Target groups*
2 NATURE OF THE CAMPAIGN
    2.1 Media
    2.2 Coverage
3 AWARENESS BY TARGET GROUPS AND OTHERS
    3.1 Those in target groups
    3.2 Others

priori codes which you have identified from existing literature, or in vivo codes derived from terms used in your data (Section 13.6). Initial use of a priori codes may also be supplemented by the subsequent development and use of in vivo codes. This process is the same as that described for Thematic Analysis in Section 13.6.

As you develop codes and code your data you will start to see how these codes may be related to each other. At this stage you will be clustering your codes as a means to group and arrange them in a hierarchical relationship. This is the process of developing themes that we described in Section 13.6 albeit that it occurs earlier in Template Analysis. This leads into the next stage where you produce an initial coding template. This template will show the clusters of codes you have produced in a hierarchical fashion to display the relationships between them, with each cluster being headed by a theme or subtheme.

Box 13.9 provides an example of an initial coding template, with a hierarchical relationship shown between the themes listed. In this example, three levels of themes have been used. The highest level is shown in capital letters (e.g. CONTEXTUAL FACTORS). The numbering system and placing of lower-level thematic codes towards the right-hand side also helps to indicate the hierarchical relationships in this coding template. Codes are also grouped together in levels 2 and 3 to show how higher-order themes are constituted.

As data collection and analysis proceeds, you will develop your template. The development of a coding template is an iterative process that involves modifying it until you devise a structure that represents all relevant ideas in your data and the relationships between them, both hierarchically and laterally where appropriate (King and Brookes 2017). The process of analysing interview transcripts or observation notes will lead to some earlier themes being revised and even changes to their level or place in the template hierarchy. Where you consider introducing a new code or theme or altering the level of an existing code or theme in the template, you need to verify this action and explore its implications in relation to your previous coding activity. This is usually more straightforward using CAQDAS (Silver and Lewins 2014). As part of this, it is helpful to use self-memos to note the reasons for these changes.

King and Brookes (2017) outline five principal ways in which a template may be reorganised and revised.

1 Insertion of a new code or theme into the hierarchy as the result of a relevant issue being identified through data collection for which there is no existing code or theme.
2 Deletion of a code or theme from the hierarchy if it is not needed.
3 Merging codes or themes that were originally considered distinctive.
4 Altering the classification of codes or themes, so that some are promoted to a higher level in the coding template, while others may be demoted.
5 Changing the scope of a code or theme. Inserted, deleted, merged and altered codes or themes may have implications for others in the coding template. This may result in the need to move a code or theme within the coding template, change its purpose or split it into two or more new codes or themes.

Box 13.10 shows how the themes and codes in the initial coding template in Box 13.9 were altered as the process of data collection and analysis progressed. Several have been deleted and new ones inserted that better reflect the terms used by participants. Some initial themes or codes have been merged. For example, the original, second-level theme, 'Reasons for campaign' has been merged with the first-level theme, 'Contextual factors' to form a new first-level theme, 'Perceiving the need for the campaign'. The original second-level themes, 'Media' and 'Coverage' have both been reclassified to become first-level themes. As a result of this reclassification, the scope of these themes has been enlarged and new subsidiary themes created to encompass this.

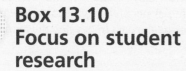

Box 13.10
Focus on student research

Part of a final template to analyse an advertising campaign's impact

As Joss continued to collect data she used her coding template to conduct analysis. The coding template was revised as these data were analysed. An extract of her final template follows:

1 PERCEIVING THE NEED FOR THE CAMPAIGN
   1.1 Market changes
      1.1.1 *Globalisation*
      1.1.2 *Competition*

      1.1.3 *Segmentation*
      1.1.4 *Technological convergence*
      1.1.5 *Compliance*
   1.2 Product promotion
      1.2.1 *Product awareness*
      1.2.2 *Product differentiation*
      1.2.3 *Product upgrades*
2 EVALUATING MEDIA
   2.1 Social media
   2.2 Television
   2.3 Radio
   2.4 Printed media
3 EXPLORING COVERAGE
   3.1 National
   3.2 Regional/Local
   3.3 Market segments

The template is likely to be revised until all data have been coded and possibly beyond. The final template should represent all units of data that are relevant to your research question so that no further changes are required to achieve this. To check this you should work through all of your codes to ensure that they are appropriately represented through the final template. Once this is achieved all of your data can then be applied to the template. This provides a basis for further analysis and interpretation, allowing the nature of the themes within the template to be fully explored and the relationships between them to be tested in the same way as we described for Thematic Analysis in Section 13.6. This will, for example, allow the relative importance of themes to be explored, the different roles that themes play in the overall structure to be recognised (for example some may contextualise others), the similarity or diversity of participant perspectives in particular themes to be evaluated, and whether predicted or expected relationships exist or are contradicted. The creation of the final form of a template is therefore not the end of the analytical and interpretive process but a means to explore this further to verify explanations and develop theory.

Evaluation

Like Thematic Analysis, Template Analysis offers a systematic, flexible and accessible approach to analyse qualitative data. It adopts a higher level of structure earlier on than Thematic Analysis through the development of an initial coding template. This may be preferred by some who like the idea of developing a very structured approach to analysing their data early on. Others may prefer to code all of their data first before playing around with analytical structures. Using a template may also help you to select a priori themes to explore and to identify emergent issues that arise through the process of data collection and analysis that you may not have intended to focus on as you commenced your research project (King and Brookes 2017).

The flexibility of developing a coding template early on and then revising this in relation to each subsequent data item or number of items allows a researcher to undertake the stages of analysis (e.g. coding, devising and linking themes, exploring relationships, sense-making) in a more holistic way. However, some researchers may feel constrained by using a template while working though transcripts and may become too focused on applying the template to the data rather than using the data to develop the template (King and Brookes 2017).

13.8 Explanation Building and Testing

In this section we outline three techniques where the nature of reaching an explanation and theorising may be differentiated from both Thematic Analysis and Template Analysis. In these three techniques the emphasis is on building (or predicting) and testing an explanation. These techniques are Analytic Induction, Deductive Explanation Building and Pattern Matching. We discuss each of these in turn.

Analytic Induction

Introduction

Analytic Induction is an inductive version of Explanation Building. A key characteristic of this technique is that it uses an incremental approach to build and test an explanation or theory. **Analytic Induction** seeks to develop and test an explanation by intensively examining the phenomenon being explored through the successive selection of purposive cases. This means that the process of collecting and analysing data will be composed of a number of repeated steps to find a valid explanation of the phenomenon being studied. Johnson (2004: 165) defines Analytic Induction as 'the intensive examination of a strategically selected number of cases so as to empirically establish the causes of a specific phenomenon'.

Analytic Induction emphasises a cycle of developing and testing propositions that are inductively grounded in participants' data rather than deductively testing existing theory, although Bansal and Roth (2000) state that this method may use such theory in conjunction with grounded data to formulate the propositions that guide each step to help to find a valid explanation. Its analytical procedures are not highly developed or formalised. As a result, where you use Analytic Induction, you may also find the generic procedures outlined for Thematic Analysis in Section 13.6 helpful to guide your analysis within each case you examine.

Procedure

Data will need to be collected from an initial purposive case study, usually by conducting exploratory interviews or observations. These data should be analysed to devise codes and themes, and to recognise relationships between them to develop an initial definition of a proposition that seeks to explain the phenomenon being studied. This initial proposition is then tested through the purposive selection of a second, related case study (Section 7.3), involving further exploratory interviews or observations.

Given the loosely defined nature of this initial proposition, it is likely that it will either need to be redefined or that the scope of the phenomenon to be explained will need to be narrowed. Redefining the proposition leads to a third iteration or step in the Analytic Induction process, involving the purposive selection of a third case study to explore the phenomenon and test this redefined proposition. If at this stage your redefined proposition appears to explain the phenomenon, you may either cease data collection on the basis that you believe you have found a valid explanation or seek to test the explanation in other purposively selected cases to see whether it is still valid.

You are likely to encounter one or more cases where your proposition is not adequate to explain the phenomenon you are studying. These are referred to as negative or deviant cases. When you encounter a negative case you will need to redefine the proposition you are testing and to test this in the context of another purposively selected case. This process may continue until a redefined proposition is generated that reasonably explains the phenomenon in relevant cases where you have collected and analysed data. In practice, several redefinitions of the proposition may be necessary to develop a valid explanation of the phenomenon being studied.

Evaluation

As an inductive and incremental way of collecting and analysing data qualitatively this technique has the capability to lead to the development of well-grounded explanations. Analytic Induction encourages the collection of data that are thorough and rich by exploring the actions and meanings of those who participate in this process, through in-depth interviews or observation, or some combination of these methods.

However, like each of the techniques in this section, it should not be thought of as a quick or easy approach to conducting qualitative analysis. While it may lead to a well-grounded and unassailable explanation, where all negative cases are either accounted for by the final revised explanation or excluded by redefining the phenomenon being studied, this outcome is only likely to occur as the result of using this technique in a thorough and rigorous way. This will involve a search for cases that are related to the phenomenon being studied, the in-depth collection of data within each case and the rigorous analysis of these data to devise a final revised proposition that explains the phenomenon being studied throughout these cases.

Analytic Induction may be criticised because of issues about its limited representativeness and generalisability. Because the final explanation of the research phenomenon will be completely grounded in the cases that give rise to it, this explanation may be without the ability to predict what may be found in other cases, even those containing the same characteristics or conditions. This is similar to criticism which is often made about other inductive research.

Two points may be made in response to such criticism. First, this type of criticism misses the point of inductive research, which is to find explanations that are well grounded in the context being researched. These explanations will exhibit high levels of reliability and internal validity. Others may subsequently seek to test these explanations in other settings. Secondly, such criticism may also be made in relation to much survey research. While survey research will be representative of a wider population, the nature of that population may be restricted to a particular case or number of cases.

In relation to Analytic Induction, you will need to select your sample of cases with care to be able to demonstrate how they relate to the phenomenon you are studying. Selecting diverse cases related to the phenomenon being studied may also help to overcome issues related to theoretical generalisability. For example, if you were seeking to explain how small enterprises respond to regulatory change you could select a sample of cases (organisations) from different business sectors and in relation to a range of regulatory changes, where feasible.

Deductive Explanation Building

Introduction

This version of Explanation Building uses a deductive approach (Yin 2018). It involves an incremental attempt to build an explanation by testing and refining a predetermined theoretical proposition. As with Analytic Induction, the process of collecting and analysing data to understand the research topic or phenomenon will be composed of a number of repeated steps to find a valid explanation.

Procedure

This explanation-building procedure follows these steps (Yin 2018):

1 Devise a theoretically based proposition, which you will then seek to test.
2 Undertake data collection through an initial, purposive case study in order to be able to compare the findings from this in relation to your theoretically based proposition.
3 Where necessary, amend the theoretically based proposition in the light of the findings from the initial case study.
4 Select a further, purposive case study to undertake a further round of data collection in order to compare the findings from this in relation to the revised proposition.
5 Where necessary, further amend the revised proposition in the light of the findings from the second case study.
6 Undertake further iterations of this process until a satisfactory explanation is derived.

Evaluation

This technique and the one discussed next, Pattern Matching, use a deductive approach involving the testing of a theoretical proposition or prediction. Where you are able to utilise existing theory to produce such a proposition or prediction (as in Pattern Matching) this may make the process of explaining the phenomenon being studied less onerous than using Analytic Induction, although use of these techniques may be just as demanding. Given the commonality of using a deductive approach in both of these techniques, we evaluate them together after outlining Pattern Matching.

Pattern Matching

Introduction

Pattern Matching involves predicting a pattern of outcomes based on theoretical propositions to explain what you expect to find from analysing your data (Yin 2018). Using this approach, you will need to develop a conceptual or analytical framework, utilising existing theory, and then test the adequacy of the framework deductively as a means to explain your findings. If the pattern of your data matches that which has been predicted through the conceptual framework you will have found an explanation, where possible threats to the validity of your conclusions can be discounted. We discuss examples related to two uses of this procedure that depend on whether you are matching patterns for the dependent or for the independent variables.

Procedure

The first use is matching patterns for dependent variables arising from another, independent variable. For example, based on theoretical propositions drawn from appropriate literature you specify a number of related outcomes (dependent variables) that you expect to find as a result of the implementation of a particular change management programme (independent variable) in an organisation where you intend to undertake research. Having specified these expected outcomes, you then engage in the process of data collection and analysis. Where your predicted outcomes are found, it is likely that your theoretically based explanation is appropriate to explain your findings. If, however, you reveal one or more outcomes that have not been predicted by your explanation, you will need to seek an alternative one (Yin 2018).

The second use is matching patterns for variables that are independent of each other. In this case you would identify two or more alternative explanations to explain the pattern of outcomes that you expect to find (Box 13.11). As a consequence, only one of these predicted explanations may be valid. If one explanation is found to explain your findings then the others may be discarded. Where you find a match between one of these predicted explanations and the data you have collected and analysed, you will have evidence to suggest that this is indeed an explanation for your findings. Further evidence that this is a correct explanation will flow from finding the same pattern of outcomes in other similar cases (Yin 2018).

Evaluation

Pattern Matching and Deductive Explanation Building both involve a defined and systematic procedure, linked to the need to specify theoretical propositions before the commencement of data collection and analysis. Even though the initial theoretical proposition in Explanation Building may need to be revised during the conduct of research, this procedure is shaped by the use of prior theory.

The use of prior theory in either procedure should enable you to develop a well-defined research question and set of objectives. It will also enable you to start with a clear framework to guide your research linked to the need to test a theoretical proposition or propositions. With regard to sampling (Section 7.3), you should be able to identify the type and number of cases to which you need access to test this proposition or these propositions. The use of prior theory should also help to shape the questions you ask during research interviews.

Use of prior theory will also help to determine an initial set of codes for analysis. Inevitably these codes will be subject to change (insertions, deletions and merging) depending on their appropriateness for the data that your participants provide. As you collect data and analyse these by attaching units of data to codes, and examine them for emergent

---

Box 13.11
Focus on student research

Alternative predicted explanations

The objective of Linzi's research project was to explain why productivity had increased in a case study organisation even though a number of factors had been held constant (technology, numbers of staff employed, pay rates and bonuses, and the order book) during the period of the increase in productivity. She developed two alternative explanations based on different theoretical propositions to explain why this increase in productivity had occurred in the organisation. Her explanations were related to the following propositions:

1 The productivity increase is due to better management, which has been able to generate greater employee engagement, where this proposition is based on theory related to strategic human resource management.

2 The productivity increase is due to fears about change and uncertainty in the future, where this proposition is based on theory related to organisational behaviour and the management of change.

These propositions offered her two possible and exclusive reasons why the described phenomenon had occurred, so that where evidence could be found to support one of these, the other, which did not match her outcomes, could be discounted.

patterns, your analysis will be guided by the theoretical propositions and explanations with which you commenced. Your propositions will still need to be tested with rigour – associated with the thoroughness with which you carry out this analytical process and by seeking negative examples and alternative explanations that do not conform to the pattern or association being tested for. The process of analysis you use will follow that outlined for Thematic Analysis in Section 13.6

The use of predicted explanations should mean that the pathway to an answer to your research question and objectives is reasonably defined. The extent to which this is the case will depend on two factors:

- your level of thoroughness in using existing theory to define clearly the theoretical propositions and conceptual framework that will guide your research project;
- the appropriateness of these theoretical propositions and the conceptual framework for the data that you reveal.

13.9 Grounded Theory Method

Introduction

Grounded Theory Method is part of a wider methodological approach. We discussed Grounded Theory in Section 5.8, recognising this as an emergent and systematic research strategy. It avoids using a priori codes derived from existing theory and commences inductively, by developing codes from the data collected (Section 13.6). Data collection and analysis are interrelated, with the concepts emerging from previously collected and analysed data being used to direct future data collection. Grounded Theory is seen as systematic, or even prescriptive, because it sets out a number of research practices that should be followed. Its use in practice is criticised when researchers only implement some of these elements, not all (Box 5.9).

We discuss the elements of Grounded Theory as a research strategy in Section 5.8. These include the early commencement of data collection, concurrent collection and analysis of data, development of codes from the data, and the use of constant comparison, self-memos, theoretical sampling, theoretical saturation and theoretical sensitivity, leading to the development of a theory that is grounded in the data. We suggest re-reading about these elements of Grounded Theory in Section 5.8 before reading further in this section.

In this section we focus on the analytical techniques used in Grounded Theory Method. A number of connected analytical techniques are defined in Grounded Theory Method but an issue arises in that the exact nature of these varies between sources that outline them (e.g. Bryant and Charmaz 2007; Charmaz 2014; Corbin and Strauss 2015; Glaser and Strauss 1967) and even between editions of the same book (Corbin and Strauss 2008, 2015; Strauss and Corbin 1998). While all subscribe to strategic research practices including concurrent collection and analysis of data, use of inductive codes, constant comparison and theoretical sampling, some versions are more structured and precisely defined (e.g. Strauss and Corbin 1998) while others are more flexible (Charmaz 2014). In the Grounded Theory Method of Strauss and Corbin (1998) the disaggregation of data into units is called open coding, the process of recognising relationships between categories is referred to as axial coding, and the integration of categories around a core category to develop a grounded theory is labelled selective coding. In the subsequent edition, open coding and axial coding have been merged and selective coding has been relabelled as integration (Corbin and

Strauss 2008). Alternatively, the more flexible approach to Grounded Theory Method of Charmaz (2014) consists of two major phases of coding: initial coding and focused coding, while she also discusses and evaluates axial coding (Strauss and Corbin 1998) and the theoretical coding approach developed by Glaser (1978, 1998).

However, rather being confused by these variations in technique, we need to step back and recognise that in its essential purpose this should not be a complicated process. Sometimes it is made to appear complicated because certain versions have elaborated elements of this method. Corbin in Corbin and Strauss (2015) succinctly summarises the process of analysing grounded data. She emphasises the central role of constant comparison which involves comparing units of data with other data to see whether these are similar or different. Similar data are given the same code in order to group these together. Similar codes are subsequently grouped together as themes, although in Grounded Theory these are often called categories. The properties or dimensions of each category are then developed as further data are collected and analysed. The categories which withstand analytical development are eventually integrated around a single category referred to as the core category. Choice of this core category will depend on your research question. This core category and its relationships to these other categories are used to develop a grounded theory.

As an introduction to the analytical techniques associated with using Grounded Theory Method, we focus on those of Strauss and Corbin (1998) and Charmaz (2014) (Figure 13.2). Where you decide to use a Grounded Theory strategy (Section 5.8) you may find it useful to consult not only these two books but also the others to which we have referred. However, the key to the success of using Grounded Theory Method is choosing one approach to this method with which you are comfortable, undertaking this without too much adaptation, and to develop your appreciation of and skills in using this method (Kenealy 2012). We would advise you to discuss this choice with your project tutor.

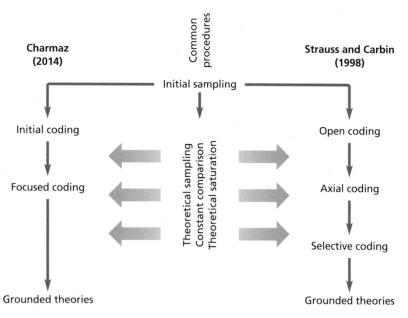

Figure 13.2 Alternative approaches to Grounded Theory Method
Source: © Mark Saunders, Philip Lewis and Adrian Thornhill 2018

Procedure

Because we outlined the elements of Grounded Theory in Section 5.8, we concentrate here on discussing the techniques used to analyse data through different levels of coding. It is important, however, to recognise that all of these elements are used in combination throughout a Grounded Theory study. Theoretical sampling (Section 7.3) is used to choose pertinent cases at each phase of data collection and analysis. An initial sample will be chosen that relates to your research question or topic. Each further case will be selected to explore analytical ideas and categories emerging from coding data in the previous case or cases. The purpose of this will be to further the development of your codes and analytical categories to be able to explore relationships between these to develop a grounded theory. Underpinning this is the process of constantly comparing the data being collected with the codes and categories being used, so as to aid the process of developing an emerging theory that will be thoroughly grounded in these data. Memo writing throughout your Grounded Theory study allows you to sum up, clarify and develop ideas that relate to the codes you develop, the categories you derive, the relationships between these, the emergence of theory and other aspects related to the conduct of your study. Theoretical sampling continues until theoretical saturation is reached. This will occur when data collection ceases to reveal new data that are relevant to a category, where the properties or dimensions of categories have become well developed and understood, and relationships between categories have been verified (Figure 13.2).

Having recognised the interrelated nature of the procedures of Grounded Theory Method we discuss coding and differences in approaches to this.

Initial coding or open coding

Initial coding or **open coding** is similar to the coding procedure outlined in Section 13.6. The data that you collect will be disaggregated into conceptual units and coded with a label. The same code will be given to similar units of data. However, because this research process commences without an explicit basis in existing theory, the result may be the creation of a multitude of conceptual codes related to the lower level of focus and structure with which you commence your research (Box 13.12). The emphasis in Grounded Theory Method is to derive meanings from the actions, interactions, subjects and settings being studied. In this way you will use in vivo codes (Section 13.6) to code your data. Charmaz (2014) also advocates **coding with gerunds** rather than coding for themes, in order to be able to stay close to the meanings in your data and to understand these through the actions

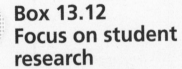

Box 13.12
Focus on student research

Using open coding

Jemma's research was concerned with Small and Medium sized Enterprises (SMEs) and their use of social media. She was particularly interested in how they used social media to communicate with potential clients and customers. At the start of her research she undertook a series of two focus groups with owner managers of SMEs. The audio-recordings of each focus group were subsequently transcribed in Microsoft Word and saved as a docx file. Within the file, Jemma labelled herself, the focus group moderator, as 'FGM'; the male participants as 'M1', 'M2' and so on; and the female participants as 'F1', 'F2' and so on. Each file was then imported into the CAQDAS software NVivo™. Open codes relating to different communication media such 'LinkedIn', 'Facebook', 'Twitter', 'Email', 'Letter' and 'Company website' were attached to the transcript, each participant's response being a separate unit of data. Codes were also attached regarding whether the participant felt the social media was 'Useful' or 'Not useful' and the frequency with which it was used.

Based upon analysis using these and other codes Jemma noticed that these SMEs were using social media sites such as LinkedIn widely and frequently to showcase their businesses and to build relationships with customers. However, she noted that clear links between the use of LinkedIn and increased revenues were difficult to establish. Facebook was used less widely in a business context than LinkedIn, being seen predominantly for personal friendships. Twitter was found to be most effective when used in conjunction with other social media such as the business' website. Jemma decided to follow up her initial findings using in-depth interviews.

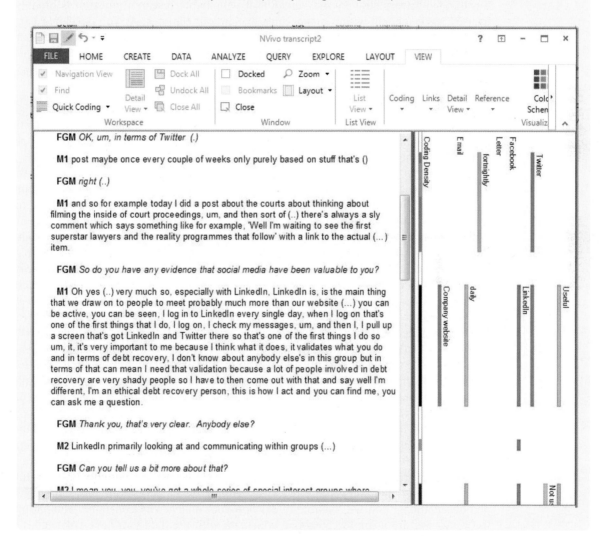

or interactions that take place in the data. A gerund is a word that ends in '-ing' which is made from a verb but used like a noun. In Box 13.5, this would result in different codes being used. In place of the thematic codes used there, codes such as, 'speaking to a HR professional', 'asking to be made redundant', 'making a choice' and 'avoiding compulsion' could have been used to reflect the actions or interactions that occurred.

In Section 13.6 we stated that a unit of data might relate to a few words, a line, a sentence or number of sentences, or a paragraph. The need to understand meanings and to generate codes to encompass these in Grounded Theory Method is likely to lead you to conduct your early analysis by looking at smaller rather than larger units of data. The resulting multitude of code labels will therefore need to be compared and placed into broader, related groupings or categories. This will allow you to produce a more manageable and focused research project and to develop the analytical process. This is discussed in focused coding and axial coding.

Coding your data should lead you to identify analytical concepts and categories and help you to consider where data collection should be focused in the future (theoretical sampling). It may also help you to develop the focus of your research question. Using a Grounded Theory strategy may mean that your initial research question is broadly focused, although still within manageable exploratory confines. As you develop a narrower focus through this process, you will be able to refine and limit the scope of your research question.

Focused coding

In Charmaz's (2014) approach, **focused coding** involves deciding which of your initial codes to use to develop the analytic and explanatory focus of your coded data. This results in a smaller number of codes being attached to larger units of data and may be seen as serving the same purpose as searching for themes in Thematic Analysis (Section 13.6). Data from various initial codes are re-coded to a smaller number of more focused codes. During initial coding some of the codes you develop may appear to have greater analytic potential, to help you to explain your data and to develop a grounded theory related to your research question. Selecting these codes will lead you to work through all of your coded data again to see if they are suitable to begin to develop a more explanatory focus. Charmaz suggests that codes with the capability to become focused codes, and to able to categorise larger units of your data, are likely to be those that proved to be the most important or frequently used during initial coding. It is worth noting that codes which are frequently used during initial coding may not necessarily prove to have the greatest analytical potential, just as codes that become important may not have initially attracted large amounts of data.

Charmaz (2014) believes that progressing from initial coding to focused coding is unlikely to be a simple, linear process. Working out and working through which initial codes may be the best ones to use as focused codes may lead you to re-code your data and develop a new set of codes. If this occurs, do not despair: it will take time but it will allow you to get closer to and understand your data through the development of greater insight. Such reflection and re-working may occur irrespective of which qualitative analytic technique you choose. As you gain insights about what your data mean, you should use these insights to evaluate which codes will have the analytical capability to become focused codes to progress your analysis. These conceptually more useful focused codes should allow you to code and compare data across different interviews and observations. You will be able to develop your analysis by constantly comparing the codes you are using to categorise your data with the data you have collected, to gain further insights and work towards an emergent explanation of what your data mean to you.

Charmaz's (2014) approach to Grounded Theory Method may be seen as being less prescriptive than other approaches. She adopts a constructivist approach, which assumes that people construct their social realities, with both the participants' and the researcher's interpretations being socially constructed. Charmaz emphasises a Grounded Theory

Method that is interactive, flexible and less prescriptive. Analysis develops from constantly comparing data to codes and codes to data, codes with other codes, and data with other data to develop higher levels of abstraction rather than necessarily using axial coding or selective coding (discussed later). Analysis is shaped by the researcher's interaction with and interpretation of these constant comparisons. As a result, this approach to Grounded Theory Method does not follow the more tightly defined prescriptive procedures of other approaches.

Axial coding is a way of rearranging the data that were fragmented during open or initial coding into a new whole, based on a hierarchical structure. In some Grounded Theory Method prescriptions, this may involve identifying structural elements such as the situation involved, the issue at the centre of this situation, the interactions that took place and the outcomes or consequences of these actions to develop a hierarchical structure. Charmaz (2014) believes that this approach may be appropriate where you wish to use a prescribed analytical framework to develop your analysis. But she believes that some will find it to be too prescriptive and will prefer to use a simpler, more flexible approach. For these, axial coding as specified by Strauss and Corbin (1998) will not be useful. Rather the use of initial coding and focused coding, combined with the use of theoretical sampling, constant comparison and theoretical saturation, will provide a more suitable and flexible approach (Figure 13.2).

Axial coding

Axial coding refers to the process of looking for relationships between the categories of data that have emerged from open coding. It indicates a process of theoretical development. As relationships between categories are recognised, they are rearranged into a hierarchical form, with the emergence of subcategories. The essence of this approach is to explore and explain a phenomenon (a subject of your research) by identifying what is happening and why, the environmental factors that affect this (such as economic, technological, political, legal, social and cultural), how it is being managed within the context being examined, and the outcomes of action that has been taken. Clearly, there will be a relationship between these aspects, or categories, and the purpose of your analysis will be to explain this.

Once these relationships have been recognised, you will then seek to verify them against actual data that you have collected. Strauss and Corbin (1998) recommend that you undertake this by formulating questions or statements, which can then be phrased as hypotheses, to test these apparent relationships. As you undertake this process you will be testing these hypotheses by looking for both supporting evidence and negative cases that demonstrate variations from these relationships.

Selective coding

Strauss and Corbin (1998) suggest that after a lengthy period of data collection, which may take several months, you will have developed a number of principal categories and related subcategories. The stage that follows is called **selective coding**. This is intended to identify one of these principal categories, which becomes known as the central or core category, in order to relate the other categories to this with the intention of integrating the research and developing a grounded theory (Corbin and Strauss 2015; Strauss and Corbin 1998). In the previous stage the emphasis was placed on recognising the relationships between categories and their subcategories. In this stage the emphasis is placed on recognising and developing the relationships between the principal categories that have emerged from this grounded approach in order to develop an explanatory theory.

Evaluation

A number of implications have emerged from this brief outline of the main procedures involved in the use of grounded theory. These may be summed up by saying that the use of Grounded Theory Method will involve you in processes that will be time-consuming, intensive and reflective.

Before you commit yourself to this method, you will need to consider the time that you have to conduct your research, the level of competence you will need, your access to data, and the logistical implications of immersing yourself in such an intensive approach to research. There may also be a concern that little of significance will emerge at the end of the research process, and this will be an important aspect for you to consider when determining the focus of your research if you use Grounded Theory Method.

Grounded Theory Method has the scope to provide you with a systematic analytical technique where you wish to use an emergent research approach that is part of a wider methodological strategy which you can follow to guide your research project from its inception, through the processes of data collection and analysis, to completion. The theory that you develop from using this approach should have the capacity to be well grounded in the meanings expressed by your participants and the context of the research setting. The successful application of this approach is likely to be related to making sure that you understand one or other of the published versions of Grounded Theory Method and your willingness to commit yourself to following its procedures.

13.10 Narrative Analysis

Introduction

We discussed Narrative Inquiry as a research strategy in Section 5.8. Our discussion here focuses on the different ways in which narrative data may be analysed. Narrative Analysis is not a specific analytical technique, such as Thematic Analysis or Template Analysis (discussed earlier). Nor is Narrative Analysis part of a wider methodological approach, as with Grounded Theory Method. Instead **Narrative Analysis** is a collection of analytical approaches to analyse different aspects of narrative. These may be combined in practice, depending on your research question and purpose, and the nature of your data.

What these analytical approaches have in common is the preservation of the data's narrative form. Unlike Thematic Analysis, Template Analysis or Grounded Theory Method, where original data are fragmented by coding and then assigned to analytical categories, narrative data are preserved and analysed as a whole unit or narrative sequence. Categories, themes and facets of content may still be identified and coded but this occurs from within a narrative. In Narrative Analysis it is important to preserve data within their narrated context to maintain the sequential and structural elements of each case.

While a narrative tends to be analysed as a whole, the nature of what constitutes a narrative varies considerably. Textual narratives may vary from a segment of text or speech to a whole life story provided by a narrator. Within this range of possibilities, analysis may focus on extracts from interview transcripts, which each provide a short narrative about a related topic or incident in which the researcher is interested. These extracts will tend to be short stories that have a clear purpose, encompassing a situation, an action and an outcome, expressed in a structure containing a beginning, middle and end. Analysis may also focus on passages of speech or dialogue, where the purpose is to analyse how the narrative is constructed. In terms of extended narratives, analysis may focus on narrated accounts of life stories or organisational events, where emphasis is likely to be placed on sequential and structural elements. Analysis may also involve a researcher constructing a narrative from fragments of data collected from multiple sources, such as different documents or research interviews. A narrative may also be constructed from other narratives to provide a unified account to further analysis, sometimes referred to as re-storying.

Narrative Analysis may use a deductive or inductive research approach. In thematic narrative analysis, prior theory can be used to develop codes and categories to help to analyse each narrative. Codes and categories may also be allowed to emerge inductively from each narrative. As in some other qualitative approaches, analysis of narratives may combine the use of deductive and inductive approaches.

Because Narrative Analysis is a collection of analytical approaches, with variations evident in each approach in terms of the way they have been used in practice by researchers, it is not sensible to describe a procedural outline as we have done in earlier sections. Instead, we briefly outline two approaches used in Narrative Analysis. These are Thematic Narrative Analysis and Structural Narrative Analysis (Maitlis 2012; Riessman, 2008).

Outline

Thematic Narrative Analysis

The purpose of **Thematic Narrative Analysis** is to identify analytical themes within narratives. This approach to Narrative Analysis focuses on the content of a narrative, rather than on the way in which it is structured. In this approach the emphasis is therefore on 'what' the narrative is about rather than 'how' it is constructed.

Thematic Narrative Analysis can be used to analyse an individual narrative or multiple, related narratives. In either approach, you will need to pay attention to the chronological sequence and contextual background of the themes you identify. Understanding sequence and context is important to be able to develop a rich and full explanation when analysing an individual narrative. Analysis of multiple narratives can commence by analysing each narrative separately or by working across all of the narratives at the same time, as we go on to describe. Multiple narratives will be related by a common focus, such as an organisational event, with each narrative provided by a different person involved in this. In analysing multiple narratives separately, the initial emphasis will be on the in-depth analysis of each narrative before then comparing and contrasting findings across them. The reason why you may wish to analyse multiple narratives individually will be to illustrate how variations in context affect the actions taken and outcomes recorded, or; to illustrate how differences in the actions taken and outcomes recorded may vary in spite of contextual similarities and to explain why (Box 13.13).

Analysis of multiple narratives can also commence by searching for themes across these narratives, rather than concentrating on the in-depth analysis of each narrative in turn in the dataset. This difference in emphasis may be more suitable where you commence your research approach deductively with a predetermined theoretical framework of analytical categories or themes for which to search. In this approach, you will be able to identify whether and which themes occur across the narratives in the dataset or parts of it, where variations occur and how contextual factors affect these. This should help you to develop an explanation that evaluates the application of prior theory to your data as well as being grounded in these data, while preserving the integrity of your narratives (Box 13.13).

Analysing narratives to identify themes while keeping each narrative intact can be achieved by adapting the method of coding we discussed earlier in this chapter. One adaptation you might use is to colour-code analytical themes in each narrative. By using a particular colour-code for a theme, you will be able to identify its occurrence across

Box 13.13
Focus on management research

Using narrative analysis to understand spousal support in relation to careers

In an article published in *Gender, Work and Organization*, Heikkinen and Lämsä (2017: 171) analysed, "the narratives of men managers to see how they perceive their wives' support in relation to their careers." One aim of this research was to understand types of spousal support and how this altered during men's careers. This research was partly conducted in response to previous studies which suggest that spousal support is often stable. Data were collected through 29 semi-structured, narrative style interviews with men who were mainly married, fathers and who

in their working lives were in the mid to late stage of their careers holding managerial posts.

Narrative analysis of this research produced three narrative groups, labelled as, 'negotiated spousal support', 'enriching spousal support' and 'declining spousal support'. In 'negotiated spousal support', negotiation of gender roles and mutual adjustments are important, allowing both the man and the woman to participate in external work and family responsibilities. In 'enriching spousal support', a traditional set of gender roles is prevalent and unchallenged; thus the 'enriching' is for the benefit of family and the man without the scope for the woman to develop a career. In 'declining spousal support', gender roles regress, shifting from more equal to more traditional, with the consequence that the man feels the woman is focusing more on their children and the household, less on supporting him while leaving him to fulfil economic expectations, hence the sense of 'declining support.' These three groups of narratives arising from this analysis challenge previous studies and point to the value of research using a narrative approach.

different narratives, without fragmenting these data. This simple procedure will allow you to compare different narrative accounts more easily as you read and re-read each one. A further adaptation that you may find useful in order to keep your narratives intact is to make several copies of each set of narratives and to code a particular theme on one set of copies. A further tactic you may use is to read each narrative transcript several times to become familiar with its content to aid your analysis.

Structural Narrative Analysis

Structural Narrative Analysis analyses the way in which a narrative is constructed. This approach to Narrative Analysis examines use of language to understand how it affects a listener or an audience. In this approach the emphasis is therefore on 'how' the narrative is constructed and language is used rather than 'what' it is about.

While Thematic Narrative Analysis is likely to be easier to use and therefore to be used more often, the use of Structural Narrative Analysis is capable of adding a further level of insight when conducting Narrative Analysis. To use this approach you will need to develop some understanding of the socio-linguistic and cognitive theories that underpin it (see the discussion in Riessman 2008). These have led to methods to analyse the structures of spoken narratives. A key method to analyse the way narrative accounts are sequenced and structured is the technique developed by Labov and Waletzky (1967) and Labov (1972), which remains a standard approach today. In this approach a researcher analyses a narrative to look for the presence of six elements and the way these have been used. These are:

- an abstract (which states the point of the story);
- an orientation (which describes the situation including when and where it took place and who was involved);

- a complicating action (which describes the sequence of events including a critical point);
- an evaluation (where the narrator explains the meaning of the narrative);
- a resolution (how the issue is solved – the outcome); and
- a coda (which ends the narrative and relates it to the present).

This analytical structure provides a framework to evaluate narratives, since not every element may be present in a narrative and the nature and sequencing of these elements are likely to vary. It is, however, worth noting that the purpose of much of the research undertaken using this and other approaches to analyse the structure of narratives is not so much to form judgemental evaluations but to understand how people in different groups form narratives. This has been undertaken to fulfil different aims: sometimes to understand how acts of speech may lead to certain actions or to falsely negative perceptions; sometimes to change professional practice.

Where you record interactions between individuals, you may consider using Structural Narrative Analysis. Potentially this encompasses a wide range of interactions; for example, between managers and other employees; across occupational groups; up and down organisational levels; across cultural and transnational boundaries, to understand the relationship between the construction of a narrative and its effect on the attitudes and subsequent actions of those who receive it. More generally, Structural Narrative Analysis may be suitable for you to analyse the narratives you collect through conducting interviews or recording naturally occurring conversations.

Evaluation

We noted that collecting data through narratives may be advantageous in certain circumstances (Section 5.8). These include research contexts where the experiences of your participants can best be understood by collecting and analysing these as complete stories or narrative sequences. The ways in which events in a narrative are linked, the actions that follow and their implications are more likely to be revealed by encouraging a participant to narrate her or his experiences than asking them to respond to a series of pre-formed questions. Narrative Analysis allows chronological connections and the sequencing of events as told by the narrator to be preserved, with the potential to enrich understanding and aid analysis.

13.11 Discourse Analysis

Introduction

'Discourse Analysis' is a term covering a variety of approaches that analyse the social effects of the use of language. In general terms 'discourse' refers to the spoken or written use of language, often referred to as talk or text. In Discourse Analysis, the emphasis is not on studying the way in which language is used for its own sake. Use of language is a key way in which people make sense of their social world. In this more specific sense, 'discourse' describes how language is used to shape this meaning-making process, to construct social reality. A **discourse** is therefore not just seen as neutrally reflecting social practice or relations but as constructing these (although the notion of 'constructing' is contentious and we return to it later). In this way, **Discourse Analysis** explores how discourses construct or constitute social reality and social relations through creating meanings and perceptions.

This conceptualisation allows the complexity and diversity of social practice and relations to be recognised through the existence of different, often competing and sometimes conflicting discourses. For example, different discourses construct perceptions about organisations and organisational relations. It also follows that language (discourse) can be used intentionally to attempt to create ideologically mounted positions, intended to be in the interests of those who produce and disseminate them. A unitarist view would emphasise the commonality of interest within an organisation (or society) and use some means (focusing on discourse) to persuade its members of this approach. By contrast, a pluralist view would see an organisation (or society) as a collection of competing interests. Even within the pluralist view, some discourses may be seen to dominate while others are marginalised.

Discourse Analysis involves studying textual sources or passages of naturally occurring talk. Textual sources may be organisational documents such as those outlined in the discussion of documentary research in Section 5.8. Discourse Analysis will often involve using multiple texts that are interrelated to understand the nature and development of a discourse. Phillips and Hardy (2002) point out that the (diffuse, interactional and often taken-for-granted) nature of a discourse means that although it cannot be explored comprehensively, by using a range of interrelated sources it should be possible to gain access to aspects of its formation, propagation and acceptance.

Transcripts of recordings of naturally occurring talk can also be used to explore a discourse. Such data may be collected through conducting and recording observation in an ethnographic study, or one incorporating ethnography (Section 5.8). As discourse occurs through naturally occurring talk, it is preferred to contrived talk through interviewing (Section 10.3) where the intervention of the researcher in asking questions, eliciting responses and analysing the data is likely to affect the authenticity of the discourse being analysed (Hepburn and Potter 2007). There may of course be a use for interview data in a subsequent, supplementary capacity.

To be able to explore the relationship between discourse and social reality also means placing emphasis on contextual and social theoretical aspects. The way in which a discourse emerges and constructs social reality through influencing social relations and practices is likely to be rooted in a particular period or event, such as the foundation of an organisation or an organisational change. Discourse Analysis may therefore require an understanding of historical context to be able to understand the ways in which discourse develops and constructs social practices. Using a range of texts may help to reveal this historical contextual development. Some approaches to Discourse Analysis also draw on existing theoretical perspectives to explore the nature of a discourse and to contextualise its impact on social practice and relations. We consider this further in the following sub-section.

Outline

Discourse Analysis encompasses a range of approaches and unlike some of the techniques we discussed earlier does not specify a particular set of procedures to conduct analysis. For this reason we briefly outline some of the approaches used in Discourse Analysis in this sub-section. Approaches to Discourse Analysis can be differentiated according to their focus and philosophical assumptions. The focus of Discourse Analysis ranges from 'finely-grained' analysis of text or talk to grand theoretical abstractions about the nature of social practice.

A finely grained approach focuses on the analysis (deconstruction) of an individual text, or of a transcript of 'talk' that occurred during a social interaction located within a particular situation. The purpose of this type of close reading of a text (or passage of talk) is to understand how the use of language indicates meaning and to categorise the nature of this discourse. Hyatt (2005, 2013) provides advice about conducting this type of analysis. His 'Critical Literacy Analysis' (2005) and 'Critical Policy Discourse Analysis' (2013) include a range of criteria for analysing text. Although these analyses are devised within the context of education, the generic analytical criteria they include are transferable or translatable to other contexts. If you are considering using Discourse Analysis you may find it useful to consult these articles.

Further (and complementary) approaches include interdiscursive and intertextual analyses. **Interdiscursivity** refers to the relation of one discourse to another, including the way one discourse may influence another discourse. For example, discourses and practices associated with the private sector have been introduced into the public sector in some societies to justify change. Box 13.14 provides an example of this in the context of the operation of the UK's passenger rail services, where discourse about private sector attributes informed discourse about operating a public rail service, with some unintended consequences. **Intertextuality** refers to the way a text or texts overtly or covertly borrow from and are informed by other texts. Overt borrowing from another text is acknowledged

Box 13.14 Focus on research in the news

East Coast rail leaves stark choice

By Tanya Powley and Jim Pickard

For the third time in less than 10 years the British government has been forced to call 'all change' on the flagship East Coast rail line between London and Edinburgh. The East Coast mainline was nationalised in 2009 and privatised in 2015. But after heavy losses the franchise is about to collapse in the latest blow to the UK's long-running policy of outsourcing public services.

The creation of a franchising system under which private companies bid to provide passenger train services was meant to cure the ills of Britain's railways when they were privatised via the break-up of British Rail in 1994.

The East Coast line has had a difficult run since privatisation, with three of its four operators forced to give up their franchises early after a series of over-optimistic passenger growth forecasts.

"The current franchise has come to a head much quicker than anyone thought," says David Begg, a transport economist.

A number of other franchises are looking increasingly vulnerable amid overly optimistic bid assumptions and slowing passenger growth, and the East Coast mainline case may tempt some to hand back their deals.

"There is a risk this is going to happen elsewhere. The contracts let out over the last few years were done on very optimistic bases . . . so we may get successive crises," Mr Wolmar [a transport historian] said.

FT *Source:* Extracts from 'East Coast rail line failure leaves Chris Grayling with stark choices', Tanya Powley and Jim Pickard (2018) *Financial Times*, 6 February. Copyright © The Financial Times Ltd

through use of quotations and citations. Covert borrowing involves adopting ideas or ideological positions and arguments from other texts without overtly acknowledging this. The focus of these types of analysis in Discourse Analysis is to analyse how discourses and texts are used in the construction of other discourses and texts, to identify how discourses change and develop, and to understand how attempts are made to give credibility to such changes or developments. These approaches to analysis point to the importance of contextual knowledge, not only to understand how discourses develop and evolve, but also to appreciate the factors that bring about change – why change occurs. Using interdiscursive and intertextual analyses therefore involves using multiple texts.

Our discussion so far has emphasised the role of social constructionism in Discourse Analysis. By this we mean the assumption that the social world is socially constructed through discourse and that Discourse Analysis analyses how use of language constructs versions of social reality (including dominant, marginalised and competing discourses). However, the extent to which social reality is socially constructed is contested. To this end, Holstein and Gubrium (2011: 342) reflect a dictum of Karl Marx in saying 'that people actively construct their worlds but not completely on, or in, their own terms'. This points to the (ontological) distinction between objectivism and subjectivism we discussed in Section 4.2. According to realist philosophical positions, objective entities exist that are external to social actors, which impact on their social constructions. It is therefore important to understand external factors that affect human attitudes and actions, whether or not social actors are aware of these influences on the ways in which they make sense of their social world.

A methodological approach to Discourse Analysis based on a realist epistemological view exists in the form of **Critical Discourse Analysis** (e.g. Fairclough, 1992, 2010). Critical Discourse Analysis adopts a critical realist approach (Section 4.4), drawing a distinction between the natural world and the social world, with the implication that social actors' understanding of the latter is affected by the former and is not entirely socially constructed. Fairclough (2010: 4–5) captures this when he writes,

> The socially constructive effects of discourse are thus a central concern, but a distinction is drawn between construal and construction; the world is discursively construed (or represented) in many and various ways, but which construals come to have socially constructive effects depends upon a range of conditions which include for instance power relations but also properties of whatever parts or aspects of the world are being construed. We cannot transform the world in any old way we happen to construe it; the world is such that some transformations are possible and others are not. So CDA is a 'moderate' or 'contingent' form of social constructionism.

Critical Discourse Analysis examines relations between discourse and other objects in the world that are recognised as existing, including the exercise of power by those who control resources (power relations). In this approach, discourse is seen as being affected or conditioned by social reality, knowingly or unknowingly, as well as socially construing it. As a result, it incorporates the need to not only analyse incidents of discourse (analysis of social interactions or text) but also to understand how wider discursive and social practices influence and are influenced by discourse. This approach, in which an incidence of discourse is 'simultaneously a piece of text, an instance of discursive practice, and an instance of social practice' (Fairclough, 1992: 4), is outlined in Figure 13.3. This approach involves analysing discourse at the level of text or social inaction (discussed earlier in this sub-section), discursive practice (including the use of interdiscursive and intertextual analyses outlined earlier) and social practice (seen as requiring an interdisciplinary or transdisciplinary approach to analysis) in order to achieve an integrated and critical understanding.

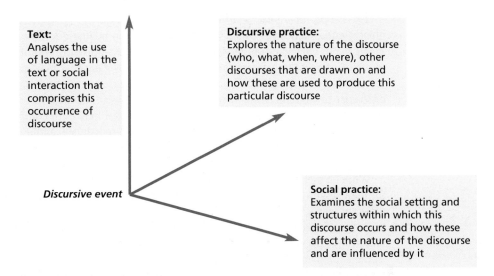

Figure 13.3 A three-dimensional analytical framework for Critical Discourse Analysis
Source: Developed from Fairclough (1992)

Evaluation

Discourse Analysis potentially provides you with a valuable analytical approach where your research involves social action and interaction within a particular setting such as an organisation. This analytical approach may be appropriate where your research is focused on a topic such as organisational communication, culture, decision making, governance, power, practices, processes, relations or trust. It may be an approach that provides you with an insightful means to analyse data resulting from the use, for example, of an Action Research, documentary or ethnographic strategy where you have transcripts relating to the use of language in discourse.

Where you consider using this approach as you formulate your research design, you will need to develop some level of familiarity with and understanding of approaches to Discourse Analysis. In particular you will need to be able to articulate your approach to Discourse Analysis and say why it is suitable for your research. Discourse Analysis, like some other analytical approaches, has developed to suit a number of purposes, incorporating different philosophical and theoretical assumptions suitable for different types of data and using different methods. Discourse Analysis can be used as your primary analytical technique, depending on your research question, research design and nature of your data, or in support of other analytical techniques where appropriate. Discourse Analysis therefore offers a potentially valuable research approach but consideration about using this approach will benefit from adequate and early preparation!

13.12 Visual Analysis

Introduction

We discuss qualitative visual research methods in Sections 8.2, 9.6 and 10.11. Visual research makes use of existing visual images, known as 'found' images, or images created by the researcher or research participants. Visual images may also be categorised as static, such as photographs and drawings; or moving, such as video, film and television.

The scope for visual research is evident through the absolute prevalence of visual objects and practices in social life, including in the business and organisational environment. In our consideration of visual research, we recognise the potentially powerful nature of visual images: as a 'way of seeing' or means to gain new insights or perspectives; as an effective way to record data including contextual data whose breadth and depth might otherwise be difficult to encapsulate and describe in a time constrained research situation; and as a representational form in their own right that may both complement and enhance textual description and analysis. However, we also recognised earlier that analysing visual data is associated with particular analytical implications that make this a problematic research method.

While 'a picture is worth a thousand words', visual images are not capable of speaking for themselves (Miles et al. 2014). All images need to be interpreted, with implications at different levels. At the practical level, interpretation involves using words to describe and analyse an image, with the consequence in many cases that the image is displaced, leaving us solely with and entirely reliant on the interpretation offered in the textual description. At the explanatory level, this interpretation will only be one of many possible. Pink (2007) says that the interpretation of an image will depend on the subjectivity of the interpreter and that any interpretation is likely to be contextual and time specific. Other people in different situations and at other times may offer different interpretations.

At the philosophical level, we may also question what the image represents. While visual images may be viewed superficially as just a way of making things visible, images are generally constructed or created by someone for an intended purpose or from a particular perspective, whether this is explicitly understood or not. The use of images, especially digital or photographic ones, as a way to capture or reveal an underlying reality is therefore contested. From this perspective, images may be constructed to justify the assumptions and practices of those who commission their creation. These images will be carefully composed or constructed to achieve this desired effect. For others, images may spontaneously capture attributes of a situation, suggesting a view into a situated reality (see the discussion in Rose 2016 and also Pink 2007). However, even where an image is apparently taken spontaneously in a natural setting, it will still be affected by its framing, depth of focus and point of view, with the consequence that different images may create different effects.

Where you use found images or those created by others, you will find yourself in the situation of making a subjective interpretation of another person's subjective representation. In doing this you will also be creating a word-based interpretation of a visual representation. Without sufficient cultural or contextual understanding this will be problematic. To undertake this task less problematically, you will need to understand:

- who took or created the image or images that you wish to analyse;
- how these images were taken or created;
- the purpose for which these images were taken or created;
- how these images have been used previously;
- any intended audience for these images, and;
- the intended effect(s) of the image maker and those who commissioned these images.

Achieving this depth of insight will necessitate you engaging reflexively during your research, where you not only seek to understand how your own preconceived ideas might influence the way you interpret visual images but also to recognise how multiple interpretations may result from the intended and unintended effects of the images you use, and from different perspectives. In recognising multiple interpretations and different perspectives, you need to make these explicit in your analysis and discussion. We defined reflexivity in Section 2.1 and have stressed its importance throughout the research process. We now briefly outline ways to analyse visual images.

Overview

There are several ways to analyse visual images, related to different analytical aims. These aims relate to analysing visual images during interviews as a means to elicit further data, analysing images as visual data in their own right, and using images as visual representations. We briefly discuss each of these aims and techniques associated with them.

Analysing visual images as a means to elicit further data

In Section 10.11 we discuss the use of visual images in interviews to elicit data from participants. This technique involves a researcher finding or creating images, or asking a participant to create images, with the intention of asking the participant to interpret what she or he sees in each image. In this way the participant is asked to analyse each image during the interview, based on his or her subjective interpretation and contextual knowledge of the setting shown. This quasi-analytical process involves visual images being used as an intermediary means to elicit further data rather than being analysed as visual data in their own right.

Analysing images as visual data in their own right

Where images are analysed as visual data in their own right a number of analytical techniques may be used, drawn from a diverse range of disciplinary domains (Bell and Davison 2013; Rose 2016). Some of these techniques to analyse visual images are data based and inductive, while others use an existing theoretical perspective through which to focus analysis. In this sub-section we briefly outline two approaches to analyse visual images. These are Content Analysis and Semiotic Analysis.

Content analysis

Content analysis is used to analyse large numbers of images and involves quantification of the visual data you derive from the images you analyse. This approach involves identifying categories of visual data in which you are interested in order to develop a systematic coding scheme, coding your visual images using this scheme and subsequently undertaking quantitative analysis. If you decide to use Content Analysis you will need to be aware of its precise analytical rules and procedure, to which you will need to adhere. We outline this in Section 12.2. Subsequent quantitative analysis ranges from calculating the frequency of different categories for a variable (Section 12.4) to examining relationships between variables created (Section 12.6). Rose (2016) outlines four stages of Content Analysis when applied to the analysis of visual images. These are finding or creating the images you wish to analyse; developing categories in order to be able to code your data; coding your data; and analysing them (Sections 12.4 and 12.6).

Semiotic analysis

Semiotics is the study of signs. A **sign** is 'something' (a word, phrase, sound, cultural artefact or visual image) that stands for (represents) something other than itself. The inclusion of 'something' twice in this definition is intentional and important, as it indicates that a sign consists of two parts. These are the signifier and the signified. The **signifier** is the word, phrase or sound used, or image or artefact shown and the **signified** is the concept or meaning suggested or implied in the sign. A simple and relatively straightforward example here might be the way in which images of some animals, birds and mythological creatures have been used in branding and advertisements as signs to indicate or represent objects such as power, strength, dependability or wisdom. There is though no automatic relationship between a signifier and what is signified. Any meaning derived will depend on the conventions held by those who see and interpret signs, and be moderated by cultural differences and assessed in relation to other, related signs. For example, it may be that the examples of animals, birds and mythological creatures each of us associates with different attributes varies by culture, while what is signified by one signifier will be altered in relation to the presence of other signs.

Approaches to semiotics propose different ways to analyse signs. These approaches are based on the work of two foundational semioticians, the Swiss linguist Ferdinand de Saussure and the American philosopher Charles Sanders Peirce, whose work on pragmatism we refer to in Section 4.4. One typology from the work of Peirce differentiates between iconic, indexical and symbolic signs. An **iconic sign** is one where the signifier resembles the object being signified. Using the example of road signs for tourist attractions, the UK's Department for Transport (2015: 100–102) use a range of icons to signify types of destination (Figure 13.4). For example, the location of a historic house is signified by the image of a large house, the location of a castle by an icon that clearly resembles a castle, and so on! An **indexical sign** inherently indicates the object being signified and we can also use the example of UK road signs for tourist attractions to illustrate this. The sign for a farm trail does not attempt to use an iconic representation (this would be too complex or confusing) but instead shows the image of a heavy horse to signify a farm. Likewise, the location of a zoo is signified by the image of an elephant and the location of a football ground by a football. Signs are often multimodal and roadside tourist signs are also a good example of this. In the UK roadside tourist

Figure 13.4 UK road signs for tourist attractions

signs have a brown background and often include text. The use of colour helps to signify the purpose of the sign and the use of text helps to anchor what is being signified. While none of the examples used so far include text, some others combine signs and text on a brown background to anchor meaning. A **symbolic sign** is more abstract while still being capable of signifying meaning to those who see it through conventional understanding. For example, some other road signs use red, which is widely accepted as signifying danger or acting as a warning. Traffic signals in many countries are based on the use of three colours, red, amber and green, indicating symbolic signs which are widely understood by convention.

Signs may also be classified as denotative and connotative. In a **denotative sign** the meaning being suggested or implied will be reasonably obvious or visible. For example, an image of a hotel bedroom on a hotel chain website will signify the quality of the furnishings and the amount of space in the room. A **connotative sign** is either a substitute for or a part of the thing it stands for: for example, in many people's minds an image of a sunlit seashore and perfectly blue sky is associated with being on holiday and such an image may be shown on a holiday company's website to stand for a relaxing holiday, while an image of a table laid for dinner with a white cloth, silver cutlery, wine glasses, candles and flowers may be used to represent a high quality dining experience. An individual sign may also signify both denotative and connotative qualities.

A further typology relates to the ways that signs work with one another. In this respect, semiotic analysis may be syntagmatic or paradigmatic. **Syntagmatic analysis** explores relations between signs and the ways in which meanings are signified as different signs are combined into structures or sequences. This approach is used in the analysis of visual images. In a static image such as a printed advertisement signs become meaningful in relation to other signs that surround them in the advert. The intention of an advertisement will be to transfer the signified meanings from one or more signs to other signs related to the product, so that, for example, signs associated with health and well-being may be projected in an advertisement for a food product that wishes to be seen as healthy and good for you. Alternatively, participant produced images (Box 13.15) can be used to explore the meanings they give to a specified activity, in this example entrepreneurship. In moving images such as video and film, signs occur sequentially and become meaningful in relation to those that occur before and after them. In a similar way to the example we have just described, filmed advertisements such as television adverts may be analysed to explore how signs are used to signify meanings in relation to the product being promoted.

Rather than focusing on structural or sequential relations between signs, **paradigmatic analysis** explores relations between signs by examining how the substitution of alternative signs for one sign will alter that sign's signified meaning in relation to other signs. Using our example of the advertisement for a healthy food product, if those who commissioned this advert wanted to project the idea of fitness and bodybuilding in relation to consuming this food instead of health and well-being, the signs used to signify this intended meaning would alter and consequently affect the market for this product.

Attempting to comprehend and analyse signified meanings and their relations to other signs is likely to be difficult. This will be due to the complex or abstract nature of some signs and the complexity involved when such signs are used in relation to one another. Complexity leads to the likelihood of multiple meanings as signs are interpreted. Semioticians use a term for this: **polysemy**, or multiple meanings, and a sign with more than one meaning is polysemic. However, while many signs and complex ones in particular are polysemic, their use and interpretation will be influenced by wider cultural and social conventions (we briefly referred to these earlier, such as the convention that red indicates danger). These conventions refer to wider systems of meaning that reflect shared understandings and expectations. For example, identifiable groups such as accountants, entrepreneurs, human resource practitioners, marketing professionals and public relations

Box 13.15
Focus on management research

Semiotic analysis of entrepreneurs' images of identity

In a paper published in the *Journal of Business Venturing* Clarke and Holt (2017) report on research to better understand entrepreneurs' entrepreneurial identity. Data were collected from 20 entrepreneurs involved in potentially high growth businesses during a training initiative. Each was asked to imagine an image or symbol that captured or expressed what their business meant to them and given an hour draw it on an A3 sheet of paper. Subsequently they were interviewed on their drawing and how it related of their experiences thereby illuminating their entrepreneurial identities.

Images were analysed using semiotic analysis. This examined the choices the entrepreneurs made about what to represent visually as salient in their drawings and how they achieved this. To do this, three interrelated components of visual grammar were examined within the images. These comprised (1) representational meaning, that is what was actually depicted of the entrepreneurial world in the image; (2) interactive meaning, that is how the image attracted the viewer's attention, and where the viewer's gaze was directed within the image; and (3) compositional meaning, that is the techniques and tools used to represent the meaning such as shading and use of jagged and dark lines. Clarke and Holt (2017: 482) explain these components in relation to an entrepreneur's drawing of: ". . . an individual/people in a fishing boat on a sea full of creatures (representational meaning) [where] the images that most capture the viewer's attention are the larger, more detailed sea creatures at the bottom of the page which dominate the image (interactional meaning), the effect [being] created by the use of charcoal, shading and contrast (compositional meaning)."

Data from each interview were analysed inductively, coding the metaphors each entrepreneur used in their discussion of their image. Early codes were used to provide signposts until the researchers noted patterns were emerging, codes being gradually reduced by rereading the coded data and looking for links between codes and removing redundant codes. In the final stage of analysis, data from the two datasets were brought together and compared. These data revealed that entrepreneurial identity was different from the ideal of a heroic individual. Rather they emphasised continuous and sometimes precarious movement, nurturing and caregiving and transformation and growth; their identities being neither singular nor fixed.

practitioners will each share a set of conventionalised understandings that are referred to as a **code**, affecting the way members of that group understand their professional world and how to interpret signs and behave within it. More broadly, codes of conventionalised understandings will operate at the societal level, affecting the ways in which signs are used and interpreted. Such codes will be influenced by prevailing **ideologies** or ways of thinking, known as **dominant codes** (Rose 2016). However, while dominant codes will underpin the way in which many signs are used with the intention of producing an intended or preferred meaning, other interpretations will still exist and some of these will encompass a critical perspective about the use of signs to promote ideological interests (for discussion of critical perspectives see Sections 4.3, 5.8 and 13.11).

Semiotic analysis is undoubtedly an important technique to help to analyse and interpret visual images but its strengths and issues need to be recognised. Rose (2016) expresses these succinctly. In relation to its strengths she says that, "A semiological analysis entails the deployment of a highly refined set of concepts that produce detailed accounts of the exact ways the meaning of an image are produced through that image" (2016: 107). In relation to its issues she says that the very richness of its analytical concepts can appear to be terminologically dense while, "for all its analytical richness, semiology does not offer a clear method for its application" (2016: 110). She does though provide her own outline to use this analytical approach, which we have developed as a Checklist in Box 13.16.

Box 13.16
Checklist

For semiotic analysis

✔ Identify the signs in an image.
✔ Assess what each sign signifies.

✔ Analyse how these signs relate to one another using the concepts outlined in this sub-section.
✔ Explore how these signs relate more widely to systems of meaning such as codes and ideologies.
✔ Evaluate the use of these signs in relation to this wider interpretation.

Developed from Rose (2016)

Using images as visual representations

Visual images may also be used to represent analytical aspects and evoke meanings that would otherwise be difficult to convey in a research project (Box 13.17). In this approach, selected images and text are combined in a research report, in order to enhance one another's ability to represent perspectives that would be difficult to describe using words alone. Where photographic images and text are combined in this way this is referred to as a **photo essay**. In a video format, voice-over narration may be used to achieve a similar effect, referred to as a **video essay**. A digital document or multimedia website may also be created that will allow both static and moving images to be integrated with text.

To produce a photo essay you need to consider a number of aspects. Your research philosophy, research strategy and approach to theory development will be likely to shape the nature and purpose of the photo essay you create. For example, your research may be designed to 'reveal' an underlying reality or it may be guided by a desire to visualise multiple realities and interpretations. Where you commence research deductively the images you use are likely to be influenced by existing theory. Where you commence research inductively the images you use are likely to be more exploratory.

A photo essay may be organised thematically or it may create a narrative account. In the first of these, a specific image, or set of images, will be included to illustrate a particular research theme (Section 13.6). These themes may be determined prior to creating images or they may emerge through the process of collecting these. A photo essay that creates a narrative account is known as a **photo novella** and will be designed to introduce a storyline into the way photographic images are used in relation to one another. In a photo novella, images and text may be presented in a similar style to those in a comic book.

You will therefore need to consider the design of the photo essay that you create. How will you arrange the images and text on a page? Will each image and its accompanying text be given equal prominence or will you choose to give prominence to a core image and arrange others in a subsidiary way? How will you present the text in relation to the images? Will images or text be more prominent, or will these have equal prominence? You may decide to use images with only brief captions, or you may incorporate a few selected images into a largely textual account. Of course there will be a limit to the latter option if you are to create a photo essay as opposed to incorporate an occasional image into a written report. An image or images may be used with only brief captions (or even without captions) to portray the perspective or experience of the photographer, while the use of longer captions provide more explanatory, reflective or theoretical comments.

Use of images by researchers as visual representations will be more likely to focus on theoretical perspectives. This will affect the way in which images and text are used in relation to one another and the balance between image and text. This is likely to involve the use of longer explanatory and theoretical captions or statements in relation to an image or set of images. For example, a longer caption or accompanying statement may explain who took the image, where it was taken, when it was taken and any significance related to the time at which it was taken, the nature and significance of any interaction or activity shown in the image, and how the image portrays an aspect or issue related to the image taker's experience or that of any person shown in the image. More theoretically, accompanying captions or statements to images may explain the nature of each theme represented by an image, why each theme shown is significant, how themes relate to one another, and how these may be integrated to generate a deeper theoretical insight. Used in this way, a researcher may create a photo essay with an explanatory and theoretical purpose (Pink 2007) (Box 13.17).

Photo essays are also produced in collaborative and participant-led visual research projects where participants analyse their own visual images and select those that represent their perspectives or experiences. In Section 10.11 we refer to approaches to participant photography in which participants engage in analysis of the images they create in order to choose those that represent ideas, issues or themes that are important to them. In photo-voice, for example, participant photographers often participate in group analysis of their images in order to choose those that represent shared issues. These images may then be used to produce photo essays.

Another participant-led narrative form that involves moving images is the video essay. In this approach, participants may produce a script for filming, record video, analyse and edit video footage and produce a video essay. The purpose and nature of a video essay may vary like that of a photo essay.

Evaluation

In this section we have addressed a concern raised in Section 9.6 about utilising the power of visual images as data in their own right and as visual representations, rather than eliminating images during an early stage of analysis, where these are literally lost from view. This will of course depend on the nature of the visual images being used and their purpose in the research project. While images such as some of those created by participants are deliberately and meaningfully used in visual interviews to elicit further data (Section 10.11), other images such as visual advertisements may be integrated in the analytical process through the use of a technique such as semiotic analysis, while others that act as visual representations may be incorporated in the output from research through the production of photo essays.

This demonstrates that you will need to think through your purpose for using visual images and related to this, your analytical aim in order to be able to analyse these appropriately. A range of techniques exist to analyse visual images but their suitability varies according to the aim of the research. Combined with the subjective nature of visual images this suggests that choice of an appropriate analytical technique to analyse visual images will be crucial. We recognised earlier in this section that the analysis of visual images should be undertaken methodically, reflexively and with a clear appreciation of your analytical purpose. To achieve this you should find it helpful to:

- think carefully about the nature of your visual images and your purpose for creating or collecting these, or those that you intend to create or collect;
- recognise your analytical aim in relation to using these visual images in your research project;
- explore possible techniques that you may use related to your analytical aim and read further about each technique as well as looking for published research that made use of these techniques to analyse visual images;
- evaluate these possible analytical techniques based on this exploration to identify one or more techniques to analyse your visual images;
- apply this technique or techniques to analyse your visual images;

Box 13.17
Focus on student research

Images from the English Riviera

Lottie's tourism research project focused on symbolism and investment in seaside tourist destinations. As part of this project she undertook visual research, visiting a number of seaside tourist destinations to create images of these locations. At the end of this research activity, she selected a number of the images she had created from each tourist destination to produce a photo-essay, which she subsequently incorporated in her project report. This photo-essay combined text with the digital images that she had created.

As her research focused on symbolism and investment in seaside tourist destinations, the images she created sought to encapsulate the relationship between these in each location she visited. One of these locations was the 'English Riviera', a tourist destination in the southwest of the UK. A selection of the images and associated text in her photo-essay for this location are reproduced here.

signifies careful planning and while the resources required to create this scene combine public and private investments, the overall effect appears intentional and symbolises an up-market tourist destination.

Lines and palms

This image was taken to combine the lines of the modern apartment block with fantastic views over the sea and the tropical sign of the feathered leaves of the palm trees. I deliberately took this image looking towards the sky so that by ignoring ground level, we may make inferences about the image and ask, where is this? We may conclude that the combination of these signs is intentional, perhaps to suggest somewhere beyond its actual location, somewhere continental.

Seafront

I took this image from the promenade to capture the blend of traditional and modern visible in this location. Beyond the railings lies the sea and beyond this is a sandy beach, a traditional symbol of a seaside town. There are only mid-rise buildings evident at either side of the image and these are coloured white which makes them appear as though they are situated somewhere around the Mediterranean. Beyond the beach in between these buildings the predominant sign is that of trees and vegetation. This image

Exotic park

This image shows exotic planting combined with defined lines and manicured spaces, and is framed by trees beyond which appear to take it out of its location in an urban area close to the sea. It appears to symbolise somewhere other than where it is and yet it also offers a safe and relaxing space. The investment to create and maintain this space and others nearby is clearly considerable and adds to the overall impression of this tourist destination.

- evaluate the use of this technique as you use it (or techniques as you use them);
- where appropriate, return to an earlier point in this list where your evaluation indicates the need to revise your approach.

13.13 Data Display and Analysis

Introduction

The Data Display and Analysis approach is based on the work of Miles et al. (2014). For them, the process of analysis consists of three concurrent sub-processes:

- data condensation;
- data display;
- drawing and verifying conclusions.

We now outline each of these.

Procedural outline

As part of the process, **data condensation** includes summarising and simplifying the data collected and/or selectively focusing on some parts of this data. The aim of this process is to transform the data and to condense it. Miles et al. (2014) outline a number of methods for condensing data. These include the production of interview or observation summaries, document summaries, coding and categorising data and perhaps constructing a narrative.

Data display involves organising and assembling your data into summary diagrammatic or visual displays. Miles et al. (2014) describe a number of ways of displaying data and refer to two main families of data display: matrices and networks. Matrices are generally tabular in form, with defined columns and rows, where data are entered selectively into the appropriate cells of such a matrix, to facilitate further data analysis (Box 13.18). A network is a collection of nodes or boxes that are joined or linked by lines, perhaps with arrows to indicate relationships. The boxes or nodes contain brief descriptions or labels to indicate variables or key points from the data.

Recognising relationships and patterns in the data, as well as drawing conclusions and verifying these, is helped by the use of data displays. A display allows you to make comparisons between the elements of the data and to identify any relationships, key themes, patterns and trends that may be evident. These will be worthy of further exploration and analysis. In this way, the use of data displays can help you to interpret your data and to draw meaning from it.

Evaluation

Miles et al. (2014) believe there are a number of advantages associated with using forms of data display. Qualitative data collection tends to produce hours of audio-recorded interviews or extensive piles of notes. Once these have been transcribed or word processed, they are generally referred to as 'extended text'. Extended text is considered an unreduced form of display that is difficult to analyse because it is both extensive and poorly ordered. Based on the logic that 'you know what you display', the analysis of data and the drawing of conclusions from these will be helped by using matrices, networks or other visual forms to display reduced or selected data drawn from your extended text. These forms of display are relatively easy to generate, can be developed to fit your data specifically, and help you to develop your analytical thinking as you work through several iterations to develop a visual form that represents your data well.

Box 13.18
Focus on student research

Using CAQDAS to explore how key words are used in context

Marcus' research was concerned with how staff were responding to the managed changes in the organisation where he worked. He had collected his data using a Web questionnaire, which contained the open question: 'If there is anything further you would like to add in relation to the changes at OrgCo, please type your comment in the box'. Marcus downloaded the responses verbatim from the online survey tool as a data file and spellchecked them, correcting words that had been misspelled or used American spellings to the English spelling. This ensured he would pick up all occurrences of particular words such as 'staff' or 'OrgCo', the pseudonym he used to anonymise the organisation. He then loaded the spellchecked data into Provalis Research's text analysis software Word-Stat. These were displayed in a tabular form. During the next stage of his analysis Marcus wanted to see which respondents had mentioned staff or staffing in their responses to the question and the context in which the words had been used. He therefore searched for the keyword 'staff' within his data.

Scanning the responses suggested that those respondents who had answered this question often appeared to talk about how staff were treated at OrgCo. Marcus decided to investigate further.

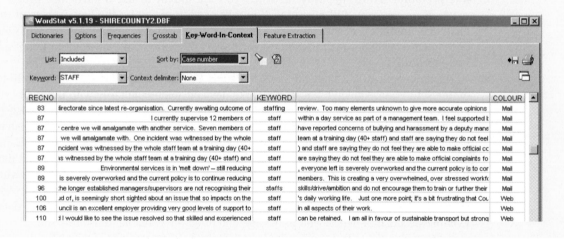

Use of Data Display and Analysis can provide you with a set of procedures to analyse your qualitative data, or alternatively one or more of the techniques that Miles et al. (2014) outline can be useful as part of your approach to analysing this type of data. They describe the analysis of qualitative data as an interactive process, and in this sense their approach includes many aspects of analysis that complement the analytical techniques we discussed earlier. Their approach is a systematic and structured one, and they recognise that the procedures they outline are often associated with a fairly high level of formalisation. However, unlike grounded theory, the exact procedures to be followed within their framework of data reduction, display and conclusion drawing and verification are not specified. Miles et al. (2014) refer to their book as a 'sourcebook', and as such they offer a number of possible techniques that may be appropriate within your overall approach to analysis. If you intend to use their book we suggest you take care in identifying what is useful for you in the context of your own research question and objectives.

Data Display and Analysis is suited to an inductive strategy to analyse qualitative data, although it is also compatible with a deductive strategy. Miles et al.'s (2014) book is useful both for its overall discussion of the analysis of qualitative data and in relation to its many analytical tools.

13.14 Using CAQDAS

Introduction

CAQDAS (Computer Assisted Qualitative Data Analysis Software, sometimes abbreviated to QDAS) refers to programs containing a range of tools to facilitate the analysis of qualitative data. The use of CAQDAS offers a number of advantages in relation to the analytical procedures we have discussed. In particular, when used systematically, it can aid continuity and increase both transparency and methodological rigour.

Silver and Lewins (2014) say that they are often asked which CAQDAS package is best; a question which they say is impossible to answer. They provide reasons for this response. First, many tools are common to all CAQDAS packages although each package will have specific characteristics, supporting particular functions in different ways. Second, they say that while there is some discussion about whether specific packages affect the way analysis is conducted, these programs are not designed to cater for particular methodological or analytical approach and it is the researcher who remains in control of the way the tools in a program are used to facilitate analysis and interpretation. Third, the way in which you are taught to use a particular program may not recognise its full potential. You will need to recognise the key aspects of the analytical approach which you wish to use (Section 13.3) and select those tools in your chosen CAQDAS package to facilitate your analysis while being aware of any that are not appropriate.

Depending on your analytical approach some CAQDAS programs may potentially be more useful. Consequently, you will need to develop some familiarity with different programs to be able to evaluate their applicability for the analytical approach you wish to use. However, attempting to achieve this may be problematic if the programs you wish to explore are not readily available. It is worth noting though that some CAQDAS programs which may be suitable for your purpose are available to download as freeware and that commercial software producers offer free downloads of trial versions. Silver and Lewins (2014) say that regardless of your preferred choice, each CAQDAS program will provide you with a range of tools to use to help you to manage and analyse your qualitative data. Even in the situation where you only have one program available to use this should provide you with tools to help you manage and analyse your data.

Function

The general function of a CAQDAS program is to facilitate the management and analysis of a qualitative research project. Its specific functions relate to its software tools that enable particular analytical processes. Based on Silver and Lewins (2014) these may be summarised as:

- *Managing the research project:* all data files can be stored in or linked through a project file created within the software, allowing access to all elements of the project and the establishment of an audit trail.
- *Writing analytic memos, comments, notes, etc.:* thoughts about the data and the research process can be recorded systematically and developmentally.
- *Exploring the data:* data can be explored prior to coding by noting and commenting on points and places of interest.
- *Searching the data initially:* can search for words, phrases etc. within and across data items to further familiarity.

- *Developing coding*: supports process of developing and applying codes, according to your research philosophy, methodological approach, approach to theory development and analytical technique.
- *Coding*: supports coding of data according to analytical approach.
- *Retrieving coded data*: offers scope to revisit and evaluate coding to data, to facilitate analysis and the future direction of data collection.
- *Revising codes and coding:* offers scope to revisit and re-code data.
- *Organising data:* offers scope to organise and re-organise the qualitative data collected to facilitate analysis.
- *Hyperlinking:* provides ability to link units of data to other units, files etc. for analytical purposes.
- *Searching and interrogating:* facilitates linking and grouping codes, conceptualising and testing relationships.
- *Mapping:* provides visualisation of relationships and representing explanations.
- *Producing outputs:* produces reports allowing you to view material in hard copy or to export it to other applications such as word-processing and spreadsheet programs, as well as producing tabular reports, charts and graphical representations.

What is not apparent from this list is that the functions contained in some CAQDAS packages are better at supporting certain types of qualitative data analysis procedures than others. A wide range of qualitative data exists and your research may involve collecting one particular type or some combination of these. Text makes up a major type of qualitative data but this comprises different types such as documents, narratives and transcripts, affecting what you wish to achieve through analysis. Audio, still images and video sources are also important types of qualitative data. This means that you may need to experiment with more than one package before you find the CAQDAS that meets your needs. Your final choice of CAQDAS package will be dependent on a range of factors, including, not least, the relative benefits you will gain relative to the time you need to invest to learn a CAQDAS program. These factors are summarised in Box 13.19 as a checklist.

Box 13.19
Checklist

Choosing a CAQDAS package

✔ How much data do you have that needs to be analysed qualitatively?

✔ How important are these qualitative data in relation to any other data you have collected for your research project and will you want to integrate any quantitative data into the qualitative software package you use?

✔ What type(s) of qualitative data do you need to analyse: audio, documentary, narratives, transcripts or visual?

✔ How much time do you have to learn how to use the package?

✔ What is the timeframe for your research project?

✔ How much support is available in your university to help you learn to use the package?

✔ What is the operating system of your computer?

✔ How much memory does your computer have?

✔ Do you want software that will allow you to take an inductive, deductive or combined approach to your analysis?

✔ Do you want a package that will help you manage your thinking and assist you in developing your own codes?

✔ Do you want a package that will allow you to explore the way language is used in your data?

✔ Do you want a package that allows you to display relationships within your data diagrammatically?

✔ Do you want a package that will allow you to quantitatively describe the content of your data?

Where you decide to use a CAQDAS program and have selected a package, you will need to familiarise yourself with it before you start collecting your data. This will avoid the problem of trying to learn the features of the package at the same time as you analyse your data, although you will of course continue to learn about these as you conduct this analysis.

Exploring the latest versions of CAQDAS

Published information about CAQDAS programs is likely to become out of date fairly quickly. Fortunately, there is a wealth of up-to-date information available from the CAQDAS Networking Project's website hosted by the University of Surrey.[1] If you are considering using CAQDAS, we would strongly recommend a visit to this website which, in addition to a wealth of useful articles, also contains web links to commercial software producers' sites including downloadable demonstration versions of the software. We would also advise you to explore the Internet sites of CAQDAS producers to obtain details and demonstrations of the latest versions of these packages and the features that they offer. Some of those most widely used are listed in Table 13.2.

Table 13.2 Internet addresses for a range of CAQDAS developers

Name	Internet address	Brief comments
ATLAS.ti	http://www.atlasti.com	Windows and MAC versions. Versatile and flexible. Supports multimedia
HyperRESEARCH™	http://www.researchware.com	Windows and MAC versions. Simple to use. Case-based structure. Supports multimedia
MAXQDA	http://www.MAXQDA.com	Windows and MAC versions. Intuitive and easy to use. Mixed methods features. Supports multimedia. Content analysis features with addition of MAXDictio in MAXQDAplus
NVivo	http://www.qsrinternational.com	Windows and MAC versions. Range of editions with added features. Versatile with large range of searching possibilities. Supports multimedia
QDA Miner	http://www.provalisresearch.com	Windows and MAC versions. Mixed methods analytical capabilities. Supportive functionality. Content analysis features with addition of WordStat
Qualrus	http://www.qualrus.com	Windows version. May also run on MAC OS using a Windows virtual machine according to the www.ideaworks website. Uses artificial intelligence to offer suggestive coding based on learning from coding trends. Supports multimedia
Transana	http://www.transana.org	Windows and MAC versions. Specifically designed for qualitative analysis of audio, still image and video data. Ability to synchronise multiple video streams during playback and to synchronise playback with transcripts

Source: Developed from QUIC Working Paper software reviews available from the CAQDAS Networking Project and Qualitative Innovations in CAQDAS Project (QUIC) website hosted by the University of Surrey and/or software producers' websites. Each comment in this table only provides a very brief indication and is not intended to promote or discourage the use of a particular software program, or to advocate the use of one program over other compatible programs. You are advised to evaluate the features and applications of current versions of CAQDAS at the time of your project in relation to the requirements of your research.

---

[1]The Internet address for the CAQDAS Networking Project is https://www.surrey.ac.uk/computer-assisted-qualitative-data-analysis.

13.15 Summary

- Qualitative data are rich and full verbal, textual and/or visual data. They may also be characterised as non-standardised and as non-numerical data.
- Data collection, analysis and interpretation are an interrelated and interactive set of processes in qualitative research. Analysis often occurs during the collection of data as well as after it.
- Understanding key aspects of different qualitative analysis techniques should help you to choose an appropriate technique, or combination of techniques, to analyse your qualitative data.
- Qualitative data need to be carefully prepared for manual or computer-assisted analysis, usually involving transcription where the spoken word is involved.
- There are a number of aids that you might use to help you through the process of qualitative analysis, including: interim summaries, event summaries, document summaries, self-memos, maintaining a research notebook and keeping a reflective diary or reflexive journal.
- A number of qualitative analysis techniques are outlined in this chapter. Analytic Induction and Grounded Theory Method commence inductively; Pattern Matching and Deductive Explanation Building commence deductively; while Thematic Analysis; Template Analysis; Narrative Analysis; Discourse Analysis; Visual Analysis; and Data Display and Analysis may commence more flexibly.
- The use of computer-assisted qualitative data analysis software (CAQDAS) can help you during qualitative analysis with regard to project management and data organisation, keeping close to your data, exploration, coding and retrieval of your data, searching and interrogating to build propositions and theorise, and recording your thoughts systematically.

Self-check questions

Help with these questions is available at the end of the chapter.

13.1 Why do we describe qualitative analysis as an 'interactive process'?

13.2 Which sorts of data will you need to retain and file while you are undertaking qualitative research?

13.3 How would you differentiate between a deductive and an inductive analytical approach?

13.4 What are the main implications of using:

a a deductive analytical approach for the way in which you conduct the process of qualitative analysis?

b an inductive analytical approach for the way in which you conduct the process of qualitative analysis?

13.5 What are the key similarities and differences between Thematic Analysis and Template Analysis?

Review and discussion questions

13.6 Assuming that you are undertaking qualitative research or proposing to do this (Section 2.5), use the Checklist in Box 13.1 to commence evaluating your choice of qualitative analysis techniques. Where your analytical technique is not specified by your choice of research strategy, work through the points in this checklist in conjunction with the material in Sections 13.6 to 13.13 to evaluate which techniques you may consider using. Draw up a shortlist of possible analytical techniques and make notes of points for and against use of each of one. Further evaluate your list of points for and against each possible technique to decide which technique(s) you will use to analyse your qualitative data. You may conduct the latter part of this evaluation with a friend to help you both to think through your respective options by discussing this. Brief each other about the nature of your respective data, your shortlists of possible analytical techniques, and lists of points for and against each possible technique before discussing these options.

13.7 With a friend, use part of a transcript that one of you has produced after undertaking a research interview to undertake the following tasks.

   a Based on the aim or purpose for undertaking this interview, or interview themes, independently code the data in this part of the transcript.

   b Compare the results of your coding.

   c Identify where your coding is similar to and different from that of your friend.

   d Where you identify differences in coding, discuss the assumptions you each made when you coded these data and why you made these.

   e By reflecting on your attempt at coding these data, which codes, if any, would you change and why?

You may repeat this process where both of you has conducted a research interview and produced transcripts.

13.8 Evaluate the scope to conduct visual research and analysis in your research project by considering the following. You may find it helpful to discuss this with a friend or tutor.

   a How would conducting visual research help you to answer your research question and address your research objectives?

   b Why would conducting visual research not be appropriate to help you to answer your research question and address your research objectives.

   c Assess your reasons for and against using visual research. Where you decide that using visual research might be helpful, continue to consider the following points.

   d How you would use this method? This more in-depth consideration will involve you re-reading Sections 8.2, 9.6 and 10.11 as well as 13.12.

   e What would be the nature and purpose of the images produced through your visual research?

   f How you will analyse these images and for what purpose?

   g How will you subsequently use these images (or not) in the way you report your research?

13.9 Visit the CAQDAS websites listed in Table 13.2. Using the information available on each website, explore the suitability of each program for the nature of your data and chosen approach to analyse these data. Find and download a demonstration version of a CAQDAS program that may be suitable for your data and analytical approach, to explore its features. Evaluate how useful you think this program will be to assist you in analysing your data.

Progressing your research project

Analysing your data qualitatively

- Review the qualitative data you have collected. These data may be in the form of documentary sources, recordings or notes of observations, visual images, interview transcripts or notes, or diary entries (Chapters 8, 9 and 10).

- Based on your earlier review of the Checklist in Box 13.1 and reading of Sections 13.2 and 13.6 to 13.13 (Review and discussion 13.6) decide which analytical technique(s) will be most appropriate to use to analyse your data.

- Prepare your data for analysis where necessary (Section 13.4) and consider how you will make use of the aids to help you during analysis (Section 13.5).
- Based on your earlier review of CAQDAS programs (Review and discussion question 13.8), decide whether you will make use of a CAQDAS program and where you decide to use one, explore whether this is available for you to use through your university.
- Following the procedural outline of your chosen analytical technique in the appropriate section

(Sections 13.6 to 13.13) together with guidance from further reading related to the use of this technique, attempt to apply this technique to your data to answer your research question and address your objectives.
- As you apply your chosen analytical technique(s) to your data to seek to answer your research questions and address your objectives, you will need to continue to evaluate use of this technique in practice and its suitability for your data.
- Use the questions in Box 1.4 to guide your reflective diary entry.

References

Bansal, P. and Roth, K. (2000) 'Why companies go green: A model of ecological responsiveness', *Academy of Management Journal,* Vol. 43, No. 4, pp. 717–736.

Bell, E. and Davison, J. (2013) 'Visual Management Studies: Empirical and Theoretical Approaches', *International Journal of Management Reviews,* Vol. 15, No. 2, pp. 167–184.

Braun, V. and Clarke, V. (2006) 'Using thematic analysis in psychology', *Qualitative Research in Psychology,* Vol. 3, No. 2, pp. 77–101.

Brekhus, W.H., Galliher, J.F. and Gubrium, J.F. (2005) 'The need for thin description', *Qualitative Inquiry,* Vol. 11, No. 6, pp. 861–79.

Brinkmann, S. and Kvale, S. (2015) *InterViews: Learning the Craft of Qualitative Research Interviewing* (3rd edn). London: Sage.

Bryant, A. and Charmaz, K. (2007) *The Sage Handbook of Grounded Theory.* London: Sage.

Charmaz, K. (2014) *Constructing Grounded Theory* (2nd edn). London: Sage.

Clarke, J. and Holt, R. (2017) 'Imagery of adventure: Understanding entrepreneurial identity through metaphor and drawing', *Journal of Business Venturing,* Vol. 32, pp. 476–497.

Corbin, J. and Strauss, A. (2008) *Basics of Qualitative Research Techniques and Procedures for Developing Grounded Theory* (3rd edn). London: Sage.

Corbin, J. and Strauss, A. (2015) *Basics of Qualitative Research Techniques and Procedures for Developing Grounded Theory* (4th edn). London: Sage.

Department for Transport (2015) *Know Your Traffic Signs* London: Department for Transport. Available at https://assets.publishing.service.gov.uk/government/uploads/system/uploads/attachment_data/file/519129/know-your-traffic-signs.pdf [Accessed 20 May 2018].

Dey, I. (1993) *Qualitative Data Analysis.* London: Routledge.

Erlandson, D.A., Harris, E.L., Skipper, B.L. and Allen, S.D. (1993) *Doing Naturalistic Inquiry.* Newbury Park, CA: Sage.

Fairclough, N. (1992) *Discourse and Social Change.* Cambridge: Polity Press.

Fairclough, N. (2010) *Critical Discourse Analysis: The Critical Study of Language* (2nd edn). Harlow: Pearson Education.

Finlay, L. (2002) 'Negotiating the swamp: The opportunity and challenge of reflexivity in research practice', *Qualitative Research,* Vol. 2, No. 2, pp. 209–30.

Gerstl-Pepin, C. and Patrizio, K. (2009) 'Learning from Dumbledore's Pensieve: Metaphor as an aid in teaching reflexivity in qualitative research', *Qualitative Research,* Vol. 9, No. 3, pp. 299–308.

Glaser, B. and Strauss, A. (1967) *The Discovery of Grounded Theory.* Chicago, IL: Aldine.

Glaser, B.G. (1978) *Theoretical Sensitivity: Advances in the Methodology of Grounded Theory.* Mill Valley, CA: Sociology Press.

Glaser, B.G. (1998) *Doing Grounded Theory: Issues and Discussions.* Mill Valley, CA: Sociology Press.

Haynes, K. (2012) 'Reflexivity in qualitative research', in G. Symon and C. Cassell (eds) *Qualitative Organizational Research: Core Methods and Current Challenges.* London: Sage.

Heikkinen, S. and Lämsä, A M. (2017) 'Narratives of Spousal Support for the Careers of Men in Managerial Posts', *Gender, Work and Organization,* Vol. 24, No. 2, pp. 171–193.

Hepburn, A. and Potter, J. (2007) 'Discourse analytic practice', in C. Seale, G. Gobo, J. F. Gubrium and D. Silverman (eds) *Qualitative Research Practice.* London: Sage.

Hodson, R. (1991) 'The active worker: Compliance and autonomy at the workplace', *Journal of Contemporary Ethnography,* Vol. 20, No. 1, pp. 47–8.

Holstein, J.A. and Gubrium, J.F. (2011) 'The constructionist analytics of interpretive practice', in N.K. Denzin and Y.S. Lincoln (eds) *The Sage Handbook of Qualitative Research.* London: Sage.

Hyatt, D. (2005) 'A critical literacy frame for UK secondary education contexts', *English in Education,* Vol. 39, No. 1, pp. 43–59.

Hyatt, D. (2013) 'The critical policy discourse analysis frame: Helping doctoral students engage with the educational policy analysis', *Teaching in Higher Education,* Vol. 18, No. 8, pp. 833–45.

Johnson, P. (2004) 'Analytic induction', in G. Symon and C. Cassell (eds) *Essential Guide to Qualitative Methods and Analysis in Organizational Research.* London: Sage, pp. 165–79.

Kenealy, G.J.J. (2012) 'Grounded theory: A theory building approach', in G. Symon and C. Cassell (eds) *Qualitative Organizational Research: Core Methods and Current Challenges.* London: Sage.

King, N. and Brookes, J.M. (2017) *Template Analysis for Business and Management Students.* London: Sage.

Labov, W. (1972) *Language in the Inner City: Studies in the Black English Vernacular.* Philadelphia: University of Pennsylvania Press.

Labov, W. and Waletzky, J. (1967) 'Narrative analysis: Oral versions of personal experience', in J. Helm (ed.) *Essays on the Verbal and Visual Arts.* Seattle, WA: University of Washington Press.

Maitlis, S. (2012) 'Narrative analysis', in G. Symon and C. Cassell (eds) *Qualitative Organizational Research: Core Methods and Current Challenges,* London: Sage, pp. 492–511.

McConville, D., Arnold, J. and Smith, A. (2016) 'Employees share ownership, psychological ownership and work attitudes and behaviours: a phenomenological analysis', *Journal of Occupational and Organizational Psychology,* Vol. 89, No. 3, pp. 634–651.

Miles, M.B., Huberman, A.M. and Saldaña, J. (2014) *Qualitative Data Analysis: A Methods Sourcebook* (3rd edn). London: Sage.

Phillips, N. and Hardy, C. (2002) *Discourse Analysis: Investigating Processes of Social Construction.* London: Sage.

Pink, S. (2007) 'Visual methods', in C. Seale, G. Gobo, J. F. Gubrium and D. Silverman (eds) *Qualitative Research Practice.* London: Sage.

Riessman, C.K. (2008) *Narrative Methods for the Human Sciences.* London: Sage.

Ritchie, J., Lewis, J., McNaughton Nicholls, C. and Ormston, R. (2014) *Qualitative Research Practice* (2nd edn). London: Sage.

Rose, G. (2016) *Visual Methodologies An Introduction to Researching with Visual Materials* (4th edn). London: Sage.

Silver, C. and Lewins, A. (2014) *Using Software in Qualitative Research: a step-by-step guide* (2nd edn). London: Sage.

Silverman, D. (2013) *A Very Short, Fairly Interesting and Reasonably Cheap Book about Qualitative Research* (2nd edn). London: Sage.

Strauss, A. and Corbin, J. (1998) *Basics of Qualitative Research* (2nd edn). Thousand Oaks, CA: Sage.

Yin, R.K. (2018) *Case Study Research and Applications: Design and Methods* (6th edn). London: Sage.

Further reading

Braun, V. and Clarke, V. (2006) 'Using thematic analysis in psychology', *Qualitative Research in Psychology,* Vol. 3, No. 2, pp. 77–101. This article provides a helpful discussion of Thematic Analysis.

Charmaz, K. (2014) *Constructing Grounded Theory* (2nd edn). London: Sage. This book provides an accessible discussion and evaluation of Grounded Theory and Grounded Theory Method.

Miles, M.B., Huberman, A.M. and Saldana, J. (2014) *Qualitative Data Analysis: A Methods Sourcebook* (3rd edn). London: Sage. This sourcebook presents a range of techniques for the analysis of qualitative data.

Riessman, C.K. (2008) *Narrative Methods for the Human Sciences.* London: Sage. This book provides a helpful discussion of approaches to Narrative Analysis.

Rose, G. (2016) *Visual Methodologies An Introduction to Researching with Visual Materials* (4th edn). London: Sage. An interesting and useful book on visual research methods with helpful chapters on semiology, content analysis and discourse analysis, and material on photo elicitation and photo essays.

Silver, C. and Lewins, A. (2014) *Using Software in Qualitative Research: a step-by-step guide* (2nd edn). London: Sage. An authoritative guide to using CAQDAS.

Symon, G. and Cassell, C. (eds) (2012) *Qualitative Organizational Research: Core Methods and Current Challenges.* London: Sage. This edited book contains a range of chapters on qualitative analysis including Template Analysis, Grounded Theory, Narrative Analysis and Discourse Analysis.

Case 13
Exploring employees experiences of remote working practices

Charlie is part of a team working in a shared service centre within a large rural county council, a public sector organisation providing services for its local region. She and her team provide human resources support and guidance to staff working across all council departments. Charlie is currently studying part time for a Masters in Business Administration and needs to carry out a work-based research project. The council has recently introduced a remote working policy as part of their 'Improving Working Lives' initiative, but the uptake by staff has been small. Charlie's line manager has asked her to investigate what makes employees choose to work remotely. Her manager is hoping the findings from this research will provide information to help the council publicise remote working and encourage more employees to adopt this working practice.

Charlie had thought about using an online questionnaire, so she could collect data from a large sample of employees. However, she was interested in finding out about employees' personal experiences of remote working and did not feel questionnaires would provide such insight. She also wanted to explore employees' opinions about why they thought the council was so keen to promote remote working. Charlie had read Miller and Glassner (2011) who argue accounts from in-depth interviews enable opportunities to explore and theorise about the social world. She found other writers described interviews as a type of conversation, which can encourage participants to reveal personal subjective experiences (Brinkmann and Kvale, 2015). This was exactly what Charlie was hoping to achieve, so she decided interviews would be the most appropriate method.

In order to recruit participants, Charlie posted a message using the council's bulletin board, on the organisation's secure intranet. She was pleased that over the next few days several employees contacted her to say they would be willing to be interviewed. Charlie was keen to conduct the interviews as soon as possible and arranged to interview the first four volunteers over the following week. There were three main questions Charlie wished to address:

1 Why do employees choose to work remotely?
2 What are the organisation's reasons for introducing remote working?
3 What are the barriers to remote working?

One week later Charlie was absolutely amazed at the wealth of data that four interviews had generated; but now her dilemma was what to do with it. She had come across thematic analysis as a popular approach to analysing qualitative data, and knew it provided a systematic, yet flexible way to analyse both small and large amounts of qualitative data (Braun and Clarke 2006). Furthermore, it was not reliant on a particular philosophical perspective.

Charlie thought that by undertaking a thematic analysis she would have the flexibility to move recursively back and forth between the different participants responses. This meant she wouldn't need to wait until she had conducted all her interviews before starting her analysis. She had begun familiarising herself with her data (the first stage in thematic analysis) from the moment she conducted the first interview. Charlie became even more immersed in her data as she transcribed the interview recordings. At this stage she began to draw out experiences, issues, behaviours, reactions, feelings and so on emerging from the data. But this was not enough, she had to go beyond this stage in order to sort, code and categorise each of these elements. This would require her to generate codes (sometimes referred to as labels or categories), based on the themes she considered to be important. Charlie would then be able develop and refine a thematic framework which would enable her in to present her findings illustratively and support further analysis, interpretation and discussion.

Below is a small extract from the first forty-minute interview Charlie transcribed. The full transcript of over 5,000 words comprised 10 word-processed A4 pages.

Within the transcript Charlie has used the following transcription conventions:

(.) A dot in between brackets indicates a gap between utterances, the greater the number of dots, the greater the gap.

(( )) Double brackets indicate the transcriber's descriptions of what is happening, rather than a transcription.

] Single right square bracket denotes point at which utterance part terminated by another.

[Single left square bracket denotes point of start of utterance overlap.

She could already see themes emerging that she felt would be helpful in beginning to answer her research questions:

Charlie: What were your reasons for choosing to work remotely?

Employee: The main one(. . .) Well I thought it would actually formalise and legitimise the working from home and because I live in Overshire, I have a long journey in and it also guaranteed that my work couldn't be spread through the week and I would have to have two, three days working from home. So that was my thinking at the time.

Charlie: And has that happened? Has it worked out that you get two]

Employee: [Yeah, generally. Because my line manager used to organise that and he was always very conscious of making sure that people's working arrangements worked out well. But yeah, it generally works fine.

Charlie: How is working remotely different to office working?

Employee: It's really not a very good deal. It's a really bad deal actually!((laughing)). You're sold this idea that it will be an advantage and you'll get a laptop and you'll get an office chair and a printer and all these things, which you do and you get a phone and stuff, but actually when you come into work you have to use a hot-desk. So you're sat in an office where you haven't got your stuff with you which is a pain in the neck. You're constantly disrupted, you can never work in a quiet environment because there are always people milling around. So that was a real difference. The working from home bit, I've got an office at home and so it takes up your home space, that's the other thing.

Charlie: So, when you work remotely is it always at home?

Employee: Yes, but I've always done some work from home to an extent, but it makes the intrusion bigger. So instead of just having a laptop and a few papers and having the bulk of things in work, I now have the bulk of stuff at home and also things like, I didn't really think about actually how would I get all of that stuff home? So I had to physically move everything myself, there was no help with moving all of the rubbish, all the boxes, files and stuff.

Charlie: OK(. . .) so what do you think are the main reasons for the council introducing remote working?

Employee: Well I think it's cost minimisation, I think it makes (. . .) If you think you've got twelve people or something sharing one office, it makes complete sense because all they've had to dish out for is for each of us a laptop. Well they would have had to provide us each with a desktop anyway. They've had to give each of us a printer, a desk chair and a phone so I think it's pretty cheap.

It's a cheap alternative really, yeah. And from what I can see, everybody works really long hours. So when you're here or working at home, I think I work longer hours at home actually.

Charlie: So what is it you like about working remotely?

Employee: I think the thing is that I quite like variety and the whole thing of actually working the same set hours and getting the same train every day and doing all of that I don't like. So I quite like having different working patterns every week and I think that's what I'd resist is going away from that, yeah. But I think it does really impinge on your working life and I think you're left to sort out your own work. So being autonomous also gives you the responsibility then to organise your work properly.

Questions

(Please refer to section 13.6 for further details on Thematic Analysis)

1   The first stage of Thematic Analysis is 'familiarisation', which involves total immersion in the data. Read through Charlie's interview transcript extract above and familiarise yourself with the contents. Make a note of any themes, patterns and meanings emerging from the data that could help Charlie answer her research questions.

2   The second stage of Thematic Analysis involves coding (or categorising) your data. Codes (labels) are used to provide a description of the key themes or patterns emerging from the data. From the familiarisation you carried out in question 1, develop a list of codes to describe the key points you have identified as important. You may find it helpful to assign a colour to your codes to assist with coding later.

3   Once you have developed your list of codes, go back to the transcript and assign each key piece of data to one of your codes. Coding is a flexible process, so as you code, link data that has a similar meaning, or data that you would like to compare and contrast. You may need to refine your codes as you work through the coding process.

4   Now the data is coded you can search for themes, patterns and relationships in your list of codes. Look at the codes you have generated. How many do you have? Organise your codes into broader themes (or categories). You may find you have main themes and sub-themes, but always remember to keep the research questions in mind. You may find it helpful to organise your themes and codes in a table or hierarchy.

5   Look at the themes you developed in question 4. Do any of your initial themes need to be merged, amended or discarded? Do you need to create new themes? What evidence and explanations are you now able to offer in answer to the research questions?

References

Braun, V. and Clarke, V. (2006) 'Using Thematic Analysis in Psychology', *Qualitative Research in Psychology* 3 (2), 77–101.

Brinkmann, S. and Kvale, S. (2015) InterViews: Learning the Craft of Qualitative Research Interviewing (3rd edition). London: Sage.

Miller, J. and Glassner, B. (2011) 'The "Inside" and the "Outside": Finding Realities in Interviews'. In Silverman, D. (Ed.) Qualitative Research (3rd edition). London: Sage. 131–148.

Additional case studies relating to material covered in this chapter are available via the book's companion website: www.pearsoned.co.uk/saunders.

They are:
- Creating environmentally friendly office spaces.
- Communicating bad news at Abco.
- Paying for competence at Investco.
- Internet abuse in universities.
- The influence of film on tourist decision making.
- Creating environmentally friendly office spaces.
- The impact of share announcements on market analysts' behaviour.

Self-check answers

13.1 There are a number of reasons why we may describe qualitative analysis as an 'interactive process'. Analysis needs to occur during the collection of data as well as after it. This helps to shape the direction of data collection, especially where you are following a grounded theory approach. The interactive nature of data collection and analysis allows you to recognise important themes, patterns and relationships as you collect data. As a result, you will be able to re-code and re-categorise your existing data to see whether emergent themes, patterns and relationships are present in the cases you have previously analysed. In addition, you will be able to adjust your future data collection approach to see whether they exist in cases where you intend to conduct your research.

13.2 You will generate three sorts of data that you will need to retain and file as the result of undertaking qualitative research.

The first of these may be referred to as raw data files. A wide range of files potentially fit within this category. These include audio-visual recordings, documents, images, original notes, written up notes and transcripts you make or collect. Electronic and word-processed versions of these files may be contained in a computer-based project file.

The second of these is analytical files containing your coded and categorised data. Alternatively, this may contain your summary or your narrative. These may also be contained in a computerised project file.

The third of these may be referred to as a supporting file, or indeed it may be different files, containing working papers, self-memos, interim reports and so forth. Again, these may also be contained in a computerised project file. You are well advised to keep all of this until the end of your research project.

Eventually you will create a fourth type of file – containing your finished work!

13.3 A *deductive* analytical approach is one where you will seek to use existing theory to shape the approach that you adopt to the qualitative research process and to aspects of data analysis. An *inductive* analytical approach is one where you will seek to build up a theory that is adequately grounded in a number of relevant cases. The design of qualitative research requires you to recognise this choice and to choose an appropriate approach to guide your research project.

13.4 a There are a number of implications of using a deductive analytical approach for the way in which you conduct the process of qualitative analysis:

- You will be in a position to commence your data collection with a well-defined research question and objectives and a clear framework and propositions, derived from the theory that you will have used.
- With regard to sampling, you will be in a position to identify the number and type of organisations to which you wish to gain access in order to undertake data collection to answer your research question and meet your objectives.
- The use of literature and the theory within it will shape the data collection questions that you wish to ask those who participate in your research project.
- You will be able to commence data collection with an initial set of categories and codes derived from your theoretical propositions/hypotheses and conceptual framework linked to your research question and objectives.
- This approach will provide you with key themes and patterns to search for in your data, and your analysis will be guided by the theoretical propositions and explanations with which you commenced.

b The main implications of using an inductive analytical approach for the process of qualitative analysis are likely to be related to:

- managing and categorising a large number of code labels, which will probably emerge from the data that you collect;
- working with smaller rather than larger units of data;
- recognising significant themes and issues during early analysis to help you to consider where data collection should be focused in the future;
- recognising the relationships between categories and rearranging these into a hierarchical form, with the emergence of subcategories;
- seeking to verify apparent relationships against the actual data that you have collected;
- understanding how negative cases broaden (or threaten) your emerging explanation;
- recognising the relationships between the principal categories that have emerged from this grounded approach in order to develop an explanatory theory;
- being rigorous in your use of the procedures that are advocated in order to be able to produce a research report that contains findings that are sufficiently 'grounded' to substantiate the analysis or theory that you are seeking to advance.

13.5 Key similarities include the important point that these are both forms of thematic analysis, as we recognise in Section 13.3. Both of these techniques to analyse data are flexible in relation to not being tied to a specific methodological or philosophical approach; they are also flexible in relation to their approach to theory development. Key differences relate to the development of themes and recognising relationships between these: in Thematic Analysis, themes are principally developed after the coding of all data has occurred; in

Template Analysis, a template is developed after an initial round of coding and themes and the relationships between these are subsequently mapped onto this emerging template. As a result, themes are developed much earlier in Template Analysis compared with Thematic Analysis. Template Analysis also emphasises the hierarchical nature of analysis and may result in more thematic levels of analysis compared to Thematic Analysis.

Get ahead using resources on the companion website at: www.pearsoned.co.uk/saunders.

- Improve your IBM SPSS Statistics with practice tutorials.
- Save time researching on the Internet with the Smarter Online Searching Guide.
- Test your progress using self-assessment questions.
- Follow live links to useful websites.

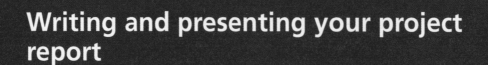

Chapter 14

Writing and presenting your project report

Learning outcomes

By the end of this chapter you should be able to:

- understand the issues about which you need to be concerned when undertaking writing for your project report;
- evaluate different ways to structure your project report;
- differentiate between a project report and a consultancy report;
- adopt an appropriate and accessible writing style for your report;
- write a project report focused on meeting the necessary assessment criteria;
- write a reflective account of your research project;
- plan a presentation of your project report using either slides or a poster.

14.1 Introduction

Some of you may view the process of writing your project report and presenting it orally as an exciting prospect. However, it is more likely that you will approach this stage of your research with some trepidation. This would be a great pity. We believe that writing about your work is the most effective way of clarifying your thoughts. Writing may be the time when we think most deeply. This suggests that writing should not be seen as the last stage of your research but, as we illustrated at the start of this book in Figure 1.2, thought of as something that is continuous throughout the research process. In this way your project report may be seen as something you develop throughout your research rather than leaving it until every other part has been completed.

Writing is a powerful way to learn. Most teachers will tell you that the best way to learn is to teach. This is because of the necessity to understand something thoroughly yourself before you can begin to explain it to others. This is the position you are in as the writer of your project report. You have to explain a highly complex set of ideas and findings to an audience that you must assume has little or no knowledge of your subject. There is another problem here, which has a parallel with teaching. Often, the more familiar you are with a subject, the more difficult

it is to explain it to others with no knowledge of that subject. You will be so familiar with your research topic that, like the teacher, you will find it difficult to put yourself in the place of the reader. The result of this is that you may fail to explain something that you assume the reader will know. Even worse, you may leave out important material that should be included.

However, why do most of us view writing with such concern? This may be because of our experience of writing. Many of us are afraid of exposing our efforts to an audience that we feel will be more likely to criticise than encourage. In our education much of our writing has been little more than rehashing the ideas of others. This has taught us to think of writing as a boring, repetitive process. Some of us are impatient. We are unwilling to devote the time and energy (and inevitable frustration) that is needed for writing.

Writing to express thoughts

If you have ever considered visiting London, you will have a list of places that you would like to visit. One that is on many people's list is the Tower of London. This is a complex of historical buildings dating from the twelfth century, which has served a number of purposes, including being a royal palace and fortress. Parts of the Tower of London have also been a prison and visitors to the Tower see 'attractions' including Traitors' Gate, the Bloody Tower, Torture at the Tower and the Scaffold Site. During the reign of England's Tudor kings and queens, important prisoners were held in the Beauchamp Tower. In the Prisoners' Room on the first floor of this tower you will see an extraordinary collection of graffiti carved into its walls. Unlike much modern graffiti these are carefully preserved as an historical record of those who were imprisoned there. These political and religious prisoners carved not only their names but also statements about their situation and their innocence.

If they had been alive today these prisoners would have wanted to send emails, instant messages and tweets and to use a range of social media to bring attention to their plight and to represent their points of view. Increasingly our world is being connected through the use of these media, so that individuals can talk, share information and coordinate their activities. Even in the isolation of a prison in a tower these people sought to express themselves through carving words in a wall. Today we have many more means to express ourselves by writing to others. The speed with which we can write and communicate with others means that we are likely to take writing for granted, without seeing this as something to be fearful about.

This fear of criticism is captured perfectly by Richards (2007), who recites the story of being asked by the distinguished sociologist Howard Becker to adopt his method of sitting down and writing what came into her head about the research she had done without even consulting her notes. Her fears of producing poor-quality material, which would be derided by colleagues who saw her work, are described vividly. It is a fear most of us experience. Set against this, most of us write a lot more than we imagine. We all have thoughts that we want to express and the desire to write about these has always been common, as the opening vignette illustrates. This vignette should be interpreted as giving you the confidence to write, even when you do this for formal reasons, rather than being fearful about writing.

This chapter looks at a number of issues that may concern you as you write your report. As we have discussed, undertaking writing remains a concern for many of us. In this chapter we begin by looking at some general issues about undertaking writing (Section 14.2). Section 14.3 focuses on a key issue about your project report – how to structure it. This section recognises that your research approach and research strategy may affect the way in which you wish to structure your project report; it discusses alternative ways to do this. Section 14.4 also focuses on structure, related to composing a consultancy report for an organisational audience.

Structural issues continue to be important after you have devised an overall structure for your project report. In Section 14.5 we look at some ways in which you may make the content of your report clear and accessible to your readers. Also critical to your ability to produce a clear and accessible project report will be your writing style. In Section 14.6 we offer some ideas about how to develop an appropriate writing style for your project report. Underpinning your choice of structure, the way in which you compose the content of your report and the writing style you use will be your concern to meet the criteria established to assess your work. In Section 14.7 we consider some generic criteria that often inform the specific criteria set by examining institutions to assess project reports.

In addition, many universities also require a reflective essay or statement as part of your project report. This can be developed from the entries you have made in your reflective diary throughout the research process when answering the questions in Box 1.4 (Section 1.5). We consider this in Section 14.8. For many of us the fear of making an oral presentation is even more daunting than writing. As we note in Section 14.9, some of this apprehension can be overcome by thorough preparation and this section examines the preparation and delivery of the oral presentation.

14.2 Undertaking writing

Writing may be approached as a continuous process throughout your research project. Before you commence your research, you will need to draft your research proposal. As you undertake your research you will be writing summaries, self-memos or entries in your research notebook and keeping a reflective diary, as we outline in Sections 1.5 and 13.5. You may also be consulting literature related to your research topic and drafting an early version of your literature review, and then revising this as your research progresses.

Approaching the task of writing as a continual process throughout the research project may be helpful to you in different ways. It should help to progress the task of producing your project report, dissertation or thesis and avoid the perception that this is a monumental chore to be undertaken at the final stage of your project. It should also help to focus your thoughts and aid your analysis. We now consider some practical hints to assist you in undertaking your writing.

Create time for your writing

Writing is not an activity that can be allocated an odd half-hour whenever it is convenient. It requires sustained effort and concentration. Some people prefer to write all day until they drop from exhaustion! Others like to set a strict timetable where a few hours a day are devoted to writing. You may find it helpful to set aside a particular period each day to write. Writing on successive days will also help to ensure the continuity of your ideas and avoid having to keep 'thinking your way back' into your research.

Write when your mind is fresh

Writing is a creative process so it is important to write at the time of day when your mind is at its freshest. All of us have jobs to do that require little or no creativity so arrange your day to do uncreative jobs when you are at your least mentally alert.

Find a regular writing place

Writing is often best undertaken in the same place. This may be because you are psychologically comfortable in a particular space. It may be for more practical reasons. If that space is your own room you will already be familiar with the need to make sure you do not disturb yourself or allow others to do this. Switching off all distractions such as your mobile phone, social media and television and putting a 'do not disturb' sign on the door may allow you to work undisturbed in your own room. However, if this doesn't work, you may be able to concentrate better if you find a neutral space, such as an area in your university's library, where you can write without your possessions or your friends being able to distract you! What is important is to know what distracts you and to remove those distractions.

Create a structure for your writing

Writing requires structure. Your research project is likely to be one of the largest pieces of written work you undertake. We discuss ways in which you may create an overall structure to write up your research project in Section 14.3. You will also need to create a structure for each chapter.

It is important to think about what you want a chapter to contain before you attempt to write it. As you work though the material you have assembled to write a chapter and jot down ideas that flow from this, you will start to work out how your ideas and this material may be grouped and how such groupings may be related to one another. Your purpose will be to create a sequential structure for the chapter you intend to write up.

Once you have a structure for the chapter composed of a number of sections and possibly sub-sections, you can start to write each section in turn. Even if you alter this structure or rearrange the order of the sections within it, you will have a framework to guide the writing of the chapter on which you are working (Box 14.1).

Set goals and achieve them

Writing may involve goal or target setting. You may decide to set yourself the goal to write a section of a chapter in a given period, or to target writing a number of words. This can be helpful where you have allocated yourself a certain amount of time to write the

Box 14.1
Focus on student research

Devising an outline structure

Andrea found the task of writing each part of her project report to be demanding. She started her literature review in the early stages of her research project. She felt that this early attempt lacked coherence and development. She returned to the planning phase of her literature review and mapped her ideas using some mind mapping software.

This process provided her with a number of discrete ideas from the literature related to her research question that she wanted to include in her review.

She worked on the order of these ideas until they matched the flow of her research objectives. This provided her with an idea or ideas for each section of her review. She then devised headings for each section and for the various sub-sections. She now had the 'skeleton' or framework of her literature review. This provided Andrea with an outline structure to start to write her literature review and she now worked on each section in turn.

The wording of some these headings changed, as did the order of some of the subheadings. However, she found the creation of this type of outline structure or framework to be very helpful, both in terms of facilitating her writing and providing targets to complete, such as a section in a given period. She used the same approach to write each of the other parts of each project report.

chapter on which you are working, to be able to judge if you are 'on time'. However, it is important to be realistic about these goals. If you are too ambitious the quality of your work may suffer as you rush to meet your target.

Finish a writing session on a high point and provide a link to a new session

Writing is about ideas. Many writers prefer to get to the end of a section before they finish writing so that they do not lose any ideas they develop during that session. This also allows them to tidy up one set of materials and possibly to lay out those for the next session of writing. The worst thing you can do is to leave a complex section half completed as it will be difficult to pick up your thoughts and ideas (Box 14.2).

Box 14.2
Focus on student research

Getting restarted

Veronika always tried to complete a section or sub-section within a writing session. This allowed her to concentrate on a set of ideas without interruption. When she did not have time to complete a section or sub-section, she made notes about her ideas to act as an aide-mémoire for her next writing session.

Veronika also found it useful to start a writing session by reading the section on which she had worked previously. Her mind was very 'clear' at the start of a new writing session and she was able to read and improve her previous work. This also had the benefit of refreshing her thoughts about what she had completed previously and directing her thoughts about what she wanted to achieve next.

Commence a new writing session by reviewing your previous session

We each find it helpful to commence a new writing session by reviewing and revising what we wrote in the previous session. If you do this it should provide you with two benefits. Firstly, it will allow you to review what you wrote previously with a fresh mind. This will allow you to revise what you wrote previously. Secondly, it will allow you to think yourself back into the ideas that you were working with previously. This should help you to progress your writing in this new writing session (Box 14.2).

Ensure you keep earlier versions and back-up copies of your work

Writing is time-consuming and enables you to develop your ideas and complete your analysis, so don't forget to create a back-up copy of the current version of your writing as well as earlier drafts. You may need them if your computer dies or you wish to revert to an earlier version (Box 14.3).

Get friends to read your work

Writing is creative and exciting, but checking our work may not be! The importance of getting someone else to read through your material cannot be overemphasised. Your project tutor should not be the first person who reads your report, even in its draft form.

Ask a friend to be constructively critical. Your friend must be prepared to tell you about things in the text that are not easy to understand – to point out omissions, spelling, punctuation and grammatical errors. Overall, your friend must tell you whether the piece of writing makes sense and achieves its purpose.

This is not an easy process for you or your critical friend. Most of us are sensitive to criticism, particularly when the consequence of it is the necessity to do a lot more work.

Box 14.3
Focus on student research

'Help, I've lost my research project'

Ross had heard of cases where others hadn't been able to submit their assignments because of computer problems. He had always found his course demanding and wondered how he would cope if the same happened to him.

This made him determined to keep at least one backup copy of every document that he created or altered. It would be disastrous if he lost any of his files without these being backed up. He very carefully followed the same routine every time he worked on his project. At the end of every session working on his project, he backed up files he had worked on or new files he had created on to a USB mass storage device that he kept specifically for his research and on the cloud. On every Sunday afternoon he also emailed all of his project files to himself.

Some weeks into his project he encountered a problem with the Netbook that he used for all of his work. He took it along to the Students' Union, where there was an IT shop. They examined the machine and told Ross that his solid state drive had failed. Ross was annoyed and shocked by this. This was another expense for Ross to have the component replaced. This left him feeling pretty low. He was reassured, however, because earlier electronic versions of his work had been saved carefully and he had a back-up copy of the most recent version.

Many of us are also hesitant about giving criticism. However, if your project report does not communicate to the reader in the way it should, you will get it back for revision work in the long run. It is much better to try to ensure that this does not happen.

14.3 Structuring your project report

There are different ways to structure a project report, dissertation or thesis. The way you write up your project report may follow the traditional structure or an alternative structure that better reflects your choice of research strategy. Whether you have a choice about how to structure your project report will depend on the requirements of your examining body. This may be something you can discuss with your project tutor.

Before you consider different ways to structure your project report, it is important to realise the structure you use will emphasise (or reflect) certain aspects of your research. Yin (2018) summarises underlying 'reporting approaches' in terms of what they emphasise or reflect. Of these, five may, potentially, be suitable for your project report. They are: linear-analytic; comparative; chronological; theory building; and suspense. We outline these before discussing the traditional and alternative ways to structure your research report.

Linear-analytic approach

In a linear-analytic approach a project report is structured logically to reflect the research process. The traditional way to structure a project report is essentially a linear-analytic approach. It is well suited to a deductive, theory-testing approach but is also adaptable to other research approaches.

Comparative approach

In a comparative approach the emphasis is placed on devising a structure that allows analytical comparisons to be made. Different types of comparisons may be made. In one type of comparative approach, the structure used will reflect the fact that the same set of data is analysed more than once using different analytical perspectives to allow the results of these analyses to then be compared. In another type of comparative approach, the structure will reflect the fact that different but related data sets are analysed so that the results of these may then be compared.

Chronological approach

In a chronological approach a structure is devised that allows the emphasis to be placed on the sequence of events evident in the data set. At its simplest, this is essentially an historical account, where it is important to use a structure that allows the data to be reported in a chronological way to understand how the order of events and contextual factors produce cause-and effect sequences.

Theory-building approach

In a theory-building approach a structure is devised that allows the emphasis to be placed on the emergence and refinement of research ideas and the development of themes, relationships and explanations as data are collected. Whereas the linear-analytic approach presents the research process in a logical, rational and 'sanitised' way, the theory-building approach is likely to present research as an emergent and messy process but which ultimately produces a convincing story and compelling theoretical explanation. This approach may resemble a chronological approach, albeit that it reports how a theory is developed rather than documenting the sequential development of explanations.

Suspense approach

In a suspense approach, the emphasis is placed on devising a structure that allows the reader to understand how an explanation has been built. Yin (2018) suggests that the explanation or answer to the research question is presented in the introduction. The structure of the project report is then devoted to exploring alternative explanations of the phenomenon being studied to be able to evaluate why the chosen explanation is the most convincing.

How might these underlying structural types affect your choice of report structure?

These reporting approaches should help you to evaluate what type of structure will best suit your project report. They should prompt you to ask yourself the following questions:

- How does my research design affect the way I might structure my project report?
- How does the way I analysed my data affect the way I might structure my project report?
- How does the purpose of my research affect the way I might structure my project report?

These and other questions you may wish to ask yourself will help you to evaluate these approaches to choosing a structure for your project report. They may also be used in combination and you may wish to devise a structure that incorporates elements from more than one approach.

Your answers to these questions may lead you to adopt the traditional structure to write up your project report, or to seek to adapt this structure, or to use an alternative structure. Whichever structure you wish to adopt, you will first need to check that this will meet two requirements. Firstly, is it permissible? Will your university allow you to use the structure you devise? You may be able to discuss this with your project tutor. Secondly, will it be clear to those who will read your project report, to allow them to understand what you have done, and will it allow you to show how you have sought to answer your research question? Where you are able to exercise some choice about how to structure your project report, you will need to think about this second requirement carefully to ensure that your proposed structure is fit for purpose.

Structuring your report

Charmaz (2014) refers to the traditional way to structure a project report as a 'logico-deductive' approach. In this approach, the report's structure reflects the logic and linear nature of the process used to undertake a deductive approach. We outline this structure in the next sub-section. There are two ways in which structures may vary from the traditional structure, related to the order and nature of the report's content. Firstly, in relation to order, content may be arranged differently, or in a more integrated way, to that of the traditional structure. For example, rather than placing the Literature Review immediately after the Introduction, as is the case in the traditional structure, it may be considered later in an alternative structure, or integrated throughout the report. Secondly, in relation to the nature of content, the material in the report will vary, perhaps so much so that the content of an alternative structure may seem, on face appearance, to bear little or limited resemblance to that of the traditional structure.

It would be unwise to suggest that a specific report structure should be used for a particular research strategy. Researchers using the same research strategy write up their work using different structures. They may choose to use the traditional structure, variations on this, or an alternative structure. However, inductive and abductive approaches are sometimes associated with alternative ways of presenting and structuring a project report.

Characteristics of the traditional structure

The traditional structure generally contains the following parts:

1 Abstract
2 Introduction
3 Literature Review
4 Method
5 Findings/Results
6 Discussion
7 Conclusions
8 References
9 Appendices

Some of these parts are likely to be required irrespective of the structure you use to write up your project report. These include an Introduction and Conclusions, even if these are titled differently, as well as an Abstract, References and any Appendices. The substantive parts in between these are likely to vary when you use an alternative structure in relation to an inductive research strategy such as Action Research, a Case Study, Ethnography, Grounded Theory or Narrative Inquiry, as we go on to discuss later.

Abstract

The **Abstract** is a short summary of the complete content of the project report. It often contains four short paragraphs with the answers to the following questions:

1 What were my research questions and why were these important?
2 How did I go about answering the research questions?
3 What did I find out in response to my research questions?
4 What conclusions do I draw regarding my research questions?

A good Abstract should be short (generally between 200 and 300 words); self-contained; a reflection of the report's content; adequate to inform your reader about the report; objective, precise and easy to read.

The academic publisher, Emerald, gives advice to potential academic authors on how to compile an abstract. This is shown in Box 14.4. Although referring to academic journal articles (papers), it is useful to consider in terms of preparation of your research report. Writing a good abstract is difficult. The obvious thing to do is to write it after you have finished the report. We suggest that you draft it at the start of your writing so that you have got your storyline abundantly clear in your mind. You can then amend the draft when you have finished the report. Box 14.5 contains an example of an abstract by Mark and colleagues.

Introduction

The **Introduction** should give the reader a clear idea about the central issue of concern in your research and why you thought that this was worth studying. It should also include a full statement of your research question(s), research aim and research objectives. If your

Box 14.4
Focus on management research

Guide to writing an abstract for publication

Abstracts should be written clearly and concisely, containing no more than 250 words and reflecting only what appears in the original paper.

Purpose

State the reason(s) for writing the paper or the research aims.

Design/methodology/approach

Describe how objectives were achieved and the main method(s) used for the research as well as the approach to the topic and the theoretical or subject scope of the paper.

Findings

Outline what was found in the research by referring to analysis and results.

Value

Discuss the contribution which the paper makes.

Research limitations/implications (if applicable)

Identify limitations in the research process and suggestions for future research.

Practical implications (if applicable)

Outline any implications for practice and impact on business or enterprise.

Social implications (if applicable)

Outline any impact on society of this research.

Source: Emerald Group Publishing (2018) Developed from advice on the Emerald website, www.emeraldgrouppublishing.com/authors/guides/write/abstracts.htm. Reproduced with permission

research is based in an organisation, we think that it is a good idea to include some brief details about the organisation, such as its history, size, products and services. This may be a general background to the more specific detail on the research setting you include in the method chapter.

It is also important to include a 'route map' to guide the reader through the rest of the report. This will give brief details of the content of each chapter and present an overview of how your storyline unfolds. You will probably find it helpful to write the Introduction after drafting the rest of your report to ensure that it accurately represents the report's content.

Literature review

Chapter 3 focuses on writing a literature review. In the traditional, logico-deductive structure this is placed before the Method chapter. The main purpose of your Literature Review is to set your study within its wider, theoretical context so the reader understands how your study relates to the work that has already been done on your topic. The Literature Review will directly inform your research questions (see Box 14.6) and any specific hypotheses or propositions that your research is designed to test. These hypotheses or propositions will also suggest a particular research approach, strategy and data collection techniques.

The title of your literature review chapter should reflect the content of the chapter and we do not recommend that you simply call it 'Literature Review'. It may be that your literature is reviewed in more than one chapter. This may be the case, for example, where you were using more than one body of literature in your research.

Box 14.5
Focus on management research

Abstract from a refereed journal article in the journal "Health"

'Standards expected by doctors' regulatory bodies in respect of the process of consent to treatment have arguably sought to restructure the nature of the doctor–patient relationship from one of the paternalism to that of shared decision-making. Yet, few studies have explored empirically, from patients' perspectives, the extent to which the process of consent to treatment enables or disables patients' participation in medical decision-making. Our article examines patients' attitudes towards the consent process, exploring how and why these attitudes influence patients' active participation in decision-making and considering possible consequent medico-legal issues. Data were collected longitudinally using semi-structured interviews and field observations involving 35 patients and 19 of their caregivers, in an English hospital between February and November 2014. These indicate that generally patients defer to the doctor in respect of treatment decision-making. Although most patients and their caregivers wanted detailed information and discussion, they did not necessarily expect that this would be provided. Furthermore, patients perceived that signing the consent form was an obligatory routine principally to protect doctors from legal action should something go wrong. Our study suggests that patients' predominantly paternalistic perceptions of the consent process can not only undermine attempts by doctors to involve them in decision-making but, as patients are now considered in law as informed actors, their perceptions of the consent form as not being in their interests could be a self-fulfilling prophecy if signing is undertaken without due consideration to the content.'

Source: Carole Doherty, Charitini Stavropoulou, Mark NK Saunders and Tracey Brown (2017) 'The consent process: Enabling or disabling patients' active participation?', *Health*, Vol. 21, No. 2, p. 205. Reproduced with permission.

Box 14.6
Focus on student research

Using the literature review to inform the research questions

Guiyan was a Chinese student studying for a master's degree. In her research dissertation she was interested to know whether Chinese managers would be able to conduct performance appraisal schemes effectively in China with Chinese employees. She was aware that there were certain aspects of Chinese culture that would make this difficult. Guiyan studied two bodies of literature: one relating to the managerial skills of performance appraisal, and a second concerned with the effects of Chinese culture on the ways in which Chinese managers manage their employees. She presented both in a literature review chapter. She structured her chapter around three questions:

1 What are the key skills needed by managers to conduct performance appraisal effectively?
2 What are the most important aspects of Chinese culture which impact upon on the ways in which Chinese managers manage their employees?
3 To what extent will the aspects of Chinese culture, explained in the answer to Question 2, affect the ability of Chinese managers to conduct performance appraisal effectively?

From this, Guiyan developed a theoretical proposition that supported her initial idea that certain aspects of Chinese culture would make the conduct of performance appraisal by Chinese managers with Chinese employees difficult. She was then ready to move on to her method chapter, which was an explanation of the way in which she would test her theoretical proposition.

Method

This should be a detailed and transparent chapter giving the reader sufficient information to understand why you chose the method you used, to assess the reliability and validity of the procedures you used, and to evaluate the trustworthiness of your findings. Box 14.7 provides a checklist of the points you should address in the Method chapter.

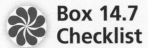

Box 14.7
Checklist

Points to address in your method chapter

Research setting

✔ What was the research setting and why did you choose it?

✔ How suitable was it to answer your research question and address your objectives?

✔ When did you conduct the research and how did its timing affect your ability to answer your research question and address your research objectives?

Selecting the sample

✔ Where probability sampling was used what was the sampling frame for your research?

- What was the size of your intended sample and how did you decide this?
- Which sampling technique did you use and why was this most appropriate?
- How representative was your actual sample in relation to the target population?

✔ Where non-probability sampling was used how did your intended sample relate to your research question and objectives?

- Which sampling technique did you use and why was this most appropriate?
- How do the characteristics of those who took part match those of your intended sample and what are the characteristics of those who declined to take part?

✔ For either type of sampling, where your research was affected by the possibility of non-response error how did you respond to this?

Data collection

✔ Which data collection method or methods was used and why?

✔ How was the method, or methods, developed and tested?

✔ How were potential participants/ respondents/ informants approached to take part?

✔ What instructions and ethical assurances were given to those from whom data were collected?

✔ How was this method (or these methods) conducted/ administered/ delivered/ completed (and where delivered how was this collected) and why?

✔ How long (on average) did each respondent/participant/informant spend providing data?

✔ What issue or issues was associated with any aspect of data collection and how was this/were these resolved?

Data analysis procedures

✔ How were the resulting data analysed?

✔ What issue or issues was associated with any aspect of data analysis and how was this/these resolved?

✔ Have you ensured that procedures (including statistical techniques) were applied correctly and, where appropriate, assumptions satisfied?

Reliability and validity or dependability and credibility/transferability

✔ Have you assessed the validity/credibility of the measures you used in the research?

✔ Have you assessed the internal validity/credibility of your findings?

✔ Have you explained how you sought to ensure reliability/dependability of your findings?

✔ Have you assessed the generalisability/transferability of your findings?

✔ Have you recognised the limitations of your research?

Ethical concerns

Which ethical issues were raised by the study and how were these addressed?

Findings/Results

This provides you with the opportunity to report your results and is probably the most straightforward part of your report to write. Where you have analysed your data quantitatively, you will include the results of your statistical analyses and use tables and graphs to illustrate your findings (do not put these in the appendices if they are important to your argument). Where data are analysed qualitatively you are likely to include illustrative quotations to convey the richness of your data and offer insights. The Findings/Results may be composed of more than one chapter. The question you should ask yourself is: 'Is more than one chapter necessary to communicate my findings/results clearly?'

There are two important points to bear in mind when writing about your findings. The first is to stress that the purpose is to present the results of your data analysis. It is normally not appropriate in this chapter to discuss these results. This is the purpose of the Discussion and Conclusions chapters. Many of us become confused about the difference between findings and discussion. One way of overcoming any confusion is to draw up a table with two columns. The first should be headed 'What I found out' and the second 'What judgements I have formed on the basis of what I found out'. The first list will be based on your data analysis (e.g. 66 per cent of responding customers indicated they preferred to receive email messages rather than mail shots) and therefore the content of your Findings/Results. The second list will be your judgements based on what you found out (e.g. it appears that electronic forms of communication are preferred to traditional) and therefore the content of your Discussion chapter.

The second point links to the first. Drawing up a table will lead you to a consideration of the way in which you present your findings. The purpose of your project report is to communicate the answer to your research question in as clear a manner as possible to your readers. Therefore you should structure your findings in a clear, logical and easily understood manner. There are many ways of doing this. One of the simplest is to return to the research objectives and let these dictate the order in which you present your findings. Alternatively, you may prefer to report your findings thematically. You could present the themes in descending order of importance. Whichever method you choose should be obvious to the reader. As with the Literature Review, the chapter(s) devoted to results should be titled in an interesting way that reflects the content of findings.

The clarity of your findings should be such that they may find their way into a news report similar to that in Box 14.8.

Discussion

Findings presented without thought run the risk of your reader asking 'so what?': what meaning do these findings have for me?; for my organisation?; for professional practice?; for the development of theory? So the main focus of the Discussion is to interpret the results you presented in the previous chapter. You should state the relation of the findings to the research questions or objectives discussed in the Introduction. In addition, the Discussion should discuss the implications of your research for the relevant theories which you detailed in your Literature Review. It is usual to discuss the strengths, weaknesses and limitations of your study. However, it is not a good idea to be too modest here and draw attention to aspects of your research which you may consider to be a limitation but that the reader is unlikely to notice!

The Discussion is where you have the opportunity to shine. It will show the degree of insight that you exhibit in reaching your conclusions. However, it is the part of the report that most of us find difficult. It is the second major opportunity in the research process to demonstrate real originality of thought (the first time being at the stage where you choose

Box 14.8 Focus on research in the news

Staff bonuses: there is no right way to reward employees

By Dylan Minor

What are the best incentives to offer the individuals and teams in your organisation? And how do you decide as a leader whether to choose between relative incentives – those based on how individuals perform compared with their peers – or team-based rewards, which are tied to collective performance?

My recent research suggests that it depends on two key factors: the nature of the work and the nature of the teams doing the work.

While there have been studies of how incentives motivate – or fail to motivate – people, few have examined the interplay between incentive types and how much the people being offered the incentives care about one another.

My study, with co-authors Pablo Hernandez-Lagos of New York University Abu Dhabi and Dana Sisak of Erasmus University Rotterdam, showed that the type of incentive, the type of work and the type of teams and the individuals within them all interact. This means there is no right answer for incentives.

Relative incentives work better for more self-focused individuals striving for non-collaborative objectives, while team-based incentives can motivate better performance among already-caring teammates.

FT *Source:* Extract from 'Staff bonuses: there is no right way to reward employees', Dylan Minor (2018) *Financial Times*, 4 April. Copyright © 2018 The Financial Times Ltd

the research topic). Because of that, we urge you to pay due attention to the Discussion. Crucially, here you are making judgements rather than reporting results, so this is where your maturity of understanding can shine through.

Conclusions

This chapter should not be used to present any new material and should be a conclusion to the whole project (not just the research findings). Check your Conclusions using the questions in Box 14.9.

You may find that the clearest way to present your Conclusions is to follow a similar structure to the one used in your Findings/Results. If that structure reflects the research

 **Box 14.9 Checklist**

Do your conclusions answer these questions?

✔ Did the research project meet your aim or answer your research question(s)?
✔ Did the research project meet your research objectives?
✔ What are the main findings of the research?

✔ Are there any recommendations for future action based on the conclusions you have drawn?
✔ Do you have any overall conclusions on the research process itself?
✔ Where should further research be focused? (Typically this will consider two points: firstly, new areas of investigation implied by developments in your project, and secondly, parts of your work which were not completed due to time constraints and/or problems encountered.)

objectives then it should make certain that your conclusions would address them. Drawing up a matrix similar to that in Figure 14.1 may help you in structuring your Findings/Results and Conclusions. The result should be a clear statement of conclusions drawn similar to that shown in Box 14.9.

An alternative approach to the matrix is to draw a 'mind map' (see Section 2.3), which places the findings randomly on a blank page and links conclusions to these findings by way of lines and arrows. For some of you this may be a more creative approach, which enables you to associate groups of findings with conclusions and vice versa.

Answering the research question(s), meeting the objectives and, if appropriate, supporting or refuting the research hypotheses or propositions is the main purpose of the Conclusions. This is where you will consider the findings presented in the previous chapter. You should also return to your literature review and ask yourself 'What do my conclusions add to the understanding of the topic displayed in the literature?'

It may be that there are practical implications of your findings. In a management report this would normally form the content of a chapter specifically devoted to recommendations. We suggest that you check your assessment criteria carefully to establish whether this is expected. In the reports that students are required to prepare on some professional courses this is an important requirement. For some academic degree programmes it is not required.

Even if you do not specify any practical implications of your research you may comment in the Conclusions chapter on what your research implies for any future research. This is a logical extension of a section in the Conclusions that should be devoted to the limitations of your research. These limitations may be about the size of sample, the snapshot nature of the research, or the restriction to one geographical area of an organisation. Virtually all research has its limitations. This section should not be seen as a confession of your weaknesses, but as a mature reflection on the degree to which your findings and conclusions can be said to be generalisable.

References

A range of conventions are used to reference other writers' material that you have cited in your text. (Appendix 1 illustrates three of the most popular of these, the Harvard, footnotes and American Psychological Association (APA) systems.) However, we suggest that you check your project assessment criteria to establish the system that is required for your project report, as many universities require their own variation of these systems.

It is a good idea to start your references section at the beginning of the writing process and add to it as you go along. It will be a tedious and time-consuming task if left until you have completed the main body of the text. If you do leave it until the end, the time spent

Research questions	Results (what factual information did I discover in relation to the specific research questions?)	Conclusions (what judgements can I make about the results in relation to the specific research questions?)
What are the operational differences between different shifts in the production plant?	Cases of indiscipline in the last six months have been twice as frequent on the night shift as on the day shift	The night shift indiscipline problems may be due to the reluctance of operators to work on this shift

Figure 14.1 Using a matrix in the planning of the content for the results and conclusions chapters

on compiling the reference section is time that would have been better spent on checking and amending your report.

At the start of your report you must acknowledge all those who have contributed to your research (including your project tutor!). In addition, you should ensure that you have cited in your reference section all those sources to which you have referred in the text. In order to avoid charges of plagiarism you should also ensure that all data and material taken verbatim (that is copied exactly) from another person's published or unpublished written or electronic work is explicitly identified and referenced to its author (see Neville 2016 and Section 3.8) giving the page numbers(s) of the copied material if possible. This also extends to work which is referred to in the written work of others. Even if this work is not quoted verbatim, the originator should be cited in your references. If you are in any doubt about this it is important that you consult your university's guidelines on how to ensure that you do not plagiarise. The proliferation of online material now is such that all academic institutions are very mindful of plagiarism and will almost certainly check your work carefully.

Appendices

In general, **appendices** should be kept to the minimum. If the material in an appendix is crucial to your reader's understanding, then it should be included in the main body of your report. If, on the other hand, the material is 'interesting to know' rather than 'essential to know' then it should be in the appendices.

Often students feel tempted to include appendices to 'pad out' a project report. Resist this temptation. Your readers will not be reading your report for relaxation. They will be pressed for time and will probably not look at your appendices. Your project report will stand or fall on the quality of the main text.

However, your appendices should include a blank copy of your questionnaire, interview or observation schedule, or participant diary. Where these have been conducted in a language different from that in which you write your submitted project report you will need to submit both this version and the translation. In addition some universities also require you to include a copy of your ethical review approval as an appendix.

Recommendations

You may have wondered why we make little reference to recommendations in the report structure. In the typical management report or consultancy report (discussed later) this may be the most important section. The hard-pressed executive reading your report may turn to your recommendations first to see what action needs to be taken to tackle the issue.

Whether you include a recommendation section depends on the objectives of your research. If you are doing exploratory research you may well write recommendations, among which will be suggestions for the pursuit of further research. However, if your research is designed to explain or describe, recommendations are less likely. For example, the research question 'Why do small engineering companies in the UK reinvest less of their profits in their businesses than their German counterparts?' may imply clear points for action.

However, strictly speaking, recommendations are outside the scope of the research question, which is to discover 'Why?' not 'What can be done about it?' The message is clear. If you want your research to change the situation that you are researching, then include the need to develop recommendations in your research objectives.

A note on tables, figures and visual images in the report

Our discussion so far in this section has focused, explicitly or implicitly, on writing your report – in other words producing text and structuring this in a way that suits your research approach. As highlighted in Section 12.3, you will also be likely to include Tables of results, findings or information, and graphs and other pictorial representations referred to as Figures in your report. Gastel and Day (2017) offer advice on when and how to use tables and figures – and not to use them!

They suggest that tables should not be constructed unless it is essential to show repetitive data. Often using text is a more effective way to present findings and where these are presented in a table they should show those that are significant rather than others that do not show any significant variation. Tables also allow a large amount of information to be included, summarised and compared through the use of several rows and columns: for example see Table 11.1 in this book. Gastel and Day (2017) advise avoiding the creation of tables that are simply lists of words. Where tables are used they advise that these should be designed to be read downwards, not across (see for example the tables in Chapter 11, which are designed to be read downwards). Tables in each chapter in a project report should be numbered sequentially (e.g. Table 1.1, 1.2 . . . 2.1, 2.2 . . . and so on).

We discuss when and how to use graphs in Section 12.4. Other types of diagrammatic representation are also shown in this book. For example, Figure 1.2 provides a pictorial representation of the research process and the use of colour in this figure allows you to distinguish between different aspects of the process. All forms of graphical and pictorial representation are labelled as figures, allowing these to be numbered sequentially in each chapter (Figure 1.1, 1.2 . . . 2.1, 2.2 . . . and so on).

Tables and figures are forms of visual representation. In this book we also discuss the use of visual images such as digital or photographic images. Where your research uses found or created images (Section 9.6) you may also consider including selected images in your research report depending on your research strategy and analytical purpose. We discuss the use of images as visual representations in Section 13.12.

Characteristics of alternative structures

Our purpose in this section is to consider how your choice of an inductive or abductive research strategy may affect the way in which you structure your project report. It is not to suggest that there is a specific way to structure your report when you use a particular strategy. Instead we look at the implications of using different strategies for structuring your project report, dissertation or thesis. The strategies whose implications we consider are Action Research, Case Study, Ethnography, Grounded Theory and Narrative Research. The implications of using these strategies may affect the structure of a project report, dissertation or thesis in one of two ways. It may lead you to use a report structure that is different to the traditional one or to use a report form that appears to be the same as or similar to the traditional structure, but where some sections within it are constructed differently. This is particularly likely to be the case with regard to the main body of the report (i.e. the 'Literature Review', 'Method' and 'Findings' in the traditional structure), as we outline in the sub-sections that follow.

You may be reading this at the time you are writing up your project report, dissertation or thesis. You may initially decide to read only the sub-section that relates to your particular research strategy. If so, we would advise you instead to read all of the following sub-sections. In writing this material, we found that it didn't really make sense to construct a single section offering ideas about alternative reporting structures for inductive and abductive research approaches. There are two related reasons for this. First, there are clear differences between research strategies that use an inductive or abductive approach, with different implications for reporting structures. Second, literature has developed for each research strategy about how to write up such a study. While our decision results in some repetition across these sub-sections, you may find ideas that are relevant and helpful to you in a sub-section that does not relate to your choice of research strategy.

Action Research

Action Research is very different to traditional, deductive research (Section 5.8). This is likely to have implications for the way you structure your Action Research project report. Given that the traditional structure is suited to reporting a logico-deductive approach, where prior theory is used to determine research hypotheses or propositions, which are then tested before being analysed and reported in a linear manner, there must be doubts whether this type of structure will be adequate to present the complexity of, and learning from, an Action Research project.

In Section 5.8 we outlined how Action Research is both emergent and iterative. It commences in a specific context, guided by an initial research question and works through several stages or cycles. Each cycle of the research involves a process of diagnosing or constructing issues, planning action, taking action and evaluating action. Learning from each cycle may lead to the focus of the question changing as the research develops. Your Action Research is likely to involve at least three such cycles. In this way, Action Research differs from other research strategies because of its explicit focus on action related to multiple stages of research. Your task in writing up this research will therefore be to devise a structure that allows you to report and evaluate this process without losing any of its richness and emergent character.

While your report will contain an Introduction and a Method (Box 14.7), the construction of these and subsequent sections will be affected by your choice of an Action Research strategy. Those who read your report will be interested to know about the context within which this Action Research project occurred and to understand why this strategy was chosen. In this way, you need to explain the setting within which this research occurs and to justify why this strategy was the most appropriate one to use. This will help to establish the credibility of using this research approach and help your readers make sense of what is to follow. Explaining the context may mean that you dedicate a separate chapter to this in your report, or you may decide to incorporate discussion of context within another chapter. Justifying your choice of an Action Research strategy and establishing the credibility of this approach will become an important part of the Method. Action Research is a participative form of research (Section 5.8) and this aspect is also relevant to consider in both your discussion of the context and method.

In our discussion of the traditional structure we noted the role of the Literature Review. In writing up deductive research the Literature Review is placed logically after the Introduction and before the Method. Theory in the existing literature is used to help to devise the research hypotheses or propositions that are subsequently tested in this approach. In an inductive or abductive approach, literature plays a different role. In Action Research, as in the other inductive or abductive approaches discussed in this section, different strands of literature become relevant at different points in this type of emergent research process. In your report you may initially wish to use literature for the following reasons. As part of your discussion of the context of your project you may wish to begin to locate your study within existing knowledge by referring to published studies that relate to your research. This can help to establish the reason for undertaking your project and why you chose to use Action Research. You will also use literature about the theory and practice of Action Research in your Method to demonstrate your understanding of this research strategy. However, unless you are required to place the Literature Review early on in your report structure, it is likely that you will need to introduce further strands of literature later in your report, as you interpret and discuss the themes which emerge from your Action Research. We return to this later in this sub-section.

The emergent nature of Action Research involving multiple stages of research is likely to mean it is inappropriate to present one section of 'findings' as is the case in the traditional structure. An alternative approach is likely to be required to present the main body of an Action Research project report. Coghlan and Brannick (2014) refer to the need to tell the story of an Action Research project. They suggest that this part of your report may first present an account of each of the Action Research cycles in your project. This will mean following a chronological approach. The purpose of this will be to provide a clear outline of the research process and its principal events. At the end of each section or chapter describing a particular cycle or stage of your Action Research, they suggest including a section of interpretation that seeks to make sense of these events and starts to theorise about them. Coghlan and Brannick (2014) state that it is important to separate description from sense-making in order to provide clarity and to help to establish the rigour and credibility of your research. While stressing the importance of separating description from sense-making, they also advise that it is important to locate the section of interpretation at the end of, or close to, the description of those events, to help readers understand the direction and flow of your work.

Following this part of the report, Coghlan and Brannick (2014) suggest the inclusion of a chapter that allows your interpretations to be drawn together into a general discussion, to allow you to make sense of the project as a whole. It will be at this stage that you will need to return to the literature to understand how your attempts to theorise about its outcomes relate to prior theory. As this is an emergent process it will be more authentic to introduce and discuss new strands of literature, which only became obvious to consult after undertaking Action Research, rather than attempting to hide this by producing one literature review chapter early in the report to imply that all literature was consulted before research commenced! Your purpose in using this literature will be to say how your Action Research links to existing knowledge, how it may be applied in other contexts and possibly how it contributes to Action Research theory and practice. The latter part of your report is also likely to include your personal reflections about having participated in an Action Research project and an account of your learning from this experience, such as questioning your assumptions and developing skills related to participation and process (Section 14.8).

Case Study

When considering how to structure a report based on case study research, you will need to reflect on how you used this research strategy. First, was the purpose of your case study research designed to be descriptive, exploratory, explanatory or evaluative? Second, was your case study research based on a deductive, inductive or abductive approach? Third, was your research based on an orthodox or emergent case study strategy? Fourth, was your case study research based on a single case or multiple cases? Fifth, did you analyse your case study or studies holistically, as whole units, or did you analyse separate analytical units within each case, such as different groups of staff or functions within a case study organisation? The purpose, nature and analysis of, and approach to, case study research is likely to affect the way in which you wish to structure your project report.

Where the purpose of your case study research is descriptive and explanatory, and you use a deductive approach, it may be appropriate to use the traditional report structure described earlier. Where the purpose of your case study research is exploratory (at least initially) and you use an inductive approach, it may be more appropriate to use an alternative structure for your project report. This may be particularly relevant where your case study strategy incorporates Action Research, Ethnographic Research, a Theory-Building Approach or Narrative Research.

Two points are relevant here in relation to the report structure. The first relates to being able to express the reality of your research process and the way in which you analysed your data. Using an inductive or abductive approach (Section 4.5) means that the conduct of your research will follow an emergent and incremental direction. In some case-based analytical approaches you will preserve the emergent and incremental nature of your research process. This will be the case when you use Analytic Induction. Analytic Induction involves successively selecting cases to be able to develop and test an explanation related to the phenomenon being studied (Section 13.8). Where you use an analytical approach that preserves the incremental nature of your research process, you may find it helpful to devise a report structure that allows you to emphasise the chronology of your research and findings, so that those who read your work can understand what you did and make a judgement about the quality of your research and conclusions. In some other inductive or abductive research methods, such as Thematic Analysis, Template Analysis and Grounded Theory Method, the emergent and incremental nature of the research process tends to be subsumed during analysis. While data are collected incrementally in these strategies, the nature of analysis means that these data are merged into the categories and themes being used to analyse them. In this approach you will probably find it helpful to devise a structure that allows you to report your research in a way that emphasises themes or theory building.

The second point relates to the place of literature and the role of theory. In an inductive research approach it is likely that the emergence of themes during data analysis will lead you to consult new strands of literature. You will be seeking to make sense of your data and relate it to existing literature. This involves a different way of working to that implied by the traditional report structure, where the Literature Review is placed after the Introduction and before the Method because in a deductive approach the theory in literature is used to construct the research hypotheses or propositions that are subsequently tested. An inductive research approach has implications for the place of literature and it may be helpful to include more than one literature chapter in your report structure where you use an inductive or abductive research approach. This may take the form of a review of the initial literature you consulted before embarking on data collection and analysis, and a later, subsequent review of literature you consulted to help to make sense of the themes that emerged from your data. It will also be important to demonstrate how your use of literature has allowed you to relate your emergent theory to existing theory. This will allow you to explain how your findings contribute to knowledge about your research subject. This suggests that it will be important to explain how you used literature throughout your research when you use an inductive or abductive approach and the structure of your report will need to reflect this.

The inclusion of a single case or multiple cases and the way in which this case or these cases are analysed will also affect the way in which you structure your project report. A traditional report structure may best suit a single case analysed as a whole unit. A case study strategy using a single case which requires embedded analytical units within it to be analysed separately, or one that includes multiple cases, suggests using a reporting structure that allows these different analytical units or cases to be compared. This may lead to the inclusion of separate chapters or sections in your report to describe the results from, or story of, each case or analytical unit. It will also be likely to necessitate the inclusion of a chapter that compares the results or stories from each case or analytical unit. Alternatively, you may choose a structure where the emphasis is placed on theory building using a cross-case analysis. In this type of report structure, each case or analytical unit is only considered in relation to the other cases or analytical units being reported and is not described and discussed separately (Yin 2018).

The structure you use will also require description of the context of the case study or case studies in your research. This contextualisation will not only describe the characteristics of the case or cases but also establish its or their importance. It will be important to establish whether and how the case or cases you selected purposively for your research are critical, extreme, typical or unique (Chapter 7.3). Where you use multiple cases it will also be important to establish whether the cases you included in your research have comparative power because they represent the same contextual variables (e.g. three marketing departments in the same industry), a similar contextual variable under different conditions (e.g. four finance departments in different industries), or different contextual variables under similar conditions (e.g. a small, medium and large enterprise operating in the same industry). However, while case study research requires a structure that permits the context of the case study to be described and its analytical importance to be established, it will be important to make sure that the structure you choose maintains an appropriate balance between description, analysis and interpretation.

Ethnography

As we noted in Section 5.8, ethnography literally means a written account of a people or group. In this way ethnography is best seen as the product of research (Watson 2011). Many ethnographies published in academic journals broadly reflect the structural outline of the traditional structure (i.e. they include an introductory section, review of contextual literature, method, main section, discussion and conclusions). However, a closer reading of ethnography reveals that its content and the conventions used to write it are different to those in a typical deductive research report. Watson (2011: 205–6) defines ethnography as a 'style of social science writing which draws upon the writer's close observation of and involvement with people in a particular social setting and relates the words spoken and the practices observed or experienced to the overall cultural framework within which they occurred'.

Van Maanen (2011a) also emphasises the textual nature of ethnography and the role of writing style in its composition, although he sees it as being composed of several styles. These styles result from the ways in which different characteristics of ethnographic research come together in practice. These characteristics include:

- the philosophical position of the research (e.g. critical realist or interpretivist);
- the relative emphasis on description, interpretation and theoretical development in the ethnography;
- whether the author of an ethnography writes herself or himself into the text (using the first person, 'I' or 'me');
- the inclusion or exclusion of reflexivity in an ethnography;
- the way in which participants or informants are referred to and their 'voice' is expressed in the ethnography (e.g. directly by quoting them or indirectly through the author's version of events); and
- the ways in which language and imagery are used in an ethnography (e.g. using 'thick' descriptions, metaphors, tropes, illustrative examples and dramatic representations).

The purpose and nature of ethnographic research will affect how these characteristics join together, with implications for the way in which ethnography is written and also for the way it is structured.

In an influential work, Van Maanen (2011b) discusses several styles of writing ethnography. We outline some of these here (Table 14.1). These descriptions are necessarily very brief. Our purpose in outlining them is not to suggest that a particular style is associated with a specific way of structuring an ethnographic report. Rather it is to recognise that each style will have implications for the content and therefore the structure of the resulting ethnography. Where you are going to write an ethnographic report we would recommend you to read Van Maanen (2011b). You might also re-read the earlier discussion of ethnography in Section 5.8.

Grounded Theory

It is possible to write up a Grounded Theory research project using the traditional structure, described earlier. However, use of this traditional structure flags up a number of issues. We briefly examine these in turn. In a Grounded Theory study, the research question is likely to be subject to refinement, initially being broad or fuzzy and later becoming much more focused. The initial literature consulted is unlikely to be the only literature used and will

Table 14.1 Categories of ethnographic writing

Account	Description
Realist	In a realist account the researcher does not write her/himself into the text and uses a detached documentary style where emphasis is placed on reporting in detail the actions and viewpoints of those being observed. The author uses his/her authorial position to interpret the data and to theorise about their meanings. 'Facts' are presented by the researcher to support her/his interpretation
Confessional	In a confessional account much greater emphasis is placed on the role of the researcher and how the research was conducted. It uses a highly personalised style of writing. When this style is used in a complete ethnography, the content will therefore reflect not only cultural descriptions but also the researcher's reflections about being there as witness or participant. This may also be embedded in another style of ethnography as an account of the methods used or as a reflective appendix
Critical	In a critical approach fieldwork is intentionally conducted within a culture affected by particular political, economic, social or technological factors, allowing the effects of these to be studied on those affected. This account commences from a theoretical framework (often a radical one) and the report will place as much emphasis on theory and theorising about the meanings in the data, as on reporting ethnographic details
Formal	In a formal account the purpose is to develop or test a theory. It places emphasis on theoretical considerations and de-emphasises description and contextualisation in the resulting ethnographic account
Structural	This is a development from and merger of critical and formal accounts with an emphasis on analysis and conceptualisation, focusing on a cultural process and incorporating first-person reporting. The resulting account blends observational reporting and theoretical explanations
Post-structural	A post-structural approach is based on a social constructionist perspective emphasising multiple interpretations. This type of account stresses uncertainty about what can be known and is inevitably inconclusive
Advocacy	In an advocacy approach fieldwork is focused on a particular issue or cause, on which the researcher takes a stance, putting forward this point of view clearly in the account produced. This is therefore one of those accounts of an ethnography that is unlikely to be appropriate for you to use, not least because theory is only likely to be used in a partial way where it supports the stance being advocated

Source: Developed from Van Maanen (2011b) with additional comments by the authors

not be used to develop research hypotheses or propositions, as is the case in a deductive research approach. Initial literature will instead be used to contextualise the research and perhaps to identify weaknesses in existing knowledge about the topic. New strands of literature will subsequently be consulted to understand how the grounded theory fits within existing theoretical perspectives. The method will also be likely to develop incrementally as the research progresses, so it may also be difficult to produce a unified draft of this that implies it was a predetermined and straightforward process. Writing up 'findings' will not simply be a case of reporting the equivalent of the results from statistical analyses and displaying these, as is the case in a quantitatively based research report. The focus of a Grounded Theory study should do exactly what it says: devise a theory grounded in the data. The 'findings' therefore need to go further than simply saying what was 'found'. The report needs to demonstrate not only what the grounded theory is but also how it was developed in order to produce a convincing explanation. Subsequently, the discussion needs to consider the relationship of this grounded theory to existing theory and how it contributes to the generation or refinement of knowledge. This raises an issue about how the continued use of literature should be reviewed in a Grounded Theory study. In summary, the concern about using the traditional structure to report a Grounded Theory study is that its incremental, iterative and emergent nature will be lost by being rearranged and 'cleaned up' to fit a logico-deductive form. This may mean that a theory is proposed without being demonstrably grounded in the data and analytical processes that gave rise to it.

A Grounded Theory report should seek to preserve 'the form and content of the analytic work' that leads to it (Charmaz 2014: 285). The purpose of a Grounded Theory project is to build theory and this analytical approach needs to be emphasised through the structure of the report. In order to preserve the form and content of the process and to emphasis its analytical nature it may therefore be useful to incorporate a chronological approach into the structure of your Grounded Theory project report. Where your research follows the Grounded Theory Method of Strauss and Corbin (1998), for example, you can adopt a report structure that allows you to outline the relationships you developed between categories during axial coding and then how you integrated these categories during selective coding. By also exploring the circumstances when these relationships appear to make sense and those when they do not, you should be able to demonstrate how and why you developed your grounded theory to produce a convincing explanation about the conditions under which it applies and those when it does not.

In a deductive research approach you develop a theoretical framework which you then test. In a Grounded Theory approach your theoretical framework is developed from the data you collect and analyse. The structure of your report will need to allow you to demonstrate how you developed your theoretical framework. The process of writing your report is also likely to allow you to continue to develop your analysis. You may not fully appreciate the analytical potential of your data until you start to write about them! For these reasons, you should find it helpful to devise a structure that preserves the analytical processes you have been engaged in, continues to encourage the development of your analysis, emphasises how it developed and evaluates it with the intention of demonstrating to your readers that your grounded theory is convincing.

Such a structure will allow you to describe the development of your analysis and grounded theory before outlining how you returned to the literature to review theoretical perspectives that relate to your grounded theory. Where you have no choice but to use the traditional structure, you may nevertheless be creative in the way you use the standard elements of this approach (e.g. Introduction, Literature Review, Method, Findings/ Results and Discussion) to ensure that your Grounded Theory project report emphasises the required qualities of being analytical, developmental and theoretical.

Narrative

Writing up a Narrative Research project may take a number of forms. Unless a particular form such as the traditional structure is prescribed, you may find that you are advised to reflect on how you might write up your study rather than being told how to do this. This is because the reporting of Narrative Research lends itself to structural experimentation. How you structure your Narrative Research project report may be influenced by the following factors:

- your purpose in using a narrative approach;
- the nature of the narratives you collect; and
- the type of Narrative Analysis you undertake.

We discuss these and consider how they may affect report structure.

In general, the use of a narrative strategy will have implications for report structure. As we note in Section 5.8, this research strategy preserves chronological connections and the sequencing of events. It enables events, the activities that compose these and their consequences to be analysed as a whole. It is associated with 'thick descriptions' of contextual detail and social relations.

More specifically, basing your Narrative Research strategy on one participant, a few participants or many participants will each be likely to affect the way in which you wish to structure your report. Your research may be based, for example, on the narrated account of one entrepreneur. In this case your structure will need to include a description of this person and a rationale for choosing her or him as your research participant. Your structure may then adopt either a chronological, event-based or thematic approach, emphasising the way this life story develops, or focusing on key events or particular themes drawn from the narrated account. Your structure may need to accommodate lengthy quotations from your participant. You will also need to interpret how this narrated account relates to wider contextual factors and to include a theoretical evaluation that draws on relevant literature.

Your research may instead be based on narrative accounts from, say, three or four participants. This choice will necessitate including a description of these participants, the context within which they operate and a rationale for choosing them. You may then decide to devote a section to each of these narrated accounts followed by a discussion that draws them together and relates themes from these accounts to relevant theories in the literature. Alternatively, you may decide to use a structure that presents a cross- narrative analysis. In this approach you would focus on key events or themes drawn from across these narrated accounts. This is likely to involve a comparative approach, which emphasises perceptions about the same event as seen from different perspectives. This approach may involve devoting a section to each theme or event you consider, within which you incorporate description, interpretation and theoretical evaluation.

These examples also illustrate how the nature of the narratives you collect can affect the structure of a project report. A contrast may be drawn between extended narratives, such as those we have just considered, and short narratives, which comprise storied segments of text you collect from conducting interviews or observations. The structure of a project report is likely to be shaped around the use of an extended narrative or narratives. A narrative structure provided by the sole narrator or by a small number of narrators may influence not only the analysis of the data provided but also the form that the report adopts. This relationship is less likely where you are dealing with a larger number of short narratives, if only because there will be many more options available to you in terms of how you seek to combine and present these narratives and the data they contain. In this case, the role of the researcher as analyst and presenter is likely to be more dominant in terms of shaping the structure of the project report.

The type of Narrative Analysis you undertake may also affect the structure you devise for your project report. In Section 13.10, we discuss two analytical approaches: Thematic Narrative Analysis and Structural Narrative Analysis. The themes you derive during Thematic Narrative Analysis may provide you with a means to structure the sections of your project report that present your analysis and discussion. Where you undertake Structural Narrative Analysis you will be interested in the way a narrative or dialogue is constructed, to examine how use of language affects others or influences the course of an interaction. This research approach may be based on prior theory, so it may be appropriate to use a traditional (logico-deductive) report structure. For both, you are likely to include examples of dialogue in your analysis and theoretical evaluation, so you will need to devise a structure to accommodate the reporting of these.

A final note about the length of the project report

You will probably have guidelines on the number of words your project report should contain. Do stick to these. However interesting your report, your tutors will have others to read, so they will not thank you for exceeding the limit. Reports that exceed the word limit are usually excessively verbose. It is more difficult to be succinct. Do not fall into the trap of writing a long report because you did not have the time to write a shorter one.

14.4 Writing reports for different audiences

In the previous section we discussed different ways to structure your project report. This may mean using the traditional structure for your report, or using a different structure that allows you to tell the story more clearly about the way in which you conducted your research and developed a theory. This section considers a situation you may face: the need to write two reports about your research, each of which may require a different structure! Many researchers of management topics face the dilemma of having to write for more than one audience. In addition to the academic audience, who will mark and grade your report, you may need to prepare a report for the management of your employing or host organisation, who will be interested in the practical benefit of your research findings.

The academic report will usually be much longer and contain contextual description that the organisational audience does not require. Similarly, those managers reading the report will probably be less interested in the literature review and the development of theory than the academic audience. They will, however, be interested in recommendations for future action and these will need to be written into the organisational version.

Fortunately, word processors make the job of compiling more than one report less time consuming. Some judicious cutting and pasting along with subsequent careful proofreading will be necessary. However, what should always be kept in mind is the audience that each specific report is addressing. Each report will need to be structured so that its content and style are suitable for its respective audience. Having discussed structures for academic project reports earlier, in the next sub-section we consider briefly the structuring and writing of consultancy reports.

The consultancy report

As you plan your consultancy report you will need to consider a number of key questions. These include:

- Who will read your consultancy report?
- What information and level of detail will they expect?
- How will they expect the report to be presented?
- How much knowledge will they already have?
- For what purpose will the report be used?
- What key messages and recommendations do you want to impart?

As with your academic project report structure, you will have a choice about how to present this consultancy report. A simplified version of the traditional structure may be appropriate, such as:

1 Executive summary;
2 Introduction;
3 Background and method;
4 Results/Findings;
5 Recommendations;
6 References;
7 Appendices.

Irrespective of the structure you use, you should avoid presenting a partial point of view and selecting only those data that support it. Where the analysis of your data lead to a complex situation suggesting alternative courses of action, you will need to devise a structure that allows you to convey these messages to the organisational audience who will read your report. Writing a consultancy report does not mean that you should produce an inferior account of your research. We recall occasions when we have presented consultancy reports to various management teams: in these situations you can always expect to be asked a range of astute and relevant questions!

Decisions about what to include in (and, just as importantly, to exclude from) the report requires care. Only information that is essential to management should go in the main body of the report; any information that is 'important' or 'of interest' should be relegated to appendices. Your readers are likely to have limited time and want only essential detail. That said, the management reader will be interested in the background to the project and in how you carried out the research. You may therefore expect to be questioned about your research methods. But the key purpose of the report is usually to provide management with clear justified recommendations. Recommendations equate with action, and managers are paid to act! As with the academic report, division of the report content into logical sections with clear subheadings will lead management through the report and show them where to find specific topics.

The Executive Summary will be the part of the report on which managers concentrate. It is important that it can be read and understood without having to look at the rest of the report. It therefore needs to provide clear information, including facts and figures. If your report includes recommendations, the executive summary should make it clear what these are and include their implications, values and costs. As with the abstract, the executive summary should be short (no more than two pages) and designed to get your main message across.

One final point may be made about the writing style of the consultancy report. The reader will not appreciate long words, complicated language, 'management speak' or a multitude of acronyms and abbreviations. If it is necessary to use complex technical terms, make sure you provide a glossary as an appendix.

As well as composing two written reports you may have to present one or both of these orally. In the final section 14.9, we now turn our attention to their oral presentation.

14.5 Making the report's content clear and accessible

The discussion in the previous two sections focused on devising an overall structure for your report or reports. In this section we make some general comments about the content of your report, irrespective of the structure you devise for it. These comments focus on the importance of choosing a title, making sure you tell a clear story throughout your report and using simple devices to make sure that your readers are able to get all of the information out of your report that they need.

Choosing a title

A good title is one that has the minimum possible number of words while describing the content of the report accurately (Gastel and Day 2017). Try choosing a title and then ask a colleague who knows your subject what they think the title describes. If their description matches your content then keep the title.

Tell a clear story

Be prepared for your project tutor to ask you 'What's your main storyline?' Your storyline (your central argument or thesis) should be clear, simple and straightforward. It should be so clear that you can stop the next person you see walking towards you and tell that person what your project report's storyline is and he or she will say 'Yes, I understand that'. This is where writing the abstract helps. It forces you to think clearly about the storyline because you have to summarise it in so few words.

Another way of checking to see whether your storyline is clear is to 'reason backwards'. An example of this is a project report that ends in clear conclusions. Start by explaining your conclusions to a tutor. This invites the question from that tutor: 'On what basis do you draw these conclusions?' Here your answer is, of course, on the findings that you established. The next question asked by the tutor is: 'How did you arrive at these findings?' in response to which you explain your method. The tutor may counter by asking you why she should take any notice of your findings. The response to this is that you took care to design a research strategy that would lead to valid and reliable findings. Moreover, that research strategy is based on a clear research question and objectives and a detailed review of the relevant literature. Such 'reasoning backwards' is a useful check to see not only whether your storyline is clear but also that it stands up to logical analysis.

Helping the reader to get all the information out that they need

Dividing your work

One of us once received the first draft of a 20,000-word project report that had virtually no section headings within the chapters. It was like looking at a road map that did not include any road numbers or towns. It was just as difficult to find your way around that report as it would be to journey between two major cities using a townless road map. The content of the project report seemed fine. However, it was hard to be sure about this because it was so difficult to spot any gaps in the material it covered. To continue with our metaphor, what were needed were some signposts and some town names. Do not think about how you can put in all your information. Instead, concentrate on helping the reader to get all the information out (Box 14.10).

The message is simple. Divide your work in such a way that it is easy for readers to find their way round it and for them always to be clear where they are, where they have come from, and where they are going. To do this you may find it helpful to return to the matrix idea in Figure 14.1. You will see that each column of the matrix represents

Box 14.10
Focus on management research

The importance of developing a storyline

In their Editors' Comments in the *Academy of Management Review,* Lange and Pfarrer (2017) illustrate the importance of developing a clear and purposeful storyline in academic writing. Based on their experience and synthesis of previous work they identify five core building blocks to achieve this. They label these 'common ground', 'complication', 'concern', 'course

of action' and 'contribution'. They explain each of these before using award winning articles to illustrate how these elements are present in effective writing.

'Common ground' is the process of establishing where the subject of interest is currently located. 'Complication' demonstrates a problem related to the established common ground. 'Concern' illustrates why this complication is important. 'Course of action' is the way in which the researcher approaches the complication in order to address and resolve it. 'Contribution' explains how this study has moved understanding about the subject forward.

Using this type of sequential structure should ensure that your work will not only makes some contribution but also demonstrates a clear and purposeful storyline.

the broad content of a chapter. The cells indicate the way in which the chapters may be divided. Each division may have a subdivision.

We hope you have noticed that we have employed a similar system in this book. Each chapter section is identified by a numbered heading made up of large, bold characters. The subheadings use slightly smaller, bold lettering, and further divisions of the content of a sub-section are denoted by bold, italicised characters. There are various textual and numerical ways of organising and signposting text. It is not important which way you do this as long as your approach is consistent and it helps the reader around the report and matches the ways specified by your examining institution.

Previewing and summarising chapters

A further way in which you can signpost your work is to 'top and tail' each chapter. This is to include a few words of introduction at the beginning of the chapter that provide a description of how the chapter is structured in relation to answering the research question and the key aspects that are covered in the chapter. At the end of each chapter it is useful to provide a brief summary of the content of the chapter and a very brief indication of how this content links to the following chapter. This may seem like repetition. However, it helps the reader on her or his journey through your report and ensures that you, the writer, are on the correct road.

Visualisation

As we introduced earlier, your reader will find your project report more accessible and easier to read if you present some of your data and ideas in tables and figures. It is not only numerical data that can be presented in tables and diagrams. You can also present ideas that can be easily compared (For example Table 11.1 and Figure 11.1). Do not be tempted to put your tables in the appendices. They will probably be some of your most important data. Include them and comment on them in the text. Your commentary should note the significant aspects of the data in the tables. It should not simply describe the table's contents. A final note of caution: to avoid confusing your reader, do make sure that, wherever possible, you have introduced the table or figure before it appears in the text.

14.6 Developing an appropriate writing style

Much of your concern in writing your project report will be about what you write. In this section of the chapter we ask you to think about the way you write. Your writing style is just as important as the structure and content of your report. That said, it is often observed that good writing cannot substitute for flawed thinking (Phillips and Pugh 2015). In fact, the clearer the writing the more flawed thinking is exposed. However, poor writing can spoil the effect of good-quality thought.

Clarity and simplicity

The . . . lack of ready intelligibility [in scholarly writing], I believe, usually has little or nothing to do with the complexity of the subject matter, and nothing at all to do with profundity of thought. It has to do almost entirely with certain confusions of the academic writer about his own status . . . To overcome the academic prose you first of all have to overcome the academic pose.

Wright Mills (1970: 239–40)

Each Christmas, Mark accompanies his Christmas cards with a family newsletter. It is written in a simple, direct and friendly manner that is easy and enjoyable to read and illustrated with a selection of photographs. Few of the project reports we read are written in such a simple, direct manner. They are more elaborate in their explanation: they use difficult words where Mark's family newsletter would use simple ones. They adopt the academic pose.

Phil tells a story that reinforces the point made by Wright Mills in the above quotation. He was asked by a student to comment on her thesis in progress, which was about the impact of a particular job advertising strategy. He thought that it was written in an over-elaborate and 'academic' way. After many suggestions for amendments Phil came across a sentence that explained that the strategy his student was studying 'was characterised by factors congruent with the results of a lifestyle analysis of the target market'. Phil thought that this was too wordy. He suggested making it simpler. His student examined the sentence at length and declared she could see no way of improving it. Phil thought that it could say 'it was a strategy that matched the lifestyles of those at whom it was aimed'. His student protested. She agreed it was shorter and clearer but protested that it was less 'academic'. We think that clarity and simplicity are more important than wishing to appear 'academic'. Your project report is a piece of communication in the same way as Mark's Christmas newsletter.

Phillips and Pugh (2015) advise that you should aim to provide readers with a report that they cannot put down until 2.00 a.m. or later for fear of spoiling the flow. (If you are reading this chapter at 2.30 a.m. we have succeeded!)

Write simple sentences

A common source of lack of clarity is the confusing sentence (see Box 14.11). This is often because it is too long. A simple rule to adopt is: one idea – one sentence. Try reading your work out loud. If your sentences are too long, you will run out of breath!

Box 14.11
Focus on student research

Writing clearer sentences

Consider the following sentence:

> While it is true to say that researchers have illusions of academic grandeur when they sit down to write their project report, and who can blame them because they have had to demonstrate skill and resilience to get to this point in their studies, they nonetheless must consider that writing a project report is an exercise in communication, and nobody likes reading a lot of ideas that are expressed in such a confusing and pretentious way that nobody can understand them, let alone the poor tutor who has to plough through it all to try and make some sense of it.

There appear to be at least six separate ideas in this sentence. It contains 101 words (when marking, we sometimes come across sentences with over 150!).

In addition, it contains a common way of introducing multiple ideas into a sentence: the embedded clause. In the sentence above the embedded clause is '. . . , and who can blame them because they have had to demonstrate skill and resilience to get to this point in their studies, . . . ' The give-away is the first word in the sentence: 'While'. This invites an embedded clause. The point here is that potentially rich ideas get buried in the literary undergrowth. Dig them up and replant them. Let them flourish in a sentence of their own.

The sentence needs to be clearer and simpler. However, it should not lose any of its meaning. Halving the number of words and dividing up the sentence into smaller, clearer sentences results in the following:

> Researchers have illusions of academic grandeur when they write their project report. This is understandable. They have demonstrated skill and resilience to reach this point in their studies. However, writing a project report is an exercise in communication. Nobody likes confusing and pretentious writing that is difficult to understand. Pity the tutor who has to make sense of it.

Avoid jargon

Jargon should not be confused with technical terminology. Some technical terms are unavoidable. To assist your reader, it is best to put a glossary of such terms in the appendices. However, do not assume that your reader will have such a full knowledge as you of the subject and, in particular, the context. Here, and in all cases, try to put yourself in the position of the reader. Phil makes this point to students who use organisations as vehicles to write assignments. He asks them to 'mark' past (anonymous) assignments. They are usually horrified at the assumptions that their fellow students make about the tutor's prior knowledge of the organisation.

What can be avoided is the sort of jargon that The Free Dictionary (2018) defines as 'gibberish'. You will know the sort of phrases: 'ongoing situation'; 'going down the route of'; 'at the end of the day'; 'the bottom line'; 'at this moment in time'. It is not just that they are ugly but they are not clear and simple. For example, 'now' is much clearer and simpler than 'at this moment in time'.

Beware of using large numbers of quotations from the literature

We believe that quotations from the literature should be used infrequently in your project report. Occasionally we receive draft projects that consist of little more than a series of quotations from books and journal articles that a student has linked together with a few sentences of her or his own. This tells us very little about the student's understanding of the concepts within the quotations. All it shows is that he or she has looked at the book or journal article and, it is hoped, can acknowledge sources correctly. In addition, by using quotations in this way the student's line of argument tends to become disjointed and less easy to follow. It is therefore usually better to explain other people's ideas in your own words.

That is not to say that you should never use quotations. As you have seen, we have used direct quotations from other people's work in this book. Rather we would advise you to use them sparingly to create maximum impact in supporting your storyline.

Check your spelling and grammar

Spelling is still a problem for many of us, in spite of spellcheckers. A spellchecker will not correct your 'moral' when you wished to say 'morale' or sort out when you should write 'practise' rather than 'practice'. This is where the friend who is reading your draft can help, provided that friend is a competent speller. Tutors tend to be more patient with errors of this kind than those that reflect carelessness. However, the point remains that spelling errors detract from the quality of your presentation and the authority of your ideas.

Avoiding common grammatical errors

Grammatical errors threaten the credibility of our writing. In Table 14.2 we outline ten of the most common errors, most of which, with some careful checking, can be avoided. It is not our intention here to conduct an English grammar lesson. Some of the common errors in Table 14.2 are self-explanatory.

You may argue that the **split infinitive** is not often thought of as an error these days. However, 'to boldly go' ahead with your project report ignoring this rule risks irritating your reader – something you can ill afford to do. You want the reader to concentrate on your ideas.

Day's (1998) 'dangling participle' warning is amusingly illustrated by the draft questionnaire shown to us by a student. This asked for 'the amount of people you employ in your

Table 14.2 Ten common grammatical errors

Often we write	The correct way is
Each pronoun should agree with their antecedent	Each pronoun should agree with its antecedent
Just between you and I, case is important	Just between you and me, case is important
A preposition is a poor word to end a sentence with	A preposition is a poor word with which to end a sentence
Verbs has to agree with their subject	Verbs have to agree with their subject
Do not use no double negatives	Do not use double negatives
Remember to never split an infinitive	Remember never to split an infinitive
When dangling, do not use participles	Do not use dangling participles
Avoid clichés like the plague	To avoid clichés like the plague!
Do not write a run-on sentence it is difficult when you have got to punctuate it so it makes sense when the reader reads what you wrote	Do not write a run-on sentence. It is difficult to punctuate it so that it makes sense to the reader
The data is included in this section	The data are included in this section

Source: Developed from Day (1998: 160)

organisation, broken down by sex'. The tutor had written: 'We haven't got people in that category: they've not got the energy when they work here!'

Some of the more obvious grammatical errors you can spot by reading your text aloud to yourself. You need not know the grammatical rules; they often just sound wrong.

Person, tense and gender

Traditionally, academic writing has been dry and unexciting. This is partly because the convention has been to write impersonally, in the past **tense** and in the **passive voice** (e.g. 'interviews were conducted following the analysis of questionnaires').

The writer was expected to be distanced from the text. This convention is no longer as strong. It is now a matter of preferred style rather than rules. The research approach and strategy that informs your methods may dictate your choice of **personal pronoun**. We noted earlier that one feature of positivism is that 'the researcher is independent of, and neither affects nor is affected by, the subject of the research', so that an impersonal style is appropriate. However where the researcher is an intrinsic part of the research process use of the first person may seem more logical. You also need to evaluate the effect of the style you adopt. Use of the term 'the author' sounds too impersonal and stilted. In contrast, excessive use of 'I' and 'we' may raise questions in your readers' minds about your ability to stand outside your data and to be objective.

Gastel and Day (2017) identify rules for the correct use of tense. When you refer to previously established knowledge from published academic papers the convention is to use the present tense (e.g. Newton identifies . . .) and the past tense when you refer to your own results (e.g. I found that . . .)'. Although Gastel and Day note exceptions to this rule, it is a useful guide to follow.

Gastel and Day (2017) argue against using the passive voice in writing ('it was found that') and champion the use of the **active voice** ('I found that'). Use of active voice is clearer, shorter and unambiguous. However, it is a good idea to check with your project tutor which form of voice is acceptable.

Finally, a note about the use of language that assumes the gender of a classification of people. The most obvious example of these is the constant reference to managers as 'he'. Not only is this inaccurate in organisations, it also gives offence to many people of both sexes. Those offended will probably include your readers! It is simple enough to avoid (e.g. 'I propose to interview each executive unless he refuses' becomes 'I propose to interview each executive unless I receive a refusal') but often less easy to spot. The further reading section in the first draft of this chapter referred to Becker as a 'master craftsman'. These notes on language and gender prompted us to change it to 'an expert in the field'. Appendix 4 gives more detailed guidance on the use of non-discriminatory language, including the use of **non-binary** (gender-neutral) pronouns to refer to individuals and groups of people.

It is a good idea to be aware of any specific discriminatory or potentially insulting concepts, terms and expressions which may be used in your research due to the particular context of the research (e.g. the industry or organisation in which you work). If your work has an international dimension, it is also a good idea to be aware of any country-specific or national guidelines on the non-discriminatory use of language.

Preserving anonymity

You may have given those people (and the organisations) from whom you collected data an undertaking that you would not disclose their identity in anything you write. In this case you will need to conceal their identities in your project report. The usual way of doing this is to invent pseudonyms for organisations and not to name individual participants. This should not detract from the impact of your report.

Similarly, your sponsoring organisation(s) may have requested sight of your report before it is submitted. Should there be misgivings about the content of the report you should be able to alleviate these by the use of pseudonyms. This is usually a better option than significant text changes.

The need for continual revision

Phil asked a group of undergraduate students how many of them wrote more than one draft of their assignment papers. He did not expect that many would reply that they did. What he did not predict was that many of them had not even thought this was necessary. Submitting the first attempt is due partly to the heavy assessment loads on many courses, which means that students are constantly having to 'keep up with the clock'. On part-time courses, students these days have so many demands in their daily work that writing an assignment just once is all that is possible. This is the way most of us learnt to write at school. The work is usually seen only by the teacher. The arrangement is a private one.

However, project reports are different. They will be seen by an audience much wider than one tutor. They may be placed in the library to be read by succeeding students. You will be judged on the quality of your work. For that reason, we urge you most strongly to polish your work with successive drafts until you are happy that you can do no better (Box 14.12).

Having been through this checklist you may decide to make minor alterations to your text. On the other hand, you may rewrite sections or move sections within chapters to other chapters. Keep asking yourself 'How can I make the reader's task easier?'

 **Box 14.12**
Checklist

To evaluate each draft of your project report

✔ Is there a clear structure?

✔ Is there a clear storyline?

✔ Does your abstract reflect the whole content of the report accurately?

✔ Does your introduction state the research question(s) and objectives clearly?

✔ Does your literature review inform the later content of the report?

✔ Are your methods clearly explained?

✔ Have you made a clear distinction between findings and conclusions in the relevant chapters?

✔ Have you checked all your references and presented these in the required manner?

✔ Is there any text material that should be in the appendices or vice versa?

✔ Does your title reflect accurately your content?

✔ Have you divided up your text throughout with suitable headings?

✔ Does each chapter have a preview and a summary?

✔ Are you happy that your writing is clear, simple and direct?

✔ Have you eliminated all jargon?

✔ Have you eliminated all unnecessary quotations?

✔ Have you checked spelling and grammar?

✔ Have you checked for assumptions about gender?

✔ Is your report in a format that will be acceptable to the assessing body?

✔ Would you be proud of your project if it was placed in the university's library as it is now?

After each successive draft do leave enough time for your thoughts to mature. It is amazing how something you wrote a few days before will now make no sense to you. However, you will also be impressed with the clarity and insight of some passages.

Having completed a second draft, you may now feel confident enough to give it to your colleague or friend to read. Ask your reader to use the checklist in Box 14.12 to which you can add specific points that you feel are important (e.g. are my arguments well-reasoned?).

14.7 Meeting the assessment criteria

Your readers will assess your work against the assessment criteria that apply to your research programme. It is therefore essential that you familiarise yourself with these criteria. More generally, Bloom's (1971) taxonomy (or classification) of educational objectives will help you understand the standard that your project report needs to meet. At the lower levels of this taxonomy, project reports should show knowledge and comprehension of the topic covered. At the intermediate levels they should contain evidence of application and analysis. Application is thought of as the ability to apply certain principles and rules in particular situations. Your method section should be the principal vehicle for demonstrating application. Analysis may be illustrated by your ability to break down your data and to clarify the nature of the component parts and the relationship between them. Whatever your assessment criteria, it is certain that you will be expected to demonstrate your ability at these lower and intermediate levels.

The higher levels of this taxonomy are synthesis and evaluation. **Synthesis** is the process of putting together or assembling various elements so as to create a new statement or conclusion. The emphasis put on conclusions and, in particular, on the development of a storyline in your project report suggests that we feel that you should be showing evidence of synthesis. **Evaluation** is the process of judging materials or methods in terms of their accuracy and internal consistency or by comparing them against external criteria. You have the chance to show this ability in the literature review and in the awareness of the limitations of your own research (see Section 14.3). Each of these levels of educational objectives should be demonstrated in your project report.

In addition to meeting these, you will also need to make sure that you meet any other assessment criteria. You will need to make sure that your project is correctly formatted, does not exceed the maximum permitted length and contains all of the elements specified for inclusion. A final, more holistic consideration that many of our students find useful is to ask yourself whether you would be proud for your project to be placed in the university's library as it is now. If your honest answer is 'no, not yet', you will have more work to do! Conversely, you will need to submit by the due date and so you will need to make sure that you do not keep polishing one part to the exclusion of completing the whole project. You will therefore need to manage your time carefully in terms of drafting the whole and then refining each part.

14.8 Writing a reflective essay or section

As we discussed in earlier chapters, being reflective and reflexive is integral to some research strategies, or particular variants of these. This is particular true of interpretive research strategies. For example, in Section 5.8 we outlined Interpretive Ethnography as an approach in which the researcher engages in continuous reflexivity. Conducting research in a reflective and reflexive way is also important in Action Research and Grounded Theory strategies. This approach involves the researcher writing himself or herself into the research by writing in the first person. Of course, not all research strategies encourage reflection and reflexivity during the research process. Neither do they encourage writing in the first person; instead they use an impersonal approach to report the research. This is often true of deductive, survey research. If being reflective and reflexive has not been integral to your research strategy, you will still be familiar with this approach if you have kept a reflective diary or journal throughout your research project. This will be very helpful in writing a reflective essay about your research, or a reflective section in your project report.

As we noted in Section 1.5, many universities require a reflective essay or section to be included in the assessment of a research project, sometimes as an appendix in the report. In Section 1.5 we discussed how reflection is a key part of learning. Your reflections about your research should be recorded throughout this process in your reflective diary or journal (Section 13.5). This will enable you to record your progress in a continuous cycle of experience, reflection, evaluation and revised practice. Your reflective diary or journal will help you to improve your practice as your research progresses and then provide you with the source material to write your reflective essay or section. It will of course be important to make regular entries in your research diary or journal and we have encouraged you to do this as you work through the 'Progressing your research project' section included in each chapter.

Box 14.13 comprises a checklist of questions that you may ask yourself to help you write your reflective essay or section.

You should be able to highlight material in your reflective diary or journal to help you to answer the questions in Box 14.13 and write your reflective essay or section. Where you have used a research strategy that incorporates a reflective and reflexive approach and written this into your project report you should also be able to draw on this material to answer these questions to produce a reflective overview. As your reflective essay or section is a personal account of your experiences, practice and learning, it will be appropriate to write this in the first person, using 'I' and 'my': such as 'my experience', 'what did I learn' and 'what I did differently'.

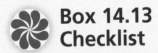

Box 14.13
Checklist

Checklist to evaluate your reflective essay or section

✔ Which aspects of my research project went well?
✔ Why do I think these aspects of my research project went well?
✔ What are my key learning points from these aspects?
✔ Which aspects of my research project did not go so well?
✔ Why do I think these aspects of my research project did not go so well?

✔ What are my key learning points from these aspects?
✔ What adjustments did I make to my research practice as a result of this learning?
✔ How well did these adjustments work in practice?
✔ What further adjustments did I make, or could I have made, to my research practice and why?
✔ How would I summarise my learning from my research project and what skills have I developed?
✔ How has my learning from this experience influenced what I would do in the event of another research project: what would I do the same and what would I do differently, and why?

14.9   Oral presentation of the report

Many students, particularly on professional courses, have to present their project report orally as part of the assessment process. The skills required here are quite different from those involved with writing. In this section we briefly consider two types of presentation, an oral presentation supported by the use of slides and perhaps a whiteboard and a poster presentation.

Slide presentations

We discuss this type of presentation under three headings: planning and preparing; the use of visual aids; and presenting, although many points outlined here will also be relevant where you prepare and make a poster presentation.

Planning and preparing

We make no apology for starting this section with the trainer's proverb: 'Failing to prepare is preparing to fail.' Your assessors will forgive any inadequacies that stem from inexperience, but they will be much less forgiving of students who have paid little attention to preparation. You can be sure of one thing about insufficient preparation: it shows, particularly to the experienced tutor.

All presentations should have clear aims and objectives. Your aim should be to give the audience members an overview of your report in such a way that it will capture their interest. Keep it clear and simple. By achieving this you will meet the most basic assessment criterion: that sometime later the tutor in the audience can remember clearly your main project storyline. Your objectives are more specific. They should start you thinking about the interests of your audience. These should be phrased in terms of what it is you want your audience members to be able to do after your presentation. Since your presentation will usually be confined to the imparting of knowledge, it is sufficient to phrase your objectives in terms of the audience members being able, for example, to define, describe, explain or clarify. It is a good idea to share the objectives with your audience members so they know about the journey on which they are being taken (Box 14.14).

Setting clear objectives for your presentation leads you neatly to deciding the content. This should be straightforward because your abstract should serve as your guide to the content. After all, the purpose of the abstract is to give the reader a brief overview of the report, which is precisely the same purpose as the presentation. How much detail you go into on each point will be determined largely by the time at your disposal. The audience member who wants more detail can always ask you to elaborate or read it in the report.

The final point to note here is to think about the general approach you will adopt in delivering your presentation. It is a good idea to involve the audience members rather than simply tell them what it is you want them to know. Thirty minutes of you talking at the audience members can seem like an age, for you and sometimes for them! Inviting them to ask questions throughout the presentation is a good way of ensuring that the talk is not all in one direction. Rarely will tutors miss the opportunity of asking you to 'dig a little deeper' to test your understanding, so don't worry that no questions will arise. However, you must be careful to ensure that you do not let questions and answers run away with time. The more you open up your presentation to debate, the less control you have of time. In general, we do not think it is a good idea to attempt to emulate tutors and turn your presentation into a teaching session. We have seen students set the audience mini-exercises to get them involved, but often these tend to fall flat. Play to your strengths and enjoy the opportunity to share your detailed knowledge with an interested audience.

Box 14.14
Focus on student research

Presenting the objectives for a project

Phil created the following slides in Microsoft Power Point as part of a lecture on project presentation. This allowed him to produce various designs of slide to meet his purpose, examples of which are shown in the following versions:

Version 1: Standard PowerPoint slide

Objectives for a presentation

- To describe the purpose of the research project
- To explain the context in which the research project research was set
- To identify the research strategy adopted and the reasons for its choice
- To list the main findings, conclusions and recommendations flowing from the research
- *N.B. Detail related to the specific project may be added*

Version 2: PowerPoint slide using a design template

Objectives for a presentation

- To describe the purpose of the research project
- To explain the context in which the research project research was set
- To identify the research strategy adopted and the reasons for its choice
- To list the main findings, conclusions and recommendations flowing from the research
- *N.B. Detail related to the specific project may be added*

Version 3: PowerPoint slide using more colour

Objectives for a presentation

- To describe the purpose of the research project
- To explain the context in which the research project research was set
- To identify the research strategy adopted and the reasons for its choice
- To list the main findings, conclusions and recommendations flowing from the research
- N.B. Detail related to the specific project may be added

Version 4: PowerPoint slide with photograph inserted

OBJECTIVES FOR A PRESENTATION

- To describe the purpose of the research project
- To explain the context in which the research project research was set
- To identify the research strategy adopted and the reasons for its choice
- To list the main findings, conclusions and recommendations flowing from the research

N.B. Detail related to the specific project may be added

Version 5: PowerPoint slide with space for the audience to add notes

OBJECTIVES FOR A PRESENTATION

- To describe the purpose of the research project
- To explain the context in which the research project research was set
- To identify the research strategy adopted and the reasons for its choice
- To list the main findings, conclusions and recommendations flowing from the research

N.B. Detail related to the specific project may be added

Using visual aids

Now another proverb: 'I hear and I forget, I see and I remember' (Rawlins 1999: 37). The use of **visual aids** will do more than enhance the understanding of your audience. It will help you to look better prepared and therefore more professional. A simple set of slides will perform the same function as a set of notes, in that it will ensure that you do not forget key points and will help you to keep your presentation on track. You will know the material so well that a key point noted on the overhead will be enough to trigger your thought process and focus the attention of the audience. Key points will also ensure that you are not tempted to read a script for your presentation, something that will not sustain the attention of your audience for very long.

Using Microsoft PowerPoint™ makes it easy to produce a highly professional presentation, using slides which can include simple illustrations to reinforce a point or add a little humour. Virtually all organisations have digital video projectors to project the slides directly from a computer, which adds to the degree of professionalism. This allows you electronically to reveal each point as you talk about it while concealing forthcoming points. However, whilst design templates and colour can be used to improve the visual appeal of individual slides (Box 14.14, versions 2 and 3), beware of using a variety of different fonts, special effects, or including illustrations that have no relevance to the presentation (Box 14.4, version 4). PowerPoint also allows you to print miniature versions of your slides as a handout or note pages (Box 14.14, version 5), which is a very useful aide-mémoire for the audience.

You may want to supplement your pre-prepared slides with the use of the whiteboard. This may be useful for explaining points in relation to questions you receive. A word of warning here: ensure that you use dry markers that can be wiped from the board. A vain attempt to erase the results of a permanent pen in front of your audience will do nothing to enhance your confidence. Ensuring that you have dry wipe markers (use only black and blue pens – red and green are too faint) and checking computers and projectors before the presentation, serve to emphasise the need for careful preparation.

Giving the presentation

The first thing to say here is: don't worry about nerves. You may expect to be a little nervous as you commence your presentation and your audience may also expect this. The best way to minimise nervousness is to have prepared your presentation carefully and to have practised it beforehand.

Be positive about your presentation and your report. Trial your presentation in front of a friend to ensure that it flows logically and smoothly. You also need to ensure that you can deliver it in the allotted time. In our experience most students put too much material in their presentations, although they worry beforehand that they have not got enough.

It is important that your presentation has a clear structure. One way to achieve this is to follow the structure of many news programmes, in which the newsreader firstly tells the audience what she or he is going to say (the 'headlines'), then elaborates on these by explaining their content and finishes by summarising them again. In a similar way your audience will want to know what to expect from your presentation, then which part they are currently observing and finally to understand your conclusions.

Finally, some practical points that will help:

- Think about whether you would prefer to sit or stand at the presentation. The former may be better to foster debate, the latter is likely to give you a sense of 'control' (Rawlins 1999). Which one you choose may depend upon the circumstances of the presentation, including the approach you wish to adopt, the room layout, the equipment you are using and your preferred style.

- Consider how you will deal with difficult questions. Try to anticipate these and how you would answer them, so that you can deal with them confidently during the presentation.
- Avoid jargon.
- Check the room before the presentation to ensure you have everything you need, you are happy and familiar with the layout, and all your equipment is working.

Poster presentations

You may be required to present your research project as a poster presentation. The purpose of a poster is not to provide a detailed explanation of your research, but to give a succinct and clear message about the main aspects. You therefore need to be selective in what you include. While some of the points we have just outlined will be relevant other points need to be considered. We consider these under two headings: planning and preparing your poster; presenting your poster.

Planning and preparing your poster

Like presentational slides, your poster needs to be well designed, clearly structured and easy for your audience to understand. Typically your poster will contain the following:

- Title;
- Summary;
- Short introduction including key literature;
- Aim and objectives/research question;
- Methodology;
- Findings/Results;
- Discussion and/or Conclusions.

Each of these sections will be succinct. Your title will need to be short and catch the reader's attention. It should be followed by your name. The introduction will briefly state what you did and the key literature on which your research draws. The method will very briefly outline how you did it. The main findings will be summarised; and the conclusions will summarise how you addressed your aim. The number of words which your poster contains will be likely to number no more than a few hundred, with a maximum of one thousand, and this will be affected by any figures or visual images also incorporated into the poster.

The poster needs to be self-explanatory, with clear headings and points of information (rather than extended blocks or paragraphs of text). It needs to be readable from two to three metres away, so ensure the font is large enough. The clarity of your poster will be aided by leaving space around points rather than making it appear complex or dense. The exact design of your poster will depend on the amount of space you have, its format and the technology you are using (Figure 14.2). The format of a poster may be either portrait or landscape. Where you have a choice about which you use, you will be able to experiment with the format that best suits your presentation. A portrait poster is often divided into two columns, while a landscape poster may be divided into three or possibly four columns, albeit with less depth.

As an alternative to preparing and using a traditional poster, you may have the opportunity to produce and use an electronic poster. This may take the form of a static image and therefore be the equivalent of a traditional poster. You may also have the opportunity to produce an electronic poster that incorporates moving images such as video clips and a short, spoken flash presentation.

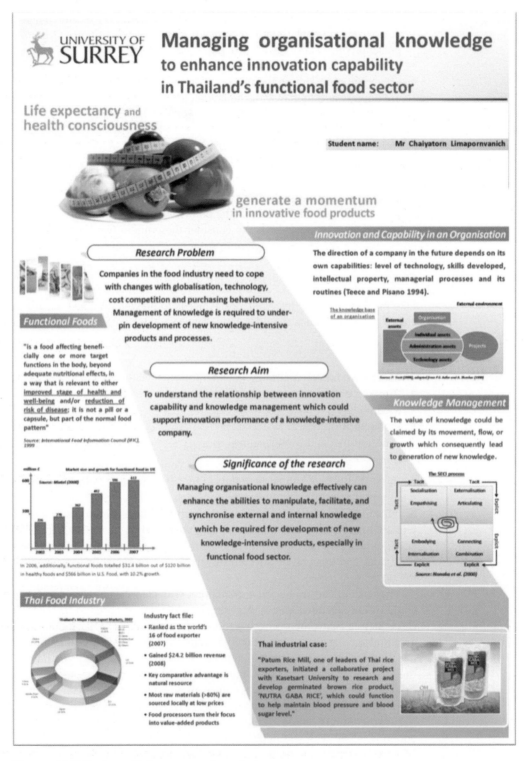

Figure 14.2 Poster outlining a research project
© Chaiyatorn Limapornvanich 2018, reproduced with permission

Presenting your poster

Your poster should be designed to 'speak' for itself. As noted it should be easy to read and easy to understand. Your role during the presentation will be, at least for some of the time it is being shown, to answer questions from those who look at and read your poster. These questions are likely to focus on seeking further information about your research. They may relate to why you chose your topic, the methods you used, the literature you read and how this informed your research, your findings, discussion and conclusions, your reflections about your research and key learning points. You therefore need to be prepared to answer a wide range of questions about your research project outside the necessarily limited scope of what you are able to include on your poster.

Like a traditional, oral presentation, you may consider practising your poster presentation by showing this to friends and inviting them to ask you questions, to see how well you can answer their questions. You may also need to provide a handout related to your poster presentation and you will need to consider the design and production of this.

14.10 Summary

- Writing is a powerful way of clarifying your thinking.
- Writing is a creative process, which needs the right conditions if it is to produce successful results.
- Your project report should have a clear structure that enables you to develop a clear storyline.
- The structure you use should be suitable for your research strategy.
- The structure you use should also be suitable for the report's audience. This audience may be an academic one or an organisational one, as is the case of a consultancy report.
- Your report should be laid out in such a way that your reader finds all the information readily accessible.
- You should try to develop a clear, simple writing style that will make reading the report an easy and enjoyable experience.
- Spelling and grammatical errors should be avoided.
- Do not think of your first draft as your last. Be prepared to rewrite your report several times until you think it is the best you can do.
- A reflective essay or section will allow you to comment on your experience, discuss your learning and improve your research practice.
- Presentations using slides or a poster should be carefully structured and purposeful, and it will help to practise it beforehand.
- Visual aids should be used to enhance the understanding of your audience and lend your presentation structure and professionalism.

Self-check questions

Help with these questions is available at the end of the chapter.

14.1 Your project tutor has returned your draft project report with the suggestion that you make a clearer distinction between your results and your conclusions. How will you go about this?

14.2 Why is it considered good practice to acknowledge the limitations of your research in the project report?

14.3 Look again at the quote from Wright Mills cited early in Section 14.6. Rewrite this so that his idea is communicated to the reader in the clearest way possible.

14.4 What are the problems that must be avoided when repositioning sections of your report in the redrafting processes?

14.5 Your friend or colleague is concerned about preparing her or his project presentation. What advice will you give to help him or her prepare this presentation?

Review and discussion questions

14.6 Draft a plan for your project report, show it to your friends and compare your plan with those they have drafted. Explain the reason for any differences between your plan and those of your friends.

14.7 Look through several of the refereed academic journals that relate to your subject area. Choose an article that is based upon some primary research and note the structure of the article. Decide whether you agree with the way in which the author has structured the article and think of ways in which you may have done this differently.

14.8 Share pieces of your writing with a group of your friends. Look at the example in Box 14.11 and subject all the pieces to the 'write clearer sentences' test.

Progressing your research project

Writing your project report

- Where you have a choice about how to structure your report, use the discussion in Section 14.3 to help you to devise a report structure that will be suitable for the research approach and research strategy you used, to allow you to tell a clear story about your project. Where you do not have a choice about how to structure your report but you feel that the given format is inappropriate for your approach and strategy, consider how you may present your research within this structure to tell a clear story about your project. Discuss this with your project tutor and ensure that the structure you use meets the expectations of your examiners.

- As you draft each part of your project report, continue to review your work to ensure that the content is clear and accessible and your writing style is appropriate. Be prepared to read your draft material very carefully and repeatedly in order to seek to improve its clarity and style. Where possible, re-read and amend drafts of a section or chapter when your mind is fresh.

- The structure you devise, related to your research approach and research strategy, will have implications for the way in which you discuss the role of literature, theory, methods, findings and conclusions in your project report. As you produce your draft, continue to evaluate how well these elements fit together without overlapping (see next point) in your report. Where the story of your research is not clear, you will need to continue to re-draft the report.

- As the draft of your report develops, ensure that you distinguish between describing events, outlining methods, reporting findings, and interpreting and theorising about what you found. This will be important irrespective of the structure you use so that your readers may distinguish between these elements in your work. Where you use an alternative structure and wish to include more than one of these elements in the same chapter, you will need to distinguish between these by, for example, using different sections with unmistakable headings.

- Give your report the 'reader-friendly' test to ensure that your style is easy to read, and the content is clear and free from avoidable errors.

- Use the questions in Box 1.4 to guide your reflective diary entry.

References

Becker, H. (2007) *Writing for Social Scientists* (2nd edn). Chicago, IL: University of Chicago Press.

Bloom, B. (ed.) (1971) *Taxonomy of Educational Objectives: Cognitive Domain*. New York: McKay.

Charmaz, K. (2014) Constructing Grounded Theory (2nd edn). London: Sage.

Coghlan, D. and Brannick, T. (2014) *Doing Action Research in Your Own Organisation* (4th edn). London: Sage.

Day, R.A. (1998) *How to Write and Publish a Scientific Paper* (5th edn). Phoenix, AZ: Oryx Press.

Emerald Group Publishing (2018) *A 6 step guide to writing an abstract.* Available at http://www .emeraldgrouppublishing.com/authors/guides/write/abstracts.htm [Accessed 04 June 2018].

Gastel, B. and Day, R.A. (2017) *How to Write and Publish a Scientific Paper* (8th edn). Cambridge: Cambridge University Press.

Lange, D. and Pfarrer, M.D. (2017) 'Editors' Comments: Sense and Structure – The Core Building Blocks of an AMR Article', *Academy of Management Review,* Vol. 42, No. 3, pp. 407–416.

Neville, C. (2016) *The Complete Guide to Referencing and Avoiding Plagiarism* (3rd edn). London: Open University Press McGraw Hill.

Phillips, E.M. and Pugh, D.S. (2015) *How to Get a PhD* (6th edn). Maidenhead: Open University Press McGraw-Hill Education.

Rawlins, K. (1999) *Presentation and Communication Skills: A Handbook for Practitioners.* London: Emap Healthcare Ltd.

Richards, P. (2007) 'Risk', in H. Becker (ed.) *Writing for Social Scientists* (2nd edn). Chicago, IL: University of Chicago Press.

Strauss, A. and Corbin, J. (1998) *Basics of Qualitative Research* (2nd edn). Thousand Oaks, CA: Sage.

The Free Dictionary (2014) 'Gibberish'. Available at http://www.thefreedictionary.com/gibberish [Accessed 03 June 2018].

Van Maanen, J. (2011a) 'Ethnography as work: Some rules of engagement', *Journal of Management Studies,* Vol. 48, No. 1, pp. 218–34.

Van Maanen, J. (2011b) *Tales of the Field: On Writing Ethnography* (2nd edn). London: University of Chicago Press.

Watson, T.J. (2011) 'Ethnography, reality, and truth: The vital need for studies of "how things work" in organizations and management', *Journal of Management Studies,* Vol. 48, No. 1, pp. 202–17.

Wright Mills, C. (1970) 'On intellectual craftsmanship', in C. Wright Mills, *The Sociological Imagination.* London: Pelican.

Yin, R.K. (2018) *Case Study Research and Applications: Design and Methods* (6th edn). London: Sage.

Further reading

Charmaz, K. (2014) *Constructing Grounded Theory* (2nd edn). London: Sage. Chapter 7 contains useful advice on writing a Grounded Theory project report.

Coghlan, D. and Brannick, T. (2014) *Doing Action Research in Your Own Organisation* (4th edn). London: Sage. Chapter 11 contains useful advice on writing an Action Research project report.

Gastel, B. and Day, R.A. (2017) *How to Write and Publish a Scientific Paper* (8th edn). Cambridge: Cambridge University Press. This takes the reader through the process, with a host of useful advice. It is funny and irreverent but nonetheless valuable for that!

Neville, C. (2016) *The Complete Guide to Referencing and Plagiarism* (3rd edn). London: Open University Press McGraw-Hill. A useful guide to both how to reference and how to help ensure you do not inadvertently plagiarise the work of others.

Van Maanen, J. (2011b) *Tales of the Field: On Writing Ethnography* (2nd edn). London: The University of Chicago Press. A fascinating read even if you are not writing an ethnography, but essential if you are to understand how it may be approached.

Yin, R.K. (2018) *Case Study Research and Applications: Design and Methods* (6th edn). London: Sage. Chapter 6 contains helpful advice on writing a Case Study project report.

Case 14
Presenting research findings to a business audience

As a master's student John had to undertake a consultancy project based on a live issue within an organisation. John was working for a large, global, fast-moving consumer goods (FMCG) producer and chose to focus on developing a learning and development (L&D) programme for a selection of key account managers (KAMs). John reviewed the literature on KAM and L&D, devised clear research objectives and conducted a number of interviews and focus groups (multi-method qualitative research). He analysed his findings using a thematic approach (Braun and Clarke, 2006) and produced a series of recommendations. All in all, John felt he had produced an academically robust piece of work, which was just within the 10,000 words limit set by his university.

Once the project report was submitted to the University, John began to focus on how he would present his work to senior colleagues in his organisation. He knew that they would not read his consultancy project in full and that, in order to ensure his research made an impact within his organisation, he would need to focus on the key aspects that would be of interest to them. John's project tutor offered to review a draft of the report for the organisation and asked John to send this to him in advance of their next meeting. John's initial draft for his employer comprised a 5,000 word version of the university project report, using the same headings:

- Introduction
- Academic literature on Key Account Management
- Academic literature on Learning and Development
- Research Methodology and Methods
- Findings and Analysis
- Conclusions and Recommendations

He intended to email this short report to work colleagues and then to make a 15-minute presentation at a future meeting using PowerPoint.

While this shortened version would be useful in an academic context, his project tutor knew that it would not meet the needs of senior colleagues. At their next meeting, his project tutor asked John to describe the forms of communication used within his organisation and to reflect on the types of communication that made the most impact.

John's project tutor then asked him to reflect on his initial plan for communicating his findings at work. John chuckled, noting that he had written the report using a similar layout to the main consultancy project, without giving due regard to the fact that the intended audiences were very different. He mentioned how he had forgotten what he had learned in the communications workshops – to focus on the needs of the audience. He now realised that he needed to find a way to cut through the volume of daily missives and to communicate the value of his research in under five minutes. He and his project tutor then discussed Customer Value Proposition (Anderson et al. 2006), a core topic in the Sales module, which John had taken, and the need for him to have a strong 'elevator pitch' – a short statement which would catch the attention of colleagues. After a few drafts they settled on:

"Hello. I have clear research findings, which will help us develop a world-class L&D programme for our KAMs which will help us to beat the competition and grow our market share. If I can have 5 minutes at our next meeting I would love to share these insights with you".

They agreed that if probed for further information John could then explain the background to the research. Once he had agreement to add an agenda item at the next meeting, John needed a way to communicate to his colleagues in an engaging manner. He mentioned that written documents presented at meetings were usually quite short, often a maximum of one page, but he questioned how impactful yet another written document would be. He also knew that a PowerPoint presentation was unlikely to be shared. John needed to think of a more engaging format.

References

Braun, V. and Clarke, V. (2006). Using thematic analysis in psychology. Qualitative Research in Psychology, 3(2), pp.77–101

Anderson, J.C., Narus, J.A. & Van Rossum, W. (2006), Customer value propositions in business markets. Harvard Business Review, 84 (3), pp. 1–8.

Questions

1 What key aspects of John's research would be likely to be of interest to his colleagues?
2 Why would a shortened version of the project report be unlikely to meet the needs of a professional audience?
3 **a** What do you think were likely to be the current communication practices in John's large global organisation?
   b Give reasons for your answer
4 **a** How do you think John should present his work?
   b Give reasons for your answer

Additional case studies relating to material covered in this chapter are available via the book's companion website: **www.pearsoned.co.uk/saunders**.
   They are:
- Writing Lata's project report.
- Amina's story.
- Akasma's draft disappointment.
- James' consultancy report on managers' financial information needs.
- Clare's research project presentation.
- Elena's research project write-up.

Self-check answers

14.1 This is easier said than done. Start by going through your results chapter, continually asking yourself 'Did I find this out?' You will probably weed out a lot of things that you have thought about that are related to points you found out. These belong in the conclusions (or discussion) chapter.

Now turn to the conclusions chapter, asking yourself the question: 'Is this a reflection of what I found out?' If the points are a repeat of what you covered in your findings section, then cut them out and make sure you write reflections on the findings.

14.2 It will demonstrate good practice in two respects. First, it will demonstrate that you have evaluated your research design. Second, it will help you to evaluate how you would alter this design if you were going to repeat your research, or if you were going to undertake further research. Remember that there is no perfect research design.

14.3 Academic writing is often difficult to understand. This is not usually because the subject matter is complex or the thoughts profound. It is because the writer thinks it necessary to write in an 'academic' way.

14.4 The 'road map' you announced in your introduction may not now be correct. The previews and summaries at the beginning and end of the relevant chapters may need changing. A more serious potential problem is that the storyline may be altered. This should not be the case. Nonetheless, it would important to re-read the whole report to ensure that any repositioning does not alter its sense of coherence.

14.5 You may emphasise the general point that preparation is very important, not least because this will help to overcome any nervousness that your friend will feel when he or she makes the presentation. You may also emphasise that she or he should think about the audience and what is it that he or she will want to tell them. You may tell her or him to make sure that the presentation has clear objectives and that it should be kept simple so that there is no danger of overloading the audience with too much information in a short period. This will mean telling the audience what they need to know and eliminating other information. You may also tell him or her that using visual aids will be important but that these should support the key points you wish to make and not be used to show off your technical skills as this may only serve to annoy or confuse your audience. Clear visual aids will also be helpful to your friend in delivering her or his presentation. You may also advise your friend to practise his or her presentation, to invite members of the audience to ask some questions during the actual performance to help to engage them but to remain mindful of the time allowed to complete it.

Get ahead using resources on the companion website at: **www.pearsoned.co .uk/saunders**.

- Improve your IBM SPSS Statistics analysis with practice tutorials.
- Save time researching on the Internet with the Smarter Online Searching Guide.
- Test your progress using self-assessment questions.
- Follow live links to useful websites.

Bibliography

A

56 Up (2012) [DVD] London: Network.

Access to Research (2018) *Access to research.* Available at http://www.accesstoresearch.org.uk/ [Accessed 20 March 2018].

Advertising Standards Canada (2012) *Guidelines for the Use of Comparative Advertising. Guidelines for the Use of Research and Survey Data to Support Comparative Advertising Claims.* Available at http://www.adstandards.com/en/ASCLibrary/guidelinesCompAdvertising-en.pdf [Accessed 9 May 2017].

Advertising Standards Canada (2016) *The Canadian Code of Advertising Standards.* Available at http://www.adstandards.com/en/standards/canCodeOfAdStandards.pdf [Accessed 9 May 2017].

Alvesson, M. and Sandberg, J. (2011) 'Generating research questions through problematization', *Academy of Management Review,* Vol. 36, No. 2, pp. 247–71.

Alvesson, M. and Sköldberg, K. (2009) *Reflexive Methodology: New Vistas for Qualitative Research* (2nd edn). London: Sage.

American Association for Public Opinion Research (2016) *Standard Definitions: Final Dispositions of Case Codes and Outcome Rates for Surveys 9th edition.* Lenexa, KA: AAPOR. Available at http://www.aapor.org/AAPOR_Main/media/publications/Standard-Definitions20169theditionfinal.pdf [Accessed 11 May 2017].

American Psychological Association (2018) *PsycTESTS* Available at http://www.apa.org/pubs/databases/psyctests/index.aspx [Accessed 3 January 2018].

Anderson, D., Lees, R. and Avery, B. (2015) 'Reviewing the literature using the Thematic Analysis Grid', *Poster presented at the European Conference on Research Methodology for Business and Management Studies,* Malta, June, 2015.

Anderson, D.R., Sweeney, D.J., Williams, T.A., Freeman, J. and Shoesmith E. (2017) *Statistics for Business and Economics* (4th edn). Andover: Cengage Learning.

Anderson, T.W. (2003) *An Introduction to Multivariate Statistical Analysis.* (3rd edn), New York: John Wiley.

Angrosino, M. and Rosenberg, J. (2011) 'Observations on observation: Continuities and challenges', in N.K. Denzin and Y.S. Lincoln (eds) *The Sage Handbook of Qualitative Research* (4th edn). London: Sage, pp. 467–78.

Anseel, F., Lievens, F., Schollaert, E. and Choragwicka, B. (2010) 'Response rates in organizational science, 1995–2008: A meta-analytic review and guidelines for survey researchers', *Journal of Business Psychology,* Vol. 25, pp. 335–49.

Arnould, E.J. and Cayla, J. (2015) 'Consumer Fetish: Commercial Ethnography and the Sovereign Consumer', *Organization Studies,* Vol. 36, No. 10, pp. 1361–1386.

B

Bakardjieva, M. and Feenberg, A. (2000) 'Involving the virtual subject', *Ethics and Information Technology,* Vol. 2, pp. 233–40.

Baker, R., Brick. J.M., Bates, N.A., Battaglia, M., Couper, M.P., Dever, J.A., Gile, K.J. and Tourangeau, R. (2013) 'Summary of the AAPOR task force on non-probability sampling', *Journal of Survey Statistics and Computing.* Vol. 1, pp. 90–143.

Banks, G.C., Pollack, J.M., Bochantin, J.E., Kirkman, B.L., Whelpley, C.E. and O'Boyle, E.H. (2016) 'Management's Science-Practice Gap: A Grand Challenge for All Stakeholders', *Academy of Management Journal,* Vol. 59, No. 6, pp. 2205–2231.

Bansal, P. and Corley, K. G. (2011) 'The coming of age for qualitative research: Embracing the diversity of qualitative methods', *Academy of Management Review,* Vol. 54, No. 2, pp. 233–7.

Bansal, P. and Roth, K. (2000) 'Why companies go green: A model of ecological responsiveness', *Academy of Management Journal,* Vol. 43, No. 4, pp. 717–736.

Barnett, V. (2002) *Sample Survey Principles and Methods* (3rd edn). Chichester: Wiley.

Barney, J.B. (1991) 'Firm resources and sustained competitive advantage', *Journal of Management,* Vol. 17, pp. 99–120.

Baruch, Y. and Holtom, B.C. (2008) 'Survey response rate levels and trends in organizational research', *Human Relations,* Vol. 61, pp. 1139–60.

Basil, M. (2011) 'Use of photography and video in observational research', *Qualitative Market Research: An International Journal,* Vol. 14, No. 3, pp. 246–57.

BBC Academy (2018) *Interviewing.* Available at http://www.bbc.co.uk/academy/journalism/skills/interviewing [Accessed 12 March 2018].

Becker, H. (2007) *Writing for Social Scientists* (2nd edn). Chicago, IL: University of Chicago Press.

Becker, H.S. (1998) *Tricks of the Trade: How to Think About Your Research While You're Doing It.* Chicago: Chicago University Press.

Bell, E. and Bryman, A. (2007) 'The ethics of management research: An exploratory content analysis', *British Journal of Management,* Vol. 18, No. 1, pp. 63–77.

Bell, E. and Davison, J. (2013) 'Visual Management Studies: Empirical and Theoretical Approaches', *International Journal of Management Reviews,* Vol. 15, No. 2, pp. 167–184.

Bell, J. and Waters, S. (2014) *Doing Your Research Project* (6th edn). Maidenhead: Open University Press.

Belzile, J.A. and Oberg, G. (2012) 'Where to begin? Grappling with how to use participant interaction in focus group design', *Qualitative Research,* Vol. 12, No. 4, pp. 459–72.

Berelson, B. (1952) *Content Analysis in Communication Research.* Glencoe, IL: Free Press.

Berman Brown, R. and Saunders, M. (2008) *Dealing with Statistics: What You Need to Know.* Maidenhead: McGraw-Hill Open University Press.

Bhaskar, R. (2008) *A Realist Theory of Science.* London: Verso (originally published by Harvester Press 1978).

Bhaskar, R. (2011) *Reclaiming Reality: A Critical Introduction to Contemporary Philosophy.* Abingdon: Routledge (originally published by Verso 1989).

Biron. M. and Van Veldhoven, M. (2016) 'When control becomes a liability rather than an asset: Comparing home and office days among part-time teleworkers', *Journal of Organizational Behaviour,* Vol. 37, pp. 1317–1337.

Bishop, L. and Kuula-Luumi, A. (2017) 'Revisiting qualitative data reuse: A decade on', *SAGE Open,* Vol. 7, No. 1, pp. 1–15.

Black, K. (2009) *Business Statistics* (6th edn). Hoboken, NJ: Wiley.

Blaikie, N. (2010) *Designing Social Research* (2nd edn). Cambridge: Polity.

Bloom, B. (ed.) (1971) *Taxonomy of Educational Objectives: Cognitive Domain.* New York: McKay.

Blumberg, B., Cooper, D.R. and Schindler, P.S. (2014) *Business Research Methods* (4th edn). Boston, MA and Burr Ridge, IL: McGraw-Hill.

Boddy, C. (2005) 'A rose by any other name may smell as sweet but "group discussion" is not another name for "focus group" nor should it be', *Qualitative Market Research,* Vol. 8, No. 3, pp. 248–55.

Böttger, T., Rudolph, T., Evanschitzky, H. and Pfrang, T. (2017) 'Customer Inspiration: Conceptualization, Scale Development, and Validation', *Journal of Marketing,* Vol. 81, November, pp.116–131.

Bourque, L.B. and Clark, V.A. (1994) 'Processing data: The survey example', in M.S. Lewis-Beck (ed.) *Research Practice.* London: Sage, pp. 1–88.

Bradley, N. (1999) 'Sampling for Internet surveys: An examination of respondent selection for Internet research', *Journal of the Market Research Society,* Vol. 41, No. 4, pp. 387–95.

Brady, S.R. (2015) 'Utilizing and adapting the Delphi method for use in qualitative research', *International Journal of Qualitative Methods,* pp. 1–6.

Brannan, M.J. and Oultram, T. (2012) 'Participant observation', in G. Symon and C. Cassell (eds) *Qualitative Organisational Research Core Methods and Current Challenges.* London: Sage, pp. 296–313.

Braun, V. and Clarke, V. (2006) 'Using thematic analysis in psychology', *Qualitative Research in Psychology,* Vol. 3, No. 2, pp. 77–101.

Breevaart, K., Baker, A.B., Demerouti, E. and Derks, D. (2016) 'Who takes the lead? A multi-source diary study on leadership, work engagement, and job performance', *Journal of Organizational Behavior,* Vol. 37, pp. 309–325.

Brekhus, W.H., Galliher, J.F. and Gubrium, J.F. (2005) 'The need for thin description', *Qualitative Inquiry,* Vol. 11, No. 6, pp. 861–79.

Bresnen, M. and Burrell, G. (2012) 'Journals à la mode? Twenty years of living alongside Mode 2 and the new production of knowledge', *Organization,* Vol. 20, No. 1, pp. 25–37.

Brinkmann, S. and Kvale, S. (2015) *InterViews: Learning the Craft of Qualitative Research Interviewing* (3rd edn). London: Sage.

Bristow, A., Robinson, S.K. and Ratle, O. (2017) 'Being an Early-Career CMS Academic in the Context of Insecurity and 'Excellence': The Dialectics of Resistance and Compliance', *Organization Studies,* Vol 38(9), pp. 1185–1207.

British Psychological Society (2009) *Code of Ethics and Conduct.* Leicester: British Psychological Society. Available at https://www.bps.org.uk/sites/bps.org.uk/files/Policy%20-%20Files/Code%20of%20Ethics%20and%20Conduct%20(2009).pdf [Accessed 12 December 2017].

British Psychological Society (2017) *Ethics Guidelines for Internet mediated Research.* INF206/04.2017 Leicester: British Psychological Society. Available at https://www.bps.org.uk/news-and-policy/ethics-guidelines-internet-mediated-research-2017 [Accessed 14 December 2017].

British Psychological Society (1988) 'Guidelines for the use of non-sexist language', *The Psychologist,* Vol. 1, No. 2, pp. 53–4.

British Psychological Society (2015) *Style Guide for Authors and Editors.* Available at https://www.bps.org.uk/news-and-policy/bps-style-guide-authors-and-editors [Accessed 4 February 2018].

British Sociological Association (2004b) *Language and the BSA: Non-Disablist.* Available at https://www.britsoc.co.uk/Equality-Diversity/ [Accessed 4 February 2018].

British Sociological Association (nd) *Language and the BSA: Ethnicity & Race.* Available at https://www.britsoc.co.uk/Equality-Diversity/ [Accessed 4 February 2018].

British Sociological Association (2017) *Statement of Ethical Practice.* Available at https://www.britsoc.co.uk/media/24310/bsa_statement_of_ethical_practice.pdf [Accessed 12 December 2017].

Broome, J. (2015) 'How Telephone Interviewers' Responsiveness Impacts Their Success', *Field Methods,* Vol. 27, No. 1, pp. 66–81.

Brozovic, D. (2018) 'Strategic Flexibility: A Review of the Literature', *International Journal of Management Reviews,* Vol. 20, No. 1, pp. 3–31.

Bruner, G.C. (2013) *Marketing Scales Handbook: The Top 20 Multi Item Measure Used in Consumer Research.* Fort Worth, TX: GBII Productions.

Bryant, A. and Charmaz, K. (2007) *The Sage Handbook of Grounded Theory.* London: Sage.

Bryman, A. (1988) *Quantity and Quality in Social Research.* London: Unwin Hyman.

Bryman, A. (1998) 'Quantitative and qualitative research strategies in knowing the social world', in T. May and M. Williams (eds), *Knowing the Social World.* Buckingham: Open University Press, pp. 138–157.

Bryman, A. (2006) 'Integrating quantitative and qualitative research: How is it done?', *Qualitative Research,* Vol. 6, No. 1, pp. 97–113.

Bryson, B. (2016) *Made in America.* London: Transworld. (originally published by Minerva 1995).

Buchanan, D., Boddy, D. and McCalman, J. (2013) 'Getting in, getting on, getting out and getting back', in A. Bryman (ed.) *Doing Research in Organisations.* London: Routledge Library Edition, pp. 53–67.

Buchanan, D.A. (2012) 'Case studies in organizational research', in G. Symon and C. Cassell (eds) *Qualitative Organisational Research Core Methods and Current Challenges.* London: Sage, pp. 351–70.

Bulmer, M., Sturgis, P.J. and Allum, N. (2009) 'Editors' introduction', in M. Bulmer, P.J. Sturgis and N. Allum (eds) *Secondary Analysis of Survey Data.* Los Angeles: Sage, pp. xviii–xxvi.

Burrell, G. and Morgan, G. (2016) *Sociological Paradigms and Organisational Analysis.* Abingdon: Routledge (originally published by Heinemann 1979).

Buzan, T. (2011) *Buzan's Study Skills: Mind Maps, Memory Techniques, Speed Reading and More.* London: BBC.

C

Calás, M. and Smircich, L. (1997) *Postmodern Management Theory.* Aldershot: Ashgate/Dartmouth.

Call for Participants (2017) *Researchers page.* Available at https://www.callforparticipants.com/ [Accessed 11 December 2017].

Carroll, L. (1989) *Alice's Adventures in Wonderland.* London: Hutchinson.

Carson, D., Gilmore, A., Perry, C. and Grønhaug, K. (2001) *Qualitative Marketing Research.* London: Sage.

Carton, A.M. (2018) "'I'm not mopping floors, I'm putting a man on the moon": How NASA Leaders enhanced the meaningfulness of work by changing the meaning of work', *Administrative Science Quarterly,* Vol. 63, No. 2, pp. 323–369.

Cassell, C. and Lee, B. (eds) (2011a) *Challenges and Controversies in Management Research.* New York: Routledge.

Cassell, C. and Lee, B. (2011b) 'Introduction: Key debates, challenges and controversies in management research', in C. Cassell and B. Lee (eds) *Challenges and Controversies in Management Research.* New York: Routledge, pp. 1–16.

Cayla, J. and Arnould, E. (2013) 'Ethnographic stories for market learning', *Journal of Marketing,* Vol. 77, July, pp. 1–16.

Center for Climate and Energy Solutions (2018) *Comments of the Center For Climate And Energy Solutions on State Guidelines for Greenhouse Gas Emissions from Existing Electric Utility Generating Units; Advance Notice Of Proposed Rulemaking. Docket Id No. EPA–HQ–OAR–2017–0545.* Available at https://www.c2es.org/site/assets/uploads/2018/01/policy-options-for-resilient-infrastructure-01-2018.pdf [Accessed 1 May 2018].

Charmaz, K. (2011) 'Grounded theory methods in social justice research', in N.K. Denzin and Y.S. Lincoln (eds) *The Sage Handbook of Qualitative Research* (4th edn). London: Sage, pp. 359–80.

Charmaz, K. (2014) *Constructing Grounded Theory* (2nd edn). London: Sage.

Charmaz, K. (2017) 'The power of constructivist grounded theory for critical inquiry', *Qualitative Inquiry,* Vol. 23, No. 1, pp. 34–45.

Chartered Institute of Library and Information Professionals (2015) *Libraries and Information Services in the United Kingdom and Republic of Ireland 2015* (38th edn). London: Facet Publishing.

Chartered Institute of Personnel and Development (2017) 'Unethical amnesia in repeat offenders', *Work,* Summer, p. 6.

Chase, S.E. (2011) 'Narrative Inquiry: Still a field in the making', in N.K. Denzin and Y.S. Lincoln (eds) *The Sage Handbook of Qualitative Research* (4th edn). London: Sage, pp. 421–34.

Chia, R. (2003) 'Organization theory as a postmodern science', in H. Tsoukas and C. Knudsen (eds) *The Oxford Handbook of Organization Theory: Meta-Theoretical Perspectives.* Oxford: Oxford University Press, pp. 113–40.

Chidlow, A., Plakoyiannaki, E. and Welch, C. (2014) 'Translation in cross-language international business research: Beyond equivalence', *Journal of International Business Studies,* Vol. 45, pp. 562–582.

Clark, A., Holland, C., Katz, J. and Peace, S. (2009) 'Learning to see: lessons from a participatory observation research project in public spaces', *International Journal of Social Research Methodology,* Vol. 12, No. 4, pp. 345–360.

Clarke, J. and Holt, R. (2017) 'Imagery of adventure: Understanding entrepreneurial identity through metaphor and drawing', *Journal of Business Venturing,* Vol. 32, pp. 476–497.

Clough, P. and Nutbrown, C. (2012) *A Student's Guide to Methodology* (3rd edn). London: Sage.

Coffey, A. and Atkinson, P. (1996) *Making Sense of Qualitative Data.* London: Sage.

Coghlan, D. (2011) 'Action Research: Exploring perspectives on a philosophy of practical knowing', *The Academy of Management Annals,* Vol. 5, No. 1, pp. 53–87.

Coghlan, D. and Brannick, T. (2014) *Doing Action Research in Your Own Organisation* (4th edn). London: Sage.

Colquitt, J.A. (2013) 'Crafting references in AMJ submissions', *Academy of Management Journal,* Vol. 56, No. 5, pp. 1221–4.

Committee of Advertising Practice (2010) *The BCAP Code: The UK Code of broadcast Advertising (Edition 1).* London: Committee of Advertising Practice. Available at https://www.asa.org.uk/asset/846F25EB-F474-47C1-AB3FF571E3DB5910/ [Accessed 9 May 2017].

Committee of Advertising Practice (2014) *The CAP Code: The UK Code of Non-broadcast Advertising and Direct & Promotional Marketing (Edition 12).* London: Committee of Advertising Practice. Available at https://www.asa.org.uk/asset/47EB51E7-028D-4509-AB3C0F4822C9A3C4/ [Accessed 9 May 2017].

Committee of Advertising Practice (2016) 'A quick guide to advertising consumer surveys' CAP News. Available at https://www.asa.org.uk/news/a-quick-guide-to-advertising-consumer-surveys.html [Accessed 9 May 2017].

Cook, T.D. and Campbell, D.T. (1979) *Quasi-experimentation: Design and Analysis Issues for Field Settings.* Chicago: Rand McNally.

Corbin, J. and Strauss, A. (2008) *Basics of Qualitative Research Techniques and Procedures for Developing Grounded Theory* (3rd edn). London: Sage.

Corbin, J. and Strauss, A. (2015) *Basics of Qualitative Research Techniques and Procedures for Developing Grounded Theory* (4th edn). London: Sage.

Corder, G.W. and Foreman, D.I. (2014) *Nonparametric statistics* (2nd edn). Hoboken, NJ: Wiley.

Corley, K.G. (2015) 'A Commentary on "What Grounded Theory Is." Engaging a Phenomenon from the Perspective of Those Living it', *Organizational Research Methods,* Vol. 18, No. 4, pp. 600–605.

Corley, K.G. and Gioia, D.A. (2011) 'Building theory about theory building: What constitutes a theoretical contribution?', *Academy of Management Review,* Vol. 36, No. 1, pp. 12–32.

Court, D. and Abbas, R. (2013) 'Whose interview is it, anyway? Methodological and ethical challenges of insider-outsider research, multiple languages, and dual-researcher cooperation', *Qualitative Inquiry,* Vol. 19, No. 6, pp. 480–8.

Cowton, C.J. (1998) 'The use of secondary data in business ethics research', *Journal of Business Ethics,* Vol. 17, No. 4, pp. 423–34.

Creswell, J.W. (2009) 'Mapping the field of mixed methods research', *Journal of Mixed Methods Research,* Vol. 3, No. 2, pp. 95–108.

Creswell, J.W. and Plano Clark, V.L. (2011) *Designing and Conducting Mixed Methods Research* (2nd edn). Thousand Oaks, CA: Sage.

Creswell, J.W. and Poth, C.N. (2017) *Qualitative Inquiry and Research Design: Choosing Among Five Approaches* (4th edn). Thousand Oaks, CA: Sage.

Crotty, M. (1998) *The Foundations of Social Research.* London: Sage.

CrowdTangle (2018) *CrowdTangle,* Available at http://www.crowdtangle.com/ [Accessed 9 May 2018].

Crozier, S.E. and Cassell, C.M. (2015) 'Methodological considerations in the use of audio diaries in work psychology: Adding to the Qualitative toolkit', *Journal of Occupational and Organizational Psychology,* Vol. 89, No. 2, pp. 396–419.

Cunliffe. A.L. (2003) 'Reflexive inquiry in organizational research: Questions and possibilities', *Human Relations,* Vol. 56, pp. 983–1003.

Cunliffe, A.L. (2010) 'Retelling tales of the field: In search of organisational ethnography 20 years on', *Organizational Research Methods,* Vol. 13, No. 2, pp. 224–39.

Cunliffe. A.L. and Scaratti. G. (2017) 'Embedding Impact in Engaged Research: Developing Socially Useful Knowledge through Dialogical Sensemaking', *British Journal of Management,* Vol 28(1), pp. 29–44.

Czarniawska, B. (1997) *Narrating the Organization: Dramas of Institutional Identity.* Chicago: University of Chicago Press.

D

Dale, A., Arber, S. and Proctor, M. (1988) *Doing Secondary Analysis*. London: Unwin Hyman.

Dale, A., Arber, S. and Procter, M. (1988) *Doing Secondary Research*. London: Unwin Hyman.

Dancey, C.P. and Reidy, J. (2017) *Statistics Without Maths for Psychology: Using SPSS for Windows* (7th edn). Harlow: Prentice Hall.

David-Barrett, E., Yakis-Douglas, B., Moss-Cowan, A. and Nguyen, Y. (2017) 'A Bitter Pill? Institutional Corruption and the Challenge of Antibribery Compliance in the Pharmaceutical Sector', *Journal of Management Inquiry*, Vol. 26, No. 3, pp. 326–347.

Davis, G.F. (2015) 'What is management research actually good for?', *Harvard Business Review*, 28 May, pp. 2–6.

Dawson, J. (2017) *Analysing Quantitative Survey Data for Business and Management Students*. London: Sage.

Day, R.A. (1998) *How to Write and Publish a Scientific Paper* (5th edn). Phoenix, AZ: Oryx Press.

Day. M and Thatcher, J. (2009) '"I'm Really Embarrassed That You're Going to Read This . . . ": Reflections on Using Diaries in Qualitative Research', *Qualitative Research in Psychology*, Vol. 6, No. 4, pp. 249–259.

De Cock, C. and Land, C. (2006) 'Organization/Literature: Exploring the seam', *Organization Studies*, Vol. 27, pp. 517–35.

De Vaus, D.A. (2014) *Surveys in Social Research* (6th edn). Abingdon: Routledge.

Dees, R. (2003) *Writing the Modern Research Paper* (4th edn). Boston, MA: Allyn and Bacon.

Delamont, S. (2007) 'Ethnography and participant observation', in C. Seale, G. Gobo, J.F. Gubrium and D. Silverman (eds) *Qualitative Research Practice*. London: Sage, pp. 205–17.

Denscombe, M. (2017) *The Good Research Guide for small-scale social research projects* (5th edn). Maidenhead: Open University Press.

Denyer, D. and Tranfield, D. (2009) 'Producing a Systematic Review', in D.A. Buchanan and A. Bryman (eds) *The Sage Handbook of Organisational Research Methods*. London: Sage, pp. 671–89.

Denzin, N.K. (2001) 'The reflexive interview and a performative social science', *Qualitative Research*, Vol. 1, No. 1, pp. 23–46.

Denzin, N.K. (2012) 'Triangulation 2.0', *Journal of Mixed Methods Research*, Vol. 6, No. 2, pp. 80–8.

Denzin, N.K. and Lincoln, Y.S. (2005) *The Sage Handbook of Qualitative Research* (3rd edn). London: Sage.

Denzin, N.K. and Lincoln, Y.S. (2018) *The Sage Handbook of Qualitative Research* (5th edn). London: Sage.

Department for Transport (2015) *Know Your Traffic Signs* London: Department for Transport. Available at https://assets.publishing.service.gov.uk/government/uploads/system/uploads/attachment_data/file/519129/know-your-traffic-signs.pdf [Accessed 20 May 2018].

Derrida J. (2016) *Of Grammatology (40th Anniversary Edition)*. Baltimore: Johns Hopkins University Press (originally published 1976).

DeVellis, R.F. (2012) *Scale Development: Theory and Applications* (3rd edn). Los Angeles: Sage.

Dey, I. (1993) *Qualitative Data Analysis*. London: Routledge.

Dick, B. (2013) 'Convergent interviewing [Online]. Available at http://www.aral.com.au/resources/coin.pdf [Accessed 23 June 2018].

Dillman, D.A., Smyth, J.D. and Christian, J.M. (2014) *Internet, Phone, Mail and Mixed Mode Surveys: The Tailored Design Method* (4th edn). Hoboken, NJ: Wiley.

Dion, D. and Borraz, S. (2017) 'Managing Status: How Luxury Brands Shape Class subjectivities in the Service Encounter', *Journal of Marketing*, Vol. 81, September, pp. 67–85.

Dochartaigh, N.O. (2012) *Internet Research Skills: How to Do Your Literature Search and Find Research Information Online*. (3rd edn) London: Sage.

Dougherty, D. (2015) 'Reflecting on the Reflective Conversation', *Organizational Research Methods*, Vol. 18, No. 4, pp. 606–611.

Dubois, A. and Gadde, L E. (2002) 'Systematic combining: An abductive approach to case research', *Journal of Business Research*, Vol. 55, pp. 553–60.

E

Easterby-Smith, M., Thorpe, R., Jackson, P. and Lowe, A. (2012) *Management Research* (4th edn). London: Sage.

Edelman (2017) *Edelman Trust Barometer™ Archive*. Available at https://www.edelman.com/insights/intellectual-property/edelman-trust-barometer-archive/ [Accessed 8 November 2017].

Eden, C. and Huxham, C. (1996) 'Action research for management research', *British Journal of Management*, Vol. 7, No. 1, pp. 75–86.

Edwards, P., Roberts, I., Clarke, M., Di Giuseppe, C., Pratap, S., Wentz, R. and Kwan, I. (2002) 'Increasing response rates to postal questionnaires: Systematic review', *British Medical Journal*, No. 324, May, pp. 1183–91.

Edwards, T., Tregaskis, O., Edwards, P., Ferner, A., Marginson, A. with Arrowsmith, J., Adam, D., Meyer, M. and Budjanovcanin, A. (2007) 'Charting the contours of multinationals in Britain: Methodological challenges arising in survey-based research', *Warwick Papers in Industrial Relations*, No. 86. Available at http://www.cbs.dk/files/cbs.dk/charting_the_contours_of_multinationals_in_britain.pdf [Accessed 14 May 2017].

Eisenhardt, K.M. (1989) 'Building theories from case study research', *Academy of Management Review*, Vol. 14, No. 4, pp. 532–50.

Eisenhardt, K.M. and Graebner, M.E. (2007) 'Theory building from cases: Opportunities and challenges', *Academy of Management Journal,* Vol. 50, No. 1, pp. 25–32.

Ekinci, Y. (2015) *Designing Research Questionnaires for Business and Management Students.* London: Sage.

Elkjaer, B. and Simpson, B. (2011) 'Pragmatism: A lived and living philosophy. What can it offer to contemporary organization theory?' in H. Tsoukas and R. Chia (eds) *Philosophy and Organization Theory.* Bradford: Emerald Publishing, pp. 55–84.

Ellis, P.D. (2010) *The Essential Guide to Effect Sizes.* Cambridge: Cambridge University Press.

Emerald Group Publishing (2018) *A 6 step guide to writing an abstract.* Available at http://www.emeraldgrouppublishing.com/authors/guides/write/abstracts.htm [Accessed 04 June 2018].

Erlandson, D.A., Harris, E.L., Skipper, B.L. and Allen, S.D. (1993) *Doing Naturalistic Inquiry.* Newbury Park, CA: Sage.

European Commission (2017) *EU Labour Force Survey - data and publication.* Available at http://ec.europa.eu/eurostat/statistics-explained/index.php/EU_labour_force_survey_%E2%80%93_data_and_publication [Accessed 9 May 2018].

Eurostat (2017) Environment and energy statistics – primary production of renewable energies. Available at https://ec.europa.eu/eurostat/web/products-datasets/-/ten00081 [Accessed 17 November 2017].

Eurostat (2017) *Eurostat Regional Yearbook 2017.* Available at http://ec.europa.eu/eurostat/en/web/products-statistical-books/-/KS-HA-17-001 [Accessed 4 May 2018].

Eurostat (2018) *Eurostat: Your Key to European Statistics.* Available at http://ec.europa.eu/eurostat/data/statistics-a-z/abc [Accessed 4 May 2018].

F

Fairclough, N. (1992) *Discourse and Social Change.* Cambridge: Polity Press.

Fairclough, N. (2010) *Critical Discourse Analysis: The Critical Study of Language* (2nd edn). Harlow: Pearson Education.

Festinger, L. (1957) *A Theory of Cognitive Dissonance.* Stanford, CA: Stanford University Press.

Field, A. (2018) *Discovering Statistics Using IBM SPSS Statistics* (5th edn). London: Sage.

Fink, A. (2016) *How to Conduct Surveys* (6th edn). Thousand Oaks, CA: Sage.

Finlay, L. (2002) 'Negotiating the swamp: The opportunity and challenge of reflexivity in research practice', *Qualitative Research,* Vol. 2, No. 2, pp. 209–30.

Fisher, C. (2010) *Researching and Writing a Dissertation for Business Students* (3rd edn). Harlow: Financial Times Prentice Hall.

Fleetwood, S. (2005) 'Ontology in organization and management studies: A critical realist perspective', *Organization,* Vol. 12, pp. 197–222.

Flyvberg, B. (2011) 'Case study', in N.K. Denzin and Y.S. Lincoln (eds) *The Sage Handbook of Qualitative Research* (4th edn). London: Sage, pp. 301–16.

Forbes (2017) *The Big (Unstructured) Data Problem* Available at https://www.forbes.com/sites/forbestechcouncil/2017/06/05/the-big-unstructured-data-problem/\#7ca6f54e493a [Accessed 2 May 2018].

Foucault, M. (1991) *Discipline and Punish: The Birth of Prison.* London: Penguin Books.

Fournier, V. and Grey, C. (2000) 'At the critical moment: Conditions and prospects for critical management studies', *Human Relations,* Vol. 53, pp. 7–32.

G

Gabriel, Y. (2015) 'Reflexivity and beyond – a plea for imagination in qualitative research methodology', *Qualitative Research in Organizations and Management: An International Journal,* Vol. 10, No. 4, pp. 332–336.

Gabriel, Y. and Griffiths, D.S. (2004) 'Stories in organizational research', in C. Cassell and G. Symon (eds) *Essential Guide to Qualitative Methods in Organizational Research.* London: Sage, pp. 114–26.

Gabriel, Y., Gray, D.E. and Goregaokar, H. (2013) 'Job loss and its aftermath among managers and professionals: Wounded, fragmented and flexible', *Work, Employment & Society,* Vol. 27, pp. 56–72.

Gastel, B. and Day, R.A. (2017) *How to Write and Publish a Scientific Paper* (8th edn). Cambridge: Cambridge University Press.

Geertz, C. (1988) *Works and Lives: The Anthropologist as Author.* Stanford, CA: Stanford University Press.

George, G, Osinga, E.C., Lavie, D. and Scott, B.A. (2016). 'Big data and data science methods for management research: From the Editors', *Academy of Management Journal,* Vol. 59, No. 5, pp. 1493–1507.

Gerstl-Pepin, C. and Patrizio, K. (2009) 'Learning from Dumbledore's Pensieve: Metaphor as an aid in teaching reflexivity in qualitative research', *Qualitative Research,* Vol. 9, No. 3, pp. 299–308.

Ghauri, P. and Grønhaug, K. (2010) *Research Methods in Business Studies: A Practical Guide* (4th edn). Harlow: Financial Times Prentice Hall.

Gibbons, M.L., Limoges, H., Nowotny, S., Schwartman, P., Scott, P. and Trow, M. (1994) *The New Production of Knowledge: The Dynamics of Science and Research in Contemporary Societies.* London: Sage.

Gill, J. and Johnson, P. (2010) *Research Methods for Managers* (4th edn). London: Sage.

Glaser, B. and Strauss, A. (1967) *The Discovery of Grounded Theory*. Chicago, IL: Aldine.

Glaser, B.G. (1978) *Theoretical Sensitivity: Advances in the Methodology of Grounded Theory*. Mill Valley, CA: Sociology Press.

Glaser, B.G. (1992) *Basics of Grounded Theory*. Mill Valley, CA: Sociology Press.

Glaser, B.G. (1998) *Doing Grounded Theory: Issues and Discussions*. Mill Valley, CA: Sociology Press.

Gobo, G. (2011) 'Glocalizing methodology? The encounter between local methodologies', *International Journal of Social Research Methodology*, Vol. 14, No. 6, pp. 417–37.

Gold, R.L. (1958) 'Roles in Sociological Field Observations', *Social Forces*, Vol. 36, No. 3, pp. 217–223.

Gray, D.E., Saunders, M.N.K. and Farrant, K. (2016) *SME Success: Winning New Business*. London: Kingston Smith LLP.

Green, S.B. (1991) 'How many subjects does it take to do a regression analysis?', *Multivariate Behavioural Research*, Vol. 26, No. 3, pp. 499–510.

Greene, J.C. (2007) *Mixed Methods in Social Inquiry*. San Francisco, CA: Jossey-Bass.

Greene, J.C., Caracelli, V.J. and Graham, W.F. (1989) 'Towards a conceptual framework for mixed-method evaluation designs', *Educational Evaluation and Policy Analysis*, Vol. 11, No. 3, pp. 255–74.

Greenwood, D.J. and Levin. M. (2007) *Introduction to Action Research* (2nd edn). London: Sage.

Griffin, M., Harding, N. and Learmonth, M. (2017) 'Whistle while you work: Disney animation, organizational readiness and gendered subjugation', *Organization Studies*, Vol. 38, No. 7, pp. 869–894.

Groves, R.M. and Peytcheva, E. (2008) 'The impact of nonresponse rates on nonresponse bias', *Public Opinion Quarterly*, Vol. 72, No. 2, pp. 167–89.

Groves, R.M., Presser, S. and Dipko, S. (2004) 'The Role of Topic Interest in Survey Participation Decisions', *Public Opinion Quarterly*, Vol. 68, No. 1, pp. 2–31.

Groves, R.M., Singer, E. and Corning, A. (2000) 'Leverage-Saliency Theory of Survey Participation', *Public Opinion Quarterly*, Vol. 64, No. 3, pp. 299–308.

Guba, E. G., & Lincoln, Y. S. (1994) 'Competing paradigms in qualitative research', in N. K. Denzin & Y S. Lincoln (Eds.), *Handbook of qualitative research*. Thousand Oaks, CA: Sage, pp. 105–116.

Guba, E.G. and Lincoln, Y.S. (1989) *Fourth Generation Evaluation*. Newbury Park, CA: Sage.

Guest, G., Bunce, A. and Johnson, L. (2006) 'How many interviews are enough? An experiment with data saturation and validity', *Field Methods*, Vol. 18, No. 1, pp. 59–82.

Gummesson, E. (2000) *Qualitative Methods in Management Research* (2nd edn). Thousand Oaks, CA: Sage.

H

Hair, J.F., Black, B., Babin, B., Anderson, R.E. and Tatham, R.L. (2014) *Multivariate Data Analysis* (7th edn). Harlow: Pearson.

Hair, J.F., Celsi, M., Money, A.H., Samouel, P. and Page, M.J. (2016) *Essentials of Business Research Methods* (3rd edn). New York: Routledge.

Hakim, C. (1982) *Secondary Analysis in Social Research*. London: Allen & Unwin.

Hakim, C. (2000) *Research Design: Successful Designs for Social and Economic Research* (2nd edn). London: Routledge.

Hall, J.F. (2018) *Journeys in Survey Research*. Available at http://surveyresearch.weebly.com/ [Accessed 12 March 2018].

Hanna, P. (2012) 'Using internet technologies (such as Skype) as a research medium: A research note', *Qualitative Research*, Vol. 12, No. 2, pp. 239–42.

Harding, R. (2017) *British Social Attitudes 34*. London: NatCen Social Research. Available at http://www.bsa.natcen.ac.uk/latest-report/british-social-attitudes-34/key-findings/context.aspx [Accessed 27 November 2017].

Hardy, B. and Ford, L.R. (2014) 'It's not me, it's you: Miscomprehension in surveys', *Organizational Research Methods*, Vol. 17, No. 2, pp. 138–162.

Harley-Davidson Inc. (2017) *Harley-Davidson Inc. Investor Relations: Motorcycle Shipments* Available at http://investor.harley-davidson.com/phoenix.zhtml%3Fc%3D87981%26p%3Dirol-shipments [Accessed 12 October 2017].

Hart, C. (2018) *Doing a Literature Review* (2nd edn). London: Sage.

Harvard College Library (2018) *Interrogating texts: 6 reading habits to develop in your first year at Harvard*. Available at https://guides.library.harvard.edu/sixreadinghabits [Accessed 17 March 2018].

Harzing, A-W. (2018) *Journal Quality List*. Available at https://harzing.com/resources/journal-quality-list [Accessed 17 March 2018].

Hatch, M.J. and Yanow, D. (2008) 'Methodology by metaphor: Ways of seeing in painting and research', *Organization Studies*, Vol. 29, No. 1, pp. 23–44.

Haynes, K. (2012) 'Reflexivity in qualitative research', in G. Symon and C. Cassell (eds) *Qualitative Organizational Research: Core Methods and Current Challenges*. London: Sage.

Hays, W.L. (1994) *Statistics* (4th edn). London: Holt-Saunders.

Healey, M.J. (1991) 'Obtaining information from businesses', in M.J. Healey (ed.) *Economic Activity and Land Use*. Harlow: Longman, pp. 193–251.

Health Research Authority (2017) *Is my study research? Decision Tool.* Available at http://www.hra-decisiontools. org.uk/research/ [Accessed 12 December 2017].

Hedrick, T.E., Bickmann, L. and Rog, D.J. (1993) *Applied Research Design.* Newbury Park, CA: Sage.

Heikkinen, S. and Lämsä, A M. (2017) 'Narratives of Spousal Support for the Careers of Men in Managerial Posts', *Gender, Work and Organization,* Vol. 24, No. 2, pp. 171–193.

Hein, W., O'Donohoe, S. and Ryan, A. (2011) 'Mobile phones as an extension of the participant observer's self', *Qualitative Market Research: An International Journal,* Vol. 14, No. 3, pp. 258–73.

Heisley, D.D. and Levy, S.J. (1991) 'Autodriving: A Photoelicitation Technique', *Journal of Consumer Research,* Vol. 18, No. 4, pp. 257–272.

Henry, G.T. (1990) *Practical Sampling.* Newbury Park, CA: Sage.

Hepburn, A. and Potter, J. (2007) 'Discourse analytic practice', in C. Seale, G. Gobo, J. F. Gubrium and D. Silverman (eds) *Qualitative Research Practice.* London: Sage.

Heron, J. (1996) *Co-operative Inquiry: Research into the Human Condition.* London: Sage.

Heron, J. and Reason, P. (1997) 'A Participatory Inquiry Paradigm', *Qualitative Inquiry,* Vol 3, Issue 3, pp. 274–294.

Herzberg, F., Mausener, B., & Snyderman, B.B. (1959). *The motivation to work.* New York: John Wiley.

Hewson, C., Yule, P., Laurent, D. and Vogel, C. (2003) *Internet Research Methods: A Practical Guide for the Social and Behavioural Sciences.* London: Sage.

Heyl, B.S. (2005) 'Ethnographic interviewing', in P. Atkinson, A. Coffey, S. Delamont, J. Lofland and L. Lofland (eds) *Handbook of Ethnography.* Thousand Oaks, CA: Sage, pp. 369–383.

Hitt, M.A.S. and Greer, C.R. (2012) 'The value of research and its evaluation in business schools: Killing the goose that laid the golden egg?', *Journal of Management Inquiry,* Vol. 21, No. 2, pp. 236–40.

Hodgkinson, G.P. and Rousseau, D. (2009) 'Bridging the rigour–relevance gap in management research. It's already happening!', *Journal of Management Studies,* Vol. 46, No. 3, pp. 534–46.

Hodgkinson, G.P. and Starkey, K. (2011) 'Not simply returning to the same answer over and over again: Reframing relevance', *British Journal of Management,* Vol. 22, pp. 355–69.

Hodgkinson, G.P., Herriot, P. and Anderson, N. (2001) 'Re-aligning the stakeholders in management research: Lessons from industrial, work and organizational psychology', *British Journal of Management,* Vol. 12, Special Issue, pp. 41–8.

Hodson, R. (1991) 'The active worker: Compliance and autonomy at the workplace', *Journal of Contemporary Ethnography,* Vol. 20, No. 1, pp. 47–8.

Holstein, J.A. and Gubrium, J.F. (2011) 'The constructionist analytics of interpretive practice', in N.K. Denzin and Y.S. Lincoln (eds) *The Sage Handbook of Qualitative Research.* London: Sage.

Holsti, O.R. (1969) *Content Analysis for the Social Sciences and Humanities.* Reading, MA: Addison-Wesley.

Holt, A. (2010) 'Using the telephone for narrative interviewing: A research note', *Qualitative Research,* Vol. 10, No. 1, pp. 113–121.

Hookway, N. (2008) 'Entering the blogosphere: Some strategies for using blogs in social research', *Qualitative Research,* Vol. 8, No. 1, pp. 91–113.

Huff, A.S. and Huff, J.O. (2001) 'Refocusing the business school agenda', *British Journal of Management,* Vol. 12, Special Issue, pp. 49–54.

Hyatt, D. (2005) 'A critical literacy frame for UK secondary education contexts', *English in Education,* Vol. 39, No. 1, pp. 43–59.

Hyatt, D. (2013) 'The critical policy discourse analysis frame: Helping doctoral students engage with the educational policy analysis', *Teaching in Higher Education,* Vol. 18, No. 8, pp. 833–45.

I

IJMR (2007) 'Special Issue on Ethnography', *International Journal of Market Research,* Vol. 49, No. 6, pp. 681–778.

Information Commissioner's Office (2012) *Anonymisation: managing data protection risk code of practice.* Wilmslow: Information Commissioner's Office. Available at https://ico.org.uk/media/for-organisations/ documents/1061/anonymisation-code.pdf [Accessed 6 May 2018].

Irvine, A. (2011) 'Duration, Dominance and Depth in Telephone and Face-to-Face Interviews: A Comparative Exploration', *International Journal of Qualitative Methods,* Vol. 10, No. 3, pp. 202–220.

Irvine, A., Drew, P. and Sainsbury, R. (2012) '"Am I not answering your questions properly?" Clarification, adequacy and responsiveness in semi-structured telephone and face-to-face interviews', *Qualitative Research,* Vol. 13, No. 1, pp. 87–106.

J

Jackson, L.A. and Taylor, M. (2015) 'Revisiting smoking bans in restaurants: Canadian employees' perspectives', *Tourism and Hospitality Research,* Vol. 15, No. 2, pp. 91–104.

Jankowicz, A.D. (2005) *Business Research Projects* (4th edn). London: Thomson Learning.

Jarzabkowski, P., LeBaron, C., Phillips, K. and Pratt, M. (2014) 'Call for papers; Feature topic: Video-based research methods', *Organizational Research Methods,* Vol. 17, No. 1, pp. 3–4.

Johnson, J.M. (1975) *Doing Field Research.* New York: Free Press.

Johnson, P. (2004) 'Analytic induction', in G. Symon and C. Cassell (eds) *Essential Guide to Qualitative Methods and Analysis in Organizational Research.* London: Sage, pp. 165–79.

Johnson, P. and Clark, M. (2006) 'Editors' introduction: Mapping the terrain: An overview of business and management research methodologies', in P. Johnson and M. Clark (eds) *Business and Management Research Methodologies.* London: Sage, pp. xxv–iv.

Jones, O. and Gatrell, C. (2014) 'Editorial: The Future of Writing and Reviewing for IJMR', *International Journal of Management Reviews,* Vol. 16, pp. 249–264.

K

Kanji, S. (2017) 'Grandparent care: A key factor in mothers' labour force participation in the UK', *Journal of Social Policy,* 1–20. Available at doi:10.1017/S004727941700071X.

Kavanagh, M.J. and Johnson, R.D. (eds) (2018) *Human Resource Information Systems: Basics, Applications, and Future Directions* (4th edn). Thousand Oaks, CA: Sage.

Keaveney, S.M. (1995) 'Customer switching behaviour in service industries: An exploratory study', *Journal of Marketing,* Vol. 59, No. 2, pp. 71–82.

Keen, K.J. (2018) *Graphics for Statistics and Data Analysis with R.* (2nd edn.) Boca Raton, FL: Chapman and Hall.

Kelemen, M. and Rumens, N. (2008) *An Introduction to Critical Management Research.* London: Sage.

Kellard, N., Millo, Y., Simon, J. and Engel, O. (2017) 'Close Communications: Hedge Funds, Brokers and the Emergence of Herding', *British Journal of Management,* Vol. 28, No. 1, pp. 84–101.

Kelly, G.A. (1955) *The Psychology of Personal Constructs.* New York: Norton.

Kenealy, G.J.J. (2012) 'Grounded theory: A theory building approach', in G. Symon and C. Cassell (eds) *Qualitative Organizational Research: Core Methods and Current Challenges.* London: Sage.

Ketokivi, M. and Mantere, S. (2010) 'Two strategies for inductive reasoning in organizational research', *Academy of Management Review,* Vol. 35, No. 2, pp. 315–33.

Kilduff, M. and Mehra, A. (1997) 'Postmodernism and organizational research', *The Academy of Management Review,* Vol. 22, pp. 453–81.

King, N. (2004) 'Using interviews in qualitative research', in C. Cassell and G. Symon (eds) *Essential Guide to Qualitative Methods in Organizational Research.* London: Sage, pp. 11–22.

King, N. and Brookes, J.M. (2017) *Template Analysis for Business and Management Students.* London: Sage.

Knoblauch, H. (2012) 'Introduction to the special issue of *Qualitative Research*: Video-analysis and videography', *Qualitative Research,* Vol. 12, No. 3, pp. 251–4.

Knudsen, C. (2003) 'Pluralism, scientific progress, and the structure of organization theory', in H. Tsoukas and C. Knudsen (eds) *The Oxford Handbook of Organization Theory: Meta-Theoretical Perspectives.* Oxford: Oxford University Press, pp. 262–86.

Kosslyn, S.M. (2006) *Graph Design for the Eye and Mind.* New York: Oxford University Press.

Kozinets, R.V. (2015) *Netnography: Redefined* (2nd edn). London: Sage.

Krueger, R.A. and Casey, M.A. (2015) *Focus Groups: A Practical Guide for Applied Research* (5th edn). London: Sage.

L

Labov, W. (1972) *Language in the Inner City: Studies in the Black English Vernacular.* Philadelphia: University of Pennsylvania Press.

Labov, W. and Waletzky, J. (1967) 'Narrative analysis: Oral versions of personal experience', in J. Helm (ed.) *Essays on the Verbal and Visual Arts.* Seattle, WA: University of Washington Press.

Lange, D. and Pfarrer, M.D. (2017) 'Editors' Comments: Sense and Structure – The Core Building Blocks of an AMR Article', *Academy of Management Review,* Vol. 42, No. 3, pp. 407–416.

LeCompte, M.D. and Goetz, J.P. (1982) 'Problems of reliability and validity in ethnographic research', *Review of Educational Research,* Vol. 52, No. 1, pp. 31–60.

Lee, B. (2012) 'Using documents in organizational research', in G. Symon and C. Cassell (eds) *Qualitative Organisational Research Core Methods and Current Challenges.* London: Sage, pp. 389–407.

Lee, B. and Saunders M.N.K. (2017) *Doing Case Study Research for Business and Management Students.* London: Sage.

Lee, R.M. (2000) *Doing Research on Sensitive Topics.* London: Sage.

Lee, W.J. (2012) 'Using documents in organizational research', in G. Symon and C. Cassell (eds) *Qualitative Organizational Research: Core Methods and Current Challenges.* London: Sage, pp. 389–407.

Lewin, K. (1946) 'Action Research and Minority Problems', *Journal of Social Issues,* Vol. 24, No. 1, pp. 34–46.

Lian, T. and Yu, C. (2017) 'Representation of online image of tourist destination: a content analysis of Huangshan', *Asia Pacific Journal of Tourism Research,* Vol. 22, No. 10, pp. 1063–1082.

Lijadi, A.A, and van Schalkwyk, G.J. (2015) 'Online Facebook Focus Group Research of Hard-to-Reach Participants', *International Journal of Qualitative Methods,* Vol. 14, No. 1, pp. 1–9.

Lincoln, Y.S. and Guba, E.G. (1985) *Naturalistic Inquiry.* Beverly Hills, CA: Sage.

Lincoln. Y.S., Lynham S.A. and Guba, E.G. (2018). 'Paradigmatic controversies, contradictions and emerging confluences revisited', in N.K. Denzin and Y.S. Lincoln (eds) *The Sage Handbook of Qualitative Research* (5th edn). Los Angeles, CA: Sage, pp. 108–150.

Little, R. and Rubin, D. (2002) *Statistical Analysis with Missing Data* (2nd edn). New York: John Wiley.

Locke, K. (2015) 'Pragmatic Reflections on a Conversation about Grounded Theory in Management and Organization Studies', *Organizational Research Methods,* Vol. 18, No. 4, pp. 612–619.

Louka, P., Maguire, M., Evans, P. and Worrell, M. (2006) '"I think that it's a pain in the ass that I have to stand outside in the cold and have a cigarette": Representations of smoking and experiences of disapproval in UK and Greek Smokers', *Journal of Health Psychology,* Vol. 11, No. 3, pp. 441–51.

Lowrey, S. (2017) A guide to non-binary pronouns and why they matter. *Huffpost.* Available at https://www.huffingtonpost.com/entry/non-binary-pronouns-why-they-matter_us_5a03107be4b0230facb8419a?guccounter=1 [Accessed 6 June 2018].

Luff, P. and Heath, C. (2012) 'Some "technical challenges" of video analysis: Social actions, objects, material realities and the problems of perspective', *Qualitative Research,* Vol. 12, No. 3, pp. 255–79.

Lumley. T., Diehr, P., Emerson, S. and Chen, L. (2002) 'The importance of the normality assumption in large public health data sets', *Annual Review of Public Health,* Vol. 23, pp. 151–169.

M

Macdonald, S. and Kam, J. (2007) 'Ring a Ring o' Roses: Quality journals and gamesmanship in management studies', *Journal of Management Studies,* Vol. 44, pp. 640–55.

MacIntosh, R. Beech, N., Bartunek, J., Mason, K. Cooke, B. and Denyer, D. (2017). 'Impact and management research: Exploring relationships between temporality, dialogue, reflexivity and praxis', *British Journal of Management,* Vol. 28, N0.1, pp. 3–13.

Macnaghten, P. and Myers, G. (2007) 'Focus groups', in C. Seale, G. Gobo, J.F. Gubrium and D. Silverman (eds) *Qualitative Research Practice.* London: Sage, pp. 65–79.

Madge, C. (2010) *Online Research Ethics.* Available at http://www.restore.ac.uk/orm/ethics/ethprint3.pdf [Accessed 25 March 2018].

Maitlis, S. (2012) 'Narrative analysis', in G. Symon and C. Cassell (eds) *Qualitative Organizational Research: Core Methods and Current Challenges,* London: Sage, pp. 492–511.

Malhotra, N.K. Nunan, D. and Birks, D.F. (2017), *Marketing Research: An Applied Approach* (5th edn). Harlow: Pearson.

Mangalindan, J.P. (2014) 'Why Amazon's fire phone failed', *Fortune.* Available at http://fortune.com/2014/09/29/why-amazons-fire-phone-failed [Accessed 24 January 2018].

Marchington, M., Wilkinson, A., Donnelly, R. and Kynighou, A. (2016) *Human Resource Management at Work* (6th edn). London: Chartered Institute of Personnel and Development, Kogan Page.

Markham, A. and Buchanan, E. (2012) *Ethical Decision-Making and Internet Research: Recommendations from the AoIR Ethics Working Committee (Version 2.0).* Available at http://aoir.org/reports/ethics2.pdf [Accessed 14 December 2017].

Marshall, C. and Rossman, G.B. (2016) *Designing Qualitative Research* (6th edn). London: Sage Publications.

Martí, I. and Fernández, P. (2013) 'The institutional work of oppression and resistance: Learning from the Holocaust', *Organization Studies,* Vol. 34, pp. 1195–223.

Martinko, M.J. and Gardner, W.L. (1985) 'Beyond Structured Observation: Methodological Issues and New Directions', *Academy of Management Review,* Vol. 10, No. 4, pp. 676–695.

Maslow, A.H. (1943) 'A theory of human motivation', *Psychological Review, 50* (4), pp. 370–396.

McAfee, A., and Brynjolfsson, E. (2012) 'Big data: The management revolution', *Harvard Business Review,* Vol. 90, No. 10, pp. 61–67.

McAreavey, R. and Muir, J. (2011) 'Research ethics committees: Values and power in higher education', *International Journal of Social Research Methodology,* Vol. 14, No. 5, pp. 391–405.

McCandless, D. (2014) *Knowledge is beautiful.* London: William Collins.

McConville, D., Arnold, J. and Smith, A. (2016) 'Employees share ownership, psychological ownership and work attitudes and behaviours: a phenomenological analysis', *Journal of Occupational and Organizational Psychology,* Vol. 89, No. 3, pp. 634–651.

McDonald, S. (2005) 'Studying actions in context: A qualitative shadowing method for organisational research', *Qualitative Research,* Vol. 5, No. 4, pp. 455–73.

Mellahi, K. and Harris, L.C. (2016) 'Response rates in Business and Management research: an overview of current practice and suggestions for future direction', *British Journal of Management,* Vol. 24, No. 2, pp. 426–37.

Meyer, A. D. (1991) 'Visual Data in Organizational Research', *Organization Science,* Vol. 2, No. 2, pp. 218–236.

Miles, M.B, Huberman, A.M. and Saldaña, J (2014) *Qualitative Data Analysis: A Methods Sourcebook* (3rd edn). London: Sage.

MindGenius (2018) *MindGenius.* Available at https://www.mindgenius.com/default.aspx [Accessed 1 April 2018].

Mingers, J. (2000) 'What is it to be critical? Teaching a critical approach to management undergraduates', *Management Learning,* Vol. 31, No. 2, pp. 219–37.

Mintzberg, H. (1973) *The Nature of Managerial Work.* New York: Harper & Row.

Mitchell, V. (1996) 'Assessing the reliability and validity of questionnaires: An empirical example', *Journal of Applied Management Studies,* Vol. 5, No. 2, pp. 199–207.

Moher, D., Liberati, A., Tetzlaff, J. and Altman, D.G. (2009) 'Preferred reporting for systematic reviews and meta-analyses: The PRISMA statement', *British Medical Journal (BMJ),* No. 338, b2535. Available at www.bmj.com/content/339/bmj.b2535.full?view=long&pmid=19622551 [Accessed 27 March 2011].

Molina-Azorin, J.F. (2011) 'The use and added value of mixed methods in management research', *Journal of Mixed Methods Research,* Vol. 5, No. 1, pp. 7–24.

Molina-Azorin, J.F., Bergh, D.D., Corley, K.G. and Ketchen, Jr., D.J. (2017) 'Mixed Methods in the Organizational Sciences: Taking Stock and Moving Forward', *Organizational Research Methods,* Vol. 20, No. 2, pp. 179–192.

Monahan, T. and Fisher, J.A. (2010) 'Benefits of "observer effects": Lessons from the field', *Qualitative Research,* Vol. 10, No. 3, pp. 357–76.

Morgan, G. (2006) *Images of Organization.* Thousand Oaks, CA: Sage (originally published in 1986).

Morris, C. (2012) *Quantitative Approaches in Business Studies* (8th edn). Harlow: Pearson.

Morse, J.M., Stern, P.N., Corbin, J., Bowers, B., Charmaz, K. and Clarke, A.E. (2009) *Developing Grounded Theory: The Second Generation,* Walnut Creek, CA: Left Coast Press.

Mortari, L. (2015) 'Reflectivity in research practice: An overview of different perspectives', *International Journal of Qualitative Methods,* pp. 1–9.

Mueller, S., Volery, T. and von Siemens, B. (2012) 'What do entrepreneurs actually do? An observational study of entrepreneurs' everyday behavior in the start-up and growth stage', *Entrepreneurship Theory and Practice,* Vol. 36, No. 5, pp. 995–1017.

Murray, S. (2017) 'Where real-life crises provide valuable lessons', *Financial Times,* 19 June.

Musson, G. (2004) 'Life histories', in C. Cassell and G. Symon (eds) *Essential Guide to Qualitative Methods in Organizational Research.* London: Sage, pp. 34–46.

N

Naipaul, V.S. (1989) *A Turn in the South.* London: Penguin.

Nastasi, B.K., Hitchcock, J.H. and Brown, L.M. (2010) 'An inclusive framework for conceptualising mixed methods typologies', in A. Tashakkori and C. Teddlie (eds) *The Sage Handbook of Mixed Methods in Social and Behavioural Research* (2nd edn). Thousand Oaks, CA: Sage.

Negrón, R. (2012) 'Audio Recording Everyday Talk', *Field Methods,* Vol. 24, No. 3, pp. 292–309.

Neuman, W.L. (2014) *Social Research Methods* (7th edn). Harlow: Pearson.

Neville, C. (2016) *The Complete Guide to Referencing and Avoiding Plagiarism* (3rd edn). London: Open University Press McGraw Hill.

Niglas, K. (2010) 'The multidimensional model of research methodology: An integrated set of continua', in A. Tashakkori and C. Teddlie (eds) *The Sage Handbook of Mixed Methods in Social and Behavioural Research.* Thousand Oaks, CA: Sage, pp. 215–36.

O

O'Reilly, M. and Parker, N. (2013) 'Unsatisfactory saturation: a critical exploration of the notion of the notion of saturated sample sizes in qualitative research', *Qualitative Research,* 13, pp. 190–197.

Oates, C. and Alevizou, P.J. (2018) *Conducting Focus Groups for Business and Management Students.* London: Sage.

Office for National Statistics (2005) *The National Statistics Socio-economic Classification User Manual.* Basingstoke: Palgrave Macmillan.

Office for National Statistics (2017) *Living Costs and Food Survey.* Available at https://www.ons.gov.uk/peoplepopulationandcommunity/personalandhouseholdfinances/incomeandwealth/methodologies/livingcostsandfoodsurvey [Accessed 9 May 2018].

Office for National Statistics (2018) *Family Spending.* Available at https://www.ons.gov.uk/peoplepopulationandcommunity/personalandhouseholdfinances/expenditure/bulletins/familyspendingintheuk/financialyearending2017 [Accessed 9 May 2018].

Office for National Statistics (n.d., a) *Census history.* Available at https://www.ons.gov.uk/census/2011census/howourcensusworks/aboutcensuses/censushistory [Accessed 2 May 2018].

Office for National Statistics (n.d., b) *200 years of the Census.* Available at https://www.ons.gov.uk/census/2011census/howourcensusworks/aboutcensuses/censushistory/200yearsofthecensus [Accessed 5 May 2018].

Office for National Statistics (n.d., c) *Annual Business Survey.* Available at https://www.ons.gov.uk/surveys/informationforbusinesses/businesssurveys/annualbusinesssurvey [Accessed 7 May 2018].

Office for National Statistics (no date a) *Standard Occupation Classification 2010 (SOC2010).* Available at https://www.ons.gov.uk/methodology/classificationsandstandards/standardoccupationalclassificationsoc/soc2010 [Accessed 27 November 2017].

Office for National Statistics (no date b) *The National Statistics Socio-economic Classification (NS-SEC rebased on the SOC2010).* Available at https://www.ons.gov.uk/methodology/classificationsandstandards/otherclassifications/thenationalstatisticssocioeconomicclassificationnssecrebasedonsoc2010 [Accessed 27 November 2017].

Office for National Statistics (no date c) *Ethnic group, national identity and religion.* Available at https://www.ons.gov.uk/methodology/classificationsandstandards/measuringequality/ethnicgroupnationalidentityandreligion [Accessed 27 November 2017].

Official Journal of the European Union (2016) *Regulation (EU) 2016/679 of The European Parliament and of The Council of 27 April 2016 on the protection of natural persons with regard to the processing of personal data and on the free movement of such data, and repealing Directive 95/46/EC.* Vol 59, L119, pp. 1–88. Available at https://eur-lex.europa.eu/legal-content/EN/TXT/PDF/?uri=OJ:L:2016:119:FULL&from=EN [Accessed 06 May 2018].

Ogbonna, E. and Harris, L.C. (2014) 'Organizational cultural perpetuation: A case study of an English Premier League football club', *British Journal of Management,* Vol. 25, No. 4, pp. 667–86.

Okumus, F., Altinay, L. and Roper, A. (2007) 'Gaining access for research: Reflections from experience', *Annals of Tourism Research,* Vol. 34, No. 1, pp. 7–26.

Ozanne, J.L., Moscato, E.M., Kunkel, D.R. (2013) 'Transformative Photography: Evaluation and Best Practices for Eliciting Social and Policy Changes', *Journal of Public Policy and Marketing,* Vol. 32, No. 1, pp. 45–65.

P

Padley, M. and Hirsch, D. (2017) *A Minimum Income Standard for the UK in 2017.* Available at file:///Users/saundmnk/Downloads/mis_2017_final_report_0.pdf [Accessed 9 May 2018].

Paechter, C. (2013) 'Researching sensitive issues online: Implications of a hybrid insider/outsider position in a retrospective ethnographic study', *Qualitative Research,* Vol. 13, No. 1, pp. 71–86.

Pallant, J. (2016) *SPSS Survival Manual: A Step-by-Step Guide to Data Analysis Using IBM SPSS* (6th edn). Maidenhead: Open University Press.

Pandza, K. and Thorpe, R. (2010) 'Management as design, but what kind of design? An appraisal of the design science analogy for management', *British Journal of Management,* Vol. 21, No. 2, pp. 171–86.

Paraskevas, A. and Saunders, M.N.K. (2012) 'Beyond consensus: an alternative use of Delphi enquiry in hospitality research', *International Journal of Contemporary Hospitality Management,* Vol. 24, No. 6, pp. 907–924.

Parker, M. (2002) *Against Management.* Cambridge: Polity Press.

Patton, M.Q. (2015) *Qualitative Research and Evaluation Methods: Integrating Theory and Practice* (4th edn). Thousand Oaks, CA: Sage.

Pearce, G., Thogersen-Ntoumani, C. and Duda, J.L. (2014) 'The development of synchronous text-based instant messaging as an online interviewing tool', *International Journal of Social Research Methodology,* Vol. 17, No. 6, pp. 677–92.

Peirce, C. S. (1896 [c.]). *Lessons of the History of Science.* MS [R] 1288. Commens: Digital Companion to C.S. Peirce, available on: http://www.commens.org/dictionary/term/retroduction [Accessed 11 September 2018].

Peticca-Harris, A., deGama, N, and Elias, S.R.S.T.A. (2016) 'A dynamic process model for finding informants and gaining access in qualitative research', *Organizational Research Methods,* Vol. 19, No. 3, pp. 376–401.

Petticrew, M. and Roberts, H. (2006) *Systematic Review in the Social Sciences: A Practical Guide.* Malden, MA: Blackwell.

Pfeffer, J. (1993). 'Barriers to the advance of organizational science: paradigm development as a dependent variable', *Academy of Management Review,* Vol. 18, pp. 599–620.

Phillips, E.M. and Pugh, D.S. (2015) *How to Get a PhD* (6th edn). Maidenhead: Open University Press McGraw-Hill Education.

Phillips, N. and Hardy, C. (2002) *Discourse Analysis: Investigating Processes of Social Construction.* London: Sage.

Pink, S. (2007) 'Visual methods', in C. Seale, G. Gobo, J. F. Gubrium and D. Silverman (eds) *Qualitative Research Practice.* London: Sage.

Plankey-Videla, N. (2012) 'Informed consent as process: Problematizing informed consent in organizational ethnographics', *Qualitative Sociology,* Vol. 35, pp. 1–21.

Podsakoff, P.M., MacKenzie, S.B. and Podsakoff, N.P. (2016) 'Recommendations for creating better concept definitions in the organizational, behavioral and social sciences', *Organizational Research Methods,* Vol. 19, No. 2, pp. 159–203.

Post-it (2018) *About Post-it® Brand.* Available at https://www.3m.co.uk/3M/en_GB/post-it-notes/contact-us/about-us/ [Accessed 7 June 2018].

Powney, J. and Watts, M. (1987) *Interviewing in Educational Research.* London: Routledge & Kegan Paul.

Prem, R., Ohly, S., Kubicek, B. and Korunka. C. (2017) 'Thriving on challenge stressors? Exploring time pressure and learning demands as antecedents of thriving at work', *Journal of Organizational Behaviour,* Vol. 38, No. 1, pp. 108–123.

Prior, D.D. and Miller, L.M. (2012) 'Webethnography: Towards a typology for quality in research design', *International Journal of Market Research,* Vol. 54, No. 4, pp. 503–20.

Prior, L. (2007) 'Documents', in C. Seale, G. Gobo, J.F. Gubrium and D. Silverman (eds) *Qualitative Research Practice.* London: Sage, 345–60.

Prosser, L. (2009) *Office for National Statistics UK Standard Industrial Classification of Activities 2007 (SIC 2007).* Basingstoke: Palgrave Macmillan. Available at http://www.ons.gov.uk/ons/guide-method/classifications/current-standard-classifications/standard-industrial-classification/index.html [Accessed 27 November 2014].

Q

Qualtrics (2017) *Qualtrics Research CORE: Sophisticated online surveys made simple.* Available at https://www.qualtrics.com/research-core/ [Accessed 27 November 2017].

Qualtrics (2018). *Qualtrics.* Available at http://www.qualtrics.com/ [Accessed 20 March 2018].

R

Raimond, P. (1993) *Management Projects.* London: Chapman & Hall.

Rawlins, K. (1999) *Presentation and Communication Skills: A Handbook for Practitioners.* London: Emap Healthcare Ltd.

Reason, P. (2006) 'Choice and quality in action research practice', *Journal of Management Inquiry,* Vol. 15, No. 2, pp. 187–202.

Reed, M. (2005) 'Reflections on the 'realist turn' in organization and management studies', *Journal of Management Studies,* Vol. 42, pp. 1621–44.

Reichertz, J. (2007) 'Abduction: The logic of discovery of grounded theory', in A. Bryant and K. Charmaz (eds) *The Sage Handbook of Grounded Theory.* London: Sage.

Reichman, C.S. (1962) *Use and Abuse of Statistics.* New York: Oxford University Press.

Reuters Institute (2017) *Reuters Institute Digital News Report 2017.* Reuters Institute and University of Oxford.

Richards, P. (2007) 'Risk', in H. Becker (ed.) *Writing for Social Scientists* (2nd edn). Chicago, IL: University of Chicago Press.

Ridder, H-G., Hoon, C. and McCandless Baluch, A. (2014) 'Entering a dialogue: Positioning case study findings towards theory', *British Journal of Management,* Vol. 25, No. 2, pp. 373–87.

Ridenour, C.S. and Newman, I. (2008) *Mixed Methods Research: Exploring the Interactive Continuum.* Carbondale, IL: South Illinois University Press.

Ridley, D. (2018) *The Literature Review: a step-by-step guide for students* (2nd edition). London: Sage.

Riessman, C.K. (2008) *Narrative Methods for the Human Sciences.* London: Sage.

Ritchie, J., Lewis, J., McNaughton Nicholls, C. and Ormston, R. (2014) *Qualitative Research Practice* (2nd edn). London: Sage.

Robson, C. and McCartan, K. (2016) *Real World Research: A Resource for Users of Social Research Methods in Applied Settings* (4th edn). Chichester: John Wiley.

Rogelberg, S.G. and Stanton, J.M. (2007) 'Introduction: Understanding and dealing with organizational survey non-response', *Organizational Research Methods,* Vol. 10, No. 2, pp. 195–209.

Rogers, C.R. (1961) *On Becoming a Person.* London: Constable.

Rose, G. (2014) 'On the relation between "visual research methods" and contemporary visual culture', *The Sociological Review,* Vol. 62, No. 1, pp. 24–46.

Rose, G. (2016) *Visual Methodologies An Introduction to Researching with Visual Materials* (4th edn). London: Sage.

Rose, S., Spinks, N. and Canhoto, I. (2015) *Management Research: Applying the Principles.* London: Routledge.

Roster, C.A., Lucianetti, L. and Albaum, G. (2015) 'Exploring slider vs. categorical response formats in web-based surveys', *Journal of Research Practice,* Vol 11, No. 1, Article D1, 15 pp.

Rousseau, D. (2006) 'Is there such a thing as "Evidence-Based Management"?', *Academy of Management Review,* Vol. 31, No. 2, pp. 256–69.

Rowlinson, K., Appleyard, L. and Gardner, J. (2016) 'Payday lending in the UK: the regul(aris)ation of a necessary evil?', *Journal of Social Policy,* Vol. 45, No. 3, pp. 527–523.

Rutherford, B.A. (2016) 'Articulating accounting principles', *Journal of Applied Accounting Research.,* Vol.17, No. 2, pp. 118–135.

S

Salmon, P. (2003) 'How do we recognise good research?', *The Psychologist,* Vol. 16, No. 1, pp. 24–7.

Saunders, M.N.K. (2011) 'The management researcher as practitioner', in B. Lee and C. Cassell (eds) *Challenges and Controversies in Management Research.* New York: Routledge, pp. 243–57.

Saunders, M.N.K. (2012) 'Choosing research participants', in G. Symons and C. Cassell (eds) *The Practice of Qualitative Organizational Research: Core Methods and Current Challenges*. London: Sage, pp. 37–55.

Saunders, M.N.K. (2012) 'Web versus mail: The influence of survey distribution mode on employees' response', *Field Methods,* Vol. 24, No. 1, pp. 56–73.

Saunders, M.N.K. and Lewis, P. (1997) 'Great ideas and blind alleys? A review of the literature on starting research', *Management Learning,* Vol. 28, No. 3, pp. 283–99.

Saunders, M.N.K. and Townsend, K. (2016), 'Reporting and justifying the number of participants in organisation and workplace research', *British Journal of Management,* Vol. 27, pp. 837–852.

Saunders, M.N.K. and Townsend, K. (2017) 'Choosing participants' in Cassell, C., Cunliffe, A., and Grandy, G. (eds) *Sage Handbook of Qualitative Business and Management Research Methods*. London: Sage. Chapter 30.

Saunders, M.N.K., Gray, D. and Goregaokor, H. (2014) 'SME innovation and learning: the role of networks and crisis event', *European Journal of Training and Development,* Vol. 38, No. ½, pp. 136–149.

Saunders, M.N.K., Gray, D.E, Tosey, P. and Sadler-Smith, E (2015) 'Concepts and theory building', in Anderson, L., Gold, J., Stewart, J. and Thorpe, R. (eds.) *Professional doctorates in business and management*. London: Sage. pp. 35–56.

Saunders, M.N.K., Gray, D.E. and Bristow, A. (2017) 'Beyond the Single Organization: Inside Insights From Gaining Access for Large Multiorganization Survey HRD Research', *Human Resource Development Quarterly,* Vol. 28, No. 3, pp. 401–425.

Schein, E. (1999) *Process Consultation Revisited: Building the Helping Relationship*. Reading, MA: Addison-Wesley.

Schoneboom, A. (2011) 'Workblogging in a Facebook age', *Work, Employment and Society,* Vol. 25, No. 1, pp. 132–40.

Schrauf, R.W. and Navarro, E. (2005) 'Using existing tests and scales in the field', *Field Methods,* Vol. 17, No. 4, pp. 373–93.

SciStatCalc (2013) *Two-sample Kolmogorov-Smirnov Test Calculator*. Available at http://scistatcalc.blogspot.co.uk/2013/11/kolmogorov-smirnov-test-calculator.html [Accessed 27 November 2017].

Sekaran, U. and Bougie, R. (2013) *Research Methods for Business: A Skill-Building Approach* (6th edn). Chichester: John Wiley.

Sekaran, U. and Bougie, R. (2016) *Research Methods for Business* (7th edn). Chichester: Wiley.

Shani, A.B. and Pasmore, W.A. (1985) 'Organization inquiry: Towards a new model of the action research process', in D.D. Warrick (ed.) *Contemporary Organization Development*. Glenview, IL: Scott Foresman, pp. 438–48.

Sharp, J.A., Peters, J. and Howard, K. (2002) *The Management of a Student Research Project* (3rd edn). Aldershot: Gower.

Sherbaum, C. and Shockley, K. (2015) *Analysing Quantitative Data for Business and Management Students*. London: Sage.

Silver, C. and Lewins, A. (2014) *Using Software in Qualitative Research: a step-by-step guide* (2nd edn). London: Sage.

Silverman, D. (2013) *A Very Short, Fairly Interesting and Reasonably Cheap Book about Qualitative Research* (2nd edn). London: Sage.

SimpleMind (2018) *SimpleMind.* Available at https://www.simpleapps.eu/ [Accessed 1 April 2018]

Smith, E. (2008) *Using Secondary Data in Educational and Social Research*. Maidenhead: Open University Press.

Snap Surveys (2018) *Snap Surveys. Software Solutions Services*. Available at www.snapsurveys.com [Accessed 5 March 2018].

Social Research Association (2001) *A Code of Practice for the Safety of Social Researchers*. Available at http://the-sra.org.uk/wp-content/uploads/safety_code_of_practice.pdf [Accessed 12 December 2017].

Sonenshein, S., DeCelles, K. and Dutton, J.E. (2014) 'It's not easy being green: The role of self evaluations in explaining the support of environmental issues', *Academy of Management Journal,* Vol. 57, No. 1, pp. 7–37.

Spano, R. (2005) 'Potential sources of observer bias in police observational data', *Social Science Research,* Vol. 34, pp. 591–617.

Speer, S.A. (2008) 'Natural and contrived data', in P. Alasuutari, L. Bickman, and J. Brannen (eds) *The Sage Handbook of Social Research Methods*. London: Sage, pp. 290–312.

Spradley, J.P. (2016) *Participant Observation*. Long Grove IL: Waveland Press.

Stake, R.E. (2005) 'Qualitative case studies', in N.K. Denzin and Y.S. Lincoln (eds) *The Sage Handbook of Qualitative Research* (3rd edn). London: Sage, pp. 443–65.

Starbuck, W. (2003) 'The origins of organization theory', in H. Tsoukas and C. Knudsen (eds) *The Oxford Handbook of Organization Theory: Meta-Theoretical Perspectives*. Oxford: Oxford University Press.

Starkey, K. and Madan, P. (2001) 'Bridging the relevance gap: Aligning stakeholders in the future of management research', *British Journal of Management,* Vol. 12, Special Issue, pp. 3–26.

Starr, R. and Fernandez, K. (2007) 'The mindcam methodology: Perceiving through the natives eye', *Qualitative Market Research,* Vol. 10, No. 2, pp. 168–82.

Stationery Office, The (1998) *Data Protection Act 1998.* London: The Stationery Office.

Stewart, D.W. and Kamins, M.A. (1993) *Secondary Research: Information Sources and Methods* (2nd edn). Newbury Park, CA: Sage.

Stokes, D. and Bergin, R. (2006) 'Methodology or "methodolatry"? An evaluation of focus groups and depth interviews', *Qualitative Market Research,* Vol. 9, No. 1, pp. 26–37.

Strauss, A. and Corbin, J. (1998) *Basics of Qualitative Research* (2nd edn). Thousand Oaks, CA: Sage.

Stutely, R. (2014) *The Economist Numbers Guide: The Essentials of Business Numeracy* (6th edn). London: Profile Books.

Suddaby, R. (2006) 'From the editors: What grounded theory is not', *Academy of Management Journal,* Vol. 49, No. 4, pp. 633–42.

SurveyMonkey (2017) *What do you want to know?* Available at https://www.surveymonkey.com/ [Accessed 27 November 2017].

SurveyMonkey (2018) *SurveyMonkey.* Available at www.surveymonkey.com [Accessed 5 March 2018].

Sutton, R. and Staw, B. (1995) 'What theory is not', *Administrative Science Quarterly,* Vol. 40, No. 3, pp. 371–84.

Swift, L. and Piff, S. (2014) *Quantitative Methods for Business, Management and Finance* (4th edn). Basingstoke: Palgrave Macmillan.

Symon, G. and Cassell, C. (eds) (2012) *Qualitative Organizational Research: Core Methods and Current Challenges.* London: Sage.

T

Tashakkori, A. and Teddlie, C. (eds) (2010) *The Sage Handbook of Mixed Methods in Social and Behavioural Research* (2nd edn). Thousand Oaks, CA: Sage.

Teddlie, C. and Tashakkori, A. (2009) *Foundations of Mixed Methods Research: Integrating Quantitative and Qualitative Approaches in the Social and Behavioural Sciences.* Thousand Oaks, CA: Sage.

Teddlie, C. and Tashakkori, A. (2011) 'Mixed methods research: Contemporary issues in an emerging field', in N.K. Denzin and Y.S. Lincoln (eds) *The Sage Handbook of Qualitative Research* (4th edn). London: Sage, pp. 285–99.

Tedlock, B. (2005) 'The observation of participation and the emergence of public ethnography', in N.K. Denzin and Y.S. Lincoln (eds) *The Sage Handbook of Qualitative Research* (3rd edn). London: Sage.

Terzidou, M., Scarles, C. and Saunders, M.N.K. (2017) 'Religiousness as tourist performances: A case study of Greek Orthodox pilgrimage', *Annals of Tourism Research,* Vol. 66, pp. 116–129.

Tharenou, P., Donohue, R. and Cooper, B. (2007) *Management Research Methods.* Melbourne: Cambridge University Press.

The Economist (2017) *The Big Mac Index: global exchange rates, to go.* Available at http://www.economist.com/content/big-mac-index [Accessed 12 November 2017].

The Free Dictionary (2014) 'Gibberish'. Available at http://www.thefreedictionary.com/gibberish [Accessed 03 June 2018].

Thomas, R. and Hardy, C. (2011) 'Reframing resistance to organizational change', *Scandinavian Journal of Management,* Vol. 27, pp. 322–31.

Tietze, S. (2012) 'Researching your own organization', in G. Symon and C. Cassell (eds) *Qualitative Organisational Research Core Methods and Current Challenges.* London: Sage, pp. 53–71.

Tinati, R., Halford, S., Carr, L. and Pope, C. (2014) 'Big Data: Methodological challenges and approaches for sociological analysis', *Sociology,* Vol. 48. No. 4, pp. 663–681.

Tranfield, D. and Denyer, D. (2004) 'Linking theory to practice: A grand challenge for management research in the 21st century?', *Organization Management Journal,* Vol. 1, No. 1, pp. 10–14.

Tranfield, D. and Starkey, K. (1998) 'The nature, social organization and promotion of management research: Towards policy', *British Journal of Management,* Vol. 9, pp. 341–53.

Tranfield, D., Denyer, D. and Smart, P. (2003) 'Towards a methodology for developing evidence-informed management knowledge by means of systematic review', *British Journal of Management,* Vol. 14, No. 3, pp. 207–22.

Trier-Bieniek, A. (2012) 'Framing the telephone interview as a participant-centred tool for qualitative research: A methodological discussion', *Qualitative Research,* Vol. 12, No. 6, pp. 630–44.

Trussell, N. and Lavrakas, P. J. (2004) 'The Influence of Incremental Increases in Token Cash Incentives on Mail Survey Response', *Public Opinion Quarterly,* Vol. 68, No. 3, pp. 349–367.

Tsoukas, H. and Chia, R. (2011) 'Research in the Sociology of Organizations', Vol. 32: *Philosophy and Organization Theory.* Bradford: Emerald Publishing.

Tucker, C. and Lepkowski, J.M. (2008) 'Telephone survey methods: Adapting to change', in J.M. Lepkowski, C. Tucker, J.M. Brick, E.D. De Leeuw, L. Japec, P.J. Lavrakas, M.W. Link and R.L. Sangster (eds), *Advances in Telephone Survey Methodology.* Hoboken, NJ: Wiley, pp. 3–28.

Tukey, J.W. (1977) *Exploratory Data Analysis.* Reading, MA: Addison-Wesley.

Tweet Archivist (2018) *Tweet Archivist,* Available at http://www.tweetarchivist.com/ [Accessed 5 May 2018].

U

UK Data Archive (2011) *Managing and Sharing Data: Best Practice for Researchers* (3rd edn). Available at http://www.data-archive.ac.uk/media/2894/managingsharing.pdf [Accessed 14 December 2017].

UK Data Archive (2017) *Create and Manage Data – Anonymisation*. Available at https://www.ukdataservice.ac.uk/manage-data/legal-ethical/anonymisation [Accessed 15 December 2017].

UK Data Archive (2018) *UK Data Archive.* Available at www.data-archive.ac.uk/ [Accessed 9 May 2018].

UK Data Service (2018) *Variable and Question Bank.* Available at http://discover.ukdataservice.ac.uk/variables [Accessed 25 Feb 2018].

University of Minnesota (2018) *Non-binary gender pronouns.* Available at http://writing.umn.edu/sws/quickhelp/grammar/nonbinary.html [Accessed 6 June 2018].

University of Oxford (2018) *Study Skills and Training: Plagiarism.* Available at https://www.ox.ac.uk/students/academic/guidance/skills/plagiarism?wssl=1 [Accessed 20 March 2018].

University of Southern California (2018) *Organising your Social Sciences Research Paper: 5. The Literature Review.* Available at http://libguides.usc.edu/writingguide/literaturereview [Accessed 7 March 2018].

Usunier, J.-C., Van Herk, H. and Lee, J.A. (2017) *International and Cross-Cultural Management Research.* (2nd edn) London: Sage.

Uy, M.A., Lin, K.J. and Ilies, R. (2017) 'Is It Better To Give Or Receive? The Role Of Help In Buffering The Depleting Effects Of Surface Acting', *Academy of Management Journal,* Vol. 60, No. 4, pp. 1442–1461.

V

Van Aken, J.E. (2005) 'Management research as a design science: Articulating the research products of Mode 2 knowledge production in management', *British Journal of Management,* Vol. 16, No. 1, pp. 19–36.

van de Heijden, P. (2017) 'The practicalities of SMS research', *Journal of Marketing Research,* Vol. 59, No. 2, pp. 157–72.

Van Maanen, J. (2011a) 'Ethnography as work: Some rules of engagement', *Journal of Management Studies,* Vol. 48, No. 1, pp. 218–34.

Van Maanen, J. (2011b) *Tales of the Field: On Writing Ethnography* (2nd edn). London: University of Chicago Press.

Van Maanen, J., Sørensen, J.B. and Mitchell, T.R. (2007) 'The interplay between theory and method', *Academy of Management Review,* Vol. 32, No. 4, pp. 1145–54.

Vartanian, T.P. (2011) *Secondary Data Analysis.* Oxford: Oxford University Press.

Vermaak, M. and de Klerk, H.M. (2017) 'Fitting room or selling room? Millennial female consumers' dressing room experiences', *International Journal of Consumer Studies,* Vol. 41, pp. 11–18.

Vogel, R.M. and Mitchell, M.S. (2017) 'The Motivational Effects of Diminished Self-Esteem for Employees Who Experience Abusive Supervision', *Journal of Management,* Vol. 43, No. 7, pp. 2218–2251.

Vogl, S. (2013) 'Telephone Versus Face-to-Face Interviews: Mode Effect on Semi-structured Interviews With Children', *Sociological Methodology,* Vol. 43, No. 1, pp. 133–177.

W

Waddington, D. (2004) 'Participant observation', in C. Cassell and G. Symon (eds) *Essential Guide to Qualitative Methods in Organizational Research.* London: Sage, pp. 154–64.

Wallace, M. and Wray, A. (2016) *Critical Reading and Writing for Postgraduates* (3rd edn). London: Sage.

Walliman, N. (2011) *Your Research Project: A Step by Step Guide for the First-Time Researcher* (3rd edn). London: Sage.

Walsh, I., Holton, J.A., Bailyn, L., Fernandez, Levina, N. and Glaser, B. (2015a) 'What Grounded Theory Is … A Critically Reflective Conversation Among Scholars', *Organizational Research Methods,* Vol. 18, No. 4, pp. 581–599.

Walsh, I., Holton, J.A., Bailyn, L., Fernandez, Levina, N. and Glaser, B. (2015b) 'Rejoinder: Moving the Management Field Forward', *Organizational Research Methods,* Vol. 18, No. 4, pp. 620–628.

Wang, H., Tong, L., Takeuchi, R. and George, G. (2016) 'Corporate Social Responsibility: An overview and new research directions', *Academy of Management Journal,* Vol. 59, No. 2, pp. 534–544.

Wang, Z., Mao, H., Li, Y.J. and Liu, F. (2017) 'Smile big or not?, Effects of smile intensity on perceptions of warmth and competence', *Journal of Consumer Research,* Vol. 43, pp.787–805.

Wasserstein R.L. and Lazar, N.A. (2016) 'The ASA's statement on p-values: context, process and pupose', *The American Statistician,* Vol. 70, No. 2, pp. 129–133.

Watson, T.J. (2011) 'Ethnography, reality, and truth: The vital need for studies of "how things work" in organizations and management', *Journal of Management Studies,* Vol. 48, No. 1, pp. 202–17.

Way, A.K., Zwier, R.K. and Tracy, S.J. (2015) 'Dialogic Interviewing and Flickers of Transformation: An Examination and Delineation of Interactional Strategies That Promote Participant Self-Reflexivity', *Qualitative Inquiry,* Vol. 2, No. 8, pp. 720–731.

Web Hosting Rating (2018) *100+ Internet Stats and Facts for 2018,* Available at https://www.websitehostingrating.com/internet-statistics-facts-2018/ [Accessed 5 May 2018].

Webspiration Pro (2018) *Webspiration Pro.* Available at https://www.webspirationpro.com/ [Accessed 1 April 2018].

Wells, P. (1994) 'Ethics in business and management research', in V.J. Wass and P.E. Wells (eds) *Principles and Practice in Business and Management Research.* Aldershot: Dartmouth, pp. 277–97.

Wensley, R. (2011) 'Seeking relevance in management research', in C. Cassell and B. Lee (eds) *Challenges and Controversies in Management Research.* New York: Routledge, pp. 258–74.

Wernicke, I.H. (2014) 'Quality of official statistics data on the economy', *Journal of Finance, Accounting and Management,* Vol. 5, No. 2, pp. 77–93.

Whetten, D. (1989) 'What constitutes a theoretical contribution?', *Academy of Management Review,* Vol. 14, No. 4, pp. 490–5.

Whiting, R. and Pritchard, K. (2018) 'Digital Ethics', in C. Cassell, A.L. Cunliffe and G. Grandy (eds) *The Sage Handbook of Qualitative Business and Management Research Methods.* Sage: London, pp. 562–579.

Whyte, W.F. (1993) *Street Corner Society: The Social Structure of an Italian Slum* (4th edn). Chicago, IL: University of Chicago Press.

Wikipedia (2018) *Wikipedia.* Available at: http://en.wikipedia.org/wiki/Wikipedia [Accessed 20 March 2018].

Williams, W. and Lewis, D. (2005) 'Convergent interviewing: a tool for strategic investigation', *Strategic Change,* Vol. 14, No. 4, pp. 219–229.

Wright Mills, C. (1970) 'On intellectual craftsmanship', in C. Wright Mills, *The Sociological Imagination.* London: Pelican.

Y

Yin, R.K. (2018) *Case Study Research and Applications: Design and Methods* (6th edn). London: Sage.

Yu, L. and Zellmer-Bruhn, M. (2018) 'Introducing team mindfulness and considering its safeguard role against transformation and social undermining', *Academy of Management Journal,* Vol. 61, No. 1, pp. 324–347.

Z

Zhang, Y., Trusov, M. Stephen, A.T. and Jamal, Z. (2017) 'Online Shopping and Social Media: Friends or Foes?', *Journal of Marketing,* Vol. 81, No. 6, pp. 24–41.

Appendix 1 Systems of referencing

Preferred styles of referencing differ both between universities and between departments within universities. Even styles that are in wide use such as 'Harvard' vary in how they are used in practice by different institutions. When this is combined with the reality that some lecturers apply an adopted style strictly, while others are more lenient, it emphasises the need for you to use the precise style prescribed in your assessment criteria. Within business and management, two author–date referencing systems predominate, the Harvard style and the American Psychological Association (APA) style, both of which are author–date systems. The alternative, numeric systems, is used far less widely.

Six points are important when referencing:

- Full credit must be given to the author or originator (the person or organisation taking main responsibility for the source) when quoting or citing others' work.
- Adequate information must be provided in the reference to enable that work to be located.
- References must be consistent, complete and accurate.
- References must be recorded using precisely the style required by your university and are often part of the marking criteria.
- Wherever you directly quote an author you should use 'quotation marks' to show this and also record the precise location (normally page number).
- If you fail to reference fully, you are likely to be accused of plagiarism (Section 3.11).

As you will see later in this appendix, when referring to an electronic document, principally a journal article, accessed online, it is becoming more usual to include that document's DOI (digital object identifier) as part of the reference. The DOI provides a permanent and unique identifier for that document. Where there is no DOI, it is usual to include the document's URL (uniform resource locator – usually its web address). As the URL is not permanent, the date when it was accessed is also included in the reference.

Author–date systems

The Harvard system

Referencing in the text

The Harvard system is an *author–date system,* a variation of which we use in this book. It appears to have its origins in a referencing practice developed by a professor of anatomy at Harvard University in the late 19th Century, although the expression 'Harvard system' was introduced by an English visitor to Harvard who was impressed by the system of referencing used in the library (Chernin 1988). The Harvard system uses the author's or originator's name and year of publication to identify cited documents within the text. All references are listed alphabetically at the end of the text in a consistent format. However, there is no definite benchmark for Harvard referencing and variations exist between institutions in its use. Common variations within the Harvard system include (Neville 2016):

- Where there are more than two authors, the names of the second and subsequent authors may or may not be replaced in the text by *et al.* This phrase may be in italics and is usually followed by a full stop to signify it is an abbreviation of *et alia.*
- Name(s) of authors or originators may or may not be in UPPER CASE in the list of references.
- The year of publication may or may not be enclosed in (brackets) in the list of references.
- Capitalisation of words in the title is usually kept to a minimum rather than being used for Many of the Words in the Title.
- The title of the publication may be in *italics* or may be underlined in the list of references.

The system for referencing work in the text and in the list of references or bibliography is outlined in Table A1.1, additional conventions for referencing in the text being given in Table A1.2.

Table A1.1 Conventions when using the Harvard system to reference

To cite	In the text		In the list of references/bibliography	
	General format	**Example**	**General format**	**Example**
Books				
Book (first edition)	*1 author:* (Family name year)	*1 author:* (Dawson 2017)	Family name, Initials. (year). *Title.* Place of publication: Publisher.	Dawson, J. (2017). *Analysing Quantitative Survey Data.* London: Sage.
	2 or 3 authors: (Family name, Family name and Family name year)	*2 or 3 authors:* (Lee and Saunders 2017)	Family name, Initials. and Family name, Initials. (year). *Title.* Place of publication: Publisher.	Lee, B. and Saunders, M. (2017). *Conducting Case Study Research.* London: Sage.
	4+ authors: (Family name et al. year)	4+ *authors:* (Millmore et al. 2010)	Family name, Initials., Family name, Initials. and Family name, Initials [can be discretionary to include more than first author] (year). *Title.* Place of publication: Publisher.	Millmore, M., Lewis, P., Saunders, M., Thornhill, A. and Morrow, T. (2007). *Strategic Human Resource Management: Contemporary Issues.* Harlow: FT Prentice Hall.
Book (other than first edition)	*As for* 'Book (first edition)'	(Saunders and Lewis, 2018)	Family name, Initials. and Family name, Initials. (year). *Title.* (# edn). Place of publication: Publisher.	Saunders, M. and Lewis, P. (2018). *Doing Research in Business and Management.* (2nd edn). Harlow: Pearson.
Book (edited)	*As for* 'Book (first edition)'	(Saunders et al. 2010)	Family name, Initials. and Family name, Initials. (eds.) (year). *Title.* Place of publication: Publisher.	Saunders, M.N.K, Skinner, D., Gillespie, N., Dietz, G. and Lewicki, R.J. (eds.) (2010). *Organizational Trust: A Cultural Perspective.* Cambridge: Cambridge University Press.

To cite	In the text		In the list of references/bibliography	
	General format	**Example**	**General format**	**Example**
Book (not in English language)	*As for* 'Book (first edition)'	(Fontaine et al. 2010)	Family name, Initials. and Family name, Initials. (year). *Title* [English translation of title]. Place of publication: Publisher.	Fontaine, C., Salti, S. and Thivard, T. (2010). *100 CV et lettres de motivation* [100 CV and cover letters]. Paris: Studyrama.
Book (translated into English)	*As for* 'Book (first edition)'	(Hugo 2003)	Family name, Initials. and Family name, Initials. (year). *Title*. (Initials of translator. Family name of translator. Trans). Place of publication: Publisher. (Original work published year).	Hugo, V. (2003). *Les Miserables*. (N. Denny. Trans.). London: Penguin. (Original work published 1862).
Republished book	*As for* 'Book (first edition)'	(Burrell and Morgan 2016)	Family name, Initials. and Family name, Initials. (year). *Title*. Place of publication: Publisher (originally published by Publisher year).	Burrell, G. and Morgan, G. (2016). *Sociological Paradigms and Organizational Analysis*. Abingdon: Routledge (originally published by Heinemann 1979).
E-book	*As for* 'Book (first edition)'	(Saunders 2013)	Family name, Initials. (year). *Title*. (# edn). [name of e-book reader]. Place of publication: Publisher.	Saunders, J.J. (2013). *The Holocaust: History in an Hour* [Kindle e-book]. London: William Collins.
Online book	*As for* 'Book (1st edition)' or 'Edited book'	(Sungsoo 2013)	Family name, Initials. and Family name, Initials. (year). *Title*. (# edn) Place of publication: Publisher. [Accessed day month year from Database name].	Burns, A.C., Veek, A. and Bush, R.F. (2017). *Marketing Research* (Global edn). Harlow: Pearson. [Accessed 6 Apr. 2018 from MyLibrary.com]
Chapters in books				
Chapter in a book	*As for* 'Book (first edition)'	(Robson and McCartan 2016)	Family name, Initials. and Family name, Initials. (year). *Title*. (# edn). Place of publication: Publisher. Chapter .	Robson, C. and McCartan, K. (2016). *Real World Research*. (4th edn). Oxford: Blackwell. Chapter 3.

(continued)

Table A1.1 (*Continued*)

To cite	In the text		In the list of references/bibliography	
	General format	**Example**	**General format**	**Example**
Chapter in an edited book containing a collection of articles (sometimes called a reader)	(Chapter author family name year)	(King et al., 2018)	Family name, Initials. (year). Chapter title. In Initials. Family name and Initials. Family name (eds) *Title*. (# edn). Place of publication: Publisher. pp. ##–###.	King, N., Brooks, J. and Tabari, S. (2018). Template Analysis in Business and Management Research. In M. Ciesielka and D. Jemielniak (eds) *Qualitative Methodologies in Organization Studies, Volume II: Methods and Possibilities*. London: Palgrave Macmillan. pp. 179–206.
Chapter in an online book	(Chapter author family name year)	(Denyer 2016)	Chapter author family name, Initials. (year). Chapter title. In Initials. Family name and Initials. Family name (eds) *Title*. (# edn). Place of publication: Publisher. pp. ##–###. [Accessed day month year from Database name].	Denyer, D. (2016). After the crisis: a systematic and critical review. In M. Saunders, P. Lewis and A. Thornhill. *Research Methods for Business Students*. (7th edn) Harlow: FT Prentice Hall. pp. 117–9. [Accessed 11 Apr. 2018 from MyLibrary.com]
Dictionaries and other reference books				
. . . where author known	*As for* 'Book (first edition)'	(Vogt and Johnson 2016)	Family name, Initials. (year). *Title*. (# edn). Place of Publication: Publisher. pp. ##–###.	Vogt, W.P. and Johnson, R.B. (2016). *The Sage Dictionary of Statistics and Methodology: A Nontechnical Guide for the Social Sciences*. (5th edn). Thousand Oaks, CA: Sage. p. 2.
. . . where no author or editor	(*Publication title* year)	(*The right word at the right time* 1985)	*Publication title*. (year). (# edn). Place of Publication: Publisher. pp. ##–###.	*The right word at the right time*. (1985). Pleasantville, NY: Readers Digest Association. pp. 563–4.
. . . where editor known and author for particular entry	(Entry author family name date)	(Watson 2008)	Entry author family name, Initials. (year). Entry title. In Initials. Family name and Initials. Family name (eds) *Title*. Place of publication: Publisher. pp. ##–###.	Watson, T. (2008). Field research. In R. Thorpe and R. Holt (eds) *The SAGE Dictionary of Qualitative Management Research*. London: Sage. pp. 99–100.

To cite	In the text		In the list of references/bibliography	
	General format	**Example**	**General format**	**Example**
. . . where accessed online and is no author or editor	(*Publication title* year)	(*Encyclopaedia Britannica Online* 2018)	*Publication title*. (year). Available at http://www.remainderoffull Internetaddress/ [Accessed day month year].	*Encyclopaedia Britannica. Online.* (2018). Available at http://www.britannica.com/ [Accessed 20 Mar. 2018].
. . . where accessed online and is editor or author for a particular entry	(Editor/entry author family name date)	(Hibbard et al. 2017)	Editor/entry author family name, Initials. (year). Title of entry. In *PublicationTitle*. Available at http://www.remainderoffull Internetaddress/ [Accessed day month year].	Hibbard, J.D., Grayson, K.A. and Kotler, P, (2017). Marketing. In *Encyclopaedia Britannica* (2017) Marketing. Available at https://www.britannica.com/topic/marketing [Accessed 27 Jan. 2018].
. . . where accessed online and no author or editor for a particular entry	(*Publication title* year)	(*Encyclopaedia Britannica Online* 2013)	*Publication title*. (year). Title of entry. Available at http://www.remainderoffull Internetaddress/ [Accessed day month year].	*Encyclopaedia Britannica Online.* (2013). Securities and Exchange Commission. Available at https://www.britannica.com/topic/Securities-and-Exchange-Commission [Accessed 27 Jan. 2018].
Reports				
Report	*As for* 'Book (first edition)'	(Gray et al. 2016)	Family name, Initials. and Family name, Initials. (year). *Title*. Place of publication: Publisher.	Gray, D.E., Saunders M.N.K. and Farrant, K. (2016). *SME Success: Winning New Business.* London: Kingston Smith LLP.
Report (no named author)	(Originator name *or Publication title* year)	(Mintel Marketing Intelligence 2018)	Originator name *or* Publication title. (year). *Title*. Place of publication: Publisher.	Mintel Marketing Intelligence. (2018). *Perceptions of Auto Brands – Canada.* London: Mintel International Group Ltd.
Organisation's annual report	(Organisation name date)	(Tesco Plc 2013)	Organisation name. (year). *Title*. Place of publication: Publisher.	Tesco Plc. (2013). *Serving Shoppers a Little Better Every Day: Annual Report and Financial Statement 2017.* Cheshunt: Tesco PLC.

(continued)

Table A1.1 (*Continued*)

To cite	In the text		In the list of references/bibliography	
	General format	**Example**	**General format**	**Example**
Online report	*As for* 'Book (first edition)'	(Thorlby et al. 2014)	Family name, Initials. and Family name, Initials. (year). *Title of report.* Available at http://www. remainderoffull Internetaddress/ [Accessed day month year].	Thorlby, R., Smith, J., Williams, S. and Dayan, M. (2014). *The Francis Report: One year on.* Available at: https://www.nuffieldtrust. org.uk/files/2017-01/francis-report-one-year-on-web-final.pdf. [Accessed 27 Jan. 2018].
Online report (no named author)	(Originator name *or Publication title* year)	(Mintel 2018)	Originator name. (year). *Title of report.* Available at http:// www.remainderoffull Internetaddress/ [Accessed day month year].	Mintel (2018) – *Beauty and Personal Care Retailing – UK – January 2018.* Available at: http://academic.mintel.com/ display/858739/ [Accessed 27 Jan, 2018].
Government and governmental bodies' publications				
Parliamentary papers including acts and bills	(Country of origin year)	(United Kingdom 2013)	Country of origin. (year). *Title.* Place of publication: Publisher.	United Kingdom. (2013). *The Financial Services (Banking Reform) Act.* London: TSO (The Stationery Office).
Parliamentary debates (Hansard)	(Country Parliament year)	(United Kingdom Parliament 2016)	Country Parliament. House of Commons (HC) or House of Lords (HL) Deb. day month year. Vol. #, No. #, Col. ##–####.	United Kingdom Parliament HC Deb. 24 Mar. 2016. Vol. 607, No. 139, Col. 1746.
Other	*As for* 'Book (first edition)'	(Francis 2013)	*As for* 'Book (first edition)'	Francis, R. (2013). *Report of the Mid Staffordshire NHS Foundation Trust Public Inquiry: Executive Summary.* London: The Stationery Office.
Other (no named author or editor)	(Department name *or* Committee name year)	(United Nations Economic and Social Commission for Asia and the Pacific 2017)	Department name or Committee name. (year). *Title.* Place of publication: Publisher.	United Nations Economic and Social Commission for Asia and the Pacific. (2017). *Towards a resource efficient, pollution-free Asia-Pacific region.* New York: United Nations.

To cite	In the text		In the list of references/bibliography	
	General format	**Example**	**General format**	**Example**
Other (online)	(Family name year)	(Edelman, 2018)	Family name, Initials. and Family name, Initials. (year). *Title of report*. Available at http://www. remainderoffull Internetaddress/ [Accessed day month year].	Edelman, R. (2018). *Research: The Battle for Truth* Available at https:// www.edelman.com/ post/the-battle-for-truth [Accessed 2 Feb. 2018].
Other (no named author or editor; online)	(Office *or* Department name *or* Committee name year)	(Office for National Statistics 2017)	Office *or* Department name or Committee name. (year). *Title*. Available at http:// www.remainderoffull Internetaddress/ [Accessed day month year].	Office for National Statistics. (2017). *Statistical bulletin: Effects of taxes and benefits on UK household income: financial year ending 2016*. Available at: https://www.ons.gov.uk/ peoplepopulationand community/ personalandhouse holdfinances/income andwealth/bulletins/the effectsoftaxesand benefitsonhouse holdincome/financial year ending 2016 [Accessed 28 Jan. 2018].
Journal articles				
Journal article (print form or facsimile of print form accessed via full text database)	*As for* 'Book (first edition)'	(Rojon et al. 2011)	Family name, Initials. and Family name, Initials. (year). Title of article. *Journal name*. Vol. #, No. #, pp. ##–####.	Rojon, C., McDowall, A. and Saunders, M.N.K. (2011). On the Experience of Conducting a Systematic Review in Industrial, Work and Organizational Psychology: Yes, It Is Worthwhile. *Journal of Personnel Psychology*. Vol. 10, No. 3, pp. 133–8.
Journal article (facsimile of print form, where full text database details required by University)	*As for* 'Book (first edition)'	(Rojon et al., 2011)	Family name, Initials. and Family name, Initials. (year). Title of article. *Journal name*. Vol. #, No. #, pp. ##–####. [Accessed day month year from Database name].	Rojon, C., McDowall, A. and Saunders, M.N.K. (2011). On the Experience of Conducting a Systematic Review in Industrial, Work and Organizational Psychology: Yes, It Is Worthwhile. *Journal of Personnel Psychology*. Vol. 10, No. 3, pp. 133–8. [Accessed 6 Apr. 2018 from PsycARTICLES].

(continued)

Table A1.1 (*Continued*)

To cite	In the text		In the list of references/bibliography	
	General format	**Example**	**General format**	**Example**
Journal article which is forthcoming but published online, prior to appearing in the journal; available in facsimile form	*As for* 'Book (first edition)'	(Walker et al., 2018)	Family name, Initials. and Family name, Initials. (year). Title of article, *Journal name.* Available at full doi *or* Internet address [Accessed day month year].	Walker, K., Zhang, Z and Ni, N. (2018). The Mirror Effect: Corporate Social Responsibility, Corporate Social Irresponsibility and Firm Performance in Coordinated Market Economies and Liberal Market Economies. *British Journal of Management.* Available at DOI: 10.1111/1467-8551.12271 [Accessed 2 Feb. 2018].
Journal article only published online, which is not published in print or facsimile form	*As for* 'Journal article made available by the publisher in advance online . . . '	(Yang and Banamah 2013)	*As for* 'Journal article made available by the publisher in advance online . . . '	Yang, K. and Banamah, A. (2013). Quota Sampling as an Alternative to Probability Sampling? An Experimental Study. *Sociological Research Online.* Vol. 18, No. 4. Available at http://www.socresonline.org.uk/19/1/29.html [Accessed 4 Mar. 2014].
Magazine articles				
Magazine article	*As for* 'Book (first edition)'	(Saunders 2004)	Family name, Initials. and Family name, Initials. (year). Title of article. *Magazine name.* Vol. #, No. # (*or* Issue *or* day *and/or* month), pp. ##–###.	Saunders, M. (2004). Land of the long white cloud. *HOG News UK.* Issue 23, Oct. pp. 24–6.
Magazine article (no named author)	(Originator name *or Publication name* year)	(*People Management* 2014)	Originator name *or* Publication *name.* (year). Title of article. *Magazine name.* Vol. #, No. # (*or* Issue *or* day *and/or* month), pp. ##–###.	People Management. (2014). Efficiency rule was misused. *People Management.* Mar. p. 17.
News articles including newspapers and online news				
Newspaper article	*As for* 'Book (first edition)'	(Frean 2014)	Family name, Initials. and Family name, Initials. Title of article. *Newspaper name,* day month year, p. ##.	Frean, A. Credit Suisse bankers 'assisted tax evasion'. *The Times.* 27 Feb. 2014, p. 35.

To cite	In the text		In the list of references/bibliography	
	General format	**Example**	**General format**	**Example**
Newspaper article (no named author)	(*Newspaper name* year)	(*The Times* 2014)	*Newspaper name.* Title of article, day month year, p. #.	*The Times.* Budweiser's early win, 27 Feb. 2014, p. 33.
Newspaper article (published online)	*As for* other News articles	(Rankin 2014)	Family name, Initials. and Family name, Initials. Title of article. *Newspaper name,* day month year. Available at http://www.full-Internetaddress/ [Accessed day month year].	Rankin J. Record number of women make 28th annual Forbes' billionaires list. *The Guardian.* 4 Mar. 2014. Available at http://www.theguardian.com/business/2014/mar/03/record-number-women-forbes-28th-billionaires-list.html?src=linkedin [Accessed 4 Mar. 2014].
Newspaper article (from electronic database)	*As for* other News articles	(Anderson 2009)	Family name, Initials. and Family name, Initials. Title of article. *Newspaper name,* day month year, p. ## (if known). [Accessed day month year from Database name].	Anderson, L. How to choose a Business School. *Financial Times,* 23 Jan. 2009. [Accessed 20 Mar. 2010 from ft.com].
News article (from news web site)	*As for* other News articles	(Gordon 2014)	Family name, Initials. and Family name, Initials. Title of article. *News web site,* day month year. Available at http://www.full-Internetaddress/ [Accessed day month year].	Gordon, O. Keeping crowdsourcing honest. Can we trust the reviews? BBC News, 14 Feb. 2014. Available at: http://www.bbc.co.uk/news/technology-26182642 [Accessed 4 Mar. 2014].
Brochures and Media/Press releases				
Brochure	(Originator name *or* Brochure title year)	(BMW AG 2017)	Originator name *or* Brochure title. (year). *Title.* Place of publication: as author.	BMW AG. (2017). *The BMW X1.* Munich: as author.
Media/press releases	(Originator name *or* Release title year).	(BBC 2014)	Originator name *or* Release title. (year). *Title.* Place of publication: as author.	BBC. (2014). *BBC Trust approves proposals for BBC store.* London: as author.

(*continued*)

Table A1.1 (*Continued*)

To cite	In the text		In the list of references/bibliography	
	General format	**Example**	**General format**	**Example**
Online/websites				
Internet site or specific site pages	(Source organisation year)	(European Commission 2018)	Source organisation. (year). *Title of site or page within site.* Available at http://www.remainderoffull Internetaddress/ [Accessed day month year].	European Commission. (2018). *Eurostat–Your Key to European Statistics.* Available at http://ec.europa. eu/eurostat/web/regions/ data/main-tables [Accessed 2 Feb. 2018].
Blogs (weblogs), web forums, Wikis				
Blogs (weblogs)	(Owners family name, year of posting)	(Kitces 2017)	Owner's family name, Owner's Initials. (year of posting). Specific subject. *Title of blog.* Day Month Year (of posting). [Blog] Available at http://www.remainderoffull Internetaddress/ [Accessed day month year].	Kitces, M. (2017). Marketing Lessons Learned from NerdWallet Ask an Advisor Shutting Down. *Nerd's Eye View.* 30 Mar. 2017. [Blog] Available at https://www. kitces.com/blog/category/20- financial-advisor-marketing/ [Accessed 2 Feb. 2018].
Web forums (Usenet groups, bulletin boards etc.)	(Author's family name, year of posting)	(MagicFajiita 2018)	Authors family name, Authors initials. (year of posting). Title of posting. *Name of forum.* Posted day month year (of posting). *Name of forum.* Posted day month year (of posting). [Web forum]. Available at http://www. remainderoffull Internetaddress/ [Accessed day month year].	MagicFajita. (2018). Adult and child foods? A British thing? *Mumsnet.* Posted 27 Jan. 2018. [Web forum] Available at https://www.mumsnet. com/Talk/am_i_being_ unreasonable/3151562- adult-and-child-foods- a-british-thing?dod=1 [Accessed 3 Feb. 2018].
Wiki	(Originator name or *Wiki title* year of posting)	(Microformats Wiki 2018)	Originator name or *Wiki title. Title of Wiki.* Day Month Year (of posting). [Wiki article]. Available at http://www.remainderoffull Internetaddress/ [Accessed day month year].	Microformats Wiki. *Chat: brainstorming.* 5 Mar. 2014. [Wiki article] Available at http://microformats.org/ wiki/chat-brainstorming [Accessed 3 Feb.. 2018].

To cite	In the text		In the list of references/bibliography	
	General format	**Example**	**General format**	**Example**
Discussion list email (where email sender known)	(Author's family name year of posting)	(Djabali 2018)	Sender's Family name, Sender's Initials. (year of posting). Re. Subject of discussion. Posted day month year. Sender's email address (see note at end of table). [Accessed day month year].	Djabali. (2018). Future Sustainability. Posted 3 Mar. 2017. fion . . . @mail.com [Accessed 2 Feb. 2018].
Letters and personal emails				
Letter	(Sender's family name year)	(Penny 2018)	Sender's family name, Sender's Initials. (year). Unpublished letter to Recipient's Initials. Recipient's Family name re. Subject matter, day, month, year.	Penny, J.J. (2018). Unpublished letter to M.N.K. Saunders re. Holocaust, 10 Sept. 2018.
Personal email	(Sender's family name year)	(Tubb 2017)	Sender's family name, Sender's initials. (year). Email to recipient's initials. recipient's family name re. Subject matter, day month year.	Tubb, V. (2017). Email to M.N.K. Saunders re. Reviewers' feedback, 27 Nov. 2017.
Online images and diagrams				
Online image or diagram	*As for* 'Book (first edition)'	(Gilroy 1936)	Author's name, Author's initials. (year of production if available). *Title of image or diagram.* [Image format] name and place of source if available. Available at http://www. remainderoffull Internetaddress/ [Accessed day month year].	Gilroy, J. (1936). *Lovely day for a Guinness.* [Advertising poster] Print Arcade. Available at https://www.printarcade. co.uk/products/guinness-poster-lovely-day-toucan-advert-art-print?utm_medium=cpc&utm_source= googlepla&gclid= CjwKCAiAtdDTBR ArEiwAPT4y-0NzKwwFm FgfqmQ_gAqw11N6s0PI7S TeeLYea8z6EQh8_KGvtCzelho Cq2AQAvD_BwE [Accessed 2 Feb. 2018].

(continued)

Table A1.1 (*Continued*)

To cite	In the text		In the list of references/bibliography	
	General format	**Example**	**General format**	**Example**
Online image or diagram (no named author)	(*Diagram or image title* year)	*Iron Maiden, A matter of life and death* 2006)	*Title of image or diagram.* (year of production if available). [Image form], name and place of source if available. Available at http://www.remainderoffull Internetaddress/ [Accessed day month year].	*Iron Maiden, A matter of life and death.* (2006). [Tour poster] Quest Poster EU. Available at https://www.amazon.co.uk/IRON-MAIDEN-POSTER-Matter-Death/dp/B005J6PUVY [Accessed 2 Feb. 2018].
Datasets				
Online data set	(Author/Provider name year)	(Eurostat 2018)	Author family name, Author's Initials/Provider name. (year). Title of data set [data form] Available at http://www.remainderoffull internetaddress/ [Retrieved day month year]	Eurostat (2018). Contributions to euro area annual inflation (in percentage points). [Datafile] Available at: http://appsso.eurostat.ec.europa.eu/nui/show.do?dataset=prc_hicp_ctrb&lang=en [Retrieved 22 June 2018]
Other data sets (published)	(Author/Provider name year)	(Inman 2002)	Author family name, Author's Initials/Provider name. (year). Title of data set [data form]. Place of publication, publisher.	Inman, G. (2002). World of noise: Essential summer sounds from road and track [CD-ROM] Peterborough, Bike Magazine.
Other data sets (un-published)	(Author/Provider name year)	(Tubb 2018)	Author family name, Author's Initials/Provider name. (year). Title of data set [data form] [Unpublished]	Tubb, V. (2018). Research Methods for Business Students Market Research [Feedback forms] [unpublished]
Conference papers				
Conference paper published as part of proceedings	*As for* 'Book (first edition)'	(Saunders 2009)	Family name, Initials. and Family name, Initials. (year). Title of paper. In Initials. Family name and Initials. Family name (eds) *Title.* Place of publication: Publisher. pp. ##–###.	Saunders, M.N.K. (2009). A real world comparison of responses to distributing questionnaire surveys by mail and web. In J. Azzopardi (Ed.) *Proceedings of the 8th European Conference on Research Methods in Business and Management.* Reading: ACI, pp. 323–30.

To cite	In the text		In the list of references/bibliography	
	General format	**Example**	**General format**	**Example**
Unpublished conference paper	*As for* 'Book (first edition)'	(Saunders et al. 2010)	Family name, Initials. and Family name, Initials. (year). *Title of paper.* Unpublished paper presented at 'Conference name'. Location of conference, day month year.	Saunders, M.N.K., Slack, R. and Bowen, D. (2010). *Location, the development of swift trust and learning: insights from two doctoral summer schools.* Unpublished paper presented at the 'EIASM 5th Workshop on Trust Within and Between Organizations'. Madrid, 28–29 January 2010.
Film, Video, TV, Radio, Downloads				
Television or radio programme	(*Television or radio programme title* year)	(*Today Programme* 2018)	*Programme title.* (year of production). Transmitting organisation and nature of transmission, day month year of transmission.	*The Today Programme.* (2018). British Broadcasting Corporation Radio broadcast, 26 Jan. 2018.
Television or radio programme that is part of a series	(*Television or radio programme series title* year)	(*The Apprentice* 2017)	*Series title.* (year of production). Episode: episode title. Transmitting organisation and nature of transmission, day month year of transmission.	*The Apprentice.* (2017). Episode: Fashion Show. British Broadcasting Corporation Television broadcast, 9 Dec. 2017.
Commercial DVD	(DVD title year)	(*7-49 Up* 2011)	*DVD title.* (Year of production). [DVD]. Place of publication: Publisher.	*7-49 Up* (2011). [DVD]. London: Network.
Commercial DVD that is part of a box-set	(DVD box set title year)	(*The Office complete series 1 and 2 and the Christmas specials* 2005)	*DVD box set title* (Year of production) Episode: Episode title. [DVD]. Place of publication: Publisher.	*The Office complete series 1 and 2 and the Christmas specials.* (2005). Episode: Series 1 Christmas Special. [DVD]. London: British Broadcasting Corporation.
Video download (e.g. YouTube)	(Company name *or* Family name year)	(Miller 2008)	Company name *or* Family name, Initials. (year). Title of audio download. *YouTube.* Available at http://www.remainderoffull Internetaddress/ [Accessed day month year].	Miller, L. (2008). Harvard style referencing made easy. *YouTube.* Available at https://www.youtube.com/watch?v=RH1lzyn7Exc [Accessed 5 Mar. 2018].

(continued)

Table A1.1 (*Continued*)

To cite	In the text		In the list of references/bibliography	
	General format	**Example**	**General format**	**Example**
Audio CD	(Family name *or* Artist *or* Group year)	(Goldratt 2005)	Family name, Initials. *or* Artist. *or* Group. (year). *Title of CD.* [Audio CD]. Place of Publication: Publisher.	Goldratt, E.M. (2005). *Beyond the goal.* [Audio CD]. Buffalo NY: Goldratt's Marketing Group.
Audio download (e.g. Podcast)	(Company name *or* Family name year)	(Friedman 2014)	Company name *or* Family name, Initials. (year). Title of audio download. *Title of series ## [Audio podcast] Available at http://www.remainderoffull Internetaddress/ [Accessed day month year].	Friedman, S.D. (2014). Is work family conflict reaching a tipping point? *Harvard Business IdeaCast 394.* [Audio podcast] Available at https://itunes.apple.com/ gb/podcast/hbr-ideacast/ id152022135?mt=2 [Accessed 9 May 2014].
Course materials and online teaching materials from virtual learning environments (VLEs)				
Lecture*	(Lecturer family name year)	(Saunders 2013)	Lecturer family name, Initials. (year). *Lecture on title of lecture.* Module title. Year (if appropriate) and course title. Place of lecture: Institution. Day month year.	Saunders, M.N.K. (2018). *Lecture on Observation and Ethnography.* Foundations in Qualitative Research. MA Social Research Methods. Birmingham: University of Birmingham. 30 Jan. 2018.
Module and course notes*	*As for* 'Book (first edition)'	(Bell 2013)	Lecturer family name, Initials. (year). *Title of material.* Module title (if appropriate). Level (if appropriate) and course title. Institution, Department or School.	Saunders, M.N.K. and Isaeva, N. (2018). *Foundations in Qualitative Research Module Handbook 2018.* MA Social Research Methods. University of Birmingham, College of Social Sciences.

To cite	In the text		In the list of references/bibliography	
	General format	**Example**	**General format**	**Example**
Materials available on a VLE*	(Author family name year)	(Saunders 2018)	Author family name, Initials. (year of production). *Title of material* [nature of material]. Module title (if appropriate). Level (if appropriate) and course title. Institution *name of VLE* [online]. Available at http://www.remainderoffull Internetaddress/ [Accessed day month year].	Saunders, MNK. (2018). *Trust, Distrust and the Management of Change* [PowerPoint slides]. Contemporary Issues in Work and Employment. University of Birmingham *Canvas* [online]. Available at https://canvas.bham.ac.uk/courses/25675/modules [Accessed 2 Feb. 2018].

Notes: Where date is not known or unclear, follow conventions outlined towards the end of Table A1.2.

Email addresses should not be included except when they are in the public domain. Even where this is the case, permission should be obtained or the email address replaced by '. . .' after the fourth character, for example: 'abcd . . . @isp.ac.uk'.

*Be warned, most lecturers consider citing of lectures as 'lazy' scholarship.

Table A1.2 Additional conventions when using the Harvard system to reference in the text

To refer to	Use the general format	For example
Work by different authors generally	(Family name year, Family name year) in alphabetical order	(Cassell 2018, Dillman 2009, Robson 2011)
Different authors with the same family name	(Family name Initial year)	(Smith J. 2017)
Different works by the same author	(Family name year, year) in ascending year order	(Saunders 2017, 2018)
Different works by the same author from the same year	(Family name year letter), make sure the letter is consistent throughout	(Tosey 2014a)
An author referred to by another author where the original has not been read (*secondary reference*)*	(Family name year, cited by Family name year)	(Cassell 2017, cited by Isaeva 2018)
A work for which the year of publication cannot be identified	(Family name or Originator name nd), where 'nd' means no date	(Woollons nd)
	(Family name or Originator name c. year) where 'c.' means circa	(Hattersley c. 2004)
A direct quotation	(Family name or Originator name year, p. ##) where 'p.' means 'page' and ## is the page in the original publication on which the quotation appears	"A card sort offers the simplest form of sorting technique" (Saunders 2012, p. 112)

*For secondary references, whilst many universities only require you to give details of the source you looked at in your list of references, you may also be required the reference for the original source in your list of references.

Referencing in the list of references or bibliography

In the list of references or bibliography all the sources are listed alphabetically in one list by the originator or author's family name, and all authors' family names and initials are normally listed in full. If there is more than one work by the same author or originator, these are listed chronologically. A system for referencing work in the list of references or bibliography is outlined in Table A1.1. While it would be impossible for us to include an example of every type of reference you might need to include, the information contained in this table should enable you to work out the required format for all your references. If there are any about which you are unsure, Colin Neville's (2016) book *The Complete Guide to Referencing and Avoiding Plagiarism* is one of the most comprehensive sources we have found.

For copies of journal articles from printed journals that you have obtained electronically online it is usually acceptable to reference these using exactly the same format as printed journal articles (Table A1.1), provided that you have obtained and read a facsimile (exact) copy of the article. Facsimile copies of journal articles have precisely the same format as the printed version, including page numbering, tables and diagrams, other than for the copy, which is published 'online first'. **Online first** refers to forthcoming articles that have been published online, prior to them appearing in journals. They therefore do not have a volume or part number, and the page numbering will not be the same as the final copy. When referencing an 'online first' copy in the list of references, you should always include the DOI. A facsimile copy is usually obtained by downloading the article as a pdf file that can be read on the screen and printed using Adobe Acrobat Reader.

Finally, remember to include a, b, c etc. immediately after the year when you are referencing different publications by the same author from the same year. Do not forget to ensure that these are consistent with the letters used for the references in the main text.

The American Psychological Association (APA) style

The 'American Psychological Association style' or 'APA style' is a variation on the author–date system and was initially developed in 1929. The latest updates are outlined in the latest edition of the American Psychological Association's (2010) *Concise Rules of the APA Style,* which is likely to be available for reference in your university's library.

Relatively small but significant differences exist between the Harvard system and APA style, and many authors adopt a combination of the two. The key differences are outlined in Table A1.3.

Numeric systems

Referencing in the text

When using a numeric system such as the Vancouver style, references within the project report are shown by a number that is either bracketed or in superscript. This number refers directly to the list of references at the end of the text, and it means it is not necessary for you to include the authors' names or year of publication:

'Research[1] indicates that . . . '

[1] Ritzer, G. *The McDonaldization of Society.* (6th edn). Thousand Oaks, CA: Sage, Pine Forge Press, 2011.

Table A1.3 Key differences between Harvard system and APA style of referencing

Harvard system	APA style	Comment
Referencing in the text		
(Lewis 2001)	(Lewis, 2001)	Note punctuation
(McDowall and Saunders 2010)	(McDowall & Saunders, 2011)	'&' not 'and'
(Altinay et al. 2014)	(Altinay, Saunders & Wang, 2014)	For first occurrence if three to five authors
(Millmore et al. 2007)	(Millmore et al., 2007)	For first occurrence if six or more authors; note punctuation and use of italics
(Tosey et al. 2012)	(Tosey et al., 2012)	For subsequent occurrences of two or more authors; note punctuation and use of italics
Referencing in the list of references or bibliography		
Berman Brown, R. and Saunders, M. (2008). *Dealing with Statistics: What You Need to Know.* Maidenhead: Open University Press.	Berman Brown, R. & Saunders, M. (2008). *Dealing with Statistics: What You Need to Know.* Maidenhead: Open University Press.	Note: use of 'and' and '&'
Varadarajan, P.R. (2003). Musings on relevance and rigour of scholarly research in marketing. *Journal of the Academy of Marketing Science.* Vol. 31, No. 4, pp. 368–76. [Accessed 6 Apr. 2010 from Business Source Complete].	Varadarajan, P.R. (2003). Musings on relevance and rigour of scholarly research in marketing. *Journal of the Academy of Marketing Science.* 31 (4): 368–376. doi: 10.1177/0092070303258240	Note: Volume, part number and page numbers; DOI (digital object identifier) number given in APA. Name of database not given in APA if DOI number given; Date accessed site not included in APA.

Referencing in the list of references

The list of references in numeric systems is sequential, referencing items in the order they are referred to in your project report. This means that they are unlikely to be in alphabetical order. When using the numeric system you need to ensure that:

- The layout of individual references is that prescribed by the style you have adopted. This is likely to differ from both the Harvard system and APA style (Table A1.3) and will be dependent upon precisely which style has been adopted. The reference to Ritzer's book in the previous sub-section (indicated by the number and the associated endnote at the end of this appendix) follows the Vancouver style. Further details of this and other numeric styles can be found in Neville's (2016) book.
- The items referred to include only those you have cited in your report. They should therefore be headed 'References' rather than 'Bibliography'.
- Only one number is used for each item, except where you refer to the same item more than once but need to refer to different pages. In such instances you use standard bibliographic abbreviations to save repeating the reference in full (Table A1.4).

Table A1.4 Bibliographic abbreviations

Abbreviation	Explanation	For example
Op. cit. (opere citato)	Meaning 'in the work cited'. This refers to a work previously referenced, and so you must give the author and year and, if necessary, the page number	Robson (2011) *op. cit.* pp. 23–4.
Loc. cit. (loco citato)	Meaning 'in the place cited'. This refers to the same page of a work previously referenced, and so you must give the author and year	Robson (2011) *loc. cit.*
Ibid. (ibidem)	Meaning 'the same work given immediately before'. This refers to the work referenced immediately before, and replaces all details of the previous reference other than a page number if necessary	*Ibid.* p. 59.

References

American Psychological Association (2010) *Concise Rules of the APA Style.* Washington, DC: American Psychological Association.

Chernin, I. (1988) 'The "Harvard System": a mystery dispelled', *BMJ.* Vol. 297, pp. 1062-3.

Neville, C. (2016) *The Complete Guide to Referencing and Avoiding Plagiarism* (3rd edn). Maidenhead: Open University Press.

Further reading

American Psychological Association (2010) *Concise Rules of the APA Style.* Washington, DC: American Psychological Association. The most recent version of this manual contains full details of how to use this form of the author–date system of referencing as well as how to lay out tables, figures, equations and other statistical data. It also provides guidance on grammar and writing.

Neville, C. (2016) *The Complete Guide to Referencing and Avoiding Plagiarism* (3rd edn). Maidenhead: Open University Press. This fully revised edition provides a comprehensive, up-to-date discussion of the layout required for a multitude of information sources including online. It includes guidance on the Harvard, American Psychological Association, numerical and other referencing styles, as well as chapters on plagiarism and answering frequently asked questions.

Taylor & Francis (nd) *Taylor & Francis Reference Style APA Quick Guide.* Available at http://www.tandf.co.uk/journals/authors/style/quickref/tf_a.pdf [Accessed 20 March 2018]. This document provides an excellent one-page guide to using the American Psychological Association author–date system as well as a direct link to a document providing full details of this style including how to cite references in the text.

University of New South Wales (2017) *Harvard Referencing Electronic Sources.* Available at https://student.unsw.edu.au/harvard-referencing-electronic-sources [Accessed 20 March 2018]. This document provides an excellent guide to referencing electronic sources and has useful 'troubleshooting' and 'frequently asked questions' sections.

Appendix 2 Calculating the minimum sample size

In some situations, such as experimental research, it is necessary for you to calculate the precise minimum sample size you require. This calculation assumes that data will be collected from all cases in the sample and is based on:

- how confident you need to be that the estimate is accurate (the level of confidence in the estimate);
- how accurate the estimate needs to be (the margin of error that can be tolerated);
- the proportion of responses you expect to have some particular attribute.

Provided that you know the level of confidence and the margin of error, it is relatively easy to estimate the proportion of responses you expect to have a particular attribute. To do this, ideally you need to collect a pilot sample of about 30 observations and from this to infer the likely proportion for your main survey. It is therefore important that the pilot sample uses the same methods as your main survey. Alternatively, you might have undertaken a very similar survey and so already have a reasonable idea of the likely proportion. If you do not, then you need either to make an informed guess or to assume that 50 per cent of the sample will have the specified attribute – the worst scenario. Most surveys will involve collecting data on more than one attribute. It is argued by De Vaus (2014) that for such multi-purpose surveys you should determine the sample size on the basis of those variables in the sample that are likely to have the greatest variability.

Once you have all the information you substitute it into the formula,

$$n = \rho\% \times q\% \times \left[\frac{z}{e\%}\right]^2$$

where:

n is the minimum sample size required
r% is the percentage belonging to the specified category
$q\%$ is the percentage not belonging to the specified category
z is the z value corresponding to the level of confidence required (see Table A2.1)
$e\%$ is the margin of error required.

Table A2.1 Levels of confidence and associated z values

Level of confidence	z value
90% certain	1.65
95% certain	1.96
99% certain	2.57

Box A2.1
Focus on student research

Calculating the minimum sample size

To answer a research question, Jon needed to estimate the proportion of a total population of 4,000 restaurant customers who had visited that restaurant at least five times in the past year. Based on his reading of the research methods literature he decided that he needed to be 95 per cent certain that his 'estimate' was accurate (the level of confidence in the estimate); this corresponded to a z score of 1.96 (Table A2.1). Based on his reading he also decided that his 'estimate' needed to be accurate to within plus or minus 5 per cent of the true percentage (the margin of error that can be tolerated).

In order to calculate the minimum sample size, Jon still needed to estimate the proportion of respondents who had visited the restaurant at least five times in the past year. From his pilot survey he discovered that 12 out of the 30 restaurant customers had visited the restaurant at least five times in the past year – in other words, that 40 per cent belonged to this specified category. This meant that 60 per cent did not.

Jon substituted these figures into the formula:

$$n = 40 \times 60 \times \left(\frac{1.96}{5}\right)^2$$
$$= 2400 \times (0.392)^2$$
$$= 2400 \times 0.154$$
$$= 369.6$$

His minimum sample size, therefore, was 370 returns.

As the total population of restaurant customers was 4,000, Jon could now calculate the adjusted minimum sample size:

$$n' = \frac{369.6}{1 + \left(\frac{369.6}{4000}\right)}$$
$$= \frac{369.6}{1 + 0.092}$$
$$= \frac{369.6}{1.092}$$
$$= 338.46$$

Because of the small total population, Jon needed a minimum sample size of only 339. However, this assumed he had a response rate of 100 per cent

Where your population is less than 10,000, a smaller sample size can be used without affecting the accuracy. This is called the *adjusted minimum sample size* (Box A2.1). It is calculated using the following formula:

$$n' = \frac{n}{1 + \left(\frac{n}{N}\right)}$$

where:
 n' is the adjusted minimum sample size
 n is the minimum sample size (as calculated above)
 N is the total population.

Reference

De Vaus, D.A. (2014) *Surveys in Social Research* (6th edn). London: Routledge.

78 41	11 62	72 18	66 69	58 71	31 90	51 36	78 09	41 00
70 50	58 19	68 26	75 69	04 00	25 29	16 72	35 73	55 85
32 78	14 47	01 55	10 91	83 21	13 32	59 53	03 38	79 32
71 60	20 53	86 78	50 57	42 30	73 48	68 09	16 35	21 87
35 30	15 57	99 96	33 25	56 43	65 67	51 45	37 99	54 89
09 08	05 41	66 54	01 49	97 34	38 85	85 23	34 62	60 58
02 59	34 51	98 71	31 54	28 85	23 84	49 07	33 71	17 88
20 13	44 15	22 95	98 97	60 02	85 07	17 57	20 51	01 67
36 26	70 11	63 81	27 31	79 71	08 11	87 74	85 53	86 78
00 30	62 19	81 68	86 10	65 61	62 22	17 22	96 83	56 37
38 41	14 59	53 03	52 86	21 88	55 87	85 59	14 90	74 87
18 89	40 84	71 04	09 82	54 44	94 23	83 89	04 59	38 29
34 38	85 56	80 74	22 31	26 39	65 63	12 38	45 75	30 35
55 90	21 71	17 88	20 08	57 64	17 93	22 34	00 55	09 78
81 43	53 96	96 88	36 86	04 33	31 40	18 71	06 00	51 45
59 69	13 03	38 31	77 08	71 20	23 28	92 43	92 63	21 74
60 24	47 44	73 93	64 37	64 97	19 82	27 59	24 20	00 04
17 04	93 46	05 70	20 95	42 25	33 95	78 80	07 57	86 58
09 55	42 30	27 05	27 93	78 10	69 11	29 56	29 79	28 66
46 69	28 64	81 02	41 89	12 03	31 20	25 16	79 93	28 22
28 94	00 91	16 15	35 12	68 93	23 71	11 55	64 56	76 95
59 10	06 29	83 84	03 68	97 65	59 21	58 54	61 59	30 54
41 04	70 71	05 56	76 66	57 86	29 30	11 31	56 76	24 13
09 81	81 80	73 10	10 23	26 29	61 15	50 00	76 37	60 16
91 55	76 68	06 82	05 33	06 75	92 35	82 21	78 15	19 43
82 69	36 73	58 69	10 92	31 14	21 08	13 78	56 53	97 77
03 59	65 34	32 06	63 43	38 04	65 30	32 82	57 05	33 95
03 96	30 87	81 54	69 39	95 69	95 69	89 33	78 90	30 07
39 91	27 38	20 90	41 10	10 80	59 68	93 10	85 25	59 25
89 93	92 10	59 40	26 14	27 47	39 51	46 70	86 85	76 02
99 16	73 21	39 05	03 36	87 58	18 52	61 61	02 92	07 24
93 13	20 70	42 59	77 69	35 59	71 80	61 95	82 96	48 84
47 32	87 68	97 86	28 51	61 21	33 02	79 65	59 49	89 93
09 75	58 00	72 49	36 58	19 45	30 61	87 74	43 01	93 91
63 24	15 65	02 05	32 92	45 61	35 43	67 64	94 45	95 66
33 58	69 42	25 71	74 31	88 80	04 50	22 60	72 01	27 88
23 25	22 78	24 88	68 48	83 60	53 59	73 73	82 43	82 66
07 17	77 20	79 37	50 08	29 79	55 13	51 90	36 77	68 69
16 07	31 84	57 22	29 54	35 14	22 22	22 60	72 15	40 90
67 90	79 28	62 83	44 96	87 70	40 64	27 22	60 19	52 54
79 52	74 68	69 74	31 75	80 59	29 28	21 69	15 97	35 88
69 44	31 09	16 38	92 82	12 25	10 57	81 32	76 71	31 61
09 47	57 04	54 00	78 75	91 99	26 20	36 19	53 29	11 55
74 78	09 25	95 80	25 72	88 85	76 02	29 89	70 78	93 84

Source: From Morris, C. (2012) *Quantitative Approaches in Business Studies* (8th edn). Reproduced by permission of Pearson Education Ltd

Reference

Morris, C. (2012) *Quantitative Approaches in Business Studies* (8th edn). Harlow: Pearson.

Appendix 4 Guidelines for non-discriminatory language

Writing in a non-discriminatory manner is important in all areas of business and management. For example, in Section 14.6 we noted how the use of language that assumes the gender of a group of people, such as referring to a clerical assistant as 'she', not only is inaccurate but also gives offence to people. There is now increasing recognition that gender is about social identity and that not all people fall under one of two categories (Lowrey 2017) and that terms used need to reflect this. Similar care needs to be exercised when referring to people from different ethnic groups and people with disabilities. Without this, the language used may reinforce beliefs and prejudices, as well as being oppressive, offensive, unfair and incorrect. The impact of this is summarised clearly by Bill Bryson (2016: 502) in his book *Made in America*, when he observes: 'at the root of the bias-free language movement lies a commendable sentiment: to make language less wounding or demeaning to those whose sex, race, physical condition or circumstances leave them vulnerable to the raw power of words'.

Therefore, although the task of ensuring that the language you use is non-discriminatory may at first seem difficult, it is important that you do so. Some universities have developed their own guidelines, which are available via their intranet or the Internet. However, if your university has not developed its own guidelines, we hope those in this appendix will help you to ensure that your language is not discriminatory.

Guidelines for gender

When referring to both sexes, it is inappropriate to use the terms 'men' or 'women' and their gender-based equivalents; in other words, do not use gender-specific terms generically. Some of the more common gender-neutral alternatives are listed in Table A4.1.

Recognising that not all people fall under one of two categories for gender or sex, we would also encourage you not to use phrases such as 'both genders. . . ', 'either gender. . . ' or refer to 'neither gender. . . ' when referring to all people. You may also wish to consider adopting the use of non-binary pronouns to refer to individuals or people. Table A4.2 lists some of those currently in use. However, beware, as the use of 'they', 'their' or 'them' to refer to a single person is considered by many to be grammatically incorrect. In addition, if your audience is not familiar with non-binary pronouns, we would recommend adding a footnote explaining why that you are using non-binary pronouns such as: 'In my project report I use the following non-binary gender pronouns [*list of all used*] because the people I am citing and/or to whom I am referring use these pronouns to refer to themselves and I wish to respect their identities.'

Table A4.1 Gender-specific terms and gender-neutral alternatives

Gender-specific term	Gender-neutral alternative
businessmen	business people, executive
chairman	chair, chairperson, convenor
conman	confidence trickster
Dear Sir	Dear Sir/Madam
disseminate	broadcast, inform, publicise
forefathers	ancestors
foreman	supervisor
layman	lay person
man	person
man hours	work hours
mankind	humanity, humankind, people
man-made	manufactured, synthetic
manning	resourcing, staffing
manpower	human resources, labour, staff, workforce
master copy	original, top copy
masterful	domineering, very skillful
policewoman/policeman	police officer
rights of man	people's/citizens' rights, rights of the individual
seminal	classical, formative
women	people
working man/working woman	worker, working people
workmanlike	efficient, skilful, through

Source: Developed from British Psychological Society (2015); British Sociological Association (2004a)

Table A4.2 Pronouns and alternative non-binary forms

Pronoun	Alternative non-binary forms			
she he	they	zie	sie	ey
her him	them	zim	sie	eir
her his	their	zir	hir	eir
hers his	their	zis	hirs	eirs
herself himself	themself	zieself	hirself	emself

Source: Developed from Lowrey (2017); University of Minnesota (2018)

Guidelines for ethnicity

Attention needs to be paid when referring to different ethnic groups. This is especially important where the term used refers to a number of ethnic groups. For example, the term 'Asian' includes a number of diverse ethnic groups that can be recognised with the terms

Table A4.3 Racist terms and race-neutral alternatives

Racist term	Race-neutral alternative
civilised/civilisation	industrialised world
developing nations	non-western nations
ethnic minority	minority ethnic
half-caste	mixed parentage, dual heritage
less developed countries	non-western countries
mixed race	mixed parentage, dual heritage
native	native-born (if used to refer to people born in a particular place)

Source: Developed from British Sociological Association (nd)

'Asian peoples' or 'Asian communities'. Similarly, the diversity of people represented by the term 'Black' can be recognised by referring to 'Black peoples' or 'Black communities'. Where possible, the individual groups within these communities should be identified separately.

'Black' is used as a term to include people who are discriminated against due to the colour of their skin. It is often used to refer to people of Caribbean, South Asian and African descent. Hyphenated terms such as 'Afro-Caribbean', 'Black-British' or 'African-American' should not be used. Rather terms such as 'African Caribbean', 'Black British' or 'African American' should be used to refer to second or subsequent generations who, although born in the country, often wish to retain their origins. Beware, the term 'British', which can imply false unity and people from England, Northern Ireland, Scotland and Wales may not wish to be identified as British.

Care should also be taken in using terms that carry racist overtones. Some of the more common race-neutral terms are listed in Table A4.3. However, if you are unsure of the term to use, then ask someone from the appropriate community for the most acceptable current term.

Guidelines for disability

Disability is also an area where terminology is constantly changing as people voice their own preferences. Despite this, general guidelines can be offered:

- Do not use medical terms as these emphasise the condition rather than the person.
- Where it is necessary to refer to a person's medical condition, make the person explicit (see Table A4.3).
- Where referring to historical and some contemporary common terms, place speech marks around each term.

There are non-disablist alternatives for the more common disablist terms. These are summarised in Table A4.4. However, if you are unsure of the term to use, ask someone from the appropriate group for the most acceptable current term.

Table A4.4 Disablist terms and non-disablist alternatives

Disablist term	Non-disablist alternative
the blind	blind and partially sighted people, visually impaired people
cripple	mobility impaired person
the deaf	deaf or hard of hearing people
the disabled, the handicapped, invalid	disabled people, people with disabilities, employees with disabilities
dumb, mute	person with a speech impairment
epileptic, epileptics	person who has epilepsy
handicap	disability
mentally handicapped	person with a learning difficulty or learning disability
mentally ill, mental patient	mental health service user
patient	person
spastic	person who has cerebral palsy
wheelchair-bound	wheelchair user
victim of, afflicted by, suffering from, crippled by	person who has, person with

Source: Adapted from British Sociological Association (2004b)

References

British Psychological Society (1988) 'Guidelines for the use of non-sexist language', *The Psychologist,* Vol. 1, No. 2, pp. 53–4.

British Psychological Society (2015) *Style Guide for Authors and Editors.* Available at https://www.bps.org.uk/news-and-policy/bps-style-guide-authors-and-editors[Accessed 4 Feb. 2018].

British Sociological Association (2004b) *Language and the BSA: Non-Disablist.* Available at https://www.britsoc.co.uk/Equality-Diversity/ [Accessed 4 Feb. 2018].

British Sociological Association (nd) *Language and the BSA: Ethnicity & Race.* Available at https://www.britsoc.co.uk/Equality-Diversity/ [Accessed 4 Feb. 2018].

Bryson, B. (2016) *Made in America.* London: Transworld. (originally published by Minerva 1995).

Lowrey, S. (2017) A guide to non-binary pronouns and why they matter. *Huffpost.* Available at https://www.huffingtonpost.com/entry/non-binary-pronouns-why-they-matter_us_5a03107be4b0230facb8419a?guccounter=1 [Accessed 6 June 2018].

University of Minnesota (2018) *Non-binary gender pronouns.* Available at http://writing.umn.edu/sws/quickhelp/grammar/nonbinary.html [Accessed 6 June 2018]

Glossary

50th percentile The middle value when all the values of a variable are arranged in rank order; usually known as the median.

A

abductive approach Approach to theory development involving the collection of data to explore a phenomenon, identify themes and explain patterns, to generate a new – or modify an existing – theory which is subsequently tested.

abstract (1) Summary, usually of an article or book, which also contains sufficient information for the original to be located. (2) Summary of the complete content of the project report.

access (1) The process involved in gaining entry into an organisation to undertake research. (2) The situation where a research participant is willing to share data with a researcher. *See also* cognitive access, continuing access, physical access.

Action Research Research strategy concerned with the management of a change and involving close collaboration between practitioners and researchers. The results flowing from Action Research should also inform other contexts.

active participation Situation where a researcher enters a research setting with the intention of participating actively in the role of an insider. *See also* participant observation, moderate participation.

active response rate Total number of responses divided by the total number in the sample after ineligible and unreachable respondents have been excluded. *See* ineligible respondent, unreachable respondent. *See also* break off, complete response, complete refusal, partial response total response rate.

active voice The voice in which the action of the verb is attributed to the person. For example, '*I* conducted interviews'.

ad hoc survey A general term normally used to describe the collection of data that only occurs once due to the specificity of focus. Although the term is normally interpreted as referring to questionnaires, it also includes other techniques such as structured observation and structured interviews. *See also* survey.

aim *see* research aim.

alpha coefficient *see* Cronbach's alpha.

alternative hypothesis Tentative, usually testable statement that there is an association, difference or relationship between two or more variables. Often referred to as H_a. *See also* hypothesis, null hypothesis.

analysis of variance Statistical test to determine the probability (likelihood) that the values of a numerical data variable for three or more independent samples or groups are different. The test assesses the likelihood of any difference between these groups occurring by chance alone.

analysis Ability to break down data and to clarify the nature of the component parts and the relationship between them.

analytic induction Analysis of qualitative data that involves the iterative examination of a number of strategically selected cases to identify the cause of a particular phenomenon.

anonymised data Personal data which if effectively anonymised mean that individuals cannot be identified. *See also* Personal data.

anonymity (1) Process of concealing the identity of participants in all documents resulting from the research. (2) Promise that even the researcher will not be able to identify by whom responses are made.

ANOVA *see* analysis of variance.

appendix A supplement to the project report. It should not normally include material that is essential for the understanding of the report itself, but additional relevant material in which the reader may be interested.

application The ability to apply certain principles and rules in particular situations.

applied research Research of direct and immediate relevance to practitioners that addresses issues they see as important and is presented in ways they can understand and act upon.

archival research Research strategy that analyses administrative records and documents as principal sources of data because they are products of day-to-day activities.

asynchronous Not undertaken in real time, working offline.

asynchronous electronic interview Electronic interview in which there are gaps in time or delays between the interviewer asking a question and the participant providing an answer. *See also* electronic interview, synchronous electronic interview.

attitude variable Variable that records data about what respondents feel about something.

autocorrelation Extent to which the value of a variable at a particular time (t) is related to its value at the previous time period ($t - 1$).

autodriving Visual interview that is 'self-driven' by the interviewee talking about visual images taken of her or him in a specific setting. *See also* photoelicitation, visual interview.

availability sampling *see* convenience sampling.

axial coding Process of recognising relationships between categories in grounded theory.

axiology Branch of philosophy concerned with the role of values and ethics within the research process.

B

bar graph/chart Graph for showing frequency distributions for a categorical or grouped discrete data variable, which highlights the highest and lowest values.

base period Period against which index numbers are calculated to facilitate comparisons of trends or changes over time. *See also* index number.

basic research Research undertaken purely to understand processes and their outcomes, predominantly in universities as a result of an academic agenda, for which the key consumer is the academic community.

behaviour variable Variable that records data about behaviours, what people did in the past, do now or will do in the future.

beneficence Actions designed to promote beneficial effects. *See also* code of ethics.

between persons analysis Analyses conducted on variations between participants' responses in a research study. *See also* within-individual level analysis.

between-subjects design Experimental design allowing a comparison of results to be made between an experimental group and a control group. *See also* experiment, within-subjects design.

bibliographic details The information needed to enable readers to find original items consulted or used for a research project. These normally include the author, date of publication, title of article, title of book or journal.

bibliography Alphabetical list of the bibliographic details for all relevant items consulted and used, including those items not referred to directly in the text. The university will specify the format of these.

big data Data sets that are massive in volume, complex in variety (often comprising both structured and unstructured data) and are being added to at high velocity. They are analysed by powerful computer techniques to reveal patterns and trends. *See also* structured data, unstructured data.

biographical interview Participant focused research interview designed to record a participant life history. *See also* in-depth interview, semi-structured interview, narrative interview.

blog A personal online journal on which an individual or group of individuals record opinions, information and the like on a regular basis for public consumption. Most blogs are interactive allowing visitors to leave comments. 'Blog' is an abbreviation of 'weblog'.

Boolean logic System by which the variety of items found in a search based on logical propositions that can be either true or false can be combined, limited or widened.

box plot Diagram that provides a pictorial representation of the distribution of the data for a variable and statistics such as median, inter-quartile range, and the highest and lowest values.

brainstorming Technique that can be used to generate and refine research ideas. It is best undertaken with a group of people.

break off Level of response to questionnaires or structured interviews in which less than 50 per cent of all questions answered other than by a refusal or no answer. Break off therefore includes complete refusal.

broker *see* gatekeeper.

C

CAQDAS Computer-Aided Qualitative Data Analysis Software.

case (1) Individual element or group member within a sample or population such as an employee. (2) Individual unit for which data have been collected.

case study Research strategy that involves the empirical investigation of a phenomenon within its real life context, using multiple sources of evidence.

categorical data Data whose values cannot be measured numerically but can either be classified into sets (categories) or placed in rank order.

categorising Process of developing categories and subsequently attaching these categories to meaningful units of data. *See also* unitising, units of data.

category question Closed question in which the respondent is offered a set of mutually exclusive categories and instructed to select one.

causal relationship Relationship between two or more variables in which the change (effect) in one variable is caused by the other variable(s).

causality Relationship between cause and effect. Everything that happens will have a cause, while each action will cause an effect.

census Collection of data from every possible case or group member in a population.

central limit theorem The larger the absolute size of a sample, the more closely its distribution will be to the normal distribution. *See* normal distribution.

central tendency measure Generic term for statistics that can be used to provide an impression of those values for a variable that are common, middling or average.

chat room Online forum operating in synchronous mode. *See also* synchronous.

chi square test Statistical test to determine the probability (likelihood) that two categorical data variables are independent. A common use is to discover whether there are statistically significant associations between the observed frequencies and the expected frequencies of two variables presented in a cross-tabulation.

classic approach to observational research Traditional observation role which claims to be objective and to rely solely on the researcher's perspective and interpretation to make sense of what is observed. *See also* complete observer, complete participant, non-participant observer, observer as participant, participant as observer.

classic experiment Experiment in which two groups are established and members assigned at random to each. *See also* experiment, experimental group.

closed question Question that provides a number of alternative answers from which the respondent is instructed to choose.

cluster sampling Probability sampling procedure in which the population is divided into discrete groups or clusters prior to sampling. A random sample (systematic or simple) of these clusters is then drawn.

code (1) Single word or short phrase, sometimes abbreviated, used to label a unit of data. (2) Number or word used to represent a response by a respondent or participant. *See also* coding, codebook, coding template unit of data. (3) Sociological term referring to conventionalised or shared understandings and expectations that operate at group and societal levels, which affect how members of a group or society make sense of their world, interpret signs and behave. *See also* dominant code, semiotics.

code of ethics Statement of principles and procedures for the design and conduct of research. *See also* privacy, research ethics, research ethics committee.

codebook Complete list of all the codes used to code data variables.

coding schedule Means to record predetermined and defined categories of behaviours, interactions or events in structured observation. *See also* structured observation.

coding template Hierarchical list of codes and themes, which is used as the central analytical tool in Template Analysis. *See also* Template Analysis.

coding Process of labelling of data using a code that symbolises or summarises the meaning of that data. *See also* axial coding, categorising, data code, focused coding, initial coding, open coding, selective coding, unitizing, unit of data.

coding with gerunds Analytical approach using verbs functioning as nouns to code actions or interactions in qualitative data. *See also* Grounded Theory Method, qualitative data.

coefficient of determination Number between 0 and 1 that enables the strength of the relationship between a numerical dependent variable and a numerical independent variable to be assessed. The coefficient represents the proportion of the variation in the dependent variable that can be explained statistically by the independent variable. A value of 1 means that all the variation in the dependent variable can be explained statistically by the independent variable. A value of 0 means that none of the variation in the dependent variable can be explained by the independent variable. *See also* regression analysis.

coefficient of multiple determination Number between 0 and 1 that enables the strength of the relationship between a numerical dependent variable and two or more numerical independent variables to be assessed. The coefficient represents the proportion of the variation in the dependent variable that can be explained statistically by the independent variables. A value of 1 means that all the variation in the dependent variable can be explained statistically by the independent variables. A value of 0 means that none of the variation in the dependent variable can be explained by the independent variables. *See also* multiple regression analysis.

coefficient of variation Statistic that compares the extent of spread of data values around the mean between two or more variables containing numerical data.

cognitive access Process of gaining access to data from intended participants. This involves participants agreeing to be interviewed or observed, within agreed limits. *See also* informed consent.

cohort study Study that collects data from the same cases over time using a series of 'snapshots'.

collaborative observation Situation where researcher does not assume a dominant research role in relation to those being observed but treats them as collaborators by involving them in many aspects of the research process. *See also* classic approach to observational research.

collinearity Extent to which two or more independent variables are correlated with each other. Also termed multicollinearity.

comparative proportional pie chart Diagram for comparing both proportions and totals for all types of data variables.

compiled data Data that have been processed, such as through some form of selection or summarising.

complete observer Observational role in which the researcher does not reveal the purpose of the research activity to those being observed. However, unlike the complete participant role, the researcher does not take part in the activities of the group being studied.

complete participant Observational role in which the researcher attempts to become a member of the group in which research is being conducted. The true purpose of the research is not revealed to the group members.

complete refusal Level of non-response to questionnaires or structured interviews in which none of the questions are answered.

complete response Level of response to questionnaires or structured interviews in which over 80 per cent of all questions answered other than by a refusal or no answer.

computer-aided personal interviewing (CAPI) Type of interviewing in which the interviewer reads questions from a computer screen and enters the respondent's answers directly into the computer.

computer-aided telephone interviewing (CATI) Type of telephone interviewing in which the interviewer reads questions from a computer screen and enters the respondent's answers directly into the computer.

conclusion Section of the project report in which judgements are made rather than just facts reported. New material is not normally introduced in the conclusion.

concurrent embedded design Mixed-methods research design where the collection of either quantitative or qualitative data is embedded within the collection of the other. *See also* concurrent mixed-methods research, embedded mixed methods research.

concurrent mixed-methods research Research using both quantitative and qualitative methods that are conducted concurrently during a single phase of data collection and analysis. *See also* concurrent embedded design,

concurrent triangulation design, mixed methods research, single-phase research design.

concurrent triangulation design Mixed-methods research design where quantitative and qualitative data are collected in the same phase so that these data can be compared to see where they converge or diverge in relation to addressing your research question. *See also* concurrent mixed methods research.

confidentiality (1) Concern relating to the right of access to the data provided by the participants and, in particular the need to keep these data secret or private. (2) Promise made by the researcher not to reveal the identity of participants or present findings in a way that enables participants to be identified.

confounding variable Extraneous but difficult to observe or measure variable than can potentially undermine the inferences drawn about the relationship between the independent variable and the dependent variable. *See also* control variable, experiment.

connotative sign Sign which is either a substitute for or a part of the thing for which it stands. *See also* denotative sign, semiotics, sign.

consent form Written agreement, signed by both parties in which the participant agrees to take part in the research and gives her or his permission for data to be used in specified ways.

consent *see* implied consent, informed consent.

constant comparison Process of constantly comparing data to analytical categories and vice versa, as well comparing data with other data and each category with other categories, to develop higher level categories and further your analysis towards the emergence of a grounded theory. *See also* inductive approach; Grounded Theory Method.

construct Attributes that, although not directly observable, can be inferred and assessed using a number of indicators.

construct validity Extent to which your measurement questions actually measure the presence of those constructs you intended them to measure. *See also* convergent validity, discriminant validity.

consultancy report *see* management report.

content analysis Analytical technique of categorising and coding text, voice and visual data using a systematic coding scheme to enable quantitative analysis. *See also:* latent content, manifest content.

content validity *see* face validity.

contextual data Additional data recorded when collecting primary or secondary data that reveals background information about the setting and the data collection process.

contingency table Technique for summarising data from two or more variables so that specific values can be read.

continuing access Gaining agreed research access to an organisation on an incremental basis.

continuous data Data whose values can theoretically take any value (sometimes within a restricted range) provided they can be measured with sufficient accuracy.

contrived data Data that result from a researcher organising an experiment, interview or survey. *See also* natural data.

control group Group in an experiment that, for the sake of comparison, does not receive the intervention in which you are interested. *See also* experiment, experimental group.

control variable Unwanted but measurable variable that needs to be kept constant to avoid it influencing the effect of the independent variable on the dependent variable. *See also* confounding variable, experiment.

controlled index language The terms and phrases used by databases to index items within the database. If search terms do not match the controlled index language, the search is likely to be unsuccessful.

convenience sampling Non-probability haphazard sampling procedure in which cases are selected only on the basis that they are easiest to obtain. *See also* haphazard sampling, non-probability sampling.

convergent interview Participant focused research interview that commences as an unstructured, in-depth interview before using more specific and focused probing questions to converge on an explanation.

convergent validity Overlap (or correlation) between two different scales that have been used to measure the same construct.

correlation coefficient Number between −1 and +1 representing the strength of the relationship between two ranked or numerical variables. A value of +1 represents a perfect positive correlation. A value of −1 represents a perfect negative correlation. Correlation coefficients between +1 and −1 represent weaker positive and negative correlations, a value of 0 meaning the variables are perfectly independent. *See also* negative correlation, Pearson's product moment correlation coefficient, positive correlation, Spearman's rank correlation coefficient.

correlation Extent to which two variables are related to each other. *See also* correlation coefficient, negative correlation, positive correlation.

coverage Extent to which a data set covers the population it is intended to cover.

covering letter Letter accompanying a questionnaire, which explains the purpose of the survey. *See also* introductory letter.

covert observation Observation where intention to observe is concealed from intended informants who are observed without being aware of this. *See also* overt observation.

covert research Research undertaken where those being researched are not aware of this fact.

Cramer's V Statistical test to measure the association between two variables within a table on a scale where 0 represents no association and 1 represents perfect association. Because the value of Cramer's V is always between 0 and 1, the relative strengths of significant associations between different pairs of variables can be compared.

creative thinking technique One of a number of techniques for generating and refining research ideas based on non-rational criteria. These may be, for example, biased heavily in favour of the individual's preferences or the spontaneous ideas of the individual or others. *See also* brainstorming, Delphi technique, relevance tree.

criterion validity Extent to which a scale, measuring instrument or question measures what it is intended to measure. *See also* internal validity.

criterion-related validity Ability of a statistical test to make accurate predictions.

critical (literature) review Detailed and justified analysis and commentary of the merits and faults of the literature within a chosen area, which demonstrates familiarity with what is already known about your research topic.

critical case sampling Non-probability purposive sampling procedure which focuses on selecting those cases on the basis of making a point dramatically or because they are important. *See also* purposive sampling, non-probability sampling.

Critical Discourse Analysis Discourse Analysis that adopts a critical realist philosophy. *See also* Discourse Analysis.

critical ethnography Ethnographic strategy that questions the status quo and often adopts an advocacy role to bring about change. *See also* ethnography, interpretive ethnography, realist ethnography.

critical incidence technique A technique in which respondents are asked to describe in detail a critical incident or number of incidents that is key to the research question. *See also* critical incident.

critical incident Activity or event where the consequences were so clear that the respondent has a definite idea regarding its effects.

critical realism Philosophical stance that what we experience are some of the manifestations of the things in the real world, rather than the actual things. *See also* direct realism, realism.

Cronbach's alpha Statistic used to measure the consistency of responses across a set of questions (scale items) designed together to measure a particular concept (scale). It consists of an alpha coefficient with a value between 0 and 1. Values of 0.7 or above suggest that the questions in the scale are internally consistent. *See also* scale item, scale.

cross-posting Receipt by individuals of multiple copies of an email, often due to the use of multiple mailing lists on which that individual appears.

cross-sectional research Study of a particular phenomenon (or phenomena) at a particular time, i.e. a 'snapshot'.

cross-tabulation *see* contingency table.

D

data cleaning Process of ensuring a transcript is accurate by correcting any transcription errors. *See also* transcript.

data display and analysis Process for the collection and analysis of qualitative data that involves three concurrent subprocesses of data reduction, data display, and drawing and verifying conclusions.

data Facts, opinions and statistics that have been collected together and recorded for reference or for analysis.

data management plan A document that outlines how data will be collected, organised, managed, stored, secured, backed-up and where applicable, shared.

data matrix Table format in which data are usually entered into analysis software consisting of rows (cases) and columns (variables).

data reduction Condensing data by summarising or simplifying these as a means to analyse them. *See also* data display and analysis.

data requirements table A table designed to ensure that, when completed, the data collected will enable the research question(s) to be answered and the objectives achieved.

data sampling Process of only transcribing those sections of an audio-recording that are pertinent to your research, having listened to it repeatedly beforehand.

data saturation Stage when any additional data collected provides few, if any, new insights.

debriefing Providing research participants with a retrospective explanation about a research project and its purpose where covert observation has occurred.

deception Deceiving participants about the nature, purpose or use of research by the researcher(s). *See also* informed consent, research ethics.

decile One of 10 sections when data are ranked and divided into 10 groups of equal size.

deductive approach Approach to theory development involving the testing of a theoretical proposition by the employment of a research strategy specifically designed for the purpose of its testing.

deliberate distortion Form of bias that occurs when data are recorded inaccurately on purpose. It is most common for secondary data sources such as organisational records.

delivery and collection questionnaire Data collection technique in which the questionnaire is delivered to each respondent. She or he then reads and answers the same set of questions in a predetermined order without an interviewer being present before the completed questionnaire is collected.

Delphi technique Technique using a group of people who are either involved or interested in the research topic to generate and select a more specific research idea.

demographic variable Variable that records data about characteristics.

denotative sign Sign in which the meaning being suggested or implied is reasonably obvious or visible. *See also* connotative sign, semiotics, sign.

deontological view View that the ends served by research can never justify research which is unethical.

dependent variable Variable that changes in response to changes in other variables.

descriptive data *see* nominal data.

descriptive observation Observation where the researcher concentrates on observing the physical setting, the key participants and their activities, particular events and their sequence and the attendant processes and emotions involved. *See also* focused observation, selective observation.

descriptive research Research for which the purpose is to produce an accurate representation of persons, events or situations.

descriptive statistics Generic term for statistics that can be used to describe variables.

descripto-explanatory study Study whose purpose is both descriptive and explanatory where, usually, description is the precursor to explanation.

deviant sampling *see* extreme case sampling.

dialogic interview Participant focused research interview designed to establish rapport with the interviewee and gain her or his trust in order to engage reflexively to allow a more open discussion to occur in which pre-conceived ideas and beliefs may be evaluated.

diary study Research project or part of a research project based on the use of research diaries. *See also* qualitative diary study, qualitative research diary, quantitative diary study, quantitative research diary, research diary.

dichotomous data Nominal data that are grouped into two categories. *See also* nominal data.

direct participation and observation Technique used in participant observation to collect data. *See also* participant observation.

direct realism Philosophical stance that what you see is what you get: what we experience through our senses portrays the world accurately. *See also* critical realism, realism.

directional hypothesis Tentative, usually testable, explanation of the direction of the association, difference or relationship between two or more variables. *See also* alternative hypothesis, hypothesis, null hypothesis.

directional null hypothesis Tentative, usually testable statement that there is no directional association, difference or relationship between two or more variables. *See also* alternative hypothesis, directional hypothesis, null hypothesis.

discourse analysis General term covering a variety of approaches to the analysis of language in its own right. It explores how language constructs and simultaneously reproduces and/or changes the social world rather than using it as a means to reveal the social world as a phenomenon.

discourse Term used in discourse analysis to describe how language is used to shape meanings and give rise to social practices and relations. *See also* discourse analysis.

discrete data Data whose values are measured in discrete units and therefore can take only one of a finite number of values from a scale that measures changes in this way.

discussion Section of the project report in which the wider implications of the findings (and conclusions) are considered.

dispersion measures Generic term for statistics that can be used to provide an impression of how the values for a variable are dispersed around the central tendency.

dissertation Usual name for research projects undertaken as part of undergraduate and taught master's degrees. Dissertations are usually written for an academic audience.

divergent validity Absence of overlap (or correlation) between different scales used to measure theoretically distinct constructs. *See also* construct validity.

document secondary data Data that, unlike the spoken word, endure physically (including digitally) as evidence allowing them to be transposed across both time and space and reanalysed for a purpose different to that for which they were originally collected. They include text, audio and visual media.

document summary Type of summary used an analytical aid. *See also* interim summary; transcript summary.

document visual data Visual data comprising two-dimensional static, two-dimensional moving and three-dimensional lived media. *See also* found visual image,

three-dimensional lived media, two-dimensional static media, two-dimensional moving media.

DOI Digital object identifier name used to uniquely identify an electronic document such as a specific journal article stored in an online database.

dominant code Conventional understandings and expectations influenced by prevailing ideology. *See also* Code (3).

double-phase research design Research involving two phases of data collection and analysis. *See also* sequential mixed methods research.

Durbin–Watson statistic Statistical test to measure the extent to which the value of a dependent variable at time t is related to its value at the previous time period, $t - 1$ (autocorrelation). The statistic ranges in value from zero to 4. A value of 2 indicates no autocorrelation. A value of towards zero indicates positive autocorrelation. A value towards 4 indicates negative autocorrelation. *See also* autocorrelation.

E

ecological validity Type of external validity referring to the extent to which findings can be generalised from one group to another. *See also* external validity.

effect size index Measure of the practical significance of a statistically significant difference, association or relationship. The statistic is normally used when the data sample is large.

electronic interview Internet- or intranet-mediated interview conducted through either a chat room, Internet forum, web conferencing or email. *See also* email interview, chat room, Internet forum.

electronic questionnaire Internet- or intranet-mediated questionnaire. *See also* Internet-mediated questionnaire, intranet-mediated questionnaire.

element Individual case or group member within a sample or population such as an employee.

elite person access When an individual who is notable in their field (but does not necessarily have an organisational affiliation) is willing to provide data to the researcher.

email interview Series of emails each containing a small number of questions rather than one email containing a series of questions.

embedded mixed-methods research Use of quantitative and qualitative methods in research design where use of one is embedded within the other. *See also* concurrent embedded design, concurrent mixed methods research.

emergent case study Case study strategy where the researcher allows the focus of the research to emerge through their engagement with the case study environment. *See also* case study.

epistemological relativism Subjectivist approach to knowledge that recognises knowledge is historically situated and that social facts are social constructions agreed on by people rather than existing independently.

epistemology Branch of philosophy concerned with assumptions about knowledge, what constitutes acceptable, valid and legitimate knowledge, and how we can communicate knowledge to others.

ethics *see* research ethics, research ethics committees, code of ethics.

ethnography Research strategy that focuses upon describing and interpreting the social world through first-hand field study.

evaluation Process of judging materials or methods in terms of internal accuracy and consistency or by comparison with external criteria.

event variable Variable that records data about events, what happened in the past, now or will happen in the future.

existing contacts Colleagues, friends, relatives or fellow students who may agree to become research informants, participants or respondents.

experiential data Data about the researcher's perceptions and feelings as the research develops.

experiential meaning Equivalence of meaning of a word or sentence for different people in their everyday experiences.

experiment Research strategy whose purpose is to study the probability of a change in an independent variable causing a change in another, dependent variable. Involves the definition of null and alternative hypotheses; random allocation of participants to either an experimental group(s) or a control group; manipulation of the independent variable; measurement of changes in the dependent variable; and control of other variables. *See also* between-subjects design, control group, experimental group, quasi-experiment.

experimental group Group in an experiment that receives the intervention in which you are interested. *See also* control group, experiment.

explanation building Deductive process for analysing qualitative data that involves the iterative examination of a number of strategically selected cases to test a theoretical proposition.

explanatory research Research that focuses on studying a situation or a problem in order to explain the relationships between variables.

exploratory data analysis (EDA) Approach to data analysis that emphasises the use of diagrams to explore and understand the data.

exploratory study Research that aims to seek new insights into phenomena, to ask questions, and to assess the phenomena in a new light.

external researcher Researcher who wishes to gain access to an organisation for which she or he does not work. *See also* access, internal researcher.

external validity Extent to which the research results from a particular study are generalisable to all relevant contexts.

extreme case sampling Non-probability purposive sampling procedure which focuses on unusual or special cases. *See also* purposive sampling, non-probability sampling.

F

fabrication Act of inventing any part of your research including but not limited to participants, data, findings and conclusions. This is a totally unacceptable and unethical course of action. *See also* falsification.

face validity Agreement that a question, scale, or measure appears logically to reflect accurately what it was intended to measure.

factual variable Variable that records factual data.

falsification Act of distorting or misrepresenting any part of your research including but not limited to data, findings and conclusions. This is a totally unacceptable and unethical course of action. *See also* fabrication.

feasibility [of access] Being able to negotiate access to conduct research.

fieldwork (1) Traditional ethnographic approach that involves the researcher physically going to the place where intended informants live, work or otherwise socially interact, to conduct observation. *See also* naturalistic observation. (2) Collection of data from respondents, participants or informants in their own settings.

filter question Closed question that identifies those respondents for whom the following question or questions are not applicable, enabling them to skip these questions.

focus group Group interview, composed of a small number of participants, facilitated by a 'moderator', in which the topic is defined clearly and precisely and there is a focus on enabling and recording interactive discussion between participants. *See also* group interview.

focused coding Analysis or reanalysis of data to identify which of the initial codes may be used as higher level codes to categorise larger units of data to further the analysis towards the emergence of a grounded theory.

focused interview Interviewer exercises direction over the interview while allowing the interviewee's opinions to emerge as he or she responds to the questions of the researcher.

focused observation Phase in an observation study when the researcher focuses her or his observations on particular events or interactions between key informants. *See also* descriptive observation, selective observation.

follow-up Contact made with respondents to thank them for completing and returning a survey and to remind non-respondents to complete and return their surveys.

forced-choice question *see* closed question.

forum *see* Internet forum.

found visual image Photograph or other still image which already exists, is accessible to the researcher and relevant to the research. *See also* document visual image, two-dimensional static media.

frequency distribution Table for summarising data from one variable so that specific values can be read.

frequency polygon Line graph connecting the mid points of the bars of a histogram or bar graph.

full-text online database Online database that indexes and provides a summary and full text of articles from a range of journals. Sometimes includes books, chapters from books, reports, theses and conference papers.

fully integrated mixed-methods research Use of both quantitative and qualitative methods throughout the research. *See also* partially integrated mixed methods research.

functionalist paradigm Paradigm concerned with rational explanations and developing sets of recommendations within the current structures such as why a particular organisational problem is occurring in terms of the functions they perform.

fundamental research *see* basic research.

G

Gantt chart Chart that provides a simple visual representation of the tasks or activities that make up a project, each being plotted against a time line.

gatekeeper Person, often in an organisation, who controls research access.

general focus research question Question that flows from the research idea and may lead to several more detailed questions or the definition of research objectives.

generalisability Extent to which the findings of a research study are applicable to other settings.

generalisation Making of more widely applicable propositions based upon the process of deduction from specific cases.

Goldilocks test Test to decide whether research questions are either too big, too small, too hot or just right. Those that are too big probably demand too many resources. Questions that are too small are likely to be of insufficient substance, while those that are too hot may be so because of sensitivities that may be aroused as a result of doing the research.

grammatical error Error of grammar that detracts from the authority of the project report.

graph Visual display that illustrates the values of one variable or the relationship between two or more variables.

grey literature *see* primary literature.

grounded theory (1) Including both Grounded Theory Methodology and Grounded Theory Method. (2) Theory that is grounded or developed using an inductive approach. *See also* Grounded Theory Methodology, Grounded Theory Method, inductive approach.

Grounded Theory (Methodology) Research strategy in which theory is developed from data collected by a series of observations or interviews principally involving an inductive approach. *See also* deductive approach, Grounded Theory Method, inductive approach.

Grounded Theory Method Data collection techniques and analytic procedures used in a Grounded Theory research strategy to derive meaning from the subjects and settings being studied. *See also* Grounded Theory (Methodology).

group interview General term to describe all non-standardised interviews conducted with two or more people.

H

habituation Situation where, in observation studies, the subjects being observed become familiar with the process of observation so that they take it for granted. This is an attempt to overcome 'observer effect' or reactivity.

haphazard sampling Non-probability sampling procedure in which cases are selected without any obvious principles of organisation. *See also* convenience sampling, non-probability sampling.

harking Hypothesizing after results are known.

hermeneutics Strand of interpretivism that focuses on the study of cultural artefacts such as texts, symbols, stories, images. *See also* intepretivism.

heterogeneous sampling Non-probability purposive sampling procedure which focuses on obtaining the maximum variation in the cases selected. *See also* purposive sampling, non-probability sampling.

heteroscedasticity Extent to which the data values for the dependent and independent variables have unequal variances. *See also* variance.

histogram Diagram for showing frequency distributions for a grouped continuous data variable in which the area of each bar represents the frequency of occurrence.

homogeneous sampling Non-probability purposive sampling procedure which focuses on selecting cases from one particular subgroup in which all the members are similar. *See also* purposive sampling, non-probability sampling.

homoscedasticity Extent to which the data values for the dependent and independent variables have equal variances. *See also* variance.

hybrid access Use of both traditional access and Internet-mediated access to conduct research.

hypothesis (1) Tentative, usually testable, explanation that there is an association, difference or relationship between two or more variables. Often referred to as H_1. *See also* alternative hypothesis, non-directional hypothesis, directional hypothesis, null hypothesis. (2) Testable proposition about the relationship between two or more events or concepts.

hypothesis testing Classical approach to assessing the statistical significance of findings from a sample. *See also* hypothesis, non-directional hypothesis, directional hypothesis.

I

iconic sign Sign in which the signifier resembles the object being signified. *See also* indexical sign, semiotics, sign, symbolic sign.

ideology *see* dominant code.

idiomatic meaning Meaning ascribed to a group of words that are natural to a native speaker, but which is not deducible from the individual words.

in-depth interview *see* unstructured interview.

incommensurability Assertion that the radical humanist, radical structuralist, interpretive and functionalist paradigms contain mutually incompatible assumptions and therefore cannot be combined. *See also* functionalist paradigm, interpretive paradigm, radical humanist paradigm, radical structuralist paradigm.

independent groups *t*-test Statistical test to determine the probability (likelihood) that the values of a numerical data variable for two independent samples or groups are different. The test assesses the likelihood of any difference between these two groups occurring by chance alone.

independent measures Use of more than one experimental group in an experiment where more than one intervention or manipulation is to be tested and measured. *See also* experiment.

independent variable Variable that causes changes to a dependent variable or variables.

index number Summary data value calculated from a base period for numerical variables, to facilitate comparisons of trends or changes over time. *See also* base period.

indexical sign Sign in which the object being signified is inherently indicated. *See also* iconic sign, semiotics, sign, symbolic sign.

individual person access When an individual, who is not affiliated to an organisation, is willing to provide data.

inductive approach Approach to theory development involving the development of a theory as a result of the observation of empirical data.

ineligible respondent Respondent selected for a sample who does not meet the requirements of the research.

inference, statistical *see* statistical inference.

inferred consent Informants, participants or respondents may or may not fully understand the implications of taking part but their consent to participate is inferred from their participating in the research. The researcher assumes that data may be recorded, analysed, used, stored or reported as she or he wishes without clarifying such issues with those who take part. *See also* informed consent.

informant error Errors that occur when informants are observed in situations that are inconsistent with their normal behaviour patterns, leading to atypical responses. *See also* informants.

informant interview Interview guided by the perceptions of the interviewee.

informant verification Form of triangulation in which the researcher presents written accounts of, for example, interview notes to informants for them to verify the content. *See also* triangulation.

informants Those who agree to be observed in participant observation or structured observation studies.

informed consent Position achieved when intended participants are fully informed about the nature, purpose and use of research to be undertaken and their role within it, and where their consent to participate, if provided, is freely given. *See also* deception, implied consent.

initial coding *see* open coding.

initial sample Purposively selected initial case from which to collect and analyse data used in Grounded Theory. *See also* Grounded Theory Method.

instrument *see* questionnaire.

integer A whole number.

inter-library loan System for borrowing a book or obtaining a copy of a journal article from another library.

inter-quartile range Difference between the upper and lower quartiles, representing the middle 50 per cent of the data when the data values for a variable have been ranked.

inter-rater reliability Extent which two coders agree when coding the same set of data.

interdiscursivity Way one discourse is introduced into another discourse within discourse analysis. *See also* discourse analysis.

interim summary Type of summary used to outline progress and to aid analysis. *See also* document summary, transcript summary.

internal researcher Person who conducts research within an organisation for which they work. *See also* cognitive access, external researcher.

internal validity Extent to which findings can be attributed to interventions rather than any flaws in your research design. *See also* measurement validity.

Internet forum Commonly referred to as web forums, message boards, discussion boards, discussion forums, discussion groups and bulletin boards. Usually only deal with one topic and discourage personal exchanges.

Internet questionnaire Data collection technique in which the questionnaire is delivered online to each respondent. She or he then reads and answers the same set of questions in a predetermined order without an interviewer being present before returning it electronically. *See also* Web questionnaire, mobile questionnaire.

Internet-mediated access Use of Internet technologies to gain virtual access to conduct research.

Internet-mediated observation Adaptation of traditional observation from oral/visual/near to textual/digital/virtual to allow researchers purely to observe or participate with members of an online community to collect data.

Internet-mediated structured observation Type of Internet-mediated observation which broadly follows the approach to structured observation. *See also* Internet-mediated observation, Internet-mediated participant observation, structured observation.

interpretive ethnography Ethnographic strategy stressing subjectivity, reflection and identifying multiple meanings. *See also* ethnography, critical ethnography, realist ethnography.

interpretive paradigm Paradigm concerned with the way humans attempt to make sense of the world around them; for example, understanding the fundamental meanings attached to organisational life.

interpretivism Philosophical stance that advocates humans are different from physical phenomena because they create meanings. Argues that human beings and their social worlds cannot be studied in the same way as physical phenomena due to the need to take account of complexity.

intertextuality Way a text or texts overtly or covertly borrow from and are informed by other texts within Discourse Analysis. *See also* Discourse Analysis.

interval data Numerical data for which the difference or 'interval' between any two data values for a particular variable can be stated, but for which the relative difference can not be stated. *See also* numerical data.

interview guide Plan for conducting a semi-structured interview containing opening comments, list of themes, questions and prompts to encourage discussion, and comments to close it. Sometimes referred to as an interview schedule, although this is more appropriate to a structured interview. See also unstructured interview, semi-structured interview, structured interview.

interview schedule *see* structured interview.

interviewee bias Attempt by an interviewee to construct an account that hides some data or when she or he presents herself or himself in a socially desirable role or situation.

interviewer bias Attempt by an interviewer to introduce bias during the conduct of an interview, or where the appearance or behaviour of the interviewer has the effect of introducing bias in the interviewee's responses.

interviewer-completed questionnaire Data collection technique in which an interviewer reads the same set of questions to the respondent in a predetermined order and records his or her responses. *See also* structured interview, telephone questionnaire.

intra-rater reliability Reliability of coding by a single coder over time.

intranet-mediated access Use of an intranet within an organisation to gain access to conduct research.

Introduction Opening to the project report, which gives the reader a clear idea of the central issue of concern of the research, states the research question(s) and research objectives, and explains the research context and the structure of the project report.

introductory letter Request for research access, addressed to an intended participant or organisational broker/gatekeeper, stating the purpose of the research, the nature of the help being sought, and the requirements of agreeing to participate. *See also* covering letter, gatekeeper.

intrusive research methods Methods that involve direct access to participants, including qualitative interviewing, observation, longitudinal research based on these methods and phenomenologically based approaches to research. *See also* access, cognitive access.

investigative question One of a number of questions that need to be answered in order to address satisfactorily each research question and meet each objective.

'in vivo' codes Names or labels for codes based on actual terms used by those who take part in research.

J

journal *see* professional journal, refereed academic journal.

judgemental sampling *see* purposive sampling.

K

Kendall's rank correlation coefficient Statistical test that assesses the strength of the relationship between two ranked data variables, especially where the data for a variable contain tied ranks. For data collected from a sample, there is also a need to calculate the probability of the correlation coefficient having occurred by chance alone.

key word Basic term selected from the controlled index language specified by the online database to describe the research question(s) and objectives to search the tertiary literature.

Kolmogorov–Smirnov test Statistical test to determine the probability (likelihood) that an observed set of values for each category of a variable differs from a specified distribution. Common uses are to discover whether a data variable's distribution differs significantly from a normal distribution, or an alternative distribution such as that of the population from which it was selected.

kurtosis Pointedness or flatness of a distribution's shape compared with the normal distribution. If a distribution is pointier or peaked, it is leptokurtic and the kurtosis value is positive. If a distribution is flatter, it is platykurtic and the kurtosis value is negative. *See also* normal distribution.

L

latent content Meanings in the data that may lie behind the manifest content and so need to be interpreted or inferred. *See also* content analysis, manifest content.

law of large numbers Samples of larger absolute size are more likely to be representative of the population from which they are drawn than smaller samples and, in particular, the mean (average) calculated for the sample is more likely to equal the mean for the population, providing the samples are not biased.

lemmatization Removal of inflectional endings, taking categories and inflections into account, to reduce a word to its base or 'lemma'.

level of access Nature and depth of access to participants required and achieved. *See also* cognitive access, continuing access, physical access.

leverage-saliency theory Theory suggesting that single design attributes will have different leverages for different individuals on the decision to respond positively or negatively to a request to participate in research. *See also* non-response.

lexical meaning Precise meaning of an individual word.

Likert-style rating question Rating question that allows the respondent to indicate how strongly she or he agrees or disagrees with a statement.

line graph Diagram for showing trends in longitudinal data for a variable.

linearity Degree to which change in a dependent variable is related to change in one or more independent variables. *See also* dependent variable, independent variable.

list question Closed question, in which the respondent is offered a list of items and instructed to select those that are appropriate.

literal replication Replication of findings across selected multiple case studies in a case study strategy. *See also* case study, theoretical replication.

literature review *see* critical (literature) review.

logical reasoning Process used in theory development to explain why relationships may exist based on what is already known.

long-term trend The overall direction of movement of numerical data values for a single variable after variations have been smoothed out. *See also* moving average.

longitudinal data Set of data repeated over time usually at regular intervals.

longitudinal study Study of a particular phenomenon (or phenomena) over an extended period of time.

lower quartile Value below which a quarter of the data values lie when the data values for a variable have been ranked.

M

mail questionnaire *see* postal questionnaire.

management report Abbreviated version of the project report, usually written for a practitioner audience. Normally includes a brief account of objectives, method, findings, conclusions and recommendations.

manifest content Components in the data that are clearly visible and can be counted. *See also* content analysis, latent content.

Mann–Whitney *U* test Statistical test to determine the probability (likelihood) that the values of a ordinal data variable for two independent samples or groups are different. The test assesses the likelihood of any difference between these two groups occurring by chance alone and is often used when the assumptions of the independent samples *t*-test are not met.

matched pair analysis Used in an experimental design to match participants in an experimental group with those in a control group before conducting the experiment where random assignment is not possible. *See also* quasi-experiment.

matrix question Series of two or more closed questions in which each respondent's answers are recorded using the same grid.

maximum variation sampling *see* heterogeneous sampling.

mean Average value calculated by adding up the values of each case for a variable and dividing by the total number of cases.

measurement validity *see* criterion validity.

median Middle value when all the values of a variable are arranged in rank order; sometimes known as the 50th percentile.

mediating variable Variable that transmits the effect of an independent variable to a dependent variable. *See also* dependent variable, independent variable.

member validation Process of allowing participants to comment on and correct data to validate these.

memo writing Key element used in Grounded Theory Method during the collection, analysis and interpretation of data, which helps to facilitate and link these stages of research and aid the development of a grounded theory. May also be used in other research strategies.

method Techniques and procedures used to obtain and analyse research data, including for example questionnaires, observation, interviews, and statistical and non-statistical techniques.

methodological rigour Strength and quality of the research method used in terms of the planning, data collection, data analysis, and subsequent reporting; and therefore the confidence that can be placed in the conclusions drawn. *See also* theoretical rigour.

methodology Theory of how research should be undertaken, including the theoretical and philosophical assumptions upon which research is based and the implications of these for the method or methods adopted.

minimal interaction Process in which the observer tries as much as possible to 'melt into the background', having as little interaction as possible with the subjects of the observation. This is an attempt to overcome observer effect. *See also* observer effect.

mixed methods research Use of both quantitative and qualitative data collection techniques and analysis procedures either at the same time (concurrent) or one after the other (sequential).

mixed-model research Combination of quantitative and qualitative data collection techniques and analysis procedures as well as combining quantitative and qualitative approaches in other phases of the research such as research question generation.

mobile questionnaire Data collection technique in which the questionnaire is delivered electronically to each respondent's mobile telephone. She or he then reads and answers the same set of questions in a predetermined order without an interviewer being present before returning it electronically. *See also* online questionnaire.

modal group Most frequently occurring category for data that have been grouped.

mode Value of a variable that occurs most frequently.

Mode 0 knowledge creation Research based on power and patronage, these being particularly visible in the close relationships between sponsor and researcher.

Mode 1 knowledge creation Research of a fundamental rather than applied nature, in which the questions are set and solved by academic interests with little, if any, focus on exploitation of research by practitioners.

Mode 2 knowledge creation Research of an applied nature, governed by the world of practice and highlighting the importance of collaboration both with and between practitioners.

Mode 3 knowledge creation Research growing out of Mode 1 and Mode 2 whose purpose is 'to assure survival and promote the common good at various levels of social aggregation' (Huff and Huff 2001:S53).

mode effect Impact of the method used to conduct an interview on its outcome; for example, the respective mode effects of face-to-face interviews, telephone interviews or electronic interviews on outcomes.

moderate participation Situation where a researcher enters a research setting with the intention of taking on some of the attributes of being an 'insider' where necessary while maintaining other characteristics of being an 'outsider'. *See also* participant observation, active participation.

moderating variable Variable that affects the relationship between an independent variable and a dependent variable. *See also* dependent variable, independent variable.

moderator Facilitator of focus group interviews. *See also* focus group, group interview.

mono method Use of a single data collection technique and corresponding analysis procedure or procedures.

moving average Statistical method of smoothing out variations in numerical data recorded for a single variable over time to enable the long-term trend to be seen more clearly. *See also* long-term trend.

multi-method Use of more than one data collection technique and corresponding analysis procedure or procedures.

multi-method qualitative study Use of more than one qualitative data collection technique and corresponding qualitative analysis procedure or procedures.

multi-method quantitative study Use of more than one quantitative data collection technique and corresponding quantitative analysis procedure or procedures.

multi-organisation access Process of gaining entry into multiple organisations to conduct research.

multi-phase research design Research involving more than two phases of data collection and analysis. *See also* sequential mixed methods research.

multi-stage sampling Sampling design that occurs in two or more successive stages and uses either probability, non-probability, or both types of sample selection techniques.

multicollinearity *see* collinearity.

multiple bar graph/chart Diagram for comparing frequency distributions for categorical or grouped discrete or continuous data variables, which highlights the highest and lowest values.

multiple line graph Diagram for comparing trends over time between numerical data variables.

multiple methods Use of more than one data collection technique and analysis procedure or procedures. *See also* mixed methods.

multiple regression analysis Process of calculating a coefficient of multiple determination and regression equation using two or more independent variables and one dependent variable. For data collected from a sample, there is also a need to calculate the probability of the regression coefficient having occurred by chance alone. *See also* multiple regression coefficient, regression analysis, regression equation.

multiple-dichotomy method Method of data coding using a separate variable for each possible response to an open question or an item in a list question. *See also* list question, open question.

multiple-response method Method of data coding using the same number of variables as the maximum number of responses to an open question or a list question by any one case. *See also* list question, open question.

multiple-source secondary data Secondary data created by combining two or more different data sets prior to the data being accessed for the research. These data sets can be based entirely on documentary or on survey data, or can be an amalgam of the two.

N

narrative Personal account that interprets an event or series of events, which is significant for the narrator and which convey meaning to the researcher, and which are narrated in a sequenced way. *See also* narrative inquiry.

Narrative Analysis Collection and analysis of qualitative data that preserves the integrity and narrative value of data collected, thereby avoiding their fragmentation.

narrative inquiry Qualitative research strategy to collect the experiences of participants as whole accounts or narratives, or which attempts to reconstruct such experiences into narratives. *See also* narrative.

narrative interview Participant focused research interview designed to generate storied accounts. *See also* in-depth interview, semi-structured interview, biographical interview.

natural data Data that are recorded from real conversations that take place in everyday, authentic situations. *See also* contrived data.

naturalistic Adopting an ethnographic strategy in which the researcher researches the phenomenon within the context in which it occurs.

naturalistic observation Type of observation conducted in a 'real world' location where intention is to conduct observation without influencing the setting being observed. *See also* fieldwork.

negative cases Cases that do not support emergent explanations, but which help the refining of these explanations and direct the selection of further cases to collect data.

negative correlation Relationship between two variables for which, as the values of one variable increase, the values of the other variable decrease. *See also* correlation coefficient.

negative skew Distribution of numerical data for a variable in which the majority of the data are found bunched to the right, with a long tail to the left.

netiquette General operating guidelines for using the Internet, including not sending junk emails.

new contacts People approached to become research informants, participants or respondents previously unknown to the researcher.

nominal data Data whose values cannot be measured numerically but can be distinguished by classifying into sets (categories).

nominalism Ontological position that asserts that the order and structures of social phenomena (and the phenomena themselves) are created by social actors through use of language, conceptual categories, perceptions and consequent actions.

non-binary pronoun Gender neutral pronoun used to refer to an individual or group of people.

non-directional hypothesis Tentative, usually testable, explanation of the association, difference or relationship between two or more variables. Also known as two-direction hypothesis. *See also* alternative hypothesis, hypothesis, null hypothesis.

non-maleficence Avoidance of harm.

non-numerical data All forms of data that are not numerical, for example text, voice and visual.

non-parametric statistic Statistic designed to be used with categorical data, that is when the data are dichotomous, nominal or ordinal.

non-participant observer Situation where researcher is detached from the event being observed and does not share any physical or virtual proximity to those being observed. *See also* collaborative observation, complete observer, complete participant, observer as participant, participant as observer.

non-probability sampling Selection of sampling techniques in which the chance or probability of each case being selected is not known.

non-random sampling *see* non-probability sampling.

non-response bias Bias in findings caused by respondent refusing to take part in the research or answer a question.

non-response error Situation where non-respondents in an intended sample differ in important ways from those who participate in the research. *See also* non-response, non-response bias.

non-response When the respondent refuses to take part in the research or answer a question.

non-standardised interview *see* semi-structured interview, unstructured interview.

normal distribution Special form of the symmetric distribution in which the numerical data for a variable can be plotted as a bell-shaped curve.

notebook of ideas Book or equivalent for noting down any interesting research ideas as you think of them.

null hypothesis Tentative, usually testable, statement stating that there is no association, difference or relationship between two or more variables. Often referred to as H_0. *See also* alternative hypothesis, directional null hypothesis, hypothesis.

numeric rating question Rating question that uses numbers as response options to identify and record the respondent's response. The end response options, and sometimes the middle, are labelled.

numerical data Data whose values can be measured numerically as quantities.

O

objectivism Ontological position that incorporates the assumptions of the natural sciences arguing that social reality is external to, and independent of, social actors concerned with their existence. *See also* ontology, subjectivism.

objectivity Avoidance of (conscious) bias and subjective selection during the conduct and reporting of research.

In some research philosophies the researcher will consider that interpretation is likely to be related to a set of values and therefore will attempt to recognise and explore this.

observation Systematic observing, recording, description, analysis and interpretation of people's behaviour. *See also* participant observation, structured observation.

observer as participant Observational role in which the researcher observes activities without taking part in those activities in the same way as the 'real' research subjects. The researcher's identity as a researcher and research purpose is clear to all concerned. *See also* participant as observer.

observer bias May occur when observers give inaccurate responses in order to distort the results of the research.

observer drift Occurs when the observer starts to redefine the way in which similar observations are interpreted leading to inconsistency.

observer effect Impact of being observed on how people act. *See also* habituation, reactivity.

observer error Systematic errors made by an observer, as a result of tiredness, for example.

one stage cluster sampling *see* cluster sampling.

one-way analysis of variance *see* analysis of variance.

online first Publication of forthcoming articles online, prior to them appearing in a journal.

online form (questionnaire) *see* Internet questionnaire.

ontology Branch of philosophy concerned with assumptions about the nature of reality or being. *See also* axiology, epistemology.

open coding Process of disaggregating data into units in grounded theory.

open question Question allowing respondents to give answers in their own way.

operationalisation Translation of concepts into tangible indicators of their existence.

opinion variable Variable that records what respondents believe about something, what they think is true or false.

opportunistic sampling Non-probability purposive sampling procedure in which new potential cases which emerge unexpectedly are recognised as potential opportunities and assessed as to their utility. *See also* purposive sampling, non-probability sampling.

ordinal data Data whose values cannot be measured numerically but which can be placed in a definite order (rank).

orthodox case study Case study strategy which is rigorously defined and highly structured before the research commences, with the intention it will be operationalised in a linear manner. *See also* case study.

outlier Case or unit of analysis that has extreme values for a variable which may distort the interpretation of data or make a statistic misleading.

overt observation Situation in which observation occurs openly following agreement by intended informants to a researcher's request. *See also* covert observation.

P

paired *t*-test Statistical test to determine the probability (likelihood) that the values of two (a pair of) numerical data variables collected for the same cases are different. The test assesses the likelihood of any difference between two variables (each half of the pair) occurring by chance alone.

paradigm Set of basic and taken-for-granted assumptions which underwrite the frame of reference, mode of theorising and ways of working in which a group operates.

paradigmatic analysis Approach used in the analysis of visual images which explores relations between signs by examining how the substitution of alternative signs for one sign will alter that sign's signified meaning in relation to other signs. *See also* semiotics, sign, syntagmatic analysis.

parametric statistic Statistic designed to be used when data are normally distributed. Used with numerical data. *See also* numerical data.

partial response Level of response to questionnaires or structured interviews in which 50 per cent to 80 per cent of all questions are answered other than by a refusal or no answer.

partially integrated mixed-methods research Use of both quantitative and qualitative methods at only one stage or at particular stages of the research. *See also* fully integrated mixed methods research.

participant Person who answers the questions, usually in an interview or group interview.

participant as observer Observational role in which the researcher takes part in and observes activities in the same way as the 'real' research subjects. The researcher's identity as a researcher and research purpose is clear to all concerned. *See also* observer as participant.

participant drawing Technique used in a visual interview when a participant is asked to create a drawing using paper and pencil to represent her or his feelings about an issue, or some aspect of his or her experience and to discuss this. *See also* visual interview.

participant information sheet Document providing information required by gatekeepers and intended participants in order for informed consent to be considered.

participant observation Observation in which the researcher attempts to participate fully in the lives and activities of the research subjects and thus becomes a member of the subjects' group(s), organisation(s) or community. *See also* complete observer, complete participant, observer as participant, participant as observer.

participant photography Participatory data collection technique in which informants are provided with digital cameras or asked to use their mobile phones as cameras to record their experiences or perspectives, including the freedom to choose the subject of each image they take. *See also* participatory video, participatory audio.

participant researcher *see* internal researcher.

participant validation *see* member validation.

participation bias Type of bias resulting from the nature of the individuals or organisational participants who agree to take part in a research study.

participation rate Proportion of respondents invited to take part in an online panel survey who provide a usable response.

participatory audio Participatory data collection technique in which informants are provided with audio recorders to let them to record their experiences or perspectives, including the freedom to choose what to record. *See also* participant photography, participatory video.

participatory video Participatory data collection technique in which informants are provided with video cameras to let them to record their experiences or perspectives, including the freedom to choose what to record. *See also* participant photography, participatory audio, video diarists, video diary.

passive voice Voice in which the subject of the sentence undergoes the action of the verb: for example, 'interviews were conducted'.

pattern matching Analysis of qualitative data involving the prediction of a pattern of outcomes based on theoretical propositions to seek to explain a set of findings.

Pearson's product moment correlation coefficient Statistical test that assesses the strength of the relationship between two numerical data variables. For data collected from a sample there is also a need to calculate the probability of the correlation coefficient having occurred by chance alone.

percentage component bar graph/chart Diagram for comparing proportions for all types of data variables.

percentile One of 100 sections when data are ranked and divided into 100 groups of equal size.

personal data Category of data, defined in law, relating to identified or identifiable persons. *See also* sensitive personal data.

personal entry Situation where the researcher needs to conduct research within an organisation, rather than rely on the use and completion of self-administered, postal questionnaires or the use of publicly available secondary data. *See* access.

personal pronoun One of the pronouns used to refer to people: I, me, you, he, she, we, us, they, him, her, them.

phenomenology Strand of interpretivism that focuses on participants' lived experience, that is the participants' recollections and interpretations of those experiences, being particularly concerned with generating meanings and gaining insights into those phenomena. *See also* interpretivism.

Phi Statistic to measure association between two variables using a scale between −1 (perfect negative association), through 0 (no association) to +1 (perfect association).

photo essay Research output that combines digital or photographic images and text to present thematic visual representations. *See also* photo novella.

photo novella Research output that combines digital or photographic images and text to present a narrative visual account. *See also* photo essay.

photoelicitation Technique used in a visual interview where a participant is given one or more photographic or digital images to interpret. *See also* visual interview.

photovoice Technique which involves participants using participant photography for research focusing on a social concern and meeting with other participants in group discussions to present, discuss and analyse images which they have created. *See also* participant photography, reflexive photography, visual interviews.

physical access Initial level of gaining access to an organisation to conduct research. *See also* cognitive access, continuing access, gatekeeper.

pictogram Diagram in which a picture or series of pictures are used to represent the data proportionally.

pie chart Diagram frequently used for showing proportions for a categorical data or a grouped continuous or discrete data variable.

pilot test Small-scale study to test data collection techniques to minimise the likelihood of problems in data collection and recording as well as allow some assessment of the validity and the reliability of the data that will be collected.

plagiarism Presenting work or ideas as if they are your own when in reality they are the work or ideas of someone else, and failing to acknowledge the original source.

pluralist view of research Belief that flexibility in the selection of both qualitative and qualitative methods is legitimate and researchers should be tolerant of others' preferred methods even when they differ from their own.

politically important sampling Non-probability purposive sampling procedure in which cases are selected or excluded on the basis of participants' connections with politically sensitive issues. *See also* purposive sampling, non-probability sampling.

polysemy Indicating multiple meanings. *See also* semiotics.

population Complete set of cases or group members. *See also* research population.

positive correlation Relationship between two variables for which, as the value of one variable increases, the values of the other variable also increase. *See also* correlation coefficient.

positive skew Distribution of numerical data for a variable in which the majority of the data are found bunched to the left, with a long tail to the right.

positivism Philosophical stance of the natural scientist entailing working with an observable social reality to produce law-like generalisations. The emphasis is on highly structured methodology to facilitate replication.

post-test Outcome measurement for the dependent variable in an experiment. *See also* pre-test.

postal questionnaire Data collection technique in which the questionnaire is delivered by post to each respondent. She or he then reads and answers the same set of questions in a predetermined order without an interviewer being present before returning it by post.

postmodernism Philosophical stance emphasising the role of language and power-relations that seeks to question accepted ways of thinking and give voice to alternative marginalised views.

PowerPoint™ Microsoft computer package that allows the presenter to design overhead slides using text, pictures, photographs etc., which lend a professional appearance.

practitioner-researcher Role occupied by a researcher when she or he is conducting research in an organisation, often her or his own, while fulfilling her or his normal working role.

pragmatism Philosophical stance that argues that concepts are only relevant where they support action. It considers research starts with a problem, and aims to contribute practical solutions that inform future practice. Pragmatists research may vary considerably in terms of how objectivist or subjectivist it is. *See also* objectivist, subjectivist.

pre-coding Process of incorporating coding schemes in questions prior to a questionnaire's administration.

pre-set codes Codes established prior to data collection and often included as part of the data collection form.

pre-survey contact Contact made with a respondent to advise them of a forthcoming survey in which she or he will be asked to take part.

pre-test Baseline measurement for the dependent variable in an experiment. *See also* post-test.

predictive validity *see* criterion-related validity.

predictor variable *see* independent variable

preliminary inquiry Process by which a research idea is refined in order to turn it into a research project. This may be simply a review of the relevant literature.

preliminary search Way of searching the literature that may be helpful in generating research ideas. It may be based, for example, on lecture notes or course textbooks.

primary data Data collected specifically for the research project being undertaken.

primary literature First occurrence of a piece of work, including published sources such as government white papers and planning documents and unpublished manuscript sources such as letters, memos and committee minutes.

primary observation Observation where the researcher notes what happened or what was said at the time. This is often done by keeping a research diary.

privacy Primary ethical concern relating to the rights of individuals not to participate in research and to their treatment where they agree to participate. *See also* research ethics, informed consent.

probability sampling Selection of sampling techniques in which the chance, or probability, of each case being selected from the population is known and is not zero.

probing questions Questions used to explore further responses that are of significance to the research topic.

professional journal Journal produced by a professional organisation for its members, often containing articles of a practical nature related to professional needs. Articles in professional journals are usually not refereed.

project report Term used in this book to refer generally to dissertations, theses and management reports. *See also* dissertation, management report, thesis.

pure research *see* basic research.

purposive sampling Non-probability sampling procedures in which the judgement of the researcher is used to select the cases that make up the sample. This can be done on the basis of criticality, extremes, heterogeneity (maximum variation), homogeneity (maximum similarity).

Q

qualitative data (1) Non-numerical data or data that have not been quantified. (2) Data derived from spoken, written, typed or printed words and still or moving visual images that have not been quantified. *See also* textual data, verbal data, visual data.

qualitative diary study Research project or part of a research project based on the use of qualitative research diaries. *See also* diary study, qualitative research diary, quantitative diary study, quantitative research diary, research diary.

qualitative interview Collective term for semi-structured and unstructured interviews aimed at generating qualitative data.

qualitative research diary Research diary created by participants writing diary entries, or audio-recording their spoken thoughts in response to pre-determined open questions at regular intervals or related to the occurrence of a particular event or activity. *See also* diary study, qualitative diary study, quantitative diary study, quantitative research diary, research diary.

qualitise Conversion of quantitative data into narrative that can be analysed qualitatively.

quantifiable data Non-numerical data that can be transformed into quantitative data.

quantitative data Data that can be recorded as numbers and analysed quantitatively.

quantitative diary study Research project or part of a research project based on the use of quantitative research diaries. *See also* diary study, qualitative diary study, qualitative research diary, quantitative research diary, research diary.

quantitative research diary Research diary composed of a series of identical, reasonably short questionnaires that are designed to be self-completed by each participant to enable repeated measurements to be obtained at regular intervals through the course of the diary study. *See also* diary study, qualitative diary study, qualitative research diary, quantitative diary study, research diary.

quantitise Conversion of qualitative data into numerical codes that can be analysed statistically.

quantity question Closed question in which the respondent's answer is recorded as a number giving the amount.

quartile One of four sections when data are ranked and divided into four groups of equal size. *See also* lower quartile, upper quartile.

quasi-experiment Experimental design using an experimental group and a control group but where experimental participants cannot be assigned randomly to each group. *See also* matched pair analysis.

questionnaire General term including all data collection techniques in which each person is asked to respond to the same set of questions in a predetermined order. *See also* delivery and collection questionnaire, interviewer-administered questionnaire, online questionnaire, postal questionnaire, self-administered questionnaire.

quota sampling Non-probability sampling procedure that ensures that the sample represents certain characteristics of the population chosen by the researcher.

R

r^2 **value** *see* coefficient of determination.

R^2 **value** *see* coefficient of multiple determination.

radical change perspective Perspective which fundamentally questions the way things are done in organisations and, through research, offers insights that would help to change the organisational and social worlds.

radical humanist paradigm Paradigm concerned with changing the status quo, focusing on issues of power and politics, domination and oppression and emphasising the importance of social construction, language, processes, and instability of structures and meanings.

radical structuralist paradigm Paradigm concerned with achieving fundamental change based upon an analysis of phenomena such as structural power relationships and patterns of conflict.

random sampling *see* simple random sampling.

range Difference between the highest and the lowest values for a variable.

ranked data *see* ordinal data.

ranking question Closed question in which the respondent is offered a list of items and instructed to place them in rank order.

rating question Closed question in which a scaling device is used to record the respondent's response. *See also* Likert-type rating question, numeric rating question, semantic differential rating question.

ratio data Numerical data for which both the difference or 'interval' and relative difference between any two data values for a particular variable can be stated. *See also* numerical data.

rational thinking technique One of a number of techniques for generating and refining research ideas based on a systematic approach such as searching the literature or examining past projects.

raw data Data for which little, if any, data processing has taken place.

re-coding The process of grouping or combining a variable's codes to form a new variable, usually with less detailed categories.

reactivity Reaction by research participants to any research intervention that affects data reliability. *See also* habituation, observer effect.

realism Epistemological position that objects exist independently of our knowledge of their existence. *See also* critical realism, direct realism.

realist ethnography Ethnographic strategy stressing objectivity, factual reporting and identifying 'true' meanings. *See also* ethnography, critical ethnography, interpretive ethnography.

reductionism Idea that problems as a whole are better understood if they are reduced to the simplest possible elements.

refereed academic journal Journal in which the articles have been evaluated by academic peers prior to publication to assess their quality and suitability. Not all academic journals are refereed.

references, list of Bibliographic details of all items referred to directly in the text. The university will specify the format required.

reflection Process of observing your own research practice and examining the way you do things.

reflective diary Diary in which the researcher notes down what has happened and lessons learnt during the research process. *See also* research notebook.

reflexive photography Technique where participants engage in participant photography and reflective interviews to explore their experiences. *See also* participant photography, photovoice, visual interviews.

reflexivity Self-examination, evaluation and interpretation of your attitudes and beliefs, reactions to data and findings, and interactions with those who take part in the research and acknowledgement of the way these affect both the processes and outcomes of the research.

regression analysis The process of calculating a regression coefficient and regression equation using one independent variable and one dependent variable. For data collected from a sample, there is also a need to calculate the probability of the regression coefficient having occurred by chance alone. *See also* multiple regression analysis, coefficient of determination, r^2 value, regression equation.

regression equation Equation used to predict the values of a dependent variable given the values of one or more independent variables. The associated coefficient of determination provides an indication of how good a predictor the regression equation is likely to be. *See* coefficient of determination.

regulation perspective Perspective concerned primarily with the need for the regulation of societies and human behavior. It seeks to explain the way in which organisational affairs are regulated and offer suggestions as to how they may be improved within the framework of the way things are done at present.

relevance tree Technique for generating research topics that starts with a broad concept from which further (usually more specific) topics are generated. Each of these topics forms a separate branch, from which further sub-branches that are more detailed can be generated.

reliability Extent to which data collection technique or techniques will yield consistent findings, similar observations would be made or conclusions reached by other researchers or there is transparency in how sense was made from the raw data.

repeated measures *see* within-subjects design.

representative sample Sample that represents exactly the population from which it is drawn.

representative sampling *see* probability sampling.

research aim Broad statement summarising the general intention or desired outcome of the research.

research approach General term for inductive, deductive or abductive research approach. *See also* abductive approach, deductive approach, inductive approach.

research design Framework for the collection and analysis of data to answer research question and meet research objectives providing reasoned justification for choice of data sources, collection methods and analysis techniques.

research diary Systematic, participant-centred research method in which participants either complete daily questionnaires to produce quantitative data, or create written, audio or audio-visual recorded entries to produce qualitative data. *See also* diary study, qualitative diary study, qualitative research diary, quantitative diary study, quantitative research diary.

research ethics Standards of the researcher's behaviour in relation to the rights of those who become the subject of a research project, or who are affected by it. *See also* code of ethics, privacy, research ethics committee.

research ethics committee Learned committee established to produce a code of research ethics, examine and approve or veto research proposals and advise in relation to the ethical dilemmas facing researchers during the conduct and reporting of research projects. *See also* code of ethics.

research idea Initial idea that may be worked up into a research project.

research interview Purposeful conversation between two or more people requiring the interviewer to establish rapport, to ask concise and unambiguous questions and to listen attentively.

research notebook Notebook in which the researcher records chronologically aspects of their research project such as useful articles they have read, notes of discussions with their project supervisor etc. and their emergent thoughts about all aspects of their research. Can be used as an analytical aid. Can incorporate a reflective diary. *See also* reflective diary; self-memo.

research objectives Clear, specific statements that identify what the researcher wishes to accomplish as a result of doing the research.

research philosophy Overarching term relating to a system of beliefs and assumptions about the development of knowledge and the nature of that knowledge in relation to research.

research proposal Structured plan of a research project, occasionally referred to as a protocol or outline.

research question The key question that the research process will address, or one of the key questions that it will address. The research question is generally the precursor of research objectives.

research strategy General plan of how the researcher will go about answering the research question(s).

research Systematic collection and interpretation of data with a clear purpose, to find things out. *See also* applied research, basic research.

researcher-completed questionnaire Data collection technique in which a researcher or research assistant reads the same set of questions to the respondent in a predetermined order and records his or her responses. *See also* structured interview, telephone questionnaire.

respondent driven sampling (RDS) Non-probability sampling procedure that is a development of snowball sampling compensating for the sample being collected in a non-random way and enabling unbiased estimates of the population to be made. *See also* snowball sampling, non-probability sampling.

respondent Person who answers the questions, usually on a questionnaire. *See also* participant.

response bias *see* interviewee bias.

response rate Total number of responses divided by the total number in the sample after ineligible respondents have been excluded. *See* ineligible respondent. *See also* active response rate, break off, complete refusal, complete response, partial response.

reverse coding Recoding the scores for negatively worded questionnaire items to ensure that high values indicates the same type of response on every item.

reverse scoring *see* reverse coding.

review article Article, normally published in a refereed academic journal, that contains both a considered review of the state of knowledge in a given topic area and pointers towards areas where further research needs to be undertaken. *See also* refereed academic journal.

review question Specific question you ask of the material you are reading, which is linked either directly or indirectly to your research question. *See also* research question.

S

sample Subgroup or part of a larger population.

sampling fraction Proportion of the total population selected for a probability sample.

sampling frame Complete list of all the cases in the population, from which a probability sample is drawn.

saturation *see* data saturation.

scale item Rating question used in combination with other rating questions to create a scale. *See* rating question, scale.

scale Measure of a concept, such as customer loyalty or organisational commitment, created by combining scores to a number of rating questions.

scale question *see* rating question.

scatter graph Diagram for showing the relationship between two numerical or ranked data variables.

scatter plot *see* scatter graph.

scientific research Research that involves the systematic observation of and experiment with phenomena.

scoping study Preliminary exploratory study undertaken as part of Systematic Review to establish whether Systematic Reviews have already been published and determine the focus of the literature search. *See also* Systematic Review.

scratch notes Initial recording of key points from a research session that serves as an immediate and condensed version of what has been observed, which later needs to be worked up into a fuller, expanded account.

search engine Automated software that searches an index of documents on the Internet using key words and Boolean logic.

search string Combination of key words or search terms used in searching online databases.

search term Basic terms that describes your research question(s) and objectives, and is used to search the tertiary literature.

secondary data Data that were originally collected for some other purpose. They can be can be further analysed to provide additional or different knowledge, interpretations

or conclusions. *See also* document secondary data, multiple source secondary data, survey-based secondary data.

secondary literature Subsequent publication of primary literature such as books and journals.

secondary observation Statement made by an observer of what happened or was said. By necessity this involves that observer's interpretations.

selective coding Process of integrating categories to produce theory in grounded theory.

selective observation Stage in participant observation where the observer develops a selective focus on which to concentrate future observation. *See also* descriptive observation, focused observation.

self-coded question Question each respondent codes her or himself as part of the process of recording their answer.

self-completed questionnaire Data collection technique in which each respondent reads and answers the same set of questions in a predetermined order without an interviewer being present.

self-memo Way of recording own ideas about research as they occur, which may then be used as an analytical aid. *See also* research notebook.

self-selection sampling Non-probability volunteer sampling procedure in which the case, usually an individual, is allowed to identify their desire to be part of the sample. *See also* non-probability sampling, volunteer sampling.

semantic differential rating question Rating question that allows the respondent to indicate his or her attitude to a concept defined by opposite adjectives or phrases.

semi-structured interview Wide-ranging category of interview in which the interviewer commences with a set of interview themes but is prepared to vary the order in which questions are asked and to ask new questions in the context of the research situation.

seminal Work that is pivotal, presenting an idea of great importance or influence. Seminal articles are likely to be referred to frequently.

semiotics The study of signs. *See also* sign.

sensitive personal data Category of data, defined in law, that refers to certain specified characteristics or beliefs relating to identified or identifiable persons.

sensitivity Level of concern on the part of a potential host organisation, informant, participant or respondent about the nature of a research project and use of data that will affect willingness to cooperate.

sequential explanatory design Mixed methods research design where initial phase of quantitative data collection is followed by second phase of explanatory qualitative data collection. *See also* sequential mixed methods research.

sequential mixed-methods research Research using both quantitative and qualitative methods that are conducted in more than one phase of data collection and analysis. *See also* double-phase research design, multi-phase research design, sequential explanatory design, sequential exploratory design.

sequential multi-phase design Mixed methods research design involving multiple phases of data collection and analysis.

serial correlation *see* autocorrelation.

shadowing Process that the researcher would follow in order to gain a better understanding of the research context. This might involve following employees who are likely to be important in the research.

Shapiro–Wilk test Statistical test to determine the probability (likelihood) that an observed set of values for each category of a variable differs from a specified distribution.

sign Something that stands for (or represents) something other than itself, indicating that a sign consists of two parts: a signifier, which is the word, phrase or sound used, or image or artefact shown, and the signified, which is the concept or meaning suggested or implied in the sign. *See also* semiotics.

signficance testing Testing the probability of a pattern such as a relationship between two variables occurring by chance alone if the null hypothesis were true.

signifier *see* sign.

simple random sampling Probability sampling procedure that ensures each case in the population has an equal chance of being included in the sample.

single-organisation access The process of gaining entry into one organisation to conduct research.

single-phase research design Research involving one phase of data collection and analysis. *See also* concurrent mixed methods research.

SMS questionnaire Data collection technique in which the questionnaire is delivered as a series of SMS (short message service) texts to each respondent. She or he then reads and answers each of the texts by replying without an interviewer being present.

snowball sampling Non-probability volunteer sampling procedure in which subsequent respondents are obtained from information provided by initial respondents. *See also* non-probability sampling, volunteer sampling.

social actors Individuals or groups who, through their actions, have the capacity to shape their world in a variety of ways by reflecting on their situation and the choices available.

social constructionism Ontological position that asserts that reality is constructed through social interaction in

which social actors create partially shared meanings and realities, in other words it is socially constructed.

social exchange theory [in relation to research access] Where a potential participant evaluates the benefits versus the costs of agreeing to take part in research.

social norm Type of behaviour that a person ought to adopt in a particular situation.

socially desirable response Answer given by a respondent due to her or his desire, either conscious or unconscious, to gain prestige or appear in a different social role.

source questionnaire Questionnaire that is to be translated from another language when translating a questionnaire.

Spearman's rank correlation coefficient Statistical test that assesses the strength of the relationship between two ranked data variables. For data collected from a sample, there is also a need to calculate the probability of the correlation coefficient having occurred by chance alone.

split infinitive Phrase consisting of an infinitive with an adverb inserted between 'to' and the verb: for example, 'to readily agree'.

stacked bar graph/chart Diagram for comparing totals and subtotals for all types of data variable.

standard deviation Statistic that describes the extent of spread of data values around the mean for a variable containing numerical data.

statistical inference Process of coming to conclusions about the population on the basis of data describing a sample drawn from that population.

statistical significance Likelihood of the pattern that is observed (or one more extreme) occurring by chance alone, if there really was no difference in the population from that which the sample was drawn.

stemming Cutting off a word's ending, to reduce it to its stem.

storyline Way in which the reader is led through the research project to the main conclusion or the answer to the research question. The storyline is, in effect, a clear theme that runs through the whole of the project report to convey a coherent and consistent message.

stratified random sampling Probability sampling procedure in which the population is divided into two or more relevant strata and a random sample (systematic or simple) is drawn from each of the strata.

structural narrative analysis Narrative Analysis that focuses on the way a narrative is constructed. *See also* Narrative Analysis.

structured data Data that are organised into a form that is easy to process such as database or spreadsheet. *See also* unstructured data.

structured interview Data collection technique in which an interviewer physically meets the respondent, reads them the same set of questions in a predetermined order, and records his or her response to each.

structured methodology Data collection methods that are easily replicated (such as the use of an observation schedule or questionnaire) to ensure high reliability.

structured observation Observation method using a high level of predetermined structure, often used to quantify observed behaviours. *See also* participant observation.

subject directory Hierarchically organised index categorised into broad topics, which, as it has been compiled by people, is likely to have its content partly censored and evaluated.

subject or participant bias Bias that may occur when research subjects are giving inaccurate responses in order to distort the results of the research.

subjectivism Ontological position that incorporates assumptions of the Arts and Humanities and asserts that social reality is made from the perceptions and consequent actions of social actors (people). *See also* ontology, objectivism.

sufficiency [of access] Being able to negotiate adequate access to conduct research.

survey Research strategy that involves the structured collection of data from a sizeable population. Although the term 'survey' is often used to describe the collection of data using questionnaires, it includes other techniques such as structured observation and structured interviews.

survey-based secondary data Data collected by surveys, such as by questionnaire, which have already been analysed for their original purpose.

symbolic interactionism Strand of interpretivism derived from pragmatist thinking that sees meaning as something that emerges out of interactions between people. It focuses on the observation and analysis of social interaction such as conversations, meetings and teamwork. *See also* interpretivism, pragmatism.

symbolic sign Abstract sign which is capable of signifying meaning to those who see it through conventional understanding. *See also* iconic sign, indexical sign, semiotics, sign.

symmetric distribution Description of the distribution of data for a variable in which the data are distributed equally either side of the highest frequency.

symmetry of potential outcomes Situation in which the results of the research will be of similar value whatever they are.

synchronous electronic interview Electronic interview conducted in real time using email, instant messaging or

web conferencing. *See also* asynchronous electronic interview, electronic interview.

synchronous Undertaken in real time, occurring at the same time.

syntagmatic analysis Approach used in the analysis of visual images which explores relations between signs and the ways in which meanings are signified as different signs are combined into structures or sequences. *See also* paradigmatic analysis, semiotics, sign.

synthesis Process of arranging and assembling various elements so as to make a new statement, or conclusion.

systematic random sampling Probability sampling procedure in which the initial sampling point is selected at random, and then the cases are selected at regular intervals.

Systematic Review Process for reviewing the literature using a comprehensive pre-planned strategy to locate existing literature, evaluate the contribution, analyse and synthesise the findings and report the evidence to allow conclusions to be reached about what is known and, also, what is not known.

systematic sampling *see* systematic random sampling.

T

t-test *see* independent groups *t*-test, paired *t*-test.

table Technique for summarising data from one or more variables so that specific values can be read. *See also* contingency table, frequency distribution.

tailored design method Approach to designing questionnaires specifying precisely how to construct and use them; previously referred to as the 'total design method'.

target population Complete set of cases or group members that is the actual focus of the research inquiry, and from which a sample may be drawn.

target questionnaire Translated questionnaire when translating from a source questionnaire.

teleological view View that the ends served by research justify the means. Consequently, the benefits of research findings are weighed against the costs of acting unethically.

telephone questionnaire Data collection technique in which an interviewer contacts the respondent and administers the questionnaire using a telephone. The interviewer reads the same set of questions to the respondent in a predetermined order and records his or her responses.

Template Analysis Analysis of qualitative data that involves creating and developing a hierarchical template of data codes or categories representing themes revealed in the data collected and the relationships between these.

tense Form taken by the verb to indicate the time of the action (i.e. past, present or future).

tertiary literature source Source designed to help locate primary and secondary literature, such as an index, abstract, encyclopaedia or bibliography.

textual data Qualitative data derived from written, typed or printed words that are either collected as notes from interviews or observations, as written diaries and participant accounts or from documents. *See also* qualitative data.

Thematic Analysis A technique used to analyse qualitative data that involves the search for themes, or patterns, occurring across a data set.

Thematic Analysis Grid (TAG) A grid for structuring your note-taking as a matrix with articles listed in rows (in date order) and each column representing a separate theme.

thematic narrative analysis Narrative Analysis that focuses on the thematic content of a narrative, rather than on the way in which it is structured. *See also* Narrative Analysis.

theme Broad category incorporating several codes that appear to be related to one another and which indicates an idea that is important to your research question.

theoretical replication Realisation or replication of predicted theoretical outcomes in selected case studies in a case study strategy. *See also* case study, literal replication.

theoretical rigour Clarity and thoroughness with which the research as reported is grounded in existing explanations of how things work. *See also* methodological rigour, theory.

theoretical sampling Non-probability purposive sampling procedure particularly associated with Grounded Theory Method which focuses on the needs of the emerging theory and the evolving story line, participants being chosen purposively to inform this. *See also* Grounded Theory Method, non-probability sampling, purposive sampling.

theoretical saturation Procedure used in Grounded Theory Method and reached when data collection ceases to reveal new data that are relevant to a category, where categories have become well developed and understood and relationships between categories have been verified. *See also* Grounded Theory Method.

theoretical sensitivity Sensitivity to meanings in the data and using *in vivo* and researcher generated codes to guide theorising activity, rather than being sensitised by concepts in existing theory.

theory Formulation that intends to explain something based on general principles that are usually independent of what is being explained, which may or may not have been tested.

thesis Usual name for research project reports undertaken for Master of Philosophy (MPhil) and Doctor of Philosophy (PhD) degrees, written for an academic audience.

three-dimensional and lived media A form of visual document data that includes architecture and clothing. *See also* document secondary data.

time error Error, usually associated with structured observations, where the time at which the observation is being conducted provides data that are untypical of the time period in which the event(s) being studied would normally occur.

time series Set of numerical data values recorded for a single variable over time usually at regular intervals. *See also* moving average.

total response rate The total number of responses divided by the total number in the sample after ineligible respondents have been excluded. *See* ineligible respondent. *See also* active response rate, break off, complete response, complete refusal, partial response.

trade journal Journal produced by a trade organisation for its members, often containing articles of a practical nature related to the trade's needs. Articles in trade journals are usually not refereed.

traditional access Use of face-to-face interactions, correspondence for postal questionnaires, 'phone conversations or visits to data archives to conduct research.

transcript summary Type of summary produced following the transcription of an interview or observation and used as an analytical aid. *See also* document summary, interim summary.

transcript Written record of what a participant (or respondent) said in response to a question, or what participants (or respondents) said to one another in conversation, in their own words.

triangulation Use of two or more independent sources of data or data-collection methods within one study in order to help ensure that the data are telling you what you think they are telling you.

trimmed mean Mean calculated after extreme values (known as outliers) have been excluded.

two-dimensional moving media Form of moving document data that include films, videos, interactive web pages and other multi-media, often being combined with audio. *See also* document secondary data.

two-dimensional static media Static form of visual document data that include photographs, pictures, cartoons, maps, graphs, logos and diagrams. *See also* document secondary data.

Type I error Error made by wrongly coming to the decision that something is true when in reality it is not.

Type II error Error made by wrongly coming to the decision that something is not true when in reality it is.

type of access Way used to gaining access to conduct research. *See also* Internet-mediated access, intranet-mediated access, hybrid access, traditional access.

typical case sampling Non-probability purposive sampling procedure which focuses on selecting cases on the basis that they are typical or illustrative. *See also* purposive sampling, non-probability sampling.

U

uninformed response Tendency for a respondent to deliberately guess where they have sufficient knowledge or experience to answer a question.

unit of data A number of words, a line of a transcript, a sentence, a number of sentences, a complete paragraph, or some other single chunk of textual data or visual image that will be coded. See *also* code, coding.

unitarist view of research Belief that there is, or should be, one legitimate method (quantitative or qualitative) and intolerance of others' preferred methods if they differ from one's own.

unitising data Process of attaching relevant 'bits' or 'chunks' of your data to the appropriate category or categories that you have devised.

unreachable respondent Respondent selected for a sample who cannot be located or who cannot be contacted.

unstructured data Data that are not easy to search or process as, in their current form, they do not follow a predefined structure. *See also* unstructured data.

unstructured interview Loosely structured and informally conducted interview that may commence with one or more themes to explore with participants but without a predetermined list of questions to work through. *See also* informant interview.

upper quartile Value above which a quarter of the data values lie when the data values for a variable have been ranked.

URL Uniform resource locator specifying where a known resource can be found.

V

validity (1) Extent to which data collection method or methods accurately measure what they were intended to measure. (2) Extent to which research findings are really about what they profess to be about. *See also* construct validity, criterion related validity, ecological validity, face validity, internal validity, measurement validity, predictive validity.

variable Individual element or attribute upon which data have been collected.

variance inflation factor (VIF) Statistic used to measure collinearity. *See* collinearity.

variance Statistic that measures the spread of data values; a measure of dispersion. The smaller the variance, the closer individual data values are to the mean. The value of the variance is the square of the standard deviation. *See also* dispersion measures, standard deviation.

verbal data Qualitiative data derived from spoken words that are collected in the form of extended speech. *See also* qualitative data.

video diarist Collaborative informant who produce a video diary during the use of participatory video. *See also* participatory video, video diary.

video diary Video produced by informant during the use of the participatory video data collection technique. *See also* participatory video, video diarist.

video essay Research output that uses video or film to analyse and interpret an experience, perspective or outcome.

videography (1) Process of recording moving images onto electronic media; (2) Ethnographic analysis of recorded video sequences.

VIF *see* variance inflation factor.

virtual access Initial level of gaining access to online communities to conduct research. *See also* cognitive access, continuing access, gatekeeper.

visual aid Item such as an overhead projector slide, whiteboard, video recording or handout that is designed to enhance professional presentation and the learning of the audience.

visual data Qualitative data derived from still or moving visual images that may be created or found in many forms including drawings, digital images and video. *See also* qualitative data.

visual interview Participant focused research interview in which visual images are used to elicit interviewee accounts and interpretations and stimulate dialogue. *See also* autodriving, participant drawing, photoelicitation.

volunteer sampling Non-probability sampling procedures in which participants are volunteered or self-select to be part of the research rather than being chosen. *See also* snowball sampling, self-selection sampling.

W

web log *see* blog.

Web questionnaire Data collection technique in which the questionnaire is delivered electronically to each respondent's email address. She or he then reads and answers the same set of questions in a predetermined order without an interviewer being present before returning it electronically. *See also* online questionnaire.

weighting Process by which data values are adjusted to reflect differences in the proportion of the population that each case represents.

within-individual level analysis Analysis conducted at the level of an individual person's responses in a research study where data are repeatedly collected from each participant, such as in a quantitative diary study. *See also* between persons analysis, quantitative diary study, quantitative research diary.

within-subjects design Experimental design using only a single group where every participant is exposed to the planned intervention or series of interventions. *See also* experiment, between-subjects design.

word cloud Visual representation of the relative frequency of occurrence of words and/or phrases in text, in which the frequency is represented by the font size, or occasionally, the colour.

Index

Note: Page numbers in bold refer to glossary entries

Index